HANDBOOK OF
U.S. LABOR
STATISTICS

Employment, Earnings, Prices, Productivity, and Other Labor Data

11th Edition
2008

HANDBOOK OF U.S. LABOR STATISTICS

Employment, Earnings, Prices, Productivity, and Other Labor Data

11th Edition
2008

Edited by Eva E. Jacobs

Associate Editor
Mary Meghan Ryan

Published in the United States of America
by Bernan Press, a wholly owned subsidiary of
The Rowman & Littlefield Publishing Group, Inc.
4501 Forbes Boulevard, Suite 200
Lanham, Maryland 20706

Bernan Press
800-865-3457
info@bernan.com
www.bernan.com

ISBN 10: 1-59888-180-9
ISBN 13: 978-1-59888-180-6

ISSN: 1526-2553

CONTENTS

LIST OF TABLES

LIST OF FIGURES

ABOUT THE EDITORS

Eva E. Jacobs has been the editor of the *Handbook of U.S. Labor Statistics* since its first edition. She served as chief of the Division of Consumer Expenditure Surveys at the Bureau of Labor Statistics (BLS) for over 20 years. As the manager of this division, Ms. Jacobs was responsible for the ongoing Consumer Expenditure Survey, which tracks the expenditure patterns of U.S. households over time. Ms. Jacobs also held positions in BLS's Productivity Division and the Economic Growth Division. More recently, she acted as an adviser on cost-of-living projects for both government and private consultants. She currently serves as chair of a panel advising the Safe Harbor Working Group on issues related to cost-of-living adjustments for federal employees in Alaska, Hawaii, Guam, Puerto Rico, and the Virgin Islands. Ms. Jacobs was the 1998 recipient of the Julius Shiskin Award, given by the National Association of Business Economists and the Washington Statistical Society for distinguished contributions to the field of economic statistics.

Mary Meghan Ryan is a data analyst with Bernan Press. She received her bachelor's degree in economics from the University of Maryland and is a former economist with the American Economics Group. Ms. Ryan has also worked as a research assistant for FRANDATA. Ms. Ryan is also an associate editor of *Business Statistics of the United States* and of *Vital Statistics of the United States*, both published by Bernan Press.

PREFACE

Bernan Press is pleased to present a compilation of Bureau of Labor Statistics (BLS) data in this 11th edition of its award-winning *Handbook of U.S. Labor Statistics*. BLS provides a treasure trove of historical information about all aspects of labor and employment in the United States. The current edition maintains the content of previous editions and updates the text with additional data and new features. The data in this *Handbook* are excellent sources of information for analysts in both government and the private sector.

In earlier editions, this publication analyzed some of the issues that were then being addressed: the decline in employment in the manufacturing sector, the high unemployment rates for young minorities, the cost of health care services and prescription drugs, the changing pension plans, the specter of inflation as a result of the rise in fuel prices, the impact of changing technology on the educational and occupational requirements of industry, and the impact of immigration on the structure of the labor force. The dramatic aging of the labor force is a major factor in current discussions about the cost of health care and changing pension plans. Policy decisions on these questions are still relevant today. Other issues include the stagnation of real wages despite an increase in productivity, which has led to concern that this trend indicates a lack of progress in improving the standard of living of workers.

It is important to examine the historical movement of various series; as a result, some tables in this publication show data back to 1913. This *Handbook* includes tables on employment and unemployment and employer costs for employee health care. Tables of projections of industry output and employment show the expected trends in the technology sector and the educational requirements of jobs in this sector. Other tables show how workers have fared in terms of wages (which have been adjusted for changing prices). The new tables from the Census Bureau that were added last year in Chapter 13 show the distribution of income which differs from wages by the addition of other income such as investment income and pension income.

FEATURES OF THIS PUBLICATION

- Approximately 200 tables present authoritative data for labor market statistics, including employment and employment costs and hours, prices, productivity, comparisons with other countries, and other labor market statistics.

- Each section is preceded by one or more figures that call attention to noteworthy trends in the data. The first edition had 8 figures, while the current edition has more than 20 figures.

- In addition to the figures, the introductory material for to each chapter also contain highlights of other salient data. For example, the highlights in Chapter 1 showcase labor force participation rates by age and the disparity in labor force participation rates for

various demographic groups. A highlight in Chapter 4 calls attention to the dramatic shift in the projected age distribution of the labor force.

- The tables in each section are also preceded by notes and definitions, which contain concise descriptions of the data sources, concepts, definitions, and methodology from which the data are derived.

- The introductory notes also include references to more comprehensive reports. These reports provide additional data and more extensive descriptions of estimation methods, sampling, and reliability measures.

ARTICLES OVERVIEW

The introduction to the text provides articles that describe current information on developments, such as the planning or introduction of new surveys, the introduction of new classification definitions, and current research on economic topics that make use of the data contained in this *Handbook*.

The first article, "The American Community Survey", describes the new American Community Survey (ACS), which is being conducted by the Census Bureau. This survey, which will run continuously on a rotating sample basis, is intended to provide data on a more timely schedule. It will include the information that has previously been obtained every ten years from the decennial census. The topics covered include demographic, housing, and economic characteristics. Such information is widely used by governments in assessing the requirements for programs and assessing the distribution of funds. The data will not only provide more current data than in the past but will also allow, by combining years, provision of data for small areas.

The second article, "Summary of Articles from the 2006 and 2007 Editions of the Monthly Labor Review" is a compilation of abstracts from articles that appeared throughout 2006 and 2007 in the *Monthly Labor Review*, a publication from BLS. All of the articles noted pertain to a chapter in this *Handbook*.

The third article, "Guidance on Differences in Employment and Unemployment Estimates from Different Sources" is a summary of a document from the Census Bureau Web site. Between BLS and the Census Bureau, there are several surveys that appear to describe the same measure. This article attempts to dispel the confusion by outlining the methodology and the uses of the various measures.

NEW TABLES IN THIS EDITION

Several major changes have taken place or are projected to take place soon as a result of new classification systems or the need for new data.

New Projections. The projections of labor force and employment have been extended to 2016.

North American Industry Classification (NAICS). More series have been converted to the new classification system. The conversion sometimes causes a problem for historical comparability, therefore, the Employment Cost Index (ECI) tables now show a shorter number of years than in previous editions of the *Handbook.* Some series have been carried back further than others. Some publications show crossover tables. See the notes and definitions in each chapter for specific information about the conversion of that particular series. There are also ongoing revisions of the NAICS system itself. While the lack of comparability over long periods of time creates a problem, the new system provides a better description of the current structure of industries. More information on NAICS is available on the BLS Web site and a summary description is in the sixth edition of this *Handbook.*

Experimental Indexes. BLS has been planning to expand the hours and earnings series to cover all private sector employees instead of production workers and non supervisory employees. These additional workers account for about 20 percent of nonfarm employment. The new series will be more comprehensive in coverage, providing improved information for analyzing economic trends. BLS began the first collection of data in 2005. There is not enough historical information yet to apply all of the review techniques used in the current series so the new series is designated as experimental. As more experience is obtained, additional detail by industry and state will be published.

Business Employment Dynamics. There is a new state table to supplement the national data.

SOURCES OF ADDITIONAL INFORMATION

BLS data are primarily derived from surveys conducted by the federal government or through federal-state cooperative arrangements. The comparability of data over time can be affected by changes in the surveys, which are essential for keeping pace with the current structure of economic institutions and for taking advantage of improved survey techniques. Revisions of current data are also periodically made as a result of the availability of new information. In addition, some tables in this *Handbook* were dropped due to the data being from a one-time survey that is now outdated—such as the data on training (1995)—or due to the survey being entirely restructured. Introductory notes to each chapter summarize specific factors that may affect the data. In the tables, the ellipsis character ("...") indicates that data are not available.

More extensive methodological information, including further discussion of the sampling and estimation procedures used for each BLS program, is contained in the *BLS Handbook of Methods.* This publication is in the process of being updated, and completed chapters are available on the BLS Web site at <http://www.bls.gov>. Other sources of current data and analytical include the *Monthly Labor Review* and a daily Internet publication, *The Editor's Desk* (TED). All of these publications can be found on the BLS Web site as well. Other relevant publications, including those from the Census Bureau, are noted in the notes and definitions in each chapter.

ACKNOWLEDGMENTS

The preparation of this publication was very much a team activity. Mary Meghan Ryan researched the data and compiled the tables. Deirdre Gaquin prepared the special tabulations of data from the Current Population Survey. Jo A. Wilson, assisted by Lateef Padgett, prepared the graphics and layout. Shana Hertz copyedited this edition. Publisher Kenneth E. Lawrence and managing editor Katherine A. DeBrandt supervised the overall editorial and production aspects of this publication. I extend my sincere gratitude to these individuals for their skills, professionalism, and cooperative effort—all of which made this publication possible.

Particular thanks also go to BLS staff members, too numerous to mention by name, who patiently answered questions and provided essential information.

OTHER PUBLICATIONS BY BERNAN PRESS

The *Handbook of U.S. Labor Statistics* is one of a number of publications in Bernan's award-winning U.S. DataBook Series. Other titles include *Business Statistics of the United States: Patterns of Economic Change; The Almanac of American Education; United States Foreign Trade Highlights: Trends in the Global Market; Datapedia of the United States, American History in Numbers; Vital Statistics of the United States: Births, Life Expectancy, Deaths, and Selected Health Data; and Crime in the United States.* Each of these titles provides the public with statistical information from official government sources.

If you have any questions or suggestions as to how we could make future editions even more useful, please contact us by e-mail at bpress@bernan.com. Please visit our Web site at <http://www.bernan.com>.

ARTICLE 1
THE AMERICAN COMMUNITY SURVEY

The following article is intended to introduce readers to the American Community Survey (ACS), a survey conducted by the Census Bureau. The following is a very brief summary. For more extensive descriptions and an evaluation of the design and methodology see "Design and Methodology: American Community Survey" available on the Census Bureau Web site at <http://www.census.gov/acs/www/Downloads/tp67.pdf> and "Using Data from the 2005 American Community Survey" at <http://www.census.gov/acs/www/UseData/advance_copy_user_guide.pdf>.

INTRODUCTION

The American Community Survey (ACS) is designed to provide communities a fresh look at how they are changing and it is a key part of the Census Bureau's Decennial Census Program. It publishes social, housing, and economic characteristics for demographic groups covering a broad spectrum of geographic areas in the United States and Puerto Rico. The ACS shifted from a demonstration program with a different sample design and sample size to the full sample size and design in 2005. It became the largest household survey in the United States with an annual sample size of about 3 million addresses.

Every year the ACS can support the release of single-year estimates for geographic areas with populations of 65,000 or more. The ACS will accumulate samples over 3-year and 5-year intervals to produce estimates for smaller geographic areas including census tracts and block groups.

WHAT TOPICS ARE INCLUDED IN THE ACS?

Demographic Characteristics

Sex, age, relationship, households by type, race, and Hispanic origin

Social Characteristics

School enrollment, educational attainment, marital status, fertility, grandparents caring for children, veteran status, disability status, residence one year ago, place of birth, U.S. citizenship status, year of entry, world region of birth of foreign born, language spoken at home, and ancestry

Economic Characteristics

Employment status, commuting to work, occupation, industry, class of worker, income and benefits, and poverty status

Housing Characteristics

Housing occupancy, units in structure, year structure built, number of rooms, number of bedrooms, housing tenure, year householder moved into unit, vehicles available, house heating fuel, utility costs, occupants per room, housing value, mortgage status, and costs

The topics covered by the ACS are virtually the same as those covered by the Census 2000 long form. Therefore, the need for the long form in the 2010 census will be eliminated. The ACS is a way to provide data the communities need every year instead of once every ten years. The 2010 census will continue to count the population to support the Constitutional mandate to provide population counts needed to apportion the seats in the U. S. House of Representatives. States develop redistricting plans based on this important information. The ACS will not provide these counts.

THE HISTORY OF THE ACS

Continuous measurement has long been viewed as a possible alternative method for collecting detailed information on the characteristics of population and housing, but it was not considered a practical alternative for the decennial census long form until 15 years ago. At that time, federal, state, and local government, as well as private sector demands for current, nationally consistent data led policymakers in government to consider the feasibility of collecting social and economic data continuously throughout the decade, instead of only once every 10 years. The benefits of current data, along with the anticipated benefits in cost savings, planning, improved census coverage, and more efficient operations led the Census Bureau to plan to implement continuous measurement in 2000, which was later renamed the American Community Survey (ACS). The need to understand the nuances of sample design, survey methods, and data products under the new program delayed implementation until after Census 2000. After additional testing, outreach to stakeholders, and an ongoing process of interaction with key data users, especially those in the statistical and demographic communities, the Census Bureau expanded the ACS to full sample size for housing units (HUs) in 2005 and for group quarters (GQ) facilities in 2006.

The history of the ACS can be divided into four distinct stages. The design and early proposals stage, 1990 to 1993, occurred when the concept of continuous measurement was first proposed. The development stage, between 1994 and 1999, occurred when the Census Bureau tested early prototypes of continuous measurement in a small number of sites. The demonstration stage, between 2000 and 2004, occurred when the Census Bureau carried out large-scale, nationwide surveys and produced reports for the country, states, and large geographic areas. The full implementation stage began in January 2005.

ARTICLE 2
SUMMARY OF ARTICLES FROM THE 2006 AND 2007 EDITIONS
OF THE MONTHLY LABOR REVIEW

In 2006 and 2007 there were many interesting articles published in the Bureau of Labor Statistics journal, The Monthly Labor Review (MLR), *which illustrate how data in this* Handbook *are used in economic research and analysis. The following is a selected list of abstracts of recent articles. The articles can be found in their entirety on the BLS Web site at* <http://www.bls.gov/opub/mlr/mlrhome.htm>. *Each abstract is followed by a reference to the relevant chapter in the* Handbook.

RELEVANT ARTICLES FROM 2007:

February: **TRENDS IN LABOR FORCE PARTICIPATION OF MARRIED MOTHERS OF INFANTS**
Written by: Sharon R. Cohany and Emy Sok
Following a long-term advance, the labor force activity of married mothers of infants began to decline in the late 1990s for a variety of demographic groups and since 2000 has been relatively stable. (See Chapter 1.)

March: **EMPLOYMENT DYNAMICS: SMALL AND LARGE FIRMS OVER THE BUSINESS CYCLE**
Written by: Jessica Helfand, Akbar Sadeghi, and David Talan
The use of the dynamic-sizing approach to measuring employment growth by size of firm provides information useful in the debate on small firm versus large firm job creation. (See Chapter 2.)

April: **ESTABLISHMENT WAGE DIFFERENTIALS**
Written by: Julia I. Lane, Laurie A. Salmon, and James R. Spletzer
Microdata from the BLS Occupational Employment Statistics program are providing researchers a new approach to use in studying how wages are influenced by the establishment in which an individual works. (See Chapter 2.)

May: **HOW DO OLDER AMERICANS SPEND THEIR TIME?**
Written by: Rachel Krantz-Kent and Jay Stewart
Older Americans' time use changes dramatically with age, but it is the lower employment rates at older ages—rather than age itself—that matter most. (See Chapter 12.)

RELEVANT ARTICLES FROM 2006:

January: **UNION MEMBERSHIP STATISTICS IN 24 COUNTRIES**
Written by: Jelle Visser
An analysis of "adjusted" union membership data in 24 countries yields past and present union density rates; the data provide explanatory factors for the differences and trends in unionization. (See Chapter 10.)

February: **UNDERSTANDING THE EMPLOYMENT MEASURES FROM THE ESTABLISHMENT AND HOUSEHOLD SURVEYS**
Written by: Mary K. Bowler and Teresa L. Morisi
The monthly BLS "Employment Situation" news release includes two distinct employment measures from two different surveys. Although these measures track well over the long term, occasional differences in trends have confounded labor market analysts. This article discusses the various differences and posits reasons that those differences may or may not affect the divergences between the two employment series. The first portion of the article offers a general background on the two surveys and a summary of past research into earlier divergences in the 1960s, 1970s, and 1980s. The second portion examines the latest BLS research into the divergences in the mid- to late 1990s through 2004. (See Chapters 1 and 2.)

March: **PROJECTED PENSION INCOME: EQUALITY OR DISPARITY FOR THE BABY-BOOM COHORT?**
Written by: James H. Moore, Jr.
This article presents data from the Modeling Income in the Near Term (MINT 3) system to address the question of what is in store for the baby-boom cohort once it reaches age 62. The primary objective is to examine disparities in projected pension eligibility and income among the various baby-boom subgenerations upon reaching 62 years. Over time, both eligibility for pensions and income from employer-sponsored pension plans will increase for baby boomers. Eligibility rates and benefit amounts are projected to be greater for late boomers overall and, within the late-boomer category, men, whites, and the more educated. (See Chapter 6.)

May: **COMPARING U.S. AND EUROPEAN INFLATION: THE CPI AND THE HICP**
Written by: Walter Lane and Mary Lynn Schmidt
This article introduces an experimental consumer price index for the United States that

follows, to the extent possible, the methods of the Harmonized Index of Consumer Prices (HICP), the European Union's (EU's) official price index. The U.S. HICP differs from the U.S. Consumer Price Index (CPI) in two major respects: HICP includes the rural population in its scope and it excludes owner-occupied housing. To construct the experimental U.S. HICP, the CPI first was expanded to cover the entire (non-institutional) U.S. population and then was narrowed to remove the owner-occupied housing costs that the HICP excludes from its scope. (See Chapter 11.)

June: **INCOME DATA QUALITY ISSUES IN THE CPS**
Written by: Daniel H. Weinberg
The Annual Social and Economic Supplement to the Current Population Survey (CPS ASEC) measures income and poverty in the United States. Based on comparisons to the National Income and Product Accounts, researchers suggest that income is underreported on the CPS ASEC, thus the estimated poverty rate is too high. This article focuses on the quality of the CPS ASEC. A close look into the questionnaire design, data collection and preparation, and post-collection data processing suggests areas for improvement. The article proposes a set of research projects that could be used to remedy many of the deficiencies identified and encourage discussion among interested researchers. (See Chapter 13.)

July: **CUTTING THE CORD: TELECOMMU-NICATIONS EMPLOYMENT SHIFTS TOWARD WIRELESS**
Written by: Christopher C. Carbone
Throughout the late 1990s and into 2000, the telecommunications industry experienced unprecedented growth. This fast-paced growth was fueled largely by changes in federal regulation, the anticipated demand for telecommunications products associated with those changes, and with rapidly developing technology. The subsequent employment downturn, one signal of the end of the "tech boom," was large and quick. Telecommunications shed 25.3 percent of its employees from the March 2001 peak through 2005. This employment bust took only 4 years, about a year less than the employment boom. This article details the telecommunications industry's growth and subsequent bust. (See Chapter 2.)

September: **INTERAREA PRICE LEVELS: AN EXPERIMENTAL METHODOLOGY**
Written by: Bettina H. Aten
Differences in relative price levels for areas of the United States can be estimated with a modified Country-Product-Dummy (CPD) method often used in international comparisons of the purchasing power of currencies; CPI observations and CE weights are used to estimate experimental price level differentials for 2003 and 2004. (See Chapter 7.)

November: **A NEW LOOK AT LONG-TERM LABOR FORCE PROJECTIONS TO 2050**
Written by: Mitra Toossi
Among the factors affecting the size, composition, and growth of the labor force over the next 50 years are the aging of the baby-boom generation, the stabilization of women's labor force participation rates, and increasing racial and ethnic diversity in the workforce. The 2005–2050 period is projected to witness the massive exit of the baby-boom generation out of the labor force, bringing to an end one of the major drivers of labor force growth over the post-World War II period. (See Chapter 4.)

November: **INCOME IMPUTATION AND ANALYSIS OF CONSUMER EXPENDITURE DATA**
Written by: Jonathan D. Fisher
The Consumer Expenditure (CE) Survey now provides imputed income data from 2004 forward for households that fail to report a specific income value. This study examines how income imputation affects analysis of the CE Survey's expenditure data. Most importantly, research that uses both income and expenditures from 2004 on will not have to restrict the sample to households that reported income. Results most sensitive to the introduction of income imputation are statistics that focus on households with lower levels of expenditures, such as the consumption expenditure poverty rate. (See Chapter 8.)

This article is excerpted from an online document on the Census Bureau's Web site. It can be found at <http://www.census .gov/hhes/www/laborfor/laborguidance082504.html>.

The federal government reports employment and unemployment (labor force) estimates from several major surveys and programs including:

- Current Population Survey (CPS)

- American Community Survey (ACS)

- Current Employment Statistics (CES) Program

These reports are compiled from three major sources:

- Household surveys, such as the CPS and the ACS, provide data (sometimes referred to as household data) that pertain to individuals, families, and households, and relate to where people live (as opposed to where they work).

- Reports based on information from employers, such as the CES, provide data from employers or establishments that pertain to jobs (people on a payroll) and relate to where those jobs are located.

- Records based on information from unemployment insurance (UI) records pertain to people who are eligible for UI benefits based on program requirements, including those who file claims, and relate to the place of insurance coverage of the establishment.

Estimates of employment and unemployment from a particular program may differ from those of other programs because of variations in definitions, coverage, methods of collection, reference periods, and estimation procedures. These variations, in turn, arise from differences in the programs' purposes. The various estimates of employment and unemployment generally complement one another, with each providing a different type of information that the others cannot suitably supply. This multiplicity of sources makes it important to understand when it is appropriate to use the data from each source.

HIGHLIGHTS

Current Population Survey (CPS)

Due to its detailed questionnaire and its interviewing staff trained to explain labor force concepts and answer questions, the CPS is a high quality source of information used to produce the official monthly estimates of employment, unemployment, and the unemployment rate for the nation and states. It is also a source of information on other labor force topics such as actual hours of work and duration of unemployment.

American Community Survey (ACS)

The ACS has an annual sample size of 3 million addresses nationwide. This makes it suitable for sub-national estimates. The ACS uses the same labor force questions as Census 2000.

Due to its large sample size, the ACS has advantages over the CPS in producing estimates in the following circumstances:

- Characterizing small geographic areas for which CPS (or Local Area Unemployment Statistics Program) estimates are not available, and for comparisons among such areas and between such areas and larger ones;

- Providing information on socioeconomic characteristics of the labor force that are not collected in the CPS, or for geographic areas below the level for which the CPS can provide this information;

- Producing tabulations of finely detailed categories, or extensive cross-tabulations of multiple characteristics of the labor force for any geographic area, including the nation, for which the CPS sample size is insufficient to produce reliable estimates;

- Studying rare characteristics of common population groups, or characteristics of uncommon population groups;

Current Employment Statistics (CES) Program

The CES program is an excellent source of information on employment, hours worked, and hourly and weekly earnings as reported by a sample of almost 400,000 establishments. Employment, hours worked, and earnings data are based on payroll reports. This survey estimates the number and characteristics of jobs held, not the number of people employed.

DETAILED COMPARISON OF SOURCES AND THEIR ESTIMATES

Household Data

The CPS is a high-quality sample survey of the population 16 years and over, conducted each month by the Census Bureau for the Bureau of Labor Statistics (BLS). It provides accurate and timely data needed for swift economic decision making by the Administration, Congress, and the Federal Reserve Board. The CPS has been the source of the official estimates of employment and unemployment for the nation for more than 50 years. The survey has been greatly expanded and improved over the years, but the basic concepts of employment and unemployment— reviewed periodically by high-ranking commissions—have remained substantially unaltered.

The CPS is specifically designed to be the official source of monthly estimates of employment and unemployment for the United States, and of annual-average estimates of these measurements for all states. It also publishes annual-average estimates for 50 large metropolitan areas (MAs) and 17 cities, but its sample is not large enough to provide reliable data for other areas. The CPS provides information on the detailed socioeconomic characteristics of the labor force for the nation, states, and published areas.

The ACS is the largest household survey in the United States. It provides direct annual estimates of employment and unemployment for the nation and states, and for counties and other governmental units of 65,000 or more population. For smaller governmental units, it will annually provide 3-year or 5-year moving averages. Eventually, the ACS will be able to measure changes over time for small areas and population groups. The ACS provides a wealth of data on socioeconomic characteristics that can be related to its labor force estimates.

Definitional and procedural differences between the CPS and the ACS are important to consider when using or comparing estimates. The remainder of this section describes differences among the household-based estimates.

The CPS program provides monthly estimates. The ACS provides annual information about the labor force for small areas (essentially all cities, counties, and metropolitan areas of 250,000 population or more during the testing phase; governmental units as small as 65,000 population when fully implemented, and all areas as small as census tracts beginning in 2010), as well as for the nation and the states.

The CPS provides a monthly snapshot of national-level employment and unemployment statistics with less than a 3-week turnaround between the end of data collection in any one month and release of the statistics for that month by the BLS. The ACS does not produce monthly estimates because it has been optimized instead to produce accurate estimates for geographic areas as small as census tracts and block groups.

The CPS computes annual averages of employment and unemployment statistics at the state level and for the New York and Los Angeles metropolitan areas. The ACS will have a large enough sample to provide annual estimates for much smaller geographic areas, with those for areas with populations under 65,000 being 3-year or 5-year moving averages.

The CPS asks a more detailed series of questions than the ACS does about labor force participation in order to obtain the accuracy required for the official labor force estimates. The CPS data are collected by field staff via personal interviews that allow for follow-up questions to clarify complicated concepts or to probe for information to implement the official definition.

Because the CPS asks detailed questions and has an overlapping sample design, it provides an estimate most consistent with the official definition of the unemployment rate, and is able to detect month-to-month changes in this key economic indicator with considerable precision, based on a sample size of 73,000 per month for labor force statistics.

The reference period for the CPS labor force estimates for a given month is the calendar week including the 12th day of the month. Employment data about the week of the 12th is collected during the week of the 19th. The week of the 12th was selected as the reference week for employment to minimize the effect of holidays and other seasonal variation. Annual CPS estimates are obtained by averaging the twelve monthly estimates. The reference period for the ACS labor force questions is also a full calendar week, but it is the week prior to the week when the respondent answers the questions rather than a specific week of the month. This week is not the same for all respondents, and, in fact, can vary over all the weeks in a year. To the extent that the labor force characteristics of people in the ACS in their reference week differ from their characteristics in the week containing the 12th, the comparability of ACS and CPS estimates is affected.

In summary, the CPS and the ACS programs are complementary rather than competing sources of employment and unemployment data. The CPS has a long history of providing consistent labor force estimates for regular, uniform, time periods. It employs trained field staff and detailed questions. The strength of the ACS is its coverage and precision of measurement for smaller geographic areas, features the CPS program can replicate, and its wealth of socioeconomic characteristics that can be reliably associated with its labor force measures.

CHAPTER ONE

POPULATION, LABOR FORCE, AND EMPLOYMENT STATUS

POPULATION, LABOR FORCE, AND EMPLOYMENT STATUS

HIGHLIGHTS

This chapter presents the detailed historical information collected in the Current Population Survey (CPS), a monthly survey of households that gathers data on the employment status of the population. Basic data on labor force, employment, and unemployment are shown for various characteristics of the population, including age, sex, race, and marital status.

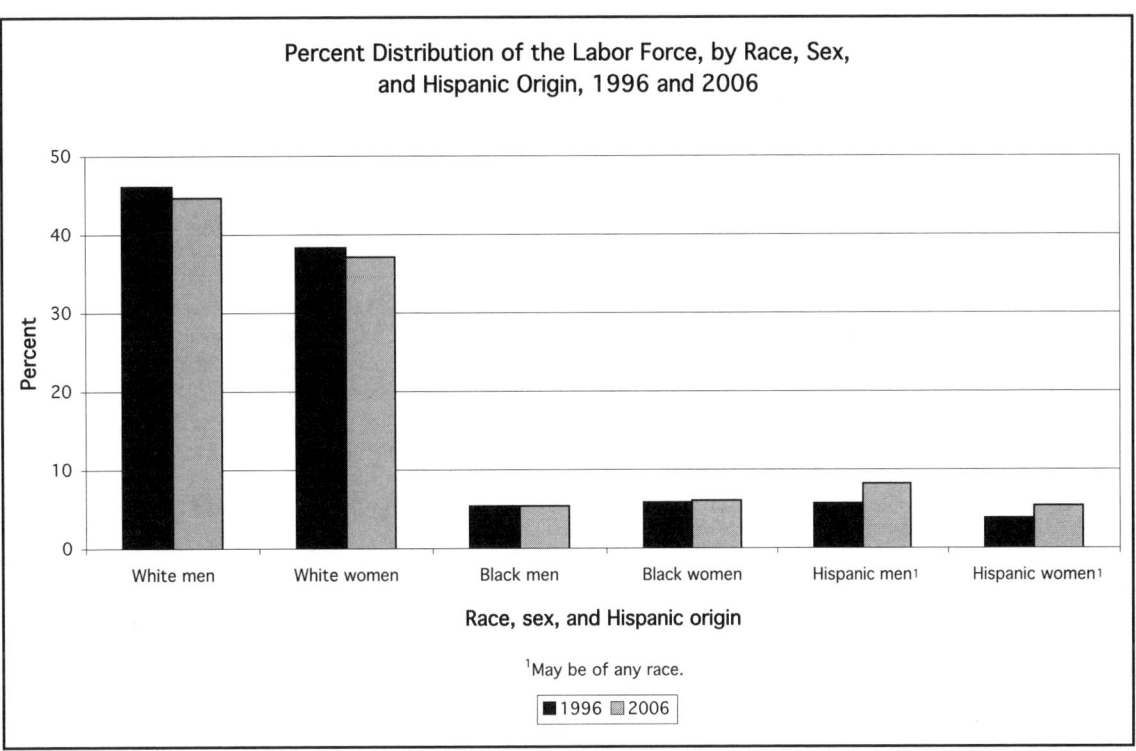

Percent Distribution of the Labor Force, by Race, Sex, and Hispanic Origin, 1996 and 2006

As evident in the figure above, the composition of the labor force changed somewhat from 1996 to 2006. The proportion of the labor force made up of Whites declined from over 84 percent to less than 82 percent during this time. Both White men and women experienced similar declines. The proportion of the labor force made up of Blacks remained stable for men and increased slightly for women. Hispanic representation changed the most significantly. From 1996 to 2006, the proportion of the labor force made up of Hispanics increased from 9.5 percent to 13.7 percent. During this period, the number of Hispanics in the labor force increased by 62 percent. Hispanics may be of any race. (See Table 1-7.)

OTHER HIGHLIGHTS

- In 2006, the labor force grew by 1.4 percent. The labor force participation rate also grew slightly after remaining stable or declining the previous two years. (See Table 1-1.)

- The labor force participation rate of persons age 65 years and over increased to 15.4 percent in 2006. This number has increased in nine of the past ten years. (See Table 1-8.)

- The labor force participation rate for married women has remained relatively constant since 1990, fluctuating between 58 percent and 61 percent. (See Table 1-4.)

- Minnesota had the highest labor force participation rate in 2006 at 73.5 percent followed by Colorado at 73.1 percent and South Dakota at 72.7 percent. West Virginia had the lowest labor force participation rate at 55.5 percent followed by Mississippi at 60.1 percent and Louisiana at 61.6 percent. The national average was 66.2 percent. (See Table 1-5.)

NOTES AND DEFINITIONS

CURRENT POPULATION SURVEY OF HOUSEHOLDS

Collection and Coverage

The Bureau of Labor Statistics (BLS) uses data from the Current Population Survey (CPS) to compile statistics on the employment status of the population and related data. The Census Bureau—using a scientifically selected sample of the civilian noninstitutional population—conducts the CPS, a monthly survey of households, for BLS.

The CPS sample has been increased from 50,000 to 60,000 households. The new sample was introduced in September 2000. However, in order to evaluate the impact of the change, the estimates of the national labor force from the additional sample were not introduced at that time. Since the estimates from the two samples were virtually the same, BLS began incorporating the additional sample into official national estimates in July 2001.

Respondents are interviewed to obtain information about the employment status of each household member age 16 years and over. The inquiry relates to the household member's employment status during the calendar week, Sunday through Saturday, that includes the 12th day of the month. This is known as the "reference week." Actual field interviewing is conducted during the following week (the week that contains the 19th day of the month).

Concepts and Definitions

The concepts and definitions underlying the labor force data have been modified—but not substantially altered—since the inception of the survey in 1940. Current definitions of some of the major concepts used in the CPS are described below.

The civilian noninstitutional population includes persons 16 years of age and over who reside in the 50 states and the District of Columbia who are not inmates of institutions (such as penal and mental facilities and homes for the aged) and who are not on active duty in the armed forces.

An *employed person* is any person who, during the reference week: (1) did any work at all (at least one hour) as a paid employees in their own business, profession, or on their own farm, or who worked 15 hours or more as an unpaid worker in an enterprise operated by a member of the family; and (2) any person who was not working but who had a job or business from which he or she was temporarily absent due to vacation, illness, bad weather, child-care problems, maternity or paternity leave, labor-management disputes, job training, or other family or personal reasons, despite whether the employee was being paid for the time off or was seeking other jobs.

Each employed person is counted only once, even if he or she holds more than one job. For purposes of occupation and industry classification, multiple jobholders are counted as being in the job at which they worked the greatest number of hours during the reference week.

Included in the total are employed citizens of foreign countries who were temporarily in the United States but not living on the premises of an embassy. Excluded are persons whose only activity during the reference week consisted of work around their own house (painting, repairing, or own home housework) or volunteer work for religious, charitable, and similar organizations.

Unemployed persons are all persons who had no employment during the reference week, but who were available for work (except for temporary illness) and had made specific efforts to find employment some time during the four-week period ending with the reference week. Persons who were waiting to be recalled to a job from which they had been laid off need not have been looking for work to be classified as unemployed.

Duration of unemployment represents the length of time (through the current reference week) that persons classified as unemployed had been looking for work. For persons on layoff, duration of unemployment represents the number of full weeks they had been on layoff. Mean duration of unemployment is the arithmetic average computed from single weeks of unemployment; median duration of unemployment is the midpoint of a distribution of weeks of unemployment.

Reasons for unemployment are divided into four major groups: (1) job losers, defined as (a) persons on temporary layoff, who have been given a date to return to work or who expect to return to work within six months; (b) permanent job losers, whose employment ended involuntarily and who began looking for work; and (c) persons who completed a temporary job and began looking for work after the job ended; (2) job leavers, defined as persons who quit or otherwise terminated their employment voluntarily and immediately began looking for work; (3) reentrants, defined as persons who previously worked but were out of the labor force prior to beginning their job search; and (4) new entrants, defined as persons who had never worked but were currently searching for work.

The *civilian labor force* comprises all civilians classified as employed or unemployed.

The *unemployment rate* is the number of unemployed persons as a percentage of the civilian labor force.

The *participation rate* represents the proportion of the civilian noninstitutional population currently in the labor force.

The *employment-population ratio* represents the proportion of the population that is currently employed.

Persons not in the labor force are all persons in the civilian noninstitutional population who are neither employed nor unemployed. Information is collected about their desire for and availability to take a job at the time of the CPS interview, job search activity during the prior year, and reason for not looking for work during the four-week period ending with the reference week. Persons not in the labor force who want and are available for a job and who have looked for work within the past 12 months (or since the end of their last job, if they had held one within the past 12 months), but who are not currently looking, are designated as *marginally attached to the labor force*. The marginally attached are divided into those not currently looking because they believe their search would be futile—so-called *discouraged workers*—and those not currently looking for other reasons, such as family responsibilities, ill health, or lack of transportation.

Discouraged workers are defined as persons not in the labor force who want and are available for a job and who have looked for work sometime in the past 12 months (or since the end of their last job, if they held one within the past 12 months), but who are not currently looking because they believe that there are no jobs available or there are none for which they would qualify. The reasons for not currently looking for work include a person's belief that no work is available in his or her line of work or area; he or she could not find any work; he or she lacks necessary schooling, training, skills, or experience; employers would think he or she is too young or too old; or he or she would encounter hiring discrimination.

Usual full- or part-time status refers to hours usually worked per week. Full-time workers are those who usually work 35 hours or more (at all jobs). This group includes some individuals who worked less than 35 hours during the reference week for economic or noneconomic reasons. Part-time workers are those who usually work less than 35 hours per week (at all jobs), regardless of the number of hours worked during the reference week. These concepts are used to differentiate a person's normal schedule from his or her specific activity during the reference week. Unemployed persons who are looking for full-time work or who are on layoff from full-time jobs are counted as part of the full-time labor force; unemployed persons who are seeking part-time work or who are on layoff from part-time jobs are counted as part of the part-time labor force.

Occupation, industry, and class of worker for members of the employed population are determined by the job held during the reference week. Persons with two or more jobs are classified as being in the job at which they worked the greatest number of hours. The unemployed are classified according to their last job. Beginning with data published in 2003, the systems used to classify occupational and industry data changed. They are currently based on the Standard Occupational Classification (SOC) system and the North American Industry Classification System (NAICS). (See the following section on historical comparability for a discussion of previous classification systems

used in the CPS.) The class-of-worker breakdown assigns workers to one of the following categories: private and government wage and salary workers, self-employed workers, and unpaid family workers. Wage and salary workers receive wages, salaries, commissions, tips, or pay in kind from a private employer or from a government unit. Self-employed workers are those who work for profit or fees in their own businesses, professions, trades, or on their own farms. Only the unincorporated self-employed are included in the self-employed category in the class-of-worker typology. Self-employed workers who respond that their businesses are incorporated are included among wage and salary workers, because they are technically paid employees of a corporation. An unpaid family worker is a person working without pay for 15 hours or more per week on a farm or in a business operated by a member of the household to whom he or she is related by birth or marriage.

A *multiple jobholder* is an employed person who, during the reference week, had two or more jobs as a wage and salary worker, was self-employed and also held a wage and salary job, or worked as an unpaid family worker and also held a wage and salary job. A person only employed in private households (as a cleaner, gardener, babysitter, etc.) who worked for two or more employers during the reference week is not counted as a multiple jobholder, since working for several employers is considered an inherent characteristic of private household work. Also excluded are self-employed persons with multiple businesses and persons with multiple jobs as unpaid family workers.

At work part-time for economic reasons, sometimes called involuntary part-time, refers to individuals who gave an economic reason for working 1 to 34 hours during the reference week. Economic reasons include slack work or unfavorable business conditions, inability to find full-time work, and seasonal declines in demand. Those who usually work part-time must also indicate that they want and are available to work full-time to be classified as working part-time for economic reasons.

At work part-time for noneconomic reasons refers to persons who usually work part-time and were at work 1 to 34 hours during the reference week for a noneconomic reason. Noneconomic reasons include illness or other medical limitations, childcare problems or other family or personal obligations, school or training, retirement or Social Security limits on earnings, and being in a job where full-time work is less than 35 hours. This also includes workers who gave an economic reason for usually working 1 to 34 hours but said they do not want to work full-time or were unavailable for full-time work.

White, Black, and Asian are terms used to describe the race of persons. Persons in these categories are those who selected that race only. Persons in the remaining race categories—American Indian or Alaskan Native, Native Hawaiian or Other Pacific Islander, and persons who selected more than one race category—are included in the estimates of total employment and unemployment but are not shown separately because the number of survey respondents is too small to develop estimates of sufficient quality for monthly publication.

Hispanic origin refers to persons who identified themselves in the enumeration process as being Spanish, Hispanic, or Latino. Persons of Hispanic or Latino origin may be of any race.

Single, never married; married, spouse present; and other marital status are the terms used to define the marital status of individuals at the time of the CPS interview. Married, spouse present, applies to a husband and wife if both were living in the same household, even though one may be temporarily absent on business, vacation, in a hospital, etc. Other marital status applies to persons who are married, spouse absent; widowed; or divorced. Married, spouse absent relates to persons who are separated due to marital problems, as well as husbands and wives living apart because one was employed elsewhere, on duty with the armed forces, or any other reason.

A *household* consists of all persons—related family members and all unrelated persons—who occupy a housing unit and have no other usual address. A house, an apartment, a group of rooms, or a single room is regarded as a housing unit when occupied or intended for occupancy as separate living quarters. A householder is the person (or one of the persons) in whose name the housing unit is owned or rented. The term is not applied to either husbands or wives in married-couple families; it refers only to persons in families maintained by either men or women without a spouse.

A *family* is defined as a group of two or more persons residing together who are related by birth, marriage, or adoption. All such persons are considered as members of one family. Families are classified as either married-couple families or families maintained by women or men without spouses.

Children refer to "own" children of the husband, wife, or person maintaining the family, including sons and daughters, stepchildren, and adopted children. Excluded are other related children, such as grandchildren, nieces, nephews, cousins, and unrelated children.

The annual CPS data on the employment characteristics of families and family members began with data for 1995. These data are not strictly comparable with family data derived from the March supplement to the CPS. The annual data are derived by averaging the data for each month of the year, whereas the March data refer to that specific month. The annual average data provide a larger sample size, while the March data provide a longer historical series.

Additional Concepts and Definitions: CPS Supplements

In addition to the above concepts and definitions, the definitions below apply to the special labor force data collected annually in the March supplement to the CPS and to the data on tenure usually collected in the February supplement to the CPS.

Persons with work experience are civilians who worked at any time during the preceding calendar year at full- or part-time jobs for pay or profit (including paid vacations and sick leave) or who worked without pay on farms or in family-operated businesses. From 1989 onward, these supplementary tables also include members of the armed forces.

Tenure refers to length of time a worker has been continuously employed by his or her current employer. These data are collected through a supplement to the CPS. All employed persons were asked how long they had been working continuously for their present employer and, if the length of time was one or two years, a follow-up question was asked about the exact number of months. The follow-up question was included for the first time in the February 1996 supplement to the CPS. CPS supplements that obtained information on tenure in the Januaries of 1983, 1987, and 1991 did not include the follow-up question. Prior to 1983, the question was asked differently. Data prior to 1983 are thus not strictly comparable to data for subsequent years.

Year-round full-time workers are workers who primarily worked at full-time jobs for 50 weeks or more during the preceding calendar year. Part-year workers worked either full- or part-time for 1 to 49 weeks.

A *spell of unemployment* is a continuous period of unemployment of at least one week's duration and is terminated by either employment or withdrawal from the labor force.

Extent of unemployment refers to the number of workers and proportion of the labor force that were unemployed at some time during the year. The number of weeks unemployed is the total number of weeks accumulated during the entire calendar year.

Earnings are all money income of $1 or more from wages and salaries and all net money income of $1 or more from farm and nonfarm self-employment.

Educational attainment refers to years of school completed in regular schools, which include graded public, private, and parochial elementary, and high schools, whether day or night school. Colleges, universities, and professional schools are also included.

Minimum wage refers to the prevailing federal minimum wage, which was $5.15 per hour in 2006. Data are for wage and salary workers who were paid hourly rates and refer to a person's earnings at the sole or principal job.

Absences are defined as instances in which persons who usually work 35 or more hours a week worked less than that during the reference period for reasons of illness or family obligations. Excluded are situations in which work was missed for vacation, holidays, or other reasons. The estimates are based on one-fourth of the sample only.

Historical Comparability

While current survey concepts and methods are very similar to those used for the inaugural CPS in 1940, a number of changes have been made over the years to improve the accuracy and usefulness of the data. Only the latest changes are described here.

Major changes to the CPS, such as the complete redesign of the questionnaire and the use of computer-assisted interviewing for the entire survey, were introduced in 1994. In addition, there were revisions to some of the labor force concepts and definitions, including the implementation of changes recommended in 1979 by the National Commission on Employment and Unemployment Statistics (NCEUS, also known as the Levitan Commission). Some of the major changes to the survey at this time were:

1) The introduction of a redesigned and automated questionnaire. The CPS questionnaire was totally redesigned in order to obtain more accurate, comprehensive, and relevant information, and to take advantage of state-of-the-art computer interviewing techniques.

2) The addition of two criteria to make the definition of discouraged workers more objective. Beginning in 1994, persons classified as discouraged must have looked for a job within the past year (or since their last job, if they worked during the year), and must have been available for work during the reference week. (A direct question on availability was added in 1994.) These changes were made because the NCEUS and others felt that the previous definition of discouraged workers was too subjective, relying mainly on an individual's stated desire for a job and not on prior testing of the labor market.

3) Similarly, the identification of persons employed part-time for economic reasons (working less than 35 hours during the reference week because of poor business conditions or an inability to find full-time work) was tightened by adding two new criteria for persons who usually work part-time: these persons must now want and be available for full-time work. (Persons who usually work full-time but worked part-time for economic reasons during the reference week are assumed to meet these criteria.)

4) Specific questions were added about the expectation of recall for persons who indicate that they are on layoff. To be classified as "on temporary layoff," persons must expect to be recalled to their jobs.

Comparability of Labor Force Levels

In addition to the refinements in concepts, definitions, and methods made over the years, other changes—made to improve the accuracy of the estimates—have also affected the comparability of the labor force data. The most important of these changes is the adjustment of the population totals as a result of new information from the decennial censuses. It is also crucial to correct for estimating errors during the intercensal years.

Beginning in January 1997, updated information on the demographic characteristics of immigrants and emigrants was introduced. This increased the overall population by about 470,000, the labor force by about 320,000, and employment by about 290,000, with similar upward adjustments for Hispanics. Unemployment and other percentage rates were not affected.

Beginning in January 1998, new estimating procedures were introduced, which reduced labor force by about 229,000 and employment by about 256,000. However, these new procedures raised unemployment by about 27,000. New information about immigration and emigration was also incorporated, which increased the Hispanic population by about 57,000. Unemployment rates were not significantly affected.

Beginning in January 1999, new information on immigration raised the population by about 310,000, with differing impacts on different demographic groups. The population of men was lowered by about 185,000, but the population of women was raised by about 490,000. The Hispanic population was lowered by about 165,000 while the rest of the population was raised by about 470,000. Hispanic labor force and employment estimates were each reduced by over 200,000. The impact on unemployment rates and other percentages was small.

Beginning in January 2003, several other changes were introduced into the CPS. These changes included the following:

1) Population controls that reflected the results of the 2000 census were introduced into the monthly CPS estimation process. These new population size controls substantially increased the size of the civilian noninstitutional population and the civilian labor force. Data from January 2000 through December 2002 were revised to reflect the higher population estimates from the 2000 census and the higher rates of population growth since the census. The entire amount of this adjustment was added to the labor force data in January 2003, resulting in the increases of about 941,000 to the civilian noninstitutional population and about 614,000 to the civilian labor force. The unemployment rate and other ratios were not substantially affected by either of these population control adjustments.

2) Questions on race and Hispanic origin were modified to comply with the new standards for maintaining, collecting, and presenting federal data on race and ethnicity for federal statistical agencies. The questions were reworded to indicate that individuals could select more than once race category and to convey more clearly that individuals should report their own perception of what race is. These changes had no impact on the overall civilian noninstitutional population and civilian labor force. However, they did reduce the population and labor force levels of Whites, Blacks, and Asians beginning in January 2003.

3) Improvements were introduced to both the second stage and composite weighting procedures. These changes adapted the weighting procedures to the new race/ethnic

classification system and enhanced the stability over time for demographic groups. The second-stage weighting procedure substantially reduced the variability of estimates and corrected, to some extent, for CPS underreporting.

Changes in the Occupational and Industrial Classification System

Beginning in January 1983, the occupational and industrial classification systems used in the 1980 census were introduced into the CPS. The 1980 census occupational classification system was so radically different in concepts and nomenclature from the 1970 system that comparisons of historical data are not possible without major adjustments.

The industrial classification system used in the 1980 census was based on the 1972 Standard Industrial Classification (SIC) system, as modified in 1977. The adoption of the new industrial system had much less of an adverse effect on historical comparability than did the new occupational system.

Beginning in January 1992, the occupational and industrial classification systems used in the 1990 census were introduced into the CPS. There were a few breaks in comparability between the 1980 and 1990 census–based sys-

tems, particularly within the technical, sales, and administrative support categories. The most notable changes in industry classification were the shift of several industries from business services to professional services and the splitting of some industries into smaller, more detailed categories.

In January 2003, the CPS adopted the 2002 census industry and occupational classification systems, which were derived, respectively, from the 2002 North American Industry Classification System (NAICS) and the 2000 Standard Occupational Classification (SOC) system. The introduction of the new industry and occupational classification systems created a complete break in comparability at all levels of industry and occupation aggregation. For more information about the January 2003 change in the CPS classification systems, see the BLS Web site at <http://www.bls.gov/cps/cpsoccind.htm>.

Sources of Additional Information

A complete description of sampling and estimation procedures and further information on the impact of historical changes in the surveys can be found in the updated version of Chapter 1 of the *BLS Handbook of Methods*. This can be found on the BLS Web site at <http://www.bls.gov/>.

Table 1-1. Employment Status of the Civilian Noninstitutional Population, 1947–2006

(Thousands of people, percent.)

Year	Civilian noninstitutional population	Civilian labor force								Not in labor force
		Total	Participation rate	Employed				Unemployed		
				Total	Percent of population	Agriculture	Nonagricultural industries	Number	Unemployment rate	
1947	101 827	59 350	58.3	57 038	56.0	7 890	49 148	2 311	3.9	42 477
1948	103 068	60 621	58.8	58 343	56.6	7 629	50 714	2 276	3.8	42 447
1949	103 994	61 286	58.9	57 651	55.4	7 658	49 993	3 637	5.9	42 708
1950	104 995	62 208	59.2	58 918	56.1	7 160	51 758	3 288	5.3	42 787
1951	104 621	62 017	59.2	59 961	57.3	6 726	53 235	2 055	3.3	42 604
1952	105 231	62 138	59.0	60 250	57.3	6 500	53 749	1 883	3.0	43 093
1953[1]	107 056	63 015	58.9	61 179	57.1	6 260	54 919	1 834	2.9	44 041
1954	108 321	63 643	58.8	60 109	55.5	6 205	53 904	3 532	5.5	44 678
1955	109 683	65 023	59.3	62 170	56.7	6 450	55 722	2 852	4.4	44 660
1956	110 954	66 552	60.0	63 799	57.5	6 283	57 514	2 750	4.1	44 402
1957	112 265	66 929	59.6	64 071	57.1	5 947	58 123	2 859	4.3	45 336
1958	113 727	67 639	59.5	63 036	55.4	5 586	57 450	4 602	6.8	46 088
1959	115 329	68 369	59.3	64 630	56.0	5 565	59 065	3 740	5.5	46 960
1960[1]	117 245	69 628	59.4	65 778	56.1	5 458	60 318	3 852	5.5	47 617
1961	118 771	70 459	59.3	65 746	55.4	5 200	60 546	4 714	6.7	48 312
1962[1]	120 153	70 614	58.8	66 702	55.5	4 944	61 759	3 911	5.5	49 539
1963	122 416	71 833	58.7	67 762	55.4	4 687	63 076	4 070	5.7	50 583
1964	124 485	73 091	58.7	69 305	55.7	4 523	64 782	3 786	5.2	51 394
1965	126 513	74 455	58.9	71 088	56.2	4 361	66 726	3 366	4.5	52 058
1966	128 058	75 770	59.2	72 895	56.9	3 979	68 915	2 875	3.8	52 288
1967	129 874	77 347	59.6	74 372	57.3	3 844	70 527	2 975	3.8	52 527
1968	132 028	78 737	59.6	75 920	57.5	3 817	72 103	2 817	3.6	53 291
1969	134 335	80 734	60.1	77 902	58.0	3 606	74 296	2 832	3.5	53 602
1970	137 085	82 771	60.4	78 678	57.4	3 463	75 215	4 093	4.9	54 315
1971	140 216	84 382	60.2	79 367	56.6	3 394	75 972	5 016	5.9	55 834
1972[1]	144 126	87 034	60.4	82 153	57.0	3 484	78 669	4 882	5.6	57 091
1973[1]	147 096	89 429	60.8	85 064	57.8	3 470	81 594	4 365	4.9	57 667
1974	150 120	91 949	61.3	86 794	57.8	3 515	83 279	5 156	5.6	58 171
1975	153 153	93 774	61.2	85 846	56.1	3 408	82 438	7 929	8.5	59 377
1976	156 150	96 158	61.6	88 752	56.8	3 331	85 421	7 406	7.7	59 991
1977	159 033	99 008	62.3	92 017	57.9	3 283	88 734	6 991	7.1	60 025
1978[1]	161 910	102 250	63.2	96 048	59.3	3 387	92 661	6 202	6.1	59 659
1979	164 863	104 962	63.7	98 824	59.9	3 347	95 477	6 137	5.8	59 900
1980	167 745	106 940	63.8	99 302	59.2	3 364	95 938	7 637	7.1	60 806
1981	170 130	108 670	63.9	100 397	59.0	3 368	97 030	8 273	7.6	61 460
1982	172 271	110 204	64.0	99 526	57.8	3 401	96 125	10 678	9.7	62 067
1983	174 215	111 550	64.0	100 834	57.9	3 383	97 450	10 717	9.6	62 665
1984	176 383	113 544	64.4	105 005	59.5	3 321	101 685	8 539	7.5	62 839
1985	178 206	115 461	64.8	107 150	60.1	3 179	103 971	8 312	7.2	62 744
1986[1]	180 587	117 834	65.3	109 597	60.7	3 163	106 434	8 237	7.0	62 752
1987	182 753	119 865	65.6	112 440	61.5	3 208	109 232	7 425	6.2	62 888
1988	184 613	121 669	65.9	114 968	62.3	3 169	111 800	6 701	5.5	62 944
1989	186 393	123 869	66.5	117 342	63.0	3 199	114 142	6 528	5.3	62 523
1990[1]	189 164	125 840	66.5	118 793	62.8	3 223	115 570	7 047	5.6	63 324
1991	190 925	126 346	66.2	117 718	61.7	3 269	114 449	8 628	6.8	64 578
1992	192 805	128 105	66.4	118 492	61.5	3 247	115 245	9 613	7.5	64 700
1993	194 838	129 200	66.3	120 259	61.7	3 115	117 144	8 940	6.9	65 638
1994[1]	196 814	131 056	66.6	123 060	62.5	3 409	119 651	7 996	6.1	65 758
1995	198 584	132 304	66.6	124 900	62.9	3 440	121 460	7 404	5.6	66 280
1996	200 591	133 943	66.8	126 708	63.2	3 443	123 264	7 236	5.4	66 647
1997[1]	203 133	136 297	67.1	129 558	63.8	3 399	126 159	6 739	4.9	66 836
1998[1]	205 220	137 673	67.1	131 463	64.1	3 378	128 085	6 210	4.5	67 547
1999[1]	207 753	139 368	67.1	133 488	64.3	3 281	130 207	5 880	4.2	68 385
2000[1]	212 577	142 583	67.1	136 891	64.4	2 464	134 427	5 692	4.0	69 994
2001	215 092	143 734	66.8	136 933	63.7	2 299	134 635	6 801	4.7	71 359
2002	217 570	144 863	66.6	136 485	62.7	2 311	134 174	8 378	5.8	72 707
2003[1]	221 168	146 510	66.2	137 736	62.3	2 275	135 461	8 774	6.0	74 658
2004[1]	223 357	147 401	66.0	139 252	62.3	2 232	137 020	8 149	5.5	75 956
2005[1]	226 082	149 320	66.0	141 730	62.7	2 197	139 532	7 591	5.1	76 762
2006[1]	228 815	151 428	66.2	144 427	63.1	2 206	142 221	7 001	4.6	77 387

[1]Not strictly comparable with data for prior years. See notes and definitions for information on historical comparability.

Table 1-2. Employment Status of the Civilian Noninstitutional Population, by Sex, 1970–2006

(Thousands of people, percent.)

Sex and year	Civilian noninstitutional population	Civilian labor force		Employed				Unemployed		Not in labor force
		Total	Participation rate	Total	Percent of population	Agriculture	Non-agricultural industries	Number	Unemployment rate	
Men										
1970	64 304	51 228	79.7	48 990	76.2	2 862	46 128	2 238	4.4	13 076
1971	65 942	52 180	79.1	49 390	74.9	2 795	46 595	2 789	5.3	13 762
1972[1]	67 835	53 555	78.9	50 896	75.0	2 849	48 047	2 659	5.0	14 280
1973[1]	69 292	54 624	78.8	52 349	75.5	2 847	49 502	2 275	4.2	14 667
1974	70 808	55 739	78.7	53 024	74.9	2 919	50 105	2 714	4.9	15 069
1975	72 291	56 299	77.9	51 857	71.7	2 824	49 032	4 442	7.9	15 993
1976	73 759	57 174	77.5	53 138	72.0	2 744	50 394	4 036	7.1	16 585
1977	75 193	58 396	77.7	54 728	72.8	2 671	52 057	3 667	6.3	16 797
1978[1]	76 576	59 620	77.9	56 479	73.8	2 718	53 761	3 142	5.3	16 956
1979	78 020	60 726	77.8	57 607	73.8	2 686	54 921	3 120	5.1	17 293
1980	79 398	61 453	77.4	57 186	72.0	2 709	54 477	4 267	6.9	17 945
1981	80 511	61 974	77.0	57 397	71.3	2 700	54 697	4 577	7.4	18 537
1982	81 523	62 450	76.6	56 271	69.0	2 736	53 534	6 179	9.9	19 073
1983	82 531	63 047	76.4	56 787	68.8	2 704	54 083	6 260	9.9	19 484
1984	83 605	63 835	76.4	59 091	70.7	2 668	56 423	4 744	7.4	19 771
1985	84 469	64 411	76.3	59 891	70.9	2 535	57 356	4 521	7.0	20 058
1986[1]	85 798	65 422	76.3	60 892	71.0	2 511	58 381	4 530	6.9	20 376
1987	86 899	66 207	76.2	62 107	71.5	2 543	59 564	4 101	6.2	20 692
1988	87 857	66 927	76.2	63 273	72.0	2 493	60 780	3 655	5.5	20 930
1989	88 762	67 840	76.4	64 315	72.5	2 513	61 802	3 525	5.2	20 923
1990[1]	90 377	69 011	76.4	65 104	72.0	2 546	62 559	3 906	5.7	21 367
1991	91 278	69 168	75.8	64 223	70.4	2 589	61 634	4 946	7.2	22 110
1992	92 270	69 964	75.8	64 440	69.8	2 575	61 866	5 523	7.9	22 306
1993	93 332	70 404	75.4	65 349	70.0	2 478	62 871	5 055	7.2	22 927
1994[1]	94 354	70 817	75.1	66 450	70.4	2 554	63 896	4 367	6.2	23 538
1995	95 178	71 360	75.0	67 377	70.8	2 559	64 818	3 983	5.6	23 818
1996	96 206	72 086	74.9	68 207	70.9	2 573	65 634	3 880	5.4	24 119
1997[1]	97 715	73 261	75.0	69 685	71.3	2 552	67 133	3 577	4.9	24 454
1998[1]	98 758	73 959	74.9	70 693	71.6	2 553	68 140	3 266	4.4	24 799
1999[1]	99 722	74 512	74.7	71 446	71.6	2 432	69 014	3 066	4.1	25 210
2000[1]	101 964	76 280	74.8	73 305	71.9	1 861	71 444	2 975	3.9	25 684
2001	103 282	76 886	74.4	73 196	70.9	1 708	71 488	3 690	4.8	26 396
2002	104 585	77 500	74.1	72 903	69.7	1 724	71 179	4 597	5.9	27 085
2003[1]	106 435	78 238	73.5	73 332	68.9	1 695	71 636	4 906	6.3	28 197
2004[1]	107 710	78 980	73.3	74 524	69.2	1 687	72 838	4 456	5.6	28 730
2005[1]	109 151	80 033	73.3	75 973	69.6	1 654	74 319	4 059	5.1	29 119
2006[1]	110 605	81 255	73.5	77 502	70.1	1 663	75 838	3 753	4.6	29 350
Women										
1970	72 782	31 543	43.3	29 688	40.8	601	29 087	1 855	5.9	41 239
1971	74 274	32 202	43.4	29 976	40.4	599	29 377	2 227	6.9	42 072
1972[1]	76 290	33 479	43.9	31 257	41.0	635	30 622	2 222	6.6	42 811
1973[1]	77 804	34 804	44.7	32 715	42.0	622	32 093	2 089	6.0	43 000
1974	79 312	36 211	45.7	33 769	42.6	596	33 173	2 441	6.7	43 101
1975	80 860	37 475	46.3	33 989	42.0	584	33 404	3 486	9.3	43 386
1976	82 390	38 983	47.3	35 615	43.2	588	35 027	3 369	8.6	43 406
1977	83 840	40 613	48.4	37 289	44.5	612	36 677	3 324	8.2	43 227
1978[1]	85 334	42 631	50.0	39 569	46.4	669	38 900	3 061	7.2	42 703
1979	86 843	44 235	50.9	41 217	47.5	661	40 556	3 018	6.8	42 608
1980	88 348	45 487	51.5	42 117	47.7	656	41 461	3 370	7.4	42 861
1981	89 618	46 696	52.1	43 000	48.0	667	42 333	3 696	7.9	42 922
1982	90 748	47 755	52.6	43 256	47.7	665	42 591	4 499	9.4	42 993
1983	91 684	48 503	52.9	44 047	48.0	680	43 367	4 457	9.2	43 181
1984	92 778	49 709	53.6	45 915	49.5	653	45 262	3 794	7.6	43 068
1985	93 736	51 050	54.5	47 259	50.4	644	46 615	3 791	7.4	42 686
1986[1]	94 789	52 413	55.3	48 706	51.4	652	48 054	3 707	7.1	42 376
1987	95 853	53 658	56.0	50 334	52.5	666	49 668	3 324	6.2	42 195
1988	96 756	54 742	56.6	51 696	53.4	676	51 020	3 046	5.6	42 014
1989	97 630	56 030	57.4	53 027	54.3	687	52 341	3 003	5.4	41 601
1990[1]	98 787	56 829	57.5	53 689	54.3	678	53 011	3 140	5.5	41 957
1991	99 646	57 178	57.4	53 496	53.7	680	52 815	3 683	6.4	42 468
1992	100 535	58 141	57.8	54 052	53.8	672	53 380	4 090	7.0	42 394
1993	101 506	58 795	57.9	54 910	54.1	637	54 273	3 885	6.6	42 711
1994[1]	102 460	60 239	58.8	56 610	55.3	855	55 755	3 629	6.0	42 221
1995	103 406	60 944	58.9	57 523	55.6	881	56 642	3 421	5.6	42 462
1996	104 385	61 857	59.3	58 501	56.0	871	57 630	3 356	5.4	42 528
1997[1]	105 418	63 036	59.8	59 873	56.8	847	59 026	3 162	5.0	42 382
1998[1]	106 462	63 714	59.8	60 771	57.1	825	59 945	2 944	4.6	42 748
1999[1]	108 031	64 855	60.0	62 042	57.4	849	61 193	2 814	4.3	43 175
2000[1]	110 613	66 303	59.9	63 586	57.5	602	62 983	2 717	4.1	44 310
2001	111 811	66 848	59.8	63 737	57.0	591	63 147	3 111	4.7	44 962
2002	112 985	67 363	59.6	63 582	56.3	587	62 995	3 781	5.6	45 621
2003[1]	114 733	68 272	59.5	64 404	56.1	580	63 824	3 868	5.7	46 461
2004[1]	115 647	68 421	59.2	64 728	56.0	546	64 182	3 694	5.4	47 225
2005[1]	116 931	69 288	59.3	65 757	56.2	544	65 213	3 531	5.1	47 643
2006[1]	118 210	70 173	59.4	66 925	56.6	543	66 382	3 247	4.6	48 037

[1]Not strictly comparable with data for prior years. See notes and definitions for information on historical comparability.

Table 1-3. Employment Status of the Civilian Noninstitutional Population, by Sex, Age, Race, and Hispanic Origin, 1986–2006

(Thousands of people.)

Characteristic	1986	1987	1988	1989	1990	1991	1992	1993	1994	1995	1996
ALL RACES											
Both Sexes											
Civilian noninstitutional population	180 587	182 753	184 613	186 393	189 164	190 925	192 805	194 838	196 814	198 584	200 591
Civilian labor force	117 834	119 865	121 669	123 869	125 840	126 346	128 105	129 200	131 056	132 304	133 943
Employed	109 597	112 440	114 968	117 342	118 793	117 718	118 492	120 259	123 060	124 900	126 708
Agriculture	3 163	3 208	3 169	3 199	3 223	3 269	3 247	3 115	3 409	3 440	3 443
Nonagricultural industries	106 434	109 232	111 800	114 142	115 570	114 449	115 245	117 144	119 651	121 460	123 264
Unemployed	8 237	7 425	6 701	6 528	7 047	8 628	9 613	8 940	7 996	7 404	7 236
Not in labor force	62 752	62 888	62 944	62 523	63 324	64 578	64 700	65 638	65 758	66 280	66 647
Men, 16 Years and Over											
Civilian noninstitutional population	85 798	86 899	87 857	88 762	90 377	91 278	92 270	93 332	94 355	95 178	96 206
Civilian labor force	65 422	66 207	66 927	67 840	69 011	69 168	69 964	70 404	70 817	71 360	72 087
Employed	60 892	62 107	63 273	64 315	65 104	64 223	64 440	65 349	66 450	67 377	68 207
Agriculture	2 511	2 543	2 493	2 513	2 546	2 589	2 575	2 478	2 554	2 559	2 573
Nonagricultural industries	58 381	59 564	60 780	61 802	62 559	61 634	61 866	62 871	63 896	64 818	65 634
Unemployed	4 530	4 101	3 655	3 525	3 906	4 946	5 523	5 055	4 367	3 983	3 880
Not in labor force	20 376	20 692	20 930	20 923	21 367	22 110	22 306	22 927	23 538	23 818	24 119
Men, 20 Years and Over											
Civilian noninstitutional population	78 523	79 565	80 553	81 619	83 030	84 144	85 247	86 256	87 151	87 811	88 606
Civilian labor force	61 320	62 095	62 768	63 704	64 916	65 374	66 213	66 642	66 921	67 324	68 044
Employed	57 569	58 726	59 781	60 837	61 678	61 178	61 496	62 355	63 294	64 085	64 897
Agriculture	2 292	2 329	2 271	2 307	2 329	2 383	2 385	2 293	2 351	2 335	2 356
Nonagricultural industries	55 277	56 397	57 510	58 530	59 349	58 795	59 111	60 063	60 943	61 750	62 541
Unemployed	3 751	3 369	2 987	2 867	3 239	4 195	4 717	4 287	3 627	3 239	3 146
Not in labor force	17 203	17 470	17 785	17 915	18 114	18 770	19 034	19 613	20 230	20 487	20 563
Women, 16 Years and Over											
Civilian noninstitutional population	94 789	95 853	96 756	97 630	98 787	99 646	100 535	101 506	102 460	103 406	104 385
Civilian labor force	52 413	53 658	54 742	56 030	56 829	57 178	58 141	58 795	60 239	60 944	61 857
Employed	48 706	50 334	51 696	53 027	53 689	53 496	54 052	54 910	56 610	57 523	58 501
Agriculture	652	666	676	687	678	680	672	637	855	881	871
Nonagricultural industries	48 054	49 668	51 020	52 341	53 011	52 815	53 380	54 273	55 755	56 642	57 630
Unemployed	3 707	3 324	3 046	3 003	3 140	3 683	4 090	3 885	3 629	3 421	3 356
Not in labor force	42 376	42 195	42 014	41 601	41 957	42 468	42 394	42 711	42 221	42 462	42 528
Women, 20 Years and Over											
Civilian noninstitutional population	87 567	88 583	89 532	90 550	91 614	92 708	93 718	94 647	95 467	96 262	97 050
Civilian labor force	48 589	49 783	50 870	52 212	53 131	53 708	54 796	55 388	56 655	57 215	58 094
Employed	45 556	47 074	48 383	49 745	50 535	50 634	51 328	52 099	53 606	54 396	55 311
Agriculture	614	622	625	642	631	639	625	598	809	830	827
Nonagricultural industries	44 943	46 453	47 757	49 103	49 904	49 995	50 702	51 501	52 796	53 566	54 484
Unemployed	3 032	2 709	2 487	2 467	2 596	3 074	3 469	3 288	3 049	2 819	2 783
Not in labor force	38 979	38 800	38 662	38 339	38 483	39 000	38 922	39 260	38 813	39 047	38 956
Both Sexes, 16 to 19 Years											
Civilian noninstitutional population	14 496	14 606	14 527	14 223	14 520	14 073	13 840	13 935	14 196	14 511	14 934
Civilian labor force	7 926	7 988	8 031	7 954	7 792	7 265	7 096	7 170	7 481	7 765	7 806
Employed	6 472	6 640	6 805	6 759	6 581	5 906	5 669	5 805	6 161	6 419	6 500
Agriculture	258	258	273	250	264	247	237	224	249	275	261
Nonagricultural industries	6 215	6 382	6 532	6 510	6 317	5 659	5 432	5 580	5 912	6 144	6 239
Unemployed	1 454	1 347	1 226	1 194	1 212	1 359	1 427	1 365	1 320	1 346	1 306
Not in labor force	6 570	6 618	6 497	6 270	6 727	6 808	6 745	6 765	6 715	6 746	7 128
WHITE[1]											
Both Sexes											
Civilian noninstitutional population	155 432	156 958	158 194	159 338	160 625	161 759	162 972	164 289	165 555	166 914	168 317
Civilian labor force	101 801	103 290	104 756	106 355	107 447	107 743	108 837	109 700	111 082	111 950	113 108
Employed	95 660	97 789	99 812	101 584	102 261	101 182	101 669	103 045	105 190	106 490	107 808
Agriculture	2 958	2 986	2 965	2 996	2 998	3 026	3 018	2 895	3 162	3 194	3 276
Nonagricultural industries	92 703	94 803	96 846	98 588	99 263	98 157	98 650	100 150	102 027	103 296	104 532
Unemployed	6 140	5 501	4 944	4 770	5 186	6 560	7 169	6 655	5 892	5 459	5 300
Not in labor force	53 631	53 669	53 349	52 983	53 178	54 061	54 135	54 589	54 473	54 965	55 209
Men, 16 Years and Over											
Civilian noninstitutional population	74 390	75 189	75 855	76 468	77 369	77 977	78 651	79 371	80 059	80 733	81 489
Civilian labor force	57 217	57 779	58 317	58 988	59 638	59 656	60 168	60 484	60 727	61 146	61 783
Employed	53 785	54 647	55 550	56 352	56 703	55 797	55 959	56 656	57 452	58 146	58 888
Agriculture	2 340	2 354	2 318	2 345	2 353	2 384	2 378	2 286	2 347	2 347	2 436
Nonagricultural industries	51 444	52 293	53 232	54 007	54 350	53 413	53 580	54 370	55 104	55 800	56 452
Unemployed	3 433	3 132	2 766	2 636	2 935	3 859	4 209	3 828	3 275	2 999	2 896
Not in labor force	17 173	17 410	17 538	17 480	17 731	18 321	18 484	18 887	19 332	19 587	19 706
Men, 20 Years and Over											
Civilian noninstitutional population	68 413	69 175	69 887	70 654	71 457	72 274	73 040	73 721	74 311	74 879	75 454
Civilian labor force	53 675	54 232	54 734	55 441	56 116	56 387	56 976	57 284	57 411	57 719	58 340
Employed	50 818	51 649	52 466	53 292	53 685	53 103	53 357	54 021	54 676	55 254	55 977
Agriculture	2 131	2 150	2 104	2 149	2 148	2 192	2 197	2 114	2 151	2 132	2 224
Nonagricultural industries	48 687	49 499	50 362	51 143	51 537	50 912	51 160	51 907	52 525	53 122	53 753
Unemployed	2 857	2 584	2 268	2 149	2 431	3 284	3 620	3 263	2 735	2 465	2 363
Not in labor force	14 738	14 942	15 153	15 213	15 340	15 887	16 064	16 436	16 900	17 161	17 114

[1]Beginning in 2003, persons who selected this race group only; persons who selected more than one race group are not included. Prior to 2003, persons who reported more than one race group were included in the group they identified as the main race.

Table 1-3. Employment Status of the Civilian Noninstitutional Population, by Sex, Age, Race, and Hispanic Origin, 1986–2006—Continued

(Thousands of people.)

Characteristic	1997	1998	1999	2000	2001	2002	2003	2004	2005	2006
ALL RACES										
Both Sexes										
Civilian noninstitutional population	203 133	205 220	207 753	212 577	215 092	217 570	221 168	223 357	226 082	228 815
Civilian labor force	136 297	137 673	139 368	142 583	143 734	144 863	146 510	147 401	149 320	151 428
Employed	129 558	131 463	133 488	136 891	136 933	136 485	137 736	139 252	141 730	144 427
Agriculture	3 399	3 378	3 281	2 464	2 299	2 311	2 275	2 232	2 197	2 206
Nonagricultural industries	126 159	128 085	130 207	134 427	134 635	134 174	135 461	137 020	139 532	142 221
Unemployed	6 739	6 210	5 880	5 692	6 801	8 378	8 774	8 149	7 591	7 001
Not in labor force	66 837	67 547	68 385	69 994	71 359	72 707	74 658	75 956	76 762	77 387
Men, 16 Years and Over										
Civilian noninstitutional population	97 715	98 758	99 722	101 964	103 282	104 585	106 435	107 710	109 151	110 605
Civilian labor force	73 261	73 959	74 512	76 280	76 886	77 500	78 238	78 980	80 033	81 255
Employed	69 685	70 693	71 446	73 305	73 196	72 903	73 332	74 524	75 973	77 502
Agriculture	2 552	2 553	2 432	1 861	1 708	1 724	1 695	1 688	1 654	1 663
Nonagricultural industries	67 133	68 140	69 014	71 444	71 488	71 179	71 636	72 836	74 319	75 838
Unemployed	3 577	3 266	3 066	2 975	3 690	4 597	4 906	4 456	4 059	3 753
Not in labor force	24 454	24 799	25 210	25 684	26 396	27 085	28 197	28 730	29 119	29 350
Men, 20 Years and Over										
Civilian noninstitutional population	89 879	90 790	91 555	93 875	95 181	96 439	98 272	99 476	100 835	102 145
Civilian labor force	69 166	69 715	70 194	72 010	72 816	73 630	74 623	75 364	76 443	77 562
Employed	66 284	67 135	67 761	69 634	69 776	69 734	70 415	71 572	73 050	74 431
Agriculture	2 356	2 350	2 244	1 756	1 613	1 629	1 614	1 596	1 577	1 579
Nonagricultural industries	63 927	64 785	65 517	67 878	68 163	68 104	68 801	69 976	71 473	72 852
Unemployed	2 882	2 580	2 433	2 376	3 040	3 896	4 209	3 791	3 392	3 131
Not in labor force	20 713	21 075	21 362	21 864	22 365	22 809	23 649	24 113	24 392	24 584
Women, 16 Years and Over										
Civilian noninstitutional population	105 418	106 462	108 031	110 613	111 811	112 985	114 733	115 647	116 931	118 210
Civilian labor force	63 036	63 714	64 855	66 303	66 848	67 363	68 272	68 421	69 288	70 173
Employed	59 873	60 771	62 042	63 586	63 737	63 582	64 404	64 728	65 757	66 925
Agriculture	847	825	849	602	591	587	580	547	544	543
Nonagricultural industries	59 026	59 945	61 193	62 983	63 147	62 995	63 824	64 181	65 213	66 382
Unemployed	3 162	2 944	2 814	2 717	3 111	3 781	3 868	3 694	3 531	3 247
Not in labor force	42 382	42 748	43 175	44 310	44 962	45 621	46 461	47 225	47 643	48 037
Women, 20 Years and Over										
Civilian noninstitutional population	97 889	98 786	100 158	102 790	103 983	105 136	106 800	107 658	108 850	109 992
Civilian labor force	59 198	59 702	60 840	62 301	63 016	63 648	64 716	64 923	65 714	66 585
Employed	56 613	57 278	58 555	60 067	60 417	60 420	61 402	61 773	62 702	63 834
Agriculture	798	768	803	567	558	557	550	515	519	520
Nonagricultural industries	55 815	56 510	57 752	59 500	59 860	59 863	60 852	61 258	62 182	63 315
Unemployed	2 585	2 424	2 285	2 235	2 599	3 228	3 314	3 150	3 013	2 751
Not in labor force	38 691	39 084	39 318	40 488	40 967	41 488	42 083	42 735	43 136	43 407
Both Sexes, 16 to 19 Years										
Civilian noninstitutional population	15 365	15 644	16 040	15 912	15 929	15 994	16 096	16 222	16 398	16 678
Civilian labor force	7 932	8 256	8 333	8 271	7 902	7 585	7 170	7 114	7 164	7 281
Employed	6 661	7 051	7 172	7 189	6 740	6 332	5 919	5 907	5 978	6 162
Agriculture	244	261	234	141	128	124	111	121	100	108
Nonagricultural industries	6 417	6 790	6 938	7 049	6 611	6 207	5 808	5 786	5 877	6 054
Unemployed	1 271	1 205	1 162	1 081	1 162	1 253	1 251	1 208	1 186	1 119
Not in labor force	7 433	7 388	7 706	7 642	8 027	8 409	8 926	9 108	9 234	9 397
WHITE[1]										
Both Sexes										
Civilian noninstitutional population	169 993	171 478	173 085	176 220	178 111	179 783	181 292	182 643	184 446	186 264
Civilian labor force	114 693	115 415	116 509	118 545	119 399	120 150	120 546	121 086	122 299	123 834
Employed	109 856	110 931	112 235	114 424	114 430	114 013	114 235	115 239	116 949	118 833
Agriculture	3 208	3 160	3 083	2 320	2 174	2 171	2 148	2 103	2 077	2 063
Nonagricultural industries	106 648	107 770	109 152	112 104	112 256	111 841	112 087	113 136	114 872	116 769
Unemployed	4 836	4 484	4 273	4 121	4 969	6 137	6 311	5 847	5 350	5 002
Not in labor force	55 301	56 064	56 577	57 675	58 713	59 633	60 746	61 558	62 148	62 429
Men, 16 Years and Over										
Civilian noninstitutional population	82 577	83 352	83 930	85 370	86 452	87 361	88 249	89 044	90 027	91 021
Civilian labor force	62 639	63 034	63 413	64 466	64 966	65 308	65 509	65 994	66 694	67 613
Employed	59 998	60 604	61 139	62 289	62 212	61 849	61 866	62 712	63 763	64 883
Agriculture	2 389	2 376	2 273	1 743	1 606	1 611	1 597	1 583	1 562	1 554
Nonagricultural industries	57 608	58 228	58 866	60 546	60 606	60 238	60 269	61 129	62 201	63 330
Unemployed	2 641	2 431	2 274	2 177	2 754	3 459	3 643	3 282	2 931	2 730
Not in labor force	19 938	20 317	20 517	20 905	21 486	22 053	22 740	23 050	23 334	23 408
Men, 20 Years and Over										
Civilian noninstitutional population	76 320	76 966	77 432	78 966	80 029	80 922	81 860	82 615	83 556	84 466
Civilian labor force	59 126	59 421	59 747	60 850	61 519	62 067	62 473	62 944	63 705	64 540
Employed	56 986	57 500	57 934	59 119	59 245	59 124	59 348	60 159	61 255	62 259
Agriculture	2 201	2 182	2 094	1 640	1 512	1 519	1 517	1 495	1 488	1 473
Nonagricultural industries	54 785	55 319	55 839	57 479	57 733	57 605	57 831	58 664	59 767	60 785
Unemployed	2 140	1 920	1 813	1 731	2 275	2 943	3 125	2 785	2 450	2 281
Not in labor force	17 194	17 545	17 685	18 116	18 510	18 855	19 386	19 671	19 851	19 927

[1]Beginning in 2003, persons who selected this race group only; persons who selected more than one race group are not included. Prior to 2003, persons who reported more than one race group were included in the group they identified as the main race.

Table 1-3. Employment Status of the Civilian Noninstitutional Population, by Sex, Age, Race, and Hispanic Origin, 1986–2006—*Continued*

(Thousands of people.)

Characteristic	1986	1987	1988	1989	1990	1991	1992	1993	1994	1995	1996
WHITE[1]											
Women, 16 Years and Over											
Civilian noninstitutional population	81 042	81 769	82 340	82 871	83 256	83 781	84 321	84 918	85 496	86 181	86 828
Civilian labor force	44 584	45 510	46 439	47 367	47 809	48 087	48 669	49 216	50 356	50 804	51 325
Employed	41 876	43 142	44 262	45 232	45 558	45 385	45 710	46 390	47 738	48 344	48 920
Agriculture	617	632	648	651	645	641	640	609	815	847	840
Nonagricultural industries	41 259	42 509	43 614	44 581	44 913	44 744	45 070	45 780	46 923	47 497	48 080
Unemployed	2 708	2 369	2 177	2 135	2 251	2 701	2 959	2 827	2 617	2 460	2 404
Not in labor force	36 458	36 258	35 901	35 504	35 447	35 695	35 651	35 702	35 141	35 377	35 503
Women, 20 Years and Over											
Civilian noninstitutional population	75 140	75 845	76 470	77 154	77 539	78 285	78 928	79 490	79 980	80 567	81 041
Civilian labor force	41 264	42 164	43 081	44 105	44 648	45 111	45 839	46 311	47 314	47 686	48 162
Employed	39 050	40 242	41 316	42 346	42 796	42 862	43 327	43 910	45 116	45 643	46 164
Agriculture	580	590	599	608	598	601	594	572	772	799	798
Nonagricultural industries	38 471	39 652	40 717	41 738	42 198	42 261	42 733	43 339	44 344	44 844	45 366
Unemployed	2 213	1 922	1 766	1 758	1 852	2 248	2 512	2 400	2 197	2 042	1 998
Not in labor force	33 876	33 681	33 389	33 050	32 891	33 174	33 089	33 179	32 666	32 881	32 879
Both Sexes, 16 to 19 Years											
Civilian noninstitutional population	11 879	11 939	11 838	11 530	11 630	11 200	11 004	11 078	11 264	11 468	11 822
Civilian labor force	6 862	6 893	6 940	6 809	6 683	6 245	6 022	6 105	6 357	6 545	6 607
Employed	5 792	5 898	6 030	5 946	5 779	5 216	4 985	5 113	5 398	5 593	5 667
Agriculture	247	246	263	239	252	233	228	209	239	262	254
Nonagricultural industries	5 545	5 652	5 767	5 707	5 528	4 984	4 757	4 904	5 158	5 331	5 413
Unemployed	1 070	995	910	863	903	1 029	1 037	992	960	952	939
Not in labor force	5 017	5 045	4 897	4 721	4 947	4 955	4 982	4 973	4 907	4 923	5 215
BLACK[1]											
Both Sexes											
Civilian noninstitutional population	19 989	20 352	20 692	21 021	21 477	21 799	22 147	22 521	22 879	23 246	23 604
Civilian labor force	12 654	12 993	13 205	13 497	13 740	13 797	14 162	14 225	14 502	14 817	15 134
Employed	10 814	11 309	11 658	11 953	12 175	12 074	12 151	12 382	12 835	13 279	13 542
Agriculture	155	164	153	150	142	160	153	143	136	101	98
Nonagricultural industries	10 659	11 145	11 505	11 803	12 034	11 914	11 997	12 239	12 699	13 178	13 444
Unemployed	1 840	1 684	1 547	1 544	1 565	1 723	2 011	1 844	1 666	1 538	1 592
Not in labor force	7 335	7 359	7 487	7 524	7 737	8 002	7 985	8 296	8 377	8 429	8 470
Men, 16 Years and Over											
Civilian noninstitutional population	8 956	9 128	9 289	9 439	9 573	9 725	9 896	10 083	10 258	10 411	10 575
Civilian labor force	6 373	6 486	6 596	6 701	6 802	6 851	6 997	7 019	7 089	7 183	7 264
Employed	5 428	5 661	5 824	5 928	5 995	5 961	5 930	6 047	6 241	6 422	6 456
Agriculture	133	142	133	127	124	139	138	128	118	93	86
Nonagricultural industries	5 295	5 519	5 691	5 802	5 872	5 822	5 791	5 919	6 122	6 329	6 371
Unemployed	946	826	771	773	806	890	1 067	971	848	762	808
Not in labor force	2 583	2 642	2 694	2 738	2 772	2 874	2 899	3 064	3 169	3 228	3 311
Men, 20 Years and Over											
Civilian noninstitutional population	7 907	8 063	8 063	8 215	8 364	8 479	8 652	8 840	9 171	9 280	9 414
Civilian labor force	5 915	6 023	6 023	6 127	6 221	6 357	6 451	6 568	6 646	6 730	6 806
Employed	5 150	5 357	5 357	5 509	5 602	5 692	5 706	5 681	5 964	6 137	6 167
Agriculture	125	135	135	129	119	117	131	131	115	89	83
Nonagricultural industries	5 025	5 222	5 222	5 381	5 483	5 576	5 575	5 550	5 849	6 048	6 084
Unemployed	765	666	666	617	619	664	745	886	682	593	639
Not in labor force	1 991	2 040	2 040	2 089	2 143	2 122	2 202	801	2 525	2 550	2 608
Women, 16 Years and Over											
Civilian noninstitutional population	11 033	11 224	11 402	11 582	11 904	12 074	12 251	12 438	12 621	12 835	13 029
Civilian labor force	6 281	6 507	6 609	6 796	6 938	6 946	7 166	7 206	7 413	7 634	7 869
Employed	5 386	5 648	5 834	6 025	6 180	6 113	6 221	6 334	6 595	6 857	7 086
Agriculture	22	22	20	24	18	21	15	15	18	8	13
Nonagricultural industries	5 364	5 626	5 814	6 001	6 162	6 092	6 206	6 320	6 577	6 849	7 073
Unemployed	894	858	776	772	758	833	944	872	818	777	784
Not in labor force	4 752	4 717	4 793	4 786	4 965	5 129	5 086	5 231	5 208	5 201	5 159
Women, 20 Years and Over											
Civilian noninstitutional population	9 945	10 126	10 298	10 482	10 760	10 959	11 152	11 332	11 496	11 682	11 833
Civilian labor force	5 855	6 071	6 190	6 352	6 517	6 572	6 778	6 824	7 004	7 175	7 405
Employed	5 128	5 365	5 548	5 727	5 884	5 874	5 978	6 095	6 320	6 556	6 762
Agriculture	22	20	18	23	18	20	15	14	17	7	12
Nonagricultural industries	5 106	5 345	5 530	5 703	5 867	5 853	5 963	6 081	6 303	6 548	6 749
Unemployed	728	706	642	625	633	698	800	729	685	620	643
Not in labor force	4 090	4 054	4 108	4 130	4 243	4 388	4 374	4 508	4 492	4 507	4 428
Both Sexes, 16 to 19 Years											
Civilian noninstitutional population	2 137	2 163	2 179	2 176	2 238	2 187	2 155	2 181	2 211	2 284	2 356
Civilian labor force	883	899	889	925	866	774	816	807	852	911	923
Employed	536	587	601	625	598	494	492	494	552	586	613
Agriculture	8	9	7	8	7	8	7	7	9	1	3
Nonagricultural industries	529	578	594	617	591	486	485	485	547	581	611
Unemployed	347	312	288	300	268	280	324	313	300	325	310
Not in labor force	1 254	1 264	1 291	1 251	1 372	1 413	1 339	1 374	1 360	1 372	1 434

[1]Beginning in 2003, persons who selected this race group only; persons who selected more than one race group are not included. Prior to 2003, persons who reported more than one race group were included in the group they identified as the main race.

Table 1-3. Employment Status of the Civilian Noninstitutional Population, by Sex, Age, Race, and Hispanic Origin, 1986–2006—Continued

(Thousands of people.)

Characteristic	1997	1998	1999	2000	2001	2002	2003	2004	2005	2006
WHITE[1]										
Women, 16 Years and Over										
Civilian noninstitutional population	87 417	88 126	89 156	90 850	91 660	92 422	93 043	93 599	94 419	95 242
Civilian labor force	52 054	52 380	53 096	54 079	54 433	54 842	55 037	55 092	55 605	56 221
Employed	49 859	50 327	51 096	52 136	52 218	52 164	52 369	52 527	53 186	53 950
Agriculture	819	784	810	578	568	560	551	520	515	510
Nonagricultural industries	49 040	49 543	50 286	51 558	51 650	51 604	51 818	52 007	52 672	53 440
Unemployed	2 195	2 053	1 999	1 944	2 215	2 678	2 668	2 565	2 419	2 271
Not in labor force	35 363	35 746	36 060	36 770	37 227	37 581	38 006	38 508	38 814	39 021
Women, 20 Years and Over										
Civilian noninstitutional population	81 492	82 073	82 953	84 718	85 526	86 266	86 905	87 430	88 200	88 942
Civilian labor force	48 847	49 029	49 714	50 740	51 218	51 717	52 099	52 212	52 643	53 286
Employed	47 063	47 342	48 098	49 145	49 369	49 448	49 823	50 040	50 589	51 359
Agriculture	771	729	765	546	537	532	522	488	492	488
Nonagricultural industries	46 292	46 612	47 333	48 599	48 831	48 916	49 301	49 552	50 097	50 871
Unemployed	1 784	1 688	1 616	1 595	1 849	2 269	2 276	2 172	2 054	1 927
Not in labor force	32 645	33 044	33 239	33 978	34 308	34 548	34 806	35 218	35 557	35 656
Both Sexes, 16 to 19 Years										
Civilian noninstitutional population	12 181	12 439	12 700	12 535	12 556	12 596	12 527	12 599	12 690	12 856
Civilian labor force	6 720	6 965	7 048	6 955	6 661	6 366	5 973	5 929	5 950	6 009
Employed	5 807	6 089	6 204	6 160	5 817	5 441	5 064	5 039	5 105	5 215
Agriculture	236	250	224	135	125	121	109	116	97	102
Nonagricultural industries	5 571	5 839	5 980	6 025	5 692	5 320	4 955	4 923	5 008	5 113
Unemployed	912	876	844	795	845	925	909	890	845	794
Not in labor force	5 462	5 475	5 652	5 581	5 894	6 230	6 554	6 669	6 739	6 847
BLACK[1]										
Both Sexes										
Civilian noninstitutional population	24 003	24 373	24 855	24 902	25 138	25 578	25 686	26 065	26 517	27 007
Civilian labor force	15 529	15 982	16 365	16 397	16 421	16 565	16 526	16 638	17 013	17 314
Employed	13 969	14 556	15 056	15 156	15 006	14 872	14 739	14 909	15 313	15 765
Agriculture	117	138	117	77	62	69	63	50	51	60
Nonagricultural industries	13 852	14 417	14 939	15 079	14 944	14 804	14 676	14 859	15 261	15 705
Unemployed	1 560	1 426	1 309	1 241	1 416	1 693	1 787	1 729	1 700	1 549
Not in labor force	8 474	8 391	8 490	8 505	8 717	9 013	9 161	9 428	9 504	9 693
Men, 16 Years and Over										
Civilian noninstitutional population	10 763	10 927	11 143	11 129	11 172	11 391	11 454	11 656	11 882	12 130
Civilian labor force	7 354	7 542	7 652	7 702	7 647	7 794	7 711	7 773	7 998	8 128
Employed	6 607	6 871	7 027	7 082	6 938	6 959	6 820	6 912	7 155	7 354
Agriculture	103	118	99	67	56	63	52	43	43	51
Nonagricultural industries	6 504	6 752	6 952	7 015	6 882	6 896	6 768	6 869	7 111	7 303
Unemployed	747	671	671	620	709	835	891	860	844	774
Not in labor force	3 409	3 386	3 386	3 427	3 525	3 597	3 743	3 884	3 884	4 002
Men, 20 Years and Over										
Civilian noninstitutional population	9 575	9 727	9 926	9 952	9 993	10 196	10 278	11 656	10 659	10 864
Civilian labor force	6 910	7 053	7 182	7 240	7 200	7 347	7 346	7 773	7 600	7 720
Employed	6 325	6 530	6 702	6 741	6 627	6 652	6 586	6 912	6 901	7 079
Agriculture	101	112	96	67	55	62	51	274	43	49
Nonagricultural industries	6 224	6 418	6 606	6 675	55	6 591	6 535	6 638	6 858	7 030
Unemployed	585	524	480	499	573	695	760	860	699	640
Not in labor force	2 665	2 673	2 743	2 711	2 792	2 848	2 932	3 884	3 060	3 144
Women, 16 Years and Over										
Civilian noninstitutional population	13 241	13 446	13 711	13 772	13 966	14 187	14 232	14 409	14 635	14 877
Civilian labor force	8 175	8 441	8 713	8 695	8 774	8 772	8 815	8 865	9 014	9 186
Employed	7 362	7 685	8 029	8 073	8 068	7 914	7 919	7 997	8 158	8 410
Agriculture	14	20	18	10	6	6	11	7	8	9
Nonagricultural industries	7 348	7 665	8 011	8 064	8 062	7 907	7 908	7 990	8 150	8 402
Unemployed	813	756	684	621	706	858	895	868	856	775
Not in labor force	5 066	5 005	4 999	5 078	5 192	5 415	5 418	5 544	5 621	5 691
Women, 20 Years and Over										
Civilian noninstitutional population	12 016	12 023	12 451	12 561	12 758	12 966	13 026	14 409	13 377	13 578
Civilian labor force	7 686	7 912	8 224	8 215	8 323	8 348	8 409	8 865	8 610	8 723
Employed	7 013	7 290	7 663	7 703	7 741	7 610	7 636	7 997	7 876	8 068
Agriculture	13	19	17	9	6	5	10	7	7	7
Nonagricultural industries	7 000	7 272	7 646	7 694	7 735	7 604	7 626	7 701	7 868	8 060
Unemployed	673	622	561	512	582	738	772	868	734	656
Not in labor force	4 330	4 291	4 226	4 346	4 434	4 618	4 618	5 544	4 768	4 854
Both Sexes, 16 to 19 Years										
Civilian noninstitutional population	2 412	2 443	2 479	2 389	2 388	2 416	2 382	2 423	2 481	2 565
Civilian labor force	933	1 017	959	941	898	870	771	762	803	871
Employed	631	736	691	711	637	611	516	520	536	618
Agriculture	3	8	4	1	1	2	1	0	1	3
Nonagricultural industries	611	728	687	710	637	609	515	520	535	614
Unemployed	310	281	268	230	260	260	255	241	267	253
Not in labor force	1 434	1 427	1 520	1 448	1 490	1 546	1 611	1 661	1 677	1 694

[1]Beginning in 2003, persons who selected this race group only; persons who selected more than one race group are not included. Prior to 2003, persons who reported more than one race group were included in the group they identified as the main race.

Table 1-3. Employment Status of the Civilian Noninstitutional Population, by Sex, Age, Race, and Hispanic Origin, 1986–2006—*Continued*

(Thousands of people.)

Characteristic	1986	1987	1988	1989	1990	1991	1992	1993	1994	1995	1996
HISPANIC[2]											
Both Sexes											
Civilian noninstitutional population	12 344	12 867	13 325	13 791	15 904	16 425	16 961	17 532	18 117	18 629	19 213
Civilian labor force	8 076	8 541	8 982	9 323	10 720	10 920	11 338	11 610	11 975	12 267	12 774
Employed	7 219	7 790	8 250	8 573	9 845	9 828	10 027	10 361	10 788	11 127	11 642
Agriculture	329	398	407	440	517	512	524	523	560	604	609
Nonagricultural industries	6 890	7 391	7 843	8 133	9 328	9 315	9 503	9 838	10 227	10 524	11 033
Unemployed	857	751	732	750	876	1 092	1 311	1 248	1 187	1 140	1 132
Not in labor force	4 268	4 327	4 342	4 468	5 184	5 506	5 623	5 922	6 142	6 362	6 439
Men, 16 Years and Over											
Civilian noninstitutional population	6 106	6 371	6 604	6 825	8 041	8 296	8 553	8 824	9 104	9 329	9 604
Civilian labor force	4 948	5 163	5 409	5 595	6 546	6 664	6 900	7 076	7 210	7 376	7 646
Employed	4 428	4 713	4 972	5 172	6 021	5 979	6 093	6 328	6 530	6 725	7 039
Agriculture	287	351	356	393	449	453	468	469	494	527	537
Nonagricultural industries	4 140	4 361	4 616	4 779	5 572	5 526	5 625	5 860	6 036	6 198	6 502
Unemployed	520	451	437	423	524	685	807	747	680	651	607
Not in labor force	1 158	1 208	1 195	1 230	1 495	1 632	1 654	1 749	1 894	1 952	1 957
Men, 20 Years and Over											
Civilian noninstitutional population	5 451	5 700	5 921	6 114	7 126	7 392	7 655	7 930	8 178	8 375	8 611
Civilian labor force	4 612	4 818	5 031	5 195	6 034	6 198	6 432	6 621	6 747	6 898	7 150
Employed	4 174	4 444	4 680	4 853	5 609	5 623	5 757	5 992	6 189	6 367	6 655
Agriculture	263	327	327	366	415	419	437	441	466	501	510
Nonagricultural industries	3 911	4 118	4 353	4 487	5 195	5 204	5 320	5 551	5 722	5 866	6 145
Unemployed	438	374	351	342	425	575	675	629	558	530	495
Not in labor force	839	882	890	919	1 092	1 194	1 223	1 309	1 431	1 477	1 461
Women, 16 Years and Over											
Civilian noninstitutional population	6 238	6 496	6 721	6 965	7 863	8 130	8 408	8 708	9 014	9 300	9 610
Civilian labor force	3 128	3 377	3 573	3 728	4 174	4 256	4 439	4 534	4 765	4 891	5 128
Employed	2 791	3 077	3 278	3 401	3 823	3 848	3 934	4 033	4 258	4 403	4 602
Agriculture	42	47	51	48	68	59	57	55	66	76	72
Nonagricultural industries	2 749	3 030	3 227	3 353	3 755	3 789	3 877	3 978	4 191	4 326	4 531
Unemployed	337	300	296	327	351	407	504	501	508	488	525
Not in labor force	3 110	3 119	3 147	3 237	3 689	3 874	3 969	4 174	4 248	4 409	4 482
Women, 20 Years and Over											
Civilian noninstitutional population	5 591	5 835	6 050	6 278	7 041	7 301	7 569	7 846	8 122	8 382	8 654
Civilian labor force	3 112	3 281	3 448	3 857	3 941	4 110	4 218	4 421	4 520	4 779	5 106
Employed	2 615	2 872	3 047	3 172	3 567	3 603	3 693	3 800	3 989	4 116	4 341
Agriculture	39	45	49	44	62	53	51	49	61	72	69
Nonagricultural industries	2 576	2 827	2 998	3 128	3 505	3 549	3 642	3 751	3 928	4 044	4 272
Unemployed	278	241	234	276	289	339	418	418	431	404	438
Not in labor force	2 698	2 723	2 769	2 830	3 184	3 360	3 459	3 628	3 701	3 863	3 875
Both Sexes, 16 to 19 Years											
Civilian noninstitutional population	1 302	1 332	1 354	1 399	1 737	1 732	1 737	1 756	1 818	1 872	1 948
Civilian labor force	571	610	671	680	829	781	796	771	807	850	845
Employed	430	474	523	548	668	602	577	570	609	645	646
Agriculture	27	27	32	31	40	41	36	33	32	31	29
Nonagricultural industries	403	447	492	517	628	562	541	537	577	614	617
Unemployed	141	136	148	132	161	179	219	201	198	205	199
Not in labor force	730	722	683	719	907	951	941	985	1 010	1 022	1 103

[2]May be of any race.

Table 1-3. Employment Status of the Civilian Noninstitutional Population, by Sex, Age, Race, and Hispanic Origin, 1986–2006—*Continued*

(Thousands of people.)

Characteristic	1997	1998	1999	2000	2001	2002	2003	2004	2005	2006
HISPANIC[2]										
Both Sexes										
Civilian noninstitutional population	20 321	21 070	21 650	23 938	24 942	25 963	27 551	28 109	29 133	30 103
Civilian labor force	13 796	14 317	14 665	16 689	17 328	17 943	18 813	19 272	19 824	20 694
Employed	12 726	13 291	13 720	15 735	16 190	16 590	17 372	17 930	18 632	19 613
Agriculture	660	742	734	536	423	448	446	441	423	428
Nonagricultural industries	12 067	12 549	12 986	15 199	15 767	16 141	16 927	17 489	18 209	19 185
Unemployed	1 069	1 026	945	954	1 138	1 353	1 441	1 342	1 191	1 081
Not in labor force	6 526	6 753	6 985	7 249	7 614	8 020	8 738	8 837	9 310	9 409
Men, 16 Years and Over										
Civilian noninstitutional population	10 368	10 734	10 713	12 174	12 695	13 221	14 098	14 417	14 962	15 473
Civilian labor force	8 309	8 571	8 546	9 923	10 279	10 609	11 288	11 587	11 985	12 488
Employed	7 728	8 018	8 067	9 428	9 668	9 845	10 479	10 832	11 337	11 887
Agriculture	571	651	642	449	345	361	350	356	350	347
Nonagricultural industries	7 157	7 367	7 425	8 979	9 323	9 484	10 129	10 476	10 987	11 540
Unemployed	582	552	480	494	611	764	809	755	647	601
Not in labor force	2 059	2 164	2 167	2 252	2 416	2 613	2 810	2 831	2 977	2 985
Men, 20 Years and Over										
Civilian noninstitutional population	9 250	9 573	9 523	10 841	11 386	11 928	12 797	13 082	13 586	14 046
Civilian labor force	7 779	8 005	7 950	9 247	9 595	9 977	10 756	11 020	11 408	11 888
Employed	7 307	7 570	7 576	8 859	9 100	9 341	10 063	10 385	10 872	11 391
Agriculture	544	621	602	423	328	345	336	335	341	337
Nonagricultural industries	6 763	6 949	6 974	8 435	8 773	8 996	9 727	10 050	10 532	11 054
Unemployed	471	436	374	388	495	636	693	635	536	497
Not in labor force	1 471	1 568	1 573	1 595	1 791	1 951	2 041	2 061	2 177	2 157
Women, 16 Years and Over										
Civilian noninstitutional population	9 953	10 335	10 937	11 764	12 247	12 742	13 452	13 692	14 172	14 630
Civilian labor force	5 486	5 746	6 119	6 767	7 049	7 334	7 525	7 685	7 839	8 206
Employed	4 999	5 273	5 653	6 307	6 522	6 744	6 894	7 098	7 295	7 725
Agriculture	89	91	92	87	77	87	96	85	73	80
Nonagricultural industries	4 910	5 182	5 561	6 220	6 445	6 657	6 798	7 013	7 222	7 645
Unemployed	488	473	466	460	527	590	631	587	544	480
Not in labor force	4 466	4 589	4 819	4 997	5 198	5 408	5 928	6 007	6 333	6 424
Women, 20 Years and Over										
Civilian noninstitutional population	8 950	9 292	9 821	10 574	11 049	11 528	12 211	12 420	12 858	13 262
Civilian labor force	5 304	5 666	6 275	6 557	6 863	7 096	7 096	7 257	7 377	7 735
Employed	4 705	4 928	5 290	5 903	6 121	6 367	6 541	6 752	6 913	7 321
Agriculture	83	85	88	81	73	84	91	78	70	77
Nonagricultural industries	4 622	4 843	5 202	5 822	6 048	6 283	6 450	6 674	6 843	7 244
Unemployed	401	376	376	371	436	496	555	504	464	414
Not in labor force	3 845	3 988	4 155	4 299	4 492	4 666	5 114	5 163	5 481	5 527
Both Sexes, 16 to 19 Years										
Civilian noninstitutional population	2 121	2 204	2 307	2 523	2 508	2 507	2 543	2 608	2 689	2 796
Civilian labor force	911	1 007	1 049	1 168	1 176	1 103	960	995	1 038	1 071
Employed	714	793	854	973	969	882	768	792	847	900
Agriculture	33	36	45	31	22	19	19	25	13	14
Nonagricultural industries	682	757	809	942	947	863	749	767	834	887
Unemployed	197	214	196	194	208	221	192	203	191	170
Not in labor force	1 210	1 197	1 257	1 355	1 331	1 404	1 583	1 612	1 651	1 725

[2]May be of any race.

Table 1-4. Employment Status of the Civilian Noninstitutional Population, by Sex, Race, and Marital Status, 1985–2006

(Thousands of people.)

Race, marital status, and year	Men				Women			
	Civilian noninstitutional population	Civilian labor force			Civilian noninstitutional population	Civilian labor force		
		Total	Employed	Unemployed		Total	Employed	Unemployed
ALL RACES								
Single								
1985	23 328	17 208	15 022	2 186	19 768	13 163	11 758	1 404
1986	23 662	17 553	15 407	2 146	20 113	13 512	12 071	1 442
1987	23 947	17 772	15 794	1 978	20 596	13 885	12 561	1 323
1988	24 572	18 345	16 521	1 824	20 961	14 194	12 979	1 215
1989	24 831	18 738	16 936	1 801	21 141	14 377	13 175	1 202
1990	25 870	19 357	17 405	1 952	21 901	14 612	13 336	1 276
1991	26 197	19 411	17 011	2 400	22 173	14 681	13 198	1 482
1992	26 436	19 709	17 098	2 611	22 475	14 872	13 263	1 609
1993	26 570	19 706	17 261	2 445	22 713	15 031	13 484	1 547
1994	26 786	19 786	17 604	2 181	23 000	15 333	13 847	1 486
1995	26 918	19 841	17 833	2 007	23 151	15 467	14 053	1 413
1996	27 387	20 071	18 055	2 016	23 623	15 842	14 403	1 439
1997	28 311	20 689	18 783	1 906	24 285	16 492	15 037	1 455
1998	28 693	21 037	19 240	1 798	24 941	17 087	15 755	1 332
1999	29 104	21 351	19 686	1 665	25 576	17 575	16 267	1 308
2000	29 887	22 002	20 339	1 663	25 920	17 849	16 628	1 221
2001	30 646	22 285	20 298	1 988	26 462	18 021	16 635	1 386
2002	31 072	22 289	19 983	2 306	26 999	18 203	16 583	1 621
2003	31 691	22 297	19 841	2 457	27 802	18 397	16 723	1 674
2004	32 422	22 776	20 395	2 381	28 228	18 616	16 995	1 621
2005	33 125	23 214	21 006	2 209	29 046	19 183	17 588	1 595
2006	33 931	23 974	21 907	2 067	29 624	19 474	17 978	1 496
Married, Spouse Present								
1985	52 128	41 014	39 248	1 767	51 832	27 894	26 336	1 558
1986	52 769	41 477	39 658	1 819	52 158	28 623	27 144	1 479
1987	53 223	41 889	40 265	1 625	52 532	29 381	28 107	1 273
1988	53 246	41 832	40 472	1 360	52 775	29 921	28 756	1 166
1989	53 530	42 036	40 760	1 276	52 885	30 548	29 404	1 145
1990	53 793	42 275	40 829	1 446	52 917	30 901	29 714	1 188
1991	54 158	42 303	40 429	1 875	53 169	31 112	29 698	1 415
1992	54 509	42 491	40 341	2 150	53 501	31 700	30 100	1 600
1993	55 178	42 834	40 935	1 899	53 838	31 980	30 499	1 482
1994	55 560	43 005	41 414	1 592	54 155	32 888	31 536	1 352
1995	56 100	43 472	42 048	1 424	54 716	33 359	32 063	1 296
1996	56 363	43 739	42 417	1 322	54 970	33 618	32 406	1 211
1997	56 396	43 808	42 642	1 167	54 915	33 802	32 755	1 047
1998	56 670	43 957	42 923	1 034	55 331	33 857	32 872	985
1999	57 089	44 244	43 254	990	56 178	34 372	33 450	921
2000	58 167	44 987	44 078	908	57 557	35 146	34 209	937
2001	58 448	45 233	44 007	1 226	57 610	35 236	34 153	1 083
2002	59 102	45 766	44 116	1 650	58 165	35 477	34 153	1 323
2003	60 063	46 404	44 653	1 751	59 069	36 046	34 695	1 352
2004	60 412	46 550	45 084	1 466	59 278	35 845	34 600	1 244
2005	60 545	46 771	45 483	1 287	59 205	35 941	34 773	1 168
2006	60 751	46 842	45 700	1 142	59 576	36 314	35 272	1 042
Divorced, Widowed, or Separated								
1985	9 013	6 190	5 621	568	22 136	9 993	9 165	828
1986	9 367	6 392	5 827	565	22 518	10 277	9 491	787
1987	9 729	6 546	6 048	498	22 726	10 393	9 665	727
1988	10 039	6 751	6 280	471	23 020	10 627	9 962	665
1989	10 401	7 066	6 618	448	23 604	11 104	10 448	656
1990	10 714	7 378	6 871	508	23 968	11 315	10 639	676
1991	10 924	7 454	6 783	671	24 304	11 385	10 600	786
1992	11 325	7 763	7 001	762	24 559	11 570	10 689	881
1993	11 584	7 864	7 153	711	24 955	11 784	10 927	856
1994	12 008	2 076	7 432	594	25 304	12 018	11 227	791
1995	12 160	2 018	7 496	551	25 539	12 118	11 407	712
1996	12 456	2 103	7 735	541	25 791	12 397	11 691	706
1997	13 009	2 316	8 260	504	26 218	12 742	12 082	660
1998	13 394	2 332	8 530	435	26 190	12 771	12 143	628
1999	13 528	2 290	8 507	411	26 276	12 909	12 324	585
2000	13 910	9 291	8 888	403	27 135	13 308	12 748	559
2001	14 188	9 367	8 892	476	27 738	13 592	12 949	642
2002	14 411	9 445	8 804	641	27 821	13 683	12 846	837
2003	14 680	9 537	8 838	699	27 862	13 828	12 986	842
2004	14 875	9 654	9 045	608	28 141	13 961	13 133	828
2005	15 481	10 048	9 484	563	28 680	14 163	13 396	768
2006	15 923	10 440	9 895	545	29 010	14 385	13 675	709

Note: See notes and definitions for information on historical comparability.

Table 1-4. Employment Status of the Civilian Noninstitutional Population, by Sex, Race, and Marital Status, 1985–2006—*Continued*

(Thousands of people.)

Race, marital status, and year	Men Civilian noninstitutional population	Men Civilian labor force Total	Men Employed	Men Unemployed	Women Civilian noninstitutional population	Women Civilian labor force Total	Women Employed	Women Unemployed
WHITE¹								
Single								
1985	19 100	14 426	12 875	1 550	15 472	10 705	9 828	877
1986	19 316	14 672	13 162	1 510	15 686	10 965	10 060	906
1987	19 526	14 850	13 449	1 401	15 990	11 196	10 382	815
1988	19 966	15 279	13 982	1 297	16 218	11 428	10 674	754
1989	20 076	15 511	14 249	1 263	16 289	11 474	10 741	734
1990	20 746	15 993	14 617	1 376	16 555	11 522	10 729	794
1991	20 899	15 989	14 233	1 756	16 569	11 497	10 557	939
1992	21 025	16 129	14 285	1 844	16 684	11 502	10 526	976
1993	20 974	16 033	14 303	1 730	16 768	11 613	10 633	980
1994	21 071	16 074	14 539	1 535	16 936	11 805	10 885	920
1995	21 132	16 080	14 674	1 406	17 046	11 830	10 967	864
1996	21 454	16 285	14 891	1 394	17 282	11 977	11 099	878
1997	22 236	16 810	15 507	1 303	17 728	12 322	11 443	879
1998	22 513	17 007	15 746	1 261	18 247	12 742	11 945	797
1999	22 788	17 272	16 116	1 157	18 635	13 029	12 206	823
2000	23 266	17 659	16 504	1 154	18 808	13 215	12 449	766
2001	23 979	17 970	16 561	1 409	19 253	13 368	12 491	877
2002	24 289	17 924	16 289	1 635	19 625	13 556	12 550	1 006
2003	24 419	17 755	16 031	1 723	19 924	13 462	12 461	1 001
2004	24 929	18 090	16 435	1 655	20 210	13 597	12 628	969
2005	25 436	18 338	16 833	1 505	20 702	13 906	12 957	949
2006	26 012	18 928	17 500	1 428	21 085	14 109	13 199	909
Married, Spouse Present								
1985	46 925	36 934	35 472	1 462	46 728	24 777	23 468	1 308
1986	47 399	37 230	35 727	1 503	46 892	25 368	24 141	1 226
1987	47 690	37 486	36 127	1 359	47 180	26 014	24 969	1 045
1988	47 685	37 429	36 304	1 125	47 364	26 499	25 540	959
1989	47 883	37 589	36 545	1 044	47 382	27 030	26 083	947
1990	47 841	37 515	36 338	1 177	47 240	27 271	26 285	986
1991	48 137	37 507	35 923	1 585	47 456	27 479	26 290	1 189
1992	48 416	37 671	35 886	1 785	47 705	27 951	26 623	1 329
1993	48 937	37 953	36 396	1 557	47 944	28 221	26 993	1 228
1994	49 169	38 008	36 719	1 288	48 120	29 017	27 888	1 129
1995	49 597	38 376	37 211	1 165	48 497	29 360	28 290	1 070
1996	49 800	38 616	37 522	1 094	48 684	29 517	28 496	1 020
1997	49 719	38 593	37 636	957	48 542	29 664	28 809	855
1998	49 901	38 629	37 793	836	48 722	29 534	28 727	808
1999	50 091	38 765	37 968	797	49 296	29 806	29 056	749
2000	50 775	39 169	38 451	717	50 194	30 344	29 582	762
2001	50 850	39 246	38 265	981	50 077	30 336	29 472	864
2002	51 284	39 580	38 261	1 319	50 489	30 511	29 463	1 048
2003	51 859	39 908	38 529	1 379	50 957	30 805	29 740	1 065
2004	51 992	39 935	38 774	1 161	50 939	30 544	29 549	996
2005	52 034	40 141	39 130	1 011	50 865	30 599	29 676	922
2006	52 035	40 103	39 207	896	51 200	30 950	30 111	839
Divorced, Widowed, or Separated								
1985	7 348	5 112	4 698	414	18 106	7 973	7 393	580
1986	7 675	5 315	4 896	420	18 463	8 251	7 675	576
1987	7 974	5 443	5 070	373	18 599	8 300	7 791	509
1988	8 204	5 608	5 265	344	18 758	8 512	8 047	464
1989	8 509	5 887	5 558	329	19 200	8 863	8 409	454
1990	8 782	6 131	5 748	382	19 461	9 016	8 544	471
1991	8 941	6 159	5 641	518	19 757	9 111	8 538	573
1992	9 210	6 368	5 788	580	19 931	9 216	8 561	654
1993	9 459	6 498	5 957	541	20 206	9 382	8 764	618
1994	9 819	6 644	6 193	451	20 439	9 533	8 965	569
1995	10 005	6 689	6 261	428	20 638	9 613	9 087	526
1996	10 234	6 883	6 474	408	20 862	9 831	9 325	506
1997	10 622	7 236	6 855	382	21 147	10 068	9 607	461
1998	10 937	7 398	7 064	334	21 157	10 104	9 656	449
1999	11 050	7 375	7 056	320	21 225	10 261	9 834	427
2000	11 329	7 638	7 333	305	21 847	10 521	10 105	416
2001	11 623	7 750	7 386	364	22 330	10 729	10 255	474
2002	11 789	7 804	7 299	505	22 308	10 775	10 151	624
2003	11 971	7 846	7 305	541	22 162	10 769	10 168	602
2004	12 124	7 969	7 503	466	22 450	10 950	10 350	600
2005	12 558	8 215	7 800	415	22 853	11 101	10 552	548
2006	12 974	8 583	8 176	407	22 957	11 162	10 640	523

Note: See notes and definitions for information on historical comparability.

¹Beginning in 2003, persons who selected this race group only; persons who selected more than one race group are not included. Prior to 2003, persons who reported more than one race group were included in the group they identified as their main race.

Table 1-4. Employment Status of the Civilian Noninstitutional Population, by Sex, Race, and Marital Status, 1985–2006—*Continued*

(Thousands of people.)

Race, marital status, and year	Men Civilian noninstitutional population	Men Civilian labor force Total	Employed	Unemployed	Women Civilian noninstitutional population	Women Civilian labor force Total	Employed	Unemployed
BLACK AND OTHER RACES¹								
Single								
1985	4 228	2 782	2 147	635	4 297	2 458	1 930	528
1986	4 345	2 881	2 245	636	4 427	2 547	2 011	536
1987	4 421	2 922	2 345	577	4 606	2 688	2 179	509
1988	4 606	3 066	2 539	527	4 743	2 766	2 304	461
1989	4 755	3 227	2 687	538	4 852	2 903	2 434	468
1990	5 124	3 364	2 788	576	5 346	3 090	2 607	482
1991	5 298	3 422	2 778	644	5 604	3 184	2 641	543
1992	5 411	3 580	2 813	767	5 791	3 370	2 737	633
1993	5 596	3 673	2 958	715	5 945	3 418	2 851	567
1994	5 715	3 712	3 065	646	6 064	3 528	2 962	566
1995	5 786	3 761	3 159	601	6 105	3 637	3 086	549
1996	5 933	3 786	3 164	622	6 341	3 865	3 304	561
1997	6 075	3 879	3 276	603	6 557	4 170	3 594	576
1998	6 180	4 030	3 494	537	6 694	4 345	3 810	535
1999	6 316	4 079	3 570	508	6 941	4 546	4 061	485
2000	6 621	4 343	3 835	509	7 112	4 634	4 179	455
2001	6 667	4 315	3 737	579	7 209	4 653	4 144	509
2002	6 783	4 365	3 694	671	7 374	4 647	4 033	615
2003	7 272	4 542	3 810	734	7 878	4 935	4 262	673
2004	7 493	4 686	3 960	726	8 018	5 019	4 367	652
2005	7 689	4 876	4 173	704	8 344	5 277	4 631	646
2006	7 919	5 046	4 407	639	8 539	5 365	4 779	587
Married, Spouse Present								
1985	5 203	4 080	3 775	305	5 104	3 118	2 868	250
1986	5 370	4 247	3 931	316	5 266	3 255	3 003	253
1987	5 534	4 403	4 137	266	5 352	3 367	3 138	228
1988	5 560	4 403	4 168	234	5 411	3 422	3 215	207
1989	5 647	4 447	4 215	232	5 503	3 518	3 321	198
1990	5 952	4 760	4 491	269	5 677	3 630	3 429	202
1991	6 021	4 796	4 506	290	5 713	3 633	3 408	226
1992	6 093	4 820	4 455	365	5 796	3 749	3 477	271
1993	6 241	4 881	4 539	342	5 894	3 759	3 506	254
1994	6 391	4 997	4 695	304	6 035	3 871	3 648	223
1995	6 503	5 096	4 837	259	6 219	3 999	3 773	226
1996	6 563	5 123	4 895	228	6 286	4 101	3 910	191
1997	6 677	5 215	5 006	210	6 373	4 138	3 946	192
1998	6 769	5 328	5 130	198	6 609	4 323	4 145	177
1999	6 998	5 479	5 286	193	6 882	4 566	4 394	172
2000	7 392	5 818	5 627	191	7 363	4 802	4 627	175
2001	7 598	5 987	5 742	245	7 533	4 900	4 681	219
2002	7 818	6 186	5 855	331	7 676	4 966	4 690	275
2003	8 204	6 496	6 124	372	8 112	5 241	4 955	287
2004	8 420	6 615	6 310	305	8 339	5 301	5 051	248
2005	8 511	6 630	6 353	276	8 340	5 342	5 097	246
2006	8 716	6 739	6 493	246	8 376	5 364	5 161	203
Divorced, Widowed, or Separated								
1985	1 665	1 078	923	155	4 030	2 020	1 772	248
1986	1 692	1 076	931	146	4 055	2 026	1 816	210
1987	1 755	1 103	977	125	4 127	2 093	1 875	218
1988	1 836	1 142	1 015	127	4 262	2 115	1 914	201
1989	1 892	1 179	1 060	119	4 404	2 241	2 039	202
1990	1 932	1 247	1 123	126	4 507	2 299	2 095	205
1991	1 983	1 295	1 142	153	4 547	2 274	2 062	213
1992	2 115	1 395	1 213	182	4 628	2 354	2 128	227
1993	2 125	1 366	1 196	170	4 749	2 402	2 163	238
1994	2 189	1 382	1 239	143	4 865	2 485	2 262	222
1995	2 155	1 358	1 235	123	4 901	2 505	2 320	186
1996	2 222	1 394	1 261	133	4 929	2 566	2 366	200
1997	2 387	1 528	1 405	122	5 071	2 674	2 475	199
1998	2 457	1 567	1 466	101	5 033	2 667	2 487	179
1999	2 478	1 543	1 451	91	5 051	2 648	2 490	158
2000	2 581	1 653	1 555	98	5 288	2 787	2 643	143
2001	2 565	1 617	1 506	112	5 408	2 863	2 694	168
2002	2 622	1 641	1 505	136	5 513	2 908	2 695	213
2003	2 709	1 691	1 533	158	5 700	3 059	2 818	240
2004	2 751	1 685	1 542	142	5 691	3 011	2 783	228
2005	2 923	1 833	1 684	148	5 827	3 062	2 844	220
2006	2 949	1 857	1 719	138	6 053	3 223	3 035	186

Note: See notes and definitions for information on historical comparability.

¹Beginning in 2003, persons who selected this race group only; persons who selected more than one race group are not included. Prior to 2003, persons who reported more than one race group were included in the group they identified as their main race.

Table 1-5. Employment Status of the Civilian Noninstitutional Population, by Region, Division, State, and Selected Territory, 2005–2006

(Thousands of people, percent.)

Region, division, and state	2005						2006					
	Civilian noninstitutional population	Civilian labor force					Civilian noninstitutional population	Civilian labor force				
		Total	Participation rate	Employed	Unemployed	Unemployment rate		Total	Participation rate	Employed	Unemployed	Unemployment rate
UNITED STATES[1]	226 082	149 320	66.0	141 730	7 591	5.1	228 815	151 428	66.2	144 427	7 001	4.6
Northeast	42 638	27 716	65.0	26 381	1 335	4.8	42 866	27 958	65.2	26 678	1 280	4.6
New England	11 188	7 552	67.5	7 199	353	4.7	11 253	7 635	67.8	7 286	349	4.6
Connecticut	2 708	1 823	67.3	1 734	88	4.9	2 728	1 844	67.6	1 765	79	4.3
Maine	1 053	703	66.8	669	34	4.8	1 061	711	67.0	679	33	4.6
Massachusetts	5 056	3 374	66.7	3 211	163	4.8	5 078	3 404	67.0	3 235	170	5.0
New Hampshire	1 028	730	71.0	703	26	3.6	1 041	737	70.8	712	25	3.4
Rhode Island	843	569	67.5	540	29	5.1	842	577	68.5	548	30	5.1
Vermont	499	354	70.9	341	12	3.4	503	361	71.8	348	13	3.6
Middle Atlantic	31 450	20 164	64.1	19 182	982	4.9	31 613	20 323	64.3	19 392	931	4.6
New Jersey	6 721	4 455	66.3	4 256	199	4.5	6 767	4 518	66.8	4 309	209	4.6
New York	15 011	9 430	62.8	8 960	470	5.0	15 070	9 499	63.0	9 073	426	4.5
Pennsylvania	9 717	6 279	64.6	5 966	313	5.0	9 776	6 306	64.5	6 010	296	4.7
Midwest	50 545	34 495	68.2	32 624	1 871	5.4	50 934	34 829	68.4	33 102	1 727	5.0
East North Central	35 378	23 708	67.0	22 328	1 380	5.8	35 620	23 963	67.3	22 682	1 281	5.3
Illinois	9 716	6 484	66.7	6 113	371	5.7	9 799	6 613	67.5	6 316	298	4.5
Indiana	4 781	3 227	67.5	3 055	173	5.3	4 830	3 271	67.7	3 109	163	5.0
Michigan	7 760	5 072	65.4	4 726	346	6.8	7 796	5 081	65.2	4 730	351	6.9
Ohio	8 835	5 892	66.7	5 547	345	5.9	8 870	5 934	66.9	5 609	325	5.5
Wisconsin	4 285	3 033	70.8	2 887	146	4.8	4 325	3 063	70.8	2 918	145	4.7
West North Central	15 168	10 787	71.1	10 296	491	4.6	15 315	10 866	71.0	10 420	446	4.1
Iowa	2 292	1 640	71.6	1 569	71	4.3	2 310	1 664	72.0	1 603	61	3.7
Kansas	2 073	1 464	70.6	1 389	75	5.1	2 090	1 466	70.1	1 400	66	4.5
Minnesota	3 951	2 916	73.8	2 797	119	4.1	3 996	2 939	73.5	2 822	117	4.0
Missouri	4 443	3 008	67.7	2 848	160	5.3	4 490	3 032	67.5	2 886	147	4.8
Nebraska	1 332	978	73.4	940	38	3.9	1 343	974	72.5	945	29	3.0
North Dakota	491	354	72.1	342	12	3.4	493	358	72.6	346	12	3.2
South Dakota	586	427	72.9	412	16	3.7	593	431	72.7	417	14	3.2
South	81 486	52 958	65.0	50 325	2 633	5.0	82 866	53 991	65.2	51 587	2 404	4.5
South Atlantic	43 108	28 158	65.3	26 882	1 276	4.5	43 941	28 893	65.8	27 714	1 179	4.1
Delaware	647	433	66.9	416	17	4.0	659	440	66.8	425	16	3.6
District of Columbia	466	314	67.4	294	20	6.5	468	316	67.5	297	19	6.0
Florida	13 929	8 711	62.5	8 376	335	3.8	14 221	8 989	63.2	8 693	296	3.3
Georgia	6 792	4 622	68.1	4 384	238	5.2	6 978	4 742	68.0	4 522	220	4.6
Maryland	4 279	2 943	68.8	2 821	122	4.2	4 319	3 009	69.7	2 893	117	3.9
North Carolina	6 587	4 340	65.9	4 113	227	5.2	6 731	4 465	66.3	4 251	214	4.8
South Carolina	3 244	2 079	64.1	1 940	140	6.7	3 309	2 126	64.2	1 988	138	6.5
Virginia	5 717	3 922	68.6	3 786	136	3.5	5 804	3 999	68.9	3 879	120	3.0
West Virginia	1 447	794	54.9	754	40	5.0	1 453	807	55.5	767	40	4.9
East South Central	13 455	8 389	62.3	7 921	468	5.6	13 623	8 536	62.7	8 097	439	5.1
Alabama	3 496	2 140	61.2	2 057	83	3.9	3 542	2 200	62.1	2 121	79	3.6
Kentucky	3 208	1 999	62.3	1 879	120	6.0	3 242	2 039	62.9	1 922	117	5.7
Mississippi	2 163	1 330	61.5	1 226	103	7.8	2 176	1 307	60.1	1 219	89	6.8
Tennessee	4 589	2 920	63.6	2 758	162	5.6	4 663	2 990	64.1	2 836	155	5.2
West South Central	24 922	16 410	65.8	15 522	889	5.4	25 301	16 562	65.5	15 776	786	4.7
Arkansas	2 120	1 345	63.4	1 277	68	5.1	2 149	1 365	63.5	1 293	72	5.3
Louisiana	3 314	2 077	62.7	1 938	139	6.7	3 229	1 990	61.6	1 910	80	4.0
Oklahoma	2 670	1 705	63.9	1 629	76	4.4	2 699	1 720	63.7	1 651	69	4.0
Texas	16 804	11 283	67.1	10 677	606	5.4	17 224	11 487	66.7	10 922	566	4.9
West	51 449	34 179	66.4	32 411	1 768	5.2	52 405	34 816	66.4	33 216	1 600	4.6
Mountain	15 236	10 325	67.8	9 851	473	4.6	15 669	10 698	68.3	10 278	420	3.9
Arizona	4 457	2 859	64.1	2 727	132	4.6	4 625	2 977	64.4	2 854	123	4.1
Colorado	3 552	2 568	72.3	2 437	131	5.1	3 630	2 652	73.1	2 537	115	4.3
Idaho	1 063	727	68.4	698	29	4.0	1 093	749	68.5	724	26	3.4
Montana	728	483	66.3	464	19	3.9	739	494	66.8	478	16	3.2
Nevada	1 831	1 230	67.2	1 178	52	4.2	1 897	1 295	68.3	1 241	54	4.2
New Mexico	1 444	915	63.4	867	48	5.3	1 472	935	63.5	896	40	4.2
Utah	1 768	1 264	71.5	1 212	52	4.1	1 815	1 311	72.2	1 273	38	2.9
Wyoming	393	278	70.7	268	10	3.7	399	285	71.4	276	9	3.2
Pacific	36 214	23 855	65.9	22 560	1 295	5.4	36 736	24 118	65.7	22 938	1 180	4.9
Alaska	477	342	71.7	318	24	6.9	485	347	71.5	324	23	6.7
California	27 096	17 740	65.5	16 782	958	5.4	27 438	17 902	65.2	17 029	873	4.9
Hawaii	956	631	66.0	614	17	2.7	969	643	66.4	628	15	2.4
Oregon	2 849	1 870	65.6	1 755	116	6.2	2 906	1 899	65.3	1 796	103	5.4
Washington	4 835	3 270	67.6	3 090	181	5.5	4 938	3 327	67.4	3 160	166	5.0
Puerto Rico[2]	2 957	1 410	47.7	1 250	160	11.3	2 982	1 407	47.2	1 261	146	10.4

Note: Data refer to place of residence. Region and division data are derived from summing the component states. Sub-national data (except for Puerto Rico) reflect revised population controls and model reestimation.

[1] Due to separate processing and weighing procedures, totals for the United States differ from the results obtained by aggregating data for regions, divisions, or states.
[2] Data from Puerto Rico are derived from a monthly household survey similar to the Current Population Survey (CPS).

Table 1-6. Civilian Noninstitutional Population, by Age, Race, Sex, and Hispanic Origin, 1948–2006

(Thousands of people.)

Race, Hispanic origin, sex, and year	16 years and over	16 to 19 years			20 years and over						
		Total	16 to 17 years	18 to 19 years	Total	20 to 24 years	25 to 34 years	35 to 44 years	45 to 54 years	55 to 64 years	65 years and over
ALL RACES											
Both Sexes											
1948	103 068	8 449	4 265	4 185	94 618	11 530	22 610	20 097	16 771	12 885	10 720
1949	103 994	8 215	4 139	4 079	95 778	11 312	22 822	20 401	17 002	13 201	11 035
1950	104 995	8 143	4 076	4 068	96 851	11 080	23 013	20 681	17 240	13 469	11 363
1951	104 621	7 865	4 096	3 771	96 755	10 167	22 843	20 863	17 464	13 692	11 724
1952	105 231	7 922	4 234	3 689	97 305	9 389	23 044	21 137	17 716	13 889	12 126
1953	107 056	8 014	4 241	3 773	99 041	8 960	23 266	21 922	17 991	13 830	13 075
1954	108 321	8 224	4 336	3 889	100 095	8 885	23 304	22 135	18 305	14 085	13 375
1955	109 683	8 364	4 440	3 925	101 318	9 036	23 249	22 348	18 643	14 309	13 728
1956	110 954	8 434	4 482	3 953	102 518	9 271	23 072	22 567	19 012	14 516	14 075
1957	112 265	8 612	4 587	4 026	103 653	9 486	22 849	22 786	19 424	14 727	14 376
1958	113 727	8 986	4 872	4 114	104 737	9 733	22 563	23 025	19 832	14 923	14 657
1959	115 329	9 618	5 337	4 282	105 711	9 975	22 201	23 207	20 203	15 134	14 985
1960	117 245	10 187	5 573	4 615	107 056	10 273	21 998	23 437	20 601	15 409	15 336
1961	118 771	10 513	5 462	5 052	108 255	10 583	21 829	23 585	20 893	15 675	15 685
1962	120 153	10 652	5 503	5 150	109 500	10 852	21 503	23 797	20 916	15 874	16 554
1963	122 416	11 370	6 301	5 070	111 045	11 464	21 400	23 948	21 144	16 138	16 945
1964	124 485	12 111	6 974	5 139	112 372	12 017	21 367	23 940	21 452	16 442	17 150
1965	126 513	12 930	6 936	5 995	113 582	12 442	21 417	23 832	21 728	16 727	17 432
1966	128 058	13 592	6 914	6 679	114 463	12 638	21 543	23 579	21 977	17 007	17 715
1967	129 874	13 480	7 003	6 480	116 391	13 421	22 057	23 313	22 256	17 310	18 029
1968	132 028	13 698	7 200	6 499	118 328	13 891	22 912	23 036	22 534	17 614	18 338
1969	134 335	14 095	7 422	6 673	120 238	14 488	23 645	22 709	22 806	17 930	18 657
1970	137 085	14 519	7 643	6 876	122 566	15 323	24 435	22 489	23 059	18 250	19 007
1971	140 216	15 022	7 849	7 173	125 193	16 345	25 337	22 274	23 244	18 581	19 406
1972	144 126	15 510	8 076	7 435	128 614	17 143	26 740	22 358	23 338	19 007	20 023
1973	147 096	15 840	8 227	7 613	131 253	17 692	28 172	22 287	23 431	19 281	20 389
1974	150 120	16 180	8 373	7 809	133 938	17 994	29 439	22 461	23 578	19 517	20 945
1975	153 153	16 418	8 419	7 999	136 733	18 595	30 710	22 526	23 535	19 844	21 525
1976	156 150	16 614	8 442	8 171	139 536	19 109	31 953	22 796	23 409	20 185	22 083
1977	159 033	16 688	8 482	8 206	142 345	19 582	33 117	23 296	23 197	20 557	22 597
1978	161 910	16 695	8 484	8 211	145 216	20 007	34 091	24 099	22 977	20 875	23 166
1979	164 863	16 657	8 389	8 268	148 205	20 353	35 261	24 861	22 752	21 210	23 767
1980	167 745	16 543	8 279	8 264	151 202	20 635	36 558	25 578	22 563	21 520	24 350
1981	170 130	16 214	8 068	8 145	153 916	20 820	37 777	26 291	22 422	21 756	24 850
1982	172 271	15 763	7 714	8 049	156 508	20 845	38 492	27 611	22 264	21 909	25 387
1983	174 215	15 274	7 385	7 889	158 941	20 799	39 147	28 932	22 167	22 003	25 892
1984	176 383	14 735	7 196	7 538	161 648	20 688	39 999	30 251	22 226	22 052	26 433
1985	178 206	14 506	7 232	7 274	163 700	20 097	40 670	31 379	22 418	22 140	26 997
1986	180 587	14 496	7 386	7 110	166 091	19 569	41 731	32 550	22 732	22 011	27 497
1987	182 753	14 606	7 501	7 104	168 147	18 970	42 297	33 755	23 183	21 835	28 108
1988	184 613	14 527	7 284	7 243	170 085	18 434	42 611	34 784	24 004	21 641	28 612
1989	186 393	14 223	6 886	7 338	172 169	18 025	42 845	35 977	24 744	21 406	29 173
1990	189 164	14 520	6 893	7 626	174 644	18 902	42 976	37 719	25 081	20 719	29 247
1991	190 925	14 073	6 901	7 173	176 852	18 963	42 688	39 116	25 709	20 675	29 700
1992	192 805	13 840	6 907	6 933	178 965	18 846	42 278	39 852	27 206	20 604	30 179
1993	194 838	13 935	7 010	6 925	180 903	18 642	41 771	40 733	28 549	20 574	30 634
1994	196 814	14 196	7 245	6 951	182 619	18 353	41 306	41 534	29 778	20 635	31 012
1995	198 584	14 511	7 407	7 104	184 073	17 864	40 798	42 254	30 974	20 735	31 448
1996	200 591	14 934	7 678	7 256	185 656	17 409	40 252	43 086	32 167	20 990	31 751
1997	203 133	15 365	7 861	7 504	187 769	17 442	39 559	43 883	33 391	21 505	31 989
1998	205 220	15 644	7 895	7 749	189 576	17 593	38 778	44 299	34 373	22 296	32 237
1999	207 753	16 040	8 060	7 979	191 713	17 968	37 976	44 635	35 587	23 064	32 484
2000	212 577	15 912	7 978	7 934	196 664	18 311	38 703	44 312	37 642	24 230	33 466
2001	215 092	15 929	8 020	7 909	199 164	18 877	38 505	44 195	38 904	25 011	33 672
2002	217 570	15 994	8 099	7 895	201 576	19 348	38 472	43 894	39 711	26 343	33 808
2003	221 168	16 096	8 561	7 535	205 072	19 801	39 021	43 746	40 522	27 728	34 253
2004	223 357	16 222	8 574	7 648	207 134	20 197	38 939	43 226	41 245	28 919	34 609
2005	226 082	16 398	8 778	7 619	209 685	20 276	39 064	43 005	42 107	30 165	35 068
2006	228 815	16 678	9 089	7 589	212 137	20 265	39 230	42 753	42 901	31 375	35 613

Table 1-6. Civilian Noninstitutional Population, by Age, Race, Sex, and Hispanic Origin, 1948–2006 —Continued

(Thousands of people.)

Race, Hispanic origin, sex, and year	16 years and over	16 to 19 years			20 years and over						
		Total	16 to 17 years	18 to 19 years	Total	20 to 24 years	25 to 34 years	35 to 44 years	45 to 54 years	55 to 64 years	65 years and over
ALL RACES											
Men											
1948	49 996	4 078	2 128	1 951	45 918	5 527	10 767	9 798	8 290	6 441	5 093
1949	50 321	3 946	2 062	1 884	46 378	5 405	10 871	9 926	8 379	6 568	5 226
1950	50 725	3 962	2 043	1 920	46 763	5 270	10 963	10 034	8 472	6 664	5 357
1951	49 727	3 725	2 039	1 687	46 001	4 451	10 709	10 049	8 551	6 737	5 503
1952	49 700	3 767	2 121	1 647	45 932	3 788	10 855	10 164	8 655	6 798	5 670
1953	50 750	3 823	2 122	1 701	46 927	3 482	11 020	10 632	8 878	6 798	6 119
1954	51 395	3 953	2 174	1 780	47 441	3 509	11 067	10 718	9 018	6 885	6 241
1955	52 109	4 022	2 225	1 798	48 086	3 708	11 068	10 804	9 164	6 960	6 380
1956	52 723	4 020	2 238	1 783	48 704	3 970	10 983	10 889	9 322	7 032	6 505
1957	53 315	4 083	2 284	1 800	49 231	4 166	10 889	10 965	9 499	7 109	6 602
1958	54 033	4 293	2 435	1 858	49 740	4 339	10 787	11 076	9 675	7 179	6 683
1959	54 793	4 652	2 681	1 971	50 140	4 488	10 625	11 149	9 832	7 259	6 785
1960	55 662	4 963	2 805	2 159	50 698	4 679	10 514	11 230	10 000	7 373	6 901
1961	56 286	5 112	2 742	2 371	51 173	4 844	10 440	11 286	10 112	7 483	7 006
1962	56 831	5 150	2 764	2 386	51 681	4 925	10 207	11 389	10 162	7 610	7 386
1963	57 921	5 496	3 162	2 334	52 425	5 240	10 165	11 476	10 274	7 740	7 526
1964	58 847	5 866	3 503	2 364	52 981	5 520	10 144	11 466	10 402	7 873	7 574
1965	59 782	6 318	3 488	2 831	53 463	5 701	10 182	11 427	10 512	7 990	7 649
1966	60 262	6 658	3 478	3 180	53 603	5 663	10 224	11 294	10 598	8 099	7 723
1967	60 905	6 537	3 528	3 010	54 367	5 977	10 495	11 161	10 705	8 218	7 809
1968	61 847	6 683	3 634	3 049	55 165	6 127	10 944	11 040	10 819	8 336	7 897
1969	62 898	6 928	3 741	3 187	55 969	6 379	11 309	10 890	10 935	8 464	7 990
1970	64 304	7 145	3 848	3 299	57 157	6 861	11 750	10 810	11 052	8 590	8 093
1971	65 942	7 430	3 954	3 477	58 511	7 511	12 227	10 721	11 129	8 711	8 208
1972	67 835	7 705	4 081	3 624	60 130	8 061	12 911	10 762	11 167	8 895	8 330
1973	69 292	7 855	4 152	3 703	61 436	8 429	13 641	10 746	11 202	8 990	8 426
1974	70 808	8 012	4 231	3 781	62 796	8 600	14 262	10 834	11 315	9 140	8 641
1975	72 291	8 134	4 252	3 882	64 158	8 950	14 899	10 874	11 298	9 286	8 852
1976	73 759	8 244	4 266	3 978	65 515	9 237	15 528	11 010	11 243	9 444	9 053
1977	75 193	8 288	4 290	4 000	66 904	9 477	16 108	11 260	11 144	9 616	9 297
1978	76 576	8 309	4 295	4 014	68 268	9 693	16 598	11 665	11 045	9 758	9 509
1979	78 020	8 310	4 251	4 060	69 709	9 873	17 193	12 046	10 944	9 907	9 746
1980	79 398	8 260	4 195	4 064	71 138	10 023	17 833	12 400	10 861	10 042	9 979
1981	80 511	8 092	4 087	4 005	72 419	10 116	18 427	12 758	10 797	10 151	10 170
1982	81 523	7 879	3 911	3 968	73 644	10 136	18 787	13 410	10 726	10 215	10 371
1983	82 531	7 659	3 750	3 908	74 872	10 140	19 143	14 067	10 689	10 261	10 573
1984	83 605	7 386	3 655	3 731	76 219	10 108	19 596	14 719	10 724	10 285	10 788
1985	84 469	7 275	3 689	3 586	77 195	9 746	19 864	15 265	10 844	10 392	11 084
1986	85 798	7 275	3 768	3 507	78 523	9 498	20 498	15 858	10 986	10 336	11 347
1987	86 899	7 335	3 824	3 510	79 565	9 195	20 781	16 475	11 215	10 267	11 632
1988	87 857	7 304	3 715	3 588	80 553	8 931	20 937	17 008	11 625	10 193	11 859
1989	88 762	7 143	3 524	3 619	81 619	8 743	21 080	17 590	11 981	10 092	12 134
1990	90 377	7 347	3 534	3 813	83 030	9 320	21 117	18 529	12 238	9 778	12 049
1991	91 278	7 134	3 548	3 586	84 144	9 367	20 977	19 213	12 554	9 780	12 254
1992	92 270	7 023	3 542	3 481	85 247	9 326	20 792	19 585	13 271	9 776	12 496
1993	93 332	7 076	3 595	3 481	86 256	9 216	20 569	20 037	13 944	9 773	12 717
1994	94 355	7 203	3 718	3 486	87 151	9 074	20 361	20 443	14 545	9 810	12 918
1995	95 178	7 367	3 794	3 573	87 811	8 835	20 079	20 800	15 111	9 856	13 130
1996	96 206	7 600	3 955	3 645	88 606	8 611	19 775	21 222	15 674	9 997	13 327
1997	97 715	7 836	4 053	3 783	89 879	8 706	19 478	21 669	16 276	10 282	13 469
1998	98 758	7 968	4 059	3 909	90 790	8 804	19 094	21 857	16 773	10 649	13 613
1999	99 722	8 167	4 143	4 024	91 555	8 899	18 565	21 969	17 335	11 008	13 779
2000	101 964	8 089	4 096	3 993	93 875	9 101	19 106	21 683	18 365	11 583	14 037
2001	103 282	8 101	4 102	3 999	95 181	9 368	19 056	21 643	18 987	11 972	14 155
2002	104 585	8 146	4 140	4 006	96 439	9 627	19 037	21 523	19 379	12 641	14 233
2003	106 435	8 163	4 365	3 797	98 272	9 878	19 347	21 463	19 784	13 305	14 496
2004	107 710	8 234	4 318	3 916	99 476	10 125	19 358	21 255	20 160	13 894	14 684
2005	109 151	8 317	4 481	3 836	100 835	10 181	19 446	21 177	20 585	14 502	14 944
2006	110 605	8 459	4 613	3 846	102 145	10 191	19 568	21 082	20 991	15 095	15 219

Table 1-6. Civilian Noninstitutional Population, by Age, Race, Sex, and Hispanic Origin, 1948–2006
—Continued

(Thousands of people.)

Race, Hispanic origin, sex, and year	16 years and over	16 to 19 years			20 years and over						
		Total	16 to 17 years	18 to 19 years	Total	20 to 24 years	25 to 34 years	35 to 44 years	45 to 54 years	55 to 64 years	65 years and over
ALL RACES											
Women											
1948	53 071	4 371	2 137	2 234	48 700	6 003	11 843	10 299	8 481	6 444	5 627
1949	53 670	4 269	2 077	2 195	49 400	5 907	11 951	10 475	8 623	6 633	5 809
1950	54 270	4 181	2 033	2 148	50 088	5 810	12 050	10 647	8 768	6 805	6 006
1951	54 895	4 140	2 057	2 084	50 754	5 716	12 134	10 814	8 913	6 955	6 221
1952	55 529	4 155	2 113	2 042	51 373	5 601	12 189	10 973	9 061	7 091	6 456
1953	56 305	4 191	2 119	2 072	52 114	5 478	12 246	11 290	9 113	7 032	6 956
1954	56 925	4 271	2 162	2 109	52 654	5 376	12 237	11 417	9 287	7 200	7 134
1955	57 574	4 342	2 215	2 127	53 232	5 328	12 181	11 544	9 479	7 349	7 348
1956	58 228	4 414	2 244	2 170	53 814	5 301	12 089	11 678	9 690	7 484	7 570
1957	58 951	4 529	2 303	2 226	54 421	5 320	11 960	11 821	9 925	7 618	7 774
1958	59 690	4 693	2 437	2 256	54 997	5 394	11 776	11 949	10 157	7 744	7 974
1959	60 534	4 966	2 656	2 311	55 570	5 487	11 576	12 058	10 371	7 875	8 200
1960	61 582	5 224	2 768	2 456	56 358	5 594	11 484	12 207	10 601	8 036	8 435
1961	62 484	5 401	2 720	2 681	57 082	5 739	11 389	12 299	10 781	8 192	8 679
1962	63 321	5 502	2 739	2 764	57 819	5 927	11 296	12 408	10 754	8 264	9 168
1963	64 494	5 874	3 139	2 736	58 620	6 224	11 235	12 472	10 870	8 398	9 419
1964	65 637	6 245	3 471	2 775	59 391	6 497	11 223	12 474	11 050	8 569	9 576
1965	66 731	6 612	3 448	3 164	60 119	6 741	11 235	12 405	11 216	8 737	9 783
1966	67 795	6 934	3 436	3 499	60 860	6 975	11 319	12 285	11 379	8 908	9 992
1967	68 968	6 943	3 475	3 470	62 026	7 445	11 562	12 152	11 551	9 092	10 220
1968	70 179	7 015	3 566	3 450	63 164	7 764	11 968	11 996	11 715	9 278	10 441
1969	71 436	7 167	3 681	3 486	64 269	8 109	12 336	11 819	11 871	9 466	10 667
1970	72 782	7 373	3 796	3 578	65 408	8 462	12 684	11 679	12 008	9 659	10 914
1971	74 274	7 591	3 895	3 697	66 682	8 834	13 110	11 553	12 115	9 870	11 198
1972	76 290	7 805	3 994	3 811	68 484	9 082	13 829	11 597	12 171	10 113	11 693
1973	77 804	7 985	4 076	3 909	69 819	9 263	14 531	11 541	12 229	10 290	11 963
1974	79 312	8 168	4 142	4 028	71 144	9 393	15 177	11 627	12 263	10 377	12 304
1975	80 860	8 285	4 168	4 117	72 576	9 645	15 811	11 652	12 237	10 558	12 673
1976	82 390	8 370	4 176	4 194	74 020	9 872	16 425	11 786	12 166	10 742	13 030
1977	83 840	8 400	4 193	4 206	75 441	10 103	17 008	12 036	12 053	10 940	13 300
1978	85 334	8 386	4 189	4 197	76 948	10 315	17 493	12 435	11 932	11 118	13 658
1979	86 843	8 347	4 139	4 208	78 496	10 480	18 070	12 815	11 808	11 303	14 021
1980	88 348	8 283	4 083	4 200	80 065	10 612	18 725	13 177	11 701	11 478	14 372
1981	89 618	8 121	3 981	4 140	81 497	10 705	19 350	13 533	11 625	11 605	14 680
1982	90 748	7 884	3 804	4 081	82 864	10 709	19 705	14 201	11 538	11 694	15 017
1983	91 684	7 616	3 635	3 981	84 069	10 660	20 004	14 865	11 478	11 742	15 319
1984	92 778	7 349	3 542	3 807	85 429	10 580	20 403	15 532	11 501	11 768	15 645
1985	93 736	7 231	3 543	3 688	86 506	10 351	20 805	16 114	11 574	11 748	15 913
1986	94 789	7 221	3 618	3 603	87 567	10 072	21 233	16 692	11 746	11 675	16 150
1987	95 853	7 271	3 677	3 594	88 583	9 776	21 516	17 279	11 968	11 567	16 476
1988	96 756	7 224	3 569	3 655	89 532	9 503	21 674	17 776	12 378	11 448	16 753
1989	97 630	7 080	3 361	3 719	90 550	9 282	21 765	18 387	12 763	11 314	17 039
1990	98 787	7 173	3 359	3 813	91 614	9 582	21 859	19 190	12 843	10 941	17 198
1991	99 646	6 939	3 353	3 586	92 708	9 597	21 711	19 903	13 155	10 895	17 446
1992	100 535	6 818	3 366	3 452	93 718	9 520	21 486	20 267	13 935	10 828	17 682
1993	101 506	6 859	3 415	3 444	94 647	9 426	21 202	20 696	14 605	10 801	17 917
1994	102 460	6 993	3 528	3 465	95 467	9 279	20 945	21 091	15 233	10 825	18 094
1995	103 406	7 144	3 613	3 531	96 262	9 029	20 719	21 454	15 862	10 879	18 318
1996	104 385	7 335	3 723	3 612	97 050	8 798	20 477	21 865	16 493	10 993	18 424
1997	105 418	7 528	3 808	3 721	97 889	8 736	20 081	22 214	17 115	11 224	18 520
1998	106 462	7 676	3 835	3 840	98 786	8 790	19 683	22 442	17 600	11 646	18 625
1999	108 031	7 873	3 917	3 955	100 158	9 069	19 411	22 666	18 251	12 056	18 705
2000	110 613	7 823	3 882	3 941	102 790	9 211	19 597	22 628	19 276	12 647	19 430
2001	111 811	7 828	3 917	3 910	103 983	9 509	19 449	22 552	19 917	13 039	19 517
2002	112 985	7 848	3 959	3 889	105 136	9 721	19 435	22 371	20 332	13 703	19 575
2003	114 733	7 934	4 195	3 738	106 800	9 924	19 674	22 283	20 738	14 423	19 758
2004	115 647	7 989	4 257	3 732	107 658	10 072	19 581	21 970	21 085	15 025	19 925
2005	116 931	8 081	4 297	3 784	108 850	10 095	19 618	21 828	21 521	15 663	20 125
2006	118 210	8 218	4 476	3 742	109 992	10 074	19 662	21 671	21 910	16 280	20 394

Table 1-6. Civilian Noninstitutional Population, by Age, Race, Sex, and Hispanic Origin, 1948–2006
—Continued

(Thousands of people.)

Race, Hispanic origin, sex, and year	16 years and over	16 to 19 years			20 years and over						
		Total	16 to 17 years	18 to 19 years	Total	20 to 24 years	25 to 34 years	35 to 44 years	45 to 54 years	55 to 64 years	65 years and over
WHITE[1]											
Both Sexes											
1954	97 705	7 180	3 786	3 394	90 524	7 794	20 818	19 915	16 569	12 993	12 438
1955	98 880	7 292	3 874	3 419	91 586	7 912	20 742	20 110	16 869	13 169	12 785
1956	99 976	7 346	3 908	3 438	92 629	8 106	20 564	20 314	17 198	13 341	13 105
1957	101 119	7 505	4 007	3 498	93 612	8 293	20 342	20 514	17 562	13 518	13 383
1958	102 392	7 843	4 271	3 573	94 547	8 498	20 063	20 734	17 924	13 681	13 645
1959	103 803	8 430	4 707	3 725	95 370	8 697	19 715	20 893	18 257	13 858	13 951
1960	105 282	8 924	4 909	4 016	96 355	8 927	19 470	21 049	18 578	14 070	14 260
1961	106 604	9 211	4 785	4 427	97 390	9 203	19 289	21 169	18 845	14 304	14 581
1962	107 715	9 343	4 818	4 526	98 371	9 484	18 974	21 293	18 872	14 450	15 297
1963	109 705	9 978	5 549	4 430	99 725	10 069	18 867	21 398	19 082	14 681	15 629
1964	111 534	10 616	6 137	4 481	100 916	10 568	18 838	21 375	19 360	14 957	15 816
1965	113 284	11 319	6 049	5 271	101 963	10 935	18 882	21 258	19 604	15 215	16 070
1966	114 566	11 862	5 993	5 870	102 702	11 094	18 989	21 005	19 822	15 469	16 322
1967	116 100	11 682	6 051	5 632	104 417	11 797	19 464	20 745	20 067	15 745	16 602
1968	117 948	11 840	6 225	5 616	106 107	12 184	20 245	20 474	20 310	16 018	16 875
1969	119 913	12 179	6 418	5 761	107 733	12 677	20 892	20 156	20 546	16 305	17 156
1970	122 174	12 521	6 591	5 931	109 652	13 359	21 546	19 929	20 760	16 591	17 469
1971	124 758	12 937	6 750	6 189	111 821	14 208	22 295	19 694	20 907	16 884	17 833
1972	127 906	13 301	6 910	6 392	114 603	14 897	23 555	19 673	20 950	17 250	18 278
1973	130 097	13 533	7 021	6 512	116 563	15 264	24 685	19 532	20 991	17 484	18 607
1974	132 417	13 784	7 114	6 671	118 632	15 502	25 711	19 628	21 061	17 645	19 085
1975	134 790	13 941	7 132	6 808	120 849	15 980	26 746	19 641	20 981	17 918	19 587
1976	137 106	14 055	7 125	6 930	123 050	16 368	27 757	19 827	20 816	18 220	20 064
1977	139 380	14 095	7 150	6 944	125 285	16 728	28 703	20 231	20 575	18 540	20 508
1978	141 612	14 060	7 132	6 928	127 552	17 038	29 453	20 932	20 322	18 799	21 007
1979	143 894	13 994	7 029	6 964	129 900	17 284	30 371	21 579	20 058	19 071	21 538
1980	146 122	13 854	6 912	6 943	132 268	17 484	31 407	22 174	19 837	19 316	22 050
1981	147 908	13 516	6 704	6 813	134 392	17 609	32 367	22 778	19 666	19 485	22 487
1982	149 441	13 076	6 383	6 693	136 366	17 579	32 863	23 910	19 478	19 591	22 945
1983	150 805	12 623	6 089	6 534	138 183	17 492	33 286	25 027	19 349	19 625	23 403
1984	152 347	12 147	5 918	6 228	140 200	17 304	33 889	26 124	19 348	19 629	23 906
1985	153 679	11 900	5 922	5 978	141 780	16 853	34 450	27 100	19 405	19 620	24 352
1986	155 432	11 879	6 036	5 843	143 553	16 353	35 293	28 062	19 587	19 477	24 780
1987	156 958	11 939	6 110	5 829	145 020	15 808	35 667	29 036	19 965	19 242	25 301
1988	158 194	11 838	5 893	5 945	146 357	15 276	35 876	29 818	20 652	18 996	25 739
1989	159 338	11 530	5 506	6 023	147 809	14 879	35 951	30 774	21 287	18 743	26 175
1990	160 625	11 630	5 464	6 166	148 996	15 538	35 661	31 739	21 535	18 204	26 319
1991	161 759	11 200	5 451	5 749	150 558	15 516	35 342	32 854	22 052	18 074	26 721
1992	162 972	11 004	5 478	5 526	151 968	15 354	34 885	33 305	23 364	17 951	27 108
1993	164 289	11 078	5 562	5 516	153 210	15 087	34 365	33 919	24 456	17 892	27 493
1994	165 555	11 264	5 710	5 554	154 291	14 708	33 865	34 582	25 435	17 924	27 776
1995	166 914	11 468	5 822	5 646	155 446	14 313	33 355	35 222	26 418	17 986	28 153
1996	168 317	11 822	6 026	5 796	156 495	13 907	32 852	35 810	27 403	18 136	28 387
1997	169 993	12 181	6 213	5 968	157 812	13 983	32 091	36 325	28 388	18 511	28 514
1998	171 478	12 439	6 264	6 176	159 039	14 138	31 286	36 610	29 132	19 231	28 642
1999	173 085	12 700	6 342	6 358	160 385	14 394	30 516	36 755	30 048	19 855	28 818
2000	176 220	12 535	6 264	6 271	163 685	14 552	30 948	36 261	31 550	20 757	29 617
2001	178 111	12 556	6 291	6 265	165 556	15 001	30 770	36 113	32 475	21 434	29 762
2002	179 783	12 596	6 346	6 250	167 187	15 360	30 676	35 750	33 012	22 540	29 849
2003	181 292	12 527	6 629	5 898	168 765	15 536	30 789	35 352	33 466	23 589	30 033
2004	182 643	12 599	6 561	6 038	170 045	15 817	30 585	34 845	34 005	24 549	30 245
2005	184 446	12 690	6 768	5 921	171 757	15 871	30 592	34 554	34 649	25 534	30 556
2006	186 264	12 856	6 981	5 875	173 408	15 848	30 661	34 217	35 228	26 486	30 968

[1]Beginning in 2003, persons who selected this race group only; persons who selected more than one race group are not included. Prior to 2003, persons who reported more than one race group were included in the group identified as their main race.

Table 1-6. Civilian Noninstitutional Population, by Age, Race, Sex, and Hispanic Origin, 1948–2006
—Continued

(Thousands of people.)

Race, Hispanic origin, sex, and year	16 years and over	16 to 19 years			20 years and over						
		Total	16 to 17 years	18 to 19 years	Total	20 to 24 years	25 to 34 years	35 to 44 years	45 to 54 years	55 to 64 years	65 years and over
WHITE¹											
Men											
1954	46 462	3 455	1 902	1 553	43 007	3 074	9 948	9 688	8 172	6 341	5 787
1955	47 076	3 507	1 945	1 563	43 569	3 241	9 936	9 768	8 303	6 398	5 923
1956	47 602	3 500	1 955	1 546	44 102	3 464	9 851	9 848	8 446	6 455	6 038
1957	48 119	3 556	2 000	1 557	44 563	3 638	9 758	9 917	8 605	6 518	6 127
1958	48 745	3 747	2 140	1 607	44 998	3 783	9 656	10 018	8 765	6 574	6 203
1959	49 408	4 079	2 370	1 710	45 329	3 903	9 499	10 081	8 909	6 639	6 298
1960	50 065	4 349	2 476	1 874	45 716	4 054	9 373	10 131	9 042	6 721	6 395
1961	50 608	4 479	2 407	2 073	46 129	4 204	9 290	10 178	9 148	6 819	6 490
1962	51 054	4 520	2 426	2 094	46 534	4 306	9 080	10 239	9 191	6 917	6 801
1963	52 031	4 827	2 792	2 036	47 204	4 610	9 039	10 309	9 297	7 031	6 919
1964	52 869	5 148	3 090	2 059	47 721	4 862	9 024	10 301	9 417	7 153	6 963
1965	53 681	5 541	3 050	2 492	48 140	5 017	9 056	10 262	9 516	7 261	7 028
1966	54 061	5 820	3 023	2 798	48 241	4 974	9 085	10 136	9 592	7 362	7 092
1967	54 608	5 671	3 058	2 613	48 937	5 257	9 339	10 013	9 688	7 474	7 167
1968	55 434	5 787	3 153	2 635	49 647	5 376	9 752	9 902	9 790	7 585	7 242
1969	56 348	6 005	3 246	2 759	50 343	5 589	10 074	9 760	9 895	7 705	7 320
1970	57 516	6 179	3 329	2 851	51 336	5 988	10 441	9 678	9 999	7 822	7 409
1971	58 900	6 420	3 412	3 008	52 481	6 546	10 841	9 578	10 066	7 933	7 517
1972	60 473	6 627	3 503	3 125	53 845	7 042	11 495	9 568	10 078	8 089	7 573
1973	61 577	6 737	3 555	3 182	54 842	7 312	12 075	9 514	10 099	8 178	7 664
1974	62 791	6 851	3 604	3 247	55 942	7 476	12 599	9 564	10 165	8 288	7 849
1975	63 981	6 929	3 609	3 320	57 052	7 766	13 131	9 578	10 134	8 413	8 031
1976	65 132	6 993	3 609	3 384	58 138	7 987	13 655	9 674	10 063	8 556	8 203
1977	66 301	7 024	3 625	3 399	59 278	8 175	14 139	9 880	9 957	8 708	8 420
1978	67 401	7 022	3 619	3 404	60 378	8 335	14 528	10 236	9 845	8 826	8 608
1979	68 547	7 007	3 568	3 439	61 540	8 470	15 008	10 563	9 730	8 949	8 820
1980	69 634	6 941	3 508	3 433	62 694	8 581	15 529	10 863	9 636	9 059	9 027
1981	70 480	6 764	3 401	3 363	63 715	8 644	16 005	11 171	9 560	9 139	9 195
1982	71 211	6 556	3 249	3 307	64 655	8 621	16 260	11 756	9 463	9 188	9 367
1983	71 922	6 340	3 098	3 242	65 581	8 597	16 499	12 314	9 408	9 208	9 556
1984	72 723	6 113	3 019	3 094	66 610	8 522	16 816	12 853	9 434	9 217	9 768
1985	73 373	5 987	3 026	2 961	67 386	8 246	17 042	13 337	9 488	9 262	10 010
1986	74 390	5 977	3 084	2 894	68 413	8 002	17 564	13 840	9 578	9 201	10 229
1987	75 189	6 015	3 125	2 890	69 175	7 729	17 754	14 338	9 771	9 101	10 481
1988	75 855	5 968	3 015	2 953	69 887	7 473	17 867	14 743	10 114	9 001	10 688
1989	76 468	5 813	2 817	2 996	70 654	7 279	17 908	15 237	10 434	8 900	10 897
1990	77 369	5 913	2 809	3 103	71 457	7 764	17 766	15 770	10 598	8 680	10 879
1991	77 977	5 704	2 805	2 899	72 274	7 748	17 615	16 340	10 856	8 640	11 074
1992	78 651	5 611	2 819	2 792	73 040	7 676	17 403	16 579	11 513	8 602	11 268
1993	79 371	5 650	2 862	2 788	73 721	7 545	17 158	16 900	12 058	8 590	11 470
1994	80 059	5 748	2 938	2 810	74 311	7 357	16 915	17 247	12 545	8 618	11 629
1995	80 733	5 854	2 995	2 859	74 879	7 163	16 653	17 567	13 028	8 653	11 815
1996	81 489	6 035	3 099	2 936	75 454	6 971	16 395	17 868	13 518	8 734	11 968
1997	82 577	6 257	3 209	3 048	76 320	7 087	16 043	18 163	14 030	8 929	12 067
1998	83 352	6 386	3 233	3 153	76 966	7 170	15 644	18 310	14 400	9 286	12 155
1999	83 930	6 498	3 266	3 232	77 432	7 244	15 150	18 340	14 834	9 581	12 283
2000	85 370	6 404	3 224	3 181	78 966	7 329	15 528	18 003	15 578	10 028	12 501
2001	86 452	6 422	3 229	3 194	80 029	7 564	15 486	17 960	16 047	10 369	12 604
2002	87 361	6 439	3 251	3 189	80 922	7 750	15 470	17 792	16 317	10 918	12 676
2003	88 249	6 390	3 378	3 012	81 860	7 856	15 569	17 620	16 555	11 442	12 818
2004	89 044	6 429	3 301	3 129	82 615	8 024	15 486	17 404	16 834	11 922	12 946
2005	90 027	6 471	3 464	3 006	83 556	8 057	15 507	17 286	17 169	12 415	13 123
2006	91 021	6 555	3 551	3 004	84 466	8 052	15 567	17 143	17 467	12 891	13 346

¹Beginning in 2003, persons who selected this race group only; persons who selected more than one race group are not included. Prior to 2003, persons who reported more than one race group were included in the group identified as their main race.

Table 1-6. Civilian Noninstitutional Population, by Age, Race, Sex, and Hispanic Origin, 1948–2006
—*Continued*

(Thousands of people.)

Race, Hispanic origin, sex, and year	16 years and over	16 to 19 years			20 years and over						
		Total	16 to 17 years	18 to 19 years	Total	20 to 24 years	25 to 34 years	35 to 44 years	45 to 54 years	55 to 64 years	65 years and over
WHITE[1]											
Women											
1954	51 242	3 725	1 884	1 841	47 517	4 720	10 870	10 227	8 397	6 652	6 651
1955	51 802	3 785	1 929	1 856	48 017	4 671	10 806	10 342	8 566	6 771	6 862
1956	52 373	3 846	1 953	1 892	48 527	4 642	10 713	10 466	8 752	6 886	7 067
1957	52 998	3 949	2 007	1 941	49 049	4 655	10 584	10 597	8 957	7 000	7 256
1958	53 645	4 096	2 131	1 966	49 549	4 715	10 407	10 716	9 159	7 107	7 442
1959	54 392	4 351	2 337	2 015	50 041	4 794	10 216	10 812	9 348	7 219	7 653
1960	55 214	4 575	2 433	2 142	50 639	4 873	10 097	10 918	9 536	7 349	7 865
1961	55 993	4 732	2 378	2 354	51 261	4 999	9 999	10 991	9 697	7 485	8 091
1962	56 660	4 823	2 392	2 432	51 837	5 178	9 894	11 054	9 681	7 533	8 496
1963	57 672	5 151	2 757	2 394	52 521	5 459	9 828	11 089	9 785	7 650	8 710
1964	58 663	5 468	3 047	2 422	53 195	5 706	9 814	11 074	9 943	7 804	8 853
1965	59 601	5 778	2 999	2 779	53 823	5 918	9 826	10 996	10 088	7 954	9 042
1966	60 503	6 042	2 970	3 072	54 461	6 120	9 904	10 869	10 230	8 107	9 230
1967	61 491	6 011	2 993	3 019	55 480	6 540	10 125	10 732	10 379	8 271	9 435
1968	62 512	6 053	3 072	2 981	56 460	6 809	10 493	10 572	10 520	8 433	9 633
1969	63 563	6 174	3 172	3 002	57 390	7 089	10 818	10 396	10 651	8 600	9 836
1970	64 656	6 342	3 262	3 080	58 315	7 370	11 105	10 251	10 761	8 769	10 060
1971	65 857	6 518	3 338	3 180	59 340	7 662	11 454	10 117	10 841	8 951	10 315
1972	67 431	6 673	3 407	3 267	60 758	7 855	12 060	10 105	10 872	9 161	10 705
1973	68 517	6 796	3 466	3 331	61 721	7 951	12 610	10 018	10 891	9 306	10 943
1974	69 623	6 933	3 510	3 424	62 690	8 026	13 112	10 064	10 896	9 356	11 236
1975	70 810	7 011	3 523	3 488	63 798	8 214	13 615	10 063	10 847	9 505	11 556
1976	71 974	7 062	3 516	3 546	64 912	8 381	14 102	10 153	10 752	9 664	11 860
1977	73 077	7 071	3 525	3 545	66 007	8 553	14 564	10 351	10 618	9 832	12 088
1978	74 213	7 038	3 513	3 524	67 174	8 704	14 926	10 696	10 476	9 974	12 399
1979	75 347	6 987	3 460	3 527	68 360	8 815	15 363	11 017	10 327	10 122	12 717
1980	76 489	6 914	3 403	3 511	69 575	8 904	15 878	11 313	10 201	10 256	13 022
1981	77 428	6 752	3 303	3 449	70 677	8 965	16 362	11 606	10 106	10 346	13 292
1982	78 230	6 519	3 134	3 385	71 711	8 959	16 603	12 154	10 015	10 402	13 579
1983	78 884	6 282	2 991	3 292	72 601	8 895	16 788	12 714	9 941	10 418	13 847
1984	79 624	6 034	2 899	3 135	73 590	8 782	17 073	13 271	9 914	10 412	14 138
1985	80 306	5 912	2 895	3 017	74 394	8 607	17 409	13 762	9 917	10 358	14 342
1986	81 042	5 902	2 953	2 949	75 140	8 351	17 728	14 223	10 009	10 277	14 551
1987	81 769	5 924	2 985	2 939	75 845	8 079	17 913	14 698	10 194	10 141	14 820
1988	82 340	5 869	2 878	2 991	76 470	7 804	18 009	15 074	10 537	9 994	15 052
1989	82 871	5 716	2 690	3 027	77 154	7 600	18 043	15 537	10 853	9 843	15 278
1990	83 256	5 717	2 654	3 063	77 539	7 774	17 895	15 969	10 937	9 524	15 440
1991	83 781	5 497	2 646	2 850	78 285	7 768	17 726	16 514	11 196	9 435	15 647
1992	84 321	5 393	2 659	2 734	78 928	7 678	17 482	16 727	11 851	9 350	15 841
1993	84 918	5 428	2 700	2 728	79 490	7 542	17 206	17 019	12 398	9 302	16 023
1994	85 496	5 516	2 772	2 744	79 980	7 351	16 950	17 335	12 890	9 306	16 148
1995	86 181	5 614	2 827	2 787	80 567	7 150	16 702	17 654	13 390	9 333	16 337
1996	86 828	5 787	2 927	2 860	81 041	6 936	16 457	17 943	13 884	9 402	16 419
1997	87 417	5 924	3 004	2 920	81 492	6 896	16 047	18 162	14 357	9 582	16 447
1998	88 126	6 053	3 031	3 023	82 073	6 969	15 642	18 300	14 732	9 944	16 486
1999	89 156	6 202	3 076	3 127	82 953	7 150	15 366	18 415	15 214	10 274	16 536
2000	90 850	6 131	3 041	3 090	84 718	7 223	15 420	18 258	15 972	10 729	17 116
2001	91 660	6 134	3 062	3 071	85 526	7 438	15 284	18 153	16 428	11 065	17 158
2002	92 422	6 157	3 096	3 061	86 266	7 611	15 207	17 958	16 695	11 622	17 173
2003	93 043	6 137	3 251	2 886	86 905	7 680	15 220	17 731	16 911	12 147	17 216
2004	93 599	6 169	3 260	2 909	87 430	7 794	15 099	17 441	17 170	12 627	17 299
2005	94 419	6 219	3 304	2 915	88 200	7 814	15 086	17 268	17 480	13 119	17 433
2006	95 242	6 301	3 429	2 871	88 942	7 796	15 094	17 074	17 760	13 596	17 623

[1]Beginning in 2003, persons who selected this race group only; persons who selected more than one race group are not included. Prior to 2003, persons who reported more than one race group were included in the group identified as their main race.

Table 1-6. Civilian Noninstitutional Population, by Age, Race, Sex, and Hispanic Origin, 1948–2006
—Continued

(Thousands of people.)

Race, Hispanic origin, sex, and year	16 years and over	16 to 19 years			20 years and over						
		Total	16 to 17 years	18 to 19 years	Total	20 to 24 years	25 to 34 years	35 to 44 years	45 to 54 years	55 to 64 years	65 years and over
BLACK[1]											
Both Sexes											
1972	14 526	2 018	1 061	956	12 508	2 027	2 809	2 329	2 139	1 601	1 605
1973	14 917	2 095	1 095	1 000	12 823	2 132	2 957	2 333	2 156	1 616	1 628
1974	15 329	2 137	1 122	1 014	13 192	2 137	3 103	2 382	2 202	1 679	1 689
1975	15 751	2 191	1 146	1 046	13 560	2 228	3 258	2 395	2 211	1 717	1 755
1976	16 196	2 264	1 165	1 098	13 932	2 303	3 412	2 435	2 220	1 736	1 826
1977	16 605	2 273	1 175	1 097	14 332	2 400	3 566	2 493	2 225	1 765	1 883
1978	16 970	2 270	1 169	1 101	14 701	2 483	3 717	2 547	2 226	1 794	1 932
1979	17 397	2 276	1 167	1 109	15 121	2 556	3 899	2 615	2 240	1 831	1 980
1980	17 824	2 289	1 171	1 119	15 535	2 606	4 095	2 687	2 249	1 870	2 030
1981	18 219	2 288	1 161	1 127	15 931	2 642	4 290	2 758	2 260	1 913	2 069
1982	18 584	2 252	1 119	1 134	16 332	2 697	4 438	2 887	2 263	1 935	2 113
1983	18 925	2 225	1 092	1 133	16 700	2 734	4 607	2 999	2 260	1 964	2 135
1984	19 348	2 161	1 056	1 105	17 187	2 783	4 789	3 167	2 288	1 977	2 183
1985	19 664	2 160	1 083	1 077	17 504	2 649	4 873	3 290	2 372	2 060	2 259
1986	19 989	2 137	1 090	1 048	17 852	2 625	5 026	3 410	2 413	2 079	2 298
1987	20 352	2 163	1 123	1 040	18 189	2 578	5 139	3 563	2 460	2 097	2 352
1988	20 692	2 179	1 130	1 049	18 513	2 527	5 234	3 716	2 524	2 110	2 402
1989	21 021	2 176	1 116	1 060	18 846	2 479	5 308	3 900	2 587	2 118	2 454
1990	21 477	2 238	1 101	1 138	19 239	2 554	5 407	4 328	2 618	1 970	2 362
1991	21 799	2 187	1 085	1 102	19 612	2 585	5 419	4 538	2 682	1 985	2 403
1992	22 147	2 155	1 086	1 069	19 992	2 615	5 404	4 722	2 809	1 996	2 446
1993	22 521	2 181	1 113	1 069	20 339	2 600	5 409	4 886	2 941	2 016	2 487
1994	22 879	2 211	1 168	1 044	20 668	2 616	5 362	5 038	3 084	2 045	2 524
1995	23 246	2 284	1 198	1 086	20 962	2 554	5 337	5 178	3 244	2 079	2 571
1996	23 604	2 356	1 238	1 118	21 248	2 519	5 311	5 290	3 408	2 110	2 609
1997	24 003	2 412	1 255	1 158	21 591	2 515	5 279	5 410	3 571	2 164	2 653
1998	24 373	2 443	1 241	1 202	21 930	2 546	5 221	5 510	3 735	2 224	2 695
1999	24 855	2 479	1 250	1 229	22 376	2 615	5 197	5 609	3 919	2 295	2 741
2000	24 902	2 389	1 205	1 183	22 513	2 611	5 089	5 488	4 168	2 407	2 750
2001	25 138	2 388	1 212	1 176	22 750	2 686	5 003	5 467	4 343	2 478	2 775
2002	25 578	2 416	1 235	1 181	23 162	2 779	5 015	5 460	4 513	2 571	2 823
2003	25 686	2 382	1 309	1 074	23 304	2 773	4 978	5 387	4 628	2 692	2 846
2004	26 065	2 423	1 350	1 072	23 643	2 821	5 020	5 335	4 739	2 827	2 899
2005	26 517	2 481	1 341	1 140	24 036	2 835	5 075	5 311	4 869	2 980	2 967
2006	27 007	2 565	1 408	1 157	24 442	2 851	5 133	5 302	4 992	3 137	3 027
BLACK[1]											
Men											
1972	6 538	978	525	453	5 559	921	1 251	1 026	963	720	679
1973	6 704	1 007	539	468	5 697	979	1 327	1 027	962	718	684
1974	6 875	1 027	554	471	5 848	956	1 381	1 055	997	753	707
1975	7 060	1 051	565	486	6 009	1 002	1 452	1 060	997	769	730
1976	7 265	1 099	579	518	6 167	1 036	1 521	1 077	999	774	756
1977	7 431	1 102	586	516	6 329	1 080	1 589	1 102	998	786	774
1978	7 577	1 093	579	514	6 484	1 120	1 657	1 128	995	794	789
1979	7 761	1 100	581	519	6 661	1 151	1 738	1 159	998	809	804
1980	7 944	1 110	583	526	6 834	1 171	1 828	1 191	999	825	822
1981	8 117	1 110	577	534	7 007	1 189	1 914	1 224	1 003	844	835
1982	8 283	1 097	556	542	7 186	1 225	1 983	1 282	1 003	848	846
1983	8 447	1 087	542	545	7 360	1 254	2 068	1 333	1 000	857	847
1984	8 654	1 055	524	531	7 599	1 292	2 164	1 411	1 012	858	861
1985	8 790	1 059	543	517	7 731	1 202	2 180	1 462	1 060	924	902
1986	8 956	1 049	548	503	7 907	1 195	2 264	1 517	1 072	934	924
1987	9 128	1 065	566	499	8 063	1 173	2 320	1 587	1 092	944	947
1988	9 289	1 074	569	505	8 215	1 151	2 367	1 656	1 121	951	970
1989	9 439	1 075	575	501	8 364	1 128	2 403	1 741	1 145	956	989
1990	9 573	1 094	555	540	8 479	1 144	2 412	1 968	1 183	855	917
1991	9 725	1 072	546	526	8 652	1 168	2 417	2 060	1 211	864	933
1992	9 896	1 056	544	512	8 840	1 194	2 409	2 150	1 268	868	951
1993	10 083	1 075	559	516	9 008	1 181	2 425	2 228	1 330	874	969
1994	10 258	1 087	586	501	9 171	1 207	2 399	2 300	1 392	889	985
1995	10 411	1 131	601	530	9 280	1 161	2 388	2 362	1 462	901	1 006
1996	10 575	1 161	623	538	9 414	1 154	2 373	2 413	1 534	914	1 025
1997	10 763	1 188	634	553	9 575	1 153	2 363	2 471	1 607	936	1 045
1998	10 927	1 201	623	578	9 727	1 166	2 335	2 520	1 682	956	1 068
1999	11 143	1 218	628	589	9 926	1 197	2 321	2 566	1 765	986	1 091
2000	11 129	1 178	605	572	9 952	1 195	2 277	2 471	1 889	1 067	1 053
2001	11 172	1 179	606	573	9 993	1 224	2 212	2 440	1 960	1 096	1 060
2002	11 391	1 195	615	580	10 196	1 281	2 223	2 437	2 042	1 137	1 075
2003	11 454	1 176	661	515	10 278	1 291	2 210	2 401	2 094	1 189	1 093
2004	11 656	1 195	680	516	10 461	1 326	2 242	2 382	2 150	1 250	1 111
2005	11 882	1 223	682	541	10 659	1 341	2 277	2 372	2 202	1 319	1 148
2006	12 130	1 266	713	552	10 864	1 355	2 318	2 369	2 261	1 390	1 170

[1]Beginning in 2003, persons who selected this race group only; persons who selected more than one race group are not included. Prior to 2003, persons who reported more than one race group were included in the group identified as their main race.

Table 1-6. Civilian Noninstitutional Population, by Age, Race, Sex, and Hispanic Origin, 1948–2006
—Continued

(Thousands of people.)

Race, Hispanic origin, sex, and year	16 years and over	16 to 19 years			20 years and over						
		Total	16 to 17 years	18 to 19 years	Total	20 to 24 years	25 to 34 years	35 to 44 years	45 to 54 years	55 to 64 years	65 years and over
BLACK[1]											
Women											
1972	7 988	1 040	536	503	6 948	1 106	1 558	1 302	1 176	881	925
1973	8 214	1 088	556	532	7 126	1 153	1 631	1 306	1 194	898	944
1974	8 454	1 110	567	542	7 344	1 181	1 723	1 327	1 206	926	981
1975	8 691	1 141	581	560	7 550	1 226	1 806	1 334	1 213	948	1 025
1976	8 931	1 165	585	580	7 765	1 266	1 890	1 357	1 220	962	1 070
1977	9 174	1 171	590	581	8 003	1 320	1 978	1 390	1 228	979	1 108
1978	9 394	1 177	589	588	8 217	1 363	2 061	1 419	1 231	999	1 143
1979	9 636	1 176	586	589	8 460	1 405	2 160	1 455	1 242	1 022	1 176
1980	9 880	1 180	587	593	8 700	1 435	2 267	1 496	1 250	1 045	1 208
1981	10 102	1 178	584	593	8 924	1 453	2 376	1 534	1 257	1 069	1 234
1982	10 300	1 155	563	592	9 146	1 472	2 455	1 605	1 260	1 087	1 267
1983	10 477	1 138	550	588	9 340	1 480	2 539	1 666	1 260	1 107	1 288
1984	10 694	1 106	532	574	9 588	1 491	2 625	1 756	1 276	1 119	1 322
1985	10 873	1 101	540	560	9 773	1 447	2 693	1 828	1 312	1 136	1 357
1986	11 033	1 088	542	545	9 945	1 430	2 762	1 893	1 341	1 145	1 374
1987	11 224	1 098	557	541	10 126	1 405	2 819	1 976	1 368	1 153	1 405
1988	11 402	1 105	561	544	10 298	1 376	2 867	2 060	1 403	1 159	1 432
1989	11 582	1 100	541	559	10 482	1 351	2 905	2 159	1 441	1 162	1 464
1990	11 904	1 144	546	598	10 760	1 410	2 995	2 360	1 435	1 114	1 446
1991	12 074	1 115	539	576	10 959	1 417	3 003	2 478	1 471	1 121	1 470
1992	12 251	1 099	542	557	11 152	1 421	2 995	2 573	1 542	1 127	1 495
1993	12 438	1 106	554	552	11 332	1 419	2 983	2 659	1 611	1 142	1 518
1994	12 621	1 125	582	543	11 496	1 410	2 963	2 738	1 692	1 156	1 538
1995	12 835	1 153	597	556	11 682	1 392	2 948	2 816	1 782	1 178	1 565
1996	13 029	1 195	615	580	11 833	1 364	2 938	2 877	1 874	1 196	1 584
1997	13 241	1 225	620	604	12 016	1 362	2 916	2 939	1 964	1 228	1 608
1998	13 446	1 243	618	624	12 203	1 380	2 886	2 991	2 053	1 268	1 626
1999	13 711	1 261	621	640	12 451	1 418	2 876	3 043	2 153	1 310	1 650
2000	13 772	1 211	600	611	12 561	1 416	2 812	3 017	2 279	1 340	1 697
2001	13 966	1 209	606	603	12 758	1 462	2 790	3 026	2 383	1 382	1 714
2002	14 187	1 221	620	601	12 966	1 498	2 792	3 023	2 471	1 434	1 747
2003	14 232	1 206	648	558	13 026	1 482	2 768	2 986	2 534	1 504	1 753
2004	14 409	1 227	670	557	13 182	1 495	2 778	2 954	2 590	1 577	1 789
2005	14 635	1 258	659	598	13 377	1 494	2 797	2 939	2 666	1 661	1 819
2006	14 877	1 299	694	605	13 578	1 495	2 815	2 933	2 731	1 747	1 857
HISPANIC[2]											
Both Sexes											
1973	6 104	867	. . .	. . .	5 238	. . .	. . .	. . .	. . .	. . .	. . .
1974	6 564	926	. . .	. . .	5 645	. . .	. . .	. . .	. . .	. . .	. . .
1975	6 862	962	. . .	. . .	5 900	. . .	. . .	. . .	. . .	. . .	. . .
1976	6 910	953	494	480	6 075	1 053	1 775	1 261	936	570	479
1977	7 362	1 024	513	508	6 376	1 163	1 869	1 283	989	587	485
1978	7 912	1 076	561	515	6 836	1 265	2 004	1 378	1 033	627	529
1979	8 207	1 095	544	551	7 113	1 296	2 117	1 458	1 015	659	566
1980	9 598	1 281	638	643	8 317	1 564	2 508	1 575	1 190	782	698
1981	10 120	1 301	641	660	8 819	1 650	2 698	1 680	1 231	832	728
1982	10 580	1 307	639	668	9 273	1 724	2 871	1 779	1 264	880	755
1983	11 029	1 304	635	670	9 725	1 790	3 045	1 883	1 298	928	781
1984	11 478	1 300	633	667	10 178	1 839	3 224	1 996	1 336	973	810
1985	11 915	1 298	638	661	10 617	1 864	3 401	2 117	1 377	1 015	843
1986	12 344	1 302	658	644	11 042	1 899	3 510	2 239	1 496	1 023	875
1987	12 867	1 332	651	681	11 536	1 910	3 714	2 464	1 492	1 061	895
1988	13 325	1 354	662	692	11 970	1 948	3 807	2 565	1 571	1 159	920
1989	13 791	1 399	672	727	12 392	1 950	3 953	2 658	1 649	1 182	1 001
1990	15 904	1 737	821	915	14 167	2 428	4 589	3 001	1 817	1 247	1 084
1991	16 425	1 732	819	913	14 693	2 481	4 674	3 243	1 879	1 283	1 134
1992	16 961	1 737	836	901	15 224	2 444	4 806	3 458	1 980	1 321	1 216
1993	17 532	1 756	855	901	15 776	2 487	4 887	3 632	2 094	1 324	1 353
1994	18 117	1 818	902	916	16 300	2 518	5 000	3 756	2 223	1 401	1 401
1995	18 629	1 872	903	969	16 757	2 528	5 050	3 965	2 294	1 483	1 437
1996	19 213	1 948	962	986	17 265	2 524	5 181	4 227	2 275	1 546	1 512
1997	20 321	2 121	1 088	1 033	18 200	2 623	5 405	4 453	2 581	1 580	1 558
1998	21 070	2 204	1 070	1 135	18 865	2 731	5 447	4 636	2 775	1 615	1 662
1999	21 650	2 307	1 113	1 194	19 344	2 700	5 512	4 833	2 868	1 713	1 718
2000	23 938	2 523	1 214	1 309	21 415	3 255	6 466	5 189	3 061	1 736	1 708
2001	24 942	2 508	1 173	1 334	22 435	3 417	6 726	5 346	3 339	1 816	1 792
2002	25 963	2 507	1 216	1 291	23 456	3 508	7 010	5 606	3 494	1 953	1 885
2003	27 551	2 543	1 346	1 197	25 008	3 533	7 506	6 003	3 845	2 093	2 027
2004	28 109	2 608	1 337	1 270	25 502	3 666	7 470	6 055	3 987	2 208	2 115
2005	29 133	2 689	1 415	1 274	26 444	3 647	7 684	6 293	4 217	2 361	2 242
2006	30 103	2 796	1 518	1 277	27 307	3 603	7 856	6 519	4 466	2 516	2 347

[1]Beginning in 2003, persons who selected this race group only; persons who selected more than one race group are not included. Prior to 2003, persons who reported more than one race group were included in the group identified as their main race.
[2]May be of any race.
. . . = Not available.

Table 1-6. Civilian Noninstitutional Population, by Age, Race, Sex, and Hispanic Origin, 1948–2006
—*Continued*

(Thousands of people.)

Race, Hispanic origin, sex, and year	16 years and over	16 to 19 years			20 years and over						
		Total	16 to 17 years	18 to 19 years	Total	20 to 24 years	25 to 34 years	35 to 44 years	45 to 54 years	55 to 64 years	65 years and over
HISPANIC[2]											
Men											
1973	2 891	. . .	. . .	. . .	2 472	. . .	. . .	. . .	. . .	. . .	. . .
1974	3 130	. . .	. . .	. . .	2 680	. . .	. . .	. . .	. . .	. . .	. . .
1975	3 219	. . .	. . .	. . .	2 741	. . .	. . .	. . .	. . .	. . .	. . .
1976	3 241	. . .	. . .	. . .	2 764	. . .	. . .	. . .	. . .	. . .	. . .
1977	3 483	. . .	. . .	. . .	2 982	. . .	. . .	. . .	. . .	. . .	. . .
1978	3 750	. . .	. . .	. . .	3 228	. . .	. . .	. . .	. . .	. . .	. . .
1979	3 917	. . .	. . .	. . .	3 362	. . .	. . .	. . .	. . .	. . .	. . .
1980	4 689	. . .	. . .	. . .	4 036	. . .	. . .	. . .	. . .	. . .	. . .
1981	4 968	. . .	. . .	. . .	4 306	. . .	. . .	. . .	. . .	. . .	. . .
1982	5 203	. . .	. . .	. . .	4 539	. . .	. . .	. . .	. . .	. . .	. . .
1983	5 432	. . .	. . .	. . .	4 771	. . .	. . .	. . .	. . .	. . .	. . .
1984	5 661	. . .	. . .	. . .	5 005	. . .	. . .	. . .	. . .	. . .	. . .
1985	5 885	. . .	. . .	. . .	5 232	. . .	. . .	. . .	. . .	. . .	. . .
1986	6 106	. . .	. . .	. . .	5 451	. . .	. . .	. . .	. . .	. . .	. . .
1987	6 371	. . .	. . .	. . .	5 700	. . .	. . .	. . .	. . .	. . .	. . .
1988	6 604	. . .	. . .	. . .	5 921	. . .	. . .	. . .	. . .	. . .	. . .
1989	6 825	. . .	. . .	. . .	6 114	. . .	. . .	. . .	. . .	. . .	. . .
1990	8 041	. . .	. . .	. . .	7 126	. . .	. . .	. . .	. . .	. . .	. . .
1991	8 296	. . .	. . .	. . .	7 392	. . .	. . .	. . .	. . .	. . .	. . .
1992	8 553	. . .	. . .	. . .	7 655	. . .	. . .	. . .	. . .	. . .	. . .
1993	8 824	. . .	. . .	. . .	7 930	. . .	. . .	. . .	. . .	. . .	. . .
1994	9 104	926	472	454	8 178	1 346	2 627	1 871	1 076	644	614
1995	9 329	954	481	473	8 375	1 337	2 657	1 966	1 127	668	619
1996	9 604	992	485	507	8 611	1 321	2 692	2 144	1 111	712	630
1997	10 368	1 119	585	534	9 250	1 439	2 872	2 275	1 266	747	651
1998	10 734	1 161	586	575	9 573	1 462	2 907	2 377	1 342	771	714
1999	10 713	1 190	571	619	9 523	1 398	2 805	2 407	1 397	767	749
2000	12 174	1 333	640	693	10 841	1 784	3 380	2 626	1 527	799	725
2001	12 695	1 310	619	690	11 386	1 846	3 529	2 765	1 650	848	749
2002	13 221	1 293	615	678	11 928	1 890	3 727	2 875	1 716	902	817
2003	14 098	1 301	674	627	12 797	1 905	4 033	3 098	1 910	989	862
2004	14 417	1 336	664	672	13 082	1 981	4 024	3 147	1 990	1 046	894
2005	14 962	1 376	730	646	13 586	1 956	4 155	3 284	2 114	1 123	953
2006	15 473	1 428	763	664	14 046	1 916	4 266	3 414	2 251	1 204	996
HISPANIC[2]											
Women											
1973	3 213	. . .	. . .	. . .	2 766	. . .	. . .	. . .	. . .	. . .	. . .
1974	3 434	. . .	. . .	. . .	2 959	. . .	. . .	. . .	. . .	. . .	. . .
1975	3 644	. . .	. . .	. . .	3 161	. . .	. . .	. . .	. . .	. . .	. . .
1976	3 669	. . .	. . .	. . .	3 263	. . .	. . .	. . .	. . .	. . .	. . .
1977	3 879	. . .	. . .	. . .	3 377	. . .	. . .	. . .	. . .	. . .	. . .
1978	4 159	. . .	. . .	. . .	3 608	. . .	. . .	. . .	. . .	. . .	. . .
1979	4 291	. . .	. . .	. . .	3 751	. . .	. . .	. . .	. . .	. . .	. . .
1980	4 909	. . .	. . .	. . .	4 281	. . .	. . .	. . .	. . .	. . .	. . .
1981	5 151	. . .	. . .	. . .	4 513	. . .	. . .	. . .	. . .	. . .	. . .
1982	5 377	. . .	. . .	. . .	4 734	. . .	. . .	. . .	. . .	. . .	. . .
1983	5 597	. . .	. . .	. . .	4 954	. . .	. . .	. . .	. . .	. . .	. . .
1984	5 816	. . .	. . .	. . .	5 173	. . .	. . .	. . .	. . .	. . .	. . .
1985	6 029	. . .	. . .	. . .	5 385	. . .	. . .	. . .	. . .	. . .	. . .
1986	6 238	. . .	. . .	. . .	5 591	. . .	. . .	. . .	. . .	. . .	. . .
1987	6 496	. . .	. . .	. . .	5 835	. . .	. . .	. . .	. . .	. . .	. . .
1988	6 721	. . .	. . .	. . .	6 050	. . .	. . .	. . .	. . .	. . .	. . .
1989	6 965	. . .	. . .	. . .	6 278	. . .	. . .	. . .	. . .	. . .	. . .
1990	7 863	. . .	. . .	. . .	7 041	. . .	. . .	. . .	. . .	. . .	. . .
1991	8 130	. . .	. . .	. . .	7 301	. . .	. . .	. . .	. . .	. . .	. . .
1992	8 408	. . .	. . .	. . .	7 569	. . .	. . .	. . .	. . .	. . .	. . .
1993	8 708	. . .	. . .	. . .	7 846	. . .	. . .	. . .	. . .	. . .	. . .
1994	9 014	892	430	462	8 122	1 173	2 373	1 885	1 147	757	787
1995	9 300	918	422	496	8 382	1 191	2 393	1 999	1 167	815	818
1996	9 610	956	477	479	8 654	1 203	2 489	2 082	1 164	834	882
1997	9 953	1 003	503	500	8 950	1 184	2 533	2 178	1 315	833	907
1998	10 335	1 044	483	560	9 292	1 269	2 539	2 259	1 433	844	948
1999	10 937	1 116	542	575	9 821	1 302	2 707	2 425	1 470	947	969
2000	11 764	1 190	574	616	10 574	1 471	3 086	2 564	1 534	937	982
2001	12 247	1 198	554	644	11 049	1 571	3 198	2 581	1 689	968	1 043
2002	12 742	1 214	601	613	11 528	1 617	3 283	2 732	1 777	1 051	1 068
2003	13 452	1 242	672	570	12 211	1 628	3 473	2 905	1 935	1 105	1 166
2004	13 692	1 272	674	598	12 420	1 685	3 447	2 908	1 997	1 162	1 221
2005	14 172	1 313	685	628	12 858	1 692	3 529	3 009	2 103	1 237	1 289
2006	14 630	1 368	755	613	13 262	1 688	3 590	3 105	2 215	1 313	1 351

[2]May be of any race.
. . . = Not available.

Table 1-7. Civilian Labor Force, by Age, Sex, Race, and Hispanic Origin, 1948–2006

(Thousands of people.)

Race, Hispanic origin, sex, and year	16 years and over	16 to 19 years			20 years and over						
		Total	16 to 17 years	18 to 19 years	Total	20 to 24 years	25 to 34 years	35 to 44 years	45 to 54 years	55 to 64 years	65 years and over
ALL RACES											
Both Sexes											
1948	60 621	4 435	1 780	2 654	56 187	7 392	14 258	13 397	10 914	7 329	2 897
1949	61 286	4 288	1 704	2 583	57 000	7 340	14 415	13 711	11 107	7 426	3 010
1950	62 208	4 216	1 659	2 557	57 994	7 307	14 619	13 954	11 444	7 633	3 036
1951	62 017	4 103	1 743	2 360	57 914	6 594	14 668	14 100	11 739	7 796	3 020
1952	62 138	4 064	1 806	2 257	58 075	5 840	14 904	14 383	11 961	7 980	3 005
1953	63 015	4 027	1 727	2 299	58 989	5 481	14 898	15 099	12 249	8 024	3 236
1954	63 643	3 976	1 643	2 300	59 666	5 475	14 983	15 221	12 524	8 269	3 192
1955	65 023	4 092	1 711	2 382	60 931	5 666	15 058	15 400	12 992	8 513	3 305
1956	66 552	4 296	1 878	2 418	62 257	5 940	14 961	15 694	13 407	8 830	3 423
1957	66 929	4 275	1 843	2 433	62 653	6 071	14 826	15 847	13 768	8 853	3 290
1958	67 639	4 260	1 818	2 442	63 377	6 272	14 668	16 028	14 179	9 031	3 199
1959	68 369	4 492	1 971	2 522	63 876	6 413	14 435	16 127	14 518	9 227	3 158
1960	69 628	4 841	2 095	2 747	64 788	6 702	14 382	16 269	14 852	9 385	3 195
1961	70 459	4 936	1 984	2 951	65 524	6 950	14 319	16 402	15 071	9 636	3 146
1962	70 614	4 916	1 919	2 997	65 699	7 082	14 023	16 589	15 096	9 757	3 154
1963	71 833	5 139	2 171	2 966	66 695	7 473	14 050	16 788	15 338	10 006	3 041
1964	73 091	5 388	2 449	2 940	67 702	7 963	14 056	16 771	15 637	10 182	3 090
1965	74 455	5 910	2 486	3 425	68 543	8 259	14 233	16 840	15 756	10 350	3 108
1966	75 770	6 558	2 664	3 893	69 219	8 410	14 458	16 738	15 984	10 575	3 053
1967	77 347	6 521	2 734	3 786	70 825	9 010	15 055	16 703	16 172	10 792	3 097
1968	78 737	6 619	2 817	3 803	72 118	9 305	15 708	16 591	16 397	10 964	3 153
1969	80 734	6 970	3 009	3 959	73 763	9 879	16 336	16 458	16 730	11 135	3 227
1970	82 771	7 249	3 135	4 115	75 521	10 597	17 036	16 437	16 949	11 283	3 222
1971	84 382	7 470	3 192	4 278	76 913	11 331	17 714	16 305	17 024	11 390	3 149
1972	87 034	8 054	3 420	4 636	78 980	12 130	18 960	16 398	16 967	11 412	3 114
1973	89 429	8 507	3 665	4 839	80 924	12 846	20 376	16 492	16 983	11 256	2 974
1974	91 949	8 871	3 810	5 059	83 080	13 314	21 654	16 763	17 131	11 284	2 934
1975	93 775	8 870	3 740	5 131	84 904	13 750	22 864	16 903	17 084	11 346	2 956
1976	96 158	9 056	3 767	5 288	87 103	14 284	24 203	17 317	16 982	11 422	2 895
1977	99 009	9 351	3 919	5 431	89 658	14 825	25 500	17 943	16 878	11 577	2 934
1978	102 251	9 652	4 127	5 526	92 598	15 370	26 703	18 821	16 891	11 744	3 070
1979	104 962	9 638	4 079	5 559	95 325	15 769	27 938	19 685	16 897	11 931	3 104
1980	106 940	9 378	3 883	5 496	97 561	15 922	29 227	20 463	16 910	11 985	3 054
1981	108 670	8 988	3 647	5 340	99 682	16 099	30 392	21 211	16 970	11 969	3 042
1982	110 204	8 526	3 336	5 189	101 679	16 082	31 186	22 431	16 889	12 062	3 030
1983	111 550	8 171	3 073	5 098	103 379	16 052	31 834	23 611	16 851	11 992	3 040
1984	113 544	7 943	3 050	4 894	105 601	16 046	32 723	24 933	17 006	11 961	2 933
1985	115 461	7 901	3 154	4 747	107 560	15 718	33 550	26 073	17 322	11 991	2 907
1986	117 834	7 926	3 287	4 639	109 908	15 441	34 591	27 232	17 739	11 894	3 010
1987	119 865	7 988	3 384	4 604	111 878	14 977	35 233	28 460	18 210	11 877	3 119
1988	121 669	8 031	3 286	4 745	113 638	14 505	35 503	29 435	19 104	11 808	3 284
1989	123 869	7 954	3 125	4 828	115 916	14 180	35 896	30 601	19 916	11 877	3 446
1990	125 840	7 792	2 937	4 856	118 047	14 700	35 929	32 145	20 248	11 575	3 451
1991	126 346	7 265	2 789	4 476	119 082	14 548	35 507	33 312	20 828	11 473	3 413
1992	128 105	7 096	2 769	4 327	121 009	14 521	35 369	33 899	22 160	11 587	3 473
1993	129 200	7 170	2 831	4 338	122 030	14 354	34 780	34 562	23 296	11 599	3 439
1994	131 056	7 481	3 134	4 347	123 576	14 131	34 353	35 226	24 318	11 713	3 834
1995	132 304	7 765	3 225	4 540	124 539	13 688	34 198	35 751	25 223	11 860	3 819
1996	133 943	7 806	3 263	4 543	126 137	13 377	33 833	36 556	26 397	12 146	3 828
1997	136 297	7 932	3 237	4 695	128 365	13 532	33 380	37 326	27 574	12 665	3 887
1998	137 673	8 256	3 335	4 921	129 417	13 638	32 813	37 536	28 368	13 215	3 847
1999	139 368	8 333	3 337	4 996	131 034	13 933	32 143	37 882	29 388	13 682	4 005
2000	142 583	8 271	3 261	5 010	134 312	14 250	32 755	37 567	31 071	14 356	4 312
2001	143 734	7 902	3 088	4 814	135 832	14 557	32 361	37 404	32 025	15 104	4 382
2002	144 863	7 585	2 870	4 715	137 278	14 781	32 196	36 926	32 597	16 309	4 469
2003	146 510	7 170	2 857	4 313	139 340	14 928	32 343	36 695	33 270	17 312	4 792
2004	147 401	7 114	2 747	4 367	140 287	15 154	32 207	36 158	33 758	18 013	4 998
2005	149 320	7 164	2 825	4 339	142 157	15 127	32 341	36 030	34 402	18 979	5 278
2006	151 428	7 281	2 952	4 329	144 147	15 113	32 573	35 848	35 146	19 984	5 484

Table 1-7. Civilian Labor Force, by Age, Sex, Race, and Hispanic Origin, 1948–2006—*Continued*

(Thousands of people.)

Race, Hispanic origin, sex, and year	16 years and over	16 to 19 years			20 years and over						
		Total	16 to 17 years	18 to 19 years	Total	20 to 24 years	25 to 34 years	35 to 44 years	45 to 54 years	55 to 64 years	65 years and over
ALL RACES											
Men											
1948	43 286	2 600	1 109	1 490	40 687	4 673	10 327	9 596	7 943	5 764	2 384
1949	43 498	2 477	1 056	1 420	41 022	4 682	10 418	9 722	8 008	5 748	2 454
1950	43 819	2 504	1 048	1 456	41 316	4 632	10 527	9 793	8 117	5 794	2 453
1951	43 001	2 347	1 081	1 266	40 655	3 935	10 375	9 799	8 205	5 873	2 469
1952	42 869	2 312	1 101	1 210	40 558	3 338	10 585	9 945	8 326	5 949	2 416
1953	43 633	2 320	1 070	1 249	41 315	3 053	10 736	10 437	8 570	5 975	2 543
1954	43 965	2 295	1 023	1 272	41 669	3 051	10 771	10 513	8 702	6 105	2 526
1955	44 475	2 369	1 070	1 299	42 106	3 221	10 806	10 595	8 838	6 122	2 526
1956	45 091	2 433	1 142	1 291	42 658	3 485	10 685	10 663	9 002	6 220	2 602
1957	45 197	2 415	1 127	1 289	42 780	3 629	10 571	10 731	9 153	6 222	2 477
1958	45 521	2 428	1 133	1 295	43 092	3 771	10 475	10 843	9 320	6 304	2 378
1959	45 886	2 596	1 206	1 390	43 289	3 940	10 346	10 899	9 438	6 345	2 322
1960	46 388	2 787	1 290	1 496	43 603	4 123	10 251	10 967	9 574	6 399	2 287
1961	46 653	2 794	1 210	1 583	43 860	4 253	10 176	11 012	9 668	6 530	2 220
1962	46 600	2 770	1 178	1 592	43 831	4 279	9 920	11 115	9 715	6 560	2 241
1963	47 129	2 907	1 321	1 586	44 222	4 514	9 876	11 187	9 836	6 675	2 135
1964	47 679	3 074	1 499	1 575	44 604	4 754	9 876	11 156	9 956	6 741	2 124
1965	48 255	3 397	1 532	1 866	44 857	4 894	9 903	11 120	10 045	6 763	2 132
1966	48 471	3 685	1 609	2 075	44 788	4 820	9 948	10 983	10 100	6 847	2 089
1967	48 987	3 634	1 658	1 976	45 354	5 043	10 207	10 859	10 189	6 937	2 118
1968	49 533	3 681	1 687	1 995	45 852	5 070	10 610	10 725	10 267	7 025	2 154
1969	50 221	3 870	1 770	2 100	46 351	5 282	10 941	10 556	10 344	7 058	2 170
1970	51 228	4 008	1 810	2 199	47 220	5 717	11 327	10 469	10 417	7 126	2 165
1971	52 180	4 172	1 856	2 315	48 009	6 233	11 731	10 347	10 451	7 155	2 090
1972	53 555	4 476	1 955	2 522	49 079	6 766	12 350	10 372	10 412	7 155	2 026
1973	54 624	4 693	2 073	2 618	49 932	7 183	13 056	10 338	10 416	7 028	1 913
1974	55 739	4 861	2 138	2 721	50 879	7 387	13 665	10 401	10 431	7 063	1 932
1975	56 299	4 805	2 065	2 740	51 494	7 565	14 192	10 398	10 401	7 023	1 914
1976	57 174	4 886	2 069	2 817	52 288	7 866	14 784	10 500	10 293	7 020	1 826
1977	58 396	5 048	2 155	2 893	53 348	8 109	15 353	10 771	10 158	7 100	1 857
1978	59 620	5 149	2 227	2 923	54 471	8 327	15 814	11 159	10 083	7 151	1 936
1979	60 726	5 111	2 192	2 919	55 615	8 535	16 387	11 531	10 008	7 212	1 943
1980	61 453	4 999	2 102	2 897	56 455	8 607	16 971	11 836	9 905	7 242	1 893
1981	61 974	4 777	1 957	2 820	57 197	8 648	17 479	12 166	9 868	7 170	1 866
1982	62 450	4 470	1 776	2 694	57 980	8 604	17 793	12 781	9 784	7 174	1 845
1983	63 047	4 303	1 621	2 682	58 744	8 601	18 038	13 398	9 746	7 119	1 842
1984	63 835	4 134	1 591	2 542	59 701	8 594	18 488	14 037	9 776	7 050	1 755
1985	64 411	4 134	1 663	2 471	60 277	8 283	18 808	14 506	9 870	7 060	1 750
1986	65 422	4 102	1 707	2 395	61 320	8 148	19 383	15 029	9 994	6 954	1 811
1987	66 207	4 112	1 745	2 367	62 095	7 837	19 656	15 587	10 176	6 940	1 899
1988	66 927	4 159	1 714	2 445	62 768	7 594	19 742	16 074	10 566	6 831	1 960
1989	67 840	4 136	1 630	2 505	63 704	7 458	19 905	16 622	10 919	6 783	2 017
1990	69 011	4 094	1 537	2 557	64 916	7 866	19 872	17 481	11 103	6 627	1 967
1991	69 168	3 795	1 452	2 343	65 374	7 820	19 641	18 077	11 362	6 550	1 924
1992	69 964	3 751	1 453	2 297	66 213	7 770	19 495	18 347	12 040	6 551	2 010
1993	70 404	3 762	1 497	2 265	66 642	7 671	19 214	18 713	12 562	6 502	1 980
1994	70 817	3 896	1 630	2 266	66 921	7 540	18 854	18 966	12 962	6 423	2 176
1995	71 360	4 036	1 668	2 368	67 324	7 338	18 670	19 189	13 421	6 504	2 201
1996	72 087	4 043	1 665	2 378	68 044	7 104	18 430	19 602	13 967	6 693	2 247
1997	73 261	4 095	1 676	2 419	69 166	7 184	18 110	20 058	14 564	6 952	2 298
1998	73 959	4 244	1 728	2 516	69 715	7 221	17 796	20 242	14 963	7 253	2 240
1999	74 512	4 318	1 732	2 587	70 194	7 291	17 318	20 382	15 394	7 477	2 333
2000	76 280	4 269	1 676	2 594	72 010	7 521	17 844	20 093	16 269	7 795	2 488
2001	76 886	4 070	1 568	2 501	72 816	7 640	17 671	20 018	16 804	8 171	2 511
2002	77 500	3 870	1 431	2 439	73 630	7 769	17 596	19 828	17 143	8 751	2 542
2003	78 238	3 614	1 405	2 209	74 623	7 906	17 767	19 762	17 352	9 144	2 692
2004	78 980	3 616	1 329	2 288	75 364	8 057	17 798	19 539	17 635	9 547	2 787
2005	80 033	3 590	1 368	2 222	76 443	8 054	17 837	19 495	18 053	10 045	2 959
2006	81 255	3 693	1 453	2 240	77 562	8 116	17 944	19 407	18 489	10 509	3 096

Table 1-7. Civilian Labor Force, by Age, Sex, Race, and Hispanic Origin, 1948–2006—*Continued*

(Thousands of people.)

Race, Hispanic origin, sex, and year	16 years and over	16 to 19 years			20 years and over						
		Total	16 to 17 years	18 to 19 years	Total	20 to 24 years	25 to 34 years	35 to 44 years	45 to 54 years	55 to 64 years	65 years and over
ALL RACES											
Women											
1948	17 335	1 835	671	1 164	15 500	2 719	3 931	3 801	2 971	1 565	513
1949	17 788	1 811	648	1 163	15 978	2 658	3 997	3 989	3 099	1 678	556
1950	18 389	1 712	611	1 101	16 678	2 675	4 092	4 161	3 327	1 839	583
1951	19 016	1 756	662	1 094	17 259	2 659	4 293	4 301	3 534	1 923	551
1952	19 269	1 752	705	1 047	17 517	2 502	4 319	4 438	3 635	2 031	589
1953	19 382	1 707	657	1 050	17 674	2 428	4 162	4 662	3 679	2 049	693
1954	19 678	1 681	620	1 028	17 997	2 424	4 212	4 708	3 822	2 164	666
1955	20 548	1 723	641	1 083	18 825	2 445	4 252	4 805	4 154	2 391	779
1956	21 461	1 863	736	1 127	19 599	2 455	4 276	5 031	4 405	2 610	821
1957	21 732	1 860	716	1 144	19 873	2 442	4 255	5 116	4 615	2 631	813
1958	22 118	1 832	685	1 147	20 285	2 501	4 193	5 185	4 859	2 727	821
1959	22 483	1 896	765	1 132	20 587	2 473	4 089	5 228	5 080	2 882	836
1960	23 240	2 054	805	1 251	21 185	2 579	4 131	5 302	5 278	2 986	908
1961	23 806	2 142	774	1 368	21 664	2 697	4 143	5 390	5 403	3 106	926
1962	24 014	2 146	741	1 405	21 868	2 803	4 103	5 474	5 381	3 197	913
1963	24 704	2 232	850	1 380	22 473	2 959	4 174	5 601	5 502	3 331	906
1964	25 412	2 314	950	1 365	23 098	3 209	4 180	5 615	5 681	3 441	966
1965	26 200	2 513	954	1 559	23 686	3 365	4 330	5 720	5 711	3 587	976
1966	27 299	2 873	1 055	1 818	24 431	3 590	4 510	5 755	5 884	3 728	964
1967	28 360	2 887	1 076	1 810	25 475	3 966	4 848	5 844	5 983	3 855	979
1968	29 204	2 938	1 130	1 808	26 266	4 235	5 098	5 866	6 130	3 939	999
1969	30 513	3 100	1 239	1 859	27 413	4 597	5 395	5 902	6 386	4 077	1 057
1970	31 543	3 241	1 325	1 916	28 301	4 880	5 708	5 968	6 532	4 157	1 056
1971	32 202	3 298	1 336	1 963	28 904	5 098	5 983	5 957	6 573	4 234	1 059
1972	33 479	3 578	1 464	2 114	29 901	5 364	6 610	6 027	6 555	4 257	1 089
1973	34 804	3 814	1 592	2 221	30 991	5 663	7 320	6 154	6 567	4 228	1 061
1974	36 211	4 010	1 672	2 338	32 201	5 926	7 989	6 362	6 699	4 221	1 002
1975	37 475	4 065	1 674	2 391	33 410	6 185	8 673	6 505	6 683	4 323	1 042
1976	38 983	4 170	1 698	2 470	34 814	6 418	9 419	6 817	6 689	4 402	1 069
1977	40 613	4 303	1 765	2 538	36 310	6 717	10 149	7 171	6 720	4 477	1 078
1978	42 631	4 503	1 900	2 603	38 128	7 043	10 888	7 662	6 807	4 593	1 134
1979	44 235	4 527	1 887	2 639	39 708	7 234	11 551	8 154	6 889	4 719	1 161
1980	45 487	4 381	1 781	2 599	41 106	7 315	12 257	8 627	7 004	4 742	1 161
1981	46 696	4 211	1 691	2 520	42 485	7 451	12 912	9 045	7 101	4 799	1 176
1982	47 755	4 056	1 561	2 495	43 699	7 477	13 393	9 651	7 105	4 888	1 185
1983	48 503	3 868	1 452	2 416	44 636	7 451	13 796	10 213	7 105	4 873	1 198
1984	49 709	3 810	1 458	2 351	45 900	7 451	14 234	10 896	7 230	4 911	1 177
1985	51 050	3 767	1 491	2 276	47 283	7 434	14 742	11 567	7 452	4 932	1 156
1986	52 413	3 824	1 580	2 244	48 589	7 293	15 208	12 204	7 746	4 940	1 199
1987	53 658	3 875	1 638	2 237	49 783	7 140	15 577	12 873	8 034	4 937	1 221
1988	54 742	3 872	1 572	2 300	50 870	6 910	15 761	13 361	8 537	4 977	1 324
1989	56 030	3 818	1 495	2 323	52 212	6 721	15 990	13 980	8 997	5 095	1 429
1990	56 829	3 698	1 400	2 298	53 131	6 834	16 058	14 663	9 145	4 948	1 483
1991	57 178	3 470	1 337	2 133	53 708	6 728	15 867	15 235	9 465	4 924	1 489
1992	58 141	3 345	1 316	2 030	54 796	6 750	15 875	15 552	10 120	5 035	1 464
1993	58 795	3 408	1 335	2 073	55 388	6 683	15 566	15 849	10 733	5 097	1 459
1994	60 239	3 585	1 504	2 081	56 655	6 592	15 499	16 259	11 357	5 289	1 658
1995	60 944	3 729	1 557	2 172	57 215	6 349	15 528	16 562	11 801	5 356	1 618
1996	61 857	3 763	1 599	2 164	58 094	6 273	15 403	16 954	12 430	5 452	1 581
1997	63 036	3 837	1 561	2 277	59 198	6 348	15 271	17 268	13 010	5 713	1 590
1998	63 714	4 012	1 607	2 405	59 702	6 418	15 017	17 294	13 405	5 962	1 607
1999	64 855	4 015	1 606	2 410	60 840	6 643	14 826	17 501	13 994	6 204	1 673
2000	66 303	4 002	1 585	2 416	62 301	6 730	14 912	17 473	14 802	6 561	1 823
2001	66 848	3 832	1 520	2 313	63 016	6 917	14 690	17 386	15 221	6 932	1 870
2002	67 363	3 715	1 439	2 277	63 648	7 012	14 600	17 098	15 454	7 559	1 926
2003	68 272	3 556	1 452	2 104	64 716	7 021	14 576	16 933	15 919	8 168	2 099
2004	68 421	3 498	1 418	2 080	64 923	7 097	14 409	16 619	16 123	8 466	2 211
2005	69 288	3 574	1 457	2 117	65 714	7 073	14 503	16 535	16 349	8 934	2 319
2006	70 173	3 588	1 499	2 089	66 585	6 997	14 628	16 441	16 656	9 475	2 388

Table 1-7. Civilian Labor Force, by Age, Sex, Race, and Hispanic Origin, 1948–2006—*Continued*

(Thousands of people.)

Race, Hispanic origin, sex, and year	16 years and over	16 to 19 years			20 years and over						
		Total	16 to 17 years	18 to 19 years	Total	20 to 24 years	25 to 34 years	35 to 44 years	45 to 54 years	55 to 64 years	65 years and over
WHITE[1]											
Both Sexes											
1954	56 816	3 501	1 448	2 054	53 315	4 752	13 226	13 540	11 258	7 591	2 946
1955	58 085	3 598	1 511	2 087	54 487	4 941	13 267	13 729	11 680	7 810	3 062
1956	59 428	3 771	1 656	2 113	55 657	5 194	13 154	14 000	12 061	8 080	3 166
1957	59 754	3 775	1 637	2 135	55 979	5 283	13 044	14 117	12 382	8 091	3 049
1958	60 293	3 757	1 615	2 144	56 536	5 449	12 884	14 257	12 727	8 254	2 964
1959	60 952	4 000	1 775	2 225	56 952	5 544	12 670	14 355	13 048	8 411	2 925
1960	61 915	4 275	1 871	2 405	57 640	5 787	12 594	14 450	13 322	8 522	2 964
1961	62 656	4 362	1 767	2 594	58 294	6 026	12 503	14 557	13 517	8 773	2 917
1962	62 750	4 354	1 709	2 645	58 396	6 164	12 218	14 695	13 551	8 856	2 912
1963	63 830	4 559	1 950	2 608	59 271	6 537	12 229	14 859	13 789	9 067	2 790
1964	64 921	4 784	2 211	2 572	60 137	6 952	12 235	14 852	14 043	9 239	2 817
1965	66 137	5 267	2 221	3 044	60 870	7 189	12 391	14 900	14 162	9 392	2 839
1966	67 276	5 827	2 367	3 460	61 449	7 324	12 591	14 785	14 370	9 583	2 793
1967	68 699	5 749	2 432	3 318	62 950	7 886	13 123	14 765	14 545	9 817	2 821
1968	69 976	5 839	2 519	3 320	64 137	8 109	13 740	14 683	14 756	9 968	2 884
1969	71 778	6 168	2 698	3 470	65 611	8 614	14 289	14 564	15 057	10 132	2 954
1970	73 556	6 442	2 824	3 617	67 113	9 238	14 896	14 525	15 269	10 255	2 930
1971	74 963	6 681	2 894	3 787	68 282	9 889	15 445	14 374	15 343	10 351	2 880
1972	77 275	7 193	3 096	4 098	70 082	10 605	16 584	14 399	15 283	10 402	2 809
1973	79 151	7 579	3 320	4 260	71 572	11 182	17 764	14 440	15 256	10 240	2 687
1974	81 281	7 899	3 441	4 459	73 381	11 600	18 862	14 644	15 375	10 241	2 656
1975	82 831	7 899	3 375	4 525	74 932	12 019	19 897	14 753	15 308	10 287	2 668
1976	84 767	8 088	3 410	4 679	76 678	12 444	20 990	15 088	15 187	10 371	2 599
1977	87 141	8 352	3 562	4 790	78 789	12 892	22 099	15 604	15 053	10 495	2 647
1978	89 634	8 555	3 715	4 839	81 079	13 309	23 067	16 353	15 004	10 602	2 745
1979	91 923	8 548	3 668	4 881	83 375	13 632	24 101	17 123	14 965	10 767	2 787
1980	93 600	8 312	3 485	4 827	85 286	13 769	25 181	17 811	14 956	10 812	2 759
1981	95 052	7 962	3 274	4 688	87 089	13 926	26 208	18 445	14 993	10 764	2 753
1982	96 143	7 518	3 001	4 518	88 625	13 866	26 814	19 491	14 879	10 832	2 742
1983	97 021	7 186	2 765	4 421	89 835	13 816	27 237	20 488	14 798	10 732	2 766
1984	98 492	6 952	2 720	4 232	91 540	13 733	27 958	21 588	14 899	10 701	2 660
1985	99 926	6 841	2 777	4 065	93 085	13 469	28 640	22 591	15 101	10 679	2 605
1986	101 801	6 862	2 895	3 967	94 939	13 176	29 497	23 571	15 379	10 583	2 732
1987	103 290	6 893	2 963	3 931	96 396	12 764	29 956	24 581	15 792	10 497	2 806
1988	104 756	6 940	2 861	4 079	97 815	12 311	30 167	25 358	16 573	10 462	2 943
1989	106 355	6 809	2 685	4 124	99 546	11 940	30 388	26 312	17 278	10 533	3 094
1990	107 447	6 683	2 543	4 140	100 764	12 397	30 174	27 265	17 515	10 290	3 123
1991	107 743	6 245	2 432	3 813	101 498	12 248	29 794	28 213	18 028	10 129	3 086
1992	108 837	6 022	2 388	3 633	102 815	12 187	29 518	28 580	19 200	10 196	3 135
1993	109 700	6 105	2 458	3 647	103 595	11 987	29 027	29 056	20 181	10 215	3 129
1994	111 082	6 357	2 681	3 677	104 725	11 688	28 580	29 626	21 026	10 319	3 486
1995	111 950	6 545	2 749	3 796	105 404	11 266	28 325	30 112	21 804	10 432	3 466
1996	113 108	6 607	2 780	3 826	106 502	11 003	27 901	30 683	22 781	10 648	3 485
1997	114 693	6 720	2 779	3 941	107 973	11 127	27 362	31 171	23 709	11 086	3 517
1998	115 415	6 965	2 860	4 105	108 450	11 244	26 707	31 221	24 282	11 548	3 448
1999	116 509	7 048	2 849	4 199	109 461	11 436	25 978	31 391	25 102	11 960	3 595
2000	118 545	6 955	2 768	4 186	111 590	11 626	26 336	30 968	26 353	12 463	3 846
2001	119 399	6 661	2 626	4 035	112 737	11 883	26 010	30 778	27 062	13 121	3 883
2002	120 150	6 366	2 445	3 921	113 784	12 073	25 908	30 286	27 405	14 148	3 965
2003	120 546	5 973	2 414	3 560	114 572	12 064	25 752	29 788	27 786	14 944	4 238
2004	121 086	5 929	2 309	3 620	115 156	12 192	25 548	29 305	28 181	15 522	4 408
2005	122 299	5 950	2 390	3 560	116 349	12 109	25 548	29 107	28 685	16 275	4 624
2006	123 834	6 009	2 473	3 536	117 825	12 128	25 681	28 849	29 231	17 132	4 805

[1]Beginning in 2003, persons who selected this race group only; persons who selected more than one race group are not included. Prior to 2003, persons who reported more than one race group were included in the group they identified as their main race.

Table 1-7. Civilian Labor Force, by Age, Sex, Race, and Hispanic Origin, 1948–2006—*Continued*

(Thousands of people.)

Race, Hispanic origin, sex, and year	16 years and over	16 to 19 years			20 years and over						
		Total	16 to 17 years	18 to 19 years	Total	20 to 24 years	25 to 34 years	35 to 44 years	45 to 54 years	55 to 64 years	65 years and over
WHITE[1]											
Men											
1954	39 759	1 989	896	1 095	37 770	2 654	9 695	9 516	7 913	5 653	2 339
1955	40 197	2 056	935	1 121	38 141	2 803	9 721	9 597	8 025	5 654	2 343
1956	40 734	2 114	1 002	1 110	38 620	3 036	9 595	9 661	8 175	5 736	2 417
1957	40 826	2 108	992	1 114	38 718	3 152	9 483	9 719	8 317	5 735	2 307
1958	41 080	2 116	1 001	1 116	38 964	3 278	9 386	9 822	8 465	5 800	2 213
1959	41 397	2 279	1 077	1 202	39 118	3 409	9 261	9 876	8 581	5 833	2 158
1960	41 743	2 433	1 140	1 293	39 310	3 559	9 153	9 919	8 689	5 861	2 129
1961	41 986	2 439	1 067	1 372	39 547	3 681	9 072	9 961	8 776	5 988	2 068
1962	41 931	2 432	1 041	1 391	39 499	3 726	8 846	10 029	8 820	5 995	2 082
1963	42 404	2 563	1 183	1 380	39 841	3 955	8 805	10 079	8 944	6 090	1 967
1964	42 894	2 716	1 345	1 371	40 178	4 166	8 800	10 055	9 053	6 161	1 942
1965	43 400	2 999	1 359	1 639	40 401	4 279	8 824	10 023	9 130	6 188	1 959
1966	43 572	3 253	1 423	1 830	40 319	4 200	8 859	9 892	9 189	6 250	1 928
1967	44 041	3 191	1 464	1 727	40 851	4 416	9 102	9 785	9 260	6 348	1 944
1968	44 553	3 236	1 504	1 732	41 318	4 432	9 477	9 662	9 340	6 427	1 981
1969	45 185	3 413	1 583	1 830	41 772	4 615	9 773	9 509	9 413	6 467	1 996
1970	46 035	3 551	1 629	1 922	42 483	4 988	10 099	9 414	9 487	6 517	1 978
1971	46 904	3 719	1 681	2 039	43 185	5 448	10 444	9 294	9 528	6 550	1 922
1972	48 118	3 980	1 758	2 223	44 138	5 937	11 039	9 278	9 473	6 562	1 846
1973	48 920	4 174	1 875	2 300	44 747	6 274	11 621	9 212	9 445	6 452	1 740
1974	49 843	4 312	1 922	2 391	45 532	6 470	12 135	9 246	9 455	6 464	1 759
1975	50 324	4 290	1 871	2 418	46 034	6 642	12 579	9 231	9 415	6 425	1 742
1976	51 033	4 357	1 869	2 489	46 675	6 890	13 092	9 289	9 310	6 437	1 657
1977	52 033	4 496	1 949	2 548	47 537	7 097	13 575	9 509	9 175	6 492	1 688
1978	52 955	4 565	2 002	2 563	48 390	7 274	13 939	9 858	9 068	6 508	1 744
1979	53 856	4 537	1 974	2 563	49 320	7 421	14 415	10 183	8 968	6 571	1 761
1980	54 473	4 424	1 881	2 543	50 049	7 479	14 893	10 455	8 877	6 618	1 727
1981	54 895	4 224	1 751	2 473	50 671	7 521	15 340	10 740	8 836	6 530	1 704
1982	55 133	3 933	1 602	2 331	51 200	7 438	15 549	11 289	8 727	6 520	1 677
1983	55 480	3 764	1 452	2 312	51 716	7 406	15 707	11 817	8 649	6 446	1 691
1984	56 062	3 609	1 420	2 189	52 453	7 370	16 037	12 348	8 683	6 410	1 606
1985	56 472	3 576	1 467	2 109	52 895	7 122	16 306	12 767	8 730	6 376	1 595
1986	57 217	3 542	1 502	2 040	53 675	6 986	16 769	13 207	8 791	6 260	1 663
1987	57 779	3 547	1 524	2 023	54 232	6 717	16 963	13 674	8 945	6 200	1 733
1988	58 317	3 583	1 487	2 095	54 734	6 468	17 018	14 068	9 285	6 108	1 787
1989	58 988	3 546	1 401	2 146	55 441	6 316	17 077	14 516	9 615	6 082	1 835
1990	59 638	3 522	1 333	2 189	56 116	6 688	16 920	15 026	9 713	5 957	1 811
1991	59 656	3 269	1 266	2 003	56 387	6 619	16 709	15 523	9 926	5 847	1 763
1992	60 168	3 192	1 260	1 932	56 976	6 542	16 512	15 701	10 570	5 821	1 830
1993	60 484	3 200	1 292	1 908	57 284	6 449	16 244	15 971	11 010	5 784	1 825
1994	60 727	3 315	1 403	1 912	57 411	6 294	15 879	16 188	11 327	5 726	1 998
1995	61 146	3 427	1 429	1 998	57 719	6 096	15 669	16 414	11 730	5 809	2 000
1996	61 783	3 444	1 421	2 023	58 340	5 922	15 475	16 728	12 217	5 943	2 054
1997	62 639	3 513	1 440	2 073	59 126	6 029	15 120	17 019	12 710	6 154	2 094
1998	63 034	3 614	1 487	2 127	59 421	6 063	14 770	17 157	13 003	6 415	2 013
1999	63 413	3 666	1 478	2 188	59 747	6 151	14 292	17 201	13 368	6 618	2 117
2000	64 466	3 615	1 422	2 193	60 850	6 244	14 666	16 880	13 977	6 840	2 243
2001	64 966	3 446	1 334	2 112	61 519	6 363	14 536	16 809	14 400	7 169	2 241
2002	65 308	3 241	1 215	2 026	62 067	6 444	14 499	16 583	14 615	7 665	2 261
2003	65 509	3 036	1 193	1 843	62 473	6 479	14 529	16 398	14 708	7 973	2 386
2004	65 994	3 050	1 127	1 923	62 944	6 586	14 429	16 192	14 934	8 326	2 478
2005	66 694	2 988	1 162	1 826	63 705	6 562	14 426	16 080	15 273	8 734	2 631
2006	67 613	3 074	1 222	1 852	64 540	6 597	14 469	15 962	15 606	9 152	2 753

[1]Beginning in 2003, persons who selected this race group only; persons who selected more than one race group are not included. Prior to 2003, persons who reported more than one race group were included in the group they identified as their main race.

Table 1-7. Civilian Labor Force, by Age, Sex, Race, and Hispanic Origin, 1948–2006—*Continued*

(Thousands of people.)

Race, Hispanic origin, sex, and year	16 years and over	16 to 19 years			20 years and over						
		Total	16 to 17 years	18 to 19 years	Total	20 to 24 years	25 to 34 years	35 to 44 years	45 to 54 years	55 to 64 years	65 years and over
WHITE[1]											
Women											
1954	17 057	1 512	552	959	15 545	2 098	3 531	4 024	3 345	1 938	607
1955	17 888	1 542	576	966	16 346	2 138	3 546	4 132	3 655	2 156	719
1956	18 694	1 657	654	1 003	17 037	2 158	3 559	4 339	3 886	2 344	749
1957	18 928	1 667	645	1 021	17 261	2 131	3 561	4 398	4 065	2 356	742
1958	19 213	1 641	614	1 028	17 572	2 171	3 498	4 435	4 262	2 454	751
1959	19 555	1 721	698	1 023	17 834	2 135	3 409	4 479	4 467	2 578	767
1960	20 172	1 842	731	1 112	18 330	2 228	3 441	4 531	4 633	2 661	835
1961	20 670	1 923	700	1 222	18 747	2 345	3 431	4 596	4 741	2 785	849
1962	20 819	1 922	668	1 254	18 897	2 438	3 372	4 666	4 731	2 861	830
1963	21 426	1 996	767	1 228	19 430	2 582	3 424	4 780	4 845	2 977	823
1964	22 027	2 068	866	1 201	19 959	2 786	3 435	4 797	4 990	3 078	875
1965	22 737	2 268	862	1 405	20 469	2 910	3 567	4 877	5 032	3 204	880
1966	23 704	2 574	944	1 630	21 130	3 124	3 732	4 893	5 181	3 333	865
1967	24 658	2 558	968	1 591	22 100	3 471	4 021	4 980	5 285	3 469	877
1968	25 423	2 603	1 015	1 588	22 821	3 677	4 263	5 021	5 416	3 541	903
1969	26 593	2 755	1 115	1 640	23 839	3 999	4 516	5 055	5 644	3 665	958
1970	27 521	2 891	1 195	1 695	24 630	4 250	4 797	5 111	5 781	3 738	952
1971	28 060	2 962	1 213	1 748	25 097	4 441	5 001	5 080	5 816	3 801	958
1972	29 157	3 213	1 338	1 875	25 945	4 668	5 544	5 121	5 810	3 839	963
1973	30 231	3 405	1 445	1 960	26 825	4 908	6 143	5 228	5 811	3 788	947
1974	31 437	3 588	1 520	2 068	27 850	5 131	6 727	5 399	5 920	3 777	897
1975	32 508	3 610	1 504	2 107	28 898	5 378	7 318	5 522	5 892	3 862	926
1976	33 735	3 731	1 541	2 189	30 004	5 554	7 898	5 799	5 877	3 935	940
1977	35 108	3 856	1 614	2 243	31 253	5 795	8 523	6 095	5 877	4 003	959
1978	36 679	3 990	1 713	2 276	32 689	6 035	9 128	6 495	5 936	4 094	1 001
1979	38 067	4 011	1 694	2 318	34 056	6 211	9 687	6 940	5 997	4 196	1 024
1980	39 127	3 888	1 605	2 284	35 239	6 290	10 289	7 356	6 079	4 194	1 032
1981	40 157	3 739	1 523	2 216	36 418	6 406	10 868	7 704	6 157	4 235	1 049
1982	41 010	3 585	1 399	2 186	37 425	6 428	11 264	8 202	6 152	4 313	1 065
1983	41 541	3 422	1 314	2 109	38 119	6 410	11 530	8 670	6 149	4 285	1 074
1984	42 431	3 343	1 300	2 043	39 087	6 363	11 922	9 240	6 217	4 292	1 054
1985	43 455	3 265	1 310	1 955	40 190	6 348	12 334	9 824	6 371	4 303	1 010
1986	44 584	3 320	1 393	1 927	41 264	6 191	12 729	10 364	6 588	4 323	1 069
1987	45 510	3 347	1 439	1 908	42 164	6 047	12 993	10 907	6 847	4 297	1 073
1988	46 439	3 358	1 374	1 984	43 081	5 844	13 149	11 291	7 288	4 354	1 156
1989	47 367	3 262	1 284	1 978	44 105	5 625	13 311	11 796	7 663	4 451	1 259
1990	47 809	3 161	1 210	1 951	44 648	5 709	13 254	12 239	7 802	4 333	1 312
1991	48 087	2 976	1 166	1 810	45 111	5 629	13 085	12 689	8 101	4 282	1 324
1992	48 669	2 830	1 128	1 702	45 839	5 645	13 006	12 879	8 630	4 375	1 305
1993	49 216	2 905	1 167	1 739	46 311	5 539	12 783	13 085	9 171	4 430	1 304
1994	50 356	3 042	1 278	1 764	47 314	5 394	12 702	13 439	9 699	4 593	1 487
1995	50 804	3 118	1 320	1 798	47 686	5 170	12 656	13 697	10 074	4 622	1 466
1996	51 325	3 163	1 360	1 803	48 162	5 081	12 426	13 955	10 563	4 706	1 431
1997	52 054	3 207	1 339	1 867	48 847	5 099	12 242	14 153	10 999	4 932	1 422
1998	52 380	3 351	1 373	1 977	49 029	5 180	11 937	14 064	11 279	5 133	1 435
1999	53 096	3 382	1 371	2 010	49 714	5 285	11 685	14 190	11 734	5 342	1 478
2000	54 079	3 339	1 346	1 993	50 740	5 381	11 669	14 088	12 376	5 623	1 602
2001	54 433	3 215	1 292	1 923	51 218	5 519	11 474	13 969	12 662	5 952	1 642
2002	54 842	3 125	1 229	1 895	51 717	5 628	11 409	13 703	12 790	6 482	1 704
2003	55 037	2 937	1 221	1 716	52 099	5 584	11 223	13 390	13 078	6 970	1 852
2004	55 092	2 879	1 182	1 697	52 212	5 606	11 119	13 114	13 247	7 197	1 930
2005	55 605	2 962	1 228	1 733	52 643	5 546	11 123	13 027	13 413	7 542	1 993
2006	56 221	2 935	1 251	1 684	53 286	5 530	11 212	12 886	13 625	7 980	2 052

[1]Beginning in 2003, persons who selected this race group only; persons who selected more than one race group are not included. Prior to 2003, persons who reported more than one race group were included in the group they identified as their main race.

Table 1-7. Civilian Labor Force, by Age, Sex, Race, and Hispanic Origin, 1948–2006—*Continued*

(Thousands of people.)

Race, Hispanic origin, sex, and year	16 years and over	16 to 19 years			20 years and over						
		Total	16 to 17 years	18 to 19 years	Total	20 to 24 years	25 to 34 years	35 to 44 years	45 to 54 years	55 to 64 years	65 years and over
BLACK[1]											
Both Sexes											
1972	8 707	788	293	496	7 919	1 393	2 107	1 735	1 496	909	281
1973	8 976	833	307	525	8 143	1 489	2 242	1 741	1 513	901	258
1974	9 167	851	317	534	8 317	1 492	2 358	1 777	1 517	917	253
1975	9 263	838	312	524	8 426	1 477	2 466	1 775	1 519	929	258
1976	9 561	837	304	532	8 724	1 544	2 646	1 824	1 518	925	268
1977	9 932	861	304	557	9 072	1 641	2 798	1 894	1 530	943	267
1978	10 432	930	341	589	9 501	1 739	2 961	1 975	1 560	978	289
1979	10 678	912	340	572	9 766	1 793	3 094	2 039	1 584	974	281
1980	10 865	891	326	565	9 975	1 802	3 259	2 081	1 596	978	257
1981	11 086	862	308	554	10 224	1 828	3 365	2 164	1 608	1 009	249
1982	11 331	824	268	556	10 507	1 849	3 492	2 303	1 610	1 012	243
1983	11 647	809	248	561	10 838	1 871	3 675	2 406	1 630	1 032	224
1984	12 033	827	268	558	11 206	1 926	3 800	2 565	1 671	1 020	224
1985	12 364	889	311	578	11 476	1 854	3 888	2 681	1 742	1 059	252
1986	12 654	883	322	562	11 770	1 881	4 028	2 793	1 793	1 051	224
1987	12 993	899	336	563	12 094	1 818	4 147	2 942	1 838	1 098	251
1988	13 205	889	344	545	12 316	1 782	4 226	3 069	1 894	1 069	276
1989	13 497	925	353	572	12 573	1 789	4 295	3 227	1 954	1 023	285
1990	13 740	866	306	560	12 874	1 758	4 307	3 566	2 003	977	262
1991	13 797	774	266	508	13 023	1 750	4 254	3 719	2 042	1 001	256
1992	14 162	816	285	532	13 346	1 763	4 309	3 843	2 142	1 029	259
1993	14 225	807	283	524	13 418	1 764	4 232	3 960	2 212	1 013	237
1994	14 502	852	351	501	13 650	1 800	4 199	4 068	2 308	1 007	267
1995	14 817	911	366	545	13 906	1 754	4 267	4 165	2 404	1 046	271
1996	15 134	923	366	556	14 211	1 738	4 305	4 287	2 553	1 073	255
1997	15 529	933	352	580	14 596	1 783	4 329	4 401	2 724	1 093	265
1998	15 982	1 017	370	646	14 966	1 797	4 332	4 531	2 863	1 163	278
1999	16 365	959	352	607	15 406	1 866	4 430	4 653	2 992	1 180	285
2000	16 397	941	356	585	15 456	1 873	4 281	4 515	3 203	1 264	320
2001	16 421	898	332	565	15 524	1 878	4 180	4 483	3 298	1 335	350
2002	16 565	870	297	574	15 695	1 908	4 134	4 458	3 435	1 407	353
2003	16 526	771	289	482	15 755	1 892	4 060	4 465	3 506	1 466	366
2004	16 638	762	272	489	15 876	1 926	4 076	4 380	3 578	1 538	380
2005	17 013	803	279	525	16 209	1 957	4 145	4 370	3 686	1 647	403
2006	17 314	871	318	553	16 443	1 960	4 197	4 348	3 785	1 739	414
BLACK[1]											
Men											
1972	4 816	453	180	272	4 364	761	1 158	935	824	522	165
1973	4 924	460	175	286	4 464	819	1 217	935	842	499	153
1974	5 020	480	189	291	4 540	798	1 279	953	838	519	152
1975	5 016	447	168	279	4 569	790	1 328	948	833	520	150
1976	5 101	454	168	285	4 648	820	1 383	969	824	504	149
1977	5 263	476	178	299	4 787	856	1 441	1 003	818	515	154
1978	5 435	491	186	306	4 943	883	1 504	1 022	829	540	166
1979	5 559	480	179	301	5 079	928	1 577	1 049	844	524	156
1980	5 612	479	181	298	5 134	935	1 659	1 061	830	509	138
1981	5 685	462	169	293	5 223	940	1 702	1 093	829	524	134
1982	5 804	436	137	300	5 368	964	1 769	1 152	824	525	135
1983	5 966	433	134	300	5 533	997	1 840	1 196	845	536	119
1984	6 126	440	141	299	5 686	1 022	1 924	1 270	847	505	118
1985	6 220	471	162	310	5 749	950	1 937	1 313	879	544	125
1986	6 373	458	164	294	5 915	957	2 029	1 359	901	552	116
1987	6 486	463	179	284	6 023	914	2 074	1 406	915	586	130
1988	6 596	469	186	283	6 127	913	2 114	1 459	936	565	139
1989	6 701	480	190	291	6 221	904	2 157	1 544	945	530	141
1990	6 802	445	161	284	6 357	879	2 142	1 733	988	496	119
1991	6 851	400	140	260	6 451	896	2 111	1 806	1 010	507	122
1992	6 997	429	149	280	6 568	900	2 121	1 859	1 037	521	130
1993	7 019	425	154	270	6 594	875	2 118	1 918	1 065	506	112
1994	7 089	443	176	266	6 646	891	2 068	1 975	1 102	484	125
1995	7 183	453	184	269	6 730	866	2 089	1 987	1 148	490	150
1996	7 264	458	182	276	6 806	848	2 077	2 036	1 204	509	132
1997	7 354	444	178	266	6 910	832	2 052	2 096	1 287	508	134
1998	7 542	488	181	307	7 053	837	2 034	2 142	1 343	548	150
1999	7 652	470	180	291	7 182	835	2 069	2 206	1 387	547	138
2000	7 702	462	181	281	7 240	875	1 999	2 105	1 497	612	151
2001	7 647	447	166	281	7 200	853	1 915	2 073	1 537	645	177
2002	7 794	446	149	297	7 347	906	1 909	2 064	1 623	664	181
2003	7 711	365	138	228	7 346	918	1 872	2 058	1 627	685	186
2004	7 773	359	128	231	7 414	927	1 931	2 000	1 654	714	188
2005	7 998	399	139	260	7 600	940	1 948	2 028	1 732	756	196
2006	8 128	409	152	256	7 720	971	1 986	1 999	1 792	777	195

[1]Beginning in 2003, persons who selected this race group only; persons who selected more than one race group are not included. Prior to 2003, persons who reported more than one race group were included in the group they identified as their main race.

Table 1-7. Civilian Labor Force, by Age, Sex, Race, and Hispanic Origin, 1948–2006—*Continued*

(Thousands of people.)

Race, Hispanic origin, sex, and year	16 years and over	16 to 19 years			20 years and over						
		Total	16 to 17 years	18 to 19 years	Total	20 to 24 years	25 to 34 years	35 to 44 years	45 to 54 years	55 to 64 years	65 years and over
BLACK[1]											
Women											
1972	3 890	335	113	224	3 555	632	949	800	672	387	116
1973	4 052	373	133	240	3 678	670	1 026	806	670	402	105
1974	4 148	371	128	243	3 777	694	1 079	824	679	398	100
1975	4 247	391	144	245	3 857	687	1 138	827	686	409	108
1976	4 460	384	136	247	4 076	723	1 264	855	694	421	119
1977	4 670	385	127	258	4 286	785	1 357	891	712	429	113
1978	4 997	439	155	283	4 558	856	1 456	953	731	439	124
1979	5 119	432	161	271	4 687	865	1 517	990	740	451	124
1980	5 253	412	144	267	4 841	867	1 600	1 020	767	469	119
1981	5 401	400	139	261	5 001	888	1 663	1 071	779	485	115
1982	5 527	387	131	256	5 140	885	1 723	1 151	786	487	108
1983	5 681	375	114	261	5 306	874	1 835	1 210	785	496	105
1984	5 907	387	127	260	5 520	904	1 876	1 294	823	515	106
1985	6 144	417	149	268	5 727	904	1 951	1 368	862	515	127
1986	6 281	425	157	268	5 855	924	1 999	1 434	892	499	107
1987	6 507	435	157	278	6 071	904	2 073	1 537	924	512	121
1988	6 609	419	158	262	6 190	869	2 112	1 610	958	504	137
1989	6 796	445	163	281	6 352	885	2 138	1 683	1 009	493	144
1990	6 938	421	145	276	6 517	879	2 165	1 833	1 015	481	143
1991	6 946	374	126	248	6 572	854	2 143	1 913	1 032	494	135
1992	7 166	387	135	252	6 778	863	2 188	1 985	1 105	508	129
1993	7 206	383	129	254	6 824	889	2 115	2 042	1 147	506	125
1994	7 413	409	174	235	7 004	909	2 131	2 093	1 206	523	142
1995	7 634	458	182	276	7 175	887	2 177	2 178	1 256	556	121
1996	7 869	464	184	280	7 405	890	2 228	2 251	1 349	565	122
1997	8 175	489	175	314	7 686	951	2 277	2 305	1 437	585	131
1998	8 441	528	189	339	7 912	960	2 298	2 390	1 520	615	128
1999	8 713	489	172	316	8 224	1 031	2 360	2 447	1 606	633	147
2000	8 695	479	175	305	8 215	998	2 282	2 409	1 706	652	168
2001	8 774	451	166	284	8 323	1 025	2 265	2 410	1 762	690	173
2002	8 772	424	148	276	8 348	1 002	2 225	2 394	1 812	743	171
2003	8 815	406	151	255	8 409	973	2 188	2 407	1 879	781	180
2004	8 865	403	144	259	8 462	999	2 144	2 380	1 924	824	192
2005	9 014	405	140	265	8 610	1 017	2 197	2 342	1 954	891	207
2006	9 186	462	166	297	8 723	989	2 211	2 349	1 993	963	218
HISPANIC[2]											
Both Sexes											
1973	3 673	407	. . .	. . .	. . .	. . .	. . .	. . .	. . .	. . .	. . .
1974	4 012	442	. . .	. . .	. . .	. . .	. . .	. . .	. . .	. . .	. . .
1975	4 171	444	. . .	. . .	. . .	. . .	. . .	. . .	. . .	. . .	. . .
1976	4 205	447	176	285	3 820	729	1 248	875	625	294	48
1977	4 536	493	184	305	4 059	813	1 325	916	656	293	55
1978	4 979	533	221	312	4 446	901	1 446	1 008	701	323	67
1979	5 219	551	207	343	4 668	960	1 532	1 062	704	339	72
1980	6 146	645	241	404	5 502	1 136	1 843	1 163	860	414	85
1981	6 492	603	215	388	5 888	1 231	2 015	1 239	886	430	87
1982	6 734	585	192	393	6 148	1 251	2 163	1 313	891	444	85
1983	7 033	590	189	401	6 442	1 282	2 267	1 380	931	495	86
1984	7 451	618	209	409	6 833	1 325	2 436	1 509	954	524	84
1985	7 698	579	199	379	7 119	1 358	2 571	1 595	985	527	82
1986	8 076	571	203	368	7 505	1 414	2 685	1 713	1 097	511	84
1987	8 541	610	206	404	7 931	1 425	2 890	1 904	1 086	545	81
1988	8 982	671	234	437	8 311	1 486	2 957	1 996	1 147	621	103
1989	9 323	680	224	456	8 643	1 483	3 118	2 092	1 205	625	120
1990	10 720	829	276	554	9 891	1 839	3 590	2 386	1 320	647	110
1991	10 920	781	249	532	10 139	1 835	3 596	2 539	1 376	681	111
1992	11 338	796	263	533	10 542	1 815	3 740	2 735	1 442	687	122
1993	11 610	771	246	525	10 839	1 811	3 800	2 865	1 534	684	145
1994	11 975	807	285	522	11 168	1 863	3 865	2 965	1 626	698	151
1995	12 267	850	291	559	11 417	1 818	3 943	3 113	1 671	720	152
1996	12 774	845	284	561	11 929	1 845	4 054	3 361	1 697	806	166
1997	13 796	911	315	596	12 884	2 004	4 298	3 601	1 945	850	186
1998	14 317	1 007	320	688	13 310	2 077	4 372	3 707	2 090	894	169
1999	14 665	1 049	333	717	13 616	2 052	4 330	3 929	2 178	927	199
2000	16 689	1 168	368	800	15 521	2 546	5 197	4 241	2 387	940	209
2001	17 328	1 176	352	824	16 152	2 616	5 380	4 377	2 583	1 000	195
2002	17 943	1 103	335	769	16 840	2 678	5 645	4 545	2 657	1 091	224
2003	18 813	960	322	638	17 853	2 672	5 960	4 867	2 894	1 201	259
2004	19 272	995	297	698	18 277	2 732	5 931	4 931	3 093	1 284	306
2005	19 824	1 038	331	708	18 785	2 651	6 080	5 110	3 256	1 378	311
2006	20 694	1 071	360	710	19 623	2 681	6 295	5 337	3 452	1 490	369

[1]Beginning in 2003, persons who selected this race group only; persons who selected more than one race group are not included. Prior to 2003, persons who reported more than one race group were included in the group they identified as their main race.
[2]May be any race.
. . . = Not available.

Table 1-7. Civilian Labor Force, by Age, Sex, Race, and Hispanic Origin, 1948–2006—*Continued*

(Thousands of people.)

Race, Hispanic origin, sex, and year	16 years and over	16 to 19 years			20 years and over						
		Total	16 to 17 years	18 to 19 years	Total	20 to 24 years	25 to 34 years	35 to 44 years	45 to 54 years	55 to 64 years	65 years and over
HISPANIC[2]											
Men											
1973	2 356	...	...	...	2 124	...	...	...	...	...	...
1974	2 556	...	...	...	2 306	...	...	...	...	...	...
1975	2 597	...	...	...	2 343	...	...	...	...	...	...
1976	2 580	260	104	155	2 326	433	771	541	398	189	34
1977	2 817	285	105	179	2 530	485	828	567	416	197	42
1978	3 041	299	129	171	2 742	546	882	620	425	217	52
1979	3 184	315	121	194	2 869	562	941	648	445	216	56
1980	3 818	392	147	245	3 426	697	1 161	713	522	270	62
1981	4 005	359	130	229	3 647	747	1 269	756	535	278	61
1982	4 148	333	111	221	3 815	759	1 361	808	539	290	58
1983	4 362	348	109	239	4 014	789	1 447	852	557	311	58
1984	4 563	345	113	232	4 218	822	1 540	910	570	325	51
1985	4 729	334	116	218	4 395	835	1 629	957	591	331	53
1986	4 948	336	114	222	4 612	888	1 669	1 015	661	323	56
1987	5 163	345	112	233	4 818	865	1 801	1 121	652	325	55
1988	5 409	378	123	255	5 031	897	1 834	1 189	686	355	69
1989	5 595	400	129	271	5 195	909	1 899	1 221	719	375	71
1990	6 546	512	165	346	6 034	1 182	2 230	1 403	775	380	65
1991	6 664	466	141	325	6 198	1 202	2 260	1 487	780	401	67
1992	6 900	468	154	314	6 432	1 141	2 366	1 593	844	414	74
1993	7 076	455	145	310	6 621	1 147	2 417	1 675	900	394	88
1994	7 210	463	163	300	6 747	1 184	2 430	1 713	922	410	89
1995	7 376	479	168	311	6 898	1 153	2 469	1 795	965	417	98
1996	7 646	496	156	340	7 150	1 132	2 510	1 966	967	469	105
1997	8 309	531	177	354	7 779	1 267	2 684	2 091	1 112	511	113
1998	8 571	565	188	377	8 005	1 288	2 733	2 173	1 164	541	106
1999	8 546	596	181	415	7 950	1 231	2 633	2 219	1 205	526	136
2000	9 923	676	204	471	9 247	1 590	3 181	2 451	1 337	555	134
2001	10 279	684	200	484	9 595	1 602	3 294	2 562	1 430	582	125
2002	10 609	632	183	449	9 977	1 627	3 484	2 647	1 478	607	134
2003	11 288	532	164	368	10 756	1 642	3 776	2 877	1 630	680	150
2004	11 587	567	156	410	11 020	1 671	3 765	2 934	1 736	728	186
2005	11 985	577	179	398	11 408	1 645	3 879	3 058	1 855	779	192
2006	12 488	600	189	411	11 888	1 646	4 014	3 203	1 960	838	228
HISPANIC[2]											
Women											
1973	1 317	...	...	...	1 142	...	...	...	...	...	...
1974	1 456	...	...	...	1 264	...	...	...	...	...	...
1975	1 574	...	...	...	1 384	...	...	...	...	...	...
1976	1 625	201	71	130	1 454	295	479	334	227	105	...
1977	1 720	204	80	125	1 523	327	497	349	240	96	...
1978	1 938	233	93	142	1 704	354	564	388	275	106	...
1979	2 035	235	86	149	1 800	397	590	413	258	124	...
1980	2 328	252	93	159	2 076	439	682	450	337	144	...
1981	2 486	244	85	159	2 242	484	745	483	351	152	...
1982	2 586	252	81	172	2 333	492	802	504	352	155	...
1983	2 671	242	80	162	2 429	493	820	529	374	184	...
1984	2 888	273	96	177	2 615	503	896	599	384	199	...
1985	2 970	245	84	161	2 725	524	943	639	394	196	...
1986	3 128	236	89	147	2 893	526	1 016	698	436	189	...
1987	3 377	265	94	171	3 112	559	1 090	783	434	220	...
1988	3 573	293	111	182	3 281	589	1 123	806	461	267	...
1989	3 728	280	95	185	3 448	574	1 219	871	486	251	...
1990	4 174	318	110	207	3 857	657	1 360	983	545	268	...
1991	4 256	315	107	207	3 941	633	1 336	1 052	596	279	44
1992	4 439	328	110	219	4 110	674	1 374	1 142	599	273	48
1993	4 534	316	101	215	4 218	664	1 383	1 190	633	290	57
1994	4 765	345	122	222	4 421	679	1 435	1 252	704	288	62
1995	4 891	371	123	249	4 520	666	1 473	1 318	706	303	54
1996	5 128	349	128	221	4 779	713	1 544	1 395	729	338	61
1997	5 486	381	138	242	5 106	737	1 614	1 510	833	338	73
1998	5 746	442	132	310	5 304	789	1 639	1 533	927	353	62
1999	6 119	453	151	302	5 666	821	1 698	1 710	973	401	63
2000	6 767	492	164	328	6 275	956	2 016	1 791	1 051	386	75
2001	7 049	492	152	340	6 557	1 014	2 086	1 815	1 153	418	70
2002	7 334	471	152	320	6 863	1 051	2 161	1 897	1 179	484	90
2003	7 525	428	158	271	7 096	1 030	2 183	1 990	1 264	520	109
2004	7 685	429	141	288	7 257	1 060	2 166	1 998	1 357	556	119
2005	7 839	462	152	310	7 377	1 005	2 201	2 052	1 401	599	119
2006	8 206	471	171	300	7 735	1 035	2 280	2 134	1 492	652	141

[2]May be any race.
. . . = Not available.

Table 1-8. Civilian Labor Force Participation Rates, by Age, Sex, Race, and Hispanic Origin, 1948–2006

(Percent.)

Race, Hispanic origin, sex, and year	16 years and over	16 to 19 years	20 years and over						
			Total	20 to 24 years	25 to 34 years	35 to 44 years	45 to 54 years	55 to 64 years	65 years and over
ALL RACES									
Both Sexes									
1948	58.8	52.5	59.4	64.1	63.1	66.7	65.1	56.9	27.0
1949	58.9	52.2	59.5	64.9	63.2	67.2	65.3	56.2	27.3
1950	59.2	51.8	59.9	65.9	63.5	67.5	66.4	56.7	26.7
1951	59.2	52.2	59.8	64.8	64.2	67.6	67.2	56.9	25.8
1952	59.0	51.3	59.7	62.2	64.7	68.0	67.5	57.5	24.8
1953	58.9	50.2	59.6	61.2	64.0	68.9	68.1	58.0	24.8
1954	58.8	48.3	59.6	61.6	64.3	68.8	68.4	58.7	23.9
1955	59.3	48.9	60.1	62.7	64.8	68.9	69.7	59.5	24.1
1956	60.0	50.9	60.7	64.1	64.8	69.5	70.5	60.8	24.3
1957	59.6	49.6	60.4	64.0	64.9	69.5	70.9	60.1	22.9
1958	59.5	47.4	60.5	64.4	65.0	69.6	71.5	60.5	21.8
1959	59.3	46.7	60.4	64.3	65.0	69.5	71.9	61.0	21.1
1960	59.4	47.5	60.5	65.2	65.4	69.4	72.2	60.9	20.8
1961	59.3	46.9	60.5	65.7	65.6	69.5	72.1	61.5	20.1
1962	58.8	46.1	60.0	65.3	65.2	69.7	72.2	61.5	19.1
1963	58.7	45.2	60.1	65.1	65.6	70.1	72.5	62.0	17.9
1964	58.7	44.5	60.2	66.3	65.8	70.0	72.9	61.9	18.0
1965	58.9	45.7	60.3	66.4	66.4	70.7	72.5	61.9	17.8
1966	59.2	48.2	60.5	66.5	67.1	71.0	72.7	62.2	17.2
1967	59.6	48.4	60.9	67.1	68.2	71.6	72.7	62.3	17.2
1968	59.6	48.3	60.9	67.0	68.6	72.0	72.8	62.2	17.2
1969	60.1	49.4	61.3	68.2	69.1	72.5	73.4	62.1	17.3
1970	60.4	49.9	61.6	69.2	69.7	73.1	73.5	61.8	17.0
1971	60.2	49.7	61.4	69.3	69.9	73.2	73.2	61.3	16.2
1972	60.4	51.9	61.4	70.8	70.9	73.3	72.7	60.0	15.6
1973	60.8	53.7	61.7	72.6	72.3	74.0	72.5	58.4	14.6
1974	61.3	54.8	62.0	74.0	73.6	74.6	72.7	57.8	14.0
1975	61.2	54.0	62.1	73.9	74.4	75.0	72.6	57.2	13.7
1976	61.6	54.5	62.4	74.7	75.7	76.0	72.5	56.6	13.1
1977	62.3	56.0	63.0	75.7	77.0	77.0	72.8	56.3	13.0
1978	63.2	57.8	63.8	76.8	78.3	78.1	73.5	56.3	13.3
1979	63.7	57.9	64.3	77.5	79.2	79.2	74.3	56.2	13.1
1980	63.8	56.7	64.5	77.2	79.9	80.0	74.9	55.7	12.5
1981	63.9	55.4	64.8	77.3	80.5	80.7	75.7	55.0	12.2
1982	64.0	54.1	65.0	77.1	81.0	81.2	75.9	55.1	11.9
1983	64.0	53.5	65.0	77.2	81.3	81.6	76.0	54.5	11.7
1984	64.4	53.9	65.3	77.6	81.8	82.4	76.5	54.2	11.1
1985	64.8	54.5	65.7	78.2	82.5	83.1	77.3	54.2	10.8
1986	65.3	54.7	66.2	78.9	82.9	83.7	78.0	54.0	10.9
1987	65.6	54.7	66.5	78.9	83.3	84.3	78.6	54.4	11.1
1988	65.9	55.3	66.8	78.7	83.3	84.6	79.6	54.6	11.5
1989	66.5	55.9	67.3	78.7	83.8	85.1	80.5	55.5	11.8
1990	66.5	53.7	67.6	77.8	83.6	85.2	80.7	55.9	11.8
1991	66.2	51.6	67.3	76.7	83.2	85.2	81.0	55.5	11.5
1992	66.4	51.3	67.6	77.0	83.7	85.1	81.5	56.2	11.5
1993	66.3	51.5	67.5	77.0	83.3	84.9	81.6	56.4	11.2
1994	66.6	52.7	67.7	77.0	83.2	84.8	81.7	56.8	12.4
1995	66.6	53.5	67.7	76.6	83.8	84.6	81.4	57.2	12.1
1996	66.8	52.3	67.9	76.8	84.1	84.8	82.1	57.9	12.1
1997	67.1	51.6	68.4	77.6	84.4	85.1	82.6	58.9	12.2
1998	67.1	52.8	68.3	77.5	84.6	84.7	82.5	59.3	11.9
1999	67.1	52.0	68.3	77.5	84.6	84.9	82.6	59.3	12.3
2000	67.1	52.0	68.3	77.8	84.6	84.8	82.5	59.2	12.9
2001	66.8	49.6	68.2	77.1	84.0	84.6	82.3	60.4	13.0
2002	66.6	47.4	68.1	76.4	83.7	84.1	82.1	61.9	13.2
2003	66.2	44.5	67.9	75.4	82.9	83.9	82.1	62.4	14.0
2004	66.0	43.9	67.7	75.0	82.7	83.6	81.8	62.3	14.4
2005	66.0	43.7	67.8	74.6	82.8	83.8	81.7	62.9	15.1
2006	66.2	43.7	67.9	74.6	83.0	83.8	81.9	63.7	15.4

Table 1-8. Civilian Labor Force Participation Rates, by Age, Sex, Race, and Hispanic Origin, 1948–2006
—*Continued*

(Percent.)

Race, Hispanic origin, sex, and year	16 years and over	16 to 19 years	20 years and over						
			Total	20 to 24 years	25 to 34 years	35 to 44 years	45 to 54 years	55 to 64 years	65 years and over
ALL RACES									
Men									
1948	86.6	63.7	88.6	84.6	95.9	97.9	95.8	89.5	46.8
1949	86.4	62.8	88.5	86.6	95.8	97.9	95.6	87.5	47.0
1950	86.4	63.2	88.4	87.9	96.0	97.6	95.8	86.9	45.8
1951	86.3	63.0	88.2	88.4	96.9	97.5	95.9	87.2	44.9
1952	86.3	61.3	88.3	88.1	97.5	97.8	96.2	87.5	42.6
1953	86.0	60.7	88.0	87.7	97.4	98.2	96.5	87.9	41.6
1954	85.5	58.0	87.8	86.9	97.3	98.1	96.5	88.7	40.5
1955	85.4	58.9	87.6	86.9	97.6	98.1	96.4	87.9	39.6
1956	85.5	60.5	87.6	87.8	97.3	97.9	96.6	88.5	40.0
1957	84.8	59.1	86.9	87.1	97.1	97.9	96.3	87.5	37.5
1958	84.2	56.6	86.6	86.9	97.1	97.9	96.3	87.8	35.6
1959	83.7	55.8	86.3	87.8	97.4	97.8	96.0	87.4	34.2
1960	83.3	56.1	86.0	88.1	97.5	97.7	95.7	86.8	33.1
1961	82.9	54.6	85.7	87.8	97.5	97.6	95.6	87.3	31.7
1962	82.0	53.8	84.8	86.9	97.2	97.6	95.6	86.2	30.3
1963	81.4	52.9	84.4	86.1	97.1	97.5	95.7	86.2	28.4
1964	81.0	52.4	84.2	86.1	97.3	97.3	95.7	85.6	28.0
1965	80.7	53.8	83.9	85.8	97.2	97.3	95.6	84.6	27.9
1966	80.4	55.3	83.6	85.1	97.3	97.2	95.3	84.5	27.1
1967	80.4	55.6	83.4	84.4	97.2	97.3	95.2	84.4	27.1
1968	80.1	55.1	83.1	82.8	96.9	97.1	94.9	84.3	27.3
1969	79.8	55.9	82.8	82.8	96.7	96.9	94.6	83.4	27.2
1970	79.7	56.1	82.6	83.3	96.4	96.9	94.3	83.0	26.8
1971	79.1	56.1	82.1	83.0	95.9	96.5	93.9	82.1	25.5
1972	78.9	58.1	81.6	83.9	95.7	96.4	93.2	80.4	24.3
1973	78.8	59.7	81.3	85.2	95.7	96.2	93.0	78.2	22.7
1974	78.7	60.7	81.0	85.9	95.8	96.0	92.2	77.3	22.4
1975	77.9	59.1	80.3	84.5	95.2	95.6	92.1	75.6	21.6
1976	77.5	59.3	79.8	85.2	95.2	95.4	91.6	74.3	20.2
1977	77.7	60.9	79.7	85.6	95.3	95.7	91.1	73.8	20.0
1978	77.9	62.0	79.8	85.9	95.3	95.7	91.3	73.3	20.4
1979	77.8	61.5	79.8	86.4	95.3	95.7	91.4	72.8	19.9
1980	77.4	60.5	79.4	85.9	95.2	95.5	91.2	72.1	19.0
1981	77.0	59.0	79.0	85.5	94.9	95.4	91.4	70.6	18.4
1982	76.6	56.7	78.7	84.9	94.7	95.3	91.2	70.2	17.8
1983	76.4	56.2	78.5	84.8	94.2	95.2	91.2	69.4	17.4
1984	76.4	56.0	78.3	85.0	94.4	95.4	91.2	68.5	16.3
1985	76.3	56.8	78.1	85.0	94.7	95.0	91.0	67.9	15.8
1986	76.3	56.4	78.1	85.8	94.6	94.8	91.0	67.3	16.0
1987	76.2	56.1	78.0	85.2	94.6	94.6	90.7	67.6	16.3
1988	76.2	56.9	77.9	85.0	94.3	94.5	90.9	67.0	16.5
1989	76.4	57.9	78.1	85.3	94.4	94.5	91.1	67.2	16.6
1990	76.4	55.7	78.2	84.4	94.1	94.3	90.7	67.8	16.3
1991	75.8	53.2	77.7	83.5	93.6	94.1	90.5	67.0	15.7
1992	75.8	53.4	77.7	83.3	93.8	93.7	90.7	67.0	16.1
1993	75.4	53.2	77.3	83.2	93.4	93.4	90.1	66.5	15.6
1994	75.1	54.1	76.8	83.1	92.6	92.8	89.1	65.5	16.8
1995	75.0	54.8	76.7	83.1	93.0	92.3	88.8	66.0	16.8
1996	74.9	53.2	76.8	82.5	93.2	92.4	89.1	67.0	16.9
1997	75.0	52.3	77.0	82.5	93.0	92.6	89.5	67.6	17.1
1998	74.9	53.3	76.8	82.0	93.2	92.6	89.2	68.1	16.5
1999	74.7	52.9	76.7	81.9	93.3	92.8	88.8	67.9	16.9
2000	74.8	52.8	76.7	82.6	93.4	92.7	88.6	67.3	17.7
2001	74.4	50.2	76.5	81.6	92.7	92.5	88.5	68.3	17.7
2002	74.1	47.5	76.3	80.7	92.4	92.1	88.5	69.2	17.9
2003	73.5	44.3	75.9	80.0	91.8	92.1	87.7	68.7	18.6
2004	73.3	43.9	75.8	79.6	91.9	91.9	87.5	68.7	19.0
2005	73.3	43.2	75.8	79.1	91.7	92.1	87.7	69.3	19.8
2006	73.5	43.7	75.9	79.6	91.7	92.1	88.1	69.6	20.3

Table 1-8. Civilian Labor Force Participation Rates, by Age, Sex, Race, and Hispanic Origin, 1948–2006
—*Continued*

(Percent.)

Race, Hispanic origin, sex, and year	16 years and over	16 to 19 years	20 years and over						
			Total	20 to 24 years	25 to 34 years	35 to 44 years	45 to 54 years	55 to 64 years	65 years and over
ALL RACES									
Women									
1948	32.7	42.0	31.8	45.3	33.2	36.9	35.0	24.3	9.1
1949	33.1	42.4	32.3	45.0	33.4	38.1	35.9	25.3	9.6
1950	33.9	41.0	33.3	46.0	34.0	39.1	37.9	27.0	9.7
1951	34.6	42.4	34.0	46.5	35.4	39.8	39.7	27.6	8.9
1952	34.7	42.2	34.1	44.7	35.4	40.4	40.1	28.7	9.1
1953	34.4	40.7	33.9	44.3	34.0	41.3	40.4	29.1	10.0
1954	34.6	39.4	34.2	45.1	34.4	41.2	41.2	30.0	9.3
1955	35.7	39.7	35.4	45.9	34.9	41.6	43.8	32.5	10.6
1956	36.9	42.2	36.4	46.3	35.4	43.1	45.5	34.9	10.8
1957	36.9	41.1	36.5	45.9	35.6	43.3	46.5	34.5	10.5
1958	37.1	39.0	36.9	46.3	35.6	43.4	47.8	35.2	10.3
1959	37.1	38.2	37.1	45.1	35.3	43.4	49.0	36.6	10.2
1960	37.7	39.3	37.6	46.1	36.0	43.4	49.9	37.2	10.8
1961	38.1	39.7	38.0	47.0	36.4	43.8	50.1	37.9	10.7
1962	37.9	39.0	37.8	47.3	36.3	44.1	50.0	38.7	10.0
1963	38.3	38.0	38.3	47.5	37.2	44.9	50.6	39.7	9.6
1964	38.7	37.0	38.9	49.4	37.2	45.0	51.4	40.2	10.1
1965	39.3	38.0	39.4	49.9	38.5	46.1	50.9	41.1	10.0
1966	40.3	41.4	40.1	51.5	39.8	46.8	51.7	41.8	9.6
1967	41.1	41.6	41.1	53.3	41.9	48.1	51.8	42.4	9.6
1968	41.6	41.9	41.6	54.5	42.6	48.9	52.3	42.4	9.6
1969	42.7	43.2	42.7	56.7	43.7	49.9	53.8	43.1	9.9
1970	43.3	44.0	43.3	57.7	45.0	51.1	54.4	43.0	9.7
1971	43.4	43.4	43.3	57.7	45.6	51.6	54.3	42.9	9.5
1972	43.9	45.8	43.7	59.1	47.8	52.0	53.9	42.1	9.3
1973	44.7	47.8	44.4	61.1	50.4	53.3	53.7	41.1	8.9
1974	45.7	49.1	45.3	63.1	52.6	54.7	54.6	40.7	8.1
1975	46.3	49.1	46.0	64.1	54.9	55.8	54.6	40.9	8.2
1976	47.3	49.8	47.0	65.0	57.3	57.8	55.0	41.0	8.2
1977	48.4	51.2	48.1	66.5	59.7	59.6	55.8	40.9	8.1
1978	50.0	53.7	49.6	68.3	62.2	61.6	57.1	41.3	8.3
1979	50.9	54.2	50.6	69.0	63.9	63.6	58.3	41.7	8.3
1980	51.5	52.9	51.3	68.9	65.5	65.5	59.9	41.3	8.1
1981	52.1	51.8	52.1	69.6	66.7	66.8	61.1	41.4	8.0
1982	52.6	51.4	52.7	69.8	68.0	68.0	61.6	41.8	7.9
1983	52.9	50.8	53.1	69.9	69.0	68.7	61.9	41.5	7.8
1984	53.6	51.8	53.7	70.4	69.8	70.1	62.9	41.7	7.5
1985	54.5	52.1	54.7	71.8	70.9	71.8	64.4	42.0	7.3
1986	55.3	53.0	55.5	72.4	71.6	73.1	65.9	42.3	7.4
1987	56.0	53.3	56.2	73.0	72.4	74.5	67.1	42.7	7.4
1988	56.6	53.6	56.8	72.7	72.7	75.2	69.0	43.5	7.9
1989	57.4	53.9	57.7	72.4	73.5	76.0	70.5	45.0	8.4
1990	57.5	51.6	58.0	71.3	73.5	76.4	71.2	45.2	8.6
1991	57.4	50.0	57.9	70.1	73.1	76.5	72.0	45.2	8.5
1992	57.8	49.1	58.5	70.9	73.9	76.7	72.6	46.5	8.3
1993	57.9	49.7	58.5	70.9	73.4	76.6	73.5	47.2	8.1
1994	58.8	51.3	59.3	71.0	74.0	77.1	74.6	48.9	9.2
1995	58.9	52.2	59.4	70.3	74.9	77.2	74.4	49.2	8.8
1996	59.3	51.3	59.9	71.3	75.2	77.5	75.4	49.6	8.6
1997	59.8	51.0	60.5	72.7	76.0	77.7	76.0	50.9	8.6
1998	59.8	52.3	60.4	73.0	76.3	77.1	76.2	51.2	8.6
1999	60.0	51.0	60.7	73.2	76.4	77.2	76.7	51.5	8.9
2000	59.9	51.2	60.6	73.1	76.1	77.2	76.8	51.9	9.4
2001	59.8	49.0	60.6	72.7	75.5	77.1	76.4	53.2	9.6
2002	59.6	47.3	60.5	72.1	75.1	76.4	76.0	55.2	9.8
2003	59.5	44.8	60.6	70.8	74.1	76.0	76.8	56.6	10.6
2004	59.2	43.8	60.3	70.5	73.6	75.6	76.5	56.3	11.1
2005	59.3	44.2	60.4	70.1	73.9	75.8	76.0	57.0	11.5
2006	59.4	43.7	60.5	69.5	74.4	75.9	76.0	58.2	11.7

Table 1-8. Civilian Labor Force Participation Rates, by Age, Sex, Race, and Hispanic Origin, 1948–2006 —*Continued*

(Percent.)

Race, Hispanic origin, sex, and year	16 years and over	16 to 19 years	20 years and over						
			Total	20 to 24 years	25 to 34 years	35 to 44 years	45 to 54 years	55 to 64 years	65 years and over
WHITE[1]									
Both Sexes									
1954	58.2	48.8	58.9	61.0	63.5	68.0	67.9	58.4	23.7
1955	58.7	49.3	59.5	62.4	64.0	68.3	69.2	59.3	23.9
1956	59.4	51.3	60.1	64.1	64.0	68.9	70.1	60.6	24.2
1957	59.1	50.3	59.8	63.7	64.1	68.8	70.5	59.9	22.8
1958	58.9	47.9	59.8	64.1	64.2	68.8	71.0	60.3	21.7
1959	58.7	47.4	59.7	63.7	64.3	68.7	71.5	60.7	21.0
1960	58.8	47.9	59.8	64.8	64.7	68.6	71.7	60.6	20.8
1961	58.8	47.4	59.9	65.5	64.8	68.8	71.7	61.3	20.0
1962	58.3	46.6	59.4	65.0	64.4	69.0	71.8	61.3	19.0
1963	58.2	45.7	59.4	64.9	64.8	69.4	72.3	61.8	17.9
1964	58.2	45.1	59.6	65.8	64.9	69.5	72.5	61.8	17.8
1965	58.4	46.5	59.7	65.7	65.6	70.1	72.2	61.7	17.7
1966	58.7	49.1	59.8	66.0	66.3	70.4	72.5	61.9	17.1
1967	59.2	49.2	60.3	66.8	67.4	71.2	72.5	62.3	17.0
1968	59.3	49.3	60.4	66.6	67.9	71.7	72.7	62.2	17.1
1969	59.9	50.6	60.9	67.9	68.4	72.3	73.3	62.1	17.2
1970	60.2	51.4	61.2	69.2	69.1	72.9	73.5	61.8	16.8
1971	60.1	51.6	61.1	69.6	69.3	73.0	73.4	61.3	16.1
1972	60.4	54.1	61.2	71.2	70.4	73.2	72.9	60.3	15.4
1973	60.8	56.0	61.4	73.3	72.0	73.9	72.7	58.6	14.4
1974	61.4	57.3	61.9	74.8	73.4	74.6	73.0	58.0	13.9
1975	61.5	56.7	62.0	75.2	74.4	75.1	73.0	57.4	13.6
1976	61.8	57.5	62.3	76.0	75.6	76.1	73.0	56.9	13.0
1977	62.5	59.3	62.9	77.1	77.0	77.1	73.2	56.6	12.9
1978	63.3	60.8	63.6	78.1	78.3	78.1	73.8	56.4	13.1
1979	63.9	61.1	64.2	78.9	79.4	79.3	74.6	56.5	12.9
1980	64.1	60.0	64.5	78.7	80.2	80.3	75.4	56.0	12.5
1981	64.3	58.9	64.8	79.1	81.0	81.0	76.2	55.2	12.2
1982	64.3	57.5	65.0	78.9	81.6	81.5	76.4	55.3	12.0
1983	64.3	56.9	65.0	79.0	81.8	81.9	76.5	54.7	11.8
1984	64.6	57.2	65.3	79.4	82.5	82.6	77.0	54.5	11.1
1985	65.0	57.5	65.7	79.9	83.1	83.4	77.8	54.4	10.7
1986	65.5	57.8	66.1	80.6	83.6	84.0	78.5	54.3	11.0
1987	65.8	57.7	66.5	80.7	84.0	84.7	79.1	54.6	11.1
1988	66.2	58.6	66.8	80.6	84.1	85.0	80.3	55.1	11.4
1989	66.7	59.1	67.3	80.2	84.5	85.5	81.2	56.2	11.8
1990	66.9	57.5	67.6	79.8	84.6	85.9	81.3	56.5	11.9
1991	66.6	55.8	67.4	78.9	84.3	85.9	81.8	56.0	11.6
1992	66.8	54.7	67.7	79.4	84.6	85.8	82.2	56.8	11.6
1993	66.8	55.1	67.6	79.5	84.5	85.7	82.5	57.1	11.4
1994	67.1	56.4	67.9	79.5	84.4	85.7	82.7	57.6	12.5
1995	67.1	57.1	67.8	78.7	84.9	85.5	82.5	58.0	12.3
1996	67.2	55.9	68.1	79.1	84.9	85.7	83.1	58.7	12.3
1997	67.5	55.2	68.4	79.6	85.3	85.8	83.5	59.9	12.3
1998	67.3	56.0	68.2	79.5	85.4	85.3	83.4	60.1	12.0
1999	67.3	55.5	68.2	79.5	85.1	85.4	83.5	60.2	12.5
2000	67.3	55.5	68.2	79.9	85.1	85.4	83.5	60.0	13.0
2001	67.0	53.1	68.1	79.2	84.5	85.2	83.3	61.2	13.0
2002	66.8	50.5	68.1	78.6	84.5	84.7	83.0	62.8	13.3
2003	66.5	47.7	67.9	77.7	83.6	84.3	83.0	63.3	14.1
2004	66.3	47.1	67.7	77.1	83.5	84.1	82.9	63.2	14.6
2005	66.3	46.9	67.7	76.3	83.5	84.2	82.8	63.7	15.1
2006	66.5	46.7	67.9	76.5	83.8	84.3	83.0	64.7	15.5

[1]Beginning in 2003, persons who selected this race group only; persons who selected more than one race group are not included. Prior to 2003, persons who reported more than one race group were included in the group they identified as their main race.

Table 1-8. Civilian Labor Force Participation Rates, by Age, Sex, Race, and Hispanic Origin, 1948–2006 —*Continued*

(Percent.)

Race, Hispanic origin, sex, and year	16 years and over	16 to 19 years	20 years and over						
			Total	20 to 24 years	25 to 34 years	35 to 44 years	45 to 54 years	55 to 64 years	65 years and over
WHITE[1]									
Men									
1954	85.6	57.6	87.8	86.3	97.5	98.2	96.8	89.1	40.4
1955	85.4	58.6	87.5	86.5	97.8	98.2	96.7	88.4	39.6
1956	85.6	60.4	87.6	87.6	97.4	98.1	96.8	88.9	40.0
1957	84.8	59.2	86.9	86.6	97.2	98.0	96.7	88.0	37.7
1958	84.3	56.5	86.6	86.7	97.2	98.0	96.6	88.2	35.7
1959	83.8	55.9	86.3	87.3	97.5	98.0	96.3	87.9	34.3
1960	83.4	55.9	86.0	87.8	97.7	97.9	96.1	87.2	33.3
1961	83.0	54.5	85.7	87.6	97.7	97.9	95.9	87.8	31.9
1962	82.1	53.8	84.9	86.5	97.4	97.9	96.0	86.7	30.6
1963	81.5	53.1	84.4	85.8	97.4	97.8	96.2	86.6	28.4
1964	81.1	52.7	84.2	85.7	97.5	97.6	96.1	86.1	27.9
1965	80.8	54.1	83.9	85.3	97.4	97.7	95.9	85.2	27.9
1966	80.6	55.9	83.6	84.4	97.5	97.6	95.8	84.9	27.2
1967	80.6	56.3	83.5	84.0	97.5	97.7	95.6	84.9	27.1
1968	80.4	55.9	83.2	82.4	97.2	97.6	95.4	84.7	27.4
1969	80.2	56.8	83.0	82.6	97.0	97.4	95.1	83.9	27.3
1970	80.0	57.5	82.8	83.3	96.7	97.3	94.9	83.3	26.7
1971	79.6	57.9	82.3	83.2	96.3	97.0	94.7	82.6	25.6
1972	79.6	60.1	82.0	84.3	96.0	97.0	94.0	81.1	24.4
1973	79.4	62.0	81.6	85.8	96.2	96.8	93.5	78.9	22.7
1974	79.4	62.9	81.4	86.6	96.3	96.7	93.0	78.0	22.4
1975	78.7	61.9	80.7	85.5	95.8	96.4	92.9	76.4	21.7
1976	78.4	62.3	80.3	86.3	95.9	96.0	92.5	75.2	20.2
1977	78.5	64.0	80.2	86.8	96.0	96.2	92.1	74.6	20.0
1978	78.6	65.0	80.1	87.3	95.9	96.3	92.1	73.7	20.3
1979	78.6	64.8	80.1	87.6	96.0	96.4	92.2	73.4	20.0
1980	78.2	63.7	79.8	87.2	95.9	96.2	92.1	73.1	19.1
1981	77.9	62.4	79.5	87.0	95.8	96.1	92.4	71.5	18.5
1982	77.4	60.0	79.2	86.3	95.6	96.0	92.2	71.0	17.9
1983	77.1	59.4	78.9	86.1	95.2	96.0	91.9	70.0	17.7
1984	77.1	59.0	78.7	86.5	95.4	96.1	92.0	69.5	16.4
1985	77.0	59.7	78.5	86.4	95.7	95.7	92.0	68.8	15.9
1986	76.9	59.3	78.5	87.3	95.5	95.4	91.8	68.0	16.3
1987	76.8	59.0	78.4	86.9	95.5	95.4	91.6	68.1	16.5
1988	76.9	60.0	78.3	86.6	95.2	95.4	91.8	67.9	16.7
1989	77.1	61.0	78.5	86.8	95.4	95.3	92.2	68.3	16.8
1990	77.1	59.6	78.5	86.2	95.2	95.3	91.7	68.6	16.6
1991	76.5	57.3	78.0	85.4	94.9	95.0	91.4	67.7	15.9
1992	76.5	56.9	78.0	85.2	94.9	94.7	91.8	67.7	16.2
1993	76.2	56.6	77.7	85.5	94.7	94.5	91.3	67.3	15.9
1994	75.9	57.7	77.3	85.5	93.9	93.9	90.3	66.4	17.2
1995	75.7	58.5	77.1	85.1	94.1	93.4	90.0	67.1	16.9
1996	75.8	57.1	77.3	85.0	94.4	93.6	90.4	68.0	17.2
1997	75.9	56.1	77.5	85.1	94.2	93.7	90.6	68.9	17.4
1998	75.6	56.6	77.2	84.6	94.4	93.7	90.3	69.1	16.6
1999	75.6	56.4	77.2	84.9	94.3	93.8	90.1	69.1	17.2
2000	75.5	56.5	77.1	85.2	94.5	93.8	89.7	68.2	17.9
2001	75.1	53.7	76.9	84.1	93.9	93.6	89.7	69.1	17.8
2002	74.8	50.3	76.7	83.2	93.7	93.2	89.6	70.2	17.8
2003	74.2	47.5	76.3	82.5	93.3	93.1	88.8	69.7	18.6
2004	74.1	47.4	76.2	82.1	93.2	93.0	88.7	69.8	19.1
2005	74.1	46.2	76.2	81.4	93.0	93.0	89.0	70.4	20.0
2006	74.3	46.9	76.4	81.9	92.9	93.1	89.3	71.0	20.6

[1]Beginning in 2003, persons who selected this race group only; persons who selected more than one race group are not included. Prior to 2003, persons who reported more than one race group were included in the group they identified as their main race.

Table 1-8. Civilian Labor Force Participation Rates, by Age, Sex, Race, and Hispanic Origin, 1948–2006
    —*Continued*

(Percent.)

Race, Hispanic origin, sex, and year	16 years and over	16 to 19 years	20 years and over						
			Total	20 to 24 years	25 to 34 years	35 to 44 years	45 to 54 years	55 to 64 years	65 years and over
WHITE[1]									
Women									
1954	33.3	40.6	32.7	44.4	32.5	39.3	39.8	29.1	9.1
1955	34.5	40.7	34.0	45.8	32.8	40.0	42.7	31.8	10.5
1956	35.7	43.1	35.1	46.5	33.2	41.5	44.4	34.0	10.6
1957	35.7	42.2	35.2	45.8	33.6	41.5	45.4	33.7	10.2
1958	35.8	40.1	35.5	46.0	33.6	41.4	46.5	34.5	10.1
1959	36.0	39.6	35.6	44.5	33.4	41.4	47.8	35.7	10.0
1960	36.5	40.3	36.2	45.7	34.1	41.5	48.6	36.2	10.6
1961	36.9	40.6	36.6	46.9	34.3	41.8	48.9	37.2	10.5
1962	36.7	39.8	36.5	47.1	34.1	42.2	48.9	38.0	9.8
1963	37.2	38.7	37.0	47.3	34.8	43.1	49.5	38.9	9.4
1964	37.5	37.8	37.5	48.8	35.0	43.3	50.2	39.4	9.9
1965	38.1	39.2	38.0	49.2	36.3	44.4	49.9	40.3	9.7
1966	39.2	42.6	38.8	51.0	37.7	45.0	50.6	41.1	9.4
1967	40.1	42.5	39.8	53.1	39.7	46.4	50.9	41.9	9.3
1968	40.7	43.0	40.4	54.0	40.6	47.5	51.5	42.0	9.4
1969	41.8	44.6	41.5	56.4	41.7	48.6	53.0	42.6	9.7
1970	42.6	45.6	42.2	57.7	43.2	49.9	53.7	42.6	9.5
1971	42.6	45.4	42.3	58.0	43.7	50.2	53.6	42.5	9.3
1972	43.2	48.1	42.7	59.4	46.0	50.7	53.4	41.9	9.0
1973	44.1	50.1	43.5	61.7	48.7	52.2	53.4	40.7	8.7
1974	45.2	51.7	44.4	63.9	51.3	53.6	54.3	40.4	8.0
1975	45.9	51.5	45.3	65.5	53.8	54.9	54.3	40.6	8.0
1976	46.9	52.8	46.2	66.3	56.0	57.1	54.7	40.7	7.9
1977	48.0	54.5	47.3	67.8	58.5	58.9	55.3	40.7	7.9
1978	49.4	56.7	48.7	69.3	61.2	60.7	56.7	41.1	8.1
1979	50.5	57.4	49.8	70.5	63.1	63.0	58.1	41.5	8.1
1980	51.2	56.2	50.6	70.6	64.8	65.0	59.6	40.9	7.9
1981	51.9	55.4	51.5	71.5	66.4	66.4	60.9	40.9	7.9
1982	52.4	55.0	52.2	71.8	67.8	67.5	61.4	41.5	7.8
1983	52.7	54.5	52.5	72.1	68.7	68.2	61.9	41.1	7.8
1984	53.3	55.4	53.1	72.5	69.8	69.6	62.7	41.2	7.5
1985	54.1	55.2	54.0	73.8	70.9	71.4	64.2	41.5	7.0
1986	55.0	56.3	54.9	74.1	71.8	72.9	65.8	42.1	7.3
1987	55.7	56.5	55.6	74.8	72.5	74.2	67.2	42.4	7.2
1988	56.4	57.2	56.3	74.9	73.0	74.9	69.2	43.6	7.7
1989	57.2	57.1	57.2	74.0	73.8	75.9	70.6	45.2	8.2
1990	57.4	55.3	57.6	73.4	74.1	76.6	71.3	45.5	8.5
1991	57.4	54.1	57.6	72.5	73.8	76.8	72.4	45.4	8.5
1992	57.7	52.5	58.1	73.5	74.4	77.0	72.8	46.8	8.2
1993	58.0	53.5	58.3	73.4	74.3	76.9	74.0	47.6	8.1
1994	58.9	55.1	59.2	73.4	74.9	77.5	75.2	49.4	9.2
1995	59.0	55.5	59.2	72.3	75.8	77.6	75.2	49.5	9.0
1996	59.1	54.7	59.4	73.3	75.5	77.8	76.1	50.1	8.7
1997	59.5	54.1	59.9	73.9	76.3	77.9	76.6	51.5	8.6
1998	59.4	55.4	59.7	74.3	76.3	76.9	76.6	51.6	8.7
1999	59.6	54.5	59.9	73.9	76.0	77.1	77.1	52.0	8.9
2000	59.5	54.5	59.9	74.5	75.7	77.2	77.5	52.4	9.4
2001	59.4	52.4	59.9	74.2	75.1	77.0	77.1	53.8	9.6
2002	59.3	50.8	60.0	74.0	75.0	76.3	76.6	55.8	9.9
2003	59.2	47.9	59.9	72.7	73.7	75.5	77.3	57.4	10.8
2004	58.9	46.7	59.7	71.9	73.6	75.2	77.1	57.0	11.2
2005	58.9	47.6	59.7	71.0	73.7	75.4	76.7	57.5	11.4
2006	59.0	46.6	59.9	70.9	74.3	75.5	76.7	58.7	11.6

[1]Beginning in 2003, persons who selected this race group only; persons who selected more than one race group are not included. Prior to 2003, persons who reported more than one race group were included in the group they identified as their main race.

Table 1-8. Civilian Labor Force Participation Rates, by Age, Sex, Race, and Hispanic Origin, 1948–2006
—Continued

(Percent.)

Race, Hispanic origin, sex, and year	16 years and over	16 to 19 years	20 years and over						
			Total	20 to 24 years	25 to 34 years	35 to 44 years	45 to 54 years	55 to 64 years	65 years and over
BLACK[1]									
Both Sexes									
1972	59.9	39.1	63.3	68.6	74.9	74.4	70.0	56.9	17.5
1973	60.2	39.8	63.4	69.7	75.7	74.5	70.3	55.9	16.0
1974	59.8	39.8	63.0	69.8	75.8	74.6	69.1	54.7	15.1
1975	58.8	38.2	62.0	66.1	75.6	74.1	69.0	54.3	14.9
1976	59.0	37.0	62.5	66.8	77.4	74.9	68.6	53.4	14.9
1977	59.8	37.9	63.2	68.2	78.3	75.9	69.0	53.7	14.5
1978	61.5	41.0	64.5	69.9	79.6	77.4	70.4	54.8	15.3
1979	61.4	40.1	64.5	70.0	79.2	77.9	71.1	53.5	14.5
1980	61.0	38.9	64.1	69.0	79.5	77.4	71.4	52.6	13.0
1981	60.8	37.7	64.2	69.2	78.5	78.4	71.2	52.8	12.0
1982	61.0	36.6	64.3	68.6	78.7	79.8	71.1	52.3	11.5
1983	61.5	36.4	64.9	68.4	79.8	80.2	72.1	52.5	10.5
1984	62.2	38.3	65.2	69.2	79.3	81.0	73.0	51.6	10.3
1985	62.9	41.2	65.6	70.0	79.8	81.5	73.4	51.4	11.2
1986	63.3	41.3	65.9	71.7	80.1	81.9	74.3	50.6	9.7
1987	63.8	41.6	66.5	70.5	80.7	82.6	74.7	52.4	10.7
1988	63.8	40.8	66.5	70.5	80.8	82.6	75.0	50.6	11.5
1989	64.2	42.5	66.7	72.2	80.9	82.7	75.5	48.3	11.6
1990	64.0	38.7	66.9	68.8	79.7	82.4	76.5	49.6	11.1
1991	63.3	35.4	66.4	67.7	78.5	82.0	76.2	50.4	10.7
1992	63.9	37.9	66.8	67.4	79.7	81.4	76.2	51.6	10.6
1993	63.2	37.0	66.0	67.8	78.3	81.0	75.2	50.2	9.5
1994	63.4	38.5	66.0	68.8	78.3	80.8	74.8	49.3	10.6
1995	63.7	39.9	66.3	68.7	80.0	80.4	74.1	50.3	10.5
1996	64.1	39.2	66.9	69.0	81.1	81.0	74.9	50.9	9.8
1997	64.7	38.7	67.6	70.9	82.0	81.4	76.3	50.5	10.0
1998	65.6	41.6	68.2	70.6	83.0	82.2	76.7	52.3	10.3
1999	65.8	38.7	68.9	71.4	85.2	83.0	76.4	51.4	10.4
2000	65.8	39.4	68.7	71.8	84.1	82.3	76.9	52.5	11.6
2001	65.3	37.6	68.2	69.9	83.6	82.0	75.9	53.9	12.6
2002	64.8	36.0	67.8	68.6	82.4	81.6	76.1	54.7	12.5
2003	64.3	32.4	67.6	68.2	81.6	82.9	75.8	54.4	12.9
2004	63.8	31.4	67.2	68.3	81.2	82.1	75.5	54.4	13.1
2005	64.2	32.4	67.4	69.0	81.7	82.3	75.7	55.3	13.6
2006	64.1	34.0	67.3	68.8	81.8	82.0	75.8	55.4	13.7
BLACK[1]									
Men									
1972	73.6	46.3	78.5	82.7	92.7	91.1	85.4	72.5	24.2
1973	73.4	45.7	78.4	83.7	91.8	91.0	87.4	69.5	22.3
1974	72.9	46.7	77.6	83.6	92.8	90.4	84.0	68.9	21.6
1975	70.9	42.6	76.0	78.7	91.6	89.4	83.5	67.7	20.7
1976	70.0	41.3	75.4	79.0	90.9	89.9	82.4	65.1	19.8
1977	70.6	43.2	75.6	79.2	90.7	91.0	82.0	65.5	20.0
1978	71.5	44.9	76.2	78.8	90.9	90.5	83.2	67.9	21.1
1979	71.3	43.6	76.3	80.7	90.8	90.4	84.5	64.8	19.5
1980	70.3	43.2	75.1	79.9	90.9	89.1	83.0	61.9	16.9
1981	70.0	41.6	74.5	79.2	88.9	89.3	82.7	62.1	16.0
1982	70.1	39.8	74.7	78.7	89.2	89.8	82.2	61.9	15.9
1983	70.6	39.9	75.2	79.4	89.0	89.7	84.5	62.6	14.0
1984	70.8	41.7	74.8	79.1	88.9	90.0	83.7	58.9	13.7
1985	70.8	44.6	74.4	79.0	88.8	89.8	83.0	58.9	13.9
1986	71.2	43.7	74.8	80.1	89.6	89.6	84.1	59.1	12.6
1987	71.1	43.6	74.7	77.8	89.4	88.6	83.7	62.1	13.7
1988	71.0	43.8	74.6	79.3	89.3	88.2	83.5	59.4	14.3
1989	71.0	44.6	74.4	80.2	89.7	88.7	82.5	55.5	14.3
1990	71.0	40.7	75.0	76.8	88.8	88.1	83.5	58.0	13.0
1991	70.4	37.3	74.6	76.7	87.3	87.7	83.4	58.7	13.0
1992	70.7	40.6	74.3	75.4	88.0	86.5	81.8	60.0	13.7
1993	69.6	39.5	73.2	74.1	87.3	86.1	80.0	57.9	11.6
1994	69.1	40.8	72.5	73.9	86.2	85.9	79.1	54.5	12.7
1995	69.0	40.1	72.5	74.6	87.5	84.1	78.5	54.4	14.9
1996	68.7	39.5	72.3	73.4	87.5	84.4	78.5	55.6	12.9
1997	68.3	37.4	72.2	72.1	86.8	84.8	80.1	54.3	12.9
1998	69.0	40.7	72.5	71.8	87.1	85.0	79.9	57.3	14.0
1999	68.7	38.6	72.4	69.8	89.2	86.0	78.5	55.5	12.7
2000	69.2	39.2	72.8	73.3	87.8	85.2	79.2	57.4	14.4
2001	68.4	37.9	72.1	69.7	86.6	84.9	78.4	58.9	16.7
2002	68.4	37.3	72.1	70.7	85.9	84.7	79.5	58.4	16.9
2003	67.3	31.1	71.5	71.1	84.7	85.7	77.7	57.6	17.0
2004	66.7	30.0	70.9	69.9	86.1	84.0	76.9	57.1	17.0
2005	67.3	32.6	71.3	70.1	85.5	85.5	78.6	57.3	17.1
2006	67.0	32.3	71.1	71.6	85.7	84.4	79.2	55.9	16.7

[1] Beginning in 2003, persons who selected this race group only; persons who selected more than one race group are not included. Prior to 2003, persons who reported more than one race group were included in the group they identified as their main race.

Table 1-8. Civilian Labor Force Participation Rates, by Age, Sex, Race, and Hispanic Origin, 1948–2006
—Continued

(Percent.)

Race, Hispanic origin, sex, and year	16 years and over	16 to 19 years	20 years and over						
			Total	20 to 24 years	25 to 34 years	35 to 44 years	45 to 54 years	55 to 64 years	65 years and over
BLACK[1]									
Women									
1972	48.7	32.2	51.2	57.0	60.8	61.4	57.2	44.0	12.6
1973	49.3	34.2	51.6	58.0	62.7	61.7	56.1	44.7	11.4
1974	49.0	33.4	51.4	58.8	62.4	62.2	56.4	42.8	10.4
1975	48.8	34.2	51.1	55.9	62.8	62.0	56.6	43.1	10.7
1976	49.8	32.9	52.5	56.9	66.7	63.0	56.8	43.7	11.3
1977	50.8	32.9	53.6	59.3	68.5	64.1	57.9	43.7	10.5
1978	53.1	37.3	55.5	62.7	70.6	67.2	59.4	43.8	11.1
1979	53.1	36.8	55.4	61.5	70.1	68.0	59.6	44.0	10.9
1980	53.1	34.9	55.6	60.2	70.5	68.1	61.4	44.8	10.2
1981	53.5	34.0	56.0	61.1	70.0	69.8	62.0	45.4	9.3
1982	53.7	33.5	56.2	60.1	70.2	71.7	62.4	44.8	8.5
1983	54.2	33.0	56.8	59.1	72.3	72.6	62.3	44.8	8.2
1984	55.2	35.0	57.6	60.7	71.5	73.7	64.5	46.1	8.0
1985	56.5	37.9	58.6	62.5	72.4	74.8	65.7	45.3	9.4
1986	56.9	39.1	58.9	64.6	72.4	75.8	66.5	43.6	7.8
1987	58.0	39.6	60.0	64.4	73.5	77.8	67.5	44.4	8.6
1988	58.0	37.9	60.1	63.2	73.7	78.1	68.3	43.4	9.6
1989	58.7	40.4	60.6	65.5	73.6	78.0	70.0	42.4	9.8
1990	58.3	36.8	60.6	62.4	72.3	77.7	70.7	43.2	9.9
1991	57.5	33.5	60.0	60.3	71.4	77.2	70.2	44.1	9.2
1992	58.5	35.2	60.8	60.8	73.1	77.1	71.7	45.1	8.6
1993	57.9	34.6	60.2	62.6	70.9	76.8	71.2	44.4	8.3
1994	58.7	36.3	60.9	64.5	71.9	76.4	71.3	45.3	9.2
1995	59.5	39.8	61.4	63.7	73.9	77.3	70.5	47.2	7.7
1996	60.4	38.9	62.6	65.2	75.9	78.2	72.0	47.2	7.7
1997	61.7	39.9	64.0	69.9	78.1	78.4	73.2	47.6	8.2
1998	62.8	42.5	64.8	69.6	79.6	79.9	74.0	48.5	7.9
1999	63.5	38.8	66.1	72.7	82.1	80.4	74.6	48.4	8.9
2000	63.1	39.6	65.4	70.5	81.1	79.9	74.9	48.6	9.9
2001	62.8	37.3	65.2	70.1	81.2	79.6	73.9	49.9	10.1
2002	61.8	34.7	64.4	66.9	79.7	79.2	73.3	51.8	9.8
2003	61.9	33.7	64.6	65.7	79.1	80.6	74.2	51.9	10.3
2004	61.5	32.8	64.2	66.8	77.2	80.6	74.3	52.3	10.7
2005	61.6	32.2	64.4	68.1	78.5	79.7	73.3	53.7	11.4
2006	61.7	35.6	64.2	66.2	78.6	80.1	73.0	55.1	11.8
HISPANIC[2]									
Both Sexes									
1973	60.2	46.9	. . .	. . .	. . .	. . .	. . .	. . .	. . .
1974	61.1	47.7	. . .	. . .	. . .	. . .	. . .	. . .	. . .
1975	60.8	46.2	. . .	. . .	. . .	. . .	. . .	. . .	. . .
1976	60.8	46.9	62.9	. . .	. . .	. . .	. . .	. . .	. . .
1977	61.6	48.2	63.7	. . .	. . .	. . .	. . .	. . .	. . .
1978	62.9	49.6	65.0	. . .	. . .	. . .	. . .	. . .	. . .
1979	63.6	50.3	65.6	. . .	. . .	. . .	. . .	. . .	. . .
1980	64.0	50.3	66.2	. . .	. . .	. . .	. . .	. . .	. . .
1981	64.1	46.4	66.8	. . .	. . .	. . .	. . .	. . .	. . .
1982	63.6	44.8	66.3	. . .	. . .	. . .	. . .	. . .	. . .
1983	63.8	45.3	66.2	. . .	. . .	. . .	. . .	. . .	. . .
1984	64.9	47.5	67.1	. . .	. . .	. . .	. . .	. . .	. . .
1985	64.6	44.6	67.1	. . .	. . .	. . .	. . .	. . .	. . .
1986	65.4	43.9	68.0	. . .	. . .	. . .	. . .	. . .	. . .
1987	66.4	45.8	68.8	. . .	. . .	. . .	. . .	. . .	. . .
1988	67.4	49.6	69.4	. . .	. . .	. . .	. . .	. . .	. . .
1989	67.6	48.6	69.7	. . .	. . .	. . .	. . .	. . .	. . .
1990	67.4	47.8	69.8	. . .	. . .	. . .	. . .	. . .	. . .
1991	66.5	45.1	69.0	. . .	. . .	. . .	. . .	. . .	. . .
1992	66.8	45.8	69.2	. . .	. . .	. . .	. . .	. . .	. . .
1993	66.2	43.9	68.7	. . .	. . .	. . .	. . .	. . .	. . .
1994	66.1	44.4	68.5	74.0	77.3	78.9	73.1	49.8	10.7
1995	65.8	45.4	68.1	71.9	78.1	78.5	72.8	48.6	10.5
1996	66.5	43.4	69.1	73.1	78.2	79.5	74.6	52.2	11.0
1997	67.9	43.0	70.8	76.4	79.5	80.9	75.4	53.8	11.9
1998	67.9	45.7	70.6	76.1	80.3	80.0	75.3	55.4	10.1
1999	67.7	45.5	70.4	76.0	78.6	81.3	75.9	54.1	11.6
2000	69.7	46.3	72.5	78.2	80.4	81.7	78.0	54.2	12.3
2001	69.5	46.9	72.0	76.6	80.0	81.9	77.4	55.1	10.9
2002	69.1	44.0	71.8	76.3	80.5	81.1	76.1	55.8	11.9
2003	68.3	37.7	71.4	75.6	79.4	81.1	75.3	57.4	12.8
2004	68.6	38.2	71.7	74.5	79.4	81.4	77.6	58.1	14.5
2005	68.0	38.6	71.0	72.7	79.1	81.2	77.2	58.4	13.9
2006	68.7	38.3	71.9	74.4	80.1	81.9	77.3	59.2	15.7

[1]Beginning in 2003, persons who selected this race group only; persons who selected more than one race group are not included. Prior to 2003, persons who reported more than one race group were included in the group they identified as their main race.
[2]May be of any race.
. . . = Not available.

Table 1-8. Civilian Labor Force Participation Rates, by Age, Sex, Race, and Hispanic Origin, 1948–2006
—Continued

(Percent.)

Race, Hispanic origin, sex, and year	16 years and over	16 to 19 years	20 years and over						
			Total	20 to 24 years	25 to 34 years	35 to 44 years	45 to 54 years	55 to 64 years	65 years and over
HISPANIC[2]									
Men									
1973	81.5	. . .	85.9	. . .	. . .	. . .	. . .	. . .	. . .
1974	81.7	. . .	86.0	. . .	. . .	. . .	. . .	. . .	. . .
1975	80.7	. . .	85.5	. . .	. . .	. . .	. . .	. . .	. . .
1976	79.6	. . .	84.2	. . .	. . .	. . .	. . .	. . .	. . .
1977	80.9	. . .	84.8	. . .	. . .	. . .	. . .	. . .	. . .
1978	81.1	. . .	84.9	. . .	. . .	. . .	. . .	. . .	. . .
1979	81.3	. . .	85.3	. . .	. . .	. . .	. . .	. . .	. . .
1980	81.4	. . .	84.9	. . .	. . .	. . .	. . .	. . .	. . .
1981	80.6	. . .	84.7	. . .	. . .	. . .	. . .	. . .	. . .
1982	79.7	. . .	84.0	. . .	. . .	. . .	. . .	. . .	. . .
1983	80.3	. . .	84.1	. . .	. . .	. . .	. . .	. . .	. . .
1984	80.6	. . .	84.3	. . .	. . .	. . .	. . .	. . .	. . .
1985	80.3	. . .	84.0	. . .	. . .	. . .	. . .	. . .	. . .
1986	81.0	. . .	84.6	. . .	. . .	. . .	. . .	. . .	. . .
1987	81.0	. . .	84.5	. . .	. . .	. . .	. . .	. . .	. . .
1988	81.9	. . .	85.0	. . .	. . .	. . .	. . .	. . .	. . .
1989	82.0	. . .	85.0	. . .	. . .	. . .	. . .	. . .	. . .
1990	81.4	. . .	84.7	. . .	. . .	. . .	. . .	. . .	. . .
1991	80.3	. . .	83.8	. . .	. . .	. . .	. . .	. . .	. . .
1992	80.7	. . .	84.0	. . .	. . .	. . .	. . .	. . .	. . .
1993	80.2	. . .	83.5	. . .	. . .	. . .	. . .	. . .	. . .
1994	79.2	50.0	82.5	88.0	92.5	91.5	85.7	63.6	14.4
1995	79.1	50.2	82.4	86.2	92.9	91.3	85.6	62.4	15.8
1996	79.6	50.0	83.0	85.7	93.2	91.7	87.0	65.9	16.7
1997	80.1	47.4	84.1	88.1	93.5	91.9	87.8	68.4	17.3
1998	79.8	48.7	83.6	88.1	94.0	91.4	86.7	70.2	14.9
1999	79.8	50.1	83.5	88.1	93.9	92.2	86.2	68.6	18.2
2000	81.5	50.7	85.3	89.1	94.1	93.3	87.6	69.4	18.5
2001	81.0	52.2	84.3	86.8	93.4	92.7	86.7	68.6	16.8
2002	80.2	48.8	83.6	86.1	93.5	92.1	86.1	67.3	16.3
2003	80.1	40.9	84.1	86.2	93.6	92.9	85.4	68.8	17.4
2004	80.4	42.4	84.2	84.4	93.6	93.2	87.2	69.6	20.8
2005	80.1	41.9	84.0	84.1	93.3	93.1	87.7	69.3	20.1
2006	80.7	42.0	84.6	85.9	94.1	93.8	87.1	69.6	22.9
HISPANIC[2]									
Women									
1973	41.0	. . .	41.3	. . .	. . .	. . .	. . .	. . .	. . .
1974	42.4	. . .	42.7	. . .	. . .	. . .	. . .	. . .	. . .
1975	43.2	. . .	43.8	. . .	. . .	. . .	. . .	. . .	. . .
1976	44.3	. . .	44.6	. . .	. . .	. . .	. . .	. . .	. . .
1977	44.3	. . .	45.1	. . .	. . .	. . .	. . .	. . .	. . .
1978	46.6	. . .	47.2	. . .	. . .	. . .	. . .	. . .	. . .
1979	47.4	. . .	48.0	. . .	. . .	. . .	. . .	. . .	. . .
1980	47.4	. . .	48.5	. . .	. . .	. . .	. . .	. . .	. . .
1981	48.3	. . .	49.7	. . .	. . .	. . .	. . .	. . .	. . .
1982	48.1	. . .	49.3	. . .	. . .	. . .	. . .	. . .	. . .
1983	47.7	. . .	49.0	. . .	. . .	. . .	. . .	. . .	. . .
1984	49.6	. . .	50.5	. . .	. . .	. . .	. . .	. . .	. . .
1985	49.3	. . .	50.6	. . .	. . .	. . .	. . .	. . .	. . .
1986	50.1	. . .	51.7	. . .	. . .	. . .	. . .	. . .	. . .
1987	52.0	. . .	53.3	. . .	. . .	. . .	. . .	. . .	. . .
1988	53.2	. . .	54.2	. . .	. . .	. . .	. . .	. . .	. . .
1989	53.5	. . .	54.9	. . .	. . .	. . .	. . .	. . .	. . .
1990	53.1	. . .	54.8	. . .	. . .	. . .	. . .	. . .	. . .
1991	52.4	. . .	54.0	. . .	. . .	. . .	. . .	. . .	. . .
1992	52.8	. . .	54.3	. . .	. . .	. . .	. . .	. . .	. . .
1993	52.1	. . .	53.8	. . .	. . .	. . .	. . .	. . .	. . .
1994	52.9	38.7	54.4	57.9	60.5	66.4	61.4	38.1	7.9
1995	52.6	40.4	53.9	55.9	61.6	65.9	60.5	37.2	6.6
1996	53.4	36.5	55.2	59.2	62.0	67.0	62.7	40.5	6.9
1997	55.1	38.0	57.0	62.3	63.7	69.3	63.3	40.6	8.1
1998	55.6	42.4	57.1	62.2	64.5	67.9	64.7	41.9	6.6
1999	55.9	40.6	57.7	63.0	62.7	70.5	66.2	42.4	6.5
2000	57.5	41.4	59.3	65.0	65.3	69.9	68.5	41.2	7.7
2001	57.6	41.1	59.3	64.6	65.2	70.3	68.3	43.2	6.7
2002	57.6	38.8	59.5	65.0	65.8	69.5	66.3	46.1	8.5
2003	55.9	34.5	58.1	63.3	62.9	68.5	65.3	47.1	9.4
2004	56.1	33.7	58.4	62.9	62.9	68.7	67.9	47.8	9.8
2005	55.3	35.2	57.4	59.4	62.4	68.2	66.6	48.4	9.3
2006	56.1	34.4	58.3	61.3	63.5	68.7	67.4	49.7	10.4

[2]May be of any race.
. . . = Not available.

Table 1-9. Employed and Unemployed Full- and Part-Time Workers, by Age, Sex, and Race, 1996–2006

(Thousands of people.)

Race, sex, age, and year	Employed[1]								Unemployed	
	Full-time workers				Part-time workers				Looking for full-time work	Looking for part-time work
		At work				At work[2]				
	Total	35 hours or more	1 to 34 hours for economic or noneco-nomic reasons	Not at work	Total	For economic reasons	For noneco-nomic reasons	Not at work		
ALL RACES										
Both Sexes, 16 Years and Over										
1996	103 537	89 020	10 381	4 137	23 170	3 080	18 459	1 631	5 803	1 433
1997	106 334	92 399	9 922	4 013	23 224	2 826	18 856	1 542	5 395	1 344
1998	108 202	91 880	12 260	4 062	23 261	2 497	19 239	1 524	4 916	1 293
1999	110 302	96 276	10 079	3 947	23 186	2 216	19 509	1 461	4 669	1 211
2000	113 846	100 533	9 125	4 188	23 044	2 003	19 548	1 493	4 538	1 154
2001	113 573	99 047	10 464	4 061	23 361	2 297	19 494	1 570	5 546	1 254
2002	112 700	99 042	9 746	3 912	23 785	2 755	19 549	1 481	7 063	1 314
2003	113 324	99 539	9 841	3 944	24 412	3 184	19 702	1 525	7 361	1 413
2004	114 518	100 496	10 053	3 969	24 734	3 113	20 109	1 513	6 762	1 388
2005	117 016	103 044	9 983	3 990	24 714	2 963	20 229	1 522	6 175	1 415
2006	119 688	105 328	10 223	4 137	24 739	2 774	20 356	1 609	5 675	1 326
Both Sexes, 20 Years and Over										
1996	101 496	87 344	10 070	4 083	18 712	2 733	14 556	1 423	5 157	773
1997	104 168	90 613	9 601	3 954	18 729	2 500	14 872	1 357	4 748	719
1998	105 882	89 966	11 915	4 001	18 530	2 197	15 007	1 326	4 332	672
1999	107 917	94 270	9 754	3 893	18 399	1 939	15 187	1 273	4 094	624
2000	111 353	98 439	8 787	4 127	18 348	1 747	15 297	1 304	3 978	632
2001	111 323	97 161	10 156	4 006	18 870	2 013	15 486	1 371	4 956	682
2002	110 679	97 342	9 474	3 862	19 475	2 448	15 704	1 322	6 395	730
2003	111 578	98 087	9 587	3 904	20 239	2 875	16 001	1 363	6 705	818
2004	112 747	99 034	9 789	3 924	20 598	2 817	16 436	1 345	6 178	764
2005	115 206	101 534	9 729	3 942	20 546	2 698	16 489	1 359	5 619	786
2006	117 844	103 779	9 974	4 090	20 421	2 510	16 478	1 433	5 117	765
Men, 16 Years and Over										
1996	60 762	53 425	5 290	2 047	7 445	1 322	5 692	431	3 276	604
1997	62 258	55 216	5 040	2 001	7 427	1 187	5 821	418	3 012	564
1998	63 189	55 080	6 136	1 973	7 504	1 063	6 026	416	2 707	559
1999	63 930	57 034	4 971	1 924	7 516	946	6 178	392	2 548	518
2000	65 930	59 345	4 555	2 030	7 375	856	6 105	414	2 486	488
2001	65 623	58 386	5 241	1 996	7 573	1 021	6 129	424	3 144	546
2002	65 205	58 318	4 971	1 916	7 697	1 246	6 050	401	4 029	568
2003	65 379	58 428	5 023	1 927	7 953	1 473	6 056	423	4 291	615
2004	66 444	59 363	5 148	1 933	8 080	1 405	6 258	417	3 843	613
2005	67 858	60 825	5 096	1 937	8 115	1 316	6 370	429	3 444	616
2006	69 307	62 087	5 237	1 984	8 194	1 232	6 510	452	3 192	561
Men, 20 Years and Over										
1996	59 543	52 411	5 117	2 015	5 354	1 155	3 859	341	2 899	248
1997	60 974	54 148	4 857	1 969	5 310	1 023	3 944	343	2 644	239
1998	61 837	53 947	5 950	1 940	5 297	925	4 050	322	2 366	214
1999	62 514	55 827	4 790	1 897	5 247	809	4 127	311	2 222	211
2000	64 464	58 095	4 370	2 000	5 170	733	4 109	328	2 162	214
2001	64 311	57 273	5 072	1 966	5 465	881	4 253	331	2 801	239
2002	64 006	57 302	4 815	1 889	5 728	1 093	4 299	336	3 642	254
2003	64 364	57 580	4 879	1 905	6 051	1 314	4 388	348	3 906	302
2004	65 377	58 471	5 000	1 906	6 196	1 251	4 600	345	3 511	281
2005	66 803	59 934	4 955	1 914	6 247	1 182	4 705	360	3 118	274
2006	68 193	61 140	5 095	1 958	6 238	1 100	4 762	376	2 861	270
Women, 16 Years and Over										
1996	42 776	35 594	5 091	2 090	15 725	1 758	12 767	1 200	2 527	829
1997	44 076	37 183	4 882	2 011	15 797	1 638	13 035	1 124	2 383	779
1998	45 014	36 800	6 124	2 090	15 757	1 435	13 214	1 108	2 210	734
1999	46 372	39 242	5 108	2 022	15 670	1 270	13 330	1 069	2 121	693
2000	47 916	41 188	4 570	2 158	15 670	1 147	13 443	1 080	2 052	666
2001	47 950	40 661	5 223	2 065	15 788	1 276	13 365	1 146	2 402	709
2002	47 494	40 723	4 775	1 996	16 088	1 509	13 498	1 080	3 034	747
2003	47 946	41 111	4 818	2 017	16 459	1 711	13 646	1 102	3 070	798
2004	48 073	41 133	4 905	2 036	16 654	1 708	13 851	1 096	2 919	775
2005	49 158	42 219	4 887	2 052	16 598	1 647	13 859	1 092	2 732	799
2006	50 380	43 241	4 986	2 153	16 545	1 542	13 846	1 157	2 483	764

Note: Beginning in January 2004, data reflect revised population controls used in the household survey. See notes and definitions for information on historical comparability.

[1]Employed persons are classified as full- or part-time workers based on their usual weekly hours at all jobs, regardless of the number of hours they were at work during the reference week. Persons absent from work are also classified according to their usual status.
[2]Includes some persons at work 35 hours or more classified by their reason for working part time.

Table 1-9. Employed and Unemployed Full- and Part-Time Workers, by Age, Sex, and Race, 1996–2006
—Continued

(Thousands of people.)

Race, sex, age, and year	Employed[1]								Unemployed	
	Full-time workers				Part-time workers					
		At work				At work[2]				
	Total	35 hours or more	1 to 34 hours for economic or noneconomic reasons	Not at work	Total	For economic reasons	For noneconomic reasons	Not at work	Looking for full-time work	Looking for part-time work
ALL RACES										
Women, 20 Years and Over										
1996	41 953	34 933	4 953	2 068	13 357	1 579	10 697	1 082	2 258	525
1997	43 194	36 465	4 744	1 985	13 419	1 477	10 927	1 015	2 105	480
1998	44 045	36 019	5 965	2 061	13 233	1 272	10 957	1 004	1 966	458
1999	45 403	38 443	4 964	1 996	13 152	1 131	11 059	962	1 872	413
2000	46 889	40 344	4 417	2 128	13 178	1 013	11 188	976	1 816	419
2001	47 012	39 889	5 083	2 040	13 405	1 132	11 233	1 040	2 155	444
2002	46 673	40 040	4 660	1 973	13 747	1 355	11 406	986	2 752	476
2003	47 215	40 507	4 708	2 000	14 188	1 560	11 613	1 015	2 799	515
2004	47 371	40 563	4 790	2 017	14 402	1 567	11 836	1 000	2 667	483
2005	48 403	41 600	4 774	2 028	14 299	1 516	11 784	999	2 501	512
2006	49 651	42 639	4 880	2 132	14 183	1 410	11 716	1 057	2 256	495
WHITE[3]										
Men, 16 Years and Over										
1996	52 527	46 208	4 547	1 772	6 361	1 046	4 941	374	2 426	470
1997	53 640	47 563	4 358	1 719	6 358	909	5 084	365	2 202	440
1998	54 206	47 239	5 257	1 709	6 398	829	5 209	360	1 999	432
1999	54 756	48 834	4 274	1 647	6 383	730	5 314	339	1 883	391
2000	56 068	50 434	3 896	1 738	6 221	656	5 213	351	1 798	379
2001	55 830	49 625	4 504	1 701	6 381	793	5 225	364	2 323	431
2002	55 369	49 459	4 267	1 644	6 480	980	5 150	350	3 017	443
2003	55 216	49 323	4 266	1 628	6 650	1 146	5 148	357	3 164	479
2004	55 926	49 891	4 396	1 638	6 786	1 092	5 331	363	2 805	477
2005	56 955	50 965	4 334	1 656	6 808	1 014	5 424	370	2 459	471
2006	58 063	51 894	4 484	1 685	6 820	947	5 481	393	2 299	432
Men, 20 Years and Over										
1996	51 442	45 300	4 397	1 745	4 534	907	3 330	297	2 167	197
1997	52 498	46 609	4 199	1 691	4 488	771	3 419	298	1 946	194
1998	53 017	46 240	5 095	1 682	4 483	716	3 487	280	1 756	164
1999	53 513	47 764	4 124	1 626	4 420	618	3 534	268	1 651	162
2000	54 778	49 335	3 733	1 710	4 341	558	3 505	278	1 566	165
2001	54 666	48 636	4 354	1 676	4 579	677	3 616	285	2 080	195
2002	54 333	48 581	4 133	1 619	4 790	857	3 640	293	2 743	200
2003	54 339	48 585	4 145	1 609	5 010	1 016	3 703	291	2 893	231
2004	55 005	49 124	4 267	1 614	5 154	961	3 895	299	2 567	217
2005	56 050	50 203	4 213	1 634	5 205	905	3 990	310	2 242	209
2006	57 108	51 081	4 365	1 662	5 150	840	3 987	324	2 074	208
Women, 16 Years and Over										
1996	35 057	29 124	4 196	1 737	13 863	1 388	11 398	1 077	1 749	656
1997	35 965	30 286	4 036	1 643	13 894	1 260	11 623	1 011	1 587	608
1998	36 553	29 792	5 039	1 722	13 774	1 089	11 695	990	1 481	572
1999	37 417	31 577	4 157	1 684	13 679	947	11 768	964	1 469	530
2000	38 438	32 942	3 729	1 767	13 698	867	11 870	961	1 422	521
2001	38 445	32 491	4 252	1 702	13 773	971	11 787	1 015	1 664	551
2002	38 152	32 623	3 896	1 633	14 011	1 152	11 903	956	2 084	595
2003	38 249	32 659	3 939	1 652	14 120	1 304	11 860	956	2 038	629
2003	38 240	32 555	4 018	1 667	14 287	1 280	12 038	969	1 968	597
2005	38 973	33 325	3 976	1 672	14 213	1 207	12 043	963	1 807	612
2006	39 813	33 980	4 082	1 751	14 137	1 157	11 967	1 013	1 670	601
Women, 20 Years and Over										
1996	34 350	28 553	4 078	1 719	11 814	1 243	9 598	973	1 570	427
1997	35 216	29 677	3 919	1 620	11 847	1 136	9 788	923	1 396	388
1998	35 738	29 130	4 910	1 698	11 604	953	9 749	902	1 318	370
1999	36 602	30 905	4 036	1 662	11 496	839	9 789	867	1 297	319
2000	37 585	32 242	3 600	1 743	11 560	754	9 935	872	1 256	339
2001	37 658	31 839	4 139	1 680	11 711	853	9 933	924	1 492	357
2002	37 467	32 049	3 803	1 615	11 981	1 029	10 079	873	1 888	381
2003	37 640	32 158	3 845	1 637	12 183	1 180	10 124	879	1 866	411
2004	37 663	32 085	3 927	1 652	12 377	1 166	10 326	885	1 795	377
2005	38 354	32 820	3 882	1 652	12 235	1 108	10 248	879	1 653	401
2006	39 232	33 500	3 998	1 733	12 128	1 050	10 151	927	1 524	402

Note: Beginning in January 2004, data reflect revised population controls used in the household survey. See notes and definitions for information on historical comparability.

[1]Employed persons are classified as full- or part-time workers based on their usual weekly hours at all jobs, regardless of the number of hours they were at work during the reference week. Persons absent from work are also classified according to their usual status.
[2]Includes some persons at work 35 hours or more classified by their reason for working part time.
[3]Beginning in 2003, persons who selected this race group only; persons who selected more than one race group are not included. Prior to 2003, persons who reported more than one race group were included in the group they identified as their main race.

Table 1-9. Employed and Unemployed Full- and Part-Time Workers, by Age, Sex, and Race, 1996–2006
     —Continued

(Thousands of people.)

	Employed[1]								Unemployed	
	Full-time workers				Part-time workers					
		At work				At work[2]				
Race, sex, age, and year	Total	35 hours or more	1 to 34 hours for economic or noneconomic reasons	Not at work	Total	For economic reasons	For noneconomic reasons	Not at work	Looking for full-time work	Looking for part-time work
BLACK[3]										
Men, 16 Years and Over										
1996	5 723	4 971	547	206	733	199	494	40	705	103
1997	5 894	5 193	490	211	713	203	474	36	648	98
1998	6 148	5 322	637	189	723	168	520	34	572	99
1999	6 263	5 574	494	196	764	163	568	33	528	97
2000	6 350	5 704	445	202	732	144	548	41	542	78
2001	6 178	5 509	468	200	761	165	557	39	626	83
2002	6 194	5 541	480	173	765	188	546	30	749	86
2003	6 055	5 414	453	188	765	221	505	39	804	87
2004	6 177	5 538	460	179	736	205	499	32	763	98
2005	6 381	5 745	463	174	773	207	533	33	742	102
2006	6 529	5 907	446	176	825	201	590	34	681	93
Men, 20 Years and Over										
1996	5 622	4 892	528	201	545	177	338	30	602	37
1997	5 790	5 111	471	208	535	179	326	30	549	35
1998	6 023	5 218	620	185	507	147	334	25	487	37
1999	6 140	5 477	471	192	561	142	392	27	446	35
2000	6 222	5 594	429	199	520	125	363	32	468	31
2001	6 069	5 417	455	197	558	145	382	31	542	31
2002	6 073	5 437	465	171	579	166	387	26	660	35
2003	5 980	5 355	439	185	607	201	372	34	717	43
2004	6 089	5 463	449	177	592	189	376	27	689	44
2005	6 287	5 662	452	174	614	189	397	28	655	44
2006	6 424	5 816	433	175	655	185	441	30	596	44
Women, 16 Years and Over										
1996	5 776	4 785	710	280	1 310	289	933	88	652	132
1997	6 026	5 085	652	289	1 336	305	952	79	677	136
1998	6 281	5 166	828	288	1 404	278	1 045	81	624	131
1999	6 641	5 651	734	256	1 388	257	1 059	72	554	130
2000	6 780	5 862	632	287	1 293	211	1 005	77	515	106
2001	6 761	5 777	715	270	1 307	223	998	85	584	122
2002	6 588	5 685	640	263	1 326	259	991	76	744	114
2003	6 552	5 709	595	247	1 367	274	1 017	76	774	121
2004	6 597	5 740	611	246	1 399	306	1 022	71	744	124
2005	6 750	5 871	619	260	1 407	320	1 018	70	723	133
2006	7 001	6 131	605	265	1 410	274	1 054	82	655	120
Women, 20 Years and Over										
1996	5 684	4 714	693	277	1 078	263	737	79	570	73
1997	5 921	5 001	634	286	1 092	273	755	64	603	70
1998	6 159	5 073	803	283	1 131	256	807	68	555	66
1999	6 519	5 549	717	252	1 145	230	850	65	486	75
2000	6 651	5 753	615	283	1 052	197	788	67	456	56
2001	6 647	5 684	695	268	1 094	203	816	75	521	61
2002	6 492	5 605	626	261	1 117	234	816	68	671	67
2003	6 468	5 639	583	246	1 168	257	842	69	698	75
2004	6 512	5 674	595	243	1 195	287	844	64	679	76
2005	6 653	5 789	606	258	1 222	298	861	63	660	74
2006	6 893	6 042	588	263	1 175	255	848	72	588	67

Note: Beginning in January 2004, data reflect revised population controls used in the household survey. See notes and definitions for information on historical comparability.

[1]Employed persons are classified as full- or part-time workers based on their usual weekly hours at all jobs, regardless of the number of hours they were at work during the reference week. Persons absent from work are also classified according to their usual status.
[2]Includes some persons at work 35 hours or more classified by their reason for working part time.
[3]Beginning in 2003, persons who selected this race group only; persons who selected more than one race group are not included. Prior to 2003, persons who reported more than one race group were included in the group they identified as their main race.

CHAPTER 1: POPULATION, LABOR FORCE, AND EMPLOYMENT STATUS 51

Table 1-10. Persons Not in the Labor Force, by Age, Sex, and Desire and Availability for Work, 2001–2006

(Thousands of people.)

Category	Total		Age						Sex			
			16 to 24 years		25 to 54 years		55 years and over		Men		Women	
	2001	2002	2001	2002	2001	2002	2001	2002	2001	2002	2001	2002
TOTAL, NOT IN THE LABOR FORCE	71 359	72 707	12 347	12 976	19 814	20 358	39 198	39 373	26 396	27 085	44 962	45 621
Do Not Want a Job Now[1]	66 769	68 029	10 616	11 254	17 797	18 286	38 355	38 489	24 403	24 994	42 366	43 035
Want a Job[1]	4 590	4 677	1 730	1 722	2 017	2 071	842	884	1 993	2 091	2 597	2 586
Did not search for work in the previous year	2 731	2 673	939	910	1 150	1 112	642	651	1 134	1 135	1 597	1 538
Searched for work in the previous year[2]	1 859	2 004	791	812	867	960	201	233	859	956	1 000	1 048
Not available to work now	593	565	300	272	256	252	37	41	228	227	365	338
Available to work now	1 266	1 439	492	540	611	708	163	191	631	729	634	710
Reason not currently looking:												
Discouragement over job prospects[3]	321	369	104	110	170	209	47	51	192	226	129	143
Reasons other than discouragement	945	1 070	388	430	441	499	116	141	440	503	505	567
Family responsibilities	133	150	32	31	89	99	13	20	29	34	105	116
In school or training	203	238	172	195	30	41	1	2	111	126	92	112
Ill health or disability	96	107	16	16	56	61	25	30	45	50	51	56
Other[4]	513	575	168	188	266	299	77	88	255	292	257	283

Category	Total		Age						Sex			
			16 to 24 years		25 to 54 years		55 years and over		Men		Women	
	2003	2004	2003	2004	2003	2004	2003	2004	2003	2004	2003	2004
TOTAL, NOT IN THE LABOR FORCE	74 658	75 956	13 800	14 151	20 980	21 288	39 878	40 517	28 197	28 730	46 461	47 225
Do Not Want a Job Now[1]	69 932	71 103	12 079	12 422	18 857	19 136	38 996	39 545	26 073	26 565	43 859	44 538
Want a Job[1]	4 726	4 852	1 721	1 729	2 124	2 152	882	971	2 124	2 165	2 603	2 687
Did not search for work in the previous year	2 631	2 715	882	886	1 129	1 145	620	684	1 127	1 126	1 503	1 590
Searched for work in the previous year[2]	2 096	2 137	838	843	995	1 006	262	288	996	1 040	1 099	1 097
Not available to work now	564	563	274	279	248	242	43	42	231	230	333	333
Available to work now	1 531	1 574	565	565	747	764	220	245	765	809	766	765
Reason not currently looking:												
Discouragement over job prospects[3]	457	466	134	142	248	240	75	84	266	288	190	178
Reasons other than discouragement	1 075	1 108	431	423	499	524	145	161	499	521	576	587
Family responsibilities	153	157	37	28	94	104	22	24	35	38	118	119
In school or training	239	244	194	199	42	43	3	2	125	131	114	112
Ill health or disability	113	123	15	18	72	71	26	35	51	56	62	67
Other[4]	570	584	184	178	292	306	94	100	288	296	282	2

Category	Total		Age						Sex			
			16 to 24 years		25 to 54 years		55 years and over		Men		Women	
	2005	2006	2005	2006	2005	2006	2005	2006	2005	2006	2005	2006
TOTAL, NOT IN THE LABOR FORCE	76 762	77 387	14 383	14 549	21 403	21 318	40 976	41 520	29 119	29 350	47 643	48 037
Do Not Want a Job Now[1]	71 777	72 602	12 585	12 867	19 238	19 221	39 954	40 514	26 926	27 248	44 851	45 354
Want a Job[1]	4 985	4 786	1 798	1 682	2 165	2 097	1 022	1 006	2 193	2 102	2 792	2 684
Did not search for work in the previous year	2 841	2 758	963	883	1 163	1 155	715	720	1 173	1 145	1 668	1 612
Searched for work in the previous year[2]	2 144	2 028	836	800	1 002	942	307	286	1 020	956	1 124	1 071
Not available to work now	599	580	285	282	260	252	54	46	231	226	368	354
Available to work now	1 545	1 448	551	518	742	690	252	240	789	731	756	717
Reason not currently looking:												
Discouragement over job prospects[3]	436	381	141	118	217	195	78	68	260	229	176	152
Reasons other than discouragement	1 109	1 067	410	399	525	495	175	172	529	502	580	565
Family responsibilities	159	152	32	31	105	97	22	24	36	35	123	117
In school or training	217	207	179	177	35	28	2	2	118	111	99	96
Ill health or disability	119	130	16	18	69	76	34	36	64	63	55	68
Other[4]	614	578	182	174	316	294	116	110	311	292	302	285

Note: Beginning in January 2004, data reflect revised population controls used in the household survey. See notes and definitions for information on historical comparability.

[1]Includes some persons who were not asked if they wanted a job.
[2]Persons who had a job during the prior 12 months must have searched since the end of that job.
[3]Includes believes no work available, could not find work, lacks necessary schooling or training, employer thinks too young or old, and other types of discrimination.
[4]Includes those who did not actively look for work in the prior four weeks for reasons such as childcare and transportation problems, as well as a small number for whom reason for nonparticipation was not ascertained.

EMPLOYMENT

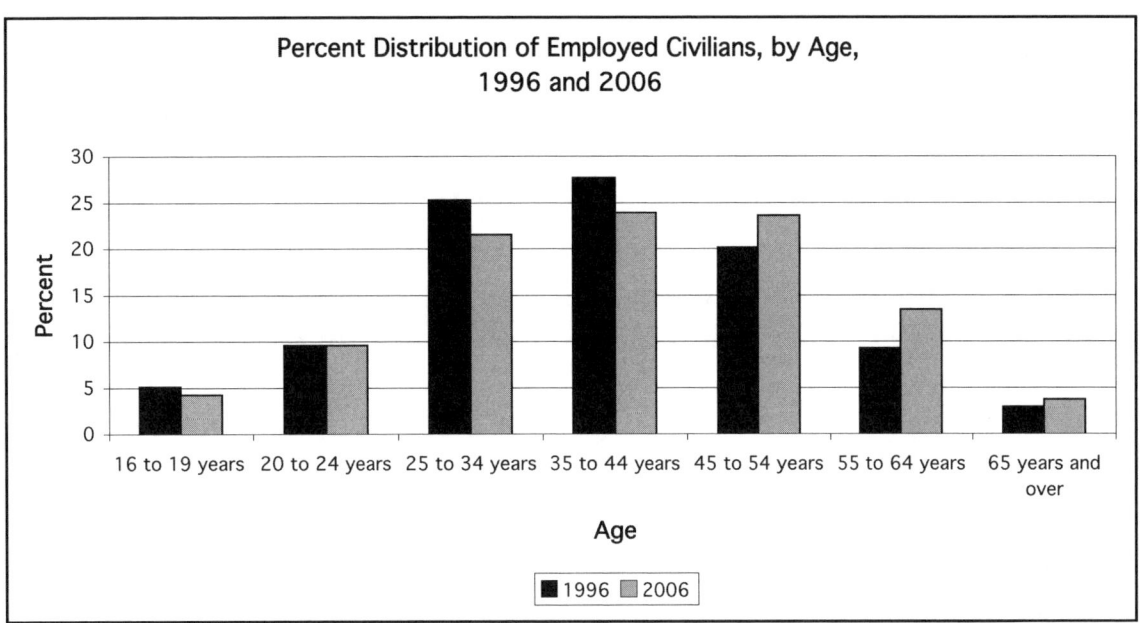

Percent Distribution of Employed Civilians, by Age, 1996 and 2006

The change in the distribution of employed civilians by age reflects, in part, the aging of the baby-boom population. From 1996 to 2006, the proportion of employed persons age 45 years and over increased significantly while the while the proportion of employed persons age 16 to 44 years declined. In 1996, workers in the 45-to 64-year-old age group made up 29 percent of employed civilians. In 2006, they made up 37 percent of employed civilians. (See Table 1-11).

OTHER HIGHLIGHTS

- Total employment increased 1.9 percent in 2006, the fastest it has grown since 2000. (See Table 1-11.)

- During the past ten years, the increase in the number of women employed (14.4 percent) has grown at a faster rate than the increase in the number of men employed (13.6 percent). (See Table 1-11.)

- The Hispanic work force continued to be younger than average: 69 percent of employed civilians were in the 20- to 44-year-old age group compared to 55 percent for all employed civilians in 2006. (See Table 1-11.)

- Although there were nearly an equal number of men and women in management, professional, and related occupations, 50 percent of the men were in management and financial occupations while 65 percent of the women were in professional and related occupations, which included teaching. (See Table 1-13.)

- Among the industries with high levels of employment, construction and healthcare and social assistance grew the most rapidly from 2005 to 2006. (See Table 1-14.)

Table 1-11. Employed Civilians, by Age, Sex, Race, and Hispanic Origin, 1948–2006

(Thousands of people.)

Race, Hispanic origin, sex, and year	16 years and over	16 to 19 years			20 years and over						
		Total	16 to 17 years	18 to 19 years	Total	20 to 24 years	25 to 34 years	35 to 44 years	45 to 54 years	55 to 64 years	65 years and over
ALL RACES											
Both Sexes											
1948	58 343	4 026	1 600	2 426	54 318	6 937	13 801	13 050	10 624	7 103	2 804
1949	57 651	3 712	1 466	2 246	53 940	6 660	13 639	13 108	10 636	7 042	2 864
1950	58 918	3 703	1 433	2 270	55 218	6 746	13 917	13 424	10 966	7 265	2 899
1951	59 961	3 767	1 575	2 192	56 196	6 321	14 233	13 746	11 421	7 558	2 917
1952	60 250	3 719	1 626	2 092	56 536	5 572	14 515	14 058	11 687	7 785	2 919
1953	61 179	3 720	1 577	2 142	57 460	5 225	14 519	14 774	11 969	7 806	3 166
1954	60 109	3 475	1 422	2 053	56 634	4 971	14 190	14 541	11 976	7 895	3 060
1955	62 170	3 642	1 500	2 143	58 528	5 270	14 481	14 879	12 556	8 158	3 185
1956	63 799	3 818	1 647	2 171	59 983	5 545	14 407	15 218	12 978	8 519	3 314
1957	64 071	3 778	1 613	2 167	60 291	5 641	14 253	15 348	13 320	8 553	3 179
1958	63 036	3 582	1 519	2 063	59 454	5 571	13 675	15 157	13 448	8 559	3 045
1959	64 630	3 838	1 670	2 168	60 791	5 870	13 709	15 454	13 915	8 822	3 023
1960	65 778	4 129	1 770	2 360	61 648	6 119	13 630	15 598	14 238	8 989	3 073
1961	65 746	4 108	1 621	2 486	61 638	6 227	13 429	15 552	14 320	9 120	2 987
1962	66 702	4 195	1 607	2 588	62 508	6 446	13 311	15 901	14 491	9 346	3 013
1963	67 762	4 255	1 751	2 504	63 508	6 815	13 318	16 114	14 749	9 596	2 915
1964	69 305	4 516	2 013	2 503	64 789	7 303	13 449	16 166	15 094	9 804	2 973
1965	71 088	5 036	2 075	2 962	66 052	7 702	13 704	16 294	15 320	10 028	3 005
1966	72 895	5 721	2 269	3 452	67 178	7 964	14 017	16 312	15 615	10 310	2 961
1967	74 372	5 682	2 334	3 348	68 690	8 499	14 575	16 281	15 789	10 536	3 011
1968	75 920	5 781	2 403	3 377	70 141	8 762	15 265	16 220	16 083	10 745	3 065
1969	77 902	6 117	2 573	3 543	71 785	9 319	15 883	16 100	16 410	10 919	3 155
1970	78 678	6 144	2 598	3 546	72 534	9 731	16 318	15 922	16 473	10 974	3 118
1971	79 367	6 208	2 596	3 613	73 158	10 201	16 781	15 675	16 451	11 009	3 040
1972	82 153	6 746	2 787	3 959	75 407	10 999	18 082	15 822	16 457	11 044	3 003
1973	85 064	7 271	3 032	4 239	77 793	11 839	19 509	16 041	16 553	10 966	2 886
1974	86 794	7 448	3 111	4 338	79 347	12 101	20 610	16 203	16 633	10 964	2 835
1975	85 846	7 104	2 941	4 162	78 744	11 885	21 087	15 953	16 190	10 827	2 801
1976	88 752	7 336	2 972	4 363	81 416	12 570	22 493	16 468	16 224	10 912	2 747
1977	92 017	7 688	3 138	4 550	84 329	13 196	23 850	17 157	16 212	11 126	2 787
1978	96 048	8 070	3 330	4 739	87 979	13 887	25 281	18 128	16 338	11 400	2 946
1979	98 824	8 083	3 340	4 743	90 741	14 327	26 492	18 981	16 357	11 585	2 999
1980	99 303	7 710	3 106	4 605	91 593	14 087	27 204	19 523	16 234	11 586	2 960
1981	100 397	7 225	2 866	4 359	93 172	14 122	28 180	20 145	16 255	11 525	2 945
1982	99 526	6 549	2 505	4 044	92 978	13 690	28 149	20 879	15 923	11 414	2 923
1983	100 834	6 342	2 320	4 022	94 491	13 722	28 756	21 960	15 812	11 315	2 927
1984	105 005	6 444	2 404	4 040	98 562	14 207	30 348	23 598	16 178	11 395	2 835
1985	107 150	6 434	2 492	3 941	100 716	13 980	31 208	24 732	16 509	11 474	2 813
1986	109 597	6 472	2 622	3 850	103 125	13 790	32 201	25 861	16 949	11 405	2 919
1987	112 440	6 640	2 736	3 905	105 800	13 524	33 105	27 179	17 487	11 465	3 041
1988	114 968	6 805	2 713	4 092	108 164	13 244	33 574	28 269	18 447	11 433	3 197
1989	117 342	6 759	2 588	4 172	110 582	12 962	34 045	29 443	19 279	11 499	3 355
1990	118 793	6 581	2 410	4 171	112 213	13 401	33 935	30 817	19 525	11 189	3 346
1991	117 718	5 906	2 202	3 704	111 812	12 975	33 061	31 593	19 882	11 001	3 300
1992	118 492	5 669	2 128	3 540	112 824	12 872	32 667	31 923	21 022	10 998	3 341
1993	120 259	5 805	2 226	3 579	114 455	12 840	32 385	32 666	22 175	11 058	3 331
1994	123 060	6 161	2 510	3 651	116 899	12 758	32 286	33 599	23 348	11 228	3 681
1995	124 900	6 419	2 573	3 846	118 481	12 443	32 356	34 202	24 378	11 435	3 666
1996	126 708	6 500	2 646	3 853	120 208	12 138	32 077	35 051	25 514	11 739	3 690
1997	129 558	6 661	2 648	4 012	122 897	12 380	31 809	35 908	26 744	12 296	3 761
1998	131 463	7 051	2 762	4 289	124 413	12 557	31 394	36 278	27 587	12 872	3 725
1999	133 488	7 172	2 793	4 379	126 316	12 891	30 865	36 728	28 635	13 315	3 882
2000	136 891	7 189	2 759	4 431	129 701	13 229	31 549	36 433	30 310	14 002	4 179
2001	136 933	6 740	2 558	4 182	130 194	13 348	30 863	36 049	31 036	14 645	4 253
2002	136 485	6 332	2 330	4 002	130 154	13 351	30 306	35 235	31 281	15 674	4 306
2003	137 736	5 919	2 312	3 607	131 817	13 433	30 383	34 881	31 914	16 598	4 608
2004	139 252	5 907	2 193	3 714	133 345	13 723	30 423	34 580	32 469	17 331	4 819
2005	141 730	5 978	2 284	3 694	135 752	13 792	30 680	34 630	33 207	18 349	5 094
2006	144 427	6 162	2 444	3 719	138 265	13 878	31 051	34 569	34 052	19 389	5 325

Table 1-11. Employed Civilians, by Age, Sex, Race, and Hispanic Origin, 1948–2006—*Continued*

(Thousands of people.)

Race, Hispanic origin, sex, and year	16 years and over	16 to 19 years			20 years and over						
		Total	16 to 17 years	18 to 19 years	Total	20 to 24 years	25 to 34 years	35 to 44 years	45 to 54 years	55 to 64 years	65 years and over
ALL RACES											
Men											
1948	41 725	2 344	996	1 348	39 382	4 349	10 038	9 363	7 742	5 587	2 303
1949	40 925	2 124	911	1 213	38 803	4 197	9 879	9 308	7 661	5 438	2 329
1950	41 578	2 186	909	1 277	39 394	4 255	10 060	9 445	7 790	5 508	2 336
1951	41 780	2 156	979	1 177	39 626	3 780	10 134	9 607	8 012	5 711	2 382
1952	41 682	2 107	985	1 121	39 578	3 183	10 352	9 753	8 144	5 804	2 343
1953	42 430	2 136	976	1 159	40 296	2 901	10 500	10 229	8 374	5 808	2 483
1954	41 619	1 985	881	1 104	39 634	2 724	10 254	10 082	8 330	5 830	2 414
1955	42 621	2 095	936	1 159	40 526	2 973	10 453	10 267	8 553	5 857	2 424
1956	43 379	2 164	1 008	1 156	41 216	3 245	10 337	10 385	8 732	6 004	2 512
1957	43 357	2 115	987	1 130	41 239	3 346	10 222	10 427	8 851	6 002	2 394
1958	42 423	2 012	948	1 064	40 411	3 293	9 790	10 291	8 828	5 955	2 254
1959	43 466	2 198	1 015	1 183	41 267	3 597	9 862	10 492	9 048	6 058	2 210
1960	43 904	2 361	1 090	1 271	41 543	3 754	9 759	10 552	9 182	6 105	2 191
1961	43 656	2 315	989	1 325	41 342	3 795	9 591	10 505	9 195	6 155	2 098
1962	44 177	2 362	990	1 372	41 815	3 898	9 475	10 711	9 333	6 260	2 138
1963	44 657	2 406	1 073	1 334	42 251	4 118	9 431	10 801	9 478	6 385	2 038
1964	45 474	2 587	1 242	1 345	42 886	4 370	9 531	10 832	9 637	6 478	2 039
1965	46 340	2 918	1 285	1 634	43 422	4 583	9 611	10 837	9 792	6 542	2 057
1966	46 919	3 253	1 389	1 863	43 668	4 599	9 709	10 764	9 904	6 668	2 024
1967	47 479	3 186	1 417	1 769	44 294	4 809	9 988	10 674	9 990	6 774	2 058
1968	48 114	3 255	1 453	1 802	44 859	4 812	10 405	10 554	10 102	6 893	2 093
1969	48 818	3 430	1 526	1 904	45 388	5 012	10 736	10 401	10 187	6 931	2 122
1970	48 990	3 409	1 504	1 905	45 581	5 237	10 936	10 216	10 170	6 928	2 094
1971	49 390	3 478	1 510	1 968	45 912	5 593	11 218	10 028	10 139	6 916	2 019
1972	50 896	3 765	1 598	2 167	47 130	6 138	11 884	10 088	10 139	6 929	1 953
1973	52 349	4 039	1 721	2 318	48 310	6 655	12 617	10 126	10 197	6 857	1 856
1974	53 024	4 103	1 744	2 359	48 922	6 739	13 119	10 135	10 181	6 880	1 869
1975	51 857	3 839	1 621	2 219	48 018	6 484	13 205	9 891	9 902	6 722	1 811
1976	53 138	3 947	1 626	2 321	49 190	6 915	13 869	10 069	9 881	6 724	1 732
1977	54 728	4 174	1 733	2 441	50 555	7 232	14 483	10 399	9 832	6 848	1 761
1978	56 479	4 336	1 800	2 535	52 143	7 559	15 124	10 845	9 806	6 954	1 855
1979	57 607	4 300	1 799	2 501	53 308	7 791	15 688	11 202	9 735	7 015	1 876
1980	57 186	4 085	1 672	2 412	53 101	7 532	15 832	11 355	9 548	6 999	1 835
1981	57 397	3 815	1 526	2 289	53 582	7 504	16 266	11 613	9 478	6 909	1 812
1982	56 271	3 379	1 307	2 072	52 891	7 197	16 002	11 902	9 234	6 781	1 776
1983	56 787	3 300	1 213	2 087	53 487	7 232	16 216	12 450	9 133	6 686	1 770
1984	59 091	3 322	1 244	2 078	55 769	7 571	17 166	13 309	9 326	6 694	1 703
1985	59 891	3 328	1 300	2 029	56 562	7 339	17 564	13 800	9 411	6 753	1 695
1986	60 892	3 323	1 352	1 971	57 569	7 250	18 092	14 266	9 554	6 654	1 753
1987	62 107	3 381	1 393	1 988	58 726	7 058	18 487	14 898	9 750	6 682	1 850
1988	63 273	3 492	1 403	2 089	59 781	6 918	18 702	15 457	10 201	6 591	1 911
1989	64 315	3 477	1 327	2 150	60 837	6 799	18 952	16 002	10 569	6 548	1 968
1990	65 104	3 427	1 254	2 173	61 678	7 151	18 779	16 771	10 690	6 378	1 909
1991	64 223	3 044	1 135	1 909	61 178	6 909	18 265	17 086	10 813	6 245	1 860
1992	64 440	2 944	1 096	1 848	61 496	6 819	17 966	17 230	11 365	6 173	1 943
1993	65 349	2 994	1 155	1 839	62 355	6 805	17 877	17 665	11 927	6 166	1 916
1994	66 450	3 156	1 288	1 868	63 294	6 771	17 741	18 111	12 439	6 142	2 089
1995	67 377	3 292	1 316	1 977	64 085	6 665	17 709	18 374	12 958	6 272	2 108
1996	68 207	3 310	1 318	1 992	64 897	6 429	17 527	18 816	13 483	6 470	2 172
1997	69 685	3 401	1 355	2 045	66 284	6 548	17 338	19 327	14 107	6 735	2 229
1998	70 693	3 558	1 398	2 161	67 135	6 638	17 097	19 634	14 544	7 052	2 171
1999	71 446	3 685	1 437	2 249	67 761	6 729	16 694	19 811	14 991	7 274	2 263
2000	73 305	3 671	1 394	2 276	69 634	6 974	17 241	19 537	15 871	7 606	2 406
2001	73 196	3 420	1 268	2 151	69 776	6 952	16 915	19 305	16 268	7 900	2 437
2002	72 903	3 169	1 130	2 040	69 734	6 978	16 573	18 932	16 419	8 378	2 455
2003	73 332	2 917	1 115	1 802	70 415	7 065	16 670	18 774	16 588	8 733	2 585
2004	74 524	2 952	1 037	1 915	71 572	7 246	16 818	18 700	16 951	9 174	2 683
2005	75 973	2 923	1 067	1 855	73 050	7 279	16 993	18 780	17 429	9 714	2 857
2006	77 502	3 071	1 182	1 888	74 431	7 412	17 134	18 765	17 920	10 192	3 008

Table 1-11. Employed Civilians, by Age, Sex, Race, and Hispanic Origin, 1948–2006—*Continued*

(Thousands of people.)

Race, Hispanic origin, sex, and year	16 years and over	16 to 19 years			20 years and over						
		Total	16 to 17 years	18 to 19 years	Total	20 to 24 years	25 to 34 years	35 to 44 years	45 to 54 years	55 to 64 years	65 years and over
ALL RACES											
Women											
1948	16 617	1 682	604	1 078	14 936	2 588	3 763	3 687	2 882	1 516	501
1949	16 723	1 588	555	1 033	15 137	2 463	3 760	3 800	2 975	1 604	535
1950	17 340	1 517	524	993	15 824	2 491	3 857	3 979	3 176	1 757	563
1951	18 181	1 611	596	1 015	16 570	2 541	4 099	4 139	3 409	1 847	535
1952	18 568	1 612	641	971	16 958	2 389	4 163	4 305	3 543	1 981	576
1953	18 749	1 584	601	983	17 164	2 324	4 019	4 545	3 595	1 998	683
1954	18 490	1 490	541	949	17 000	2 247	3 936	4 459	3 646	2 065	646
1955	19 551	1 547	564	984	18 002	2 297	4 028	4 612	4 003	2 301	761
1956	20 419	1 654	639	1 015	18 767	2 300	4 070	4 833	4 246	2 515	802
1957	20 714	1 663	626	1 037	19 052	2 295	4 031	4 921	4 469	2 551	785
1958	20 613	1 570	571	999	19 043	2 278	3 885	4 866	4 620	2 604	791
1959	21 164	1 640	655	985	19 524	2 273	3 847	4 962	4 867	2 764	813
1960	21 874	1 768	680	1 089	20 105	2 365	3 871	5 046	5 056	2 884	882
1961	22 090	1 793	632	1 161	20 296	2 432	3 838	5 047	5 125	2 965	889
1962	22 525	1 833	617	1 216	20 693	2 548	3 836	5 190	5 158	3 086	875
1963	23 105	1 849	678	1 170	21 257	2 697	3 887	5 313	5 271	3 211	877
1964	23 831	1 929	771	1 158	21 903	2 933	3 918	5 334	5 457	3 326	934
1965	24 748	2 118	790	1 328	22 630	3 119	4 093	5 457	5 528	3 486	948
1966	25 976	2 468	880	1 589	23 510	3 365	4 308	5 548	5 711	3 642	937
1967	26 893	2 496	917	1 579	24 397	3 690	4 587	5 607	5 799	3 762	953
1968	27 807	2 526	950	1 575	25 281	3 950	4 860	5 666	5 981	3 852	972
1969	29 084	2 687	1 047	1 639	26 397	4 307	5 147	5 699	6 223	3 988	1 033
1970	29 688	2 735	1 094	1 641	26 952	4 494	5 382	5 706	6 303	4 046	1 023
1971	29 976	2 730	1 086	1 645	27 246	4 609	5 563	5 647	6 313	4 093	1 021
1972	31 257	2 980	1 188	1 792	28 276	4 861	6 197	5 734	6 318	4 115	1 051
1973	32 715	3 231	1 310	1 920	29 484	5 184	6 893	5 915	6 356	4 109	1 029
1974	33 769	3 345	1 367	1 978	30 424	5 363	7 492	6 068	6 451	4 084	966
1975	33 989	3 263	1 320	1 943	30 726	5 401	7 882	6 061	6 288	4 105	989
1976	35 615	3 389	1 346	2 043	32 226	5 655	8 624	6 400	6 343	4 188	1 017
1977	37 289	3 514	1 403	2 110	33 775	5 965	9 367	6 758	6 380	4 279	1 027
1978	39 569	3 734	1 530	2 204	35 836	6 328	10 157	7 282	6 532	4 446	1 091
1979	41 217	3 783	1 541	2 242	37 434	6 538	10 802	7 779	6 622	4 569	1 124
1980	42 117	3 625	1 433	2 192	38 492	6 555	11 370	8 168	6 686	4 587	1 125
1981	43 000	3 411	1 340	2 070	39 590	6 618	11 914	8 532	6 777	4 616	1 133
1982	43 256	3 170	1 198	1 972	40 086	6 492	12 147	8 977	6 689	4 634	1 147
1983	44 047	3 043	1 107	1 935	41 004	6 490	12 540	9 510	6 678	4 629	1 157
1984	45 915	3 122	1 161	1 962	42 793	6 636	13 182	10 289	6 852	4 700	1 133
1985	47 259	3 105	1 193	1 913	44 154	6 640	13 644	10 933	7 097	4 721	1 118
1986	48 706	3 149	1 270	1 879	45 556	6 540	14 109	11 595	7 395	4 751	1 165
1987	50 334	3 260	1 343	1 917	47 074	6 466	14 617	12 281	7 737	4 783	1 191
1988	51 696	3 313	1 310	2 003	48 383	6 326	14 872	12 811	8 246	4 841	1 286
1989	53 027	3 282	1 261	2 021	49 745	6 163	15 093	13 440	8 711	4 950	1 388
1990	53 689	3 154	1 156	1 998	50 535	6 250	15 155	14 046	8 835	4 811	1 437
1991	53 496	2 862	1 067	1 794	50 634	6 066	14 796	14 507	9 069	4 756	1 440
1992	54 052	2 724	1 032	1 692	51 328	6 053	14 701	14 693	9 657	4 825	1 398
1993	54 910	2 811	1 071	1 740	52 099	6 035	14 508	15 002	10 248	4 892	1 414
1994	56 610	3 005	1 222	1 783	53 606	5 987	14 545	15 488	10 908	5 085	1 592
1995	57 523	3 127	1 258	1 869	54 396	5 779	14 647	15 828	11 421	5 163	1 558
1996	58 501	3 190	1 328	1 862	55 311	5 709	14 549	16 235	12 031	5 269	1 518
1997	59 873	3 260	1 293	1 967	56 613	5 831	14 471	16 581	12 637	5 561	1 532
1998	60 771	3 493	1 364	2 128	57 278	5 919	14 298	16 644	13 043	5 820	1 554
1999	62 042	3 487	1 357	2 130	58 555	6 163	14 171	16 917	13 644	6 041	1 619
2000	63 586	3 519	1 364	2 154	60 067	6 255	14 308	16 897	14 438	6 396	1 773
2001	63 737	3 320	1 289	2 031	60 417	6 396	13 948	16 744	14 768	6 745	1 815
2002	63 582	3 162	1 200	1 962	60 420	6 374	13 733	16 303	14 863	7 296	1 851
2003	64 404	3 002	1 197	1 805	61 402	6 367	13 714	16 106	15 326	7 866	2 023
2004	64 728	2 955	1 156	1 799	61 773	6 477	13 605	15 880	15 518	8 157	2 135
2005	65 757	3 055	1 217	1 838	62 702	6 513	13 687	15 850	15 779	8 635	2 238
2006	66 925	3 091	1 261	1 830	63 834	6 467	13 917	15 804	16 132	9 198	2 316

Table 1-11. Employed Civilians, by Age, Sex, Race, and Hispanic Origin, 1948–2006—*Continued*

(Thousands of people.)

Race, Hispanic origin, sex, and year	16 years and over	16 to 19 years			20 years and over						
		Total	16 to 17 years	18 to 19 years	Total	20 to 24 years	25 to 34 years	35 to 44 years	45 to 54 years	55 to 64 years	65 years and over
WHITE[1]											
Both Sexes											
1954	53 957	3 078	1 257	1 822	50 879	4 358	12 616	13 000	10 811	7 262	2 831
1955	55 833	3 225	1 330	1 896	52 608	4 637	12 855	13 327	11 322	7 510	2 957
1956	57 269	3 389	1 465	1 922	53 880	4 897	12 748	13 637	11 706	7 822	3 068
1957	57 465	3 374	1 442	1 931	54 091	4 952	12 619	13 716	12 009	7 829	2 951
1958	56 613	3 216	1 370	1 847	53 397	4 908	12 128	13 571	12 113	7 849	2 828
1959	58 006	3 475	1 520	1 955	54 531	5 138	12 144	13 830	12 552	8 063	2 805
1960	58 850	3 700	1 598	2 103	55 150	5 331	12 021	13 930	12 820	8 192	2 855
1961	58 913	3 693	1 472	2 220	55 220	5 460	11 835	13 905	12 906	8 335	2 778
1962	59 698	3 774	1 447	2 327	55 924	5 676	11 703	14 173	13 066	8 511	2 795
1963	60 622	3 851	1 600	2 250	56 771	6 036	11 689	14 341	13 304	8 718	2 683
1964	61 922	4 076	1 846	2 230	57 846	6 444	11 794	14 380	13 596	8 916	2 717
1965	63 446	4 562	1 892	2 670	58 884	6 752	11 992	14 473	13 804	9 116	2 748
1966	65 021	5 176	2 052	3 124	59 845	6 986	12 268	14 449	14 072	9 356	2 713
1967	66 361	5 114	2 121	2 993	61 247	7 493	12 763	14 429	14 224	9 596	2 746
1968	67 750	5 195	2 193	3 002	62 555	7 687	13 410	14 386	14 487	9 781	2 804
1969	69 518	5 508	2 347	3 161	64 010	8 182	13 935	14 270	14 788	9 947	2 888
1970	70 217	5 571	2 386	3 185	64 645	8 559	14 326	14 092	14 854	9 979	2 835
1971	70 878	5 670	2 404	3 266	65 208	9 000	14 713	13 858	14 843	10 014	2 780
1972	73 370	6 173	2 581	3 592	67 197	9 718	15 904	13 940	14 845	10 077	2 714
1973	75 708	6 623	2 806	3 816	69 086	10 424	17 099	14 083	14 886	9 983	2 610
1974	77 184	6 796	2 881	3 916	70 388	10 676	18 040	14 196	14 948	9 958	2 568
1975	76 411	6 487	2 721	3 770	69 924	10 546	18 485	13 979	14 555	9 827	2 533
1976	78 853	6 724	2 762	3 962	72 129	11 119	19 662	14 407	14 549	9 923	2 470
1977	81 700	7 068	2 926	4 142	74 632	11 696	20 844	14 984	14 483	10 107	2 518
1978	84 936	7 367	3 085	4 282	77 569	12 251	22 008	15 809	14 550	10 311	2 642
1979	87 259	7 356	3 079	4 278	79 904	12 594	23 033	16 578	14 522	10 477	2 699
1980	87 715	7 021	2 861	4 161	80 694	12 405	23 653	17 071	14 405	10 475	2 684
1981	88 709	6 588	2 645	3 943	82 121	12 477	24 551	17 617	14 414	10 386	2 676
1982	87 903	5 984	2 317	3 667	81 918	12 097	24 531	18 268	14 083	10 283	2 656
1983	88 893	5 799	2 156	3 643	83 094	12 138	24 955	19 194	13 961	10 169	2 678
1984	92 120	5 836	2 209	3 627	86 284	12 451	26 235	20 552	14 239	10 227	2 580
1985	93 736	5 768	2 270	3 498	87 968	12 235	26 945	21 552	14 459	10 247	2 530
1986	95 660	5 792	2 386	3 406	89 869	12 027	27 746	22 515	14 750	10 176	2 654
1987	97 789	5 898	2 468	3 431	91 890	11 748	28 429	23 596	15 216	10 164	2 738
1988	99 812	6 030	2 424	3 606	93 782	11 438	28 796	24 468	16 054	10 153	2 874
1989	101 584	5 946	2 278	3 668	95 638	11 084	29 091	25 442	16 775	10 223	3 024
1990	102 261	5 779	2 141	3 638	96 481	11 498	28 773	26 282	16 933	9 960	3 035
1991	101 182	5 216	1 971	3 246	95 966	11 116	27 989	26 883	17 269	9 719	2 990
1992	101 669	4 985	1 904	3 081	96 684	11 031	27 552	27 097	18 285	9 701	3 019
1993	103 045	5 113	1 990	3 123	97 932	10 931	27 274	27 645	19 273	9 772	3 037
1994	105 190	5 398	2 210	3 188	99 792	10 736	27 101	28 442	20 247	9 912	3 354
1995	106 490	5 593	2 273	3 320	100 897	10 400	27 014	28 951	21 127	10 070	3 335
1996	107 808	5 667	2 325	3 343	102 141	10 149	26 678	29 566	22 071	10 313	3 364
1997	109 856	5 807	2 341	3 466	104 049	10 362	26 294	30 137	23 061	10 785	3 411
1998	110 931	6 089	2 436	3 653	104 842	10 512	25 729	30 320	23 662	11 272	3 347
1999	112 235	6 204	2 435	3 769	106 032	10 716	25 113	30 548	24 507	11 657	3 491
2000	114 424	6 160	2 383	3 777	108 264	10 944	25 500	30 151	25 762	12 169	3 738
2001	114 430	5 817	2 224	3 593	108 613	11 054	24 948	29 793	26 301	12 743	3 774
2002	114 013	5 441	2 037	3 404	108 572	11 096	24 568	29 049	26 401	13 630	3 828
2003	114 235	5 064	1 999	3 065	109 171	11 052	24 399	28 501	26 762	14 375	4 083
2004	115 239	5 039	1 895	3 145	110 199	11 233	24 337	28 176	27 228	14 965	4 260
2005	116 949	5 105	1 999	3 106	111 844	11 231	24 443	28 102	27 801	15 788	4 480
2006	118 833	5 215	2 099	3 117	113 618	11 296	24 652	27 929	28 419	16 652	4 670

[1]Beginning in 2003, persons who selected this race group only; persons who selected more than one race group are not included. Prior to 2003, persons who reported more than one race group were included in the group they identified as the main race.

Table 1-11. Employed Civilians, by Age, Sex, Race, and Hispanic Origin, 1948–2006—*Continued*

(Thousands of people.)

Race, Hispanic origin, sex, and year	16 years and over	16 to 19 years			20 years and over						
		Total	16 to 17 years	18 to 19 years	Total	20 to 24 years	25 to 34 years	35 to 44 years	45 to 54 years	55 to 64 years	65 years and over
WHITE[1]											
Men											
1954	37 846	1 723	771	953	36 123	2 394	9 287	9 175	7 614	5 412	2 241
1955	38 719	1 824	821	1 004	36 895	2 607	9 461	9 351	7 792	5 431	2 254
1956	39 368	1 893	890	1 002	37 475	2 850	9 330	9 449	7 950	5 559	2 336
1957	39 349	1 865	874	990	37 484	2 930	9 226	9 480	8 067	5 542	2 234
1958	38 591	1 783	852	932	36 808	2 896	8 861	9 386	8 061	5 501	2 103
1959	39 494	1 961	915	1 046	37 533	3 153	8 911	9 560	8 261	5 588	2 060
1960	39 755	2 092	973	1 119	37 663	3 264	8 777	9 589	8 372	5 618	2 043
1961	39 588	2 055	891	1 164	37 533	3 311	8 630	9 566	8 394	5 670	1 961
1962	40 016	2 098	883	1 215	37 918	3 426	8 514	9 718	8 512	5 749	1 998
1963	40 428	2 156	972	1 184	38 272	3 646	8 463	9 782	8 650	5 844	1 887
1964	41 115	2 316	1 128	1 188	38 799	3 856	8 538	9 800	8 787	5 945	1 872
1965	41 844	2 612	1 159	1 453	39 232	4 025	8 598	9 795	8 924	5 998	1 892
1966	42 331	2 913	1 245	1 668	39 418	4 028	8 674	9 719	9 029	6 096	1 871
1967	42 833	2 849	1 278	1 571	39 985	4 231	8 931	9 632	9 093	6 208	1 892
1968	43 411	2 908	1 319	1 589	40 503	4 226	9 315	9 522	9 198	6 316	1 926
1969	44 048	3 070	1 385	1 685	40 978	4 401	9 608	9 379	9 279	6 359	1 953
1970	44 178	3 066	1 374	1 692	41 112	4 601	9 784	9 202	9 271	6 340	1 914
1971	44 595	3 157	1 393	1 764	41 438	4 935	10 026	9 026	9 256	6 339	1 856
1972	45 944	3 416	1 470	1 947	42 528	5 431	10 664	9 047	9 236	6 363	1 786
1973	47 085	3 660	1 590	2 071	43 424	5 863	11 268	9 046	9 257	6 299	1 689
1974	47 674	3 728	1 611	2 117	43 946	5 965	11 701	9 027	9 242	6 304	1 706
1975	46 697	3 505	1 502	2 002	43 192	5 770	11 783	8 818	9 005	6 160	1 656
1976	47 775	3 604	1 501	2 103	44 171	6 140	12 362	8 944	8 968	6 176	1 579
1977	49 150	3 824	1 607	2 217	45 326	6 437	12 893	9 212	8 898	6 279	1 605
1978	50 544	3 950	1 664	2 286	46 594	6 717	13 413	9 608	8 840	6 339	1 677
1979	51 452	3 904	1 654	2 250	47 546	6 868	13 888	9 930	8 748	6 406	1 707
1980	51 127	3 708	1 534	2 174	47 419	6 652	14 009	10 077	8 586	6 412	1 684
1981	51 315	3 469	1 402	2 066	47 846	6 652	14 398	10 307	8 518	6 309	1 662
1982	50 287	3 079	1 214	1 865	47 209	6 372	14 164	10 593	8 267	6 188	1 624
1983	50 621	3 003	1 124	1 879	47 618	6 386	14 297	11 062	8 152	6 084	1 637
1984	52 462	3 001	1 140	1 861	49 461	6 647	15 045	11 776	8 320	6 108	1 564
1985	53 046	2 985	1 185	1 800	50 061	6 428	15 374	12 214	8 374	6 118	1 552
1986	53 785	2 966	1 225	1 741	50 818	6 340	15 790	12 620	8 442	6 012	1 612
1987	54 647	2 999	1 252	1 747	51 649	6 150	16 084	13 138	8 596	5 991	1 690
1988	55 550	3 084	1 248	1 836	52 466	5 987	16 241	13 590	8 992	5 909	1 748
1989	56 352	3 060	1 171	1 889	53 292	5 839	16 383	14 046	9 335	5 891	1 797
1990	56 703	3 018	1 119	1 899	53 685	6 179	16 124	14 496	9 383	5 744	1 760
1991	55 797	2 694	1 017	1 677	53 103	5 942	15 644	14 743	9 488	5 578	1 707
1992	55 959	2 602	990	1 612	53 357	5 855	15 357	14 842	10 027	5 503	1 772
1993	56 656	2 634	1 031	1 603	54 021	5 830	15 230	15 178	10 497	5 514	1 772
1994	57 452	2 776	1 144	1 632	54 676	5 738	15 052	15 562	10 910	5 490	1 925
1995	58 146	2 892	1 169	1 723	55 254	5 613	14 958	15 793	11 359	5 609	1 921
1996	58 888	2 911	1 161	1 750	55 977	5 444	14 820	16 136	11 834	5 755	1 987
1997	59 998	3 011	1 206	1 806	56 986	5 590	14 567	16 470	12 352	5 972	2 037
1998	60 604	3 103	1 233	1 870	57 500	5 659	14 259	16 715	12 661	6 251	1 955
1999	61 139	3 205	1 254	1 951	57 934	5 753	13 851	16 781	13 046	6 447	2 056
2000	62 289	3 169	1 205	1 965	59 119	5 876	14 238	16 477	13 675	6 678	2 175
2001	62 212	2 967	1 102	1 865	59 245	5 870	13 989	16 280	13 987	6 941	2 178
2002	61 849	2 725	987	1 738	59 124	5 882	13 727	15 910	14 060	7 360	2 184
2003	61 866	2 518	972	1 546	59 348	5 890	13 731	15 675	14 117	7 640	2 295
2004	62 712	2 553	903	1 650	60 159	6 026	13 735	15 572	14 418	8 018	2 390
2005	63 763	2 508	942	1 566	61 255	6 041	13 840	15 544	14 810	8 471	2 550
2006	64 883	2 625	1 020	1 605	62 259	6 114	13 903	15 480	15 189	8 893	2 680

[1]Beginning in 2003, persons who selected this race group only; persons who selected more than one race group are not included. Prior to 2003, persons who reported more than one race group were included in the group they identified as the main race.

Table 1-11. Employed Civilians, by Age, Sex, Race, and Hispanic Origin, 1948–2006—*Continued*

(Thousands of people.)

Race, Hispanic origin, sex, and year	16 years and over	16 to 19 years			20 years and over						
		Total	16 to 17 years	18 to 19 years	Total	20 to 24 years	25 to 34 years	35 to 44 years	45 to 54 years	55 to 64 years	65 years and over
WHITE[1]											
Women											
1954	16 111	1 355	486	869	14 756	1 964	3 329	3 825	3 197	1 850	590
1955	17 114	1 401	509	892	15 713	2 030	3 394	3 976	3 530	2 079	703
1956	17 901	1 496	575	920	16 405	2 047	3 418	4 188	3 756	2 263	732
1957	18 116	1 509	568	941	16 607	2 022	3 393	4 236	3 942	2 287	717
1958	18 022	1 433	518	915	16 589	2 012	3 267	4 185	4 052	2 348	725
1959	18 512	1 514	605	909	16 998	1 985	3 233	4 270	4 291	2 475	745
1960	19 095	1 608	625	984	17 487	2 067	3 244	4 341	4 448	2 574	812
1961	19 325	1 638	581	1 056	17 687	2 149	3 205	4 339	4 512	2 665	817
1962	19 682	1 676	564	1 112	18 006	2 250	3 189	4 455	4 554	2 762	797
1963	20 194	1 695	628	1 066	18 499	2 390	3 226	4 559	4 654	2 874	796
1964	20 807	1 760	718	1 042	19 047	2 588	3 256	4 580	4 809	2 971	845
1965	21 602	1 950	733	1 217	19 652	2 727	3 394	4 678	4 880	3 118	856
1966	22 690	2 263	807	1 456	20 427	2 958	3 594	4 730	5 043	3 260	842
1967	23 528	2 265	843	1 422	21 263	3 262	3 832	4 797	5 131	3 388	854
1968	24 339	2 287	874	1 413	22 052	3 461	4 095	4 864	5 289	3 465	878
1969	25 470	2 438	962	1 476	23 032	3 781	4 327	4 891	5 509	3 588	935
1970	26 039	2 505	1 012	1 493	23 534	3 959	4 542	4 890	5 582	3 640	921
1971	26 283	2 513	1 011	1 502	23 770	4 065	4 687	4 831	5 588	3 675	924
1972	27 426	2 755	1 111	1 645	24 669	4 286	5 240	4 893	5 608	3 714	928
1973	28 623	2 962	1 217	1 746	25 661	4 562	5 831	5 036	5 628	3 684	920
1974	29 511	3 069	1 269	1 799	26 442	4 711	6 340	5 169	5 706	3 654	862
1975	29 714	2 983	1 215	1 767	26 731	4 775	6 701	5 161	5 550	3 667	877
1976	31 078	3 120	1 260	1 860	27 958	4 978	7 300	5 462	5 580	3 746	891
1977	32 550	3 244	1 319	1 923	29 306	5 259	7 950	5 772	5 585	3 829	912
1978	34 392	3 416	1 420	1 996	30 975	5 535	8 595	6 201	5 710	3 972	964
1979	35 807	3 451	1 423	2 027	32 357	5 726	9 145	6 648	5 773	4 071	993
1980	36 587	3 314	1 327	1 986	33 275	5 753	9 644	6 994	5 818	4 064	1 001
1981	37 394	3 119	1 242	1 877	34 275	5 826	10 153	7 311	5 896	4 077	1 013
1982	37 615	2 905	1 103	1 802	34 710	5 724	10 367	7 675	5 816	4 095	1 032
1983	38 272	2 796	1 032	1 764	35 476	5 751	10 659	8 132	5 809	4 084	1 041
1984	39 659	2 835	1 069	1 766	36 823	5 804	11 190	8 776	5 920	4 118	1 015
1985	40 690	2 783	1 085	1 698	37 907	5 807	11 571	9 338	6 084	4 128	978
1986	41 876	2 825	1 160	1 665	39 050	5 687	11 956	9 895	6 307	4 164	1 042
1987	43 142	2 900	1 216	1 684	40 242	5 598	12 345	10 459	6 620	4 172	1 047
1988	44 262	2 946	1 176	1 770	41 316	5 450	12 555	10 878	7 062	4 244	1 126
1989	45 232	2 886	1 107	1 779	42 346	5 245	12 708	11 395	7 440	4 332	1 227
1990	45 558	2 762	1 023	1 739	42 796	5 319	12 649	11 785	7 551	4 217	1 275
1991	45 385	2 523	954	1 569	42 862	5 174	12 344	12 139	7 781	4 141	1 283
1992	45 710	2 383	915	1 468	43 327	5 176	12 195	12 254	8 258	4 198	1 246
1993	46 390	2 479	959	1 520	43 910	5 101	12 044	12 467	8 776	4 258	1 265
1994	47 738	2 622	1 066	1 556	45 116	4 997	12 049	12 880	9 338	4 423	1 429
1995	48 344	2 701	1 104	1 597	45 643	4 787	12 056	13 157	9 768	4 461	1 415
1996	48 920	2 756	1 164	1 592	46 164	4 705	11 858	13 430	10 237	4 558	1 376
1997	49 859	2 796	1 136	1 660	47 063	4 773	11 727	13 667	10 709	4 813	1 374
1998	50 327	2 986	1 203	1 783	47 342	4 853	11 470	13 604	11 001	5 021	1 392
1999	51 096	2 999	1 181	1 817	48 098	4 963	11 262	13 767	11 461	5 211	1 435
2000	52 136	2 991	1 178	1 813	49 145	5 068	11 262	13 674	12 087	5 490	1 564
2001	52 218	2 850	1 122	1 727	49 369	5 184	10 959	13 513	12 314	5 802	1 597
2002	52 164	2 716	1 050	1 665	49 448	5 214	10 842	13 138	12 341	6 269	1 644
2003	52 369	2 546	1 027	1 519	49 823	5 161	10 668	12 826	12 645	6 735	1 788
2004	52 527	2 486	991	1 495	50 040	5 207	10 602	12 604	12 810	6 947	1 870
2005	53 186	2 597	1 057	1 540	50 589	5 190	10 603	12 558	12 991	7 317	1 930
2006	53 950	2 590	1 079	1 512	51 359	5 182	10 750	12 449	13 230	7 758	1 991

[1]Beginning in 2003, persons who selected this race group only; persons who selected more than one race group are not included. Prior to 2003, persons who reported more than one race group were included in the group they identified as the main race.

Table 1-11. Employed Civilians, by Age, Sex, Race, and Hispanic Origin, 1948–2006—*Continued*

(Thousands of people.)

Race, Hispanic origin, sex, and year	16 years and over	16 to 19 years			20 years and over						
		Total	16 to 17 years	18 to 19 years	Total	20 to 24 years	25 to 34 years	35 to 44 years	45 to 54 years	55 to 64 years	65 years and over
BLACK[1]											
Both Sexes											
1972	7 802	509	180	329	7 292	1 166	1 924	1 629	1 434	872	269
1973	8 128	570	194	378	7 559	1 258	2 062	1 659	1 460	872	249
1974	8 203	554	190	364	7 649	1 231	2 157	1 682	1 452	884	243
1975	7 894	507	183	325	7 386	1 115	2 145	1 617	1 393	874	241
1976	8 227	508	170	338	7 719	1 193	2 309	1 679	1 416	870	252
1977	8 540	508	169	339	8 031	1 244	2 443	1 754	1 448	892	251
1978	9 102	571	191	380	8 531	1 359	2 641	1 848	1 479	932	273
1979	9 359	579	204	376	8 780	1 424	2 759	1 902	1 502	927	266
1980	9 313	547	192	356	8 765	1 376	2 827	1 910	1 487	925	239
1981	9 355	505	170	335	8 849	1 346	2 872	1 957	1 489	954	231
1982	9 189	428	138	290	8 761	1 283	2 830	2 025	1 469	928	225
1983	9 375	416	123	294	8 959	1 280	2 976	2 107	1 456	937	204
1984	10 119	474	146	328	9 645	1 423	3 223	2 311	1 533	945	209
1985	10 501	532	175	356	9 969	1 399	3 325	2 427	1 598	985	235
1986	10 814	536	183	353	10 278	1 429	3 464	2 524	1 666	982	214
1987	11 309	587	203	385	10 722	1 421	3 614	2 695	1 714	1 036	241
1988	11 658	601	223	378	11 057	1 433	3 725	2 839	1 783	1 018	261
1989	11 953	625	237	388	11 328	1 467	3 801	2 981	1 844	970	265
1990	12 175	598	194	404	11 577	1 409	3 803	3 287	1 897	933	248
1991	12 074	494	161	334	11 580	1 373	3 714	3 401	1 892	957	243
1992	12 151	492	157	335	11 659	1 343	3 699	3 441	1 964	965	246
1993	12 382	494	171	323	11 888	1 377	3 700	3 584	2 059	941	226
1994	12 835	552	224	328	12 284	1 449	3 732	3 722	2 178	953	251
1995	13 279	586	223	363	12 693	1 443	3 844	3 861	2 288	1 004	253
1996	13 542	613	233	380	12 929	1 411	3 851	3 974	2 426	1 025	241
1997	13 969	631	229	401	13 339	1 456	3 903	4 094	2 588	1 048	249
1998	14 556	736	246	490	13 820	1 496	3 967	4 238	2 739	1 118	262
1999	15 056	691	243	448	14 365	1 594	4 091	4 404	2 872	1 134	271
2000	15 156	711	260	451	14 444	1 593	3 993	4 261	3 073	1 226	300
2001	15 006	637	230	408	14 368	1 571	3 840	4 200	3 139	1 283	335
2002	14 872	611	193	417	14 262	1 543	3 726	4 109	3 220	1 332	332
2003	14 739	516	196	320	14 222	1 516	3 618	4 080	3 289	1 373	346
2004	14 909	520	169	351	14 389	1 572	3 635	4 039	3 332	1 452	359
2005	15 313	536	164	372	14 776	1 599	3 722	4 060	3 464	1 555	375
2006	15 765	618	215	402	15 147	1 643	3 809	4 072	3 570	1 659	394
BLACK[1]											
Men											
1972	4 368	309	114	195	4 058	648	1 074	890	793	499	156
1973	4 527	330	112	220	4 197	711	1 142	898	816	483	148
1974	4 527	322	114	209	4 204	668	1 176	912	803	500	145
1975	4 275	276	98	179	3 998	595	1 159	865	755	487	137
1976	4 404	283	100	184	4 120	635	1 217	897	763	472	137
1977	4 565	291	105	186	4 273	659	1 271	940	777	484	143
1978	4 796	312	106	206	4 483	697	1 357	969	788	516	155
1979	4 923	316	111	205	4 606	754	1 425	983	801	498	147
1980	4 798	299	109	191	4 498	713	1 438	975	770	478	126
1981	4 794	273	95	178	4 520	693	1 457	991	764	492	123
1982	4 637	223	65	158	4 414	660	1 414	997	750	471	122
1983	4 753	222	64	158	4 531	684	1 483	1 034	749	477	105
1984	5 124	252	79	173	4 871	750	1 635	1 138	780	460	108
1985	5 270	278	92	186	4 992	726	1 669	1 187	795	501	114
1986	5 428	278	96	182	5 150	732	1 756	1 211	831	507	112
1987	5 661	304	109	195	5 357	728	1 821	1 283	853	547	124
1988	5 824	316	122	193	5 509	736	1 881	1 348	878	536	131
1989	5 928	327	124	202	5 602	742	1 931	1 415	886	498	131
1990	5 995	303	99	204	5 692	702	1 895	1 586	926	469	114
1991	5 961	255	85	170	5 706	695	1 859	1 634	923	481	114
1992	5 930	249	78	170	5 681	679	1 819	1 650	930	478	124
1993	6 047	254	88	166	5 793	674	1 858	1 717	978	461	106
1994	6 241	276	107	169	5 964	718	1 850	1 795	1 030	455	115
1995	6 422	285	111	174	6 137	714	1 895	1 836	1 085	468	138
1996	6 456	289	109	180	6 167	685	1 867	1 878	1 129	482	126
1997	6 607	282	108	174	6 325	668	1 874	1 955	1 215	487	127
1998	6 871	341	120	221	6 530	686	1 886	2 008	1 284	524	142
1999	7 027	325	120	205	6 702	700	1 926	2 092	1 327	525	131
2000	7 082	341	129	211	6 741	730	1 865	1 984	1 425	596	142
2001	6 938	311	115	196	6 627	703	1 757	1 931	1 452	614	170
2002	6 959	306	95	212	6 652	725	1 729	1 899	1 503	624	172
2003	6 820	234	89	145	6 586	726	1 660	1 868	1 518	638	176
2004	6 912	231	76	155	6 681	739	1 720	1 840	1 534	668	180
2005	7 155	254	76	178	6 901	748	1 759	1 886	1 616	711	182
2006	7 354	275	99	175	7 079	804	1 797	1 882	1 680	734	184

[1]Beginning in 2003, persons who selected this race group only; persons who selected more than one race group are not included. Prior to 2003, persons who reported more than one race group were included in the group they identified as the main race.

Table 1-11. Employed Civilians, by Age, Sex, Race, and Hispanic Origin, 1948–2006—*Continued*

(Thousands of people.)

Race, Hispanic origin, sex, and year	16 years and over	16 to 19 years			20 years and over						
		Total	16 to 17 years	18 to 19 years	Total	20 to 24 years	25 to 34 years	35 to 44 years	45 to 54 years	55 to 64 years	65 years and over
BLACK[1]											
Women											
1972	3 433	200	65	134	3 233	519	850	739	641	373	113
1973	3 601	239	81	158	3 362	546	920	761	644	389	101
1974	3 677	232	77	155	3 445	562	981	770	649	383	98
1975	3 618	231	85	146	3 388	520	985	752	638	387	104
1976	3 823	224	70	154	3 599	558	1 092	782	653	398	115
1977	3 975	217	64	153	3 758	585	1 172	814	671	408	109
1978	4 307	260	85	175	4 047	662	1 283	879	691	416	118
1979	4 436	263	92	171	4 174	670	1 333	919	702	428	119
1980	4 515	248	82	165	4 267	663	1 389	936	717	448	113
1981	4 561	232	75	157	4 329	653	1 415	966	725	462	108
1982	4 552	205	73	132	4 347	623	1 416	1 028	719	457	103
1983	4 622	194	59	136	4 428	596	1 493	1 073	707	460	99
1984	4 995	222	67	155	4 773	673	1 588	1 173	753	485	101
1985	5 231	254	83	171	4 977	673	1 656	1 240	804	484	121
1986	5 386	259	87	171	5 128	696	1 708	1 313	835	475	102
1987	5 648	283	93	190	5 365	693	1 793	1 412	860	489	117
1988	5 834	285	101	184	5 548	697	1 844	1 491	905	482	129
1989	6 025	298	113	185	5 727	725	1 870	1 566	959	472	134
1990	6 180	296	96	200	5 884	707	1 907	1 701	971	464	135
1991	6 113	239	76	164	5 874	677	1 855	1 768	969	476	129
1992	6 221	243	79	164	5 978	664	1 880	1 791	1 034	487	123
1993	6 334	239	82	157	6 095	703	1 842	1 867	1 081	480	121
1994	6 595	275	117	158	6 320	731	1 882	1 926	1 147	497	136
1995	6 857	301	112	189	6 556	729	1 949	2 025	1 202	536	114
1996	7 086	324	124	200	6 762	726	1 984	2 096	1 297	543	115
1997	7 362	349	122	227	7 013	789	2 029	2 139	1 373	561	122
1998	7 685	395	126	268	7 290	810	2 081	2 230	1 455	594	120
1999	8 029	366	123	243	7 663	893	2 165	2 312	1 545	609	139
2000	8 073	370	131	240	7 703	862	2 128	2 277	1 647	630	158
2001	8 068	327	115	212	7 741	868	2 084	2 269	1 686	668	165
2002	7 914	304	99	205	7 610	819	1 997	2 209	1 717	708	160
2003	7 919	283	107	175	7 636	790	1 959	2 211	1 770	735	171
2004	7 997	289	93	196	7 707	833	1 914	2 199	1 798	784	179
2005	8 158	282	88	194	7 876	852	1 964	2 175	1 848	844	193
2006	8 410	343	116	227	8 068	839	2 012	2 191	1 890	925	210
HISPANIC[2]											
Both Sexes											
1973	. . .	325	. . .	. . .	. . .	. . .	. . .	. . .	. . .	. . .	. . .
1974	. . .	355	. . .	. . .	. . .	. . .	. . .	. . .	. . .	. . .	. . .
1975	. . .	322	. . .	. . .	. . .	. . .	. . .	. . .	. . .	. . .	. . .
1976	3 777	341	124	230	3 436	614	1 135	803	573	269	42
1977	4 096	381	135	245	3 715	715	1 212	860	608	269	50
1978	4 527	423	159	264	4 104	803	1 330	942	661	307	62
1979	4 785	445	152	292	4 340	860	1 430	996	666	319	69
1980	5 528	500	174	325	5 028	998	1 675	1 074	811	389	80
1981	5 813	459	155	304	5 354	1 060	1 837	1 147	829	399	82
1982	5 804	410	119	291	5 394	1 030	1 896	1 173	816	399	80
1983	6 072	423	125	297	5 649	1 068	1 997	1 224	837	441	81
1984	6 650	468	148	320	6 182	1 160	2 201	1 385	883	474	79
1985	6 887	438	144	294	6 449	1 187	2 316	1 473	913	486	75
1986	7 219	430	146	284	6 789	1 231	2 427	1 570	1 011	474	76
1987	7 790	474	149	325	7 316	1 273	2 668	1 775	1 010	512	76
1988	8 250	523	171	353	7 727	1 341	2 749	1 876	1 078	585	97
1989	8 573	548	165	383	8 025	1 325	2 900	1 968	1 129	589	114
1990	9 845	668	208	460	9 177	1 672	3 327	2 229	1 235	611	103
1991	9 827	602	169	433	9 225	1 622	3 264	2 333	1 266	637	103
1992	10 027	577	169	408	9 450	1 575	3 350	2 468	1 316	628	112
1993	10 362	570	160	410	9 792	1 574	3 446	2 605	1 402	630	135
1994	10 787	609	195	415	10 178	1 643	3 517	2 737	1 495	647	139
1995	11 128	645	194	450	10 483	1 609	3 618	2 889	1 565	666	135
1996	11 642	646	199	447	10 996	1 628	3 758	3 115	1 595	748	152
1997	12 726	714	228	487	12 012	1 798	4 029	3 371	1 846	794	173
1998	13 291	793	230	563	12 498	1 883	4 113	3 504	1 994	846	158
1999	13 720	854	254	600	12 866	1 881	4 097	3 738	2 074	886	190
2000	15 735	973	285	688	14 762	2 356	4 950	4 052	2 308	898	197
2001	16 190	969	268	701	15 221	2 404	5 065	4 149	2 472	944	187
2002	16 590	882	254	628	15 708	2 413	5 272	4 273	2 511	1 029	209
2003	17 372	768	242	525	16 604	2 399	5 541	4 573	2 711	1 132	249
2004	17 930	792	211	581	17 138	2 477	5 560	4 671	2 932	1 210	288
2005	18 632	847	253	595	17 785	2 423	5 756	4 879	3 114	1 317	296
2006	19 612	900	287	614	18 712	2 487	6 001	5 106	3 324	1 441	354

[1]Beginning in 2003, persons who selected this race group only; persons who selected more than one race group are not included. Prior to 2003, persons who reported more than one race group were included in the group they identified as the main race.
[2]May be of any race.
. . . = Not available.

Table 1-11. Employed Civilians, by Age, Sex, Race, and Hispanic Origin, 1948–2006—*Continued*

(Thousands of people.)

Race, Hispanic origin, sex, and year	16 years and over	16 to 19 years			20 years and over						
		Total	16 to 17 years	18 to 19 years	Total	20 to 24 years	25 to 34 years	35 to 44 years	45 to 54 years	55 to 64 years	65 years and over
HISPANIC[2]											
Men											
1973	2 198	...	...	...	2 010	...	...	...	...	...	...
1974	2 369	...	...	...	2 165	...	...	...	...	...	...
1975	2 301	...	...	...	2 117	...	...	...	...	...	...
1976	2 303	199	74	125	2 109	364	708	504	369	173	...
1977	2 564	225	78	147	2 335	427	763	540	394	184	...
1978	2 808	241	93	147	2 568	494	824	590	405	207	...
1979	2 962	260	93	168	2 701	511	891	615	427	205	...
1980	3 448	306	109	198	3 142	611	1 065	662	491	254	...
1981	3 597	272	90	182	3 325	642	1 157	707	504	259	...
1982	3 583	229	66	162	3 354	621	1 192	729	498	261	...
1983	3 771	248	71	177	3 523	655	1 280	760	499	275	...
1984	4 083	258	78	180	3 825	718	1 398	841	530	292	...
1985	4 245	251	82	169	3 994	727	1 473	888	550	308	...
1986	4 428	254	82	172	4 174	773	1 510	929	614	297	...
1987	4 713	268	81	188	4 444	777	1 664	1 044	606	303	...
1988	4 972	292	87	205	4 680	815	1 706	1 120	645	331	...
1989	5 172	319	94	225	4 853	821	1 787	1 152	676	350	...
1990	6 021	412	126	286	5 609	1 083	2 076	1 312	722	355	...
1991	5 979	356	94	263	5 623	1 063	2 050	1 360	719	369	...
1992	6 093	336	97	238	5 757	985	2 127	1 437	768	372	...
1993	6 328	337	95	242	5 992	1 003	2 200	1 527	822	360	...
1994	6 530	341	109	233	6 189	1 056	2 227	1 600	847	379	79
1995	6 725	358	110	248	6 367	1 030	2 284	1 675	908	384	85
1996	7 039	384	107	277	6 655	1 015	2 345	1 842	918	438	96
1997	7 728	420	130	290	7 307	1 142	2 547	1 978	1 059	477	105
1998	8 018	449	133	315	7 570	1 173	2 592	2 077	1 115	512	101
1999	8 067	491	139	352	7 576	1 135	2 524	2 135	1 151	502	130
2000	9 428	570	159	411	8 859	1 486	3 063	2 358	1 295	532	126
2001	9 668	568	149	419	9 100	1 473	3 142	2 446	1 375	545	119
2002	9 845	504	141	363	9 341	1 476	3 271	2 503	1 396	569	125
2003	10 479	415	121	294	10 063	1 485	3 537	2 724	1 533	639	144
2004	10 832	446	108	338	10 385	1 514	3 557	2 801	1 654	687	174
2005	11 337	465	137	328	10 872	1 511	3 711	2 939	1 781	748	183
2006	11 887	496	146	350	11 391	1 535	3 845	3 088	1 894	809	220
HISPANIC[2]											
Women											
1973	1 198	...	...	...	1 060	...	...	...	...	...	...
1974	1 319	...	...	...	1 166	...	...	...	...	...	...
1975	1 362	...	...	...	1 224	...	...	...	...	...	...
1976	1 417	155	50	106	1 288	249	427	300	204	96	...
1977	1 516	155	57	98	1 370	288	449	320	214	86	...
1978	1 719	182	65	117	1 537	308	506	352	256	99	...
1979	1 824	185	60	125	1 638	349	539	381	241	115	...
1980	2 079	193	65	128	1 886	387	610	412	320	136	...
1981	2 216	187	65	122	2 029	418	680	440	326	139	...
1982	2 222	181	52	129	2 040	409	704	444	318	139	...
1983	2 301	175	54	120	2 127	413	717	464	338	166	...
1984	2 568	211	71	140	2 357	442	804	544	354	181	...
1985	2 642	187	62	125	2 456	460	843	585	362	178	...
1986	2 791	176	64	112	2 615	458	917	641	397	177	...
1987	3 077	206	69	137	2 872	496	1 004	732	405	209	...
1988	3 278	231	84	147	3 047	526	1 042	756	434	254	...
1989	3 401	229	71	158	3 172	504	1 114	816	453	239	...
1990	3 823	256	82	174	3 567	588	1 251	917	513	256	...
1991	3 848	246	76	170	3 603	559	1 214	972	548	268	...
1992	3 934	242	72	170	3 693	591	1 223	1 031	548	256	...
1993	4 033	233	65	168	3 800	571	1 246	1 077	581	269	...
1994	4 258	268	86	182	3 989	587	1 290	1 137	648	268	59
1995	4 403	287	85	202	4 116	579	1 334	1 213	657	282	50
1996	4 602	261	92	169	4 341	612	1 412	1 273	677	310	56
1997	4 999	294	98	196	4 705	656	1 482	1 393	787	318	69
1998	5 273	345	97	247	4 928	710	1 521	1 428	879	334	57
1999	5 653	363	115	248	5 290	746	1 574	1 603	923	384	60
2000	6 307	404	127	277	5 903	870	1 887	1 695	1 013	366	72
2001	6 522	401	119	282	6 121	931	1 923	1 703	1 097	398	67
2002	6 744	378	113	265	6 367	937	2 001	1 770	1 114	460	84
2003	6 894	353	121	231	6 541	914	2 004	1 849	1 178	493	105
2004	7 098	346	103	243	6 752	964	2 003	1 870	1 279	523	114
2005	7 295	382	116	266	6 913	912	2 045	1 940	1 333	569	113
2006	7 725	404	140	264	7 321	951	2 155	2 018	1 430	632	135

[2]May be of any race.
. . . = Not available.

Table 1-12. Civilian Employment-Population Ratios, by Sex, Age, Race, and Hispanic Origin, 1948–2006

(Percent.)

Race, Hispanic origin, and year	Both sexes			Men			Women		
	16 years and over	16 to 19 years	20 years and over	16 years and over	16 to 19 years	20 years and over	16 years and over	16 to 19 years	20 years and over
ALL RACES									
1948	56.6	47.7	57.4	83.5	57.5	85.8	31.3	38.5	30.7
1949	55.4	45.2	56.3	81.3	53.8	83.7	31.2	37.2	30.6
1950	56.1	45.5	57.0	82.0	55.2	84.2	32.0	36.3	31.6
1951	57.3	47.9	58.1	84.0	57.9	86.1	33.1	38.9	32.6
1952	57.3	46.9	58.1	83.9	55.9	86.2	33.4	38.8	33.0
1953	57.1	46.4	58.0	83.6	55.9	85.9	33.3	37.8	32.9
1954	55.5	42.3	56.6	81.0	50.2	83.5	32.5	34.9	32.3
1955	56.7	43.5	57.8	81.8	52.1	84.3	34.0	35.6	33.8
1956	57.5	45.3	58.5	82.3	53.8	84.6	35.1	37.5	34.9
1957	57.1	43.9	58.2	81.3	51.8	83.8	35.1	36.7	35.0
1958	55.4	39.9	56.8	78.5	46.9	81.2	34.5	33.5	34.6
1959	56.0	39.9	57.5	79.3	47.2	82.3	35.0	33.0	35.1
1960	56.1	40.5	57.6	78.9	47.6	81.9	35.5	33.8	35.7
1961	55.4	39.1	56.9	77.6	45.3	80.8	35.4	33.2	35.6
1962	55.5	39.4	57.1	77.7	45.9	80.9	35.6	33.3	35.8
1963	55.4	37.4	57.2	77.1	43.8	80.6	35.8	31.5	36.3
1964	55.7	37.3	57.7	77.3	44.1	80.9	36.3	30.9	36.9
1965	56.2	38.9	58.2	77.5	46.2	81.2	37.1	32.0	37.6
1966	56.9	42.1	58.7	77.9	48.9	81.5	38.3	35.6	38.6
1967	57.3	42.2	59.0	78.0	48.7	81.5	39.0	35.9	39.3
1968	57.5	42.2	59.3	77.8	48.7	81.3	39.6	36.0	40.0
1969	58.0	43.4	59.7	77.6	49.5	81.1	40.7	37.5	41.1
1970	57.4	42.3	59.2	76.2	47.7	79.7	40.8	37.1	41.2
1971	56.6	41.3	58.4	74.9	46.8	78.5	40.4	36.0	40.9
1972	57.0	43.5	58.6	75.0	48.9	78.4	41.0	38.2	41.3
1973	57.8	45.9	59.3	75.5	51.4	78.6	42.0	40.5	42.2
1974	57.8	46.0	59.2	74.9	51.2	77.9	42.6	41.0	42.8
1975	56.1	43.3	57.6	71.7	47.2	74.8	42.0	39.4	42.3
1976	56.8	44.2	58.3	72.0	47.9	75.1	43.2	40.5	43.5
1977	57.9	46.1	59.2	72.8	50.4	75.6	44.5	41.8	44.8
1978	59.3	48.3	60.6	73.8	52.2	76.4	46.4	44.5	46.6
1979	59.9	48.5	61.2	73.8	51.7	76.5	47.5	45.3	47.7
1980	59.2	46.6	60.6	72.0	49.5	74.6	47.7	43.8	48.1
1981	59.0	44.6	60.5	71.3	47.1	74.0	48.0	42.0	48.6
1982	57.8	41.5	59.4	69.0	42.9	71.8	47.7	40.2	48.4
1983	57.9	41.5	59.5	68.8	43.1	71.4	48.0	40.0	48.8
1984	59.5	43.7	61.0	70.7	45.0	73.2	49.5	42.5	50.1
1985	60.1	44.4	61.5	70.9	45.7	73.3	50.4	42.9	51.0
1986	60.7	44.6	62.1	71.0	45.7	73.3	51.4	43.6	52.0
1987	61.5	45.5	62.9	71.5	46.1	73.8	52.5	44.8	53.1
1988	62.3	46.8	63.6	72.0	47.8	74.2	53.4	45.9	54.0
1989	63.0	47.5	64.2	72.5	48.7	74.5	54.3	46.4	54.9
1990	62.8	45.3	64.3	72.0	46.6	74.3	54.3	44.0	55.2
1991	61.7	42.0	63.2	70.4	42.7	72.7	53.7	41.2	54.6
1992	61.5	41.0	63.0	69.8	41.9	72.1	53.8	40.0	54.8
1993	61.7	41.7	63.3	70.0	42.3	72.3	54.1	41.0	55.0
1994	62.5	43.4	64.0	70.4	43.8	72.6	55.3	43.0	56.2
1995	62.9	44.2	64.4	70.8	44.7	73.0	55.6	43.8	56.5
1996	63.2	43.5	64.7	70.9	43.6	73.2	56.0	43.5	57.0
1997	63.8	43.4	65.5	71.3	43.4	73.7	56.8	43.3	57.8
1998	64.1	45.1	65.6	71.6	44.7	73.9	57.1	45.5	58.0
1999	64.3	44.7	65.9	71.6	45.1	74.0	57.4	44.3	58.5
2000	64.4	45.2	66.0	71.9	45.4	74.2	57.5	45.0	58.4
2001	63.7	42.3	65.4	70.9	42.2	73.3	57.0	42.4	58.1
2002	62.7	39.6	64.6	69.7	38.9	72.3	56.3	40.3	57.5
2003	62.3	36.8	64.3	68.9	35.7	71.7	56.1	37.8	57.5
2004	62.3	36.4	64.4	69.2	35.9	71.9	56.0	37.0	57.4
2005	62.7	36.5	64.7	69.6	35.1	72.4	56.2	37.8	57.6
2006	63.1	36.9	65.2	70.1	36.3	72.9	56.6	37.6	58.0

Table 1-12. Civilian Employment-Population Ratios, by Sex, Age, Race, and Hispanic Origin, 1948–2006
—*Continued*

(Percent.)

Race, Hispanic origin, and year	Both sexes			Men			Women		
	16 years and over	16 to 19 years	20 years and over	16 years and over	16 to 19 years	20 years and over	16 years and over	16 to 19 years	20 years and over
WHITE[1]									
1954	55.2	42.9	56.2	81.5	49.9	84.0	31.4	36.4	31.1
1955	56.5	44.2	57.4	82.2	52.0	84.7	33.0	37.0	32.7
1956	57.3	46.1	58.2	82.7	54.1	85.0	34.2	38.9	33.8
1957	56.8	45.0	57.8	81.8	52.4	84.1	34.2	38.2	33.9
1958	55.3	41.0	56.5	79.2	47.6	81.8	33.6	35.0	33.5
1959	55.9	41.2	57.2	79.9	48.1	82.8	34.0	34.8	34.0
1960	55.9	41.5	57.2	79.4	48.1	82.4	34.6	35.1	34.5
1961	55.3	40.1	56.7	78.2	45.9	81.4	34.5	34.6	34.5
1962	55.4	40.4	56.9	78.4	46.4	81.5	34.7	34.8	34.7
1963	55.3	38.6	56.9	77.7	44.7	81.1	35.0	32.9	35.2
1964	55.5	38.4	57.3	77.8	45.0	81.3	35.5	32.2	35.8
1965	56.0	40.3	57.8	77.9	47.1	81.5	36.2	33.7	36.5
1966	56.8	43.6	58.3	78.3	50.1	81.7	37.5	37.5	37.5
1967	57.2	43.8	58.7	78.4	50.2	81.7	38.3	37.7	38.3
1968	57.4	43.9	59.0	78.3	50.3	81.6	38.9	37.8	39.1
1969	58.0	45.2	59.4	78.2	51.1	81.4	40.1	39.5	40.1
1970	57.5	44.5	59.0	76.8	49.6	80.1	40.3	39.5	40.4
1971	56.8	43.8	58.3	75.7	49.2	79.0	39.9	38.6	40.1
1972	57.4	46.4	58.6	76.0	51.5	79.0	40.7	41.3	40.6
1973	58.2	48.9	59.3	76.5	54.3	79.2	41.8	43.6	41.6
1974	58.3	49.3	59.3	75.9	54.4	78.6	42.4	44.3	42.2
1975	56.7	46.5	57.9	73.0	50.6	75.7	42.0	42.5	41.9
1976	57.5	47.8	58.6	73.4	51.5	76.0	43.2	44.2	43.1
1977	58.6	50.1	59.6	74.1	54.4	76.5	44.5	45.9	44.4
1978	60.0	52.4	60.8	75.0	56.3	77.2	46.3	48.5	46.1
1979	60.6	52.6	61.5	75.1	55.7	77.3	47.5	49.4	47.3
1980	60.0	50.7	61.0	73.4	53.4	75.6	47.8	47.9	47.8
1981	60.0	48.7	61.1	72.8	51.3	75.1	48.3	46.2	48.5
1982	58.8	45.8	60.1	70.6	47.0	73.0	48.1	44.6	48.4
1983	58.9	45.9	60.1	70.4	47.4	72.6	48.5	44.5	48.9
1984	60.5	48.0	61.5	72.1	49.1	74.3	49.8	47.0	50.0
1985	61.0	48.5	62.0	72.3	49.9	74.3	50.7	47.1	51.0
1986	61.5	48.8	62.6	72.3	49.6	74.3	51.7	47.9	52.0
1987	62.3	49.4	63.4	72.7	49.9	74.7	52.8	49.0	53.1
1988	63.1	50.9	64.1	73.2	51.7	75.1	53.8	50.2	54.0
1989	63.8	51.6	64.7	73.7	52.6	75.4	54.6	50.5	54.9
1990	63.7	49.7	64.8	73.3	51.0	75.1	54.7	48.3	55.2
1991	62.6	46.6	63.7	71.6	47.2	73.5	54.2	45.9	54.8
1992	62.4	45.3	63.6	71.1	46.4	73.1	54.2	44.2	54.9
1993	62.7	46.2	63.9	71.4	46.6	73.3	54.6	45.7	55.2
1994	63.5	47.9	64.7	71.8	48.3	73.6	55.8	47.5	56.4
1995	63.8	48.8	64.9	72.0	49.4	73.8	56.1	48.1	56.7
1996	64.1	47.9	65.3	72.3	48.2	74.2	56.3	47.6	57.0
1997	64.6	47.7	65.9	72.7	48.1	74.7	57.0	47.2	57.8
1998	64.7	48.9	65.9	72.7	48.6	74.7	57.1	49.3	57.7
1999	64.8	48.8	66.1	72.8	49.3	74.8	57.3	48.3	58.0
2000	64.9	49.1	66.1	73.0	49.5	74.9	57.4	48.8	58.0
2001	64.2	46.3	65.6	72.0	46.2	74.0	57.0	46.5	57.7
2002	63.4	43.2	64.9	70.8	42.3	73.1	56.4	44.1	57.3
2003	63.0	40.4	64.7	70.1	39.4	72.5	56.3	41.5	57.3
2004	63.1	40.0	64.8	70.4	39.7	72.8	56.1	40.3	57.2
2005	63.4	40.2	65.1	70.8	38.8	73.3	56.3	41.8	57.4
2006	63.8	40.6	65.5	71.3	40.0	73.7	56.6	41.1	57.7

[1]Beginning in 2003, persons who selected this race group only; persons who selected more than one race group are not included. Prior to 2003, persons who reported more than one race group were included in the group they identified as their main race.

Table 1-12. Civilian Employment-Population Ratios, by Sex, Age, Race, and Hispanic Origin, 1948–2006
—Continued

(Percent.)

Race, Hispanic origin, and year	Both sexes 16 years and over	16 to 19 years	20 years and over	Men 16 years and over	16 to 19 years	20 years and over	Women 16 years and over	16 to 19 years	20 years and over
BLACK[1]									
1972	53.7	25.2	58.3	66.8	31.6	73.0	43.0	19.2	46.5
1973	54.5	27.2	58.9	67.5	32.8	73.7	43.8	22.0	47.2
1974	53.5	25.9	58.0	65.8	31.4	71.9	43.5	20.9	46.9
1975	50.1	23.1	54.5	60.6	26.3	66.5	41.6	20.2	44.9
1976	50.8	22.4	55.4	60.6	25.8	66.8	42.8	19.2	46.4
1977	51.4	22.3	56.0	61.4	26.4	67.5	43.3	18.5	47.0
1978	53.6	25.2	58.0	63.3	28.5	69.1	45.8	22.1	49.3
1979	53.8	25.4	58.1	63.4	28.7	69.1	46.0	22.4	49.3
1980	52.3	23.9	56.4	60.4	27.0	65.8	45.7	21.0	49.1
1981	51.3	22.1	55.5	59.1	24.6	64.5	45.1	19.7	48.5
1982	49.4	19.0	53.6	56.0	20.3	61.4	44.2	17.7	47.5
1983	49.5	18.7	53.6	56.3	20.4	61.6	44.1	17.0	47.4
1984	52.3	21.9	56.1	59.2	23.9	64.1	46.7	20.1	49.8
1985	53.4	24.6	57.0	60.0	26.3	64.6	48.1	23.1	50.9
1986	54.1	25.1	57.6	60.6	26.5	65.1	48.8	23.8	51.6
1987	55.6	27.1	58.9	62.0	28.5	66.4	50.3	25.8	53.0
1988	56.3	27.6	59.7	62.7	29.4	67.1	51.2	25.8	53.9
1989	56.9	28.7	60.1	62.8	30.4	67.0	52.0	27.1	54.6
1990	56.7	26.7	60.2	62.6	27.7	67.1	51.9	25.8	54.7
1991	55.4	22.6	59.0	61.3	23.8	65.9	50.6	21.5	53.6
1992	54.9	22.8	58.3	59.9	23.6	64.3	50.8	22.1	53.6
1993	55.0	22.6	58.4	60.0	23.6	64.3	50.9	21.6	53.8
1994	56.1	24.9	59.4	60.8	25.4	65.0	52.3	24.5	55.0
1995	57.1	25.7	60.5	61.7	25.2	66.1	53.4	26.1	56.1
1996	57.4	26.0	60.8	61.1	24.9	65.5	54.4	27.1	57.1
1997	58.2	26.1	61.8	61.4	23.7	66.1	55.6	28.5	58.4
1998	59.7	30.1	63.0	62.9	28.4	67.1	57.2	31.8	59.7
1999	60.6	27.9	64.2	63.1	26.7	67.5	58.6	29.0	61.5
2000	60.9	29.8	64.2	63.6	28.9	67.7	58.6	30.6	61.3
2001	59.7	26.7	63.2	62.1	26.4	66.3	57.8	27.0	60.7
2002	58.1	25.3	61.6	61.1	25.6	65.2	55.8	24.9	58.7
2003	57.4	21.7	61.0	59.5	19.9	64.1	55.6	23.4	58.6
2004	57.2	21.5	60.9	59.3	19.3	63.9	55.5	23.6	58.5
2005	57.7	21.6	61.5	60.2	20.8	64.7	55.7	22.4	58.9
2006	58.4	24.1	62.0	60.6	21.7	65.2	56.5	26.4	59.4
HISPANIC[2]									
1973	55.6	. . .	55.6	. . .	. . .	. . .	. . .	. . .	. . .
1974	56.2	. . .	56.2	. . .	. . .	. . .	. . .	. . .	. . .
1975	53.4	. . .	53.4	. . .	. . .	. . .	. . .	. . .	. . .
1976	53.8	. . .	53.8	. . .	. . .	. . .	. . .	. . .	. . .
1977	55.4	. . .	55.4	. . .	. . .	. . .	. . .	. . .	. . .
1978	57.2	. . .	57.2	. . .	. . .	. . .	. . .	. . .	. . .
1979	58.3	. . .	58.3	. . .	. . .	. . .	. . .	. . .	. . .
1980	57.6	. . .	57.6	. . .	. . .	. . .	. . .	. . .	. . .
1981	57.4	. . .	57.4	. . .	. . .	. . .	. . .	. . .	. . .
1982	54.9	. . .	54.9	. . .	. . .	. . .	. . .	. . .	. . .
1983	55.1	. . .	55.1	. . .	. . .	. . .	. . .	. . .	. . .
1984	57.9	. . .	57.9	. . .	. . .	. . .	. . .	. . .	. . .
1985	57.8	. . .	57.8	. . .	. . .	. . .	. . .	. . .	. . .
1986	58.5	. . .	58.5	. . .	. . .	. . .	. . .	. . .	. . .
1987	60.5	. . .	60.5	. . .	. . .	. . .	. . .	. . .	. . .
1988	61.9	. . .	61.9	. . .	. . .	. . .	. . .	. . .	. . .
1989	62.2	. . .	62.2	. . .	. . .	. . .	. . .	. . .	. . .
1990	61.9	. . .	61.9	. . .	. . .	. . .	. . .	. . .	. . .
1991	59.8	. . .	59.8	. . .	. . .	. . .	. . .	. . .	. . .
1992	59.1	. . .	59.1	. . .	. . .	. . .	. . .	. . .	. . .
1993	59.1	. . .	59.1	. . .	. . .	. . .	. . .	. . .	. . .
1994	59.5	33.5	59.5	71.7	36.8	. . .	47.2	30.1	. . .
1995	59.7	34.4	59.7	72.1	37.5	. . .	47.3	31.3	. . .
1996	60.6	33.1	60.6	73.3	38.8	. . .	47.9	27.3	. . .
1997	62.6	33.7	62.6	74.5	37.6	. . .	50.2	29.3	. . .
1998	63.1	36.0	63.1	74.7	38.6	. . .	51.0	33.0	. . .
1999	63.4	37.0	63.4	75.3	41.2	. . .	51.7	32.5	. . .
2000	65.7	38.6	65.7	77.4	42.8	81.7	53.6	33.9	55.8
2001	64.9	38.6	64.9	76.2	43.3	79.9	53.3	33.5	55.4
2002	63.9	35.2	63.9	74.5	39.0	78.3	52.9	31.1	55.2
2003	63.1	30.2	63.1	74.3	31.9	78.6	51.2	28.4	53.6
2004	63.8	30.4	63.8	75.1	33.4	79.4	51.8	27.2	54.4
2005	64.0	31.5	64.0	75.8	33.8	80.0	51.5	29.1	53.8
2006	65.2	32.2	65.2	76.8	34.8	81.1	52.8	29.5	55.2

[1]Beginning in 2003, persons who selected this race group only; persons who selected more than one race group are not included. Prior to 2003, persons who reported more than one race group were included in the group they identified as their main race.
[2]May be of any race.
. . . = Not available.

Table 1-13. Employed Civilians, by Sex, Race, Hispanic Origin, and Occupation, 2004–2006

(Thousands of people.)

Year and occupation	Total	Men	Women	White[1]	Black[1]	Hispanic[2]
2004						
All Occupations	139 252	74 524	64 728	115 239	14 909	17 930
Management, professional, and related	48 532	24 136	24 396	41 027	3 949	3 101
Management, business, and financial operations	20 235	11 718	8 517	17 590	1 408	1 290
Professional and related	28 297	12 418	15 879	23 438	2 541	1 811
Life, physical, and social sciences	1 365	777	588	1 143	76	69
Community and social services	2 170	845	1 325	1 650	415	203
Services	22 720	9 826	12 894	17 544	3 543	4 336
Health care support	2 921	311	2 609	1 991	758	384
Protective services	2 847	2 230	616	2 197	510	315
Food preparation and serving related	7 279	3 196	4 084	5 854	835	1 405
Building and grounds cleaning and maintenance	5 185	3 085	2 100	4 094	773	1 661
Personal care and services	4 488	1 004	3 484	3 407	667	571
Sales and office	35 464	12 805	22 660	29 399	3 918	3 818
Office and administrative support	19 481	4 700	14 781	15 842	2 487	2 164
Natural resources, construction, and maintenance	14 582	13 930	652	12 928	1 012	3 229
Farming, fishing, and forestry	991	786	204	885	53	387
Construction and extraction	8 522	8 306	216	7 642	572	2 127
Installation, maintenance, and repair	5 069	4 838	231	4 401	387	715
Production, transportation, and material moving	17 954	13 827	4 126	14 340	2 488	3 446
Transportation and material moving	8 491	7 240	1 251	6 746	1 364	1 552
2005						
All Occupations	141 730	75 973	65 757	116 949	15 313	18 632
Management, professional, and related	49 245	24 349	24 896	41 475	3 985	3 174
Management, business, and financial operations	20 450	11 761	8 689	17 668	1 451	1 330
Professional and related	28 795	12 588	16 207	23 807	2 533	1 844
Life, physical, and social sciences	1 406	808	598	1 171	71	63
Community and social services	2 138	827	1 311	1 654	365	209
Services	23 133	9 882	13 251	17 817	3 656	4 434
Health care support	3 092	339	2 753	2 121	766	426
Protective services	2 894	2 246	648	2 195	560	300
Food preparation and serving related	7 374	3 202	4 173	5 888	857	1 519
Building and grounds cleaning and maintenance	5 241	3 111	2 130	4 130	828	1 605
Personal care and services	4 531	984	3 548	3 484	645	584
Sales and office	35 962	13 190	22 772	29 658	4 033	4 000
Office and administrative support	19 529	4 829	14 700	15 777	2 526	2 258
Natural resources, construction, and maintenance	15 348	14 635	713	13 582	1 086	3 552
Farming, fishing, and forestry	976	756	220	882	50	394
Construction and extraction	9 145	8 871	274	8 158	643	2 450
Installation, maintenance, and repair	5 226	5 008	219	4 542	394	709
Production, transportation, and material moving	18 041	13 917	4 124	14 418	2 552	3 473
Transportation and material moving	8 664	7 377	1 286	6 892	1 393	1 597
2006						
All Occupations	144 427	77 502	66 925	118 833	15 765	19 613
Management, professional, and related	50 420	24 928	25 492	42 177	4 252	3 337
Management, business, and financial operations	21 233	12 347	8 886	18 298	1 547	1 477
Professional and related	29 187	12 581	16 606	23 879	2 704	1 860
Life, physical, and social sciences	1 434	813	620	1 146	81	59
Community and social services	2 156	829	1 327	1 631	402	184
Services	23 811	10 159	13 653	18 310	3 797	4 649
Health care support	3 132	333	2 799	2 137	774	410
Protective services	2 939	2 284	654	2 239	578	301
Food preparation and serving related	7 606	3 297	4 309	6 071	892	1 608
Building and grounds cleaning and maintenance	5 381	3 230	2 151	4 264	840	1 712
Personal care and services	4 754	1 014	3 740	3 600	714	618
Sales and office	36 141	13 275	22 866	29 798	4 051	4 154
Office and administrative support	19 500	4 797	14 703	15 772	2 548	2 314
Natural resources, construction, and maintenance	15 830	15 079	752	14 025	1 079	3 893
Farming, fishing, and forestry	961	750	212	870	47	382
Construction and extraction	9 507	9 216	292	8 481	624	2 790
Installation, maintenance, and repair	5 362	5 114	248	4 674	408	721
Production, transportation, and material moving	18 224	14 061	4 163	14 522	2 586	3 580
Transportation and material moving	8 846	7 533	1 313	6 974	1 438	1 645

[1]Beginning in 2003, persons who selected this race group only; persons who selected more than one race group are not included. Prior to 2003, persons who reported more than one race group were included in the group they identified as the main race.
[2]May be of any race.

Table 1-14. Employed Civilians, by Selected Occupation and Industry, 2004–2006

(Thousands of people.)

Year and industry	Total employed	Management, professional, and related occupations	Life, physical, and social science occupations	Service occupations	Sales and office occupations	Natural resources, construction, and maintenance occupations	Production, transportation, and material moving occupations
2004							
All Industries	139 252	48 532	1 365	22 720	35 464	14 582	17 954
Agriculture, forestry, fishing, and hunting	2 232	1 092	28	95	106	837	103
Mining	539	118	13	5	51	232	133
Construction	10 768	1 696	5	70	732	7 743	527
Manufacturing	16 484	4 719	265	225	2 185	1 151	8 203
Durable goods	10 329	3 202	53	113	1 247	771	4 996
Nondurable goods	6 155	1 517	212	113	938	380	3 207
Wholesale trade	4 600	754	12	60	2 553	292	940
Retail trade	16 269	1 759	16	571	11 295	815	1 830
Transportation and warehousing	5 844	593	3	277	1 636	383	2 955
Utilities	1 168	373	35	22	266	276	231
Information	3 463	1 766	19	93	1 102	341	161
Finance and insurance	6 940	3 311	17	69	3 495	34	30
Real estate and rental and leasing	3 029	931	2	280	1 502	201	115
Professional and technical services	8 386	6 333	326	108	1 651	139	156
Management, administrative, and waste services	5 722	1 050	26	2 503	1 249	278	642
Education services	12 058	9 036	170	1 298	1 201	184	338
Health care and social assistance	16 661	8 756	211	4 860	2 634	127	285
Arts, entertainment, and recreation	2 690	898	15	1 266	372	86	67
Accommodation and food services	9 131	1 286	4	6 487	1 000	70	289
Other services	6 903	1 467	16	2 408	1 082	1 134	812
Public administration	6 365	2 594	181	2 021	1 354	259	138
2005							
All Industries	141 730	49 245	1 406	23 133	35 962	15 348	18 041
Agriculture, forestry, fishing, and hunting	2 197	1 086	29	82	96	836	97
Mining	624	141	23	6	64	264	150
Construction	11 197	1 688	5	76	736	8 208	489
Manufacturing	16 253	4 612	247	242	2 127	1 179	8 092
Durable goods	10 333	3 170	60	112	1 216	787	5 048
Nondurable goods	5 919	1 443	187	130	911	392	3 044
Wholesale trade	4 579	751	21	55	2 479	295	1 000
Retail trade	16 825	1 817	14	559	11 790	830	1 830
Transportation and warehousing	6 184	650	4	270	1 678	414	3 172
Utilities	1 176	353	31	23	234	307	261
Information	3 402	1 717	13	90	1 096	336	164
Finance and insurance	7 035	3 408	14	72	3 497	33	25
Real estate and rental and leasing	3 168	980	1	284	1 588	206	110
Professional and technical services	8 584	6 545	329	113	1 610	172	144
Management, administrative, and waste services	5 709	1 005	25	2 542	1 260	268	635
Education services	12 264	9 197	179	1 318	1 222	202	323
Health care and social assistance	16 910	8 805	230	5 047	2 653	146	259
Arts, entertainment, and recreation	2 765	979	17	1 256	358	102	71
Accommodation and food services	9 306	1 367	2	6 535	1 045	61	297
Other services	7 020	1 498	15	2 448	1 078	1 219	778
Public administration	6 530	2 646	207	2 115	1 353	272	144
2006							
All Industries	144 427	50 420	1 434	23 811	36 141	15 830	18 224
Agriculture, forestry, fishing, and hunting	2 206	1 089	35	89	96	830	102
Mining	687	165	22	6	63	320	133
Construction	11 749	1 892	13	63	729	8 596	469
Manufacturing	16 377	4 673	238	262	2 117	1 195	8 130
Durable goods	10 499	3 170	54	144	1 265	811	5 110
Nondurable goods	5 877	1 503	184	118	852	384	3 021
Wholesale trade	4 561	785	19	50	2 437	321	968
Retail trade	16 767	1 797	11	610	11 763	814	1 783
Transportation and warehousing	6 269	668	6	289	1 702	377	3 233
Utilities	1 186	351	26	21	245	293	275
Information	3 573	1 804	13	101	1 095	405	169
Finance and insurance	7 254	3 506	20	66	3 602	41	38
Real estate and rental and leasing	3 237	997	1	269	1 635	216	119
Professional and technical services	8 776	6 734	364	128	1 616	159	138
Management, administrative, and waste services	6 092	1 082	23	2 709	1 279	309	713
Education services	12 522	9 371	217	1 408	1 216	219	309
Health care and social assistance	17 416	9 112	215	5 239	2 638	163	265
Arts, entertainment, and recreation	2 671	880	9	1 249	379	91	72
Accommodation and food services	9 474	1 389	2	6 624	1 048	71	342
Other services	7 088	1 466	15	2 533	1 135	1 136	818
Public administration	6 524	2 659	186	2 095	1 346	275	149

Table 1-15. Employed Civilians in Agriculture and Nonagricultural Industries, by Class of Worker and Sex, 1985–2006

(Thousands of people.)

Sex and year	Total employed	Agriculture				Nonagricultural industries						
		Total	Wage and salary workers	Self-employed workers	Unpaid family workers	Total	Wage and salary workers				Self-employed workers	Unpaid family workers
							Total	Government	Private household	Other private		
Both Sexes												
1985	107 150	3 179	1 535	1 458	185	103 971	95 871	16 031	1 249	78 591	7 811	289
1986	109 597	3 163	1 547	1 447	169	106 434	98 299	16 342	1 235	80 722	7 881	255
1987	112 440	3 208	1 632	1 423	153	109 232	100 771	16 800	1 208	82 763	8 201	260
1988	114 969	3 169	1 621	1 398	150	111 800	103 021	17 114	1 153	84 754	8 519	260
1989	117 341	3 199	1 665	1 403	131	114 142	105 259	17 469	1 101	86 689	8 605	279
1990	118 793	3 223	1 740	1 378	105	115 570	106 598	17 769	1 027	87 802	8 719	253
1991	117 718	3 269	1 729	1 423	118	114 449	105 373	17 934	1 010	86 429	8 851	226
1992	118 492	3 247	1 750	1 385	112	115 245	106 437	18 136	1 135	87 166	8 575	233
1993	120 259	3 115	1 689	1 320	106	117 144	107 966	18 579	1 126	88 261	8 959	218
1994	123 060	3 409	1 715	1 645	49	119 651	110 517	18 293	966	91 258	9 003	131
1995	124 900	3 440	1 814	1 580	45	121 460	112 448	18 362	963	93 123	8 902	110
1996	126 707	3 443	1 869	1 518	56	123 264	114 171	18 217	928	95 026	8 971	122
1997	129 558	3 399	1 890	1 457	51	126 159	116 983	18 131	915	97 937	9 056	120
1998	131 463	3 378	2 000	1 341	38	128 085	119 019	18 383	962	99 674	8 962	103
1999	133 488	3 281	1 944	1 297	40	130 207	121 323	18 903	933	101 487	8 790	95
2000	136 891	2 464	1 421	1 010	33	134 427	125 114	19 248	718	105 148	9 205	108
2001	136 933	2 299	1 283	988	28	134 635	125 407	19 335	694	105 378	9 121	107
2002	136 485	2 311	1 282	1 003	26	134 174	125 156	19 636	757	104 764	8 923	95
2003	137 736	2 275	1 299	951	25	135 461	126 015	19 634	764	105 616	9 344	101
2004	139 252	2 232	1 242	964	27	137 020	127 463	19 983	779	106 701	9 467	90
2005	141 730	2 197	1 212	955	30	139 532	129 931	20 357	812	108 761	9 509	93
2006	144 427	2 206	1 287	901	18	142 221	132 449	20 337	803	111 309	9 685	87
Men												
1985	59 891	2 535	1 230	1 244	60	57 356	52 111	7 757	170	44 184	5 207	38
1986	60 892	2 511	1 230	1 227	54	58 381	53 075	7 805	180	45 090	5 271	35
1987	62 107	2 543	1 290	1 194	58	59 564	54 102	8 013	180	45 909	5 423	39
1988	63 273	2 493	1 268	1 174	50	60 780	55 177	8 074	157	46 946	5 564	39
1989	64 315	2 513	1 302	1 167	44	61 802	56 202	8 116	156	47 930	5 562	38
1990	65 105	2 546	1 355	1 151	39	62 559	56 913	8 245	149	48 519	5 597	48
1991	64 223	2 589	1 359	1 185	45	61 634	55 899	8 300	143	47 456	5 700	35
1992	64 441	2 575	1 371	1 164	40	61 866	56 212	8 348	156	47 708	5 613	41
1993	65 349	2 478	1 323	1 117	39	62 871	56 926	8 435	146	48 345	5 894	50
1994	66 450	2 554	1 330	1 197	27	63 896	58 300	8 327	99	49 874	5 560	37
1995	67 377	2 559	1 395	1 138	26	64 818	59 332	8 267	96	50 969	5 461	25
1996	68 207	2 573	1 418	1 124	31	65 634	60 133	8 110	99	51 924	5 465	36
1997	69 685	2 552	1 439	1 084	29	67 133	61 595	8 015	81	53 499	5 506	31
1998	70 693	2 553	1 526	1 005	23	68 140	62 630	8 178	86	54 366	5 480	29
1999	71 446	2 432	1 450	962	20	69 014	63 624	8 278	74	55 272	5 366	25
2000	73 305	1 861	1 116	725	20	71 444	65 838	8 309	71	57 458	5 573	33
2001	73 196	1 708	990	703	15	71 488	65 930	8 342	63	57 524	5 527	31
2002	72 903	1 724	979	731	14	71 179	65 726	8 437	76	57 212	5 425	29
2003	73 332	1 695	991	694	11	71 636	65 871	8 368	59	57 444	5 736	30
2004	74 525	1 687	970	702	15	72 838	66 951	8 616	60	58 275	5 860	27
2005	75 973	1 654	949	688	17	74 319	68 345	8 760	67	59 518	5 944	30
2006	77 502	1 663	989	664	10	75 838	69 811	8 696	60	61 055	6 004	23
Women												
1985	47 259	644	305	214	125	46 615	43 761	8 274	1 078	34 409	2 603	251
1986	48 706	652	317	220	115	48 054	45 225	8 537	1 055	35 633	2 610	219
1987	50 334	666	342	229	95	49 668	46 669	8 788	1 029	36 852	2 778	221
1988	51 696	676	353	224	99	51 020	47 844	9 039	996	37 809	2 955	220
1989	53 028	687	363	236	87	52 341	49 057	9 353	945	38 759	3 043	240
1990	53 689	678	385	227	66	53 011	49 685	9 524	879	39 282	3 122	205
1991	53 495	680	369	237	73	52 815	49 474	9 635	867	38 972	3 150	191
1992	54 052	672	379	221	73	53 380	50 225	9 788	979	39 458	2 963	192
1993	54 910	637	367	204	67	54 273	51 040	10 144	979	39 916	3 065	168
1994	56 610	855	384	448	23	55 755	52 217	9 965	867	41 385	3 443	95
1995	57 523	881	419	442	20	56 642	53 115	10 095	867	42 153	3 440	86
1996	58 501	871	452	394	25	57 630	54 037	10 107	830	43 100	3 506	87
1997	59 873	847	451	373	23	59 026	55 388	10 116	834	44 438	3 550	89
1998	60 770	825	474	336	15	59 945	56 389	10 205	876	45 308	3 482	74
1999	62 042	849	494	335	20	61 193	57 699	10 625	859	46 215	3 424	70
2000	63 586	602	305	285	12	62 983	59 277	10 939	647	47 690	3 631	76
2001	63 737	591	293	284	13	63 147	59 477	10 993	630	47 853	3 594	75
2002	63 582	587	303	272	12	62 995	59 431	11 199	680	47 552	3 499	66
2003	64 404	580	309	257	14	63 824	60 144	11 267	705	48 172	3 609	72
2004	64 728	546	271	262	12	64 182	60 512	11 367	719	48 426	3 607	63
2005	65 757	544	263	267	13	65 213	61 586	11 598	745	49 243	3 565	63
2006	66 925	543	298	237	8	66 382	62 638	11 641	742	50 254	3 681	64

Note: See notes and definitions for information on historical comparabilty.

Table 1-16. Number of Employed Persons Age 25 Years and Over, by Educational Attainment, Sex, Race, and Hispanic Origin, 1996–2006

(Thousands of people.)

Race, Hispanic origin, sex, and year	Total	Less than a high school diploma	High school graduate, no college	Some college, no degree	Associate's degree	College graduate or higher	
						Total	Bachelor's degree only
All Races							
1996	108 070	11 317	36 300	20 590	9 404	31 459	20 742
1997	110 518	11 546	36 163	20 678	9 643	32 488	21 524
1998	111 855	11 673	35 976	20 626	9 850	33 730	22 260
1999	113 425	11 294	36 017	21 129	10 079	34 905	22 973
2000	116 473	11 692	36 452	21 601	10 707	36 020	23 706
2001	116 846	11 669	36 078	21 459	11 127	36 514	23 907
2002	116 802	11 535	35 779	20 928	11 166	37 395	24 570
2003	118 385	11 537	35 857	21 107	11 313	38 570	25 188
2004	119 622	11 408	35 944	21 284	11 693	39 293	25 484
2005	121 960	11 712	36 398	21 380	12 245	40 225	26 027
2006	124 386	11 892	36 702	21 630	12 514	41 649	26 960
Men							
1996	58 468	7 058	18 639	10 759	4 416	17 596	11 266
1997	59 736	7 210	19 124	10 876	4 517	18 010	11 587
1998	60 497	7 238	19 188	10 684	4 731	18 656	12 028
1999	61 032	6 921	19 125	10 941	4 838	19 208	12 343
2000	62 661	7 199	19 388	11 260	5 013	19 800	12 742
2001	62 824	7 188	19 274	11 076	5 226	20 060	12 872
2002	62 756	7 220	19 154	10 811	5 221	20 350	13 076
2003	63 349	7 290	19 200	10 858	5 231	20 770	13 354
2004	64 326	7 276	19 535	10 896	5 426	21 192	13 575
2005	65 772	7 487	20 127	10 993	5 739	21 427	13 687
2006	67 019	7 614	20 345	11 110	5 835	22 114	14 138
Women							
1996	49 602	4 259	16 661	9 831	4 988	13 863	9 475
1997	50 782	4 336	17 039	9 802	5 126	14 478	9 937
1998	51 359	4 435	16 788	9 943	5 119	15 074	10 231
1999	52 392	4 372	16 893	10 189	5 242	15 697	10 630
2000	53 812	4 493	17 064	10 341	5 694	16 220	10 964
2001	54 021	4 480	16 804	10 383	5 901	16 453	11 035
2002	54 046	4 315	16 624	10 117	5 945	17 045	11 493
2003	55 035	4 248	16 657	10 249	6 081	17 800	11 834
2004	55 296	4 132	16 409	10 387	6 267	18 101	11 908
2005	56 188	4 226	16 271	10 388	6 506	18 798	12 340
2006	57 367	4 278	16 357	10 520	6 678	19 535	12 822
White[1]							
1996	91 992	9 258	30 042	17 249	8 072	27 371	17 978
1997	93 687	9 414	30 552	17 302	8 271	28 148	18 801
1998	94 330	9 510	30 249	17 101	8 426	29 044	19 107
1999	95 316	9 235	30 211	17 388	8 556	29 925	19 668
2000	97 320	9 544	30 438	17 770	9 075	30 493	20 078
2001	97 560	9 550	30 126	17 671	9 393	30 821	20 136
2002	97 476	9 394	29 836	17 209	9 440	31 597	20 670
2003	98 120	9 437	29 645	17 227	9 476	32 335	21 103
2004	98 967	9 335	29 571	17 445	9 817	32 799	21 299
2005	100 613	9 579	29 911	17 515	10 256	33 352	21 550
2006	102 322	9 720	30 188	17 632	10 424	34 357	22 272
Black[1]							
1996	11 518	1 534	4 192	2 640	969	2 183	1 539
1997	11 882	1 578	4 409	2 681	984	2 230	1 591
1998	12 324	1 579	4 504	2 776	1 020	2 446	1 741
1999	12 771	1 488	4 631	2 924	1 108	2 621	1 814
2000	12 852	1 499	4 571	2 910	1 160	2 713	1 866
2001	12 797	1 492	4 492	2 871	1 216	2 727	1 921
2002	12 719	1 498	4 453	2 843	1 210	2 715	1 955
2003	12 706	1 376	4 465	2 780	1 199	2 887	2 056
2004	12 817	1 326	4 606	2 717	1 195	2 973	2 097
2005	13 177	1 369	4 742	2 720	1 288	3 057	2 106
2006	13 504	1 389	4 697	2 816	1 338	3 263	2 243
Hispanic[2]							
1996	9 368	3 450	2 746	1 453	568	1 151	813
1997	10 214	3 738	2 945	1 603	611	1 316	926
1998	10 615	3 889	3 018	1 622	660	1 427	1 007
1999	10 985	3 926	3 213	1 696	660	1 491	1 034
2000	12 406	4 468	3 658	1 828	756	1 696	1 198
2001	12 817	4 601	3 796	1 916	781	1 723	1 223
2002	13 294	4 744	3 921	1 900	823	1 906	1 370
2003	14 205	5 073	4 169	2 037	889	2 039	1 468
2004	14 661	5 135	4 330	2 137	931	2 127	1 538
2005	15 362	5 367	4 535	2 230	997	2 232	1 595
2006	16 225	5 620	4 801	2 282	1 095	2 428	1 698

[1]Beginning in 2003, persons who selected this race group only; persons who selected more than one race group are not included. Prior to 2003, persons who reported more than one race group were included in the group they identified as their main race.
[2]May be of any race.

Table 1-16. Number of Employed Persons Age 25 Years and Over, by Educational Attainment, Sex, Race, and Hispanic Origin, 1996–2006—Continued

(Thousands of people.)

Race, Hispanic origin, sex, and year	Total	Less than a high school diploma	High school graduate, no college	Some college, no degree	Associate's degree	College graduate or higher	
						Total	Bachelor's degree only
White Men[1]							
1996	50 533	5 920	15 995	9 197	3 861	15 559	9 965
1997	51 397	6 049	16 330	9 245	3 941	15 832	10 191
1998	51 842	6 123	16 308	9 009	4 118	16 284	10 490
1999	52 180	5 883	16 193	9 182	4 160	16 763	10 806
2000	53 243	6 085	16 373	9 435	4 320	17 030	11 029
2001	53 375	6 080	16 292	9 344	4 501	17 158	11 060
2002	53 242	6 072	16 148	9 102	4 497	17 423	11 217
2003	53 458	6 192	16 068	9 042	4 431	17 725	11 461
2004	54 133	6 188	16 297	9 125	4 613	17 910	11 555
2005	55 214	6 368	16 750	9 225	4 851	18 021	11 551
2006	56 145	6 448	17 018	9 244	4 952	18 483	11 881
White Women[1]							
1996	41 459	3 337	14 046	8 052	4 211	11 812	8 012
1997	42 290	3 365	14 222	8 058	4 330	12 316	8 410
1998	42 488	3 387	13 941	8 092	4 308	12 760	8 618
1999	43 135	3 352	14 018	8 207	4 396	13 162	8 862
2000	44 077	3 459	14 065	8 335	4 755	13 463	9 049
2001	44 184	3 469	13 834	8 327	4 891	13 663	9 075
2002	44 234	3 322	13 688	8 107	4 944	14 173	9 453
2003	44 662	3 245	13 576	8 185	5 045	14 610	9 643
2004	44 834	3 146	13 275	8 320	5 203	14 888	9 744
2005	45 399	3 211	13 162	8 290	5 405	15 331	9 999
2006	46 177	3 272	13 171	8 388	5 473	15 874	10 391
Black Men[1]							
1996	5 483	861	2 104	1 177	382	960	666
1997	5 658	868	2 181	1 241	385	983	710
1998	5 844	811	2 248	1 267	413	1 104	802
1999	6 001	741	2 339	1 313	469	1 140	789
2000	6 011	755	2 253	1 326	466	1 210	828
2001	5 924	762	2 232	1 258	486	1 186	834
2002	5 928	785	2 212	1 264	482	1 185	855
2003	5 860	693	2 190	1 256	492	1 230	890
2004	5 942	676	2 287	1 172	503	1 305	931
2005	6 153	697	2 417	1 171	558	1 310	938
2006	6 276	720	2 338	1 249	535	1 433	1 002
Black Women[1]							
1996	6 035	673	2 088	1 463	587	1 224	873
1997	6 225	710	2 229	1 439	600	1 247	882
1998	6 480	768	2 256	1 509	607	1 341	939
1999	6 770	746	2 292	1 612	639	1 481	1 025
2000	6 841	743	2 318	1 583	694	1 503	1 038
2001	6 873	730	2 260	1 612	729	1 541	1 087
2002	6 791	713	2 241	1 579	729	1 530	1 101
2003	6 846	683	2 275	1 524	707	1 657	1 166
2004	6 874	650	2 319	1 545	691	1 668	1 166
2005	7 024	672	2 325	1 549	730	1 748	1 169
2006	7 228	669	2 359	1 567	803	1 830	1 241
Hispanic Men[2]							
1996	5 640	2 320	1 588	790	271	671	456
1997	6 165	2 502	1 714	899	302	747	502
1998	6 397	2 594	1 764	913	336	790	547
1999	6 441	2 554	1 839	917	334	797	540
2000	7 373	2 937	2 128	995	397	916	634
2001	7 628	3 041	2 174	1 082	386	945	669
2002	7 865	3 141	2 244	1 029	415	1 035	732
2003	8 578	3 424	2 461	1 105	451	1 137	806
2004	8 872	3 508	2 583	1 158	468	1 155	837
2005	9 361	3 639	2 775	1 251	503	1 193	847
2006	9 856	3 823	2 932	1 260	547	1 293	891
Hispanic Women[2]							
1996	3 729	1 131	1 159	663	297	480	357
1997	4 049	1 236	1 231	704	309	569	425
1998	4 219	1 295	1 254	708	325	637	459
1999	4 544	1 372	1 373	778	327	694	494
2000	5 033	1 531	1 529	833	359	780	564
2001	5 190	1 560	1 622	834	395	778	553
2002	5 429	1 604	1 676	871	408	871	638
2003	5 627	1 649	1 708	932	438	901	661
2004	5 789	1 628	1 746	980	463	972	701
2005	6 000	1 728	1 759	979	495	1 039	748
2006	6 370	1 797	1 868	1 021	548	1 135	807

[1]Beginning in 2003, persons who selected this race group only; persons who selected more than one race group are not included. Prior to 2003, persons who reported more than one race group were included in the group they identified as their main race.
[2]May be of any race.

Table 1-17. Multiple Jobholders and Multiple Jobholding Rates, by Selected Characteristics, May of Selected Years, 1970–2007

(Thousands of people, percent, not seasonally adjusted.)

Year	Total employed	Multiple jobholders				Multiple jobholding rate[1]						
		Total	Men	Women		Total	Men	Women	White	Black[2]	Asian	Hispanic[3]
				Number	Percent of all multiple jobholders							
1970	78 358	4 048	3 412	636	15.7	5.2	7.0	2.2	5.3	4.4	. . .	. . .
1971	78 708	4 035	3 270	765	19.0	5.1	6.7	2.6	5.3	3.8	. . .	. . .
1972	81 224	3 770	3 035	735	19.5	4.6	6.0	2.4	4.8	3.7	. . .	. . .
1973	83 758	4 262	3 393	869	20.4	5.1	6.6	2.7	5.1	4.7	. . .	. . .
1974	85 786	3 889	3 022	867	22.3	4.5	5.8	2.6	4.6	3.8	. . .	. . .
1975	84 146	3 918	2 962	956	24.4	4.7	5.8	2.9	4.8	3.7	. . .	. . .
1976	87 278	3 948	3 037	911	23.1	4.5	5.8	2.6	4.7	2.8	. . .	. . .
1977	90 482	4 558	3 317	1 241	27.2	5.0	6.2	3.4	5.3	2.6	. . .	. . .
1978	93 904	4 493	3 212	1 281	28.5	4.8	5.8	3.3	5.0	3.1	. . .	. . .
1979	96 327	4 724	3 317	1 407	29.8	4.9	5.9	3.5	5.1	3.0	. . .	. . .
1980	96 809	4 759	3 210	1 549	32.5	4.9	5.8	3.8	5.1	3.2	. . .	. . .
1985	106 878	5 730	3 537	2 192	38.3	5.4	5.9	4.7	5.7	3.2	. . .	. . .
1989	117 084	7 225	4 115	3 109	43.0	6.2	6.4	5.9	6.5	4.3	. . .	. . .
1991	116 626	7 183	4 054	3 129	43.6	6.2	6.4	5.9	6.4	4.9	. . .	. . .
1994	122 946	7 316	3 973	3 343	45.7	6.0	6.0	5.9	6.1	4.9	. . .	3.8
1995	124 554	7 952	4 225	3 727	46.9	6.4	6.3	6.5	6.6	5.2	. . .	3.6
1996	126 391	7 846	4 352	3 494	44.5	6.2	6.4	6.0	6.4	5.1	. . .	4.0
1997	129 565	8 197	4 398	3 800	46.4	6.3	6.3	6.4	6.5	5.7	. . .	4.1
1998	131 476	8 126	4 438	3 688	45.4	6.2	6.3	6.1	6.3	5.5	. . .	4.4
1999	133 411	7 895	4 117	3 778	47.9	5.9	5.8	6.1	6.0	5.5	. . .	3.6
2000	136 685	7 751	4 084	3 667	47.3	5.7	5.6	5.8	5.9	4.9	. . .	3.2
2001	137 121	7 540	3 914	3 626	48.1	5.5	5.3	5.7	5.6	5.3	. . .	3.4
2002	136 559	7 247	3 736	3 511	48.4	5.3	5.1	5.5	5.5	4.7	. . .	3.8
2003	137 567	7 338	3 841	3 498	47.7	5.3	5.3	5.4	5.5	4.3	. . .	3.4
2004	138 867	7 258	3 653	3 605	49.7	5.2	4.9	5.6	5.3	5.1	. . .	3.4
2005	141 591	7 348	3 741	3 607	49.1	5.2	4.9	5.5	5.4	4.4	. . .	2.8
2006	144 041	7 641	3 863	3 778	49.4	5.3	5.0	5.7	5.3	5.4	. . .	3.1
2007	145 864	7 693	3 835	3 858	50.1	5.3	4.9	5.7	5.5	4.4	. . .	3.0

Note: Data prior to 1985 reflect 1970 census–based population controls; years 1985–1991 reflect 1980 census–based controls; years 1994–1999 reflect 1990 census–based controls adjusted for the estimated undercount; and data for years 2000–2002 have been revised to incorporate population controls from the 2000 census. Prior to 1994, data on multiple jobholders were collected only through special periodic supplements to the Current Population Survey (CPS) in May of various years; these supplemental surveys were not conducted in 1981–1984, 1986–1988, 1990, or 1992–1993. Beginning in 1994, data reflect the introduction of a major redesign of the CPS, including the the collection of monthly data on multiple jobholders.

[1]Multiple jobholders as a percent of all employed persons in specified group.
[2]Data for years prior to 1977 refer to the Black-and-Other population group.
[3]May be of any race.
. . . = Not available.

Table 1-18. Multiple Jobholders, by Sex, Age, Marital Status, Race, Hispanic Origin, and Job Status, 2003–2006

(Thousands of people, percent.)

Characteristic	Both sexes Number 2003	2004	Both sexes Rate[1] 2003	2004	Men Number 2003	2004	Men Rate[1] 2003	2004	Women Number 2003	2004	Women Rate[1] 2003	2004
Age												
Total, 16 years and over[2]	7 315	7 473	5.3	5.4	3 716	3 835	5.1	5.1	3 599	3 638	5.6	5.6
16 to 19 years	280	274	4.7	4.6	107	107	3.7	3.6	173	167	5.7	5.7
20 to 24 years	778	795	5.8	5.8	350	377	5.0	5.2	428	419	6.7	6.5
25 to 34 years	. . .	1 608	. . .	5.3	. . .	853	. . .	5.1	696	755	5.1	5.6
35 to 44 years	. . .	1 898	. . .	5.5	. . .	1 012	. . .	5.4	920	886	5.7	5.6
45 to 54 years	. . .	1 855	. . .	5.7	. . .	935	. . .	5.5	908	920	5.9	5.9
55 to 64 years	837	869	5.0	5.0	430	451	4.9	4.9	407	417	5.2	5.1
65 years and over	154	173	3.3	3.6	87	100	3.4	3.7	67	74	3.3	3.4
Marital Status												
Single	1 978	2 044	5.4	5.5	907	964	4.6	4.7	1 070	1 080	6.4	6.4
Married, spouse present	4 067	4 125	5.1	5.2	2 398	2 408	5.4	5.3	1 669	1 718	4.8	5.0
Widowed, divorced, or separated	1 270	1 303	5.8	5.9	410	463	4.6	5.1	860	840	6.6	6.4
Race and Hispanic Origin												
White[3]	6 273	6 357	5.5	5.5	3 190	3 266	5.2	5.2	3 083	3 091	5.9	5.9
Black[3]	645	705	4.4	4.7	328	360	4.8	5.2	317	345	4.0	4.3
Hispanic[4]	554	612	3.2	3.4	325	363	3.1	3.4	229	248	3.3	3.5
Full- or Part-time Status												
Primary job full time, secondary job part time	3 825	3 908	. . .	. . .	2 164	2 210	. . .	. . .	1 661	1 697	. . .	. . .
Primary and secondary jobs, both part time	1 651	1 678	. . .	. . .	510	540	. . .	. . .	1 141	1 138	. . .	. . .
Primary and secondary jobs, both full time	273	286	. . .	. . .	187	187	. . .	. . .	86	100	. . .	. . .
Hours vary on primary or secondary job	1 523	1 564	. . .	. . .	831	879	. . .	. . .	692	685	. . .	. . .

Characteristic	Both sexes Number 2005	2006	Both sexes Rate[1] 2005	2006	Men Number 2005	2006	Men Rate[1] 2005	2006	Women Number 2005	2006	Women Rate[1] 2005	2006
Age												
Total, 16 years and over[2]	7 546	7 576	5.3	5.2	3 855	3 822	5.1	4.9	3 691	3 753	5.6	5.6
16 to 19 years	298	270	5.0	4.4	118	103	4.0	3.4	180	167	5.9	5.4
20 to 24 years	798	774	5.8	5.6	373	341	5.1	4.6	425	432	6.5	6.7
25 to 34 years	1 582	1 577	5.2	5.1	827	850	4.9	5.0	755	727	5.5	5.2
35 to 44 years	1 900	1 856	5.5	5.4	1 016	969	5.4	5.2	884	887	5.6	5.6
45 to 54 years	1 879	1 934	5.7	5.7	939	940	5.4	5.2	940	994	6.0	6.2
55 to 64 years	900	988	4.9	5.1	473	517	4.9	5.1	426	471	4.9	5.1
65 years and over	189	176	3.7	3.3	109	101	3.8	3.4	80	75	3.6	3.2
Marital Status												
Single	2 113	2 131	5.5	5.3	987	962	4.7	4.4	1 125	1 169	6.4	6.5
Married, spouse present	4 109	4 136	5.1	5.1	2 416	2 420	5.3	5.3	1 693	1 716	4.9	4.9
Widowed, divorced, or separated	1 324	1 308	5.8	5.6	452	440	4.8	4.4	872	868	6.5	6.3
Race and Hispanic Origin												
White[3]	6 342	6 321	5.4	5.3	3 268	3 199	5.1	4.9	3 074	3 122	5.8	5.8
Black[3]	763	818	5.0	5.2	363	404	5.1	5.5	400	415	4.9	4.9
Hispanic[4]	582	598	3.1	3.0	333	337	2.9	2.8	248	261	3.4	3.4
Full- or Part-time Status												
Primary job full time, secondary job part time	3 942	3 981	. . .	. . .	2 219	2 233	. . .	. . .	1 724	1 748	. . .	. . .
Primary and secondary jobs, both part time	1 708	1 676	. . .	. . .	570	508	. . .	. . .	1 138	1 168	. . .	. . .
Primary and secondary jobs, both full time	294	310	. . .	. . .	188	208	. . .	. . .	105	102	. . .	. . .
Hours vary on primary or secondary job	1 558	1 564	. . .	. . .	859	849	. . .	. . .	698	715	. . .	. . .

Note: Estimates for the above race groups (White or Black) do not sum to totals because data are not presented for all races. Beginning in January 2003, data reflect the revised population controls used in the household survey.

[1] Multiple jobholders as a percent of all employed persons in specified group.
[2] Includes a small number of persons who work part time at their primary job and full time at their secondary job(s), not shown separately.
[3] Beginning in 2003, persons who selected this race group only; persons who selected more than one race group are not included. Prior to 2003, persons who reported more than one race group were included in the group they identified as their main race.
[4] May be of any race.
. . . = Not available.

Table 1-19. Multiple Jobholders, by Sex and Industry of Principal Secondary Job, Annual Averages, 2004–2006

(Thousands of people.)

Year and industry of secondary job	Both sexes	Men	Women
2004			
All Nonagricultural Industries, Wage and Salary Workers	5 149	2 444	2 705
Mining	9	6	4
Construction	246	196	49
Manufacturing	169	102	67
Durable goods	92	60	32
Nondurable goods	77	42	35
Wholesale and retail trade	1 137	488	648
Wholesale trade	89	48	40
Retail trade	1 048	440	608
Transportation and utilities	185	137	49
Transportation and warehousing	172	127	45
Utilities	13	10	3
Information	197	123	74
Financial activities	371	224	147
Professional and business services	850	483	366
Education and health services	1 455	511	945
Leisure and hospitality	1 114	560	554
Other services	533	235	298
Other services, except private households	455	228	226
Other servces, private households	79	7	71
Public administration	196	133	63
2005			
All Nonagricultural Industries, Wage and Salary Workers	5 209	2 458	2 751
Mining	7	3	4
Construction	239	199	40
Manufacturing	195	122	73
Durable goods	124	86	38
Nondurable goods	72	36	36
Wholesale and retail trade	1 126	464	661
Wholesale trade	112	78	34
Retail trade	1 014	387	627
Transportation and utilities	186	138	48
Transportation and warehousing	172	131	41
Utilities	14	7	7
Information	175	113	62
Financial activities	369	225	144
Professional and business services	836	499	337
Education and health services	1 527	535	992
Leisure and hospitality	1 120	547	573
Other services	536	245	291
Other services, except private households	453	235	218
Other servces, private households	84	10	73
Public administration	215	130	85
2006			
All Nonagricultural Industries, Wage and Salary Workers	5 219	2 453	2 766
Mining	3	3	0
Construction	275	224	50
Manufacturing	175	111	64
Durable goods	106	76	30
Nondurable goods	68	34	34
Wholesale and retail trade	1 105	472	633
Wholesale trade	89	54	35
Retail trade	1 015	418	598
Transportation and utilities	178	138	41
Transportation and warehousing	171	131	40
Utilities	8	7	1
Information	195	115	80
Financial activities	416	245	171
Professional and business services	831	484	347
Education and health services	1 550	530	1 020
Leisure and hospitality	1 076	549	527
Other services	525	219	306
Other services, except private households	438	209	229
Other servces, private households	86	10	77
Public administration	214	138	77

Table 1-20. Employment and Unemployment in Families, by Race and Hispanic Origin, Annual Averages, 1996–2006

(Thousands of people, percent.)

Characteristic	1996	1997	1998	1999	2000	2001	2002	2003	2004	2005	2006
ALL RACES											
Total Families	69 203	69 714	70 218	71 250	71 680	73 306	74 169	75 301	75 872	76 443	77 017
With employed member(s)	56 342	57 289	57 986	59 185	59 626	60 707	61 121	61 761	62 424	62 933	63 492
As percent of total families	81.4	82.2	82.6	83.1	83.2	82.8	82.4	82.0	82.3	82.3	82.4
Some usually work full time[1]	52 249	53 226	53 945	55 123	55 683	56 519	56 742	57 229	57 813	58 276	58 918
With no employed member	12 860	12 425	12 232	12 065	12 054	12 600	13 048	13 540	13 447	13 509	13 525
As percent of total families	18.6	17.8	17.4	16.9	16.8	17.2	17.6	18.0	17.7	17.7	17.6
With unemployed member(s)	5 270	4 913	4 503	4 260	4 110	4 847	5 809	6 079	5 593	5 318	4 913
As percent of total families	7.6	7.0	6.4	6.0	5.7	6.6	7.8	8.1	7.4	7.0	6.4
Some member(s) employed	3 678	3 445	3 177	3 091	2 973	3 494	4 126	4 285	3 915	3 717	3 419
As percent of families with unemployed member(s)	69.8	70.1	70.6	72.6	72.3	72.1	71.0	70.5	70.0	69.9	69.6
Some usually work full time[1]	3 265	3 070	2 830	2 771	2 675	3 122	3 668	3 790	3 494	3 310	3 049
As percent of families with unemployed member(s)	62.0	62.5	62.8	65.0	65.1	64.4	63.1	62.3	62.5	62.2	62.1
WHITE[2]											
Total Families	58 315	58 514	58 930	59 661	59 918	60 921	61 494	61 995	62 250	62 567	62 977
With employed member(s)	47 882	48 378	48 850	49 632	49 877	50 505	50 785	51 002	51 350	51 645	52 054
As percent of total families	82.1	82.7	82.9	83.2	83.2	83.0	82.6	82.3	82.5	82.5	82.7
Some usually work full time[1]	44 522	45 069	45 567	46 333	46 639	47 060	47 193	47 356	47 620	47 883	48 395
With no employed member	10 434	10 135	10 080	10 029	10 042	10 416	10 709	10 993	10 900	10 922	10 923
As percent of total families	17.9	17.3	17.1	16.8	16.8	17.0	17.4	17.7	17.5	17.5	17.3
With unemployed member(s)	3 896	3 566	3 299	3 134	3 010	3 553	4 275	4 411	4 078	3 801	3 556
As percent of total families	6.7	6.1	5.6	5.3	5.0	5.8	7.0	7.1	6.6	6.1	5.6
Some member(s) employed	2 875	2 632	2 463	2 374	2 276	2 661	3 164	3 245	3 000	2 782	2 582
As percent of families with unemployed member(s)	73.8	73.8	74.7	75.8	75.6	74.9	74.0	73.6	73.6	73.2	72.6
Some usually work full time[1]	2 557	2 353	2 204	2 132	2 052	2 379	2 808	2 873	2 677	2 477	2 306
As percent of families with unemployed member(s)	65.6	66.0	66.8	68.0	68.2	67.0	65.7	65.1	65.7	65.2	64.8
BLACK[2]											
Total Families	8 149	8 308	8 317	8 498	8 600	8 674	8 845	8 869	8 860	8 952	9 058
With employed member(s)	6 137	6 409	6 554	6 847	6 964	6 933	6 987	6 906	6 920	6 986	7 078
As percent of total families	75.3	77.1	78.8	80.6	81.0	80.0	79.0	77.9	78.1	78.0	78.1
Some usually work full time[1]	5 563	5 810	5 953	6 249	6 401	6 373	6 390	6 270	6 292	6 353	6 437
With no employed member	2 012	1 899	1 763	1 652	1 636	1 742	1 858	1 963	1 940	1 966	1 980
As percent of total families	24.7	22.9	21.2	19.4	19.0	20.1	21.0	22.1	21.9	22.0	21.9
With unemployed member(s)	1 121	1 104	984	905	881	990	1 162	1 213	1 127	1 140	1 036
As percent of total families	13.8	13.3	11.8	10.6	10.2	11.4	13.1	13.7	12.7	12.7	11.4
Some member(s) employed	627	631	555	551	535	596	689	695	625	657	596
As percent of families with unemployed member(s)	55.9	57.2	56.4	60.9	60.8	60.2	59.3	57.3	55.5	57.7	57.6
Some usually work full time[1]	553	553	485	486	476	533	611	612	556	583	526
As percent of families with unemployed member(s)	49.3	50.1	49.3	53.7	54.1	53.8	52.6	50.5	49.3	51.1	50.8
HISPANIC[3]											
Total Families	6 465	6 779	7 025	7 403	7 581	8 140	8 650	9 185	9 305	9 603	9 905
With employed member(s)	5 312	5 701	5 947	6 405	6 633	7 100	7 485	7 907	8 071	8 312	8 641
As percent of total families	82.2	84.1	84.7	86.5	87.5	87.2	86.5	86.1	86.7	86.6	87.2
Some usually work full time[1]	4 917	5 285	5 545	6 017	6 255	6 692	6 989	7 383	7 566	7 786	8 129
With no employed member	1 153	1 078	1 078	998	947	1 040	1 165	1 277	1 235	1 291	1 264
As percent of total families	17.8	15.9	15.3	13.5	12.5	12.8	13.5	13.9	13.3	13.4	12.8
With unemployed member(s)	841	789	744	715	679	809	965	1 020	950	860	793
As percent of total families	13.0	11.6	10.6	9.7	9.0	9.9	11.2	11.1	10.2	9.0	8.0
Some member(s) employed	563	532	522	518	493	592	686	715	664	606	544
As percent of families with unemployed member(s)	66.9	67.4	70.2	72.4	72.7	73.2	71.1	70.1	69.9	70.5	68.6
Some usually work full time[1]	497	473	467	467	446	537	615	640	594	544	491
As percent of families with unemployed member(s)	59.1	59.9	62.8	65.3	65.8	66.4	63.7	62.7	62.5	63.2	61.9

Note: The race or ethnicity of the family is determined by the race of the householder. Estimates for the above race groups (White or Black) do not sum to totals because data are not presented for all races. Detail may not sum to total due to rounding. Data for 2003 reflect the revised population controls used in the Current Population Survey (CPS).

[1]Usually work 35 hours or more a week at all jobs.
[2]Beginning in 2003, families where the householder selected this race group only; families where the householder selected more than one race group are excluded. Prior to 2003, families where the householder selected more than one race group were included in the group that the householder identified as the main race.
[3]May be of any race.

Table 1-21. Families, by Presence and Relationship of Employed Members and Family Type, Annual Averages, 2000–2006

(Thousands of people, percent.)

Characteristic	Number of families							Percent distribution						
	2000	2001	2002	2003	2004	2005	2006	2000	2001	2002	2003	2004	2005	2006
MARRIED-COUPLE FAMILIES														
Total	54 704	55 749	56 280	57 074	57 188	57 167	57 509	100.0	100.0	100.0	100.0	100.0	100.0	100.0
Member(s) employed, total	45 967	46 680	46 976	47 535	47 767	47 895	48 196	84.0	83.7	83.5	83.3	83.5	83.8	83.8
Husband only	10 500	10 833	11 174	11 403	11 712	11 562	11 399	19.2	19.4	19.9	20.0	20.5	20.2	19.8
Wife only	2 946	3 257	3 613	3 863	3 843	3 715	3 754	5.4	5.8	6.4	6.8	6.7	6.5	6.5
Husband and wife	29 128	29 241	28 873	29 077	28 991	29 330	29 799	53.2	52.5	51.3	50.9	50.7	51.3	51.8
Other employment combinations	3 394	3 350	3 317	3 193	3 222	3 288	3 244	6.2	6.0	5.9	5.6	5.6	5.8	5.6
No member(s) employed	8 737	9 068	9 303	9 539	9 420	9 272	9 313	16.0	16.3	16.5	16.7	16.5	16.2	16.2
FAMILIES MAINTAINED BY WOMEN[1]														
Total	12 775	13 037	13 215	13 450	13 614	14 035	14 208	100.0	100.0	100.0	100.0	100.0	100.0	100.0
Member(s) employed, total	10 026	10 131	10 169	10 187	10 358	10 609	10 796	78.5	77.7	77.0	75.7	76.1	75.6	76.0
Householder only	5 581	5 667	5 944	5 987	6 021	6 052	6 103	43.7	43.5	45.0	44.5	44.2	43.1	43.0
Householder and other member(s)	2 806	2 778	2 559	2 539	2 701	2 830	2 955	22.0	21.3	19.4	18.9	19.8	20.2	20.8
Other member(s), not householder	1 639	1 686	1 666	1 660	1 636	1 727	1 738	12.8	12.9	12.6	12.3	12.0	12.3	12.2
No member(s) employed	2 749	2 906	3 047	3 263	3 255	3 426	3 412	21.5	22.3	23.1	24.3	23.9	24.4	24.0
FAMILIES MAINTAINED BY MEN[1]														
Total	4 200	4 521	4 674	4 777	5 071	5 242	5 300	100.0	100.0	100.0	100.0	100.0	100.0	100.0
Member(s) employed, total	3 632	3 895	3 976	4 039	4 299	4 430	4 500	86.5	86.2	85.1	84.6	84.8	84.5	84.9
Householder only	1 761	1 875	1 939	1 954	2 060	2 093	2 089	41.9	41.5	41.5	40.9	40.6	39.9	39.4
Householder and other member(s)	1 358	1 450	1 440	1 427	1 557	1 639	1 715	32.3	32.1	30.8	29.9	30.7	31.3	32.4
Other member(s), not householder	514	570	598	658	682	698	696	12.2	12.6	12.8	13.8	13.5	13.3	13.1
No member(s) employed	567	625	698	739	772	812	800	13.5	13.8	14.9	15.5	15.2	15.5	15.1

Note: Detail may not sum to total due to rounding.

[1]No spouse present.

Table 1-22. Unemployment in Families, by Presence and Relationship of Employed Members and Family Type, Annual Averages, 2000–2006

(Thousands of people, percent.)

Characteristic	Number							Percent distribution						
	2000	2001	2002	2003	2004	2005	2006	2000	2001	2002	2003	2004	2005	2006
MARRIED-COUPLE FAMILIES														
With Unemployed Member(s), Total	2 584	3 081	3 772	3 857	3 521	3 243	2 968	100.0	100.0	100.0	100.0	100.0	100.0	100.0
No member employed	411	531	676	713	615	580	526	17.2	17.9	18.5	17.5	17.9	17.9	17.7
Some member(s) employed	2 174	2 550	3 096	3 144	2 906	2 664	2 442	82.8	82.1	81.5	82.5	82.1	82.1	82.3
Husband unemployed	836	1 160	1 523	1 600	1 333	1 190	1 061	37.7	40.4	41.5	37.9	36.7	36.7	35.7
Wife employed	531	736	993	1 023	850	753	679	23.9	26.3	26.5	24.2	23.2	23.2	22.9
Wife unemployed	789	918	1 117	1 129	1 041	1 004	898	29.8	29.6	29.3	29.6	31.0	31.0	30.3
Husband employed	694	809	969	991	913	873	772	26.3	25.7	25.7	25.9	26.9	26.9	26.0
Other family member unemployed	959	1 003	1 133	1 129	1 147	1 049	1 010	32.6	30.0	29.3	32.6	32.4	32.4	34.0
FAMILIES MAINTAINED BY WOMEN[1]														
With Unemployed Member(s), Total	1 194	1 324	1 504	1 612	1 521	1 539	1 429	100.0	100.0	100.0	100.0	100.0	100.0	100.0
No member employed	587	643	787	842	829	797	753	48.6	52.3	52.2	54.5	51.8	51.8	52.7
Some member(s) employed	607	681	717	770	692	743	675	51.4	47.7	47.8	45.5	48.2	48.2	47.3
Householder unemployed	522	593	737	791	758	746	688	44.8	49.0	49.1	49.8	48.5	48.5	48.2
Other member(s) employed	102	129	147	162	146	161	132	9.7	9.8	10.0	9.6	10.5	10.5	9.3
Other member(s) unemployed	672	731	767	821	764	793	740	55.2	51.0	50.9	50.2	51.5	51.5	51.8
FAMILIES MAINTAINED BY MEN[1]														
With Unemployed Member(s), Total	331	442	533	610	551	536	516	100.0	100.0	100.0	100.0	100.0	100.0	100.0
No member employed	139	178	220	239	234	225	215	40.3	41.3	39.2	42.5	42.1	42.1	41.7
Some member(s) employed	192	264	313	371	316	310	301	59.7	58.7	60.8	57.5	57.9	57.9	58.3
Householder unemployed	173	234	303	340	296	301	284	52.9	56.8	55.7	53.7	56.1	56.1	55.0
Other member(s) employed	67	96	129	158	117	122	118	21.7	24.2	25.9	21.3	22.8	22.8	22.8
Other member(s) unemployed	158	208	230	270	255	235	232	47.1	43.2	44.3	46.3	43.9	43.9	45.0

Note: Detail may not sum to total due to rounding.

[1]No spouse present.

Table 1-23. Employment Status of the Population, by Sex, Marital Status, and Presence and Age of Own Children Under 18 Years, Annual Averages, 2000–2006

(Thousands of people, percent.)

Characteristic	2000			2001			2002			2003		
	Both sexes	Men	Women	Both sexes	Men	Women	Both sexes	Men	Women	Both sexes	Men	Women
With Own Children Under 18 Years, Total												
Civilian noninstitutional population	63 267	27 673	35 595	64 100	28 076	36 024	64 399	28 137	36 263	64 932	28 402	36 530
Civilian labor force	51 944	26 202	25 742	52 489	26 551	25 938	52 566	26 529	26 036	52 727	26 739	25 988
Participation rate	82.1	94.7	72.3	81.9	94.6	72.0	81.6	94.3	71.8	81.2	94.1	71.1
Employed	50 259	25 622	24 637	50 455	25 750	24 704	50 022	25 474	24 549	50 103	25 638	24 466
Employment-population ratio	79.4	92.6	69.2	78.7	91.7	68.6	77.7	90.5	67.7	77.2	90.3	67.0
Full-time workers[1]	43 365	24 922	18 443	43 424	24 964	18 460	42 884	24 644	18 240	42 880	24 762	18 118
Part-time workers[2]	6 894	699	6 195	7 031	787	6 244	7 138	829	6 308	7 223	876	6 347
Unemployed	1 685	581	1 104	2 034	801	1 233	2 543	1 056	1 488	2 624	1 101	1 523
Unemployment rate	3.2	2.2	4.3	3.9	3.0	4.8	4.8	4.0	5.7	5.0	4.1	5.9
Married, Spouse Present												
Civilian noninstitutional population	51 415	25 540	25 874	51 981	25 796	26 185	51 947	25 781	26 166	52 476	26 049	26 427
Civilian labor force	42 361	24 290	18 072	42 712	24 512	18 201	42 492	24 425	18 067	42 776	24 638	18 138
Participation rate	82.4	95.1	69.8	82.2	95.0	69.5	81.8	94.7	69.0	81.5	94.6	68.6
Employed	41 357	23 816	17 541	41 431	23 849	17 581	40 867	23 533	17 334	41 128	23 712	17 416
Employment-population ratio	80.4	93.2	67.8	79.7	92.5	67.1	78.7	91.3	66.2	78.4	91.0	65.9
Full-time workers[1]	35 793	23 212	12 581	35 772	23 169	12 603	35 180	22 825	12 356	35 315	22 954	12 360
Part-time workers[2]	5 564	604	4 960	5 659	680	4 979	5 687	708	4 979	5 813	757	5 056
Unemployed	1 004	474	531	1 282	662	619	1 625	893	733	1 648	926	722
Unemployment rate	2.4	2.0	2.9	3.0	2.7	3.4	3.8	3.7	4.1	3.9	3.8	4.0
Other Marital Status[3]												
Civilian noninstitutional population	11 853	2 132	9 720	12 119	2 280	9 839	12 452	2 355	10 096	12 455	2 354	10 102
Civilian labor force	9 583	1 913	7 670	9 777	2 039	7 737	10 073	2 103	7 970	9 950	2 100	7 850
Participation rate	80.8	89.7	78.9	80.7	89.4	78.6	80.9	89.3	78.9	79.9	89.2	77.7
Employed	8 902	1 806	7 096	9 024	1 902	7 123	9 155	1 941	7 215	8 975	1 926	7 050
Employment-population ratio	75.1	84.7	73.0	74.5	83.4	72.4	73.5	82.4	71.5	72.1	81.8	69.8
Full-time workers[1]	7 572	1 710	5 862	7 652	1 795	5 857	7 704	1 820	5 885	7 566	1 807	5 759
Part-time workers[2]	1 330	96	1 234	1 372	107	1 265	1 451	122	1 329	1 411	118	1 291
Unemployed	681	107	574	752	138	614	918	163	755	976	175	800
Unemployment rate	7.1	5.6	7.5	7.7	6.8	7.9	9.1	7.8	9.5	9.8	8.3	10.2
With Own Children 6 to 17 Years, None Younger												
Civilian noninstitutional population	34 737	15 165	19 572	35 523	15 486	20 038	35 829	15 580	20 250	35 943	15 653	20 290
Civilian labor force	29 576	14 178	15 398	30 182	14 489	15 693	30 371	14 541	15 830	30 362	14 572	15 790
Participation rate	85.1	93.5	78.7	85.0	93.6	78.3	84.8	93.3	78.2	84.5	93.1	77.8
Employed	28 744	13 877	14 868	29 174	14 096	15 078	29 122	14 023	15 099	29 040	14 008	15 032
Employment-population ratio	82.7	91.5	76.0	82.1	91.0	75.2	81.3	90.0	74.6	80.8	89.5	74.1
Full-time workers[1]	25 042	13 513	11 529	25 382	13 689	11 693	25 225	13 586	11 638	25 116	13 558	11 557
Part-time workers[2]	3 703	364	3 339	3 792	407	3 385	3 898	437	3 461	3 925	450	3 475
Unemployed	832	302	530	1 008	393	615	1 249	518	731	1 322	564	758
Unemployment rate	2.8	2.1	3.4	3.3	2.7	3.9	4.1	3.6	4.6	4.4	3.9	4.8
With Own Children Under 6 Years												
Civilian noninstitutional population	28 530	12 508	16 022	28 577	12 590	15 986	28 570	12 557	16 013	28 988	12 749	16 240
Civilian labor force	22 368	12 024	10 344	22 307	12 062	10 245	22 194	11 988	10 206	22 365	12 167	10 198
Participation rate	78.4	96.1	64.6	78.1	95.8	64.1	77.7	95.5	63.7	77.2	95.4	62.8
Employed	21 515	11 745	9 770	21 280	11 654	9 626	20 900	11 450	9 450	21 063	11 630	9 433
Employment-population ratio	75.4	93.9	61.0	74.5	92.6	60.2	73.2	91.2	59.0	72.7	91.2	58.1
Full-time workers[1]	18 323	11 410	6 914	18 041	11 274	6 767	17 660	11 058	6 602	17 764	11 203	6 561
Part-time workers[2]	3 191	335	2 856	3 239	380	2 859	3 240	392	2 848	3 299	426	2 872
Unemployed	853	279	574	1 026	408	619	1 294	538	757	1 302	538	765
Unemployment rate	3.8	2.3	5.6	4.6	3.4	6.0	5.8	4.5	7.4	5.8	4.4	7.5
With No Own Children Under 18 Years												
Civilian noninstitutional population	145 199	71 825	73 374	149 643	73 857	75 786	151 715	74 993	76 722	154 714	76 510	78 204
Civilian labor force	88 014	48 140	39 874	90 171	49 249	40 922	90 971	49 644	41 327	92 319	50 036	42 284
Participation rate	60.6	67.0	54.3	60.3	66.7	54.0	60.0	66.2	53.9	59.7	65.4	54.1
Employed	84 058	45 781	38 278	85 421	46 371	39 050	85 187	46 154	39 034	86 233	46 294	39 939
Employment-population ratio	57.9	63.7	52.2	57.1	62.8	51.5	56.1	61.5	50.9	55.7	60.5	51.1
Full-time workers[1]	68 046	39 136	28 910	69 074	39 596	29 478	68 574	39 319	29 254	69 073	39 245	29 827
Part-time workers[2]	16 012	6 645	9 367	16 347	6 776	9 572	16 614	6 834	9 779	17 160	7 049	10 111
Unemployed	3 956	2 359	1 596	4 750	2 878	1 872	5 784	3 491	2 293	6 087	3 741	2 345
Unemployment rate	4.5	4.9	4.0	5.3	5.8	4.6	6.4	7.0	5.5	6.6	7.5	5.5

Note: Own children include sons, daughters, stepchildren, and adopted children. Not included are nieces, nephews, grandchildren, and other related and unrelated children. Detail may not sum to total due to rounding.

[1] Usually work 35 hours or more a week at all jobs.
[2] Usually work less than 35 hours a week at all jobs.
[3] Includes never-married, divorced, separated, and widowed persons.

Table 1-23. Employment Status of the Population, by Sex, Marital Status, and Presence and Age of Own Children Under 18 Years, Annual Averages, 2000–2006—*Continued*

(Thousands of people, percent.)

Characteristic	2004			2005			2006		
	Both sexes	Men	Women	Both sexes	Men	Women	Both sexes	Men	Women
With Own Children Under 18 Years, Total									
Civilian noninstitutional population	64 758	28 272	36 486	64 482	28 065	36 417	64 680	28 188	36 492
Civilian labor force	52 288	26 607	25 681	52 056	26 399	25 657	52 391	26 530	25 861
Participation rate	80.7	94.1	70.4	80.7	94.1	70.5	81.0	94.1	70.9
Employed	49 957	25 696	24 261	49 882	25 587	24 294	50 388	25 774	24 614
Employment-population ratio	77.1	90.9	66.5	77.4	91.2	66.7	77.9	91.4	67.4
Full-time workers[1]	42 758	24 794	17 964	42 852	24 713	18 139	43 485	24 884	18 601
Part-time workers[2]	7 200	902	6 298	7 029	875	6 155	6 902	890	6 013
Unemployed	2 331	911	1 420	2 174	811	1 363	2 004	756	1 247
Unemployment rate	4.5	3.4	5.5	4.2	3.1	5.3	3.8	2.9	4.8
Married, Spouse Present									
Civilian noninstitutional population	52 109	25 852	26 258	51 519	25 578	25 942	51 670	25 648	26 022
Civilian labor force	42 247	24 449	17 798	41 905	24 215	17 690	42 136	24 295	17 842
Participation rate	81.1	94.6	67.8	81.3	94.7	68.2	81.5	94.7	68.6
Employed	40 847	23 703	17 144	40 614	23 556	17 058	40 960	23 680	17 280
Employment-population ratio	78.4	91.7	65.3	78.8	92.1	65.8	79.3	92.3	66.4
Full-time workers[1]	35 141	22 935	12 206	35 086	22 808	12 278	35 500	22 925	12 575
Part-time workers[2]	5 706	768	4 938	5 528	748	4 780	5 460	755	4 705
Unemployed	1 400	747	653	1 291	659	632	1 176	614	562
Unemployment rate	3.3	3.1	3.7	3.1	2.7	3.6	2.8	2.5	3.1
Other Marital Status[3]									
Civilian noninstitutional population	12 649	2 420	10 229	12 963	2 487	10 475	13 010	2 541	10 470
Civilian labor force	10 042	2 158	7 883	10 151	2 184	7 967	10 255	2 236	8 019
Participation rate	79.4	89.2	77.1	78.3	87.8	76.1	78.8	88.0	76.6
Employed	9 110	1 993	7 117	9 268	2 032	7 236	9 427	2 094	7 333
Employment-population ratio	72.0	82.4	69.6	71.5	81.7	69.1	72.5	82.4	70.0
Full-time workers[1]	7 617	1 859	5 757	7 766	1 905	5 861	7 985	1 960	6 026
Part-time workers[2]	1 494	134	1 360	1 502	127	1 375	1 442	134	1 308
Unemployed	931	165	766	883	152	731	827	142	686
Unemployment rate	9.3	7.6	9.7	8.7	7.0	9.2	8.1	6.3	8.5
With Own Children 6 to 17 Years, None Younger									
Civilian noninstitutional population	35 874	15 597	20 277	35 937	15 590	20 348	35 912	15 594	20 318
Civilian labor force	30 182	14 516	15 666	30 068	14 496	15 572	30 100	14 515	15 585
Participation rate	84.1	93.1	77.3	83.7	93.0	76.5	83.8	93.1	76.7
Employed	29 013	14 056	14 957	28 953	14 066	14 887	29 076	14 124	14 952
Employment-population ratio	80.9	90.1	73.8	80.6	90.2	73.2	81.0	90.6	73.6
Full-time workers[1]	25 069	13 597	11 473	25 074	13 606	11 468	25 277	13 648	11 629
Part-time workers[2]	3 944	459	3 485	3 880	460	3 419	3 799	476	3 323
Unemployed	1 170	460	709	1 115	430	684	1 024	392	632
Unemployment rate	3.9	3.2	4.5	3.7	3.0	4.4	3.4	2.7	4.1
With Own Children Under 6 Years									
Civilian noninstitutional population	28 884	12 675	16 210	28 545	12 475	16 070	28 768	12 594	16 174
Civilian labor force	22 106	12 091	10 014	21 988	11 903	10 085	22 291	12 015	10 276
Participation rate	76.5	95.4	61.8	77.0	95.4	62.8	77.5	95.4	63.5
Employed	20 944	11 640	9 304	20 928	11 521	9 407	21 311	11 650	9 661
Employment-population ratio	72.5	91.8	57.4	73.3	92.4	58.5	74.1	92.5	59.7
Full-time workers[1]	17 689	11 197	6 491	17 778	11 107	6 671	18 208	11 236	6 972
Part-time workers[2]	3 256	443	2 813	3 150	414	2 736	3 103	414	2 689
Unemployed	1 162	451	710	1 060	381	678	980	365	615
Unemployment rate	5.3	3.7	7.1	4.8	3.2	6.7	4.4	3.0	6.0
With No Own Children Under 18 Years									
Civilian noninstitutional population	156 900	77 739	79 160	159 751	79 237	80 514	162 438	80 719	81 718
Civilian labor force	93 511	50 771	42 740	95 545	51 914	43 631	97 427	53 115	44 312
Participation rate	59.6	65.3	54.0	59.8	65.5	54.2	60.0	65.8	54.2
Employed	87 748	47 282	40 467	90 171	48 709	41 462	92 460	50 148	42 312
Employment-population ratio	55.9	60.8	51.1	56.4	61.5	51.5	56.9	62.1	51.8
Full-time workers[1]	70 244	40 134	30 110	72 515	41 496	31 019	74 638	42 859	31 780
Part-time workers[2]	17 505	7 148	10 357	17 657	7 213	10 444	17 821	7 289	10 532
Unemployed	5 763	3 489	2 274	5 374	3 205	2 169	4 967	2 967	2 000
Unemployment rate	6.2	6.9	5.3	5.6	6.2	5.0	5.1	5.6	4.5

Note: Own children include sons, daughters, stepchildren, and adopted children. Not included are nieces, nephews, grandchildren, and other related and unrelated children. Detail may not sum to total due to rounding.

[1] Usually work 35 hours or more a week at all jobs.
[2] Usually work less than 35 hours a week at all jobs.
[3] Includes never-married, divorced, separated, and widowed persons.

Table 1-24. Employment Status of Mothers with Own Children Under 3 Years of Age, by Age of Youngest Child and Marital Status, Annual Averages, 2002–2006

(Thousands of people, percent.)

Year and characteristic	Civilian noninsti- tutional population	Civilian labor force		Employed				Unemployed	
		Total	Percent of population	Total	Percent of population	Full-time workers[1]	Part-time workers[2]	Number	Percent of labor force
2002									
Total Mothers with Own Children Under 3 Years	9 350	5 632	60.2	5 181	55.4	3 513	1 667	451	8.0
2 years	2 949	1 895	64.3	1 758	59.6	1 234	524	137	7.2
1 year	3 310	2 003	60.5	1 852	56.0	1 241	610	151	7.5
Under 1 year	3 091	1 734	56.1	1 571	50.8	1 038	533	163	9.4
Married, Spouse Present with Own Children Under 3 Years	7 073	4 071	57.6	3 869	54.7	2 572	1 297	203	5.0
2 years	2 201	1 333	60.6	1 274	57.9	870	404	59	4.4
1 year	2 509	1 446	57.6	1 379	55.0	902	477	67	4.6
Under 1 year	2 363	1 292	54.7	1 216	51.5	800	416	77	6.0
Other Marital Status with Own Children Under 3 Years[3]	2 278	1 562	68.6	1 313	57.6	941	372	248	15.9
2 years	748	562	75.1	484	64.7	364	120	77	13.7
1 year	802	557	69.5	473	59.0	340	134	84	15.1
Under 1 year	728	443	60.9	356	48.9	237	118	87	19.6
2003									
Total Mothers with Own Children Under 3 Years	9 450	5 563	58.9	5 115	54.1	3 430	1 685	446	8.0
2 years	2 987	1 896	63.5	1 752	58.7	1 205	547	143	7.5
1 year	3 353	1 997	59.6	1 842	54.9	1 223	619	154	7.7
Under 1 year	3 110	1 670	53.7	1 521	48.9	1 002	519	149	8.9
Married, Spouse Present with Own Children Under 3 Years	7 165	4 068	56.8	3 872	54.0	2 529	1 342	197	4.8
2 years	2 243	1 350	60.2	1 281	57.1	853	428	69	5.1
1 year	2 541	1 458	57.4	1 395	54.9	906	488	64	4.4
Under 1 year	2 381	1 260	52.9	1 196	50.2	770	426	64	5.1
Other Marital Status with Own Children Under 3 Years[3]	2 287	1 495	65.4	1 244	54.4	902	341	250	16.7
2 years	744	546	73.4	471	63.3	352	118	75	13.7
1 year	813	539	66.3	448	55.1	317	131	91	16.9
Under 1 year	730	410	56.2	325	44.5	233	92	84	20.5
2004									
Total Mothers with Own Children Under 3 Years	9 345	5 377	57.5	4 964	53.1	3 360	1 604	414	7.7
2 years	2 813	1 746	62.1	1 630	57.9	1 152	477	116	6.6
1 year	3 273	1 906	58.2	1 759	53.7	1 172	587	147	7.7
Under 1 year	3 259	1 725	52.9	1 575	48.3	1 035	540	151	8.7
Married, Spouse Present with Own Children Under 3 Years	7 071	3 910	55.3	3 740	52.9	2 513	1 227	170	4.4
2 years	2 111	1 246	59.0	1 200	56.8	839	361	46	3.7
1 year	2 519	1 401	55.6	1 337	53.1	877	459	65	4.6
Under 1 year	2 441	1 262	51.7	1 203	49.3	797	406	59	4.7
Other Marital Status with Own Children Under 3 Years[3]	2 274	1 467	64.5	1 224	53.8	847	377	243	16.6
2 years	702	499	71.1	430	61.2	314	116	70	13.9
1 year	754	505	66.9	422	56.0	295	127	82	16.3
Under 1 year	818	463	56.6	372	45.4	238	134	91	19.7
2005									
Total Mothers with Own Children Under 3 Years	9 365	5 470	58.4	5 077	54.2	3 501	1 576	393	7.2
2 years	2 845	1 773	62.3	1 654	58.1	1 162	492	119	6.7
1 year	3 287	1 958	59.6	1 823	55.5	1 247	576	135	6.9
Under 1 year	3 233	1 740	53.8	1 600	49.5	1 092	508	140	8.0
Married, Spouse Present with Own Children Under 3 Years	6 951	3 939	56.7	3 776	54.3	2 588	1 188	164	4.2
2 years	2 118	1 268	59.9	1 214	57.3	840	374	55	4.3
1 year	2 435	1 389	57.0	1 337	54.9	901	436	52	3.7
Under 1 year	2 398	1 282	53.5	1 225	51.1	847	378	58	4.5
Other Marital Status with Own Children Under 3 Years[3]	2 414	1 531	63.4	1 301	53.9	913	388	230	15.0
2 years	726	504	69.5	440	60.6	322	118	64	12.7
1 year	852	569	66.8	486	57.0	346	139	83	14.6
Under 1 year	836	457	54.7	375	44.9	245	130	82	18.0
2006									
Total Mothers with Own Children Under 3 Years	9 431	5 675	60.2	5 315	56.4	3 751	1 564	360	6.3
2 years	2 864	1 847	64.5	1 746	61.0	1 280	466	101	5.5
1 year	3 318	2 006	60.5	1 883	56.7	1 305	577	123	6.1
Under 1 year	3 248	1 822	56.1	1 686	51.9	1 166	520	136	7.4
Married, Spouse Present with Own Children Under 3 Years	6 998	4 076	58.2	3 933	56.2	2 756	1 177	143	3.5
2 years	2 114	1 305	61.7	1 265	59.8	910	354	40	3.1
1 year	2 494	1 456	58.4	1 404	56.3	962	442	52	3.6
Under 1 year	2 390	1 315	55.0	1 264	52.9	883	381	51	3.9
Other Marital Status with Own Children Under 3 Years[3]	2 433	1 600	65.7	1 382	56.8	996	386	217	13.6
2 years	750	543	72.3	481	64.2	369	112	61	11.3
1 year	824	550	66.7	479	58.1	344	135	71	13.0
Under 1 year	859	507	59.0	422	49.2	283	139	85	16.7

Note: Own children include sons, daughters, stepchildren, and adopted children. Not included are nieces, nephews, grandchildren, and other related and unrelated children. Detail may not sum to total due to rounding. Data for 2003 reflect the revised population controls used in the Current Population Survey (CPS).

[1]Usually work 35 hours or more a week at all jobs.
[2]Usually work less than 35 hours a week at all jobs.
[3]Includes never-married, divorced, separated, and widowed persons.

UNEMPLOYMENT

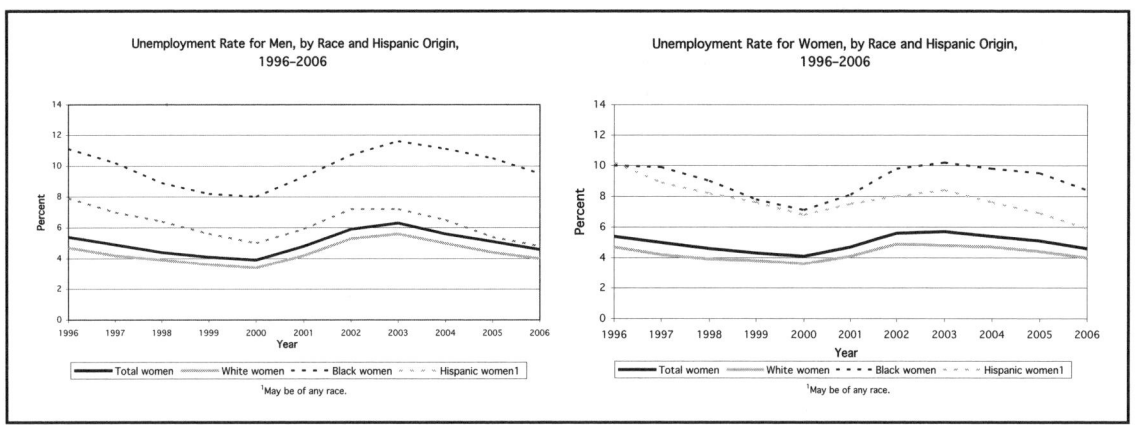

The unemployment rate continued to decline in 2006, dropping to 4.6 percent, the lowest it has been since 2000. The unemployment rate dropped for all groups. However, the rates for Black men and women continued to be more than double the rates for White men and women. (See Table 1-27.)

OTHER HIGHLIGHTS

- The number of unemployed persons dropped by more than 500,000 for the third consecutive year in 2006. (See Table 1-28.)

- Younger workers experience higher levels of unemployment. The 16- to 19-year-old group had the highest unemployment rate at 15.4 percent followed by the 20- to 24-year-old age group at 8.2 percent. For Whites, the unemployment rate dropped from 13.2 percent for persons age 16 to 19 years to 6.9 percent for persons age 20 to 24 years. For Blacks, the unemployment rate also fell but still remained extremely high, declining from 29.1 percent for persons age 16 to 19 to 16.2 percent for persons age 20 to 24 years. (See Table 1-27.)

- The median duration of unemployment dropped again in 2006, declining from 8.9 to 8.3 weeks. (See Table 1-30.)

- Among the states, Michigan had the highest unemployment rate in 2006 at 6.9 percent, followed by Mississippi at 6.8 percent and Alaska at 6.7 percent. Hawaii had the lowest unemployment rate at 2.4 percent. Utah, with an unemployment rate of 2.9 percent, was the only other state with an unemployment rate under 3.0 percent. (See Table 1-5.)

Table 1-25. Unemployment Rate, by Selected Characteristics, 1948–2006

(Unemployment as a percent of civilian labor force.)

Year	All civilian workers	Both sexes, 16 to 19 years	Men, 20 years and over	Women, 20 years and over	White[1]	Black[1]	Asian[1]	Hispanic[2]	Married men, spouse present	Married women, spouse present	Women who maintain families
1948	3.8	9.2	3.2	3.6	...	...	...	...	...	...	...
1949	5.9	13.4	5.4	5.3	...	...	...	...	...	...	...
1950	5.3	12.2	4.7	5.1	...	...	...	...	...	...	...
1951	3.3	8.2	2.5	4.0	...	...	...	...	...	...	...
1952	3.0	8.5	2.4	3.2	...	...	...	...	...	...	...
1953	2.9	7.6	2.5	2.9	...	...	...	...	...	...	...
1954	5.5	12.6	4.9	5.5	5.0	...	...	...	...	...	...
1955	4.4	11.0	3.8	4.4	3.9	...	...	...	2.6	3.7	...
1956	4.1	11.1	3.4	4.2	3.6	...	...	...	2.3	3.6	...
1957	4.3	11.6	3.6	4.1	3.8	...	...	...	2.8	4.3	...
1958	6.8	15.9	6.2	6.1	6.1	...	...	...	5.1	6.5	...
1959	5.5	14.6	4.7	5.2	4.8	...	...	...	3.6	5.2	...
1960	5.5	14.7	4.7	5.1	5.0	...	...	...	3.7	5.2	...
1961	6.7	16.8	5.7	6.3	6.0	...	...	...	4.6	6.4	...
1962	5.5	14.7	4.6	5.4	4.9	...	...	...	3.6	5.4	...
1963	5.7	17.2	4.5	5.4	5.0	...	...	...	3.4	5.4	...
1964	5.2	16.2	3.9	5.2	4.6	...	...	...	2.8	5.1	...
1965	4.5	14.8	3.2	4.5	4.1	...	...	...	2.4	4.5	...
1966	3.8	12.8	2.5	3.8	3.4	...	...	...	1.9	3.7	...
1967	3.8	12.9	2.3	4.2	3.4	...	...	...	1.8	4.5	4.9
1968	3.6	12.7	2.2	3.8	3.2	...	...	...	1.6	3.9	4.4
1969	3.5	12.2	2.1	3.7	3.1	...	...	...	1.5	3.9	4.4
1970	4.9	15.3	3.5	4.8	4.5	...	...	...	2.6	4.9	5.4
1971	5.9	16.9	4.4	5.7	5.4	...	...	...	3.2	5.7	7.3
1972	5.6	16.2	4.0	5.4	5.1	10.4	...	...	2.8	5.4	7.2
1973	4.9	14.5	3.3	4.9	4.3	9.4	...	7.5	2.3	4.7	7.1
1974	5.6	16.0	3.8	5.5	5.0	10.5	...	8.1	2.7	5.3	7.0
1975	8.5	19.9	6.8	8.0	7.8	14.8	...	12.2	5.1	7.9	10.0
1976	7.7	19.0	5.9	7.4	7.0	14.0	...	11.5	4.2	7.1	10.1
1977	7.1	17.8	5.2	7.0	6.2	14.0	...	10.1	3.6	6.5	9.4
1978	6.1	16.4	4.3	6.0	5.2	12.8	...	9.1	2.8	5.5	8.5
1979	5.8	16.1	4.2	5.7	5.1	12.3	...	8.3	2.8	5.1	8.3
1980	7.1	17.8	5.9	6.4	6.3	14.3	...	10.1	4.2	5.8	9.2
1981	7.6	19.6	6.3	6.8	6.7	15.6	...	10.4	4.3	6.0	10.4
1982	9.7	23.2	8.8	8.3	8.6	18.9	...	13.8	6.5	7.4	11.7
1983	9.6	22.4	8.9	8.1	8.4	19.5	...	13.7	6.5	7.0	12.2
1984	7.5	18.9	6.6	6.8	6.5	15.9	...	10.7	4.6	5.7	10.3
1985	7.2	18.6	6.2	6.6	6.2	15.1	...	10.5	4.3	5.6	10.4
1986	7.0	18.3	6.1	6.2	6.0	14.5	...	10.6	4.4	5.2	9.8
1987	6.2	16.9	5.4	5.4	5.3	13.0	...	8.8	3.9	4.3	9.2
1988	5.5	15.3	4.8	4.9	4.7	11.7	...	8.2	3.3	3.9	8.1
1989	5.3	15.0	4.5	4.7	4.5	11.4	...	8.0	3.0	3.7	8.1
1990	5.6	15.5	5.0	4.9	4.8	11.4	...	8.2	3.4	3.8	8.3
1991	6.8	18.7	6.4	5.7	6.1	12.5	...	10.0	4.4	4.5	9.3
1992	7.5	20.1	7.1	6.3	6.6	14.2	...	11.6	5.1	5.0	10.0
1993	6.9	19.0	6.4	5.9	6.1	13.0	...	10.8	4.4	4.6	9.7
1994	6.1	17.6	5.4	5.4	5.3	11.5	...	9.9	3.7	4.1	8.9
1995	5.6	17.3	4.8	4.9	4.9	10.4	...	9.3	3.3	3.9	8.0
1996	5.4	16.7	4.6	4.8	4.7	10.5	...	8.9	3.0	3.6	8.2
1997	4.9	16.0	4.2	4.4	4.2	10.0	...	7.7	2.7	3.1	8.1
1998	4.5	14.6	3.7	4.1	3.9	8.9	...	7.2	2.4	2.9	7.2
1999	4.2	13.9	3.5	3.8	3.7	8.0	...	6.4	2.2	2.7	6.4
2000	4.0	13.1	3.3	3.6	3.5	7.6	3.6	5.7	2.0	2.7	5.9
2001	4.7	14.7	4.2	4.1	4.2	8.6	4.5	6.6	2.7	3.1	6.6
2002	5.8	16.5	5.3	5.1	5.1	10.2	5.9	7.5	3.6	3.7	8.0
2003	6.0	17.5	5.6	5.1	5.2	10.8	6.0	7.7	3.8	3.7	8.5
2004	5.5	17.0	5.0	4.9	4.8	10.4	4.4	7.0	3.1	3.5	8.0
2005	5.1	16.6	4.4	4.6	4.4	10.0	4.0	6.0	2.8	3.3	7.8
2006	4.6	15.4	4.0	4.1	4.0	8.9	3.0	5.2	2.4	2.9	7.1

Note: See notes and definitions for information on historical comparability.

[1]Beginning in 2003, persons who selected this race group only; persons who selected more than one race group are not included. Prior to 2003, persons who reported more than one race group were included in the group they identified as their main race.
[2]May be of any race.
. . . = Not available.

Table 1-26. Unemployed Persons, by Age, Sex, Race, and Hispanic Origin, 1948–2006

(Thousands of people.)

Race, Hispanic origin, sex, and year	16 years and over	16 to 19 years			20 years and over						
		Total	16 to 17 years	18 to 19 years	Total	20 to 24 years	25 to 34 years	35 to 44 years	45 to 54 years	55 to 64 years	65 years and over
ALL RACES											
Both Sexes											
1948	2 276	409	180	228	1 869	455	457	347	290	226	93
1949	3 637	576	238	337	3 060	680	776	603	471	384	146
1950	3 288	513	226	287	2 776	561	702	530	478	368	137
1951	2 055	336	168	168	1 718	273	435	354	318	238	103
1952	1 883	345	180	165	1 539	268	389	325	274	195	86
1953	1 834	307	150	157	1 529	256	379	325	280	218	70
1954	3 532	501	221	247	3 032	504	793	680	548	374	132
1955	2 852	450	211	239	2 403	396	577	521	436	355	120
1956	2 750	478	231	247	2 274	395	554	476	429	311	109
1957	2 859	497	230	266	2 362	430	573	499	448	300	111
1958	4 602	678	299	379	3 923	701	993	871	731	472	154
1959	3 740	654	301	354	3 085	543	726	673	603	405	135
1960	3 852	712	325	387	3 140	583	752	671	614	396	122
1961	4 714	828	363	465	3 886	723	890	850	751	516	159
1962	3 911	721	312	409	3 191	636	712	688	605	411	141
1963	4 070	884	420	462	3 187	658	732	674	589	410	126
1964	3 786	872	436	437	2 913	660	607	605	543	378	117
1965	3 366	874	411	463	2 491	557	529	546	436	322	103
1966	2 875	837	395	441	2 041	446	441	426	369	265	92
1967	2 975	839	400	438	2 140	511	480	422	383	256	86
1968	2 817	838	414	426	1 978	543	443	371	314	219	88
1969	2 832	853	436	416	1 978	560	453	358	320	216	72
1970	4 093	1 106	537	569	2 987	866	718	515	476	309	104
1971	5 016	1 262	596	665	3 755	1 130	933	630	573	381	109
1972	4 882	1 308	633	676	3 573	1 132	878	576	510	368	111
1973	4 365	1 235	634	600	3 130	1 008	866	451	430	290	88
1974	5 156	1 422	699	722	3 733	1 212	1 044	559	498	321	99
1975	7 929	1 767	799	968	6 161	1 865	1 776	951	893	520	155
1976	7 406	1 719	796	924	5 687	1 714	1 710	849	758	510	147
1977	6 991	1 663	781	881	5 330	1 629	1 650	785	666	450	147
1978	6 202	1 583	796	787	4 620	1 483	1 422	694	552	345	123
1979	6 137	1 555	739	816	4 583	1 442	1 446	705	540	346	104
1980	7 637	1 669	778	890	5 969	1 835	2 024	940	676	399	94
1981	8 273	1 763	781	981	6 510	1 976	2 211	1 065	715	444	98
1982	10 678	1 977	831	1 145	8 701	2 392	3 037	1 552	966	647	107
1983	10 717	1 829	753	1 076	8 888	2 330	3 078	1 650	1 039	677	114
1984	8 539	1 499	646	854	7 039	1 838	2 374	1 335	828	566	97
1985	8 312	1 468	662	806	6 844	1 738	2 341	1 340	813	518	93
1986	8 237	1 454	665	789	6 783	1 651	2 390	1 371	790	489	91
1987	7 425	1 347	648	700	6 077	1 453	2 129	1 281	723	412	78
1988	6 701	1 226	573	653	5 475	1 261	1 929	1 166	657	375	87
1989	6 528	1 194	537	657	5 333	1 218	1 851	1 159	637	379	91
1990	7 047	1 212	527	685	5 835	1 299	1 995	1 328	723	386	105
1991	8 628	1 359	587	772	7 269	1 573	2 447	1 719	946	473	113
1992	9 613	1 427	641	787	8 186	1 649	2 702	1 976	1 138	589	132
1993	8 940	1 365	606	759	7 575	1 514	2 395	1 896	1 121	541	108
1994	7 996	1 320	624	696	6 676	1 373	2 067	1 627	971	485	153
1995	7 404	1 346	652	695	6 058	1 244	1 841	1 549	844	425	153
1996	7 236	1 306	617	689	5 929	1 239	1 757	1 505	883	406	139
1997	6 739	1 271	589	683	5 467	1 152	1 571	1 418	830	369	127
1998	6 210	1 205	573	632	5 005	1 081	1 419	1 258	782	343	122
1999	5 880	1 162	544	618	4 718	1 042	1 278	1 154	753	367	124
2000	5 692	1 081	502	579	4 611	1 022	1 207	1 133	762	355	132
2001	6 801	1 162	531	632	5 638	1 209	1 498	1 355	989	458	129
2002	8 378	1 253	540	714	7 124	1 430	1 890	1 691	1 315	635	163
2003	8 774	1 251	545	706	7 523	1 495	1 960	1 815	1 356	713	183
2004	8 149	1 208	554	653	6 942	1 431	1 784	1 578	1 288	682	179
2005	7 591	1 186	541	645	6 405	1 335	1 661	1 400	1 195	630	184
2006	7 001	1 119	509	610	5 882	1 234	1 521	1 279	1 094	595	159

Table 1-26. Unemployed Persons, by Age, Sex, Race, and Hispanic Origin, 1948–2006—*Continued*

(Thousands of people.)

Race, Hispanic origin, sex, and year	16 years and over	16 to 19 years			20 years and over						
		Total	16 to 17 years	18 to 19 years	Total	20 to 24 years	25 to 34 years	35 to 44 years	45 to 54 years	55 to 64 years	65 years and over
ALL RACES											
Men											
1948	1 559	256	113	142	1 305	324	289	233	201	. . .	. . .
1949	2 572	353	145	207	2 219	485	539	414	347	310	125
1950	2 239	318	139	179	1 922	377	467	348	327	286	117
1951	1 221	191	102	89	1 029	155	241	192	193	162	87
1952	1 185	205	116	89	980	155	233	192	182	145	73
1953	1 202	184	94	90	1 019	152	236	208	196	167	60
1954	2 344	310	142	168	2 035	327	517	431	372	275	112
1955	1 854	274	134	140	1 580	248	353	328	285	265	102
1956	1 711	269	134	135	1 442	240	348	278	270	216	90
1957	1 841	300	140	159	1 541	283	349	304	302	220	83
1958	3 098	416	185	231	2 681	478	685	552	492	349	124
1959	2 420	398	191	207	2 022	343	484	407	390	287	112
1960	2 486	426	200	225	2 060	369	492	415	392	294	96
1961	2 997	479	221	258	2 518	458	585	507	473	375	122
1962	2 423	408	188	220	2 016	381	445	404	382	300	103
1963	2 472	501	248	252	1 971	396	445	386	358	290	97
1964	2 205	487	257	230	1 718	384	345	324	319	263	85
1965	1 914	479	247	232	1 435	311	292	283	253	221	75
1966	1 551	432	220	212	1 120	221	239	219	196	179	65
1967	1 508	448	241	207	1 060	235	219	185	199	163	60
1968	1 419	426	234	193	993	258	205	171	165	132	61
1969	1 403	440	244	196	963	270	205	155	157	127	48
1970	2 238	599	306	294	1 638	479	391	253	247	198	71
1971	2 789	693	346	347	2 097	640	513	320	313	239	71
1972	2 659	711	357	355	1 948	628	466	284	272	227	73
1973	2 275	653	352	300	1 624	528	439	211	219	171	57
1974	2 714	757	394	362	1 957	649	546	266	250	183	63
1975	4 442	966	445	521	3 476	1 081	986	507	499	302	103
1976	4 036	939	443	496	3 098	951	914	431	411	296	94
1977	3 667	874	421	453	2 794	877	869	373	326	252	97
1978	3 142	813	426	388	2 328	768	691	314	277	198	81
1979	3 120	811	393	418	2 308	744	699	329	272	196	67
1980	4 267	913	429	485	3 353	1 076	1 137	482	357	243	58
1981	4 577	962	431	531	3 615	1 144	1 213	552	390	261	55
1982	6 179	1 090	469	621	5 089	1 407	1 791	879	550	393	69
1983	6 260	1 003	408	595	5 257	1 369	1 822	947	613	433	73
1984	4 744	812	348	464	3 932	1 023	1 322	728	450	356	53
1985	4 521	806	363	443	3 715	944	1 244	706	459	307	55
1986	4 530	779	355	424	3 751	899	1 291	763	440	301	58
1987	4 101	732	353	379	3 369	779	1 169	689	426	258	49
1988	3 655	667	311	356	2 987	676	1 040	617	366	240	49
1989	3 525	658	303	355	2 867	660	953	619	351	234	49
1990	3 906	667	283	384	3 239	715	1 092	711	413	249	59
1991	4 946	751	317	433	4 195	911	1 375	990	550	305	64
1992	5 523	806	357	449	4 717	951	1 529	1 118	675	378	67
1993	5 055	768	342	426	4 287	865	1 338	1 049	636	336	64
1994	4 367	740	342	398	3 627	768	1 113	855	522	281	88
1995	3 983	744	352	391	3 239	673	961	815	464	233	94
1996	3 880	733	347	387	3 146	675	903	786	484	223	76
1997	3 577	694	321	373	2 882	636	772	732	457	217	69
1998	3 266	686	330	355	2 580	583	699	609	420	201	69
1999	3 066	633	295	338	2 433	562	624	571	403	203	70
2000	2 975	599	281	317	2 376	547	602	557	398	189	83
2001	3 690	650	300	350	3 040	688	756	714	536	272	74
2002	4 597	700	301	399	3 896	792	1 023	897	725	373	87
2003	4 906	697	291	407	4 209	841	1 097	988	764	412	107
2004	4 456	664	292	372	3 791	811	980	839	684	373	104
2005	4 059	667	300	367	3 392	775	844	715	624	331	102
2006	3 753	622	271	352	3 131	705	810	642	569	318	88

. . . = Not available.

Table 1-26. Unemployed Persons, by Age, Sex, Race, and Hispanic Origin, 1948–2006—*Continued*

(Thousands of people.)

Race, Hispanic origin, sex, and year	16 years and over	16 to 19 years			20 years and over						
		Total	16 to 17 years	18 to 19 years	Total	20 to 24 years	25 to 34 years	35 to 44 years	45 to 54 years	55 to 64 years	65 years and over
ALL RACES											
Women											
1948	717	153	67	86	564	131	168	114	89	49	12
1949	1 065	223	93	130	841	195	237	189	124	74	21
1950	1 049	195	87	108	854	184	235	182	151	82	20
1951	834	145	66	79	689	118	194	162	125	76	16
1952	698	140	64	76	559	113	156	133	92	50	13
1953	632	123	56	67	510	104	143	117	84	51	10
1954	1 188	191	79	79	997	177	276	249	176	99	20
1955	998	176	77	99	823	148	224	193	151	90	18
1956	1 039	209	97	112	832	155	206	198	159	95	19
1957	1 018	197	90	107	821	147	224	195	146	80	28
1958	1 504	262	114	148	1 242	223	308	319	239	123	30
1959	1 320	256	110	147	1 063	200	242	266	213	118	23
1960	1 366	286	125	162	1 080	214	260	256	222	102	26
1961	1 717	349	142	207	1 368	265	305	343	278	141	37
1962	1 488	313	124	189	1 175	255	267	284	223	111	38
1963	1 598	383	172	210	1 216	262	287	288	231	120	29
1964	1 581	385	179	207	1 195	276	262	281	224	115	32
1965	1 452	395	164	231	1 056	246	237	263	183	101	28
1966	1 324	405	175	229	921	225	202	207	173	86	27
1967	1 468	391	159	231	1 078	277	261	237	184	93	26
1968	1 397	412	180	233	985	285	238	200	149	87	27
1969	1 429	413	192	220	1 015	290	248	203	163	89	24
1970	1 855	506	231	275	1 349	387	327	262	229	111	33
1971	2 227	568	250	318	1 658	489	420	310	260	142	38
1972	2 222	598	276	322	1 625	503	413	293	237	141	38
1973	2 089	583	282	301	1 507	480	427	240	212	119	31
1974	2 441	665	305	360	1 777	564	497	294	248	137	36
1975	3 486	802	355	447	2 684	783	791	444	395	219	52
1976	3 369	780	352	429	2 588	763	795	417	346	214	53
1977	3 324	789	361	428	2 535	752	782	412	340	198	50
1978	3 061	769	370	399	2 292	714	731	381	275	148	43
1979	3 018	743	346	396	2 276	697	748	375	268	150	38
1980	3 370	755	349	407	2 615	760	886	459	318	155	36
1981	3 696	800	350	450	2 895	833	998	513	325	184	43
1982	4 499	886	362	524	3 613	985	1 246	673	416	254	38
1983	4 457	825	344	481	3 632	961	1 255	703	427	244	41
1984	3 794	687	298	390	3 107	815	1 052	607	378	211	45
1985	3 791	661	298	363	3 129	794	1 098	634	355	211	39
1986	3 707	675	310	365	3 032	752	1 099	609	350	189	33
1987	3 324	616	295	321	2 709	674	960	592	298	155	30
1988	3 046	558	262	297	2 487	585	889	550	291	136	38
1989	3 003	536	234	302	2 467	558	897	540	286	144	41
1990	3 140	544	243	301	2 596	584	902	617	310	137	46
1991	3 683	608	270	338	3 074	662	1 071	728	396	168	49
1992	4 090	621	283	338	3 469	698	1 173	858	463	210	66
1993	3 885	597	264	333	3 288	648	1 058	847	485	205	45
1994	3 629	580	282	298	3 049	605	954	772	449	204	66
1995	3 421	602	299	303	2 819	571	880	735	381	193	60
1996	3 356	573	270	303	2 783	564	854	720	399	183	63
1997	3 162	577	268	310	2 585	516	800	686	373	152	58
1998	2 944	519	242	277	2 424	498	720	650	362	141	53
1999	2 814	529	249	280	2 285	480	654	584	350	163	54
2000	2 717	483	221	262	2 235	475	604	577	364	165	50
2001	3 111	512	230	282	2 599	521	742	641	453	187	55
2002	3 781	553	238	315	3 228	638	866	795	591	263	76
2003	3 868	554	255	299	3 314	654	863	827	592	302	76
2004	3 694	543	262	281	3 150	619	804	739	605	309	75
2005	3 531	519	240	278	3 013	560	817	685	571	299	82
2006	3 247	496	238	258	2 751	530	711	637	524	277	71

Table 1-26. Unemployed Persons, by Age, Sex, Race, and Hispanic Origin, 1948–2006—*Continued*

(Thousands of people.)

Race, Hispanic origin, sex, and year	16 years and over	16 to 19 years			20 years and over						
		Total	16 to 17 years	18 to 19 years	Total	20 to 24 years	25 to 34 years	35 to 44 years	45 to 54 years	55 to 64 years	65 years and over
WHITE[1]											
Both Sexes											
1954	2 859	423	191	232	2 436	394	610	540	447	329	115
1955	2 252	373	181	191	1 879	304	412	402	358	300	105
1956	2 159	382	191	191	1 777	297	406	363	355	258	98
1957	2 289	401	195	204	1 888	331	425	401	373	262	98
1958	3 680	541	245	297	3 139	541	756	686	614	405	136
1959	2 946	525	255	270	2 421	406	526	525	496	348	120
1960	3 065	575	273	302	2 490	456	573	520	502	330	109
1961	3 743	669	295	374	3 074	566	668	652	611	438	139
1962	3 052	580	262	318	2 472	488	515	522	485	345	117
1963	3 208	708	350	358	2 500	501	540	518	485	349	107
1964	2 999	708	365	342	2 291	508	441	472	447	323	100
1965	2 691	705	329	374	1 986	437	399	427	358	276	91
1966	2 255	651	315	336	1 604	338	323	336	298	227	80
1967	2 338	635	311	325	1 703	393	360	336	321	221	75
1968	2 226	644	326	318	1 582	422	330	297	269	187	80
1969	2 260	660	351	309	1 601	432	354	294	269	185	66
1970	3 339	871	438	432	2 468	679	570	433	415	275	95
1971	4 085	1 011	491	521	3 074	887	732	517	500	338	100
1972	3 906	1 021	515	506	2 885	887	679	459	439	324	95
1973	3 442	955	513	443	2 486	758	664	358	371	257	77
1974	4 097	1 104	561	544	2 993	925	821	448	427	283	88
1975	6 421	1 413	657	755	5 007	1 474	1 413	774	753	460	136
1976	5 914	1 364	649	715	4 550	1 326	1 329	682	637	448	128
1977	5 441	1 284	636	648	4 157	1 195	1 255	621	569	388	129
1978	4 698	1 189	631	558	3 509	1 059	1 059	543	453	290	104
1979	4 664	1 193	589	603	3 472	1 038	1 068	545	443	290	87
1980	5 884	1 291	625	666	4 593	1 364	1 528	740	550	335	74
1981	6 343	1 374	629	745	4 968	1 449	1 658	827	578	379	77
1982	8 241	1 534	683	851	6 707	1 770	2 283	1 223	796	549	86
1983	8 128	1 387	609	778	6 741	1 678	2 282	1 294	837	563	88
1984	6 372	1 116	510	605	5 256	1 282	1 723	1 036	660	475	81
1985	6 191	1 074	507	567	5 117	1 235	1 695	1 039	642	432	75
1986	6 140	1 070	509	561	5 070	1 149	1 751	1 056	629	407	78
1987	5 501	995	495	500	4 506	1 017	1 527	984	576	333	68
1988	4 944	910	437	473	4 033	874	1 371	890	520	309	69
1989	4 770	863	407	456	3 908	856	1 297	871	503	311	70
1990	5 186	903	401	502	4 283	899	1 401	983	582	330	88
1991	6 560	1 029	461	568	5 532	1 132	1 805	1 330	759	410	96
1992	7 169	1 037	484	553	6 132	1 156	1 967	1 483	915	495	116
1993	6 655	992	468	523	5 663	1 057	1 754	1 411	907	442	92
1994	5 892	960	471	489	4 933	952	1 479	1 184	779	407	132
1995	5 459	952	476	476	4 507	866	1 311	1 161	676	362	131
1996	5 300	939	456	484	4 361	854	1 223	1 117	709	336	122
1997	4 836	912	438	475	3 924	765	1 068	1 035	648	302	106
1998	4 484	876	424	451	3 608	731	978	901	620	276	101
1999	4 273	844	414	430	3 429	720	865	843	595	303	104
2000	4 121	795	386	409	3 326	682	835	817	591	294	107
2001	4 969	845	402	443	4 124	829	1 062	985	761	378	109
2002	6 137	925	407	518	5 212	977	1 340	1 237	1 004	518	137
2003	6 311	909	414	495	5 401	1 012	1 354	1 287	1 025	569	155
2004	5 847	890	414	476	4 957	959	1 211	1 130	953	557	148
2005	5 350	845	391	454	4 505	878	1 106	1 006	884	488	144
2006	5 002	794	375	419	4 208	832	1 029	920	813	480	135

[1]Beginning in 2003, persons who selected this race group only; persons who selected more than one race group are not included. Prior to 2003, persons who reported more than one race group were included in the group they identified as their main race.

Table 1-26. Unemployed Persons, by Age, Sex, Race, and Hispanic Origin, 1948–2006—*Continued*

(Thousands of people.)

Race, Hispanic origin, sex, and year	16 years and over	16 to 19 years			20 years and over						
		Total	16 to 17 years	18 to 19 years	Total	20 to 24 years	25 to 34 years	35 to 44 years	45 to 54 years	55 to 64 years	65 years and over
WHITE[1]											
Men											
1954	1 913	266	125	142	1 647	260	408	341	299	241	98
1955	1 478	232	114	117	1 246	196	260	246	233	223	89
1956	1 366	221	112	108	1 145	186	265	212	225	177	81
1957	1 477	243	118	124	1 234	222	257	239	250	193	73
1958	2 489	333	149	184	2 156	382	525	436	404	299	110
1959	1 903	318	162	156	1 585	256	350	316	320	245	98
1960	1 988	341	167	174	1 647	295	376	330	317	243	86
1961	2 398	384	176	208	2 014	370	442	395	382	318	107
1962	1 915	334	158	176	1 581	300	332	311	308	246	84
1963	1 976	407	211	196	1 569	309	342	297	294	246	80
1964	1 779	400	217	183	1 379	310	262	255	266	216	70
1965	1 556	387	200	186	1 169	254	226	228	206	190	67
1966	1 241	340	178	162	901	172	185	173	160	154	57
1967	1 208	342	186	156	866	185	171	153	167	140	52
1968	1 142	328	185	143	814	206	162	140	142	111	55
1969	1 137	343	198	145	794	214	165	130	134	108	43
1970	1 857	485	255	230	1 372	388	316	212	216	177	64
1971	2 309	562	288	275	1 747	513	418	268	272	211	66
1972	2 173	564	288	276	1 610	506	375	231	237	199	60
1973	1 836	513	284	229	1 323	411	353	166	188	153	51
1974	2 169	584	311	274	1 585	505	434	218	213	161	53
1975	3 627	785	369	416	2 841	871	796	412	411	265	86
1976	3 258	754	368	385	2 504	750	730	346	341	259	78
1977	2 883	672	342	330	2 211	660	682	297	276	213	82
1978	2 411	615	338	277	1 797	558	525	250	227	169	68
1979	2 405	633	319	313	1 773	553	526	253	220	165	56
1980	3 345	716	347	369	2 629	827	884	378	291	206	44
1981	3 580	755	349	406	2 825	869	943	433	317	221	42
1982	4 846	854	387	467	3 991	1 066	1 385	696	460	331	53
1983	4 859	761	328	433	4 098	1 019	1 410	755	497	362	54
1984	3 600	608	280	328	2 992	722	991	572	363	302	42
1985	3 426	592	282	310	2 834	694	931	553	356	257	43
1986	3 433	576	276	299	2 857	645	978	586	349	248	51
1987	3 132	548	272	276	2 584	568	879	536	350	209	43
1988	2 766	499	239	260	2 268	480	777	477	293	200	40
1989	2 636	487	230	257	2 149	476	694	470	280	191	38
1990	2 935	504	214	290	2 431	510	796	530	330	214	51
1991	3 859	575	249	327	3 284	677	1 064	780	438	269	55
1992	4 209	590	270	319	3 620	686	1 155	858	543	318	58
1993	3 828	565	261	305	3 263	619	1 015	793	512	270	53
1994	3 275	540	259	280	2 735	555	827	626	417	236	74
1995	2 999	535	260	275	2 465	483	711	621	371	200	79
1996	2 896	532	260	273	2 363	478	655	592	383	188	67
1997	2 641	502	234	268	2 140	439	553	549	358	182	58
1998	2 431	510	254	257	1 920	405	512	441	342	164	58
1999	2 274	461	223	237	1 813	398	441	419	322	172	61
2000	2 177	446	217	229	1 731	368	428	403	302	162	68
2001	2 754	479	232	247	2 275	494	547	529	413	229	64
2002	3 459	516	228	288	2 943	562	772	672	554	305	77
2003	3 643	518	221	298	3 125	589	798	723	591	333	91
2004	3 282	497	224	274	2 785	560	694	620	516	307	88
2005	2 931	480	220	260	2 450	522	586	536	463	263	81
2006	2 730	449	202	247	2 281	483	567	482	417	259	73

[1]Beginning in 2003, persons who selected this race group only; persons who selected more than one race group are not included. Prior to 2003, persons who reported more than one race group were included in the group they identified as their main race.

Table 1-26. Unemployed Persons, by Age, Sex, Race, and Hispanic Origin, 1948–2006—*Continued*

(Thousands of people.)

Race, Hispanic origin, sex, and year	16 years and over	16 to 19 years			20 years and over						
		Total	16 to 17 years	18 to 19 years	Total	20 to 24 years	25 to 34 years	35 to 44 years	45 to 54 years	55 to 64 years	65 years and over
WHITE[1]											
Women											
1954	946	157	66	90	789	134	202	199	148	88	17
1955	774	141	67	74	633	108	152	156	125	77	16
1956	793	161	79	83	632	111	141	151	130	81	17
1957	812	158	77	80	654	109	168	162	123	69	25
1958	1 191	208	96	113	983	159	231	250	210	106	26
1959	1 043	207	93	114	836	150	176	209	176	103	22
1960	1 077	234	106	128	843	161	197	190	185	87	23
1961	1 345	285	119	166	1 060	196	226	257	229	120	32
1962	1 137	246	104	142	891	188	183	211	177	99	33
1963	1 232	301	139	162	931	192	198	221	191	103	27
1964	1 220	308	148	159	912	198	179	217	181	107	30
1965	1 135	318	129	188	817	183	173	199	152	86	24
1966	1 014	311	137	174	703	166	138	163	138	73	23
1967	1 130	293	125	169	837	209	189	183	154	81	23
1968	1 084	316	141	175	768	216	168	157	127	76	25
1969	1 123	317	153	164	806	218	189	164	135	77	23
1970	1 482	386	183	202	1 096	291	254	221	199	98	31
1971	1 777	449	203	246	1 328	376	314	249	228	126	34
1972	1 733	457	227	230	1 275	381	304	227	202	125	35
1973	1 606	442	228	214	1 164	347	311	192	183	104	26
1974	1 927	519	250	270	1 408	420	387	230	214	122	35
1975	2 794	628	288	340	2 166	602	617	362	342	195	49
1976	2 656	611	280	330	2 045	577	598	336	296	188	49
1977	2 558	612	294	318	1 946	536	573	323	293	175	47
1978	2 287	574	292	281	1 713	500	533	294	226	122	37
1979	2 260	560	270	290	1 699	485	542	293	223	125	32
1980	2 540	576	278	298	1 964	537	645	362	259	129	31
1981	2 762	620	281	339	2 143	580	715	394	261	158	36
1982	3 395	680	296	384	2 715	704	898	527	337	217	33
1983	3 270	626	282	345	2 643	659	872	539	340	201	33
1984	2 772	508	231	277	2 264	559	731	464	297	173	39
1985	2 765	482	225	257	2 283	541	763	486	286	175	32
1986	2 708	495	233	262	2 213	504	773	470	281	159	27
1987	2 369	447	223	224	1 922	449	648	448	227	124	25
1988	2 177	412	198	214	1 766	393	594	413	227	110	30
1989	2 135	376	177	199	1 758	380	603	401	223	120	32
1990	2 251	399	187	212	1 852	389	605	453	251	116	37
1991	2 701	453	212	241	2 248	455	741	550	320	141	41
1992	2 959	447	214	233	2 512	469	811	625	372	177	58
1993	2 827	426	208	219	2 400	438	739	618	395	172	39
1994	2 617	420	211	208	2 197	397	652	558	361	170	58
1995	2 460	418	216	201	2 042	384	600	540	306	162	52
1996	2 404	407	196	211	1 998	376	568	525	326	148	55
1997	2 195	411	204	207	1 784	326	515	486	290	119	49
1998	2 053	365	171	195	1 688	327	467	460	279	112	43
1999	1 999	383	190	193	1 616	322	423	423	273	131	43
2000	1 944	349	168	180	1 595	314	407	414	289	133	39
2001	2 215	366	170	196	1 849	335	515	456	348	150	45
2002	2 678	409	179	230	2 269	415	567	565	449	213	60
2003	2 668	391	194	197	2 276	423	555	564	434	235	64
2004	2 565	393	191	202	2 172	399	516	510	437	250	60
2005	2 419	365	172	193	2 054	356	520	469	421	225	63
2006	2 271	345	173	172	1 927	349	462	437	395	222	62

[1]Beginning in 2003, persons who selected this race group only; persons who selected more than one race group are not included. Prior to 2003, persons who reported more than one race group were included in the group they identified as their main race.

Table 1-26. Unemployed Persons, by Age, Sex, Race, and Hispanic Origin, 1948–2006—*Continued*

(Thousands of people.)

Race, Hispanic origin, sex, and year	16 years and over	16 to 19 years			20 years and over						
		Total	16 to 17 years	18 to 19 years	Total	20 to 24 years	25 to 34 years	35 to 44 years	45 to 54 years	55 to 64 years	65 years and over
BLACK[1]											
Both Sexes											
1972	906	279	113	167	627	226	183	106	62	37	12
1973	846	262	114	148	584	231	181	82	53	29	9
1974	965	297	127	170	666	261	201	95	65	33	10
1975	1 369	330	130	200	1 040	362	321	157	126	54	17
1976	1 334	330	134	195	1 005	350	338	145	101	54	16
1977	1 393	354	135	218	1 040	397	355	140	81	51	16
1978	1 330	360	150	210	972	379	320	127	82	47	17
1979	1 319	333	137	197	986	369	335	137	82	48	15
1980	1 553	343	134	210	1 209	426	433	171	109	53	18
1981	1 731	357	138	219	1 374	483	493	207	119	55	17
1982	2 142	396	130	266	1 747	565	662	278	141	84	17
1983	2 272	392	125	267	1 879	591	700	299	174	95	21
1984	1 914	353	122	230	1 561	504	577	253	138	75	15
1985	1 864	357	135	221	1 507	455	562	254	143	74	18
1986	1 840	347	138	209	1 493	453	564	269	127	69	10
1987	1 684	312	134	178	1 373	397	533	247	124	62	10
1988	1 547	288	121	167	1 259	349	502	230	111	51	15
1989	1 544	300	116	184	1 245	322	494	246	109	53	20
1990	1 565	268	112	156	1 297	349	505	278	106	44	14
1991	1 723	280	105	175	1 443	378	539	318	151	44	13
1992	2 011	324	127	197	1 687	421	610	402	178	64	13
1993	1 844	313	112	201	1 530	387	532	376	153	72	11
1994	1 666	300	127	173	1 366	351	468	346	130	55	16
1995	1 538	325	143	182	1 213	311	423	303	116	42	18
1996	1 592	310	133	177	1 282	327	454	313	127	48	13
1997	1 560	302	123	179	1 258	327	426	307	136	45	16
1998	1 426	281	124	156	1 146	301	366	294	125	45	16
1999	1 309	268	109	159	1 041	273	339	249	121	46	14
2000	1 241	230	96	134	1 011	281	289	254	131	38	20
2001	1 416	260	102	158	1 155	307	340	283	159	52	15
2002	1 693	260	103	156	1 433	365	407	349	215	76	21
2003	1 787	255	93	162	1 532	375	442	385	217	93	20
2004	1 729	241	103	138	1 487	353	441	341	245	86	21
2005	1 700	267	115	152	1 433	358	423	310	222	92	28
2006	1 549	253	102	151	1 296	318	388	276	214	81	19
BLACK[1]											
Men											
1972	448	143	66	77	305	113	84	45	31	23	9
1973	395	128	62	66	267	108	75	37	27	16	5
1974	494	159	75	82	336	129	103	41	35	19	8
1975	741	170	71	100	571	195	169	83	78	33	13
1976	698	170	69	103	528	185	166	73	60	32	13
1977	698	187	73	114	512	197	170	63	40	31	12
1978	641	180	80	101	462	185	148	53	40	24	11
1979	636	164	68	97	473	174	152	66	44	27	10
1980	815	179	72	108	636	222	222	88	60	32	12
1981	891	188	73	115	703	248	245	102	65	32	10
1982	1 167	213	72	141	954	304	355	154	74	54	12
1983	1 213	211	70	142	1 002	313	358	162	96	59	14
1984	1 003	188	62	126	815	272	289	132	67	45	9
1985	951	193	69	124	757	224	268	127	85	43	11
1986	946	180	68	112	765	225	273	148	70	44	5
1987	826	160	70	90	666	186	253	122	61	39	6
1988	771	154	64	90	617	177	233	111	58	30	8
1989	773	153	65	88	619	162	226	129	59	33	10
1990	806	142	62	80	664	177	247	146	62	27	6
1991	890	145	54	91	745	201	252	172	87	25	7
1992	1 067	180	71	109	886	221	301	208	107	42	6
1993	971	170	66	104	801	201	260	201	87	46	7
1994	848	167	69	97	682	173	218	180	72	29	10
1995	762	168	73	95	593	153	195	150	63	21	11
1996	808	169	73	96	639	163	210	158	75	26	7
1997	747	162	70	92	585	165	178	141	72	22	7
1998	671	147	61	86	524	151	148	133	60	24	8
1999	626	145	60	85	480	135	143	114	60	22	7
2000	620	121	52	70	499	145	134	121	72	17	9
2001	709	136	51	85	573	150	159	142	84	31	7
2002	835	140	54	85	695	181	180	165	120	40	9
2003	891	132	49	83	760	192	212	189	109	47	10
2004	860	128	52	75	733	188	211	160	120	46	8
2005	844	145	63	82	699	192	189	143	116	45	14
2006	774	134	53	81	640	167	189	118	112	43	11

[1]Beginning in 2003, persons who selected this race group only; persons who selected more than one race group are not included. Prior to 2003, persons who reported more than one race group were included in the group they identified as their main race.

Table 1-26. Unemployed Persons, by Age, Sex, Race, and Hispanic Origin, 1948–2006—*Continued*

(Thousands of people.)

Race, Hispanic origin, sex, and year	16 years and over	16 to 19 years			20 years and over						
		Total	16 to 17 years	18 to 19 years	Total	20 to 24 years	25 to 34 years	35 to 44 years	45 to 54 years	55 to 64 years	65 years and over
BLACK[1]											
Women											
1972	458	136	47	90	322	113	99	61	31	14	3
1973	451	134	51	82	317	123	105	45	26	13	4
1974	470	139	51	87	331	132	98	55	30	14	2
1975	629	160	60	100	469	167	153	75	48	22	4
1976	637	160	66	93	477	165	172	73	41	23	3
1977	695	167	63	104	528	200	185	77	41	21	4
1978	690	179	70	110	510	194	173	74	41	23	6
1979	683	169	69	100	513	195	183	71	38	21	5
1980	738	164	62	102	574	204	211	83	49	21	6
1981	840	169	65	104	671	235	248	105	54	23	7
1982	975	182	58	124	793	261	307	123	67	29	5
1983	1 059	181	56	125	878	278	342	137	77	36	7
1984	911	165	60	104	747	231	288	121	71	30	5
1985	913	164	66	98	750	231	295	127	58	31	7
1986	894	167	70	97	728	228	291	121	57	25	5
1987	858	152	64	88	706	211	280	125	63	23	4
1988	776	134	57	78	642	172	269	118	53	22	7
1989	772	147	51	96	625	160	267	118	50	21	9
1990	758	126	49	76	633	172	258	132	44	17	8
1991	833	135	51	84	698	177	288	145	64	19	6
1992	944	144	56	88	800	200	308	194	71	22	6
1993	872	143	46	97	729	186	272	175	66	26	5
1994	818	133	57	76	685	178	249	166	59	26	6
1995	777	157	. . .	87	620	158	228	153	53	20	. . .
1996	784	141	60	80	643	164	244	155	52	21	7
1997	813	140	53	87	673	163	248	166	64	24	9
1998	756	134	63	71	622	150	218	160	65	21	8
1999	684	123	49	74	561	138	196	135	61	25	7
2000	621	109	44	65	512	136	154	132	59	22	10
2001	706	124	52	72	582	157	181	141	75	21	8
2002	858	120	49	71	738	183	228	185	95	35	12
2003	895	123	44	79	772	183	230	195	109	46	10
2004	868	114	51	63	755	166	230	180	126	40	13
2005	856	123	52	70	734	166	233	168	106	47	14
2006	775	120	50	70	656	150	199	158	102	38	8
HISPANIC[2]											
Both Sexes											
1973	277	80	. . .	. . .	. . .	. . .	. . .	. . .	. . .	. . .	. . .
1974	325	88	. . .	. . .	. . .	. . .	. . .	. . .	. . .	. . .	. . .
1975	508	123	. . .	. . .	. . .	. . .	. . .	. . .	. . .	. . .	. . .
1976	485	106	51	55	385	116	113	72	53	26	6
1977	456	113	50	60	344	98	114	56	48	24	5
1978	452	110	63	47	342	98	116	65	41	16	5
1979	434	106	54	51	329	100	102	65	37	20	4
1980	620	145	66	79	474	138	168	90	49	24	5
1981	678	144	60	84	533	171	178	92	57	31	5
1982	929	175	73	102	754	221	267	140	75	45	6
1983	961	167	64	104	793	214	270	156	93	54	5
1984	800	149	60	88	651	164	235	124	71	51	5
1985	811	141	55	85	670	171	256	123	73	41	7
1986	857	141	57	84	716	183	258	143	85	38	9
1987	751	136	57	79	615	152	222	128	75	33	5
1988	732	148	63	84	585	145	209	120	69	36	6
1989	750	132	59	73	618	158	218	124	76	36	6
1990	876	161	68	94	714	167	263	156	85	36	7
1991	1 092	179	79	99	913	214	332	206	110	44	8
1992	1 311	219	94	124	1 093	240	390	267	126	59	10
1993	1 248	201	86	115	1 047	237	354	261	132	54	10
1994	1 187	198	90	108	989	220	348	227	132	51	12
1995	1 140	205	96	109	934	209	325	224	106	54	16
1996	1 132	199	85	114	933	217	296	246	101	59	14
1997	1 069	197	87	110	872	206	269	229	99	56	13
1998	1 026	214	89	125	812	194	260	203	96	48	11
1999	945	196	79	117	750	171	233	190	104	42	10
2000	954	194	83	112	759	190	247	189	79	42	12
2001	1 138	208	84	123	931	212	315	228	111	56	9
2002	1 353	221	81	140	1 132	265	373	271	146	62	15
2003	1 441	192	79	113	1 249	273	419	294	183	69	10
2004	1 342	203	86	117	1 139	255	371	261	161	74	18
2005	1 191	191	78	113	1 000	227	324	231	142	61	15
2006	1 081	170	74	97	911	194	294	231	128	49	14

[1]Beginning in 2003, persons who selected this race group only; persons who selected more than one race group are not included. Prior to 2003, persons who reported more than one race group were included in the group they identified as their main race.
[2]May be of any race.
. . . = Not available.

Table 1-26. Unemployed Persons, by Age, Sex, Race, and Hispanic Origin, 1948–2006—*Continued*

(Thousands of people.)

Race, Hispanic origin, sex, and year	16 years and over	16 to 19 years			20 years and over						
		Total	16 to 17 years	18 to 19 years	Total	20 to 24 years	25 to 34 years	35 to 44 years	45 to 54 years	55 to 64 years	65 years and over
HISPANIC[2]											
Men											
1973	158	...	...	...	114	...	...	...	...	...	...
1974	187	...	...	...	139	...	...	...	...	...	...
1975	296	...	...	...	225	...	...	...	...	...	...
1976	278	60	30	31	217	69	63	38	29	16	...
1977	253	60	27	33	195	57	65	28	22	15	...
1978	234	59	35	24	175	51	59	30	20	10	...
1979	223	55	29	27	168	52	50	33	19	11	...
1980	370	86	39	47	284	85	96	51	31	16	...
1981	408	87	40	47	321	105	113	49	31	19	...
1982	565	104	45	59	461	138	169	80	40	29	...
1983	591	100	38	62	491	134	168	92	57	36	...
1984	480	87	36	51	393	103	142	69	41	33	...
1985	483	82	34	49	401	108	156	69	40	23	...
1986	520	82	33	50	438	115	159	86	46	26	...
1987	451	77	32	45	374	88	137	77	46	22	...
1988	437	86	36	50	351	83	128	70	42	24	...
1989	423	81	36	45	342	88	113	69	43	25	...
1990	524	100	40	60	425	99	154	91	53	25	...
1991	685	110	47	62	575	139	210	126	62	33	...
1992	807	132	56	75	675	156	239	156	75	42	...
1993	747	118	50	68	629	144	217	148	79	33	...
1994	680	121	54	67	558	128	203	113	75	30	9
1995	651	121	59	63	530	123	185	120	57	33	13
1996	607	112	49	63	495	117	165	124	49	31	9
1997	582	110	47	63	471	125	137	113	54	35	8
1998	552	117	54	62	436	115	142	97	49	29	5
1999	480	106	42	63	374	96	109	83	54	24	7
2000	494	106	46	60	388	105	118	93	42	23	8
2001	611	117	52	65	495	129	152	116	55	36	6
2002	764	127	42	86	636	151	213	144	82	38	8
2003	809	116	42	74	693	157	239	153	98	41	5
2004	755	120	48	72	635	158	207	133	82	41	13
2005	647	112	42	70	536	134	168	119	74	31	9
2006	601	104	43	61	497	110	169	114	66	29	8
HISPANIC[2]											
Women											
1973	119	...	...	...	83	...	...	...	...	...	...
1974	137	...	...	...	98	...	...	...	...	...	...
1975	212	...	...	...	160	...	...	...	...	...	...
1976	207	45	22	24	166	47	52	33	22	10	...
1977	204	50	23	27	153	40	49	28	25	11	...
1978	219	51	28	23	168	46	58	36	20	8	...
1979	211	50	26	24	160	48	52	32	18	10	...
1980	249	59	28	31	190	53	72	39	18	8	...
1981	269	57	20	37	212	65	65	43	25	13	...
1982	364	71	28	43	293	83	98	60	35	16	...
1983	369	68	26	42	302	80	102	65	36	18	...
1984	320	62	25	37	258	61	93	55	30	17	...
1985	327	58	22	37	269	63	100	54	32	18	...
1986	337	59	25	35	278	68	99	57	39	12	...
1987	300	59	25	34	241	64	85	51	29	11	...
1988	296	62	27	34	234	63	81	50	27	12	...
1989	327	51	23	28	276	70	105	55	33	11	...
1990	351	62	28	34	289	68	109	65	32	11	...
1991	407	69	32	37	339	74	122	80	48	12	...
1992	504	87	38	49	418	84	151	111	51	17	...
1993	501	83	36	47	418	93	136	113	53	21	...
1994	508	77	36	40	431	92	145	115	57	21	2
1995	488	84	38	46	404	86	140	104	50	21	3
1996	525	88	36	52	438	100	131	122	52	27	5
1997	488	87	40	46	401	81	132	117	46	21	4
1998	473	98	35	63	376	80	118	106	48	19	5
1999	466	90	36	54	376	75	124	107	50	17	3
2000	460	88	37	51	371	86	129	96	38	19	4
2001	527	91	33	58	436	83	163	112	56	20	3
2002	590	94	39	54	496	113	160	127	65	24	7
2003	631	76	37	39	555	116	180	141	86	28	5
2004	587	83	38	45	504	97	164	128	78	32	5
2005	544	80	36	43	464	93	156	112	68	30	6
2006	480	67	31	36	414	84	125	116	62	20	6

[2]May be of any race.
. . . = Not available.

Table 1-27. Unemployment Rates of Civilian Workers, by Age, Sex, Race, and Hispanic Origin, 1948–2006

(Percent of labor force.)

Race, Hispanic origin, sex, and year	16 years and over	16 to 19 years			20 years and over						
		Total	16 to 17 years	18 to 19 years	Total	20 to 24 years	25 to 34 years	35 to 44 years	45 to 54 years	55 to 64 years	65 years and over
ALL RACES											
Both Sexes											
1948	3.8	9.2	10.1	8.6	3.3	6.2	3.2	2.6	2.7	3.1	3.2
1949	5.9	13.4	14.0	13.0	5.4	9.3	5.4	4.4	4.2	5.2	4.9
1950	5.3	12.2	13.6	11.2	4.8	7.7	4.8	3.8	4.2	4.8	4.5
1951	3.3	8.2	9.6	7.1	3.0	4.1	3.0	2.5	2.7	3.1	3.4
1952	3.0	8.5	10.0	7.3	2.7	4.6	2.6	2.3	2.3	2.4	2.9
1953	2.9	7.6	8.7	6.8	2.6	4.7	2.5	2.2	2.3	2.7	2.2
1954	5.5	12.6	13.5	10.7	5.1	9.2	5.3	4.5	4.4	4.5	4.1
1955	4.4	11.0	12.3	10.0	3.9	7.0	3.8	3.4	3.4	4.2	3.6
1956	4.1	11.1	12.3	10.2	3.7	6.6	3.7	3.0	3.2	3.5	3.2
1957	4.3	11.6	12.5	10.9	3.8	7.1	3.9	3.1	3.3	3.4	3.4
1958	6.8	15.9	16.4	15.5	6.2	11.2	6.8	5.4	5.2	5.2	4.8
1959	5.5	14.6	15.3	14.0	4.8	8.5	5.0	4.2	4.2	4.4	4.3
1960	5.5	14.7	15.5	14.1	4.8	8.7	5.2	4.1	4.1	4.2	3.8
1961	6.7	16.8	18.3	15.8	5.9	10.4	6.2	5.2	5.0	5.4	5.1
1962	5.5	14.7	16.3	13.6	4.9	9.0	5.1	4.1	4.0	4.2	4.5
1963	5.7	17.2	19.3	15.6	4.8	8.8	5.2	4.0	3.8	4.1	4.1
1964	5.2	16.2	17.8	14.9	4.3	8.3	4.3	3.6	3.5	3.7	3.8
1965	4.5	14.8	16.5	13.5	3.6	6.7	3.7	3.2	2.8	3.1	3.3
1966	3.8	12.8	14.8	11.3	2.9	5.3	3.1	2.5	2.3	2.5	3.0
1967	3.8	12.9	14.6	11.6	3.0	5.7	3.2	2.5	2.4	2.4	2.8
1968	3.6	12.7	14.7	11.2	2.7	5.8	2.8	2.2	1.9	2.0	2.8
1969	3.5	12.2	14.5	10.5	2.7	5.7	2.8	2.2	1.9	1.9	2.2
1970	4.9	15.3	17.1	13.8	4.0	8.2	4.2	3.1	2.8	2.7	3.2
1971	5.9	16.9	18.7	15.5	4.9	10.0	5.3	3.9	3.4	3.3	3.5
1972	5.6	16.2	18.5	14.6	4.5	9.3	4.6	3.5	3.0	3.2	3.6
1973	4.9	14.5	17.3	12.4	3.9	7.8	4.2	2.7	2.5	2.6	3.0
1974	5.6	16.0	18.3	14.3	4.5	9.1	4.8	3.3	2.9	2.8	3.4
1975	8.5	19.9	21.4	18.9	7.3	13.6	7.8	5.6	5.2	4.6	5.2
1976	7.7	19.0	21.1	17.5	6.5	12.0	7.1	4.9	4.5	4.5	5.1
1977	7.1	17.8	19.9	16.2	5.9	11.0	6.5	4.4	3.9	3.9	5.0
1978	6.1	16.4	19.3	14.2	5.0	9.6	5.3	3.7	3.3	2.9	4.0
1979	5.8	16.1	18.1	14.7	4.8	9.1	5.2	3.6	3.2	2.9	3.4
1980	7.1	17.8	20.0	16.2	6.1	11.5	6.9	4.6	4.0	3.3	3.1
1981	7.6	19.6	21.4	18.4	6.5	12.3	7.3	5.0	4.2	3.7	3.2
1982	9.7	23.2	24.9	22.1	8.6	14.9	9.7	6.9	5.7	5.4	3.5
1983	9.6	22.4	24.5	21.1	8.6	14.5	9.7	7.0	6.2	5.6	3.7
1984	7.5	18.9	21.2	17.4	6.7	11.5	7.3	5.4	4.9	4.7	3.3
1985	7.2	18.6	21.0	17.0	6.4	11.1	7.0	5.1	4.7	4.3	3.2
1986	7.0	18.3	20.2	17.0	6.2	10.7	6.9	5.0	4.5	4.1	3.0
1987	6.2	16.9	19.1	15.2	5.4	9.7	6.0	4.5	4.0	3.5	2.5
1988	5.5	15.3	17.4	13.8	4.8	8.7	5.4	4.0	3.4	3.2	2.7
1989	5.3	15.0	17.2	13.6	4.6	8.6	5.2	3.8	3.2	3.2	2.6
1990	5.6	15.5	17.9	14.1	4.9	8.8	5.6	4.1	3.6	3.3	3.0
1991	6.8	18.7	21.0	17.2	6.1	10.8	6.9	5.2	4.5	4.1	3.3
1992	7.5	20.1	23.1	18.2	6.8	11.4	7.6	5.8	5.1	5.1	3.8
1993	6.9	19.0	21.4	17.5	6.2	10.5	6.9	5.5	4.8	4.7	3.2
1994	6.1	17.6	19.9	16.0	5.4	9.7	6.0	4.6	4.0	4.1	4.0
1995	5.6	17.3	20.2	15.3	4.9	9.1	5.4	4.3	3.3	3.6	4.0
1996	5.4	16.7	18.9	15.2	4.7	9.3	5.2	4.1	3.3	3.3	3.6
1997	4.9	16.0	18.2	14.5	4.3	8.5	4.7	3.8	3.0	2.9	3.3
1998	4.5	14.6	17.2	12.8	3.9	7.9	4.3	3.4	2.8	2.6	3.2
1999	4.2	13.9	16.3	12.4	3.6	7.5	4.0	3.0	2.6	2.7	3.1
2000	4.0	13.1	15.4	11.6	3.4	7.2	3.7	3.0	2.5	2.5	3.1
2001	4.7	14.7	17.2	13.1	4.2	8.3	4.6	3.6	3.1	3.0	2.9
2002	5.8	16.5	18.8	15.1	5.2	9.7	5.9	4.6	4.0	3.9	3.6
2003	6.0	17.5	19.1	16.4	5.4	10.0	6.1	4.9	4.1	4.1	3.8
2004	5.5	17.0	20.2	15.0	4.9	9.4	5.5	4.4	3.8	3.8	3.6
2005	5.1	16.6	19.1	14.9	4.5	8.8	5.1	3.9	3.5	3.3	3.5
2006	4.6	15.4	17.2	14.1	4.1	8.2	4.7	3.6	3.1	3.0	2.9

Table 1-27. Unemployment Rates of Civilian Workers, by Age, Sex, Race, and Hispanic Origin, 1948–2006
    —Continued

(Percent of labor force.)

Race, Hispanic origin, sex, and year	16 years and over	16 to 19 years			20 years and over						
		Total	16 to 17 years	18 to 19 years	Total	20 to 24 years	25 to 34 years	35 to 44 years	45 to 54 years	55 to 64 years	65 years and over
ALL RACES											
Men											
1948	3.6	9.8	10.2	9.5	3.2	6.9	2.8	2.4	2.5	3.1	3.4
1949	5.9	14.3	13.7	14.6	5.4	10.4	5.2	4.3	4.3	5.4	5.1
1950	5.1	12.7	13.3	12.3	4.7	8.1	4.4	3.6	4.0	4.9	4.8
1951	2.8	8.1	9.4	7.0	2.5	3.9	2.3	2.0	2.4	2.8	3.5
1952	2.8	8.9	10.5	7.4	2.4	4.6	2.2	1.9	2.2	2.4	3.0
1953	2.8	7.9	8.8	7.2	2.5	5.0	2.2	2.0	2.3	2.8	2.4
1954	5.3	13.5	13.9	13.2	4.9	10.7	4.8	4.1	4.3	4.5	4.4
1955	4.2	11.6	12.5	10.8	3.8	7.7	3.3	3.1	3.2	4.3	4.0
1956	3.8	11.1	11.7	10.5	3.4	6.9	3.3	2.6	3.0	3.5	3.5
1957	4.1	12.4	12.4	12.3	3.6	7.8	3.3	2.8	3.3	3.5	3.4
1958	6.8	17.1	16.3	17.8	6.2	12.7	6.5	5.1	5.3	5.5	5.2
1959	5.2	15.3	15.8	14.9	4.7	8.7	4.7	3.7	4.1	4.5	4.8
1960	5.4	15.3	15.5	15.0	4.7	8.9	4.8	3.8	4.1	4.6	4.2
1961	6.4	17.1	18.3	16.3	5.7	10.8	5.7	4.6	4.9	5.7	5.5
1962	5.2	14.7	16.0	13.8	4.6	8.9	4.5	3.6	3.9	4.6	4.6
1963	5.2	17.2	18.8	15.9	4.5	8.8	4.5	3.5	3.6	4.3	4.5
1964	4.6	15.8	17.1	14.6	3.9	8.1	3.5	2.9	3.2	3.9	4.0
1965	4.0	14.1	16.1	12.4	3.2	6.4	2.9	2.5	2.5	3.3	3.5
1966	3.2	11.7	13.7	10.2	2.5	4.6	2.4	2.0	1.9	2.6	3.1
1967	3.1	12.3	14.5	10.5	2.3	4.7	2.1	1.7	2.0	2.3	2.8
1968	2.9	11.6	13.9	9.7	2.2	5.1	1.9	1.6	1.6	1.9	2.8
1969	2.8	11.4	13.8	9.3	2.1	5.1	1.9	1.5	1.5	1.8	2.2
1970	4.4	15.0	16.9	13.4	3.5	8.4	3.5	2.4	2.4	2.8	3.3
1971	5.3	16.6	18.7	15.0	4.4	10.3	4.4	3.1	3.0	3.3	3.4
1972	5.0	15.9	18.3	14.1	4.0	9.3	3.8	2.7	2.6	3.2	3.6
1973	4.2	13.9	17.0	11.4	3.3	7.3	3.4	2.0	2.1	2.4	3.0
1974	4.9	15.6	18.4	13.3	3.8	8.8	4.0	2.6	2.4	2.6	3.3
1975	7.9	20.1	21.6	19.0	6.8	14.3	6.9	4.9	4.8	4.3	5.4
1976	7.1	19.2	21.4	17.6	5.9	12.1	6.2	4.1	4.0	4.2	5.1
1977	6.3	17.3	19.5	15.6	5.2	10.8	5.7	3.5	3.2	3.6	5.2
1978	5.3	15.8	19.1	13.3	4.3	9.2	4.4	2.8	2.7	2.8	4.2
1979	5.1	15.9	17.9	14.3	4.2	8.7	4.3	2.9	2.7	2.7	3.4
1980	6.9	18.3	20.4	16.7	5.9	12.5	6.7	4.1	3.6	3.4	3.1
1981	7.4	20.1	22.0	18.8	6.3	13.2	6.9	4.5	4.0	3.6	2.9
1982	9.9	24.4	26.4	23.1	8.8	16.4	10.1	6.9	5.6	5.5	3.7
1983	9.9	23.3	25.2	22.2	8.9	15.9	10.1	7.1	6.3	6.1	3.9
1984	7.4	19.6	21.9	18.3	6.6	11.9	7.2	5.2	4.6	5.0	3.0
1985	7.0	19.5	21.9	17.9	6.2	11.4	6.6	4.9	4.6	4.3	3.1
1986	6.9	19.0	20.8	17.7	6.1	11.0	6.7	5.1	4.4	4.3	3.2
1987	6.2	17.8	20.2	16.0	5.4	9.9	5.9	4.4	4.2	3.7	2.6
1988	5.5	16.0	18.2	14.6	4.8	8.9	5.3	3.8	3.5	3.5	2.5
1989	5.2	15.9	18.6	14.2	4.5	8.8	4.8	3.7	3.2	3.5	2.4
1990	5.7	16.3	18.4	15.0	5.0	9.1	5.5	4.1	3.7	3.8	3.0
1991	7.2	19.8	21.8	18.5	6.4	11.6	7.0	5.5	4.8	4.6	3.3
1992	7.9	21.5	24.6	19.5	7.1	12.2	7.8	6.1	5.6	5.8	3.3
1993	7.2	20.4	22.9	18.8	6.4	11.3	7.0	5.6	5.1	5.2	3.2
1994	6.2	19.0	21.0	17.6	5.4	10.2	5.9	4.5	4.0	4.4	4.0
1995	5.6	18.4	21.1	16.5	4.8	9.2	5.1	4.2	3.5	3.6	4.3
1996	5.4	18.1	20.8	16.3	4.6	9.5	4.9	4.0	3.5	3.3	3.4
1997	4.9	16.9	19.1	15.4	4.2	8.9	4.3	3.6	3.1	3.1	3.0
1998	4.4	16.2	19.1	14.1	3.7	8.1	3.9	3.0	2.8	2.8	3.1
1999	4.1	14.7	17.0	13.1	3.5	7.7	3.6	2.8	2.6	2.7	3.0
2000	3.9	14.0	16.8	12.2	3.3	7.3	3.4	2.8	2.4	2.4	3.3
2001	4.8	16.0	19.1	14.0	4.2	9.0	4.3	3.6	3.2	3.3	3.0
2002	5.9	18.1	21.1	16.4	5.3	10.2	5.8	4.5	4.2	4.3	3.4
2003	6.3	19.3	20.7	18.4	5.6	10.6	6.2	5.0	4.4	4.5	4.0
2004	5.6	18.4	22.0	16.3	5.0	10.1	5.5	4.3	3.9	3.9	3.7
2005	5.1	18.6	22.0	16.5	4.4	9.6	4.7	3.7	3.5	3.3	3.4
2006	4.6	16.9	18.6	15.7	4.0	8.7	4.5	3.3	3.1	3.0	2.8

Table 1-27. Unemployment Rates of Civilian Workers, by Age, Sex, Race, and Hispanic Origin, 1948–2006
—Continued

(Percent of labor force.)

Race, Hispanic origin, sex, and year	16 years and over	16 to 19 years			20 years and over						
		Total	16 to 17 years	18 to 19 years	Total	20 to 24 years	25 to 34 years	35 to 44 years	45 to 54 years	55 to 64 years	65 years and over
ALL RACES											
Women											
1948	4.1	8.3	10.0	7.4	3.6	4.8	4.3	. . .	. . .	3.1	2.3
1949	6.0	12.3	14.4	11.2	5.3	7.3	5.9	4.7	4.0	4.4	3.8
1950	5.7	11.4	14.2	9.8	5.1	6.9	5.7	4.4	4.5	4.5	3.4
1951	4.4	8.3	10.0	7.2	4.0	4.4	4.5	3.8	3.5	4.0	2.9
1952	3.6	8.0	9.1	7.3	3.2	4.5	3.6	3.0	2.5	2.5	2.2
1953	3.3	7.2	8.5	6.4	2.9	4.3	3.4	2.5	2.3	2.5	1.4
1954	6.0	11.4	12.7	7.7	5.5	7.3	6.6	5.3	4.6	4.6	3.0
1955	4.9	10.2	12.0	9.1	4.4	6.1	5.3	4.0	3.6	3.8	2.3
1956	4.8	11.2	13.2	9.9	4.2	6.3	4.8	3.9	3.6	3.6	2.3
1957	4.7	10.6	12.6	9.4	4.1	6.0	5.3	3.8	3.2	3.0	3.4
1958	6.8	14.3	16.6	12.9	6.1	8.9	7.3	6.2	4.9	4.5	3.7
1959	5.9	13.5	14.4	13.0	5.2	8.1	5.9	5.1	4.2	4.1	2.8
1960	5.9	13.9	15.5	12.9	5.1	8.3	6.3	4.8	4.2	3.4	2.9
1961	7.2	16.3	18.3	15.1	6.3	9.8	7.4	6.4	5.1	4.5	4.0
1962	6.2	14.6	16.7	13.5	5.4	9.1	6.5	5.2	4.1	3.5	4.2
1963	6.5	17.2	20.2	15.2	5.4	8.9	6.9	5.1	4.2	3.6	3.2
1964	6.2	16.6	18.8	15.2	5.2	8.6	6.3	5.0	3.9	3.3	3.3
1965	5.5	15.7	17.2	14.8	4.5	7.3	5.5	4.6	3.2	2.8	2.9
1966	4.8	14.1	16.6	12.6	3.8	6.3	4.5	3.6	2.9	2.3	2.8
1967	5.2	13.5	14.8	12.8	4.2	7.0	5.4	4.1	3.1	2.4	2.7
1968	4.8	14.0	15.9	12.9	3.8	6.7	4.7	3.4	2.4	2.2	2.7
1969	4.7	13.3	15.5	11.8	3.7	6.3	4.6	3.4	2.6	2.2	2.3
1970	5.9	15.6	17.4	14.4	4.8	7.9	5.7	4.4	3.5	2.7	3.1
1971	6.9	17.2	18.7	16.2	5.7	9.6	7.0	5.2	4.0	3.3	3.6
1972	6.6	16.7	18.8	15.2	5.4	9.4	6.2	4.9	3.6	3.3	3.5
1973	6.0	15.3	17.7	13.5	4.9	8.5	5.8	3.9	3.2	2.8	2.9
1974	6.7	16.6	18.2	15.4	5.5	9.5	6.2	4.6	3.7	3.2	3.6
1975	9.3	19.7	21.2	18.7	8.0	12.7	9.1	6.8	5.9	5.1	5.0
1976	8.6	18.7	20.8	17.4	7.4	11.9	8.4	6.1	5.2	4.9	5.0
1977	8.2	18.3	20.5	16.9	7.0	11.2	7.7	5.7	5.1	4.4	4.7
1978	7.2	17.1	19.5	15.3	6.0	10.1	6.7	5.0	4.0	3.2	3.8
1979	6.8	16.4	18.3	15.0	5.7	9.6	6.5	4.6	3.9	3.2	3.3
1980	7.4	17.2	19.6	15.6	6.4	10.4	7.2	5.3	4.5	3.3	3.1
1981	7.9	19.0	20.7	17.9	6.8	11.2	7.7	5.7	4.6	3.8	3.6
1982	9.4	21.9	23.2	21.0	8.3	13.2	9.3	7.0	5.9	5.2	3.2
1983	9.2	21.3	23.7	19.9	8.1	12.9	9.1	6.9	6.0	5.0	3.4
1984	7.6	18.0	20.4	16.6	6.8	10.9	7.4	5.6	5.2	4.3	3.8
1985	7.4	17.6	20.0	16.0	6.6	10.7	7.4	5.5	4.8	4.3	3.3
1986	7.1	17.6	19.6	16.3	6.2	10.3	7.2	5.0	4.5	3.8	2.8
1987	6.2	15.9	18.0	14.3	5.4	9.4	6.2	4.6	3.7	3.1	2.4
1988	5.6	14.4	16.6	12.9	4.9	8.5	5.6	4.1	3.4	2.7	2.9
1989	5.4	14.0	15.7	13.0	4.7	8.3	5.6	3.9	3.2	2.8	2.9
1990	5.5	14.7	17.4	13.1	4.9	8.5	5.6	4.2	3.4	2.8	3.1
1991	6.4	17.5	20.2	15.9	5.7	9.8	6.8	4.8	4.2	3.4	3.3
1992	7.0	18.6	21.5	16.6	6.3	10.3	7.4	5.5	4.6	4.2	4.5
1993	6.6	17.5	19.8	16.1	5.9	9.7	6.8	5.3	4.5	4.0	3.1
1994	6.0	16.2	18.7	14.3	5.4	9.2	6.2	4.7	4.0	3.9	4.0
1995	5.6	16.1	19.2	14.0	4.9	9.0	5.7	4.4	3.2	3.6	3.7
1996	5.4	15.2	16.9	14.0	4.8	9.0	5.5	4.2	3.2	3.4	4.0
1997	5.0	15.0	17.2	13.6	4.4	8.1	5.2	4.0	2.9	2.7	3.6
1998	4.6	12.9	15.1	11.5	4.1	7.8	4.8	3.8	2.7	2.4	3.3
1999	4.3	13.2	15.5	11.6	3.8	7.2	4.4	3.3	2.5	2.6	3.2
2000	4.1	12.1	13.9	10.8	3.6	7.1	4.1	3.3	2.5	2.5	2.7
2001	4.7	13.4	15.2	12.2	4.1	7.5	5.1	3.7	3.0	2.7	2.9
2002	5.6	14.9	16.6	13.8	5.1	9.1	5.9	4.6	3.8	3.5	3.9
2003	5.7	15.6	17.5	14.2	5.1	9.3	5.9	4.9	3.7	3.7	3.6
2004	5.4	15.5	18.5	13.5	4.9	8.7	5.6	4.4	3.7	3.6	3.4
2005	5.1	14.5	16.5	13.1	4.6	7.9	5.6	4.1	3.5	3.3	3.5
2006	4.6	13.8	15.9	12.4	4.1	7.6	4.9	3.9	3.1	2.9	3.0

. . . = Not available.

Table 1-27. Unemployment Rates of Civilian Workers, by Age, Sex, Race, and Hispanic Origin, 1948–2006
  —Continued

(Percent of labor force.)

Race, Hispanic origin, sex, and year	16 years and over	16 to 19 years			20 years and over						
		Total	16 to 17 years	18 to 19 years	Total	20 to 24 years	25 to 34 years	35 to 44 years	45 to 54 years	55 to 64 years	65 years and over
WHITE[1]											
Both Sexes											
1954	5.0	12.1	13.2	11.3	4.6	8.3	4.6	4.0	4.0	4.3	3.9
1955	3.9	10.4	12.0	9.2	3.4	6.2	3.1	2.9	3.1	3.8	3.4
1956	3.6	10.1	11.5	9.0	3.2	5.7	3.1	2.6	2.9	3.2	3.1
1957	3.8	10.6	11.9	9.6	3.4	6.3	3.3	2.8	3.0	3.2	3.2
1958	6.1	14.4	15.2	13.9	5.6	9.9	5.9	4.8	4.8	4.9	4.6
1959	4.8	13.1	14.4	12.1	4.3	7.3	4.2	3.7	3.8	4.1	4.1
1960	5.0	13.5	14.6	12.6	4.3	7.9	4.5	3.6	3.8	3.9	3.7
1961	6.0	15.3	16.7	14.4	5.3	9.4	5.3	4.5	4.5	5.0	4.8
1962	4.9	13.3	15.3	12.0	4.2	7.9	4.2	3.6	3.6	3.9	4.0
1963	5.0	15.5	17.9	13.7	4.2	7.7	4.4	3.5	3.5	3.8	3.8
1964	4.6	14.8	16.5	13.3	3.8	7.3	3.6	3.2	3.2	3.5	3.5
1965	4.1	13.4	14.8	12.3	3.3	6.1	3.2	2.9	2.5	2.9	3.2
1966	3.4	11.2	13.3	9.7	2.6	4.6	2.6	2.3	2.1	2.4	2.9
1967	3.4	11.0	12.8	9.8	2.7	5.0	2.7	2.3	2.2	2.3	2.7
1968	3.2	11.0	12.9	9.6	2.5	5.2	2.4	2.0	1.8	1.9	2.8
1969	3.1	10.7	13.0	8.9	2.4	5.0	2.5	2.0	1.8	1.8	2.2
1970	4.5	13.5	15.5	11.9	3.7	7.3	3.8	3.0	2.7	2.7	3.2
1971	5.4	15.1	17.0	13.8	4.5	9.0	4.7	3.6	3.3	3.3	3.5
1972	5.1	14.2	16.6	12.3	4.1	8.4	4.1	3.2	2.9	3.1	3.4
1973	4.3	12.6	15.4	10.4	3.5	6.8	3.7	2.5	2.4	2.5	2.9
1974	5.0	14.0	16.3	12.2	4.1	8.0	4.4	3.1	2.8	2.8	3.3
1975	7.8	17.9	19.5	16.7	6.7	12.3	7.1	5.2	4.9	4.5	5.1
1976	7.0	16.9	19.0	15.3	5.9	10.7	6.3	4.5	4.2	4.3	4.9
1977	6.2	15.4	17.9	13.5	5.3	9.3	5.7	4.0	3.8	3.7	4.9
1978	5.2	13.9	17.0	11.5	4.3	8.0	4.6	3.3	3.0	2.7	3.8
1979	5.1	14.0	16.1	12.4	4.2	7.6	4.4	3.2	3.0	2.7	3.1
1980	6.3	15.5	17.9	13.8	5.4	9.9	6.1	4.2	3.7	3.1	2.7
1981	6.7	17.3	19.2	15.9	5.7	10.4	6.3	4.5	3.9	3.5	2.8
1982	8.6	20.4	22.8	18.8	7.6	12.8	8.5	6.3	5.4	5.1	3.1
1983	8.4	19.3	22.0	17.6	7.5	12.1	8.4	6.3	5.7	5.2	3.2
1984	6.5	16.0	18.8	14.3	5.7	9.3	6.2	4.8	4.4	4.4	3.0
1985	6.2	15.7	18.3	13.9	5.5	9.2	5.9	4.6	4.3	4.0	2.9
1986	6.0	15.6	17.6	14.1	5.3	8.7	5.9	4.5	4.1	3.8	2.9
1987	5.3	14.4	16.7	12.7	4.7	8.0	5.1	4.0	3.7	3.2	2.4
1988	4.7	13.1	15.3	11.6	4.1	7.1	4.5	3.5	3.1	3.0	2.4
1989	4.5	12.7	15.2	11.1	3.9	7.2	4.3	3.3	2.9	3.0	2.3
1990	4.8	13.5	15.8	12.1	4.3	7.3	4.6	3.6	3.3	3.2	2.8
1991	6.1	16.5	19.0	14.9	5.5	9.2	6.1	4.7	4.2	4.0	3.1
1992	6.6	17.2	20.3	15.2	6.0	9.5	6.7	5.2	4.8	4.9	3.7
1993	6.1	16.2	19.0	14.4	5.5	8.8	6.0	4.9	4.5	4.3	3.0
1994	5.3	15.1	17.6	13.3	4.7	8.1	5.2	4.0	3.7	3.9	3.8
1995	4.9	14.5	17.3	12.5	4.3	7.7	4.6	3.9	3.1	3.5	3.8
1996	4.7	14.2	16.4	12.6	4.1	7.8	4.4	3.6	3.1	3.2	3.5
1997	4.2	13.6	15.8	12.0	3.6	6.9	3.9	3.3	2.7	2.7	3.0
1998	3.9	12.6	14.8	11.0	3.3	6.5	3.7	2.9	2.6	2.4	2.9
1999	3.7	12.0	14.5	10.2	3.1	6.3	3.3	2.7	2.4	2.5	2.9
2000	3.5	11.4	13.9	9.8	3.0	5.9	3.2	2.6	2.2	2.4	2.8
2001	4.2	12.7	15.3	11.0	3.7	7.0	4.1	3.2	2.8	2.9	2.8
2002	5.1	14.5	16.7	13.2	4.6	8.1	5.2	4.1	3.7	3.7	3.5
2003	5.2	15.2	17.2	13.9	4.7	8.4	5.3	4.3	3.7	3.8	3.7
2004	4.8	15.0	17.9	13.1	4.3	7.9	4.7	3.9	3.4	3.6	3.3
2005	4.4	14.2	16.4	12.7	3.9	7.2	4.3	3.5	3.1	3.0	3.1
2006	4.0	13.2	15.1	11.9	3.6	6.9	4.0	3.2	2.8	2.8	2.8

[1]Beginning in 2003, persons who selected this race group only; persons who selected more than one race group are not included. Prior to 2003, persons who reported more than one race group were included in the group they identified as their main race.

Table 1-27. Unemployment Rates of Civilian Workers, by Age, Sex, Race, and Hispanic Origin, 1948–2006 —Continued

(Percent of labor force.)

Race, Hispanic origin, sex, and year	16 years and over	16 to 19 years			20 years and over						
		Total	16 to 17 years	18 to 19 years	Total	20 to 24 years	25 to 34 years	35 to 44 years	45 to 54 years	55 to 64 years	65 years and over
WHITE[1]											
Men											
1954	4.8	13.4	14.0	13.0	4.4	9.8	4.2	3.6	3.8	4.3	4.2
1955	3.7	11.3	12.2	10.4	3.3	7.0	2.7	2.6	2.9	3.9	3.8
1956	3.4	10.5	11.2	9.7	3.0	6.1	2.8	2.2	2.8	3.1	3.4
1957	3.6	11.5	11.9	11.1	3.2	7.0	2.7	2.5	3.0	3.4	3.2
1958	6.1	15.7	14.9	16.5	5.5	11.7	5.6	4.4	4.8	5.2	5.0
1959	4.6	14.0	15.0	13.0	4.1	7.5	3.8	3.2	3.7	4.2	4.5
1960	4.8	14.0	14.6	13.5	4.2	8.3	4.1	3.3	3.6	4.1	4.0
1961	5.7	15.7	16.5	15.2	5.1	10.1	4.9	4.0	4.4	5.3	5.2
1962	4.6	13.7	15.2	12.7	4.0	8.1	3.8	3.1	3.5	4.1	4.0
1963	4.7	15.9	17.8	14.2	3.9	7.8	3.9	2.9	3.3	4.0	4.1
1964	4.1	14.7	16.1	13.3	3.4	7.4	3.0	2.5	2.9	3.5	3.6
1965	3.6	12.9	14.7	11.3	2.9	5.9	2.6	2.3	2.3	3.1	3.4
1966	2.8	10.5	12.5	8.9	2.2	4.1	2.1	1.7	1.7	2.5	3.0
1967	2.7	10.7	12.7	9.0	2.1	4.2	1.9	1.6	1.8	2.2	2.7
1968	2.6	10.1	12.3	8.3	2.0	4.6	1.7	1.4	1.5	1.7	2.8
1969	2.5	10.0	12.5	7.9	1.9	4.6	1.7	1.4	1.4	1.7	2.2
1970	4.0	13.7	15.7	12.0	3.2	7.8	3.1	2.3	2.3	2.7	3.2
1971	4.9	15.1	17.1	13.5	4.0	9.4	4.0	2.9	2.9	3.2	3.4
1972	4.5	14.2	16.4	12.4	3.6	8.5	3.4	2.5	2.5	3.0	3.3
1973	3.8	12.3	15.2	10.0	3.0	6.6	3.0	1.8	2.0	2.4	2.9
1974	4.4	13.5	16.2	11.5	3.5	7.8	3.6	2.4	2.2	2.5	3.0
1975	7.2	18.3	19.7	17.2	6.2	13.1	6.3	4.5	4.4	4.1	5.0
1976	6.4	17.3	19.7	15.5	5.4	10.9	5.6	3.7	3.7	4.0	4.7
1977	5.5	15.0	17.6	13.0	4.7	9.3	5.0	3.1	3.0	3.3	4.9
1978	4.6	13.5	16.9	10.8	3.7	7.7	3.8	2.5	2.5	2.6	3.9
1979	4.5	13.9	16.1	12.2	3.6	7.5	3.7	2.5	2.5	2.5	3.2
1980	6.1	16.2	18.5	14.5	5.3	11.1	5.9	3.6	3.3	3.1	2.5
1981	6.5	17.9	19.9	16.4	5.6	11.6	6.1	4.0	3.6	3.4	2.4
1982	8.8	21.7	24.2	20.0	7.8	14.3	8.9	6.2	5.3	5.1	3.2
1983	8.8	20.2	22.6	18.7	7.9	13.8	9.0	6.4	5.7	5.6	3.2
1984	6.4	16.8	19.7	15.0	5.7	9.8	6.2	4.6	4.2	4.7	2.6
1985	6.1	16.5	19.2	14.7	5.4	9.7	5.7	4.3	4.1	4.0	2.7
1986	6.0	16.3	18.4	14.7	5.3	9.2	5.8	4.4	4.0	4.0	3.0
1987	5.4	15.5	17.9	13.7	4.8	8.4	5.2	3.9	3.9	3.4	2.5
1988	4.7	13.9	16.1	12.4	4.1	7.4	4.6	3.4	3.2	3.3	2.2
1989	4.5	13.7	16.4	12.0	3.9	7.5	4.1	3.2	2.9	3.1	2.1
1990	4.9	14.3	16.1	13.2	4.3	7.6	4.7	3.5	3.4	3.6	2.8
1991	6.5	17.6	19.7	16.3	5.8	10.2	6.4	5.0	4.4	4.6	3.1
1992	7.0	18.5	21.5	16.5	6.4	10.5	7.0	5.5	5.1	5.5	3.2
1993	6.3	17.7	20.2	16.0	5.7	9.6	6.2	5.0	4.7	4.7	2.9
1994	5.4	16.3	18.5	14.7	4.8	8.8	5.2	3.9	3.7	4.1	3.7
1995	4.9	15.6	18.2	13.8	4.3	7.9	4.5	3.8	3.2	3.4	4.0
1996	4.7	15.5	18.3	13.5	4.1	8.1	4.2	3.5	3.1	3.2	3.2
1997	4.2	14.3	16.3	12.9	3.6	7.3	3.7	3.2	2.8	3.0	2.7
1998	3.9	14.1	17.1	12.1	3.2	6.7	3.5	2.6	2.6	2.6	2.9
1999	3.6	12.6	15.1	10.8	3.0	6.5	3.1	2.4	2.4	2.6	2.9
2000	3.4	12.3	15.3	10.4	2.8	5.9	2.9	2.4	2.2	2.4	3.0
2001	4.2	13.9	17.4	11.7	3.7	7.8	3.8	3.1	2.9	3.2	2.8
2002	5.3	15.9	18.8	14.2	4.7	8.7	5.3	4.1	3.8	4.0	3.4
2003	5.6	17.1	18.5	16.1	5.0	9.1	5.5	4.4	4.0	4.2	3.8
2004	5.0	16.3	19.8	14.2	4.4	8.5	4.8	3.8	3.5	3.7	3.5
2005	4.4	16.1	18.9	14.3	3.8	7.9	4.1	3.3	3.0	3.0	3.1
2006	4.0	14.6	16.5	13.4	3.5	7.3	3.9	3.0	2.7	2.8	2.7

[1]Beginning in 2003, persons who selected this race group only; persons who selected more than one race group are not included. Prior to 2003, persons who reported more than one race group were included in the group they identified as their main race.

Table 1-27. Unemployment Rates of Civilian Workers, by Age, Sex, Race, and Hispanic Origin, 1948–2006
—*Continued*

(Percent of labor force.)

Race, Hispanic origin, sex, and year	16 years and over	16 to 19 years			20 years and over						
		Total	16 to 17 years	18 to 19 years	Total	20 to 24 years	25 to 34 years	35 to 44 years	45 to 54 years	55 to 64 years	65 years and over
WHITE[1]											
Women											
1954	5.5	10.4	12.0	9.4	5.1	6.4	5.7	4.9	4.4	4.5	2.8
1955	4.3	9.1	11.6	7.7	3.9	5.1	4.3	3.8	3.4	3.6	2.2
1956	4.2	9.7	12.1	8.3	3.7	5.1	4.0	3.5	3.3	3.5	2.3
1957	4.3	9.5	11.9	7.8	3.8	5.1	4.7	3.7	3.0	2.9	3.4
1958	6.2	12.7	15.6	11.0	5.6	7.3	6.6	5.6	4.9	4.3	3.5
1959	5.3	12.0	13.3	11.1	4.7	7.0	5.2	4.7	3.9	4.0	2.9
1960	5.3	12.7	14.5	11.5	4.6	7.2	5.7	4.2	4.0	3.3	2.8
1961	6.5	14.8	17.0	13.6	5.7	8.4	6.6	5.6	4.8	4.3	3.8
1962	5.5	12.8	15.6	11.3	4.7	7.7	5.4	4.5	3.7	3.5	4.0
1963	5.8	15.1	18.1	13.2	4.8	7.4	5.8	4.6	3.9	3.5	3.3
1964	5.5	14.9	17.1	13.2	4.6	7.1	5.2	4.5	3.6	3.5	3.4
1965	5.0	14.0	15.0	13.4	4.0	6.3	4.9	4.1	3.0	2.7	2.7
1966	4.3	12.1	14.5	10.7	3.3	5.3	3.7	3.3	2.7	2.2	2.7
1967	4.6	11.5	12.9	10.6	3.8	6.0	4.7	3.7	2.9	2.3	2.6
1968	4.3	12.1	13.9	11.0	3.4	5.9	3.9	3.1	2.3	2.1	2.8
1969	4.2	11.5	13.7	10.0	3.4	5.5	4.2	3.2	2.4	2.1	2.4
1970	5.4	13.4	15.3	11.9	4.4	6.9	5.3	4.3	3.4	2.6	3.3
1971	6.3	15.1	16.7	14.1	5.3	8.5	6.3	4.9	3.9	3.3	3.6
1972	5.9	14.2	17.0	12.3	4.9	8.2	5.5	4.4	3.5	3.3	3.7
1973	5.3	13.0	15.8	10.9	4.3	7.1	5.1	3.7	3.2	2.7	2.8
1974	6.1	14.5	16.4	13.0	5.1	8.2	5.8	4.3	3.6	3.2	3.9
1975	8.6	17.4	19.2	16.1	7.5	11.2	8.4	6.5	5.8	5.0	5.3
1976	7.9	16.4	18.2	15.1	6.8	10.4	7.6	5.8	5.0	4.8	5.3
1977	7.3	15.9	18.2	14.2	6.2	9.3	6.7	5.3	5.0	4.4	4.9
1978	6.2	14.4	17.1	12.4	5.2	8.3	5.8	4.5	3.8	3.0	3.7
1979	5.9	14.0	15.9	12.5	5.0	7.8	5.6	4.2	3.7	3.0	3.1
1980	6.5	14.8	17.3	13.1	5.6	8.5	6.3	4.9	4.3	3.1	3.0
1981	6.9	16.6	18.4	15.3	5.9	9.1	6.6	5.1	4.2	3.7	3.4
1982	8.3	19.0	21.2	17.6	7.3	10.9	8.0	6.4	5.5	5.0	3.1
1983	7.9	18.3	21.4	16.4	6.9	10.3	7.6	6.2	5.5	4.7	3.1
1984	6.5	15.2	17.8	13.6	5.8	8.8	6.1	5.0	4.8	4.0	3.7
1985	6.4	14.8	17.2	13.1	5.7	8.5	6.2	4.9	4.5	4.1	3.1
1986	6.1	14.9	16.7	13.6	5.4	8.1	6.1	4.5	4.3	3.7	2.6
1987	5.2	13.4	15.5	11.7	4.6	7.4	5.0	4.1	3.3	2.9	2.4
1988	4.7	12.3	14.4	10.8	4.1	6.7	4.5	3.7	3.1	2.5	2.6
1989	4.5	11.5	13.8	10.1	4.0	6.8	4.5	3.4	2.9	2.7	2.5
1990	4.7	12.6	15.5	10.9	4.1	6.8	4.6	3.7	3.2	2.7	2.8
1991	5.6	15.2	18.2	13.3	5.0	8.1	5.7	4.3	4.0	3.3	3.1
1992	6.1	15.8	18.9	13.7	5.5	8.3	6.2	4.9	4.3	4.0	4.5
1993	5.7	14.7	17.8	12.6	5.2	7.9	5.8	4.7	4.3	3.9	3.0
1994	5.2	13.8	16.6	11.8	4.6	7.4	5.1	4.2	3.7	3.7	3.9
1995	4.8	13.4	16.4	11.2	4.3	7.4	4.7	3.9	3.0	3.5	3.5
1996	4.7	12.9	14.4	11.7	4.1	7.4	4.6	3.8	3.1	3.1	3.8
1997	4.2	12.8	15.2	11.1	3.7	6.4	4.2	3.4	2.6	2.4	3.4
1998	3.9	10.9	12.4	9.8	3.4	6.3	3.9	3.3	2.5	2.2	3.0
1999	3.8	11.3	13.9	9.6	3.3	6.1	3.6	3.0	2.3	2.5	2.9
2000	3.6	10.4	12.5	9.0	3.1	5.8	3.5	2.9	2.3	2.4	2.4
2001	4.1	11.4	13.1	10.2	3.6	6.1	4.5	3.3	2.7	2.5	2.7
2002	4.9	13.1	14.6	12.1	4.4	7.4	5.0	4.1	3.5	3.3	3.5
2003	4.8	13.3	15.9	11.5	4.4	7.6	4.9	4.2	3.3	3.4	3.5
2004	4.7	13.6	16.1	11.9	4.2	7.1	4.6	3.9	3.3	3.5	3.1
2005	4.4	12.3	14.0	11.1	3.9	6.4	4.7	3.6	3.1	3.0	3.2
2006	4.0	11.7	13.8	10.2	3.6	6.3	4.1	3.4	2.9	2.8	3.0

[1]Beginning in 2003, persons who selected this race group only; persons who selected more than one race group are not included. Prior to 2003, persons who reported more than one race group were included in the group they identified as their main race.

Table 1-27. Unemployment Rates of Civilian Workers, by Age, Sex, Race, and Hispanic Origin, 1948–2006
—Continued

(Percent of labor force.)

Race, Hispanic origin, sex, and year	16 years and over	16 to 19 years			20 years and over						
		Total	16 to 17 years	18 to 19 years	Total	20 to 24 years	25 to 34 years	35 to 44 years	45 to 54 years	55 to 64 years	65 years and over
BLACK[1]											
Both Sexes											
1972	10.4	35.4	38.7	33.6	7.9	16.3	8.7	6.1	4.2	4.1	4.3
1973	9.4	31.5	37.0	28.1	7.2	15.5	8.1	4.7	3.5	3.2	3.5
1974	10.5	35.0	40.0	31.8	8.0	17.5	8.5	5.4	4.3	3.6	3.9
1975	14.8	39.5	41.6	38.1	12.3	24.5	13.0	8.9	8.3	5.9	6.6
1976	14.0	39.3	44.2	36.7	11.5	22.7	12.8	8.0	6.7	5.9	5.9
1977	14.0	41.1	44.5	39.2	11.5	24.2	12.7	7.4	5.3	5.5	5.9
1978	12.8	38.7	43.9	35.7	10.2	21.8	10.8	6.4	5.2	4.8	5.8
1979	12.3	36.5	40.2	34.4	10.1	20.6	10.8	6.7	5.2	4.9	5.3
1980	14.3	38.5	41.1	37.1	12.1	23.6	13.3	8.2	6.8	5.4	6.9
1981	15.6	41.4	44.8	39.5	13.4	26.4	14.7	9.5	7.4	5.5	7.0
1982	18.9	48.0	48.6	47.8	16.6	30.6	19.0	12.1	8.7	8.3	7.1
1983	19.5	48.5	50.5	47.6	17.3	31.6	19.0	12.4	10.7	9.2	9.2
1984	15.9	42.7	45.7	41.2	13.9	26.1	15.2	9.9	8.2	7.4	6.5
1985	15.1	40.2	43.6	38.3	13.1	24.5	14.5	9.5	8.2	7.0	7.0
1986	14.5	39.3	43.0	37.2	12.7	24.1	14.0	9.6	7.1	6.6	4.5
1987	13.0	34.7	39.7	31.6	11.3	21.8	12.8	8.4	6.8	5.6	3.9
1988	11.7	32.4	35.1	30.7	10.2	19.6	11.9	7.5	5.9	4.8	5.5
1989	11.4	32.4	32.9	32.2	9.9	18.0	11.5	7.6	5.6	5.2	6.9
1990	11.4	30.9	36.5	27.8	10.1	19.9	11.7	7.8	5.3	4.6	5.3
1991	12.5	36.1	39.5	34.4	11.1	21.6	12.7	8.5	7.4	4.4	5.2
1992	14.2	39.7	44.7	37.1	12.6	23.8	14.2	10.5	8.3	6.2	4.9
1993	13.0	38.8	39.7	38.4	11.4	21.9	12.6	9.5	6.9	7.1	4.7
1994	11.5	35.2	36.1	34.6	10.0	19.5	11.1	8.5	5.6	5.4	6.2
1995	10.4	35.7	39.1	33.4	8.7	17.7	9.9	7.3	4.8	4.0	6.7
1996	10.5	33.6	36.3	31.7	9.0	18.8	10.5	7.3	5.0	4.4	5.3
1997	10.0	32.4	35.0	30.8	8.6	18.3	9.9	7.0	5.0	4.2	6.1
1998	8.9	27.6	33.6	24.2	7.7	16.8	8.4	6.5	4.4	3.9	5.6
1999	8.0	27.9	31.0	26.2	6.8	14.6	7.6	5.3	4.0	3.9	5.0
2000	7.6	24.5	26.9	22.9	6.5	15.0	6.7	5.6	4.1	3.0	6.1
2001	8.6	29.0	30.8	27.9	7.4	16.3	8.1	6.3	4.8	3.9	4.3
2002	10.2	29.8	34.9	27.2	9.1	19.1	9.9	7.8	6.3	5.4	5.9
2003	10.8	33.0	32.2	33.5	9.7	19.8	10.9	8.6	6.2	6.3	5.4
2004	10.4	31.7	37.8	28.3	9.4	18.4	10.8	7.8	6.9	5.6	5.5
2005	10.0	33.3	41.2	29.0	8.8	18.3	10.2	7.1	6.0	5.6	6.9
2006	8.9	29.1	32.2	27.3	7.9	16.2	9.3	6.3	5.7	4.6	4.7
BLACK[1]											
Men											
1972	9.3	31.7	36.7	28.4	7.0	14.9	7.2	4.8	3.8	4.4	5.4
1973	8.0	27.8	35.7	23.0	6.0	13.2	6.2	3.9	3.2	3.2	3.3
1974	9.8	33.1	39.9	28.3	7.4	16.2	8.1	4.3	4.2	3.6	5.3
1975	14.8	38.1	41.9	35.9	12.5	24.7	12.7	8.7	9.3	6.3	8.7
1976	13.7	37.5	40.8	36.0	11.4	22.6	12.0	7.5	7.3	6.3	8.7
1977	13.3	39.2	41.0	38.2	10.7	23.0	11.8	6.2	4.9	6.0	7.8
1978	11.8	36.7	43.0	32.9	9.3	21.0	9.8	5.1	4.9	4.4	6.6
1979	11.4	34.2	37.9	32.2	9.3	18.7	9.6	6.3	5.2	5.1	6.4
1980	14.5	37.5	39.7	36.2	12.4	23.7	13.4	8.2	7.2	6.2	8.7
1981	15.7	40.7	43.2	39.2	13.5	26.4	14.4	9.3	7.8	6.1	7.5
1982	20.1	48.9	52.7	47.1	17.8	31.5	20.1	13.4	9.0	10.3	9.3
1983	20.3	48.8	52.2	47.3	18.1	31.4	19.4	13.5	11.4	11.0	11.8
1984	16.4	42.7	44.0	42.2	14.3	26.6	15.0	10.4	7.9	8.9	7.9
1985	15.3	41.0	42.9	40.0	13.2	23.5	13.8	9.6	9.7	7.9	8.9
1986	14.8	39.3	41.4	38.2	12.9	23.5	13.5	10.9	7.8	8.0	4.3
1987	12.7	34.4	39.0	31.6	11.1	20.3	12.2	8.7	6.7	6.6	4.3
1988	11.7	32.7	34.4	31.7	10.1	19.4	11.0	7.6	6.2	5.2	5.6
1989	11.5	31.9	34.4	30.3	10.0	17.9	10.5	8.4	6.2	6.2	7.4
1990	11.9	31.9	38.8	28.0	10.4	20.1	11.5	8.4	6.3	5.4	4.6
1991	13.0	36.3	39.0	34.8	11.5	22.4	11.9	9.5	8.6	5.0	6.1
1992	15.2	42.0	47.5	39.1	13.5	24.6	14.2	11.2	10.3	8.1	4.9
1993	13.8	40.1	42.7	38.6	12.1	23.0	12.3	10.5	8.1	9.0	5.8
1994	12.0	37.6	39.3	36.5	10.3	19.4	10.6	9.1	6.5	6.0	8.2
1995	10.6	37.1	39.7	35.4	8.8	17.6	9.3	7.6	5.5	4.4	7.6
1996	11.1	36.9	39.9	34.9	9.4	19.2	10.1	7.8	6.3	5.2	5.0
1997	10.2	36.5	39.5	34.4	8.5	19.8	8.7	6.7	5.6	4.2	5.5
1998	8.9	30.1	33.9	27.9	7.4	18.0	7.3	6.2	4.4	4.5	5.2
1999	8.2	30.9	33.3	29.4	6.7	16.2	6.9	5.2	4.3	3.9	5.0
2000	8.0	26.2	28.5	24.7	6.9	16.6	6.7	5.8	4.8	2.7	6.3
2001	9.3	30.4	30.5	30.4	8.0	17.6	8.3	6.9	5.5	4.8	4.0
2002	10.7	31.3	36.6	28.7	9.5	20.0	9.4	8.0	7.4	6.1	5.0
2003	11.6	36.0	35.6	36.3	10.3	20.9	11.3	9.2	6.7	6.8	5.6
2004	11.1	35.6	40.8	32.7	9.9	20.3	10.9	8.0	7.2	6.4	4.2
2005	10.5	36.3	45.1	31.5	9.2	20.5	9.7	7.0	6.7	5.9	7.1
2006	9.5	32.7	34.8	31.5	8.3	17.2	9.5	5.9	6.3	5.5	5.8

[1]Beginning in 2003, persons who selected this race group only; persons who selected more than one race group are not included. Prior to 2003, persons who reported more than one race group were included in the group they identified as their main race.

Table 1-27. Unemployment Rates of Civilian Workers, by Age, Sex, Race, and Hispanic Origin, 1948–2006
—*Continued*

(Percent of labor force.)

Race, Hispanic origin, sex, and year	16 years and over	16 to 19 years			20 years and over						
		Total	16 to 17 years	18 to 19 years	Total	20 to 24 years	25 to 34 years	35 to 44 years	45 to 54 years	55 to 64 years	65 years and over
BLACK[1]											
Women											
1972	11.8	40.5	42.0	40.1	9.0	17.9	10.5	7.6	4.6	3.7	2.6
1973	11.1	36.1	38.6	34.2	8.6	18.4	10.3	5.6	3.9	3.3	3.7
1974	11.3	37.4	40.2	36.0	8.8	19.0	9.0	6.6	4.4	3.6	1.9
1975	14.8	41.0	41.2	40.6	12.2	24.3	13.4	9.0	7.0	5.3	3.6
1976	14.3	41.6	48.4	37.6	11.7	22.8	13.6	8.5	5.9	5.4	2.4
1977	14.9	43.4	49.5	40.4	12.3	25.5	13.6	8.7	5.8	4.8	3.4
1978	13.8	40.8	45.0	38.7	11.2	22.7	11.9	7.8	5.6	5.2	4.7
1979	13.3	39.1	42.7	36.9	10.9	22.6	12.1	7.2	5.2	4.7	3.9
1980	14.0	39.8	42.9	38.2	11.9	23.5	13.2	8.2	6.4	4.5	4.9
1981	15.6	42.2	46.5	39.8	13.4	26.4	14.9	9.8	6.9	4.7	6.0
1982	17.6	47.1	44.2	48.6	15.4	29.6	17.8	10.7	8.5	6.1	4.5
1983	18.6	48.2	48.6	48.0	16.5	31.8	18.6	11.4	9.9	7.3	6.3
1984	15.4	42.6	47.5	40.2	13.5	25.6	15.4	9.4	8.6	5.9	4.9
1985	14.9	39.2	44.3	36.4	13.1	25.6	15.1	9.3	6.8	6.0	5.2
1986	14.2	39.2	44.6	36.1	12.4	24.7	14.6	8.5	6.4	5.0	4.9
1987	13.2	34.9	40.5	31.7	11.6	23.3	13.5	8.1	6.9	4.5	3.4
1988	11.7	32.0	35.9	29.6	10.4	19.8	12.7	7.4	5.6	4.3	5.4
1989	11.4	33.0	31.1	34.0	9.8	18.1	12.5	7.0	5.0	4.2	6.4
1990	10.9	29.9	34.1	27.6	9.7	19.6	11.9	7.2	4.3	3.6	5.9
1991	12.0	36.0	40.1	33.9	10.6	20.7	13.4	7.6	6.2	3.8	4.4
1992	13.2	37.2	41.7	34.8	11.8	23.1	14.1	9.8	6.4	4.2	5.0
1993	12.1	37.4	36.1	38.1	10.7	20.9	12.9	8.6	5.8	5.1	3.6
1994	11.0	32.6	32.9	32.5	9.8	19.6	11.7	8.0	4.9	4.9	4.4
1995	10.2	34.3	38.5	31.5	8.6	17.8	10.5	7.0	4.2	3.6	. . .
1996	10.0	30.3	32.8	28.6	8.7	18.4	11.0	6.9	3.8	3.8	5.6
1997	9.9	28.7	30.3	27.8	8.8	17.1	10.9	7.2	4.4	4.1	6.6
1998	9.0	25.3	33.2	20.9	7.9	15.7	9.5	6.7	4.3	3.4	6.1
1999	7.8	25.1	28.5	23.3	6.8	13.4	8.3	5.5	3.8	3.9	5.0
2000	7.1	22.8	25.3	21.3	6.2	13.6	6.8	5.5	3.4	3.3	6.0
2001	8.1	27.5	31.2	25.4	7.0	15.3	8.0	5.8	4.3	3.1	4.6
2002	9.8	28.3	33.2	25.6	8.8	18.3	10.2	7.7	5.3	4.7	6.9
2003	10.2	30.3	29.1	31.1	9.2	18.8	10.5	8.1	5.8	5.9	5.3
2004	9.8	28.2	35.2	24.3	8.9	16.6	10.7	7.6	6.5	4.8	6.8
2005	9.5	30.3	37.3	26.6	8.5	16.3	10.6	7.2	5.4	5.3	6.6
2006	8.4	25.9	29.9	23.6	7.5	15.2	9.0	6.7	5.1	3.9	3.7
HISPANIC[2]											
Both Sexes											
1973	7.5	19.7	23.4	17.3	6.0	8.5	5.7	5.6	4.7	5.5	3.9
1974	8.1	19.8	23.5	17.2	6.6	9.8	6.3	5.9	4.6	6.1	6.3
1975	12.2	27.7	30.0	26.5	10.3	16.7	9.9	8.6	8.1	7.7	9.9
1976	11.5	23.8	29.2	19.2	10.1	15.9	9.1	8.2	8.4	8.8	12.6
1977	10.1	22.9	27.0	19.6	8.5	12.0	8.6	6.1	7.3	8.2	9.2
1978	9.1	20.7	28.3	15.1	7.7	10.9	8.0	6.5	5.8	5.0	7.5
1979	8.3	19.2	26.0	14.9	7.0	10.4	6.7	6.2	5.2	6.0	5.7
1980	10.1	22.5	27.6	19.5	8.6	12.1	9.1	7.7	5.7	5.9	6.0
1981	10.4	23.9	28.0	21.7	9.1	13.9	8.8	7.4	6.4	7.3	5.4
1982	13.8	29.9	38.1	25.9	12.3	17.7	12.3	10.7	8.4	10.1	6.5
1983	13.7	28.4	33.8	25.8	12.3	16.7	11.9	11.3	10.0	10.9	5.8
1984	10.7	24.1	28.9	21.6	9.5	12.4	9.7	8.2	7.5	9.7	6.1
1985	10.5	24.3	27.8	22.5	9.4	12.6	9.9	7.7	7.4	7.8	8.1
1986	10.6	24.7	28.1	22.9	9.5	12.9	9.6	8.4	7.8	7.3	10.1
1987	8.8	22.3	27.7	19.5	7.8	10.6	7.7	6.7	6.9	6.0	6.5
1988	8.2	22.0	27.1	19.3	7.0	9.8	7.1	6.0	6.0	5.8	5.6
1989	8.0	19.4	26.4	16.0	7.2	10.7	7.0	5.9	6.3	5.8	5.3
1990	8.2	19.5	24.5	16.9	7.2	9.1	7.3	6.6	6.4	5.6	6.0
1991	10.0	22.9	31.9	18.7	9.0	11.6	9.2	8.1	8.0	6.5	7.0
1992	11.6	27.5	35.7	23.4	10.4	13.2	10.4	9.8	8.8	8.6	8.1
1993	10.8	26.1	35.1	21.8	9.7	13.1	9.3	9.1	8.6	8.0	6.6
1994	9.9	24.5	31.7	20.6	8.9	11.8	9.0	7.7	8.1	7.3	7.9
1995	9.3	24.1	33.1	19.5	8.2	11.5	8.2	7.2	6.4	7.5	10.6
1996	8.9	23.6	30.0	20.3	7.8	11.8	7.3	7.3	6.0	7.3	8.2
1997	7.7	21.6	27.7	18.4	6.8	10.3	6.3	6.4	5.1	6.5	6.8
1998	7.2	21.3	28.0	18.1	6.1	9.4	5.9	5.5	4.6	5.3	6.4
1999	6.4	18.6	23.7	16.3	5.5	8.3	5.4	4.8	4.8	4.5	5.0
2000	5.7	16.6	22.5	13.9	4.9	7.5	4.8	4.5	3.3	4.5	5.7
2001	6.6	17.7	24.0	15.0	5.8	8.1	5.9	5.2	4.3	5.6	4.5
2002	7.5	20.1	24.2	18.2	6.7	9.9	6.6	6.0	5.5	5.7	6.8
2003	7.7	20.0	24.6	17.7	7.0	10.2	7.0	6.0	6.3	5.7	3.9
2004	7.0	20.4	29.0	16.8	6.2	9.3	6.3	5.3	5.2	5.8	6.0
2005	6.0	18.4	23.6	16.0	5.3	8.6	5.3	4.5	4.4	4.4	4.9
2006	5.2	15.9	20.4	13.6	4.6	7.2	4.7	4.3	3.7	3.3	3.9

[1]Beginning in 2003, persons who selected this race group only; persons who selected more than one race group are not included. Prior to 2003, persons who reported more than one race group were included in the group they identified as their main race.
[2]May be of any race.
. . . = Not available.

Table 1-27. Unemployment Rates of Civilian Workers, by Age, Sex, Race, and Hispanic Origin, 1948–2006
—Continued

(Percent of labor force.)

Race, Hispanic origin, sex, and year	16 years and over	16 to 19 years			20 years and over						
		Total	16 to 17 years	18 to 19 years	Total	20 to 24 years	25 to 34 years	35 to 44 years	45 to 54 years	55 to 64 years	65 years and over
HISPANIC[2]											
Men											
1973	6.7	19.0	20.9	17.7	5.4	8.2	5.0	4.2	4.5	5.4	...
1974	7.3	19.0	22.0	17.1	6.0	9.9	5.5	5.0	4.3	5.4	...
1975	11.4	27.6	29.3	26.5	9.6	16.3	9.6	7.9	7.0	6.8	...
1976	10.8	23.3	28.7	19.7	9.4	16.0	8.1	7.0	7.4	8.7	...
1977	9.0	20.9	25.9	18.2	7.7	11.7	7.9	4.9	5.4	7.4	...
1978	7.7	19.7	27.5	13.9	6.4	9.4	6.6	4.8	4.8	4.4	...
1979	7.0	17.5	23.5	13.8	5.8	9.2	5.3	5.1	4.4	5.0	...
1980	9.7	21.9	26.2	19.3	8.3	12.2	8.3	7.1	6.0	5.9	...
1981	10.2	24.3	30.9	20.3	8.8	14.1	8.9	6.5	5.9	6.7	...
1982	13.6	31.3	40.2	26.8	12.1	18.2	12.4	9.9	7.5	10.0	...
1983	13.6	28.7	34.7	25.9	12.2	17.0	11.6	10.8	10.3	11.7	...
1984	10.5	25.2	31.5	22.2	9.3	12.5	9.2	7.6	7.2	10.2	...
1985	10.2	24.7	29.1	22.4	9.1	12.9	9.6	7.2	6.8	7.0	...
1986	10.5	24.5	28.5	22.4	9.5	13.0	9.5	8.5	7.0	8.0	...
1987	8.7	22.2	28.2	19.3	7.8	10.2	7.6	6.9	7.1	6.7	...
1988	8.1	22.7	29.5	19.5	7.0	9.2	7.0	5.9	6.1	6.7	...
1989	7.6	20.2	27.6	16.8	6.6	9.7	5.9	5.7	6.0	6.6	...
1990	8.0	19.5	24.0	17.4	7.0	8.4	6.9	6.5	6.8	6.5	...
1991	10.3	23.5	33.6	19.2	9.3	11.6	9.3	8.5	7.9	8.1	...
1992	11.7	28.2	36.6	24.0	10.5	13.7	10.1	9.8	8.9	10.2	...
1993	10.6	25.9	34.5	21.9	9.5	12.6	9.0	8.8	8.8	8.5	...
1994	9.4	26.3	33.3	22.5	8.3	10.8	8.4	6.6	8.1	7.4	10.5
1995	8.8	25.3	34.8	20.2	7.7	10.6	7.5	6.7	5.9	7.9	12.9
1996	7.9	22.5	31.5	18.4	6.9	10.3	6.6	6.3	5.1	6.7	8.3
1997	7.0	20.8	26.5	17.9	6.1	9.8	5.1	5.4	4.8	6.8	7.2
1998	6.4	20.6	29.0	16.4	5.4	8.9	5.2	4.5	4.2	5.3	5.0
1999	5.6	17.8	23.4	15.3	4.7	7.8	4.1	3.8	4.5	4.6	5.0
2000	5.0	15.7	22.3	12.8	4.2	6.6	3.7	3.8	3.1	4.1	6.2
2001	5.9	17.1	25.8	13.4	5.2	8.1	4.6	4.5	3.8	6.3	4.8
2002	7.2	20.2	22.9	19.1	6.4	9.3	6.1	5.4	5.5	6.2	6.3
2003	7.2	21.9	25.9	20.1	6.4	9.6	6.3	5.3	6.0	6.0	3.6
2004	6.5	21.2	30.7	17.6	5.8	9.4	5.5	4.5	4.7	5.7	6.9
2005	5.4	19.3	23.4	17.5	4.7	8.2	4.3	3.9	4.0	4.0	4.8
2006	4.8	17.3	22.6	14.8	4.2	6.7	4.2	3.6	3.4	3.5	3.7
HISPANIC[2]											
Women											
1973	9.0	20.7	26.8	16.7	7.3	9.0	6.9	8.3	5.1	5.6	...
1974	9.4	20.8	25.3	17.4	7.7	9.7	7.7	7.5	5.3	7.5	...
1975	13.5	27.9	31.0	26.4	11.5	17.2	10.5	9.9	10.0	9.3	...
1976	12.7	22.2	30.3	18.7	11.4	15.8	10.8	10.0	9.8	9.0	...
1977	11.9	24.4	28.5	21.9	10.1	12.1	9.8	8.2	10.6	11.0	...
1978	11.3	21.8	29.9	16.6	9.8	13.0	10.3	9.2	7.4	7.2	...
1979	10.3	21.2	30.0	15.8	8.9	12.1	8.9	7.7	7.1	7.9	...
1980	10.7	23.4	29.7	19.8	9.2	12.0	10.6	8.6	5.3	5.8	...
1981	10.8	23.4	23.5	23.4	9.5	13.5	8.7	8.9	7.2	8.4	...
1982	14.1	28.2	35.1	25.0	12.5	16.8	12.2	11.9	9.9	10.4	...
1983	13.8	28.0	32.5	25.7	12.4	16.2	12.5	12.2	9.7	9.6	...
1984	11.1	22.8	26.1	21.0	9.9	12.2	10.3	9.1	7.9	8.8	...
1985	11.0	23.8	26.2	22.6	9.9	12.1	10.6	8.5	8.1	9.2	...
1986	10.8	25.1	27.6	23.6	9.6	12.9	9.8	8.2	8.9	6.2	...
1987	8.9	22.4	27.1	19.9	7.7	11.4	7.8	6.5	6.7	5.0	...
1988	8.3	21.0	24.5	18.9	7.1	10.7	7.2	6.2	5.9	4.6	...
1989	8.8	18.2	24.7	14.9	8.0	12.2	8.6	6.3	6.7	4.5	...
1990	8.4	19.4	25.4	16.2	7.5	10.4	8.0	6.7	6.0	4.3	...
1991	9.6	21.9	29.6	17.9	8.6	11.7	9.1	7.6	8.1	4.1	...
1992	11.4	26.4	34.5	22.4	10.2	12.4	11.0	9.7	8.5	6.2	...
1993	11.0	26.3	36.0	21.7	9.9	14.0	9.9	9.5	8.3	7.2	...
1994	10.7	22.2	29.7	18.1	9.8	13.5	10.1	9.2	8.0	7.1	3.6
1995	10.0	22.6	30.7	18.7	8.9	13.0	9.5	7.9	7.0	6.8	6.4
1996	10.2	25.1	28.2	23.3	9.2	14.1	8.5	8.7	7.2	8.1	8.0
1997	8.9	22.7	29.2	19.1	7.9	11.0	8.2	7.7	5.5	6.1	6.0
1998	8.2	22.1	26.4	20.2	7.1	10.1	7.2	6.9	5.1	5.4	8.8
1999	7.6	19.8	24.0	17.7	6.6	9.1	7.3	6.3	5.1	4.3	4.8
2000	6.8	18.0	22.7	15.6	5.9	9.0	6.4	5.4	3.6	5.0	4.8
2001	7.5	18.5	21.6	17.1	6.6	8.2	7.8	6.2	4.8	4.8	4.0
2002	8.0	19.9	25.8	17.0	7.2	10.8	7.4	6.7	5.5	5.0	7.5
2003	8.4	17.7	23.2	14.4	7.8	11.3	8.2	7.1	6.8	5.3	4.4
2004	7.6	19.3	27.0	15.5	7.0	9.1	7.6	6.4	5.8	5.8	4.6
2005	6.9	17.2	23.8	14.0	6.3	9.2	7.1	5.5	4.8	5.0	5.1
2006	5.9	14.1	18.1	11.9	5.3	8.1	5.5	5.5	4.2	3.1	4.2

[2]May be of any race.
. . . = Not available.

Table 1-28. Unemployed Persons and Unemployment Rates, by Selected Occupation, 2000–2006

(Thousands of people, percent of civilian labor force.)

Occupation	2000	2001	2002	2003	2004	2005	2006
Total Unemployed Persons, 16 Years and Over[1]	5 692	6 801	8 378	8 774	8 149	7 591	7 001
Management, professional, and related	827	1 102	1 482	1 556	1 346	1 172	1 065
Management, business, and financial operations	320	455	622	627	544	464	427
Professional and related	507	647	859	929	801	708	638
Services	1 132	1 311	1 544	1 681	1 617	1 587	1 485
Sales and office	1 446	1 652	2 110	2 070	1 937	1 820	1 667
Sales and related	673	779	998	995	912	874	812
Office and administrative support	773	873	1 112	1 076	1 025	946	856
Natural resources, construction, and maintenance	758	943	1 155	1 244	1 140	1 069	1 007
Farming, fishing, and forestry	133	163	142	136	132	103	101
Construction and extraction	507	626	788	814	786	751	699
Installation, maintenance, and repair	119	154	225	295	222	214	207
Production, transportation, and material moving	1 081	1 318	1 530	1 555	1 393	1 245	1 127
Production	575	759	848	807	714	677	544
Transportation and material moving	505	559	682	748	679	568	583
Total Unemployment Rate, 16 Years and Over[1]	4.0	4.7	5.8	6.0	5.5	5.1	4.6
Management, professional, and related	1.8	2.3	3.0	3.1	2.7	2.3	2.1
Management, business, and financial operations	1.6	2.2	3.0	3.1	2.6	2.2	2.0
Professional and related	1.9	2.3	3.0	3.2	2.8	2.4	2.1
Services	5.2	5.8	6.6	7.1	6.6	6.4	5.9
Sales and office	3.8	4.4	5.6	5.5	5.2	4.8	4.4
Sales and related	4.1	4.7	5.9	5.9	5.4	5.0	4.7
Office and administrative support	3.6	4.2	5.4	5.2	5.0	4.6	4.2
Natural resources, construction, and maintenance	5.3	6.4	7.8	8.1	7.3	6.5	6.0
Farming, fishing, and forestry	10.2	13.4	12.0	11.4	11.8	9.6	9.5
Construction and extraction	6.2	7.3	9.1	9.1	8.4	7.6	6.8
Installation, maintenance, and repair	2.4	3.2	4.6	5.5	4.2	3.9	3.7
Production, transportation, and material moving	5.1	6.4	7.6	7.9	7.2	6.5	5.8
Production	4.8	6.6	7.8	7.7	7.0	6.7	5.5
Transportation and material moving	5.6	6.2	7.4	8.2	7.4	6.2	6.2

[1]Includes persons with no work experience and persons whose last job was in the armed forces.

Table 1-29. Unemployed Persons and Unemployment Rates, by Class of Worker and Industry, 2000–2006

(Thousands of people, percent.)

Class of worker and industry	2000	2001	2002	2003	2004	2005	2006
Total Unemployed Persons, 16 Years and Over	5 692	6 801	8 378	8 774	8 149	7 591	7 001
Nonagricultural private wage and salary workers	4 483	5 540	6 926	7 131	6 484	5 989	5 523
Mining	21	23	33	37	21	20	22
Construction	513	609	800	810	769	712	671
Manufacturing	691	992	1 205	1 166	966	812	699
Durable goods	400	630	789	762	590	485	410
Nondurable goods	290	362	416	404	375	326	289
Wholesale trade and retail trade	837	945	1 202	1 237	1 197	1 137	1 039
Transportation and utilities	193	236	274	283	236	232	229
Information	124	190	253	246	189	163	126
Financial activities	208	252	320	319	332	272	264
Professional and business services	573	768	1 009	1 042	861	792	746
Education and health services	383	463	570	640	617	627	568
Leisure and hospitality	720	833	961	1 006	972	921	865
Other services	219	229	301	347	324	301	293
Agriculture and related private wage and salary workers	134	153	139	140	129	104	95
Government workers	422	430	512	568	548	534	473
Self-employed and unpaid family workers	219	218	265	294	303	298	293
Total Unemployment Rate, 16 Years and Over[1]	4.0	4.7	5.8	6.0	5.5	5.1	4.6
Nonagricultural private wage and salary workers	4.1	5.0	6.2	6.3	5.7	5.2	4.7
Mining	4.4	4.2	6.3	6.7	3.9	3.1	3.2
Construction	6.2	7.1	9.2	9.3	8.4	7.4	6.7
Manufacturing	3.5	5.2	6.7	6.6	5.7	4.9	4.2
Durable goods	3.2	5.2	6.9	6.9	5.5	4.6	3.9
Nondurable goods	4.0	5.2	6.2	6.1	5.9	5.3	4.8
Wholesale trade and retail trade	4.3	4.9	6.1	6.0	5.8	5.4	4.9
Transportation and utilities	3.4	4.3	4.9	5.3	4.4	4.1	4.0
Information	3.2	4.9	6.9	6.8	5.7	5.0	3.7
Financial activities	2.4	2.9	3.5	3.5	3.6	2.9	2.7
Professional and business services	4.8	6.1	7.9	8.2	6.8	6.2	5.6
Education and health services	2.5	2.8	3.4	3.6	3.4	3.4	3.0
Leisure and hospitality	6.6	7.5	8.4	8.7	8.3	7.8	7.3
Other services	3.9	4.0	5.1	5.7	5.3	4.8	4.7
Agriculture and related private wage and salary workers	9.0	11.2	10.1	10.2	9.9	8.3	7.2
Government workers	2.1	2.2	2.5	2.8	2.7	2.6	2.3
Self-employed and unpaid family workers	2.1	2.1	2.6	2.7	2.8	2.7	2.7

Note: See notes and definitions for information on historical comparability.

[1]Includes persons with no work experience and persons whose last job was in the armed forces.

Table 1-30. Unemployed Persons, by Duration of Unemployment, 1948–2006

(Thousands of people, number of weeks.)

Year	Total unemployed	Duration of unemployment					Average duration, in weeks	Median duration, in weeks
		Less than 5 weeks	5 to 14 weeks	15 weeks and over				
				Total	15 to 26 weeks	27 weeks and over		
1948	2 276	1 300	669	309	193	116	8.6	. . .
1949	3 637	1 756	1 194	684	428	256	10.0	. . .
1950	3 288	1 450	1 055	782	425	357	12.1	. . .
1951	2 055	1 177	574	303	166	137	9.7	. . .
1952	1 883	1 135	516	232	148	84	8.4	. . .
1953	1 834	1 142	482	210	132	78	8.0	. . .
1954	3 532	1 605	1 116	812	495	317	11.8	. . .
1955	2 852	1 335	815	702	366	336	13.0	. . .
1956	2 750	1 412	805	533	301	232	11.3	. . .
1957	2 859	1 408	891	560	321	239	10.5	. . .
1958	4 602	1 753	1 396	1 452	785	667	13.9	. . .
1959	3 740	1 585	1 114	1 040	469	571	14.4	. . .
1960	3 852	1 719	1 176	957	503	454	12.8	. . .
1961	4 714	1 806	1 376	1 532	728	804	15.6	. . .
1962	3 911	1 663	1 134	1 119	534	585	14.7	. . .
1963	4 070	1 751	1 231	1 088	535	553	14.0	. . .
1964	3 786	1 697	1 117	973	491	482	13.3	. . .
1965	3 366	1 628	983	755	404	351	11.8	. . .
1966	2 875	1 573	779	526	287	239	10.4	. . .
1967	2 975	1 634	893	448	271	177	8.7	2.3
1968	2 817	1 594	810	412	256	156	8.4	4.5
1969	2 832	1 629	827	375	242	133	7.8	4.4
1970	4 093	2 139	1 290	663	428	235	8.6	4.9
1971	5 016	2 245	1 585	1 187	668	519	11.3	6.3
1972	4 882	2 242	1 472	1 167	601	566	12.0	6.2
1973	4 365	2 224	1 314	826	483	343	10.0	5.2
1974	5 156	2 604	1 597	955	574	381	9.8	5.2
1975	7 929	2 940	2 484	2 505	1 303	1 203	14.2	8.4
1976	7 406	2 844	2 196	2 366	1 018	1 348	15.8	8.2
1977	6 991	2 919	2 132	1 942	913	1 028	14.3	7.0
1978	6 202	2 865	1 923	1 414	766	648	11.9	5.9
1979	6 137	2 950	1 946	1 241	706	535	10.8	5.4
1980	7 637	3 295	2 470	1 871	1 052	820	11.9	6.5
1981	8 273	3 449	2 539	2 285	1 122	1 162	13.7	6.9
1982	10 678	3 883	3 311	3 485	1 708	1 776	15.6	8.7
1983	10 717	3 570	2 937	4 210	1 652	2 559	20.0	10.1
1984	8 539	3 350	2 451	2 737	1 104	1 634	18.2	7.9
1985	8 312	3 498	2 509	2 305	1 025	1 280	15.6	6.8
1986	8 237	3 448	2 557	2 232	1 045	1 187	15.0	6.9
1987	7 425	3 246	2 196	1 983	943	1 040	14.5	6.5
1988	6 701	3 084	2 007	1 610	801	809	13.5	5.9
1989	6 528	3 174	1 978	1 375	730	646	11.9	4.8
1990	7 047	3 265	2 257	1 525	822	703	12.0	5.3
1991	8 628	3 480	2 791	2 357	1 246	1 111	13.7	6.8
1992	9 613	3 376	2 830	3 408	1 453	1 954	17.7	8.7
1993	8 940	3 262	2 584	3 094	1 297	1 798	18.0	8.3
1994	7 996	2 728	2 408	2 860	1 237	1 623	18.8	9.2
1995	7 404	2 700	2 342	2 363	1 085	1 278	16.6	8.3
1996	7 236	2 633	2 287	2 316	1 053	1 262	16.7	8.3
1997	6 739	2 538	2 138	2 062	995	1 067	15.8	8.0
1998	6 210	2 622	1 950	1 637	763	875	14.5	6.7
1999	5 880	2 568	1 832	1 480	755	725	13.4	6.4
2000	5 692	2 558	1 815	1 318	669	649	12.6	5.9
2001	6 801	2 853	2 196	1 752	951	801	13.1	6.8
2002	8 378	2 893	2 580	2 904	1 369	1 535	16.6	9.1
2003	8 774	2 785	2 612	3 378	1 442	1 936	19.2	10.1
2004	8 149	2 696	2 382	3 072	1 293	1 779	19.6	9.8
2005	7 591	2 667	2 304	2 619	1 130	1 490	18.4	8.9
2006	7 001	2 614	2 121	2 266	1 031	1 235	16.8	8.3

. . . = Not available.

Table 1-31. Long-Term Unemployment, by Industry and Selected Occupation, 2000–2006

(Thousands of people.)

Length of unemployment, industry, and occupation	2000	2001	2002	2003	2004	2005	2006
UNEMPLOYED 15 WEEKS AND OVER							
Total	1 318	1 752	2 904	3 378	3 072	2 619	2 266
Wage and Salary Workers, by Industry							
Agriculture and related	32	44	39	44	38	29	30
Mining	7	7	11	17	8	8	5
Construction	107	130	236	262	248	216	177
Manufacturing	184	303	528	575	467	326	257
Durable goods	99	183	348	389	293	199	140
Nondurable goods	86	120	180	186	174	127	116
Wholesale and retail trade	186	241	423	472	455	415	337
Transportation and utilities	57	71	124	132	114	91	87
Information	33	52	119	128	87	76	55
Financial activities	58	75	131	144	139	91	103
Professional and business services	143	217	377	440	345	299	266
Education and health services	124	149	232	300	304	271	263
Leisure and hospitality	146	196	279	328	321	277	259
Other services	54	58	95	132	126	117	97
Public administration	41	36	51	59	72	62	34
Experienced Workers, by Occupation							
Management, professional, and related	213	313	603	692	571	436	373
Services	246	323	447	564	565	511	464
Sales and office	331	419	759	810	750	641	561
Natural resources, construction, and maintenance	161	212	346	424	386	341	294
Production, transportation, and material moving	273	360	575	654	561	461	380
UNEMPLOYED 27 WEEKS AND OVER							
Total	649	801	1 535	1 936	1 779	1 490	1 235
Wage and Salary Workers, by Industry							
Agriculture and related	13	16	18	21	18	16	13
Mining	4	3	5	10	6	4	3
Construction	44	60	111	132	133	108	92
Manufacturing	100	132	291	366	302	195	140
Durable goods	50	75	191	255	196	124	75
Nondurable goods	50	57	100	111	106	71	64
Wholesale and retail trade	80	114	226	261	261	230	183
Transportation and utilities	27	33	67	74	63	50	42
Information	18	21	62	80	58	41	30
Financial activities	32	34	131	88	79	56	56
Professional and business services	67	90	377	262	193	172	144
Education and health services	63	71	232	167	168	156	144
Leisure and hospitality	69	90	279	166	169	158	135
Other services	26	31	95	71	76	74	51
Public administration	23	18	51	33	44	38	21
Experienced Workers, by Occupation							
Management, professional, and related	101	135	340	429	356	269	206
Services	128	156	225	295	307	284	249
Sales and office	151	185	397	459	419	354	299
Natural resources, construction, and maintenance	74	96	164	229	221	186	158
Production, transportation, and material moving	140	162	313	388	336	261	206

Note: Beginning in January 2004, data reflect revised population controls used in the household survey. See notes and definitions for information on historical comparability.

Table 1-32. Unemployed Persons and Unemployment Rates, by Reason for Unemployment, Sex, and Age, 1970–2006

(Thousands of people, percent.)

Sex, age, and year	Number of unemployed					Unemployed as a percent of the total civilian labor force			
	Total	Job losers	Job leavers	Entrants		Job losers	Job leavers	Entrants	
				Reentrants	New entrants			Reentrants	New entrants
Both Sexes, 16 Years and Over									
1970	4 093	1 811	550	1 228	504	2.2	0.7	1.5	0.6
1971	5 016	2 323	590	1 472	630	2.8	0.7	1.7	0.7
1972	4 882	2 108	641	1 456	677	2.4	0.7	1.7	0.8
1973	4 365	1 694	683	1 340	649	1.9	0.8	1.5	0.7
1974	5 156	2 242	768	1 463	681	2.4	0.8	1.6	0.7
1975	7 929	4 386	827	1 892	823	4.7	0.9	2.0	0.9
1976	7 406	3 679	903	1 928	895	3.8	0.9	2.0	0.9
1977	6 991	3 166	909	1 963	953	3.2	0.9	2.0	1.0
1978	6 202	2 585	874	1 857	885	2.5	0.9	1.8	0.9
1979	6 137	2 635	880	1 806	817	2.5	0.8	1.7	0.8
1980	7 637	3 947	891	1 927	872	3.7	0.8	1.8	0.8
1981	8 273	4 267	923	2 102	981	3.9	0.8	1.9	0.9
1982	10 678	6 268	840	2 384	1 185	5.7	0.8	2.2	1.1
1983	10 717	6 258	830	2 412	1 216	5.6	0.7	2.2	1.1
1984	8 539	4 421	823	2 184	1 110	3.9	0.7	1.9	1.0
1985	8 312	4 139	877	2 256	1 039	3.6	0.8	2.0	0.9
1986	8 237	4 033	1 015	2 160	1 029	3.4	0.9	1.8	0.9
1987	7 425	3 566	965	1 974	920	3.0	0.8	1.6	0.8
1988	6 701	3 092	983	1 809	816	2.5	0.8	1.5	0.7
1989	6 528	2 983	1 024	1 843	677	2.4	0.8	1.5	0.5
1990	7 047	3 387	1 041	1 930	688	2.7	0.8	1.5	0.5
1991	8 628	4 694	1 004	2 139	792	3.7	0.8	1.7	0.6
1992	9 613	5 389	1 002	2 285	937	4.2	0.8	1.8	0.7
1993	8 940	4 848	976	2 198	919	3.8	0.8	1.7	0.7
1994	7 996	3 815	791	2 786	604	2.9	0.6	2.1	0.5
1995	7 404	3 476	824	2 525	579	2.6	0.6	1.9	0.4
1996	7 236	3 370	774	2 512	580	2.5	0.6	1.9	0.4
1997	6 739	3 037	795	2 338	569	2.2	0.6	1.7	0.4
1998	6 210	2 822	734	2 132	520	2.1	0.5	1.5	0.4
1999	5 880	2 622	783	2 005	469	1.9	0.6	1.4	0.3
2000	5 692	2 517	780	1 961	434	1.8	0.5	1.4	0.3
2001	6 801	3 476	835	2 031	459	2.4	0.6	1.4	0.3
2002	8 378	4 607	866	2 368	536	3.2	0.6	1.6	0.4
2003	8 774	4 838	818	2 477	641	3.3	0.6	1.7	0.4
2004	8 149	4 197	858	2 408	686	2.8	0.6	1.6	0.5
2005	7 591	3 667	872	2 386	666	2.5	0.6	1.6	0.4
2006	7 001	3 321	827	2 237	616	2.2	0.5	1.5	0.4
Both Sexes, 16 to 19 Years									
1970	1 106	200	126	378	401	2.8	1.7	5.2	5.5
1971	1 262	233	117	410	501	3.1	1.6	5.5	6.7
1972	1 308	248	129	395	536	3.1	1.6	4.9	6.6
1973	1 235	212	146	364	513	2.4	1.7	4.3	6.0
1974	1 422	280	173	436	533	3.1	2.0	4.9	6.0
1975	1 767	450	155	529	634	5.1	1.7	6.0	7.1
1976	1 719	387	153	496	683	4.3	1.7	5.5	7.5
1977	1 663	318	156	477	711	3.4	1.7	5.1	7.6
1978	1 583	300	167	455	660	3.1	1.7	4.7	6.8
1979	1 555	319	184	452	599	3.3	1.9	4.7	6.2
1980	1 669	388	156	481	643	4.1	1.7	5.1	6.9
1981	1 763	385	162	487	728	4.3	1.8	5.4	8.1
1982	1 977	460	134	509	874	5.4	1.6	6.0	10.2
1983	1 829	370	110	482	867	4.6	1.3	5.9	10.6
1984	1 499	271	114	370	745	3.4	1.4	4.7	9.4
1985	1 468	275	113	390	689	3.5	1.4	4.9	8.7
1986	1 454	240	145	374	695	3.0	1.8	4.7	8.8
1987	1 347	210	146	375	617	2.7	1.8	4.7	7.7
1988	1 226	207	159	310	550	2.6	2.0	3.9	6.8
1989	1 194	198	200	345	452	2.5	2.5	4.3	5.7
1990	1 212	233	181	338	460	3.0	2.3	4.3	5.9
1991	1 359	289	180	365	524	4.0	2.5	5.0	7.2
1992	1 427	259	149	377	643	3.6	2.1	5.3	9.1
1993	1 365	233	151	353	628	3.3	2.1	4.9	8.8
1994	1 320	185	84	634	416	2.5	1.1	8.5	5.6
1995	1 346	214	102	615	415	2.8	1.3	7.9	5.3
1996	1 306	182	91	625	409	2.3	1.2	8.0	5.2
1997	1 271	174	104	606	388	2.2	1.3	7.6	4.9
1998	1 205	181	86	577	361	2.2	1.0	7.0	4.4
1999	1 162	173	114	547	328	2.1	1.4	6.6	3.9
2000	1 081	157	109	516	299	1.9	1.3	6.2	3.6
2001	1 162	185	98	568	311	2.3	1.2	7.2	3.9
2002	1 253	197	91	597	368	2.6	1.2	7.9	4.9
2003	1 251	188	85	554	424	2.6	1.2	7.7	5.9
2004	1 208	165	76	510	456	2.3	1.1	7.2	6.4
2005	1 186	155	76	489	466	2.2	1.1	6.8	6.5
2006	1 119	145	78	461	435	2.0	1.1	6.3	6.0

Note: See notes and definitions for information on historical comparability.

Table 1-32. Unemployed Persons and Unemployment Rates, by Reason for Unemployment, Sex, and Age, 1970–2006—*Continued*

(Thousands of people, percent.)

Sex, age, and year	Number of unemployed					Unemployed as a percent of the total civilian labor force			
	Total	Job losers	Job leavers	Entrants		Job losers	Job leavers	Entrants	
				Reentrants	New entrants			Reentrants	New entrants
Men, 20 Years and Over									
1970	1 638	1 066	209	318	44	2.2	0.4	0.7	0.1
1971	2 097	1 391	239	411	57	2.9	0.5	0.9	0.1
1972	1 948	1 219	248	420	60	2.5	0.5	0.9	0.1
1973	1 624	959	258	350	56	1.9	0.5	0.7	0.1
1974	1 957	1 276	276	356	48	2.5	0.5	0.7	0.1
1975	3 476	2 598	298	506	76	5.0	0.6	1.0	0.1
1976	3 098	2 167	323	521	86	4.1	0.6	1.0	0.2
1977	2 794	1 816	335	540	103	3.4	0.6	1.0	0.2
1978	2 328	1 433	337	471	86	2.6	0.6	0.9	0.2
1979	2 308	1 464	325	446	73	2.6	0.6	0.8	0.1
1980	3 353	2 389	359	516	90	4.2	0.6	0.9	0.2
1981	3 615	2 565	356	592	102	4.5	0.6	1.0	0.2
1982	5 089	3 965	327	678	119	6.8	0.6	1.2	0.2
1983	5 257	4 088	336	695	138	6.9	0.6	1.2	0.2
1984	3 932	2 800	324	663	146	4.7	0.5	1.1	0.2
1985	3 715	2 568	352	671	124	4.3	0.6	1.1	0.2
1986	3 751	2 568	444	611	128	4.1	0.7	1.0	0.2
1987	3 369	2 289	413	558	108	3.7	0.7	0.9	0.2
1988	2 987	1 939	416	534	98	3.1	0.7	0.9	0.2
1989	2 867	1 843	394	541	88	2.9	0.6	0.8	0.1
1990	3 239	2 100	431	626	82	3.2	0.7	1.0	0.1
1991	4 195	2 982	411	698	105	4.6	0.6	1.1	0.2
1992	4 717	3 420	421	765	111	5.2	0.6	1.2	0.2
1993	4 287	2 996	429	747	114	4.5	0.6	1.1	0.2
1994	3 627	2 296	367	898	65	3.4	0.5	1.3	0.1
1995	3 239	2 051	356	775	57	3.0	0.5	1.2	0.1
1996	3 146	2 043	322	731	51	3.0	0.5	1.1	0.1
1997	2 882	1 795	358	675	55	2.6	0.5	1.0	0.1
1998	2 580	1 588	318	611	63	2.3	0.5	0.9	0.1
1999	2 433	1 459	336	592	46	2.1	0.5	0.8	0.1
2000	2 376	1 416	328	577	55	2.0	0.5	0.8	0.1
2001	3 040	1 999	372	612	56	2.7	0.5	0.8	0.1
2002	3 896	2 702	386	743	65	3.7	0.5	1.0	0.1
2003	4 209	2 899	376	846	88	3.9	0.5	1.1	0.1
2004	3 791	2 503	398	791	99	3.3	0.5	1.0	0.1
2005	4 059	2 188	445	1 067	359	2.7	0.5	1.0	0.1
2006	3 131	1 927	368	757	78	2.5	0.5	1.0	0.1
Women, 20 Years and Over									
1970	1 349	546	214	531	58	1.9	0.8	1.9	0.2
1971	1 658	700	235	651	72	2.5	0.8	2.3	0.2
1972	1 625	641	264	641	80	2.2	0.9	2.1	0.3
1973	1 507	522	280	625	80	1.6	0.9	2.0	0.3
1974	1 777	685	319	673	100	2.1	1.0	2.1	0.3
1975	2 684	1 339	375	858	114	4.0	1.1	2.6	0.3
1976	2 588	1 124	427	912	126	3.2	1.2	2.6	0.4
1977	2 535	1 031	419	945	140	2.8	1.2	2.6	0.4
1978	2 292	852	371	930	138	2.2	1.0	2.4	0.4
1979	2 276	851	370	908	145	2.1	0.9	2.3	0.4
1980	2 615	1 170	376	930	139	2.8	0.9	2.3	0.3
1981	2 895	1 317	404	1 023	151	3.1	1.0	2.4	0.4
1982	3 613	1 844	379	1 197	192	4.2	0.9	2.7	0.4
1983	3 632	1 801	384	1 235	212	4.0	0.9	2.8	0.5
1984	3 107	1 350	386	1 151	220	2.9	0.8	2.5	0.5
1985	3 129	1 296	412	1 195	227	2.7	0.9	2.5	0.5
1986	3 032	1 225	426	1 175	206	2.5	0.9	2.4	0.4
1987	2 709	1 067	406	1 041	194	2.2	0.8	2.1	0.4
1988	2 487	946	408	965	168	1.9	0.8	1.9	0.3
1989	2 467	942	430	958	137	1.8	0.8	1.8	0.3
1990	2 596	1 054	429	966	146	2.0	0.8	1.8	0.3
1991	3 074	1 423	413	1 075	163	2.6	0.8	2.0	0.3
1992	3 469	1 710	433	1 142	183	3.1	0.8	2.1	0.3
1993	3 288	1 619	395	1 098	176	2.9	0.7	2.0	0.3
1994	3 049	1 334	339	1 253	122	2.4	0.6	2.2	0.2
1995	2 819	1 211	366	1 135	107	2.1	0.6	2.0	0.2
1996	2 783	1 145	361	1 156	120	2.0	0.6	2.0	0.2
1997	2 585	1 069	333	1 057	126	1.8	0.6	1.8	0.2
1998	2 424	1 053	330	944	97	1.8	0.6	1.6	0.2
1999	2 285	990	333	866	96	1.6	0.5	1.4	0.2
2000	2 235	943	343	868	80	1.5	0.6	1.4	0.1
2001	2 599	1 291	365	850	92	2.0	0.6	1.3	0.1
2002	3 228	1 708	389	1 028	102	2.7	0.6	1.6	0.2
2003	3 314	1 751	357	1 076	130	2.7	0.6	1.7	0.2
2004	3 150	1 529	384	1 107	131	2.4	0.6	1.7	0.2
2005	3 013	1 417	391	1 103	101	2.2	0.6	1.7	0.2
2006	2 751	1 249	380	1 019	103	1.9	0.6	1.5	0.2

Note: See notes and definitions for information on historical comparability.

Table 1-33. Percent of the Population with Work Experience During the Year, by Age and Sex, 1987–2006

(Percent.)

Sex and year	Total	16 to 17 years	18 to 19 years	20 to 24 years	25 to 34 years	35 to 44 years	45 to 54 years	55 to 59 years	60 to 64 years	65 to 69 years	70 years and over
Both Sexes											
1987	69.7	51.8	76.6	85.5	85.7	86.1	81.6	69.4	51.3	26.2	10.2
1988	70.2	50.6	75.5	85.7	86.0	86.8	82.2	70.5	52.2	27.9	10.3
1989	70.5	51.9	75.4	84.9	86.6	86.9	82.8	70.4	52.5	28.4	10.0
1990	70.2	48.6	74.2	84.1	86.2	87.0	82.8	70.9	53.4	28.3	10.2
1991	69.5	43.4	70.8	83.4	85.9	86.6	83.0	70.3	52.9	27.2	9.8
1992	69.1	43.8	69.9	82.7	85.2	85.9	82.8	70.8	53.5	25.5	9.8
1993	69.2	42.1	70.4	82.0	85.0	85.3	82.8	71.6	51.6	27.5	10.7
1994	69.6	44.1	71.5	82.5	85.5	85.6	83.8	72.2	52.8	27.5	10.0
1995	69.6	44.4	71.2	82.0	85.6	85.9	83.4	72.2	53.3	28.0	10.2
1996	69.9	43.3	70.5	83.1	86.1	85.7	84.3	73.3	54.3	27.8	10.4
1997	70.1	43.6	70.5	83.0	87.1	85.9	84.4	73.8	53.8	28.5	10.0
1998	70.1	42.1	69.9	82.9	86.7	86.3	84.2	73.7	54.5	29.2	10.6
1999	70.7	43.7	71.2	82.7	87.3	86.9	85.0	72.3	55.8	30.5	11.6
2000	70.5	42.2	69.6	82.6	87.1	87.0	84.6	72.9	55.1	30.8	11.4
2001	69.4	37.7	66.7	80.8	86.1	85.8	83.7	73.5	56.7	30.6	10.5
2002	68.5	34.5	62.8	78.5	84.4	85.0	83.7	74.7	56.8	33.1	10.4
2003	67.8	32.0	61.7	77.5	83.7	84.0	82.9	73.9	56.5	33.2	11.4
2004	67.7	32.6	59.8	76.9	83.3	84.2	82.6	73.9	57.0	32.7	12.2
2005	67.8	31.1	60.1	77.3	83.7	84.1	82.8	74.4	58.2	32.0	12.1
2006	67.9	30.9	58.3	76.9	84.4	84.3	82.8	74.5	58.2	33.6	12.6
Men											
1987	78.9	52.4	77.4	90.4	94.3	94.1	91.9	83.3	63.2	34.2	15.4
1988	79.1	51.8	78.9	90.7	94.3	94.6	91.6	82.1	63.1	35.6	15.6
1989	79.4	53.2	77.7	89.9	94.7	94.7	91.9	82.0	64.2	35.4	15.1
1990	78.9	50.3	76.7	88.7	94.4	94.7	91.3	82.0	65.8	35.8	14.0
1991	77.9	45.4	72.2	87.9	93.5	93.6	91.3	81.5	63.6	35.0	14.4
1992	77.4	46.6	73.7	87.1	93.3	92.8	89.9	80.9	63.2	32.4	14.3
1993	76.8	43.9	71.4	86.6	92.5	92.0	89.3	79.8	59.1	34.3	15.3
1994	77.2	44.4	74.7	87.2	92.9	92.0	90.0	81.3	61.4	33.9	14.8
1995	77.0	43.7	73.6	86.4	92.6	92.2	89.7	81.5	62.1	34.5	14.9
1996	77.2	44.1	71.8	86.7	93.4	92.1	90.4	81.8	62.5	33.6	15.2
1997	77.1	43.4	70.3	86.6	94.1	92.3	90.7	81.4	62.9	33.8	13.9
1998	76.9	40.4	71.6	86.4	93.5	92.7	90.1	81.7	63.5	35.5	14.7
1999	77.3	44.7	72.3	85.5	93.9	93.2	89.9	79.2	65.1	37.4	16.5
2000	77.1	42.1	70.2	85.1	93.4	93.6	89.8	80.6	64.4	38.4	16.0
2001	76.3	37.4	67.7	84.8	93.2	92.2	89.1	80.4	64.3	37.8	14.5
2002	75.2	34.7	62.8	82.1	91.6	91.8	88.9	80.7	64.3	39.3	14.6
2003	74.3	32.8	61.7	80.2	90.8	90.9	87.7	80.9	63.1	37.3	15.8
2004	74.2	32.1	58.9	80.2	91.0	91.1	87.9	80.1	64.5	37.1	16.7
2005	74.6	31.1	60.7	80.8	91.3	91.6	88.2	80.1	64.3	37.6	17.0
2006	74.5	30.9	57.9	80.1	91.9	91.8	88.0	80.6	64.1	38.3	17.3
Women											
1987	61.3	51.1	75.8	81.0	77.3	78.5	71.9	56.7	41.0	19.6	6.8
1988	62.1	49.3	72.2	81.0	78.1	79.4	73.5	60.0	42.5	21.4	6.8
1989	62.3	50.6	73.1	80.2	78.6	79.3	74.2	59.9	42.4	22.5	6.7
1990	62.2	46.8	71.7	79.6	78.0	79.6	74.9	60.4	42.5	22.1	7.7
1991	61.8	41.4	69.4	79.0	78.3	79.9	75.3	59.9	43.6	20.6	6.7
1992	61.5	40.9	66.1	78.4	77.2	79.1	76.1	61.5	44.4	20.0	6.7
1993	62.1	40.3	69.4	77.5	77.6	78.7	76.5	63.9	44.7	22.1	7.7
1994	62.5	43.7	68.4	77.8	78.1	79.4	78.0	63.9	45.0	22.2	6.8
1995	62.8	45.2	68.7	77.7	78.8	79.8	77.6	63.2	45.6	22.4	7.1
1996	63.2	42.5	69.2	79.5	78.9	79.5	78.4	65.4	46.9	23.0	7.1
1997	63.6	43.9	70.7	79.5	80.1	79.6	78.4	66.7	45.6	24.0	7.3
1998	63.7	44.1	68.2	79.4	80.1	80.0	78.6	66.3	46.2	23.8	7.8
1999	64.5	42.6	70.1	79.9	80.9	80.7	80.3	66.2	47.3	24.4	8.2
2000	64.3	42.3	69.0	80.2	80.9	80.5	79.5	65.7	47.0	23.9	8.2
2001	63.1	38.1	65.7	76.9	79.2	79.5	78.6	67.1	49.8	24.2	7.9
2002	62.3	34.3	62.8	74.9	77.2	78.4	78.7	69.1	50.0	27.8	7.4
2003	61.7	31.2	61.6	74.6	76.6	77.2	78.4	67.3	50.7	29.6	8.3
2004	61.5	33.1	60.7	73.7	75.6	77.4	77.5	68.2	50.3	28.7	9.0
2005	61.4	31.2	59.6	73.7	76.1	76.8	77.6	68.9	52.7	27.1	8.7
2006	61.6	30.9	58.7	73.7	76.9	76.9	77.9	68.8	53.0	29.5	9.3

Note: See notes and definitions for information on historical comparability.

Table 1-34. Persons with Work Experience During the Year, by Industry and Class of Worker of Job Held the Longest, 2002–2006

(Thousands of people.)

Industry and class of worker	2002	2003	2004	2005	2006
TOTAL	151 546	151 553	153 024	155 127	157 352
Agriculture	2 490	2 521	2 492	2 344	2 332
Wage and salary workers	1 583	1 605	1 549	1 501	1 495
Self-employed workers	875	894	918	829	812
Unpaid family workers	33	22	25	14	25
Nonagricultural Industries	149 055	149 032	150 532	152 783	155 021
Wage and salary workers	139 909	139 747	140 885	143 002	145 152
Mining	594	576	630	696	758
Construction	9 488	9 423	10 076	10 423	10 989
Manufacturing	17 660	17 349	17 196	17 243	17 112
Durable goods	11 013	10 622	10 814	10 930	10 995
Nondurable goods	6 647	6 727	6 382	6 313	6 116
Wholesale and retail trade	21 615	21 650	22 091	22 479	21 822
Wholesale trade	4 402	4 691	4 470	4 517	4 395
Retail trade	17 213	16 959	17 621	17 962	17 427
Transportation and utilities	7 039	6 934	7 040	7 248	7 413
Transportation and warehousing	5 745	5 736	5 827	6 095	6 197
Utilities	1 294	1 198	1 213	1 153	1 216
Information	3 989	3 755	3 359	3 495	3 710
Financial activities	9 591	9 822	9 956	9 748	10 101
Finance and insurance	6 986	7 135	7 192	7 011	7 190
Real estate and rental and leasing	2 605	2 687	2 764	2 737	2 912
Professional and business services	13 883	13 485	13 277	13 537	14 412
Professional, scientific, and technical services	7 989	7 855	7 793	7 768	8 294
Management, administration, and waste management services	5 894	5 629	5 484	5 769	6 118
Education and health services	29 343	29 571	29 814	30 552	31 314
Education services	12 765	13 026	13 169	13 282	13 659
Health care and social assistance services	16 578	16 544	16 645	17 270	17 655
Leisure and hospitality	13 260	13 110	13 345	13 405	13 455
Arts, entertainment, and recreation	2 852	2 789	2 888	2 877	2 797
Accommodation and food services	10 408	10 321	10 457	10 528	10 658
Other services and private household	6 416	6 529	6 473	6 490	6 341
Private households	873	897	907	866	912
Public administration	6 290	6 734	6 897	6 917	7 076
Self-employed workers	9 023	9 169	9 520	9 658	9 733
Unpaid family workers	124	116	128	123	135

Note: See notes and definitions for information on historical comparability.

Table 1-35. Number of Persons with Work Experience During the Year, by Extent of Employment and Sex, 1987–2006

(Thousands of people.)

Sex and year	Total	Full-time workers				Part-time workers			
		Total	50 to 52 weeks	27 to 49 weeks	1 to 26 weeks	Total	50 to 52 weeks	27 to 49 weeks	1 to 26 weeks
Both Sexes									
1987	128 315	100 288	77 015	13 361	9 912	28 027	10 973	6 594	10 460
1988	130 451	102 131	79 627	12 875	9 629	28 320	11 384	6 624	10 312
1989	132 817	104 876	81 117	14 271	9 488	27 941	11 275	6 987	9 679
1990	133 535	105 323	80 932	14 758	9 633	28 212	11 507	7 012	9 693
1991	133 410	104 472	80 385	14 491	9 596	28 938	11 946	7 003	9 989
1992	133 912	104 813	81 523	13 587	9 703	29 099	12 326	6 841	9 932
1993	136 354	106 299	83 384	13 054	9 861	30 055	12 818	6 777	10 460
1994	138 468	108 141	85 764	13 051	9 326	30 327	12 936	6 956	10 435
1995	139 724	110 063	88 173	12 970	8 920	29 661	12 725	6 831	10 105
1996	142 201	112 313	90 252	12 997	9 064	29 888	13 382	6 643	9 863
1997	143 968	113 879	92 631	12 508	8 740	30 089	13 810	6 565	9 714
1998	145 566	116 412	95 772	12 156	8 484	29 155	13 538	6 480	9 137
1999	148 295	119 096	97 941	12 294	8 861	29 199	13 680	6 317	9 202
2000	149 361	120 591	100 349	12 071	8 171	28 770	13 865	6 161	8 744
2001	151 042	121 921	100 357	13 172	8 392	29 121	14 038	6 139	8 944
2002	151 546	121 726	100 659	12 544	8 523	29 819	14 635	6 184	9 000
2003	151 553	121 158	100 700	11 972	8 486	30 395	15 333	6 027	9 035
2004	153 024	122 404	102 427	11 862	8 115	30 621	15 552	6 077	8 992
2005	155 127	124 683	104 876	11 816	7 991	30 444	15 374	6 161	8 909
2006	157 352	127 340	107 734	11 736	7 870	30 012	15 131	6 223	8 657
Men									
1987	69 144	59 736	47 040	7 503	5 193	9 408	3 260	2 191	3 957
1988	70 021	60 504	48 299	7 329	4 876	9 517	3 468	2 199	3 850
1989	71 640	62 108	49 693	7 642	4 773	9 532	3 619	2 254	3 659
1990	71 953	62 319	49 175	8 188	4 956	9 634	3 650	2 322	3 662
1991	71 700	61 636	47 895	8 324	5 417	10 064	3 820	2 342	3 902
1992	72 007	61 722	48 300	7 965	5 457	10 285	3 864	2 354	4 067
1993	72 872	62 513	49 832	7 317	5 364	10 359	4 005	2 144	4 210
1994	73 958	63 634	51 582	7 094	4 958	10 324	3 948	2 358	4 018
1995	74 381	64 145	52 671	6 973	4 501	10 236	4 034	2 257	3 945
1996	75 760	65 356	53 795	6 891	4 670	10 404	4 321	2 136	3 947
1997	76 408	66 089	54 918	6 638	4 533	10 319	4 246	2 274	3 799
1998	76 918	67 250	56 953	6 208	4 089	9 669	4 197	2 090	3 382
1999	78 145	68 347	57 520	6 401	4 426	9 797	4 297	2 062	3 438
2000	78 804	68 925	58 756	6 094	4 075	9 879	4 485	1 957	3 437
2001	79 971	70 074	58 715	7 087	4 272	9 897	4 306	1 989	3 602
2002	80 282	70 132	58 765	6 804	4 563	10 151	4 519	2 042	3 590
2003	80 317	69 766	58 778	6 479	4 509	10 551	5 042	1 872	3 637
2004	81 261	70 780	60 096	6 428	4 256	10 482	4 987	1 992	3 503
2005	82 735	72 056	61 510	6 299	4 247	10 679	5 153	2 074	3 452
2006	83 767	73 578	63 058	6 373	4 147	10 189	4 747	2 046	3 396
Women									
1987	59 171	40 552	29 975	5 858	4 719	18 619	7 713	4 403	6 503
1988	60 430	41 627	31 328	5 546	4 753	18 803	7 916	4 425	6 462
1989	61 178	42 768	31 424	6 629	4 715	18 410	7 656	4 733	6 021
1990	61 582	43 004	31 757	6 570	4 677	18 578	7 857	4 690	6 031
1991	61 712	42 837	32 491	6 167	4 179	18 875	8 126	4 662	6 087
1992	61 904	43 090	33 223	5 621	4 246	18 814	8 462	4 487	5 865
1993	63 481	43 785	33 552	5 736	4 497	19 696	8 813	4 633	6 250
1994	64 511	44 508	34 182	5 957	4 369	20 003	8 988	4 598	6 417
1995	65 342	45 917	35 502	5 997	4 418	19 425	8 691	4 574	6 160
1996	66 439	46 955	36 457	6 105	4 393	19 484	9 061	4 507	5 916
1997	67 559	47 790	37 713	5 870	4 207	19 769	9 564	4 291	5 914
1998	68 648	49 162	38 819	5 948	4 395	19 486	9 341	4 390	5 755
1999	70 150	50 748	40 421	5 892	4 435	19 402	9 383	4 255	5 764
2000	70 556	51 665	41 593	5 977	4 095	18 891	9 380	4 204	5 307
2001	71 071	51 848	41 642	6 085	4 120	19 223	9 731	4 150	5 342
2002	71 263	51 593	41 893	5 741	3 959	19 671	10 117	4 143	5 411
2003	71 236	51 391	41 921	5 493	3 977	19 844	10 291	4 155	5 398
2004	71 763	51 624	42 331	5 434	3 859	20 139	10 565	4 085	5 489
2005	72 392	52 627	43 366	5 517	3 744	19 765	10 222	4 087	5 456
2006	73 585	53 762	44 676	5 364	3 723	19 823	10 384	4 178	5 261

Note: See notes and definitions for information on historical comparability.

Table 1-36. Percent Distribution of the Population with Work Experience During the Year, by Extent of Employment and Sex, 1987–2006

(Percent of total people with work experience.)

Sex and year	Total	Full-time workers				Part-time workers			
		Total	50 to 52 weeks	27 to 49 weeks	1 to 26 weeks	Total	50 to 52 weeks	27 to 49 weeks	1 to 26 weeks
Both Sexes									
1987	100.0	78.1	60.0	10.4	7.7	21.9	8.6	5.1	8.2
1988	100.0	78.3	61.0	9.9	7.4	21.7	8.7	5.1	7.9
1989	100.0	78.9	61.1	10.7	7.1	21.1	8.5	5.3	7.3
1990	100.0	78.9	60.6	11.1	7.2	21.2	8.6	5.3	7.3
1991	100.0	78.4	60.3	10.9	7.2	21.7	9.0	5.2	7.5
1992	100.0	78.2	60.9	10.1	7.2	21.7	9.2	5.1	7.4
1993	100.0	78.0	61.2	9.6	7.2	22.1	9.4	5.0	7.7
1994	100.0	78.0	61.9	9.4	6.7	21.8	9.3	5.0	7.5
1995	100.0	78.8	63.1	9.3	6.4	21.2	9.1	4.9	7.2
1996	100.0	79.0	63.5	9.1	6.4	21.0	9.4	4.7	6.9
1997	100.0	79.1	64.3	8.7	6.1	20.9	9.6	4.6	6.7
1998	100.0	80.0	65.8	8.4	5.8	20.1	9.3	4.5	6.3
1999	100.0	80.3	66.0	8.3	6.0	19.7	9.2	4.3	6.2
2000	100.0	80.8	67.2	8.1	5.5	19.3	9.3	4.1	5.9
2001	100.0	80.7	66.4	8.7	5.6	19.3	9.3	4.1	5.9
2002	100.0	80.3	66.4	8.3	5.6	19.7	9.7	4.1	5.9
2003	100.0	79.9	66.4	7.9	5.6	20.1	10.1	4.0	6.0
2004	100.0	80.0	66.9	7.8	5.3	20.1	10.2	4.0	5.9
2005	100.0	80.4	67.6	7.6	5.2	19.6	9.9	4.0	5.7
2006	100.0	80.9	68.5	7.5	5.0	19.1	9.6	4.0	5.5
Men									
1987	100.0	86.4	68.0	10.9	7.5	13.6	4.7	3.2	5.7
1988	100.0	86.5	69.0	10.5	7.0	13.6	5.0	3.1	5.5
1989	100.0	86.8	69.4	10.7	6.7	13.3	5.1	3.1	5.1
1990	100.0	86.6	68.3	11.4	6.9	13.4	5.1	3.2	5.1
1991	100.0	86.0	66.8	11.6	7.6	14.0	5.3	3.3	5.4
1992	100.0	85.8	67.1	11.1	7.6	14.3	5.4	3.3	5.6
1993	100.0	85.8	68.4	10.0	7.4	14.2	5.5	2.9	5.8
1994	100.0	86.0	69.7	9.6	6.7	13.9	5.3	3.2	5.4
1995	100.0	86.3	70.8	9.4	6.1	13.7	5.4	3.0	5.3
1996	100.0	86.3	71.0	9.1	6.2	13.7	5.7	2.8	5.2
1997	100.0	86.5	71.9	8.7	5.9	13.6	5.6	3.0	5.0
1998	100.0	87.4	74.0	8.1	5.3	12.6	5.5	2.7	4.4
1999	100.0	87.5	73.6	8.2	5.7	12.5	5.5	2.6	4.4
2000	100.0	87.5	74.6	7.7	5.2	12.6	5.7	2.5	4.4
2001	100.0	87.6	73.4	8.9	5.3	12.4	5.4	2.5	4.5
2002	100.0	87.4	73.2	8.5	5.7	12.6	5.6	2.5	4.5
2003	100.0	86.9	73.2	8.1	5.6	13.1	6.3	2.3	4.5
2004	100.0	87.1	74.0	7.9	5.2	12.9	6.1	2.5	4.3
2005	100.0	87.0	74.3	7.6	5.1	12.9	6.2	2.5	4.2
2006	100.0	87.8	75.3	7.6	5.0	12.2	5.7	2.4	4.1
Women									
1987	100.0	68.6	50.7	9.9	8.0	31.4	13.0	7.4	11.0
1988	100.0	68.9	51.8	9.2	7.9	31.1	13.1	7.3	10.7
1989	100.0	69.9	51.4	10.8	7.7	30.0	12.5	7.7	9.8
1990	100.0	69.9	51.6	10.7	7.6	30.2	12.8	7.6	9.8
1991	100.0	69.4	52.6	10.0	6.8	30.7	13.2	7.6	9.9
1992	100.0	69.7	53.7	9.1	6.9	30.4	13.7	7.2	9.5
1993	100.0	69.0	52.9	9.0	7.1	31.0	13.9	7.3	9.8
1994	100.0	69.0	53.0	9.2	6.8	30.9	13.9	7.1	9.9
1995	100.0	70.3	54.3	9.2	6.8	29.7	13.3	7.0	9.4
1996	100.0	70.7	54.9	9.2	6.6	29.3	13.6	6.8	8.9
1997	100.0	70.7	55.8	8.7	6.2	29.4	14.2	6.4	8.8
1998	100.0	71.6	56.5	8.7	6.4	28.4	13.6	6.4	8.4
1999	100.0	72.3	57.6	8.4	6.3	27.7	13.4	6.1	8.2
2000	100.0	73.2	58.9	8.5	5.8	26.8	13.3	6.0	7.5
2001	100.0	73.0	58.6	8.6	5.8	27.0	13.7	5.8	7.5
2002	100.0	72.5	58.8	8.1	5.6	27.6	14.2	5.8	7.6
2003	100.0	72.1	58.8	7.7	5.6	27.8	14.4	5.8	7.6
2004	100.0	72.0	59.0	7.6	5.4	28.0	14.7	5.7	7.6
2005	100.0	72.7	59.9	7.6	5.2	27.2	14.1	5.6	7.5
2006	100.0	73.1	60.7	7.3	5.1	26.9	14.1	5.7	7.1

Note: See notes and definitions for information on historical comparability.

Table 1-37. Extent of Unemployment During the Year, by Sex, 1995–2006

(Thousands of people, percent.)

Sex and extent of unemployment	1995	1996	1997	1998	1999	2000	2001	2002	2003	2004	2005	2006
BOTH SEXES												
Total Who Worked or Looked for Work	142 413	144 528	146 096	147 295	149 798	150 786	153 056	154 205	154 315	155 576	157 549	159 259
Percent with unemployment	12.7	11.6	10.7	9.5	8.7	8.1	10.4	10.9	10.7	9.7	9.2	9.1
Total with Unemployment	18 067	16 789	15 637	14 044	13 068	12 269	15 843	16 824	16 462	15 074	14 558	14 447
Did not work but looked for work	2 690	2 329	2 129	1 729	1 503	1 425	2 014	2 660	2 762	2 551	2 422	1 907
Worked during the year	15 377	14 460	13 508	12 316	11 566	10 845	13 829	14 164	13 699	12 522	12 136	12 540
Year-round workers with 1 or 2 weeks of unemployment	715	589	611	630	562	573	602	584	534	465	431	450
Part-year workers with unemployment	14 662	13 871	12 897	11 686	11 004	10 272	13 227	13 580	13 165	12 057	11 705	10 996
1 to 4 weeks	2 812	2 550	2 582	2 323	2 361	2 233	2 368	2 002	1 839	1 985	1 941	2 601
5 to 10 weeks	2 725	2 671	2 601	2 495	2 218	2 014	2 557	2 373	2 264	2 100	2 170	2 107
11 to 14 weeks	2 147	2 020	1 822	1 701	1 594	1 505	2 038	1 970	1 749	1 773	1 698	1 615
15 to 26 weeks	4 013	3 662	3 378	3 019	2 803	2 641	3 683	3 848	3 778	3 448	3 349	3 176
27 weeks or more	2 965	2 968	2 514	2 148	2 028	1 879	2 582	3 387	3 535	2 751	2 547	2 592
With 2 or more spells of unemployment	4 468	4 237	4 044	3 628	3 225	3 079	3 421	3 226	3 093	2 896	3 095	3 076
2 spells	1 963	1 982	1 853	1 650	1 449	1 397	1 643	1 556	1 585	1 344	1 477	1 564
3 or more spells	2 505	2 255	2 191	1 978	1 776	1 682	1 779	1 670	1 508	1 552	1 618	1 513
MEN												
Total Who Worked or Looked for Work	75 698	76 786	77 385	77 704	78 905	79 546	80 975	81 651	81 804	82 478	83 951	84 736
Percent with unemployment	13.2	11.9	11.1	9.4	9.0	8.6	11.0	11.8	11.4	10.0	9.7	9.6
Total with Unemployment	9 996	9 157	8 604	7 284	7 091	6 806	8 928	9 621	9 339	8 256	8 116	8 115
Did not work but looked for work	1 317	1 026	978	787	760	742	1 004	1 369	1 487	1 217	1 216	969
Worked during the year	8 679	8 130	7 626	6 497	6 332	6 064	7 924	8 252	7 854	7 039	6 899	7 146
Year-round workers with 1 or 2 weeks of unemployment	462	395	382	386	373	379	421	365	359	289	296	295
Part-year workers with unemployment	8 217	7 735	7 244	6 111	5 959	5 685	7 502	7 887	7 495	6 750	6 603	6 850
1 to 4 weeks	1 398	1 272	1 275	1 085	1 166	1 070	1 247	1 075	958	1 028	1 052	1 283
5 to 10 weeks	1 434	1 478	1 474	1 363	1 168	1 135	1 446	1 342	1 314	1 170	1 209	1 267
11 to 14 weeks	1 253	1 258	1 068	980	937	880	1 207	1 186	1 039	1 021	1 024	961
15 to 26 weeks	2 439	2 076	1 949	1 585	1 655	1 595	2 191	2 282	2 178	2 065	1 923	1 868
27 weeks or more	1 693	1 651	1 478	1 098	1 033	1 005	1 412	2 002	2 006	1 466	1 395	1 472
With 2 or more spells of unemployment	2 793	2 554	2 437	2 014	1 845	1 809	2 100	1 920	1 882	1 828	1 975	1 936
2 spells	1 110	1 109	1 078	880	787	804	1 002	914	946	808	940	945
3 or more spells	1 683	1 445	1 359	1 134	1 058	1 005	1 099	1 006	936	1 020	1 035	991
WOMEN												
Total Who Worked or Looked for Work	66 716	67 742	68 710	69 591	70 893	71 240	72 081	72 554	72 511	73 097	73 598	74 523
Percent with unemployment	12.1	11.3	10.2	9.7	8.4	7.7	9.6	9.9	9.8	9.3	8.8	8.5
Total with Unemployment	8 070	7 632	7 033	6 760	5 976	5 463	6 915	7 203	7 123	6 818	6 442	6 332
Did not work but looked for work	1 373	1 303	1 151	942	743	683	1 010	1 291	1 275	1 334	1 206	938
Worked during the year	6 696	6 330	5 882	5 816	5 234	4 779	5 905	5 913	5 848	5 484	5 236	5 394
Year-round workers with 1 or 2 weeks of unemployment	253	194	229	243	189	193	180	220	176	177	136	154
Part-year workers with unemployment	6 443	6 136	5 653	5 573	5 045	4 586	5 725	5 693	5 672	5 307	5 100	5 240
1 to 4 weeks	1 413	1 279	1 307	1 237	1 194	1 164	1 121	927	882	957	888	1 317
5 to 10 weeks	1 291	1 192	1 127	1 131	1 050	878	1 111	1 031	950	929	961	840
11 to 14 weeks	893	762	754	721	657	625	831	784	710	752	674	655
15 to 26 weeks	1 574	1 586	1 429	1 434	1 148	1 045	1 492	1 566	1 600	1 384	1 426	1 307
27 weeks or more	1 272	1 317	1 036	1 050	996	874	1 170	1 385	1 530	1 285	1 151	1 120
With 2 or more spells of unemployment	1 675	1 682	1 607	1 614	1 379	1 270	1 321	1 306	1 211	1 069	1 120	1 140
2 spells	853	872	775	770	662	593	641	642	639	537	537	619
3 or more spells	822	810	832	844	717	677	680	664	572	532	583	521

Note: See notes and definitions for information on historical comparability.

Table 1-38. Percent Distribution of Persons with Unemployment During the Year, by Sex and Extent of Unemployment, 1995–2006

(Percent.)

Sex and extent of unemployment	1995	1996	1997	1998	1999	2000	2001	2002	2003	2004	2005	2006
BOTH SEXES												
Total with Unemployment Who Worked During the Year	100.0	100.0	100.0	100.0	100.0	100.0	100.0	100.0	100.0	100.0	100.0	100.0
Year-round workers with 1 or 2 weeks of unemployment	4.6	4.1	4.5	5.1	4.9	5.3	4.4	4.1	3.9	3.7	3.6	3.6
Part-year workers with unemployment	95.4	96.0	95.5	95.0	95.1	94.8	95.6	95.9	96.1	96.3	96.4	96.4
1 to 4 weeks	18.3	17.6	19.1	18.9	20.4	20.6	17.1	14.1	13.4	15.9	16.0	20.7
5 to 10 weeks	17.7	18.5	19.3	20.3	19.2	18.6	18.5	16.8	16.5	16.8	17.9	16.8
11 to 14 weeks	14.0	14.0	13.5	13.8	13.8	13.9	14.7	13.9	12.8	14.2	14.0	12.9
15 to 26 weeks	26.1	25.3	25.0	24.5	24.2	24.4	26.6	27.2	27.6	27.5	27.6	25.3
27 weeks or more	19.3	20.6	18.6	17.5	17.5	17.3	18.7	23.9	25.8	22.0	20.9	20.7
With 2 or more spells of unemployment	29.1	29.3	29.9	29.5	27.9	28.4	24.8	22.8	22.6	23.1	25.5	24.5
2 spells	12.8	13.7	13.7	13.4	12.5	12.9	11.9	11.0	11.6	10.7	12.2	12.5
3 or more spells	16.3	15.6	16.2	16.1	15.4	15.5	12.9	11.8	11.0	12.4	13.3	12.1
MEN												
Total with Unemployment Who Worked During the Year	100.0	100.0	100.0	100.0	100.0	99.9	100.0	100.0	100.0	100.0	100.0	100.0
Year-round workers with 1 or 2 weeks of unemployment	5.3	4.9	5.0	5.9	5.9	6.3	5.3	4.4	4.6	4.1	4.3	4.1
Part-year workers with unemployment	94.7	95.1	95.1	94.1	94.0	93.6	94.7	95.6	95.4	95.9	95.7	95.9
1 to 4 weeks	16.1	15.6	16.7	16.7	18.4	17.6	15.7	13.0	12.2	14.6	15.3	18.0
5 to 10 weeks	16.5	18.2	19.3	21.0	18.4	18.7	18.2	16.3	16.7	16.6	17.5	17.7
11 to 14 weeks	14.4	15.5	14.0	15.1	14.8	14.5	15.2	14.4	13.2	14.5	14.8	13.4
15 to 26 weeks	28.1	25.5	25.6	24.4	26.1	26.3	27.6	27.7	27.7	29.3	27.9	26.1
27 weeks or more	19.5	20.3	19.4	16.9	16.3	16.5	17.8	24.3	25.5	20.8	20.2	20.6
With 2 or more spells of unemployment	32.2	31.4	31.9	31.0	29.1	29.9	26.5	23.3	24.0	26.0	28.6	27.1
2 spells	12.8	13.6	14.1	13.5	12.4	13.3	12.6	11.1	12.1	11.5	13.6	13.2
3 or more spells	19.4	17.8	17.8	17.5	16.7	16.6	13.9	12.2	11.9	14.5	15.0	13.9
WOMEN												
Total With Unemployment Who Worked During the Year	100.0	100.0	100.0	100.0	100.0	100.0	100.0	100.0	100.0	100.0	100.0	100.0
Year-round workers with 1 or 2 weeks of unemployment	3.8	3.1	3.9	4.2	3.6	4.0	3.1	3.7	3.0	3.2	2.6	2.9
Part-year workers with unemployment	96.2	96.9	96.1	95.8	96.4	96.0	96.9	96.3	97.0	96.8	97.4	97.1
1 to 4 weeks	21.1	20.2	22.2	21.3	22.8	24.3	19.0	15.7	15.1	17.4	17.0	24.4
5 to 10 weeks	19.3	18.8	19.2	19.4	20.1	18.4	18.8	17.4	16.2	16.9	18.4	15.6
11 to 14 weeks	13.3	12.0	12.8	12.4	12.6	13.1	14.1	13.3	12.1	13.7	12.9	12.1
15 to 26 weeks	23.5	25.1	24.3	24.7	21.9	21.9	25.3	26.5	27.4	25.2	27.2	24.2
27 weeks or more	19.0	20.8	17.6	18.0	19.0	18.3	19.8	23.4	26.2	23.5	22.0	20.8
With 2 or more spells of unemployment	25.0	26.6	27.3	27.7	26.3	26.6	22.4	22.1	20.7	19.5	21.4	21.1
2 spells	12.7	13.8	13.2	13.2	12.6	12.4	10.9	10.9	10.9	9.8	10.3	11.5
3 or more spells	12.3	12.8	14.1	14.5	13.7	14.2	11.5	11.2	9.8	9.7	11.1	9.7

Note: See notes and definitions for information on historical comparability.

Table 1-39. Number and Median Annual Earnings of Year-Round, Full-Time Wage and Salary Workers, by Age, Sex, and Race, 1995–2006

(Thousands of people, dollars.)

Sex, age, and race	1995	1996	1997	1998	1999	2000	2001	2002	2003	2004	2005	2006
NUMBER												
Both Sexes, 16 Years and Over	83 407	85 611	86 905	89 748	91 722	94 359	94 531	94 526	94 731	96 098	98 632	101 353
16 to 24 years	6 892	6 809	7 063	7 618	7 631	8 384	7 989	7 903	7 631	7 702	7 956	8 113
25 to 44 years	48 695	49 225	49 513	50 264	50 532	51 159	49 939	49 120	48 343	48 421	49 149	50 056
25 to 34 years	23 310	23 071	23 186	23 048	22 952	23 044	22 744	22 657	22 512	22 405	22 808	23 613
35 to 44 years	25 385	26 154	26 327	27 216	27 580	28 115	27 195	26 463	25 831	26 016	26 341	26 443
45 to 54 years	18 436	19 714	20 109	21 274	22 375	23 307	23 855	23 999	24 507	25 074	25 661	26 338
55 to 64 years	8 122	8 455	8 901	9 273	9 594	9 870	10 948	11 584	12 207	12 812	13 605	14 340
65 years and over	1 263	1 408	1 318	1 318	1 590	1 639	1 800	1 921	2 042	2 090	2 262	2 507
Men, 16 Years and Over	49 334	50 407	50 772	52 509	53 132	54 477	54 630	54 420	54 575	55 610	57 020	58 533
16 to 24 years	4 094	3 942	4 021	4 479	4 347	4 602	4 605	4 570	4 421	4 493	4 663	4 812
25 to 44 years	28 940	29 282	29 453	29 763	29 738	30 080	29 271	28 855	28 499	28 763	29 151	29 589
25 to 34 years	13 844	13 817	13 735	13 612	13 471	13 497	13 386	13 400	13 288	13 430	13 629	13 933
35 to 44 years	15 096	15 465	15 718	16 151	16 267	16 583	15 885	15 455	15 211	15 333	15 522	15 655
45 to 54 years	10 589	11 372	11 388	12 030	12 546	13 045	13 363	13 330	13 616	13 975	14 382	14 758
55 to 64 years	4 884	4 908	5 133	5 438	5 498	5 693	6 253	6 502	6 872	7 165	7 489	7 905
65 years and over	827	903	775	801	1 003	1 057	1 138	1 163	1 165	1 213	1 334	1 469
Women, 16 Years and Over	34 073	35 203	36 133	37 239	38 591	39 887	39 901	40 106	40 156	40 488	41 613	42 820
16 to 24 years	2 798	2 867	3 041	3 140	3 285	3 782	3 384	3 333	3 210	3 209	3 293	3 301
25 to 44 years	19 755	19 942	20 060	20 503	20 794	21 081	20 668	20 264	19 844	19 656	19 997	20 467
25 to 34 years	9 467	9 254	9 451	9 437	9 481	9 548	9 358	9 257	9 224	8 974	9 179	9 679
35 to 44 years	10 288	10 688	10 609	11 066	11 313	11 533	11 310	11 007	10 620	10 682	10 818	10 788
45 to 54 years	7 847	8 343	8 721	9 244	9 829	10 263	10 493	10 669	10 891	11 099	11 279	11 580
55 to 64 years	3 238	3 547	3 767	3 836	4 096	4 178	4 695	5 082	5 335	5 647	6 116	6 434
65 years and over	436	505	543	517	586	583	662	758	877	877	927	1 038
White, 16 Years and Over	70 430	72 068	72 650	75 046	76 203	77 790	78 306	77 632	77 545	78 236	80 546	82 411
Men	42 608	43 554	43 429	44 901	45 211	46 105	46 373	45 823	45 816	46 317	47 790	48 897
Women	27 822	28 514	29 221	30 145	30 992	31 685	31 933	31 809	31 729	31 919	32 756	33 513
Black, 16 Years and Over	9 446	9 706	10 248	10 532	11 145	11 899	11 001	10 966	10 979	11 301	11 417	11 988
Men	4 686	4 682	5 026	5 202	5 411	5 636	5 281	5 150	5 196	5 470	5 402	5 679
Women	4 759	5 024	5 222	5 329	5 734	6 264	5 720	5 816	5 783	5 832	6 015	6 309
MEDIAN ANNUAL EARNINGS												
Both Sexes, 16 Years and Over	27 000	28 000	30 000	30 000	31 000	32 000	34 000	35 000	35 000	35 672	36 400	38 000
16 to 24 years	15 500	15 600	16 000	18 000	18 000	19 000	20 000	20 000	20 000	20 000	20 000	21 000
25 to 34 years	25 000	25 300	27 000	28 500	30 000	30 000	31 000	31 800	32 000	33 000	33 000	35 000
35 to 44 years	30 000	31 000	32 000	33 000	34 992	35 000	36 000	37 000	39 000	40 000	40 000	41 000
45 to 54 years	32 000	33 000	35 000	35 000	36 000	38 000	39 500	40 000	40 000	40 000	42 000	44 000
55 to 64 years	30 000	30 000	32 000	34 000	35 000	35 000	36 400	39 145	40 000	40 000	41 000	43 000
65 years and over	29 600	26 496	28 200	26 000	30 000	32 000	32 000	33 000	32 000	35 000	35 000	35 001
Men, 16 Years and Over	31 000	32 000	34 000	35 000	36 000	37 600	38 500	40 000	40 000	40 000	40 051	42 000
16 to 24 years	16 000	17 000	17 000	18 720	19 000	20 000	20 000	20 000	20 800	20 800	20 800	22 000
25 to 34 years	27 000	28 000	29 852	30 000	32 000	33 500	34 000	34 740	35 000	35 000	35 000	36 000
35 to 44 years	35 000	36 000	37 000	38 000	40 000	40 000	42 000	43 000	43 900	45 000	45 000	48 000
45 to 54 years	40 000	40 000	41 000	42 000	44 616	45 000	45 000	47 000	48 000	48 000	50 000	50 000
55 to 64 years	36 000	36 000	39 000	40 000	40 853	44 000	45 000	47 000	50 000	50 000	50 000	50 000
65 years and over	36 000	33 000	36 400	35 000	36 000	35 999	35 000	37 861	42 000	40 000	41 000	44 000
Women, 16 Years and Over	23 000	24 000	25 000	25 000	26 000	27 500	29 000	30 000	30 000	30 001	32 000	33 000
16 to 24 years	15 000	15 000	15 000	17 000	17 000	18 000	19 000	19 000	20 000	20 000	20 000	20 000
25 to 34 years	22 000	23 000	24 000	25 000	26 000	27 000	28 080	29 500	30 000	30 000	30 000	31 000
35 to 44 years	25 000	25 000	26 000	27 200	28 000	29 000	30 000	30 400	32 000	32 800	35 000	35 000
45 to 54 years	25 000	26 000	27 040	28 132	30 000	30 000	32 000	32 000	33 466	34 771	35 000	36 000
55 to 64 years	22 500	24 000	24 800	25 775	27 000	28 000	30 000	31 410	32 000	33 000	33 000	35 000
65 years and over	23 290	20 800	24 000	22 000	20 800	24 000	25 000	28 000	26 000	27 000	28 768	27 878
White, 16 Years and Over	28 000	29 000	30 000	31 000	32 000	34 000	35 000	35 000	36 000	37 000	38 000	40 000
Men	32 000	33 000	35 000	36 000	37 200	39 000	40 000	40 000	40 000	42 000	42 000	44 707
Women	23 000	24 000	25 000	26 000	27 000	28 000	30 000	30 000	31 000	31 800	32 000	34 000
Black, 16 Years and Over	22 000	23 784	24 000	25 000	25 760	26 000	28 500	29 000	30 000	30 000	30 000	31 000
Men	24 500	26 000	26 000	27 000	30 000	30 000	30 000	30 000	32 000	30 000	33 000	34 000
Women	20 000	21 000	22 000	23 000	24 000	25 000	26 000	26 000	27 000	28 000	29 141	30 000

Note: Detail for the race groups will not sum to totals because data for other race groups are not presented. See notes and definitions for information on historical comparability.

Table 1-40. Number and Median Annual Earnings of Year-Round, Full-Time Wage and Salary Workers, by Sex and Occupation of Job Held the Longest, 2002–2006

(Thousands of people, dollars.)

Sex and occupation	2002	2003	2004	2005	2006
Both Sexes, Number of Workers					
Management, business, and financial operations	15 707	15 552	15 575	16 299	16 806
Management	11 350	11 102	11 125	11 685	11 866
Business and financial operations	4 357	4 450	4 451	4 613	4 941
Professional and related	19 149	19 607	19 592	20 093	21 268
Computer and mathematical	2 644	2 598	2 680	2 779	2 888
Architecture and engineering	2 257	2 273	2 349	2 361	2 491
Life, physical, and social sciences	1 094	1 010	999	1 096	1 142
Community and social services	1 694	1 698	1 632	1 728	1 835
Legal	1 006	1 149	1 087	1 093	1 168
Education, training, and library	4 606	4 918	4 742	4 894	5 195
Arts, design, entertainment, sports, and media	1 453	1 374	1 416	1 362	1 633
Health care practitioner and technical	4 395	4 586	4 688	4 780	4 916
Services	12 011	11 990	12 457	13 117	13 236
Health care support	1 767	1 703	1 781	2 027	2 081
Protective services	2 042	2 385	2 406	2 429	2 506
Food preparation and serving related	3 592	3 223	3 383	3 586	3 646
Building and grounds cleaning and maintenance	2 843	2 942	3 116	3 285	3 120
Personal care and services	1 767	1 735	1 771	1 790	1 883
Sales and office	23 791	23 766	23 619	24 010	24 467
Sales and related	9 929	9 804	9 951	10 251	10 497
Office and administrative support	13 862	13 962	13 668	13 758	13 970
Natural resources, construction, and maintenance	9 823	9 709	10 574	10 864	11 295
Farming, fishing, and forestry	573	562	629	556	585
Construction and extraction	5 256	5 070	5 711	6 145	6 484
Installation, maintenance, and repair	3 994	4 077	4 234	4 163	4 226
Production, transportation, and material moving	13 386	13 391	13 648	13 586	13 704
Production	7 736	7 670	7 787	7 623	7 762
Transportation and material moving	5 650	5 721	5 861	5 963	5 942
Armed forces	658	717	632	664	576
Both Sexes, Median Annual Earnings					
Management, business, and financial operations	50 000	52 000	55 000	57 000	60 000
Management	55 000	58 000	60 000	60 000	62 500
Business and financial operations	44 000	45 000	45 000	49 000	50 000
Professional and related	46 000	46 000	48 000	50 000	50 000
Computer and mathematical	60 000	60 000	62 000	62 400	68 000
Architecture and engineering	59 400	62 000	60 000	65 000	69 000
Life, physical, and social sciences	50 000	50 000	50 000	53 500	57 000
Community and social services	34 000	34 349	36 000	36 000	36 780
Legal	61 860	75 000	70 000	72 000	70 000
Education, training, and library	38 000	39 000	40 000	40 000	40 282
Arts, design, entertainment, sports, and media	43 500	40 000	40 000	42 000	45 000
Health care practitioner and technical	46 000	48 000	50 000	50 000	52 000
Services	22 000	22 000	22 000	23 000	24 000
Health care support	22 100	22 000	22 000	22 000	23 000
Protective services	38 000	42 000	42 000	42 000	45 000
Food preparation and serving related	18 000	18 000	18 000	19 656	19 000
Building and grounds cleaning and maintenance	20 000	20 000	20 000	21 000	23 000
Personal care and services	21 840	20 678	22 537	23 000	23 000
Sales and office	30 000	30 000	30 000	31 200	32 002
Sales and related	35 000	35 000	35 000	35 000	37 000
Office and administrative support	28 000	29 000	30 000	30 000	30 000
Natural resources, construction, and maintenance	33 000	34 000	35 000	35 000	35 000
Farming, fishing, and forestry	20 000	20 000	20 000	21 000	20 000
Construction and extraction	31 200	32 000	33 000	32 000	35 000
Installation, maintenance, and repair	36 000	38 000	38 300	40 000	40 000
Production, transportation, and material moving	28 704	30 000	30 000	30 200	30 000
Production	28 000	30 000	30 000	30 000	30 000
Transportation and material moving	29 000	30 000	30 000	30 800	30 000
Armed forces	36 000	36 000	40 000	39 000	40 000

Note: See notes and definitions for information on historical comparability.

Table 1-40. Number and Median Annual Earnings of Year-Round, Full-Time Wage and Salary Workers, by Sex and Occupation of Job Held the Longest, 2002–2006—*Continued*

(Thousands of people, dollars.)

Sex and occupation	2002	2003	2004	2005	2006
Men, Number of Workers					
Management, business, and financial operations	9 178	8 961	8 849	9 496	9 519
Management	7 145	6 991	6 911	7 477	7 361
Business and financial operations	2 033	1 970	1 938	2 019	2 157
Professional and related	9 299	9 535	9 497	9 561	10 387
Computer and mathematical	1 953	1 913	1 972	2 060	2 159
Architecture and engineering	1 984	2 004	2 049	2 041	2 174
Life, physical, and social sciences	667	668	626	668	748
Community and social services	726	730	705	713	756
Legal	490	610	537	490	546
Education, training, and library	1 407	1 476	1 386	1 421	1 587
Arts, design, entertainment, sports, and media	847	811	848	789	953
Health care practitioner and technical	1 225	1 323	1 374	1 378	1 464
Services	5 988	6 204	6 314	6 658	6 715
Health care support	181	178	208	240	252
Protective services	1 689	1 967	1 906	1 919	1 998
Food preparation and serving related	1 836	1 638	1 716	1 873	1 991
Building and grounds cleaning and maintenance	1 788	1 914	2 002	2 153	1 939
Personal care and services	494	508	482	473	535
Sales and office	9 453	9 398	9 380	9 464	9 747
Sales and related	5 933	5 891	5 892	5 896	6 125
Office and administrative support	3 520	3 507	3 488	3 568	3 622
Natural resources, construction, and maintenance	9 434	9 348	10 178	10 503	10 904
Farming, fishing, and forestry	463	470	536	469	482
Construction and extraction	5 156	4 972	5 576	6 026	6 344
Installation, maintenance, and repair	3 815	3 905	4 065	4 008	4 078
Production, transportation, and material moving	10 472	10 492	10 812	10 747	10 733
Production	5 517	5 513	5 637	5 503	5 525
Transportation and material moving	4 955	4 979	5 176	5 244	5 208
Armed forces	600	636	580	591	528
Men, Median Annual Earnings					
Management, business, and financial operations	60 000	60 200	65 000	69 000	68 000
Management	65 000	65 000	70 000	70 000	70 000
Business and financial operations	52 000	51 000	55 000	60 000	60 000
Professional and related	55 000	58 000	58 000	60 000	61 000
Computer and mathematical	60 000	65 000	65 000	65 000	70 000
Architecture and engineering	60 000	64 558	61 785	66 921	70 000
Life, physical, and social sciences	52 000	50 801	55 000	62 000	61 000
Community and social services	35 000	35 000	38 000	40 000	39 000
Legal	100 000	100 000	101 000	108 000	100 000
Education, training, and library	45 600	48 000	47 000	50 000	50 000
Arts, design, entertainment, sports, and media	46 000	45 000	45 000	50 000	50 000
Health care practitioner and technical	72 000	65 500	70 000	70 000	72 000
Services	25 000	26 000	25 000	26 000	29 000
Health care support	24 000	22 537	20 400	22 880	25 000
Protective services	40 000	44 000	44 000	45 000	46 886
Food preparation and serving related	20 000	18 720	18 720	20 000	20 000
Building and grounds cleaning and maintenance	24 500	22 156	24 000	24 000	25 000
Personal care and services	30 000	28 559	26 000	30 000	30 000
Sales and office	38 000	39 000	40 000	40 000	40 000
Sales and related	41 600	41 000	44 000	42 000	45 000
Office and administrative support	32 000	32 000	34 000	34 000	35 000
Natural resources, construction, and maintenance	33 592	34 283	35 000	35 000	35 674
Farming, fishing, and forestry	22 000	22 000	22 000	22 500	20 000
Construction and extraction	31 304	32 000	33 000	32 000	35 000
Installation, maintenance, and repair	36 000	38 000	38 870	40 000	40 000
Production, transportation, and material moving	30 000	32 000	33 000	34 000	33 358
Production	30 360	32 000	34 000	35 000	35 000
Transportation and material moving	30 000	30 000	32 000	32 760	32 000
Armed forces	36 000	36 000	40 000	40 000	40 000

Note: See notes and definitions for information on historical comparability.

Table 1-40. Number and Median Annual Earnings of Year-Round, Full-Time Wage and Salary Workers, by Sex and Occupation of Job Held the Longest, 2002–2006—*Continued*

(Thousands of people, dollars.)

Sex and occupation	2002	2003	2004	2005	2006
Women, Number of Workers					
Management, business, and financial operations	6 529	6 591	6 726	6 803	7 287
Management	4 205	4 111	4 214	4 209	4 504
Business and financial operations	2 324	2 479	2 512	2 594	2 783
Professional and related	9 851	10 071	10 095	10 532	10 881
Computer and mathematical	691	685	708	718	729
Architecture and engineering	273	269	300	320	317
Life, physical, and social sciences	428	342	373	428	394
Community and social services	968	968	927	1 015	1 079
Legal	516	539	550	603	622
Education, training, and library	3 199	3 441	3 356	3 473	3 608
Arts, design, entertainment, sports, and media	606	563	568	573	681
Health care practitioner and technical	3 170	3 263	3 314	3 403	3 452
Services	6 026	5 786	6 144	6 459	6 522
Health care support	1 586	1 525	1 573	1 787	1 829
Protective services	354	419	500	510	509
Food preparation and serving related	1 757	1 585	1 668	1 713	1 655
Building and grounds cleaning and maintenance	1 055	1 029	1 115	1 132	1 181
Personal care and services	1 274	1 228	1 289	1 317	1 349
Sales and office	14 338	14 368	14 239	14 546	14 720
Sales and related	3 996	3 913	4 060	4 355	4 372
Office and administrative support	10 342	10 455	10 180	10 191	10 348
Natural resources, construction, and maintenance	391	361	396	360	391
Farming, fishing, and forestry	111	92	93	87	104
Construction and extraction	100	97	135	119	140
Installation, maintenance, and repair	180	172	169	155	148
Production, transportation, and material moving	2 914	2 899	2 835	2 839	2 971
Production	2 219	2 157	2 150	2 120	2 237
Transportation and material moving	695	742	685	719	734
Armed forces	58	81	52	73	48
Women, Median Annual Earnings					
Management, business, and financial operations	41 000	43 000	43 000	46 000	50 000
Management	44 000	47 000	46 000	50 000	52 000
Business and financial operations	38 500	40 000	40 000	41 000	46 000
Professional and related	40 000	40 000	40 000	42 000	43 000
Computer and mathematical	51 627	52 000	57 000	57 000	60 000
Architecture and engineering	50 000	48 000	47 500	55 000	52 000
Life, physical, and social sciences	44 000	45 000	45 995	50 000	48 000
Community and social services	33 000	33 000	35 000	35 000	36 000
Legal	45 000	45 000	46 000	47 500	50 000
Education, training, and library	35 000	35 000	37 000	38 000	38 632
Arts, design, entertainment, sports, and media	40 000	35 000	36 000	35 000	38 000
Health care practitioner and technical	41 000	43 000	45 000	46 000	48 000
Services	20 000	20 000	20 000	20 000	20 500
Health care support	22 000	22 000	22 000	21 000	23 000
Protective services	30 900	32 000	32 000	34 344	37 896
Food preparation and serving related	16 160	17 000	16 000	18 000	18 000
Building and grounds cleaning and maintenance	16 491	16 000	16 866	18 000	19 000
Personal care and services	20 000	20 000	21 000	20 800	20 000
Sales and office	26 989	28 000	28 000	29 000	30 000
Sales and related	25 000	26 000	26 000	26 000	26 000
Office and administrative support	27 000	28 000	28 000	29 800	30 000
Natural resources, construction, and maintenance	26 000	28 000	30 000	30 200	27 000
Farming, fishing, and forestry	17 000	16 000	15 700	18 000	18 808
Construction and extraction	26 000	29 500	40 000	31 200	24 980
Installation, maintenance, and repair	34 000	37 000	33 000	36 000	40 000
Production, transportation, and material moving	22 000	22 100	23 000	23 000	23 000
Production	21 632	22 000	23 000	23 400	23 000
Transportation and material moving	22 000	22 710	23 000	21 000	24 000
Armed forces	40 000	32 000	35 100	32 652	32 000

Note: See notes and definitions for information on historical comparability.

Table 1-41. Wage and Salary Workers Paid Hourly Rates with Earnings at or Below the Prevailing Federal Minimum Wage, by Selected Characteristics, 2005–2006

(Thousands of people, percent.)

Characteristic	Workers paid hourly rates				
	Total	Below prevailing federal minimum wage	At prevailing federal minimum wage	Total at or below prevailing federal minimum wage	
				Number	Percent of hourly-paid workers
2005					
Age and Sex					
Both sexes, 16 years and over	75 609	1 403	479	1 882	2.5
16 to 24 years	16 374	720	283	1 002	6.1
25 years and over	59 235	683	196	880	1.5
Men, 16 years and over	37 652	459	189	648	1.7
16 to 24 years	8 288	223	130	353	4.3
25 years and over	29 364	236	60	296	1.0
Women, 16 years and over	37 957	944	290	1 234	3.3
16 to 24 years	8 086	496	153	650	8.0
25 years and over	29 871	447	137	584	2.0
Race, Sex, and Hispanic Origin					
White, 16 years and over	60 978	1 188	349	1 537	2.5
Men	30 901	352	133	485	1.6
Women	30 078	836	216	1 053	3.5
Black, 16 years and over	9 793	119	96	215	2.2
Men	4 421	63	42	105	2.4
Women	5 372	57	54	111	2.1
Asian, 16 years and over	2 720	51	14	65	2.4
Men	1 283	25	5	30	2.3
Women	1 437	26	9	35	2.4
Hispanic,[1] 16 years and over	12 527	210	71	282	2.2
Men	7 467	85	29	114	1.5
Women	5 060	125	42	167	3.3
Full- and Part-Time Status[2] and Sex					
Full-time workers	57 385	608	143	752	1.3
Men	31 911	252	69	321	1.0
Women	25 474	356	74	430	1.7
Part-time workers	18 084	790	336	1 126	6.2
Men	5 669	207	120	327	5.8
Women	12 415	583	216	799	6.4
2006					
Age and Sex					
Both sexes, 16 years and over	76 514	1 283	409	1 692	2.2
16 to 24 years	16 649	619	247	866	5.2
25 years and over	59 865	664	162	826	1.4
Men, 16 years and over	38 193	422	146	569	1.5
16 to 24 years	8 583	198	98	296	3.4
25 years and over	29 609	224	49	273	0.9
Women, 16 years and over	38 321	861	263	1 124	2.9
16 to 24 years	8 065	421	149	570	7.1
25 years and over	30 256	440	114	553	1.8
Race, Sex, and Hispanic Origin					
White, 16 years and over	61 907	1 105	329	1 435	2.3
Men	31 403	354	115	469	1.5
Women	30 504	751	215	966	3.2
Black, 16 years and over	9 903	111	62	173	1.8
Men	4 485	40	28	67	1.5
Women	5 419	72	34	106	2.0
Asian, 16 years and over	2 654	30	8	38	1.4
Men	1 259	13	1	14	1.1
Women	1 395	17	7	24	1.7
Hispanic,[1] 16 years and over	13 121	155	68	223	1.7
Men	7 780	67	29	96	1.2
Women	5 341	88	40	127	2.4
Full- and Part-Time Status[2] and Sex					
Full-time workers	58 452	554	99	653	1.1
Men	32 477	213	35	247	0.8
Women	25 975	341	64	406	1.6
Part-time workers	17 930	724	310	1 034	5.8
Men	5 652	205	112	317	5.6
Women	12 278	519	198	717	5.8

Note: The prevailing federal minimum wage was $5.15 per hour in 2006. Data are for wage and salary workers, excluding the incorporated self-employed. They refer to a person's earnings for their sole or principal job and pertain only to workers who are paid hourly rates. Salaried workers and other non-hourly workers are not included. The presence of workers with hourly earnings below the minimum wage does not necessarily indicate violations of the Fair Labor Standards Act, as there are exceptions to the minimum wage provisions of the law. In addition, some survey respondents might have rounded hourly earnings to the nearest dollar, and, as a result, reported hourly earnings below the minimum wage even though they earned the minimum wage or higher. Beginning in January 2005, data reflect the revised population controls used in the household survey.

[1]May be of any race.
[2]The distinction between full- and part-time workers is based on the hours usually worked. These data will not sum to totals because full- or part-time status on the principal job is not identifiable for a small number of multiple jobholders.

Table 1-42. Absences from Work of Employed Full-Time Wage and Salary Workers, by Age and Sex, 2004–2006

(Thousands of people, percent.)

Year, sex, and age	Total employed	Absence rate[1]			Lost worktime rate[2]		
		Total	Illness or injury	Other reasons	Total	Illness or injury	Other reasons
2004							
Both Sexes, 16 Years and Over	101 011	3.2	2.3	0.9	1.7	1.2	0.5
16 to 19 years	1 663	3.2	2.4	0.8	1.7	1.2	0.5
20 to 24 years	9 191	3.1	2.0	1.1	1.6	0.9	0.6
25 years and over	90 157	3.2	2.3	0.9	1.8	1.3	0.5
25 to 54 years	76 458	3.1	2.2	1.0	1.7	1.2	0.5
55 years and over	13 699	3.5	2.9	0.7	2.1	1.8	0.3
Men, 16 Years and Over	56 922	2.3	1.8	0.5	1.2	1.0	0.2
16 to 19 years	1 015	2.9	2.4	0.5	1.7	1.4	0.3
20 to 24 years	5 242	2.2	1.6	0.5	1.1	0.8	0.2
25 years and over	50 665	2.3	1.8	0.5	1.3	1.0	0.2
25 to 54 years	43 177	2.2	1.7	0.5	1.2	0.9	0.2
55 years and over	7 489	3.0	2.4	0.5	1.9	1.6	0.2
Women, 16 Years and Over	44 088	4.4	2.9	1.4	2.4	1.5	0.9
16 to 19 years	648	3.7	2.3	1.3	1.8	0.9	0.9
20 to 24 years	3 949	4.4	2.6	1.8	2.3	1.1	1.2
25 years and over	39 492	4.4	3.0	1.4	2.4	1.6	0.8
25 to 54 years	33 282	4.4	2.9	1.5	2.4	1.5	0.9
55 years and over	6 210	4.2	3.4	0.9	2.4	2.0	0.4
2005							
Both Sexes, 16 Years and Over	103 410	3.3	2.4	0.9	1.8	1.3	0.5
16 to 19 years	1 691	2.8	1.9	0.9	1.5	0.9	0.5
20 to 24 years	9 376	3.2	2.2	1.0	1.6	1.0	0.6
25 years and over	92 344	3.4	2.4	0.9	1.8	1.3	0.5
25 to 54 years	77 674	3.3	2.3	1.0	1.8	1.2	0.5
55 years and over	14 670	3.8	3.1	0.7	2.1	1.8	0.3
Men, 16 Years and Over	58 287	2.5	1.9	0.6	1.3	1.1	0.3
16 to 19 years	997	1.8	1.4	0.4	0.8	0.7	0.1
20 to 24 years	5 343	2.3	1.8	0.5	1.1	0.9	0.2
25 years and over	51 947	2.5	1.9	0.6	1.4	1.1	0.3
25 to 54 years	43 953	2.4	1.8	0.6	1.3	1.0	0.3
55 years and over	7 994	3.1	2.6	0.6	1.8	1.6	0.3
Women, 16 Years and Over	45 123	4.4	3.0	1.4	2.4	1.5	0.8
16 to 19 years	694	4.2	2.6	1.6	2.4	1.3	1.1
20 to 24 years	4 033	4.4	2.7	1.8	2.3	1.1	1.2
25 years and over	40 397	4.5	3.1	1.4	2.4	1.6	0.8
25 to 54 years	33 720	4.4	2.9	1.5	2.4	1.5	0.9
55 years and over	6 676	4.5	3.6	0.9	2.4	2.1	0.4
2006							
Both Sexes, 16 Years and Over	105 785	3.2	2.3	0.9	1.8	1.2	0.5
16 to 19 years	1 741	3.0	2.1	0.9	1.4	1.1	0.4
20 to 24 years	9 490	2.8	1.9	0.9	1.4	0.9	0.5
25 years and over	94 555	3.3	2.3	0.9	1.8	1.3	0.5
25 to 54 years	78 821	3.2	2.2	1.0	1.7	1.2	0.6
55 years and over	15 733	3.6	3.0	0.7	2.0	1.7	0.3
Men, 16 Years and Over	59 633	2.4	1.8	0.6	1.3	1.0	0.3
16 to 19 years	1 059	2.1	1.7	0.5	1.1	1.0	0.2
20 to 24 years	5 462	2.2	1.6	0.6	1.0	0.8	0.2
25 years and over	53 111	2.4	1.9	0.6	1.3	1.0	0.3
25 to 54 years	44 601	2.3	1.7	0.6	1.2	0.9	0.3
55 years and over	8 510	3.2	2.7	0.5	1.9	1.7	0.2
Women, 16 Years and Over	46 152	4.3	2.8	1.4	2.4	1.5	0.9
16 to 19 years	681	4.4	2.9	1.5	2.0	1.2	0.8
20 to 24 years	4 027	3.8	2.3	1.4	2.0	1.0	1.0
25 years and over	41 443	4.3	2.9	1.4	2.4	1.6	0.9
25 to 54 years	34 221	4.3	2.8	1.5	2.5	1.5	1.0
55 years and over	7 223	4.2	3.3	0.9	2.3	1.8	0.4

Note: Beginning in January 2003, data reflect the revised population controls used in the household survey.

[1]Absences are defined as instances when persons who usually work 35 or more hours a week worked less than 35 hours during the reference week for reasons including own illness, injury, or medical problems; childcare problems; other family or personal obligations; civic or military duty; and maternity or paternity leave. Excluded are situations in which work was missed due to vacation or personal days, holidays, labor disputes, and other reasons. For multiple jobholders, absence data refer only to work missed at their main jobs. The absence rate is the ratio of workers with absences to total full-time wage and salary employment. The estimates of full-time wage and salary employment shown in this table do not match those in other tables because the estimates in this table are based on the full Current Population Survey (CPS) sample. Those in the other tables are based on a quarter of the sample only.
[2]Hours absent as a percentage of hours usually worked.

Table 1-43. Median Years of Tenure with Current Employer for Employed Wage and Salary Workers, by Age and Sex, Selected Years, February 1996–January 2006

(Number of years.)

Sex and age	February 1996	February 1998	February 2000	January 2002	January 2004	January 2006
Both Sexes						
16 years and over	3.8	3.6	3.5	3.7	4.0	4.0
16 to 17 years	0.7	0.6	0.6	0.7	0.7	0.6
18 to 19 years	0.7	0.7	0.7	0.8	0.8	0.7
20 to 24 years	1.2	1.1	1.1	1.2	1.3	1.3
25 years and over	5.0	4.7	4.7	4.7	4.9	4.9
25 to 34 years	2.8	2.7	2.6	2.7	2.9	2.9
35 to 44 years	5.3	5.0	4.8	4.6	4.9	4.9
45 to 54 years	8.3	8.1	8.2	7.6	7.7	7.3
55 to 64 years	10.2	10.1	10.0	9.9	9.6	9.3
65 years and over	8.4	7.8	9.4	8.6	9.0	8.8
Men						
16 years and over	4.0	3.8	3.8	3.9	4.1	4.1
16 to 17 years	0.6	0.6	0.6	0.8	0.7	0.7
18 to 19 years	0.7	0.7	0.7	0.8	0.8	0.7
20 to 24 years	1.2	1.2	1.2	1.4	1.3	1.4
25 years and over	5.3	4.9	4.9	4.9	5.1	5.0
25 to 34 years	3.0	2.8	2.7	2.8	3.0	2.9
35 to 44 years	6.1	5.5	5.3	5.0	5.2	5.1
45 to 54 years	10.1	9.4	9.5	9.1	9.6	8.1
55 to 64 years	10.5	11.2	10.2	10.2	9.8	9.5
65 years and over	8.3	7.1	9.0	8.1	8.2	8.3
Women						
16 years and over	3.5	3.4	3.3	3.4	3.8	3.9
16 to 17 years	0.7	0.6	0.6	0.7	0.6	0.6
18 to 19 years	0.7	0.7	0.7	0.8	0.8	0.7
20 to 24 years	1.2	1.1	1.0	1.1	1.3	1.2
25 years and over	4.7	4.4	4.4	4.4	4.7	4.8
25 to 34 years	2.7	2.5	2.5	2.5	2.8	2.8
35 to 44 years	4.8	4.5	4.3	4.2	4.5	4.6
45 to 54 years	7.0	7.2	7.3	6.5	6.4	6.7
55 to 64 years	10.0	9.6	9.9	9.6	9.2	9.2
65 years and over	8.4	8.7	9.7	9.4	9.6	9.5

Note: Data for 1996 and 1998 are based on population controls from the 1990 census. Data beginning in 2000 reflect the introduction of Census 2000 population controls and are not strictly comparable with data for prior years. In addition, data for 2004 reflect the introduction of revised population controls in January 2003 and January 2004, and data for January 2006 reflect the introduction of revisions to the population controls in January 2005 and 2006.

Table 1-44. Median Years of Tenure with Current Employer for Employed Wage and Salary Workers, by Industry, Selected Years, February 2000–January 2006

(Number of years.)

Industry	February 2000	January 2002	January 2004	January 2006
TOTAL, 16 YEARS AND OVER	3.5	3.7	4.0	4.0
Private Sector	3.2	3.3	3.5	3.6
Agriculture and related industries	3.7	4.2	3.7	3.8
Nonagricultural industries	3.2	3.3	3.5	3.6
Mining	4.8	4.5	5.2	3.8
Construction	2.7	3.0	3.0	3.0
Manufacturing	4.9	5.4	5.8	5.5
Durable goods manufacturing	4.8	5.5	6.0	5.6
Nonmetallic mineral product	5.5	5.3	4.8	5.0
Primary metals and fabricated metal product	5.0	6.3	6.4	6.2
Machinery manufacturing	5.3	6.8	6.4	6.6
Computers and electronic product	3.9	4.7	5.2	5.9
Electrical equipment and appliances	5.0	5.5	9.8	6.2
Transportation equipment	6.4	7.0	7.7	7.2
Wood product	3.7	4.3	5.0	4.7
Furniture and fixtures	4.4	4.7	4.7	4.2
Miscellaneous manufacturing	3.7	4.5	4.6	3.9
Nondurable goods manufacturing	5.0	5.3	5.5	5.4
Food manufacturing	4.6	5.0	4.9	5.2
Beverage and tobacco product	5.5	4.6	8.0	5.4
Textiles, apparel, and leather	4.7	5.0	5.0	4.4
Paper and printing	5.1	6.2	6.9	6.3
Petroleum and coal product	9.5	9.8	11.4	5.0
Chemicals	6.0	5.7	5.3	6.1
Plastics and rubber product	4.6	5.3	5.7	5.0
Wholesale and retail trade	2.7	2.8	3.1	3.1
Wholesale trade	3.9	3.9	4.3	4.6
Retail trade	2.5	2.6	2.8	2.8
Transportation and utilities	4.7	4.9	5.3	4.9
Transportation and warehousing	4.0	4.3	4.7	4.3
Utilities	11.5	13.4	13.3	10.4
Information[1]	3.4	3.3	4.3	4.8
Publishing, except Internet	4.2	4.8	4.7	5.3
Motion picture and sound recording industries	1.6	2.3	2.2	1.9
Broadcasting, except Internet	3.6	3.1	4.0	4.6
Telecommunications	4.3	3.4	4.6	5.3
Financial activities	3.5	3.6	3.9	4.0
Finance and insurance	3.6	3.9	4.1	4.1
Finance	3.3	3.6	4.0	3.9
Insurance	4.4	4.5	4.4	4.7
Real estate and rental and leasing	3.1	3.0	3.3	3.4
Real estate	3.1	3.2	3.5	3.5
Rental and leasing services	3.0	2.2	2.9	3.1
Professional and business services	2.4	2.7	3.2	3.2
Professional and technical services	2.6	3.1	3.6	3.8
Management, administrative, and waste services[1]	2.0	2.1	2.6	2.5
Administrative and support services	1.8	1.9	2.4	2.4
Waste management and remediation services	3.6	4.3	3.4	4.1
Education and health services	3.4	3.5	3.6	4.0
Education services	3.2	3.6	3.8	4.0
Health care and social assistance	3.5	3.5	3.6	4.1
Hospitals	5.1	4.9	4.7	5.2
Health services, except hospitals	3.2	3.1	3.3	3.6
Social assistance	2.4	2.5	2.8	3.1
Leisure and hospitality	1.7	1.8	2.0	1.9
Arts, entertainment, and recreation	2.6	2.3	2.8	3.1
Accommodation and food services	1.5	1.6	1.9	1.6
Accommodation	2.8	2.7	3.1	2.5
Food services and drinking places	1.4	1.4	1.6	1.4
Other services	3.1	3.3	3.3	3.2
Other services, except private households	3.2	3.3	3.5	3.3
Repair and maintenance	3.0	3.0	3.2	2.9
Personal and laundry services	2.7	2.8	3.4	2.8
Membership associations and organizations	4.0	4.1	3.9	4.2
Other services, private households	3.0	2.7	2.3	2.8
Public Sector	7.1	6.7	6.9	6.9
Federal government	11.5	11.3	10.4	9.9
State government	5.5	5.4	6.4	6.3
Local government	6.7	6.2	6.4	6.6

Note: Data for January 2004 reflect the introduction of revisions to the population controls in January 2003 and 2004. Data for January 2006 reflect the introduction of revisions to the population controls in January 2005 and 2006.

[1]Includes other industries not shown separately.

Table 1-45. Employment Status of the Population, by Sex and Marital Status, March 1990–March 2007

(Thousands of people, percent.)

Marital status and year	Men						Women					
	Population	Labor force					Population	Labor force				
		Total		Employed	Unemployed			Total		Employed	Unemployed	
		Number	Percent of population		Number	Percent of labor force		Number	Percent of population		Number	Percent of labor force
Single												
1990	25 757	18 829	73.1	16 893	1 936	10.3	21 088	14 003	66.4	12 856	1 147	8.2
1991	26 220	19 014	72.5	16 418	2 596	13.7	21 688	14 125	65.1	12 887	1 238	8.8
1992	26 529	19 229	72.5	16 401	2 828	14.7	21 738	14 072	64.7	12 793	1 279	9.1
1993	26 951	19 625	72.8	16 858	2 767	14.1	21 848	14 091	64.5	12 711	1 380	9.8
1994	28 350	20 365	71.8	17 826	2 539	12.5	22 885	14 903	65.1	13 419	1 484	10.0
1995	28 318	20 449	72.2	18 286	2 163	10.6	22 853	14 974	65.5	13 673	1 301	8.7
1996	28 695	20 561	71.7	18 097	2 464	12.0	23 632	15 417	65.2	14 084	1 333	8.6
1997	29 294	20 942	71.5	18 683	2 259	10.8	24 215	16 178	66.8	14 747	1 431	8.8
1998	29 558	21 255	71.9	19 124	2 131	10.0	24 808	16 885	68.1	15 626	1 259	7.5
1999	29 883	21 329	71.4	19 465	1 864	8.7	25 674	17 486	68.1	16 185	1 301	7.4
2000	30 232	21 641	71.6	19 823	1 818	8.4	25 863	17 749	68.6	16 446	1 303	7.3
2001	30 968	22 232	71.8	20 239	1 993	9.0	26 180	17 900	68.4	16 631	1 269	7.1
2002	32 220	22 761	70.6	20 066	2 695	11.8	26 942	18 079	67.1	16 499	1 580	8.7
2003	32 852	22 821	69.5	20 194	2 627	11.5	27 527	17 901	65.0	16 219	1 682	9.4
2004	33 786	23 212	68.7	20 434	2 778	12.0	28 033	18 089	64.5	16 506	1 583	8.8
2005	34 069	23 335	68.5	20 831	2 504	10.7	28 508	18 554	65.1	16 902	1 652	8.9
2006	34 906	24 369	69.8	21 961	2 408	9.9	29 357	18 989	64.7	17 444	1 545	8.1
2007	35 359	24 506	69.3	22 224	2 281	9.3	29 695	19 218	64.7	17 935	1 284	6.7
Married, Spouse Present												
1990	52 464	41 020	78.2	39 562	1 458	3.6	53 207	30 967	58.2	29 870	1 097	3.5
1991	52 460	40 883	77.9	38 843	2 040	5.0	53 176	31 103	58.5	29 668	1 435	4.6
1992	52 780	40 930	77.5	38 650	2 280	5.6	53 464	31 686	59.3	30 130	1 556	4.9
1993	53 488	41 255	77.1	39 069	2 186	5.3	54 146	32 158	59.4	30 757	1 401	4.4
1994	53 436	40 993	76.7	39 085	1 908	4.7	54 198	32 863	60.6	31 397	1 466	4.5
1995	54 166	41 806	77.2	40 262	1 544	3.7	54 902	33 563	61.1	32 267	1 296	3.9
1996	53 996	41 837	77.5	40 356	1 481	3.5	54 640	33 382	61.1	32 258	1 124	3.4
1997	53 981	41 967	77.7	40 628	1 339	3.2	54 611	33 907	62.1	32 836	1 071	3.2
1998	54 685	42 288	77.3	41 039	1 249	3.0	55 241	34 136	61.8	33 028	1 108	3.2
1999	55 256	42 557	77.0	41 476	1 081	2.5	55 801	34 349	61.6	33 403	946	2.8
2000	55 897	43 254	77.4	42 261	993	2.3	56 432	34 959	61.9	33 998	961	2.7
2001	56 152	43 463	77.4	42 245	1 218	2.8	56 740	35 234	62.1	34 273	961	2.7
2002	57 325	44 271	77.2	42 508	1 763	4.0	57 883	35 624	61.5	34 295	1 329	3.7
2003	57 940	44 700	77.1	42 797	1 903	4.3	58 545	36 185	61.8	34 806	1 379	3.8
2004	58 395	44 860	76.8	43 247	1 613	3.6	59 008	35 918	60.9	34 582	1 336	3.7
2005	58 854	45 263	76.9	43 763	1 500	3.3	59 449	35 809	60.2	34 738	1 071	3.0
2006	58 850	45 082	76.6	43 877	1 205	2.7	59 476	36 192	60.9	35 185	1 007	2.8
2007	60 126	46 129	76.7	44 813	1 317	2.9	60 656	37 335	61.6	36 370	965	2.6
Widowed, Divorced, or Separated												
1990	11 152	7 513	67.4	6 959	554	7.4	23 857	11 168	46.8	10 530	638	5.7
1991	11 588	7 804	67.3	6 985	819	10.5	24 105	11 145	46.2	10 386	759	6.8
1992	11 927	8 049	67.5	7 140	909	11.3	24 582	11 486	46.7	10 610	876	7.6
1993	11 861	7 956	67.1	7 055	901	11.3	24 661	11 308	45.9	10 528	780	6.9
1994	12 239	8 156	66.6	7 382	774	9.5	25 098	11 879	47.3	10 995	884	7.4
1995	12 410	8 315	67.0	7 632	683	8.2	25 373	12 001	47.3	11 308	693	5.8
1996	13 176	8 697	66.0	7 976	721	8.3	25 786	12 430	48.2	11 742	688	5.5
1997	14 113	9 420	66.7	8 715	705	7.5	26 301	12 814	48.7	12 071	743	5.8
1998	14 166	9 482	66.9	8 954	528	5.6	26 092	12 880	49.4	12 235	645	5.0
1999	14 225	9 449	66.4	8 971	478	5.1	26 199	12 951	49.4	12 307	644	5.0
2000	14 289	9 623	67.3	9 152	471	4.9	26 354	13 228	50.2	12 657	571	4.3
2001	14 392	9 421	65.5	8 927	494	5.2	26 747	13 454	50.3	12 887	567	4.2
2002	14 617	9 650	66.0	8 931	719	7.5	27 802	13 716	49.3	12 855	861	6.3
2003	15 180	9 855	64.9	9 020	835	8.5	28 240	14 154	50.1	13 240	914	6.5
2004	15 059	9 789	65.0	9 059	730	7.5	28 228	14 194	50.3	13 324	870	6.1
2005	15 779	10 256	65.0	9 569	687	6.7	28 576	14 233	49.8	13 472	761	5.3
2006	16 405	10 815	65.9	10 141	674	6.2	28 981	14 220	49.1	13 539	681	4.8
2007	16 247	10 799	66.5	10 150	650	6.0	28 950	14 320	49.5	13 620	700	4.9

Note: See notes and definitions for information on historical comparability.

Table 1-45. Employment Status of the Population, by Sex and Marital Status, March 1990–March 2007 —Continued

(Thousands of people, percent.)

Marital status and year	Men						Women					
	Population	Labor force					Population	Labor force				
		Total		Employed	Unemployed			Total		Employed	Unemployed	
		Number	Percent of population		Number	Percent of labor force		Number	Percent of population		Number	Percent of labor force
Widowed												
1990	2 331	519	22.3	490	29	5.6	11 477	2 243	19.5	2 149	94	4.2
1991	2 385	486	20.4	448	38	7.8	11 288	2 150	19.0	2 044	106	4.9
1992	2 529	566	22.4	501	65	11.5	11 325	2 131	18.8	2 029	102	4.8
1993	2 468	596	24.1	535	61	10.2	11 214	1 961	17.5	1 856	105	5.4
1994	2 220	474	21.4	440	34	7.2	11 073	1 945	17.6	1 825	120	6.2
1995	2 282	496	21.7	469	27	5.4	11 080	1 941	17.5	1 844	97	5.0
1996	2 476	487	19.7	466	21	4.3	11 070	1 916	17.3	1 820	96	5.0
1997	2 686	559	20.8	529	30	5.4	11 058	2 018	18.2	1 926	92	4.6
1998	2 567	563	21.9	551	12	2.1	11 027	2 157	19.6	2 071	86	4.0
1999	2 540	562	22.1	532	30	5.3	10 943	2 039	18.6	1 942	97	4.8
2000	2 601	583	22.4	547	36	6.2	11 061	2 011	18.2	1 911	100	5.0
2001	2 638	568	21.5	546	22	3.9	11 182	2 137	19.1	2 045	92	4.3
2002	2 635	629	23.9	581	48	7.6	11 411	2 001	17.5	1 887	114	5.7
2003	2 694	628	23.3	588	40	6.4	11 295	2 087	18.5	1 991	96	4.6
2004	2 651	581	21.9	558	23	4.0	11 159	2 157	19.3	2 048	109	5.1
2005	2 729	618	22.6	590	28	4.5	11 125	2 111	19.0	2 005	106	5.0
2006	2 626	610	23.2	563	47	7.7	11 305	2 164	19.1	2 094	70	3.2
2007	2 697	631	23.4	588	43	6.8	11 220	2 058	18.3	1 971	87	4.2
Divorced												
1990	6 256	5 004	80.0	4 639	365	7.3	8 845	6 678	75.5	6 333	345	5.2
1991	6 586	5 262	79.9	4 722	540	10.3	9 152	6 779	74.1	6 365	414	6.1
1992	6 743	5 418	80.3	4 823	595	11.0	9 569	7 076	73.9	6 578	498	7.0
1993	6 770	5 330	78.7	4 736	594	11.1	9 879	7 183	72.7	6 736	447	6.2
1994	7 222	5 548	76.8	5 028	520	9.4	10 113	7 473	73.9	6 962	511	6.8
1995	7 343	5 739	78.2	5 266	473	8.2	10 262	7 559	73.7	7 206	353	4.7
1996	7 734	5 954	77.0	5 468	486	8.2	10 508	7 829	74.5	7 468	361	4.6
1997	8 191	6 298	76.9	5 851	447	7.1	11 102	8 092	72.9	7 666	426	5.3
1998	8 307	6 378	76.8	6 045	333	5.2	11 065	8 038	72.6	7 687	351	4.4
1999	8 529	6 481	76.0	6 151	330	5.1	11 130	8 171	73.4	7 841	330	4.0
2000	8 532	6 583	77.2	6 279	304	4.6	11 061	8 505	76.9	8 217	288	3.4
2001	8 580	6 403	74.6	6 074	329	5.1	11 719	8 662	73.9	8 335	327	3.8
2002	8 643	6 519	75.4	6 053	466	7.1	12 227	8 902	72.8	8 416	486	5.5
2003	8 938	6 621	74.1	6 052	569	8.6	12 653	9 191	72.6	8 673	518	5.6
2004	8 942	6 622	74.1	6 104	518	7.8	12 817	9 246	72.1	8 706	540	5.8
2005	9 196	6 754	73.4	6 281	473	7.0	12 950	9 253	71.5	8 836	417	4.5
2006	9 646	7 065	73.2	6 631	434	6.1	13 107	9 188	70.1	8 799	389	4.2
2007	9 608	7 110	74.0	6 679	431	6.1	13 214	9 334	70.6	8 896	439	4.7
Separated												
1990	2 565	1 990	77.6	1 830	160	8.0	3 535	2 247	63.6	2 048	199	8.9
1991	2 616	2 057	78.6	1 816	241	11.7	3 665	2 216	60.5	1 977	239	10.8
1992	2 655	2 065	77.8	1 816	249	12.1	3 688	2 279	61.8	2 003	276	12.1
1993	2 623	2 030	77.4	1 784	246	12.1	3 568	2 165	60.7	1 937	228	10.5
1994	2 797	2 134	76.3	1 914	220	10.3	3 911	2 461	62.9	2 208	253	10.3
1995	2 784	2 081	74.7	1 898	183	8.8	4 031	2 501	62.0	2 258	243	9.7
1996	2 966	2 255	76.0	2 041	214	9.5	4 209	2 684	63.8	2 453	231	8.6
1997	3 236	2 563	79.2	2 335	228	8.9	4 141	2 705	65.3	2 480	225	8.3
1998	3 293	2 542	77.2	2 358	184	7.2	4 000	2 683	67.1	2 476	207	7.7
1999	3 156	2 405	76.2	2 287	118	4.9	4 126	2 740	66.4	2 523	217	7.9
2000	3 157	2 456	77.8	2 326	130	5.3	4 012	2 711	67.6	2 528	183	6.8
2001	3 174	2 450	77.2	2 307	143	5.8	3 846	2 654	69.0	2 507	147	5.5
2002	3 339	2 502	74.9	2 297	205	8.2	4 164	2 812	67.5	2 551	261	9.3
2003	3 548	2 606	73.4	2 380	226	8.7	4 293	2 877	67.0	2 576	301	10.5
2004	3 466	2 586	74.6	2 397	189	7.3	4 251	2 791	65.7	2 569	222	8.0
2005	3 855	2 884	74.8	2 698	186	6.4	4 501	2 870	63.8	2 632	238	8.3
2006	4 132	3 141	76.0	2 947	194	6.2	4 569	2 869	62.8	2 647	222	7.7
2007	3 943	3 058	77.6	2 883	176	5.7	4 516	2 927	64.8	2 753	174	6.0

Note: See notes and definitions for information on historical comparability.

Table 1-46. Employment Status of All Women and Single Women, by Presence and Age of Children, March 1990–March 2007

(Thousands of women, percent.)

Presence and age of children and year	All women						Single women					
	Civilian labor force	Civilian labor force as percent of population	Employed		Unemployed		Civilian labor force	Civilian labor force as percent of population	Employed		Unemployed	
			Number	Percent full time	Percent part time	Number	Percent of labor force			Number	Percent full time	Percent part time	Number	Percent of labor force

Presence and age of children and year	Civilian labor force	Civilian labor force as percent of population	Number	Percent full time	Percent part time	Number	Percent of labor force	Civilian labor force	Civilian labor force as percent of population	Number	Percent full time	Percent part time	Number	Percent of labor force
Women with No Children Under 18 Years														
1990	33 942	52.3	32 391	74.4	25.6	1 551	4.6	12 478	68.1	11 611	65.9	34.1	866	6.9
1991	34 047	52.0	32 167	74.0	26.0	1 880	5.5	12 472	67.0	11 529	66.2	33.8	943	7.6
1992	34 487	52.3	32 481	74.3	25.7	2 006	5.8	12 355	66.9	11 374	66.6	33.4	982	7.9
1993	34 495	52.1	32 476	74.6	25.4	2 020	5.9	12 223	66.4	11 201	66.1	33.9	1 022	8.4
1994	35 454	53.1	33 343	72.7	27.3	2 110	6.0	12 737	66.8	11 674	64.5	35.5	1 063	8.3
1995	35 843	52.9	34 054	72.9	27.1	1 789	5.0	12 870	67.1	11 919	64.5	35.5	951	7.4
1996	36 509	53.0	34 698	73.3	26.7	1 811	5.0	13 172	66.1	12 255	64.6	35.4	918	7.0
1997	37 295	53.6	35 572	73.7	26.3	1 723	4.6	13 405	66.5	12 442	64.0	36.0	964	7.2
1998	38 253	54.1	36 680	74.1	25.9	1 573	4.1	13 888	67.2	13 082	64.8	35.2	806	5.8
1999	39 316	54.3	37 589	74.6	25.4	1 727	4.4	14 435	67.1	13 491	65.6	34.4	944	6.5
2000	40 142	54.8	38 408	75.4	24.6	1 733	4.3	14 677	67.6	13 713	66.6	33.4	964	6.6
2001	40 836	54.9	39 219	75.7	24.3	1 617	4.0	14 877	67.4	13 993	67.3	32.7	884	5.9
2002	41 278	54.0	39 038	75.1	24.9	2 241	5.4	14 855	65.6	13 682	65.9	34.1	1 173	7.9
2003	42 039	54.1	39 667	74.8	25.2	2 372	5.6	14 678	63.5	13 430	65.1	34.9	1 249	8.5
2004	42 289	53.8	40 000	74.6	25.4	2 289	5.4	14 828	63.0	13 670	65.5	34.5	1 157	7.8
2005	42 039	54.1	39 667	74.8	25.2	2 372	5.6	14 678	63.5	13 430	65.1	34.9	1 249	8.5
2006	43 392	53.6	41 440	75.3	24.7	1 952	4.5	15 673	63.4	14 547	66.5	33.5	1 125	7.2
2007	44 039	53.9	42 279	75.3	24.7	1 760	4.0	15 704	63.4	14 801	66.4	33.6	903	5.7
Women with Children Under 18 Years														
1990	22 196	66.7	20 865	73.0	27.0	1 331	6.0	1 525	55.2	1 244	79.1	20.9	280	18.4
1991	22 327	66.6	20 774	73.0	27.0	1 552	7.0	1 654	53.6	1 358	76.4	23.6	296	17.9
1992	22 756	67.2	21 052	73.8	26.2	1 704	7.5	1 716	52.5	1 420	75.9	24.1	297	17.3
1993	23 063	66.9	21 521	73.9	26.1	1 541	6.7	1 869	54.4	1 510	74.8	25.2	359	19.2
1994	24 191	68.4	22 467	70.8	29.2	1 724	7.1	2 166	56.9	1 745	73.9	26.1	421	19.4
1995	24 695	69.7	23 195	71.7	28.3	1 500	6.1	2 104	57.5	1 754	73.6	26.4	350	16.6
1996	24 720	70.2	23 386	72.6	27.4	1 334	5.4	2 245	60.5	1 829	73.5	26.5	416	18.5
1997	25 604	72.1	24 082	74.1	25.9	1 522	5.9	2 772	68.1	2 305	76.6	23.4	467	16.8
1998	25 647	72.3	24 209	74.0	26.0	1 438	5.6	2 997	72.5	2 544	75.6	24.4	453	15.1
1999	25 469	72.1	24 305	74.1	25.9	1 165	4.6	3 051	73.4	2 694	75.8	24.2	357	11.7
2000	25 795	72.9	24 693	74.6	25.4	1 102	4.3	3 073	73.9	2 734	79.7	20.3	339	11.0
2001	25 751	73.1	24 572	75.6	24.4	1 179	4.6	3 022	73.8	2 638	81.8	18.2	385	12.7
2002	26 140	72.2	24 612	74.8	25.2	1 529	5.8	3 224	75.3	2 818	79.1	20.9	406	12.6
2003	26 202	71.7	24 598	74.3	25.7	1 603	6.1	3 222	73.1	2 789	79.5	20.5	433	13.4
2004	25 913	70.7	24 413	74.2	25.8	1 501	5.8	3 262	72.6	2 836	76.8	23.2	426	13.1
2005	26 202	71.7	24 598	74.3	25.7	1 603	6.1	3 222	73.1	2 789	79.5	20.5	433	13.4
2006	26 009	70.6	24 728	75.6	24.4	1 281	4.9	3 317	71.5	2 896	77.8	22.2	420	12.7
2007	26 834	71.3	25 646	75.2	24.8	1 188	4.4	3 514	71.4	3 133	76.4	23.6	381	10.8
Women with Children Under 6 Years														
1990	9 397	58.2	8 732	69.6	30.4	664	7.1	929	48.7	736	75.0	25.0	194	20.9
1991	9 636	58.4	8 758	69.5	30.5	878	9.1	1 050	48.8	819	72.2	27.8	231	22.0
1992	9 573	58.0	8 662	70.2	29.8	911	9.5	1 029	45.8	829	73.2	26.8	200	19.4
1993	9 621	57.9	8 764	70.1	29.9	857	8.9	1 125	47.4	869	70.0	30.0	257	22.8
1994	10 328	60.3	9 394	67.1	32.9	935	9.1	1 379	52.2	1 062	70.0	30.0	317	23.0
1995	10 395	62.3	9 587	67.5	32.5	809	7.8	1 328	53.0	1 069	68.6	31.4	259	19.5
1996	10 293	62.3	9 592	68.4	31.6	701	6.8	1 378	55.1	1 099	67.3	32.7	279	20.2
1997	10 610	65.0	9 800	70.5	29.5	810	7.6	1 755	65.1	1 424	71.6	28.4	330	18.8
1998	10 619	65.2	9 839	69.8	30.2	780	7.3	1 755	67.3	1 448	71.7	28.3	307	17.5
1999	10 322	64.4	9 674	69.0	31.0	648	6.3	1 811	68.1	1 565	71.0	29.0	246	13.6
2000	10 316	65.3	9 763	70.5	29.5	553	5.4	1 835	70.5	1 603	75.3	24.7	232	12.6
2001	10 200	64.9	9 618	71.2	28.8	582	5.7	1 783	69.7	1 542	79.1	20.9	242	13.6
2002	10 193	64.1	9 441	70.4	29.6	752	7.4	1 819	71.0	1 568	74.5	25.5	251	13.8
2003	10 209	62.9	9 433	70.0	30.0	776	7.6	1 893	70.2	1 614	75.2	24.8	279	14.7
2004	10 131	62.2	9 407	69.4	30.6	724	7.1	1 885	68.4	1 605	70.1	29.9	279	14.8
2005	10 209	62.9	9 433	70.0	30.0	776	7.6	1 893	70.2	1 614	75.2	24.8	279	14.7
2006	10 430	63.0	9 779	72.0	28.0	651	6.2	1 934	68.6	1 659	72.8	27.2	276	14.3
2007	10 894	63.5	10 305	71.9	28.1	589	5.4	2 066	67.4	1 827	72.7	27.3	239	11.6

Note: See notes and definitions for information on historical comparability.

Table 1-47. Employment Status of Ever-Married Women and Married Women, Spouse Present, by Presence and Age of Children, March 1990–March 2007

(Thousands of women, percent.)

Presence and age of children and year	Ever-married women[1] Civilian labor force	Civilian labor force as percent of population	Employed Number	Percent full time	Percent part time	Unemployed Number	Percent of labor force	Married women, spouse present Civilian labor force	Civilian labor force as percent of population	Employed Number	Percent full time	Percent part time	Unemployed Number	Percent of labor force
Women with No Children Under 18 Years														
1990	21 464	46.1	20 779	79.1	20.9	685	3.2	14 467	51.1	14 068	77.3	22.7	399	2.8
1991	21 575	46.1	20 637	78.4	21.6	937	4.3	14 529	51.2	13 976	77.6	22.4	552	3.8
1992	22 132	46.6	21 108	78.5	21.5	1 024	4.6	14 851	51.9	14 247	77.8	22.2	604	4.1
1993	22 273	46.6	21 275	79.0	21.0	998	4.5	15 211	52.4	14 630	77.6	22.4	581	3.8
1994	22 716	47.6	21 669	77.1	22.9	1 047	4.6	15 234	53.2	14 641	75.6	24.4	593	3.9
1995	22 973	47.3	22 134	77.4	22.6	839	3.7	15 594	53.2	15 072	76.3	23.7	522	3.3
1996	23 337	47.7	22 444	78.1	21.9	893	3.8	15 628	53.4	15 123	76.8	23.2	506	3.2
1997	23 890	48.3	23 130	78.9	21.1	760	3.2	15 750	54.2	15 315	77.7	22.3	435	2.8
1998	24 366	48.7	23 598	79.3	20.7	767	3.1	16 007	54.1	15 581	78.3	21.7	426	2.7
1999	24 881	48.9	24 098	79.7	20.3	783	3.1	16 484	54.4	16 061	78.2	21.8	423	2.6
2000	25 465	49.4	24 695	80.3	19.7	769	3.0	16 786	54.7	16 357	79.1	20.9	429	2.6
2001	25 959	49.6	25 226	80.4	19.6	733	2.8	16 909	54.8	16 528	78.7	21.3	381	2.3
2002	26 423	49.1	25 356	80.0	20.0	1 068	4.0	17 353	54.8	16 780	78.4	21.6	573	3.3
2003	27 361	50.1	26 238	79.7	20.3	1 123	4.1	17 901	55.7	17 273	78.6	21.4	628	3.5
2004	27 461	49.8	26 329	79.3	20.7	1 131	4.1	17 965	55.0	17 367	78.6	21.4	598	3.3
2005	27 361	50.1	26 238	79.7	20.3	1 123	4.1	17 901	55.7	17 273	78.6	21.4	628	3.5
2006	27 719	49.3	26 893	80.1	19.9	827	3.0	18 124	54.8	17 691	79.3	20.7	434	2.4
2007	28 335	49.8	27 477	80.1	19.9	858	3.0	18 766	55.4	18 326	79.6	20.4	441	2.3
Women with Children Under 18 Years														
1990	20 671	67.8	19 621	72.6	27.4	1 051	5.1	16 500	66.3	15 803	69.8	30.2	698	4.2
1991	20 673	67.9	19 416	72.8	27.2	1 257	6.1	16 575	66.8	15 692	70.1	29.9	883	5.3
1992	21 040	68.8	19 633	73.6	26.4	1 407	6.7	16 835	67.8	15 884	71.3	28.7	952	5.7
1993	21 194	68.3	20 011	73.9	26.1	1 183	5.6	16 947	67.5	16 127	71.4	28.6	820	4.8
1994	22 025	69.8	20 722	70.5	29.5	1 303	5.9	17 628	69.0	16 755	68.0	32.0	873	5.0
1995	22 591	71.1	21 441	71.5	28.5	1 150	5.1	17 969	70.2	17 195	68.8	31.2	774	4.3
1996	22 475	71.4	21 556	72.5	27.5	919	4.1	17 754	70.0	17 136	69.6	30.4	618	3.5
1997	22 831	72.6	21 777	73.9	26.1	1 054	4.6	18 157	71.1	17 521	71.6	28.4	636	3.5
1998	22 650	72.3	21 665	73.8	26.2	985	4.3	18 129	70.6	17 447	71.5	28.5	682	3.8
1999	22 419	71.9	21 611	73.9	26.1	808	3.6	17 865	70.1	17 342	71.5	28.5	523	2.9
2000	22 722	72.7	21 960	74.0	26.0	763	3.4	18 174	70.6	17 641	71.7	28.3	533	2.9
2001	22 729	73.0	21 934	74.9	25.1	795	3.5	18 325	70.8	17 745	72.6	27.4	580	3.2
2002	22 917	71.8	21 794	74.3	25.7	1 122	4.9	18 271	69.6	17 515	71.7	28.3	756	4.1
2003	22 979	71.5	21 809	73.7	26.3	1 170	5.1	18 284	69.2	17 533	71.0	29.0	751	4.1
2004	22 651	70.5	21 576	73.8	26.2	1 075	4.7	17 953	68.2	17 215	71.3	28.7	738	4.1
2005	22 979	71.5	21 809	73.7	26.3	1 170	5.1	18 284	69.2	17 533	71.0	29.0	751	4.1
2006	22 692	70.5	21 831	75.3	24.7	861	3.8	18 067	68.4	17 494	73.0	27.0	574	3.2
2007	23 320	71.3	22 513	75.0	25.0	807	3.5	18 569	69.3	18 045	72.6	27.4	524	2.8
Women with Children Under 6 Years														
1990	8 467	59.5	7 996	69.1	30.9	471	5.6	7 247	58.9	6 901	67.4	32.6	346	4.8
1991	8 585	59.9	7 938	69.2	30.8	647	7.5	7 434	59.9	6 933	67.5	32.5	501	6.7
1992	8 544	60.0	7 832	69.9	30.1	711	8.3	7 333	59.9	6 819	68.5	31.5	514	7.0
1993	8 496	59.6	7 895	70.2	29.8	600	7.1	7 289	59.6	6 840	68.8	31.2	450	6.2
1994	8 949	61.8	8 332	66.7	33.3	617	6.9	7 723	61.7	7 291	65.4	34.6	432	5.6
1995	9 067	63.9	8 517	67.4	32.6	550	6.1	7 759	63.5	7 349	66.1	33.9	409	5.3
1996	8 915	63.6	8 493	68.6	31.4	422	4.7	7 590	62.7	7 297	66.5	33.5	293	3.9
1997	8 856	64.9	8 376	70.3	29.7	480	5.4	7 582	63.6	7 252	69.1	30.9	330	4.4
1998	8 864	64.8	8 391	69.5	30.5	473	5.3	7 655	63.7	7 309	68.1	31.9	346	4.5
1999	8 511	63.7	8 109	68.6	31.4	402	4.7	7 246	61.8	6 979	67.1	32.9	267	3.7
2000	8 481	64.3	8 159	69.5	30.5	321	3.8	7 341	62.8	7 087	68.1	31.9	254	3.5
2001	8 417	64.0	8 077	69.7	30.3	340	4.0	7 319	62.5	7 062	68.5	31.5	257	3.5
2002	8 373	62.8	7 873	69.6	30.4	501	6.0	7 166	60.8	6 804	67.7	32.3	363	5.1
2003	8 315	61.4	7 818	68.9	31.1	497	6.0	7 175	59.8	6 826	67.1	32.9	349	4.9
2004	8 246	61.0	7 801	69.3	30.7	445	5.4	7 107	59.3	6 774	68.1	31.9	332	4.7
2005	8 315	61.4	7 818	68.9	31.1	497	6.0	7 175	59.8	6 826	67.1	32.9	349	4.9
2006	8 496	61.9	8 121	71.8	28.2	375	4.4	7 366	60.3	7 092	70.6	29.4	274	3.7
2007	8 829	62.7	8 479	71.7	28.3	350	4.0	7 664	61.5	7 407	70.8	29.2	257	3.4

[1]Ever-married women are women who are, or have ever been, married.

Table 1-48. Employment Status of Women Who Maintain Families, by Marital Status and Presence and Age of Children, March 1990–March 2007

(Thousands of women, percent.)

Marital status, age of children, and year	Civilian noninstitutional population	Civilian labor force					Not in the labor force
		Number	Percent of the population	Employed	Unemployed		
					Number	Percent of the labor force	
Total, Women Who Maintain Families							
1990	11 309	7 088	62.7	6 471	617	8.7	4 221
1991	11 765	7 329	62.3	6 657	672	9.2	4 436
1992	12 214	7 517	61.5	6 798	719	9.6	4 697
1993	12 489	7 777	62.3	7 093	684	8.8	4 712
1994	12 963	8 214	63.4	7 413	801	9.8	4 750
1995	12 762	8 192	64.2	7 527	665	8.1	4 570
1996	12 993	8 460	65.1	7 832	628	7.4	4 532
1997	13 258	8 998	67.9	8 192	806	9.0	4 260
1998	13 102	8 976	68.5	8 309	667	7.4	4 127
1999	13 191	9 213	69.8	8 596	617	6.7	3 978
2000	13 145	9 226	70.2	8 592	634	6.9	3 918
2001	12 930	9 034	69.9	8 453	581	6.4	3 897
2002	13 489	9 523	70.6	8 755	768	8.1	3 966
2003	14 000	9 759	69.7	8 898	861	8.8	4 241
2004	14 165	9 869	69.7	9 054	815	8.3	4 297
2005	14 391	9 941	69.1	9 140	801	8.1	4 450
2006	14 485	9 966	68.8	9 227	739	7.4	4 520
2007	14 833	10 172	68.6	9 510	661	6.5	4 662
Women with No Children Under 18 Years							
1990	4 290	2 227	51.9	2 132	95	4.3	2 062
1991	4 447	2 364	53.2	2 231	133	5.6	2 083
1992	4 651	2 427	52.2	2 307	120	4.9	2 223
1993	4 708	2 466	52.4	2 339	127	5.2	2 242
1994	4 758	2 609	54.8	2 489	120	4.6	2 149
1995	4 610	2 471	53.6	2 394	77	3.1	2 139
1996	4 847	2 552	52.7	2 462	90	3.5	2 295
1997	4 909	2 663	54.2	2 571	92	3.5	2 246
1998	4 952	2 649	53.5	2 578	71	2.7	2 303
1999	4 942	2 667	54.0	2 556	111	4.2	2 275
2000	5 097	2 707	53.1	2 546	161	5.9	2 390
2001	5 185	2 772	53.5	2 668	104	3.8	2 413
2002	5 119	2 764	54.0	2 628	136	4.9	2 355
2003	5 457	2 934	53.8	2 728	206	7.0	2 522
2004	5 551	3 052	55.0	2 855	197	6.5	2 499
2005	5 692	3 095	54.4	2 961	134	4.3	2 597
2006	5 693	3 088	54.2	2 945	143	4.6	2 604
2007	5 823	3 124	53.7	2 990	134	4.3	2 699
Women with Children Under 18 Years							
1990	7 018	4 860	69.3	4 338	522	10.7	2 159
1991	7 318	4 965	67.8	4 426	539	10.9	2 353
1992	7 564	5 090	67.3	4 491	599	11.8	2 473
1993	7 781	5 311	68.3	4 755	556	10.5	2 470
1994	8 205	5 604	68.3	4 924	680	12.1	2 601
1995	8 152	5 720	70.2	5 132	588	10.3	2 431
1996	8 146	5 908	72.5	5 370	538	9.1	2 237
1997	8 348	6 335	75.9	5 621	714	11.3	2 014
1998	8 151	6 327	77.6	5 731	596	9.4	1 823
1999	8 248	6 546	79.4	6 040	506	7.7	1 702
2000	8 048	6 520	81.0	6 046	474	7.3	1 528
2001	7 746	6 261	80.8	5 785	476	7.6	1 484
2002	8 370	6 759	80.8	6 127	632	9.4	1 611
2003	8 543	6 825	79.9	6 170	655	9.6	1 718
2004	8 614	6 817	79.1	6 199	618	9.1	1 798
2005	8 699	6 846	78.7	6 179	667	9.7	1 853
2006	8 793	6 878	78.2	6 282	596	8.7	1 915
2007	9 010	7 047	78.2	6 520	527	7.5	1 963
Single Women with No Children Under 18 Years							
1990	642	450	70.1	425	25	5.6	192
1991	682	469	68.8	441	28	6.0	214
1992	745	505	67.8	475	30	5.9	241
1993	752	531	70.6	494	37	7.0	221
1994	704	490	69.6	451	39	8.0	213
1995	779	534	68.5	508	26	4.9	245
1996	895	588	65.7	572	16	2.7	308
1997	860	585	68.0	563	22	3.8	275
1998	893	637	71.3	613	24	3.8	256
1999	969	674	69.6	638	36	5.3	295
2000	1 004	720	71.7	642	78	10.8	284
2001	1 096	787	71.8	756	31	3.9	309
2002	1 154	796	69.0	747	49	6.2	358
2003	1 254	814	64.9	713	101	12.4	440
2004	1 381	977	70.7	887	90	9.2	404
2005	1 388	926	66.7	855	71	7.7	463
2006	1 370	933	68.1	861	72	7.7	437
2007	1 413	986	69.8	930	57	5.7	427

Note: See notes and definitions for information on historical comparability.

Table 1-48. Employment Status of Women Who Maintain Families, by Marital Status and Presence and Age of Children, March 1990–March 2007—*Continued*

(Thousands of women, percent.)

Marital status, age of children, and year	Civilian noninstitutional population	Civilian labor force					Not in the labor force
		Number	Percent of the population	Employed	Unemployed		
					Number	Percent of the labor force	
Single Women with Children Under 18 Years							
1990	1 953	1 095	56.1	874	221	20.2	858
1991	2 208	1 187	53.8	985	202	17.0	1 021
1992	2 376	1 256	52.9	1 067	189	15.0	1 120
1993	2 445	1 414	57.8	1 161	253	17.9	1 031
1994	2 790	1 625	58.2	1 328	297	18.3	1 165
1995	2 613	1 510	57.8	1 261	249	16.5	1 102
1996	2 639	1 633	61.9	1 346	287	17.6	1 006
1997	3 012	2 087	69.3	1 749	338	16.2	925
1998	3 083	2 280	74.0	1 960	320	14.0	803
1999	3 163	2 415	76.4	2 146	269	11.1	748
2000	3 167	2 413	76.2	2 151	262	10.9	754
2001	3 097	2 351	75.9	2 055	296	12.6	745
2002	3 315	2 566	77.4	2 241	325	12.7	749
2003	3 421	2 584	75.5	2 272	312	12.1	837
2004	3 414	2 568	75.2	2 233	335	13.0	846
2005	3 591	2 708	75.4	2 325	383	14.1	882
2006	3 671	2 710	73.8	2 370	340	12.5	961
2007	3 748	2 782	74.2	2 491	291	10.4	966
Widowed, Divorced, or Separated Women with No Children Under 18 Years							
1990	3 648	1 778	48.7	1 708	70	3.9	1 870
1991	3 765	1 896	50.4	1 791	105	5.5	1 869
1992	3 905	1 923	49.2	1 832	91	4.7	1 982
1993	3 956	1 935	48.9	1 845	90	4.7	2 021
1994	4 054	2 118	52.2	2 037	81	3.8	1 936
1995	3 831	1 938	50.6	1 887	51	2.6	1 894
1996	3 952	1 964	49.7	1 890	74	3.8	1 988
1997	4 049	2 077	51.3	2 008	69	3.3	1 971
1998	4 058	2 011	49.6	1 965	46	2.3	2 047
1999	3 974	1 993	50.2	1 918	75	3.8	1 980
2000	4 093	1 987	48.5	1 904	83	4.2	2 106
2001	4 088	1 985	48.6	1 912	73	3.7	2 104
2002	3 964	1 968	49.6	1 882	86	4.4	1 997
2003	4 203	2 121	50.5	2 016	105	5.0	2 082
2004	4 170	2 075	49.8	1 968	107	5.2	2 095
2005	4 304	2 170	50.4	2 106	64	2.9	2 135
2006	4 323	2 156	49.9	2 084	72	3.3	2 168
2007	4 410	2 138	48.5	2 061	77	3.6	2 272
Widowed, Divorced, or Separated Women with Children Under 18 Years							
1990	5 065	3 765	74.3	3 464	301	8.0	1 301
1991	5 109	3 778	73.9	3 441	337	8.9	1 331
1992	5 187	3 834	73.9	3 424	410	10.7	1 353
1993	5 336	3 897	73.0	3 594	303	7.8	1 439
1994	5 415	3 979	73.5	3 596	383	9.6	1 436
1995	5 539	4 210	76.0	3 871	339	8.1	1 329
1996	5 507	4 275	77.6	4 024	251	5.9	1 231
1997	5 337	4 248	79.6	3 872	376	8.9	1 089
1998	5 068	4 047	79.9	3 771	276	6.8	1 020
1999	5 086	4 131	81.2	3 894	237	5.7	955
2000	4 881	4 107	84.1	3 895	212	5.2	774
2001	4 649	3 910	84.1	3 730	180	4.6	739
2002	5 056	4 193	82.9	3 886	307	7.3	862
2003	5 122	4 241	82.8	3 898	343	8.1	881
2004	5 201	4 249	81.7	3 966	283	6.7	952
2005	5 108	4 137	81.0	3 854	283	6.8	971
2006	5 121	4 167	81.4	3 912	255	6.1	955
2007	5 262	4 266	81.1	4 029	237	5.5	997

Note: See notes and definitions for information on historical comparability.

Table 1-49. Number and Age of Children in Families, by Type of Family and Labor Force Status of Mother, March 1990–March 2007

(Thousands of children.)

Age of children and year	Total children	Mother in labor force	Mother not in labor force	Married-couple families			Families maintained by women			Families maintained by men
				Total	Mother in labor force	Mother not in labor force	Total	Mother in labor force	Mother not in labor force	
Children Under 18 Years										
1990	59 596	36 712	21 110	45 898	29 077	16 820	11 925	7 635	4 290	1 774
1991	60 330	36 968	21 526	45 912	29 056	16 856	12 582	7 912	4 670	1 836
1992	61 262	38 081	21 176	45 966	29 882	16 084	13 291	8 199	5 093	2 005
1993	62 020	38 542	21 444	46 499	30 054	16 445	13 487	8 488	4 999	2 034
1994	63 407	40 186	21 188	47 247	31 279	15 968	14 127	8 907	5 220	2 033
1995	63 989	41 365	20 421	47 675	32 190	15 486	14 111	9 176	4 935	2 202
1996	64 506	41 573	20 449	47 484	31 764	15 720	14 538	9 809	4 729	2 484
1997	64 710	42 747	19 223	47 529	32 263	15 265	14 441	10 483	3 958	2 740
1998	65 043	43 156	19 069	47 909	32 533	15 376	14 317	10 623	3 694	2 818
1999	65 191	43 419	19 074	47 945	32 193	15 752	14 547	11 226	3 322	2 699
2000	65 601	44 188	18 674	48 902	33 149	15 753	13 960	11 039	2 921	2 739
2001	65 777	44 051	18 864	49 352	33 436	15 916	13 563	10 615	2 948	2 862
2002	65 978	43 821	19 243	48 836	32 673	16 163	14 228	11 149	3 079	2 914
2003	66 521	43 769	19 782	49 004	32 411	16 593	14 547	11 359	3 189	2 970
2004	66 386	43 144	20 229	48 656	31 892	16 764	14 717	11 252	3 465	3 014
2005	66 526	43 239	20 179	48 688	31 886	16 802	14 729	11 352	3 377	3 108
2006	66 883	43 278	20 440	48 853	31 946	16 908	14 865	11 332	3 532	3 165
2007	67 228	44 116	20 073	48 927	32 496	16 431	15 263	11 620	3 643	3 038
Children 6 to 17 Years										
1990	39 095	25 805	12 079	29 726	20 067	9 659	8 157	5 737	2 420	1 211
1991	39 470	25 806	12 392	29 598	19 907	9 691	8 599	5 899	2 701	1 272
1992	40 064	26 666	12 067	29 673	20 586	9 087	9 060	6 079	2 980	1 331
1993	40 622	27 046	12 291	30 233	20 796	9 437	9 104	6 249	2 854	1 285
1994	41 795	28 179	12 287	30 895	21 663	9 233	9 570	6 516	3 054	1 329
1995	42 423	28 931	12 000	31 298	22 239	9 059	9 633	6 692	2 941	1 492
1996	42 964	29 381	11 897	31 231	22 092	9 139	10 047	7 289	2 758	1 685
1997	43 488	30 308	11 400	31 509	22 602	8 906	10 199	7 705	2 493	1 781
1998	43 771	30 579	11 367	31 707	22 706	9 001	10 238	7 873	2 365	1 826
1999	44 110	30 885	11 370	31 975	22 706	9 269	10 281	8 179	2 101	1 855
2000	44 562	31 531	11 198	32 732	23 393	9 339	9 997	8 138	1 859	1 833
2001	44 458	31 411	11 153	32 957	23 599	9 358	9 608	7 813	1 795	1 894
2002	44 865	31 437	11 510	32 799	23 296	9 504	10 148	8 142	2 006	1 918
2003	45 273	31 559	11 635	32 782	23 160	9 622	10 412	8 399	2 013	2 080
2004	45 066	31 040	11 968	32 506	22 736	9 769	10 502	8 304	2 199	2 058
2005	45 027	30 930	11 995	32 412	22 565	9 847	10 514	8 366	2 148	2 102
2006	45 039	30 591	12 250	32 311	22 315	9 996	10 530	8 276	2 254	2 198
2007	45 155	31 252	11 855	32 417	22 788	9 629	10 690	8 464	2 226	2 048
Children Under 6 Years										
1990	20 502	10 907	9 031	16 171	9 010	7 161	3 767	1 897	1 870	563
1991	20 860	11 162	9 134	16 313	9 148	7 165	3 983	2 013	1 969	563
1992	21 198	11 415	9 109	16 293	9 296	6 997	4 232	2 119	2 112	674
1993	21 398	11 496	9 153	16 266	9 258	7 008	4 383	2 239	2 145	749
1994	21 612	12 007	8 901	16 352	9 617	6 735	4 556	2 391	2 166	704
1995	21 566	12 435	8 421	16 377	9 951	6 427	4 478	2 484	1 995	710
1996	21 542	12 192	8 552	16 253	9 672	6 581	4 491	2 520	1 971	799
1997	21 222	12 439	7 823	16 020	9 661	6 359	4 243	2 778	1 464	959
1998	21 272	12 577	7 703	16 201	9 827	6 375	4 079	2 751	1 328	992
1999	21 081	12 533	7 704	15 971	9 487	6 484	4 267	3 046	1 220	844
2000	21 039	12 657	7 476	16 170	9 757	6 413	3 963	2 901	1 062	906
2001	21 318	12 640	7 711	16 395	9 837	6 558	3 956	2 802	1 153	968
2002	21 113	12 384	7 733	16 037	9 377	6 660	4 080	3 007	1 073	996
2003	21 248	12 210	8 147	16 222	9 251	6 971	4 136	2 960	1 176	890
2004	21 321	12 104	8 261	16 151	9 156	6 995	4 214	2 948	1 266	956
2005	21 498	12 308	8 184	16 276	9 321	6 955	4 216	2 987	1 229	1 006
2006	21 844	12 687	8 190	16 542	9 631	6 911	4 335	3 057	1 278	968
2007	22 073	12 864	8 218	16 509	9 708	6 802	4 572	3 156	1 416	991

Note: See notes and definitions for information on historical comparability.

Table 1-50. Number of Families and Median Family Income, by Type of Family and Earner Status of Members, 1995–2006

(Thousands of families, dollars.)

Number and type of families and median family income	1995	1996	1997	1998	1999	2000	2001	2002	2003	2004	2005	2006
NUMBER OF FAMILIES												
Married-Couple Families, Total	53 621	53 654	54 362	54 829	55 352	55 650	56 798	57 362	57 767	58 180	58 225	59 050
No earners	7 276	7 145	7 286	7 257	7 160	7 297	7 662	7 803	8 043	7 998	8 017	8 091
One earner	11 708	11 493	11 700	12 246	12 290	12 450	12 852	13 503	14 061	14 385	14 301	14 562
Husband	8 792	8 611	8 770	9 173	9 062	9 319	9 573	10 121	10 478	10 853	10 611	10 706
Wife	2 251	2 207	2 298	2 411	2 585	2 545	2 689	2 821	3 027	2 993	3 097	3 264
Other family member	666	674	632	662	643	586	590	560	557	539	593	591
Two earners	27 180	27 260	27 712	27 593	28 010	28 329	28 779	28 891	28 693	28 806	28 802	29 216
Husband and wife	25 274	25 274	25 731	25 696	26 134	26 447	26 829	26 966	26 860	26 758	26 833	27 241
Husband and other family member	1 393	1 483	1 406	1 306	1 325	1 277	1 424	1 391	1 322	1 462	1 376	1 358
Husband not an earner	513	502	575	590	552	605	526	534	511	586	594	616
Three earners or more	7 456	7 756	7 664	7 733	7 892	7 575	7 504	7 165	6 970	6 991	7 104	7 181
Husband and wife	6 770	7 126	7 023	7 102	7 220	6 917	6 859	6 565	6 349	6 459	6 535	6 620
Husband, not wife	531	479	478	456	528	537	530	455	467	381	445	397
Husband not an earner	155	150	163	176	144	120	115	145	154	152	124	165
Families Maintained by Women, Total	13 007	13 277	13 115	13 206	13 164	12 950	13 517	14 033	14 196	14 404	14 505	14 852
No earners	2 664	2 574	2 332	2 143	1 883	1 786	2 076	2 228	2 451	2 610	2 616	2 627
One earner	6 815	7 027	7 091	7 351	7 441	7 462	7 693	8 153	8 012	8 074	8 052	8 303
Householder	5 590	5 817	5 841	6 167	6 127	6 132	6 436	6 832	6 725	6 788	6 724	6 904
Other family member	1 225	1 211	1 251	1 183	1 314	1 331	1 257	1 321	1 286	1 285	1 329	1 398
Two earners or more	3 527	3 675	3 692	3 712	3 840	3 702	3 748	3 652	3 733	3 720	3 836	3 923
Householder and other family member(s)	3 225	3 431	3 398	3 399	3 508	3 376	3 442	3 290	3 364	3 399	3 468	3 547
Householder not an earner	302	245	294	313	332	325	306	362	369	321	368	376
Families Maintained by Men, Total	3 557	3 924	3 982	4 041	4 086	4 316	4 499	4 747	4 778	4 953	5 193	5 119
No earners	357	359	344	381	376	380	461	466	530	492	537	555
One earner	1 800	1 972	2 104	2 027	2 044	2 223	2 319	2 434	2 466	2 573	2 661	2 584
Householder	1 548	1 667	1 791	1 725	1 721	1 879	1 911	2 026	2 053	2 152	2 196	2 155
Other family member	253	305	313	302	323	344	408	408	413	421	464	429
Two earners or more	1 400	1 593	1 534	1 634	1 666	1 713	1 719	1 847	1 782	1 888	1 995	1 979
Householder and other family member(s)	1 302	1 469	1 427	1 532	1 522	1 585	1 629	1 709	1 625	1 736	1 848	1 828
Householder not an earner	98	124	107	102	143	128	90	138	157	152	147	152
MEDIAN FAMILY INCOME												
Married-Couple Families, Total	47 000	49 614	51 475	54 043	56 792	59 200	60 100	61 000	62 388	63 627	65 586	69 300
No earners	21 888	22 622	23 782	24 525	25 262	25 356	25 900	25 954	26 312	26 798	28 376	30 000
One earner	35 100	36 468	39 140	40 519	41 261	44 424	44 400	45 000	46 546	47 749	50 000	50 400
Husband	36 052	38 150	40 300	42 000	44 200	47 010	47 500	48 004	48 948	50 000	52 000	53 360
Wife	32 098	30 301	34 050	35 625	35 546	36 458	36 140	39 072	41 180	41 000	43 505	45 000
Other family member	37 784	39 644	40 317	42 414	41 120	45 492	44 270	40 927	45 936	46 324	50 263	49 352
Two earners	53 500	56 000	58 020	61 300	64 007	67 500	69 543	71 282	73 309	75 100	76 960	81 500
Husband and wife	53 626	56 392	58 564	61 900	64 950	68 132	70 000	72 150	74 500	76 000	77 539	82 762
Husband and other family member	52 530	49 610	53 854	57 680	53 541	56 503	65 240	62 848	60 100	66 120	67 350	68 828
Husband not an earner	47 121	46 990	47 979	50 955	52 466	53 430	58 725	54 840	58 000	63 050	65 622	63 657
Three earners or more	68 996	70 400	75 593	78 973	81 940	83 990	86 090	88 632	93 000	94 212	98 000	103 803
Husband and wife	69 371	71 148	76 105	79 907	83 000	84 634	87 000	89 962	94 353	95 524	99 800	104 045
Husband, not wife	60 360	61 824	68 890	71 001	69 561	79 050	76 230	82 180	77 316	87 000	79 417	91 965
Husband not an earner	61 196	55 495	62 684	63 205	69 275	68 050	80 661	68 400	91 771	73 137	84 638	97 510
Families Maintained by Women, Total	19 306	19 416	20 470	21 875	23 100	25 000	25 064	26 000	26 000	26 400	27 000	28 218
No earners	7 440	7 092	7 476	7 737	8 010	8 988	8 160	8 808	8 344	8 400	8 228	8 657
One earner	18 824	18 500	19 000	20 000	20 092	22 306	23 008	24 597	24 752	25 040	25 308	26 393
Householder	17 890	18 000	18 000	18 800	19 000	21 400	22 001	23 760	23 832	24 505	24 505	25 381
Other family member	23 166	21 000	22 870	25 981	26 800	27 524	28 476	29 524	28 857	29 700	31 700	31 462
Two earners or more	35 000	36 400	39 275	40 000	41 144	43 035	45 244	46 580	47 576	48 549	50 000	52 400
Householder and other family member(s)	34 674	36 400	39 000	39 713	40 855	43 000	44 842	46 000	46 701	47 974	48 989	51 479
Householder not an earner	39 444	38 249	47 471	43 725	48 004	45 600	51 000	51 248	57 267	56 799	64 805	61 699
Families Maintained by Men, Total	30 000	31 500	32 984	35 000	37 000	37 040	36 000	37 440	37 914	40 000	40 293	41 130
No earners	12 240	12 030	14 252	15 468	13 752	14 946	12 840	15 200	15 408	14 167	13 950	15 462
One earner	25 337	26 100	26 897	29 125	31 038	30 160	30 800	30 139	32 097	35 000	35 001	35 100
Householder	25 069	25 874	27 000	29 125	30 483	30 816	30 500	30 014	31 355	35 000	35 075	35 011
Other family member	27 291	28 584	25 486	28 241	34 756	29 118	31 052	32 000	33 525	35 438	35 000	37 840
Two earners or more	43 100	44 275	49 900	51 288	51 040	55 010	55 024	55 000	57 840	57 600	60 024	61 000
Householder and other family member(s)	43 000	43 065	50 000	50 954	50 960	55 400	54 850	55 220	57 400	57 058	60 000	61 000
Householder not an earner	55 133	47 001	44 786	68 257	57 407	51 945	61 824	49 852	64 658	65 400	70 879	62 000

Note: See notes and definitions for information on historical comparability.

Table 1-51. Employment Status of the Foreign-Born and Native-Born Populations, by Selected Characteristics, 2005–2006

(Thousands of people, percent.)

Year and characteristic	Civilian noninstitutional population	Civilian labor force				
		Total	Participation rate	Employed	Unemployed	
					Number	Rate
2005						
TOTAL						
Both sexes, 16 years and over	226 082	149 320	66.0	141 730	7 591	5.1
Men	109 151	80 033	73.3	75 973	4 059	5.1
Women	116 931	69 288	59.3	65 757	3 531	5.1
FOREIGN BORN						
Both sexes, 16 years and over	32 558	22 042	67.7	21 022	1 020	4.6
Men	16 321	13 263	81.3	12 720	544	4.1
Women	16 236	8 779	54.1	8 302	477	5.4
Age						
16 to 24 years	4 168	2 469	59.2	2 277	192	7.8
25 to 34 years	7 902	6 094	77.1	5 824	270	4.4
35 to 44 years	7 620	6 162	80.9	5 930	232	3.8
45 to 54 years	5 578	4 473	80.2	4 285	188	4.2
55 to 64 years	3 499	2 278	65.1	2 163	115	5.1
65 years and over	3 791	566	14.9	542	24	4.2
Race and Hispanic Origin						
White, non-Hispanic	7 239	4 351	60.1	4 187	165	3.8
Black, non-Hispanic	2 360	1 746	74.0	1 631	115	6.6
Asian, non-Hispanic	7 289	4 922	67.5	4 728	194	3.9
Hispanic[1]	15 360	10 794	70.3	10 252	541	5.0
Educational Attainment						
Total, 25 years and over	28 389	19 573	68.9	18 745	828	4.2
Less than a high school diploma	9 053	5 545	61.2	5 227	318	5.7
High school graduate, no college[2]	7 106	4 804	67.6	4 599	205	4.3
Some college or associate's degree	4 354	3 181	73.1	3 064	118	3.7
Bachelor's degree or higher[3]	7 876	6 043	76.7	5 856	188	3.1
NATIVE BORN						
Both sexes, 16 years and over	193 525	127 278	65.8	120 708	6 570	5.2
Men	92 830	66 769	71.9	63 254	3 516	5.3
Women	100 695	60 509	60.1	57 454	3 055	5.0
Age						
16 to 24 years	32 505	19 821	61.0	17 493	2 328	11.7
25 to 34 years	31 162	26 247	84.2	24 856	1 391	5.3
35 to 44 years	35 385	29 868	84.4	28 699	1 168	3.9
45 to 54 years	36 529	29 930	81.9	28 922	1 008	3.4
55 to 64 years	26 666	16 701	62.6	16 186	515	3.1
65 years and over	31 278	4 712	15.1	4 552	160	3.4
Race and Hispanic Origin						
White, non-Hispanic	150 155	99 539	66.3	95 430	4 109	4.1
Black, non-Hispanic	23 283	14 694	63.1	13 155	1 538	10.5
Asian, non-Hispanic	2 444	1 496	61.2	1 434	62	4.2
Hispanic[1]	13 773	9 030	65.6	8 380	650	7.2
Educational Attainment						
Total, 25 years and over	161 019	107 457	66.7	103 215	4 242	3.9
Less than a high school diploma	18 818	7 135	37.9	6 485	649	9.1
High school graduates, no college[2]	53 302	33 392	62.6	31 799	1 593	4.8
Some college or associate's degree	43 915	31 793	72.4	30 561	1 232	3.9
Bachelor's degree or higher[3]	44 984	35 137	78.1	34 369	768	2.2

Note: Due to the introduction of revised population controls in January 2006, estimated levels for 2006 are not strictly comparable with those for 2005. Data for race/ethnicity groups do not sum to total because data are not presented for all races.

[1]May be of any race.
[2]Includes persons with a high school diploma or equivalent.
[3]Includes persons with bachelor's, master's, professional, and doctoral degrees.

Table 1-51. Employment Status of the Foreign-Born and Native-Born Populations, by Selected Characteristics, 2005–2006—*Continued*

(Thousands of people, percent.)

Year and characteristic	Civilian noninstitutional population	Civilian labor force				
		Total	Participation rate	Employed	Unemployed	
					Number	Rate
2006						
TOTAL						
Both sexes, 16 years and over	228 815	151 428	66.2	144 427	7 001	4.6
Men	110 605	81 255	73.5	77 502	3 753	4.6
Women	118 210	70 173	59.4	66 925	3 247	4.6
FOREIGN BORN						
Both sexes, 16 years and over	33 733	23 148	68.6	22 225	923	4.0
Men	16 989	13 885	81.7	13 395	491	3.5
Women	16 743	9 263	55.3	8 831	432	4.7
Age						
16 to 24 years	4 156	2 501	60.2	2 318	183	7.3
25 to 34 years	7 997	6 267	78.4	6 027	240	3.8
35 to 44 years	8 022	6 552	81.7	6 325	227	3.5
45 to 54 years	5 896	4 740	80.4	4 575	165	3.5
55 to 64 years	3 707	2 428	65.5	2 340	87	3.6
65 years and over	3 955	660	16.7	640	20	3.1
Race and Hispanic Origin						
White, non-Hispanic	7 329	4 503	61.4	4 344	159	3.5
Black, non-Hispanic	2 450	1 807	73.7	1 708	99	5.5
Asian, non-Hispanic	7 481	5 060	67.6	4 917	142	2.8
Hispanic[1]	16 156	11 549	71.5	11 034	514	4.5
Educational Attainment						
Total, 25 years and over	29 576	20 647	69.8	19 908	739	3.6
Less than a high school diploma	9 361	5 865	62.7	5 566	299	5.1
High school graduates, no college[2]	7 358	5 032	68.4	4 855	177	3.5
Some college or associate degree	4 511	3 346	74.2	3 232	114	3.4
Bachelor's degree and higher[3]	8 347	6 405	76.7	6 255	149	2.3
NATIVE BORN						
Both sexes, 16 years and over	195 082	128 280	65.8	122 202	6 078	4.7
Men	93 615	67 370	72.0	64 107	3 263	4.8
Women	101 467	60 910	60.0	58 095	2 815	4.6
Age						
16 to 24 years	32 787	19 893	60.7	17 723	2 170	10.9
25 to 34 years	31 233	26 305	84.2	25 024	1 282	4.9
35 to 44 years	34 731	29 296	84.3	28 244	1 051	3.6
45 to 54 years	37 005	30 405	82.2	29 477	928	3.1
55 to 64 years	27 668	17 557	63.5	17 049	508	2.9
65 years and over	31 658	4 824	15.2	4 685	139	2.9
Race and Hispanic Origin						
White, non-Hispanic	150 979	100 126	66.3	96 262	3 864	3.9
Black, non-Hispanic	23 668	14 905	63.0	13 500	1 405	9.4
Asian, non-Hispanic	2 522	1 552	61.5	1 493	59	3.8
Hispanic[1]	13 947	9 145	65.6	8 578	567	6.2
Educational Attainment						
Total, 25 years and over	162 295	108 387	66.8	104 479	3 908	3.6
Less than a high school diploma	18 181	6 893	37.9	6 326	567	8.2
High school graduates, no college[2]	53 390	33 322	62.4	31 847	1 475	4.4
Some college or associate degree	44 500	32 064	72.1	30 911	1 152	3.6
Bachelor's degree or higher[3]	46 224	36 108	78.1	35 394	714	2.0

Note: Due to the introduction of revised population controls in January 2006, estimated levels for 2006 are not strictly comparable with those for 2005. Data for race/ethnicity groups do not sum to total because data are not presented for all races.

[1]May be of any race.
[2]Includes persons with a high school diploma or equivalent.
[3]Includes persons with bachelor's, master's, professional, and doctoral degrees.

Table 1-52. Employment Status of the Foreign-Born and Native-Born Populations Age 16 Years and Over, by Sex and Presence and Age of Youngest Child, Annual Averages, 2005–2006

(Thousands of people, percent.)

Characteristic	2005			2006		
	Both sexes	Men	Women	Both sexes	Men	Women
FOREIGN BORN						
With Own Children Under 18 Years						
Civilian noninstitutional population	12 781	6 084	6 697	13 239	6 283	6 956
Civilian labor force	9 653	5 737	3 916	10 068	5 912	4 155
Participation rate	75.5	94.3	58.5	76.0	94.1	59.7
Employed	9 247	5 547	3 700	9 674	5 731	3 943
Employment-population ratio	72.3	91.2	55.2	73.1	91.2	56.7
Unemployed	406	190	216	394	182	212
Unemployment rate	4.2	3.3	5.5	3.9	3.1	5.1
With Own Children 6 to 17 Years, None Younger						
Civilian noninstitutional population	6 353	2 950	3 403	6 604	3 050	3 554
Civilian labor force	5 053	2 750	2 303	5 256	2 828	2 428
Participation rate	79.5	93.2	67.7	79.6	92.7	68.3
Employed	4 852	2 658	2 194	5 052	2 737	2 315
Employment-population ratio	76.4	90.1	64.5	76.5	89.7	65.1
Unemployed	201	93	108	204	91	113
Unemployment rate	4.0	3.4	4.7	3.9	3.2	4.6
With Own Children Under 6 Years						
Civilian noninstitutional population	6 428	3 134	3 294	6 635	3 233	3 402
Civilian labor force	4 600	2 987	1 613	4 812	3 084	1 727
Participation rate	71.6	95.3	49.0	72.5	95.4	50.8
Employed	4 395	2 889	1 505	4 622	2 994	1 628
Employment-population ratio	68.4	92.2	45.7	69.7	92.6	47.8
Unemployed	206	98	108	190	90	100
Unemployment rate	4.5	3.3	6.7	3.9	2.9	5.8
With Own Children Under 3 Years						
Civilian noninstitutional population	3 732	1 841	1 891	3 805	1 845	1 961
Civilian labor force	2 595	1 760	835	2 658	1 758	900
Participation rate	69.5	95.6	44.2	69.8	95.3	45.9
Employed	2 489	1 711	778	2 552	1 706	846
Employment-population ratio	66.7	93.0	41.1	67.1	92.5	43.1
Unemployed	106	49	57	105	51	54
Unemployment rate	4.1	2.8	6.8	4.0	2.9	6.0
With No Own Children Under 18 Years						
Civilian noninstitutional population	19 777	10 237	9 539	20 493	10 706	9 787
Civilian labor force	12 389	7 526	4 863	13 080	7 973	5 107
Participation rate	62.6	73.5	51.0	63.8	74.5	52.2
Employed	11 775	7 173	4 603	12 552	7 664	4 888
Employment-population ratio	59.5	70.1	48.2	61.2	71.6	49.9
Unemployed	614	354	260	529	309	220
Unemployment rate	5.0	4.7	5.4	4.0	3.9	4.3

Note: Due to the introduction of revised population controls in January 2006, estimated levels for 2006 are not strictly comparable with those for 2005.

Table 1-52. Employment Status of the Foreign-Born and Native-Born Populations Age 16 Years and Over, by Sex and Presence and Age of Youngest Child, Annual Averages, 2005–2006—*Continued*

(Thousands of people, percent.)

Characteristic	2005			2006		
	Both sexes	Men	Women	Both sexes	Men	Women
NATIVE BORN						
With Own Children Under 18 Years						
Civilian noninstitutional population	52 845	23 226	29 619	52 551	23 118	29 433
Civilian labor force	43 521	21 852	21 669	43 400	21 774	21 626
Participation rate	82.4	94.1	73.2	82.6	94.2	73.5
Employed	41 727	21 202	20 524	41 768	21 176	20 592
Employment-population ratio	79.0	91.3	69.3	79.5	91.6	70.0
Unemployed	1 794	650	1 145	1 632	598	1 034
Unemployment rate	4.1	3.0	5.3	3.8	2.7	4.8
With Own Children 6 to 17 Years, None Younger						
Civilian noninstitutional population	30 095	13 252	16 843	29 775	13 114	16 662
Civilian labor force	25 526	12 329	13 197	25 296	12 219	13 077
Participation rate	84.8	93.0	78.4	85.0	93.2	78.5
Employed	24 600	11 977	12 623	24 471	11 912	12 559
Employment-population ratio	81.7	90.4	74.9	82.2	90.8	75.4
Unemployed	926	351	574	825	307	518
Unemployment rate	3.6	2.9	4.4	3.3	2.5	4.0
With Own Children Under 6 Years						
Civilian noninstitutional population	22 749	9 974	12 776	22 776	10 004	12 772
Civilian labor force	17 995	9 524	8 472	18 104	9 555	8 549
Participation rate	79.1	95.5	66.3	79.5	95.5	66.9
Employed	17 127	9 225	7 901	17 297	9 264	8 033
Employment-population ratio	75.3	92.5	61.8	75.9	92.6	62.9
Unemployed	869	298	570	807	291	516
Unemployment rate	4.8	3.1	6.7	4.5	3.0	6.0
With Own Children Under 3 Years						
Civilian noninstitutional population	13 384	5 910	7 474	13 433	5 963	7 470
Civilian labor force	10 285	5 650	4 635	10 481	5 706	4 775
Participation rate	76.8	95.6	62.0	78.0	95.7	63.9
Employed	9 769	5 470	4 299	9 992	5 523	4 469
Employment-population ratio	73.0	92.6	57.5	74.4	92.6	59.8
Unemployed	516	180	336	489	183	306
Unemployment rate	5.0	3.2	7.3	4.7	3.2	6.4
With No Own Children Under 18 Years						
Civilian noninstitutional population	140 680	69 605	71 076	142 531	70 497	72 034
Civilian labor force	83 757	44 917	38 840	84 880	45 596	39 284
Participation rate	59.5	64.5	54.6	59.6	64.7	54.5
Employed	78 981	42 051	36 930	80 434	42 931	37 503
Employment-population ratio	56.1	60.4	52.0	56.4	60.9	52.1
Unemployed	4 776	2 866	1 910	4 446	2 665	1 781
Unemployment rate	5.7	6.4	4.9	5.2	5.8	4.5

Note: Due to the introduction of revised population controls in January 2006, estimated levels for 2006 are not strictly comparable with those for 2005.

Table 1-53. Employment Status of the Foreign-Born and Native-Born Populations Age 25 Years and Over, by Educational Attainment, Race, and Hispanic Origin, Annual Averages, 2005–2006

(Thousands of people, percent.)

Characteristic	2005				2006			
	Less than a high school diploma	High school graduate, no college[1]	Some college or associate's degree	Bachelor's degree or higher[2]	Less than a high school diploma	High school graduate, no college[1]	Some college or associate's degree	Bachelor's degree or higher[2]
FOREIGN BORN								
White, Non-Hispanic								
Civilian noninstitutional population	928	1 869	1 258	2 525	940	1 803	1 296	2 647
Civilian labor force	345	988	797	1 862	349	971	848	1 969
Participation rate	37.1	52.8	63.4	73.8	37.1	53.8	65.4	74.4
Employed	325	955	766	1 805	331	937	819	1 920
Employment-population ratio	35.0	51.1	60.9	71.5	35.2	52.0	63.1	72.6
Unemployed	19	33	31	57	18	33	30	48
Unemployment rate	5.6	3.4	3.9	3.1	5.3	3.4	3.5	2.5
Black, Non-Hispanic								
Civilian noninstitutional population	361	641	499	558	357	648	507	608
Civilian labor force	219	490	407	468	226	477	416	510
Participation rate	60.7	76.5	81.5	83.9	63.2	73.7	81.9	83.9
Employed	203	458	382	452	207	453	398	495
Employment-population ratio	56.1	71.5	76.6	80.9	57.8	69.9	78.4	81.4
Unemployed	17	32	25	17	19	25	18	15
Unemployment rate	7.5	6.5	6.1	3.6	8.6	5.2	4.3	3.0
Asian, Non-Hispanic								
Civilian noninstitutional population	857	1 332	998	3 385	858	1 340	1 016	3 575
Civilian labor force	402	845	725	2 606	391	862	742	2 743
Participation rate	46.9	63.5	72.7	77.0	45.6	64.3	73.0	76.7
Employed	378	804	702	2 524	376	834	721	2 684
Employment-population ratio	44.1	60.4	70.3	74.6	43.8	62.3	71.0	75.1
Unemployed	24	41	23	82	15	27	21	58
Unemployment rate	5.9	4.9	3.2	3.2	3.9	3.2	2.8	2.1
Hispanic[3]								
Civilian noninstitutional population	6 870	3 207	1 534	1 309	7 167	3 506	1 615	1 424
Civilian labor force	4 558	2 437	1 202	1 026	4 875	2 677	1 279	1 111
Participation rate	66.4	76.0	78.3	78.4	68.0	76.4	79.2	78.0
Employed	4 301	2 340	1 164	997	4 631	2 587	1 234	1 085
Employment-population ratio	62.6	72.9	75.9	76.2	64.6	73.8	76.4	76.1
Unemployed	257	98	38	29	243	90	46	27
Unemployment rate	5.6	4.0	3.1	2.9	5.0	3.4	3.6	2.4
NATIVE BORN								
White, Non-Hispanic								
Civilian noninstitutional population	12 313	42 100	34 792	38 847	11 847	42 087	35 100	39 751
Civilian labor force	4 479	25 768	24 879	30 102	4 369	25 714	24 931	30 787
Participation rate	36.4	61.2	71.5	77.5	36.9	61.1	71.0	77.4
Employed	4 157	24 740	24 058	29 490	4 079	24 773	24 157	30 200
Employment-population ratio	33.8	58.8	69.1	75.9	34.4	58.9	68.8	76.0
Unemployed	322	1 027	821	612	289	941	774	586
Unemployment rate	7.2	4.0	3.3	2.0	6.6	3.7	3.1	1.9
Black, Non-Hispanic								
Civilian noninstitutional population	3 464	6 778	5 039	3 211	3 396	6 801	5 215	3 379
Civilian labor force	1 277	4 538	3 780	2 617	1 236	4 488	3 885	2 762
Participation rate	36.9	66.9	75.0	81.5	36.4	66.0	74.5	81.7
Employed	1 077	4 135	3 518	2 528	1 065	4 115	3 634	2 687
Employment-population ratio	31.1	61.0	69.8	78.7	31.4	60.5	69.7	79.5
Unemployed	200	403	263	89	171	373	251	75
Unemployment rate	15.7	8.9	6.9	3.4	13.8	8.3	6.5	2.7
Asian, Non-Hispanic								
Civilian noninstitutional population	158	303	380	859	152	339	391	880
Civilian labor force	57	162	257	680	55	188	276	710
Participation rate	36.3	53.5	67.8	79.2	36.4	55.4	70.6	80.7
Employed	56	158	249	664	53	183	265	696
Employment-population ratio	35.3	52.0	65.5	77.3	35.1	54.0	67.7	79.2
Unemployed	2	5	9	17	2	5	11	13
Unemployment rate	2.8	2.8	3.4	2.4	3.4	2.6	4.1	1.9
Hispanic[3]								
Civilian noninstitutional population	2 455	3 182	2 735	1 504	2 352	3 232	2 781	1 626
Civilian labor force	1 163	2 313	2 164	1 272	1 073	2 331	2 222	1 373
Participation rate	47.4	72.7	79.1	84.5	45.6	72.1	79.9	84.4
Employed	1 066	2 195	2 064	1 235	989	2 214	2 143	1 344
Employment-population ratio	43.4	69.0	75.5	82.1	42.0	68.5	77.1	82.6
Unemployed	97	118	100	36	85	117	79	29
Unemployment rate	8.4	5.1	4.6	2.9	7.9	5.0	3.6	2.1

Note: Due to the introduction of revised population controls in January 2006, estimated levels for 2006 are not strictly comparable with those for 2005. Data for race/ethnicity groups do not sum to total because data are not presented for all races.

[1] Includes persons with a high school diploma or equivalent.
[2] Includes persons with bachelor's, master's, professional, and doctoral degrees.
[3] May be of any race.

Table 1-54. Employed Foreign-Born and Native-Born Persons Age 16 Years and Over, by Occupation and Sex, 2006 Averages

(Thousands of people, percent.)

Occupation	Foreign born			Native born		
	Both sexes	Male	Female	Both sexes	Male	Female
TOTAL EMPLOYED	22 225	13 395	8 831	122 202	64 107	58 095
Percent Employed	100.0	100.0	100.0	100.0	100.0	100.0
Management, professional, and related	26.4	24.3	29.6	36.4	33.8	39.4
Management, business, and financial operations	10.0	10.1	9.9	15.5	17.1	13.8
Management	7.2	8.0	5.9	11.2	13.4	8.7
Business and financial operations	2.9	2.1	4.0	4.4	3.8	5.1
Professional and related	16.4	14.2	19.7	20.9	16.7	25.6
Computer and mathematical	3.1	3.9	2.0	2.1	2.9	1.2
Architecture and engineering	2.0	2.7	1.1	1.9	3.2	0.5
Life, physical, and social sciences	1.1	1.1	1.1	1.0	1.0	0.9
Community and social services	0.8	0.6	1.1	1.6	1.2	2.1
Legal	0.4	0.3	0.7	1.3	1.2	1.4
Education, training, and library	3.1	1.8	5.0	6.1	2.9	9.6
Arts, design, entertainment, sports, and media	1.2	1.1	1.5	2.0	2.0	2.1
Health care practitioner and technical	4.6	2.7	7.3	4.9	2.4	7.8
Services	22.5	17.2	30.4	15.4	12.2	18.9
Health care support	2.5	0.6	5.5	2.1	0.4	4.0
Protective services	0.8	1.0	0.4	2.3	3.4	1.1
Food preparation and serving related	7.7	7.4	8.1	4.8	3.6	6.2
Building and grounds cleaning and maintenance	7.9	7.0	9.3	3.0	3.6	2.3
Personal care and services	3.6	1.3	7.1	3.2	1.3	5.4
Sales and office	17.9	12.9	25.6	26.3	18.0	35.5
Sales and related	9.2	7.9	11.3	11.9	11.6	12.3
Office and administrative support	8.7	5.0	14.2	14.4	6.4	23.1
Natural resources, construction, and maintenance	16.5	26.1	1.9	10.0	18.1	1.0
Farming, fishing, and forestry	1.6	2.1	1.0	0.5	0.7	0.2
Construction and extraction	11.8	19.0	0.7	5.6	10.4	0.4
Installation, maintenance, and repair	3.1	4.9	0.2	3.8	6.9	0.4
Production, transportation, and material moving	16.7	19.5	12.5	11.9	17.9	5.3
Production	9.7	9.7	9.6	5.9	8.2	3.4
Transportation and material moving	7.0	9.8	2.9	6.0	9.7	1.8

Note: Due to the introduction of revised population controls in January 2006, estimated levels for 2006 are not strictly comparable with those for 2005.

Table 1-55. Median Usual Weekly Earnings of Full-Time Wage and Salary Workers for the Foreign-Born and Native-Born Populations, by Selected Characteristics, Annual Averages, 2005–2006

(Thousands of people, dollars, percent.)

Year and characteristic	Foreign born		Native born		Earnings of foreign born as a percent of earnings of native born[1]
	Number	Median weekly earnings	Number	Median weekly earnings	
2005					
Both Sexes, 16 Years and Over	16 340	511	87 220	677	75.6
Men	10 396	523	48 011	760	68.9
Women	5 945	487	39 210	596	81.7
Age					
16 to 24 years	1 578	353	9 529	404	87.3
25 to 34 years	4 831	495	20 181	633	78.3
35 to 44 years	4 700	587	22 403	755	77.8
45 to 54 years	3 352	563	22 299	772	73.0
55 to 64 years	1 582	607	11 192	757	80.2
65 years and over	297	494	1 616	578	85.4
Race and Hispanic Origin					
White, non-Hispanic	2 978	733	67 458	720	101.8
Black, non-Hispanic	1 326	521	10 671	521	100.0
Asian, non-Hispanic	3 541	747	1 041	777	96.1
Hispanic[2]	8 331	412	6 343	555	74.2
Educational Attainment					
Total, 25 years and over	14 762	543	77 691	724	74.9
Less than a high school diploma	4 305	385	4 557	442	87.0
High school graduate, no college[3]	3 589	496	23 926	594	83.4
Some college	2 316	592	23 155	679	87.2
Bachelor's degree or higher[4]	4 553	960	26 053	1 023	93.8
2006					
Both Sexes, 16 Years and Over	17 267	532	88 839	698	76.2
Men	10 931	563	48 816	782	72.0
Women	6 336	502	40 022	611	82.1
Age					
16 to 24 years	1 608	379	9 753	414	91.5
25 to 34 years	5 008	508	20 407	647	78.4
35 to 44 years	5 035	597	22 159	776	76.9
45 to 54 years	3 567	612	22 814	801	76.4
55 to 64 years	1 703	608	11 919	787	77.3
65 years and over	345	554	1 787	588	94.3
Race and Hispanic Origin					
White, non-Hispanic	3 051	765	68 410	740	103.3
Black, non-Hispanic	1 349	563	10 939	557	101.1
Asian, non-Hispanic	3 685	790	1 066	789	100.1
Hispanic[2]	9 010	430	6 683	572	75.1
Educational Attainment					
Total, 25 years and over	15 659	575	79 085	743	77.4
Less than a high school diploma	4 542	396	4 487	462	85.8
High school graduates, no college[3]	3 813	507	24 210	607	83.5
Some college	2 446	613	23 580	701	87.4
Bachelor's degree and higher[4]	4 857	1 024	26 808	1 042	98.2

Note: Due to the introduction of revised population controls in January 2006, estimated levels for 2006 are not strictly comparable with those for 2005. Data for race/ethnicity groups do not sum to total because data are not presented for all races.

[1]These figures are computed using unrounded medians and may differ slightly from percentages computed using the rounded medians displayed in this table.
[2]May be of any race.
[3]Includes persons with a high school diploma or equivalent.
[4]Includes persons with bachelor's, master's, professional, and doctoral degrees.

Table 1-56. Percent Distribution of the Civilian Labor Force Age 25 to 64 Years, by Educational Attainment, Sex, and Race, March 1990–March 2007

(Thousands of people, percent.)

Sex, race, and year	Civilian labor force	Percent distribution				
		Total	Less than a high school diploma	4 years of high school only	1 to 3 years of college	4 or more years of college
Both Sexes						
1990	99 175	100.0	13.4	39.5	20.7	26.4
1991	100 480	100.0	13.0	39.4	21.1	26.5
1992	102 387	100.0	12.2	36.2	25.2	26.4
1993	103 504	100.0	11.5	35.2	26.3	27.0
1994	104 868	100.0	11.0	34.0	27.7	27.3
1995	106 519	100.0	10.8	33.1	27.8	28.3
1996	108 037	100.0	10.9	32.9	27.7	28.5
1997	110 514	100.0	10.9	33.0	27.4	28.6
1998	111 857	100.0	10.7	32.8	27.4	29.1
1999	112 542	100.0	10.3	32.3	27.4	30.0
2000	114 052	100.0	9.8	31.8	27.9	30.4
2001	115 073	100.0	9.8	31.4	28.1	30.7
2002	117 738	100.0	10.1	30.6	27.7	31.6
2003	119 261	100.0	10.1	30.1	27.8	31.9
2004	119 392	100.0	9.7	30.1	27.8	32.4
2005	120 461	100.0	9.8	30.1	27.8	32.3
2006	122 541	100.0	9.8	29.6	28.0	32.6
2007	124 581	100.0	9.8	29.3	27.3	33.6
Men						
1990	54 476	100.0	15.1	37.2	19.7	28.0
1991	55 165	100.0	14.7	37.5	20.2	27.6
1992	55 917	100.0	13.9	34.7	23.8	27.5
1993	56 544	100.0	13.2	33.9	24.7	28.1
1994	56 633	100.0	12.7	32.9	25.8	28.6
1995	57 454	100.0	12.2	32.3	25.7	29.7
1996	58 121	100.0	12.7	32.2	26.0	29.1
1997	59 268	100.0	12.8	32.2	25.8	29.2
1998	59 905	100.0	12.3	32.3	25.8	29.6
1999	60 030	100.0	11.7	32.0	25.8	30.5
2000	60 510	100.0	11.1	31.8	26.1	30.9
2001	61 091	100.0	11.0	31.6	26.3	31.1
2002	62 794	100.0	11.8	30.6	25.9	31.7
2003	63 466	100.0	12.0	30.1	25.8	32.1
2004	63 699	100.0	11.5	30.5	25.8	32.2
2005	64 562	100.0	11.6	31.4	25.4	31.6
2006	65 708	100.0	11.8	30.7	25.7	31.8
2007	66 742	100.0	11.7	30.6	25.1	32.7
Women						
1990	44 699	100.0	11.3	42.4	21.9	24.5
1991	45 315	100.0	10.9	41.6	22.2	25.2
1992	46 469	100.0	10.2	37.9	26.9	25.0
1993	46 961	100.0	9.3	36.7	28.2	25.8
1994	48 235	100.0	9.1	35.3	29.8	25.8
1995	49 065	100.0	9.1	34.1	30.2	26.6
1996	49 916	100.0	8.8	33.7	29.7	27.8
1997	51 246	100.0	8.7	34.0	29.3	28.0
1998	51 953	100.0	8.8	33.3	29.3	28.6
1999	52 512	100.0	8.7	32.7	29.2	29.5
2000	53 541	100.0	8.4	31.8	30.0	29.8
2001	53 982	100.0	8.5	31.1	30.1	30.2
2002	54 944	100.0	8.2	30.6	29.7	31.5
2003	55 795	100.0	8.0	30.1	30.1	31.8
2004	55 693	100.0	7.7	29.6	30.2	32.5
2005	55 899	100.0	7.8	28.6	30.5	33.1
2006	56 833	100.0	7.6	28.2	30.6	33.6
2007	57 839	100.0	7.5	27.9	29.9	34.6

Table 1-56. Percent Distribution of the Civilian Labor Force Age 25 to 64 Years, by Educational Attainment, Sex, and Race, March 1990–March 2007—*Continued*

(Thousands of people, percent.)

Sex, race, and year	Civilian labor force	Percent distribution				
		Total	Less than a high school diploma	4 years of high school only	1 to 3 years of college	4 or more years of college
White[1]						
1990	85 238	100.0	12.6	39.6	20.6	27.1
1991	86 344	100.0	12.2	39.3	21.1	27.4
1992	87 656	100.0	11.3	36.1	25.5	27.1
1993	88 457	100.0	10.7	35.0	26.4	27.9
1994	89 009	100.0	10.5	33.7	27.7	28.1
1995	90 192	100.0	10.0	32.8	27.8	29.3
1996	91 506	100.0	10.4	32.8	27.5	29.3
1997	93 179	100.0	10.4	32.8	27.3	29.5
1998	93 527	100.0	10.2	32.7	27.4	29.8
1999	94 216	100.0	9.8	32.2	27.2	30.8
2000	95 073	100.0	9.5	31.8	27.7	31.0
2001	95 562	100.0	9.5	31.0	28.0	31.4
2002	97 699	100.0	9.8	30.6	27.6	32.0
2003	98 241	100.0	9.9	30.0	27.7	32.4
2004	98 030	100.0	9.5	29.8	27.8	32.9
2005	98 581	100.0	9.7	29.8	27.8	32.7
2006	100 205	100.0	9.7	29.3	28.1	32.9
2007	101 548	100.0	9.7	29.1	27.3	33.9
Black[1]						
1990	10 537	100.0	19.9	42.5	22.1	15.5
1991	10 650	100.0	19.5	42.9	22.1	15.4
1992	10 936	100.0	19.2	40.3	24.9	15.6
1993	11 051	100.0	16.8	39.5	27.6	16.1
1994	11 368	100.0	14.5	39.3	29.2	17.0
1995	11 695	100.0	14.1	38.6	29.6	17.7
1996	11 891	100.0	14.2	37.2	31.2	17.4
1997	12 253	100.0	14.3	37.8	31.3	16.6
1998	12 893	100.0	14.3	37.3	30.1	18.2
1999	12 945	100.0	13.0	37.2	30.4	19.5
2000	13 383	100.0	11.8	36.1	31.5	20.7
2001	13 617	100.0	12.0	37.1	31.1	19.8
2002	13 319	100.0	12.4	34.5	32.0	21.0
2003	13 315	100.0	11.3	35.6	31.5	21.6
2004	13 372	100.0	11.0	36.6	30.5	21.9
2005	13 635	100.0	11.2	37.3	29.9	21.6
2006	13 855	100.0	10.9	35.6	30.4	23.0
2007	14 186	100.0	10.1	35.4	31.4	23.1

[1]Beginning in 2003, persons who selected this race group only; persons who selected more than one race group are not included. Prior to 2003, persons who reported more than one race group were included in the group they identified as their main race.

Table 1-57. Labor Force Participation Rates of Persons Age 25 to 64 Years, by Educational Attainment, Sex, and Race, March 1990–March 2007

(Civilian labor force as a percent of the civilian noninstitutional population.)

Sex, race, and year	Participation rates				
	Total	Less than a high school diploma	4 years of high school only	1 to 3 years of college	4 or more years of college
Both Sexes					
1990	78.6	60.7	78.2	83.3	88.4
1991	78.6	60.7	78.1	83.2	88.4
1992	79.0	60.3	78.3	83.5	88.4
1993	78.9	59.6	77.7	82.9	88.3
1994	78.9	58.3	77.8	83.2	88.2
1995	79.3	59.8	77.3	83.2	88.7
1996	79.4	60.2	77.9	83.7	87.8
1997	80.1	61.7	78.5	83.7	88.5
1998	80.2	63.0	78.4	83.5	88.0
1999	80.0	62.7	78.1	83.0	87.6
2000	80.3	62.7	78.4	83.2	87.8
2001	80.2	63.5	78.4	83.0	87.0
2002	79.7	63.5	77.7	82.1	86.7
2003	79.4	64.1	76.9	81.9	86.2
2004	78.8	63.2	76.1	81.2	85.9
2005	78.5	62.9	75.7	81.1	85.7
2006	78.7	63.2	75.9	81.0	85.9
2007	79.0	63.7	76.3	81.1	85.9
Men					
1990	88.8	75.1	89.9	91.5	94.5
1991	88.6	75.1	89.3	92.0	94.2
1992	88.6	75.1	89.0	91.8	93.7
1993	88.1	74.9	88.1	90.6	93.7
1994	87.0	71.5	86.8	90.3	93.2
1995	87.4	72.0	86.9	90.1	93.8
1996	87.5	74.3	86.9	90.0	92.9
1997	87.7	75.2	86.4	90.6	93.5
1998	87.8	75.3	86.7	90.0	93.4
1999	87.5	74.4	86.6	89.4	93.0
2000	87.5	74.9	86.2	88.9	93.3
2001	87.4	75.4	85.8	89.1	92.9
2002	87.0	75.5	85.3	88.8	92.4
2003	86.4	76.1	84.3	87.5	92.2
2004	85.9	75.2	83.8	87.0	91.9
2005	86.0	75.7	83.7	87.5	91.7
2006	86.0	76.3	83.4	87.8	91.7
2007	86.2	75.7	83.9	87.2	92.4
Women					
1990	68.9	46.2	68.7	75.9	81.1
1991	69.1	46.2	68.6	75.2	81.8
1992	70.0	45.6	69.1	76.2	82.2
1993	70.0	44.2	68.8	76.1	82.2
1994	71.1	44.7	70.0	77.0	82.5
1995	71.5	47.2	68.9	77.3	82.8
1996	71.8	45.7	69.8	78.1	82.3
1997	72.8	47.1	71.4	77.6	83.2
1998	73.0	49.8	70.9	77.8	82.3
1999	72.8	50.5	70.4	77.4	81.9
2000	73.5	50.4	71.2	78.3	82.0
2001	73.4	51.7	71.3	77.7	80.9
2002	72.7	50.4	70.4	76.4	81.0
2003	72.6	50.5	69.8	77.1	80.1
2004	72.0	49.7	68.6	76.2	80.0
2005	71.4	48.7	67.4	75.8	79.8
2006	71.7	48.3	68.2	75.3	80.4
2007	72.1	49.6	68.4	76.0	79.7

Table 1-57. Labor Force Participation Rates of Persons Age 25 to 64 Years, by Educational Attainment, Sex, and Race, March 1990–March 2007—*Continued*

(Civilian labor force as a percent of the civilian noninstitutional population.)

Sex, race, and year	Participation rates				
	Total	Less than a high school diploma	4 years of high school only	1 to 3 years of college	4 or more years of college
White[1]					
1990	79.2	62.5	78.4	83.3	88.3
1991	79.4	62.5	78.3	83.1	88.6
1992	79.8	61.5	78.7	83.8	88.7
1993	79.7	61.1	78.2	83.1	88.8
1994	79.8	60.3	78.3	83.5	88.5
1995	80.1	61.6	77.9	83.4	88.8
1996	80.4	62.5	78.6	83.9	88.2
1997	81.0	63.8	79.2	83.9	89.0
1998	80.6	63.8	78.6	83.5	88.3
1999	80.6	64.2	78.5	83.3	87.9
2000	80.8	64.2	78.7	83.1	87.9
2001	80.7	64.5	78.7	83.1	87.2
2002	80.3	65.0	78.2	82.4	87.0
2003	80.1	65.7	77.5	82.3	86.5
2004	79.5	64.6	76.7	81.6	86.2
2005	79.2	63.8	76.4	81.5	86.1
2006	79.5	65.1	76.5	81.4	86.2
2007	79.6	65.1	77.2	81.4	86.1
Black[1]					
1990	74.6	54.5	78.2	84.2	92.0
1991	73.9	53.9	77.1	84.1	90.2
1992	74.4	55.4	76.9	83.4	89.1
1993	73.8	53.4	74.7	83.0	89.6
1994	73.5	49.4	75.2	82.4	89.5
1995	74.2	51.0	74.5	82.8	90.9
1996	73.7	50.1	74.3	83.0	87.9
1997	74.9	52.9	75.0	83.8	89.0
1998	77.7	59.3	77.0	85.0	88.8
1999	76.5	55.1	76.5	82.9	88.6
2000	77.9	55.5	77.0	84.2	90.3
2001	78.1	58.7	76.8	83.0	90.5
2002	76.4	56.6	75.0	81.7	88.9
2003	75.8	55.4	73.9	81.2	88.2
2004	75.0	55.2	73.4	79.0	87.9
2005	75.2	58.2	72.6	79.5	87.2
2006	75.0	54.0	73.3	79.6	87.7
2007	75.6	55.3	72.5	80.7	88.0

[1]Beginning in 2003, persons who selected this race group only; persons who selected more than one race group are not included. Prior to 2003, persons who reported more than one race group were included in the group they identified as their main race.

Table 1-58. Unemployment Rates of Persons Age 25 to 64 Years, by Educational Attainment and Sex, March 1990–March 2007

(Unemployment as a percent of the civilian labor force.)

Sex, race, and year	Unemployment rates				
	Total	Less than a high school diploma	4 years of high school only	1 to 3 years of college	4 or more years of college
Both Sexes					
1990	4.5	9.6	4.9	3.7	1.9
1991	6.1	12.3	6.7	5.0	2.9
1992	6.7	13.5	7.7	5.9	2.9
1993	6.4	13.0	7.3	5.5	3.2
1994	5.8	12.6	6.7	5.0	2.9
1995	4.8	10.0	5.2	4.5	2.5
1996	4.8	10.9	5.5	4.1	2.2
1997	4.4	10.4	5.1	3.8	2.0
1998	4.0	8.5	4.8	3.6	1.8
1999	3.5	7.7	4.0	3.1	1.9
2000	3.3	7.9	3.8	3.0	1.5
2001	3.5	8.1	4.2	2.9	2.0
2002	5.0	10.2	6.1	4.5	2.8
2003	5.3	9.9	6.4	5.2	3.0
2004	5.1	10.5	5.9	4.9	2.9
2005	4.4	9.0	5.5	4.1	2.3
2006	4.1	8.3	4.7	3.9	2.3
2007	3.9	8.5	4.7	3.7	1.8
Men					
1990	4.8	9.6	5.3	3.9	2.1
1991	6.8	13.4	7.7	5.2	3.2
1992	7.5	14.8	8.8	6.4	3.2
1993	7.3	14.1	8.7	6.3	3.4
1994	6.2	12.8	7.2	5.3	2.9
1995	5.1	10.9	5.7	4.4	2.6
1996	5.3	11.0	6.4	4.5	2.3
1997	4.7	9.9	5.6	4.0	2.1
1998	4.1	8.0	5.1	3.7	1.7
1999	3.5	7.0	4.1	3.2	1.9
2000	3.3	7.1	3.9	3.1	1.6
2001	3.7	7.5	4.6	3.2	1.9
2002	5.5	9.9	6.7	4.9	3.0
2003	5.8	9.5	6.9	6.0	3.2
2004	5.4	9.4	6.6	5.4	3.0
2005	4.7	7.9	6.0	4.3	2.5
2006	4.3	7.6	5.0	4.2	2.4
2007	4.3	8.4	5.5	3.9	1.9
Women					
1990	4.2	9.5	4.6	3.5	1.7
1991	5.2	10.7	5.5	4.8	2.5
1992	5.7	11.4	6.5	5.3	2.5
1993	5.2	11.2	5.8	4.6	2.9
1994	5.4	12.4	6.2	4.7	2.9
1995	4.4	8.6	4.6	4.5	2.4
1996	4.1	10.7	4.4	3.8	2.1
1997	4.1	11.3	4.5	3.6	2.0
1998	3.9	9.3	4.4	3.5	1.9
1999	3.5	8.8	3.9	3.0	1.9
2000	3.2	9.1	3.6	2.9	1.4
2001	3.3	8.9	3.8	2.6	2.0
2002	4.6	10.6	5.4	4.1	2.6
2003	4.8	10.6	5.9	4.4	2.8
2004	4.7	12.2	5.2	4.3	2.9
2005	4.2	10.9	4.8	4.0	2.2
2006	3.8	9.4	4.4	3.7	2.1
2007	3.4	8.5	3.8	3.6	1.8

Table 1-58. Unemployment Rates of Persons Age 25 to 64 Years, by Educational Attainment and Sex, March 1990–March 2007—*Continued*

(Unemployment as a percent of the civilian labor force.)

Sex, race, and year	Unemployment rates				
	Total	Less than a high school diploma	4 years of high school only	1 to 3 years of college	4 or more years of college
White[1]					
1990	4.0	8.3	4.4	3.3	1.8
1991	5.6	11.6	6.2	4.6	2.7
1992	6.0	12.9	6.8	5.3	2.7
1993	5.8	12.4	6.5	5.0	3.1
1994	5.2	11.7	5.8	4.5	2.6
1995	4.3	9.2	4.6	4.2	2.3
1996	4.2	10.2	4.6	3.7	2.1
1997	3.9	9.4	4.6	3.4	1.8
1998	3.5	7.5	4.2	3.2	1.7
1999	3.1	7.0	3.4	2.8	1.7
2000	3.0	7.5	3.3	2.7	1.4
2001	3.1	7.2	3.6	2.7	1.8
2002	4.6	9.1	5.5	4.1	2.6
2003	4.7	9.0	5.7	4.5	2.7
2004	4.6	9.6	5.4	4.4	2.8
2005	3.9	7.7	4.9	3.6	2.2
2006	3.5	7.1	4.0	3.5	2.1
2007	3.5	7.8	4.2	3.3	1.7
Black[1]					
1990	8.6	15.9	8.6	6.5	1.9
1991	10.1	15.9	10.3	8.0	5.2
1992	12.4	17.2	14.1	10.7	4.8
1993	10.9	17.3	12.4	8.7	4.1
1994	10.6	17.4	12.2	8.3	4.9
1995	7.7	13.7	8.4	6.3	4.1
1996	8.9	15.3	10.8	6.9	3.3
1997	8.1	16.6	8.2	6.1	4.4
1998	7.3	13.4	8.4	6.4	2.1
1999	6.3	12.0	6.7	5.2	3.3
2000	5.4	10.4	6.3	4.3	2.5
2001	6.5	14.0	7.7	4.3	3.3
2002	8.1	15.4	9.7	6.0	4.1
2003	9.0	14.7	9.9	8.9	4.7
2004	8.4	15.8	9.3	7.9	3.7
2005	8.3	17.9	8.6	7.5	3.6
2006	7.8	16.4	9.0	6.5	3.6
2007	6.5	14.0	7.7	5.7	2.5

[1]Beginning in 2003, persons who selected this race group only; persons who selected more than one race group are not included. Prior to 2003, persons who reported more than one race group were included in the group they identified as their main race.

Table 1-59. Workers Age 25 to 64 Years, by Educational Attainment, Occupation of Longest Job Held, and Sex, 2005–2006

(Thousands of people with work experience during the year.)

Year, sex, and occupation	Total	Less than a high school diploma	4 years of high school only	1 to 3 years of college	4 or more years of college
2005					
Both Sexes	125 664	12 170	37 080	35 438	40 976
Management, business, and financial operations	19 624	442	3 348	5 132	10 702
Management	14 083	394	2 633	3 674	7 382
Business and financial operations	5 541	48	715	1 458	3 320
Professional and related	26 851	173	2 245	6 184	18 249
Computer and mathematical	3 116	19	258	799	2 040
Architecture and engineering	2 509	3	253	662	1 592
Life, physical, and social sciences	1 317	. . .	87	172	1 057
Community and social services	1 992	18	163	361	1 449
Legal	1 389	6	96	237	1 050
Education, training, and library	7 659	33	574	1 030	6 022
Arts, design, entertainment, sports, and media	2 400	62	304	682	1 352
Health care practitioner and technical	6 469	30	510	2 240	3 688
Services	18 586	3 336	7 499	5 425	2 325
Health care support	2 772	301	1 092	1 044	335
Protective services	2 576	84	691	1 179	621
Food preparation and serving related	4 771	1 034	2 132	1 124	481
Building and grounds cleaning and maintenance	4 787	1 492	2 143	847	304
Personal care and services	3 680	425	1 441	1 231	584
Sales and office	29 770	1 653	9 939	10 963	7 214
Sales and related	12 984	917	3 998	4 052	4 016
Office and administrative support	16 786	736	5 941	6 912	3 198
Natural resources, construction, and maintenance	13 977	3 287	5 964	3 684	1 042
Farming, fishing, and forestry	818	431	262	74	51
Construction and extraction	8 430	2 263	3 679	1 917	571
Installation, maintenance, and repair	4 729	594	2 023	1 693	420
Production, transportation, and material moving	16 255	3 273	7 955	3 806	1 221
Production	8 835	1 887	4 220	2 098	631
Transportation and material moving	7 420	1 386	3 736	1 708	590
Armed forces	602	7	129	244	222
Men	67 099	7 739	20 592	17 354	21 416
Management, business, and financial operations	11 244	309	1 846	2 618	6 472
Management	8 840	287	1 646	2 127	4 780
Business and financial operations	2 403	21	199	491	1 692
Professional and related	11 428	75	790	2 281	8 282
Computer and mathematical	2 271	16	179	562	1 514
Architecture and engineering	2 165	3	217	590	1 355
Life, physical, and social sciences	728	. . .	57	103	568
Community and social services	751	5	47	116	583
Legal	636	3	4	12	618
Education, training, and library	1 958	3	51	162	1 742
Arts, design, entertainment, sports, and media	1 266	33	156	418	658
Health care practitioner and technical	1 652	12	78	318	1 244
Services	7 824	1 386	2 990	2 286	1 162
Health care support	296	12	98	108	78
Protective services	1 959	61	523	895	479
Food preparation and serving related	2 007	482	804	490	231
Building and grounds cleaning and maintenance	2 781	761	1 288	541	191
Personal care and services	781	70	276	252	183
Sales and office	10 528	583	3 076	3 500	3 369
Sales and related	6 688	329	1 826	2 131	2 403
Office and administrative support	3 840	254	1 250	1 369	967
Natural resources, construction, and maintenance	13 326	3 115	5 761	3 479	971
Farming, fishing, and forestry	612	321	209	47	35
Construction and extraction	8 185	2 215	3 597	1 830	543
Installation, maintenance, and repair	4 529	579	1 955	1 603	392
Production, transportation, and material moving	12 222	2 266	6 011	2 986	960
Production	5 988	1 106	2 861	1 570	451
Transportation and material moving	6 234	1 160	3 150	1 416	509
Armed forces	527	5	118	204	200
Women	58 567	4 432	16 488	18 085	19 561
Management, business, and financial operations	8 380	133	1 502	2 514	4 231
Management	5 243	107	986	1 547	2 602
Business and financial operations	3 138	26	516	967	1 628
Professional and related	15 424	98	1 455	3 903	9 967
Computer and mathematical	846	3	79	237	527
Architecture and engineering	344	. . .	36	72	237
Life, physical, and social sciences	589	. . .	30	69	489
Community and social services	1 241	13	116	245	866
Legal	753	4	92	225	432
Education, training, and library	5 701	31	523	869	4 279
Arts, design, entertainment, sports, and media	1 134	29	148	264	693
Health care practitioner and technical	4 817	18	432	1 922	2 444
Services	10 762	1 949	4 510	3 139	1 163
Health care support	2 476	289	994	936	257
Protective services	617	23	168	284	142
Food preparation and serving related	2 765	552	1 328	634	250
Building and grounds cleaning and maintenance	2 005	731	855	306	113
Personal care and services	2 899	355	1 165	979	400
Sales and office	19 242	1 070	6 863	7 464	3 845
Sales and related	6 296	589	2 173	1 921	1 614
Office and administrative support	12 946	481	4 690	5 543	2 232
Natural resources, construction, and maintenance	651	172	203	205	71
Farming, fishing, and forestry	206	110	53	28	16
Construction and extraction	245	48	82	87	28
Installation, maintenance, and repair	200	15	68	90	28
Production, transportation, and material moving	4 033	1 008	1 944	820	261
Production	2 847	781	1 359	528	179
Transportation and material moving	1 186	226	585	293	82
Armed forces	75	2	11	40	23

. . . = Not available.

Table 1-59. Workers Age 25 to 64 Years, by Educational Attainment, Occupation of Longest Job Held, and Sex, 2005–2006—*Continued*

(Thousands of people with work experience during the year.)

Year, sex, and occupation	Total	Less than a high school diploma	4 years of high school only	1 to 3 years of college	4 or more years of college
2006					
Both Sexes	127 402	12 394	37 276	34 978	42 755
Management, business, and financial operations	20 041	483	3 334	5 058	11 166
Management	14 133	422	2 592	3 573	7 546
Business and financial operations	5 908	61	742	1 484	3 620
Professional and related	27 923	202	2 266	5 999	19 456
Computer and mathematical	3 122	17	254	717	2 134
Architecture and engineering	2 664	8	213	620	1 823
Life, physical, and social sciences	1 345	. . .	113	139	1 093
Community and social services	2 155	17	192	431	1 515
Legal	1 455	14	123	217	1 101
Education, training, and library	8 012	50	571	1 068	6 322
Arts. design. entertainment. sports. and media	2 557	48	321	660	1 527
Health care practitioner and technical	6 614	47	479	2 147	3 941
Services	18 354	3 378	7 184	5 406	2 387
Health care support	2 763	297	1 064	1 090	312
Protective services	2 616	82	740	1 117	677
Food preparation and serving related	4 698	1 081	1 990	1 160	467
Building and grounds cleaning and maintenance	4 661	1 480	2 032	811	338
Personal care and services	3 616	438	1 357	1 227	594
Sales and office	29 825	1 653	10 132	10 716	7 323
Sales and related	13 234	892	3 981	4 103	4 259
Office and administrative support	16 590	761	6 151	6 613	3 065
Natural resources, construction, and maintenance	14 350	3 305	6 306	3 712	1 027
Farming, fishing, and forestry	820	396	273	104	48
Construction and extraction	8 903	2 346	3 973	1 985	599
Installation, maintenance, and repair	4 627	563	2 061	1 623	380
Production, transportation, and material moving	16 398	3 363	7 935	3 867	1 233
Production	8 813	1 874	4 170	2 119	650
Transportation and material moving	7 585	1 489	3 766	1 748	583
Armed forces	511	10	118	220	164
Men	67 964	7 957	20 673	17 141	22 194
Management, business, and financial operations	11 171	325	1 852	2 570	6 424
Management	8 672	295	1 636	2 074	4 668
Business and financial operations	2 499	30	216	497	1 756
Professional and related	12 072	90	792	2 162	9 028
Computer and mathematical	2 295	12	164	523	1 596
Architecture and engineering	2 291	4	171	539	1 576
Life, physical, and social sciences	832	. . .	69	91	672
Community and social services	787	10	77	151	549
Legal	683	12	9	12	650
Education, training, and library	2 139	11	59	183	1 885
Arts, design, entertainment, sports, and media	1 374	33	159	379	803
Health care practitioner and technical	1 672	7	84	283	1 297
Services	7 577	1 419	2 717	2 273	1 167
Health care support	270	25	76	115	55
Protective services	1 992	62	526	901	504
Food preparation and serving related	2 011	516	729	521	245
Building and grounds cleaning and maintenance	2 607	758	1 158	479	212
Personal care and services	696	59	229	257	152
Sales and office	10 674	629	3 099	3 436	3 510
Sales and related	6 948	375	1 811	2 104	2 659
Office and administrative support	3 726	254	1 289	1 332	851
Natural resources, construction, and maintenance	13 724	3 152	6 098	3 509	966
Farming, fishing, and forestry	619	305	213	65	36
Construction and extraction	8 660	2 305	3 874	1 903	577
Installation, maintenance, and repair	4 446	542	2 011	1 541	353
Production, transportation, and material moving	12 280	2 333	6 001	2 992	954
Production	5 956	1 112	2 852	1 548	445
Transportation and material moving	6 323	1 222	3 149	1 445	509
Armed forces	466	8	114	199	145
Women	59 438	4 437	16 603	17 837	20 561
Management, business, and financial operations	8 869	158	1 482	2 487	4 742
Management	5 461	127	956	1 500	2 878
Business and financial operations	3 409	31	526	988	1 864
Professional and related	15 852	112	1 475	3 837	10 428
Computer and mathematical	827	5	90	193	538
Architecture and engineering	373	4	42	81	247
Life, physical, and social sciences	513	. . .	44	49	420
Community and social services	1 369	7	115	280	966
Legal	772	2	114	205	451
Education, training, and library	5 873	39	512	886	4 436
Arts, design, entertainment, sports, and media	1 183	16	162	280	725
Health care practitioner and technical	4 942	40	395	1 864	2 644
Services	10 777	1 958	4 467	3 133	1 220
Health care support	2 492	272	989	975	257
Protective services	624	20	215	216	173
Food preparation and serving related	2 687	565	1 261	639	222
Building and grounds cleaning and maintenance	2 054	722	874	332	126
Personal care and services	2 920	379	1 128	970	442
Sales and office	19 151	1 024	7 033	7 281	3 813
Sales and related	6 286	517	2 170	1 999	1 600
Office and administrative support	12 865	507	4 863	5 281	2 214
Natural resources, construction, and maintenance	625	153	208	204	61
Farming, fishing, and forestry	201	91	59	39	12
Construction and extraction	243	41	99	82	22
Installation, maintenance, and repair	181	21	50	82	27
Production, transportation, and material moving	4 119	1 030	1 935	875	279
Production	2 857	763	1 318	571	205
Transportation and material moving	1 262	267	617	304	74
Armed forces	45	2	4	21	18

. . . = Not available.

Table 1-60. Percent Distribution of Workers Age 25 to 64 Years, by Educational Attainment, Occupation of Longest Job Held, and Sex, 2005–2006

(Percent of total workers in occupation.)

Year, sex, and occupation	Total	Less than a high school diploma	4 years of high school only	1 to 3 years of college	4 or more years of college
2005					
Both Sexes	100.0	9.7	29.5	28.2	32.6
Management, business, and financial operations	100.0	2.3	17.1	26.2	54.5
Management	100.0	2.8	18.7	26.1	52.4
Business and financial operations	100.0	0.9	12.9	26.3	59.9
Professional and related	100.0	0.6	8.4	23.0	68.0
Computer and mathematical	100.0	0.6	8.3	25.6	65.5
Architecture and engineering	100.0	0.1	10.1	26.4	63.4
Life, physical, and social sciences	100.0	. . .	6.6	13.1	80.3
Community and social services	100.0	0.9	8.2	18.1	72.7
Legal	100.0	0.5	6.9	17.1	75.6
Education, training, and library	100.0	0.4	7.5	13.5	78.6
Arts, design, entertainment, sports, and media	100.0	2.6	12.7	28.4	56.3
Health care practitioner and technical	100.0	0.5	7.9	34.6	57.0
Services	100.0	17.9	40.4	29.2	12.5
Health care support	100.0	10.8	39.4	37.7	12.1
Protective services	100.0	3.3	26.8	45.8	24.1
Food preparation and serving related	100.0	21.7	44.7	23.6	10.1
Building and grounds cleaning and maintenance	100.0	31.2	44.8	17.7	6.4
Personal care and services	100.0	11.6	39.2	33.4	15.9
Sales and office	100.0	5.6	33.4	36.8	24.2
Sales and related	100.0	7.1	30.8	31.2	30.9
Office and administrative support	100.0	4.4	35.4	41.2	19.1
Natural resources, construction, and maintenance	100.0	23.5	42.7	26.4	7.5
Farming, fishing, and forestry	100.0	52.7	32.0	9.1	6.2
Construction and extraction	100.0	26.8	43.6	22.7	6.8
Installation, maintenance, and repair	100.0	12.6	42.8	35.8	8.9
Production, transportation, and material moving	100.0	20.1	48.9	23.4	7.5
Production	100.0	21.4	47.8	23.7	7.1
Transportation and material moving	100.0	18.7	50.3	23.0	8.0
Armed forces	100.0	1.1	21.4	40.5	37.0
Men	. . .	. . .	. . .	. . .	. . .
Management, business, and financial operations	100.0	2.7	16.4	23.3	57.6
Management	100.0	3.3	18.6	24.1	54.1
Business and financial operations	100.0	0.9	8.3	20.4	70.4
Professional and related	100.0	0.7	6.9	20.0	72.5
Computer and mathematical	100.0	0.7	7.9	24.7	66.7
Architecture and engineering	100.0	0.1	10.0	27.2	62.6
Life, physical, and social sciences	100.0	. . .	7.8	14.1	78.0
Community and social services	100.0	0.7	6.3	15.4	77.6
Legal	100.0	0.4	0.6	1.9	97.0
Education, training, and library	100.0	0.1	2.6	8.3	89.0
Arts, design, entertainment, sports, and media	100.0	2.6	12.4	33.0	52.0
Health care practitioner and technical	100.0	0.7	4.7	19.3	75.3
Services	100.0	17.7	38.2	29.2	14.8
Health care support	100.0	4.1	33.0	36.5	26.4
Protective services	100.0	3.1	26.7	45.7	24.5
Food preparation and serving related	100.0	24.0	40.1	24.4	11.5
Building and grounds cleaning and maintenance	100.0	27.4	46.3	19.4	6.9
Personal care and services	100.0	9.0	35.4	32.2	23.4
Sales and office	100.0	5.5	29.2	33.2	32.0
Sales and related	100.0	4.9	27.3	31.9	35.9
Office and administrative support	100.0	6.6	32.6	35.6	25.2
Natural resources, construction, and maintenance	100.0	23.4	43.2	26.1	7.3
Farming, fishing, and forestry	100.0	52.4	34.2	7.6	5.8
Construction and extraction	100.0	27.1	43.9	22.4	6.6
Installation, maintenance, and repair	100.0	12.8	43.2	35.4	8.7
Production, transportation, and material moving	100.0	18.5	49.2	24.4	7.9
Production	100.0	18.5	47.8	26.2	7.5
Transportation and material moving	100.0	18.6	50.5	22.7	8.2
Armed forces	100.0	0.9	22.5	38.7	37.9
Women	. . .	. . .	. . .	. . .	. . .
Management, business, and financial operations	100.0	1.6	17.9	30.0	50.5
Management	100.0	2.0	18.8	29.5	49.6
Business and financial operations	100.0	0.8	16.4	30.8	51.9
Professional and related	100.0	0.6	9.4	25.3	64.6
Computer and mathematical	100.0	0.4	9.3	28.0	62.3
Architecture and engineering	100.0	. . .	10.4	20.9	68.7
Life, physical, and social sciences	100.0	. . .	5.1	11.8	83.1
Community and social services	100.0	1.1	9.3	19.8	69.8
Legal	100.0	0.5	12.2	29.9	57.4
Education, training, and library	100.0	0.5	9.2	15.2	75.1
Arts, design, entertainment, sports, and media	100.0	2.6	13.0	23.3	61.1
Health care practitioner and technical	100.0	0.4	9.0	39.9	50.7
Services	100.0	18.1	41.9	29.2	10.8
Health care support	100.0	11.7	40.1	37.8	10.4
Protective services	100.0	3.8	27.2	46.0	23.0
Food preparation and serving related	100.0	20.0	48.0	22.9	9.1
Building and grounds cleaning and maintenance	100.0	36.5	42.6	15.3	5.6
Personal care and services	100.0	12.2	40.2	33.8	13.8
Sales and office	100.0	5.6	35.7	38.8	20.0
Sales and related	100.0	9.4	34.5	30.5	25.6
Office and administrative support	100.0	3.7	36.2	42.8	17.2
Natural resources, construction, and maintenance	100.0	26.5	31.1	31.5	10.9
Farming, fishing, and forestry	100.0	53.4	25.6	13.5	7.6
Construction and extraction	100.0	19.5	33.6	35.6	11.4
Installation, maintenance, and repair	100.0	7.4	33.9	45.0	13.8
Production, transportation, and material moving	100.0	25.0	48.2	20.3	6.5
Production	100.0	27.4	47.7	18.5	6.3
Transportation and material moving	100.0	19.1	49.4	24.7	6.9
Armed forces	100.0	2.2	14.2	53.4	30.3

. . . = Not available.

Table 1-60. Percent Distribution of Workers Age 25 to 64 Years, by Educational Attainment, Occupation of Longest Job Held, and Sex, 2005–2006—*Continued*

(Percent of total workers in occupation.)

Year, sex, and occupation	Total	Less than a high school diploma	4 years of high school only	1 to 3 years of college	4 or more years of college
2006					
Both Sexes	100.0	9.7	29.3	27.5	33.6
Management, business, and financial operations	100.0	2.4	16.6	25.2	55.7
Management	100.0	3.0	18.3	25.3	53.4
Business and financial operations	100.0	1.0	12.6	25.1	61.3
Professional and related	100.0	0.7	8.1	21.5	69.7
Computer and mathematical	100.0	0.5	8.1	23.0	68.4
Architecture and engineering	100.0	0.3	8.0	23.3	68.4
Life, physical, and social sciences	100.0	0.0	8.4	10.4	81.2
Community and social services	100.0	0.8	8.9	20.0	70.3
Legal	100.0	1.0	8.4	14.9	75.7
Education, training, and library	100.0	0.6	7.1	13.3	78.9
Arts, design, entertainment, sports, and media	100.0	1.9	12.6	25.8	59.7
Health care practitioner and technical	100.0	0.7	7.2	32.5	59.6
Services	100.0	18.4	39.1	29.5	13.0
Health care support	100.0	10.7	38.5	39.5	11.3
Protective services	100.0	3.1	28.3	42.7	25.9
Food preparation and serving related	100.0	23.0	42.4	24.7	9.9
Building and grounds cleaning and maintenance	100.0	31.8	43.6	17.4	7.2
Personal care and services	100.0	12.1	37.5	33.9	16.4
Sales and office	100.0	5.5	34.0	35.9	24.6
Sales and related	100.0	6.7	30.1	31.0	32.2
Office and administrative support	100.0	4.6	37.1	39.9	18.5
Natural resources, construction, and maintenance	100.0	23.0	43.9	25.9	7.2
Farming, fishing, and forestry	100.0	48.3	33.2	12.7	5.8
Construction and extraction	100.0	26.4	44.6	22.3	6.7
Installation, maintenance, and repair	100.0	12.2	44.5	35.1	8.2
Production, transportation, and material moving	100.0	20.5	48.4	23.6	7.5
Production	100.0	21.3	47.3	24.0	7.4
Transportation and material moving	100.0	19.6	49.6	23.0	7.7
Armed forces	100.0	1.9	23.1	43.0	32.0
Men	100.0	11.7	30.4	25.2	32.7
Management, business, and financial operations	100.0	2.9	16.6	23.0	57.5
Management	100.0	3.4	18.9	23.9	53.8
Business and financial operations	100.0	1.2	8.7	19.9	70.3
Professional and related	100.0	0.7	6.6	17.9	74.8
Computer and mathematical	100.0	0.5	7.1	22.8	69.5
Architecture and engineering	100.0	0.2	7.5	23.5	68.8
Life, physical, and social sciences	100.0	0.0	8.3	10.9	80.8
Community and social services	100.0	1.3	9.7	19.2	69.7
Legal	100.0	1.8	1.3	1.8	95.1
Education, training, and library	100.0	0.5	2.8	8.5	88.2
Arts, design, entertainment, sports, and media	100.0	2.4	11.6	27.6	58.4
Health care practitioner and technical	100.0	0.4	5.0	17.0	77.6
Services	100.0	18.7	35.9	30.0	15.4
Health care support	100.0	9.2	28.0	42.5	20.3
Protective services	100.0	3.1	26.4	45.2	25.3
Food preparation and serving related	100.0	25.7	36.2	25.9	12.2
Building and grounds cleaning and maintenance	100.0	29.1	44.4	18.4	8.1
Personal care and services	100.0	8.4	32.9	36.9	21.9
Sales and office	100.0	5.9	29.0	32.2	32.9
Sales and related	100.0	5.4	26.1	30.3	38.3
Office and administrative support	100.0	6.8	34.6	35.8	22.8
Natural resources, construction, and maintenance	100.0	23.0	44.4	25.6	7.0
Farming, fishing, and forestry	100.0	49.3	34.5	10.5	5.8
Construction and extraction	100.0	26.6	44.7	22.0	6.7
Installation, maintenance, and repair	100.0	12.2	45.2	34.6	7.9
Production, transportation, and material moving	100.0	19.0	48.9	24.4	7.8
Production	100.0	18.7	47.9	26.0	7.5
Transportation and material moving	100.0	19.3	49.8	22.8	8.0
Armed forces	100.0	1.7	24.5	42.7	31.1
Women	100.0	7.5	27.9	30.0	34.6
Management, business, and financial operations	100.0	1.8	16.7	28.0	53.5
Management	100.0	2.3	17.5	27.5	52.7
Business and financial operations	100.0	0.9	15.4	29.0	54.7
Professional and related	100.0	0.7	9.3	24.2	65.8
Computer and mathematical	100.0	0.6	10.9	23.4	65.1
Architecture and engineering	100.0	1.0	11.3	21.6	66.1
Life, physical, and social sciences	100.0	0.0	8.6	9.5	81.9
Community and social services	100.0	0.5	8.4	20.4	70.6
Legal	100.0	0.2	14.8	26.5	58.5
Education, training, and library	100.0	0.7	8.7	15.1	75.5
Arts, design, entertainment, sports, and media	100.0	1.3	13.7	23.7	61.3
Health care practitioner and technical	100.0	0.8	8.0	37.7	53.5
Services	100.0	18.2	41.4	29.1	11.3
Health care support	100.0	10.9	39.7	39.1	10.3
Protective services	100.0	3.3	34.4	34.6	27.7
Food preparation and serving related	100.0	21.0	46.9	23.8	8.3
Building and grounds cleaning and maintenance	100.0	35.1	42.6	16.2	6.1
Personal care and services	100.0	13.0	38.6	33.2	15.1
Sales and office	100.0	5.3	36.7	38.0	19.9
Sales and related	100.0	8.2	34.5	31.8	25.4
Office and administrative support	100.0	3.9	37.8	41.1	17.2
Natural resources, construction, and maintenance	100.0	24.4	33.3	32.6	9.7
Farming, fishing, and forestry	100.0	45.1	29.5	19.5	5.9
Construction and extraction	100.0	16.8	40.6	33.7	8.9
Installation, maintenance, and repair	100.0	11.7	27.6	45.6	15.1
Production, transportation, and material moving	100.0	25.0	47.0	21.2	6.8
Production	100.0	26.7	46.1	20.0	7.2
Transportation and material moving	100.0	21.2	48.9	24.1	5.9
Armed forces	100.0	3.4	9.2	46.5	41.0

Table 1-61. Median Annual Earnings of Year-Round, Full-Time Wage and Salary Workers Age 25 to 64 Years, by Educational Attainment and Sex, 2000–2006

(Thousands of workers, dollars.)

Year and sex	Total	Less than a high school diploma	4 years of high school only	1 to 3 years of college	4 or more years of college
2000					
Both Sexes					
Number of workers	84 337	7 354	26 144	24 064	26 775
Median annual earnings	35 000	20 000	28 600	34 000	50 000
Men					
Number of workers	48 816	4 738	15 057	13 242	15 780
Median annual earnings	40 000	22 500	33 000	40 000	60 000
Women					
Number of workers	35 521	2 616	11 087	10 822	10 995
Median annual earnings	29 000	16 000	24 000	28 000	40 000
2001					
Both Sexes					
Number of workers	84 743	7 623	25 522	23 719	27 879
Median annual earnings	35 000	20 800	29 000	35 000	50 000
Men					
Number of workers	48 887	5 049	14 655	12 968	16 215
Median annual earnings	40 000	24 000	33 800	40 000	60 000
Women					
Number of workers	35 856	2 574	10 867	10 751	11 664
Median annual earnings	30 000	17 000	24 000	30 000	42 000
2002					
Both Sexes					
Number of workers	84 702	7 578	25 078	23 604	28 443
Median annual earnings	36 000	21 000	30 000	35 100	52 000
Men					
Number of workers	48 687	5 102	14 306	12 677	16 602
Median annual earnings	41 000	23 400	34 000	41 500	61 000
Women					
Number of workers	36 015	2 476	10 772	10 927	11 841
Median annual earnings	30 000	18 000	25 000	30 000	43 500
2003					
Both Sexes					
Number of workers	85 058	7 245	25 352	23 702	28 759
Median annual earnings	37 752	21 000	30 000	36 000	53 000
Men					
Number of workers	48 988	4 879	14 657	12 766	16 686
Median annual earnings	42 000	24 000	35 000	42 000	62 000
Women					
Number of workers	36 070	2 366	10 695	10 936	12 073
Median annual earnings	32 000	18 000	25 111	31 000	45 000
2004					
Both Sexes					
Number of workers	86 306	7 648	25 786	23 897	28 976
Median annual earnings	38 000	21 840	30 000	37 000	55 000
Men					
Number of workers	49 904	5 178	15 263	12 822	16 642
Median annual earnings	42 900	24 000	35 000	43 000	65 000
Women					
Number of workers	36 402	2 470	10 523	11 074	12 334
Median annual earnings	32 000	18 000	25 280	31 200	45 000
2005					
Both Sexes					
Number of workers	88 415	7 758	26 023	24 623	30 012
Median annual earnings	39 768	22 880	31 000	38 000	55 000
Men					
Number of workers	51 022	5 376	15 451	13 199	16 996
Median annual earnings	44 000	25 000	35 360	45 000	65 000
Women					
Number of workers	37 393	2 381	10 571	11 424	13 016
Median annual earnings	33 644	18 200	26 000	32 000	46 700
2006					
Both Sexes					
Number of workers	90 733	7 951	26 233	24 737	31 812
Median annual earnings	40 000	23 000	32 000	39 482	57 588
Men					
Number of workers	52 252	5 485	15 525	13 204	18 038
Median annual earnings	45 000	25 000	36 665	45 000	68 000
Women					
Number of workers	38 481	2 466	10 708	11 533	13 774
Median annual earnings	35 000	19 000	26 800	33 000	49 000

NOTES AND DEFINITIONS

CONTINGENT AND ALTERNATIVE EMPLOYMENT

Data on contingent workers is collected through a supplement to the Current Population Survey (CPS), a monthly survey of about 60,000 households that provides data on employment and unemployment for the nation. The purpose of this supplement is to obtain information from workers on whether they held contingent jobs (jobs expected to last for only a limited period of time). Information is also collected on several alternative employment arrangements, namely working on call and as independent contractors, as well as working through temporary help agencies or contract firms.

Several major changes introduced into the CPS in 2003 affect the data that is presented in this *Handbook*. These include the introduction of Census 2000 population controls, the use of new questions about race and Hispanic or Latino ethnicity, the presentation of data for Asians, and the introduction of new industry and occupational classification systems. All employed persons, except unpaid family workers, were included in the February 2005 supplement. For persons holding more than one job, the questions referred to the characteristics of their main job—the job at which they worked the most hours. Similar surveys were conducted in Februaries of 1995, 1997, 1999, and 2001, and 2005.

Defining and Estimating the Contingent Workforce

Contingent workers are defined as those who do not have an explicit or implicit contract for long-term employment. Several pieces of data are collected in the supplement; these allow the existence of a contingent employment arrangement to be discerned. Included information consists of the following: whether the job is temporary or not expected to continue, how long the worker expects to be able to hold the job, and how long the worker has held the job. For workers who have a job with an intermediary (namely a temporary help agency or a contract company), information is collected about their employment at the place they are assigned to work by the intermediary as well as about their employment with the intermediary itself.

The key factor used to determine whether a worker's job fits the conceptual definition of contingent is whether the job is temporary or not expected to continue. The first questions in the supplement ask: (1) "Some people are in temporary jobs that last only for a limited time or until the completion of a project. Is your job temporary?" (2) "Provided the economy does not change and your job performance is adequate, can you continue to work for your current employer as long as you wish?" Respondents who answer "yes" to the first question or "no" to the second are then asked a series of questions designed to distinguish persons in temporary jobs from those who, for personal reasons, are temporarily holding jobs that offer the opportunity of ongoing employment. For example, students holding part-time jobs in fast-food restaurants while in school might view those jobs as temporary if they intend to leave them at the end of the school year. Other workers, however, would be available to fill those jobs themselves once the students leave.

To assess the impact of altering some of the defining factors on the estimated size of the contingent workforce, three measures of contingent employment were developed:

1) Estimate one, which is the narrowest of the three estimates, measures contingent workers as wage and salary workers who expect to work in their current job for one year or less and who have worked for their current employer for one year or less. Self-employed workers, both incorporated and unincorporated, and independent contractors are excluded from the count of contingent workers under estimate one; individuals who work for temporary help agencies or contract companies are considered contingent under estimate one only if they expect their employment arrangement with the temporary help or contract company to last for one year or less and they have worked for the company for one year or less.

2) Estimate two expands the measure of the contingent work force by including the self-employed—both the incorporated and the unincorporated—and independent contractors who expect to be, and have been, in such employment arrangements for one year or less. (The questions asked of the self-employed are different from those asked of wage and salary workers.) In addition, temporary help and contract company workers are classified as contingent under estimate two if they have worked and expect to work with customers to whom they have been assigned for one year or less.

3) Estimate three expands the count of contingency by removing the one-year requirement on both expected duration of the job and current tenure for wage and salary workers. The estimate effectively includes all the wage and salary workers who do not expect their employment to last, except for those who, for personal reasons, expect to leave jobs that they would otherwise be able to keep. Thus, a worker who has held a job for five years could be considered contingent if he or she now views the job as temporary. These conditions on expected and current tenure are not relaxed for the self-employed and independent contractors because they are asked a different set of questions than wage and salary workers.

Sources of Additional Information

A complete description of the survey and additional tables are available from BLS news release USDL 05-1433, "Contingent and Alternative Employment Arrangements, February 2005" at <http://www.bls.gov>.

Table 1-62. Employed Contingent and Noncontingent Workers, by Selected Characteristics, February 2005

(Thousands of people.)

Characteristic	Total employed	Contingent workers			Noncontingent workers
		Estimate 1	Estimate 2	Estimate 3	
Age and Sex					
Both sexes, 16 years and over	138 952	2 504	3 177	5 705	133 247
16 to 19 years	5 510	308	338	476	5 035
20 to 24 years	13 114	606	688	1 077	12 036
25 to 34 years	30 103	693	874	1 447	28 656
35 to 44 years	34 481	415	580	1 044	33 437
45 to 54 years	32 947	263	387	875	32 072
55 to 64 years	17 980	143	198	536	17 445
65 years and over	4 817	76	111	250	4 567
Men, 16 years and over	73 946	1 325	1 648	2 914	71 032
16 to 19 years	2 579	145	157	229	2 351
20 to 24 years	6 928	358	394	597	6 331
25 to 34 years	16 624	395	512	829	15 794
35 to 44 years	18 523	245	303	540	17 983
45 to 54 years	17 193	95	140	368	16 825
55 to 64 years	9 485	70	107	261	9 224
65 years and over	2 615	17	35	92	2 523
Women, 16 years and over	65 006	1 180	1 529	2 790	62 216
16 to 19 years	2 931	163	182	247	2 684
20 to 24 years	6 186	249	294	481	5 705
25 to 34 years	13 480	298	362	618	12 862
35 to 44 years	15 958	171	277	504	15 454
45 to 54 years	15 754	168	247	508	15 247
55 to 64 years	8 495	73	91	275	8 220
65 years and over	2 202	58	76	158	2 044
Race and Hispanic Origin					
White	115 043	2 007	2 534	4 521	110 522
Black	14 688	296	387	660	14 028
Asian	6 083	121	161	350	5 733
Hispanic[1]	18 062	603	704	1 185	16 876
Full- or Part-Time Status					
Full-time workers	113 798	1 367	1 812	3 410	110 387
Part-time workers	25 154	1 137	1 364	2 294	22 860

Note: Noncontingent workers are those who do not fall into any estimate of contingent workers. Estimates for the above race groups (White, Black, and Asian) do not sum to total because data are not presented for all races. Detail for other characteristics may not sum to total due to rounding.

[1]May be of any race.

Table 1-63. Employed Contingent and Noncontingent Workers, by Occupation and Industry, February 2005

(Thousands of people, percent.)

Characteristic	Contingent workers			Noncontingent workers
	Estimate 1	Estimate 2	Estimate 3	
OCCUPATION				
Total, 16 years and over	2 504	3 177	5 705	133 247
Percent Distribution	100.0	100.0	100.0	100.0
Management, professional, and related	28.4	30.7	35.9	35.2
Management, business, and financial operations	5.5	8.0	8.7	14.6
Professional and related	22.8	22.6	27.2	20.6
Services	17.3	17.6	15.7	15.6
Sales and office	24.3	22.5	20.6	26.0
Sales and related	4.9	6.0	5.7	12.1
Office and administrative support	19.4	16.5	14.8	13.9
Natural resources, construction, and maintenance	16.5	16.7	16.1	10.2
Farming, fishing, and forestry	2.4	2.0	2.1	0.5
Construction and extraction	11.4	12.3	11.1	5.8
Installation, maintenance, and repair	2.7	2.4	2.9	3.8
Production, transportation, and material moving	13.6	12.5	11.7	13.1
Production	4.5	4.0	5.2	6.8
Transportation and material moving	9.1	8.5	6.5	6.2
INDUSTRY				
Total, 16 years and over	2 504	3 177	5 705	133 247
Percent Distribution	100.0	100.0	100.0	100.0
Agriculture and related industries	2.5	2.3	1.7	1.3
Mining	0.7	0.6	0.4	0.4
Construction	13.0	14.0	12.3	7.2
Manufacturing	6.7	6.0	6.4	11.9
Wholesale trade	3.2	2.9	2.2	3.2
Retail trade	6.4	6.7	6.4	12.4
Transportation and utilities	5.0	4.7	3.7	5.3
Information	1.6	1.3	2.1	2.3
Financial activities	1.4	2.6	3.1	7.7
Professional and business services	18.2	20.7	18.2	9.7
Education and health services	23.5	21.8	27.1	20.8
Leisure and hospitality	10.1	8.9	7.4	8.1
Other services	5.0	5.3	4.9	4.7
Public administration	2.8	2.3	4.0	4.9

Note: Noncontingent workers are those who do not fall into any estimate of contingent workers. See notes and definitions for more information on contingent and noncontingent workers. Detail may not sum to total due to rounding.

Table 1-64. Employed Workers with Alternative and Traditional Work Arrangements, by Selected Characteristics, February 2005

(Thousands of people.)

Characteristic	Total employed	Workers with alternative arrangements				Workers with traditional arrangements
		Independent contractors	On-call workers	Temporary help agency workers	Workers provided by contract firms	
Age and Sex						
Both sexes, 16 years and over	138 952	10 342	2 454	1 217	813	123 843
16 to 19 years	5 510	89	133	33	7	5 194
20 to 24 years	13 114	356	355	202	87	12 055
25 to 34 years	30 103	1 520	535	362	205	27 427
35 to 44 years	34 481	2 754	571	253	196	30 646
45 to 54 years	32 947	2 799	417	200	186	29 324
55 to 64 years	17 980	1 943	267	135	114	15 496
65 years and over	4 817	881	175	33	18	3 701
Men, 16 years and over	73 946	6 696	1 241	574	561	64 673
16 to 19 years	2 579	32	82	24	7	2 389
20 to 24 years	6 928	194	200	107	61	6 331
25 to 34 years	16 624	1 006	299	185	138	14 950
35 to 44 years	18 523	1 824	252	120	140	16 130
45 to 54 years	17 193	1 764	209	71	143	15 003
55 to 64 years	9 485	1 287	108	52	70	7 954
65 years and over	2 615	589	91	16	3	1 917
Women, 16 years and over	65 006	3 647	1 212	643	252	59 170
16 to 19 years	2 931	57	52	9	0	2 805
20 to 24 years	6 186	162	155	95	27	5 724
25 to 34 years	13 480	514	236	177	67	12 477
35 to 44 years	15 958	930	319	133	57	14 516
45 to 54 years	15 754	1 035	208	129	43	14 322
55 to 64 years	8 495	656	158	83	44	7 542
65 years and over	2 202	292	84	17	15	1 785
Race and Hispanic Origin						
White	115 043	9 169	2 097	840	637	102 052
Black	14 688	583	212	276	121	13 471
Asian	6 083	370	64	63	43	5 538
Hispanic[1]	18 062	951	385	255	133	16 202
Full- or Part-Time Status						
Full-time workers	113 798	7 732	1 370	979	695	102 889
Part-time workers	25 154	2 611	1 084	238	119	20 954

Note: Workers with traditional arrangements are those who do not fall into any of the "alternative arrangements" categories. Detail may not add to totals because the total employed includes day laborers (an alternative arrangement not shown separately) and a small number of workers who were both "on call" and "provided by contract firms." Estimates for the above race groups (White, Black, and Asian) do not sum to totals because data are not presented for all races. Detail for other characteristics may not sum to total due to rounding.

[1]May be of any race.

Table 1-65. Employed Contingent and Noncontingent Workers and Those with Alternative and Traditional Work Arrangements, by Health Insurance Coverage and Eligibility for Employer-Provided Pension Plans, February 2005

(Thousands of people, percent.)

Characteristic	Total employed	Percent with health insurance coverage		Percent eligible for employer-provided pension plan[1]	
		Total	Provided by employer[2]	Total	Included in employer-provided pension plan
Contingent Workers					
Estimate 1	2 504	51.8	9.4	9.2	4.6
Estimate 2	3 177	52.5	7.9	8.3	4.1
Estimate 3	5 705	59.1	18.1	18.6	12.4
Noncontingent Workers	133 247	79.4	52.1	49.6	44.7
With Alternative Arrangements					
Independent contractors	10 342	69.3	X	2.6	1.9
On-call workers	2 454	66.9	25.7	33.2	27.8
Temporary help agency workers	1 217	39.7	8.3	8.9	3.8
Workers provided by contract firms	813	80.2	48.9	42.6	33.5
With Traditional Arrangements	123 843	80.0	56.0	52.9	47.7

Note: Noncontingent workers are those who do not fall into any estimate of contingent workers. Workers with traditional arrangements are those who do not fall into any of the "alternative arrangements" categories. See notes and definitions for more information on contingent and noncontingent workers.

[1]Excludes the self-employed (incorporated and unincorporated); includes independent contractors who were self-employed.
[2]Excludes the self-employed (incorporated and unincorporated) and independent contractors.
X = Not applicable.

Table 1-66. Median Usual Weekly Earnings of Full- and Part-Time Contingent Wage and Salary Workers and Those with Alternative Work Arrangements, by Sex, Race, and Hispanic Origin, February 2005

(Dollars.)

Characteristic	Contingent workers			Workers with alternative arrangements			
	Estimate 1	Estimate 2	Estimate 3	Independent contractors	On-call workers	Temporary help agency workers	Workers provided by contract firms
Full-Time Workers							
Total, 16 years and over	405	411	488	716	519	414	756
Men	427	440	505	794	586	405	860
Women	376	383	423	462	394	424	595
White	413	421	498	731	561	418	772
Black	344	375	387	474	303	375	([1])
Asian	([1])	([1])	619	889	([1])	([1])	([1])
Hispanic[2]	335	331	370	603	417	311	513
Part-Time Workers							
Total, 16 years and over	152	152	161	253	173	224	204
Men	165	169	183	330	206	253	([1])
Women	142	138	149	216	159	202	([1])
White	154	154	163	252	177	247	([1])
Black	133	133	145	196	([1])	([1])	([1])
Asian	([1])	([1])	190	([1])	([1])	([1])	0
Hispanic[2]	152	153	175	207	249	([1])	([1])

Note: Earnings data for contingent workers exclude the incorporated self-employed and independent contractors. Data for independent contractors include the incorporated and unincorporated self-employed. However, these groups are excluded from the data for workers with other arrangements. Full- or part-time status is determined by hours usually worked at the sole or primary job. See notes and definitions for more information on contingent and noncontingent workers.

[1]Data not shown where base is less than 100,000.
[2]May be of any race.

NOTES AND DEFINITIONS

FLEXIBLE WORKERS

These data and other information on work schedules were obtained from a supplement to the May 2004 Current Population Survey (CPS). This was the first time since 2001 that the supplemental survey was conducted. Respondents to the May 2004 supplement answered questions about flexible and shift schedules, their reasons for working particular shifts, the beginning and ending hours of work, the availability of formal flextime programs and home-based work, and other related topics. The data cover the incidence and nature of flexible and shift schedules and pertain to wage and salary workers who usually work 35 hours or more per week at their principal job. The data exclude all self-employed persons, regardless of whether or not their businesses were incorporated.

Sources of Additional Information

For further information see BLS new release USDL 05-1198, "Workers on Flexible and Shift Schedules in May 2004," at <http://www.bls.gov>.

Table 1-67. Flexible Schedules: Full-Time Wage and Salary Workers, by Selected Characteristics, May 2004

(Thousands of people, percent.)

Characteristic	Both sexes			Men			Women		
	Total[1]	With flexible schedules		Total[1]	With flexible schedules		Total[1]	With flexible schedules	
		Number	Percent of total		Number	Percent of total		Number	Percent of total
Age									
Total, 16 years and over	99 778	27 411	27.5	56 412	15 853	28.1	43 366	11 558	26.7
16 to 19 years	1 427	336	23.6	903	185	20.5	524	151	28.9
20 years and over	98 351	27 075	27.5	55 509	15 668	28.2	42 842	11 406	26.6
20 to 24 years	9 004	2 058	22.9	5 147	1 065	20.7	3 856	993	25.8
25 to 34 years	24 640	6 902	28.0	14 358	4 051	28.2	10 283	2 851	27.7
35 to 44 years	26 766	7 807	29.2	15 424	4 605	29.9	11 342	3 202	28.2
45 to 54 years	24 855	6 651	26.8	13 440	3 769	28.0	11 415	2 882	25.2
55 to 64 years	11 745	3 181	27.1	6 383	1 865	29.2	5 361	1 316	24.5
65 years and over	1 341	475	35.4	757	314	41.4	585	161	27.6
Race and Hispanic Origin									
White	80 498	23 121	28.7	46 222	13 582	29.4	34 276	9 539	27.8
Black	12 578	2 476	19.7	6 447	1 193	18.5	6 131	1 283	20.9
Asian	4 136	1 132	27.4	2 300	720	31.3	1 836	412	22.4
Hispanic[2]	14 110	2 596	18.4	8 621	1 430	16.6	5 489	1 166	21.2
Marital Status									
Married, spouse present	57 630	16 270	28.2	34 926	10 382	29.7	22 704	5 888	25.9
Not married	42 148	11 141	26.4	21 486	5 471	25.5	20 662	5 670	27.4
Never married	25 144	6 693	26.6	14 469	3 605	24.9	10 676	3 088	28.9
Other marital status	17 004	4 448	26.2	7 018	1 866	26.6	9 986	2 582	25.9
Presence and Age of Children									
Without own children under 18 years	61 761	16 759	27.1	34 680	9 410	27.1	27 081	7 349	27.1
With own children under 18 years	38 018	10 652	28.0	21 733	6 443	29.6	16 285	4 209	25.8
With youngest child 6 to 17 years	21 739	5 960	27.4	11 477	3 341	29.1	10 262	2 619	25.5
With youngest child under 6 years	16 279	4 692	28.8	10 256	3 102	30.2	6 023	1 590	26.4

Note: Data relate to the sole or principal job of full-time wage and salary workers and exclude all self-employed persons, regardless of whether or not their businesses were incorporated. Detail for the above race and Hispanic origin groups will not sum to total because data for the "other races" group are not presented. Own children include sons, daughters, stepchildren, and adopted children. Not included are nieces, nephews, grandchildren, and other related and unrelated children.

[1]Includes persons who did not provide information on flexible schedules.
[2]May be of any race.

Table 1-68. Flexible Schedules: Full-Time Wage and Salary Workers, by Sex, Occupation, and Industry, May 2004

(Thousands of people, percent.)

Occupation and industry	Both sexes			Men			Women		
	Total[1]	With flexible schedules		Total[1]	With flexible schedules		Total[1]	With flexible schedules	
		Number	Percent of total		Number	Percent of total		Number	Percent of total
Occupation									
Total, 16 years and over	99 778	27 411	27.5	56 412	15 853	28.1	43 366	11 558	26.7
Management, professional, and related	36 200	13 325	36.8	17 911	7 832	43.7	18 289	5 492	30.0
Management, business, and financial operations	14 496	6 483	44.7	7 969	3 741	46.9	6 527	2 742	42.0
Management	10 036	4 598	45.8	6 000	2 862	47.7	4 035	1 736	43.0
Business and financial operations	4 461	1 885	42.3	1 969	879	44.7	2 492	1 006	40.4
Professional and related	21 704	6 842	31.5	9 942	4 091	41.1	11 762	2 751	23.4
Computer and mathematical	2 683	1 405	52.4	2 023	1 085	53.6	660	320	48.5
Architecture and engineering	2 478	1 080	43.6	2 147	917	42.7	330	163	49.3
Life, physical, and social sciences	1 016	483	47.5	640	285	44.6	376	198	52.6
Community and social services	1 866	860	46.1	786	430	54.7	1 080	430	39.8
Legal	1 118	497	44.5	536	312	58.2	582	185	31.8
Education, training, and library	6 414	843	13.1	1 779	374	21.0	4 635	469	10.1
Arts, design, entertainment, sports, and media	1 502	613	40.8	915	396	43.3	587	217	37.0
Health care practitioner and technical	4 626	1 060	22.9	1 115	291	26.1	3 511	769	21.9
Services	13 423	2 849	21.2	6 858	1 339	19.5	6 566	1 510	23.0
Health care support	1 908	315	16.5	199	37	18.7	1 708	278	16.3
Protective services	2 224	419	18.8	1 807	312	17.2	417	107	25.7
Food preparation and serving related	3 881	972	25.0	2 086	524	25.1	1 795	448	25.0
Building and grounds cleaning and maintenance	3 481	531	15.2	2 260	318	14.1	1 221	213	17.4
Personal care and services	1 929	612	31.7	505	148	29.2	1 424	465	32.6
Sales and office	24 359	7 196	29.5	9 561	3 069	32.1	14 798	4 127	27.9
Sales and related	9 634	3 669	38.1	5 683	2 305	40.6	3 952	1 364	34.5
Office and administrative support	14 724	3 527	24.0	3 878	764	19.7	10 847	2 763	25.5
Natural resources, construction, and maintenance	10 848	1 908	17.6	10 403	1 820	17.5	445	88	19.8
Farming, fishing, and forestry	744	172	23.1	591	132	22.4	152	39	25.7
Construction and extraction	5 825	942	16.2	5 750	925	16.1	74	17	([2])
Installation, maintenance, and repair	4 280	795	18.6	4 061	762	18.8	218	32	14.7
Production, transportation, and material moving	14 948	2 133	14.3	11 679	1 793	15.3	3 268	340	10.4
Production	8 281	1 030	12.4	5 928	806	13.6	2 353	224	9.5
Transportation and material moving	6 666	1 102	16.5	5 751	986	17.1	915	116	12.7
Industry									
Private sector	82 870	23 978	28.9	48 724	14 119	29.0	34 145	9 859	28.9
Agriculture and related industries	888	233	26.3	702	180	25.6	186	53	28.7
Nonagricultural industries	81 982	23 745	29.0	48 023	13 939	29.0	33 959	9 806	28.9
Mining	446	102	22.9	416	84	20.2	30	18	([2])
Construction	6 617	1 341	20.3	6 059	1 153	19.0	558	188	33.7
Manufacturing	15 125	3 631	24.0	10 659	2 638	24.7	4 466	993	22.2
Durable goods	9 249	2 351	25.4	6 881	1 794	26.1	2 368	558	23.6
Nondurable goods	5 875	1 280	21.8	3 777	844	22.3	2 098	436	20.8
Wholesale and retail trade	14 008	4 100	29.3	8 717	2 544	29.2	5 291	1 557	29.4
Wholesale trade	3 771	1 209	32.1	2 698	910	33.7	1 072	300	27.9
Retail trade	10 237	2 891	28.2	6 019	1 634	27.1	4 219	1 257	29.8
Transportation and utilities	4 226	1 086	25.7	3 454	906	26.2	771	179	23.2
Transportation and warehousing	3 482	912	26.2	2 858	767	26.8	624	145	23.3
Utilities	744	173	23.3	596	139	23.4	147	34	23.0
Information[3]	2 716	948	34.9	1 674	600	35.8	1 041	348	33.4
Publishing, except Internet	648	274	42.3	364	165	45.4	284	109	38.4
Motion picture and sound recording industries	211	74	35.3	162	62	38.5	49	12	([2])
Broadcasting, except Internet	512	116	22.7	319	79	24.7	193	37	19.4
Telecommunications	1 180	419	35.5	732	254	34.7	448	164	36.7
Financial activities	7 341	2 767	37.7	3 117	1 323	42.4	4 224	1 444	34.2
Finance and insurance	5 537	2 056	37.1	2 100	943	44.9	3 437	1 113	32.4
Finance	3 633	1 218	33.5	1 443	584	40.5	2 190	633	28.9
Insurance	1 904	838	44.0	657	359	54.6	1 247	480	38.5
Real estate and rental and leasing	1 805	711	39.4	1 017	380	37.3	787	332	42.1
Professional and business services	8 997	3 381	37.6	5 342	2 072	38.8	3 655	1 309	35.8
Professional and technical services	5 476	2 570	46.9	3 113	1 596	51.3	2 364	974	41.2
Management, administrative, and waste services	3 521	811	23.0	2 229	477	21.4	1 292	335	25.9
Education and health services	12 485	3 202	25.6	2 969	862	29.0	9 517	2 339	24.6
Education services	2 260	541	23.9	812	246	30.3	1 448	295	20.4
Health care and social assistance	10 226	2 661	26.0	2 157	616	28.6	8 069	2 045	25.3
Leisure and hospitality	6 111	1 686	27.6	3 458	956	27.6	2 653	730	27.5
Arts, entertainment, and recreation	1 134	312	27.5	630	165	26.2	504	147	29.2
Accommodation and food services	4 977	1 374	27.6	2 828	791	28.0	2 149	583	27.1
Accommodation	1 123	252	22.4	546	147	26.9	577	105	18.2
Food services and drinking places	3 854	1 122	29.1	2 282	644	28.2	1 572	478	30.4
Other services	3 911	1 502	38.4	2 158	801	37.1	1 753	701	40.0
Other services, except private households	3 584	1 370	38.2	2 140	792	37.0	1 444	577	40.0
Other services, private households	327	132	40.4	18	9	([2])	309	123	39.9
Public sector	16 909	3 433	20.3	7 688	1 734	22.6	9 221	1 699	18.4
Federal government	2 786	803	28.8	1 617	453	28.0	1 169	351	30.0
State government	4 724	1 340	28.4	2 089	640	30.7	2 635	700	26.6
Local government	9 399	1 289	13.7	3 982	641	16.1	5 417	648	12.0

Note: Data relate to the sole or principal job of full-time wage and salary workers and exclude all self-employed persons, regardless of whether or not their businesses were incorporated.

[1] Includes persons who did not provide information on flexible schedules.
[2] Percent not shown where base is less than 75,000.
[3] Includes other industries not shown separately.

Table 1-69. Flexible Schedules: Full-Time Wage and Salary Workers, by Formal Flextime Program Status, Occupation, and Industry, May 2004

(Thousands of people, percent.)

Occupation and industry	Total[1]	With flexible schedules	With a formal flextime program		
			Number	Percent of total employed	Percent of workers with flexible schedules
Occupation					
Total, 16 years and over	99 778	27 411	10 642	10.7	38.8
Management, professional, and related	36 200	13 325	5 137	14.2	38.6
Management, business, and financial operations	14 496	6 483	2 293	15.8	35.4
Management	10 036	4 598	1 436	14.3	31.2
Business and financial operations	4 461	1 885	857	19.2	45.5
Professional and related	21 704	6 842	2 844	13.1	41.6
Computer and mathematical	2 683	1 405	729	27.1	51.8
Architecture and engineering	2 478	1 080	509	20.5	47.1
Life, physical, and social sciences	1 016	483	203	19.9	42.0
Community and social services	1 866	860	325	17.4	37.8
Legal	1 118	497	140	12.6	28.2
Education, training, and library	6 414	843	278	4.3	33.0
Arts, design, entertainment, sports, and media	1 502	613	272	18.1	44.4
Health care practitioner and technical	4 626	1 060	389	8.4	36.6
Services	13 423	2 849	1 188	8.9	41.7
Health care support	1 908	315	139	7.3	44.3
Protective services	2 224	419	192	8.6	45.8
Food preparation and serving related	3 881	972	423	10.9	43.5
Building and grounds cleaning and maintenance	3 481	531	178	5.1	33.5
Personal care and services	1 929	612	256	13.3	41.8
Sales and office	24 359	7 196	2 734	11.2	38.0
Sales and related	9 634	3 669	1 175	12.2	32.0
Office and administrative support	14 724	3 527	1 559	10.6	44.2
Natural resources, construction, and maintenance	10 848	1 908	697	6.4	36.5
Farming, fishing, and forestry	744	172	47	6.3	27.1
Construction and extraction	5 825	942	416	7.1	44.2
Installation, maintenance, and repair	4 280	795	234	5.5	29.5
Production, transportation, and material moving	14 948	2 133	885	5.9	41.5
Production	8 281	1 030	490	5.9	47.6
Transportation and material moving	6 666	1 102	395	5.9	35.8
Industry					
Private sector	82 870	23 978	8 816	10.6	36.8
Agriculture and related industries	888	233	53	6.0	22.9
Nonagricultural industries	81 982	23 745	8 762	10.7	36.9
Mining	446	102	47	10.5	46.1
Construction	6 617	1 341	493	7.5	36.8
Manufacturing	15 125	3 631	1 618	10.7	44.6
Durable goods	9 249	2 351	1 061	11.5	45.1
Nondurable goods	5 875	1 280	557	9.5	43.5
Wholesale and retail trade	14 008	4 100	1 302	9.3	31.8
Wholesale trade	3 771	1 209	300	8.0	24.8
Retail trade	10 237	2 891	1 002	9.8	34.6
Transportation and utilities	4 226	1 086	432	10.2	39.8
Transportation and warehousing	3 482	912	335	9.6	36.7
Utilities	744	173	97	13.0	55.9
Information[2]	2 716	948	371	13.7	39.2
Publishing, except Internet	648	274	102	15.8	37.3
Motion picture and sound recording industries	211	74	33	15.9	(3)
Broadcasting, except Internet	512	116	43	8.4	37.2
Telecommunications	1 180	419	170	14.4	40.5
Financial activities	7 341	2 767	1 066	14.5	38.5
Finance and insurance	5 537	2 056	868	15.7	42.2
Finance	3 633	1 218	425	11.7	34.9
Insurance	1 904	838	443	23.3	52.9
Real estate and rental and leasing	1 805	711	198	11.0	27.9
Professional and business services	8 997	3 381	1 294	14.4	38.3
Professional and technical services	5 476	2 570	991	18.1	38.6
Management, administrative, and waste services	3 521	811	303	8.6	37.3
Education and health services	12 485	3 202	1 118	9.0	34.9
Education services	2 260	541	156	6.9	28.8
Health care and social assistance	10 226	2 661	962	9.4	36.2
Leisure and hospitality	6 111	1 686	598	9.8	35.4
Arts, entertainment, and recreation	1 134	312	84	7.4	27.1
Accommodation and food services	4 977	1 374	513	10.3	37.4
Accommodation	1 123	252	105	9.3	41.5
Food services and drinking places	3 854	1 122	408	10.6	36.4
Other services	3 911	1 502	422	10.8	28.1
Other services, except private households	3 584	1 370	404	11.3	29.5
Other services, private households	327	132	18	5.5	13.6
Public sector	16 909	3 433	1 826	10.8	53.2
Federal government	2 786	803	561	20.1	69.9
State government	4 724	1 340	665	14.1	49.6
Local government	9 399	1 289	600	6.4	46.5

Note: Data relate to the sole or principal job of full-time wage and salary workers and exclude all self-employed persons, regardless of whether or not their businesses were incorporated.

[1]Includes persons who did not provide information on flexible schedules.
[2]Includes other industries not shown separately.
[3]Percent not shown where base is less than 75,000.

Table 1-70. Shift Usually Worked: Full-Time Wage and Salary Workers, by Selected Characteristics, May 2004

(Thousands of people, percent.)

Characteristic	Total[1]	Regular daytime schedule	Shift workers						
			Total	Evening shift	Night shift	Rotating shift	Split shift	Employer-arranged irregular schedule	Other shift
Age and Sex									
Both sexes, 16 years and over	99 778	84.6	14.8	4.7	3.2	2.5	0.5	3.1	0.7
16 to 19 years	1 427	64.9	34.6	14.5	4.4	6.1	1.0	8.3	0.2
20 years and over	98 351	84.9	14.6	4.6	3.2	2.5	0.5	3.0	0.7
20 to 24 years	9 004	76.8	22.3	8.8	3.7	3.3	0.9	4.6	0.9
25 to 34 years	24 640	84.1	15.2	5.0	3.4	2.7	0.5	2.8	0.8
35 to 44 years	26 766	85.4	14.1	4.1	3.2	2.5	0.4	3.1	0.7
45 to 54 years	24 855	86.8	12.8	3.6	3.2	2.3	0.5	2.5	0.7
55 to 64 years	11 745	87.1	12.5	3.8	2.6	2.0	0.4	3.0	0.7
65 years and over	1 341	88.8	10.3	3.5	1.8	1.4	0.5	2.9	0.2
Men	56 412	82.7	16.7	5.2	3.6	2.8	0.5	3.6	0.9
Women	43 366	87.0	12.4	4.1	2.8	2.2	0.5	2.4	0.4
Race and Hispanic Origin									
White	80 498	85.8	13.7	4.1	3.0	2.3	0.5	3.1	0.7
Black	12 578	78.0	20.8	7.9	4.5	4.1	0.4	3.0	0.7
Asian	4 136	83.6	15.7	5.4	4.1	1.6	1.2	2.6	0.8
Hispanic[2]	14 110	83.1	16.0	5.8	3.9	2.1	0.6	2.6	0.9
Marital Status and Presence and Age of Children									
Men									
Married, spouse present	34 926	84.8	14.9	3.9	3.3	2.9	0.5	3.4	0.9
Not married	21 486	79.5	19.7	7.4	3.9	2.6	0.7	4.0	1.0
Never married	14 469	78.6	20.6	8.1	3.8	2.6	0.8	4.2	1.0
Other marital status	7 018	81.4	17.8	5.9	4.2	2.8	0.4	3.6	1.0
Without own children under 18 years	34 680	81.8	17.6	6.0	3.6	2.7	0.6	3.8	0.9
With own children under 18 years	21 733	84.3	15.3	4.0	3.6	3.0	0.5	3.2	1.0
With youngest child 6 to 17 years	11 477	85.1	14.6	3.9	3.2	3.1	0.2	3.4	0.8
With youngest child under 6 years	10 256	83.5	16.1	4.2	3.9	2.9	0.8	3.0	1.2
Women									
Married, spouse present	22 704	90.4	9.2	2.8	2.4	1.4	0.3	1.9	0.3
Not married	20 662	83.2	16.0	5.6	3.2	3.0	0.6	2.9	0.6
Never married	10 676	81.2	17.9	6.3	3.0	3.6	0.8	3.6	0.6
Other marital status	9 986	85.5	13.9	4.8	3.5	2.3	0.4	2.1	0.6
Without own children under 18 years	27 081	86.4	13.0	4.1	2.7	2.5	0.6	2.7	0.4
With own children under 18 years	16 285	87.9	11.5	4.3	2.9	1.7	0.3	1.9	0.4
With youngest child 6 to 17 years	10 262	89.1	10.5	3.4	3.0	1.6	0.2	1.8	0.5
With youngest child under 6 years	6 023	86.0	13.2	5.8	2.7	1.8	0.4	2.1	0.4

Note: Data relate to the sole or principal job of full-time wage and salary workers and exclude all self-employed persons, regardless of whether or not their businesses were incorporated. Detail for the above race and Hispanic origin groups will not sum to total because data for the "other races" group are not presented. Own children include sons, daughters, stepchildren, and adopted children. Not included are nieces, nephews, grandchildren, and other related and unrelated children.

[1]Includes persons who did not provide information on shift usually worked.
[2]May be of any race.

Table 1-71. Shift Usually Worked: Full-Time Wage and Salary Workers, by Occupation and Industry, May 2004

(Thousands of people, civilian labor force as a percent of the civilian noninstitutional population.)

Occupation and industry	Total[1]	Regular daytime schedule	Shift workers						
			Total	Evening shift	Night shift	Rotating shift	Split shift	Employer-arranged irregular schedule	Other shift
Occupation									
Total, 16 years and over	99 778	84.6	14.8	4.7	3.2	2.5	0.5	3.1	0.7
Management, professional, and related	36 200	91.9	7.6	1.7	1.6	1.3	0.3	2.2	0.5
Management, business, and financial operations	14 496	94.6	5.0	1.1	0.5	0.9	0.2	2.0	0.3
Management	10 036	93.6	6.1	1.4	0.5	1.1	0.3	2.4	0.4
Business and financial operations	4 461	96.8	2.7	0.5	0.6	0.4	0.1	0.9	0.2
Professional and related	21 704	90.1	9.4	2.1	2.4	1.6	0.3	2.3	0.7
Computer and mathematical	2 683	95.2	4.1	1.1	1.3	0.8	0.3	0.4	0.4
Architecture and engineering	2 478	95.7	3.9	0.9	1.2	0.7	0.1	0.7	0.4
Life, physical, and social sciences	1 016	93.9	5.8	1.1	1.4	2.0	0.0	1.2	0.1
Community and social services	1 866	87.0	12.7	1.9	1.3	2.2	0.3	4.9	2.0
Legal	1 118	97.4	1.8	0.0	0.0	0.0	0.2	1.4	0.2
Education, training, and library	6 414	97.3	2.3	0.6	0.1	0.2	0.4	0.9	0.2
Arts, design, entertainment, sports, and media	1 502	84.7	14.7	3.1	1.6	2.2	0.4	6.0	1.2
Health care practitioner and technical	4 626	74.5	24.6	5.8	8.3	4.4	0.5	4.4	1.1
Services	13 423	66.5	32.6	12.5	6.2	5.2	1.4	5.5	1.7
Health care support	1 908	70.4	28.0	12.5	7.1	3.8	0.7	3.1	0.7
Protective services	2 224	48.3	50.6	14.4	12.9	11.9	0.6	6.2	4.3
Food preparation and serving related	3 881	58.7	40.4	17.6	3.4	5.8	3.3	8.9	1.1
Building and grounds cleaning and maintenance	3 481	82.1	17.5	8.3	5.4	1.5	0.5	1.1	0.7
Personal care and services	1 929	70.9	28.1	7.3	4.6	4.5	1.0	8.1	2.7
Sales and office	24 359	87.3	12.0	3.5	2.6	2.3	0.3	2.8	0.3
Sales and related	9 634	83.8	15.2	3.5	1.9	3.8	0.6	5.0	0.4
Office and administrative support	14 724	89.6	9.9	3.6	3.0	1.4	0.2	1.4	0.3
Natural resources, construction, and maintenance	10 848	92.0	7.5	2.1	1.9	1.3	0.1	1.5	0.5
Farming, fishing, and forestry	744	89.8	9.8	0.6	2.4	1.4	1.0	2.4	2.0
Construction and extraction	5 825	95.1	4.4	0.8	0.8	1.2	0.1	1.3	0.3
Installation, maintenance, and repair	4 280	88.2	11.4	4.3	3.4	1.5	0.0	1.7	0.5
Production, transportation, and material moving	14 948	73.3	26.2	9.1	6.5	4.2	0.8	4.6	1.1
Production	8 281	75.0	24.4	10.1	7.1	4.7	0.3	1.4	0.8
Transportation and material moving	6 666	71.2	28.5	7.8	5.7	3.7	1.4	8.4	1.5
Industry									
Private sector	82 870	84.0	15.4	5.0	3.3	2.6	0.5	3.3	0.7
Agriculture and related industries	888	90.1	9.9	1.4	2.3	1.1	1.0	3.2	1.0
Nonagricultural industries	81 982	83.9	15.5	5.1	3.3	2.6	0.5	3.3	0.7
Mining	446	68.0	31.9	3.6	4.9	15.1	0.2	6.1	2.1
Construction	6 617	96.6	2.9	0.5	0.5	0.3	0.0	1.3	0.2
Manufacturing	15 125	81.5	18.1	7.2	5.2	3.3	0.3	1.2	0.8
Durable goods	9 249	85.3	14.4	6.7	4.2	1.9	0.2	0.7	0.7
Nondurable goods	5 875	75.6	23.8	8.1	6.8	5.4	0.5	1.9	1.1
Wholesale and retail trade	14 008	82.9	16.3	4.4	3.2	3.6	0.4	4.1	0.5
Wholesale trade	3 771	91.5	8.0	2.7	1.8	0.7	0.1	2.3	0.2
Retail trade	10 237	79.8	19.4	5.0	3.7	4.6	0.5	4.8	0.6
Transportation and utilities	4 226	71.4	27.9	5.0	4.8	4.0	1.7	11.0	1.3
Transportation and warehousing	3 482	67.5	31.8	5.6	5.6	3.9	1.9	13.1	1.4
Utilities	744	89.5	9.5	1.9	0.8	4.4	0.9	1.1	0.5
Information[2]	2 716	87.3	11.7	4.2	2.4	1.7	0.1	2.6	0.6
Publishing, except Internet	648	87.6	10.3	2.3	3.6	0.8	0.3	2.0	1.3
Motion picture and sound recording industries	211	85.0	15.0	5.5	2.2	1.8	0.0	5.5	0.0
Broadcasting, except Internet	512	84.4	15.0	6.4	0.1	2.9	0.3	3.3	1.3
Telecommunications	1 180	88.8	10.5	3.6	2.7	1.9	0.0	2.3	0.0
Financial activities	7 341	94.0	5.4	2.0	0.6	0.6	0.1	1.8	0.3
Finance and insurance	5 537	96.7	2.8	1.2	0.4	0.5	0.1	0.5	0.1
Finance	3 633	96.8	2.6	1.2	0.5	0.5	0.0	0.3	0.1
Insurance	1 904	96.5	3.1	1.2	0.3	0.4	0.2	0.8	0.2
Real estate and rental and leasing	1 805	85.6	13.4	4.3	1.4	1.0	0.2	5.9	0.7
Professional and business services	8 997	92.0	7.8	2.7	2.4	0.7	0.1	1.4	0.5
Professional and technical services	5 476	96.5	3.2	0.6	0.5	0.4	0.1	1.3	0.4
Management, administrative, and waste services ...	3 521	84.9	15.0	6.1	5.3	1.1	0.2	1.5	0.8
Education and health services	12 485	83.2	16.0	5.5	4.5	2.4	0.5	2.3	0.7
Education services	2 260	93.9	5.6	3.0	0.4	0.3	0.5	1.3	0.2
Health care and social assistance	10 226	80.9	18.3	6.0	5.4	2.9	0.5	2.6	0.8
Leisure and hospitality	6 111	60.8	38.3	15.2	4.8	5.2	2.4	9.4	1.2
Arts, entertainment, and recreation	1 134	67.7	31.9	10.2	7.9	1.6	0.7	9.2	2.1
Accommodation and food services	4 977	59.3	39.8	16.4	4.1	6.0	2.9	9.5	1.0
Accommodation	1 123	70.2	29.4	11.1	6.6	4.2	0.7	5.9	0.9
Food services and drinking places	3 854	56.1	42.8	17.9	3.3	6.6	3.5	10.5	1.0
Other services	3 911	88.9	10.6	1.5	1.0	1.9	0.3	4.8	1.0
Other services, except private households	3 584	89.3	10.3	1.4	1.0	1.9	0.3	4.9	0.8
Other services, private households	327	85.0	14.1	3.3	0.6	2.7	0.6	4.0	3.0
Public sector	16 909	87.6	11.9	3.4	2.9	2.4	0.4	1.9	0.9
Federal government	2 786	84.8	14.7	4.4	4.9	1.2	0.2	3.1	0.7
State government	4 724	87.9	11.5	3.8	3.3	1.9	0.4	1.4	0.7
Local government	9 399	88.3	11.3	2.9	2.0	3.0	0.4	1.8	1.1

Note: Data relate to the sole or principal job of full-time wage and salary workers and exclude all self-employed persons, regardless of whether or not their businesses were incorporated.

[1]Includes persons who did not provide information on shift usually worked.
[2]Includes other industries not shown seperately.

CHAPTER 2

EMPLOYMENT, HOURS, AND EARNINGS

EMPLOYMENT AND HOURS

HIGHLIGHTS

The employment, hours, and earnings data in this section are presented by industry and state and are derived from the Current Employment Statistics (CES) survey, which covers 400,000 establishments. The employment numbers differ from those presented in from the household survey in Chapter 1 because of dissimilarities in methodology, concepts, definitions, and coverage. As the CES survey data are obtained from payroll records, they are consistent for industry classifications. The data on hours and earnings are also likely to be more accurate.

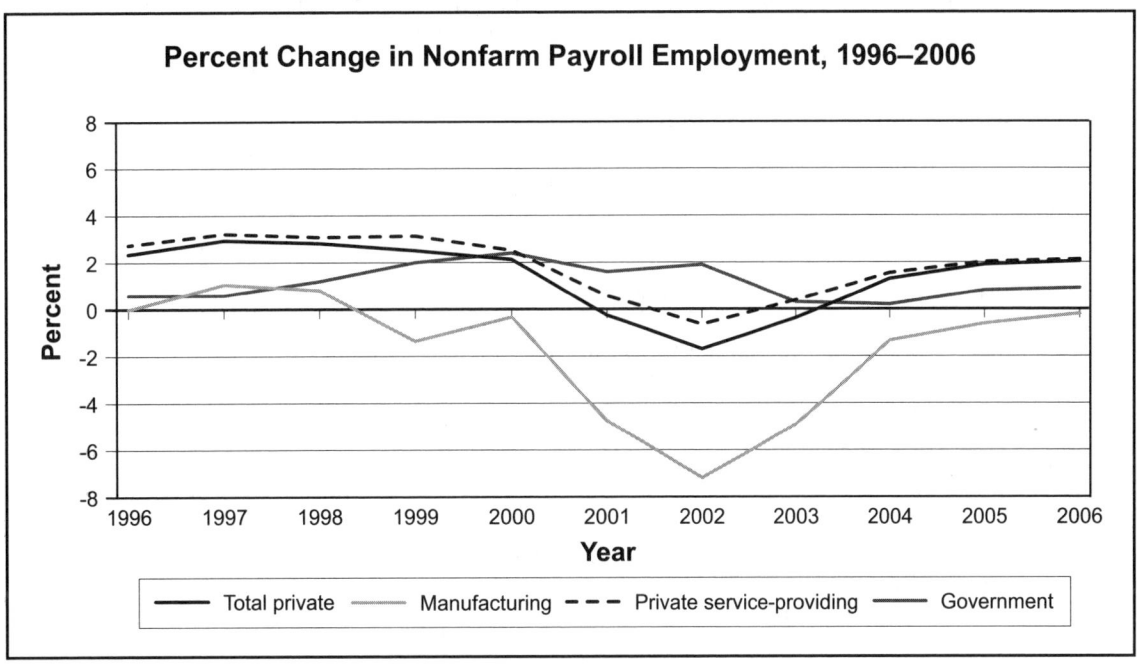

Total employment rose 1.8 percent in 2006, which was slightly higher than the increase in 2005. Employment was relatively stagnant from 2000 to 2003. Private employment rose 2.0 percent, while employment in government grew a slight 0.9 percent. (See Table 2-1.)

OTHER HIGHLIGHTS

- The private sector provided an increase of almost 2.3 million jobs in 2006, which accounted for almost 93 percent of the overall increase. (See Table 2-1.)

- In 2006, construction employment increased 4.8 percent, which was down slightly from the 5.2 percent increase in 2005. Manufacturing continued to decline. Employment in information remained about the same; however, there was a small decline in telecommunications employment. (See Table 2-1.)

- While government employment increased, federal government employment declined for the seventh time in a decade. (See Table 2-1.)

- Average weekly hours in manufacturing increased slightly in 2006. For the total private non-farm sector, the increase in average hours was very small, but aggregate weekly hours increased 3.0 percent. (See Tables 2-6 and 2-9.)

NOTES AND DEFINITIONS

EMPLOYMENT, HOURS, AND EARNINGS

Collection and Coverage

The Bureau of Labor Statistics (BLS) works with State Employment Security Agencies (SESAs) to conduct the Current Employment Statistics (CES), or establishment, survey. This survey collects monthly data on employment, hours, and earnings from a sample of nonfarm establishments (including government). The CES sample includes about 160,000 businesses and government agencies and covers approximately 400,000 individual worksites. The active CES sample includes approximately one-third of all nonfarm payroll workers. From these data, a large number of employment, hours, and earnings series with considerable industrial and geographic detail are prepared and published.

The most frequently used data collection method is the touchtone data entry (TDE) system. Under the TDE system, the respondent uses a touchtone telephone to call a toll-free number and activate an interview session. Other frequently used data collection methods include computer-assisted telephone interviewing (CATI), electronic files transmission (EDI), and interviews over the Internet.

Establishment survey data are adjusted annually to accord with comprehensive counts of employment in March of the preceding year; these adjustments are called "benchmarks." All estimates back to the most recent benchmark month are subject to revision each year when new benchmarks become available. National benchmarks are published 11 months after the benchmark month (March). The benchmarks are derived mainly from employment reports from all employers subject to unemployment insurance. The related series on production and nonsupervisory workers, hours, and earnings are recalculated to be consistent with the employment benchmarks.

Concepts and Definitions

Industry classification

The CES survey completed a conversion from its original quota sample design to a probability-based sample survey design, and switched from the Standard Industrial Classification (SIC) system to the North American Industry Classification System (NAICS) in 2003. The industry-coding update included reconstruction of historical estimates in order to preserve time series for data users. The foundation of industrial classification with NAICS has changed how establishments are classified into industries and how businesses, as they exist today, are recognized.

Establishments reporting on BLS Form 790 are classified into industries on the basis of their primary activities. Those that use comparable capital equipment, labor, and raw material inputs are classified together. This information is collected on a supplement to the quarterly unemployment insurance tax reports filed by employers.

For an establishment engaging in more than one activity, the entire employment of the establishment is included under the industry indicated by the principal activity.

Industry employment

Employment data refer to persons on establishment payrolls who received pay for any part of the pay period containing the 12th day of the month. The data exclude proprietors, the self-employed, unpaid volunteer or family workers, farm workers, and domestic workers. Salaried officers of corporations are included. Government employment covers only civilian employees; military personnel are excluded. Employees of the Central Intelligence Agency, the National Security Agency, the National Imagery and Mapping Agency, and the Defense Intelligence Agency are also excluded.

Persons on establishment payrolls who were on paid sick leave (for cases in which pay is received directly from the firm), paid holiday, or vacation leave, or who work during part of the pay period despite being unemployed or on strike during the rest of the period were counted as employed. Not counted as employed were persons on layoff, on leave without pay, on strike for the entire period, or who had been hired but had not yet reported during to their new jobs.

Beginning with the June 2003 publication of May 2003 data, the CES national federal government employment series has been estimated from a sample of federal establishments and benchmarked annually to counts from unemployment insurance tax records. It reflects employee counts as of the pay period containing the 12th day of the month, which is consistent with other CES industry series. Previously, the national series was an end-of-month count produced by the Office of Personnel Management.

The exclusion of farm employment, self-employment, and domestic service employment accounts from the payroll survey accounts for the differences in employment figures between the household and payroll surveys. The payroll survey also excludes workers on leave without pay. (These workers are counted as employed in the household survey.) Persons who worked in more than one establishment during the reporting period are counted each time their names appear on payrolls; these persons are only counted once in the household survey.

Production and related workers. This category includes working supervisors and all nonsupervisory workers (including group leaders and trainees) engaged in fabricating, processing, assembling, inspecting, receiving, storing, handling, packing, warehousing, shipping, trucking, hauling, maintenance, repair, janitorial, guard services, product development, auxiliary production for plant's own use (such as a power plant), record- keeping, and other services closely associated with production operations.

Construction workers. This group includes the following employees in the construction division: working supervisors, qualified craft workers, mechanics, apprentices, helpers, and laborers engaged in new work, alterations, demolition, repair, maintenance, and the like, whether working at the site of construction or at jobs in shops or yards at jobs (such as precutting and pre-assembling) ordinarily performed by members of the construction trades.

Nonsupervisory workers. This category consists of employees such as office and clerical workers, repairers, salespersons, operators, drivers, physicians, lawyers, accountants, nurses, social workers, research aides, teachers, drafters, photographers, beauticians, musicians, restaurant workers, custodial workers, attendants, line installers and repairers, laborers, janitors, guards, and other employees at similar occupational levels whose services are closely associated with those of the employees listed. It excludes persons in executive, managerial, and supervisory positions.

Payroll. This refers to payments made to full- and part-time production, construction, or nonsupervisory workers who received pay for any part of the pay period containing the 12th day of the month. The payroll is reported before deductions of any kind, such as those for old age and unemployment insurance, group insurance, withholding tax, bonds, or union dues. Also included is pay for overtime, holidays, and vacation, as well as for sick leave paid directly by the firm. Bonuses (unless earned and paid regularly each pay period), other pay not earned in the pay period reported (such as retroactive pay), tips, and the value of free rent, fuel, meals, or other payment-in-kind are excluded. Employee benefits (such as health and other types of insurance and contributions to retirement, as paid by the employer) are also excluded.

Total hours. During the pay period, total hours include all hours worked (including overtime hours), hours paid for standby or reporting time, and equivalent hours for which employees received pay directly from the employer for sick leave, holidays, vacations, and other leave. Overtime and other premium pay hours are not converted to straight-time equivalent hours. The concept of total hours differs from those of scheduled hours and hours worked. The average weekly hours derived from paid total hours reflect the effects of such factors as unpaid absenteeism, labor turnover, part-time work, and work stoppages, as well as fluctuations in work schedules.

Overtime hours. These are hours worked by production or related workers for which overtime premiums were paid because the hours were in excess of the number of hours of either the straight-time workday or the total workweek. Weekend and holiday hours are included only if overtime premiums were paid. Hours for which only shift differential, hazard, incentive, or other similar types of premiums were paid are excluded.

Average weekly hours. The workweek information relates to the average hours for which pay was received and is different from standard or scheduled hours. Such factors as unpaid absenteeism, labor turnover, part-time work, and

work stoppages cause average weekly hours to be lower than scheduled hours of work for an establishment. Group averages further reflect changes in the workweeks of component industries.

Industry hours and earnings. Average hours and earnings data are derived from reports of payrolls and hours for production and related workers in manufacturing and natural resources and mining, construction workers in construction, and nonsupervisory employees in private service-providing industries.

Indexes of aggregate weekly hours and payrolls. The indexes of aggregate weekly hours are calculated by dividing the current month's aggregate by the average of the 12 monthly figures for 1982. For basic industries, the hours aggregates are the product of average weekly hours and production worker or nonsupervisory worker employment. At all higher levels of industry aggregation, hours aggregates are the sum of the component aggregates.

The indexes of aggregate weekly payrolls are calculated by dividing the current month's aggregate by the average of the 12 monthly figures for 1982. For basic industries, the payroll aggregates are the product of average hourly earnings and aggregate weekly hours. At all higher levels of industry aggregation, payroll aggregates are the sum of the component aggregates.

Average overtime hours. Overtime hours represent the portion of average weekly hours that exceeded regular hours and for which overtime premiums were paid. If an employee worked during a paid holiday at regular rates, receiving as total compensation his or her holiday pay plus straight-time pay for hours worked that day, no overtime hours would be reported.

Since overtime hours are premium hours by definition, weekly hours and overtime hours do not necessarily move in the same direction from month to month. Factors such as work stoppages, absenteeism, and labor turnover may not have the same influence on overtime hours as on average hours. Diverse trends at the industry group level may also be caused by a marked change in hours for a component industry in which little or no overtime was worked in both the previous and current months.

Average hourly earnings. Average hourly earnings are on a "gross" basis. They reflect not only changes in basic hourly and incentive wage rates, but also such variable factors as premium pay for overtime and late-shift work and changes in output of workers paid on an incentive plan. They also reflect shifts in the number of employees between relatively high-paid and low-paid work and changes in workers' earnings in individual establishments. Averages for groups and divisions further reflect changes in average hourly earnings for individual industries.

Averages of hourly earnings differ from wage rates. Earnings are the actual return to the worker for a stated period; rates are the amount stipulated for a given unit of work or time. The earnings series do not measure the level of total labor costs on the part of the employer because the following items are excluded: irregular bonuses, retroactive items, payroll taxes paid by employers, and earnings for those employees not covered under the definitions of production workers, construction workers, or nonsupervisory employees.

Average hourly earnings, excluding overtime-premium pay, are computed by dividing the total production worker payroll for the industry group by the sum of total production worker hours and one-half of total overtime hours. No adjustments are made for other premium payment provisions, such as holiday pay, late-shift premiums, and overtime rates other than time and one-half.

Average weekly earnings. These estimates are derived by multiplying average weekly hours estimates by average hourly earnings estimates. Therefore, weekly earnings are affected not only by changes in average hourly earnings but also by changes in the length of the workweek. Monthly variations in factors, such as the proportion of part-time workers, work stoppages, labor turnover during the survey period, and absenteeism for which employees are not paid may cause the average workweek to fluctuate.

Long-term trends of average weekly earnings can be affected by structural changes in the makeup of the workforce. For example, persistent long-term increases in the proportion of part-time workers in retail trade and many of the services industries have reduced average workweeks in these industries and have affected the average weekly earnings series.

These earnings are in constant dollars and are calculated from the earnings averages for the current month using a deflator derived from the Consumer Price Index for Urban Wage Earnings and Clerical Workers (CPI-W). The reference year for these series is 1982.

Experimental All Employee Hours and Earnings Series from the Current Employment Statistics Program

Background

The Current Employment Statistics (CES) program began work in 2005 to add new series on hours and earnings. New series have been developed to measure the average hourly earnings, average weekly hours, and gross monthly earnings of all nonfarm private sector employees. The new hours and earnings series are more comprehensive in coverage, thereby providing improved information for analyzing economic trends and improved input to productivity and personal income series.

Additionally, CES is adding average overtime hours in manufacturing. Historically, the CES program has published average hours and earnings series for production workers in the goods-producing industries and nonsupervisory workers in the service-providing industries. These workers account for about 80 percent of total private nonfarm employment.

Experimental designation and future publication plans

BLS is designating the first release of these new series as experimental because of the limited experience to date with the editing and review of the sample reports and the resultant estimates. BLS began the first collection of the all employee payroll, hours, and gross monthly earnings data from respondents late in 2005. There is not yet enough historical information to apply all of the edit and review techniques used in the published CES data to these new series, nor is there sufficient data to allow seasonal adjustment of the new series.

The first release of experimental series on April 6, 2007, included national-level estimates at a total private-sector level and limited industry detail from March 2006 through January 2007. As BLS and data users gain more experience with these new data series, additional industry detail may be released, and publication of first and second preliminary estimates may be added over the next two to three years.

Beginning in March 2008, BLS plans to publish experimental all employee hours and earnings series in limited industry detail for all states. Total private gross monthly earnings will also be published at the statewide level. For metropolitan statistical areas (MSAs), BLS will publish total private all employee hours and earnings; in some cases, limited industry detail also will be available. There will be no gross monthly earnings data published for MSAs.

By the end of 2009, BLS should have sufficient historical data to seasonally adjust the all employee payroll and hours series. Beginning in February 2010, the bureau and is planning to publish them as official CES data in the "Employment Situation" news release and other BLS publications.

Definitions and Methodology

In order to publish all employee average weekly hours, average hourly earnings, and average weekly earnings, BLS is collecting all employees total payroll and all employees total hours from survey respondents. The definitions of these data items parallel the definitions used for the production worker payroll and hours data; the only difference is that they cover all employees, rather than just production or nonsupervisory workers. More detailed information on current estimation formulas can be found at <http://www.bls.gov/web/cestn1.htm>.

Sources of Additional Information

For further information on sampling and estimation methods see the updated version of Chapter 2 in the *BLS Handbook of Methods*, BLS news releases, and the publication *Employment and Earnings*. All of these resources are available on the BLS Web site at <http://www.bls.gov>.

Table 2-1. Employees on Nonfarm Payrolls, by Super Sector and Selected Component Groups, NAICS Basis, 1995–2006

(Thousands of people.)

Industry	1995	1996	1997	1998	1999	2000	2001	2002	2003	2004	2005	2006
TOTAL	117 298	119 708	122 776	125 930	128 993	131 785	131 826	130 341	129 999	131 435	133 703	136 174
Total Private	97 866	100 169	103 113	106 021	108 686	110 996	110 707	108 828	108 416	109 814	111 899	114 184
Goods-Producing	23 156	23 410	23 886	24 354	24 465	24 649	23 873	22 557	21 816	21 882	22 190	22 570
Natural Resources and Mining	641	637	654	645	598	599	606	583	572	591	628	684
Mining	558	556	571	565	517	520	533	512	503	523	562	619
Logging	83	81	82	80	81	79	74	70	69	68	65	65
Construction	5 274	5 536	5 813	6 149	6 545	6 787	6 826	6 716	6 735	6 976	7 336	7 689
Construction of buildings	1 325	1 380	1 435	1 509	1 586	1 633	1 589	1 575	1 576	1 630	1 712	1 806
Heavy and civil engineering	775	800	825	865	909	937	953	931	903	907	951	983
Specialty trade contractors	3 174	3 355	3 553	3 775	4 050	4 217	4 284	4 210	4 256	4 439	4 673	4 900
Manufacturing	17 241	17 237	17 419	17 560	17 322	17 263	16 441	15 259	14 510	14 315	14 226	14 197
Durable goods	10 372	10 485	10 704	10 910	10 830	10 876	10 335	9 483	8 963	8 924	8 955	9 001
Wood product	574	583	595	609	620	613	574	555	538	550	559	560
Nonmetallic mineral product	513	517	526	535	541	554	545	516	494	506	505	508
Primary metals	642	639	639	642	625	622	571	509	477	467	466	462
Fabricated metal product	1 623	1 648	1 696	1 740	1 728	1 753	1 676	1 549	1 479	1 497	1 522	1 554
Machinery	1 440	1 467	1 494	1 512	1 466	1 455	1 368	1 230	1 149	1 143	1 163	1 191
Computer and electronic product	1 688	1 747	1 803	1 831	1 781	1 820	1 749	1 507	1 355	1 323	1 316	1 316
Electrical equipment and appliances	593	591	586	592	588	591	557	497	460	445	434	436
Transportation equipment	1 977	1 974	2 026	2 077	2 087	2 056	1 938	1 829	1 774	1 766	1 771	1 765
Furniture and related product	607	604	615	641	665	680	642	604	573	573	565	556
Miscellaneous manufacturing	715	716	723	732	729	733	715	688	663	656	652	652
Nondurable goods	6 869	6 752	6 716	6 650	6 492	6 388	6 107	5 775	5 547	5 391	5 272	5 197
Food manufacturing	1 560	1 562	1 558	1 555	1 550	1 553	1 551	1 526	1 518	1 494	1 478	1 484
Beverage and tobacco product	203	204	206	209	208	207	209	207	200	195	192	195
Textile mills	469	443	436	425	397	378	333	291	261	237	218	196
Textile product mills	219	216	217	217	217	216	206	195	179	176	170	161
Apparel	814	743	700	639	556	497	427	360	312	286	257	238
Paper and paper product	640	631	631	625	616	605	578	547	516	496	484	469
Printing and related support activities	817	816	821	828	815	807	768	707	681	663	646	636
Petroleum and coal product	140	137	136	135	128	123	121	118	114	112	112	114
Chemicals	988	985	987	993	983	980	959	928	906	887	872	869
Plastics and rubber product	915	920	934	943	948	952	897	848	815	806	803	797
Private Service-Providing	74 710	76 759	79 227	81 667	84 221	86 346	86 834	86 271	86 599	87 932	89 709	91 615
Trade, Transportation, and Utilities	23 834	24 239	24 700	25 186	25 771	26 225	25 983	25 497	25 287	25 533	25 959	26 231
Wholesale Trade	5 433	5 522	5 664	5 795	5 893	5 933	5 773	5 652	5 608	5 663	5 764	5 898
Durable goods	2 909	2 978	3 072	3 162	3 220	3 251	3 130	3 008	2 941	2 951	2 999	3 077
Nondurable goods	1 969	1 978	2 008	2 033	2 061	2 065	2 031	2 015	2 005	2 010	2 022	2 040
Electronic markets, agents, and brokers	555	567	584	600	612	618	611	629	662	702	743	781
Retail Trade	13 897	14 143	14 389	14 609	14 970	15 280	15 239	15 025	14 917	15 058	15 280	15 319
Motor vehicle and parts dealers	1 627	1 686	1 723	1 741	1 797	1 847	1 855	1 879	1 883	1 902	1 919	1 908
Furniture and home furnishing stores	461	474	485	499	524	544	541	539	547	563	576	589
Electronic and appliance stores	449	470	494	510	542	564	555	525	512	516	536	538
Building material and garden supply stores	982	1 007	1 043	1 062	1 101	1 142	1 152	1 177	1 185	1 227	1 276	1 323
Food and beverage stores	2 880	2 928	2 957	2 966	2 985	2 993	2 951	2 882	2 838	2 822	2 818	2 828
Health and personal care stores	812	826	853	876	898	928	952	939	938	941	954	956
Gasoline stations	922	946	956	961	944	936	925	896	882	876	871	861
Clothing and clothing accessories stores	1 246	1 221	1 236	1 269	1 307	1 322	1 321	1 313	1 305	1 364	1 415	1 439
Sporting goods, hobby, and music stores	606	614	626	635	664	686	679	661	647	641	647	647
General merchandise stores	2 635	2 657	2 658	2 687	2 752	2 820	2 842	2 812	2 822	2 863	2 934	2 913
Miscellaneous store retailers	841	874	913	950	986	1 007	993	960	931	914	900	885
Nonstore retailers	435	439	445	453	472	492	474	444	427	429	435	434
Transportation and Warehousing	3 838	3 935	4 027	4 168	4 300	4 410	4 372	4 224	4 185	4 249	4 361	4 466
Air transportation	511	526	542	563	586	614	615	564	528	515	501	487
Rail transportation	233	225	221	225	229	232	227	218	218	226	228	225
Water transportation	51	51	51	51	52	56	54	53	55	56	61	64
Truck transportation	1 249	1 282	1 308	1 354	1 392	1 406	1 387	1 339	1 326	1 352	1 398	1 437
Transit and ground passenger transportation	328	339	350	363	371	372	375	381	382	385	389	394
Pipeline transportation	54	51	50	48	47	46	45	42	40	38	38	39
Scenic and sightseeing transportation	22	23	25	25	26	28	29	26	27	27	29	27
Support activities for transportation	430	446	473	497	518	537	539	525	520	535	552	571
Couriers and messengers	517	540	546	568	586	605	587	561	562	557	571	585
Warehousing and storage	444	452	462	474	494	514	514	517	528	558	595	636

Table 2-1. Employees on Nonfarm Payrolls, by Super Sector and Selected Component Groups, NAICS Basis, 1995–2006—*Continued*

(Thousands of people.)

Industry	1995	1996	1997	1998	1999	2000	2001	2002	2003	2004	2005	2006
Utilities	666	640	621	613	609	601	599	596	577	564	554	549
Information	2 843	2 940	3 084	3 218	3 419	3 631	3 629	3 395	3 188	3 118	3 061	3 055
Publishing industries, except Internet	911	927	956	982	1 005	1 035	1 021	964	925	909	904	904
Motion picture and sound recording industry	311	335	353	370	384	383	377	388	376	385	378	378
Broadcasting, except Internet	298	309	313	321	329	344	345	334	324	325	328	331
Internet publishing and broadcasting	19	21	24	27	37	51	46	34	29	30	32	35
Telecommunications	976	997	1 060	1 108	1 180	1 263	1 302	1 187	1 082	1 035	992	973
ISPs, search portals, and data processing	291	312	339	369	439	510	494	441	402	384	378	383
Other information services	38	39	40	41	44	46	46	47	49	51	51	51
Financial Activities	6 827	6 969	7 178	7 462	7 648	7 687	7 807	7 847	7 977	8 031	8 153	8 363
Finance and insurance	5 072	5 154	5 305	5 532	5 668	5 680	5 773	5 817	5 923	5 949	6 023	6 184
Monetary authorities, central bank	23	23	22	22	23	23	23	23	23	22	21	22
Credit intermediation	2 314	2 368	2 434	2 532	2 591	2 548	2 598	2 686	2 792	2 817	2 869	2 937
Securities, commodity contracts, and investments	562	590	636	692	737	805	831	789	758	766	786	816
Insurance carriers and related activities	2 108	2 108	2 144	2 209	2 236	2 221	2 234	2 233	2 266	2 259	2 259	2 316
Funds, trusts, and other financial vehicles	64	66	70	77	82	85	88	85	84	85	88	93
Real estate and rental and leasing	1 755	1 814	1 873	1 930	1 979	2 007	2 035	2 030	2 054	2 082	2 130	2 180
Real estate	1 179	1 206	1 241	1 274	1 299	1 312	1 340	1 353	1 384	1 415	1 457	1 503
Rental and leasing services	557	588	610	631	653	667	666	649	643	641	646	647
Lessors of nonfinancial intangible assets	19	21	23	25	27	28	29	28	27	26	27	29
Professional and Business Services	12 844	13 462	14 335	15 147	15 957	16 666	16 476	15 976	15 987	16 395	16 954	17 552
Professional and technical services	5 101	5 337	5 656	6 021	6 375	6 734	6 902	6 676	6 630	6 774	7 053	7 372
Management of companies and enterprises	1 686	1 703	1 730	1 756	1 774	1 796	1 779	1 705	1 687	1 724	1 759	1 809
Administrative and waste services	6 057	6 422	6 950	7 369	7 807	8 136	7 795	7 595	7 670	7 896	8 142	8 371
Administrative and support services	5 783	6 140	6 659	7 070	7 497	7 823	7 478	7 277	7 348	7 567	7 804	8 024
Waste management and remediation services	273	282	291	299	311	313	317	318	322	329	338	347
Education and Health Services	13 289	13 683	14 087	14 446	14 798	15 109	15 645	16 199	16 588	16 953	17 372	17 838
Education services	2 010	2 078	2 155	2 233	2 320	2 390	2 511	2 643	2 695	2 763	2 836	2 918
Health care and social assistance	11 278	11 605	11 932	12 214	12 477	12 718	13 134	13 556	13 893	14 190	14 536	14 920
Ambulatory health care services	3 768	3 940	4 093	4 161	4 227	4 320	4 462	4 633	4 786	4 952	5 114	5 283
Hospitals	3 734	3 773	3 822	3 892	3 936	3 954	4 051	4 160	4 245	4 285	4 345	4 427
Nursing and residential health facilities	2 308	2 380	2 443	2 487	2 529	2 583	2 676	2 743	2 786	2 818	2 855	2 901
Social assistance	1 470	1 512	1 574	1 673	1 786	1 860	1 946	2 020	2 075	2 135	2 222	2 309
Leisure and Hospitality	10 501	10 777	11 018	11 232	11 543	11 862	12 036	11 986	12 173	12 493	12 816	13 143
Arts, entertainment, and recreation	1 459	1 522	1 600	1 645	1 709	1 788	1 824	1 783	1 813	1 850	1 892	1 927
Performing arts and spectator sports	308	329	350	350	361	382	382	364	372	368	376	399
Museums, historical sites	84	89	94	97	103	110	115	114	115	118	121	124
Amusements, gambling, and recreation	1 068	1 105	1 157	1 198	1 245	1 296	1 327	1 305	1 327	1 364	1 395	1 404
Accommodation and food services	9 042	9 254	9 418	9 586	9 834	10 074	10 211	10 203	10 360	10 643	10 923	11 216
Accommodation	1 653	1 699	1 730	1 774	1 832	1 884	1 852	1 779	1 775	1 790	1 819	1 833
Food services and drinking places	7 389	7 555	7 689	7 813	8 002	8 189	8 359	8 425	8 584	8 854	9 104	9 383
Other Services	4 572	4 690	4 825	4 976	5 087	5 168	5 258	5 372	5 401	5 409	5 395	5 432
Repair and maintenance	1 079	1 136	1 169	1 189	1 222	1 242	1 257	1 247	1 234	1 229	1 236	1 249
Personal and laundry services	1 144	1 166	1 180	1 206	1 220	1 243	1 255	1 257	1 264	1 273	1 277	1 284
Membership associations and organizations	2 349	2 389	2 475	2 581	2 644	2 683	2 746	2 868	2 904	2 908	2 882	2 899
Government	19 432	19 539	19 664	19 909	20 307	20 790	21 118	21 513	21 583	21 621	21 804	21 990
Federal	2 949	2 877	2 806	2 772	2 769	2 865	2 764	2 766	2 761	2 730	2 732	2 728
Federal, excluding U.S. Postal Service	2 099	2 010	1 940	1 891	1 880	1 985	1 891	1 924	1 952	1 948	1 957	1 958
State	4 635	4 606	4 582	4 612	4 709	4 786	4 905	5 029	5 002	4 982	5 032	5 080
State, excluding education	2 716	2 695	2 678	2 690	2 726	2 756	2 792	2 786	2 748	2 744	2 772	2 785
Local	11 849	12 056	12 276	12 525	12 829	13 139	13 449	13 718	13 820	13 909	14 041	14 182
Local, excluding education	5 396	5 464	5 517	5 604	5 709	5 845	5 970	6 063	6 110	6 144	6 185	6 243

Table 2-2. Women Employees on Nonfarm Payrolls, by Super Sector and Selected Component Groups, NAICS Basis, 1995–2006

(Thousands of people.)

Industry	1995	1996	1997	1998	1999	2000	2001	2002	2003	2004	2005	2006
TOTAL NONFARM	56 213	57 406	58 914	60 309	61 810	63 222	63 683	63 360	63 237	63 739	64 718	65 571
Total Private	45 514	46 573	47 923	49 144	50 358	51 452	51 669	51 033	50 901	51 404	52 329	53 338
Goods-Producing	6 225	6 214	6 294	6 353	6 299	6 297	5 961	5 486	5 192	5 117	5 104	5 097
Natural resources and mining	98	96	99	100	96	92	90	85	80	80	79	82
Construction	666	700	730	769	818	846	832	827	822	841	890	945
Manufacturing	5 462	5 417	5 466	5 484	5 386	5 359	5 039	4 574	4 290	4 197	4 136	4 070
Private Service-Providing	39 289	40 360	41 629	42 791	44 059	45 155	45 708	45 547	45 709	46 287	47 225	48 241
Trade, transportation, and utilities	9 870	10 043	10 230	10 413	10 658	10 859	10 768	10 466	10 321	10 364	10 535	10 601
Wholesale trade	1 668	1 701	1 746	1 778	1 809	1 827	1 770	1 718	1 700	1 714	1 738	1 794
Retail trade	7 021	7 142	7 272	7 380	7 543	7 680	7 635	7 449	7 339	7 387	7 524	7 565
Transportation and warehousing	1 018	1 043	1 060	1 103	1 154	1 202	1 212	1 149	1 134	1 117	1 130	1 096
Utilities	163	157	153	152	152	151	151	150	147	146	143	146
Information	1 380	1 433	1 481	1 514	1 600	1 697	1 684	1 554	1 428	1 366	1 333	1 312
Financial activities	4 164	4 241	4 359	4 515	4 605	4 638	4 726	4 755	4 830	4 831	4 896	5 053
Professional and business services	5 979	6 273	6 705	7 030	7 370	7 680	7 591	7 314	7 248	7 360	7 574	7 774
Education and health services	10 181	10 474	10 779	11 042	11 323	11 586	12 037	12 474	12 786	13 073	13 408	13 769
Leisure and hospitality	5 382	5 520	5 640	5 760	5 933	6 082	6 224	6 215	6 319	6 516	6 708	6 921
Other services	2 333	2 376	2 435	2 517	2 570	2 614	2 677	2 769	2 779	2 776	2 772	2 810
Government	10 698	10 832	10 991	11 164	11 452	11 771	12 015	12 327	12 337	12 335	12 389	12 233
Federal	1 285	1 261	1 240	1 184	1 174	1 231	1 148	1 155	1 173	1 168	1 177	1 193
State	2 326	2 316	2 324	2 354	2 412	2 464	2 534	2 621	2 599	2 562	2 575	2 634
Local	7 088	7 255	7 426	7 627	7 866	8 076	8 333	8 551	8 565	8 606	8 637	8 407

Table 2-3. Production Workers on Private Nonfarm Payrolls, by Super Sector, NAICS Basis, 1995–2006

(Thousands of people.)

Industry	1995	1996	1997	1998	1999	2000	2001	2002	2003	2004	2005	2006
TOTAL PRIVATE	79 845	81 773	84 158	86 316	88 430	90 336	89 983	88 393	87 658	88 937	91 135	93 503
Goods-Producing	17 137	17 318	17 698	18 008	18 067	18 169	17 466	16 400	15 732	15 821	16 145	16 586
Natural resources and mining	458	461	479	473	438	446	457	436	420	440	473	518
Construction	4 113	4 325	4 546	4 807	5 105	5 295	5 332	5 196	5 123	5 309	5 611	5 900
Manufacturing	12 566	12 532	12 673	12 729	12 524	12 428	11 677	10 768	10 190	10 072	10 060	10 168
Private Service-Providing	62 708	64 455	66 460	68 308	70 363	72 167	72 517	71 993	71 926	73 116	74 990	76 917
Trade, transportation, and utilities	19 984	20 325	20 698	21 059	21 576	21 965	21 709	21 337	21 078	21 319	21 830	22 126
Wholesale trade	4 361	4 423	4 523	4 605	4 673	4 686	4 555	4 474	4 396	4 444	4 584	4 719
Retail trade	11 841	12 057	12 274	12 440	12 772	13 040	12 952	12 774	12 655	12 788	13 030	13 080
Transportation and warehousing	3 260	3 339	3 407	3 522	3 642	3 753	3 718	3 611	3 563	3 637	3 774	3 885
Utilities	522	506	494	492	489	485	483	478	464	450	443	442
Information	2 007	2 096	2 181	2 217	2 351	2 502	2 530	2 398	2 347	2 371	2 386	2 412
Financial activities	5 165	5 279	5 415	5 605	5 728	5 737	5 810	5 872	5 967	5 989	6 090	6 307
Professional and business services	10 645	11 161	11 896	12 566	13 184	13 790	13 588	13 049	12 910	13 287	13 854	14 435
Education and health services	11 765	12 123	12 478	12 791	13 089	13 362	13 846	14 311	14 532	14 771	15 129	15 549
Leisure and hospitality	9 330	9 565	9 780	9 947	10 216	10 516	10 662	10 576	10 666	10 955	11 263	11 599
Other services	3 812	3 907	4 013	4 124	4 219	4 296	4 373	4 449	4 426	4 425	4 438	4 489

Table 2-4. Production Workers on Durable Goods Manufacturing Payrolls, by Industry, NAICS Basis, 1995–2006

(Thousands of people.)

Industry	1995	1996	1997	1998	1999	2000	2001	2002	2003	2004	2005	2006
Total Durable Goods	7 351	7 425	7 597	7 720	7 650	7 658	7 163	6 529	6 152	6 139	6 219	6 369
Wood product	478	485	497	508	514	506	468	449	433	444	453	451
Nonmetallic mineral product	400	405	413	421	426	440	427	399	375	388	387	390
Primary metals	500	500	502	505	492	490	447	396	370	364	363	361
Fabricated metal product	1 223	1 242	1 285	1 320	1 305	1 326	1 254	1 147	1 093	1 109	1 129	1 163
Machinery	969	983	1 006	1 015	977	960	889	785	731	728	748	776
Computer and electronic product	890	915	951	965	933	949	876	744	673	656	700	761
Electrical equipment and appliances	438	434	428	432	433	433	402	352	320	307	300	305
Transportation equipment	1 471	1 480	1 521	1 529	1 525	1 497	1 398	1 309	1 269	1 264	1 276	1 302
Furniture and related product	480	478	490	512	532	544	509	475	444	444	435	432
Miscellaneous manufacturing	502	503	507	514	512	513	493	473	445	435	428	429

Table 2-5. Production Workers on Nondurable Goods Manufacturing Payrolls, by Industry, NAICS Basis, 1995–2006

(Thousands of people.)

Industry	1995	1996	1997	1998	1999	2000	2001	2002	2003	2004	2005	2006
Total Nondurable Goods	5 215	5 107	5 076	5 009	4 873	4 770	4 514	4 239	4 038	3 933	3 841	3 799
Food manufacturing	1 221	1 228	1 228	1 228	1 229	1 228	1 221	1 202	1 193	1 178	1 170	1 176
Beverage and tobacco product	117	120	121	123	120	117	116	120	106	107	112	115
Textile mills	393	372	367	357	334	315	276	242	217	194	174	158
Textile product mills	176	173	175	174	173	172	164	154	141	141	138	130
Apparel	719	650	612	550	472	415	351	294	249	225	198	187
Leather and allied product	89	79	74	67	60	55	47	40	35	33	31	29
Paper and paper product	494	488	489	484	474	468	446	421	393	374	365	357
Printing and related support	599	594	597	598	585	576	544	493	471	460	447	448
Petroleum and coal product	89	87	88	87	85	83	81	78	74	77	75	73
Chemicals	598	595	593	601	595	588	562	532	525	520	510	509
Plastics and rubber product	720	721	733	740	747	754	705	663	634	626	621	617

Table 2-6. Average Weekly Hours of Production Workers on Private Nonfarm Payrolls, by Super Sector, NAICS Basis, 1995–2006

(Hours.)

Industry	1995	1996	1997	1998	1999	2000	2001	2002	2003	2004	2005	2006
TOTAL PRIVATE	34.3	34.3	34.5	34.5	34.3	34.3	34.0	33.9	33.7	33.7	33.8	33.9
Goods-Producing	40.8	40.8	41.1	40.8	40.8	40.7	39.9	39.9	39.8	40.0	40.1	40.5
Natural resources and mining	45.3	46.0	46.2	44.9	44.2	44.4	44.6	43.2	43.6	44.5	45.6	45.6
Construction	38.8	38.9	38.9	38.8	39.0	39.2	38.7	38.4	38.4	38.3	38.6	39.0
Manufacturing	41.3	41.3	41.7	41.4	41.4	41.3	40.3	40.5	40.4	40.8	40.7	41.1
Private Service-Providing	32.6	32.6	32.8	32.8	32.7	32.7	32.5	32.5	32.4	32.3	32.4	32.5
Trade, transportation, and utilities	34.1	34.1	34.3	34.2	33.9	33.8	33.5	33.6	33.6	33.5	33.4	33.4
Wholesale trade	38.6	38.6	38.8	38.6	38.6	38.8	38.4	38.0	37.9	37.8	37.7	38.0
Retail trade	30.8	30.7	30.9	30.9	30.8	30.7	30.7	30.9	30.9	30.7	30.6	30.5
Transportation and warehousing	38.9	39.1	39.4	38.7	37.6	37.4	36.7	36.8	36.8	37.2	37.0	36.9
Utilities	42.3	42.0	42.0	42.0	42.0	42.0	41.4	40.9	41.1	40.9	41.1	41.4
Information	36.0	36.4	36.3	36.6	36.7	36.8	36.9	36.5	36.2	36.3	36.5	36.6
Financial activities	35.5	35.5	35.7	36.0	35.8	35.9	35.8	35.6	35.5	35.5	35.9	35.8
Professional and business services	34.0	34.1	34.3	34.3	34.4	34.5	34.2	34.2	34.1	34.2	34.2	34.6
Education and health services	32.0	31.9	32.2	32.2	32.1	32.2	32.3	32.4	32.3	32.4	32.6	32.5
Leisure and hospitality	25.9	25.9	26.0	26.2	26.1	26.1	25.8	25.8	25.6	25.7	25.7	25.7
Other services	32.6	32.5	32.7	32.6	32.5	32.5	32.3	32.0	31.4	31.0	30.9	30.9

Table 2-7. Average Weekly Hours of Production Workers on Manufacturing Payrolls, by Industry, NAICS Basis, 1995–2006

(Hours.)

Industry	1995	1996	1997	1998	1999	2000	2001	2002	2003	2004	2005	2006
DURABLE GOODS												
Total	42.1	42.1	42.6	42.1	41.9	41.8	40.6	40.8	40.8	41.3	41.1	41.4
Wood product	41.0	41.2	41.4	41.4	41.3	41.0	40.2	39.9	40.4	40.7	40.0	39.8
Nonmetallic mineral product	41.8	42.0	41.9	42.2	42.1	41.6	41.6	42.0	42.2	42.3	42.2	43.0
Primary metals	43.4	43.6	44.3	43.5	43.8	44.2	42.4	42.4	42.3	43.1	43.1	43.6
Fabricated metal product	41.9	41.9	42.3	41.9	41.7	41.9	40.6	40.6	40.7	41.1	41.0	41.4
Machinery	43.5	43.3	44.0	43.1	42.3	42.3	40.9	40.5	40.8	41.9	42.1	42.4
Computer and electronic product	42.2	41.9	42.5	41.8	41.5	41.4	39.8	39.7	40.4	40.4	40.0	40.5
Electrical equipment and appliances	41.9	42.1	42.1	41.8	41.8	41.6	39.8	40.1	40.6	40.7	40.6	41.0
Transportation equipment	43.7	43.8	44.2	43.2	43.6	43.3	41.9	42.5	41.9	42.5	42.4	42.7
Furniture and related product	38.5	38.3	39.1	39.4	39.3	39.2	38.3	39.2	38.9	39.5	39.2	38.8
Miscellaneous manufacturing	39.2	39.1	39.7	39.2	39.3	39.0	38.8	38.6	38.4	38.5	38.7	38.7
NONDURABLE GOODS												
Total	40.1	40.1	40.5	40.5	40.4	40.3	39.9	40.1	39.8	40.0	39.9	40.6
Food manufacturing	39.6	39.5	39.8	40.1	40.2	40.1	39.6	39.6	39.3	39.3	39.0	40.1
Beverage and tobacco product	39.3	39.7	40.0	40.3	41.0	42.0	40.9	39.4	39.1	39.2	40.1	40.7
Textile mills	40.9	40.8	41.6	41.0	41.0	41.4	40.0	40.6	39.1	40.1	40.3	40.6
Textile product mills	39.1	39.2	39.6	39.5	39.4	39.0	38.6	39.2	39.6	38.9	39.0	40.0
Apparel	35.3	35.2	35.5	35.5	35.4	35.7	36.0	36.7	35.6	36.0	35.7	36.5
Leather and allied product	37.7	37.8	38.2	37.4	37.2	37.5	36.4	37.5	39.3	38.4	38.4	38.9
Paper and paper product	43.4	43.5	43.9	43.6	43.6	42.8	42.1	41.9	41.5	42.1	42.5	42.9
Printing and related support	39.1	39.1	39.5	39.3	39.1	39.2	38.7	38.4	38.2	38.4	38.4	39.2
Petroleum and coal product	43.7	43.7	43.1	43.6	42.6	42.7	43.8	43.0	44.5	44.9	45.5	45.0
Chemicals	43.3	43.3	43.4	43.2	42.7	42.2	41.9	42.3	42.4	42.8	42.3	42.5
Plastics and rubber product	41.1	41.0	41.4	41.3	41.3	40.8	40.0	40.6	40.4	40.4	40.0	40.6

Table 2-8. Average Weekly Overtime Hours of Production Workers on Manufacturing Payrolls, by Industry, NAICS Basis, 1995–2006

(Hours.)

Industry	1995	1996	1997	1998	1999	2000	2001	2002	2003	2004	2005	2006
TOTAL MANUFACTURING	4.7	4.8	5.1	4.8	4.8	4.7	4.0	4.2	4.2	4.6	4.6	4.4
Total Durable Goods	5.0	5.0	5.4	5.0	5.0	4.8	3.9	4.2	4.3	4.7	4.6	4.4
Wood product	3.9	4.0	4.0	4.0	4.2	4.1	3.7	3.9	4.1	4.4	4.1	3.8
Nonmetallic mineral product	5.7	6.1	6.0	6.4	6.1	6.1	5.5	5.9	5.8	6.1	6.3	5.7
Primary metals	5.7	5.8	6.3	5.9	6.3	6.5	5.5	5.6	5.5	6.5	6.3	6.3
Fabricated metal product	4.8	4.8	5.3	4.9	4.8	4.9	4.1	4.1	4.1	4.5	4.6	4.5
Machinery	5.3	5.2	5.8	5.1	5.0	5.1	3.9	4.0	4.2	4.8	5.0	4.6
Computer and electronic product	4.9	4.7	5.2	4.8	4.6	4.6	3.2	3.4	3.8	3.7	3.6	3.5
Electrical equipment and appliances	3.5	3.7	3.9	3.6	3.6	3.7	3.0	3.1	3.4	4.0	3.8	4.1
Transportation equipment	6.5	6.7	7.2	6.4	6.1	5.5	4.5	5.1	5.0	5.5	5.0	4.9
Furniture and related product	2.8	2.9	3.3	3.0	3.9	3.5	2.7	3.4	3.5	3.6	3.2	3.0
Miscellaneous manufacturing	3.4	3.4	3.7	3.4	3.7	3.1	2.8	2.9	2.7	3.2	3.3	2.9
Total Nondurable Goods	4.3	4.4	4.6	4.5	4.6	4.4	4.1	4.2	4.1	4.4	4.4	4.4
Food manufacturing	4.4	4.4	4.6	4.8	5.0	4.8	4.6	4.6	4.4	4.7	4.7	4.8
Beverage and tobacco product	4.8	5.0	4.8	5.0	5.3	5.8	4.9	4.8	4.0	4.3	5.7	5.5
Textile mills	5.0	5.0	5.5	5.2	5.0	4.8	3.8	4.2	4.0	4.4	3.9	3.8
Textile product mills	3.4	3.8	4.1	4.1	4.1	3.5	2.7	3.3	3.2	3.0	4.4	4.3
Apparel	2.2	2.3	2.4	2.2	2.4	2.1	1.8	2.3	2.0	2.2	2.1	2.3
Leather and allied product	4.0	4.0	4.7	4.7	4.1	4.6	2.2	2.9	2.7	2.2	2.2	3.6
Paper and paper product	5.5	5.7	6.0	5.8	5.9	5.7	4.9	5.1	5.1	5.4	5.6	5.6
Printing and related support	3.8	3.8	4.2	3.9	3.6	3.7	3.4	3.4	3.2	3.4	3.3	3.5
Petroleum and coal product	6.3	6.4	6.4	6.8	6.6	6.5	7.9	7.0	8.3	8.2	8.5	7.7
Chemicals	5.6	5.7	5.8	5.6	5.2	5.0	4.6	4.7	4.5	4.9	4.6	4.1
Plastics and rubber product	3.9	4.0	4.3	4.2	4.2	3.9	3.6	3.9	3.9	4.2	4.0	3.9

Table 2-9. Indexes of Aggregate Weekly Hours of Production Workers on Private Nonfarm Payrolls, by Super Sector, NAICS Basis, 1995–2006

(2002 = 100.)

Industry	1995	1996	1997	1998	1999	2000	2001	2002	2003	2004	2005	2006
TOTAL PRIVATE	91.6	93.8	97.1	99.4	101.5	103.6	102.1	100.0	98.7	100.2	102.8	105.9
Goods-Producing	106.8	108.1	111.2	112.3	112.6	113.1	106.6	100.0	95.8	96.8	98.9	102.7
Natural resources and mining	110.2	112.7	117.6	112.8	102.9	105.1	108.3	100.0	97.4	104.0	114.7	125.7
Construction	79.9	84.3	88.6	93.4	99.7	104.0	103.2	100.0	98.4	101.7	108.3	115.3
Manufacturing	119.0	118.8	121.4	121.0	118.9	117.7	108.1	100.0	94.5	94.3	93.9	95.9
Private Service-Providing	87.3	89.7	93.1	95.8	98.4	101.0	100.8	100.0	99.5	101.1	103.8	106.7
Trade, transportation, and utilities	95.1	96.6	98.8	100.3	101.9	103.5	101.5	100.0	98.6	99.6	101.6	103.1
Wholesale trade	99.2	100.7	103.4	104.8	106.2	107.1	102.9	100.0	98.0	98.9	101.8	105.6
Retail trade	92.3	93.7	95.9	97.2	99.5	101.3	100.5	100.0	98.9	99.4	100.8	100.8
Transportation and warehousing	95.6	98.3	101.0	102.7	103.2	105.6	102.8	100.0	98.8	101.9	105.2	107.9
Utilities	112.9	108.6	106.1	105.8	105.0	104.2	102.4	100.0	97.4	94.2	93.1	93.8
Information	82.5	86.9	90.4	92.6	98.5	104.9	106.6	100.0	97.0	98.2	99.4	100.8
Financial activities	87.8	89.8	92.6	96.5	98.0	98.5	99.5	100.0	101.5	101.9	104.8	107.9
Professional and business services	81.2	85.2	91.5	96.7	101.7	106.6	104.0	100.0	98.7	101.8	106.3	112.0
Education and health services	81.2	83.4	86.7	88.9	90.6	92.8	96.6	100.0	101.4	103.3	106.4	109.0
Leisure and hospitality	88.5	90.8	93.4	95.5	97.9	100.6	100.7	100.0	100.1	103.0	106.3	109.1
Other services	87.1	89.1	91.9	94.3	96.3	97.8	99.1	100.0	97.5	96.1	96.2	97.4

Table 2-10. Indexes of Aggregate Weekly Hours of Production Workers on Manufacturing Payrolls, by Industry, NAICS Basis, 1995–2006

(2002 = 100.)

Industry	1995	1996	1997	1998	1999	2000	2001	2002	2003	2004	2005	2006
DURABLE GOODS												
Total	116.3	117.5	121.6	122.0	120.6	120.4	109.3	100.0	94.3	95.2	96.1	99.1
Wood product	109.3	111.6	114.8	117.5	118.6	115.8	105.0	100.0	97.8	100.9	101.3	100.3
Nonmetallic mineral product	99.7	101.5	103.2	105.8	106.9	109.1	106.1	100.0	94.3	98.0	97.5	100.1
Primary metals	129.3	129.9	132.3	131.1	128.4	128.9	113.0	100.0	93.4	93.3	93.1	93.8
Fabricated metal product	109.9	111.6	116.6	118.6	116.7	119.1	109.3	100.0	95.3	97.7	99.3	103.2
Machinery	132.3	133.8	139.0	137.4	129.9	127.6	114.1	100.0	93.6	95.9	98.8	103.3
Computer and electronic product	127.1	129.9	136.8	136.7	131.1	133.0	117.9	100.0	92.1	89.7	94.8	104.3
Electrical equipment and appliances	130.3	129.4	127.7	127.8	128.3	127.8	113.4	100.0	92.0	88.7	86.4	88.6
Transportation equipment	115.4	116.4	120.7	118.7	119.5	116.4	105.3	100.0	95.4	96.5	97.3	99.9
Furniture and related product	99.3	98.3	102.9	108.5	112.6	114.8	104.8	100.0	93.0	94.3	91.8	90.1
Miscellaneous manufacturing	107.7	107.7	110.0	110.3	110.3	109.5	104.8	100.0	93.6	91.8	90.6	90.9
NONDURABLE GOODS												
Total	123.1	120.5	120.9	119.4	116.1	113.3	106.0	100.0	94.7	92.7	90.2	90.8
Food manufacturing	101.6	101.8	102.6	103.4	103.8	103.5	101.5	100.0	98.4	97.1	95.8	99.0
Beverage and tobacco product	97.9	101.4	103.1	104.9	104.7	104.2	100.3	100.0	88.4	88.8	94.8	99.5
Textile mills	163.5	154.1	155.2	148.9	139.1	132.4	112.2	100.0	86.3	79.0	71.3	65.2
Textile product mills	114.4	112.8	114.8	114.1	113.5	111.1	105.0	100.0	92.9	91.0	89.2	86.6
Apparel	235.4	211.9	201.4	181.2	154.7	137.4	117.1	100.0	81.9	75.1	65.7	63.3
Leather and allied product	221.8	197.5	187.1	166.6	148.3	138.4	113.3	100.0	91.3	83.6	79.0	75.4
Paper and paper product	121.4	120.1	121.5	119.5	117.1	113.4	106.6	100.0	92.4	89.2	87.9	86.7
Printing and related support	123.9	122.8	124.6	124.3	120.9	119.4	111.5	100.0	95.3	93.4	90.9	92.7
Petroleum and coal product	115.5	113.5	112.7	113.4	107.6	105.8	105.6	100.0	98.7	102.6	102.4	97.8
Chemicals	115.4	114.7	114.6	115.4	113.1	110.4	104.7	100.0	98.9	99.0	95.9	96.4
Plastics and rubber product	109.9	110.1	112.7	113.8	114.6	114.3	105.0	100.0	95.2	94.2	92.4	93.1

Table 2-11. Employees on Total Nonfarm Payrolls, by State and Selected Territory, 1966–2006

(Thousands of people.)

State	1966	1967	1968	1969	1970	1971	1972	1973	1974	1975	1976	1977	1978	1979	1980
UNITED STATES	64 020	65 931	68 023	70 512	71 006	71 335	73 798	76 912	78 389	77 069	79 502	82 593	86 826	89 932	90 528
Alabama	936	952	970	1 000	1 010	1 022	1 072	1 136	1 170	1 155	1 207	1 269	1 337	1 362	1 356
Alaska	73	77	80	87	93	98	104	110	128	162	172	163	164	167	169
Arizona	435	446	473	517	547	581	646	714	746	729	759	809	895	980	1 014
Arkansas	490	501	515	534	536	551	582	615	641	624	660	696	733	750	742
California	6 145	6 368	6 642	6 932	6 946	6 917	7 210	7 622	7 834	7 847	8 154	8 600	9 200	9 665	9 849
Colorado	631	656	687	721	750	787	869	936	960	964	1 003	1 058	1 150	1 218	1 251
Connecticut	1 095	1 130	1 158	1 194	1 198	1 164	1 190	1 239	1 264	1 223	1 240	1 282	1 346	1 398	1 427
Delaware	193	197	203	212	217	225	232	239	233	230	237	239	248	257	259
District of Columbia	587	595	583	575	567	567	572	574	580	577	576	579	596	613	616
Florida	1 727	1 816	1 932	2 070	2 152	2 276	2 513	2 779	2 864	2 746	2 784	2 933	3 181	3 381	3 576
Georgia	1 338	1 395	1 456	1 532	1 558	1 603	1 695	1 803	1 828	1 756	1 839	1 927	2 050	2 128	2 159
Hawaii	232	242	255	276	294	302	313	328	336	343	349	359	377	394	404
Idaho	185	188	193	201	208	217	237	252	267	273	291	307	331	338	330
Illinois	4 095	4 210	4 285	4 376	4 346	4 296	4 315	4 467	4 546	4 419	4 565	4 656	4 789	4 880	4 850
Indiana	1 737	1 777	1 817	1 880	1 849	1 841	1 922	2 028	2 031	1 942	2 024	2 114	2 206	2 236	2 130
Iowa	804	833	852	873	877	883	912	961	999	999	1 037	1 079	1 119	1 132	1 110
Kansas	634	653	672	687	679	678	718	763	790	801	835	871	913	947	945
Kentucky	804	837	869	896	910	932	718	1 039	1 066	1 058	1 103	1 148	1 210	1 245	1 210
Louisiana	958	997	1 021	1 033	1 034	1 056	718	1 176	1 221	1 250	1 314	1 365	1 464	1 517	1 579
Maine	309	317	323	330	332	332	718	355	362	357	375	388	406	416	418
Maryland	1 132	1 179	1 224	1 272	1 349	1 372	718	1 472	1 494	1 479	1 498	1 546	1 626	1 691	1 712
Massachusetts	2 097	2 148	2 188	2 249	2 244	2 211	718	2 333	2 354	2 273	2 324	2 416	2 526	2 604	2 654
Michigan	2 861	2 901	2 960	3 081	2 999	2 995	718	3 284	3 278	3 137	3 283	3 442	3 609	3 637	3 443
Minnesota	1 148	1 200	1 243	1 300	1 315	1 310	718	1 436	1 481	1 474	1 521	1 597	1 689	1 767	1 770
Mississippi	522	535	552	573	584	602	718	693	711	692	728	766	814	838	829
Missouri	1 554	1 596	1 631	1 672	1 668	1 661	718	1 771	1 789	1 741	1 798	1 862	1 953	2 011	1 970
Montana	185	188	193	196	199	205	718	224	234	238	251	265	280	284	280
Nebraska	434	449	459	474	484	491	718	541	562	558	572	594	610	631	628
Nevada	162	166	177	194	203	211	718	245	256	263	280	308	350	384	400
New Hampshire	235	244	252	259	259	260	718	298	300	293	313	337	360	379	385
New Jersey	2 359	2 422	2 485	2 570	2 606	2 608	718	2 760	2 783	2 700	2 754	2 837	2 962	3 027	3 060
New Mexico	272	273	277	288	293	306	328	346	360	370	390	415	444	461	465
New York	6 710	6 858	7 002	7 182	7 157	7 011	7 039	7 132	7 077	6 830	6 790	6 858	7 045	7 179	7 207
North Carolina	1 534	1 601	1 679	1 747	1 783	1 814	718	2 018	2 048	1 980	2 083	2 171	2 278	2 373	2 380
North Dakota	148	152	156	158	164	167	718	184	194	204	215	221	234	244	245
Ohio	3 537	3 620	3 751	3 887	3 881	3 840	718	4 113	4 169	4 016	4 095	4 230	4 395	4 485	4 367
Oklahoma	676	700	720	748	763	774	718	852	887	900	931	972	1 036	1 088	1 138
Oregon	640	652	679	709	711	729	718	816	838	837	879	937	1 009	1 056	1 045
Pennsylvania	4 077	4 171	4 264	4 375	4 352	4 291	718	4 507	4 515	4 436	4 513	4 565	4 716	4 806	4 753
Rhode Island	330	338	343	346	344	343	718	366	367	349	367	382	396	400	398
South Carolina	735	755	783	820	842	863	718	984	1 016	983	1 038	1 082	1 138	1 176	1 189
South Dakota	160	164	168	173	175	179	718	199	207	209	219	227	237	241	238
Tennessee	1 184	1 219	1 264	1 310	1 328	1 357	718	1 531	1 558	1 506	1 575	1 648	1 737	1 777	1 747
Texas	3 109	3 259	3 424	3 597	3 625	3 684	718	4 142	4 360	4 463	4 684	4 907	5 272	5 602	5 851
Utah	317	327	335	348	357	369	718	415	434	440	463	489	525	548	551
Vermont	131	136	140	146	148	148	718	161	163	162	168	178	191	198	200
Virginia	1 285	1 330	1 385	1 436	1 519	1 567	718	1 753	1 805	1 779	1 848	1 930	2 034	2 115	2 157
Washington	989	1 045	1 099	1 120	1 079	1 064	718	1 152	1 199	1 226	1 283	1 367	1 485	1 581	1 608
West Virginia	495	504	508	512	517	520	718	562	572	575	596	612	633	659	646
Wisconsin	1 394	1 431	1 472	1 525	1 530	1 525	718	1 661	1 703	1 677	1 726	1 799	1 887	1 960	1 938
Wyoming	...	...	103	107	108	111	718	126	137	146	157	171	187	201	210
Puerto Rico	...	...	...	...	...	...	...	...	...	...	...	...	...	...	693
Virgin Islands	...	...	...	...	...	...	...	...	...	33	31	32	34	36	37

. . . = Not available.

Table 2-11. Employees on Total Nonfarm Payrolls, by State and Selected Territory, 1966–2006—*Continued*

(Thousands of people.)

State	1981	1982	1983	1984	1985	1986	1987	1988	1989	1990	1991	1992	1993
UNITED STATES	91 289	89 677	90 280	94 530	97 511	99 474	102 088	105 345	108 014	109 487	108 374	108 726	110 844
Alabama	1 348	1 313	1 329	1 388	1 427	1 463	1 508	1 559	1 601	1 636	1 642	1 674	1 717
Alaska	186	200	214	226	231	221	210	214	227	238	243	247	253
Arizona	1 041	1 030	1 078	1 182	1 279	1 338	1 386	1 419	1 455	1 483	1 491	1 517	1 584
Arkansas	740	720	741	780	797	814	837	865	893	924	937	963	994
California	9 985	9 810	9 918	10 390	10 770	11 086	11 473	11 912	12 239	12 500	12 359	12 154	12 045
Colorado	1 295	1 317	1 327	1 402	1 419	1 408	1 413	1 436	1 482	1 521	1 545	1 597	1 671
Connecticut	1 438	1 429	1 444	1 517	1 558	1 598	1 638	1 667	1 666	1 620	1 557	1 526	1 531
Delaware	259	259	266	280	293	303	321	334	345	347	342	341	349
District of Columbia	611	598	597	614	629	640	656	674	681	686	677	674	670
Florida	3 736	3 762	3 905	4 204	4 410	4 599	4 848	5 067	5 261	5 376	5 283	5 348	5 560
Georgia	2 199	2 202	2 280	2 449	2 570	2 672	2 782	2 876	2 941	2 992	2 938	2 987	3 109
Hawaii	405	399	406	413	426	439	460	478	506	528	539	543	539
Idaho	328	312	318	331	336	328	333	349	366	385	398	415	433
Illinois	4 732	4 593	4 531	4 672	4 755	4 791	4 928	5 098	5 214	5 288	5 233	5 235	5 330
Indiana	2 115	2 028	2 030	2 122	2 169	2 222	2 305	2 396	2 479	2 522	2 507	2 554	2 627
Iowa	1 089	1 042	1 040	1 075	1 074	1 074	1 109	1 156	1 200	1 226	1 238	1 253	1 279
Kansas	950	921	922	961	968	985	1 005	1 035	1 064	1 092	1 097	1 116	1 135
Kentucky	1 196	1 161	1 152	1 214	1 250	1 274	1 328	1 382	1 433	1 471	1 475	1 509	1 548
Louisiana	1 631	1 607	1 565	1 602	1 591	1 519	1 484	1 512	1 539	1 588	1 611	1 625	1 657
Maine	419	416	425	446	458	477	501	527	542	535	514	512	519
Maryland	1 716	1 676	1 724	1 814	1 888	1 952	2 028	2 102	2 155	2 173	2 103	2 084	2 104
Massachusetts	2 672	2 642	2 697	2 856	2 931	2 992	3 071	3 138	3 118	2 988	2 824	2 798	2 843
Michigan	3 364	3 193	3 223	3 381	3 562	3 657	3 736	3 819	3 922	3 947	3 884	3 919	3 999
Minnesota	1 761	1 707	1 718	1 820	1 866	1 893	1 963	2 028	2 087	2 136	2 146	2 194	2 252
Mississippi	819	791	793	821	839	848	864	896	919	937	938	960	1 002
Missouri	1 957	1 923	1 937	2 033	2 095	2 143	2 198	2 259	2 315	2 345	2 309	2 334	2 395
Montana	282	274	276	281	279	275	274	283	291	297	304	317	326
Nebraska	623	610	611	635	651	653	667	688	708	730	739	750	767
Nevada	411	401	403	426	446	468	500	538	581	621	629	639	672
New Hampshire	395	394	410	442	466	490	513	529	529	508	482	487	502
New Jersey	3 099	3 093	3 165	3 329	3 414	3 488	3 576	3 651	3 690	3 635	3 499	3 458	3 493
New Mexico	476	474	480	503	520	526	529	548	562	580	585	602	626
New York	7 287	7 255	7 313	7 570	7 751	7 908	8 059	8 187	8 247	8 212	7 886	7 730	7 759
North Carolina	2 392	2 347	2 419	2 565	2 651	2 744	2 863	2 987	3 074	3 122	3 076	3 140	3 243
North Dakota	249	250	251	253	252	250	252	257	260	266	271	277	285
Ohio	4 318	4 124	4 093	4 260	4 373	4 472	4 583	4 701	4 818	4 882	4 819	4 848	4 918
Oklahoma	1 201	1 217	1 171	1 180	1 165	1 124	1 109	1 132	1 164	1 202	1 217	1 228	1 253
Oregon	1 019	961	967	1 007	1 030	1 059	1 100	1 153	1 206	1 256	1 254	1 277	1 318
Pennsylvania	4 729	4 580	4 524	4 655	4 730	4 791	4 915	5 042	5 139	5 170	5 084	5 076	5 123
Rhode Island	401	391	396	416	429	443	452	459	462	454	424	424	430
South Carolina	1 197	1 162	1 189	1 263	1 296	1 338	1 392	1 449	1 500	1 540	1 510	1 525	1 568
South Dakota	236	230	235	247	249	252	257	266	276	289	296	308	318
Tennessee	1 755	1 703	1 719	1 812	1 868	1 930	2 012	2 092	2 167	2 193	2 184	2 245	2 328
Texas	6 180	6 263	6 194	6 492	6 663	6 564	6 517	6 678	6 840	7 102	7 181	7 276	7 488
Utah	558	561	567	601	624	634	640	660	691	724	745	769	810
Vermont	204	203	206	215	225	234	246	256	262	258	249	251	257
Virginia	2 161	2 146	2 207	2 333	2 455	2 558	2 680	2 773	2 862	2 894	2 829	2 848	2 919
Washington	1 612	1 569	1 586	1 660	1 710	1 770	1 852	1 941	2 047	2 143	2 177	2 222	2 253
West Virginia	629	608	582	597	597	598	599	610	615	630	629	640	652
Wisconsin	1 923	1 867	1 867	1 949	1 983	2 024	2 090	2 169	2 236	2 292	2 302	2 358	2 413
Wyoming	224	218	203	204	207	196	183	189	193	199	203	206	210
Puerto Rico	680	642	646	684	693	728	764	818	837	846	838	858	872
Virgin Islands	38	37	36	37	37	38	40	42	42	43	44	45	49

Table 2-11. Employees on Total Nonfarm Payrolls, by State and Selected Territory, 1966–2006—*Continued*

(Thousands of people.)

State	1994	1995	1996	1997	1998	1999	2000	2001	2002	2003	2004	2005	2006
UNITED STATES	114 291	117 298	119 708	122 776	125 930	128 993	131 785	131 826	130 341	129 999	131 435	133 703	136 174
Alabama	1 759	1 804	1 829	1 866	1 898	1 920	1 931	1 909	1 883	1 876	1 902	1 945	1 982
Alaska	259	262	264	269	275	278	284	289	295	299	304	310	315
Arizona	1 692	1 793	1 892	1 985	2 075	2 163	2 243	2 265	2 265	2 296	2 381	2 509	2 644
Arkansas	1 034	1 070	1 087	1 105	1 122	1 142	1 159	1 154	1 146	1 145	1 158	1 178	1 200
California	12 160	12 422	12 743	13 130	13 596	13 992	14 488	14 602	14 458	14 392	14 530	14 798	15 073
Colorado	1 756	1 835	1 901	1 980	2 058	2 133	2 214	2 227	2 184	2 153	2 180	2 226	2 279
Connecticut	1 544	1 562	1 582	1 608	1 643	1 669	1 693	1 681	1 665	1 645	1 650	1 662	1 680
Delaware	356	366	376	388	400	413	420	419	415	415	424	431	436
District of Columbia	659	643	623	618	614	627	650	654	664	666	674	682	688
Florida	5 788	5 985	6 172	6 403	6 625	6 816	7 070	7 160	7 169	7 250	7 499	7 800	8 007
Georgia	3 266	3 402	3 527	3 614	3 741	3 855	3 949	3 943	3 870	3 845	3 901	4 003	4 086
Hawaii	536	533	531	532	531	535	551	555	557	568	583	602	617
Idaho	459	475	489	506	521	539	560	568	568	572	588	611	640
Illinois	5 463	5 593	5 685	5 771	5 899	5 959	6 045	5 995	5 884	5 811	5 816	5 862	5 935
Indiana	2 713	2 787	2 814	2 858	2 917	2 970	3 000	2 933	2 901	2 895	2 929	2 955	2 973
Iowa	1 320	1 358	1 383	1 407	1 443	1 469	1 478	1 466	1 447	1 440	1 457	1 481	1 503
Kansas	1 167	1 200	1 228	1 270	1 314	1 328	1 346	1 349	1 336	1 313	1 325	1 333	1 354
Kentucky	1 597	1 643	1 672	1 711	1 753	1 795	1 827	1 805	1 789	1 783	1 799	1 825	1 845
Louisiana	1 720	1 770	1 808	1 848	1 887	1 894	1 918	1 915	1 896	1 906	1 918	1 892	1 857
Maine	532	538	542	554	569	586	604	608	607	607	612	612	615
Maryland	2 148	2 184	2 213	2 269	2 326	2 392	2 455	2 472	2 480	2 487	2 518	2 556	2 588
Massachusetts	2 907	2 980	3 039	3 114	3 184	3 243	3 329	3 339	3 259	3 198	3 195	3 212	3 243
Michigan	4 142	4 269	4 353	4 439	4 514	4 585	4 677	4 561	4 487	4 414	4 395	4 390	4 341
Minnesota	2 320	2 388	2 443	2 500	2 564	2 622	2 685	2 690	2 665	2 660	2 681	2 723	2 760
Mississippi	1 056	1 075	1 089	1 107	1 134	1 153	1 154	1 130	1 124	1 115	1 125	1 130	1 142
Missouri	2 470	2 521	2 567	2 639	2 684	2 727	2 749	2 730	2 699	2 681	2 695	2 735	2 774
Montana	340	352	362	367	376	384	391	392	396	401	411	421	434
Nebraska	796	817	837	857	880	897	914	920	912	914	922	935	947
Nevada	738	786	843	891	926	983	1 027	1 051	1 052	1 088	1 153	1 223	1 282
New Hampshire	523	540	554	570	589	606	622	627	618	618	627	636	639
New Jersey	3 553	3 601	3 639	3 725	3 801	3 901	3 995	3 997	3 984	3 979	3 999	4 039	4 075
New Mexico	657	682	695	708	720	730	745	757	766	776	790	809	833
New York	7 831	7 892	7 938	8 067	8 236	8 455	8 635	8 591	8 458	8 406	8 461	8 533	8 612
North Carolina	3 351	3 451	3 536	3 653	3 759	3 849	3 915	3 894	3 836	3 789	3 836	3 915	4 021
North Dakota	295	302	309	314	319	324	328	330	330	333	338	345	353
Ohio	5 076	5 221	5 296	5 392	5 482	5 564	5 625	5 543	5 445	5 398	5 408	5 427	5 441
Oklahoma	1 286	1 322	1 360	1 400	1 445	1 466	1 493	1 507	1 487	1 458	1 474	1 512	1 552
Oregon	1 372	1 428	1 485	1 537	1 563	1 586	1 618	1 606	1 585	1 574	1 607	1 655	1 702
Pennsylvania	5 192	5 253	5 306	5 406	5 495	5 586	5 691	5 683	5 641	5 611	5 644	5 702	5 753
Rhode Island	434	439	441	450	458	466	477	478	479	484	489	491	493
South Carolina	1 605	1 644	1 673	1 718	1 783	1 830	1 859	1 823	1 804	1 807	1 833	1 867	1 903
South Dakota	331	342	347	353	360	370	378	379	377	378	383	390	399
Tennessee	2 423	2 499	2 533	2 584	2 638	2 685	2 729	2 688	2 664	2 663	2 706	2 743	2 783
Texas	7 758	8 029	8 263	8 614	8 944	9 160	9 432	9 514	9 416	9 370	9 497	9 741	10 053
Utah	860	908	954	994	1 023	1 049	1 075	1 081	1 073	1 074	1 104	1 148	1 203
Vermont	264	270	275	279	285	292	299	302	299	299	303	306	307
Virginia	3 004	3 070	3 136	3 232	3 320	3 412	3 517	3 517	3 494	3 498	3 584	3 664	3 726
Washington	2 304	2 347	2 416	2 515	2 595	2 649	2 711	2 697	2 654	2 658	2 701	2 777	2 859
West Virginia	674	688	699	708	719	726	736	735	733	728	737	747	756
Wisconsin	2 491	2 559	2 601	2 656	2 718	2 784	2 834	2 814	2 782	2 775	2 807	2 842	2 861
Wyoming	217	219	221	225	228	233	239	245	248	250	255	264	277
Puerto Rico	898	930	973	989	997	1 011	1 025	1 009	1 005	1 022	1 046	1 048	1 043
Virgin Islands	44	42	41	42	42	41	42	44	43	42	43	44	45

Table 2-12. Employees on Manufacturing Payrolls, by State and Selected Territory, NAICS Basis, 1990–2006

(Thousands of people.)

State	1990	1991	1992	1993	1994	1995	1996	1997	1998	1999	2000	2001	2002	2003	2004	2005	2006
UNITED STATES	17 695	17 068	16 799	16 774	17 021	17 241	17 237	17 419	17 560	17 322	17 263	16 441	15 259	14 510	14 315	14 226	14 197
Alabama	364	354	357	359	362	370	362	364	365	358	351	326	307	294	292	299	303
Alaska	14	15	16	15	14	15	14	14	13	12	12	12	11	12	12	13	13
Arizona	177	171	167	170	182	191	199	205	211	207	210	202	184	175	177	182	187
Arkansas	219	219	224	231	240	246	241	241	242	241	240	227	214	206	203	201	199
California	1 969	1 895	1 796	1 704	1 692	1 724	1 783	1 833	1 864	1 837	1 864	1 791	1 645	1 555	1 533	1 514	1 505
Colorado	170	165	164	167	172	179	181	187	191	187	189	180	164	154	152	150	149
Connecticut	301	286	274	262	254	249	245	245	248	240	236	227	211	200	197	195	194
Delaware	46	46	44	44	43	43	41	43	44	44	42	39	37	36	35	33	34
District of Columbia	7	6	5	5	5	5	5	4	4	4	4	3	3	3	2	2	2
Florida	494	464	458	464	460	465	471	472	468	464	463	441	414	396	397	402	403
Georgia	523	499	508	518	533	547	552	555	553	550	538	505	471	452	448	450	449
Hawaii	21	20	19	18	17	16	16	16	16	16	16	16	15	15	15	15	15
Idaho	53	55	58	61	63	63	66	68	69	69	70	69	66	62	62	64	66
Illinois	915	876	855	860	878	894	899	902	906	882	871	815	754	714	697	688	683
Indiana	606	587	597	611	628	653	647	652	658	666	665	615	588	573	572	571	566
Iowa	219	216	216	221	230	237	235	239	251	253	251	240	227	220	223	229	231
Kansas	178	175	174	172	176	180	186	198	206	204	201	195	184	175	177	180	183
Kentucky	273	267	271	279	289	299	298	302	307	309	310	292	275	265	264	262	261
Louisiana	177	178	177	177	179	182	183	185	185	181	177	172	161	156	153	152	152
Maine	93	88	84	83	83	83	81	81	81	81	80	75	68	64	63	61	60
Maryland	200	188	180	176	176	176	173	175	175	173	173	168	156	147	142	140	136
Massachusetts	480	447	432	420	413	412	411	412	413	400	403	389	349	324	313	305	299
Michigan	837	792	795	804	847	871	864	872	888	896	895	820	760	716	697	677	648
Minnesota	342	339	343	351	361	375	381	391	397	395	397	379	356	343	343	347	347
Mississippi	230	231	236	239	244	241	231	228	234	233	223	201	188	179	180	178	176
Missouri	392	373	366	365	366	377	376	377	378	373	365	345	325	314	311	309	307
Montana	20	19	20	20	21	21	22	22	22	22	22	21	20	19	19	20	20
Nebraska	97	97	98	100	105	110	111	112	114	113	114	111	106	102	101	101	102
Nevada	24	25	26	29	33	36	38	40	41	41	43	44	43	44	46	48	51
New Hampshire	99	92	90	91	94	97	99	102	104	101	103	97	85	80	80	80	77
New Jersey	530	498	474	463	456	449	437	435	429	422	422	401	368	350	338	330	325
New Mexico	38	38	37	39	42	43	43	43	43	41	42	41	38	37	36	36	38
New York	983	910	870	836	816	810	797	797	792	773	751	708	652	613	597	581	568
North Carolina	824	792	803	820	824	828	809	800	796	777	758	704	644	599	577	565	553
North Dakota	16	16	17	18	19	20	20	22	22	23	24	24	24	24	25	26	26
Ohio	1 060	1 018	993	980	1 003	1 037	1 030	1 027	1 030	1 028	1 021	953	885	843	822	812	797
Oklahoma	156	156	152	156	158	161	162	168	175	177	177	170	152	143	142	145	149
Oregon	204	196	193	195	203	211	218	227	229	224	225	216	202	195	200	204	207
Pennsylvania	950	911	890	879	880	881	867	871	874	864	864	822	760	712	691	679	672
Rhode Island	95	87	85	84	83	80	77	76	75	72	71	68	62	59	57	55	53
South Carolina	348	334	338	342	345	347	339	339	341	336	336	314	290	276	268	261	252
South Dakota	34	34	36	38	41	44	44	44	44	44	44	41	38	38	39	40	42
Tennessee	498	484	497	508	519	524	507	503	504	500	493	454	429	413	412	409	400
Texas	948	936	929	942	966	995	1 017	1 045	1 077	1 063	1 068	1 027	949	900	891	897	926
Utah	104	103	102	106	112	117	122	126	127	126	126	122	114	112	115	118	123
Vermont	43	40	40	40	40	41	43	44	45	45	46	46	41	38	37	37	36
Virginia	387	376	373	370	371	373	371	374	376	367	364	341	320	305	299	296	289
Washington	336	329	325	317	312	311	325	350	361	343	332	316	285	267	264	273	286
West Virginia	82	79	78	79	77	78	78	77	78	77	76	72	69	65	63	62	61
Wisconsin	523	513	517	526	546	567	568	579	593	595	594	560	528	504	503	505	505
Wyoming	9	9	9	10	10	10	10	10	10	10	10	10	10	9	9	10	10
Puerto Rico	. . .	. . .	. . .	. . .	. . .	. . .	. . .	. . .	. . .	. . .	132	121	118	118	115	110
Virgin Islands	2	2	3	3	3	2	2	2	2	2	2	2	2	2	2	2	2

. . . = Not available.

Table 2-13. Employees on Government Payrolls, by State and Selected Territory, NAICS Basis, 1990–2006

(Thousands of people.)

State	1990	1991	1992	1993	1994	1995	1996	1997	1998	1999	2000	2001	2002	2003	2004	2005	2006
UNITED STATES	18 415	18 545	18 787	18 989	19 275	19 432	19 539	19 664	19 909	20 307	20 790	21 118	21 513	21 583	21 621	21 804	21 990
Alabama	327	333	338	341	346	343	343	346	347	351	352	352	355	358	359	363	371
Alaska	71	72	73	75	74	73	73	73	74	74	74	79	81	82	81	81	82
Arizona	273	285	291	295	303	310	318	328	341	354	367	378	390	394	399	403	410
Arkansas	159	163	167	170	173	177	180	183	185	187	191	194	195	199	200	204	208
California	2 075	2 091	2 096	2 081	2 093	2 107	2 113	2 141	2 166	2 239	2 318	2 382	2 447	2 426	2 396	2 417	2 447
Colorado	277	283	291	297	299	304	309	316	322	328	337	344	355	356	359	363	368
Connecticut	210	208	207	211	217	221	223	226	228	235	242	244	249	246	243	244	246
Delaware	48	48	49	50	50	51	52	53	54	55	57	57	57	57	58	59	61
District of Columbia	277	281	286	285	270	255	240	233	226	222	224	226	232	231	231	234	233
Florida	847	859	870	882	911	918	928	942	955	966	1 002	1 023	1 039	1 053	1 066	1 081	1 098
Georgia	532	537	537	548	564	570	570	577	586	590	597	610	625	632	637	650	663
Hawaii	106	109	111	112	112	111	111	112	112	113	115	115	118	119	120	120	121
Idaho	81	84	88	90	93	96	97	100	103	105	109	110	112	113	114	115	116
Illinois	766	771	774	774	786	799	809	808	816	826	840	850	861	853	845	846	846
Indiana	375	376	384	387	387	387	386	387	394	398	405	410	417	423	426	426	426
Iowa	219	221	221	222	227	230	233	235	236	239	243	245	244	245	245	245	247
Kansas	214	219	226	230	233	237	234	236	240	240	245	248	251	250	251	251	254
Kentucky	260	267	273	277	281	287	289	291	295	301	308	312	315	313	310	314	318
Louisiana	326	332	340	342	351	358	362	364	367	370	373	374	375	379	382	374	348
Maine	96	96	96	95	94	93	93	93	95	97	100	102	103	104	105	105	105
Maryland	422	419	417	419	422	423	423	423	433	444	450	457	465	462	463	466	471
Massachusetts	410	398	391	396	398	404	409	414	422	428	435	440	436	426	422	425	429
Michigan	631	633	636	638	639	641	644	647	656	667	681	685	687	685	680	674	670
Minnesota	348	354	362	371	380	387	389	389	391	397	408	409	414	413	412	415	414
Mississippi	203	204	208	210	214	215	217	219	223	227	234	238	240	241	242	241	240
Missouri	370	371	371	377	385	390	401	413	414	421	426	429	431	432	429	429	433
Montana	71	72	74	74	77	78	79	80	81	82	84	84	85	86	87	86	87
Nebraska	143	146	148	149	152	151	151	152	151	151	154	157	159	160	160	161	162
Nevada	76	81	86	89	92	97	101	107	112	117	122	127	131	135	139	144	150
New Hampshire	73	72	73	74	76	76	78	79	80	82	84	86	88	90	90	91	91
New Jersey	577	572	572	571	573	573	571	570	572	578	589	603	614	622	633	642	649
New Mexico	150	152	156	159	163	166	171	177	178	180	183	186	191	195	198	201	198
New York	1 473	1 445	1 428	1 433	1 436	1 416	1 400	1 406	1 424	1 445	1 467	1 467	1 492	1 487	1 484	1 489	1 487
North Carolina	492	502	514	527	539	551	561	576	594	604	622	636	642	641	652	663	675
North Dakota	68	68	69	70	70	71	70	70	70	71	73	73	74	75	75	75	76
Ohio	722	728	735	736	741	749	752	758	763	772	785	794	800	803	802	800	801
Oklahoma	262	265	270	270	270	270	271	276	278	283	288	296	301	296	302	312	318
Oregon	232	235	240	242	245	250	257	260	266	272	279	282	286	280	282	285	287
Pennsylvania	699	695	693	702	706	712	713	715	712	716	725	728	739	746	744	745	746
Rhode Island	62	61	61	61	62	61	61	63	63	63	64	65	66	66	66	65	65
South Carolina	282	286	292	296	295	294	295	299	309	315	323	323	326	326	325	328	330
South Dakota	63	65	67	69	71	69	69	69	69	70	71	73	74	74	75	75	75
Tennessee	351	353	357	362	371	373	382	380	386	390	399	403	410	411	415	413	415
Texas	1 263	1 288	1 334	1 376	1 414	1 446	1 458	1 483	1 504	1 535	1 562	1 586	1 626	1 646	1 656	1 684	1 712
Utah	151	154	157	159	161	164	167	172	177	180	185	190	195	197	199	202	204
Vermont	44	44	44	44	45	45	45	46	46	48	49	50	51	52	52	53	54
Virginia	578	581	589	598	603	598	596	597	602	611	625	629	635	638	651	662	674
Washington	398	412	424	430	437	444	451	458	466	474	483	505	516	521	524	527	529
West Virginia	127	128	132	133	137	136	139	139	141	141	143	141	143	143	143	144	145
Wisconsin	343	346	357	362	367	379	384	387	393	399	406	414	415	413	412	415	416
Wyoming	55	56	57	57	58	58	58	58	58	59	61	62	63	64	65	65	66
Puerto Rico	. . .	. . .	. . .	. . .	. . .	. . .	. . .	. . .	. . .	. . .	282	295	301	307	305	299
Virgin Islands	14	13	14	14	14	14	14	14	14	13	13	12	13	13	12	12	12

. . . = Not available.

Table 2-14. Average Weekly Hours of Production Workers on Manufacturing Payrolls, by State and Selected Territory, NAICS Basis, 2001–2006

(Hours.)

State	2001	2002	2003	2004	2005	2006
UNITED STATES	40.3	40.5	40.4	40.8	40.7	41.1
Alabama	41.0	41.4	41.0	40.8	40.8	40.9
Alaska	43.1	37.4	43.0	40.6	32.9	40.5
Arizona	40.3	40.0	40.4	40.5	40.7	40.6
Arkansas	39.9	39.7	39.6	39.9	39.9	41.0
California	39.6	39.6	39.7	40.0	39.9	40.4
Colorado	40.7	40.6	40.4	40.4	38.5	39.2
Connecticut	41.7	41.6	41.4	41.8	42.2	42.2
Delaware	39.7	40.0	40.3	40.1	39.7	39.9
District of Columbia	. . .	. . .	. . .	. . .	. . .	. . .
Florida	40.6	42.1	41.0	41.1	41.7	41.5
Georgia	40.4	40.9	39.8	39.2	39.0	39.5
Hawaii	36.0	35.6	37.2	37.9	38.4	38.6
Idaho	39.1	39.6	41.3	40.5	40.3	41.7
Illinois	41.0	41.4	40.6	41.0	40.8	41.1
Indiana	41.0	42.4	42.1	42.1	41.9	41.7
Iowa	40.9	41.3	41.7	42.2	41.6	41.9
Kansas	40.7	40.8	40.5	41.0	41.1	43.0
Kentucky	41.5	42.2	41.7	40.8	40.6	41.1
Louisiana	43.1	43.9	44.1	43.9	42.0	43.0
Maine	39.8	39.9	40.0	39.6	39.6	41.4
Maryland	. . .	. . .	39.5	40.1	40.1	40.6
Massachusetts	40.3	40.8	40.6	41.1	41.5	40.7
Michigan	. . .	. . .	42.1	42.4	41.7	42.2
Minnesota	39.6	39.7	40.2	40.9	40.9	41.0
Mississippi	39.7	40.6	39.9	40.1	40.1	39.4
Missouri	40.3	39.3	40.5	40.2	39.6	39.3
Montana	38.8	38.2	38.4	38.3	40.1	40.0
Nebraska	41.2	41.9	41.6	41.6	40.0	40.9
Nevada	38.7	38.8	39.0	40.1	39.8	39.4
New Hampshire	40.6	39.8	40.0	40.0	41.2	41.2
New Jersey	40.6	40.9	41.0	42.1	42.0	42.1
New Mexico	39.0	39.9	39.4	39.6	39.1	39.2
New York	39.8	40.3	40.0	39.7	39.6	41.1
North Carolina	39.4	40.2	39.8	40.3	40.0	40.0
North Dakota	40.9	40.2	40.0	39.3	39.2	39.0
Ohio	41.2	41.4	41.0	41.7	41.4	41.4
Oklahoma	39.4	39.2	39.3	40.5	39.4	39.9
Oregon	39.1	39.1	39.3	39.1	40.2	40.5
Pennsylvania	40.4	40.3	40.0	40.3	40.5	40.8
Rhode Island	39.4	38.7	39.3	39.2	38.4	38.9
South Carolina	. . .	. . .	41.3	39.5	39.7	41.0
South Dakota	41.7	42.3	42.5	42.0	42.3	42.1
Tennessee	38.9	40.1	39.8	40.0	39.2	39.4
Texas	41.6	41.1	41.4	39.8	40.0	40.9
Utah	38.4	37.8	39.7	38.1	39.2	41.1
Vermont	39.6	40.0	40.0	40.2	39.2	39.6
Virginia	40.1	40.8	40.8	41.5	41.4	41.3
Washington	40.0	40.1	39.5	40.0	39.7	40.6
West Virginia	. . .	. . .	41.3	41.4	41.4	41.3
Wisconsin	40.2	40.5	40.3	40.3	40.4	40.7
Wyoming	38.6	39.3	40.2	39.7	40.5	41.2
Puerto Rico	39.9	40.6	40.9	41.0	40.8	40.5
Virgin Islands	43.9	43.7	42.8	46.4	43.7	43.9

. . . = Not available.

Table 2-15. Average Weekly Hours of All Employees on Private Nonfarm Payrolls, by Major Industry Sector and Selected Industry Detail, Not Seasonally Adjusted, 2006

(Hours.)

Industry	January	February	March	April	May	June	July	August	September	October	November	December
TOTAL PRIVATE	. . .	. . .	34.2	34.6	34.3	34.6	34.9	34.6	34.5	34.9	34.4	34.6
Goods-Producing	. . .	. . .	39.0	38.8	39.3	39.7	39.4	39.7	39.6	39.7	39.3	39.6
Natural resources and mining	. . .	. . .	42.1	42.9	42.5	43.1	43.2	43.3	43.1	42.6	42.2	42.6
Construction	. . .	. . .	37.2	37.3	37.8	38.4	38.3	38.7	38.1	38.6	37.8	38.1
Manufacturing	. . .	. . .	39.7	39.4	39.9	40.2	39.9	40.1	40.2	40.2	40.0	40.3
Overtime hours	. . .	. . .	3.3	2.9	3.4	3.5	3.3	3.5	3.4	3.3	3.3	3.5
Durable goods	. . .	. . .	40.2	39.7	40.4	40.6	40.3	40.6	40.5	40.6	40.2	40.7
Overtime hours	. . .	. . .	3.4	2.8	3.4	3.5	3.3	3.5	3.4	3.3	3.3	3.5
Nondurable goods	. . .	. . .	39.0	38.8	39.1	39.4	39.3	39.3	39.6	39.5	39.4	39.5
Overtime hours	. . .	. . .	3.2	3.0	3.4	3.5	3.4	3.4	3.5	3.4	3.5	3.4
Private Service-Providing	. . .	. . .	33.0	33.6	33.1	33.4	33.8	33.4	33.3	33.7	33.3	33.4
Trade, transportation, and utilities	. . .	. . .	33.6	34.4	34.0	34.3	34.8	34.5	34.4	34.7	34.3	34.7
Wholesale trade	. . .	. . .	37.3	38.0	37.4	37.7	38.1	37.5	37.5	38.2	37.7	37.8
Retail trade	. . .	. . .	30.8	31.6	31.3	31.6	32.2	31.9	31.7	31.9	31.6	32.2
Transportation and warehousing	. . .	. . .	37.7	38.1	37.9	38.3	38.6	38.4	38.5	38.8	38.5	38.5
Utilities	. . .	. . .	40.7	41.5	41.2	41.4	41.8	41.4	41.4	41.7	41.5	41.6
Information	. . .	. . .	36.0	36.8	36.0	36.3	37.2	36.5	36.2	36.7	35.9	36.0
Financial activities	. . .	. . .	36.5	37.5	36.3	36.5	37.3	36.3	36.3	37.3	36.2	36.4
Professional and business services	. . .	. . .	34.9	35.4	35.0	35.5	35.5	35.1	35.2	35.8	35.3	35.3
Education and health services	. . .	. . .	33.2	33.5	33.2	33.3	33.6	33.3	33.4	33.6	33.4	33.4
Leisure and hospitality	. . .	. . .	25.9	26.4	26.1	26.5	27.2	26.8	26.0	26.4	25.9	26.0
Other services	. . .	. . .	33.0	33.3	32.9	33.1	33.3	33.2	32.9	33.2	32.9	32.9

. . . = Not available.

EARNINGS

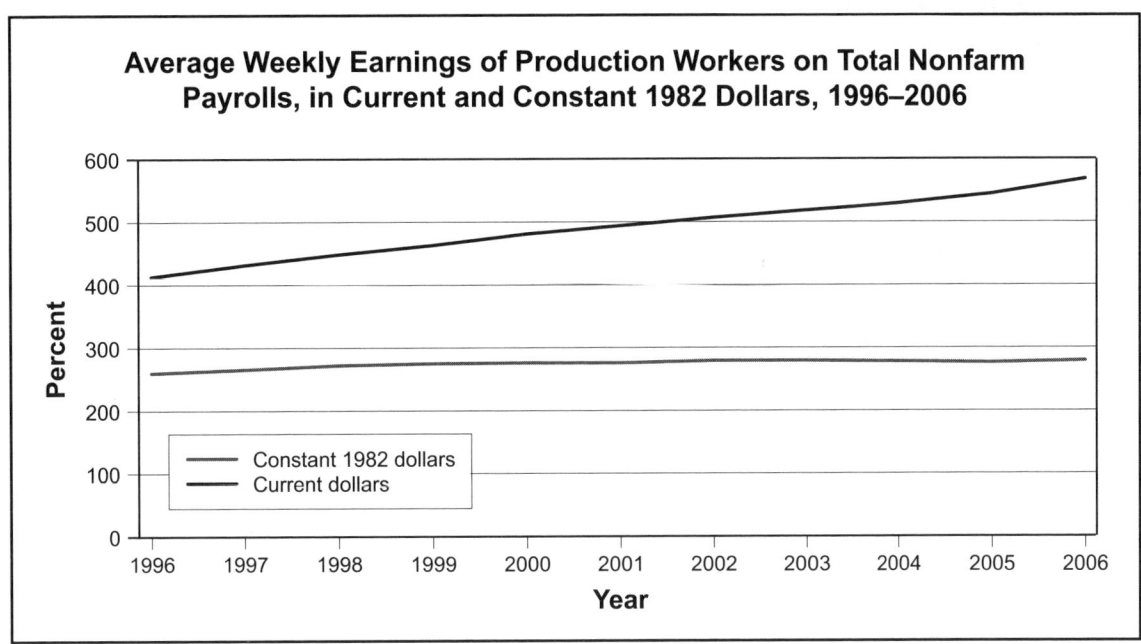

Average Weekly Earnings of Production Workers on Total Nonfarm Payrolls, in Current and Constant 1982 Dollars, 1996–2006

Weekly earnings of production workers adjusted for inflation rose for the first time since 2002. Current dollar earnings rose 4.3 percent and prices for urban wage earners and clerical workers rose 3.2 percent, leading to an increase in real earnings of 1.1 percent. (See Table 2-18.)

OTHER HIGHLIGHTS

• In the manufacturing sector, real weekly earning of production workers decreased slightly. The largest increase in current dollar earnings was in professional and business services, which rose by 7.0 percent. (See Table 2-18.)

• Production workers in utilities had the highest average weekly earnings at $1,136.08 in 2006—double the average weekly earnings of all private workers. (See Table 2-18.) Although average weekly earnings were $690.83 in the manufacturing sector, the highest level within that sector was in the petroleum and coal product industry ($1,084.83), while the lowest was in the apparel industry ($387.27). (See Tables 2-18 and 2-19.)

• For all covered workers, the highest average annual pay was in the utilities sector at $78,341. Within the government sector, the federal government had the highest annual pay at $62,274, while local government the lowest average annual pay at $39,179. (See Table 2-23.)

Table 2-16. Average Hourly Earnings of Production Workers on Private Nonfarm Payrolls, by Super Sector, NAICS Basis, 1995–2006

(Dollars.)

Industry	1995	1996	1997	1998	1999	2000	2001	2002	2003	2004	2005	2006
TOTAL PRIVATE	11.65	12.04	12.51	13.01	13.49	14.02	14.54	14.97	15.37	15.69	16.13	16.76
Goods-Producing	12.96	13.38	13.82	14.23	14.71	15.27	15.78	16.33	16.80	17.19	17.60	18.02
Natural resources and mining	14.78	15.10	15.57	16.20	16.33	16.55	17.00	17.19	17.56	18.07	18.72	19.90
Construction	14.73	15.11	15.67	16.23	16.80	17.48	18.00	18.52	18.95	19.23	19.46	20.02
Manufacturing	12.34	12.75	13.14	13.45	13.85	14.32	14.76	15.29	15.74	16.15	16.56	16.80
Private Service-Providing	11.21	11.59	12.07	12.61	13.09	13.62	14.18	14.59	14.99	15.29	15.74	16.42
Trade, transportation, and utilities	11.10	11.46	11.90	12.39	12.82	13.31	13.70	14.02	14.34	14.58	14.92	15.40
Wholesale trade	13.34	13.80	14.41	15.07	15.62	16.28	16.77	16.98	17.36	17.65	18.16	18.91
Retail trade	8.85	9.21	9.59	10.05	10.45	10.86	11.29	11.67	11.90	12.08	12.36	12.58
Transportation and warehousing	13.18	13.45	13.78	14.12	14.55	15.05	15.33	15.76	16.25	16.52	16.70	17.28
Utilities	19.19	19.78	20.59	21.48	22.03	22.75	23.58	23.96	24.77	25.61	26.68	27.42
Information	15.68	16.30	17.14	17.67	18.40	19.07	19.80	20.20	21.01	21.40	22.06	23.23
Financial activities	12.28	12.71	13.22	13.93	14.47	14.98	15.59	16.17	17.14	17.52	17.94	18.80
Professional and business services	12.53	13.00	13.57	14.27	14.85	15.52	16.33	16.81	17.21	17.48	18.08	19.12
Education and health services	11.80	12.17	12.56	13.00	13.44	13.95	14.64	15.21	15.64	16.15	16.71	17.38
Leisure and hospitality	6.79	6.99	7.32	7.67	7.96	8.32	8.57	8.81	9.00	9.15	9.38	9.75
Other services	10.51	10.85	11.29	11.79	12.26	12.73	13.27	13.72	13.84	13.98	14.34	14.77

Table 2-17. Average Hourly Earnings of Production Workers on Manufacturing Payrolls, by Industry, NAICS Basis, 1995–2006

(Dollars.)

Industry	1995	1996	1997	1998	1999	2000	2001	2002	2003	2004	2005	2006
DURABLE GOODS												
Total	13.05	13.45	13.83	14.07	14.46	14.93	15.38	16.02	16.45	16.82	17.33	17.67
Wood product	9.92	10.24	10.53	10.85	11.18	11.63	11.99	12.33	12.71	13.03	13.16	13.40
Nonmetallic mineral product	12.39	12.80	13.17	13.59	13.97	14.53	14.86	15.40	15.76	16.25	16.61	16.59
Primary metals	14.75	15.12	15.40	15.66	16.00	16.64	17.06	17.68	18.13	18.57	18.94	19.35
Fabricated metal product	11.91	12.26	12.64	12.97	13.34	13.77	14.19	14.68	15.01	15.31	15.80	16.17
Machinery	13.14	13.49	13.94	14.24	14.77	15.22	15.49	15.92	16.30	16.68	17.03	17.20
Computer and electronic product	12.29	12.75	13.24	13.85	14.37	14.73	15.42	16.20	16.69	17.27	18.39	18.96
Electrical equipment and appliances	11.25	11.80	12.24	12.51	12.90	13.23	13.78	13.98	14.36	14.90	15.24	15.53
Transportation equipment	17.21	17.67	18.00	17.92	18.24	18.89	19.48	20.64	21.23	21.49	22.10	22.41
Furniture and related product	9.75	10.08	10.50	10.88	11.27	11.72	12.14	12.61	12.98	13.16	13.45	13.79
Miscellaneous manufacturing	10.23	10.60	10.89	11.18	11.56	11.93	12.46	12.91	13.30	13.84	14.08	14.36
NONDURABLE GOODS												
Total	11.30	11.68	12.04	12.45	12.85	13.31	13.75	14.15	14.63	15.05	15.27	15.32
Food manufacturing	10.27	10.50	10.77	11.09	11.40	11.77	12.18	12.55	12.80	12.98	13.04	13.13
Beverage and tobacco product	15.40	15.73	16.00	16.03	16.54	17.40	17.67	17.73	17.96	19.14	18.76	18.19
Textile mills	9.63	9.88	10.22	10.58	10.90	11.23	11.40	11.73	11.99	12.13	12.38	12.55
Textile product mills	8.76	9.12	9.45	9.75	10.18	10.43	10.60	10.96	11.23	11.39	11.67	11.94
Apparel	7.22	7.45	7.76	8.05	8.35	8.60	8.82	9.10	9.56	9.75	10.24	10.61
Leather and allied product	8.50	8.94	9.31	9.68	9.93	10.35	10.69	11.00	11.66	11.63	11.50	11.44
Paper and paper product	13.94	14.38	14.76	15.20	15.58	15.91	16.38	16.85	17.33	17.91	17.99	18.01
Printing and related support	12.08	12.41	12.78	13.20	13.67	14.09	14.48	14.93	15.37	15.71	15.74	15.80
Petroleum and coal product	20.24	20.18	21.10	21.75	22.22	22.80	22.90	23.04	23.63	24.39	24.47	24.08
Chemicals	14.86	15.37	15.78	16.23	16.40	17.09	17.57	17.97	18.50	19.17	19.67	19.60
Plastics and rubber product	10.86	11.17	11.48	11.79	12.25	12.69	13.21	13.55	14.18	14.59	14.80	14.96

Table 2-18. Average Weekly Earnings of Production Workers on Nonfarm Payrolls, by Industry, in Current and Constant 1982 Dollars, NAICS Basis, 1995–2006

(Dollars.)

Industry	1995	1996	1997	1998	1999	2000	2001	2002	2003	2004	2005	2006
TOTAL PRIVATE												
Current dollars	400.07	413.28	431.86	448.56	463.15	481.01	493.79	506.72	518.06	529.09	544.33	567.87
Constant 1982 dollars	258.78	259.92	265.60	272.18	275.03	275.97	275.71	279.18	279.13	277.88	276.17	279.19
Goods-Producing												
Current dollars	528.62	546.48	568.43	580.99	599.99	621.86	630.04	651.61	669.13	688.17	705.31	729.87
Constant 1982 dollars	341.93	343.70	349.59	352.54	356.29	356.78	351.78	359.01	360.52	361.43	357.84	358.83
Natural resources and mining												
Current dollars	670.32	695.07	720.11	727.28	721.74	734.92	757.92	741.97	765.94	803.82	853.71	908.01
Constant 1982 dollars	433.58	437.15	442.87	441.31	428.59	421.64	423.18	408.80	412.68	422.17	433.14	446.42
Construction												
Current dollars	571.57	588.48	609.48	629.75	655.11	685.78	695.89	711.82	726.83	735.55	750.22	781.04
Constant 1982 dollars	369.71	370.11	374.83	382.13	389.02	393.45	388.55	392.19	391.61	386.32	380.63	383.99
Manufacturing												
Current dollars	509.26	526.55	548.22	557.12	573.17	590.65	595.19	618.75	635.99	658.59	673.37	690.83
Constant 1982 dollars	329.40	331.16	337.16	338.06	340.36	338.87	332.32	340.91	342.67	345.90	341.64	339.64
Private Service-Providing												
Current dollars	364.80	377.37	395.51	413.50	427.98	445.74	461.08	473.80	484.81	494.22	509.58	532.84
Constant 1982 dollars	235.96	237.34	243.24	250.91	254.14	255.73	257.44	261.05	261.21	259.57	258.54	261.97
Trade, transportation, and utilities												
Current dollars	378.79	390.64	407.57	423.30	434.31	449.88	459.53	471.27	481.14	488.42	498.43	514.61
Constant 1982 dollars	245.01	245.69	250.66	256.86	257.90	258.11	256.58	259.65	259.23	256.52	252.88	253.00
Wholesale trade												
Current dollars	515.14	533.29	559.39	582.21	602.77	631.40	643.45	644.38	657.29	667.09	685.00	718.30
Constant 1982 dollars	333.21	335.40	344.03	353.28	357.94	362.25	359.27	355.03	354.14	350.36	347.54	353.15
Retail trade												
Current dollars	272.56	282.76	295.97	310.34	321.63	333.38	346.16	360.81	367.15	371.13	377.58	383.16
Constant 1982 dollars	176.30	177.84	182.02	188.31	190.99	191.27	193.28	198.79	197.82	194.92	191.57	188.38
Transportation and warehousing												
Current dollars	513.37	525.60	542.55	546.86	547.97	562.31	562.70	579.75	598.41	614.82	618.58	637.14
Constant 1982 dollars	332.06	330.57	333.67	331.83	325.40	322.61	314.18	319.42	322.42	322.91	313.84	313.24
Utilities												
Current dollars	811.52	830.74	865.26	902.94	924.59	955.66	977.18	979.09	1 017.27	1 048.44	1 095.90	1 136.08
Constant 1982 dollars	524.92	522.48	532.14	547.90	549.04	548.28	545.61	539.44	548.10	550.65	556.01	558.54
Information												
Current dollars	564.98	592.68	622.40	646.52	675.32	700.89	731.11	738.17	760.81	777.05	805.00	850.81
Constant 1982 dollars	365.45	372.75	382.78	392.31	401.02	402.12	408.21	406.71	409.92	408.11	408.42	418.29
Financial activities												
Current dollars	436.12	451.49	472.37	500.95	517.57	537.37	558.02	575.51	609.08	622.87	645.10	672.40
Constant 1982 dollars	282.10	283.96	290.51	303.97	307.35	308.30	311.57	317.09	328.17	327.14	327.30	330.58
Professional and business services												
Current dollars	426.44	442.81	465.51	490.00	510.99	535.07	557.84	574.66	587.02	597.56	618.87	662.23
Constant 1982 dollars	275.83	278.50	286.29	297.33	303.44	306.98	311.47	316.62	316.28	313.84	313.99	325.58
Education and health services												
Current dollars	377.73	388.27	404.65	418.82	431.35	449.29	473.39	492.74	505.69	523.78	544.59	564.95
Constant 1982 dollars	244.33	244.19	248.86	254.14	256.15	257.77	264.32	271.48	272.46	275.09	276.30	277.75
Leisure and hospitality												
Current dollars	175.74	180.98	190.52	200.82	208.05	217.20	220.73	227.17	230.42	234.86	241.36	250.11
Constant 1982 dollars	113.67	113.82	117.17	121.86	123.55	124.61	123.24	125.16	124.15	123.35	122.46	122.96
Other services												
Current dollars	342.36	352.62	368.63	384.25	398.77	413.41	428.64	439.76	434.41	433.04	443.37	456.60
Constant 1982 dollars	221.45	221.77	226.71	233.16	236.80	237.18	239.33	242.29	234.06	227.44	224.95	224.48

Table 2-19. Average Weekly Earnings of Production Workers on Manufacturing Payrolls, by Industry, NAICS Basis, 1995–2006

(Dollars.)

Industry	1995	1996	1997	1998	1999	2000	2001	2002	2003	2004	2005	2006
TOTAL MANUFACTURING	509.26	526.55	548.22	557.12	573.17	590.65	595.19	618.75	635.99	658.59	673.37	690.83
Total Durable Goods	549.49	566.53	589.10	591.68	606.67	624.38	624.54	652.97	671.21	694.13	712.95	731.81
Wood product	406.51	422.32	435.78	449.78	461.61	477.23	481.36	492.00	514.10	530.15	526.65	533.44
Nonmetallic mineral product	517.68	537.81	552.02	572.96	587.53	604.88	618.79	646.91	664.92	688.20	700.78	713.34
Primary metals	639.70	658.68	681.47	681.64	700.76	734.62	723.95	749.32	767.60	799.78	815.78	842.94
Fabricated metal product	498.48	513.57	534.48	543.20	555.86	576.68	576.60	596.38	610.37	628.80	647.34	668.84
Machinery	571.25	584.69	613.49	613.87	625.40	643.92	632.77	645.55	664.79	699.59	716.55	728.99
Computer and electronic product	518.25	534.42	562.69	579.70	596.25	609.70	613.07	642.87	674.72	697.83	735.59	767.86
Electrical equipment and appliances	471.63	496.69	515.73	522.51	538.98	550.56	548.00	560.24	583.23	606.97	618.97	635.87
Transportation equipment	751.74	773.95	795.82	774.82	796.25	817.98	817.08	877.87	889.48	912.98	938.03	957.43
Furniture and related product	375.06	385.68	410.38	428.50	443.38	459.69	464.57	494.01	505.30	519.62	527.35	535.35
Miscellaneous manufacturing	400.85	414.13	431.89	437.99	454.56	465.02	483.44	499.13	510.82	533.07	545.21	556.16
Total Nondurable Goods	452.83	467.88	487.04	503.99	519.91	536.82	548.41	566.84	582.61	602.53	608.95	621.78
Food manufacturing	406.66	414.74	428.58	444.81	458.63	472.09	481.67	496.91	502.92	509.55	508.55	526.02
Beverage and tobacco product	605.00	624.82	639.69	646.26	679.06	730.35	721.68	698.39	702.45	751.20	751.54	741.31
Textile mills	394.17	403.08	425.53	434.15	447.38	464.51	456.64	476.52	469.33	486.68	498.47	509.41
Textile product mills	342.17	356.90	373.95	385.13	401.01	406.24	408.56	429.01	444.70	443.12	455.52	477.56
Apparel	254.85	261.90	275.61	286.07	295.20	307.00	317.15	333.66	340.12	351.56	366.17	387.27
Leather and allied product	319.98	337.86	355.63	361.87	369.80	388.46	388.83	412.99	457.83	446.66	441.96	445.50
Paper and paper product	604.74	625.38	647.55	662.20	679.24	681.34	690.06	705.62	719.73	754.14	764.04	772.26
Printing and related support	472.37	484.99	504.46	518.32	534.15	552.15	560.89	573.05	587.58	603.97	604.73	618.81
Petroleum and coal product	883.68	881.24	908.50	949.28	947.60	973.53	1 003.34	990.88	1 052.32	1 095.00	1 114.51	1 084.03
Chemicals	644.30	666.00	685.26	700.53	700.45	721.90	735.54	759.53	783.95	819.73	831.76	833.59
Plastics and rubber product	445.91	458.15	474.87	487.00	505.31	517.74	528.69	549.85	572.26	589.84	591.58	607.82

Table 2-20. Average Hourly Earnings of Production Workers on Manufacturing Payrolls, by State and Selected Territory, NAICS Basis, 2001–2006

(Dollars.)

State	2001	2002	2003	2004	2005	2006
UNITED STATES	14.76	15.29	15.74	16.15	16.56	16.80
Alabama	12.76	13.10	13.56	14.33	14.93	15.56
Alaska	11.70	13.24	12.18	12.01	14.22	14.30
Arizona	13.80	14.16	14.38	14.20	14.55	14.88
Arkansas	12.90	13.30	13.55	13.49	13.71	13.35
California	14.69	14.89	15.04	15.36	15.70	15.95
Colorado	14.72	15.44	16.89	16.46	15.91	16.58
Connecticut	16.42	17.24	17.74	18.35	18.96	19.78
Delaware	16.56	16.60	16.91	17.66	17.74	18.13
District of Columbia	. . .	. . .	. . .	. . .	. . .	. . .
Florida	12.68	13.30	14.09	13.84	13.89	14.75
Georgia	12.50	13.38	14.08	14.54	14.56	14.74
Hawaii	13.18	13.07	12.90	13.50	14.34	15.89
Idaho	13.85	13.80	13.72	14.15	14.96	16.89
Illinois	14.66	14.99	15.20	15.61	15.84	16.03
Indiana	16.42	17.15	17.84	17.92	18.14	18.57
Iowa	14.67	15.32	15.70	16.17	16.25	16.40
Kansas	15.48	15.98	15.83	16.57	17.14	17.68
Kentucky	15.44	15.73	16.01	16.50	16.65	16.92
Louisiana	16.18	17.03	16.86	16.40	17.30	17.94
Maine	14.71	15.55	16.28	16.97	17.28	18.57
Maryland	. . .	. . .	15.74	16.47	16.98	17.87
Massachusetts	15.75	16.25	16.53	16.89	17.66	18.26
Michigan	. . .	. . .	21.20	21.51	21.50	21.83
Minnesota	14.76	15.06	15.43	16.04	16.63	17.23
Mississippi	11.93	12.32	12.89	13.12	13.53	13.78
Missouri	16.11	16.80	18.22	17.92	17.42	17.16
Montana	14.03	14.43	14.02	14.87	15.62	15.90
Nebraska	13.64	14.05	14.86	15.19	15.44	15.04
Nevada	13.79	14.62	14.63	14.60	14.98	15.47
New Hampshire	13.98	14.21	14.85	15.48	15.87	16.56
New Jersey	14.74	15.19	15.45	15.89	16.33	16.55
New Mexico	13.27	13.41	13.19	13.13	13.66	14.06
New York	16.24	16.75	16.78	17.29	17.77	18.29
North Carolina	12.81	13.18	13.66	14.25	14.38	14.57
North Dakota	12.77	13.17	14.04	14.35	15.29	14.97
Ohio	16.79	17.49	17.99	18.47	19.07	19.16
Oklahoma	13.66	14.11	14.13	14.24	14.56	14.77
Oregon	14.74	15.06	15.20	15.34	15.49	15.57
Pennsylvania	14.37	14.75	14.99	15.16	15.26	15.37
Rhode Island	12.68	12.75	12.88	13.03	13.12	13.42
South Carolina	. . .	. . .	14.19	14.73	15.23	15.03
South Dakota	12.11	12.60	13.13	13.37	13.47	13.75
Tennessee	12.88	13.15	13.56	13.84	14.02	14.04
Texas	14.04	13.93	13.94	13.98	14.03	14.01
Utah	13.76	14.12	14.90	15.38	14.73	15.25
Vermont	14.18	14.33	14.54	14.60	15.06	15.79
Virginia	14.50	15.20	15.90	16.11	16.40	16.75
Washington	17.96	18.15	18.02	18.28	18.83	19.90
West Virginia	. . .	. . .	16.05	16.57	17.14	17.89
Wisconsin	15.44	15.86	16.12	16.19	16.29	16.54
Wyoming	17.26	17.72	16.75	16.58	17.08	17.44
Puerto Rico	9.84	10.30	10.46	10.84	11.10	11.47
Virgin Islands	22.57	22.98	23.37	23.35	23.49	26.53

. . . = Not available.

Table 2-21. Average Weekly Earnings of Production Workers on Manufacturing Payrolls, by State and Selected Territory, NAICS Basis, 2001–2006

(Dollars.)

State	2001	2002	2003	2004	2005	2006
UNITED STATES	595.19	618.75	635.99	658.59	673.37	690.83
Alabama	523.16	542.34	555.96	584.66	609.14	636.40
Alaska	504.27	495.18	523.74	487.61	467.84	579.15
Arizona	556.14	566.40	580.95	575.10	592.19	604.13
Arkansas	514.71	528.01	536.58	538.25	547.03	547.35
California	581.72	589.64	597.09	614.40	626.43	644.38
Colorado	599.10	626.86	682.36	664.98	612.54	649.94
Connecticut	684.71	717.18	734.44	767.03	800.11	834.72
Delaware	657.43	664.00	681.47	708.17	704.28	723.39
District of Columbia	. . .	. . .	. . .	. . .	. . .	. . .
Florida	514.81	559.93	577.69	568.82	579.21	612.13
Georgia	505.00	547.24	560.38	569.97	567.84	582.23
Hawaii	474.48	465.29	479.88	511.65	550.66	613.35
Idaho	541.54	546.48	566.64	573.08	602.89	704.31
Illinois	601.06	620.59	617.12	640.01	646.27	658.83
Indiana	673.22	727.16	751.06	754.43	760.07	774.37
Iowa	600.00	632.72	654.69	682.37	676.00	687.16
Kansas	630.04	651.98	641.12	679.37	704.45	760.24
Kentucky	640.76	663.81	667.62	673.20	675.99	695.41
Louisiana	697.36	747.62	743.53	719.96	726.60	771.42
Maine	585.46	620.45	651.20	672.01	684.29	768.80
Maryland	. . .	. . .	621.73	660.45	680.90	725.52
Massachusetts	634.73	663.00	671.12	694.18	732.89	743.18
Michigan	. . .	. . .	892.52	912.02	896.55	921.23
Minnesota	584.50	597.88	620.29	656.04	680.17	706.43
Mississippi	473.62	500.19	514.31	526.11	542.55	542.93
Missouri	649.23	660.24	737.91	720.38	689.83	674.39
Montana	544.36	551.23	538.37	569.52	626.36	636.00
Nebraska	561.97	588.70	618.18	631.90	617.60	615.14
Nevada	533.67	567.26	570.57	585.46	596.20	609.52
New Hampshire	567.59	565.56	594.00	619.20	653.84	682.27
New Jersey	598.44	621.27	633.45	668.97	685.86	696.76
New Mexico	517.53	535.06	519.69	519.95	534.11	551.15
New York	646.35	675.03	671.20	686.41	703.69	751.72
North Carolina	504.71	529.84	543.67	574.28	575.20	582.80
North Dakota	522.29	529.43	561.60	563.96	599.37	583.83
Ohio	691.75	724.09	737.59	770.20	789.50	793.22
Oklahoma	538.20	553.11	555.31	576.72	573.66	589.32
Oregon	576.33	588.85	597.36	599.79	622.70	630.59
Pennsylvania	580.55	594.43	599.60	610.95	618.03	627.10
Rhode Island	499.59	493.43	506.18	510.78	503.81	522.04
South Carolina	. . .	. . .	586.05	581.84	604.63	616.23
South Dakota	504.99	532.98	558.03	561.54	569.78	578.88
Tennessee	501.03	527.32	539.69	553.60	549.58	553.18
Texas	584.06	572.52	577.12	556.40	561.20	573.01
Utah	528.38	533.74	591.53	585.98	577.42	626.78
Vermont	561.53	573.20	581.60	586.92	590.35	625.28
Virginia	581.30	621.30	647.70	668.57	678.96	691.78
Washington	718.40	727.82	711.79	731.20	747.55	807.94
West Virginia	. . .	. . .	662.87	686.00	709.60	738.86
Wisconsin	620.69	642.33	649.64	652.46	658.12	673.18
Wyoming	666.24	696.40	673.35	658.23	691.74	718.53
Puerto Rico	392.62	418.18	427.81	444.44	452.88	464.54
Virgin Islands	990.82	1 004.23	1 000.24	1 083.44	1 026.51	1 164.67

. . . = Not available.

Table 2-22. Average Hourly Earnings of All Employees on Private Nonfarm Payrolls, by Industry Sector and Selected Industry Detail, Not Seasonally Adjusted, Experimental Series, 2006

(Dollars.)

Industry	January	February	March	April	May	June	July	August	September	October	November	December
TOTAL PRIVATE	. . .	. . .	20.02	20.32	20.02	20.01	20.24	20.09	20.31	20.47	20.40	20.56
Goods-Producing	. . .	. . .	21.16	21.41	21.18	21.25	21.44	21.36	21.53	21.69	21.69	21.96
Natural resources and mining	. . .	. . .	22.91	23.64	23.22	23.47	23.77	23.40	23.64	24.32	24.84	24.80
Construction	. . .	. . .	21.84	22.02	21.93	22.05	22.19	22.20	22.43	22.54	22.50	22.75
Manufacturing	. . .	. . .	20.75	20.98	20.69	20.70	20.91	20.80	20.94	21.10	21.10	21.41
Private Service-Providing	. . .	. . .	19.69	20.01	19.68	19.64	19.89	19.71	19.95	20.11	20.03	20.16
Trade, transportation, and utilities	. . .	. . .	18.24	18.53	18.22	18.25	18.46	18.20	18.38	18.40	18.20	18.24
Wholesale trade	. . .	. . .	22.83	23.33	22.90	22.90	23.51	23.13	23.49	23.54	23.51	23.87
Retail trade	. . .	. . .	15.26	15.44	15.20	15.22	15.28	15.08	15.20	15.18	14.96	14.91
Transportation and warehousing	. . .	. . .	19.10	19.42	19.18	19.31	19.50	19.25	19.22	19.26	19.15	19.26
Utilities	. . .	. . .	29.26	29.75	29.18	28.92	29.30	28.91	29.20	29.66	29.52	29.42
Information	. . .	. . .	26.69	27.22	26.99	26.91	27.19	27.05	27.46	27.55	27.32	27.50
Financial activities	. . .	. . .	23.92	24.85	24.28	24.21	24.90	24.69	24.71	25.14	25.12	25.11
Professional and business services	. . .	. . .	23.40	23.87	23.24	23.15	23.68	23.32	23.65	23.97	23.82	24.23
Education and health services	. . .	. . .	19.90	19.99	19.92	20.00	20.16	20.14	20.19	20.18	20.23	20.33
Leisure and hospitality	. . .	. . .	11.54	11.59	11.65	11.55	11.54	11.58	11.77	11.92	12.01	12.16
Other services	. . .	. . .	17.20	17.33	17.25	17.14	17.13	17.13	17.33	17.36	17.36	17.49

. . . = Not available.

NOTES AND DEFINITIONS

QUARTERLY CENSUS OF EMPLOYMENT AND WAGES

The Quarterly Census of Employment and Wages (QCEW), also called the ES-202 program, is a cooperative endeavor of the Bureau of Labor Statistics (BLS) and the State Employment Security Agencies (SESAs). Using quarterly data submitted by the agencies, BLS summarizes the employment and wage data for workers covered by state unemployment insurance laws and civilian workers covered by the Unemployment Compensation for Federal Employees (UCFE) program.

The QCEW tables use the 2002 version of the North American Industry Classification System (NAICS) as the basis for the assignment and tabulation of economic data by industry. The structure of NAICS is significantly different than that of the 1987 Standard Industrial Classification (SIC) system, which was previously used for industry classification purposes. Due to these differences, results in NAICS-based data are not directly comparable with historical SIC-based data. The NAICS classification system was described in the sixth edition of this *Handbook* and more information on NAICS can be found on the BLS Web site at <http://www.bls.gov/bls/naics.htm>.

The QCEW data series is the most complete universe of employment and wage information by industry, county, and state. These data serve as the basic source of benchmark information for employment by industry in the Current Employment Statistics (CES) survey, which is described in the first section of notes in this chapter. Therefore, the entire employment series is not presented here. The wage series is presented because the CES only provides earnings only for production and nonsupervisory employees. The QCEW is more comprehensive. BLS aggregates the data by industry and ownership; these aggregations are available at the national, state, county, and metropolitan statistical area (MSA) levels.

Collection and Coverage

Employment data under the QCEW program represent the number of covered workers who worked during (or received pay for) the pay period containing the 12th of the month. Excluded are members of the armed forces, the self-employed, proprietors, domestic workers, unpaid family workers, and railroad workers covered by the railroad unemployment insurance system.

Annual pay data are compiled from reports submitted by employers subject to state and federal unemployment insurance (UI) laws, covering approximately 131.6 million full- and part-time workers. Average annual pay is computed by dividing total annual payrolls of employees covered by UI programs by the average monthly number of these employees. Pay differences among states reflect the varying composition of employment by occupation, industry, hours of work, and other factors, and pay differences among industries are similarly affected. For example, the relatively large share of part-time workers reduces average annual pay levels in retail trade industries. Correspondingly, pay levels in construction industries reflect the prevalence of part-year employment due to weather and seasonal factors. Over-the-year pay changes may reflect shifts in the composition of employment, as well as changes in the average level of pay.

Total wages, for purposes of the quarterly UI reports submitted by private industry employers in private industry in most states, include gross wages and salaries, bonuses, stock options, tips and other gratuities, and the value of meals and lodging (when supplied). In some of the states, employer contributions to certain deferred compensation plans, such as 401(k) plans, are included in total wages. Total wages, however, do not include employer contributions to Old-Age, Survivors', and Disability Insurance (OASDI), health insurance, unemployment insurance, workers' compensation, and private pension and welfare funds.

In most states, firms report the total wages paid during the calendar quarter, regardless of the timing of the services performed. However, under the laws of a few states, the employers report total wages earned during the quarter (payable) rather than actual amounts paid. For federal workers, wages represent the gross amount of all payrolls for all pay periods paid within the quarter. This gross amount includes cash allowances and the cash equivalent of any type of remuneration. It includes all lump-sum payments for terminal leave, withholding taxes, and retirement deductions. Federal employee remuneration generally covers the same types of services as those for workers in private industry.

Sources of Additional Information

Additional information and the sub-national data are available in the BLS publication, *Employment and Wages, Annual Averages*, which can be found on the BLS Web site at <http://www.bls.gov>.

Table 2-23. Employment and Average Annual Pay for All Covered Workers,[1] by Industry, NAICS Basis, 2001–2006

(Number, dollars.)

Industry	2001		2002		2003	
	Employment	Average annual pay	Employment	Average annual pay	Employment	Average annual pay
Total Private	109 304 802	36 157	107 577 281	36 539	107 065 553	37 508
Agriculture, forestry, fishing, and hunting	1 170 570	20 188	1 155 890	20 890	1 156 242	21 366
Natural resources and mining	1 705 759	32 580	1 661 870	32 917	1 656 345	33 729
Construction	6 773 512	38 412	6 683 553	39 027	6 672 360	39 509
Manufacturing	16 386 001	42 969	15 209 192	44 097	14 459 712	45 916
Wholesale trade	5 730 294	48 791	5 617 456	49 241	5 589 032	50 835
Retail trade	15 179 753	22 667	15 018 588	23 232	14 930 765	23 804
Transportation and warehousing	4 138 146	36 189	3 989 116	36 823	3 946 170	37 436
Utilities	599 899	65 561	592 152	67 374	575 877	68 651
Information	3 591 995	57 288	3 364 485	56 103	3 180 752	58 002
Financial activities	7 678 974	55 515	7 706 265	55 172	7 826 930	57 143
Professional and business services	16 324 890	43 566	15 939 596	43 899	15 858 457	45 052
Education and health services	14 849 666	32 718	15 346 718	33 931	15 738 013	35 071
Leisure and hospitality	11 884 966	15 426	11 995 950	15 777	12 162 238	16 138
Other services	4 206 345	23 220	4 246 011	23 784	4 261 165	24 348
Total Government	20 330 998	36 549	20 656 638	37 935	20 730 273	39 094
Federal	2 752 619	48 940	2 758 627	52 050	2 764 275	54 239
State	4 452 237	37 814	4 485 071	39 212	4 481 845	40 057
Local	13 126 143	33 521	13 412 941	34 605	13 484 153	35 669

Industry	2004		2005		2006	
	Employment	Average annual pay	Employment	Average annual pay	Employment	Average annual pay
Total Private	108 490 066	39 134	110 611 016	40 505	112 718 858	42 414
Agriculture, forestry, fishing, and hunting	1 155 106	22 337	1 163 629	23 117	1 160 179	24 132
Natural resources and mining	1 675 038	36 086	1 724 044	39 080	1 776 777	42 904
Construction	6 916 398	40 521	7 269 317	42 100	7 602 148	44 496
Manufacturing	14 257 380	47 861	14 190 394	49 287	14 110 663	51 427
Wholesale trade	5 642 537	53 310	5 752 802	55 262	5 885 194	58 046
Retail trade	15 060 686	24 415	15 256 340	24 930	15 370 040	25 567
Transportation and warehousing	4 009 165	38 834	4 098 553	39 515	4 204 514	40 848
Utilities	563 931	72 403	550 593	75 208	546 521	78 341
Information	3 099 633	60 722	3 056 431	62 853	3 040 577	65 962
Financial activities	7 890 786	61 487	8 037 850	64 398	8 162 063	68 901
Professional and business services	16 294 776	47 401	16 869 852	49 574	17 469 679	51 974
Education and health services	16 084 963	36 548	16 479 482	37 654	16 916 228	39 115
Leisure and hospitality	12 467 597	16 624	12 739 466	17 068	13 024 615	17 781
Other services	4 287 999	25 152	4 324 015	25 883	4 364 889	26 923
Total Government	20 788 110	40 500	20 960 607	41 585	21 114 976	43 180
Federal	2 739 596	57 782	2 733 675	59 864	2 728 974	62 274
State	4 484 997	41 118	4 527 514	42 249	4 565 908	43 875
Local	13 563 517	36 805	13 699 418	37 718	13 820 093	39 179

[1]Includes workers covered by unemployment insurance (UI) and Unemployment Compensation for Federal Employees (UCFE) programs.

Table 2-24. Employment and Average Annual Pay for All Covered Workers,[1] by State and Selected Territory, 2001–2006

(Number, dollars.)

State	2001		2002		2003	
	Employment	Average annual pay	Employment	Average annual pay	Employment	Average annual pay
UNITED STATES	129 635 800	36 219	128 233 919	36 764	127 795 827	37 765
Alabama	1 854 462	30 102	1 830 620	31 163	1 823 573	32 236
Alaska	283 033	36 170	287 231	37 134	291 797	37 804
Arizona	2 243 652	33 411	2 240 234	34 036	2 272 393	35 056
Arkansas	1 127 151	27 260	1 119 428	28 074	1 115 891	28 893
California	14 981 757	41 327	14 837 334	41 419	14 807 656	42 592
Colorado	2 201 379	37 952	2 153 857	38 005	2 117 773	38 942
Connecticut	1 665 607	46 993	1 648 547	46 852	1 625 801	48 328
Delaware	406 736	38 427	401 971	39 684	402 166	40 954
District of Columbia	635 749	55 908	650 515	57 914	651 088	60 417
Florida	7 153 589	31 553	7 164 523	32 426	7 248 097	33 544
Georgia	3 871 763	35 136	3 807 915	35 734	3 783 232	36 626
Hawaii	557 146	31 253	558 651	32 671	569 532	33 742
Idaho	571 314	27 768	571 869	28 163	575 889	28 677
Illinois	5 886 248	39 083	5 771 132	39 688	5 698 184	40 540
Indiana	2 871 236	31 779	2 832 553	32 603	2 821 879	33 379
Iowa	1 429 543	28 837	1 412 203	29 668	1 404 377	30 708
Kansas	1 083 162	30 153	1 064 161	30 825	1 048 871	31 489
Kentucky	1 736 575	30 021	1 717 975	30 904	1 714 060	31 855
Louisiana	1 869 966	29 131	1 847 754	30 115	1 855 554	30 782
Maine	593 166	28 815	591 052	29 736	591 372	30 750
Maryland	2 421 899	38 253	2 427 257	39 382	2 434 245	40 686
Massachusetts	3 276 224	44 975	3 202 323	44 954	3 141 089	46 323
Michigan	4 476 659	37 391	4 390 209	38 135	4 321 094	39 433
Minnesota	2 609 669	36 587	2 585 650	37 458	2 576 452	38 610
Mississippi	1 111 255	25 923	1 104 225	26 665	1 096 802	27 591
Missouri	2 652 876	32 421	2 627 082	33 118	2 615 848	33 788
Montana	383 905	25 195	388 161	26 001	393 541	26 907
Nebraska	883 920	28 377	874 063	29 448	875 251	30 382
Nevada	1 043 748	33 121	1 045 012	33 993	1 080 624	35 329
New Hampshire	610 192	35 481	603 234	36 176	604 340	37 321
New Jersey	3 876 194	44 320	3 855 419	45 182	3 850 590	46 351
New Mexico	729 422	28 702	737 418	29 431	745 935	30 202
New York	8 423 312	46 727	8 272 274	46 328	8 224 387	47 247
North Carolina	3 805 498	32 024	3 751 648	32 689	3 719 444	33 532
North Dakota	311 632	25 707	311 800	26 550	314 283	27 628
Ohio	5 434 769	33 283	5 332 891	34 214	5 281 390	35 153
Oklahoma	1 463 622	28 016	1 439 701	28 654	1 411 640	29 699
Oregon	1 596 753	33 204	1 573 057	33 684	1 563 725	34 450
Pennsylvania	5 552 366	34 978	5 504 553	35 808	5 471 255	36 995
Rhode Island	468 952	33 603	468 557	34 810	472 586	36 415
South Carolina	1 786 899	29 255	1 765 717	30 003	1 766 861	30 750
South Dakota	364 715	25 601	363 292	26 360	364 263	27 210
Tennessee	2 625 746	31 520	2 601 518	32 531	2 598 748	33 581
Texas	9 350 770	36 045	9 261 089	36 248	9 208 473	36 968
Utah	1 050 674	30 077	1 041 707	30 585	1 041 938	31 106
Vermont	298 020	30 238	295 443	31 041	294 395	32 086
Virginia	3 436 172	36 733	3 404 760	37 222	3 410 834	38 585
Washington	2 689 507	37 459	2 643 754	38 242	2 653 237	39 021
West Virginia	685 754	27 981	683 183	28 612	677 901	29 284
Wisconsin	2 717 660	31 540	2 690 830	32 464	2 687 919	33 425
Wyoming	237 278	28 043	239 615	28 975	241 699	29 924
Puerto Rico	1 007 919	19 728	992 529	20 662	1 023 102	21 548
Virgin Islands	44 330	29 210	43 070	30 506	41 961	30 994

[1]Includes workers covered by the unemployment insurance (UI) and Unemployment Compensation for Federal Employees (UCFE) programs.

Table 2-24. Employment and Average Annual Pay for All Covered Workers,[1] by State and Selected Territory, 2001–2006—*Continued*

(Number, dollars.)

State	2004		2005		2006	
	Employment	Average annual pay	Employment	Average annual pay	Employment	Average annual pay
UNITED STATES	129 278 176	39 354	131 571 623	40 677	133 833 834	42 535
Alabama	1 851 769	33 414	1 894 616	34 598	1 928 281	36 204
Alaska	296 292	39 062	302 330	40 216	307 637	41 750
Arizona	2 354 660	36 646	2 489 462	38 154	2 614 344	40 019
Arkansas	1 129 018	30 245	1 147 615	31 266	1 167 925	32 389
California	14 953 022	44 641	15 234 188	46 211	15 503 144	48 345
Colorado	2 142 352	40 276	2 189 516	41 601	2 242 012	43 506
Connecticut	1 631 240	51 007	1 644 274	52 954	1 672 109	54 814
Delaware	411 298	42 487	417 692	44 622	422 187	46 285
District of Columbia	659 542	63 887	667 512	66 696	671 143	70 151
Florida	7 463 255	35 186	7 747 729	36 800	7 952 023	38 485
Georgia	3 840 663	37 866	3 932 315	39 096	4 024 699	40 370
Hawaii	585 131	35 198	603 668	36 353	618 178	37 799
Idaho	591 355	29 871	614 548	30 777	643 671	32 580
Illinois	5 700 643	42 277	5 748 355	43 744	5 821 022	45 650
Indiana	2 848 873	34 694	2 873 795	35 431	2 892 419	36 553
Iowa	1 422 454	32 097	1 446 568	33 070	1 470 742	34 320
Kansas	1 058 858	32 738	1 067 241	33 864	1 085 952	35 696
Kentucky	1 729 015	33 165	1 757 997	33 965	1 779 202	35 201
Louisiana	1 865 164	31 880	1 841 046	33 566	1 807 563	36 604
Maine	597 238	31 906	594 481	32 701	598 525	33 794
Maryland	2 459 362	42 579	2 497 487	44 368	2 530 011	46 162
Massachusetts	3 138 738	48 916	3 159 934	50 095	3 194 914	52 435
Michigan	4 301 743	40 373	4 297 017	41 214	4 235 650	42 157
Minnesota	2 600 360	40 398	2 640 326	40 800	2 670 222	42 185
Mississippi	1 105 915	28 535	1 111 269	29 763	1 122 474	31 194
Missouri	2 627 401	34 845	2 664 447	35 951	2 699 860	37 143
Montana	403 432	27 830	413 460	29 150	426 182	30 596
Nebraska	882 263	31 507	892 397	32 422	902 383	33 814
Nevada	1 145 762	37 106	1 215 783	38 763	1 271 634	40 070
New Hampshire	613 310	39 176	620 893	40 551	627 371	42 447
New Jersey	3 873 787	48 064	3 917 397	49 471	3 951 210	51 645
New Mexico	760 449	31 411	778 233	32 605	807 063	34 567
New York	8 271 927	49 941	8 348 739	51 937	8 429 519	55 479
North Carolina	3 777 872	34 791	3 856 748	35 912	3 965 479	37 439
North Dakota	321 108	28 987	328 097	29 956	335 718	31 316
Ohio	5 292 088	36 441	5 308 808	37 333	5 314 572	38 568
Oklahoma	1 427 618	30 743	1 465 969	31 721	1 507 196	34 022
Oregon	1 595 003	35 630	1 652 773	36 588	1 699 932	38 077
Pennsylvania	5 496 599	38 555	5 552 301	39 661	5 607 139	41 349
Rhode Island	475 628	37 651	477 420	38 751	480 570	40 454
South Carolina	1 789 447	31 839	1 819 217	32 927	1 855 842	34 281
South Dakota	369 632	28 281	375 707	29 149	383 876	30 291
Tennessee	2 644 749	34 925	2 685 491	35 879	2 728 694	37 564
Texas	9 323 537	38 511	9 583 457	40 150	9 922 313	42 458
Utah	1 071 855	32 171	1 115 375	33 328	1 170 587	35 130
Vermont	298 454	33 274	300 919	34 197	303 205	35 542
Virginia	3 495 767	40 534	3 578 558	42 287	3 636 417	44 051
Washington	2 694 933	39 361	2 766 451	40 721	2 850 073	42 897
West Virginia	686 936	30 382	695 382	31 347	705 189	32 728
Wisconsin	2 714 847	34 743	2 744 006	35 471	2 767 141	36 821
Wyoming	248 051	31 210	254 418	33 251	266 894	36 662
Puerto Rico	1 043 949	22 259	1 048 004	22 859	1 036 802	23 707
Virgin Islands	43 156	31 846	44 464	33 404	45 114	35 357

[1]Includes workers covered by the unemployment insurance (UI) and Unemployment Compensation for Federal Employees (UCFE) programs.

BUSINESS EMPLOYMENT DYNAMICS

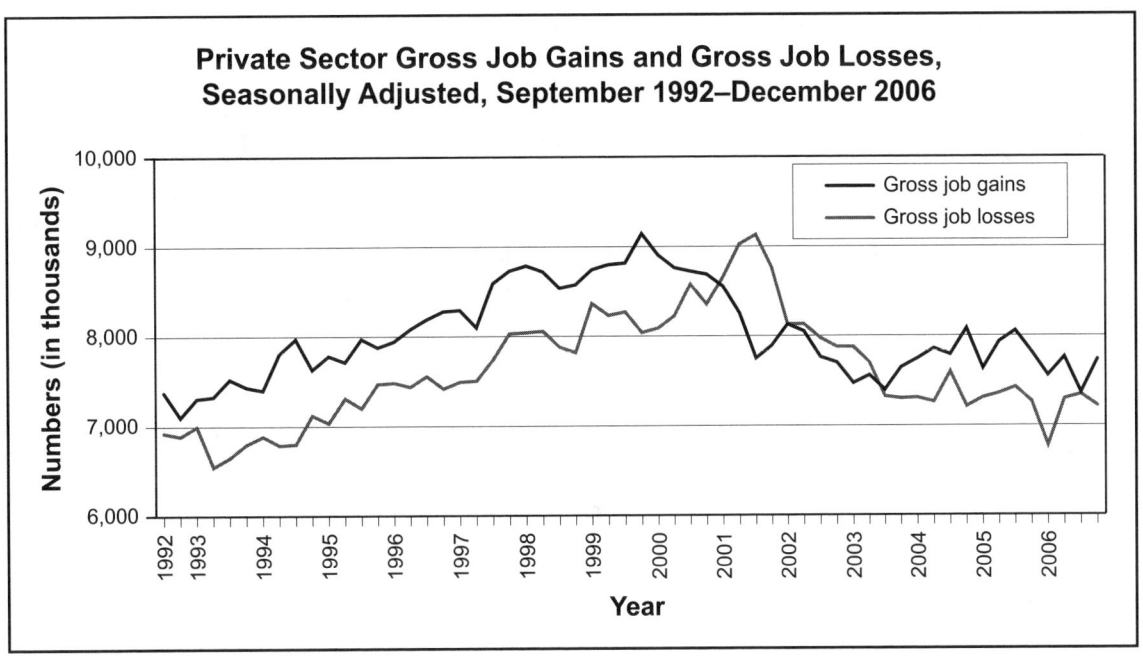

Private Sector Gross Job Gains and Gross Job Losses, Seasonally Adjusted, September 1992–December 2006

The change in the number of jobs is the net result of the gross increase in the number of jobs from expanding and opening establishments and the gross decrease in jobs from contracting and closing establishments. The net gain of 512,000 in the fourth quarter of 2006 resulted from 7.809 million gross job gains and 7.297 million gross job losses. There was a net increase of 501,000 jobs from the third quarter of 2006. However, the net gain in the fourth quarter of 2006 was still somewhat lower than the net gain in the fourth quarter of 2005. (See Table 2-25.)

OTHER HIGHLIGHTS

- The number of gross jobs gained from expanding establishments and opening establishments was similar in the fourth quarter 2005 as it was in the fourth quarter of 2006. In 2005, expanding establishments accounted for 6.293 millions jobs, while opening establishments accounted for 1.525 million jobs. In 2006, they accounted for 6.271 million jobs and 1.538 million jobs, respectively. (See Table 2-25.)

- The service-providing sector had a net gain of 595,000 jobs in the fourth quarter of 2006, with gains exceeding losses by about 10.7 percent. The goods-producing sector, which is much smaller, showed a net loss of 83,000 jobs, with most of the net loss in manufacturing. There was a net gain in natural resources and mining jobs in the fourth quarter of 2006. (See Table 2-27.)

- In March 2007, the net change—the difference between total gross job gains and total gross job losses—was negative in 11 states. Michigan had a net loss of over 17,000 jobs, while Texas (81,080) and Washington State (36,005) and had the largest net gains. (See Table 2-28.)

NOTES AND DEFINITIONS

BUSINESS EMPLOYMENT DYNAMICS (BED)

The Business Employment Dynamics (BED) data are a product of a federal-state cooperative program known as the Quarterly Census of Employment and Wages (QCEW), or the ES-202 program. The Bureau of Labor Statistics (BLS) compiles the BED data from existing quarterly state unemployment insurance (UI) records. Most employers in the United States are required to file quarterly reports on the employment and wages of workers covered by UI laws and to pay quarterly UI taxes. The quarterly UI reports are sent by the State Workforce Agencies (SWAs) to BLS. These reports form the basis of the BLS establishment universe-sampling frame.

In the BED program, the quarterly UI records are linked across quarters to provide a longitudinal history for each establishment. The linkage process allows the tracking of net employment changes at the establishment level, which in turn allows estimations of jobs gained at opening and expanding establishments and of jobs lost at closing and contracting establishments. BLS publishes three different establishment-based employment measures for every given quarter. Each of these measures—the Current Employment Statistics (CES) survey, the QCEW program, and the BED data each make use of the quarterly UI employment reports. However, each measure has somewhat different types of universal coverage, estimation procedures, and publication products. (See the notes and corresponding tables for CES and QCEW in earlier sections of this chapter.)

Concepts and Definitions

The BED data measure the net change in employment at the establishment level. These changes can come about in four different ways. A net increase in employment can come from either opening establishments or ex- panding establishments. A net decrease in employment can come from either closing establishments or contracting establishments.

Gross job gains include the sum of all jobs added at either opening or expanding establishments.

Gross job losses include the sum of all jobs lost in either closing or contracting establishments. The net change in employment is the difference between gross job gains and gross job losses.

Openings consist of establishments with positive third-month em-ployment for the first time in the current quarter, with no links to the prior quarter, or with positive third-month employment in the current quarter, following zero employment in the previous quarter.

Expansions include establishments with positive employment in the third month in both the previous and current quarters, with a net increase in employment over this period.

Closings consist of establishments with positive third-month employment in the previous quarter, with no employment or zero employment reported in the current quarter.

Contractions include establishments with positive employment in the third month in both the previous and current quarters, with a net decrease in employment over this period.

Sources of Additional Information

For additional information, see BLS news release 07-1244, "Business Employment Dynamics: Fourth Quarter 2006." An extensive article on the BED data appeared in the April 2004 edition of the *Monthly Labor Review*. These resources can be found on the BLS Web site at <http://www.bls.gov>.

Table 2-25. Private Sector Gross Job Gains and Job Losses, Seasonally Adjusted, September 1992–December 2006

(Thousands of jobs.)

Year and month	Net change[1]	Gross job gains			Gross job losses		
		Total	Expanding establishments	Opening establishments	Total	Contracting establishments	Closing establishments
1992							
September	455	7 377	5 632	1 745	6 922	5 351	1 571
December	216	7 101	5 465	1 636	6 885	5 487	1 398
1993							
March	313	7 309	5 410	1 899	6 996	5 354	1 642
June	786	7 330	5 794	1 536	6 544	5 136	1 408
September	874	7 523	5 881	1 642	6 649	5 316	1 333
December	641	7 436	5 840	1 596	6 795	5 420	1 375
1994							
March	517	7 400	5 807	1 593	6 883	5 435	1 448
June	1 021	7 807	6 060	1 747	6 786	5 295	1 491
September	1 175	7 972	6 227	1 745	6 797	5 493	1 304
December	507	7 630	5 998	1 632	7 123	5 647	1 476
1995							
March	746	7 782	6 129	1 653	7 036	5 660	1 376
June	402	7 714	6 017	1 697	7 312	5 839	1 473
September	771	7 970	6 291	1 679	7 199	5 680	1 519
December	407	7 877	6 153	1 724	7 470	5 934	1 536
1996							
March	460	7 943	6 190	1 753	7 483	5 957	1 526
June	642	8 080	6 302	1 778	7 438	5 894	1 544
September	632	8 189	6 326	1 863	7 557	5 998	1 559
December	861	8 278	6 409	1 869	7 417	5 889	1 528
1997							
March	799	8 292	6 448	1 844	7 493	5 900	1 593
June	594	8 098	6 342	1 756	7 504	5 925	1 579
September	854	8 593	6 680	1 913	7 739	5 981	1 758
December	702	8 731	6 727	2 004	8 029	6 068	1 961
1998							
March	747	8 788	6 633	2 155	8 041	6 107	1 934
June	666	8 722	6 569	2 153	8 056	6 218	1 838
September	659	8 539	6 574	1 965	7 880	6 161	1 719
December	759	8 576	6 778	1 798	7 817	6 060	1 757
1999							
March	380	8 744	6 733	2 011	8 364	6 466	1 898
June	569	8 800	6 788	2 012	8 231	6 419	1 812
September	548	8 817	6 871	1 946	8 269	6 397	1 872
December	1 105	9 144	7 112	2 032	8 039	6 264	1 775
2000							
March	818	8 906	6 988	1 918	8 088	6 361	1 727
June	541	8 764	6 975	1 789	8 223	6 509	1 714
September	146	8 724	6 834	1 890	8 578	6 719	1 859
December	336	8 690	6 862	1 828	8 354	6 582	1 772
2001							
March	-101	8 555	6 768	1 787	8 656	6 756	1 900
June	-771	8 254	6 439	1 815	9 025	7 149	1 876
September	-1 380	7 749	5 990	1 759	9 129	7 174	1 955
December	-871	7 893	6 055	1 838	8 764	6 995	1 769
2002							
March	-1	8 128	6 324	1 804	8 129	6 400	1 729
June	-80	8 050	6 246	1 804	8 130	6 411	1 719
September	-211	7 763	6 083	1 680	7 974	6 345	1 629
December	-175	7 702	6 059	1 643	7 877	6 267	1 610
2003							
March	-404	7 472	5 932	1 540	7 876	6 321	1 555
June	-142	7 560	6 033	1 527	7 702	6 138	1 564
September	72	7 396	5 897	1 499	7 324	5 893	1 431
December	344	7 646	6 063	1 583	7 302	5 816	1 486
2004							
March	435	7 745	6 231	1 514	7 310	5 871	1 439
June	594	7 857	6 292	1 565	7 263	5 726	1 537
September	191	7 789	6 123	1 666	7 598	5 953	1 645
December	869	8 081	6 365	1 716	7 212	5 727	1 485
2005							
March	325	7 635	6 171	1 464	7 310	5 852	1 458
June	574	7 932	6 311	1 621	7 358	5 873	1 485
September	628	8 055	6 423	1 632	7 427	5 915	1 512
December	551	7 818	6 293	1 525	7 267	5 888	1 379
2006							
March	774	7 679	6 261	1 418	6 905	5 633	1 272
June	416	7 811	6 292	1 519	7 395	6 015	1 380
September	11	7 473	6 032	1 441	7 462	6 110	1 352
December	512	7 809	6 271	1 538	7 297	5 943	1 354

[1]Net change is the difference between total gross job gains and total gross job losses.

Table 2-26. Private Sector Gross Job Gains and Job Losses, as a Percent of Employment,[1] Seasonally Adjusted, September 1992–December 2006

(Percent.)

Year and month	Net change[2]	Gross job gains			Gross job losses		
		Total	Expanding establishments	Opening establishments	Total	Contracting establishments	Closing establishments
1992							
September	0.5	8.3	6.3	2.0	7.8	6.0	1.8
December	0.2	7.9	6.1	1.8	7.7	6.1	1.6
1993							
March	0.3	8.1	6.0	2.1	7.8	6.0	1.8
June	0.8	8.1	6.4	1.7	7.3	5.7	1.6
September	0.9	8.2	6.4	1.8	7.3	5.8	1.5
December	0.6	8.0	6.3	1.7	7.4	5.9	1.5
1994							
March	0.5	8.0	6.3	1.7	7.5	5.9	1.6
June	1.1	8.4	6.5	1.9	7.3	5.7	1.6
September	1.2	8.4	6.6	1.8	7.2	5.8	1.4
December	0.6	8.0	6.3	1.7	7.4	5.9	1.5
1995							
March	0.8	8.1	6.4	1.7	7.3	5.9	1.4
June	0.5	8.0	6.2	1.8	7.5	6.0	1.5
September	0.8	8.2	6.5	1.7	7.4	5.8	1.6
December	0.4	8.1	6.3	1.8	7.7	6.1	1.6
1996							
March	0.4	8.1	6.3	1.8	7.7	6.1	1.6
June	0.6	8.2	6.4	1.8	7.6	6.0	1.6
September	0.7	8.3	6.4	1.9	7.6	6.0	1.6
December	0.9	8.3	6.4	1.9	7.4	5.9	1.5
1997							
March	0.7	8.2	6.4	1.8	7.5	5.9	1.6
June	0.5	7.9	6.2	1.7	7.4	5.8	1.6
September	0.8	8.4	6.5	1.9	7.6	5.9	1.7
December	0.6	8.4	6.5	1.9	7.8	5.9	1.9
1998							
March	0.7	8.5	6.4	2.1	7.8	5.9	1.9
June	0.6	8.4	6.3	2.1	7.8	6.0	1.8
September	0.7	8.2	6.3	1.9	7.5	5.9	1.6
December	0.7	8.1	6.4	1.7	7.4	5.7	1.7
1999							
March	0.3	8.2	6.3	1.9	7.9	6.1	1.8
June	0.6	8.3	6.4	1.9	7.7	6.0	1.7
September	0.5	8.2	6.4	1.8	7.7	6.0	1.7
December	1.1	8.5	6.6	1.9	7.4	5.8	1.6
2000							
March	0.8	8.2	6.4	1.8	7.4	5.8	1.6
June	0.4	7.9	6.3	1.6	7.5	5.9	1.6
September	0.1	7.9	6.2	1.7	7.8	6.1	1.7
December	0.3	7.9	6.2	1.7	7.6	6.0	1.6
2001							
March	-0.1	7.7	6.1	1.6	7.8	6.1	1.7
June	-0.8	7.4	5.8	1.6	8.2	6.5	1.7
September	-1.3	7.1	5.5	1.6	8.4	6.6	1.8
December	-0.8	7.3	5.6	1.7	8.1	6.5	1.6
2002							
March	0.1	7.6	5.9	1.7	7.5	5.9	1.6
June	-0.1	7.5	5.8	1.7	7.6	6.0	1.6
September	-0.1	7.3	5.7	1.6	7.4	5.9	1.5
December	-0.2	7.1	5.6	1.5	7.3	5.8	1.5
2003							
March	-0.5	6.9	5.5	1.4	7.4	5.9	1.5
June	-0.2	7.0	5.6	1.4	7.2	5.7	1.5
September	0.1	6.9	5.5	1.4	6.8	5.5	1.3
December	0.4	7.2	5.7	1.5	6.8	5.4	1.4
2004							
March	0.4	7.2	5.8	1.4	6.8	5.5	1.3
June	0.5	7.2	5.8	1.4	6.7	5.3	1.4
September	0.2	7.2	5.7	1.5	7.0	5.5	1.5
December	0.7	7.4	5.8	1.6	6.7	5.3	1.4
2005							
March	0.3	6.9	5.6	1.3	6.6	5.3	1.3
June	0.6	7.2	5.7	1.5	6.6	5.3	1.3
September	0.5	7.3	5.8	1.5	6.8	5.4	1.4
December	0.6	7.1	5.7	1.4	6.5	5.3	1.2
2006							
March	0.8	6.9	5.6	1.3	6.1	5.0	1.1
June	0.4	6.9	5.6	1.3	6.5	5.3	1.2
September	0.1	6.7	5.4	1.3	6.6	5.4	1.2
December	0.5	7.0	5.6	1.4	6.5	5.3	1.2

[1]The rates measure gross job gains and job losses as a percentage of the average of the previous and current employment.
[2]Net change is the difference between total gross job gains and total gross job losses.

Table 2-27. Three-Month Private Sector Job Gains and Losses, by Industry, Seasonally Adjusted, March 2005–December 2006

(Thousands of jobs.)

Industry	Gross job gains (3 months ended)				Gross job losses (3 months ended)			
	March 2005	June 2005	September 2005	December 2005	March 2005	June 2005	September 2005	December 2005
TOTAL PRIVATE[1]	7 635	7 932	8 055	7 818	7 310	7 358	7 427	7 267
Goods-Producing	1 720	1 713	1 698	1 722	1 686	1 679	1 663	1 606
Natural resources and mining	307	288	265	279	284	285	265	265
Construction	844	859	868	862	806	786	782	774
Manufacturing	569	566	565	581	596	608	616	567
Service-Providing[1]	5 915	6 219	6 357	6 096	5 624	5 679	5 764	5 661
Wholesale trade	319	337	338	320	310	300	311	302
Retail trade	1 020	1 047	1 074	1 058	980	989	1 063	1 015
Transportation and warehousing	243	248	254	268	231	262	236	231
Utilities	15	15	13	14	15	18	12	16
Information	143	155	170	152	164	153	154	156
Financial activities	452	475	480	472	443	439	413	434
Professional and business services	1 370	1 456	1 523	1 432	1 304	1 332	1 311	1 303
Education and health services	741	800	811	766	704	701	691	699
Leisure and hospitality	1 138	1 212	1 202	1 175	1 131	1 135	1 219	1 165
Other services	302	309	297	289	297	300	309	296

Industry	Gross job gains (3 months ended)				Gross job losses (3 months ended)			
	March 2006	June 2006	September 2006	December 2006	March 2006	June 2006	September 2006	December 2006
TOTAL PRIVATE[1]	7 679	7 811	7 473	7 809	6 905	7 395	7 462	7 297
Goods-Producing	1 737	1 692	1 572	1 636	1 572	1 667	1 739	1 719
Natural resources and mining	283	293	269	287	277	268	263	266
Construction	924	838	791	825	757	841	868	845
Manufacturing	530	561	512	524	538	558	608	608
Service-Providing[1]	5 942	6 119	5 901	6 173	5 333	5 728	5 723	5 578
Wholesale trade	315	332	311	322	290	292	305	303
Retail trade	1 056	1 062	1 030	1 081	986	1 100	1 085	1 004
Transportation and warehousing	240	247	241	269	230	232	224	225
Utilities	11	15	15	19	11	13	15	18
Information	143	150	148	167	149	144	171	146
Financial activities	429	457	446	457	419	442	445	444
Professional and business services	1 329	1 438	1 335	1 427	1 202	1 287	1 279	1 313
Education and health services	791	787	784	795	662	713	674	692
Leisure and hospitality	1 226	1 210	1 180	1 223	1 064	1 182	1 184	1 105
Other services	298	313	295	299	283	287	305	291

[1]Includes unclassified sector, not shown separately.

Table 2-28. Private Sector Gross Job Gains and Losses, by State and Selected Territory, Seasonally Adjusted, March 2006–March 2007

(Number.)

State	Gross job gains (3 months ended)					Gross job losses (3 months ended)				
	March 2006	June 2006	September 2006	December 2006	March 2007	March 2006	June 2006	September 2006	December 2006	March 2007
UNITED STATES	7 679 000	7 811 000	7 473 000	7 809 000	7 509 000	6 905 000	7 395 000	7 462 000	7 297 000	7 071 000
Alabama	103 596	100 840	100 446	106 892	112 765	93 285	100 349	103 700	104 477	89 364
Alaska	26 202	28 861	22 123	25 702	24 244	22 112	23 040	26 742	26 432	22 400
Arizona	172 977	170 647	174 546	161 693	156 804	128 109	154 963	152 200	165 067	153 133
Arkansas	63 662	59 654	58 160	62 275	60 704	53 032	60 404	63 784	58 778	52 796
California	935 087	955 811	910 172	982 478	947 540	914 176	926 329	927 374	907 888	912 613
Colorado	137 903	149 241	142 546	150 220	146 688	127 514	132 280	142 570	138 889	131 774
Connecticut	79 072	87 841	81 794	85 126	75 957	75 076	80 456	82 496	77 497	81 107
Delaware	25 605	28 310	23 470	26 159	29 733	24 123	26 663	27 718	23 392	28 414
District of Columbia	25 795	29 069	27 044	25 599	28 423	23 511	26 424	25 381	26 443	23 213
Florida	487 572	526 449	508 541	501 285	464 050	413 474	495 061	493 363	522 827	451 580
Georgia	252 674	257 404	247 388	263 872	249 091	222 660	233 395	251 362	252 232	227 479
Hawaii	27 726	29 136	28 211	27 446	27 483	25 165	24 918	26 129	26 250	26 630
Idaho	47 870	46 245	45 061	47 395	48 396	38 960	42 628	41 378	40 019	40 735
Illinois	282 837	306 757	278 177	293 431	281 177	265 446	263 652	288 515	281 099	268 855
Indiana	153 735	149 946	148 107	153 325	145 342	139 656	151 845	154 760	148 985	140 603
Iowa	78 930	79 031	75 093	79 518	72 577	70 936	73 192	74 910	73 886	73 448
Kansas	70 596	72 012	78 985	85 024	78 808	62 938	72 548	74 864	68 067	67 661
Kentucky	100 762	88 851	92 740	106 958	101 623	83 028	94 323	96 675	90 552	95 549
Louisiana	151 997	123 125	120 127	123 095	121 990	108 712	112 380	108 558	104 159	99 462
Maine	35 790	40 612	35 951	40 832	37 283	37 017	37 701	39 975	37 567	37 189
Maryland	142 555	136 710	131 708	136 491	130 873	124 678	136 422	136 408	130 083	125 994
Massachusetts	158 389	181 498	167 647	166 346	154 124	157 177	158 219	169 849	163 458	157 024
Michigan	217 382	246 077	226 583	229 109	216 604	240 704	237 059	255 227	261 024	234 035
Minnesota	150 980	155 378	138 439	146 430	140 915	139 748	150 512	165 270	147 210	133 393
Mississippi	69 320	63 581	68 823	67 302	60 198	57 864	66 289	62 884	58 428	62 486
Missouri	147 042	150 269	137 786	151 637	148 426	133 236	143 796	142 506	144 042	133 861
Montana	32 383	30 383	27 503	32 922	32 066	26 344	27 899	29 606	26 893	26 215
Nebraska	45 650	45 693	47 050	47 973	44 773	40 465	45 424	44 754	45 236	41 131
Nevada	83 071	79 576	73 442	80 115	79 439	65 159	72 527	76 814	77 068	70 468
New Hampshire	39 074	41 230	37 381	39 715	36 043	36 571	39 132	40 708	37 503	37 188
New Jersey	220 345	238 571	217 626	226 397	200 823	201 996	228 241	230 836	221 251	216 208
New Mexico	50 814	56 728	46 361	49 483	45 658	40 539	46 459	46 285	45 992	39 391
New York	453 399	497 341	451 199	491 296	439 880	450 140	450 660	454 776	436 426	450 887
North Carolina	230 967	230 531	228 819	271 718	238 694	195 552	216 862	222 867	209 905	203 669
North Dakota	21 355	19 942	19 561	19 077	19 613	17 434	19 436	17 615	18 029	17 877
Ohio	276 942	280 652	266 494	273 486	259 261	268 183	279 071	286 805	285 789	260 711
Oklahoma	86 999	86 252	85 999	87 109	85 616	72 308	86 973	80 220	80 850	73 657
Oregon	107 378	103 093	103 167	107 374	104 745	95 893	97 275	94 670	97 684	96 037
Pennsylvania	294 436	292 189	281 640	286 900	282 273	266 079	277 751	278 525	278 568	266 506
Rhode Island	25 198	29 960	28 749	28 621	25 073	25 959	25 774	28 340	28 374	27 137
South Carolina	112 697	112 410	124 764	109 561	113 532	97 125	110 062	103 809	97 192	98 842
South Dakota	22 210	21 897	21 559	22 548	21 003	20 193	19 443	20 198	19 873	19 153
Tennessee	146 716	149 007	143 225	156 388	148 938	127 034	152 368	143 136	157 013	144 012
Texas	556 703	555 610	545 573	566 668	542 825	451 599	508 951	480 295	476 908	461 745
Utah	83 821	78 264	77 218	79 960	80 804	63 988	65 772	68 620	64 989	62 978
Vermont	17 022	19 375	16 515	18 861	16 966	18 312	17 694	18 832	18 099	18 899
Virginia	194 262	196 604	181 450	193 009	192 908	168 421	193 525	196 437	181 525	174 760
Washington	177 761	187 676	176 707	184 842	190 639	158 900	161 486	170 405	166 948	154 634
West Virginia	43 348	38 485	37 841	40 697	38 687	35 457	39 828	40 489	36 849	37 621
Wisconsin	142 738	151 415	143 515	146 759	144 613	135 231	143 378	146 137	143 350	141 179
Wyoming	23 117	19 438	20 984	22 692	22 362	16 596	18 839	19 491	16 482	18 199
Puerto Rico	48 421	46 809	50 294	56 039	43 159	54 363	55 110	56 054	47 988	55 059
Virgin Islands	2 492	2 243	2 727	2 358	2 091	1 899	2 287	2 766	1 980	2 501

CHAPTER 3

OCCUPATIONAL EMPLOYMENT AND WAGES

OCCUPATIONAL EMPLOYMENT AND WAGES

HIGHLIGHTS

This chapter presents employment and wage statistics from the Bureau of Labor Statistics's Occupational Employment Statistics (OES) program.

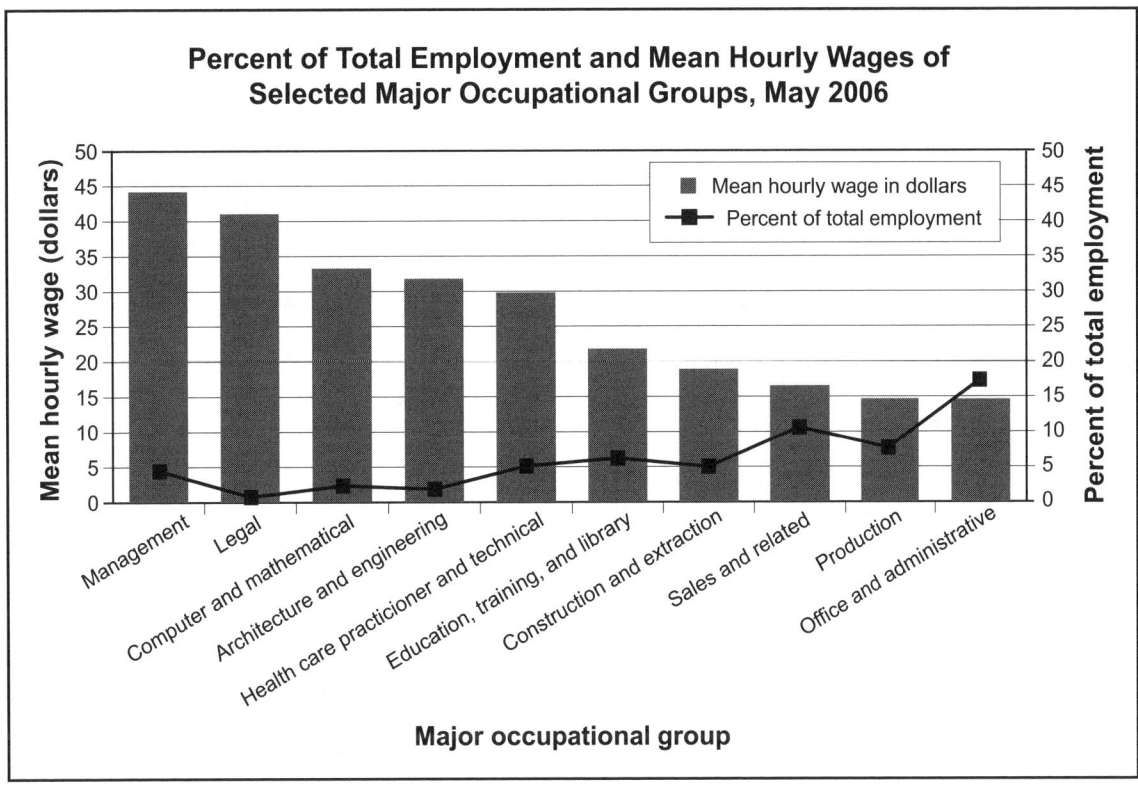

Percent of Total Employment and Mean Hourly Wages of Selected Major Occupational Groups, May 2006

The distribution of wages and employment changed little from 2005 to 2006. Office and administration support occupations continued to employ the largest percentage of workers of any major group (17.4 percent). Average hourly wages for this group increased by less than the average (2.2 percent compared with 3.5 percent). Management occupations made up 4.4 percent of total employment, while their mean hourly wage increased faster than the average (4.0 percent). This increased the wage disparity between the higher- and lower-paid occupations. (See Table 3-1.)

OTHER HIGHLIGHTS

- Food preparation and serving occupations, which accounted for 8.3 percent of total employment in 2006, continued to be the lowest-paying occupational group in 2006, with a mean hourly wage of only $8.86 per hour (less than half the mean hourly wage for all occupations). (See Table 3-1.)

- Meanwhile, management occupations continued to have the highest mean hourly wage in 2006 at $44.20 per hour, followed by legal occupations at $41.04 per hour. However, the mean hourly wage for legal occupations increased by a greater amount (5.3 percent) than that for management occupations (4.0 percent). (See Table 3-1.)

- Surgeons and anesthesiologists were the most highly paid occupations, with average salaries of over $180,000 in 2006. The largest group of health support workers—nursing aides, orderlies, and attendants—earned less than $23,000 per year. (See Table 3-3.)

- There was a wider variation in the mean annual wages of postsecondary school teachers with a range of salaries mostly between $55,000 and $95,000 a year. For elementary school teachers, the average wage was about $49,000 per year. (See Table 3-3.)

NOTES AND DEFINITIONS

COLLECTION AND COVERAGE

The Occupational Employment Statistics (OES) survey is a federal-state cooperative program conducted by the Bureau of Labor Statistics (BLS) and the State Workforce Agencies (SWAs). The OES survey provides estimates of employment and hourly and annual wages for wage and salary workers in 22 major occupational groups and 801 detailed occupations. BLS funds the survey and provides procedural and technical support, while the SWAs collect the necessary data.

Scope of the Survey

In 1999, the OES survey began using the Standard Occupational Classification (SOC) system. The SOC system is the first occupational classification system for federal agencies required by the Office of Management and Budget (OMB). The SOC system consists of 821 detailed occupations grouped into 449 broad occupations, 96 minor occupational groups, and 23 major occupational groups. The OES survey uses 22 of the 23 major occupational groups from the SOC to categorize workers into 801 detailed occupations. Military-specific occupations, which are not covered by the OES survey, are not included.

Prior to 2002, the OES survey was conducted annually by mail and measured occupational employment and occupational wage rates for wage and salary workers in nonfarm establishments by industry. The survey sampled and contacted approximately 400,000 establishments in the fourth quarter of each year.

Beginning in November 2002 the OES survey became a semi-annual survey that sampled approximately 200,000 establishments per panel. The OES survey also switched from the Standard Industrial Classification System (SIC) to the North American Industry Classification System (NAICS) in 2002. More information about NAICS can be found on the BLS Web site at <http://www.bls.gov/bls/naics.htm>.

May 2006 employment and wage estimates are based on all data collected from establishments in the May 2006, November 2005, May 2005, November 2004, May 2004, and November 2003 semi-annual samples. Approximately 1.2 million establishments are sampled over the course of a 3-year cycle.

Concepts and Definitions

Employment is the estimate of total wage and salary employment in an occupation across the industries in which it was reported. The OES survey defines employment as the number of workers who can be classified as full-time or part-time employees, including workers on paid vacations or other types of leave; workers on unpaid short-term absences; employees who are salaried officers, executives, or staff members of incorporated firms; employees temporarily assigned to other units; and employees for whom the reporting unit is their permanent duty station regardless of whether that unit prepares their paycheck. Self-employed owners, partners in unincorporated firms, household workers, and unpaid family workers are excluded.

Occupations are classified based on work performed and required skills. Employees are assigned to an occupation based on the work they perform and not on their education or training. For example, an employee trained as an engineer but working as a drafter is reported as a drafter. Employees who perform the duties of two or more occupations are reported as being in either the occupation that requires the highest level of skill or the occupation in which the most time is spent (if there is no measurable difference in skill requirements).

The OES survey form sent to an establishment contains between 50 and 225 SOC occupations selected on the basis of the industry classification and size class of the sampled establishment. To reduce paperwork and respondent burden, no survey form contains every SOC occupation. Data for specific occupations are thus primarily collected from establishments within the industries that are the predominant employers of labor for these occupations. However, each survey form is structured to allow a respondent to provide information for each detailed occupation employed at the establishment; unlisted occupations can be added to the survey form.

Wages are money that is paid or received for work or services performed in a specified period. Base rate, cost-of-living allowances, guaranteed pay, hazardous-duty pay, incentive pay (including commissions and production bonuses), tips, and on-call pay are included. Excluded are back pay, jury duty pay, overtime pay, severance pay, shift differentials, nonproduction bonuses, employer cost of supplementary benefits, and tuition reimbursements.

Mean wage refers to an average wage; an occupational mean wage estimate is calculated by summing the wages of all the employees in a given occupation and then dividing the total wages by the number of employees.

An *establishment* is defined as an economic unit that processes goods or provides services, such as a factory, store, or mine. The establishment is generally at a single physical location and is primarily engaged in one type of economic activity.

Additional Information

For additional data including area data, see BLS news release USDL 07-0712, "Occupational Employment and Wages, May 2006," and special reports on the BLS Web site at <http://www.bls.gov>.

Table 3-1. Employment and Wages, by Major Occupational Group, May 2005 and May 2006

(Number, percent, dollars.)

Occupation	May 2005				May 2006			
	Employment		Mean hourly wage	Mean annual wage[1]	Employment		Mean hourly wage	Mean annual wage[1]
	Number	Percent			Number	Percent		
All Occupations	130 307 850	100.0	18.21	37 870	132 604 980	100.0	18.84	39 190
Management	5 960 560	4.6	42.52	88 450	5 892 900	4.4	44.20	91 930
Business and financial operations	5 410 410	4.2	27.85	57 930	5 826 140	4.4	28.85	60 000
Computer and mathematical sciences	2 952 740	2.3	32.26	67 100	3 076 200	2.3	33.29	69 240
Architecture and engineering	2 382 480	1.8	30.73	63 910	2 430 250	1.8	31.82	66 190
Life, physical, and social sciences	1 185 730	0.9	27.90	58 030	1 231 070	0.9	28.68	59 660
Community and social services	1 692 950	1.3	18.04	37 530	1 749 210	1.3	18.75	39 000
Legal	986 740	0.8	38.98	81 070	976 740	0.7	41.04	85 360
Education, training, and library	8 078 500	6.2	20.89	43 450	8 206 440	6.2	21.79	45 320
Arts, design, entertainment, sports, and media	1 683 310	1.3	21.30	44 310	1 727 380	1.3	22.17	46 110
Health care practitioner and technical	6 547 350	5.0	28.45	59 170	6 713 780	5.1	29.82	62 030
Health care support	3 363 800	2.6	11.47	23 850	3 483 270	2.6	11.83	24 610
Protective services	3 056 660	2.3	17.19	35 750	3 024 840	2.3	17.81	37 040
Food preparation and serving related	10 797 700	8.3	8.58	17 840	11 029 280	8.3	8.86	18 430
Building and grounds cleaning and maintenance	4 342 550	3.3	10.55	21 930	4 396 250	3.3	10.86	22 580
Personal care and services	3 188 850	2.4	10.67	22 180	3 249 760	2.5	11.02	22 920
Sales and related	13 930 320	10.7	15.77	32 800	14 114 860	10.6	16.52	34 350
Office and administrative support	22 784 330	17.5	14.28	29 710	23 077 190	17.4	14.60	30 370
Farming, fishing, and forestry	443 070	0.3	10.10	21 010	450 040	0.3	10.49	21 810
Construction and extraction	6 370 400	4.9	18.39	38 260	6 680 710	5.0	18.89	39 290
Installation, maintenance, and repair	5 305 260	4.1	18.30	38 050	5 352 420	4.0	18.78	39 060
Production	10 249 220	7.9	14.37	29 890	10 268 510	7.7	14.65	30 480
Transportation and material moving	9 594 920	7.4	13.85	28 820	9 647 730	7.3	14.16	29 460

[1]The annual wage has been calculated by multiplying the hourly mean wage by a "year-round, full-time" hours figure of 2,080 hours; for occupations with no published hourly mean wage, the annual wage has been directly calculated from the reported survey data.

Table 3-2. Distribution of Employment, by Wage Range and Occupational Group, May 2006

(Percent distribution.)

Occupation	Total	Wage range								
		Under $9.50	$9.50 to $11.99	$12.00 to $15.24	$15.25 to $19.24	$19.25 to $24.49	$24.50 to $30.99	$31.00 to $39.24	$39.25 to $49.74	$49.75 and over
Management	100.0	1.2	1.1	2.8	5.4	9.6	13.7	16.8	17.3	32.0
Business and financial operations	100.0	1.7	2.4	7.4	13.8	20.1	20.7	16.5	9.8	7.6
Computer and mathematical sciences	100.0	0.7	1.6	4.2	8.3	14.1	18.8	21.8	18.1	12.3
Architecture and engineering	100.0	0.8	2.0	4.9	9.2	15.5	20.5	20.6	16.2	10.4
Life, physical, and social sciences	100.0	2.0	3.7	9.0	14.1	18.1	18.2	15.2	10.5	9.1
Community and social services	100.0	7.8	11.8	19.3	21.3	18.5	12.8	6.0	1.9	0.6
Legal	100.0	1.3	2.6	6.6	10.7	13.6	12.9	11.3	11.1	30.0
Education, training, and library	100.0	11.9	9.0	11.1	16.0	19.3	15.3	9.7	4.4	3.4
Arts, design, entertainment, sports, and media	100.0	13.9	9.9	13.3	15.7	15.8	12.5	8.6	5.2	5.0
Health care practitioner and technical	100.0	2.7	5.0	8.7	12.9	18.9	20.1	13.8	7.3	10.4
Health care support	100.0	30.1	30.5	22.7	11.1	4.1	1.1	0.3	0.1	-
Protective services	100.0	19.1	15.1	15.1	14.0	14.3	12.0	7.1	2.7	0.7
Food preparation and serving related	100.0	71.3	15.1	8.1	3.5	1.5	0.5	0.1	-	-
Building and grounds cleaning and maintenance	100.0	47.2	23.5	15.4	8.2	4.1	1.2	0.3	0.1	-
Personal care and services	100.0	53.8	20.1	11.4	6.5	3.8	2.3	1.0	0.7	0.3
Sales and related	100.0	39.4	14.9	11.3	9.3	8.0	6.0	4.3	3.0	3.9
Office and administrative support	100.0	18.4	20.0	23.6	18.6	13.0	4.5	1.4	0.4	0.1
Farming, fishing, and forestry	100.0	60.7	14.8	10.4	7.3	4.2	1.7	0.6	0.2	-
Construction and extraction	100.0	8.3	13.3	19.3	19.1	17.2	12.6	7.3	2.3	0.6
Installation, maintenance, and repair	100.0	8.5	11.4	17.4	20.3	20.4	14.2	6.0	1.4	0.3
Production	100.0	21.9	20.0	21.1	16.8	11.1	6.3	2.1	0.6	0.1
Transportation and material moving	100.0	29.8	19.1	18.7	14.5	10.0	4.8	1.6	0.6	0.9

- = Quantity represents or rounds to zero.

Table 3-3. Employment and Wages, by Occupation, May 2005 and May 2006

(Number of people, dollars.)

Occupation	May 2005				May 2006			
	Employ-ment	Median hourly wage	Mean hourly wage	Mean annual wage[1]	Employ-ment	Median hourly wage	Mean hourly wage	Mean annual wage[1]
ALL OCCUPATIONS	130 307 840	14.15	18.21	37 870	132 604 980	14.61	18.84	39 190
Management								
Chief executives	321 300	68.48	67.22	139 810	299 520	([2])	69.52	144 600
General and operations managers	1 663 810	39.17	45.90	95 470	1 663 280	40.97	47.73	99 280
Legislators	61 060	([3])	([3])	31 320	62 020	([3])	([3])	32 730
Advertising and promotions managers	41 710	33.10	39.06	81 250	38 130	35.12	40.93	85 140
Marketing managers	166 470	44.56	49.03	101 990	159 950	47.46	51.74	107 610
Sales managers	317 970	42.11	47.36	98 510	307 960	44.02	49.39	102 730
Public relations managers	43 770	36.75	41.26	85 820	44 010	39.51	44.35	92 250
Administrative services managers	239 410	30.78	33.44	69 540	232 410	32.54	35.02	72 840
Computer and information systems managers	259 330	46.41	49.21	102 360	251 210	48.84	51.56	107 250
Financial managers	471 950	41.48	46.45	96 620	468 270	43.74	48.77	101 450
Compensation and benefits managers	51 470	33.23	36.68	76 300	46 640	35.94	39.43	82 010
Training and development managers	28 720	35.66	38.55	80 180	27 450	38.58	41.67	86 670
Human resources managers, all other	57 830	40.47	43.24	89 950	55 280	42.55	45.63	94 910
Industrial production managers	153 950	36.34	39.41	81 960	153 410	37.34	40.37	83 970
Purchasing managers	69 300	36.67	39.16	81 440	66 490	39.22	41.35	86 020
Transportation, storage, and distribution managers	84 870	33.23	36.12	75 130	89 010	35.14	37.77	78 560
Farm, ranch, and other agricultural managers	4 070	24.60	26.81	55 760	3 300	25.03	28.15	58 550
Farmers and ranchers	350	16.41	19.09	39 720	300	17.85	20.92	43 520
Construction managers	192 610	34.74	39.31	81 760	207 630	35.43	39.79	82 760
Education administrators, preschool and childcare center/programs	47 670	17.79	20.51	42 670	46 890	18.15	20.88	43 430
Education administrators, elementary and secondary schools	213 250	([3])	([3])	76 890	215 630	([3])	([3])	79 200
Education administrators, postsecondary	105 360	33.82	37.78	78 590	103 330	35.57	39.82	82 820
Education administrators, all other	24 710	30.85	33.38	69 430	26 570	32.03	34.38	71 520
Engineering managers	187 410	48.44	50.71	105 470	183 960	50.69	52.90	110 030
Food service managers	191 420	19.87	21.60	44 930	189 050	20.68	22.49	46 780
Funeral directors	21 960	22.90	27.04	56 240	22 810	23.86	27.53	57 250
Gaming managers	3 310	28.82	31.69	65 920	3 330	30.20	32.38	67 340
Lodging managers	31 040	19.53	22.80	47 420	31 300	20.35	23.83	49 560
Medical and health services managers	230 130	33.51	37.09	77 140	232 920	35.26	39.02	81 160
Natural sciences managers	40 400	44.75	47.66	99 140	38 660	48.11	51.91	107 970
Postmasters and mail superintendents	26 120	25.34	25.83	53 740	26 580	26.82	26.74	55 630
Property, real estate, and community association managers	154 230	20.14	24.31	50 570	156 880	20.71	25.14	52 290
Social and community service managers	112 910	23.80	25.92	53 920	112 360	25.03	26.97	56 090
Managers, all other	340 720	38.06	40.16	83 530	326 390	39.66	41.95	87 250
Business and Financial Operations								
Agents and business managers of artists, performers, and athletes	10 640	25.87	33.68	70 060	11 130	31.01	40.42	84 070
Purchasing agents and buyers, farm products	12 970	22.44	25.47	52 970	13 110	22.49	25.83	53 730
Wholesale and retail buyers, except farm products	132 900	20.61	23.58	49 050	137 310	21.46	24.52	51 010
Purchasing agents, except wholesale, retail, and farm products	267 410	23.57	25.27	52 560	275 910	24.39	26.04	54 160
Claims adjusters, examiners, and investigators	234 030	22.21	23.66	49 210	279 240	24.36	25.36	52 750
Insurance appraisers, auto damage	12 900	23.12	23.43	48 740	12 630	23.65	24.03	49 980
Compliance officers, except agriculture, construction, health and safety, and transportation	161 810	23.73	25.63	53 320	222 080	22.62	24.47	50 890
Cost estimators	204 330	25.01	26.91	55 980	216 900	25.45	27.32	56 820
Emergency management specialists	11 240	22.10	23.90	49 720	11 330	22.79	24.26	50 450
Employment, recruitment, and placement specialists	181 260	20.08	23.31	48 470	186 620	20.40	24.07	50 070
Compensation, benefits, and job analysis specialists	97 740	23.49	24.88	51 750	103 870	24.15	25.72	53 500
Training and development specialists	206 860	22.05	23.58	49 060	197 050	22.99	24.57	51 100
Human resources, training, and labor relations specialists, all other	171 880	23.29	24.27	50 480	204 290	25.13	26.30	54 700
Logisticians	52 220	28.90	30.30	63 010	79 570	30.49	31.56	65 640
Management analysts	441 000	31.91	36.06	75 000	476 070	32.72	37.15	77 270
Meeting and convention planners	40 040	19.85	21.44	44 590	42 510	20.28	21.92	45 580
Business operations specialists, all other	916 290	26.22	28.38	59 030	983 340	26.76	28.96	60 240
Accountants and auditors	1 051 220	25.10	27.89	58 020	1 092 960	26.26	29.17	60 670
Appraisers and assessors of real estate	63 800	20.88	23.96	49 830	66 420	21.38	24.57	51 110
Budget analysts	53 510	28.32	29.89	62 180	58 100	29.53	30.73	63 920
Credit analysts	61 500	24.22	27.94	58 110	66 690	25.17	28.94	60 190
Financial analysts	180 910	30.70	35.16	73 130	196 960	32.02	37.16	77 280
Personal financial advisers	108 640	30.53	39.89	82 970	119 690	31.79	41.70	86 730
Insurance underwriters	98 970	24.65	27.15	56 480	99 430	25.17	27.86	57 960
Financial examiners	22 160	30.33	32.74	68 090	24 430	31.43	34.25	71 240
Loan counselors	28 030	17.15	20.85	43 370	30 430	17.21	20.12	41 840
Loan officers	332 690	23.77	28.53	59 350	359 260	24.89	29.77	61 930
Tax examiners, collectors, and revenue agents	72 290	21.26	23.78	49 460	75 160	21.93	23.89	49 690
Tax preparers	58 850	12.36	14.90	31 000	62 860	13.15	15.94	33 160
Financial specialists, all other	122 320	24.64	27.47	57 130	120 790	25.81	28.65	59 600

[1]Annual wages have been calculated by multiplying the hourly mean wage by a "year-round, full-time" hours figure of 2,080 hours; for occupations with no published hourly mean wage, the annual wage has been directly calculated from the reported survey data.
[2]Median hourly wage is equal to or greater than $70.00 per hour.
[3]Wages for some occupations that do not generally entail year-round, full-time employment are reported as either hourly wages or annual salaries (depending on how employees are typically paid).

Table 3-3. Employment and Wages, by Occupation, May 2005 and May 2006—*Continued*

(Number of people, dollars.)

Occupation	May 2005				May 2006			
	Employment	Median hourly wage	Mean hourly wage	Mean annual wage[1]	Employment	Median hourly wage	Mean hourly wage	Mean annual wage[1]
Computer and Mathematical Sciences								
Computer and information scientists, research	25 890	43.86	45.21	94 030	27 650	45.17	46.36	96 440
Computer programmers	389 090	30.49	32.40	67 400	396 020	31.50	33.42	69 500
Computer software engineers, applications	455 980	37.06	38.24	79 540	472 520	38.36	39.42	82 000
Computer software engineers, systems software	320 720	39.48	40.54	84 310	329 060	41.04	41.95	87 250
Computer support specialists	499 860	19.52	20.86	43 380	514 460	19.94	21.32	44 350
Computer systems analysts	492 120	32.84	33.86	70 430	446 460	33.54	34.73	72 230
Database administrators	99 380	30.41	31.54	65 590	109 840	31.09	32.43	67 460
Network and computer systems administrators	270 330	28.81	30.39	63 210	289 520	29.87	31.37	65 260
Network systems and data communications analysts	185 190	29.69	31.23	64 970	203 710	31.06	32.43	67 460
Computer specialists, all other	116 760	28.57	30.38	63 190	180 270	32.97	33.35	69 370
Actuaries	15 770	39.25	43.63	90 760	16 620	39.81	44.14	91 810
Mathematicians	2 930	38.90	39.02	81 150	2 840	41.79	41.72	86 780
Operations research analysts	52 530	29.90	31.70	65 940	56 170	31.08	33.22	69 100
Statisticians	17 480	30.02	31.79	66 130	19 660	31.60	33.21	69 080
Mathematical technicians	1 430	17.54	22.23	46 230	1 210	18.21	22.12	46 010
Mathematical scientists, all other	7 320	29.74	29.60	61 560	10 190	30.56	31.21	64 920
Architecture and Engineering								
Architects, except landscape and naval	96 740	30.22	32.96	68 560	101 010	30.84	33.54	69 760
Landscape architects	20 220	26.07	28.62	59 540	22 130	26.51	29.08	60 480
Cartographers and photogrammetrists	11 260	23.20	24.68	51 340	11 430	23.19	25.29	52 600
Surveyors	54 220	22.05	23.53	48 950	56 820	23.22	24.71	51 390
Aerospace engineers	81 100	40.43	41.08	85 450	86 720	42.12	42.92	89 260
Agricultural engineers	3 170	31.20	31.91	66 370	3 050	31.75	32.60	67 810
Biomedical engineers	11 660	34.54	36.24	75 380	14 030	35.54	37.51	78 030
Chemical engineers	27 550	37.09	38.09	79 230	29 060	37.91	39.23	81 600
Civil engineers	229 700	31.82	33.41	69 480	236 690	32.98	34.67	72 120
Computer hardware engineers	78 580	40.59	41.91	87 170	74 480	42.54	43.88	91 280
Electrical engineers	144 920	35.34	36.57	76 060	147 670	36.50	37.93	78 900
Electronics engineers, except computer	130 050	37.52	38.46	79 990	131 880	38.97	39.82	82 820
Environmental engineers	50 140	32.74	34.00	70 720	51 370	33.63	34.90	72 590
Health and safety engineers, except mining safety engineers and inspectors	25 330	31.35	32.33	67 240	24 620	31.87	32.89	68 400
Industrial engineers	191 640	32.05	32.93	68 500	198 340	32.99	33.96	70 630
Marine engineers and naval architects	6 550	35.06	35.73	74 320	7 810	35.09	36.25	75 400
Materials engineers	20 950	33.49	34.32	71 390	21 230	35.57	36.52	75 960
Mechanical engineers	220 750	32.49	33.65	70 000	217 500	33.58	34.89	72 580
Mining and geological engineers, including mining safety engineers	5 680	33.69	36.09	75 070	6 810	34.69	37.32	77 620
Nuclear engineers	14 290	42.45	43.60	90 690	14 870	43.38	44.25	92 040
Petroleum engineers	14 860	44.71	46.80	97 350	15 060	47.30	48.86	101 620
Engineers, all other	152 940	37.09	37.29	77 570	155 620	39.26	39.30	81 750
Architectural and civil drafters	101 040	19.42	20.24	42 110	107 110	20.17	21.11	43 900
Electrical and electronics drafters	30 270	21.90	23.27	48 410	32 440	22.51	23.85	49 610
Mechanical drafters	74 650	20.84	21.87	45 490	72 950	21.01	22.10	45 960
Drafters, all other	20 870	20.34	21.84	45 420	22 800	20.70	21.87	45 480
Aerospace engineering and operations technicians	9 950	25.22	26.31	54 720	8 280	25.62	26.19	54 480
Civil engineering technicians	90 390	18.85	19.61	40 780	86 730	19.50	20.37	42 380
Electrical and electronic engineering technicians	165 850	23.10	23.42	48 710	166 340	24.35	24.44	50 840
Electromechanical technicians	15 130	21.10	21.96	45 670	15 310	21.50	22.37	46 540
Environmental engineering technicians	19 900	19.14	20.16	41 940	20 600	19.50	20.72	43 100
Industrial engineering technicians	73 310	21.77	23.67	49 220	73 640	22.51	24.48	50 920
Mechanical engineering technicians	46 580	21.55	22.37	46 520	46 660	22.04	22.94	47 710
Engineering technicians, except drafters, all other	78 300	25.25	25.19	52 400	78 260	26.08	25.89	53 850
Surveying and mapping technicians	63 910	15.04	16.05	33 390	70 940	15.55	16.63	34 590
Life, Physical, and Social Sciences								
Animal scientists	3 000	20.76	22.88	47 600	3 930	22.98	25.59	53 230
Food scientists and technologists	7 570	24.73	27.33	56 840	8 770	25.87	28.49	59 260
Soil and plant scientists	10 100	26.22	27.90	58 040	10 720	26.96	28.52	59 330
Biochemists and biophysicists	17 690	34.14	36.21	75 320	18 680	36.69	38.90	80 900
Microbiologists	15 250	27.34	30.46	63 360	15 730	27.87	31.35	65 200
Zoologists and wildlife biologists	16 440	25.02	26.58	55 280	18 000	25.63	26.98	56 120
Biological scientists, all other	26 200	28.94	30.61	63 670	25 220	29.30	30.56	63 560
Conservation scientists	15 540	25.65	26.27	54 640	16 000	26.43	26.64	55 410
Foresters	10 750	23.40	24.53	51 030	10 760	24.61	25.22	52 450
Epidemiologists	3 630	25.08	27.09	56 340	4 120	27.25	28.99	60 290
Medical scientists, except epidemiologists	73 670	29.68	33.24	69 140	78 210	29.66	33.82	70 350
Life scientists, all other	12 790	27.10	31.04	64 570	12 830	27.39	31.00	64 480
Astronomers	970	50.32	48.73	101 360	1 430	46.03	45.67	95 000
Physicists	15 160	43.18	43.98	91 480	15 420	45.31	45.95	95 580
Atmospheric and space scientists	7 050	35.55	35.11	73 020	8 250	37.09	37.41	77 810
Chemists	76 540	27.83	30.51	63 470	80 500	28.78	31.75	66 040
Materials scientists	7 880	34.35	35.74	74 350	9 390	35.87	37.02	77 010
Environmental scientists and specialists, including health	72 000	25.30	27.63	57 470	77 720	26.97	29.38	61 120
Geoscientists, except hydrologists and geographers	27 430	34.44	38.46	79 990	28 980	34.93	38.41	79 890
Hydrologists	8 360	30.68	32.33	67 260	7 740	31.86	32.80	68 230

[1]Annual wages have been calculated by multiplying the hourly mean wage by a "year-round, full-time" hours figure of 2,080 hours; for occupations with no published hourly mean wage, the annual wage has been directly calculated from the reported survey data.

Table 3-3. Employment and Wages, by Occupation, May 2005 and May 2006—Continued

(Number of people, dollars.)

Occupation	May 2005				May 2006			
	Employ-ment	Median hourly wage	Mean hourly wage	Mean annual wage[1]	Employ-ment	Median hourly wage	Mean hourly wage	Mean annual wage[1]
Life, Physical, and Social Sciences—*Continued*								
Physical scientists, all other	23 800	40.05	40.57	84 380	21 380	40.12	41.01	85 310
Economists	12 470	35.43	38.90	80 900	12 970	37.03	40.14	83 500
Market research analysts	195 710	27.55	30.95	64 370	213 590	28.28	31.70	65 930
Survey researchers	21 650	14.97	18.13	37 710	24 140	16.04	19.08	39 680
Clinical, counseling, and school psychologists	98 820	27.49	30.75	63 960	97 330	28.58	31.78	66 110
Industrial-organizational psychologists	1 070	40.72	43.26	89 980	1 140	41.55	43.23	89 920
Psychologists, all other	6 750	35.70	35.70	74 250	7 960	36.69	38.63	80 360
Sociologists	3 500	25.37	29.66	61 700	3 440	28.99	32.83	68 300
Urban and regional planners	31 650	26.53	27.70	57 620	32 640	27.22	28.33	58 940
Anthropologists and archeologists	4 790	22.07	24.07	50 060	4 960	24.00	25.43	52 900
Geographers	810	30.56	31.07	64 620	960	30.28	30.64	63 720
Historians	2 850	21.35	23.86	49 620	3 090	23.33	25.36	52 750
Political scientists	5 010	40.43	40.78	84 820	3 970	43.34	41.52	86 370
Social scientists and related workers, all other	31 900	30.12	31.27	65 040	31 110	31.21	32.56	67 720
Agricultural and food science technicians	19 340	15.08	15.99	33 260	19 220	15.26	16.20	33 700
Biological technicians	67 080	16.47	17.54	36 480	71 590	17.17	18.38	38 240
Chemical technicians	59 790	18.51	19.29	40 120	59 900	18.87	19.70	40 970
Geological and petroleum technicians	11 130	21.03	23.82	49 550	11 280	22.19	24.76	51 490
Nuclear technicians	6 050	29.39	28.77	59 840	6 400	31.49	31.14	64 760
Social science research assistants	16 320	16.32	17.29	35 960	15 840	16.28	17.23	35 840
Environmental science and protection technicians, including health	32 460	17.43	18.52	38 520	34 790	18.31	19.36	40 260
Forensic science technicians	11 030	21.44	22.79	47 390	12 310	21.79	23.14	48 130
Forest and conservation technicians	29 940	13.72	15.13	31 480	30 580	14.84	16.24	33 780
Life, physical, and social science technicians, all other	63 810	19.25	21.72	45 180	58 080	18.23	19.65	40 870
Community and Social Services								
Substance abuse and behavioral disorder counselors	72 210	15.66	16.73	34 800	75 940	16.36	17.28	35 950
Educational, vocational, and school counselors	214 160	22.33	23.33	48 530	226 720	22.85	23.92	49 760
Marriage and family therapists	18 500	20.34	21.90	45 550	21 330	20.78	21.49	44 700
Mental health counselors	87 220	16.35	18.01	37 470	91 830	16.53	18.19	37 840
Rehabilitation counselors	117 230	13.62	15.07	31 350	121 380	14.04	15.80	32 870
Counselors, all other	21 390	17.91	19.01	39 540	24 260	18.37	19.37	40 280
Child, family, and school social workers	256 430	17.00	18.65	38 780	262 830	18.02	19.54	40 640
Medical and public health social workers	112 230	19.77	20.52	42 690	116 750	20.69	21.48	44 690
Mental health and substance abuse social workers	120 140	16.54	17.75	36 920	114 820	17.02	18.26	37 980
Social workers, all other	60 940	19.85	20.54	42 720	61 270	20.95	21.61	44 950
Health educators	51 970	19.10	20.89	43 440	57 900	19.87	21.81	45 370
Probation officers and correctional treatment specialists	90 600	19.33	20.92	43 510	89 650	20.43	22.18	46 130
Social and human service assistants	313 210	12.03	12.79	26 600	318 620	12.30	13.08	27 200
Community and social service specialists, all other	99 860	15.83	16.85	35 060	107 380	16.93	17.99	37 410
Clergy	36 590	18.53	20.05	41 700	37 820	19.07	20.70	43 060
Directors, religious activities and education	13 610	15.64	17.09	35 540	14 750	16.47	18.06	37 570
Religious workers, all other	6 670	11.43	13.48	28 050	5 990	11.70	14.11	29 350
Legal								
Lawyers	529 190	47.56	53.13	110 520	547 710	49.26	54.65	113 660
Administrative law judges, adjudicators, and hearing officers	15 350	33.98	36.89	76 730	14 470	34.90	37.37	77 730
Arbitrators, mediators, and conciliators	5 780	26.14	28.78	59 870	8 110	23.80	28.27	58 790
Judges, magistrate judges, and magistrates	25 330	46.91	43.99	91 500	25 870	48.89	45.98	95 640
Paralegals and legal assistants	217 700	19.79	20.92	43 510	229 430	20.69	21.86	45 460
Court reporters	17 130	20.02	21.84	45 420	16 940	21.93	23.25	48 370
Law clerks	40 620	17.12	17.78	36 980	31 890	17.48	18.85	39 210
Title examiners, abstractors, and searchers	64 580	16.88	19.26	40 070	63 410	17.32	19.55	40 660
Legal support workers, all other	71 060	21.06	22.54	46 890	38 910	21.70	24.29	50 520
Education, Training, and Library								
Business teachers, postsecondary	67 420	(3)	(3)	67 500	67 390	(3)	(3)	70 220
Computer science teachers, postsecondary	38 520	(3)	(3)	60 330	36 630	(3)	(3)	65 000
Mathematical science teachers, postsecondary	44 660	(3)	(3)	58 850	44 570	(3)	(3)	62 790
Architecture teachers, postsecondary	6 110	(3)	(3)	65 740	5 820	(3)	(3)	67 390
Engineering teachers, postsecondary	34 500	(3)	(3)	78 780	31 950	(3)	(3)	82 080
Agricultural sciences teachers, postsecondary	11 460	(3)	(3)	73 680	10 120	(3)	(3)	77 190
Biological science teachers, postsecondary	59 540	(3)	(3)	77 690	51 950	(3)	(3)	82 110
Forestry and conservation science teachers, postsecondary	2 990	(3)	(3)	67 550	2 630	(3)	(3)	66 970
Atmospheric, earth, marine, and space sciences teachers, postsecondary	8 810	(3)	(3)	70 960	8 670	(3)	(3)	74 880
Chemistry teachers, postsecondary	19 520	(3)	(3)	65 400	19 560	(3)	(3)	70 100
Environmental science teachers, postsecondary	4 340	(3)	(3)	66 020	4 310	(3)	(3)	71 980
Physics teachers, postsecondary	13 310	(3)	(3)	71 020	12 340	(3)	(3)	74 650
Anthropology and archeology teachers, postsecondary	5 320	(3)	(3)	66 700	5 040	(3)	(3)	68 240
Area, ethnic, and cultural studies teachers, postsecondary	7 970	(3)	(3)	62 480	7 350	(3)	(3)	63 710
Economics teachers, postsecondary	12 670	(3)	(3)	74 600	12 330	(3)	(3)	79 370

[1]Annual wages have been calculated by multiplying the hourly mean wage by a "year-round, full-time" hours figure of 2,080 hours; for occupations with no published hourly mean wage, the annual wage has been directly calculated from the reported survey data.
[3]Wages for some occupations that do not generally entail year-round, full-time employment are reported as either hourly wages or annual salaries (depending on how employees are typically paid).

Table 3-3. Employment and Wages, by Occupation, May 2005 and May 2006—*Continued*

(Number of people, dollars.)

Occupation	May 2005				May 2006			
	Employ-ment	Median hourly wage	Mean hourly wage	Mean annual wage[1]	Employ-ment	Median hourly wage	Mean hourly wage	Mean annual wage[1]
Education, Training, and Library–*Continued*								
Geography teachers, postsecondary	4 250	(3)	(3)	61 790	4 070	(3)	(3)	62 850
Political science teachers, postsecondary	13 710	(3)	(3)	65 760	13 850	(3)	(3)	69 040
Psychology teachers, postsecondary	30 240	(3)	(3)	61 980	29 690	(3)	(3)	64 580
Sociology teachers, postsecondary	14 980	(3)	(3)	59 030	16 110	(3)	(3)	63 160
Social sciences teachers, postsecondary, all other	6 330	(3)	(3)	66 060	5 750	(3)	(?)	69 640
Health specialties teachers, postsecondary	108 680	(3)	(3)	82 450	116 370	(3)	(?)	91 260
Nursing instructors and teachers, postsecondary	37 020	(3)	(3)	56 840	39 350	(3)	(?)	58 690
Education teachers, postsecondary	51 320	(?)	(3)	54 790	53 470	(3)	(?)	57 410
Library science teachers, postsecondary	3 960	(3)	(3)	56 630	3 830	(3)	(?)	57 550
Criminal justice and law enforcement teachers, postsecondary	9 880	(3)	(3)	52 930	10 430	(3)	(3)	55 310
Law teachers, postsecondary	13 560	(3)	(3)	95 570	11 870	(3)	(3)	94 290
Social work teachers, postsecondary	7 440	(3)	(3)	56 520	7 860	(3)	(3)	57 990
Art, drama, and music teachers, postsecondary	69 260	(3)	(3)	55 340	72 100	(3)	(3)	58 250
Communications teachers, postsecondary	22 320	(3)	(3)	. . .	23 560	(3)	(3)	56 600
English language and literature teachers, postsecondary	58 710	(3)	(3)	53 950	59 320	(3)	(3)	57 320
Foreign language and literature teachers, postsecondary	23 830	(3)	(3)	53 400	24 680	(3)	(3)	60 050
History teachers, postsecondary	20 520	(3)	(3)	59 450	20 980	(3)	(3)	63 200
Philosophy and religion teachers, postsecondary	18 340	(3)	(3)	57 960	17 840	(3)	(3)	60 180
Graduate teaching assistants	117 970	(3)	(3)	29 170	112 830	(3)	(3)	30 190
Home economics teachers, postsecondary	4 010	(3)	(3)	51 760	4 330	(3)	(3)	60 630
Recreation and fitness studies teachers, postsecondary	16 530	(3)	(3)	48 960	17 110	(3)	(3)	54 020
Vocational education teachers, postsecondary	105 980	20.07	(3)	45 110	109 360	21.11	22.65	47 110
Postsecondary teachers, all other	267 280	(3)	(3)	67 540	272 410	(3)	(3)	72 310
Preschool teachers, except special education	348 690	10.57	12.09	25 150	361 600	10.91	12.45	25 900
Kindergarten teachers, except special education	171 290	(3)	(3)	45 250	165 780	(3)	(3)	47 040
Elementary school teachers, except special education	1 486 650	(3)	(3)	46 990	1 509 180	(3)	(3)	48 700
Middle school teachers, except special and vocational education	637 340	(3)	(3)	47 890	652 700	(3)	(3)	49 470
Vocational education teachers, middle school	15 380	(3)	(3)	46 080	15 740	(3)	(3)	46 650
Secondary school teachers, except special and vocational education	1 015 740	(3)	(3)	49 400	1 030 780	(3)	(3)	51 150
Vocational education teachers, secondary school	96 600	(3)	(3)	49 240	95 040	(3)	(3)	51 050
Special education teachers, preschool, kindergarten, and elementary school	214 060	(3)	(3)	47 820	216 930	(3)	(3)	49 710
Special education teachers, middle school	103 480	(3)	(3)	50 340	101 420	(3)	(3)	52 550
Special education teachers, secondary school	136 290	(3)	(3)	50 880	136 870	(3)	(3)	52 520
Adult literacy, remedial education, and GED teachers and instructors	66 070	19.84	21.21	44 110	71 740	21.11	22.45	46 690
Self-enrichment education teachers	141 650	15.56	17.68	36 760	149 700	16.08	18.50	38 470
Teachers and instructors, all other	530 670	(3)	(3)	33 510	576 840	(3)	(3)	35 370
Archivists	5 410	17.99	19.64	40 850	5 460	19.58	21.35	44 400
Curators	8 790	21.75	23.64	49 180	9 520	22.26	24.03	49 980
Museum technicians and conservators	9 370	16.39	17.94	37 320	9 810	16.51	18.30	38 060
Librarians	146 740	22.79	23.61	49 110	148 610	23.59	24.45	50 860
Library technicians	115 770	12.33	12.95	26 940	113 940	12.77	13.42	27 910
Audio-visual collections specialists	6 910	19.36	19.76	41 100	6 520	19.49	20.23	42 090
Farm and home management advisers	12 620	20.14	22.05	45 860	12 390	20.06	22.59	46 990
Instructional coordinators	112 880	24.24	25.66	53 360	117 630	25.38	26.72	55 570
Teacher assistants	1 260 400	(3)	(3)	21 100	1 246 030	(3)	(3)	21 860
Education, training, and library workers, all other	72 450	14.37	16.33	33 970	84 390	15.46	17.14	35 640
Arts, Design, Entertainment, Sports, and Media								
Art directors	29 350	30.75	35.48	73 790	31 030	32.74	37.70	78 420
Craft artists	4 300	10.78	13.15	27 360	4 870	11.58	13.75	28 610
Fine artists, including painters, sculptors, and illustrators	10 390	19.85	22.44	46 670	11 260	20.18	22.65	47 100
Multimedia artists and animators	23 790	24.18	27.53	57 270	26 260	24.69	27.90	58 030
Artists and related workers, all other	5 290	15.01	17.73	36 880	7 870	20.19	23.51	48 890
Commercial and industrial designers	31 650	25.10	27.30	56 780	33 540	26.23	28.53	59 340
Fashion designers	12 980	29.26	32.39	67 370	15 670	30.10	33.30	69 270
Floral designers	63 920	10.12	10.77	22 410	61 320	10.43	11.08	23 040
Graphic designers	178 530	18.46	20.45	42 530	190 880	19.18	21.07	43 830
Interior designers	50 020	19.88	22.60	47 010	52 440	20.32	23.08	48 000
Merchandise displayers and window trimmers	64 320	10.86	12.10	25 170	62 580	11.45	12.77	26 550
Set and exhibit designers	8 380	17.98	20.15	41 920	8 320	20.11	21.93	45 620
Designers, all other	12 410	20.96	22.99	47 810	11 390	21.09	23.50	48 890
Actors	59 590	13.60	23.73	(?)	51 880	11.61	21.84	(?)
Producers and directors	59 070	25.89	33.16	68 970	63 840	27.07	34.72	72 210
Athletes and sports competitors	12 230	(3)	(3)	71 900	12 500	(3)	(3)	74 440
Coaches and scouts	145 440	(3)	(3)	32 050	154 350	(3)	(3)	33 290
Umpires, referees, and other sports officials	12 800	(3)	(3)	27 150	13 790	(3)	(3)	27 450
Dancers	16 240	8.92	13.22	(?)	16 010	9.55	13.86	(?)
Choreographers	16 150	15.84	18.26	37 970	16 340	16.67	18.42	38 320

[1]Annual wages have been calculated by multiplying the hourly mean wage by a "year-round, full-time" hours figure of 2,080 hours; for occupations with no published hourly mean wage, the annual wage has been directly calculated from the reported survey data.
[3]Wages for some occupations that do not generally entail year-round, full-time employment are reported as either hourly wages or annual salaries (depending on how employees are typically paid).
. . . = Not available.

Table 3-3. Employment and Wages, by Occupation, May 2005 and May 2006—*Continued*

(Number of people, dollars.)

Occupation	May 2005				May 2006			
	Employ-ment	Median hourly wage	Mean hourly wage	Mean annual wage[1]	Employ-ment	Median hourly wage	Mean hourly wage	Mean annual wage[1]
Arts, Design, Entertainment, Sports, and Media—*Continued*								
Music directors and composers	8 610	16.74	20.90	43 470	9 470	19.11	25.63	53 320
Musicians and singers	50 410	17.90	25.16	([3])	46 600	19.73	27.51	([3])
Entertainers and performers, sports and related workers, all other	68 540	15.73	17.92	([3])	59 450	15.11	16.84	([3])
Radio and television announcers	41 090	11.60	17.11	35 600	40 020	11.69	17.36	36 120
Public address system and other announcers	8 150	11.20	14.98	31 160	8 300	12.02	16.33	33 970
Broadcast news analysts	6 680	20.58	30.73	63 920	6 770	22.46	32.17	66 910
Reporters and correspondents	52 920	15.52	19.41	40 370	53 060	16.09	20.14	41 900
Public relations specialists	191 430	21.64	24.56	51 080	209 560	22.76	25.85	53 760
Editors	96 270	21.88	24.88	51 750	100 170	22.59	25.59	53 220
Technical writers	46 250	26.52	27.75	57 720	45 330	27.91	29.25	60 850
Writers and authors	43 020	22.32	25.89	53 850	43 260	23.38	27.93	58 080
Interpreters and translators	29 240	16.73	18.41	38 300	30 910	17.10	19.11	39 750
Media and communication workers, all other	25 660	20.14	22.13	46 030	22 970	20.47	22.26	46 310
Audio and video equipment technicians	40 390	15.84	17.48	36 350	40 360	16.75	18.61	38 710
Broadcast technicians	30 730	14.62	17.00	35 350	32 070	14.75	17.09	35 540
Radio operators	1 190	17.42	18.21	37 880	1 220	18.22	18.69	38 870
Sound engineering technicians	12 680	18.46	22.98	47 790	14 080	20.68	24.16	50 260
Photographers	58 260	12.55	15.10	31 410	60 300	12.58	15.30	31 830
Camera operators, television, video, and motion picture	22 530	20.01	22.13	46 040	22 230	19.26	22.19	46 150
Film and video editors	15 200	22.56	26.31	54 730	17 380	22.44	27.93	58 100
Media and communication equipment workers, all other	17 200	22.95	24.81	51 610	17 740	25.03	25.59	53 230
Health Care Practitioner and Technical								
Chiropractors	24 290	32.31	39.45	82 060	25 470	31.36	38.97	81 070
Dentists, general	86 270	60.24	64.27	133 680	86 110	63.53	67.76	140 950
Oral and maxillofacial surgeons	5 120	([2])	77.24	160 660	5 320	([2])	79.21	164 760
Orthodontists	4 820	([2])	78.56	163 410	5 200	([2])	85.05	176 900
Prosthodontists	560	([2])	70.23	146 080	480	([2])	76.42	158 940
Dentists, all other specialists	3 480	45.48	55.60	115 640	4 560	43.85	52.09	108 340
Dietitians and nutritionists	48 850	21.61	22.09	45 950	51 230	22.59	23.02	47 890
Optometrists	23 720	42.33	45.91	95 500	24 220	43.77	47.38	98 550
Pharmacists	229 740	43.18	42.62	88 650	239 920	45.44	44.95	93 500
Anesthesiologists	27 970	([2])	83.77	174 240	29 890	([2])	88.63	184 340
Family and general practitioners	112 150	67.50	67.49	140 370	109 400	([2])	72.04	149 850
Internists, general	48 210	([2])	75.27	156 550	48 700	([2])	77.34	160 860
Obstetricians and gynecologists	21 910	([2])	82.60	171 810	22 520	([2])	85.60	178 040
Pediatricians, general	26 400	65.67	66.94	139 230	28 930	66.41	68.00	141 440
Psychiatrists	23 450	([2])	70.26	146 150	24 730	([2])	72.11	149 990
Surgeons	52 930	([2])	85.43	177 690	51 900	([2])	88.53	184 150
Physicians and surgeons, all other	180 210	68.98	66.79	138 910	208 960	([2])	68.38	142 220
Physician assistants	63 350	34.63	34.17	71 070	62 960	36.05	35.71	74 270
Podiatrists	8 290	48.34	53.49	111 250	9 020	52.03	56.97	118 500
Registered nurses	2 368 070	26.28	27.35	56 880	2 417 150	27.54	28.71	59 730
Audiologists	10 330	25.72	27.72	57 660	10 910	27.46	29.38	61 110
Occupational therapists	87 430	27.34	28.41	59 100	88 570	29.07	30.05	62 510
Physical therapists	151 280	30.33	31.42	65 350	156 100	31.83	32.72	68 050
Radiation therapists	14 120	29.97	30.59	63 620	14 290	31.81	32.49	67 580
Recreational therapists	23 260	16.10	16.90	35 150	24 130	16.82	17.55	36 510
Respiratory therapists	95 320	21.70	22.24	46 270	99 330	22.80	23.37	48 610
Speech-language pathologists	94 660	26.38	27.89	58 000	98 690	27.74	29.25	60 840
Therapists, all other	9 730	20.22	21.96	45 680	11 660	20.31	21.67	45 070
Veterinarians	47 870	33.13	37.36	77 710	49 750	34.61	39.18	81 490
Health diagnosing and treating practitioners, all other	57 880	27.64	42.13	87 630	53 270	29.60	39.96	83 110
Medical and clinical laboratory technologists	155 250	22.94	23.37	48 600	160 760	23.90	24.30	50 550
Medical and clinical laboratory technicians	142 330	15.24	15.95	33 170	144 710	15.79	16.65	34 620
Dental hygienists	161 140	29.28	29.15	60 620	166 380	30.19	30.01	62 430
Cardiovascular technologists and technicians	43 560	19.43	19.99	41 580	43 870	20.34	21.15	43 990
Diagnostic medical sonographers	43 590	26.14	26.65	55 430	44 340	27.48	27.94	58 110
Nuclear medicine technologists	18 280	28.69	29.10	60 530	19 270	29.95	30.29	63 000
Radiologic technologists and technicians	184 580	22.09	22.60	47 010	190 180	23.16	23.71	49 320
Emergency medical technicians and paramedics	196 880	12.54	13.68	28 440	196 190	13.01	14.13	29 390
Dietetic technicians	23 780	11.28	12.20	25 380	24 450	11.56	12.55	26 090
Pharmacy technicians	266 790	11.73	12.19	25 350	282 450	12.32	12.75	26 510
Psychiatric technicians	62 040	12.87	14.04	29 210	58 940	13.36	14.64	30 450
Respiratory therapy technicians	22 060	18.37	18.57	38 620	18 710	18.81	19.17	39 860
Surgical technologists	83 680	16.75	17.27	35 920	84 330	17.35	17.97	37 370
Veterinary technologists and technicians	63 860	12.34	12.84	26 710	69 700	12.88	13.34	27 750
Licensed practical and licensed vocational nurses	710 020	16.94	17.41	36 210	720 380	17.57	18.05	37 530

[1]Annual wages have been calculated by multiplying the hourly mean wage by a "year-round, full-time" hours figure of 2,080 hours; for occupations with no published hourly mean wage, the annual wage has been directly calculated from the reported survey data.
[2]Median hourly wage is equal to or greater than $70.00 per hour.
[3]Wages for some occupations that do not generally entail year-round, full-time employment are reported as either hourly wages or annual salaries (depending on how employees are typically paid).

Table 3-3. Employment and Wages, by Occupation, May 2005 and May 2006—*Continued*

(Number of people, dollars.)

Occupation	May 2005				May 2006			
	Employ-ment	Median hourly wage	Mean hourly wage	Mean annual wage[1]	Employ-ment	Median hourly wage	Mean hourly wage	Mean annual wage[1]
Health Care Practitioner and Technical—*Continued*								
Medical records and health information technicians	160 450	12.83	13.81	28 720	164 700	13.48	14.49	30 140
Opticians, dispensing	70 090	13.94	14.80	30 770	65 190	14.57	15.49	32 220
Orthotists and prosthetists	5 190	25.85	28.87	60 050	5 290	28.36	29.86	62 110
Health technologists and technicians, all other	71 140	16.49	18.04	37 520	72 180	16.89	18.39	38 260
Occupational health and safety specialists	35 460	25.82	26.83	55 800	42 220	27.90	28.50	59 270
Occupational health and safety technicians	9 510	20.75	22.17	46 120	10 020	20.27	21.32	44 340
Athletic trainers	15 110	(3)	(3)	36 520	15 440	(3)	(3)	38 860
Health care practitioners and technical workers, all other	50 880	16.12	19.03	39 590	50 690	17.89	21.68	45 090
Health Care Support								
Home health aides	663 280	9.04	9.34	19 420	751 480	9.34	9.66	20 100
Nursing aides, orderlies, and attendants	1 391 430	10.31	10.67	22 200	1 376 660	10.67	11.04	22 960
Psychiatric aides	56 150	11.02	11.47	23 860	57 000	11.49	12.01	24 990
Occupational therapist assistants	22 160	19.11	19.13	39 800	23 700	20.22	20.25	42 110
Occupational therapist aides	6 220	11.69	13.20	27 450	7 780	12.03	13.35	27 760
Physical therapist assistants	58 670	18.98	18.98	39 490	59 350	19.88	19.91	41 410
Physical therapist aides	41 930	10.34	11.01	22 900	45 520	10.61	11.20	23 290
Massage therapists	37 670	15.81	19.33	40 210	41 920	16.06	18.93	39 380
Dental assistants	270 720	14.19	14.41	29 970	277 040	14.53	14.83	30 850
Medical assistants	382 720	12.19	12.58	26 160	409 570	12.64	13.07	27 190
Medical equipment preparers	41 790	11.96	12.42	25 830	42 740	12.47	12.97	26 980
Medical transcriptionists	90 380	13.98	14.36	29 880	86 790	14.40	14.74	30 660
Pharmacy aides	46 610	9.09	9.76	20 310	47 810	9.35	10.07	20 950
Veterinary assistants and laboratory animal caretakers	69 890	9.43	9.90	20 590	70 310	9.60	10.13	21 060
Health care support workers, all other	184 200	12.51	13.05	27 150	185 580	12.98	13.55	28 170
Protective Services								
First-line supervisors/managers of correctional officers	37 530	23.35	24.37	50 700	37 400	25.28	26.27	54 630
First-line supervisors/managers of police and detectives	91 320	31.52	32.33	67 240	89 170	33.32	33.76	70 230
First-line supervisors/managers of fire fighting and prevention workers	53 490	29.25	30.06	62 510	50 810	30.24	31.27	65 030
First-line supervisors/managers of protective service workers, all other	49 330	19.78	21.95	45 650	45 170	19.99	22.28	46 350
Firefighters	282 180	18.80	19.43	40 420	283 630	19.80	20.37	42 370
Fire inspectors and investigators	12 820	22.64	23.44	48 760	13 360	23.10	24.02	49 950
Forest fire inspectors and prevention specialists	1 720	16.48	18.44	38 360	1 710	15.84	17.21	35 810
Bailiffs	17 160	16.25	16.90	35 160	17 890	16.45	17.43	36 260
Correctional officers and jailers	411 080	16.39	17.60	36 600	417 810	17.19	18.42	38 310
Detectives and criminal investigators	85 270	26.82	28.24	58 750	100 110	28.01	29.03	60 390
Fish and game wardens	6 300	20.60	20.85	43 360	7 520	21.01	21.25	44 200
Parking enforcement workers	10 140	13.98	14.72	30 620	10 090	14.50	15.03	31 260
Police and sheriff's patrol officers	624 130	22.25	22.73	47 270	624 380	22.82	23.27	48 410
Transit and railroad police	5 090	23.49	24.20	50 330	5 320	22.63	23.86	49 620
Animal control workers	13 940	12.87	13.50	28 090	14 600	13.42	14.12	29 370
Private detectives and investigators	33 720	15.70	17.78	36 980	35 980	16.23	18.41	38 290
Gaming surveillance officers and gaming investigators	8 730	12.44	13.82	28 740	8 470	13.04	14.65	30 470
Security guards	994 220	9.98	10.91	22 690	1 004 130	10.35	11.35	23 620
Crossing guards	69 390	9.64	10.21	21 230	67 750	10.13	10.71	22 270
Lifeguards, ski patrol, and other recreational protective service workers	107 620	8.13	8.67	18 020	108 870	8.25	8.85	18 410
Protective service workers, all other	141 480	14.77	15.90	33 070	80 680	12.94	14.63	30 420
Food Preparation and Serving Related								
Chefs and head cooks	115 850	15.54	17.23	35 840	104 080	16.52	18.21	37 880
First-line supervisors/managers of food preparation and serving workers	748 550	12.53	13.44	27 960	769 320	12.97	13.88	28 870
Cooks, fast food	631 190	7.25	7.45	15 500	612 020	7.41	7.67	15 960
Cooks, institution and cafeteria	393 500	9.44	9.88	20 550	375 210	9.81	10.25	21 320
Cooks, private household	830	10.01	11.18	23 250	900	11.00	13.64	28 370
Cooks, restaurant	791 450	9.54	9.86	20 510	825 840	9.78	10.11	21 020
Cooks, short order	203 350	8.28	8.64	17 980	189 610	8.59	8.99	18 710
Cooks, all other	12 100	10.48	11.40	23 720	12 940	10.39	11.34	23 590
Food preparation workers	880 360	8.19	8.68	18 060	871 470	8.37	8.88	18 480
Bartenders	480 010	7.62	8.48	17 640	485 120	7.86	8.91	18 540
Combined food preparation and serving workers, including fast food	2 298 010	7.11	7.48	15 550	2 461 890	7.24	7.66	15 930
Counter attendants, cafeteria, food concession, and coffee shop	501 390	7.60	7.88	16 380	524 410	7.76	8.15	16 950
Waiters and waitresses	2 274 770	6.83	7.84	16 310	2 312 930	7.14	8.27	17 190
Food servers, nonrestaurant	188 750	8.28	8.98	18 680	183 700	8.70	9.48	19 710
Dining room and cafeteria attendants and bartender helpers	391 320	7.23	7.59	15 800	401 790	7.36	7.84	16 320
Dishwashers	498 620	7.45	7.58	15 760	502 770	7.57	7.78	16 190
Hosts and hostesses, restaurant, lounge, and coffee shop	328 930	7.62	7.90	16 430	340 390	7.78	8.10	16 860
Food preparation and serving related workers, all other	58 730	8.38	9.14	19 000	54 900	8.55	9.31	19 360

[1]Annual wages have been calculated by multiplying the hourly mean wage by a "year-round, full-time" hours figure of 2,080 hours; for occupations with no published hourly mean wage, the annual wage has been directly calculated from the reported survey data.
[3]Wages for some occupations that do not generally entail year-round, full-time employment are reported as either hourly wages or annual salaries (depending on how employees are typically paid).

Table 3-3. Employment and Wages, by Occupation, May 2005 and May 2006—*Continued*

(Number of people, dollars.)

Occupation	May 2005				May 2006			
	Employ-ment	Median hourly wage	Mean hourly wage	Mean annual wage[1]	Employ-ment	Median hourly wage	Mean hourly wage	Mean annual wage[1]
Building and Grounds Cleaning and Maintenance								
First-line supervisors/managers of housekeeping and janitorial workers	186 870	14.58	15.66	32 570	182 690	15.04	16.16	33 610
First-line supervisors/managers of landscaping, lawn service, and groundskeeping workers	106 280	17.46	18.82	39 150	111 100	17.93	19.35	40 240
Janitors and cleaners, except maids and housekeeping cleaners	2 107 360	9.32	10.15	21 120	2 124 860	9.58	10.45	21 730
Maids and housekeeping cleaners	893 820	8.21	8.74	18 180	900 040	8.45	8.99	18 700
Building cleaning workers, all other	15 610	11.25	12.99	27 020	14 390	12.06	13.78	28 670
Pest control workers	62 400	13.06	13.89	28 880	62 710	13.41	14.11	29 350
Landscaping and groundskeeping workers	896 690	9.94	10.74	22 350	924 330	10.22	11.06	23 010
Pesticide handlers, sprayers, and applicators, vegetation	25 770	12.56	13.22	27 500	25 880	12.84	13.73	28 560
Tree trimmers and pruners	29 790	13.42	14.35	29 850	28 300	13.58	14.38	29 910
Grounds maintenance workers, all other	17 960	10.04	11.78	24 510	21 930	9.82	11.77	24 490
Personal Care and Services								
First-line supervisors/managers of personal service workers	24 180	19.38	19.87	41 320	23 860	19.79	20.38	42 390
Gaming supervisors	14 700	10.64	11.65	24 230	13 450	10.92	12.16	25 300
Slot key persons	125 760	15.09	16.53	34 390	125 430	15.77	17.35	36 090
Animal trainers	8 320	11.92	14.19	29 510	10 020	12.65	14.39	29 920
Nonfarm animal caretakers	100 550	8.52	9.64	20 050	108 130	8.72	9.73	20 230
Gaming dealers	82 320	6.85	7.71	16 040	82 960	7.08	8.18	17 010
Gaming and sports book writers and runners	19 290	8.87	9.58	19 930	17 780	9.04	10.02	20 850
Gaming service workers, all other	16 070	10.37	11.53	23 980	. . .	10.52	11.59	24 110
Motion picture projectionists	10 230	8.07	9.30	19 340	10 620	8.39	9.70	20 180
Ushers, lobby attendants, and ticket takers	102 330	7.41	8.05	16 740	101 530	7.64	8.41	17 500
Amusement and recreation attendants	232 030	7.65	8.15	16 950	235 670	7.83	8.43	17 530
Costume attendants	3 900	12.19	13.94	28 990	4 150	12.37	14.20	29 540
Locker room, coatroom, and dressing room attendants	20 340	8.63	9.02	18 760	18 770	8.95	9.50	19 760
Embalmers	9 840	17.77	19.01	39 550	8 860	18.19	19.43	40 410
Funeral attendants	30 220	9.48	10.39	21 600	32 250	9.78	10.56	21 970
Barbers	13 630	10.46	11.88	24 700	11 500	11.13	12.76	26 540
Hairdressers, hairstylists, and cosmetologists	338 910	9.91	11.36	. . .	344 900	10.25	11.80	24 550
Makeup artists, theatrical and performance	1 070	11.29	15.70	32 660	1 250	15.30	17.66	36 730
Manicurists and pedicurists	42 960	8.79	9.81	20 400	47 450	9.23	10.23	21 280
Shampooers	16 040	7.49	7.85	16 320	15 580	7.78	8.20	17 050
Skin care specialists	22 740	11.22	12.90	26 830	22 620	12.58	14.21	29 550
Baggage porters and bellhops	51 300	8.46	10.03	20 870	48 450	8.83	10.37	21 580
Concierges	16 810	11.30	12.08	25 130	19 150	11.83	12.50	26 000
Tour guides and escorts	28 320	9.61	10.42	21 670	30 390	9.82	10.73	22 310
Travel guides	3 120	14.06	15.03	31 270	3 220	13.68	14.83	30 840
Flight attendants	99 590	(3)	(3)	53 740	96 760	(3)	(3)	56 150
Transportation attendants, except flight attendants and baggage porters	24 810	9.28	9.88	20 550	20 790	9.65	10.17	21 140
Childcare workers	557 680	8.20	8.74	18 180	572 950	8.48	9.05	18 820
Personal and home care aides	566 860	8.34	8.52	17 710	578 290	8.54	8.74	18 180
Fitness trainers and aerobics instructors	189 220	12.43	14.93	31 060	205 970	12.46	15.24	31 710
Recreation workers	264 840	9.67	10.78	22 420	273 280	9.84	11.03	22 950
Residential advisers	50 490	10.51	11.39	23 690	48 470	10.90	11.79	24 520
Personal care and service workers, all other	60 260	8.91	10.20	21 210	58 440	9.12	10.40	21 640
Sales and Related								
First-line supervisors/managers of retail sales workers	1 083 890	15.79	18.08	37 600	1 111 740	16.33	18.67	38 830
First-line supervisors/managers of non-retail sales workers	294 010	29.79	35.42	73 670	285 690	31.49	36.94	76 840
Cashiers	3 481 420	7.82	8.32	17 300	3 479 390	8.08	8.62	17 930
Gaming change persons and booth cashiers	28 590	9.64	9.92	20 630	26 700	9.94	10.32	21 470
Counter and rental clerks	473 090	9.12	10.83	22 530	468 900	9.41	11.22	23 340
Parts salespersons	235 190	12.72	13.94	28 990	234 770	13.19	14.43	30 010
Retail salespersons	4 344 770	9.20	11.14	23 170	4 374 230	9.50	11.51	23 940
Advertising sales agents	153 890	20.08	24.23	50 400	159 640	20.55	24.70	51 370
Insurance sales agents	299 470	20.36	27.38	56 960	311 380	21.09	28.10	58 450
Securities, commodities, and financial services sales agents	251 710	32.28	42.30	87 990	260 360	32.93	43.45	90 380
Travel agents	88 590	13.78	14.78	30 750	87 600	14.05	15.12	31 460
Sales representatives, services, all other	439 450	22.50	26.07	54 230	501 850	23.12	27.13	56 420
Sales representatives, wholesale and manufacturing, technical and scientific products	379 890	29.21	33.14	68 940	390 280	30.98	34.95	72 700
Sales representatives, wholesale and manufacturing, except technical and scientific products	1 436 800	22.78	26.90	55 940	1 488 990	23.85	28.14	58 540
Demonstrators and product promoters	86 050	9.96	11.81	24 570	82 830	10.65	12.39	25 770
Models	1 430	10.92	13.26	27 570	1 470	11.22	13.45	27 980
Real estate brokers	41 760	27.49	36.98	76 930	46 950	29.23	38.57	80 230
Real estate sales agents	150 200	18.87	25.04	52 090	168 400	19.12	26.13	54 350
Sales engineers	69 770	35.68	38.16	79 370	75 150	37.37	39.94	83 080
Telemarketers	400 860	9.79	11.30	23 500	385 700	10.09	11.63	24 190
Door-to-door sales workers, news and street vendors, and related workers	10 970	9.83	12.19	25 350	11 140	9.71	12.92	26 880
Sales and related workers, all other	178 480	15.77	19.05	39 610	161 700	16.47	19.63	40 820

[1]Annual wages have been calculated by multiplying the hourly mean wage by a "year-round, full-time" hours figure of 2,080 hours; for occupations with no published hourly mean wage, the annual wage has been directly calculated from the reported survey data.
[3]Wages for some occupations that do not generally entail year-round, full-time employment are reported as either hourly wages or annual salaries (depending on how employees are typically paid).
. . . = Not available.

Table 3-3. Employment and Wages, by Occupation, May 2005 and May 2006—*Continued*

(Number of people, dollars.)

Occupation	May 2005				May 2006			
	Employ-ment	Median hourly wage	Mean hourly wage	Mean annual wage[1]	Employ-ment	Median hourly wage	Mean hourly wage	Mean annual wage[1]
Office and Adminstrative Support								
First-line supervisors/managers of office and administrative support workers	1 352 130	20.38	21.89	45 540	1 351 180	20.92	22.37	46 530
Switchboard operators, including answering service	194 980	10.61	11.07	23 020	172 060	10.88	11.37	23 640
Telephone operators	29 290	15.09	14.92	31 030	26 350	16.41	15.73	32 710
Communications equipment operators, all other	3 870	15.64	16.36	34 030	4 220	15.23	15.93	33 130
Bill and account collectors	431 280	13.54	14.36	29 860	423 090	13.97	14.73	30 640
Billing and posting clerks and machine operators	513 020	13.36	13.87	28 860	517 750	13.87	14.39	29 930
Bookkeeping, accounting, and auditing clerks	1 815 340	14.18	14.76	30 700	1 856 890	14.69	15.28	31 780
Gaming cage workers	18 730	10.76	11.28	23 460	17 970	11.13	11.62	24 170
Payroll and timekeeping clerks	205 600	15.08	15.44	32 120	205 970	15.58	15.93	33 140
Procurement clerks	71 390	15.49	15.64	32 530	74 370	15.91	16.13	33 540
Tellers	599 220	10.24	10.59	22 020	603 150	10.64	10.97	22 810
Brokerage clerks	70 110	17.04	18.34	38 140	72 400	17.50	18.89	39 280
Correspondence clerks	17 990	13.66	14.51	30 180	16 260	13.80	14.35	29 850
Court, municipal, and license clerks	102 060	14.09	15.02	31 230	107 100	14.89	15.66	32 580
Credit authorizers, checkers, and clerks	65 410	14.10	14.90	30 990	67 400	14.41	15.25	31 710
Customer service representatives	2 067 700	13.22	14.27	29 680	2 147 770	13.62	14.61	30 400
Eligibility interviewers, government programs	85 550	16.22	16.53	34 390	106 210	18.05	18.16	37 770
File clerks	229 830	10.30	10.98	22 840	223 090	10.62	11.32	23 540
Hotel, motel, and resort desk clerks	207 190	8.56	9.05	18 820	214 110	8.88	9.37	19 480
Interviewers, except eligibility and loan	201 790	12.07	12.54	26 070	211 500	12.64	13.07	27 190
Library assistants, clerical	104 650	10.16	10.76	22 380	109 090	10.40	11.03	22 940
Loan interviewers and clerks	231 700	14.52	15.33	31 880	248 050	14.89	15.71	32 680
New accounts clerks	82 450	13.18	13.69	28 460	80 770	13.65	14.19	29 510
Order clerks	259 760	12.30	13.18	27 410	264 520	12.66	13.52	28 130
Human resources assistants, except payroll and timekeeping	161 870	15.74	16.24	33 790	159 750	16.23	16.70	34 740
Receptionists and information clerks	1 088 400	10.65	11.12	23 120	1 112 350	11.01	11.45	23 810
Reservation and transportation ticket agents and travel clerks	160 120	13.52	14.45	30 050	157 650	13.72	14.48	30 120
All other information and record clerks	288 730	16.16	19.10	39 720	230 990	14.98	15.82	32 900
Cargo and freight agents	78 730	17.24	17.97	37 380	84 340	17.84	18.54	38 560
Couriers and messengers	106 520	10.03	10.80	22 460	105 070	10.36	11.14	23 170
Police, fire, and ambulance dispatchers	94 060	14.45	15.03	31 270	94 710	15.13	15.67	32 590
Dispatchers, except police, fire, and ambulance	172 550	15.09	16.15	33 590	185 410	15.48	16.56	34 450
Meter readers, utilities	46 920	14.09	14.92	31 030	45 770	14.58	15.41	32 040
Postal service clerks	78 710	23.23	22.51	46 820	81 670	21.54	21.13	43 950
Postal service mail carriers	347 180	22.27	21.38	44 460	346 990	21.32	21.03	43 750
Postal service mail sorters, processors, and processing machine operators	208 600	20.88	20.01	41 620	203 110	21.10	19.75	41 070
Production, planning, and expediting clerks	287 980	18.07	18.71	38 920	286 160	18.57	19.23	40 000
Shipping, receiving, and traffic clerks	759 910	12.10	12.80	26 620	763 350	12.53	13.21	27 480
Stock clerks and order fillers	1 625 430	9.66	10.60	22 060	1 705 450	9.83	10.79	22 440
Weighers, measurers, checkers, and samplers, record-keeping	79 050	12.17	12.99	27 030	77 520	12.20	13.14	27 330
Executive secretaries and administrative assistants	1 442 040	17.29	18.18	37 810	1 487 310	17.90	18.83	39 160
Legal secretaries	265 000	18.15	18.78	39 070	268 170	18.36	19.07	39 670
Medical secretaries	381 020	13.13	13.65	28 390	394 330	13.51	14.05	29 220
Secretaries, except legal, medical, and executive	1 744 380	12.82	13.35	27 780	1 750 600	13.20	13.68	28 460
Computer operators	129 160	15.42	16.15	33 580	123 750	16.13	16.83	35 010
Data entry keyers	296 700	11.45	11.98	24 910	295 650	11.87	12.33	25 640
Word processors and typists	153 580	13.95	14.49	30 140	153 530	14.15	14.68	30 540
Desktop publishers	29 910	15.77	16.72	34 770	30 440	16.41	17.36	36 120
Insurance claims and policy processing clerks	239 120	14.49	15.24	31 700	238 210	14.96	15.74	32 740
Mail clerks and mail machine operators, except postal service	148 330	10.99	11.59	24 120	141 170	11.45	12.05	25 060
Office clerks, general	2 997 370	11.09	11.82	24 580	3 026 710	11.40	12.12	25 200
Office machine operators, except computer	87 900	11.53	12.24	25 460	91 810	11.80	12.51	26 010
Proofreaders and copy markers	18 070	12.30	13.30	27 660	16 960	13.20	14.12	29 380
Statistical assistants	18 700	13.92	15.04	31 270	19 680	15.02	15.84	32 950
Office and administrative support workers, all other	287 270	12.52	13.50	28 070	277 310	13.08	14.07	29 260
Farming, Fishing, and Forestry								
First-line supervisors/managers of farming, fishing, and forestry workers	19 750	17.32	18.65	38 790	19 670	18.15	19.33	40 210
Farm labor contractors	2 310	9.52	12.14	25 240	2 060	11.32	13.87	28 850
Agricultural inspectors	11 730	15.79	16.75	34 840	14 790	18.32	18.67	38 820
Animal breeders	1 860	12.90	15.23	31 690	2 060	13.02	15.37	31 970
Graders and sorters, agricultural products	45 010	8.06	8.74	18 170	45 890	8.27	8.95	18 610
Agricultural equipment operators	19 940	9.36	10.06	20 930	21 140	9.72	10.55	21 950
Farmworkers and laborers, crop, nursery, and greenhouse	227 750	7.91	8.35	17 370	230 780	7.95	8.48	17 630
Farmworkers, farm and ranch animals	49 740	8.76	9.56	19 890	47 870	9.17	9.92	20 630
Agricultural workers, all other	8 970	10.61	11.60	24 140	8 550	10.80	12.05	25 070
Fishers and related fishing workers	770	12.08	13.94	29 000	880	13.10	13.71	28 510
Forest and conservation workers	8 700	9.46	11.19	23 280	8 530	10.01	11.97	24 890
Fallers	9 780	13.64	15.26	31 740	8 790	13.80	15.84	32 960
Logging equipment operators	26 880	13.91	14.28	29 700	28 300	14.28	14.85	30 880
Log graders and scalers	4 520	13.31	14.21	29 550	4 810	14.06	14.90	30 980
Logging workers, all other	5 330	15.24	15.04	31 290	5 880	15.32	15.25	31 720

[1]Annual wages have been calculated by multiplying the hourly mean wage by a "year-round, full-time" hours figure of 2,080 hours; for occupations with no published hourly mean wage, the annual wage has been directly calculated from the reported survey data.

Table 3-3. Employment and Wages, by Occupation, May 2005 and May 2006—*Continued*

(Number of people, dollars.)

Occupation	May 2005				May 2006			
	Employ-ment	Median hourly wage	Mean hourly wage	Mean annual wage[1]	Employ-ment	Median hourly wage	Mean hourly wage	Mean annual wage[1]
Construction and Extraction								
First-line supervisors/managers of construction trades and extraction workers	555 380	24.98	26.79	55 720	574 870	25.89	27.64	57 500
Boilermakers	17 760	23.10	23.62	49 130	17 240	22.58	23.37	48 600
Brickmasons and blockmasons	115 950	20.13	20.60	42 850	118 080	20.66	21.33	44 370
Stonemasons	17 030	16.66	17.53	36 450	18 210	17.29	18.29	38 040
Carpenters	935 920	17.11	18.62	38 720	985 990	17.57	19.20	39 930
Carpet installers	37 050	16.13	17.84	37 100	36 840	16.62	18.40	38 280
Floor layers, except carpet, wood, and hard tiles	14 520	15.87	17.92	37 270	14 910	16.44	18.81	39 120
Floor sanders and finishers	5 950	13.14	14.34	29 830	7 480	13.89	15.29	31 810
Tile and marble setters	47 410	17.56	18.81	39 130	51 330	17.59	18.92	39 360
Cement masons and concrete finishers	204 720	15.40	16.64	34 610	218 170	15.70	17.13	35 630
Terrazzo workers and finishers	5 440	15.40	16.69	34 720	6 550	15.21	16.78	34 900
Construction laborers	934 000	12.22	13.97	29 050	1 016 530	12.66	14.39	29 930
Paving, surfacing, and tamping equipment operators	63 220	14.58	15.93	33 140	63 090	15.05	16.45	34 210
Pile-driver operators	4 410	23.51	24.27	50 490	5 280	22.20	24.02	49 950
Operating engineers and other construction equipment operators	378 720	17.23	18.85	39 210	393 090	17.74	19.50	40 560
Drywall and ceiling tile installers	126 810	16.70	18.07	37 580	140 630	17.38	18.66	38 810
Tapers	38 570	19.17	19.91	41 410	40 090	19.85	20.48	42 590
Electricians	606 500	20.57	21.94	45 630	617 370	20.97	22.41	46 620
Glaziers	49 310	16.12	17.75	36 920	51 990	16.64	18.30	38 060
Insulation workers, floor, ceiling, and wall	34 250	15.08	16.59	34 510	31 450	14.67	16.48	34 280
Insulation workers, mechanical	22 100	17.07	19.16	39 840	27 900	17.74	20.07	41 740
Painters, construction and maintenance	249 850	14.81	16.08	33 450	263 390	15.00	16.45	34 220
Paperhangers	7 710	16.08	17.65	36 720	6 160	16.21	17.42	36 230
Pipelayers	56 280	13.83	15.53	32 290	58 330	14.58	16.21	33 710
Plumbers, pipefitters, and steamfitters	420 770	20.27	21.56	44 850	435 960	20.56	22.03	45 830
Plasterers and stucco masons	47 760	16.08	17.40	36 200	50 700	16.68	17.91	37 260
Reinforcing iron and rebar workers	30 270	16.78	19.32	40 190	30 180	18.38	20.35	42 330
Roofers	120 070	15.01	16.14	33 570	125 030	15.51	16.99	35 340
Sheet metal workers	174 550	17.50	19.03	39 570	177 540	17.96	19.61	40 780
Structural iron and steel workers	68 900	19.51	20.93	43 540	67 560	19.46	21.13	43 950
Helpers—brickmasons, blockmasons, stonemasons, and tile and marble setters	58 690	11.83	13.14	27 340	62 290	12.19	13.39	27 850
Helpers—carpenters	101 870	10.57	11.11	23 100	104 200	11.09	11.63	24 190
Helpers—electricians	90 370	11.17	11.86	24 670	100 550	11.42	12.05	25 050
Helpers—painters, paperhangers, plasterers, and stucco masons	21 820	9.88	10.61	22 070	23 390	10.25	10.87	22 620
Helpers—pipelayers, plumbers, pipefitters, and steamfitters	77 630	10.97	11.84	24 630	81 510	11.50	12.22	25 430
Helpers—roofers	20 510	9.97	10.41	21 660	21 050	10.46	10.93	22 740
Helpers—construction trades, all other	37 590	10.40	11.55	24 020	35 880	10.94	11.93	24 820
Construction and building inspectors	87 820	21.50	22.51	46 830	96 630	22.39	23.37	48 620
Elevator installers and repairers	21 000	28.46	28.12	58 500	21 700	30.59	29.78	61 930
Fence erectors	22 600	11.99	12.74	26 490	24 610	12.69	13.53	28 130
Hazardous materials removal workers	38 260	16.20	17.90	37 240	38 740	17.04	18.43	38 340
Highway maintenance workers	140 600	14.54	14.88	30 950	138 670	15.17	15.56	32 370
Rail-track laying and maintenance equipment operators	13 510	19.23	18.81	39 120	13 680	19.23	19.06	39 640
Septic tank servicers and sewer pipe cleaners	17 940	14.64	15.38	31 980	22 090	15.11	15.65	32 560
Segmental pavers	330	12.02	12.82	26 670	880	13.80	13.75	28 600
Construction and related workers, all other	63 340	14.36	15.50	32 230	56 130	14.65	15.81	32 880
Derrick operators, oil and gas	13 270	16.29	17.16	35 690	16 920	17.42	18.23	37 930
Rotary drill operators, oil and gas	15 500	18.03	19.18	39 880	18 010	18.49	20.36	42 350
Service unit operators, oil, gas, and mining	19 530	14.74	16.61	34 560	25 360	15.82	17.37	36 120
Earth drillers, except oil and gas	18 800	16.23	17.20	35 770	19 070	16.59	17.80	37 030
Explosives workers, ordnance handling experts, and blasters	4 800	18.65	19.33	40 210	5 110	19.18	19.83	41 240
Continuous mining machine operators	9 000	18.80	18.67	38 830	9 660	19.44	19.38	40 310
Mine cutting and channeling machine operators	6 080	18.64	18.12	37 680	7 700	19.23	18.71	38 930
Mining machine operators, all other	2 450	17.37	18.26	37 970	2 880	17.97	18.50	38 490
Rock splitters, quarry	3 600	13.10	13.56	28 200	3 790	13.05	13.91	28 940
Roof bolters, mining	4 140	18.91	18.84	39 180	4 240	19.83	20.29	42 200
Roustabouts, oil and gas	33 570	11.96	12.71	26 430	41 120	12.36	12.93	26 890
Helpers—extraction workers	25 550	13.19	13.76	28 620	23 980	13.79	14.65	30 460
Extraction workers, all other	9 060	16.35	17.32	36 010	8 880	17.04	18.49	38 470
Installation, Maintenance, and Repair								
First-line supervisors/managers of mechanics, installers, and repairers	455 690	24.99	26.15	54 390	450 710	25.91	26.98	56 110
Computer, automated teller, and office machine repairers	138 210	17.34	18.10	37 640	139 770	17.54	18.29	38 050
Radio mechanics	6 170	18.25	18.78	39 070	6 250	18.12	19.17	39 880
Telecommunications equipment installers and repairers, except line installers	198 350	24.33	23.72	49 330	190 130	25.21	24.33	50 610
Avionics technicians	22 490	22.42	22.57	46 940	15 360	22.57	22.78	47 380
Electric motor, power tool, and related repairers	20 070	16.09	16.77	34 880	22 100	15.80	16.74	34 810
Electrical and electronics installers and repairers, transportation equipment	20 560	19.95	20.20	42 010	20 480	20.72	20.98	43 650
Electrical and electronics repairers, commercial and industrial equipment	69 620	21.21	21.32	44 350	78 570	21.72	21.96	45 670
Electrical and electronics repairers, powerhouse, substation, and relay	21 250	26.43	26.26	54 620	22 090	27.60	27.34	56 870
Electronic equipment installers and repairers, motor vehicles	17 650	13.19	14.94	31 080	19 510	13.57	14.99	31 190

[1]Annual wages have been calculated by multiplying the hourly mean wage by a "year-round, full-time" hours figure of 2,080 hours; for occupations with no published hourly mean wage, the annual wage has been directly calculated from the reported survey data.

Table 3-3. Employment and Wages, by Occupation, May 2005 and May 2006—*Continued*

(Number of people, dollars.)

Occupation	May 2005				May 2006			
	Employ-ment	Median hourly wage	Mean hourly wage	Mean annual wage[1]	Employ-ment	Median hourly wage	Mean hourly wage	Mean annual wage[1]
Installation, Maintenance, and Repair—*Continued*								
Electronic home entertainment equipment installers and repairers	35 360	13.91	14.83	30 840	35 310	14.42	15.25	31 710
Security and fire alarm systems installers	49 470	16.21	17.06	35 480	51 740	16.73	17.51	36 410
Aircraft mechanics and service technicians	115 120	22.74	23.68	49 260	118 210	22.95	23.70	49 300
Automotive body and related repairers	158 160	16.74	18.23	37 920	155 500	16.92	18.38	38 230
Automotive glass installers and repairers	17 760	14.18	14.67	30 510	18 650	14.77	15.41	32 050
Automotive service technicians and mechanics	654 800	15.89	16.90	35 140	642 360	16.24	17.34	36 070
Bus and truck mechanics and diesel engine specialists	248 280	17.61	17.96	37 360	254 850	18.11	18.48	38 440
Farm equipment mechanics	30 800	13.81	14.17	29 480	29 500	14.16	14.58	30 320
Mobile heavy equipment mechanics, except engines	117 500	18.95	19.32	40 190	119 060	19.44	19.90	41 390
Rail car repairers	24 270	20.45	20.32	42 270	23 810	20.82	20.68	43 010
Motorboat mechanics	18 190	15.76	16.31	33 920	18 550	15.96	16.55	34 430
Motorcycle mechanics	16 140	14.16	15.11	31 430	16 700	14.45	15.39	32 000
Outdoor power equipment and other small engine mechanics	24 680	12.41	12.95	26 930	25 560	12.94	13.44	27 950
Bicycle repairers	7 980	10.05	10.33	21 490	8 350	10.48	10.87	22 610
Recreational vehicle service technicians	13 540	14.65	15.43	32 100	13 560	15.15	16.00	33 280
Tire repairers and changers	100 860	10.08	10.72	22 300	103 120	10.26	10.96	22 790
Mechanical door repairers	14 400	14.57	15.81	32 890	15 130	15.20	16.38	34 060
Control and valve installers and repairers, except mechanical door	38 640	21.21	21.21	44 120	42 270	21.84	21.77	45 290
Heating, air-conditioning, and refrigeration mechanics and installers	241 380	17.81	18.64	38 770	250 970	18.11	19.09	39 710
Home appliance repairers	43 110	15.86	16.38	34 060	42 810	16.28	16.99	35 350
Industrial machinery mechanics	234 650	19.11	19.74	41 060	250 810	19.74	20.47	42 570
Maintenance and repair workers, general	1 307 820	15.01	15.70	32 650	1 310 580	15.34	16.11	33 510
Maintenance workers, machinery	83 220	16.18	16.96	35 270	81 580	16.61	17.50	36 390
Millwrights	53 080	21.53	22.33	46 450	53 320	21.94	22.99	47 820
Refractory materials repairers, except brickmasons	3 250	19.35	19.74	41 070	3 340	19.61	19.61	40 790
Electrical power line installers and repairers	106 060	24.11	23.65	49 200	110 520	24.41	23.99	49 900
Telecommunications line installers and repairers	142 560	20.39	20.66	42 970	156 440	22.25	21.99	45 740
Camera and photographic equipment repairers	3 160	16.78	17.37	36 130	3 470	16.76	17.60	36 600
Medical equipment repairers	27 940	19.02	20.04	41 680	32 100	19.51	20.69	43 040
Musical instrument repairers and tuners	4 830	13.73	15.33	31 880	5 120	14.04	15.31	31 850
Watch repairers	3 080	15.21	16.00	33 280	3 050	14.86	15.75	32 760
Precision instrument and equipment repairers, all other	12 870	21.37	22.11	45 980	12 980	22.23	22.71	47 230
Coin, vending, and amusement machine servicers and repairers	39 570	13.56	14.11	29 340	39 440	13.80	14.33	29 820
Commercial divers	2 310	18.25	20.15	41 910	2 680	19.03	21.83	45 410
Fabric menders, except garment	2 140	16.77	16.37	34 040	1 280	13.64	14.55	30 260
Locksmiths and safe repairers	16 080	14.85	15.67	32 600	17 870	15.39	16.14	33 560
Manufactured building and mobile home installers	10 120	11.09	12.05	25 070	9 520	12.06	12.79	26 600
Riggers	11 840	17.79	18.17	37 790	12 010	18.85	19.07	39 670
Signal and track switch repairers	6 100	23.65	23.25	48 370	5 980	24.11	23.98	49 870
Helpers—installation, maintenance, and repair workers	158 520	10.21	11.17	23 230	159 110	10.71	11.64	24 210
Installation, maintenance, and repair workers, all other	135 560	16.39	17.43	36 260	130 260	15.84	17.10	35 560
Production								
First-line supervisors/managers of production and operating workers	679 930	22.18	23.66	49 210	676 640	22.74	24.27	50 480
Aircraft structure, surfaces, rigging, and systems assemblers	22 820	21.15	20.45	42 530	27 680	21.83	21.09	43 860
Coil winders, tapers, and finishers	23 190	12.32	12.65	26 320	22 560	12.64	12.94	26 910
Electrical and electronic equipment assemblers	207 270	12.08	13.05	27 150	211 460	12.29	13.23	27 510
Electromechanical equipment assemblers	57 200	12.97	13.71	28 520	59 760	13.25	13.91	28 930
Engine and other machine assemblers	49 430	16.72	17.38	36 150	45 120	15.99	17.02	35 400
Structural metal fabricators and fitters	93 490	14.56	15.09	31 390	99 680	14.56	15.11	31 440
Fiberglass laminators and fabricators	30 560	12.13	12.64	26 300	32 510	12.49	12.96	26 960
Team assemblers	1 242 370	11.60	12.50	26 000	1 250 120	11.63	12.59	26 180
Timing device assemblers, adjusters, and calibrators	2 460	13.54	14.23	29 600	2 460	13.86	14.68	30 530
Assemblers and fabricators, all other	258 240	12.62	14.49	30 140	288 370	12.85	14.90	31 000
Bakers	144 110	10.35	11.13	23 150	139 700	10.59	11.40	23 710
Butchers and meat cutters	128 660	12.78	13.37	27 810	128 350	12.95	13.61	28 310
Meat, poultry, and fish cutters and trimmers	136 690	9.53	9.99	20 780	139 830	9.79	10.22	21 260
Slaughterers and meat packers	132 000	10.20	10.33	21 490	118 610	10.43	10.55	21 940
Food and tobacco roasting, baking, and drying machine operators and tenders	18 160	11.17	12.15	25 280	18 510	11.30	12.36	25 710
Food batchmakers	89 400	10.82	11.61	24 140	92 590	11.11	11.92	24 790
Food cooking machine operators and tenders	43 100	10.29	11.03	22 950	44 060	10.23	10.94	22 750
Computer-controlled machine tool operators, metal and plastic	136 490	14.91	15.41	32 060	139 580	15.23	15.78	32 820
Numerical tool and process control programmers	17 860	20.11	21.15	43 990	17 800	20.42	21.54	44 810
Extruding and drawing machine setters, operators, and tenders, metal and plastic	87 290	13.46	13.84	28 790	93 810	13.58	14.10	29 330
Forging machine setters, operators, and tenders, metal and plastic	33 850	13.93	14.53	30 220	31 050	13.94	14.41	29 980
Rolling machine setters, operators, and tenders, metal and plastic	37 500	14.65	15.02	31 240	34 710	14.93	15.43	32 080
Cutting, punching, and press machine setters, operators, and tenders, metal and plastic	265 480	12.49	13.13	27 310	269 640	12.66	13.33	27 730
Drilling and boring machine tool setters, operators, and tenders, metal and plastic	43 180	13.85	14.72	30 610	42 480	14.36	15.21	31 640
Grinding, lapping, polishing, and buffing machine tool setters, operators, and tenders, metal and plastic	101 530	13.34	14.23	29 600	100 010	13.50	14.32	29 780
Lathe and turning machine tool setters, operators, and tenders, metal and plastic	71 410	15.26	15.74	32 750	65 840	15.46	15.98	33 250
Milling and planing machine setters, operators, and tenders, metal and plastic	29 140	15.13	15.44	32 120	29 040	15.18	15.52	32 280
Machinists	368 380	16.51	17.00	35 350	385 690	16.71	17.22	35 810
Metal refining furnace operators and tenders	17 960	15.83	16.26	33 820	18 430	15.69	16.14	33 560

[1]Annual wages have been calculated by multiplying the hourly mean wage by a "year-round, full-time" hours figure of 2,080 hours; for occupations with no published hourly mean wage, the annual wage has been directly calculated from the reported survey data.

Table 3-3. Employment and Wages, by Occupation, May 2005 and May 2006—*Continued*

(Number of people, dollars.)

Occupation	May 2005				May 2006			
	Employ-ment	Median hourly wage	Mean hourly wage	Mean annual wage[1]	Employ-ment	Median hourly wage	Mean hourly wage	Mean annual wage[1]
Production—*Continued*								
Pourers and casters, metal	14 340	14.02	14.73	30 650	14 880	14.22	14.87	30 930
Model makers, metal and plastic	8 120	21.62	22.26	46 300	8 370	20.22	21.22	44 130
Patternmakers, metal and plastic	6 850	16.57	17.74	36 900	7 070	17.01	18.31	38 090
Foundry mold and coremakers	15 890	13.95	14.87	30 920	14 460	13.82	14.40	29 950
Molding, coremaking, and casting machine setters, operators, and tenders, metal and plastic	157 080	12.05	12.82	26 680	155 670	12.29	13.14	27 330
Multiple machine tool setters, operators, and tenders, metal and plastic	98 120	14.32	15.17	31 550	96 480	14.68	15.45	32 140
Tool and die makers	99 680	20.95	21.61	44 940	96 960	21.29	21.95	45 650
Welders, cutters, solderers, and brazers	358 050	14.90	15.52	32 280	376 630	15.10	15.81	32 880
Welding, soldering, and brazing machine setters, operators, and tenders	45 220	14.63	15.55	32 350	48 770	14.90	16.08	33 440
Heat treating equipment setters, operators, and tenders, metal and plastic	26 310	14.57	14.97	31 130	27 050	14.83	15.27	31 750
Lay out workers, metal and plastic	10 970	16.03	16.56	34 440	9 960	16.15	16.87	35 080
Plating and coating machine setters, operators, and tenders, metal and plastic	40 550	12.86	13.67	28 420	41 500	13.21	14.08	29 280
Tool grinders, filers, and sharpeners	18 180	15.05	15.64	32 530	17 620	14.73	15.49	32 210
Metal workers and plastic workers, all other	49 650	17.06	17.97	37 380	47 760	16.69	18.14	37 730
Bindery workers	64 330	12.04	12.92	26 880	63 700	12.29	13.16	27 370
Bookbinders	7 660	14.04	14.52	30 200	7 120	14.55	15.49	32 210
Job printers	50 580	15.35	16.02	33 320	46 200	15.58	16.36	34 020
Prepress technicians and workers	72 050	15.79	16.53	34 380	70 890	16.01	16.70	34 730
Printing machine operators	192 520	14.77	15.61	32 470	191 610	14.90	15.79	32 840
Laundry and dry-cleaning workers	218 360	8.38	8.87	18 450	217 580	8.58	9.08	18 890
Pressers, textile, garment, and related materials	78 620	8.45	8.76	18 220	75 150	8.56	8.88	18 470
Sewing machine operators	233 130	8.82	9.55	19 860	219 080	9.04	9.78	20 340
Shoe and leather workers and repairers	7 680	9.62	10.11	21 030	7 450	9.83	10.41	21 660
Shoe machine operators and tenders	3 850	9.90	10.31	21 440	4 080	10.54	10.92	22 710
Sewers, hand	11 090	9.51	10.61	22 060	9 750	9.79	10.43	21 680
Tailors, dressmakers, and custom sewers	30 150	10.95	11.79	24 530	30 000	11.01	11.91	24 770
Textile bleaching and dyeing machine operators and tenders	21 660	10.80	11.16	23 200	20 070	11.20	11.50	23 920
Textile cutting machine setters, operators, and tenders	21 420	10.30	10.83	22 530	19 140	10.39	10.93	22 740
Textile knitting and weaving machine setters, operators, and tenders	42 760	11.40	11.41	23 740	38 900	11.68	11.80	24 530
Textile winding, twisting, and drawing-out machine setters, operators, and tenders	47 670	11.04	11.30	23 510	44 210	11.08	11.32	23 550
Extruding and forming machine setters, operators, and tenders, synthetic and glass fibers	23 040	13.82	14.20	29 540	17 860	13.78	14.38	29 910
Fabric and apparel patternmakers	9 650	15.07	17.62	36 660	8 840	15.74	18.45	38 380
Upholsterers	41 040	12.84	13.46	27 990	40 340	13.09	13.70	28 500
Textile, apparel, and furnishings workers, all other	24 740	11.01	11.35	23 610	22 890	11.03	11.91	24 770
Cabinetmakers and bench carpenters	121 660	12.51	13.29	27 650	127 780	12.99	13.83	28 760
Furniture finishers	24 610	11.83	12.60	26 200	24 890	12.02	12.83	26 680
Model makers, wood	2 280	13.46	15.71	32 680	1 920	13.69	15.86	33 000
Patternmakers, wood	2 000	13.78	15.16	31 540	2 270	15.15	16.20	33 690
Sawing machine setters, operators, and tenders, wood	60 280	11.15	11.72	24 380	60 230	11.67	12.20	25 380
Woodworking machine setters, operators, and tenders, except sawing	94 690	11.25	11.83	24 610	97 700	11.51	12.07	25 110
Woodworkers, all other	10 550	10.20	11.13	23 150	11 350	10.86	12.03	25 030
Nuclear power reactor operators	3 730	31.84	32.17	66 900	3 750	33.35	34.04	70 800
Power distributors and dispatchers	7 520	28.44	28.61	59 510	8 420	30.09	30.12	62 640
Power plant operators	33 650	25.56	25.65	53 350	34 200	26.44	26.60	55 340
Stationary engineers and boiler operators	43 110	21.44	21.94	45 640	42 730	22.13	22.59	46 990
Water and liquid waste treatment plant and system operators	102 940	16.79	17.34	36 060	106 550	17.34	17.88	37 180
Chemical plant and system operators	58 640	22.45	22.55	46 900	52 970	23.60	23.53	48 930
Gas plant operators	10 530	24.96	25.15	52 310	12 120	25.80	25.90	53 870
Petroleum pump system operators, refinery operators, and gaugers	40 470	24.55	24.19	50 320	40 880	25.18	25.20	52 410
Plant and system operators, all other	13 920	21.57	21.50	44 730	13 820	22.25	22.33	46 450
Chemical equipment operators and tenders	50 610	18.77	19.05	39 620	50 570	19.37	19.85	41 300
Separating, filtering, clarifying, precipitating, and still machine setters, operators, and tenders	41 250	16.66	17.15	35 680	43 660	16.81	17.37	36 130
Crushing, grinding, and polishing machine setters, operators, and tenders	41 480	13.21	13.89	28 900	41 910	13.50	14.22	29 570
Grinding and polishing workers, hand	44 890	11.28	12.03	25 010	43 980	11.48	12.24	25 460
Mixing and blending machine setters, operators, and tenders	129 440	13.89	14.52	30 200	140 710	14.10	14.80	30 790
Cutters and trimmers, hand	28 360	10.50	11.57	24 070	28 790	10.73	11.72	24 370
Cutting and slicing machine setters, operators, and tenders	78 030	13.25	14.04	29 210	77 960	13.43	14.23	29 610
Extruding, forming, pressing, and compacting machine setters, operators, and tenders	80 420	13.36	14.15	29 420	81 000	13.32	14.06	29 230
Furnace, kiln, oven, dryer, and kettle operators and tenders	28 140	14.62	15.36	31 940	27 100	14.58	15.25	31 720
Inspectors, testers, sorters, samplers, and weighers	506 160	14.04	15.51	32 250	483 020	14.14	15.48	32 190
Jewelers and precious stone and metal workers	28 100	14.15	15.79	32 830	26 220	14.30	16.01	33 300
Dental laboratory technicians	45 600	15.50	16.47	34 260	45 840	15.67	16.79	34 910
Medical appliance technicians	10 810	13.98	15.61	32 460	10 610	14.99	16.56	34 450
Ophthalmic laboratory technicians	26 740	11.89	12.81	26 640	29 130	12.24	13.35	27 770
Packaging and filling machine operators and tenders	396 270	11.02	11.94	24 840	384 160	11.06	12.02	25 000
Coating, painting, and spraying machine setters, operators, and tenders	100 830	12.82	13.50	28 080	102 210	12.90	13.57	28 230
Painters, transportation equipment	52 650	16.75	18.14	37 720	52 170	17.15	18.57	38 630
Painting, coating, and decorating workers	27 830	10.89	12.15	25 280	29 950	11.04	12.14	25 260
Photographic process workers	28 000	10.51	12.05	25 070	24 180	11.19	12.84	26 710
Photographic processing machine operators	53 970	9.26	10.16	21 120	50 040	9.38	10.35	21 540

[1]Annual wages have been calculated by multiplying the hourly mean wage by a "year-round, full-time" hours figure of 2,080 hours; for occupations with no published hourly mean wage, the annual wage has been directly calculated from the reported survey data.

Table 3-3. Employment and Wages, by Occupation, May 2005 and May 2006—*Continued*

(Number of people, dollars.)

Occupation	May 2005				May 2006			
	Employ-ment	Median hourly wage	Mean hourly wage	Mean annual wage[1]	Employ-ment	Median hourly wage	Mean hourly wage	Mean annual wage[1]
Production—*Continued*								
Semiconductor processors	44 720	14.92	15.80	32 870	41 520	15.80	16.70	34 730
Cementing and gluing machine operators and tenders	25 650	11.78	12.45	25 900	23 540	12.10	12.90	26 840
Cleaning, washing, and metal pickling equipment operators and tenders	15 250	10.95	12.19	25 350	15 500	10.99	12.22	25 420
Cooling and freezing equipment operators and tenders	9 640	11.13	12.16	25 290	10 050	11.48	12.48	25 970
Etchers and engravers	10 050	12.04	13.35	27 760	11 390	12.30	13.34	27 750
Molders, shapers, and casters, except metal and plastic	41 250	11.39	12.33	25 640	42 610	12.03	12.85	26 730
Paper goods machine setters, operators, and tenders	107 560	14.98	15.32	31 870	113 930	15.14	15.68	32 610
Tire builders	19 860	17.68	17.80	37 020	23 210	18.33	18.38	38 220
Helpers—production	528 610	9.80	10.45	21 730	539 350	9.97	10.63	22 120
Production workers, all other	296 340	11.36	13.49	28 070	288 470	11.97	13.82	28 740
Transportation and Material Moving								
Aircraft cargo handling supervisors	6 210	16.78	19.73	41 030	5 620	19.16	21.85	45 440
First-line supervisors/managers of helpers, laborers, and material movers, hand	176 030	18.75	19.81	41 210	178 820	19.02	20.16	41 940
First-line supervisors/managers of transportation and material moving machine and vehicle operators	221 520	22.85	24.63	51 230	220 570	23.24	24.51	50 990
Airline pilots, copilots, and flight engineers	76 240	(3)	(3)	135 040	75 810	(3)	(3)	140 380
Commercial pilots	24 860	(3)	(3)	65 560	27 120	(3)	(3)	66 720
Air traffic controllers	21 590	(3)	(3)	105 820	23 240	56.37	53.02	110 270
Airfield operations specialists	4 510	17.95	20.30	42 230	4 760	18.09	19.90	41 400
Ambulance drivers and attendants, except emergency medical technicians	18 320	9.03	9.72	20 220	21 100	9.79	10.54	21 930
Bus drivers, transit and intercity	183 450	14.91	15.37	31 960	191 120	15.43	15.89	33 050
Bus drivers, school	465 880	11.57	11.71	24 350	456 570	11.93	12.08	25 130
Driver/sales workers	400 530	9.67	11.44	23 800	396 680	9.99	11.72	24 380
Truck drivers, heavy and tractor-trailer	1 624 740	16.48	17.05	35 460	1 673 950	16.85	17.46	36 320
Truck drivers, light or delivery services	938 280	11.92	12.99	27 020	941 590	12.17	13.23	27 520
Taxi drivers and chauffeurs	144 280	9.60	10.36	21 550	154 490	9.78	10.62	22 080
Motor vehicle operators, all other	76 500	10.71	12.29	25 570	71 880	10.92	12.76	26 550
Locomotive engineers	37 390	26.69	28.96	60 230	36 870	27.88	29.74	61 850
Locomotive firers	540	18.65	20.54	42 710	560	19.85	21.96	45 680
Rail yard engineers, dinkey operators, and hostlers	6 970	18.28	18.99	39 500	5 820	18.21	19.24	40 020
Railroad brake, signal, and switch operators	20 700	23.89	25.07	. . .	22 810	23.49	25.05	52 110
Railroad conductors and yardmasters	38 330	25.98	27.50	57 200	37 110	26.70	28.31	58 880
Subway and streetcar operators	7 430	22.84	22.43	46 660	6 740	23.55	22.20	46 180
Rail transportation workers, all other	7 500	18.74	18.32	38 100	6 360	18.82	18.43	38 330
Sailors and marine oilers	31 090	14.11	15.19	31 590	31 690	14.73	15.73	32 710
Captains, mates, and pilots of water vessels	28 570	24.49	25.55	53 140	29 170	25.69	27.43	57 060
Motorboat operators	2 700	16.48	17.14	35 650	2 450	15.55	16.74	34 810
Ship engineers	13 240	25.38	27.54	57 290	14 190	26.36	28.53	59 340
Bridge and lock tenders	3 620	18.26	17.44	36 270	3 700	18.76	17.27	35 930
Parking lot attendants	124 250	8.14	8.64	17 970	131 870	8.33	8.87	18 450
Service station attendants	96 340	8.32	8.94	18 590	94 780	8.53	9.21	19 150
Traffic technicians	6 990	17.82	18.21	37 870	6 560	17.86	18.68	38 840
Transportation inspectors	25 570	23.79	25.59	53 230	23 790	24.22	26.62	55 370
Transportation workers, all other	54 010	15.68	15.98	33 240	42 130	14.51	15.55	32 350
Conveyor operators and tenders	49 220	12.81	13.24	27 530	50 080	13.09	13.45	27 970
Crane and tower operators	43 690	18.69	19.65	40 860	45 740	18.77	19.93	41 450
Dredge operators	1 720	14.92	16.08	33 450	1 780	16.26	17.81	37 050
Excavating and loading machine and dragline operators	66 030	15.57	16.64	34 610	67 590	15.83	17.19	35 740
Loading machine operators, underground mining	2 390	17.15	17.47	36 330	2 480	17.91	19.37	40 290
Hoist and winch operators	3 110	15.66	17.52	36 440	2 990	16.16	17.56	36 530
Industrial truck and tractor operators	627 060	13.02	13.86	28 830	629 100	13.11	13.99	29 090
Cleaners of vehicles and equipment	333 350	8.47	9.48	19 720	334 560	8.68	9.68	20 130
Laborers and freight, stock, and material movers, hand	2 363 960	9.91	10.80	22 460	2 372 130	10.20	11.08	23 050
Machine feeders and offbearers	145 740	10.74	11.41	23 730	150 600	10.88	11.58	24 080
Packers and packagers, hand	840 410	8.36	9.13	18 990	827 470	8.48	9.30	19 340
Gas compressor and gas pumping station operators	3 950	21.07	20.91	43 500	3 900	21.83	21.52	44 760
Pump operators, except wellhead pumpers	9 970	17.38	18.47	38 410	10 030	19.13	19.55	40 670
Wellhead pumpers	10 190	18.12	17.86	37 150	13 280	17.38	17.67	36 760
Refuse and recyclable material collectors	133 930	13.68	14.50	30 160	125 770	13.93	14.96	31 110
Shuttle car operators	3 100	18.42	18.28	38 030	2 860	18.78	18.92	39 350
Tank car, truck, and ship loaders	15 950	15.06	16.34	33 990	15 360	15.37	16.44	34 200
Material moving workers, all other	52 970	14.53	15.65	32 550	52 120	14.55	15.87	33 000

[1]Annual wages have been calculated by multiplying the hourly mean wage by a "year-round, full-time" hours figure of 2,080 hours; for occupations with no published hourly mean wage, the annual wage has been directly calculated from the reported survey data.
[3]Wages for some occupations that do not generally entail year-round, full-time employment are reported as either hourly wages or annual salaries (depending on how employees are typically paid).
. . . = Not available.

CHAPTER 4

LABOR FORCE AND EMPLOYMENT
PROJECTIONS BY INDUSTRY
AND OCCUPATION

LABOR FORCE AND EMPLOYMENT PROJECTIONS
BY INDUSTRY AND OCCUPATION

HIGHLIGHTS

Every two years, the Bureau of Labor Statistics (BLS) develops decade-long projections for industry output, employment, and occupations. This chapter presents the employment outlook for the 2006–2016 period. The projections are based on a set of explicit assumptions and an application of a model of economic relationships.

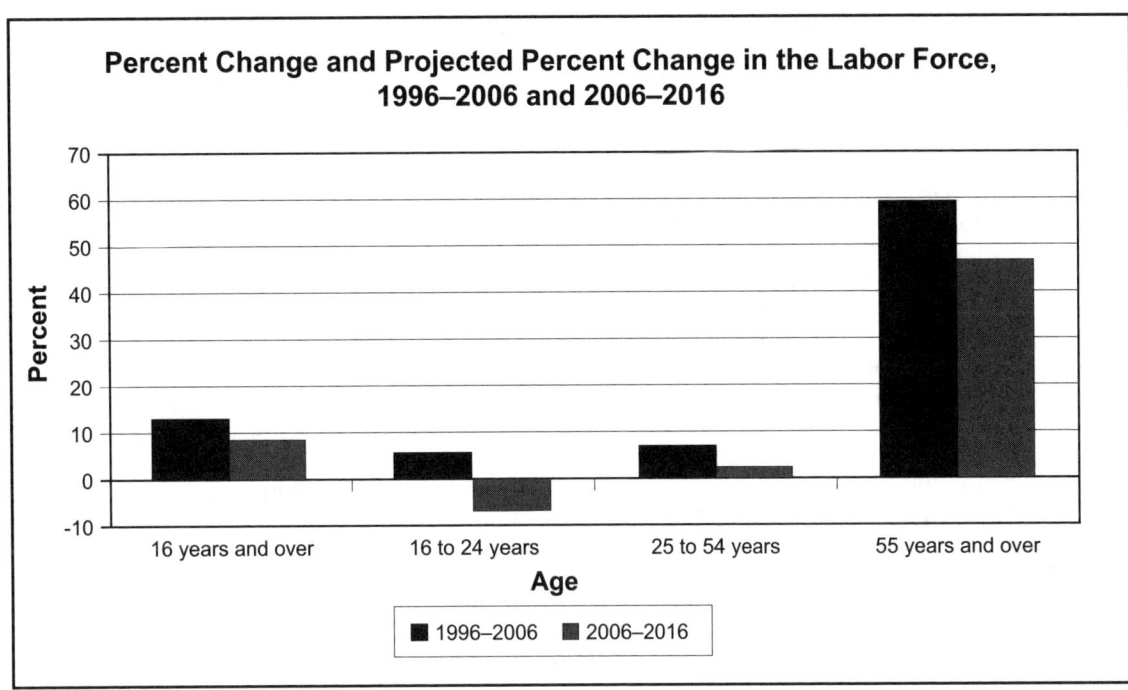

The labor force is projected to grow by 8.5 percent from 2006 to 2016, a slower rate than the 13.1 percent increase from 1996 to 2006. The aging of baby boomers has lead to a significant projected increase in the labor force of older workers. The labor force of those age 55 years and over is expected to grow by 46.7 percent, while the labor force of those age 65 years and over is expected to increase by over 80 percent. Meanwhile, the labor force made up of the 25- to 54-year-old age group is expected to increase by only 2.4 percent. (See Table 4-1.)

OTHER HIGHLIGHTS

- The increase in the number of workers age 55 years and over represents more than 90 percent of the total projected increase of the labor force during the 2006–2016 period. The shares of workers in the 16- to 24-year-old age group and the 35- to 54-year-old age group are actually expected to decline. (See Table 4-1.)

- The proportion of men in the labor force is expected to decrease slightly during the 2006–2016 period, continuing the decline from the 1986–1996 and 1996–2006 periods. (See Table 4-1.)

- The Hispanic labor force is projected to continue to increase but at a much slower rate (2.9 percent per year compared to 6.2 percent per year from 1996–2006); and it is projected to comprise 16.4 percent of the labor force by 2016. (See Table 4-1.)

NOTES AND DEFINITIONS

NOTES AND DEFINITIONS

Concepts, Definitions, and Procedures

The Bureau of Labor Statistics (BLS) employment projections are carried out as a staged set of methodologies that move from the determination of labor supply and aggregate economic activity to the determination of jobs at a detailed industry level, and the demand for specific occupations within each of the detailed industries. The following notes include a general discussion of the methods used; greater detail on the projection techniques is presented in the *BLS Handbook of Methods*.

The labor force projections are a function of two components—projections of the population and projections of labor force participation rates. Population projections are provided by the Census Bureau for detailed age, sex, race, and ethnicity groupings. BLS extrapolates participation rates for these same categories by applying well-specified smoothing and time series techniques to historical time series for the detailed participation rates.

The extrapolation results are multiplied by the projected population to arrive at initial estimates of the labor force categories. Both the participation rate and the labor force projections are carefully examined by senior staff to ensure that relationships among the various categories do not change in unexplained ways over the forecast horizon. The total of all the categories in the labor force is used as one of the critical demographic assumptions in the next stage of the projections: the determination of aggregate economic activity.

The aggregate economic projections are carried out using the Macroeconomic Advisers, LLC's (MA) quarterly model of the U.S. economy. MA is a team of economists based in St. Louis, MO, that provides monthly short-term forecasts of the U.S. economy as well as quarterly long-term projections. The MA macroeconomic model comprises 744 variables descriptive of the U.S. economy. Of these, 134 are behavioral equations, 409 are identities. The remaining 201 variables are exogenous and must be supplied to the model in order to calculate a solution for the projections horizon.

The industry projections involve two primary tasks. The first is to translate the gross domestic product (GDP) categories from the aggregate economic model into a detailed commodity-by-category matrix. This redistribution of GDP, carried out using an eclectic grouping of models, techniques, and expert judgments, provides the demand component of an interindustry model of the U.S. economy. Approximately 200 commodities and 160 categories of demand are identified for this exercise. The second task is to derive input-output tables for the projection year, which when combined with the final demand matrix, yield estimates of both commodity and industry total output necessary to produce that level of GDP. Industry total output, also referred to as gross duplicated output, com-

bines industry sales to final users with sales to intermediate users (other industries) in the economy and is the primary determinant of the factors of production (labor and capital) necessary to produce that total output.

The determination of detailed employment estimates begins with the specification of a production function for each of the 200 industries for which employment estimates are carried out. The production function is solved for the labor input component, and the resulting set of equations determines total hours paid as a function of industry output, sector wage rates, the unemployment rate, and a trend variable standing in as a proxy for technological change. A separate set of trend equations is estimated for industry-specific measures of average annual hours. Dividing hours paid by average hours yields a count of jobs by industry. The final stage of the industry employment projections process is to extrapolate the 200 industries to a full, 4-digit North American Industry Classification System (NAICS) level of detail (about 310 industries) for input to occupational demand.

The occupational projections also involve two basic tasks. The first is to extrapolate the latest historical industry-by occupation staffing pattern matrix to the projection year. A staffing pattern matrix presents the proportional distribution of detailed occupations within each of the 310 4-digit NAICS industries. Analysts must determine whether each occupational ratio should remain unchanged, increase, or decrease relative to all the other ratios within a given industry. Straightforward balancing procedures are applied to ensure that the changed ratios still account for exactly 100 percent of industry employment. The projected industry employments from the previous step are then applied to the projected staffing pattern matrix and result in estimates of new job growth for about 700 detailed occupations. Estimates of job growth for the self-employed are carried out as a separate step.

In addition to the job growth estimates, analysts must also carry out estimates of replacement demand for individuals who have died, retired, or moved on to other occupations during the intervening decade. These estimates are based on relationships derived from the Current Population Survey (CPS), which is based on household employment behavior. In terms of occupational job opportunities, replacement demand often exceeds new job growth; thus, basing the analysis on measurements of new jobs alone could seriously underestimate job opportunities for many occupations.

A detailed review process is carried out during this entire process. Review feedback can affect occupational ratios, industry outputs, and/or employment totals; it could even impose changes at the aggregate level of detail. The purpose of the detailed review process is to derive a set of estimates which are consistent at all levels of detail, from the aggregate level to the most detailed occupational level. The ultimate review, of course, occurs when historical data finally overtakes the projected years. BLS has been carrying out and publishing these types of reviews since the 1970 projections. It has pointed the way toward improvements in the process and has allowed users to determine for themselves the places where weak points might impact their use of the projections.

Sources of Additional Information

A complete presentation of the projections, including analysis of results and additional tables and a comprehensive description of the methodology, can be found in the November 2007 edition of the *Monthly Labor Review*. See "An Overview of BLS Projections to 2016," written by James C. Franklin, for specific detail. A more detailed description of methods can be found in Chapter 13 of the *BLS Handbook of Methods* and in the 2006–2007 edition of *Occupational Projections and Training Data*. All of these resources are available on the BLS Web site at <http://www.bls.gov>.

Table 4-1. Civilian Labor Force, by Age, Sex, Race, and Hispanic Origin, 1986, 1996, 2006, and Projected 2016

(Numbers in thousands, percent.)

Age, sex, race, and Hispanic origin	Labor force				Change			Percent change		
	1986	1996	2006	2016	1986–1996	1996–2006	2006–2016	1986–1996	1996–2006	2006–2016
Both Sexes, 16 Years and Over	117 834	133 943	151 428	164 232	16 109	17 485	12 804	13.7	13.1	8.5
16 to 24 years	23 367	21 183	22 394	20 852	-2 184	1 211	-1 542	-9.3	5.7	-6.9
16 to 19 years	7 926	7 806	7 281	5 896	-120	-525	-1 385	-1.5	-6.7	-19.0
20 to 24 years	15 441	13 377	15 113	14 955	-2 064	1 736	-158	-13.4	13.0	-1.0
25 to 54 years	79 563	96 786	103 566	106 026	17 223	6 780	2 460	21.6	7.0	2.4
25 to 34 years	34 591	33 833	32 573	37 289	-758	-1 260	4 716	-2.2	-3.7	14.5
35 to 44 years	27 232	36 556	35 848	33 654	9 324	-708	-2 194	34.2	-1.9	-6.1
45 to 54 years	17 739	26 397	35 146	35 083	8 658	8 749	-63	48.8	33.1	-0.2
55 years and over	14 904	15 974	25 468	37 354	1 070	9 494	11 886	7.2	59.4	46.7
55 to 64 years	11 894	12 146	19 984	27 288	252	7 838	7 304	2.1	64.5	36.5
65 to 74 years	2 594	3 194	4 404	8 076	600	1 210	3 672	23.1	37.9	83.4
75 years and over	417	634	1 080	1 990	217	446	910	52.0	70.3	84.3
Men, 16 Years and Over	65 422	72 087	81 255	87 781	6 665	9 168	6 526	10.2	12.7	8.0
16 to 24 years	12 250	11 147	11 810	10 915	-1 103	663	-895	-9.0	5.9	-7.6
16 to 19 years	4 102	4 043	3 693	2 923	-59	-350	-770	-1.4	-8.7	-20.9
20 to 24 years	8 148	7 104	8 116	7 992	-1 044	1 012	-124	-12.8	14.2	-1.5
25 to 54 years	44 406	51 999	55 840	57 491	7 593	3 841	1 651	17.1	7.4	3.0
25 to 34 years	19 383	18 430	17 944	20 913	-953	-486	2 969	-4.9	-2.6	16.5
35 to 44 years	15 029	19 602	19 407	18 373	4 573	-195	-1 034	30.4	-1.0	-5.3
45 to 54 years	9 994	13 967	18 489	18 205	3 973	4 522	-284	39.8	32.4	-1.5
55 years and over	8 765	8 941	13 605	19 376	176	4 664	5 771	2.0	52.2	42.4
55 to 64 years	6 954	6 693	10 509	13 865	-261	3 816	3 356	-3.8	57.0	31.9
65 to 74 years	1 552	1 872	2 466	4 387	320	594	1 921	20.6	31.7	77.9
75 years and over	260	375	630	1 124	115	255	494	44.2	68.0	78.4
Women, 16 Years and Over	52 413	61 856	70 173	76 450	9 443	8 317	6 277	18.0	13.4	8.9
16 to 24 years	11 117	10 036	10 584	9 937	-1 081	548	-647	-9.7	5.5	-6.1
16 to 19 years	3 824	3 763	3 588	2 974	-61	-175	-614	-1.6	-4.7	-17.1
20 to 24 years	7 293	6 273	6 997	6 963	-1 020	724	-34	-14.0	11.5	-0.5
25 to 54 years	35 158	44 787	47 726	48 534	9 629	2 939	808	27.4	6.6	1.7
25 to 34 years	15 208	15 403	14 628	16 376	195	-775	1 748	1.3	-5.0	11.9
35 to 44 years	12 204	16 954	16 441	15 281	4 750	-513	-1 160	38.9	-3.0	-7.1
45 to 54 years	7 746	12 430	16 656	16 877	4 684	4 226	221	60.5	34.0	1.3
55 years and over	6 139	7 033	11 863	17 979	894	4 830	6 116	14.6	68.7	51.6
55 to 64 years	4 940	5 452	9 475	13 423	512	4 023	3 948	10.4	73.8	41.7
65 to 74 years	1 042	1 321	1 937	3 689	279	616	1 752	26.8	46.6	90.4
75 years and over	159	260	451	867	101	191	416	63.5	73.5	92.2
White, 16 Years and Over	101 801	113 108	123 834	130 665	11 307	10 726	6 831	11.1	9.5	5.5
Men	57 217	61 783	67 613	71 283	4 566	5 830	3 670	8.0	9.4	5.4
Women	44 584	51 325	56 221	59 382	6 741	4 896	3 161	15.1	9.5	5.6
Black, 16 Years and Over	12 654	15 134	17 314	20 121	2 480	2 180	2 807	19.6	14.4	16.2
Men	6 373	7 264	8 128	9 420	891	864	1 292	14.0	11.9	15.9
Women	6 281	7 869	9 186	10 701	1 588	1 317	1 515	25.3	16.7	16.5
Asian, 16 Years and Over	3 379	5 701	6 727	8 741	2 322	1 026	2 014	68.7	18.0	29.9
Men	1 831	3 039	3 621	4 600	1 208	582	979	66.0	19.2	27.0
Women	1 548	2 662	3 106	4 141	1 114	444	1 035	72.0	16.7	33.3
All Other Groups,[1] 16 Years and Over	...	...	3 553	4 705	...	...	1 152	...	...	32.4
Men	...	...	1 893	2 478	...	...	585	...	...	30.9
Women	...	...	1 660	2 227	...	...	567	...	...	34.2
Hispanic,[2] 16 Years and Over	8 076	12 774	20 694	26 889	4 698	7 920	6 195	58.2	62.0	29.9
Men	4 948	7 646	12 488	15 802	2 698	4 842	3 314	54.5	63.3	26.5
Women	3 128	5 128	8 206	11 087	2 000	3 078	2 881	63.9	60.0	35.1
Non-Hispanic, 16 Years and Over	109 758	121 169	130 734	137 343	11 411	9 565	6 609	10.4	7.9	5.1
Men	60 474	64 441	68 767	71 979	3 967	4 326	3 212	6.6	6.7	4.7
Women	49 285	56 728	61 967	65 363	7 443	5 239	3 396	15.1	9.2	5.5
White Non-Hispanic, 16 Years and Over	94 027	100 915	104 629	106 133	6 888	3 714	1 504	7.3	3.7	1.4
Men	52 447	54 451	55 953	56 791	2 004	1 502	838	3.8	2.8	1.5
Women	41 579	46 464	48 676	49 342	4 885	2 212	666	11.7	4.8	1.4

[1]The "All other groups" category includes respondents who reported the racial categories of "American Indian and Alaska Native" or "Native Hawaiian and Other Pacific Islander," as well as those who reported two or more races. This category was not defined prior to 2003.
[2]May be of any race.
. . . = Not available.

Table 4-1. Civilian Labor Force, by Age, Sex, Race, and Hispanic Origin, 1986, 1996, 2006, and Projected 2016—*Continued*

(Numbers in thousands, percent.)

Age, sex, race, and Hispanic origin	Percent distribution				Annual growth rate (percent)		
	1986	1996	2006	2016	1986–1996	1996–2006	2006–2016
Both Sexes, 16 Years and Over	100.0	100.0	100.0	100.0	1.3	1.2	0.8
16 to 24 years	19.8	15.8	14.8	12.7	-1.0	0.6	-0.7
16 to 19 years	6.7	5.8	4.8	3.6	-0.2	-0.7	-2.1
20 to 24 years	13.1	10.0	10.0	9.1	-1.4	1.2	-0.1
25 to 54 years	67.5	72.3	68.4	64.6	2.0	0.7	0.2
25 to 34 years	29.4	25.3	21.5	22.7	-0.2	-0.4	1.4
35 to 44 years	23.1	27.3	23.7	20.5	3.0	-0.2	-0.6
45 to 54 years	15.1	19.7	23.2	21.4	4.1	2.9	0.0
55 years and over	12.6	11.9	16.8	22.7	0.7	4.8	3.9
55 to 64 years	10.1	9.1	13.2	16.6	0.2	5.1	3.2
65 to 74 years	2.2	2.4	2.9	4.9	2.1	3.3	6.3
75 years and over	0.4	0.5	0.7	1.2	4.3	5.5	6.3
Men, 16 Years and Over	55.5	53.8	53.7	53.4	1.0	1.2	0.8
16 to 24 years	10.4	8.3	7.8	6.6	-0.9	0.6	-0.8
16 to 19 years	3.5	3.0	2.4	1.8	-0.1	-0.9	-2.3
20 to 24 years	6.9	5.3	5.4	4.9	-1.4	1.3	-0.2
25 to 54 years	37.7	38.8	36.9	35.0	1.6	0.7	0.3
25 to 34 years	16.4	13.8	11.8	12.7	-0.5	-0.3	1.5
35 to 44 years	12.8	14.6	12.8	11.2	2.7	-0.1	-0.5
45 to 54 years	8.5	10.4	12.2	11.1	3.4	2.8	-0.2
55 years and over	7.4	6.7	9.0	11.8	0.2	4.3	3.6
55 to 64 years	5.9	5.0	6.9	8.4	-0.4	4.6	2.8
65 to 74 years	1.3	1.4	1.6	2.7	1.9	2.8	5.9
75 years and over	0.2	0.3	0.4	0.7	3.7	5.3	6.0
Women, 16 Years and Over	44.5	46.2	46.3	46.6	1.7	1.3	0.9
16 to 24 years	9.4	7.5	7.0	6.1	-1.0	0.5	-0.6
16 to 19 years	3.2	2.8	2.4	1.8	-0.2	-0.5	-1.9
20 to 24 years	6.2	4.7	4.6	4.2	-1.5	1.1	0.0
25 to 54 years	29.8	33.4	31.5	29.6	2.5	0.6	0.2
25 to 34 years	12.9	11.5	9.7	10.0	0.1	-0.5	1.1
35 to 44 years	10.4	12.7	10.9	9.3	3.3	-0.3	-0.7
45 to 54 years	6.6	9.3	11.0	10.3	4.8	3.0	0.1
55 years and over	5.2	5.3	7.8	10.9	1.4	5.4	4.2
55 to 64 years	4.2	4.1	6.3	8.2	1.0	5.7	3.5
65 to 74 years	0.9	1.0	1.3	2.2	2.4	3.9	6.7
75 years and over	0.1	0.2	0.3	0.5	5.0	5.7	6.8
White, 16 Years and Over	86.4	84.4	81.8	79.6	1.1	0.9	0.5
Men	48.6	46.1	44.7	43.4	0.8	0.9	0.5
Women	37.8	38.3	37.1	36.2	1.4	0.9	0.5
Black, 16 Years and Over	10.7	11.3	11.4	12.3	1.8	1.4	1.5
Men	5.4	5.4	5.4	5.7	1.3	1.1	1.5
Women	5.3	5.9	6.1	6.5	2.3	1.6	1.5
Asian, 16 Years and Over	2.9	4.3	4.4	5.3	5.4	1.7	2.7
Men	1.6	2.3	2.4	2.8	5.2	1.8	2.4
Women	1.3	2.0	2.1	2.5	5.6	1.6	2.9
All Other Groups,[1] 16 Years and Over	. . .	. . .	2.3	2.9	. . .	. . .	2.8
Men	. . .	. . .	1.3	1.5	. . .	. . .	2.7
Women	. . .	. . .	1.1	1.4	. . .	. . .	3.0
Hispanic,[2] 16 Years and Over	6.9	9.5	13.7	16.4	4.7	4.9	2.7
Men	4.2	5.7	8.2	9.6	4.4	5.0	2.4
Women	2.7	3.8	5.4	6.8	5.1	4.8	3.1
Non-Hispanic, 16 Years and Over	93.1	90.5	86.3	83.6	1.0	0.8	0.5
Men	51.3	48.1	45.4	43.8	0.6	0.7	0.5
Women	41.8	42.4	40.9	39.8	1.4	0.9	0.5
White Non-Hispanic, 16 Years and Over	79.8	75.3	69.1	64.6	0.7	0.4	0.1
Men	44.5	40.7	37.0	34.6	0.4	0.3	0.1
Women	35.3	34.7	32.1	30.0	1.1	0.5	0.1

[1]The "All other groups" category includes respondents who reported the racial categories of "American Indian and Alaska Native" or "Native Hawaiian and Other Pacific Islander," as well as those who reported two or more races. This category was not defined prior to 2003.
[2]May be of any race.
. . . = Not available.

PROJECTED EMPLOYMENT

The 10 Fastest Growing Occupations, 2006–2016

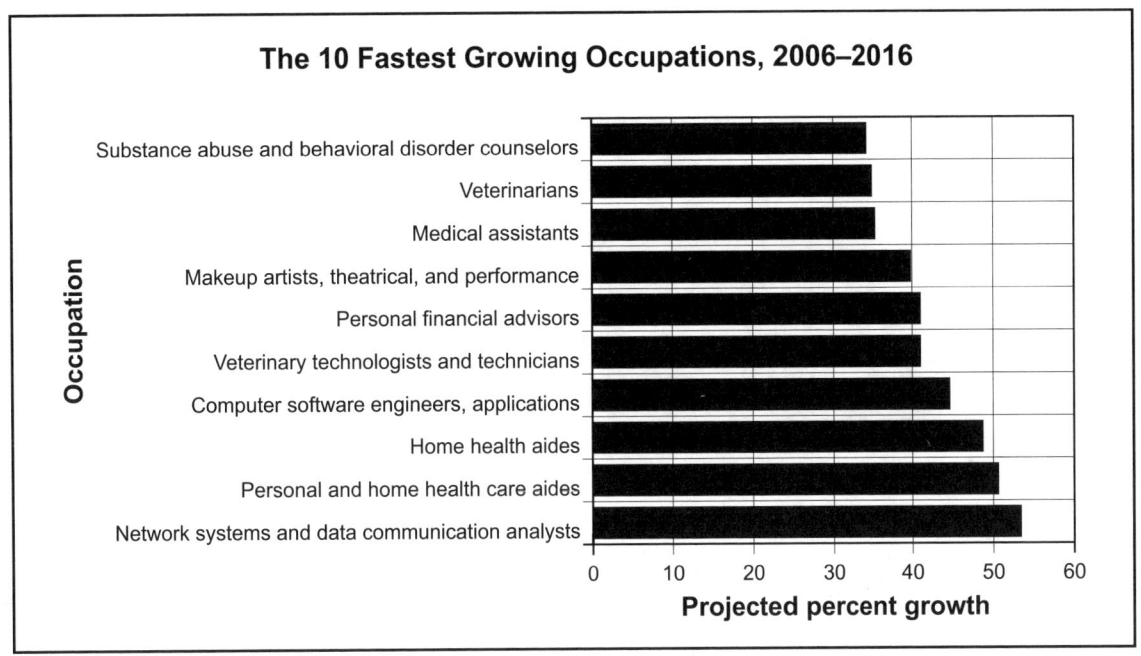

Only two of the top ten fastest-growing occupations are associated with computers. Four are in the health care industry and two are concerned with veterinary activities. (See Table 4-2.)

OTHER HIGHLIGHTS

- The fastest-growing occupations do not necessarily provide the largest amount of additional jobs. The network systems and data communication analyst group is expected to be the fastest-growing occupation, however, it will still only employ approximately 402,000 people in 2016 (up from 262,000 in 2006). (See Table 4-2.)

- Of the ten occupations with the fastest job growth, five require a bachelor's degree or more. Only three require short-term or moderate-term on-the-job training. (See Table 4-2.)

- Of the ten occupations with the largest job growth, seven require only short-term or moderate-term on-the-job training, indicating that these are relatively low-paying jobs. (See Table 4-3.)

- By 2016, there are expected to be approximately 51,000 job openings (due to growth plus net replacements). Nearly one-third will due to growth, while the rest will be due to replacements. (See Table 4-7.)

Table 4-2. Fastest-Growing Occupations, 2006–2016

(Numbers in thousands, percent.)

Occupation	Occupational group	Employment		Change		Most significant source of postsecondary education or training[1]
		2006	2016	Number	Percent	
Network systems and data communications analysts	Professional and related	262	402	140	53.4	Bachelor's degree
Personal and home care aides	Service	767	1 156	389	50.6	Short-term on-the-job training
Home health aides	Service	787	1 171	384	48.7	Short-term on-the-job training
Computer software engineers, applications	Professional and related	507	733	226	44.6	Bachelor's degree
Veterinary technologists and technicians	Professional and related	71	100	29	41.0	Associate's degree
Personal financial advisers	Management, business, and financial	176	248	72	41.0	Bachelor's degree
Makeup artists, theatrical and performance	Service	2	3	1	39.8	Postsecondary vocational award
Medical assistants	Service	417	565	148	35.4	Moderate-term on-the-job training
Veterinarians	Professional and related	62	84	22	35.0	First professional degree
Substance abuse and behavioral disorder counselors	Professional and related	83	112	29	34.3	Bachelor's degree
Skin care specialists	Service	38	51	13	34.3	Postsecondary vocational award
Financial analysts	Management, business, and financial	221	295	75	33.8	Bachelor's degree
Social and human service assistants	Professional and related	339	453	114	33.6	Moderate-term on-the-job training
Gaming surveillance officers and gaming investigators	Service	9	12	3	33.6	Moderate-term on-the-job training
Physical therapist assistants	Service	60	80	20	32.4	Associate's degree
Pharmacy technicians	Professional and related	285	376	91	32.0	Moderate-term on-the-job training
Forensic science technicians	Professional and related	13	17	4	30.7	Bachelor's degree
Dental hygienists	Professional and related	167	217	50	30.1	Associate's degree
Mental health counselors	Professional and related	100	130	30	30.0	Master's degree
Mental health and substance abuse social workers	Professional and related	122	159	37	29.9	Master's degree
Marriage and family therapists	Professional and related	25	32	7	29.8	Master's degree
Dental assistants	Service	280	362	82	29.2	Moderate-term on-the-job training
Computer systems analysts	Professional and related	504	650	146	29.0	Bachelor's degree
Database administrators	Professional and related	119	154	34	28.6	Bachelor's degree
Computer software engineers, systems software	Professional and related	350	449	99	28.2	Bachelor's degree
Gaming and sports book writers and runners	Service	18	24	5	28.0	Short-term on-the-job training
Environmental science and protection technicians, including health	Professional and related	36	47	10	28.0	Associate's degree
Manicurists and pedicurists	Service	78	100	22	27.6	Postsecondary vocational degree
Physical therapists	Professional and related	173	220	47	27.1	Master's degree
Physician assistants	Professional and related	66	83	18	27.0	Master's degree

[1]An occupation is placed into one of 11 categories that best describes the education or training needed by most workers to become fully qualified in that occupation.

Table 4-3. Occupations with the Largest Job Growth, 2006–2016

(Numbers in thousands, percent.)

Occupation	Occupational group	Employment		Change		Most significant source of postsecondary education or training[1]
		2006	2016	Number	Percent	
Registered nurses	Professional and related	2 505	3 092	587	23.5	Associate's degree
Retail salespersons	Sales and related	4 477	5 034	557	12.4	Short-term on-the-job training
Customer service representatives	Office and administrative	2 202	2 747	545	24.8	Moderate-term on-the-job training
Combined food preparation and serving workers, including fast food	Service	2 503	2 955	452	18.1	Short-term on-the-job training
Office clerks, general	Office and administrative	3 200	3 604	404	12.6	Short-term on-the-job training
Personal and home care aides	Service	767	1 156	389	50.6	Short-term on-the-job training
Home health aides	Service	787	1 171	384	48.7	Short-term on-the-job training
Postsecondary teachers	Professional and related	1 672	2 054	382	22.9	Doctoral degree
Janitors and cleaners, except maids and housekeeping cleaners	Service	2 387	2 732	345	14.5	Short-term on-the-job training
Nursing aides, orderlies, and attendants	Service	1 447	1 711	264	18.2	Postsecondary vocational award
Bookkeeping, accounting, and auditing clerks	Office and administrative	2 114	2 377	264	12.5	Moderate-term on-the-job training
Waiters and waitresses	Service	2 361	2 615	255	10.8	Short-term on-the-job training
Childcare workers	Service	1 388	1 636	248	17.8	Short-term on-the-job training
Executive secretaries and administrative assistants	Office and administrative	1 618	1 857	239	14.8	Work experience
Computer software engineers, applications	Professional and related	507	733	226	44.6	Bachelor's degree
Accountants and auditors	Management, business, and financial	1 274	1 500	226	17.7	Bachelor's degree
Landscaping and groundskeeping workers	Service	1 220	1 441	221	18.1	Short-term on-the-job training
Elementary school teachers, except special education	Professional and related	1 540	1 749	209	13.6	Bachelor's degree
Receptionists and information clerks	Office and administrative	1 173	1 375	202	17.2	Short-term on-the-job training
Truck drivers, heavy and tractor-trailer	Transportation and material moving	1 860	2 053	193	10.4	Moderate-term on-the-job training
Maids and housekeeping cleaners	Service	1 470	1 656	186	12.7	Short-term on-the-job training
Security guards	Service	1 040	1 216	175	16.9	Short-term on-the-job training
Carpenters	Construction and extraction	1 462	1 612	150	10.3	Long-term on-the-job training
Management analysts	Management and business	678	827	149	21.9	Bachelor's degree or higher
Medical assistants	Service	417	565	148	35.4	Moderate-term on-the-job training
Computer systems analysts	Professional and related	504	650	146	29.0	Bachelor's degree
Maintenance and repair workers, general	Installation, maintenance, and repair	1 391	1 531	140	10.1	Moderate-term on-the-job training
Network systems and data communications analysts	Professional and related	262	402	140	53.4	Bachelor's degree
Food preparation workers	Service	902	1 040	138	15.3	Short-term on-the-job training
Teacher assistants	Professional and related	1 312	1 449	137	10.4	Short-term on-the-job training

[1]An occupation is placed into one of 11 categories that best describes the education or training needed by most workers to become fully qualified in that occupation.

Table 4-4. Industries with the Largest Output Growth and Declines, 2006–2016

(Dollars, number, percent.)

Industry	Billions of chained (2000) dollars		Change, 2006–2016	Average annual rate of change, 2006–2016
	2006	2016		
Largest Growth				
Computer and peripheral equipment manufacturing	134.5	867.0	732.5	20.5
Wholesale trade	1 041.9	1 702.7	660.8	5.0
Securities, commodity contracts, and other financial investments and related activities	351.2	958.3	607.1	10.6
Retail trade	1 305.3	1 892.1	586.8	3.8
Semiconductor and other electronic component manufacturing	162.6	543.4	380.8	12.8
Owner-occupied dwellings	919.8	1 229.4	309.6	2.9
Telecommunications	469.6	758.5	288.9	4.9
Monetary authorities, credit intermediation, and related activities	659.5	946.0	286.5	3.7
Software publishers	153.3	419.8	266.5	10.6
Offices of health practitioners	432.8	643.0	210.2	4.0
Real estate	847.0	1 007.4	160.4	1.7
Management of companies and enterprises	435.0	591.7	156.7	3.1
Management, scientific, and technical consulting services	171.0	317.8	146.8	6.4
Hospitals, private	397.2	542.6	145.4	3.2
Lessors of nonfinancial intangible assets (except copyrighted works)	138.6	278.4	139.8	7.2
Internet and other information services	109.4	248.2	138.8	8.5
Construction	899.1	1 031.1	131.9	1.4
Motor vehicle manufacturing	277.6	384.7	107.1	3.3
Air transportation	144.4	236.5	92.0	5.1
Scientific research and development services	126.8	216.1	89.3	5.5
Largest Declines				
Tobacco manufacturing	39.2	22.1	-17.1	-5.6
Cut and sew apparel manufacturing	27.6	15.1	-12.5	-5.9
Printing and related support activities	83.6	73.2	-10.4	-1.3
Natural gas distribution	51.9	45.4	-6.5	-1.3
Fabric mills	15.0	10.6	-4.4	-3.4
Pesticide, fertilizer, and other agricultural chemical manufacturing	20.8	16.7	-4.1	-2.1
Industrial machinery manufacturing	34.4	30.4	-3.9	-1.2
Pipeline transportation	23.8	20.7	-3.1	-1.4
Textile and fabric finishing and fabric coating mills	8.6	6.4	-2.2	-3.0
Converted paper product manufacturing	77.3	75.1	-2.2	-0.3
Logging	25.0	22.9	-2.1	-0.9
Apparel knitting mills	5.4	3.3	-2.1	-4.8
Pulp, paper, and paperboard mills	70.2	68.1	-2.1	-0.3
Commercial and service industry machinery manufacturing	21.7	19.6	-2.0	-1.0
Fishing, hunting and trapping	5.7	4.2	-1.5	-2.9
Leather and hide tanning and finishing, and other leather and allied product manufacturing	3.4	2.1	-1.2	-4.5
Hardware manufacturing	9.6	8.4	-1.1	-1.3
Footwear manufacturing	1.8	0.7	-1.0	-8.4
Apparel accessories and other apparel manufacturing	2.6	1.8	-0.8	-3.8
Cutlery and hand tool manufacturing	9.3	8.6	-0.7	-0.8
Other textile product mills	9.0	8.3	-0.7	-0.8

Table 4-5. Employment and Total Job Openings, by Education Cluster, 2006–2016

(Numbers in thousands, percent, dollars.)

Education cluster	Employment				Change in employment, 2006–2016		Total job openings due to growth and net replacements[1]		May 2006 median annual wages[2]
	Number		Percent distribution		Number	Percent	Number	Percent distribution	
	2006	2016	2006	2016					
Total, all occupations	150 620	166 220	100.0	100.0	15 600	10.4	50 732	100.0	30 400
First professional degree	1 970	2 247	1.3	1.4	277	14.0	638	1.3	112 070
Doctoral degree	2 025	2 462	1.3	1.5	437	21.6	793	1.6	57 640
Master's degree	2 167	2 575	1.4	1.5	409	18.9	819	1.6	51 380
Bachelor's or higher degree, plus work experience	6 524	7 117	4.3	4.3	592	9.1	2 008	4.0	81 280
Bachelor's degree	18 585	21 659	12.3	13.0	3 074	16.5	6 706	13.2	53 550
Associate's degree	5 812	6 899	3.9	4.2	1 087	18.7	2 240	4.4	50 240
Postsecondary vocational award	7 901	8 973	5.2	5.4	1 072	13.6	2 491	4.9	29 520
Work experience in a related occupation	14 579	15 889	9.7	9.6	1 310	9.0	4 126	8.1	43 480
Long-term on-the-job training	11 489	12 200	7.6	7.3	711	6.2	3 272	6.5	37 360
Moderate-term on-the-job training	27 230	29 248	18.1	17.6	2 018	7.4	7 516	14.8	29 100
Short-term on-the-job training	52 339	56 951	34.7	34.3	4 613	8.8	20 123	39.7	19 620

[1]Total job openings are given by the sum of net employment increases and net replacements. If employment change is negative, job openings due to growth are zero and total job openings equal net replacements.

[2] Data for wage and salary workers are derived from the Occupational Employment Statistics Survey.

Table 4-6. Employment and Output, by Industry, 1996, 2006, and Projected 2016

(Number, percent, dollars.)

Industry	Employment							Output				
	Number of jobs (thousands)			Change		Average annual rate of change (percent)		Billions of chained (2000) dollars			Average annual rate of change (percent)	
	1996	2006	2016	1996–2006	2006–2016	1996–2006	2006–2016	1996	2006	2016	1996–2006	2006–2016
TOTAL[1,2]	134 690	150 620	166 220	15 930	15 600	1.1	1.0	15 120	20 265	27 094	3.0	2.9
Nonagriculture Wage and Salary Workers[3]	120 371	136 912	151 962	16 541	15 050	1.3	1.0	14 880	19 998	26 757	3.0	3.0
Mining	556	619	608	62	-10	1.1	-0.2	213	242	269	1.3	1.0
Oil and gas extraction	147	136	134	-11	-2	-0.8	-0.2	144	142	152	-0.1	0.7
Mining (except oil and gas)	249	221	231	-28	10	-1.2	0.4	47	52	66	1.0	2.4
Coal mining	90	79	79	-12	0.2	-1.4	0.0	21	23	27	1.1	1.4
Metal ore mining	50	32	35	-18	3	-4.3	0.8	9	8	11	-2.2	4.3
Nonmetallic mineral mining and quarrying	108	110	116	1	6	0.1	0.6	17	21	27	2.4	2.2
Mining support activities	160	262	244	102	-17	5.0	-0.7	24	46	52	6.5	1.2
Utilities	640	548	518	-91	-31	-1.5	-0.6	309	323	354	0.5	0.9
Electric power generation, transmission, and distribution	464	397	376	-67	-21	-1.5	-0.5	230	266	303	1.5	1.3
Natural gas distribution	136	106	87	-30	-19	-2.5	-1.9	74	52	45	-3.4	-1.3
Water, sewage, and other systems	39	46	54	7	8	1.6	1.7	6	7	10	1.2	2.7
Construction	5 536	7 689	8 470	2 153	781	3.3	1.0	741	899	1 031	2.0	1.4
Manufacturing	17 237	14 197	12 694	-3 039	-1 503	-1.9	-1.1	3 610	4 146	5 264	1.4	2.4
Food	1 562	1 484	1 489	-78	5	-0.5	0.0	385	461	551	1.8	1.8
Animal food	56	50	42	-6	-8	-1.0	-1.7	20	26	35	2.8	3.0
Grain and oilseed milling	69	60	51	-8	-9	-1.3	-1.6	38	43	52	1.2	1.8
Sugar and confectionery product	99	75	61	-24	-14	-2.8	-2.0	23	24	28	0.7	1.5
Fruit and vegetable preserving and specialty food	210	177	156	-32	-22	-1.7	-1.3	46	52	66	1.4	2.3
Dairy product	134	132	127	-2	-5	-0.1	-0.4	58	65	76	1.2	1.6
Animal slaughtering and processing	486	509	569	23	60	0.5	1.1	99	127	155	2.6	2.0
Seafood product preparation and packaging	53	40	36	-13	-4	-2.7	-1.2	9	10	11	1.6	1.2
Bakery and tortilla	306	280	285	-26	4	-0.9	0.1	43	52	58	1.9	1.2
Other food	149	160	162	11	2	0.7	0.2	52	61	70	1.7	1.4
Beverage and tobacco product	204	195	171	-10	-24	-0.5	-1.3	134	118	109	-1.3	-0.8
Beverage	166	171	156	5	-16	0.3	-1.0	70	80	89	1.4	1.1
Tobacco	38	23	16	-15	-8	-4.8	-4.0	66	39	22	-5.1	-5.6
Textile mills	443	196	134	-248	-62	-7.8	-3.7	52	32	25	-4.7	-2.4
Fiber, yarn, and thread mills	87	48	38	-38	-10	-5.7	-2.3	12	8	8	-3.1	-0.3
Fabric mills	233	90	61	-143	-29	-9.1	-3.8	28	15	11	-6.0	-3.4
Textile fabric finishing/fabric coating mills	124	58	34	-66	-23	-7.3	-5.0	12	9	6	-3.4	-3.0
Textile product mills	216	161	141	-55	-20	-2.9	-1.3	29	30	31	0.4	0.4
Textile furnishings mills	126	90	79	-36	-11	-3.3	-1.3	19	21	23	1.3	0.8
Other textile product mills	90	71	62	-20	-9	-2.4	-1.3	10	9	8	-1.3	-0.8
Apparel	743	238	110	-505	-129	-10.7	-7.5	67	36	20	-6.2	-5.5
Apparel knitting mills	98	34	20	-64	-14	-10.0	-5.1	12	5	3	-7.6	-4.8
Cut and sew apparel	605	186	77	-419	-108	-11.1	-8.4	51	28	15	-5.9	-5.9
Apparel accessories and other apparel	40	19	12	-22	-6	-7.3	-4.1	5	3	2	-5.8	-3.8
Leather and allied product	94	37	20	-57	-17	-8.8	-6.0	10	5	3	-6.2	-5.7
Leather and hide tanning and finishing[4]	46	20	12	-26	-8	-8.0	-4.9	6	3	2	-5.0	-4.5
Footwear	48	17	8	-31	-9	-9.7	-7.3	4	2	1	-8.2	-8.4
Wood product	583	560	527	-22	-33	-0.4	-0.6	85	95	104	1.1	1.0
Sawmills and wood preservation	133	118	94	-15	-24	-1.2	-2.3	26	27	27	0.5	0.0
Veneer, plywood, and engineered wood product	110	120	131	10	10	0.9	0.8	19	20	24	1.0	1.7
Other wood product	339	322	302	-18	-19	-0.5	-0.6	40	47	53	1.5	1.2
Paper	631	469	367	-162	-102	-2.9	-2.4	159	147	143	-0.8	-0.3
Pulp, paper, and paperboard mills	216	136	94	-80	-42	-4.5	-3.6	72	70	68	-0.2	-0.3
Converted paper product	415	333	274	-82	-60	-2.2	-2.0	87	77	75	-1.2	-0.3
Printing and related support activities	816	636	497	-180	-138	-2.5	-2.4	99	84	73	-1.7	-1.3
Petroleum and coal product	137	114	88	-23	-26	-1.8	-2.6	223	268	295	1.9	1.0
Chemical	984	869	848	-116	-21	-1.2	-0.2	398	450	556	1.2	2.1
Basic chemical	224	148	124	-77	-23	-4.1	-1.7	102	115	130	1.2	1.2
Resin, synthetic rubber, and artificial and synthetic fiber and filament	141	105	84	-36	-21	-2.9	-2.3	62	63	67	0.1	0.7
Pesticide, fertilizer, and other agricultural chemical	50	39	30	-11	-8	-2.4	-2.4	21	21	17	-0.2	-2.1
Pharmaceutical and medicine	229	292	362	64	69	2.5	2.2	99	123	186	2.1	4.3
Paint, coating, and adhesive	76	67	62	-9	-5	-1.2	-0.8	26	25	27	-0.3	0.9
Soap, cleaning compound, and toilet preparation	127	113	104	-15	-8	-1.2	-0.8	52	67	87	2.6	2.7
Other chemical product and preparation	137	105	82	-32	-23	-2.6	-2.5	36	37	41	0.4	1.0
Plastics and rubber product	920	797	764	-123	-33	-1.4	-0.4	150	168	239	1.1	3.6
Plastics product	708	638	650	-71	13	-1.0	0.2	118	139	208	1.6	4.1
Rubber product	212	159	114	-52	-46	-2.8	-3.3	32	29	30	-0.9	0.3
Nonmetallic mineral product	517	508	507	-9	-1	-0.2	0.0	88	98	114	1.2	1.5
Clay product and refractory	84	61	54	-23	-6	-3.2	-1.1	10	9	10	-1.1	1.2
Glass and glass product	142	103	87	-39	-16	-3.1	-1.6	21	25	28	1.5	1.2
Cement and concrete product	200	248	266	48	18	2.2	0.7	36	43	52	1.7	1.8
Lime and gypsum product[3]	92	96	99	4	4	0.4	0.4	20	22	26	1.1	1.4
Primary metal	639	462	336	-177	-126	-3.2	-3.1	157	150	157	-0.5	0.5
Iron and steel mills ferroalloy	153	94	64	-58	-31	-4.7	-3.9	52	55	58	0.6	0.6
Steel product from purchased steel	70	60	52	-10	-8	-1.6	-1.4	18	15	16	-1.8	0.8
Alumina and aluminum production and processing	99	73	50	-26	-22	-3.0	-3.6	33	34	33	0.1	-0.2
Nonferrous (except aluminum) production and processing	102	73	50	-29	-23	-3.3	-3.7	27	18	19	-3.7	0.2
Foundries	216	162	120	-54	-42	-2.8	-3.0	27	29	30	0.9	0.4

[1]Employment data for wage and salary workers are from the BLS Current Employment Statistics (CES) Survey, which counts jobs, whereas data for self-employed, unpaid family workers and agriculture, forestry, fishing, and hunting workers are from the Current Population Survey (CPS, or household, survey), which counts workers.
[2]Output subcategories do not necessarily add to higher categories as a by-product of chain weighting.
[3]Includes wage and salary data from the CES Survey, except data for private households. Logging workers are excluded.
[4]Employment data are based on estimates from the CES Survey.

Table 4-6. Employment and Output, by Industry, 1996, 2006, and Projected 2016—*Continued*

(Number, percent, dollars.)

Industry	Employment							Output				
	Number of jobs (thousands)			Change		Average annual rate of change (percent)		Billions of chained (2000) dollars			Average annual rate of change (percent)	
	1996	2006	2016	1996–2006	2006–2016	1996–2006	2006–2016	1996	2006	2016	1996–2006	2006–2016
Manufacturing—*Continued*												
Fabricated metal product	1 648	1 554	1 365	-94	-189	-0.6	-1.3	234	246	278	0.5	1.2
Forging and stamping	139	113	86	-26	-27	-2.0	-2.7	23	24	25	0.8	0.2
Cutlery and handtool	78	54	40	-24	-14	-3.6	-3.0	12	9	9	-2.5	-0.8
Architectural and structural metals	370	414	437	45	23	1.1	0.5	49	59	71	2.0	1.8
Boiler, tank, and shipping container	107	92	82	-16	-10	-1.5	-1.1	22	21	22	-0.7	0.6
Hardware	53	34	24	-19	-10	-4.4	-3.6	11	10	8	-1.5	-1.3
Spring and wire product	82	58	42	-23	-16	-3.3	-3.2	8	8	8	-0.1	0.2
Machine shops; turned product; and screw, nut, and bolt	343	352	283	9	-69	0.3	-2.2	42	45	61	0.8	3.0
Coating, engraving, heat treating, and allied activities	158	149	120	-9	-29	-0.6	-2.2	18	20	24	1.4	1.4
Other fabricated metal product	318	287	252	-31	-36	-1.0	-1.3	50	49	50	-0.1	0.2
Machinery	1 467	1 192	1 045	-275	-146	-2.1	-1.3	248	281	335	1.3	1.8
Agriculture, construction, and mining machinery	220	222	207	1	-15	0.1	-0.7	48	60	84	2.4	3.4
Industrial machinery	169	123	101	-46	-22	-3.2	-2.0	36	34	30	-0.6	-1.2
Commercial and service industry machinery	146	111	97	-34	-14	-2.7	-1.3	25	22	20	-1.5	-1.0
Ventilation, heating, air-conditioning, and commercial refrigeration	187	160	145	-27	-15	-1.6	-1.0	30	35	46	1.8	2.7
Metalworking machinery	280	203	166	-77	-37	-3.2	-2.0	29	27	29	-0.7	0.5
Engine, turbine, and power transmission equipment	113	100	84	-12	-16	-1.1	-1.8	23	38	48	5.0	2.4
Other general purpose machinery	352	273	246	-79	-27	-2.5	-1.0	56	64	76	1.3	1.7
Computer and electronic product	1 747	1 316	1 159	-430	-157	-2.8	-1.3	321	493	1 214	4.4	9.4
Computer and peripheral equipment	305	199	132	-106	-66	-4.2	-4.0	52	134	867	9.9	20.5
Communications equipment	238	144	145	-93	1	-4.9	0.0	66	78	116	1.6	4.1
Audio and video equipment	53	32	25	-21	-7	-5.0	-2.3	8	10	13	1.8	3.1
Semiconductor and other electronic component	607	463	399	-144	-64	-2.7	-1.5	107	163	543	4.3	12.8
Navigational, measuring, electromedical, and control instruments	489	438	418	-52	-20	-1.1	-0.5	87	107	140	2.1	2.7
Manufacturing and reproducing magnetic and optical media	56	41	40	-15	-2	-3.0	-0.4	8	12	15	3.7	2.3
Electrical equipment, appliance, and component	591	436	354	-155	-81	-3.0	-2.0	106	105	116	-0.1	1.1
Electric lighting equipment	82	59	42	-23	-16	-3.2	-3.2	12	13	14	1.0	0.6
Household appliance	111	82	61	-29	-21	-3.0	-2.9	20	25	30	2.4	1.8
Electrical equipment	217	156	126	-61	-29	-3.3	-2.1	35	30	32	-1.6	0.6
Other electrical equipment and component	181	139	125	-42	-14	-2.6	-1.1	39	37	42	-0.5	1.2
Transportation equipment	1 974	1 765	1 651	-209	-114	-1.1	-0.7	525	657	863	2.3	2.8
Motor vehicle	285	236	226	-49	-10	-1.9	-0.4	193	278	385	3.7	3.3
Motor vehicle body and trailer	155	180	176	25	-4	1.5	-0.2	22	27	36	1.7	2.9
Motor vehicle parts	800	654	516	-146	-138	-2.0	-2.3	166	190	204	1.3	0.7
Aerospace product and parts	514	472	497	-43	25	-0.9	0.5	111	122	166	1.0	3.1
Railroad rolling stock	33	28	23	-5	-5	-1.7	-1.8	7	7	10	-0.4	3.9
Ship and boat building	145	156	174	10	18	0.7	1.1	16	21	35	2.8	5.0
Other transportation equipment	40	40	40	-1	0	-0.2	0.0	9	14	23	4.1	5.3
Furniture and related product	604	556	521	-47	-36	-0.8	-0.7	58	79	93	3.1	1.6
Household and institutional furniture and kitchen cabinet	397	374	346	-24	-28	-0.6	-0.8	35	46	51	2.8	1.2
Office furniture (including fixtures)	158	132	123	-25	-9	-1.7	-0.7	18	26	31	3.7	2.0
Other furniture related product	49	50	52	1	1	0.2	0.2	6	8	10	2.9	2.6
Miscellaneous	716	652	600	-64	-52	-0.9	-0.8	101	147	219	3.9	4.0
Medical equipment and supplies	298	309	312	11	4	0.4	0.1	44	77	117	5.8	4.3
Other miscellaneous	418	343	287	-75	-56	-2.0	-1.8	57	70	102	2.1	3.8
Wholesale Trade	5 522	5 898	6 326	376	428	0.7	0.7	654	1 042	1 703	4.8	5.0
Retail Trade	14 143	15 319	16 006	1 177	687	0.8	0.4	824	1 305	1 892	4.7	3.8
Transportation and Warehousing	3 936	4 466	4 962	530	496	1.3	1.1	523	670	890	2.5	2.9
Air transportation	526	486	522	-39	35	-0.8	0.7	97	144	236	4.0	5.1
Rail transportation	225	225	213	0.1	-12	0.0	-0.5	43	37	49	-1.4	2.7
Water transportation	51	64	76	13	12	2.3	1.7	29	22	29	-2.6	2.7
Truck transportation	1 282	1 437	1 595	155	158	1.1	1.0	179	261	338	3.8	2.6
Transit and ground passenger transportation	339	394	438	55	44	1.5	1.1	26	32	39	2.3	1.8
Pipeline transportation	51	39	26	-12	-13	-2.7	-3.8	27	24	21	-1.4	-1.4
Scenic and sightseeing transportation	23	27	35	4	8	1.5	2.5	2	2	2	0.8	1.1
Support activities for transportation	446	571	668	125	97	2.5	1.6	41	48	54	1.6	1.1
Couriers and messengers	540	585	603	46	18	0.8	0.3	47	63	83	2.9	2.8
Warehousing and storage	452	636	786	185	150	3.5	2.1	31	40	58	2.4	3.8
Information	2 940	3 055	3 267	115	212	0.4	0.7	634	1 006	1 683	4.7	5.3
Publishing industries, except Internet	927	904	932	-24	28	-0.3	0.3	165	274	461	5.2	5.3
Newspaper, periodical, book, and directory publishers	752	660	611	-92	-49	-1.3	-0.8	118	132	167	1.1	2.4
Software publishers	175	243	321	69	78	3.4	2.8	49	153	420	12.0	10.6
Motion picture, video, and sound recording industries	335	378	414	43	36	1.2	0.9	70	81	116	1.5	3.7
Broadcasting, except Internet	309	331	363	22	31	0.7	0.9	59	73	99	2.1	3.1
Telecommunications	997	973	1 022	-24	49	-0.2	0.5	301	470	758	4.6	4.9
Internet and other information services	372	469	536	97	67	2.3	1.3	41	109	248	10.3	8.5
Financial Activities	6 969	8 363	9 570	1 395	1 207	1.8	1.4	1 726	2 621	3 762	4.3	3.7
Monetary authorities, credit intermediation, and related activities	2 391	2 958	3 196	567	238	2.2	0.8	415	660	946	4.7	3.7
Securities, commodity contracts, and other financial investments and related activities	590	816	1 192	227	376	3.3	3.9	112	351	958	12.1	10.6
Insurance carriers	1 382	1 428	1 463	46	35	0.3	0.2	288	355	406	2.1	1.3
Agencies, brokerages, and other insurance-related activities	726	888	1 025	162	137	2.0	1.4	88	104	153	1.6	4.0
Funds, trusts, and other financial vehicles	66	93	122	28	29	3.6	2.8	57	72	90	2.4	2.2
Real estate	1 206	1 503	1 796	298	293	2.2	1.8	664	847	1 007	2.5	1.7
Automotive equipment rental and leasing	180	200	229	20	30	1.0	1.4	26	30	34	1.2	1.2
Consumer goods rental and general rental centers	320	326	361	6	35	0.2	1.0	20	24	34	1.7	3.6
Commercial and industrial machinery and equipment rental and leasing	88	122	148	34	27	3.3	2.0	33	43	54	2.9	2.3
Lessors of nonfinancial intangible assets (except copyrighted works)	21	29	37	8	8	3.3	2.4	63	139	278	8.3	7.2

Table 4-6. Employment and Output, by Industry, 1996, 2006, and Projected 2016—Continued

(Number, percent, dollars.)

Industry	Employment — Number of jobs (thousands) 1996	2006	2016	Change 1996–2006	2006–2016	Avg annual rate of change (pct) 1996–2006	2006–2016	Output — Billions of chained (2000) dollars 1996	2006	2016	Avg annual rate of change (pct) 1996–2006	2006–2016
Professional, Scientific, and Technical Services	5 337	7 372	9 494	2 035	2 122	3.3	2.6	770	1 149	1 607	4.1	3.4
Legal services	968	1 173	1 285	205	111	1.9	0.9	172	192	214	1.1	1.1
Accounting, tax preparation, bookkeeping, and payroll services	730	889	1 072	160	183	2.0	1.9	82	97	110	1.7	1.3
Architectural, engineering, and related services	1 025	1 386	1 731	361	345	3.1	2.3	136	210	276	4.4	2.8
Specialized design services	107	136	179	29	44	2.4	2.8	18	27	40	4.0	4.2
Computer systems design and related services	701	1 278	1 768	577	489	6.2	3.3	97	156	230	4.8	4.0
Management, scientific, and technical consulting services	517	921	1 639	404	718	5.9	5.9	87	171	318	7.0	6.4
Scientific research and development services	472	593	649	121	55	2.3	0.9	59	127	216	7.9	5.5
Advertising and related services	414	458	520	44	62	1.0	1.3	57	77	97	3.1	2.3
Other professional, scientific, and technical services	402	537	651	135	114	2.9	1.9	63	96	132	4.3	3.3
Management of companies and enterprises	1 703	1 809	2 080	107	270	0.6	1.4	226	435	592	6.7	3.1
Administrative and support and waste management and remediation services	6 422	8 370	10 070	1 948	1 700	2.7	1.9	348	553	800	4.8	3.8
Administrative and support services	6 140	8 023	9 646	1 883	1 623	2.7	1.9	302	494	724	5.0	3.9
Office administrative services	247	363	456	116	93	3.9	2.3	30	74	129	9.2	5.7
Facilities support services	80	123	179	43	56	4.4	3.8	8	11	12	3.0	0.8
Employment services	2 601	3 657	4 348	1 056	692	3.5	1.7	83	134	186	4.9	3.4
Business support services	678	791	950	112	160	1.5	1.9	41	61	93	4.1	4.3
Travel arrangement and reservation services	294	227	230	-67	3	-2.6	0.1	26	30	30	1.5	0.1
Investigation and and security services	612	760	923	149	163	2.2	2.0	22	36	58	4.7	4.9
Services to buildings and dwellings	1 362	1 797	2 161	436	364	2.8	1.9	62	106	162	5.5	4.4
Other support services	266	305	399	39	94	1.4	2.7	30	43	55	3.7	2.6
Waste management and remediation services	282	347	424	65	77	2.1	2.0	46	59	75	2.6	2.4
Waste collection	92	130	157	38	26	3.5	1.9	24	30	36	2.4	1.8
Waste treatment and disposal and waste management services	190	217	267	27	50	1.4	2.1	22	29	39	2.8	2.9
Education services	2 078	2 918	3 527	841	609	3.5	1.9	124	157	191	2.4	2.0
Elementary and secondary schools	599	847	1 001	248	154	3.5	1.7	26	30	34	1.5	1.2
Junior colleges, colleges, universities, and professional schools	1 170	1 537	1 824	368	287	2.8	1.7	72	95	114	2.8	1.8
Other education services	309	534	702	225	168	5.6	2.8	26	33	44	2.4	2.9
Health care and social assistance	11 605	14 920	18 954	3 315	4 034	2.5	2.4	865	1 211	1 720	3.4	3.6
Ambulatory health care services	3 940	5 283	6 844	1 343	1 561	3.0	2.6	401	593	890	4.0	4.1
Offices of health practitioners	2 629	3 508	4 365	879	857	2.9	2.2	286	433	643	4.2	4.0
Home health care services	667	867	1 348	200	480	2.7	4.5	36	48	83	3.0	5.6
Outpatient, laboratory, and other ambulatory services	644	908	1 130	264	223	3.5	2.2	79	112	164	3.5	3.8
Hospitals, private	3 773	4 427	5 119	654	692	1.6	1.5	292	397	543	3.1	3.2
Nursing and residential care facilities	2 380	2 901	3 588	521	687	2.0	2.1	98	119	146	1.9	2.1
Nursing care facilities	1 448	1 584	1 758	136	174	0.9	1.0	64	72	84	1.2	1.6
Residential care facilities	932	1 317	1 829	385	512	3.5	3.3	34	47	62	3.2	2.9
Social assistance	1 512	2 309	3 404	797	1 095	4.3	4.0	74	103	149	3.4	3.8
Individual and family services	545	974	1 687	429	713	6.0	5.7	30	44	68	3.7	4.5
Community, and vocational rehabilitation services	408	529	638	120	110	2.6	1.9	14	22	32	4.2	4.0
Child day care services	559	807	1 078	248	272	3.7	2.9	29	38	50	2.8	2.8
Arts, entertainment, and recreation	1 522	1 927	2 522	405	595	2.4	2.7	130	185	274	3.5	4.0
Performing arts, spectator sports, and related industries	329	399	478	70	79	2.0	1.8	56	62	84	1.1	3.0
Performing arts companies	115	121	120	5	-1	0.5	-0.1	10	9	10	-0.8	0.8
Spectator sports	109	131	162	22	31	1.9	2.1	18	24	31	2.5	2.8
Promoters of events, and agents and managers	72	100	131	28	31	3.3	2.8	11	14	18	2.0	2.9
Independent artists, writers, and performers	32	47	65	15	18	3.9	3.3	16	16	24	-0.1	4.5
Museums, historical sites, and similar institutions	89	124	167	35	44	3.4	3.1	5	7	10	2.8	3.7
Amusement, gambling, and recreation industries	1 104	1 404	1 877	300	472	2.4	2.9	70	116	182	5.2	4.6
Accommodation and food services	9 254	11 216	12 494	1 962	1 278	1.9	1.1	427	555	635	2.6	1.4
Accommodation	1 699	1 833	2 088	134	254	0.8	1.3	115	139	170	2.0	2.0
Food services and drinking places	7 556	9 383	10 406	1 827	1 024	2.2	1.0	312	415	465	2.9	1.1
Other services	5 435	6 235	7 077	800	843	1.4	1.3	370	439	550	1.7	2.3
Repair and maintenance	1 136	1 248	1 453	113	204	1.0	1.5	144	176	223	2.0	2.4
Automotive repair and maintenance	781	887	1 094	106	207	1.3	2.1	90	106	132	1.7	2.2
Electronic and precision equipment repair and maintenance	110	104	94	-6	-10	-0.5	-1.0	18	20	20	0.8	0.2
Commercial and industrial machinery and equipment (except automotive and electronic) repair and maintenance	160	179	191	18	12	1.1	0.7	17	29	45	5.5	4.4
Personal and household goods repair and maintenance	84	78	73	-6	-5	-0.7	-0.6	19	21	26	0.7	2.2
Personal and laundry services	1 166	1 284	1 415	118	131	1.0	1.0	96	122	167	2.5	3.1
Personal care services	454	585	649	131	64	2.6	1.0	29	40	56	3.5	3.3
Death care services	126	137	154	10	18	0.8	1.2	13	11	12	-1.5	0.6
Dry-cleaning and laundry services	378	344	346	-34	2	-0.9	0.1	20	21	23	0.3	1.0
Other personal services	207	218	265	12	47	0.6	2.0	33	50	76	4.1	4.3
Religious, grantmaking, civic, professional, and similar organizations	2 389	2 899	3 373	510	474	2.0	1.5	118	128	147	0.8	1.4
Religious organizations	1 310	1 666	1 981	356	316	2.4	1.7	47	49	56	0.5	1.3
Grantmaking and giving services and social advocacy organizations	251	321	367	70	46	2.5	1.4	15	18	22	2.3	1.9
Civic, social, professional, and similar organizations	828	913	1 025	85	112	1.0	1.2	57	60	69	0.5	1.4
Private households	744	802	837	58	34	0.8	0.4	13	13	15	0.4	0.9
Federal Government	2 877	2 728	2 626	-149	-103	-0.5	-0.4	580	715	761	2.1	0.6
Postal Service	867	770	757	-97	-13	-1.2	-0.2	58	58	62	-0.1	0.7
Federal electric utilities	26	22	23	-4	0.3	-1.5	0.1	9	10	12	1.4	1.5
Federal enterprises except Postal Service and electric utilities	97	45	26	-52	-19	-7.3	-5.2	8	7	8	-1.3	1.2
Federal government except enterprises	1 887	1 891	1 819	4	-71	0.0	-0.4	506	640	680	2.4	0.6
Federal defense government	597	492	434	-105	-58	-1.9	-1.3	274	358	385	2.7	0.7
Federal non-defense government except enterprises	1 290	1 398	1 386	109	-13	0.8	-0.1	152	192	192	2.4	0.0
Federal government capital services	. . .	. . .	. . .	. . .	. . .	. . .	. . .	80	90	102	1.1	1.3

. . . = Not available.

Table 4-6. Employment and Output, by Industry, 1996, 2006, and Projected 2016—*Continued*

(Number, percent, dollars.)

Industry	Employment							Output				
	Number of jobs (thousands)			Change		Average annual rate of change (percent)		Billions of chained (2000) dollars			Average annual rate of change (percent)	
	1996	2006	2016	1996–2006	2006–2016	1996–2006	2006–2016	1996	2006	2016	1996–2006	2006–2016
State and Local Government	16 662	19 262	20 696	2 600	1 434	1.5	0.7	1 159	1 436	1 749	2.2	2.0
Local government passenger transit	206	256	317	50	61	2.2	2.2	7	9	10	1.6	1.8
Local government enterprises except passenger transit	3 746	4 311	4 542	565	231	1.4	0.5	111	132	176	1.8	2.9
Local government hospitals	648	650	679	2	30	0.0	0.4	47	65	87	3.4	2.9
Local government educational services	6 592	7 938	8 450	1 346	512	1.9	0.6	349	418	449	1.8	0.7
Local government excluding enterprises, educational services, and hospitals	864	1 027	1 347	163	320	1.7	2.7	277	350	437	2.4	2.2
State government enterprises	1 824	1 876	1 879	52	4	0.3	0.0	15	19	25	2.2	2.9
State government hospitals	376	361	346	-15	-14	-0.4	-0.4	34	47	61	3.5	2.5
State government educational services	1 911	2 295	2 586	384	291	1.8	1.2	125	159	189	2.4	1.8
State government excluding enterprises, educational services, and hospitals	496	549	549	53	0	1.0	0.0	124	135	179	0.8	2.9
State and local government capital services	...	...	...	...	...	...	...	71	103	140	3.9	3.0
Owner-Occupied Dwellings	...	...	...	...	...	...	...	680	920	1 229	3.1	2.9
Agriculture, Forestry, Fishing, and Hunting[5]	2 731	2 139	1 966	-592	-173	-2.4	-0.8	236	267	331	1.3	2.2
Crop production	1 166	898	758	-268	-139	-2.6	-1.7	88	107	148	1.9	3.3
Animal production	1 238	922	904	-316	-18	-2.9	-0.2	96	112	138	1.6	2.1
Forestry	18	19	21	1	1	0.5	0.6	5	5	4	-1.4	-0.4
Logging	121	95	76	-26	-19	-2.4	-2.2	27	25	23	-0.9	-0.9
Fishing, hunting and trapping	62	49	39	-13	-10	-2.3	-2.2	7	6	4	-1.5	-2.9
Support activities for agriculture and forestry	126	155	167	29	12	2.1	0.7	13	12	14	-0.4	1.1
Nonagriculture Self-Employed and Unpaid Family Workers[6]	9 368	9 772	10 462	404	690	0.4	0.7	...	...	...	...	...
Secondary Wage and Salary Jobs in Agriculture and Private Household Industries[7]	177	178	185	2	7	0.1	0.4	...	...	...	...	...
Secondary Jobs as Self-Employed or Unpaid Family Workers[8]	2 043	1 619	1 646	-425	27	-2.3	0.2	...	...	...	...	...

[5]Includes agriculture, forestry, fishing, and hunting wage and salary, self-employed, and unpaid family worker data from the household survey (except logging, which is from the CES Survey). Government wage and salary workers are excluded.
[6]Comparable estimate of output growth is not available.
[7]Workers who hold a secondary wage and salary job in agricultural production, forestry, fishing, and private household industries.
[8]Wage and salary workers who hold a secondary job as a self-employed or unpaid family worker.
. . . = Not available.

Table 4-7. Employment, by Occupation, 2006 and Projected 2016

(Numbers in thousands, percent.)

Occupation	Employment				Change, 2006–2016		Total job openings due to growth and net replacements, 2006–2016[1]
	Number		Percent distribution		Number	Percent	
	2006	2016	2006	2016			
ALL OCCUPATIONS	150 620	166 220	100.0	100.0	15 600	10.4	50 732
Management, Business, and Financial	15 397	16 993	10.2	10.2	1 596	10.4	4 575
Management	8 789	9 322	5.8	5.6	533	6.1	2 373
Top executives	2 187	2 222	1.5	1.3	35	1.6	572
Chief executives	402	410	0.3	0.2	8	2.1	118
General and operations managers	1 720	1 746	1.1	1.1	26	1.5	441
Legislators	65	65	0.0	0.0	1	1.0	13
Advertising, marketing, promotions, public relations, and sales managers	583	651	0.4	0.4	68	11.7	198
Advertising and promotions managers	47	50	0.0	0.0	3	6.2	13
Marketing and sales managers	486	542	0.3	0.3	57	11.7	165
Marketing managers	167	192	0.1	0.1	24	14.4	61
Sales managers	318	351	0.2	0.2	33	10.2	103
Public relations managers	50	58	0.0	0.0	8	16.9	20
Operations specialties managers	1 474	1 628	1.0	1.0	154	10.5	473
Administrative services managers	247	276	0.2	0.2	29	11.7	94
Computer and information systems managers	264	307	0.2	0.2	43	16.4	86
Financial managers	506	570	0.3	0.3	64	12.6	138
Human resources managers	136	153	0.1	0.1	17	12.5	43
Compensation and benefits managers	49	55	0.0	0.0	6	12.0	15
Training and development managers	29	33	0.0	0.0	5	15.6	10
Human resources managers, all other	58	65	0.0	0.0	7	11.4	18
Industrial production managers	157	148	0.1	0.1	-9	-5.9	54
Purchasing managers	70	72	0.0	0.0	2	3.4	22
Transportation, storage, and distribution managers	94	102	0.1	0.1	8	8.4	36
Other management occupations	4 545	4 821	3.0	2.9	276	6.1	1 130
Agricultural managers	1 317	1 230	0.9	0.7	-87	-6.6	117
Farm, ranch, and other agricultural managers	258	261	0.2	0.2	3	1.1	22
Farmers and ranchers	1 058	969	0.7	0.6	-90	-8.5	95
Construction managers	487	564	0.3	0.3	77	15.7	152
Education administrators	443	496	0.3	0.3	53	11.9	176
Education administrators, preschool and childcare center/program	56	69	0.0	0.0	13	23.5	29
Education administrators, elementary and secondary school	226	243	0.1	0.1	17	7.6	80
Education administrators, postsecondary	131	150	0.1	0.1	19	14.2	55
Education administrators, all other	30	33	0.0	0.0	4	12.6	12
Engineering managers	187	201	0.1	0.1	14	7.3	51
Food service managers	350	368	0.2	0.2	18	5.0	100
Funeral directors	29	32	0.0	0.0	4	12.5	10
Gaming managers	4	5	0.0	0.0	1	24.4	2
Lodging managers	71	80	0.0	0.0	9	12.2	24
Medical and health services managers	262	305	0.2	0.2	43	16.4	92
Natural sciences managers	41	45	0.0	0.0	5	11.4	14
Postmasters and mail superintendents	26	26	0.0	0.0	0	-0.8	6
Property, real estate, and community association managers	329	379	0.2	0.2	50	15.1	95
Social and community service managers	130	162	0.1	0.1	32	24.7	57
Managers, all other	870	930	0.6	0.6	60	6.9	233
Business and Financial Operations	6 608	7 671	4.4	4.6	1 063	16.1	2 203
Business operations specialists	3 860	4 466	2.6	2.7	606	15.7	1 276
Agents and business managers of artists, performers, and athletes	25	27	0.0	0.0	2	9.6	9
Buyers and purchasing agents	460	459	0.3	0.3	-1	-0.3	99
Purchasing agents and buyers, farm products	16	15	0.0	0.0	-1	-8.6	2
Wholesale and retail buyers, except farm products	157	156	0.1	0.1	0	-0.1	35
Purchasing agents, except wholesale, retail, and farm products	287	288	0.2	0.2	0	0.1	62
Claims adjusters, appraisers, examiners, and investigators	319	347	0.2	0.2	29	9.1	110
Claims adjusters, examiners, and investigators	305	332	0.2	0.2	27	8.9	105
Insurance appraisers, auto damage	13	15	0.0	0.0	2	12.5	5
Compliance officers, except agriculture, construction, health and safety, and transportation	237	249	0.2	0.1	12	4.9	39
Cost estimators	221	262	0.1	0.2	41	18.5	86
Emergency management specialists	12	13	0.0	0.0	1	12.3	3
Human resources, training, and labor relations specialists	732	862	0.5	0.5	130	17.8	288
Employment, recruitment, and placement specialists	197	233	0.1	0.1	36	18.4	79
Compensation, benefits, and job analysis specialists	110	130	0.1	0.1	20	18.4	44
Training and development specialists	210	249	0.1	0.1	38	18.3	84
Human resources, training, and labor relations specialists, all other	214	250	0.1	0.2	35	16.5	81
Logisticians	83	98	0.1	0.1	14	17.3	27
Management analysts	678	827	0.5	0.5	149	21.9	264
Meeting and convention planners	51	61	0.0	0.0	10	19.9	20
Business operation specialists, all other	1 043	1 261	0.7	0.8	218	20.9	330
Financial specialists	2 748	3 204	1.8	1.9	457	16.6	927
Accountants and auditors	1 274	1 500	0.8	0.9	226	17.7	450
Appraisers and assessors of real estate	101	118	0.1	0.1	17	16.9	37
Budget analysts	62	66	0.0	0.0	4	7.1	19
Credit analysts	67	68	0.0	0.0	1	1.9	27
Financial analysts and advisers	501	655	0.3	0.4	153	30.6	210
Financial analysts	221	295	0.1	0.2	75	33.8	87
Personal financial advisers	176	248	0.1	0.1	72	41.0	88
Insurance underwriters	104	111	0.1	0.1	7	6.3	35
Financial examiners	26	28	0.0	0.0	3	10.7	7
Loan counselors and officers	406	450	0.3	0.3	44	10.8	88
Loan counselors	33	35	0.0	0.0	1	4.0	5
Loan officers	373	415	0.2	0.2	43	11.5	83
Tax examiners, collectors, preparers, and revenue agents	181	174	0.1	0.1	-7	-3.7	40
Tax examiners, collectors, and revenue agents	81	82	0.1	0.0	2	2.1	22
Tax preparers	100	92	0.1	0.1	-8	-8.4	18
Financial specialists, all other	129	144	0.1	0.1	15	11.8	50

Note: Data may not sum to totals or 100 percent due to rounding.

[1]Total job openings represent the sum of employment increases and net replacements. If employment change is negative, job openings due to growth are zero and total job openings equal net replacements.

Table 4-7. Employment, by Occupation, 2006 and Projected 2016—*Continued*

(Numbers in thousands, percent.)

Occupation	Employment				Change, 2006–2016		Total job openings due to growth and net replacements, 2006–2016[1]
	Number		Percent distribution		Number	Percent	
	2006	2016	2006	2016			
Computer and Mathematical Sciences	3 313	4 135	2.2	2.5	822	24.8	1 568
Computer specialists	3 200	4 006	2.1	2.4	807	25.2	1 524
Computer and information scientists, research	25	31	0.0	0.0	5	21.5	12
Computer programmers	435	417	0.3	0.3	-18	-4.1	91
Computer software engineers	857	1 181	0.6	0.7	324	37.9	449
Computer software engineers, applications	507	733	0.3	0.4	226	44.6	300
Computer software engineers, systems software	350	449	0.2	0.3	99	28.2	150
Computer support specialists	552	624	0.4	0.4	71	12.9	242
Computer systems analysts	504	650	0.3	0.4	146	29.0	280
Database administrators	119	154	0.1	0.1	34	28.6	47
Network and computer systems administrators	309	393	0.2	0.2	83	26.9	154
Network systems and data communications analysts	262	402	0.2	0.2	140	53.4	193
Computer specialists, all other	136	157	0.1	0.1	21	15.1	57
Mathematical science occupations	114	129	0.1	0.1	15	13.2	44
Actuaries	18	22	0.0	0.0	4	23.7	11
Mathematicians	3	3	0.0	0.0	0	10.2	1
Operations research analysts	58	65	0.0	0.0	6	10.6	18
Statisticians	22	24	0.0	0.0	2	8.5	9
Miscellaneous mathematical science occupations	12	14	0.0	0.0	2	19.8	5
Mathematical technicians	1	1	0.0	0.0	0	7.9	0
Mathematical scientists, all other	10	13	0.0	0.0	2	21.3	5
Architecture and engineering	2 583	2 852	1.7	1.7	268	10.4	852
Architects, surveyors, and cartographers	232	277	0.2	0.2	45	19.2	97
Architects, except naval	160	188	0.1	0.1	28	17.5	58
Architects, except landscape and naval	132	155	0.1	0.1	23	17.7	48
Landscape architects	28	32	0.0	0.0	5	16.4	10
Surveyors, cartographers, and photogrammetrists	72	89	0.0	0.1	17	23.1	39
Cartographers and photogrammetrists	12	15	0.0	0.0	2	20.3	6
Surveyors	60	74	0.0	0.0	14	23.7	33
Engineers	1 512	1 671	1.0	1.0	160	10.6	505
Aerospace engineers	90	99	0.1	0.1	9	10.2	27
Agricultural engineers	3	3	0.0	0.0	0	8.6	1
Biomedical engineers	14	17	0.0	0.0	3	21.1	6
Chemical engineers	30	33	0.0	0.0	2	7.9	10
Civil engineers	256	302	0.2	0.2	46	18.0	114
Computer hardware engineers	79	82	0.1	0.0	4	4.6	28
Electrical and electronics engineers	291	306	0.2	0.2	15	5.0	82
Electrical engineers	153	163	0.1	0.1	10	6.3	45
Electronics engineers, except computer	138	143	0.1	0.1	5	3.7	37
Environmental engineers	54	68	0.0	0.0	14	25.4	30
Industrial engineers, including health and safety	227	270	0.2	0.2	43	19.1	98
Health and safety engineers, except mining safety engineers and inspectors	25	28	0.0	0.0	2	9.6	9
Industrial engineers	201	242	0.1	0.1	41	20.3	89
Marine engineers and naval architects	9	10	0.0	0.0	1	10.9	3
Materials engineers	22	22	0.0	0.0	1	4.0	6
Mechanical engineers	226	235	0.1	0.1	9	4.2	58
Mining and geological engineers, including mining safety engineers	7	8	0.0	0.0	1	10.0	2
Nuclear engineers	15	16	0.0	0.0	1	7.2	5
Petroleum engineers	17	18	0.0	0.0	1	5.2	5
Engineers, all other	170	180	0.1	0.1	9	5.5	29
Drafters, engineering, and mapping technicians	840	904	0.6	0.5	64	7.6	250
Drafters	253	268	0.2	0.2	15	6.0	88
Architectural and civil drafters	116	123	0.1	0.1	7	6.1	40
Electrical and electronics drafters	35	36	0.0	0.0	1	4.1	11
Mechanical drafters	78	82	0.1	0.0	4	5.2	26
Drafters, all other	25	27	0.0	0.0	3	11.0	10
Engineering technicians, except drafters	511	545	0.3	0.3	34	6.7	134
Aerospace engineering and operations technicians	9	9	0.0	0.0	1	10.4	3
Civil engineering technicians	91	100	0.1	0.1	9	10.2	27
Electrical and electronic engineering technicians	170	177	0.1	0.1	6	3.6	39
Electromechanical technicians	16	16	0.0	0.0	0	2.7	3
Environmental engineering technicians	21	26	0.0	0.0	5	24.8	9
Industrial engineering technicians	75	82	0.0	0.0	7	9.9	22
Mechanical engineering technicians	48	51	0.0	0.0	3	6.4	12
Engineering technicians, except drafters, all other	82	83	0.1	0.1	2	2.0	18
Surveying and mapping technicians	76	90	0.1	0.1	15	19.4	29
Life, Physical, and Social Sciences	1 407	1 610	0.9	1.0	203	14.4	538
Life scientists	258	292	0.2	0.2	33	12.8	103
Agricultural and food scientists	33	36	0.0	0.0	3	9.3	13
Animal scientists	5	6	0.0	0.0	1	9.9	2
Food scientists and technologists	12	13	0.0	0.0	1	10.4	5
Soil and plant scientists	16	17	0.0	0.0	1	8.4	6
Biological scientists	87	95	0.1	0.1	8	9.2	26
Biochemists and biophysicists	20	23	0.0	0.0	3	15.9	7
Microbiologists	17	19	0.0	0.0	2	11.2	5
Zoologists and wildlife biologists	20	22	0.0	0.0	2	8.7	6
Biological scientists, all other	29	30	0.0	0.0	1	3.7	7
Conservation scientists and foresters	33	35	0.0	0.0	2	5.3	11
Conservation scientists	20	21	0.0	0.0	1	5.3	7
Foresters	13	14	0.0	0.0	1	5.2	5
Medical scientists	92	110	0.1	0.1	18	19.9	47
Epidemiologists	5	5	0.0	0.0	1	13.6	2
Medical scientists, except epidemiologists	87	105	0.1	0.1	18	20.2	45
Life scientists, all other	14	16	0.0	0.0	2	15.3	6

Note: Data may not sum to totals or 100 percent due to rounding.

[1]Total job openings represent the sum of employment increases and net replacements. If employment change is negative, job openings due to growth are zero and total job openings equal net replacements.

Table 4-7. Employment, by Occupation, 2006 and Projected 2016—*Continued*

(Numbers in thousands, percent.)

Occupation	Employment				Change, 2006–2016		Total job openings due to growth and net replacements, 2006–2016[1]
	Number		Percent distribution		Number	Percent	
	2006	2016	2006	2016			
Life, Physical, and Social Sciences—*Continued*							
Physical scientists	267	309	0.2	0.2	42	15.7	109
Astronomers and physicists	18	19	0.0	0.0	1	6.7	6
Astronomers	2	2	0.0	0.0	0	5.5	0
Physicists	17	18	0.0	0.0	1	6.8	5
Atmospheric and space scientists	9	10	0.0	0.0	1	10.6	3
Chemists and materials scientists	93	102	0.1	0.1	8	9.1	33
Chemists	84	91	0.1	0.1	8	9.1	30
Materials scientists	10	11	0.0	0.0	1	8.7	3
Environmental scientists and geoscientists	123	152	0.1	0.1	30	24.2	61
Environmental scientists and specialists, including health	83	104	0.1	0.1	21	25.1	42
Geoscientists, except hydrologists and geologists	31	38	0.0	0.0	7	21.9	15
Hydrologists	8	10	0.0	0.0	2	24.3	4
Physical scientists, all other	24	25	0.0	0.0	1	6.2	6
Social scientists and related	530	616	0.4	0.4	86	16.3	160
Economists	15	16	0.0	0.0	1	7.5	5
Market and survey researchers	261	313	0.2	0.2	51	19.7	69
Market research analysts	234	281	0.2	0.2	47	20.1	63
Survey researchers	27	31	0.0	0.0	4	15.9	6
Psychologists	166	191	0.1	0.1	25	15.3	51
Clinical, counseling, and school psychologists	152	176	0.1	0.1	24	15.8	47
Industrial-organizational psychologists	2	2	0.0	0.0	0	21.3	1
Psychologists, all other	12	13	0.0	0.0	1	7.9	3
Sociologists	4	4	0.0	0.0	0	10.0	1
Urban and regional planners	34	39	0.0	0.0	5	14.5	15
Miscellaneous social scientists and related workers	51	54	0.0	0.0	3	6.1	19
Anthropologists and archeologists	6	6	0.0	0.0	1	15.0	3
Geographers	1	1	0.0	0.0	0	6.1	0
Historians	3	4	0.0	0.0	0	7.8	1
Political scientists	5	5	0.0	0.0	0	5.3	2
Social scientists and related workers, all other	36	38	0.0	0.0	2	4.7	13
Life, physical, and social science technicians	351	393	0.2	0.2	42	11.8	165
Agricultural and food science technicians	26	28	0.0	0.0	2	6.6	6
Biological technicians	79	91	0.1	0.1	13	16.0	41
Chemical technicians	61	65	0.0	0.0	4	5.8	24
Geological and petroleum technicians	12	13	0.0	0.0	1	8.6	5
Nuclear technicians	7	7	0.0	0.0	0	6.7	3
Social science research assistants	18	20	0.0	0.0	2	12.4	9
Other life, physical, and social science technicians	150	170	0.1	0.1	20	13.4	78
Environmental science and protection technicians, including health	37	47	0.0	0.0	10	27.9	24
Forensic science technicians	13	17	0.0	0.0	4	30.7	9
Forest and conservation technicians	34	33	0.0	0.0	-1	-2.0	13
Life, physical, and social science technicians, all other	66	73	0.0	0.0	7	9.9	32
Community and Social Services	2 386	2 927	1.6	1.8	541	22.7	945
Counselors, social workers, and other community and social service specialists	1 843	2 280	1.2	1.4	438	23.8	760
Counselors	635	771	0.4	0.5	136	21.3	261
Substance abuse and behavioral disorder counselors	83	112	0.1	0.1	29	34.4	45
Educational, vocational, and school counselors	260	292	0.2	0.2	33	12.6	84
Marriage and family therapists	25	32	0.0	0.0	7	29.8	12
Mental health counselors	100	130	0.1	0.1	30	30.0	50
Rehabilitation counselors	141	173	0.1	0.1	32	23.0	60
Counselors, all other	27	32	0.0	0.0	5	16.6	10
Social workers	595	727	0.4	0.4	132	22.2	258
Child, family, and school social workers	282	336	0.2	0.2	54	19.1	114
Medical and public health social workers	124	154	0.1	0.1	30	24.2	56
Mental health and substance abuse social workers	122	159	0.1	0.1	37	29.9	62
Social workers, all other	66	78	0.0	0.0	12	17.8	26
Miscellaneous community and social service specialists	613	783	0.4	0.5	170	27.7	241
Health educators	62	78	0.0	0.0	16	26.2	23
Probation officers and correctional treatment specialists	94	105	0.1	0.1	10	10.9	21
Social and human service assistants	339	453	0.2	0.3	114	33.6	153
Community and social service specialists, all other	118	148	0.1	0.1	30	25.1	43
Religious workers	543	646	0.4	0.4	104	19.1	185
Clergy	404	481	0.3	0.3	76	18.9	130
Directors, religious activities and education	99	119	0.1	0.1	20	19.7	42
Religious workers, all other	39	47	0.0	0.0	8	19.7	12
Legal	1 222	1 367	0.8	0.8	145	11.8	360
Lawyers, judges, and related workers	812	898	0.5	0.5	86	10.6	240
Lawyers	761	844	0.5	0.5	84	11.0	228
Judges, magistrates, and other judicial workers	51	53	0.0	0.0	2	4.5	12
Administrative law judges, adjudicators, and hearing officers	15	15	0.0	0.0	0	0.1	3
Arbitrators, mediators, and conciliators	8	9	0.0	0.0	1	10.6	3
Judges, magistrate judges, and magistrates	27	29	0.0	0.0	1	5.1	7
Legal support workers	410	469	0.3	0.3	59	14.3	120
Paralegals and legal assistants	238	291	0.2	0.2	53	22.2	84
Miscellaneous legal support workers	173	179	0.1	0.1	6	3.4	36
Court reporters	19	24	0.0	0.0	5	24.6	8
Law clerks	37	36	0.0	0.0	0	-1.2	6
Title examiners, abstractors, and searchers	69	68	0.0	0.0	-1	-1.2	11
Legal support workers, all other	48	50	0.0	0.0	2	5.1	10

Note: Data may not sum to totals or 100 percent due to rounding.

[1]Total job openings represent the sum of employment increases and net replacements. If employment change is negative, job openings due to growth are zero and total job openings equal net replacements.

Table 4-7. Employment, by Occupation, 2006 and Projected 2016—*Continued*

(Numbers in thousands, percent.)

Occupation	Employment				Change, 2006–2016		Total job openings due to growth and net replacements, 2006–2016[1]
	Number		Percent distribution		Number	Percent	
	2006	2016	2006	2016			
Education, Training, and Library	9 034	10 298	6.0	6.2	1 265	14.0	3 050
Postsecondary teachers	1 672	2 054	1.1	1.2	382	22.9	662
Primary, secondary, and special education teachers	4 413	4 963	2.9	3.0	550	12.5	1 578
Preschool and kindergarten teachers	607	750	0.4	0.5	143	23.5	243
Preschool teachers, except special education	437	552	0.3	0.3	115	26.3	187
Kindergarten teachers, except special education	170	198	0.1	0.1	28	16.3	56
Elementary and middle school teachers	2 214	2 496	1.5	1.5	282	12.7	766
Elementary school teachers, except special education	1 540	1 749	1.0	1.1	209	13.6	545
Middle school teachers, except special and vocational education	658	732	0.4	0.4	74	11.2	217
Vocational education teachers, middle school	16	15	0.0	0.0	-1	-5.1	3
Secondary school teachers	1 133	1 187	0.8	0.7	54	4.8	396
Secondary school teachers, except special and vocational education	1 038	1 096	0.7	0.7	59	5.6	368
Vocational education teachers, secondary school	96	91	0.1	0.1	-4	-4.6	28
Special education teachers	459	530	0.3	0.3	71	15.5	173
Special education teachers, preschool, kindergarten, and elementary school	219	262	0.1	0.2	43	19.6	92
Special education teachers, middle school	102	118	0.1	0.1	16	15.8	39
Special education teachers, secondary school	138	150	0.1	0.1	12	8.5	42
Other teachers and instructors	1 078	1 214	0.7	0.7	136	12.6	251
Adult literacy, remedial education, and GED teachers and instructors	76	87	0.1	0.1	11	14.2	19
Self-enrichment education teachers	261	322	0.2	0.2	60	23.1	88
Teachers and instructors, all other	741	805	0.5	0.5	64	8.7	144
Archivists, curators, and librarians	307	328	0.2	0.2	21	6.9	135
Archivists, curators, and museum technicians	27	33	0.0	0.0	5	18.3	17
Archivists	6	7	0.0	0.0	1	14.4	4
Curators	10	13	0.0	0.0	2	23.3	7
Museum technicians and conservators	11	12	0.0	0.0	2	15.9	6
Librarians	158	164	0.1	0.1	6	3.6	49
Library technicians	121	132	0.1	0.1	10	8.5	69
Other education, training, and library	1 563	1 739	1.0	1.0	176	11.2	425
Audio-visual collections specialists	7	6	0.0	0.0	-1	-13.8	1
Farm and home management advisers	15	16	0.0	0.0	1	5.1	3
Instructional coordinators	129	159	0.1	0.1	29	22.5	47
Teacher assistants	1 312	1 449	0.9	0.9	137	10.4	350
Education, training, and library workers, all other	99	110	0.1	0.1	10	10.5	24
Arts, Design, Entertainment, Sports, and Media	2 677	2 982	1.8	1.8	305	11.4	968
Art and design	821	905	0.5	0.5	84	10.2	303
Artists and related workers	218	253	0.1	0.2	34	15.8	85
Art directors	78	85	0.1	0.1	7	9.0	25
Craft artists	9	10	0.0	0.0	1	8.0	3
Fine artists, including painters, sculptors, and illustrators	30	33	0.0	0.0	3	9.9	10
Multimedia artists and animators	87	110	0.1	0.1	23	25.8	43
Artists and related workers, all other	14	15	0.0	0.0	1	8.4	4
Designers	603	653	0.4	0.4	50	8.2	218
Commercial and industrial designers	48	51	0.0	0.0	3	7.2	16
Fashion designers	20	21	0.0	0.0	1	5.0	6
Floral designers	87	79	0.1	0.0	-8	-8.9	23
Graphic designers	261	286	0.2	0.2	26	9.8	95
Interior designers	72	86	0.0	0.1	14	19.5	33
Merchandise displayers and window trimmers	87	96	0.1	0.1	9	10.7	32
Set and exhibit designers	12	14	0.0	0.0	2	17.8	5
Designers, all other	16	18	0.0	0.0	2	11.8	6
Entertainers and performers, sports and related	798	897	0.5	0.5	100	12.5	307
Actors, producers, and directors	163	182	0.1	0.1	18	11.3	60
Actors	70	78	0.0	0.0	8	11.6	23
Producers and directors	93	103	0.1	0.1	10	11.1	38
Athletes, coaches, umpires, and related workers	253	291	0.2	0.2	38	15.1	103
Athletes and sports competitors	18	21	0.0	0.0	3	19.2	8
Coaches and scouts	217	249	0.1	0.1	32	14.7	87
Umpires, referees, and other sports officials	19	22	0.0	0.0	3	16.0	8
Dancers and choreographers	40	43	0.0	0.0	2	5.9	25
Dancers	20	22	0.0	0.0	2	9.5	13
Choreographers	20	21	0.0	0.0	0	2.4	12
Musicians, singers, and related workers	264	293	0.2	0.2	29	10.8	82
Music directors and composers	68	77	0.0	0.0	9	12.9	23
Musicians and singers	196	216	0.1	0.1	20	10.1	60
Entertainers and performers, sports and related, all other	77	89	0.1	0.1	12	15.8	37
Media and communication	764	847	0.5	0.5	83	10.8	245
Announcers	71	66	0.0	0.0	-5	-6.9	24
Radio and television announcers	59	54	0.0	0.0	-5	-8.3	20
Public address system and other announcers	12	12	0.0	0.0	0	-0.2	4
News analysts, reporters, and correspondents	67	68	0.0	0.0	1	1.8	22
Broadcast news analysts	8	8	0.0	0.0	0	6.0	3
Reporters and correspondents	59	60	0.0	0.0	1	1.2	19
Public relations specialists	243	286	0.2	0.2	43	17.6	61
Writers and editors	306	336	0.2	0.2	30	9.7	105
Editors	122	124	0.1	0.1	3	2.3	39
Technical writers	49	59	0.0	0.0	10	19.5	24
Writers and authors	135	153	0.1	0.1	17	12.8	42
Miscellaneous media and communication workers	77	91	0.1	0.1	14	18.1	32
Interpreters and translators	41	51	0.0	0.0	10	23.6	20
Media and communication workers, all other	36	40	0.0	0.0	4	11.7	13

Note: Data may not sum to totals or 100 percent due to rounding.

[1]Total job openings represent the sum of employment increases and net replacements. If employment change is negative, job openings due to growth are zero and total job openings equal net replacements.

Table 4-7. Employment, by Occupation, 2006 and Projected 2016—*Continued*

(Numbers in thousands, percent.)

Occupation	Employment				Change, 2006–2016		Total job openings due to growth and net replacements, 2006–2016[1]
	Number		Percent distribution		Number	Percent	
	2006	2016	2006	2016			
Arts, Design, Entertainment, Sports, and Media—*Continued*							
Media and communication equipment occupations	294	332	0.2	0.2	38	13.0	113
Broadcast and sound engineering technicians and radio operators	105	123	0.1	0.1	18	17.0	52
Audio and video equipment technicians	50	62	0.0	0.0	12	24.2	28
Broadcast technicians	38	42	0.0	0.0	5	12.1	17
Radio operators	2	1	0.0	0.0	0	-16.3	1
Sound engineering technicians	16	18	0.0	0.0	1	9.1	7
Photographers	122	135	0.1	0.1	13	10.3	40
Television, video, and motion picture camera operators and editors	47	53	0.0	0.0	6	12.0	15
Camera operators, television, video, and motion picture	27	30	0.0	0.0	3	11.5	8
Film and video editors	21	23	0.0	0.0	3	12.7	6
Media and communication equipment workers, all other	19	21	0.0	0.0	2	10.2	7
Health Care Practitioner and Technical	7 198	8 620	4.8	5.2	1 423	19.8	2 785
Health diagnosing and treating practitioners	4 460	5 383	3.0	3.2	923	20.7	1 670
Chiropractors	53	60	0.0	0.0	8	14.4	13
Dentists	161	176	0.1	0.1	15	9.1	46
Dentists, general	136	149	0.1	0.1	13	9.2	39
Oral and maxillofacial surgeons	8	8	0.0	0.0	1	9.1	2
Orthodontists	9	10	0.0	0.0	1	9.2	3
Prosthodontists	1	1	0.0	0.0	0	10.7	0
Dentists, all other specialists	7	7	0.0	0.0	0	6.8	2
Dietitians and nutritionists	57	62	0.0	0.0	5	8.6	19
Optometrists	33	36	0.0	0.0	4	11.3	9
Pharmacists	243	296	0.2	0.2	53	21.7	95
Physicians and surgeons	633	723	0.4	0.4	90	14.2	204
Physician assistants	66	83	0.0	0.1	18	27.0	27
Podiatrists	12	13	0.0	0.0	1	9.5	5
Registered nurses	2 505	3 092	1.7	1.9	587	23.4	1 001
Therapists	570	684	0.4	0.4	114	19.9	197
Audiologists	12	13	0.0	0.0	1	9.8	3
Occupational therapists	99	122	0.1	0.1	23	23.1	37
Physical therapists	173	220	0.1	0.1	47	27.1	68
Radiation therapists	15	18	0.0	0.0	4	24.8	6
Recreational therapists	25	26	0.0	0.0	1	3.7	5
Respiratory therapists	102	126	0.1	0.1	23	22.6	38
Speech-language pathologists	110	121	0.1	0.1	12	10.6	33
Therapists, all other	35	38	0.0	0.0	3	10.0	8
Veterinarians	62	84	0.0	0.1	22	35.0	34
Health diagnosing and treating practitioners, all other	65	73	0.0	0.0	8	11.8	19
Health technologists and technicians	2 612	3 094	1.7	1.9	482	18.5	1 074
Clinical laboratory technologists and technicians	319	362	0.2	0.2	43	13.6	92
Medical and clinical laboratory technologists	167	188	0.1	0.1	21	12.4	46
Medical and clinical laboratory technicians	151	174	0.1	0.1	23	15.0	46
Dental hygienists	167	217	0.1	0.1	50	30.1	82
Diagnostic related technologists and technicians	307	360	0.2	0.2	53	17.2	95
Cardiovascular technologists and technicians	45	57	0.0	0.0	12	25.5	18
Diagnostic medical sonographers	46	54	0.0	0.0	9	19.1	15
Nuclear medicine technologists	20	23	0.0	0.0	3	14.8	6
Radiologic technologists and technicians	196	226	0.1	0.1	30	15.1	56
Emergency medical technicians and paramedics	201	240	0.1	0.1	39	19.2	62
Health diagnosing and treating practitioner support technicians	549	692	0.4	0.4	143	26.1	313
Dietetic technicians	25	29	0.0	0.0	4	14.8	11
Pharmacy technicians	285	376	0.2	0.2	91	32.0	178
Psychiatric technicians	62	60	0.0	0.0	-2	-3.3	19
Respiratory therapy technicians	19	19	0.0	0.0	0	0.9	6
Surgical technologists	86	107	0.1	0.1	21	24.4	47
Veterinary technologists and technicians	71	100	0.0	0.1	29	41.0	51
Licensed practical and licensed vocational nurses	749	854	0.5	0.5	105	14.0	309
Medical records and health information technicians	170	200	0.1	0.1	30	17.8	76
Opticians, dispensing	66	72	0.0	0.0	6	8.7	27
Miscellaneous health technologists and technicians	85	98	0.1	0.1	13	14.7	19
Orthotists and prosthetists	6	6	0.0	0.0	1	11.8	1
Health care technologists and technicians, all other	79	91	0.1	0.1	12	15.0	18
Other health care practitioner and technical	126	143	0.1	0.1	17	13.7	41
Occupational health and safety specialists and technicians	56	61	0.0	0.0	5	9.3	16
Occupational health and safety specialists	45	49	0.0	0.0	4	8.1	12
Occupational health and safety technicians	10	12	0.0	0.0	2	14.6	4
Miscellaneous health care practitioner and technical	70	82	0.0	0.0	12	17.1	25
Athletic trainers	17	21	0.0	0.0	4	24.3	7
Health care practitioner and technical workers, all other	53	61	0.0	0.0	8	14.8	18
Health Care Support	3 724	4 721	2.5	2.8	997	26.8	1 399
Nursing, psychiatric, and home health aides	2 296	2 944	1.5	1.8	647	28.2	853
Home health aides	787	1 171	0.5	0.7	384	48.7	454
Nursing aides, orderlies, and attendants	1 447	1 711	1.0	1.0	264	18.2	393
Psychiatric aides	62	62	0.0	0.0	0	-0.1	6
Occupational and physical therapist assistants and aides	140	179	0.1	0.1	39	27.9	58
Occupational therapist assistants and aides	33	41	0.0	0.0	8	24.5	13
Occupational therapist assistants	25	31	0.0	0.0	6	25.4	10
Occupational therapist aides	8	10	0.0	0.0	2	21.9	3
Physical therapist assistants and aides	107	137	0.1	0.1	31	28.9	44
Physical therapist assistants	60	80	0.0	0.0	20	32.4	27
Physical therapist aides	46	58	0.0	0.0	11	24.4	17

Note: Data may not sum to totals or 100 percent due to rounding.

[1]Total job openings represent the sum of employment increases and net replacements. If employment change is negative, job openings due to growth are zero and total job openings equal net replacements.

Table 4-7. Employment, by Occupation, 2006 and Projected 2016—*Continued*

(Numbers in thousands, percent.)

Occupation	Employment				Change, 2006–2016		Total job openings due to growth and net replacements, 2006–2016[1]
	Number		Percent distribution		Number	Percent	
	2006	2016	2006	2016			
Health Care Support—*Continued*							
Other health care support	1 287	1 598	0.9	1.0	311	24.2	489
Massage therapists	118	142	0.1	0.1	24	20.3	37
Miscellaneous health care support	1 170	1 457	0.8	0.9	287	24.5	452
Dental assistants	280	362	0.2	0.2	82	29.2	130
Medical assistants	417	565	0.3	0.3	148	35.4	199
Medical equipment preparers	45	52	0.0	0.0	6	14.2	12
Medical transcriptionists	98	112	0.1	0.1	13	13.5	26
Pharmacy aides	50	45	0.0	0.0	-6	-11.1	6
Veterinary assistants and laboratory animal caretakers	75	86	0.0	0.1	12	15.7	21
Health care support workers, all other	204	236	0.1	0.1	32	15.6	57
Protective Services	3 163	3 616	2.1	2.2	453	14.3	1 327
First-line supervisors/managers of protective service workers	233	260	0.2	0.2	26	11.4	91
First-line supervisors/managers of law enforcement workers	133	146	0.1	0.1	13	10.2	53
First-line supervisors/managers of correctional officers	40	45	0.0	0.0	5	12.5	16
First-line supervisors/managers of police and detectives	93	102	0.1	0.1	9	9.2	38
First-line supervisors/managers of fire fighting and prevention workers	52	58	0.0	0.0	6	11.5	22
First-line supervisors/managers of protective service workers, all other	48	55	0.0	0.0	7	14.5	15
Fire fighting and prevention workers	308	345	0.2	0.2	37	12.0	147
Firefighters	293	328	0.2	0.2	35	12.1	142
Fire inspectors	16	17	0.0	0.0	2	10.0	5
Fire inspectors and investigators	14	15	0.0	0.0	2	11.0	5
Forest fire inspectors and prevention specialists	2	2	0.0	0.0	0	2.1	0
Law enforcement workers	1 239	1 406	0.8	0.8	167	13.5	475
Bailiffs, correctional officers, and jailers	460	537	0.3	0.3	77	16.6	182
Bailiffs	19	21	0.0	0.0	2	11.2	6
Correctional officers and jailers	442	516	0.3	0.3	75	16.9	175
Detectives and criminal investigators	106	125	0.1	0.1	18	17.3	42
Fish and game wardens	8	8	0.0	0.0	0	-0.2	2
Parking enforcement workers	11	12	0.0	0.0	1	12.3	4
Police officers	654	724	0.4	0.4	70	10.8	245
Police and sheriff's patrol officers	648	719	0.4	0.4	70	10.8	243
Transit and railroad police	6	6	0.0	0.0	0	6.4	2
Other protective services	1 382	1 605	0.9	1.0	223	16.1	615
Animal control workers	15	17	0.0	0.0	2	12.5	5
Private detectives and investigators	52	61	0.0	0.0	9	18.2	19
Security guards and gaming surveillance officers	1 049	1 227	0.7	0.7	178	17.0	391
Gaming surveillance officers and gaming investigators	9	12	0.0	0.0	3	33.6	5
Security guards	1 040	1 216	0.7	0.7	175	16.9	387
Miscellaneous protective services	266	299	0.2	0.2	33	12.4	199
Crossing guards	69	71	0.0	0.0	1	1.9	21
Lifeguards, ski patrol, and other recreational protective service workers	114	136	0.1	0.1	21	18.7	106
Protective service workers, all other	83	93	0.1	0.1	10	12.6	72
Food Preparation and Serving Related	11 352	12 789	7.5	7.7	1 436	12.7	5 382
Supervisors of food preparation and serving workers	932	1 033	0.6	0.6	101	10.9	177
Chefs and head cooks	115	124	0.1	0.1	9	7.6	23
First-line supervisors/managers of food preparation and serving workers	817	909	0.5	0.5	92	11.3	154
Cooks and food preparation workers	2 998	3 340	2.0	2.0	342	11.4	1 223
Cooks	2 097	2 301	1.4	1.4	204	9.7	772
Cooks, fast food	629	681	0.4	0.4	52	8.3	223
Cooks, institution and cafeteria	401	445	0.3	0.3	43	10.9	152
Cooks, private household	5	5	0.0	0.0	0	8.8	2
Cooks, restaurant	850	948	0.6	0.6	98	11.5	328
Cooks, short order	195	205	0.1	0.1	9	4.8	62
Cooks, all other	16	16	0.0	0.0	1	3.4	5
Food preparation workers	902	1 040	0.6	0.6	138	15.3	451
Food and beverage serving workers	6 081	6 927	4.0	4.2	846	13.9	3 182
Bartenders	495	551	0.3	0.3	56	11.2	236
Fast food and counter workers	3 036	3 542	2.0	2.1	506	16.7	1 350
Combined food preparation and serving workers, including fast food	2 503	2 955	1.7	1.8	452	18.1	927
Counter attendants, cafeteria, food concession, and coffee shop	533	587	0.4	0.4	54	10.2	424
Waiters and waitresses	2 361	2 615	1.6	1.6	255	10.8	1 537
Food servers, nonrestaurant	189	219	0.1	0.1	30	15.8	59
Other food preparation and serving related workers	1 341	1 488	0.9	0.9	147	11.0	800
Dining room and cafeteria attendants and bartender helpers	416	466	0.3	0.3	49	11.8	223
Dishwashers	517	571	0.3	0.3	54	10.4	265
Hosts and hostesses, restaurant, lounge, and coffee shop	351	388	0.2	0.2	37	10.4	277
Food preparation and serving related workers, all other	56	64	0.0	0.0	7	13.0	35
Building and Grounds Cleaning and Maintenance	5 745	6 595	3.8	4.0	850	14.8	1 833
Supervisors of building and grounds cleaning and maintenance workers	484	555	0.3	0.3	71	14.7	127
First-line supervisors/managers of housekeeping and janitorial workers	282	318	0.2	0.2	36	12.7	77
First-line supervisors/managers of landscaping, lawn service, and groundskeeping workers	202	237	0.1	0.1	36	17.6	49
Building cleaning and pest control workers	3 941	4 486	2.6	2.7	544	13.8	1 298
Building cleaning workers	3 872	4 405	2.6	2.7	533	13.8	1 270
Janitors and cleaners, except maids and housekeeping workers	2 387	2 732	1.6	1.6	345	14.5	802
Maids and housekeeping cleaners	1 470	1 656	1.0	1.0	186	12.7	463
Building cleaning workers, all other	16	18	0.0	0.0	2	15.1	5
Pest control workers	70	81	0.0	0.0	11	15.5	28
Grounds maintenance	1 319	1 554	0.9	0.9	235	17.8	409
Landscaping and groundskeeping	1 220	1 441	0.8	0.9	221	18.1	382
Pesticide handlers, sprayers, and applicators, vegetation	31	35	0.0	0.0	4	14.0	8
Tree trimmers and pruners	41	45	0.0	0.0	5	11.1	10
Grounds maintenance workers, all other	28	33	0.0	0.0	5	16.6	8

Note: Data may not sum to totals or 100 percent due to rounding.

[1]Total job openings represent the sum of employment increases and net replacements. If employment change is negative, job openings due to growth are zero and total job openings equal net replacements.

Table 4-7. Employment, by Occupation, 2006 and Projected 2016—*Continued*

(Numbers in thousands, percent.)

Occupation	Employment				Change, 2006–2016		Total job openings due to growth and net replacements, 2006–2016[1]
	Number		Percent distribution		Number	Percent	
	2006	2016	2006	2016			
Personal Care and Services	4 966	6 060	3.3	3.6	1 094	22.0	2 276
Supervisors of personal care and service workers	268	312	0.2	0.2	43	16.2	100
First-line supervisors/managers of gaming workers	54	64	0.0	0.0	10	18.9	20
Gaming supervisors	34	42	0.0	0.0	8	23.4	14
Slot key persons	20	22	0.0	0.0	2	11.1	6
First-line supervisors/managers of personal service workers	215	248	0.1	0.1	33	15.5	80
Animal care and service workers	200	238	0.1	0.1	39	19.3	71
Animal trainers	43	53	0.0	0.0	10	22.7	17
Nonfarm animal caretakers	157	185	0.1	0.1	29	18.4	54
Entertainment attendants and related workers	546	667	0.4	0.4	120	22.1	378
Gaming services workers	117	146	0.1	0.1	29	25.0	53
Gaming dealers	84	104	0.1	0.1	20	24.1	37
Gaming and sports book writers and runners	18	24	0.0	0.0	5	28.0	9
Gaming service workers, all other	15	18	0.0	0.0	4	26.2	7
Motion picture projectionists	11	11	0.0	0.0	-1	-8.4	5
Ushers, lobby attendants, and ticket takers	103	121	0.1	0.1	17	16.9	90
Miscellaneous entertainment attendants and related workers	315	390	0.2	0.2	75	23.8	230
Amusement and recreation attendants	247	308	0.2	0.2	60	24.3	182
Costume attendants	4	5	0.0	0.0	1	14.1	3
Locker room, coatroom, and dressing room attendants	19	24	0.0	0.0	4	21.6	14
Funeral service	42	48	0.0	0.0	6	14.3	16
Embalmers	9	10	0.0	0.0	1	14.3	3
Funeral attendants	33	37	0.0	0.0	5	14.3	12
Personal appearance	825	942	0.5	0.6	117	14.2	217
Barbers and cosmetologists	677	755	0.4	0.5	77	11.4	162
Barbers	60	61	0.0	0.0	1	1.1	12
Hairdressers, hairstylists, and cosmetologists	617	694	0.4	0.4	77	12.4	151
Miscellaneous personal appearance	148	187	0.1	0.1	39	26.7	55
Makeup artists, theatrical and performance	2	3	0.0	0.0	1	39.8	1
Manicurists and pedicurists	78	100	0.1	0.1	22	27.6	30
Shampooers	29	33	0.0	0.0	4	13.3	7
Skin care specialists	38	51	0.0	0.0	13	34.3	17
Transportation, tourism, and lodging attendants	232	261	0.2	0.2	29	12.7	77
Baggage porters, bellhops, and concierges	69	76	0.0	0.0	7	10.4	16
Baggage porters and bellhops	49	54	0.0	0.0	4	9.0	11
Concierges	20	23	0.0	0.0	3	14.1	5
Tour and travel guides	45	54	0.0	0.0	9	20.1	27
Tour guides and escorts	40	49	0.0	0.0	9	21.2	25
Travel guides	5	5	0.0	0.0	0	10.5	2
Transportation attendants	118	131	0.1	0.1	13	11.2	34
Flight attendants	97	107	0.1	0.1	10	10.6	27
Transportation attendants, except flight attendants and baggage porters	21	24	0.0	0.0	3	14.0	7
Other personal care and services	2 853	3 593	1.9	2.2	739	25.9	1 418
Childcare workers	1 388	1 636	0.9	1.0	248	17.9	646
Personal and home care aides	767	1 156	0.5	0.7	389	50.6	519
Recreation and fitness workers	555	658	0.4	0.4	104	18.7	208
Fitness trainers and aerobics instructors	235	298	0.2	0.2	63	26.8	107
Recreation workers	320	360	0.2	0.2	41	12.7	101
Residential advisers	57	67	0.0	0.0	11	18.5	27
Personal care and service workers, all other	86	75	0.1	0.0	-11	-12.9	19
Sales and Related	15 985	17 203	10.6	10.3	1 218	7.6	6 171
Supervisors of sales workers	2 206	2 296	1.5	1.4	91	4.1	519
First-line supervisors/managers of retail sales workers	1 676	1 747	1.1	1.1	71	4.2	423
First-line supervisors/managers of non-retail sales workers	530	549	0.4	0.3	19	3.7	96
Retail sales	8 719	9 263	5.8	5.6	544	6.2	3 932
Cashiers	3 527	3 411	2.3	2.1	-116	-3.3	1 679
Cashiers, except gaming	3 500	3 382	2.3	2.0	-118	-3.4	1 664
Gaming change persons and booth cashiers	27	29	0.0	0.0	2	6.7	15
Counter and rental clerks and parts salespersons	715	819	0.5	0.5	104	14.6	318
Counter and rental clerks	477	586	0.3	0.4	109	22.9	291
Parts salespersons	238	233	0.2	0.1	-5	-2.2	27
Retail salespersons	4 477	5 034	3.0	3.0	557	12.4	1 935
Sales representatives, services	1 567	1 889	1.0	1.1	322	20.6	663
Advertising sales agents	170	205	0.1	0.1	35	20.3	64
Insurance sales agents	436	492	0.3	0.3	56	12.9	151
Securities, commodities, and financial services sales agents	320	399	0.2	0.2	79	24.8	161
Travel agents	101	102	0.1	0.1	1	1.0	8
Sales representatives, services, all other	540	690	0.4	0.4	151	27.9	278
Sales representatives, wholesale and manufacturing	1 973	2 155	1.3	1.3	182	9.2	617
Sales representatives, wholesale and manufacturing, technical and scientific products	411	462	0.3	0.3	51	12.4	142
Sales representatives, wholesale and manufacturing, except technical and scientific products	1 562	1 693	1.0	1.0	131	8.4	476
Other sales and related workers	1 520	1 599	1.0	1.0	79	5.2	440
Models, demonstrators, and product promoters	107	126	0.1	0.1	19	17.9	49
Demonstrators and product promoters	105	124	0.1	0.1	19	18.0	49
Models	2	2	0.0	0.0	0	9.8	1
Real estate brokers and sales agents	564	624	0.4	0.4	60	10.7	150
Real estate brokers	131	146	0.1	0.1	15	11.1	36
Real estate sales agents	432	478	0.3	0.3	46	10.6	115
Sales engineers	76	82	0.1	0.0	6	8.5	26
Telemarketers	395	356	0.3	0.2	-39	-9.9	139

Note: Data may not sum to totals or 100 percent due to rounding.

[1] Total job openings represent the sum of employment increases and net replacements. If employment change is negative, job openings due to growth are zero and total job openings equal net replacements.

Table 4-7. Employment, by Occupation, 2006 and Projected 2016—*Continued*

(Numbers in thousands, percent.)

Occupation	Employment				Change, 2006–2016		Total job openings due to growth and net replacements, 2006–2016[1]
	Number		Percent distribution		Number	Percent	
	2006	2016	2006	2016			
Sales and Related—*Continued*							
Miscellaneous sales and related	379	412	0.3	0.2	33	8.6	76
Door-to-door sales workers, news and street vendors, and related workers	200	207	0.1	0.1	7	3.7	34
Sales and related workers, all other	180	205	0.1	0.1	25	14.0	41
Office and Administrative Support	24 344	26 089	16.2	15.7	1 745	7.2	7 424
Supervisors of office and administrative support workers	1 418	1 500	0.9	0.9	82	5.8	374
First-line supervisors/managers of office and administrative support workers	1 418	1 500	0.9	0.9	82	5.8	374
Communications equipment operators	209	183	0.1	0.1	-25	-12.1	42
Switchboard operators, including answering service	177	163	0.1	0.1	-15	-8.4	37
Telephone operators	27	16	0.0	0.0	-11	-39.5	3
Communications equipment operators, all other	4	5	0.0	0.0	0	7.4	1
Financial clerks	4 007	4 482	2.7	2.7	476	11.9	1 283
Bill and account collectors	434	534	0.3	0.3	99	22.9	165
Billing and posting clerks and machine operators	542	566	0.4	0.3	24	4.4	93
Bookkeeping, accounting, and auditing clerks	2 114	2 377	1.4	1.4	264	12.5	594
Gaming cage workers	18	20	0.0	0.0	2	11.3	7
Payroll and timekeeping clerks	214	220	0.1	0.1	7	3.1	61
Procurement clerks	78	76	0.1	0.0	-2	-2.1	16
Tellers	608	689	0.4	0.4	82	13.5	347
Information and record clerks	5 738	6 389	3.8	3.8	651	11.4	2 320
Brokerage clerks	73	88	0.0	0.1	15	20.0	38
Correspondence clerks	17	20	0.0	0.0	2	12.0	7
Court, municipal, and license clerks	115	125	0.1	0.1	10	8.8	36
Credit authorizers, checkers, and clerks	69	63	0.0	0.0	-6	-8.4	21
Customer service representatives	2 202	2 747	1.5	1.7	545	24.8	1 158
Eligibility interviewers, government programs	112	116	0.1	0.1	3	3.1	23
File clerks	234	137	0.2	0.1	-97	-41.3	62
Hotel, motel, and resort desk clerks	219	257	0.1	0.2	38	17.4	127
Interviewers, except eligibility and loan	221	242	0.1	0.1	21	9.5	79
Library assistants, clerical	116	125	0.1	0.1	9	7.9	46
Loan interviewers and clerks	256	254	0.2	0.2	-2	-0.9	44
New accounts clerks	81	68	0.1	0.0	-13	-16.3	24
Order clerks	271	205	0.2	0.1	-66	-24.4	57
Human resources assistants, except payroll and timekeeping	168	187	0.1	0.1	19	11.3	31
Receptionists and information clerks	1 173	1 375	0.8	0.8	202	17.2	489
Reservation and transportation ticket agents and travel clerks	165	167	0.1	0.1	2	1.1	38
Information and record clerks, all other	245	213	0.2	0.1	-32	-12.9	39
Material recording, scheduling, dispatching, and distributing occupations	4 016	3 931	2.7	2.4	-86	-2.1	1 050
Cargo and freight agents	86	100	0.1	0.1	14	16.5	38
Couriers and messengers	134	134	0.1	0.1	0	-0.2	36
Dispatchers	289	306	0.2	0.2	16	5.7	89
Police, fire, and ambulance dispatchers	99	113	0.1	0.1	13	13.6	38
Dispatchers, except police, fire, and ambulance	190	193	0.1	0.1	3	1.5	51
Meter readers, utilities	47	42	0.0	0.0	-5	-10.3	15
Postal service workers	615	603	0.4	0.4	-12	-2.0	142
Postal service clerks	80	80	0.1	0.0	1	1.2	19
Postal service mail carriers	338	341	0.2	0.2	4	1.1	102
Postal service mail sorters, processors, and processing machine operators	198	181	0.1	0.1	-17	-8.4	21
Production, planning, and expediting clerks	293	305	0.2	0.2	12	4.2	92
Shipping, receiving, and traffic clerks	769	797	0.5	0.5	28	3.7	213
Stock clerks and order fillers	1 705	1 574	1.1	0.9	-131	-7.7	405
Weighers, measurers, checkers, and samplers, recordkeeping	79	70	0.1	0.0	-9	-11.3	21
Secretaries and administrative assistants	4 241	4 603	2.8	2.8	362	8.5	1 037
Executive secretaries and administrative assistants	1 618	1 857	1.1	1.1	239	14.8	497
Legal secretaries	275	308	0.2	0.2	32	11.7	76
Medical secretaries	408	477	0.3	0.3	68	16.7	133
Secretaries, except legal, medical, and executive	1 940	1 962	1.3	1.2	22	1.2	331
Other office and administrative support	4 715	5 001	3.1	3.0	286	6.1	1 318
Computer operators	130	98	0.1	0.1	-32	-24.7	21
Data entry and information processing	492	457	0.3	0.3	-35	-7.2	111
Data entry keyers	313	299	0.2	0.2	-15	-4.7	77
Word processors and typists	179	158	0.1	0.1	-21	-11.6	34
Desktop publishers	32	32	0.0	0.0	0	1.0	7
Insurance claims and policy processing clerks	254	251	0.2	0.2	-3	-1.3	31
Mail clerks and mail machine operators, except postal service	152	134	0.1	0.1	-18	-11.6	40
Office clerks, general	3 200	3 604	2.1	2.2	404	12.6	991
Office machine operators, except computer	94	91	0.1	0.1	-3	-2.7	31
Proofreaders and copy markers	18	19	0.0	0.0	1	6.4	5
Statistical assistants	23	24	0.0	0.0	2	7.6	12
Office and administrative support workers, all other	320	290	0.2	0.2	-30	-9.3	71
Farming, Fishing, and Forestry	1 039	1 010	0.7	0.6	-29	-2.8	251
Supervisors of farming, fishing, and forestry workers	53	53	0.0	0.0	0	-0.4	10
Agricultural workers	859	838	0.6	0.5	-21	-2.4	214
Agricultural inspectors	16	16	0.0	0.0	0	-1.1	4
Animal breeders	11	11	0.0	0.0	0	4.4	3
Graders and sorters, agricultural products	42	41	0.0	0.0	-1	-1.8	6
Miscellaneous agricultural	790	769	0.5	0.5	-20	-2.6	201
Agricultural equipment operators	59	56	0.0	0.0	-3	-5.0	15
Farmworkers and laborers, crop, nursery, and greenhouse	603	583	0.4	0.4	-20	-3.4	151
Farmworkers, farm and ranch animals	107	110	0.1	0.1	3	2.7	30
Agricultural workers, all other	20	20	0.0	0.0	0	0.1	5
Fishing and hunting	39	33	0.0	0.0	-6	-16.2	5
Fishers and related fishing	38	32	0.0	0.0	-6	-16.1	5
Hunters and trappers	0	0	0.0	0.0	0	-19.0	0

Note: Data may not sum to totals or 100 percent due to rounding.

[1]Total job openings represent the sum of employment increases and net replacements. If employment change is negative, job openings due to growth are zero and total job openings equal net replacements.

Table 4-7. Employment, by Occupation, 2006 and Projected 2016—*Continued*

(Numbers in thousands, percent.)

Occupation	Employment				Change, 2006–2016		Total job openings due to growth and net replacements, 2006–2016[1]
	Number		Percent distribution		Number	Percent	
	2006	2016	2006	2016			
Farming, Fishing, and Forestry—*Continued*							
Forest, conservation, and logging	88	87	0.1	0.1	-1	-1.4	23
Forest and conservation	20	21	0.0	0.0	1	5.5	9
Logging	69	66	0.0	0.0	-2	-3.4	14
Fallers	13	12	0.0	0.0	-1	-7.4	3
Logging equipment operators	40	40	0.0	0.0	-1	-1.3	8
Log graders and scalers	7	7	0.0	0.0	0	-5.3	1
Logging workers, all other	8	7	0.0	0.0	0	-5.9	2
Construction and Extraction	8 295	9 079	5.5	5.5	785	9.5	2 249
Supervisors of construction and extraction workers	772	842	0.5	0.5	70	9.1	178
First-line supervisors/managers of construction and extraction workers	772	842	0.5	0.5	70	9.1	178
Construction trades and related	6 422	7 044	4.3	4.2	622	9.7	1 719
Boilermakers	18	20	0.0	0.0	2	14.0	9
Brickmasons, blockmasons, and stonemasons	182	200	0.1	0.1	18	9.7	56
Brickmasons and blockmasons	158	174	0.1	0.1	15	9.7	48
Stonemasons	24	26	0.0	0.0	2	10.0	7
Carpenters	1 462	1 612	1.0	1.0	150	10.3	348
Carpet, floor, and tile installers and finishers	196	203	0.1	0.1	8	3.9	41
Carpet installers	73	72	0.0	0.0	-1	-1.2	11
Floor layers, except carpet, wood, and hard tiles	29	25	0.0	0.0	-4	-12.2	4
Floor sanders and finishers	14	14	0.0	0.0	0	-1.8	2
Tile and marble setters	79	91	0.1	0.1	12	15.4	24
Cement masons, concrete finishers, and terrazzo workers	228	254	0.2	0.2	26	11.4	92
Cement masons and concrete finishers	222	247	0.1	0.1	25	11.4	89
Terrazzo workers and finishers	7	8	0.0	0.0	1	10.9	3
Construction laborers	1 232	1 366	0.8	0.8	134	10.9	227
Construction equipment operators	494	536	0.3	0.3	42	8.5	138
Paving, surfacing, and tamping equipment operators	64	70	0.0	0.0	6	9.0	19
Pile-driver operators	6	6	0.0	0.0	0	8.3	2
Operating engineers and other construction equipment operators	424	460	0.3	0.3	35	8.4	118
Drywall installers, ceiling tile installers, and tapers	240	258	0.2	0.2	17	7.2	50
Drywall and ceiling tile installers	186	199	0.1	0.1	14	7.3	39
Tapers	54	58	0.0	0.0	4	7.1	11
Electricians	705	757	0.5	0.5	52	7.4	234
Glaziers	55	62	0.0	0.0	7	11.9	16
Insulation workers	61	66	0.0	0.0	5	8.5	19
Insulation workers, floor, ceiling, and wall	32	35	0.0	0.0	3	8.4	10
Insulation workers, mechanical	28	31	0.0	0.0	2	8.6	9
Painters and paperhangers	473	526	0.3	0.3	53	11.3	138
Painters, construction and maintenance	463	517	0.3	0.3	54	11.8	137
Paperhangers	10	9	0.0	0.0	-1	-12.2	2
Pipelayers, plumbers, pipefitters, and steamfitters	569	628	0.4	0.4	59	10.4	176
Pipelayers	67	72	0.0	0.0	6	8.7	20
Plumbers, pipefitters, and steamfitters	502	555	0.3	0.3	53	10.6	157
Plasterers and stucco masons	61	66	0.0	0.0	5	8.1	19
Reinforcing iron and rebar workers	30	34	0.0	0.0	3	11.5	11
Roofers	156	179	0.1	0.1	22	14.3	58
Sheet metal workers	189	201	0.1	0.1	13	6.8	59
Structural iron and steel workers	72	76	0.0	0.0	4	6.0	28
Helpers—construction trades	448	491	0.3	0.3	43	9.6	157
Helpers—brickmasons, blockmasons, stonemasons, and tile and marble setters	65	73	0.0	0.0	7	11.0	24
Helpers—carpenters	109	122	0.1	0.1	13	11.7	40
Helpers—electricians	105	112	0.1	0.1	7	6.8	34
Helpers—painters, paperhangers, plasterers, and stucco masons	24	24	0.0	0.0	0	-0.7	6
Helpers—pipelayers, plumbers, pipefitters, and steamfitters	85	95	0.1	0.1	10	11.9	32
Helpers—roofers	22	23	0.0	0.0	1	6.7	7
Helpers—construction trades, all other	38	42	0.0	0.0	5	12.6	14
Other construction and related	451	502	0.3	0.3	51	11.4	144
Construction and building inspectors	110	130	0.1	0.1	20	18.2	40
Elevator installers and repairers	22	24	0.0	0.0	2	8.8	8
Fence erectors	32	36	0.0	0.0	3	10.6	10
Hazardous materials removal	39	44	0.0	0.0	4	11.2	13
Highway maintenance	145	158	0.1	0.1	13	8.9	39
Rail-track laying and maintenance equipment operators	15	15	0.0	0.0	1	4.8	4
Septic tank servicers and sewer pipe cleaners	24	26	0.0	0.0	2	10.2	7
Miscellaneous construction and related	63	69	0.0	0.0	6	8.9	22
Segmental pavers	1	1	0.0	0.0	0	10.3	0
Construction and related workers, all other	62	68	0.0	0.0	6	8.8	22
Extraction workers	202	200	0.1	0.1	-2	-0.8	52
Derrick, rotary drill, and service unit operators, oil, gas, and mining	67	63	0.0	0.0	-4	-5.5	7
Derrick operators, oil and gas	19	18	0.0	0.0	-1	-5.8	2
Rotary drill operators, oil and gas	20	19	0.0	0.0	-1	-5.4	2
Service unit operators, oil, gas, and mining	28	26	0.0	0.0	-2	-5.4	3
Earth drillers, except oil and gas	22	23	0.0	0.0	1	6.5	8
Explosives workers, ordnance handling experts, and blasters	5	5	0.0	0.0	0	1.4	2
Mining machine operators	21	22	0.0	0.0	1	4.3	9
Continuous mining machine operators	10	11	0.0	0.0	0	4.6	4
Mine cutting and channeling machine operators	8	8	0.0	0.0	0	3.8	3
Mining machine operators, all other	3	3	0.0	0.0	0	4.9	1
Rock splitters, quarry	4	5	0.0	0.0	1	25.1	2
Roof bolters, mining	4	4	0.0	0.0	0	1.2	1
Roustabouts, oil and gas	44	43	0.0	0.0	-1	-3.2	13
Helpers—extraction workers	25	25	0.0	0.0	0	-0.2	7
Extraction workers, all other	10	10	0.0	0.0	0	0.4	2

Note: Data may not sum to totals or 100 percent due to rounding.

[1]Total job openings represent the sum of employment increases and net replacements. If employment change is negative, job openings due to growth are zero and total job openings equal net replacements.

Table 4-7. Employment, by Occupation, 2006 and Projected 2016—*Continued*

(Numbers in thousands, percent.)

Occupation	Employment				Change, 2006–2016		Total job openings due to growth and net replacements, 2006–2016[1]
	Number		Percent distribution		Number	Percent	
	2006	2016	2006	2016			
Installation, Maintenance, and Repair	5 883	6 433	3.9	3.9	550	9.3	1 502
Supervisors of installation, maintenance, and repair workers	465	499	0.3	0.3	34	7.3	143
First-line supervisors/managers of mechanics, installers, and repairers	465	499	0.3	0.3	34	7.3	143
Electrical and electronic equipment mechanics, installers, and repairers	661	690	0.4	0.4	29	4.4	170
Computer, automated teller, and office machine repairers	175	180	0.1	0.1	5	3.0	26
Radio and telecommunications equipment installers and reporters	205	209	0.1	0.1	5	2.3	55
Radio mechanics	7	6	0.0	0.0	0	-4.1	2
Telecommunications equipment installers and repairers, except line installers	198	203	0.1	0.1	5	2.6	54
Miscellaneous electrical and electronic equipment mechanics, installers, and repairers	281	301	0.2	0.2	19	6.8	89
Avionics technicians	16	17	0.0	0.0	1	8.1	3
Electric motor, power tool, and related repairers	25	24	0.0	0.0	-1	-4.2	10
Electrical and electronics installers and repairers, transportation equipment	21	22	0.0	0.0	1	4.3	5
Electrical and electronics repairers, commercial and industrial equipment	80	86	0.1	0.1	5	6.8	33
Electrical and electronics repairers, powerhouse, substation, and relay	22	21	0.0	0.0	-1	-4.7	8
Electronic equipment installers and repairers, motor vehicles	20	21	0.0	0.0	1	4.6	7
Electronic home entertainment equipment installers and repairers	40	41	0.0	0.0	1	3.0	5
Security and fire alarm systems installers	57	68	0.0	0.0	11	20.2	19
Vehicle and mobile equipment mechanics, installers, and repairers	1 771	2 003	1.2	1.2	232	13.1	589
Aircraft mechanics and service technicians	122	135	0.1	0.1	13	10.6	25
Automotive technicians and repairers	979	1 115	0.6	0.7	136	13.9	343
Automotive body and related repairers	183	204	0.1	0.1	21	11.6	64
Automotive glass installers and repairers	24	28	0.0	0.0	4	18.7	13
Automotive service technicians and mechanics	773	883	0.5	0.5	110	14.3	265
Bus and truck mechanics and diesel engine specialists	275	306	0.2	0.2	32	11.5	91
Heavy vehicle and mobile equipment service technicians and mechanics	188	206	0.1	0.1	18	9.5	55
Farm equipment mechanics	31	31	0.0	0.0	0	1.4	6
Mobile heavy equipment mechanics, except engines	131	147	0.1	0.1	16	12.3	42
Rail car repairers	27	28	0.0	0.0	1	5.1	7
Small engine mechanics	78	87	0.1	0.1	9	11.6	25
Motorboat mechanics	24	29	0.0	0.0	5	19.0	9
Motorcycle mechanics	21	24	0.0	0.0	3	12.5	7
Outdoor power equipment and other small engine mechanics	33	35	0.0	0.0	2	5.5	8
Miscellaneous vehicle and mobile equipment mechanics, installers, and repairers	128	153	0.1	0.1	25	19.1	50
Bicycle repairers	9	9	0.0	0.0	1	7.2	2
Recreational vehicle service technicians	14	17	0.0	0.0	3	18.2	5
Tire repairers and changers	106	127	0.1	0.1	21	20.2	42
Other installation, maintenance, and repair occupations	2 987	3 241	2.0	1.9	254	8.5	599
Control and valve installers and repairers	58	61	0.0	0.0	2	4.2	13
Mechanical door repairers	15	18	0.0	0.0	2	14.9	5
Control and valve installers and repairers, except mechanical door	43	43	0.0	0.0	0	0.3	8
Heating, air-conditioning, and refrigeration mechanics and installers	292	317	0.2	0.2	25	8.7	77
Home appliance repairers	57	58	0.0	0.0	1	1.5	14
Industrial machinery installation, repair, and maintenance	1 794	1 960	1.2	1.2	165	9.2	265
Industrial machinery mechanics	261	284	0.2	0.2	24	9.0	67
Maintenance and repair workers, general	1 391	1 531	0.9	0.9	140	10.1	174
Maintenance workers, machinery	84	83	0.1	0.1	-1	-1.1	14
Millwrights	55	58	0.0	0.0	3	5.8	10
Refractory materials repairers, except brickmasons	3	3	0.0	0.0	0	-11.5	1
Line installers and repairers	275	290	0.2	0.2	16	5.7	93
Electrical power line installers and repairers	112	120	0.1	0.1	8	7.2	43
Telecommunications line installers and repairers	162	170	0.1	0.1	7	4.6	50
Precision instrument and equipment repairers	68	77	0.0	0.0	9	12.8	28
Camera and photographic equipment repairers	4	4	0.0	0.0	0	-2.1	1
Medical equipment repairers	38	46	0.0	0.0	8	21.7	19
Musical instrument repairers and tuners	6	6	0.0	0.0	0	2.8	2
Watch repairers	4	4	0.0	0.0	0	-5.1	1
Precision instrument and equipment repairers, all other	16	17	0.0	0.0	1	4.3	5
Miscellaneous installation, maintenance, and repair	442	478	0.3	0.3	36	8.2	109
Coin, vending, and amusement machine servicers and repairers	48	46	0.0	0.0	-1	-3.0	13
Commercial divers	3	4	0.0	0.0	1	17.7	1
Fabric menders, except garment	2	2	0.0	0.0	0	-1.6	0
Locksmiths and safe repairers	26	32	0.0	0.0	6	22.1	11
Manufactured building and mobile home installers	12	11	0.0	0.0	0	-2.9	2
Riggers	12	12	0.0	0.0	0	-0.3	1
Signal and track switch repairers	7	7	0.0	0.0	0	-5.1	0
Helpers—installation, maintenance, and repair	163	183	0.1	0.1	19	11.8	58
Installation, maintenance, and repair workers, all other	168	181	0.1	0.1	13	7.5	24
Production	10 675	10 147	7.1	6.1	-528	-4.9	2 323
Supervisors of production workers	699	665	0.5	0.4	-34	-4.8	117
First-line supervisors/managers of production and operating workers	699	665	0.5	0.4	-34	-4.8	117
Assemblers and fabricators	2 075	1 982	1.4	1.2	-93	-4.5	424
Aircraft structure, surfaces, rigging, and systems assemblers	28	32	0.0	0.0	4	12.8	9
Electrical, electronics, and electromechanical assemblers	297	227	0.2	0.1	-70	-23.5	50
Coil winders, tapers, and finishers	23	16	0.0	0.0	-7	-30.5	4
Electrical and electronic equipment assemblers	213	156	0.1	0.1	-57	-26.8	36
Electromechanical equipment assemblers	60	55	0.0	0.0	-5	-9.1	10
Engine and other machine assemblers	45	41	0.0	0.0	-4	-8.6	11
Structural metal fabricators and fitters	103	103	0.1	0.1	0	-0.2	18
Miscellaneous assemblers and fabricators	1 602	1 579	1.1	0.9	-23	-1.4	336
Fiberglass laminators and fabricators	33	35	0.0	0.0	2	6.2	9
Team assemblers	1 274	1 275	0.8	0.8	1	0.1	265
Timing device assemblers, adjusters, and calibrators	3	2	0.0	0.0	0	-7.6	1
Assemblers and fabricators, all other	292	266	0.2	0.2	-25	-8.7	61

Note: Data may not sum to totals or 100 percent due to rounding.

[1]Total job openings represent the sum of employment increases and net replacements. If employment change is negative, job openings due to growth are zero and total job openings equal net replacements.

Table 4-7. Employment, by Occupation, 2006 and Projected 2016—*Continued*

(Numbers in thousands, percent.)

Occupation	Employment				Change, 2006–2016		Total job openings due to growth and net replacements, 2006–2016¹
	Number		Percent distribution		Number	Percent	
	2006	2016	2006	2016			
Production—*Continued*							
Food processing	705	764	0.5	0.5	59	8.4	267
Bakers	149	164	0.1	0.1	15	10.1	47
Butchers and other meat, poultry, and fish processing	398	431	0.3	0.3	34	8.5	160
Butchers and meat cutters	131	134	0.1	0.1	3	1.9	44
Meat, poultry, and fish cutters and trimmers	144	160	0.1	0.1	16	10.9	61
Slaughterers and meat packers	122	138	0.1	0.1	16	12.7	54
Miscellaneous food processing	158	169	0.1	0.1	10	6.5	61
Food and tobacco roasting, baking, and drying machine operators and tenders	19	21	0.0	0.0	2	10.8	9
Food batchmakers	95	105	0.1	0.1	10	10.9	35
Food cooking machine operators and tenders	44	42	0.0	0.0	-2	-4.7	17
Metal workers and plastic	2 258	2 087	1.5	1.3	-171	-7.6	455
Computer control programmers and operators	158	153	0.1	0.1	-6	-3.6	19
Computer-controlled machine tool operators, metal and plastic	141	136	0.1	0.1	-4	-3.0	17
Numerical tool and process control programmers	18	16	0.0	0.0	-2	-8.4	2
Forming machine setters, operators, and tenders, metal and plastic	161	140	0.1	0.1	-20	-12.7	43
Extruding and drawing machine setters, operators, and tenders, metal and plastic	94	87	0.1	0.1	-7	-7.2	26
Forging machine setters, operators, and tenders, metal and plastic	31	22	0.0	0.0	-9	-30.4	10
Rolling machine setters, operators, and tenders, metal and plastic	36	32	0.0	0.0	-4	-11.8	7
Machine tool cutting setters, operators, and tenders, metal and plastic	513	425	0.3	0.3	-88	-17.1	100
Cutting, punching, and press machine setters, operators, and tenders, metal and plastic	272	231	0.2	0.1	-40	-14.9	65
Drilling and boring machine tool setters, operators, and tenders, metal and plastic	43	33	0.0	0.0	-9	-22.2	9
Grinding, lapping, polishing, and buffing machine, tool setters, operators, and tenders, metal and plastic	101	85	0.1	0.1	-16	-15.7	10
Lathe and turning machine tool setters, operators, and tenders, metal and plastic	68	52	0.0	0.0	-16	-23.3	13
Milling and planing machine setters, operators, and tenders, metal and plastic	29	23	0.0	0.0	-6	-21.0	3
Machinists	397	384	0.3	0.2	-12	-3.1	61
Metal furnace and kiln operators and tenders	33	27	0.0	0.0	-6	-18.3	5
Metal-refining furnace operators and tenders	18	15	0.0	0.0	-3	-19.0	3
Pourers and casters, metal	15	12	0.0	0.0	-3	-17.4	2
Model makers and patternmakers, metal and plastic	16	15	0.0	0.0	-1	-5.9	4
Model makers, metal and plastic	9	8	0.0	0.0	-1	-6.3	2
Patternmakers, metal and plastic	7	7	0.0	0.0	0	-5.5	2
Molders and molding machine setters, operators, and tenders, metal and plastic	171	148	0.1	0.1	-23	-13.6	40
Foundry mold and coremakers	15	11	0.0	0.0	-3	-22.7	3
Molding, coremaking, and casting machine setters, operators and tenders, metal and plastic	157	137	0.1	0.1	-20	-12.8	37
Multiple machine tool setters, operators, and tenders, metal and plastic	97	97	0.1	0.1	0	0.3	20
Tool and die makers	101	91	0.1	0.1	-10	-9.6	13
Welding, soldering, and brazing	462	484	0.3	0.3	22	4.8	120
Welders, cutters, solderers, and brazers	409	430	0.3	0.3	21	5.1	107
Welding, soldering, and brazing machine setters, operators, and tenders	53	54	0.0	0.0	2	3.0	13
Miscellaneous metalworkers and plastic	150	122	0.1	0.1	-28	-18.4	30
Heat treating equipment setters, operators, and tenders, matal and plastic	27	23	0.0	0.0	-4	-14.8	5
Lay out workers, metal and plastic	10	8	0.0	0.0	-2	-19.8	2
Plating and coating machine setters, operators, and tenders, metal and plastic	42	37	0.0	0.0	-5	-12.2	12
Tool grinders, filers, and sharpeners	22	18	0.0	0.0	-4	-19.4	4
Metal workers and plastic workers, all other	49	36	0.0	0.0	-12	-25.1	8
Printing occupations	389	343	0.3	0.2	-46	-11.9	70
Bookbinders and bindery workers	72	57	0.0	0.0	-15	-21.3	10
Bindery workers	65	51	0.0	0.0	-14	-21.8	9
Bookbinders	7	6	0.0	0.0	-1	-16.9	1
Printers	317	286	0.2	0.2	-31	-9.7	59
Job printers	48	44	0.0	0.0	-4	-9.3	5
Prepress technicians and workers	71	56	0.0	0.0	-15	-21.1	11
Printing machine operators	198	186	0.1	0.1	-11	-5.7	44
Textile, apparel, and furnishings occupations	873	777	0.6	0.5	-97	-11.1	169
Laundry and dry-cleaning	239	262	0.2	0.2	23	9.7	77
Pressers, textile, garment, and related materials	77	74	0.1	0.0	-3	-4.4	6
Sewing machine operators	233	170	0.2	0.1	-63	-27.2	22
Shoe and leather	20	17	0.0	0.0	-3	-15.6	4
Shoe and leather workers and repairers	16	14	0.0	0.0	-2	-10.3	3
Shoe machine operators and tenders	4	3	0.0	0.0	-1	-35.7	0
Tailors, dressmakers, and sewers	77	76	0.1	0.0	-2	-2.4	14
Sewers, hand	23	21	0.0	0.0	-3	-12.2	4
Tailors, dressmakers, and custom sewers	54	55	0.0	0.0	1	1.9	10
Textile machine setters, operators, and tenders	122	88	0.1	0.1	-34	-27.9	27
Textile bleaching and dyeing machine operators and tenders	19	14	0.0	0.0	-6	-30.2	3
Textile cutting machine setters, operators, and tenders	19	14	0.0	0.0	-5	-27.4	6
Textile knitting and weaving machine setters, operators, and tenders	40	28	0.0	0.0	-12	-30.9	12
Textile winding, twisting, and drawing out machine setters, operators, and tenders	43	33	0.0	0.0	-11	-24.3	6
Miscellaneous textile, apparel, and furnishings workers	106	92	0.1	0.1	-14	-13.5	20
Extruding and forming machine setters, operators, and tenders, synthetic or glass fibers	18	15	0.0	0.0	-3	-17.6	4
Fabric and apparel patternmakers	9	7	0.0	0.0	-3	-28.6	2
Upholsterers	55	50	0.0	0.0	-5	-9.0	9
Textile, apparel, and furnishings workers, all other	24	21	0.0	0.0	-4	-14.8	6
Woodworkers	370	380	0.2	0.2	11	2.9	106
Cabinetmakers and bench carpenters	149	153	0.1	0.1	4	2.8	48
Furniture finishers	31	30	0.0	0.0	-1	-3.1	6
Model makers and patternmakers, wood	4	2	0.0	0.0	-2	-40.3	1
Model makers, wood	2	1	0.0	0.0	-1	-40.8	0
Patternmakers, wood	2	1	0.0	0.0	-1	-39.9	0
Woodworking machine setters, operators, and tenders	165	173	0.1	0.1	9	5.4	47
Sawing machine setters, operators, and tenders, wood	65	68	0.0	0.0	2	3.8	15
Woodworking machine setters, operators, and tenders, except sawing	100	106	0.1	0.1	6	6.4	31

Note: Data may not sum to totals or 100 percent due to rounding.

¹Total job openings represent the sum of employment increases and net replacements. If employment change is negative, job openings due to growth are zero and total job openings equal net replacements.

Table 4-7. Employment, by Occupation, 2006 and Projected 2016—*Continued*

(Numbers in thousands, percent.)

Occupation	Employment				Change, 2006–2016		Total job openings due to growth and net replacements, 2006–2016[1]
	Number		Percent distribution		Number	Percent	
	2006	2016	2006	2016			
Production—*Continued*							
Woodworkers, all other	20	21	0.0	0.0	0	1.6	5
Plant and system operators	325	327	0.2	0.2	2	0.8	95
Power plant operators, distributors, and dispatchers	47	48	0.0	0.0	1	2.0	18
Nuclear power reactor operators	4	4	0.0	0.0	0	10.6	2
Power distributors and dispatchers	9	8	0.0	0.0	0	-4.9	3
Power plant operators	35	36	0.0	0.0	1	2.7	13
Stationary engineers and boiler operators	45	47	0.0	0.0	2	3.4	9
Water and liquid waste treatment plant and system operators	111	126	0.1	0.1	15	13.8	35
Miscellaneous plant and system operators	122	106	0.1	0.1	-15	-12.6	34
Chemical plant and system operators	53	45	0.0	0.0	-8	-15.3	15
Gas plant operators	12	11	0.0	0.0	-1	-9.9	3
Petroleum pump system operators, refinery operators, and gaugers	42	36	0.0	0.0	-6	-13.4	12
Plant and system operators, all other	14	14	0.0	0.0	0	-2.6	4
Other production	2 981	2 822	2.0	1.7	-159	-5.3	619
Chemical processing machine setters, operators, and tenders	97	94	0.1	0.1	-3	-3.6	22
Chemical equipment operators and tenders	53	51	0.0	0.0	-2	-3.9	12
Separating, filtering, clarifying, precipitating, and still machine setters, operators, and tenders	44	43	0.0	0.0	-1	-3.2	10
Crushing, grinding, polishing, mixing, and blending	230	215	0.2	0.1	-16	-6.8	38
Crushing, grinding, and polishing machine setters, operators, and tenders	42	37	0.0	0.0	-5	-11.9	7
Grinding and polishing workers, hand	45	42	0.0	0.0	-3	-7.1	7
Mixing and blending machine setters, operators, and tenders	143	136	0.1	0.1	-7	-5.1	23
Cutting	107	98	0.1	0.1	-9	-8.4	16
Cutters and trimmers, hand	29	27	0.0	0.0	-2	-6.1	4
Cutting and slicing machine setters, operators, and tenders	79	71	0.1	0.0	-7	-9.3	12
Extruding, forming, pressing, and compacting machine setters, operators, and tenders	81	75	0.1	0.0	-7	-8.1	15
Furnace, kiln, oven, drier, and kettle operators and tenders	32	29	0.0	0.0	-3	-8.7	9
Inspectors, testers, sorters, samplers, and weighers	491	457	0.3	0.3	-35	-7.0	73
Jewelers and precious stone and metal	52	51	0.0	0.0	-1	-2.2	9
Medical, dental, and ophthalmic laboratory technicians	95	100	0.1	0.1	5	5.3	23
Dental laboratory technicians	53	55	0.0	0.0	2	3.7	12
Medical appliance technicians	12	13	0.0	0.0	1	9.5	3
Ophthalmic laboratory technicians	29	31	0.0	0.0	2	6.6	7
Packaging and filling machine operators and tenders	386	365	0.3	0.2	-21	-5.4	72
Painting workers	192	184	0.1	0.1	-8	-4.2	43
Coating, painting, and spraying machine setters, operators, and tenders	106	93	0.1	0.1	-14	-12.9	21
Painters, transportation equipment	54	59	0.0	0.0	5	8.4	15
Painting, coating, and decorating workers	31	32	0.0	0.0	1	3.6	7
Photographic process workers and processing machine operators	73	40	0.0	0.0	-33	-45.4	25
Photographic process workers	24	15	0.0	0.0	-9	-36.3	8
Photographic processing machine operators	49	25	0.0	0.0	-25	-49.8	17
Semiconductor processors	42	37	0.0	0.0	-5	-12.9	7
Miscellaneous production	1 102	1 078	0.7	0.6	-23	-2.1	268
Cementing and gluing machine operators and tenders	23	21	0.0	0.0	-2	-9.2	6
Cleaning, washing, and metal pickling equipment operators, and tenders	16	14	0.0	0.0	-2	-9.8	5
Cooling and freezing equipment operators and tenders	11	10	0.0	0.0	-1	-6.8	2
Etchers and engravers	14	13	0.0	0.0	-1	-4.8	3
Molders, shapers, and casters, except metal and plastic	56	57	0.0	0.0	1	1.3	13
Paper goods machine setters, operators, and tenders	113	93	0.1	0.1	-21	-18.2	27
Tire builders	23	20	0.0	0.0	-3	-12.0	8
Helpers—production	542	539	0.4	0.3	-3	-0.5	133
Production workers, all other	305	312	0.2	0.2	7	2.3	70
Transportation and Material Moving	10 233	10 695	6.8	6.4	462	4.5	2 952
Supervisors of transportation and material moving workers	414	461	0.3	0.3	47	11.4	132
Aircraft cargo handling supervisors	6	7	0.0	0.0	1	23.3	3
First-line supervisors/managers of helpers, laborers, and material movers, hand	182	205	0.1	0.1	23	12.5	60
First-line supervisors/managers of transportation and material moving machine and vehicle operators	226	249	0.2	0.1	23	10.2	69
Air transportation	137	154	0.1	0.1	17	12.4	57
Aircraft pilots and flight engineers	107	121	0.1	0.1	14	13.0	45
Airline pilots, copilots, and flight engineers	79	90	0.1	0.1	10	12.9	33
Commercial pilots	28	31	0.0	0.0	4	13.2	12
Air traffic controllers and airfield operations specialists	30	33	0.0	0.0	3	10.5	11
Air traffic controllers	25	28	0.0	0.0	3	10.2	9
Airfield operations specialists	5	5	0.0	0.0	1	11.8	2
Motor vehicle operators	4 335	4 704	2.9	2.8	368	8.5	1 117
Ambulance drivers and attendants, except emergency medical technicians	22	26	0.0	0.0	5	21.7	7
Bus drivers	653	721	0.4	0.4	67	10.3	153
Bus drivers, transit and intercity	198	223	0.1	0.1	25	12.5	51
Bus drivers, school	455	497	0.3	0.3	42	9.3	102
Driver/sales workers and truck drivers	3 356	3 614	2.2	2.2	258	7.7	877
Driver/sales workers	445	421	0.3	0.3	-24	-5.3	79
Truck drivers, heavy and tractor trailer	1 860	2 053	1.2	1.2	193	10.4	523
Truck drivers, light or delivery services	1 051	1 140	0.7	0.7	89	8.5	275
Taxi drivers and chauffeurs	229	258	0.2	0.2	30	13.0	59
Motor vehicle operators, all other	76	85	0.1	0.1	9	11.4	21

Note: Data may not sum to totals or 100 percent due to rounding.

[1]Total job openings represent the sum of employment increases and net replacements. If employment change is negative, job openings due to growth are zero and total job openings equal net replacements.

Table 4-7. Employment, by Occupation, 2006 and Projected 2016—*Continued*

(Numbers in thousands, percent.)

Occupation	Employment				Change, 2006–2016		Total job openings due to growth and net replacements, 2006–2016[1]
	Number		Percent distribution		Number	Percent	
	2006	2016	2006	2016			
Transportation and Material Moving—*Continued*							
Rail transportation	125	127	0.1	0.1	2	1.4	51
Locomotive engineers and operators	47	48	0.0	0.0	1	2.9	17
Railroad brake, signal, and switch operators	25	22	0.0	0.0	-3	-11.4	9
Railroad conductors and yardmasters	40	44	0.0	0.0	4	9.1	19
Subway and streetcar operators	7	8	0.0	0.0	1	12.1	3
Rail transportation workers, all other	7	6	0.0	0.0	-1	-18.7	2
Water transportation	84	98	0.1	0.1	14	16.1	39
Sailors and marine oilers	33	38	0.0	0.0	5	15.7	17
Ship and boat captains and operators	37	43	0.0	0.0	6	17.3	16
Captains, mates, and pilots of water vessels	34	40	0.0	0.0	6	17.9	15
Motorboat operators	3	3	0.0	0.0	0	10.9	1
Ship engineers	15	17	0.0	0.0	2	14.1	6
Other transportation	312	351	0.2	0.2	39	12.6	139
Bridge and lock tenders	4	4	0.0	0.0	0	-3.2	1
Parking lot attendants	135	152	0.1	0.1	16	12.1	53
Service station attendants	96	108	0.1	0.1	12	12.6	56
Traffic technicians	7	8	0.0	0.0	1	9.9	2
Transportation inspectors	26	31	0.0	0.0	4	16.4	13
Transportation workers, all other	44	49	0.0	0.0	6	13.3	14
Material moving	4 825	4 800	3.2	2.9	-25	-0.5	1 417
Conveyor operators and tenders	50	46	0.0	0.0	-4	-7.4	9
Crane and tower operators	46	48	0.0	0.0	1	2.8	10
Dredge, excavating, and loading machine operators	85	92	0.1	0.1	7	8.1	20
Dredge operators	2	2	0.0	0.0	0	6.7	0
Excavating and loading machine and dragline operators	80	87	0.1	0.1	7	8.3	19
Loading machine operators, underground mining	3	3	0.0	0.0	0	4.5	1
Hoist and winch operators	3	3	0.0	0.0	0	-1.2	1
Industrial truck and tractor operators	637	624	0.4	0.4	-13	-2.0	161
Laborers and material movers, hand	3 766	3 741	2.5	2.3	-25	-0.7	1 143
Cleaners of vehicles and equipment	368	420	0.2	0.3	52	14.0	192
Laborers and freight, stock, and material movers, hand	2 416	2 466	1.6	1.5	50	2.1	823
Machine feeders and offbearers	148	125	0.1	0.1	-22	-15.2	26
Packers and packagers, hand	834	730	0.6	0.4	-104	-12.4	102
Pumping station operators	29	25	0.0	0.0	-4	-12.9	12
Gas compressor and gas pumping station operators	4	3	0.0	0.0	-1	-17.5	2
Pump operators, except wellhead pumpers	11	9	0.0	0.0	-1	-12.5	4
Wellhead pumpers	14	13	0.0	0.0	-2	-11.9	6
Refuse and recyclable material collectors	136	146	0.1	0.1	10	7.4	47
Shuttle car operators	3	3	0.0	0.0	0	-8.3	1
Tank car, truck, and ship loaders	16	18	0.0	0.0	2	9.2	4
Material moving workers, all other	54	54	0.0	0.0	0	0.7	10

Note: Data may not sum to totals or 100 percent due to rounding.

[1]Total job openings represent the sum of employment increases and net replacements. If employment change is negative, job openings due to growth are zero and total job openings equal net replacements.

CHAPTER 5

PRODUCTIVITY AND COSTS

PRODUCTIVITY AND COSTS

HIGHLIGHTS

This chapter covers two kinds of productivity measures produced by the Bureau of Labor Statistics (BLS): output per hour (or labor productivity) and multifactor productivity. Multifactor productivity is designed to combine the joint influence of technological change, efficiency improvements, returns to scale, and other factors on economic growth. Industry data are based on the North American Industry Classification System (NAICS).

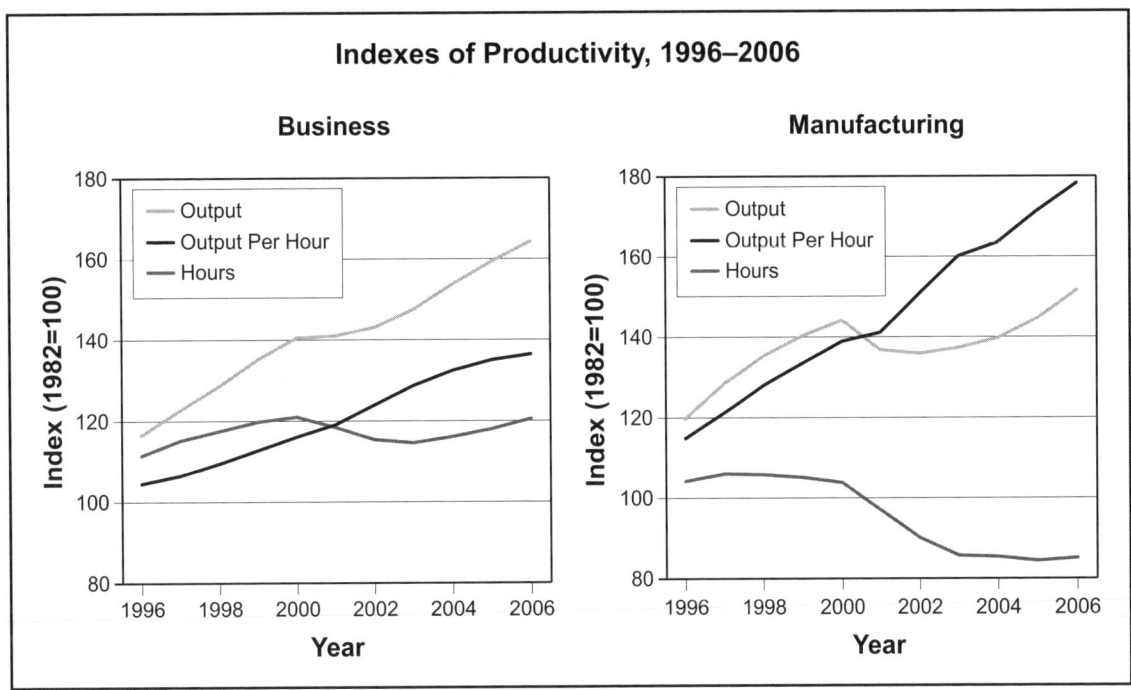

The levels of the output indexes for business and manufacturing are not directly comparable because of different sources of the data. However, trends can be examined in output per hour. The upward trend in manufacturing output per hour is much steeper than that the trend for business. In 2006, output per hour in business increased by only 1.0 percent. In contrast, hours in manufacturing increased slightly while its output increased substantially, leading to a 4.0 percent increase in output per hour. (See Table 5-1.)

OTHER HIGHLIGHTS:

- Unit labor costs in the business sector rose faster than the previous year—2.8 percent, compared with 2.0 percent. (See Table 5-1.)

- Output per hour in wholesale trade rose 4.3 percent in 2006, which was much faster than the previous year's increase of 0.6 percent. In retail trade, output per hour also increased more rapidly than it did the previous year (4.9 percent compared with 3.4 percent). (See Table 5-3.)

- Output per hour continued to decline in mining, decreasing by 10.1 percent in 2005. (See Table 5-2.)

- Multifactor productivity in the nonfarm business sector increased slowly in 2006, rising only 1.0 percent. Output per hour increased 1.6 percent, while output per unit of capital increased 0.7 percent. (See Table 5-4.)

NOTES AND DEFINITIONS

Concepts and Definitions

Measures of output per hour for the business, nonfarm business, and manufacturing sectors describe the relationship between real output and the labor time involved in production. The output measures for the business sectors and nonfinancial corporations are based on series prepared by the Bureau of Economic Analysis (BEA) of the U.S. Department of Commerce as part of the national income and product accounts (NIPAs). The Bureau of Labor Statistics (BLS) derives manufacturing output indexes by combining data from the Census Bureau, BEA, and the Federal Reserve Board. All of the output measures are chain-type annual-weighted indexes. This means that the relative prices (weights) used to combine output changes into an aggregate output measure are revised annually, thus minimizing the bias that arises from using fixed weights over long periods of time.

Business sector output is constructed by excluding the following outputs from gross domestic product (GDP): general government, nonprofit institutions, paid employees of private households, and the rental value of owner-occupied dwellings. Corresponding exclusions are also made in labor inputs. These activities are excluded because theoretical or practical difficulties make it impossible to use them as a basis for the computation of meaningful productivity measures. Business output accounted for about 78 percent of GDP and nonfarm business output accounted for about 77 percent of GDP in 2000. Manufacturing indexes are constructed by deflating current-dollar industry value of production data from the Census Bureau with deflators from BLS. These deflators are based on data from the BLS producer price program and other sources. To avoid duplication, intrasector transactions are removed when industry shipments are aggregated.

Productivity measures show the changes from period to period in the amount of goods and services produced per hour. Although these measures relate output to hours of persons engaged in a sector, they do not measure the specific contributions of labor, capital, or any other factor of production. Rather, they reflect the joint effects of many influences, including changes in technology, capital, economies of scale, utilization of capacity, the substitution of capital or intermediates for labor, the organization of production, managerial skill, and the characteristics and effort of the work force.

Measures of labor input are based mainly on the monthly BLS survey of nonagricultural establishments. Measures of employment and average weekly hours paid for employees of these establishments are drawn from this survey. Weekly hours paid are adjusted to hours at work using information from the National Compensation Survey program for 2000 onward and the annual Hours at Work Survey for years prior to 2000. (The Hours at Work Survey was terminated in 2000.) Supplementary informa-

tion for farm workers, the self-employed, and unpaid family workers is obtained from the Current Population Survey, the monthly survey of households conducted by the Census Bureau for BLS.

The *indexes of hourly compensation* are based mainly on the BLS hours data, discussed above, and employee compensation data from the NIPAs. Compensation includes wages and salaries and supplemental payments such as employer contributions to Social Security and private health and pension funds. The all persons' compensation data include estimates of proprietors' salaries and contributions for supplementary benefits. Real compensation per hour is derived by adjusting the compensation data with the Consumer Price Index Research Series Using Current Methods (CPI-U-RS) in order to reflect changes in purchasing power.

The *indexes of unit labor costs* are computed by dividing compensation per hour by output per hour.

Nonlabor payments are calculated by subtracting total compensation from current dollar output and thus include profits, depreciation, interest, and indirect taxes.

The *implicit deflator* reflects changes in all of the costs of production and distribution (unit labor costs plus unit nonlabor payments). To construct the implicit price deflator, the current-dollar measure of output in a sector is divided by the real output series.

Output per Hour and Related Series in Selected Industries

The BLS industry productivity program produces annual indexes of labor productivity, labor compensation, and unit labor costs for selected 4-, 5-, and 6-digit NAICS industries. These data series cover 60 percent of employment in the private nonfarm business sector and 100 percent of employment in the manufacturing, retail trade, and wholesale trade sectors. The data sources used in the industry measures differ from those used in the productivity and cost measures for the major sectors.

Output per hour indexes are obtained by dividing an output index by an index of aggregate hours. Although the measures relate output to one input (labor time), they do not measure the specific contribution of labor or any other factor of production. Rather, they reflect the joint effect of a number of interrelated influences, such as changes in technology, capital investment per worker, and capacity utilization. Caution is necessary when analyzing year-to-year changes in output per hour; the annual changes can be irregular and are not necessarily indicative of long-term trends. Conversely, long-term trends are not necessarily applicable to any one year or period in the future.

An *output index* for a particular industry is calculated using a Tornqvist index formula that aggregates the growth rates of the industry products between two periods of time, with weights based on the products' shares in industry value of production. The weight for each product equals its average value share in the two periods. The formula yields the ratio of output in a given period to that in the previous period. The ratios for successive years must be chained together to form a time series. The quantities of products used in the output index are measured with either deflated values of production or actual quantities. For most industries, output indexes are developed in two stages. First, comprehensive data from the Economic Census (conducted by the Census Bureau every five years) are used to develop benchmark indexes. Second, less comprehensive data are used to prepare annual indexes. The latter indexes are adjusted to the benchmark indexes by means of linear interpolation. Annual indexes are linked to the most recent benchmark index for the period following the most recent census year.

Indexes of labor input are employee hours indexes or all-person hours indexes. In manufacturing industries, employee hours are used. In nonmanufacturing industries where self-employed workers play a significant role, all person hours are used. For most industries, the hours series are based on hours paid. Total hours are calculated by multiplying the number of workers by average weekly hours. Employee hours are treated as homogenous and additive, with no distinction made between the hours worked by different groups. Annual indexes are developed by dividing the aggregate hours for each year by the base period aggregate.

Indexes of unit labor costs are calculated as the ratio of total labor compensation to real output, or equivalently as the ratio of hourly compensation to labor productivity (output per hour). Unit labor costs measure the cost of labor input required to produce one unit of output.

Indexes of total compensation measure the change in the total costs to the employer of securing labor. Compensation is defined as payroll plus supplemental payments. Payroll includes salaries, wages, commissions, dismissal pay, bonuses, vacation and sick-leave pay, and compensation-in-kind. Supplemental payments are divided into legally required expenditures and payments for voluntary programs. The legally required expenditures include employers' contributions to Social Security, unemployment insurance taxes, and workers' compensation. Payments for voluntary programs include all programs not specifically required by legislation, such as the employer portion of private health insurance and pension plans.

Multifactor Productivity

BLS calculates the annual growth of multifactor productivity for the U.S. private business sector. This measure is generally released about 14 months after the end of the measured, or target, year. The lag occurs because the process of calculating multifactor productivity requires detailed data from many sources. BLS uses a simplified methodology to make preliminary estimates of private business sector multifactor productivity changes available within a few months after the end of target year.

Annual measures of output per unit of combined labor and capital input (multifactor productivity) and related measures are produced for the private business and private nonfarm business sectors. The private business and private nonfarm business sectors for which multifactor productivity indexes are prepared exclude government enterprises.

Multifactor productivity measures refer to the ratio of an output index to an index of combined labor and capital services inputs.

Multifactor productivity growth reflects the amount of output growth that cannot be accounted for by the growth of weighted labor and capital inputs. The weights are associated cost shares. Labor's share is the ratio of compensation to current-dollar output. Capital's share is equal to the ratio of capital cost to current-dollar output. As with the output measures, the multifactor productivity growth weights are updated annually.

Capital services measure the services derived from the stock of physical assets and software. Physical assets included are fixed business equipment, structures, inventories, and land. Structures include nonresidential structures and residential capital that is rented out by profit-making firms or persons. Software includes prepackaged, custom, and own-account software. Financial assets are excluded, as are owner-occupied residential structures. Data on investments in physical assets and gross product originating by industry, which are used in measuring the rental prices, are obtained from BEA.

Labor input in private business and private nonfarm business is obtained by weighting the hours worked by all persons, classified by education, work experience, gender, and their shares of labor compensation. Additional information concerning data sources and methods of measuring labor composition can be found in BLS Bulletin 2426 (December 1993), "Labor Composition and U.S. Productivity Growth, 1948-90."

The *manufacturing multifactor productivity index* is derived by dividing an output index by a weighted index of combined hours, capital services, energy, materials and purchased business services. Weights (shares of total costs) are updated annually. The labor hours for the manufacturing measure are directly added and thus do not include the effect of changing labor composition, unlike those used for business multifactor productivity. The manufacturing sector coverage is the same in both the multifactor and the labor productivity series.

Sources of Additional Information

Productivity concepts and methodology are described in Chapters 10 and 11 of the *BLS Handbook of Methods*. More information on productivity can be found in BLS news releases. Additional information on multifactor productivity can be found in the June 2005 edition of the *Monthly Labor Review*. All of these resources can be found on the BLS Web site at <http://www.bls.gov>.

Table 5-1. Indexes of Productivity and Related Data, 1947–2006

(1992 = 100.)

Year	Business											
	Output per hour	Output	Hours	Hourly compensation	Real hourly compensation	Unit labor costs	Unit nonlabor payments	Implicit price deflator	Employment	Output per person	Compensation in current dollars	Nonlabor payments in current dollars
1947	32.2	20.4	63.4	7.0	41.1	21.8	18.6	20.6	55.7	36.7	4.4	3.8
1948	33.7	21.5	63.8	7.6	41.2	22.6	20.6	21.8	56.3	38.2	4.9	4.4
1949	34.5	21.3	61.8	7.7	42.3	22.4	20.4	21.6	55.1	38.7	4.8	4.4
1950	37.3	23.4	62.6	8.3	44.7	22.1	21.5	21.9	55.6	42.0	5.2	5.0
1951	38.5	24.9	64.6	9.0	45.4	23.5	23.7	23.6	57.1	43.6	5.8	5.9
1952	39.6	25.7	64.8	9.6	47.3	24.2	23.2	23.8	57.3	44.8	6.2	5.9
1953	41.0	26.9	65.6	10.2	50.0	24.9	22.6	24.0	58.1	46.3	6.7	6.1
1954	41.9	26.6	63.4	10.5	51.2	25.2	22.5	24.2	56.7	46.8	6.7	6.0
1955	43.6	28.7	65.8	10.8	52.7	24.8	24.0	24.5	58.3	49.2	7.1	6.9
1956	43.6	29.1	66.8	11.5	55.3	26.4	23.5	25.3	59.5	49.0	7.7	6.8
1957	45.0	29.6	65.8	12.3	57.0	27.2	24.2	26.1	59.4	49.9	8.1	7.2
1958	46.3	29.1	62.9	12.8	57.9	27.7	24.7	26.6	57.1	50.9	8.1	7.2
1959	48.0	31.4	65.5	13.3	59.9	27.8	25.2	26.8	58.9	53.4	8.7	7.9
1960	48.9	32.0	65.6	13.9	61.3	28.4	24.9	27.1	59.2	54.1	9.1	8.0
1961	50.6	32.7	64.6	14.4	63.1	28.5	25.3	27.3	58.6	55.8	9.3	8.3
1962	52.9	34.8	65.8	15.1	65.2	28.5	26.1	27.6	59.3	58.6	9.9	9.1
1963	55.0	36.4	66.2	15.6	66.6	28.4	26.6	27.7	59.6	61.0	10.3	9.7
1964	56.8	38.7	68.1	16.2	68.3	28.5	27.3	28.1	60.8	63.7	11.0	10.6
1965	58.8	41.4	70.4	16.8	69.7	28.6	28.4	28.5	62.5	66.3	11.8	11.8
1966	61.2	44.2	72.3	17.9	72.3	29.3	29.0	29.2	64.3	68.8	13.0	12.8
1967	62.5	45.1	72.1	19.0	74.1	30.3	29.5	30.0	65.2	69.1	13.7	13.3
1968	64.7	47.3	73.2	20.5	76.9	31.7	30.4	31.2	66.5	71.2	15.0	14.4
1969	65.0	48.8	75.0	21.9	78.0	33.7	30.8	32.6	68.6	71.1	16.4	15.0
1970	66.3	48.7	73.5	23.6	79.5	35.6	31.5	34.1	68.4	71.3	17.4	15.3
1971	69.0	50.6	73.3	25.1	80.9	36.3	34.1	35.5	68.5	73.9	18.4	17.3
1972	71.2	53.9	75.6	26.7	83.3	37.4	35.7	36.8	70.5	76.4	20.2	19.2
1973	73.4	57.6	78.5	28.9	85.1	39.4	37.5	38.7	73.5	78.4	22.7	21.6
1974	72.3	56.8	78.7	31.7	84.0	43.9	40.0	42.4	74.7	76.1	24.9	22.7
1975	74.8	56.3	75.3	34.9	84.8	46.7	46.3	46.6	72.4	77.7	26.3	26.1
1976	77.1	60.0	77.8	38.0	87.1	49.2	48.7	49.0	74.7	80.3	29.5	29.2
1977	78.5	63.3	80.7	41.0	88.3	52.2	51.5	52.0	77.9	81.3	33.1	32.6
1978	79.3	67.3	84.9	44.5	89.7	56.2	54.8	55.6	82.2	81.9	37.8	36.9
1979	79.3	69.6	87.7	48.9	89.9	61.6	58.2	60.4	85.4	81.5	42.9	40.5
1980	79.2	68.8	87.0	54.1	89.6	68.4	61.3	65.8	85.6	80.4	47.1	42.2
1981	80.8	70.7	87.6	59.3	89.6	73.5	69.1	71.8	86.4	81.8	52.0	48.9
1982	80.1	68.6	85.6	63.6	90.6	79.4	70.1	75.9	85.0	80.7	54.4	48.1
1983	83.0	72.3	87.1	66.3	90.6	79.8	76.3	78.5	85.8	84.3	57.7	55.2
1984	85.2	78.6	92.2	69.1	90.7	81.1	80.2	80.8	90.1	87.2	63.7	63.0
1985	87.1	82.2	94.3	72.5	91.9	83.2	82.0	82.7	92.3	89.0	68.4	67.4
1986	89.7	85.3	95.1	76.1	94.9	84.9	82.6	84.1	93.9	90.8	72.4	70.4
1987	90.1	88.3	97.9	79.0	95.2	87.6	83.1	85.9	96.4	91.5	77.3	73.3
1988	91.5	92.1	100.6	83.0	96.5	90.7	85.1	88.6	99.3	92.7	83.5	78.4
1989	92.4	95.4	103.3	85.2	95.0	92.2	91.3	91.9	101.5	94.0	88.0	87.1
1990	94.4	96.9	102.7	90.6	96.2	96.0	93.7	95.1	102.2	94.8	93.0	90.8
1991	95.9	96.1	100.2	95.1	97.5	99.1	96.7	98.2	100.6	95.6	95.3	92.9
1992	100.0	100.0	100.0	100.0	100.0	100.0	100.0	100.0	100.0	100.0	100.0	100.0
1993	100.4	103.1	102.7	102.2	99.7	101.8	102.6	102.1	102.1	101.0	105.0	105.8
1994	101.3	108.2	106.8	103.6	99.0	102.3	106.7	103.9	105.6	102.5	110.7	115.5
1995	101.5	111.4	109.7	105.8	98.7	104.2	108.3	105.7	108.5	102.6	116.1	120.6
1996	104.5	116.5	111.5	109.5	99.5	104.8	111.9	107.4	110.9	105.0	122.0	130.4
1997	106.5	122.7	115.2	113.0	100.5	106.1	113.8	109.0	113.9	107.7	130.2	139.7
1998	109.5	128.6	117.5	119.9	105.2	109.5	110.0	109.7	116.2	110.7	140.8	141.4
1999	112.8	135.2	119.8	125.8	108.0	111.5	109.4	110.7	118.1	114.5	150.7	147.9
2000	116.1	140.5	121.0	134.7	112.0	116.0	107.2	112.7	120.1	117.0	163.0	150.7
2001	119.1	141.0	118.4	140.4	113.5	117.9	110.0	114.9	119.0	118.4	166.1	155.0
2002	123.9	143.1	115.4	145.3	115.7	117.3	114.1	116.1	116.3	123.0	167.8	163.3
2003	128.7	147.5	114.6	151.2	117.7	117.5	118.3	117.8	116.0	127.1	173.4	174.5
2004	132.4	153.7	116.1	156.9	118.9	118.5	124.6	120.8	117.6	130.7	182.2	191.6
2005	135.0	159.3	118.0	163.2	119.7	120.9	130.8	124.5	119.7	133.1	192.5	208.3
2006	136.4	164.3	120.5	169.6	120.4	124.3	134.6	128.2	122.0	134.7	204.3	221.1

Table 5-1. Indexes of Productivity and Related Data, 1947–2006—*Continued*

(1992 = 100.)

Year	Nonfarm business											
	Output per hour	Output	Hours	Hourly compensation	Real hourly compensation	Unit labor costs	Unit nonlabor payments	Implicit price deflator	Employment	Output per person	Compensation in current dollars	Nonlabor payments in current dollars
1947	37.0	20.1	54.2	7.5	43.7	20.2	17.8	19.3	47.1	42.5	4.0	3.6
1948	38.0	20.9	55.1	8.1	43.9	21.3	19.4	20.6	48.2	43.5	4.5	4.1
1949	39.3	20.8	53.0	8.3	45.8	21.2	20.0	20.8	46.8	44.5	4.4	4.2
1950	41.9	22.9	54.7	8.8	47.9	21.1	20.8	21.0	47.9	47.8	4.8	4.8
1951	43.0	24.6	57.2	9.6	48.3	22.3	22.5	22.4	50.1	49.2	5.5	5.5
1952	43.8	25.3	57.9	10.1	49.9	23.1	22.3	22.8	50.7	50.0	5.9	5.6
1953	44.8	26.6	59.3	10.7	52.3	23.9	22.2	23.3	52.2	50.9	6.3	5.9
1954	45.6	26.1	57.3	11.0	53.6	24.2	22.3	23.5	50.8	51.5	6.3	5.8
1955	47.5	28.3	59.6	11.4	55.8	24.1	23.7	23.9	52.3	54.1	6.8	6.7
1956	47.2	28.8	61.1	12.1	58.3	25.8	23.1	24.8	53.8	53.5	7.4	6.6
1957	48.4	29.4	60.7	12.8	59.7	26.6	23.8	25.6	54.1	54.3	7.8	7.0
1958	49.4	28.7	58.2	13.4	60.4	27.0	24.1	26.0	52.2	55.1	7.8	6.9
1959	51.3	31.2	60.9	13.9	62.3	27.1	25.0	26.3	54.1	57.7	8.5	7.8
1960	51.9	31.8	61.2	14.5	63.9	27.9	24.3	26.6	54.7	58.1	8.9	7.7
1961	53.5	32.4	60.6	15.0	65.3	28.0	24.8	26.8	54.3	59.7	9.1	8.0
1962	55.9	34.6	61.9	15.6	67.3	27.8	25.8	27.1	55.3	62.6	9.6	8.9
1963	57.8	36.2	62.6	16.1	68.7	27.8	26.3	27.3	55.9	64.8	10.1	9.5
1964	59.6	38.7	64.9	16.6	69.9	27.9	27.2	27.6	57.3	67.5	10.8	10.5
1965	61.4	41.4	67.4	17.1	71.1	27.9	28.1	28.0	59.3	69.9	11.6	11.6
1966	63.6	44.4	69.8	18.2	73.2	28.6	28.7	28.6	61.6	72.0	12.7	12.7
1967	64.7	45.1	69.7	19.2	75.2	29.7	29.2	29.5	62.6	72.1	13.4	13.2
1968	66.9	47.5	71.0	20.7	77.8	31.0	30.2	30.7	64.1	74.1	14.7	14.4
1969	67.0	48.9	73.0	22.1	78.8	33.0	30.5	32.1	66.4	73.7	16.2	14.9
1970	68.0	48.9	71.9	23.7	79.8	34.9	31.2	33.5	66.4	73.6	17.0	15.2
1971	70.7	50.7	71.7	25.2	81.4	35.7	33.8	35.0	66.6	76.1	18.1	17.1
1972	73.1	54.1	74.0	26.9	84.0	36.8	34.9	36.1	68.6	78.8	19.9	18.9
1973	75.3	58.0	77.0	29.1	85.5	38.6	35.3	37.4	71.7	81.0	22.4	20.5
1974	74.2	57.3	77.2	31.9	84.5	43.0	38.1	41.2	72.8	78.6	24.6	21.8
1975	76.2	56.3	73.9	35.1	85.2	46.0	44.9	45.6	70.7	79.6	25.9	25.3
1976	78.7	60.2	76.5	38.1	87.4	48.3	47.8	48.1	73.2	82.3	29.1	28.8
1977	80.0	63.6	79.5	41.2	88.7	51.5	50.7	51.2	76.5	83.1	32.7	32.3
1978	81.0	67.8	83.7	44.8	90.3	55.3	53.4	54.6	80.7	84.0	37.5	36.2
1979	80.7	70.0	86.6	49.1	90.2	60.8	56.5	59.2	84.2	83.1	42.5	39.5
1980	80.6	69.2	85.9	54.4	90.0	67.5	60.4	64.9	84.4	82.0	46.7	41.8
1981	81.7	70.7	86.6	59.7	90.2	73.1	67.7	71.1	85.4	82.8	51.7	47.9
1982	80.8	68.4	84.7	63.9	91.1	79.1	69.3	75.5	84.0	81.4	54.1	47.4
1983	84.5	72.9	86.3	66.6	91.1	78.9	76.1	77.9	84.9	85.9	57.5	55.4
1984	86.1	78.9	91.6	69.5	91.1	80.7	79.2	80.1	89.4	88.2	63.6	62.4
1985	87.5	82.2	94.0	72.6	92.1	83.0	81.5	82.5	92.0	89.4	68.2	67.0
1986	90.2	85.4	94.7	76.4	95.2	84.7	82.4	83.9	93.6	91.2	72.3	70.3
1987	90.6	88.4	97.6	79.2	95.5	87.4	82.8	85.7	96.2	91.9	77.3	73.2
1988	92.1	92.4	100.4	83.1	96.7	90.2	85.0	88.3	99.3	93.1	83.4	78.6
1989	92.8	95.7	103.1	85.3	95.1	91.9	90.9	91.5	101.5	94.3	87.9	87.0
1990	94.5	97.1	102.7	90.4	96.0	95.7	93.5	94.9	102.2	95.0	92.9	90.8
1991	96.1	96.3	100.2	95.0	97.4	98.9	96.8	98.1	100.6	95.8	95.2	93.2
1992	100.0	100.0	100.0	100.0	100.0	100.0	100.0	100.0	100.0	100.0	100.0	100.0
1993	100.4	103.4	102.9	102.0	99.5	101.6	103.1	102.1	102.4	101.0	105.0	106.5
1994	101.5	108.3	106.6	103.7	99.1	102.1	107.3	104.0	105.7	102.5	110.6	116.1
1995	102.0	111.8	109.6	105.9	98.8	103.8	109.3	105.8	108.7	102.9	116.0	122.2
1996	104.7	116.8	111.5	109.4	99.5	104.5	112.1	107.3	111.2	105.0	122.0	130.9
1997	106.4	122.8	115.4	112.8	100.4	106.0	114.5	109.1	114.3	107.4	130.2	140.7
1998	109.4	128.9	117.9	119.6	104.9	109.3	111.0	109.9	116.9	110.3	140.9	143.1
1999	112.5	135.6	120.5	125.2	107.5	111.3	110.9	111.1	119.0	113.9	150.8	150.4
2000	115.7	140.8	121.7	134.2	111.6	116.0	108.7	113.3	121.1	116.3	163.3	153.1
2001	118.6	141.3	119.2	139.5	112.8	117.7	111.6	115.4	120.2	117.6	166.3	157.7
2002	123.5	143.4	116.1	144.6	115.1	117.1	116.0	116.7	117.4	122.2	167.9	166.4
2003	128.0	147.8	115.4	150.4	117.1	117.5	119.6	118.3	117.2	126.1	173.6	176.8
2004	131.5	153.9	117.0	155.9	118.2	118.5	125.5	121.1	118.8	129.6	182.4	193.1
2005	134.1	159.5	118.9	162.1	118.9	120.9	132.4	125.1	121.0	131.8	192.8	211.1
2006	135.4	164.5	121.5	168.5	119.7	124.5	136.5	128.9	123.3	133.4	204.8	224.5

Table 5-1. Indexes of Productivity and Related Data, 1947–2006—*Continued*

(1992 = 100.)

Year	Nonfinancial corporations												
	Output per hour	Output	Hours	Hourly compen-sation	Real hourly compen-sation	Unit labor costs	Unit nonlabor costs	Unit profits	Implicit price deflator	Employment	Output per person	Compen-sation in current dollars	Nonlabor payments in current dollars
1947	...	...	...	...	...	...	...	...	...	...	...	...	...
1948	...	...	...	...	...	...	...	...	...	...	...	...	...
1949	...	...	...	...	...	...	...	...	...	...	...	...	...
1950	...	...	...	...	...	...	...	...	...	...	...	...	...
1951	...	...	...	...	...	...	...	...	...	...	...	...	...
1952	...	...	...	...	...	...	...	...	...	...	...	...	...
1953	...	...	...	...	...	...	...	...	...	...	...	...	...
1954	...	...	...	...	...	...	...	...	...	...	...	...	...
1955	...	...	...	...	...	...	...	...	...	...	...	...	...
1956	...	...	...	...	...	...	...	...	...	...	...	...	...
1957	...	...	...	...	...	...	...	...	...	...	...	...	...
1958	52.8	25.4	48.0	15.0	67.8	28.4	23.5	47.2	28.9	43.6	58.2	7.2	7.6
1959	55.3	28.2	50.9	15.6	69.9	28.1	22.3	55.8	29.2	45.6	61.8	7.9	8.8
1960	56.2	29.1	51.7	16.2	71.4	28.8	23.3	50.2	29.4	46.6	62.4	8.4	8.9
1961	57.9	29.7	51.3	16.7	73.0	28.8	23.8	50.3	29.5	46.3	64.2	8.6	9.2
1962	60.4	32.2	53.3	17.4	75.1	28.7	23.4	54.5	29.7	47.8	67.3	9.3	10.2
1963	62.6	34.1	54.5	17.9	76.4	28.6	23.4	57.3	29.9	48.8	69.9	9.8	11.1
1964	63.6	36.5	57.4	18.2	76.8	28.7	23.3	59.7	30.1	50.6	72.1	10.5	12.1
1965	65.1	39.5	60.7	18.8	77.8	28.8	23.1	64.1	30.6	53.3	74.1	11.4	13.5
1966	66.2	42.3	63.9	19.8	79.9	29.9	23.3	63.6	31.3	56.3	75.2	12.7	14.4
1967	67.1	43.4	64.6	20.9	81.8	31.2	24.7	59.9	32.2	57.9	74.9	13.5	14.8
1968	69.5	46.1	66.4	22.5	84.5	32.4	26.2	60.0	33.4	59.9	76.9	14.9	16.3
1969	69.5	47.9	69.0	24.0	85.6	34.6	28.6	54.0	34.8	62.7	76.5	16.6	16.9
1970	69.8	47.4	67.9	25.7	86.6	36.9	32.2	44.4	36.4	62.8	75.5	17.5	16.8
1971	72.7	49.3	67.8	27.3	88.1	37.6	33.6	50.5	37.8	63.0	78.4	18.5	18.8
1972	74.2	53.1	71.6	28.8	90.0	38.8	33.9	54.1	39.0	66.1	80.3	20.6	20.9
1973	74.8	56.3	75.2	31.0	91.2	41.4	35.7	54.9	41.2	69.7	80.7	23.3	23.0
1974	73.3	55.3	75.5	33.9	90.0	46.3	41.1	48.4	45.2	71.1	77.8	25.6	23.8
1975	76.2	54.6	71.7	37.3	90.5	49.0	46.6	63.1	49.6	68.4	79.8	26.7	27.8
1976	78.6	58.9	75.0	40.3	92.6	51.3	46.4	71.4	51.9	71.5	82.4	30.2	31.3
1977	80.6	63.2	78.4	43.5	93.8	54.0	48.4	77.3	54.7	75.1	84.2	34.1	35.5
1978	81.7	67.4	82.5	47.6	95.9	58.2	51.2	79.1	58.4	79.3	84.9	39.2	39.5
1979	81.0	69.5	85.8	51.9	95.5	64.1	55.8	74.0	62.9	83.3	83.4	44.6	42.2
1980	80.8	68.8	85.2	57.2	94.7	70.8	64.9	66.9	69.0	83.6	82.3	48.7	45.0
1981	82.9	71.6	86.4	62.4	94.3	75.3	73.5	81.0	75.4	85.1	84.2	53.9	54.0
1982	83.1	69.9	84.1	66.5	94.7	80.0	81.3	75.2	79.9	83.1	84.0	55.9	55.7
1983	85.7	73.1	85.3	68.9	94.3	80.4	81.6	91.2	81.7	83.5	87.6	58.8	61.6
1984	87.8	79.7	90.8	71.9	94.3	81.9	81.3	107.6	84.1	88.4	90.1	65.3	70.4
1985	89.6	83.2	92.9	75.2	95.4	83.9	83.6	102.3	85.5	90.9	91.5	69.8	73.7
1986	91.4	85.2	93.2	78.9	98.3	86.3	86.3	90.2	86.6	92.2	92.3	73.5	74.4
1987	93.3	89.7	96.1	81.6	98.3	87.4	85.8	100.1	88.1	94.8	94.6	78.4	80.4
1988	95.7	94.9	99.1	84.9	98.8	88.7	86.8	111.6	90.3	97.9	96.9	84.2	88.6
1989	94.6	96.6	102.2	87.0	97.0	92.0	93.3	101.2	93.2	100.4	96.2	88.9	92.2
1990	95.4	97.8	102.5	91.1	96.8	95.5	97.3	96.9	96.1	102.2	95.8	93.4	95.1
1991	97.4	97.0	99.6	95.5	97.9	98.0	102.7	93.2	98.7	100.0	97.1	95.1	97.2
1992	100.0	100.0	100.0	100.0	100.0	100.0	100.0	100.0	100.0	100.0	100.0	100.0	100.0
1993	100.3	102.8	102.4	101.8	99.3	101.4	99.9	114.1	102.2	102.0	100.8	104.2	106.6
1994	102.2	109.2	106.8	103.5	98.9	101.3	100.8	131.7	103.9	105.7	103.2	110.6	119.1
1995	103.3	114.3	110.6	105.3	98.3	101.9	101.2	136.9	104.9	109.5	104.4	116.5	126.6
1996	107.1	120.6	112.6	108.5	98.6	101.3	100.0	150.0	105.3	112.3	107.4	122.1	136.7
1997	109.9	128.4	116.9	111.7	99.4	101.7	99.7	154.3	105.9	115.8	110.9	130.6	146.9
1998	113.7	135.8	119.5	118.3	103.8	104.1	99.5	137.0	105.9	118.7	114.5	141.4	148.8
1999	117.9	144.0	122.2	124.1	106.6	105.3	100.4	129.1	106.2	121.2	118.8	151.7	155.6
2000	122.4	151.5	123.7	133.0	110.6	108.6	104.2	108.7	107.5	123.6	122.6	164.5	159.7
2001	124.7	150.2	120.4	138.6	112.1	111.2	112.6	82.2	108.9	122.1	123.0	166.9	156.9
2002	129.7	151.5	116.8	143.6	114.3	110.7	110.8	98.0	109.6	118.6	127.7	167.7	162.7
2003	134.6	154.8	115.0	149.5	116.3	111.0	111.1	109.9	110.9	117.4	131.9	171.9	171.5
2004	139.3	162.4	116.6	153.9	116.7	110.5	109.5	145.1	113.3	118.9	136.7	179.4	193.3
2005	140.8	166.9	118.5	159.8	117.2	113.5	112.8	155.2	117.0	121.2	137.7	189.3	207.1
2006	142.6	172.8	121.2	165.4	117.5	116.0	113.8	162.9	119.6	123.5	139.9	200.4	219.3

. . . = Not available.

Table 5-1. Indexes of Productivity and Related Data, 1947–2006—*Continued*

(1992 = 100.)

Year		Manufacturing										
	Output per hour	Output	Hours	Hourly compen-sation	Real hourly compen-sation	Unit labor costs	Unit nonlabor payments	Implicit price deflator	Employment	Output per person	Compen-sation in current dollars	Nonlabor payments in current dollars
1947	. . .	. . .	. . .	. . .	. . .	. . .	. . .	. . .	. . .	. . .	. . .	. . .
1948	. . .	. . .	. . .	. . .	. . .	. . .	. . .	. . .	. . .	. . .	. . .	. . .
1949	. . .	. . .	. . .	. . .	. . .	. . .	. . .	. . .	. . .	. . .	. . .	. . .
1950	. . .	. . .	. . .	. . .	. . .	. . .	. . .	. . .	. . .	. . .	. . .	. . .
1951	. . .	. . .	. . .	. . .	. . .	. . .	. . .	. . .	. . .	. . .	. . .	. . .
1952	. . .	. . .	. . .	. . .	. . .	. . .	. . .	. . .	. . .	. . .	. . .	. . .
1953	. . .	. . .	. . .	. . .	. . .	. . .	. . .	. . .	. . .	. . .	. . .	. . .
1954	. . .	. . .	. . .	. . .	. . .	. . .	. . .	. . .	. . .	. . .	. . .	. . .
1955	. . .	. . .	. . .	. . .	. . .	. . .	. . .	. . .	. . .	. . .	. . .	. . .
1956	. . .	. . .	. . .	. . .	. . .	. . .	. . .	. . .	. . .	. . .	. . .	. . .
1957	. . .	. . .	. . .	. . .	. . .	. . .	. . .	. . .	. . .	. . .	. . .	. . .
1958	. . .	. . .	. . .	. . .	. . .	. . .	. . .	. . .	. . .	. . .	. . .	. . .
1959	. . .	. . .	. . .	. . .	. . .	. . .	. . .	. . .	. . .	. . .	. . .	. . .
1960	. . .	. . .	. . .	. . .	. . .	. . .	. . .	. . .	. . .	. . .	. . .	. . .
1961	. . .	. . .	. . .	. . .	. . .	. . .	. . .	. . .	. . .	. . .	. . .	. . .
1962	. . .	. . .	. . .	. . .	. . .	. . .	. . .	. . .	. . .	. . .	. . .	. . .
1963	. . .	. . .	. . .	. . .	. . .	. . .	. . .	. . .	. . .	. . .	. . .	. . .
1964	. . .	. . .	. . .	. . .	. . .	. . .	. . .	. . .	. . .	. . .	. . .	. . .
1965	. . .	. . .	. . .	. . .	. . .	. . .	. . .	. . .	. . .	. . .	. . .	. . .
1966	. . .	. . .	. . .	. . .	. . .	. . .	. . .	. . .	. . .	. . .	. . .	. . .
1967	. . .	. . .	. . .	. . .	. . .	. . .	. . .	. . .	. . .	. . .	. . .	. . .
1968	. . .	. . .	. . .	. . .	. . .	. . .	. . .	. . .	. . .	. . .	. . .	. . .
1969	. . .	. . .	. . .	. . .	. . .	. . .	. . .	. . .	. . .	. . .	. . .	. . .
1970	. . .	. . .	. . .	. . .	. . .	. . .	. . .	. . .	. . .	. . .	. . .	. . .
1971	. . .	. . .	. . .	. . .	. . .	. . .	. . .	. . .	. . .	. . .	. . .	. . .
1972	. . .	. . .	. . .	. . .	. . .	. . .	. . .	. . .	. . .	. . .	. . .	. . .
1973	. . .	. . .	. . .	. . .	. . .	. . .	. . .	. . .	. . .	. . .	. . .	. . .
1974	. . .	. . .	. . .	. . .	. . .	. . .	. . .	. . .	. . .	. . .	. . .	. . .
1975	. . .	. . .	. . .	. . .	. . .	. . .	. . .	. . .	. . .	. . .	. . .	. . .
1976	. . .	. . .	. . .	. . .	. . .	. . .	. . .	. . .	. . .	. . .	. . .	. . .
1977	. . .	. . .	. . .	. . .	. . .	. . .	. . .	. . .	. . .	. . .	. . .	. . .
1978	. . .	. . .	. . .	. . .	. . .	. . .	. . .	. . .	. . .	. . .	. . .	. . .
1979	. . .	. . .	. . .	. . .	. . .	. . .	. . .	. . .	. . .	. . .	. . .	. . .
1980	. . .	. . .	. . .	. . .	. . .	. . .	. . .	. . .	. . .	. . .	. . .	. . .
1981	. . .	. . .	. . .	. . .	. . .	. . .	. . .	. . .	. . .	. . .	. . .	. . .
1982	. . .	. . .	. . .	. . .	. . .	. . .	. . .	. . .	. . .	. . .	. . .	. . .
1983	. . .	. . .	. . .	. . .	. . .	. . .	. . .	. . .	. . .	. . .	. . .	. . .
1984	. . .	. . .	. . .	. . .	. . .	. . .	. . .	. . .	. . .	. . .	. . .	. . .
1985	. . .	. . .	. . .	. . .	. . .	. . .	. . .	. . .	. . .	. . .	. . .	. . .
1986	. . .	. . .	. . .	. . .	. . .	. . .	. . .	. . .	. . .	. . .	. . .	. . .
1987	89.0	92.4	103.8	81.3	98.0	91.3	86.8	88.3	104.6	88.4	84.4	80.3
1988	90.9	97.2	106.9	84.1	97.8	92.5	90.1	90.9	106.4	91.4	90.0	87.6
1989	91.8	98.8	107.6	86.6	96.6	94.3	95.2	94.9	107.0	92.4	93.2	94.1
1990	93.9	98.5	104.9	90.5	96.1	96.4	99.0	98.1	105.4	93.4	94.9	97.5
1991	96.3	96.8	100.5	95.6	98.0	99.2	98.5	98.8	101.7	95.2	96.0	95.4
1992	100.0	100.0	100.0	100.0	100.0	100.0	100.0	100.0	100.0	100.0	100.0	100.0
1993	102.5	103.9	101.3	102.0	99.5	99.5	101.1	100.6	100.1	103.8	103.4	105.1
1994	106.1	110.1	103.7	105.3	100.6	99.2	102.6	101.5	101.4	108.6	109.2	112.9
1995	110.9	115.8	104.4	107.3	100.1	96.7	106.3	103.1	102.8	112.7	112.0	123.1
1996	114.9	119.8	104.2	109.3	99.4	95.1	108.0	103.8	102.7	116.7	113.9	129.4
1997	121.3	128.6	106.0	112.2	99.8	92.5	107.6	102.7	103.6	124.1	119.0	138.4
1998	127.9	135.2	105.8	118.7	104.2	92.9	102.6	99.4	104.5	129.5	125.6	138.8
1999	133.5	140.3	105.1	123.4	106.0	92.4	102.9	99.5	102.9	136.4	129.7	144.5
2000	138.9	144.2	103.8	134.7	112.0	97.0	103.5	101.4	102.7	140.3	139.8	149.2
2001	141.1	136.8	97.0	137.8	111.5	97.7	102.0	100.6	97.9	139.8	133.7	139.6
2002	150.8	135.9	90.1	147.8	117.7	98.0	100.2	99.5	90.9	149.6	133.2	136.2
2003	160.1	137.3	85.7	158.2	123.1	98.8	102.8	101.5	86.6	158.5	135.6	141.1
2004	163.5	139.7	85.4	161.5	122.4	98.7	109.5	106.0	85.6	163.3	137.9	152.9
2005	171.3	144.6	84.4	168.3	123.4	98.2	118.0	111.5	85.0	170.0	142.0	170.6
2006	178.2	151.7	85.1	172.4	122.5	96.8	. . .	. . .	84.6	179.3	146.8	. . .

. . . = Not available.

Table 5-2. Average Annual Percent Change in Output Per Hour and Related Series, 1987–2005 and 2004–2005

(Number, percent.)

Industry	NAICS code	2005 employment (thousands)	Average annual percent change, 1987–2005			Annual percent change, 2004–2005		
			Output per hour	Output	Hours	Output per hour	Output	Hours
Mining								
Mining	21	562	0.6	-0.4	-1.0	-10.1	-2.1	8.9
Oil and gas extraction	211	126	1.7	-1.1	-2.7	-3.4	-3.6	-0.2
Mining, except oil and gas	212	213	2.7	1.1	-1.6	-1.9	3.5	5.5
Coal mining	2121	74	3.4	0.1	-3.2	-4.6	1.7	6.6
Metal ore mining	2122	29	3.4	1.9	-1.5	-4.3	-1.6	2.9
Nonmetallic mineral mining and quarrying	2123	110	1.6	1.5	0.0	2.2	7.8	5.4
Utilities								
Power generation and supply	2211	401	3.1	1.3	-1.8	6.2	5.2	-1.0
Natural gas distribution	2212	107	3.4	1.3	-2.0	4.4	-1.0	-5.1
Manufacturing								
Food	311	1 478	1.5	1.7	0.2	5.5	3.6	-1.8
Animal food	3111	49	3.9	2.5	-1.3	11.1	8.8	-2.0
Grain and oilseed milling	3112	61	3.0	1.8	-1.2	5.7	5.9	0.2
Sugar and confectionery product	3113	79	2.3	1.2	-1.0	11.1	2.5	-7.7
Fruit and vegetable preserving and specialty	3114	174	2.0	1.6	-0.4	4.6	0.2	-4.2
Dairy product	3115	132	1.6	1.0	-0.5	2.0	5.3	3.2
Animal slaughtering and processing	3116	504	1.0	2.4	1.3	8.7	5.2	-3.3
Seafood product preparation and packaging	3117	41	2.3	1.1	-1.2	14.8	5.1	-8.4
Bakery and tortilla manufacturing	3118	280	0.7	0.8	0.0	1.4	0.9	-0.5
Other food product	3119	159	0.9	2.1	1.2	-3.3	0.1	3.5
Beverage and tobacco product	312	192	1.4	0.3	-1.1	5.6	5.0	-0.6
Beverages	3121	167	2.5	1.8	-0.6	4.6	5.2	0.6
Tobacco and tobacco product	3122	25	1.5	-2.0	-3.4	13.0	4.5	-7.5
Textile mills	313	218	3.9	-1.1	-4.9	6.6	-1.3	-7.5
Fiber, yarn, and thread mills	3131	50	4.6	0.1	-4.3	-2.4	-3.4	-1.1
Fabric mills	3132	104	4.5	-1.5	-5.8	8.6	-3.0	-10.7
Textile and fabric finishing mills	3133	63	2.4	-1.3	-3.6	9.5	1.9	-7.0
Textile product mills	314	170	2.1	1.0	-1.0	8.8	5.3	-3.2
Textile furnishings mills	3141	96	2.2	1.1	-1.1	10.5	5.6	-4.4
Other textile product mills	3149	74	1.8	0.9	-0.9	6.2	4.6	-1.5
Apparel	315	257	2.5	-4.9	-7.2	7.6	-3.4	-10.2
Apparel knitting mills	3151	37	2.5	-3.9	-6.3	23.7	11.0	-10.2
Cut and sew apparel	3152	200	2.7	-5.1	-7.6	4.3	-6.7	-10.5
Accessories and other apparel	3159	21	-1.0	-4.2	-3.2	15.2	6.5	-7.5
Leather and allied product	316	40	2.9	-4.0	-6.8	9.8	4.2	-5.1
Leather and hide tanning and finishing	3161	7	0.7	-3.5	-4.2	10.3	-0.7	-10.0
Footwear	3162	18	1.9	-6.8	-8.5	6.9	2.2	-4.4
Other leather product	3169	15	2.5	-2.4	-4.8	14.1	10.1	-3.5
Wood product	321	560	1.4	1.3	-0.2	6.5	6.7	0.2
Sawmills and wood preservation	3211	119	2.8	1.4	-1.4	8.2	7.7	-0.5
Plywood and engineered wood product	3212	123	0.6	1.6	1.0	7.2	8.1	0.8
Other wood product	3219	317	1.1	1.0	-0.1	5.2	5.4	0.2
Paper and paper product	322	484	2.1	0.6	-1.5	1.5	0.5	-1.1
Pulp, paper, and paperboard mills	3221	142	3.4	0.3	-3.0	0.6	0.0	-0.6
Converted paper product	3222	343	1.4	0.7	-0.7	2.1	0.8	-1.2
Printing and related support activities	323	646	1.1	0.3	-0.8	4.5	2.3	-2.2
Petroleum and coal product	324	112	3.1	1.3	-1.8	0.3	0.2	-0.1
Chemicals	325	872	2.4	1.8	-0.6	5.5	1.9	-3.4
Basic chemicals	3251	150	3.1	0.5	-2.5	5.7	-0.7	-6.0
Resin, rubber, and artificial fibers	3252	108	2.8	1.3	-1.5	4.8	3.8	-1.0
Agricultural chemicals	3253	40	2.9	1.5	-1.3	14.2	9.6	-4.1
Pharmaceuticals and medicines	3254	288	1.2	4.0	2.8	3.6	0.8	-2.7
Paints, coatings, and adhesives	3255	68	1.8	0.7	-1.1	3.6	1.3	-2.3
Soaps, cleaning compounds, and toiletries	3256	114	3.3	2.7	-0.6	12.8	7.7	-4.5
Other chemical product and preparations	3259	104	2.8	0.6	-2.1	1.8	-1.2	-3.0
Plastics and rubber product	326	804	2.8	2.8	0.0	3.1	1.2	-1.9
Plastics product	3261	635	2.8	3.2	0.4	2.7	1.2	-1.5
Rubber product	3262	168	2.6	1.4	-1.2	4.3	0.8	-3.4
Nonmetallic mineral product	327	505	1.5	1.4	-0.1	5.4	4.0	-1.3
Clay product and refractories	3271	62	1.6	-0.2	-1.8	6.6	2.9	-3.5

Table 5-2. Average Annual Percent Change in Output Per Hour and Related Series, 1987–2005 and 2004–2005—*Continued*

(Number, percent.)

Industry	NAICS code	2005 employment (thousands)	Average annual percent change, 1987–2005			Annual percent change, 2004–2005		
			Output per hour	Output	Hours	Output per hour	Output	Hours
Manufacturing—*Continued*								
Glass and glass product	3272	108	2.2	0.8	-1.4	7.8	0.3	-6.9
Cement and concrete product	3273	240	0.7	2.0	1.3	2.6	4.8	2.1
Lime and gypsum product	3274	20	1.6	0.7	-0.9	12.1	7.4	-4.2
Other nonmetallic mineral product	3279	76	2.0	1.5	-0.5	6.9	5.6	-1.2
Primary metal	331	466	2.8	0.8	-2.0	1.8	1.8	0.0
Iron and steel mills and ferroalloy production	3311	96	5.2	1.9	-3.1	-2.6	-1.9	0.7
Steel product from purchased steel	3312	61	0.7	0.1	-0.6	2.1	4.2	2.0
Alumina and aluminum production	3313	73	3.0	0.7	-2.2	12.0	11.4	-0.6
Other nonferrous metal production	3314	72	1.3	-0.8	-2.1	-0.5	1.5	2.0
Foundries	3315	164	2.5	1.1	-1.4	3.3	1.4	-1.8
Fabricated metal product	332	1 522	1.6	1.4	-0.2	2.6	4.2	1.6
Forging and stamping	3321	111	3.0	2.0	-1.1	3.3	4.2	0.9
Cutlery and hand tools	3322	56	1.7	-0.1	-1.7	8.2	2.7	-5.0
Architectural and structural metal	3323	398	1.1	1.8	0.7	2.5	6.8	4.2
Boilers, tanks, and shipping containers	3324	91	0.5	-0.5	-1.0	0.4	-0.4	-0.9
Hardware	3325	36	2.3	-1.0	-3.2	5.1	-4.5	-9.2
Spring and wire product	3326	59	3.3	1.6	-1.6	9.3	2.7	-6.0
Machine shops and threaded product	3327	345	2.3	3.3	1.0	0.6	5.3	4.6
Coating, engraving, and heat treating metal	3328	145	3.3	3.6	0.3	8.5	9.7	1.1
Other fabricated metal product	3329	282	1.2	0.3	-0.9	1.3	2.1	0.8
Machinery	333	1 163	2.7	1.9	-0.9	5.3	6.9	1.5
Agriculture, construction, and mining machinery	3331	208	3.2	3.2	0.0	4.3	12.5	7.8
Industrial machinery	3332	124	2.7	1.9	-0.8	-3.6	-2.1	1.6
Commercial and service industry machinery	3333	111	1.5	-0.3	-1.8	6.6	0.6	-5.6
HVAC and commercial refrigeration equipment	3334	153	2.8	2.4	-0.4	3.7	4.5	0.9
Metalworking machinery	3335	202	2.2	0.8	-1.4	8.1	7.2	-0.8
Turbine and power transmission equipment	3336	98	2.8	2.1	-0.7	3.7	9.2	5.2
Other general purpose machinery	3339	268	2.8	1.9	-0.9	7.9	8.8	0.9
Computer and electronic product	334	1 306	13.1	10.4	-2.4	6.2	6.5	0.3
Computer and peripheral equipment	3341	205	24.6	19.5	-4.1	38.4	28.0	-7.5
Communications equipment	3342	147	7.4	4.8	-2.5	-2.7	-1.7	1.0
Audio and video equipment	3343	32	7.8	4.2	-3.3	0.0	0.4	0.4
Semiconductors and electronic components	3344	452	19.0	17.2	-1.5	7.1	6.6	-0.4
Electronic instruments	3345	436	3.9	1.4	-2.4	-3.9	1.2	5.3
Magnetic media manufacturing and reproduction	3346	35	2.9	2.8	-0.1	0.7	-3.2	-3.9
Electrical equipment and appliances	335	434	3.1	0.6	-2.4	5.3	2.1	-3.1
Electric lighting equipment	3351	61	2.2	0.5	-1.6	8.9	4.2	-4.3
Household appliances	3352	85	4.6	2.0	-2.5	3.4	-0.4	-3.7
Electrical equipment	3353	152	3.0	0.0	-2.9	5.4	1.5	-3.6
Other electrical equipment and components	3359	136	2.4	0.3	-2.1	5.2	3.7	-1.5
Transportation equipment	336	1 772	2.9	1.9	-1.1	4.1	4.4	0.3
Motor vehicles	3361	248	3.8	2.5	-1.2	3.5	-0.2	-3.6
Motor vehicle bodies and trailers	3362	171	1.7	3.0	1.3	3.2	6.0	2.8
Motor vehicle parts	3363	678	3.4	3.8	0.3	4.7	1.3	-3.2
Aerospace product and parts	3364	455	2.1	-1.2	-3.2	11.3	16.2	4.4
Railroad rolling stock	3365	27	4.4	4.8	0.3	-8.0	3.2	12.2
Ship and boat building	3366	153	1.9	1.1	-0.8	-4.0	2.5	6.7
Other transportation equipment	3369	40	5.2	5.5	0.3	8.7	9.9	1.1
Furniture and related product	337	566	2.2	1.8	-0.4	5.6	3.8	-1.7
Household and institutional furniture	3371	380	2.0	1.6	-0.4	6.8	4.2	-2.4
Office furniture and fixtures	3372	133	2.6	1.7	-0.9	4.3	3.6	-0.7
Other furniture-related product	3379	52	2.0	2.6	0.6	1.7	2.0	0.4
Miscellaneous manufacturing	339	652	3.3	3.3	0.0	8.3	7.7	-0.5
Medical equipment and supplies	3391	305	3.8	4.8	1.0	7.8	10.9	2.9
Other miscellaneous manufacturing	3399	348	2.7	2.0	-0.7	8.1	4.4	-3.4

Table 5-2. Average Annual Percent Change in Output Per Hour and Related Series, 1987–2005 and 2004–2005—*Continued*

(Number, percent.)

Industry	NAICS code	2005 employment (thousands)	Average annual percent change, 1987–2005			Annual percent change, 2004–2005		
			Output per hour	Output	Hours	Output per hour	Output	Hours
Transportation and Warehousing								
Air transportation	481	472	2.9	3.6	0.6	7.7	5.3	-2.2
Line-haul railroads	482111	182	4.9	2.5	-2.3	-5.4	0.2	5.9
General freight trucking, long distance	48412	901	1.5	3.4	1.8	1.7	5.1	3.3
Used household and office goods, moving	48421	106	-1.0	0.6	1.6	-0.2	5.4	5.6
Postal service	491	774	1.1	1.2	0.1	1.1	1.2	0.2
Couriers and messengers	492	612	-1.0	2.4	3.4	-1.7	-0.6	1.2
Information								
Publishing	511	953	4.3	5.0	0.7	4.1	3.6	-0.6
Newspaper, book, and directory publishers	5111	714	0.2	-0.3	-0.5	1.6	0.5	-1.1
Software publishers	5112	239	17.0	25.2	7.1	6.5	7.6	1.1
Motion picture and video exhibition	51213	135	0.7	2.0	1.3	-1.1	-6.6	-5.5
Broadcasting, except Internet	515	341	0.9	2.4	1.5	4.6	6.6	1.9
Radio and television broadcasting	5151	249	0.2	0.5	0.3	5.1	5.1	0.0
Cable and other subscription programming	5152	92	2.4	8.2	5.6	2.4	9.1	6.5
Wired telecommunications carriers	5171	519	5.1	3.6	-1.5	4.7	-1.8	-6.1
Wireless telecommunications carriers	5172	194	9.6	24.3	13.5	34.4	28.2	-4.6
Cable and other program distribution	5175	137	0.3	5.8	5.5	-2.9	5.4	8.5
Finance and Insurance								
Commercial banking	52211	1 296	2.2	2.0	-0.2	-0.1	2.2	2.4
Real Estate Rental and Leasing								
Passenger car rental	532111	129	1.0	3.7	2.7	-6.6	3.2	10.5
Truck, trailer, and RV rental and leasing	53212	63	5.0	4.8	-0.2	7.3	9.0	1.6
Videotape and disc rental	53223	151	4.0	6.8	2.7	0.7	-3.0	-3.7
Professional and Technical Services								
Tax preparation services	541213	142	1.4	4.4	2.9	6.9	6.3	-0.6
Architectural services	54131	219	1.8	4.1	2.3	4.8	10.9	5.9
Engineering services	54133	879	1.3	3.5	2.1	5.9	13.3	6.9
Advertising agencies	54181	184	1.8	1.7	0.0	-1.4	1.2	2.6
Photography studios, portrait	541921	80	-0.3	2.7	3.0	0.4	4.3	3.9
Administrative and Support Services								
Travel agencies	56151	124	4.2	3.3	-0.9	12.4	9.2	-2.9
Janitorial services	56172	1 146	2.7	4.6	1.8	4.7	5.4	0.7
Health Care and Social Assistance[1]								
Medical and diagnostic laboratories	6215	204	3.9	7.2	3.2	-1.4	3.7	5.2
Medical laboratories	621511	140	3.0	5.9	2.8	-2.7	2.6	5.5
Diagnostic imaging centers	621512	64	5.1	9.4	4.1	0.9	5.3	4.4
Accommodation and Food Services								
Traveler accommodations	7211	1 794	1.7	2.9	1.1	-4.1	0.6	4.9
Other Services								
Automotive repair and maintenance	8111	1 182	1.5	2.6	1.1	0.5	2.2	1.7
Hair, nail, and skin care services	81211	909	2.5	3.5	1.0	4.3	4.3	0.0
Funeral homes and funeral services	81221	111	-0.6	0.3	0.9	0.3	0.4	0.1
Dry-cleaning and laundry services	8123	362	1.2	0.6	-0.7	9.2	2.7	-5.9
Photofinishing	81292	32	0.9	-4.3	-5.2	10.9	-14.8	-23.2

[1]For NAICS industries 6215, 621511, and 621512, average annual percent changes are for 1994–2005.

Table 5-3. Average Annual Percent Change in Output Per Hour and Related Series: Retail Trade, Wholesale Trade, and Food Services and Drinking Places, 1987–2006 and 2005–2006

(Number, percent.)

Industry	NAICS code	2006 employment (thousands)	Average annual percent change, 1987–2006			Annual percent change, 2005–2006		
			Output per hour	Output	Hours	Output per hour	Output	Hours
Wholesale Trade	42	6 118	3.5	4.2	0.7	4.3	6.6	2.2
Durable goods	423	3 185	5.6	6.2	0.5	5.1	8.3	3.0
Motor vehicles and parts	4231	365	4.3	4.2	-0.1	13.0	12.7	-0.2
Furniture and furnishings	4232	123	2.8	3.0	0.2	7.4	8.7	1.2
Lumber and construction supplies	4233	274	1.2	3.3	2.0	-2.5	2.8	5.5
Commercial equipment	4234	667	15.6	16.4	0.6	10.0	14.0	3.6
Metals and minerals	4235	128	-0.1	0.4	0.5	-3.1	1.0	4.2
Electric goods	4236	351	9.1	8.9	-0.2	10.6	9.5	-0.9
Hardware and plumbing	4237	260	1.3	2.8	1.4	0.9	5.6	4.7
Machinery and supplies	4238	694	2.7	2.8	0.1	3.8	6.1	2.2
Miscellaneous durable goods	4239	324	1.5	2.7	1.1	-10.2	-2.6	8.5
Nondurable goods	424	2 143	1.3	1.7	0.3	2.7	4.3	1.5
Paper and paper product	4241	161	2.5	2.0	-0.5	-1.3	0.9	2.2
Druggists' goods	4242	217	2.8	5.3	2.4	6.7	9.2	2.4
Apparel and piece goods	4243	166	3.0	2.8	-0.2	6.8	8.5	1.6
Grocery and related product	4244	747	0.9	1.9	1.0	0.7	3.6	2.8
Farm product (raw materials)	4245	77	2.1	-0.6	-2.7	11.8	6.3	-4.9
Chemicals	4246	137	-0.1	0.8	0.9	1.3	-0.8	-2.1
Petroleum	4247	103	3.3	0.4	-2.9	3.4	3.4	0.0
Alcoholic beverages	4248	155	0.4	2.0	1.5	2.6	5.1	2.4
Miscellaneous nondurable goods	4249	382	0.7	0.8	0.1	2.0	3.1	1.1
Electronic markets and agents and brokers	425	790	2.0	4.7	2.6	7.2	8.2	0.9
Retail Trade	44-45	16 389	3.4	4.2	0.8	4.9	4.1	-0.8
Motor vehicle and parts dealers	441	2 002	2.7	3.8	1.1	2.2	0.5	-1.6
Automobile dealers	4411	1 306	2.5	3.7	1.2	2.4	1.1	-1.3
Other motor vehicle dealers	4412	181	3.5	6.0	2.4	0.8	-3.5	-4.3
Auto parts, accessory, and tire stores	4413	516	2.5	3.0	0.5	-0.1	-1.7	-1.6
Furniture and home furnishings stores	442	650	4.2	5.4	1.2	7.4	8.0	0.6
Furniture stores	4421	322	3.7	4.6	0.9	8.4	5.6	-2.6
Home furnishings stores	4422	328	4.8	6.4	1.5	6.6	10.9	4.0
Electronics and appliance stores	443	571	13.4	15.6	1.9	12.6	17.0	3.9
Building material and garden supply stores	444	1 378	3.4	5.5	2.0	6.5	7.9	1.3
Building material and supplies dealers	4441	1 208	3.3	5.7	2.3	5.9	7.5	1.5
Lawn and garden equipment and supplies stores	4442	169	4.3	4.4	0.0	10.7	10.9	0.2
Food and beverage stores	445	2 933	0.5	0.4	-0.1	3.2	2.8	-0.5
Grocery stores	4451	2 524	0.4	0.4	0.0	1.8	2.1	0.3
Specialty food stores	4452	255	0.5	0.4	-0.2	20.0	10.1	-8.3
Beer, wine, and liquor stores	4453	154	2.5	0.9	-1.6	5.0	7.7	2.6
Health and personal care stores	446	987	2.7	3.9	1.2	4.9	4.1	-0.7
Gasoline stations	447	882	2.0	1.5	-0.4	-2.3	-1.3	1.0
Clothing and clothing accessories stores	448	1 537	4.9	5.0	0.1	10.5	6.2	-3.9
Clothing stores	4481	1 142	5.0	5.5	0.5	10.9	6.5	-4.0
Shoe stores	4482	185	4.4	3.0	-1.4	12.3	5.9	-5.7
Jewelry, luggage, and leather goods stores	4483	210	4.5	4.8	0.3	7.1	4.6	-2.3
Sporting goods, hobby, book, and music stores	451	726	4.6	5.1	0.5	6.3	7.0	0.7
Sporting goods and musical instrument stores	4511	520	5.5	5.9	0.4	11.8	12.2	0.4
Book, periodical, and music stores	4512	207	2.4	3.2	0.8	-6.6	-5.4	1.3
General merchandise stores	452	2 944	3.9	5.6	1.6	5.1	5.0	0.0
Department stores	4521	1 563	1.4	2.5	1.1	2.9	-0.5	-3.4
Other general merchandise stores	4529	1 381	7.3	9.6	2.1	5.4	8.8	3.3
Miscellaneous store retailers	453	1 084	4.8	5.2	0.4	12.2	8.2	-3.6
Florists	4531	119	2.6	0.2	-2.3	3.9	-4.6	-8.2
Office supply, stationery, and gift stores	4532	421	6.8	7.1	0.2	14.7	10.3	-3.8
Used merchandise stores	4533	191	5.1	6.5	1.3	4.4	11.0	6.3
Other miscellaneous store retailers	4539	353	2.9	4.4	1.4	14.5	7.6	-6.1
Nonstore retailers	454	695	8.9	9.3	0.4	17.3	10.1	-6.2
Electronic shopping and mail-order houses	4541	296	12.0	16.0	3.6	18.2	14.7	-2.9
Vending machine operators	4542	66	0.8	-1.5	-2.3	5.4	-4.8	-9.6
Direct selling establishments	4543	333	3.5	2.4	-1.1	11.6	1.9	-8.7
Food Services and Drinking Places	722	9 656	0.8	2.5	1.7	2.4	4.9	2.4
Full-service restaurants	7221	4 495	0.9	2.7	1.8	2.9	5.7	2.8
Limited-service eating places	7222	4 082	0.8	2.7	2.0	3.2	5.4	2.1
Special food services	7223	700	1.4	2.5	1.1	-2.4	2.8	5.3
Drinking places, alcoholic beverages	7224	380	-0.5	-0.5	0.0	2.6	-2.3	-4.8

Table 5-4. Indexes of Multifactor Productivity and Related Measures, 1987–2006

(2000 = 100.)

Sector	1987	1988	1989	1990	1991	1992	1993	1994	1995	1996	1997
PRIVATE BUSINESS											
Productivity											
Output per hour of all persons	77.3	78.5	79.3	81.0	82.4	86.0	86.4	87.2	87.4	90.0	91.7
Output per unit of capital	106.5	107.2	107.0	105.5	102.0	103.9	104.0	105.6	104.4	104.5	104.7
Multifactor productivity	89.7	90.3	90.6	91.2	90.6	93.0	93.2	93.9	93.7	95.3	96.2
Output	62.4	65.2	67.6	68.6	68.1	70.9	73.2	76.8	79.2	82.8	87.2
Inputs											
Labor input	75.4	78.1	80.6	80.5	79.4	80.2	82.6	86.3	88.8	90.6	94.2
Capital services	58.6	60.8	63.1	65.1	66.8	68.3	70.3	72.8	75.8	79.2	83.3
Combined units of labor and capital inputs	69.6	72.2	74.6	75.2	75.2	76.2	78.5	81.8	84.5	86.9	90.7
Capital services per hour for all persons	72.5	73.2	74.1	76.8	80.8	82.7	83.0	82.6	83.8	86.1	87.6
PRIVATE NONFARM BUSINESS											
Productivity											
Output per hour of all persons	78.0	79.3	79.9	81.4	82.9	86.3	86.7	87.7	88.2	90.5	92.0
Output per unit of capital	108.3	109.4	108.9	107.1	103.3	104.9	105.2	106.5	105.5	105.3	105.1
Multifactor productivity	90.6	91.4	91.5	91.9	91.3	93.4	93.7	94.5	94.5	95.8	96.4
Output	62.4	65.3	67.6	68.6	68.1	70.8	73.2	76.7	79.3	82.8	87.2
Inputs											
Labor input	74.7	77.5	80.0	80.0	78.9	79.8	82.3	85.7	88.2	90.2	93.9
Capital services	57.7	59.7	62.1	64.1	65.9	67.5	69.6	72.1	75.2	78.7	82.9
Combined units of labor and capital inputs	68.9	71.5	73.9	74.7	74.6	75.7	78.1	81.2	83.9	86.5	90.4
Capital services per hour for all persons	72.0	72.5	73.3	76.1	80.2	82.2	82.4	82.4	83.6	86.0	87.5
MANUFACTURING											
Productivity											
Output per hour of all persons	63.9	65.2	65.9	67.3	69.1	71.7	73.5	76.1	79.4	82.4	86.9
Output per unit of capital	95.4	98.7	98.2	95.2	91.5	92.3	93.6	96.6	98.2	97.6	100.2
Multifactor productivity	84.8	86.3	85.8	85.2	85.0	84.5	86.7	89.0	90.6	91.0	93.6
Output	64.1	67.4	68.5	68.3	67.1	69.4	72.1	76.4	80.4	83.1	89.2
Inputs											
Hours at work of all persons	100.3	103.4	104.0	101.5	97.2	96.7	98.0	100.3	101.2	100.8	102.6
Capital services	67.2	68.3	69.8	71.7	73.4	75.1	77.0	79.0	81.8	85.2	89.0
Energy	99.3	103.3	103.0	105.2	104.8	103.8	107.1	110.4	113.7	110.3	108.2
Non-energy materials	62.9	63.8	65.1	66.0	65.6	71.3	71.9	74.8	78.8	86.0	92.9
Purchased business services	65.3	71.0	75.3	76.6	76.0	81.5	81.7	84.7	88.9	88.5	92.1
Combined units of all inputs	75.6	78.1	79.9	80.1	79.0	82.1	83.1	85.8	88.7	91.3	95.3

Table 5-4. Indexes of Multifactor Productivity and Related Measures, 1987–2006 —*Continued*

(2000 = 100.)

Sector	1998	1999	2000	2001	2002	2003	2004	2005	2006
PRIVATE BUSINESS									
Productivity									
Output per hour of all persons	94.3	97.2	100.0	102.8	107.1	111.2	114.7	117.1	119.1
Output per unit of capital	103.3	102.2	100.0	96.1	95.0	95.9	98.0	99.1	99.9
Multifactor productivity	97.4	98.7	100.0	100.2	101.9	104.6	107.3	109.2	110.4
Output	91.5	96.2	100.0	100.5	102.0	105.2	109.9	114.1	118.4
Inputs									
Labor input	96.4	99.0	100.0	98.6	97.2	96.9	98.4	100.2	102.8
Capital services	88.5	94.2	100.0	104.5	107.4	109.7	112.2	115.1	118.6
Combined units of labor and capital inputs	93.9	97.5	100.0	100.3	100.2	100.6	102.4	104.5	107.3
Capital services per hour for all persons	91.2	95.1	100.0	106.9	112.7	116.0	117.1	118.1	119.2
PRIVATE NONFARM BUSINESS									
Productivity									
Output per hour of all persons	94.5	97.3	100.0	102.7	107.1	111.0	114.4	116.8	118.7
Output per unit of capital	103.7	102.4	100.0	96.1	94.9	95.7	97.7	99.1	99.8
Multifactor productivity	97.7	98.8	100.0	100.1	101.9	104.4	107.1	109.1	110.2
Output	91.5	96.3	100.0	100.5	102.1	105.2	109.9	114.1	118.4
Inputs									
Labor input	96.2	99.0	100.0	98.7	97.2	97.1	98.6	100.4	103.0
Capital services	88.2	94.0	100.0	104.6	107.6	110.0	112.4	115.1	118.7
Combined units of labor and capital inputs	93.7	97.5	100.0	100.4	100.2	100.7	102.5	104.6	107.5
Capital services per hour for all persons	91.1	95.0	100.0	106.9	112.8	116.1	117.0	117.9	119.0
MANUFACTURING									
Productivity									
Output per hour of all persons	91.7	95.8	100.0	101.5	108.6	115.3	117.9	123.4	. . .
Output per unit of capital	100.5	100.3	100.0	93.6	92.5	93.5	95.9	99.6	. . .
Multifactor productivity	95.8	96.5	100.0	98.7	102.4	105.3	109.2	113.0	. . .
Output	93.8	97.4	100.0	94.9	94.3	95.2	96.9	100.3	. . .
Inputs									
Hours at work of all persons	102.3	101.6	100.0	93.5	86.8	82.6	82.2	81.3	. . .
Capital services	93.4	97.1	100.0	101.4	101.9	101.8	101.1	100.7	. . .
Energy	105.4	105.5	100.0	90.6	89.3	84.4	81.1	78.5	. . .
Non-energy materials	97.7	102.6	100.0	93.3	88.3	87.7	85.5	86.3	. . .
Purchased business services	95.0	100.0	100.0	100.7	98.2	99.1	95.2	96.5	. . .
Combined units of all inputs	98.0	100.9	100.0	96.2	92.1	90.5	88.7	88.8	. . .

. . . = Not available.

Table 5-5. Indexes of Multifactor Productivity and Related Measures, Manufacturing Industries, 1987–2005

(2000 = 100.)

Industry	1987	1988	1989	1990	1991	1992	1993	1994	1995	1996
Total Nondurable Goods										
Output per hour of all persons	75.1	76.5	77.2	78.8	80.8	82.3	83.1	85.0	87.1	89.1
Output per unit of capital	111.4	113.8	113.6	110.9	108.1	107.8	107.4	108.3	107.3	104.6
Multifactor productivity	99.7	100.3	99.4	97.9	97.8	96.3	99.5	101.1	101.3	100.1
Sector output	79.9	82.8	84.5	85.1	85.4	87.7	89.7	92.7	94.4	94.5
Hours of all persons at work	106.4	108.3	109.5	108.0	105.7	106.6	108.0	109.1	108.4	106.1
Capital services	71.7	72.8	74.4	76.7	79.0	81.4	83.5	85.6	88.0	90.3
Energy	93.4	96.4	97.6	100.6	100.9	102.0	105.1	107.3	111.4	108.1
Non-energy materials	79.5	80.4	81.6	83.1	82.8	88.0	85.7	87.7	88.5	92.8
Purchased business services	60.3	67.9	75.0	80.7	83.4	88.8	85.1	85.8	89.5	87.9
Combined units of all inputs	80.1	82.6	85.0	86.9	87.3	91.0	90.2	91.7	93.2	94.4
Food, Beverage, and Tobacco Product										
Output per hour of all persons	88.3	89.8	90.0	90.1	93.6	95.5	94.6	96.2	97.3	97.3
Output per unit of capital	102.9	104.5	104.4	102.2	101.5	100.8	99.2	100.4	102.0	99.4
Multifactor productivity	106.8	107.5	106.0	101.5	100.8	98.5	106.0	106.3	109.7	105.3
Sector output	82.1	84.6	86.0	86.4	88.0	89.7	90.1	92.5	95.4	94.3
Hours of all persons at work	93.1	94.1	95.6	96.0	94.0	93.9	95.3	96.1	98.1	96.9
Capital services	79.9	80.9	82.4	84.6	86.7	89.0	90.8	92.1	93.5	94.9
Energy	88.2	89.7	90.3	88.4	91.6	89.6	88.8	91.6	96.1	93.8
Non-energy materials	78.0	78.3	79.5	83.3	85.1	90.4	82.1	85.3	83.8	89.0
Purchased business services	59.3	66.3	74.4	83.2	89.1	93.8	82.9	82.5	83.7	83.1
Combined units of all inputs	77.0	78.6	81.2	85.1	87.2	91.1	85.1	87.0	87.0	89.5
Textile Mills										
Output per hour of all persons	72.5	71.9	72.9	73.4	73.6	78.4	79.3	81.0	84.6	84.9
Output per unit of capital	97.7	96.9	98.4	93.7	92.1	97.2	100.5	103.8	100.9	98.0
Multifactor productivity	87.7	89.4	90.1	90.1	89.6	90.9	91.0	91.9	93.4	93.2
Sector output	90.3	89.7	91.3	87.4	85.9	90.9	94.8	99.8	98.8	96.4
Hours of all persons at work	124.7	124.7	125.2	119.1	116.7	116.0	119.6	123.3	116.9	113.5
Capital services	92.4	92.5	92.8	93.3	93.3	93.5	94.3	96.2	98.0	98.4
Energy	107.5	107.7	106.0	101.8	103.6	116.2	122.9	128.5	132.1	122.7
Non-energy materials	103.3	96.9	96.7	91.4	88.9	93.8	98.9	104.0	101.2	99.5
Purchased business services	58.7	66.5	75.9	77.8	84.3	96.5	99.9	104.3	103.8	99.8
Combined units of all inputs	103.0	100.3	101.3	97.1	95.9	100.0	104.2	108.6	105.8	103.4
Apparel and Leather										
Output per hour of all persons	61.6	61.7	59.7	62.6	63.9	65.8	68.8	71.2	75.5	79.3
Output per unit of capital	144.3	139.9	136.4	132.7	134.4	135.1	133.5	131.9	125.1	126.6
Multifactor productivity	83.9	83.8	82.7	84.0	87.9	85.6	86.4	90.9	96.4	93.9
Sector output	123.6	122.1	117.5	115.4	115.4	119.7	122.3	124.0	123.0	119.9
Hours of all persons at work	200.7	197.8	196.7	184.4	180.7	181.8	177.8	174.1	162.9	151.1
Capital services	85.6	87.3	86.1	87.0	85.9	88.6	91.6	94.0	98.3	94.7
Energy	139.1	141.5	124.0	117.7	119.7	158.8	166.6	155.5	157.1	141.6
Non-energy materials	172.0	165.9	156.4	150.5	137.8	150.2	155.0	144.0	130.0	136.1
Purchased business services	75.6	83.3	88.5	91.7	91.2	106.2	107.4	104.6	97.2	104.0
Combined units of all inputs	147.3	145.7	142.1	137.4	131.3	139.8	141.6	136.3	127.5	127.6
Paper Product										
Output per hour of all persons	79.9	81.6	81.0	81.6	83.5	84.6	86.3	89.3	90.9	90.2
Output per unit of capital	109.1	111.3	108.0	103.6	99.9	99.8	100.6	103.3	103.4	99.2
Multifactor productivity	101.0	102.4	100.3	99.9	100.0	100.0	103.4	104.0	99.2	100.3
Sector output	84.5	87.9	88.6	88.8	89.0	91.3	93.5	97.2	98.2	96.2
Hours of all persons at work	105.8	107.7	109.4	108.8	106.7	108.0	108.3	108.9	108.1	106.7
Capital services	77.5	79.0	82.0	85.8	89.1	91.5	92.9	94.1	95.0	97.0
Energy	84.1	85.9	88.0	93.3	93.9	95.2	97.1	99.3	103.2	97.7
Non-energy materials	78.6	79.0	80.2	79.7	79.5	81.9	80.7	85.1	91.6	89.0
Purchased business services	72.3	83.3	93.1	93.2	93.7	97.9	92.7	96.3	116.5	101.7
Combined units of all inputs	83.7	85.8	88.4	89.0	89.0	91.3	90.5	93.5	99.0	95.9
Printing and Support										
Output per hour of all persons	93.3	90.7	89.8	91.8	91.6	96.7	94.8	92.8	91.2	94.5
Output per unit of capital	123.7	122.8	118.4	118.4	111.7	115.3	113.7	114.6	113.5	112.8
Multifactor productivity	98.3	99.2	99.9	100.2	98.8	101.2	98.1	99.6	98.2	98.9
Sector output	85.8	88.4	88.7	91.6	88.4	93.2	93.1	94.1	95.4	95.9
Hours of all persons at work	91.9	97.5	98.8	99.8	96.5	96.4	98.2	101.4	104.6	101.6
Capital services	69.4	72.0	74.9	77.4	79.1	80.9	81.9	82.1	84.1	85.0
Energy	115.4	123.2	121.9	127.7	126.2	132.1	137.3	141.9	149.7	143.9
Non-energy materials	94.6	93.1	90.1	93.9	92.2	97.0	100.9	96.3	97.1	99.5
Purchased business services	69.4	70.1	70.4	73.0	70.2	75.1	78.8	79.1	85.9	85.6
Combined units of all inputs	87.2	89.1	88.8	91.4	89.5	92.2	94.9	94.5	97.2	97.0
Chemical Product										
Output per hour of all persons	79.6	80.5	80.4	81.0	80.8	81.0	82.5	87.3	87.4	87.7
Output per unit of capital	131.2	135.2	134.3	129.6	122.4	119.2	117.3	116.9	112.4	107.7
Multifactor productivity	106.8	106.1	105.1	104.2	102.3	99.4	99.4	102.4	100.1	99.7
Sector output	80.3	84.2	86.1	86.8	86.0	87.3	89.3	92.3	92.0	91.9
Hours of all persons at work	100.8	104.6	107.1	107.3	106.4	107.9	108.2	105.7	105.2	104.7
Capital services	61.2	62.3	64.1	67.0	70.3	73.2	76.1	79.0	81.8	85.3
Energy	102.1	106.8	109.4	114.3	113.4	113.1	118.5	120.8	123.5	123.4
Non-energy materials	82.8	85.7	86.0	85.3	83.8	88.7	91.1	91.2	91.2	91.9
Purchased business services	57.5	67.2	74.4	77.6	80.2	85.5	86.5	86.2	90.5	87.2
Combined units of all inputs	75.2	79.3	81.9	83.3	84.0	87.8	89.8	90.1	91.9	92.2

Table 5-5. Indexes of Multifactor Productivity and Related Measures, Manufacturing Industries, 1987–2005
—Continued

(2000 = 100.)

Industry	1997	1998	1999	2000	2001	2002	2003	2004	2005
Total Nondurable Goods									
Output per hour of all persons	92.8	95.2	96.1	100.0	102.3	108.2	113.3	117.4	123.0
Output per unit of capital	105.8	103.6	101.1	100.0	96.3	96.2	96.7	98.5	100.7
Multifactor productivity	101.1	100.1	99.5	100.0	98.8	101.8	104.2	106.9	110.2
Sector output	98.4	99.4	99.3	100.0	96.8	97.1	97.5	98.6	100.5
Hours of all persons at work	106.0	104.4	103.3	100.0	94.6	89.8	86.0	84.0	81.7
Capital services	93.0	95.9	98.2	100.0	100.5	100.9	100.7	100.1	99.8
Energy	105.3	102.2	103.2	100.0	92.9	91.3	83.9	82.0	77.9
Non-energy materials	98.3	101.3	100.4	100.0	95.3	92.3	91.8	91.2	90.9
Purchased business services	90.2	94.1	96.4	100.0	104.1	102.2	99.9	98.1	96.7
Combined units of all inputs	97.3	99.4	99.8	100.0	97.9	95.4	93.5	92.3	91.2
Food, Beverage, and Tobacco Product									
Output per hour of all persons	97.8	101.6	98.1	100.0	101.1	103.4	106.6	107.7	114.4
Output per unit of capital	100.9	101.5	99.5	100.0	100.5	100.3	102.4	102.9	107.7
Multifactor productivity	104.0	101.6	100.4	100.0	101.9	101.5	102.0	100.5	105.0
Sector output	96.6	99.5	98.5	100.0	100.2	100.2	101.8	101.4	105.4
Hours of all persons at work	98.8	98.0	100.5	100.0	99.1	96.9	95.6	94.1	92.1
Capital services	95.8	98.0	99.0	100.0	99.7	99.9	99.4	98.5	97.9
Energy	100.7	108.0	101.9	100.0	94.8	97.6	94.2	97.8	92.6
Non-energy materials	94.7	100.5	100.2	100.0	95.0	97.9	101.0	100.9	101.5
Purchased business services	83.8	92.2	91.9	100.0	103.9	100.8	101.9	107.1	106.5
Combined units of all inputs	92.9	97.9	98.1	100.0	98.4	98.7	99.9	100.8	100.4
Textile Mills									
Output per hour of all persons	91.1	92.4	98.6	100.0	101.6	109.2	119.7	126.5	136.9
Output per unit of capital	103.5	100.9	100.7	100.0	91.4	94.8	93.5	96.7	102.9
Multifactor productivity	97.7	97.4	97.9	100.0	96.0	98.8	105.7	109.4	119.9
Sector output	103.2	101.5	101.5	100.0	89.4	89.4	86.3	85.4	87.0
Hours of all persons at work	113.3	109.9	102.9	100.0	88.0	81.9	72.1	67.6	63.5
Capital services	99.7	100.6	100.7	100.0	97.8	94.4	92.3	88.4	84.6
Energy	116.4	117.5	110.7	100.0	85.3	91.8	72.2	69.8	56.3
Non-energy materials	103.6	101.8	104.4	100.0	94.2	91.7	85.1	81.4	76.3
Purchased business services	99.6	102.3	103.2	100.0	98.6	102.4	85.7	85.7	74.7
Combined units of all inputs	105.6	104.2	103.7	100.0	93.0	90.5	81.7	78.1	72.5
Apparel and Leather									
Output per hour of all persons	85.6	86.7	92.2	100.0	98.7	84.3	91.7	88.7	93.6
Output per unit of capital	126.6	115.3	107.0	100.0	87.7	68.6	64.9	58.2	58.7
Multifactor productivity	93.4	93.6	93.3	100.0	102.7	96.9	104.9	105.6	105.6
Sector output	119.4	111.3	105.4	100.0	86.1	64.6	60.5	52.2	51.0
Hours of all persons at work	139.5	128.3	114.3	100.0	87.2	76.6	65.9	58.9	54.5
Capital services	94.3	96.5	98.5	100.0	98.1	94.2	93.2	89.7	86.9
Energy	125.9	113.7	113.8	100.0	76.7	54.3	41.3	31.2	30.9
Non-energy materials	144.1	129.9	119.4	100.0	73.2	50.4	40.9	33.0	33.6
Purchased business services	105.6	101.6	109.1	100.0	88.1	62.3	53.5	42.3	45.0
Combined units of all inputs	127.9	118.9	113.0	100.0	83.8	66.6	57.6	49.5	48.3
Paper Product									
Output per hour of all persons	92.6	96.0	96.0	100.0	100.7	108.9	113.4	116.6	118.9
Output per unit of capital	101.4	101.0	101.5	100.0	95.6	97.5	97.1	100.8	104.4
Multifactor productivity	102.7	101.1	101.2	100.0	96.5	99.8	103.3	108.4	111.7
Sector output	99.6	100.8	101.7	100.0	94.3	95.0	92.6	93.3	93.7
Hours of all persons at work	107.6	105.0	105.9	100.0	93.7	87.2	81.7	80.0	78.8
Capital services	98.2	99.8	100.2	100.0	98.6	97.4	95.4	92.5	89.8
Energy	96.3	94.2	99.2	100.0	93.9	82.4	76.3	71.3	66.9
Non-energy materials	91.4	97.3	98.4	100.0	98.3	99.1	93.2	90.1	88.3
Purchased business services	98.3	101.4	99.8	100.0	104.4	101.0	94.3	85.5	81.3
Combined units of all inputs	96.9	99.7	100.5	100.0	97.8	95.2	89.6	86.1	83.9
Printing and Support									
Output per hour of all persons	93.9	96.3	98.1	100.0	100.9	106.8	106.0	108.7	115.4
Output per unit of capital	110.5	108.2	103.9	100.0	93.2	87.8	84.3	84.6	85.6
Multifactor productivity	97.8	98.2	98.7	100.0	98.3	100.8	102.1	105.4	114.4
Sector output	97.8	98.6	99.4	100.0	94.9	91.1	87.9	88.5	90.5
Hours of all persons at work	104.1	102.3	101.3	100.0	94.1	85.3	83.0	81.5	78.4
Capital services	88.5	91.1	95.7	100.0	101.9	103.8	104.4	104.6	105.8
Energy	104.1	106.0	102.1	100.0	94.4	90.4	80.6	72.8	61.3
Non-energy materials	102.0	102.5	102.9	100.0	94.9	89.2	82.1	80.1	73.3
Purchased business services	93.5	97.0	97.6	100.0	104.0	98.2	92.5	86.7	77.9
Combined units of all inputs	99.9	100.3	100.7	100.0	96.6	90.4	86.2	84.0	79.1
Chemical Product									
Output per hour of all persons	94.1	92.9	95.3	100.0	99.6	108.6	111.6	118.4	123.8
Output per unit of capital	108.9	103.3	101.4	100.0	95.3	100.7	102.1	107.7	109.6
Multifactor productivity	101.6	98.1	99.5	100.0	98.2	104.4	104.0	109.6	115.5
Sector output	97.3	96.9	98.6	100.0	96.6	103.0	104.5	109.7	111.8
Hours of all persons at work	103.4	104.3	103.6	100.0	97.0	94.9	93.6	92.7	90.4
Capital services	89.3	93.8	97.3	100.0	101.3	102.3	102.4	101.9	102.0
Energy	114.7	112.1	103.2	100.0	88.0	87.9	92.2	93.8	87.2
Non-energy materials	98.2	100.0	100.0	100.0	93.4	94.5	97.5	100.2	94.3
Purchased business services	91.7	96.8	96.0	100.0	104.2	105.1	109.7	105.7	101.7
Combined units of all inputs	95.8	98.8	99.2	100.0	98.4	98.7	100.5	100.1	96.8

Table 5-5. Indexes of Multifactor Productivity and Related Measures, Manufacturing Industries, 1987–2005
—Continued

(2000 = 100.)

Industry	1987	1988	1989	1990	1991	1992	1993	1994	1995	1996
Petroleum and Coal										
Output per hour of all persons	63.6	65.7	67.1	67.4	67.9	69.8	74.6	76.5	81.1	83.3
Output per unit of capital	89.0	91.5	92.3	93.1	92.0	92.7	94.4	93.4	92.4	92.3
Multifactor productivity	95.8	96.2	95.4	95.7	97.5	98.5	100.2	99.4	98.8	98.6
Sector output	82.5	84.4	84.8	85.6	85.1	87.1	90.2	90.7	92.3	94.8
Hours of all persons at work	129.8	128.5	126.4	127.1	125.5	124.7	120.9	118.5	113.8	113.9
Capital services	92.7	92.3	91.9	91.9	92.6	93.9	95.5	97.1	99.8	102.8
Energy	93.9	98.1	99.0	111.1	108.3	104.4	107.0	104.2	109.2	105.0
Non-energy materials	84.7	86.7	87.5	86.7	84.6	86.5	89.1	90.5	92.7	95.0
Purchased business services	64.7	66.6	76.1	91.7	84.6	78.8	74.2	76.7	81.9	92.1
Combined units of all inputs	86.1	87.7	88.9	89.5	87.4	88.4	90.0	91.2	93.4	96.2
Plastics and Rubber Product										
Output per hour of all persons	72.9	73.2	74.1	76.7	78.2	80.4	81.0	82.9	84.1	87.1
Output per unit of capital	99.6	100.9	100.4	99.2	95.3	99.3	103.0	106.7	103.6	101.8
Multifactor productivity	89.4	89.4	91.4	91.2	92.8	91.2	92.6	94.1	93.9	95.8
Sector output	60.8	63.1	64.8	66.3	65.5	70.2	75.1	81.1	82.8	85.2
Hours of all persons at work	83.4	86.2	87.5	86.5	83.8	87.4	92.8	97.8	98.4	97.8
Capital services	61.1	62.5	64.6	66.9	68.8	70.7	73.0	76.0	79.9	83.7
Energy	81.1	84.7	86.9	88.3	86.5	88.3	94.9	100.9	106.5	103.5
Non-energy materials	66.6	68.1	66.8	69.2	65.6	74.1	78.1	83.5	84.4	85.7
Purchased business services	50.8	56.9	59.9	63.7	64.0	74.3	77.7	84.1	89.3	87.7
Combined units of all inputs	68.1	70.5	70.9	72.7	70.6	77.0	81.1	86.2	88.2	88.9
Total Durable Goods										
Output per hour of all persons	56.0	57.3	57.7	58.8	59.9	63.3	65.8	69.0	73.1	77.2
Output per unit of capital	86.2	89.8	88.8	85.7	81.3	83.4	86.0	90.6	93.6	94.2
Multifactor productivity	75.6	77.5	77.3	77.5	77.1	77.4	78.8	81.5	83.8	85.4
Sector output	54.3	57.7	58.3	57.5	55.3	57.6	60.7	65.8	71.0	75.5
Hours of all persons at work	96.9	100.6	100.9	97.8	92.3	91.0	92.3	95.4	97.1	97.8
Capital services	63.0	64.2	65.6	67.1	68.1	69.1	70.6	72.6	75.9	80.2
Energy	108.7	114.3	111.6	112.5	110.9	106.8	110.4	115.3	117.4	113.9
Non-energy materials	51.5	52.5	53.3	53.4	52.3	58.0	61.9	66.0	72.2	80.6
Purchased business services	69.3	73.5	75.5	73.3	70.2	75.7	79.0	83.9	88.4	89.1
Combined units of all inputs	71.9	74.4	75.4	74.3	71.7	74.5	77.1	80.8	84.8	88.4
Wood Product										
Output per hour of all persons	91.8	90.2	90.3	92.4	95.1	96.3	92.3	91.6	92.1	94.4
Output per unit of capital	96.4	97.6	97.1	95.9	90.3	95.8	97.7	102.1	101.5	101.3
Multifactor productivity	103.0	104.7	106.1	106.2	106.6	104.0	98.5	98.4	99.7	98.7
Sector output	84.5	84.5	83.1	81.8	76.2	80.0	81.3	86.5	88.6	91.7
Hours of all persons at work	92.0	93.7	92.0	88.6	80.2	83.0	88.1	94.4	96.2	97.2
Capital services	87.6	86.5	85.6	85.4	84.4	83.4	83.2	84.7	87.3	90.6
Energy	95.1	100.2	98.0	98.7	98.9	92.3	102.1	108.2	114.1	110.8
Non-energy materials	80.4	77.5	73.5	72.6	66.7	74.2	77.8	84.0	84.9	90.9
Purchased business services	55.8	54.2	58.6	58.5	56.2	65.0	93.4	95.5	91.2	93.3
Combined units of all inputs	82.0	80.7	78.3	77.1	71.5	76.9	82.6	87.9	88.9	93.0
Furniture and Related Product										
Output per hour of all persons	83.6	80.8	81.0	82.1	82.1	85.5	86.4	86.9	88.7	90.7
Output per unit of capital	113.9	108.9	107.9	103.7	96.9	104.0	106.0	107.5	104.4	102.4
Multifactor productivity	96.2	94.4	94.7	93.8	93.6	96.8	98.1	97.6	96.8	97.2
Sector output	75.3	74.3	74.7	72.7	67.3	72.7	75.9	78.8	80.4	81.4
Hours of all persons at work	90.0	91.9	92.2	88.5	81.9	85.0	87.8	90.7	90.6	89.8
Capital services	66.1	68.3	69.2	70.1	69.4	69.9	71.5	73.3	77.0	79.5
Energy	86.1	89.3	92.8	87.9	86.8	87.1	91.4	93.7	98.4	94.5
Non-energy materials	69.0	68.7	69.0	69.6	64.5	68.6	70.5	75.2	78.9	81.1
Purchased business services	88.6	85.9	84.2	80.9	72.0	74.8	77.2	79.2	81.1	80.1
Combined units of all inputs	78.3	78.7	78.9	77.5	71.9	75.1	77.3	80.8	83.0	83.8
Primary Metal										
Output per hour of all persons	81.1	84.0	82.2	83.4	83.4	88.1	91.7	93.8	95.2	97.2
Output per unit of capital	79.9	87.9	85.7	85.2	79.7	82.7	87.2	94.7	95.3	97.0
Multifactor productivity	93.9	94.7	94.2	96.9	96.6	96.5	97.8	98.0	97.6	95.5
Sector output	84.0	91.6	88.9	88.0	82.1	84.5	88.4	95.1	95.9	97.8
Hours of all persons at work	103.5	109.0	108.2	105.5	98.5	95.9	96.4	101.4	100.8	100.6
Capital services	105.2	104.2	103.7	103.3	103.0	102.3	101.3	100.5	100.6	100.8
Energy	140.7	159.7	146.7	150.8	152.8	140.9	140.1	156.6	141.3	140.5
Non-energy materials	74.3	80.5	77.6	73.5	68.5	75.0	79.9	87.4	89.3	98.1
Purchased business services	98.7	118.9	118.8	109.9	96.1	97.9	99.4	109.7	118.5	115.9
Combined units of all inputs	89.5	96.7	94.4	90.8	85.0	87.6	90.4	97.1	98.2	102.4
Fabricated Metal										
Output per hour of all persons	83.5	84.2	81.6	82.3	82.5	86.4	87.5	90.0	92.3	93.7
Output per unit of capital	98.8	102.4	100.1	97.4	92.2	93.7	95.1	100.4	101.7	101.3
Multifactor productivity	95.1	96.6	95.0	94.8	93.5	93.6	94.1	97.9	99.4	99.5
Sector output	73.0	76.4	75.5	74.7	71.4	73.5	75.7	81.8	86.0	88.7
Hours of all persons at work	87.4	90.7	92.6	90.7	86.6	85.1	86.5	90.9	93.1	94.6
Capital services	73.9	74.6	75.5	76.6	77.4	78.5	79.6	81.5	84.5	87.5
Energy	95.9	100.3	100.3	99.9	99.0	94.4	98.5	102.2	109.0	105.9
Non-energy materials	67.2	68.4	67.6	67.7	66.1	71.4	74.0	76.1	78.8	83.3
Purchased business services	76.9	81.8	82.5	79.9	75.5	80.2	81.6	85.3	90.0	90.8
Combined units of all inputs	76.8	79.1	79.5	78.8	76.3	78.6	80.4	83.5	86.4	89.1

Table 5-5. Indexes of Multifactor Productivity and Related Measures, Manufacturing Industries, 1987–2005
—Continued

(2000 = 100.)

Industry	1997	1998	1999	2000	2001	2002	2003	2004	2005
Petroleum and Coal									
Output per hour of all persons	90.2	90.0	94.5	100.0	98.1	103.8	106.7	109.2	106.4
Output per unit of capital	94.8	97.4	97.2	100.0	98.5	98.1	98.8	100.7	100.5
Multifactor productivity	100.3	107.9	100.6	100.0	96.5	99.1	106.6	106.5	101.4
Sector output	98.3	100.0	98.8	100.0	99.0	100.4	101.6	104.3	104.5
Hours of all persons at work	108.9	111.1	104.5	100.0	100.9	96.7	95.2	95.5	98.2
Capital services	103.7	102.7	101.6	100.0	100.6	102.3	102.8	103.5	104.0
Energy	104.2	67.5	107.5	100.0	104.1	105.7	57.3	50.0	58.2
Non-energy materials	97.4	94.7	96.3	100.0	101.0	99.2	97.6	101.9	107.6
Purchased business services	93.7	66.7	105.7	100.0	121.8	123.1	73.5	65.6	76.9
Combined units of all inputs	97.9	92.7	98.2	100.0	102.6	101.3	95.3	97.9	103.1
Plastics and Rubber Product									
Output per hour of all persons	90.5	92.9	96.3	100.0	102.5	110.5	115.2	118.2	121.3
Output per unit of capital	102.8	102.0	102.4	100.0	92.7	94.4	94.1	95.5	96.5
Multifactor productivity	97.8	97.6	98.2	100.0	97.8	100.9	101.1	105.9	106.0
Sector output	90.3	93.7	98.5	100.0	94.4	97.2	97.1	98.4	99.6
Hours of all persons at work	99.8	100.9	102.4	100.0	92.1	87.9	84.3	83.3	82.1
Capital services	87.9	91.8	96.2	100.0	101.9	102.9	103.2	103.1	103.2
Energy	103.6	104.7	106.1	100.0	95.5	98.4	96.6	85.7	84.6
Non-energy materials	89.1	94.4	100.4	100.0	95.2	95.5	96.7	94.1	95.7
Purchased business services	92.6	95.8	100.7	100.0	102.6	107.1	108.9	98.7	103.0
Combined units of all inputs	92.3	96.0	100.4	100.0	96.5	96.3	96.1	93.0	94.0
Total Durable Goods									
Output per hour of all persons	82.5	88.9	95.3	100.0	100.5	108.1	115.8	117.8	123.8
Output per unit of capital	97.5	98.9	100.0	100.0	91.0	89.4	90.5	93.5	98.5
Multifactor productivity	88.8	93.0	94.7	100.0	98.7	102.7	105.8	110.5	114.2
Sector output	83.0	89.9	95.9	100.0	93.3	92.1	93.4	95.6	100.3
Hours of all persons at work	100.7	101.1	100.7	100.0	92.8	85.2	80.6	81.2	81.1
Capital services	85.2	90.9	95.9	100.0	102.6	103.0	103.2	102.2	101.8
Energy	113.0	110.5	109.2	100.0	86.8	86.0	85.3	79.6	79.5
Non-energy materials	88.4	94.1	103.2	100.0	91.5	86.7	86.0	83.5	86.3
Purchased business services	93.6	95.9	103.0	100.0	97.9	94.9	98.3	92.7	96.4
Combined units of all inputs	93.5	96.6	101.3	100.0	94.6	89.6	88.3	86.5	87.9
Wood Product									
Output per hour of all persons	96.3	96.6	98.6	100.0	101.0	110.4	113.3	112.3	118.0
Output per unit of capital	101.3	103.2	104.1	100.0	93.2	96.6	98.1	100.6	106.2
Multifactor productivity	98.9	98.5	98.4	100.0	101.6	103.5	105.4	106.4	110.9
Sector output	94.5	98.4	101.7	100.0	93.8	96.7	96.8	99.2	105.8
Hours of all persons at work	98.1	101.8	103.1	100.0	92.9	87.6	85.4	88.3	89.6
Capital services	93.3	95.3	97.7	100.0	100.6	100.2	98.6	98.6	99.6
Energy	98.9	99.5	108.9	100.0	80.7	79.0	77.0	74.2	75.2
Non-energy materials	94.3	99.6	104.6	100.0	90.8	94.8	93.5	95.2	98.3
Purchased business services	98.5	101.7	102.8	100.0	92.6	100.5	99.1	97.1	99.5
Combined units of all inputs	95.6	99.9	103.4	100.0	92.3	93.5	91.8	93.2	95.4
Furniture and Related Product									
Output per hour of all persons	95.8	98.7	98.0	100.0	100.0	109.6	112.6	115.3	122.5
Output per unit of capital	106.1	108.0	104.6	100.0	91.5	94.5	90.5	93.3	96.5
Multifactor productivity	99.3	98.7	98.7	100.0	96.7	98.7	103.7	108.8	107.1
Sector output	89.3	95.6	98.5	100.0	94.0	98.7	96.8	99.7	103.4
Hours of all persons at work	93.2	96.8	100.5	100.0	94.0	90.1	86.0	86.4	84.4
Capital services	84.1	88.5	94.2	100.0	102.8	104.4	107.0	106.8	107.2
Energy	103.4	112.7	107.7	100.0	92.1	105.3	91.8	83.6	91.8
Non-energy materials	88.5	97.7	100.4	100.0	97.5	103.4	92.9	90.3	100.9
Purchased business services	90.0	100.4	100.0	100.0	101.5	113.7	104.4	97.5	111.5
Combined units of all inputs	89.9	96.9	99.8	100.0	97.2	100.0	93.4	91.6	96.6
Primary Metal									
Output per hour of all persons	99.1	102.7	101.3	100.0	100.4	113.5	117.7	131.4	133.4
Output per unit of capital	100.2	101.1	100.4	100.0	89.9	93.0	92.5	106.0	110.0
Multifactor productivity	95.5	95.3	96.5	100.0	97.4	100.7	102.6	111.3	113.7
Sector output	101.3	102.3	101.2	100.0	88.3	89.3	86.2	95.9	97.6
Hours of all persons at work	102.2	99.6	99.9	100.0	88.0	78.7	73.2	72.9	73.2
Capital services	101.1	101.3	100.9	100.0	98.2	96.1	93.2	90.4	88.7
Energy	133.0	123.1	112.6	100.0	83.9	78.8	77.2	82.2	78.8
Non-energy materials	104.6	111.0	108.2	100.0	90.7	95.8	89.5	94.0	95.0
Purchased business services	120.2	114.4	106.6	100.0	94.1	86.1	87.3	89.9	87.0
Combined units of all inputs	106.1	107.4	104.9	100.0	90.7	88.7	84.1	86.1	85.9
Fabricated Metal									
Output per hour of all persons	93.8	95.8	97.5	100.0	99.4	105.4	108.3	106.9	110.3
Output per unit of capital	102.6	101.8	99.3	100.0	91.9	89.7	88.7	90.7	94.8
Multifactor productivity	98.8	97.7	97.8	100.0	96.2	97.2	99.2	104.5	109.3
Sector output	92.6	95.7	96.4	100.0	93.0	90.8	89.6	90.5	94.4
Hours of all persons at work	98.7	99.9	98.8	100.0	93.6	86.1	82.8	84.7	85.5
Capital services	90.2	94.0	97.0	100.0	101.2	101.2	101.1	99.8	99.6
Energy	107.8	109.5	105.1	100.0	89.4	91.7	89.4	73.3	69.7
Non-energy materials	89.1	96.7	98.0	100.0	96.3	93.6	88.3	84.0	82.3
Purchased business services	96.2	99.3	100.4	100.0	101.3	103.1	103.6	86.5	87.2
Combined units of all inputs	93.7	97.9	98.6	100.0	96.7	93.4	90.4	86.6	86.3

Table 5-5. Indexes of Multifactor Productivity and Related Measures, Manufacturing Industries, 1987–2005
—Continued

(2000 = 100.)

Industry	1987	1988	1989	1990	1991	1992	1993	1994	1995	1996
Machinery										
Output per hour of all persons	72.3	74.7	76.2	76.2	74.3	75.8	78.1	82.5	83.9	86.5
Output per unit of capital	142.7	152.3	150.5	142.3	130.0	128.4	133.1	138.4	138.6	132.2
Multifactor productivity	110.3	114.1	115.6	113.6	108.1	104.9	104.5	105.9	103.7	99.5
Sector output	67.7	74.4	76.8	74.6	69.6	69.6	74.8	82.0	87.6	90.1
Hours of all persons at work	93.7	99.6	100.8	97.9	93.6	91.8	95.8	99.5	104.4	104.1
Capital services	47.5	48.9	51.0	52.4	53.5	54.2	56.2	59.3	63.2	68.1
Energy	106.7	110.1	115.1	115.5	114.4	104.7	108.6	115.9	119.2	115.3
Non-energy materials	39.9	43.0	43.6	44.1	44.5	48.9	55.5	62.5	72.1	83.6
Purchased business services	77.6	82.1	83.4	79.3	74.9	77.6	83.9	92.1	97.5	100.4
Combined units of all inputs	61.4	65.3	66.4	65.7	64.4	66.4	71.6	77.5	84.5	90.5
Computer and Electronic Equipment										
Output per hour of all persons	15.9	17.1	17.5	19.1	21.0	24.1	26.9	31.6	39.2	46.9
Output per unit of capital	41.6	44.1	43.1	43.5	43.0	45.0	47.2	52.1	61.3	67.0
Multifactor productivity	25.9	28.2	28.5	30.5	32.0	33.7	35.9	40.5	48.0	55.3
Sector output	17.0	18.6	19.0	20.1	20.6	22.7	24.9	29.2	37.6	45.9
Hours of all persons at work	106.9	109.2	108.5	104.9	98.5	94.2	92.6	92.5	95.8	98.0
Capital services	40.9	42.2	44.0	46.1	48.0	50.3	52.8	56.0	61.3	68.5
Energy	91.2	94.2	95.3	98.1	96.0	92.8	95.9	98.4	105.3	102.3
Non-energy materials	49.1	46.9	47.2	47.8	49.0	54.5	57.9	60.2	68.0	77.0
Purchased business services	58.3	60.0	61.1	59.4	57.8	62.8	66.0	70.9	77.6	78.6
Combined units of all inputs	65.7	66.0	66.6	65.8	64.5	67.3	69.4	72.1	78.2	83.0
Electrical Equipment, Appliances, and Components										
Output per hour of all persons	67.8	68.1	67.1	67.5	67.5	72.7	77.2	80.6	83.1	84.9
Output per unit of capital	98.9	101.3	95.3	89.1	83.6	87.5	91.3	96.0	94.4	93.0
Multifactor productivity	123.9	122.1	119.2	116.0	112.5	112.2	114.2	113.8	105.5	99.3
Sector output	75.5	78.2	75.6	72.4	68.1	72.3	77.3	83.2	84.8	87.2
Hours of all persons at work	111.3	114.8	112.6	107.3	100.9	99.4	100.2	103.2	102.1	102.8
Capital services	76.3	77.2	79.3	81.2	81.5	82.6	84.7	86.7	89.8	93.8
Energy	97.6	100.4	99.4	100.7	99.2	96.3	101.4	105.5	106.2	104.2
Non-energy materials	32.6	35.4	34.8	35.0	34.9	40.8	45.3	51.8	63.5	76.8
Purchased business services	60.6	65.1	63.8	60.2	55.4	61.7	64.9	73.8	83.2	86.3
Combined units of all inputs	60.9	64.0	63.4	62.4	60.5	64.4	67.7	73.1	80.4	87.9
Transportation Equipment										
Output per hour of all persons	77.3	77.2	78.9	77.9	77.6	82.4	84.9	86.4	84.9	86.2
Output per unit of capital	133.9	134.7	135.1	123.8	113.8	118.2	119.2	121.9	116.2	110.4
Multifactor productivity	105.0	104.2	103.3	99.7	99.4	98.7	100.4	100.3	98.4	97.4
Sector output	77.9	80.9	83.0	78.5	73.5	76.6	78.7	82.7	82.3	83.2
Hours of all persons at work	100.8	104.7	105.2	100.7	94.7	93.0	92.7	95.7	97.0	96.6
Capital services	58.2	60.0	61.4	63.4	64.6	64.8	66.0	67.8	70.9	75.4
Energy	109.4	107.1	105.7	104.6	100.9	105.1	111.9	113.2	118.3	112.2
Non-energy materials	63.2	65.6	68.4	67.4	61.7	67.2	68.4	73.5	74.7	78.5
Purchased business services	69.1	76.9	84.2	83.4	82.1	91.3	91.6	96.2	95.9	93.6
Combined units of all inputs	74.2	77.6	80.3	78.7	74.0	77.6	78.3	82.4	83.7	85.5
Miscellaneous Manufacturing										
Output per hour of all persons	71.3	72.8	72.4	75.3	76.6	77.8	79.0	79.4	83.7	88.2
Output per unit of capital	85.5	91.1	89.8	91.1	90.6	90.6	93.1	94.1	96.2	98.1
Multifactor productivity	83.6	87.9	88.4	89.8	89.8	87.4	87.4	88.6	91.1	93.8
Sector output	62.3	67.6	68.4	71.1	72.0	74.5	78.2	79.1	81.9	85.7
Hours of all persons at work	87.4	92.9	94.5	94.5	94.1	95.8	98.9	99.7	97.8	97.2
Capital services	72.9	74.2	76.1	78.1	79.4	82.2	83.9	84.1	85.2	87.4
Energy	108.0	110.9	113.2	115.4	113.3	104.9	116.1	116.5	128.9	119.6
Non-energy materials	57.4	57.8	57.5	61.7	65.3	74.1	79.4	79.1	80.9	85.4
Purchased business services	82.9	85.3	84.1	83.3	81.0	87.0	92.3	90.8	92.9	92.5
Combined units of all inputs	74.6	76.9	77.4	79.2	80.2	85.3	89.4	89.3	89.9	91.4

Table 5-5. Indexes of Multifactor Productivity and Related Measures, Manufacturing Industries, 1987–2005
—*Continued*

(2000 = 100.)

Industry	1997	1998	1999	2000	2001	2002	2003	2004	2005
Machinery									
Output per hour of all persons	87.4	90.4	92.4	100.0	98.1	105.2	112.4	114.4	120.4
Output per unit of capital	126.2	115.9	102.8	100.0	83.5	77.3	77.3	81.3	86.5
Multifactor productivity	98.5	102.0	98.1	100.0	98.9	100.2	100.1	106.4	108.1
Sector output	94.6	97.1	94.7	100.0	89.1	85.1	85.2	89.0	95.1
Hours of all persons at work	108.2	107.4	102.5	100.0	90.8	80.9	75.8	77.8	79.0
Capital services	74.9	83.8	92.1	100.0	106.7	110.1	110.3	109.5	110.0
Energy	115.0	104.2	103.0	100.0	81.6	83.4	86.6	73.7	76.9
Non-energy materials	91.7	89.4	92.3	100.0	84.9	79.7	82.0	81.7	87.8
Purchased business services	100.8	95.1	97.9	100.0	91.4	91.8	98.4	87.5	96.6
Combined units of all inputs	96.1	95.2	96.6	100.0	90.1	84.9	85.1	83.6	88.0
Computer and Electronic Equipment									
Output per hour of all persons	56.2	65.9	82.0	100.0	100.3	103.8	119.4	133.2	144.5
Output per unit of capital	74.1	79.0	87.9	100.0	86.4	74.9	81.0	90.3	98.6
Multifactor productivity	64.6	76.5	85.2	100.0	100.3	106.9	117.1	128.2	135.5
Sector output	57.0	67.1	81.0	100.0	93.1	82.1	86.7	94.1	100.2
Hours of all persons at work	101.5	101.8	98.7	100.0	92.8	79.2	72.5	70.7	69.3
Capital services	76.9	84.9	92.1	100.0	107.7	109.7	106.9	104.2	101.6
Energy	106.6	93.0	103.1	100.0	87.1	76.3	73.3	69.2	64.3
Non-energy materials	82.7	77.5	89.4	100.0	85.8	63.6	61.6	64.0	68.2
Purchased business services	83.1	83.1	96.4	100.0	97.4	83.8	85.1	83.8	84.2
Combined units of all inputs	88.2	87.8	95.0	100.0	92.8	76.8	74.0	73.4	73.9
Electrical Equipment, Appliances, and Components									
Output per hour of all persons	89.4	91.7	94.5	100.0	98.8	101.2	105.7	110.7	115.9
Output per unit of capital	92.4	95.0	96.0	100.0	86.3	81.2	80.3	83.2	86.1
Multifactor productivity	96.2	93.7	97.3	100.0	99.9	103.7	108.4	107.4	108.4
Sector output	89.6	92.9	95.0	100.0	90.0	82.5	80.7	82.1	83.9
Hours of all persons at work	100.2	101.3	100.6	100.0	91.1	81.5	76.4	74.2	72.4
Capital services	97.0	97.8	99.1	100.0	104.4	101.6	100.5	98.8	97.4
Energy	107.8	112.5	103.8	100.0	82.7	70.3	64.7	63.6	63.2
Non-energy materials	86.6	97.3	94.7	100.0	82.5	66.3	59.3	66.4	69.4
Purchased business services	93.6	101.1	98.3	100.0	91.7	83.6	78.9	80.9	84.3
Combined units of all inputs	93.1	99.2	97.7	100.0	90.1	79.5	74.5	76.5	77.3
Transportation Equipment									
Output per hour of all persons	92.2	102.1	107.6	100.0	104.2	116.4	126.1	124.0	129.5
Output per unit of capital	113.2	113.5	113.9	100.0	94.9	99.9	101.4	100.6	106.0
Multifactor productivity	99.1	101.3	99.6	100.0	99.2	105.7	105.5	104.4	106.3
Sector output	92.0	101.5	110.3	100.0	95.9	102.3	105.4	104.2	108.7
Hours of all persons at work	99.8	99.4	102.5	100.0	92.0	87.9	83.6	84.0	84.0
Capital services	81.3	89.5	96.8	100.0	101.0	102.4	103.9	103.6	102.6
Energy	116.5	120.7	125.2	100.0	92.4	99.4	103.2	94.8	95.2
Non-energy materials	88.4	100.0	115.5	100.0	97.5	98.1	104.7	106.4	110.2
Purchased business services	101.5	109.3	121.3	100.0	100.3	107.5	118.4	112.8	118.9
Combined units of all inputs	92.8	100.2	110.7	100.0	96.6	96.8	99.9	99.8	102.3
Miscellaneous Manufacturing									
Output per hour of all persons	85.8	91.1	92.9	100.0	100.7	108.5	115.7	115.2	124.8
Output per unit of capital	97.5	98.2	97.1	100.0	96.7	98.3	100.5	100.4	107.7
Multifactor productivity	93.5	93.5	94.4	100.0	98.5	98.1	101.7	107.6	113.9
Sector output	87.7	92.4	94.4	100.0	98.5	100.9	103.8	104.1	112.1
Hours of all persons at work	102.2	101.5	101.6	100.0	97.9	93.0	89.7	90.3	89.8
Capital services	90.0	94.1	97.1	100.0	101.9	102.6	103.3	103.6	104.1
Energy	104.7	109.5	105.5	100.0	97.0	107.2	106.1	90.3	92.2
Non-energy materials	86.5	96.5	99.1	100.0	97.6	109.0	108.8	96.5	99.8
Purchased business services	92.9	101.1	100.2	100.0	107.4	116.6	119.8	105.5	112.0
Combined units of all inputs	93.8	98.8	99.9	100.0	100.1	102.9	102.0	96.7	98.4

CHAPTER SIX

COMPENSATION OF EMPLOYEES

COMPENSATION OF EMPLOYEES

HIGHLIGHTS

This chapter discusses the Employment Cost Index (ECI), which covers changes in wages and salaries and benefits; the Employer Costs for Employee Compensation (ECEC); the experimental estimates of compensation levels and trends for workers in the 15 largest metropolitan areas; employee participation in various benefit plans; and occupational wages from the National Compensation Survey (NCS).

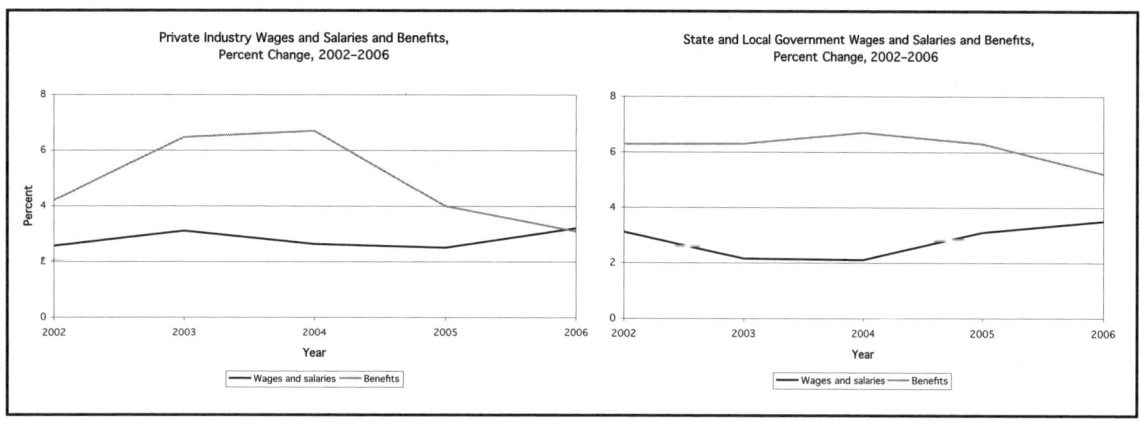

In 2006, the ECI for all private workers increased by 3.2 percent for wages and salaries and 3.1 percent for benefits, narrowing the gap from previous years. In 2005, it increased by 2.5 percent for wages and salaries and 3.9 percent for benefits. However, for state and local governments, the increase in benefit costs continued to be considerably higher than the increase for wages and salaries—5.2 percent compared to 3.5 percent. (See Tables 6-1, 6-3, and 6-4.)

OTHER HIGHLIGHTS

- From 2001 to 2006, the ECI for wages and salaries rose by almost 15 percent for both private industry workers and government workers. During the same period, the ECI for benefits rose 26.9 percent in private industry and 34.5 percent in state and local government (See Tables 6-1, 6-3, and 6-4.)

- In goods-producing industries, wages and salaries constituted 66.6 percent of total compensation with benefits making up 33.4 percent. In service-providing industries, wages and salaries made up 71.9 percent of total compensation while total benefits made up 28.1 percent. (See Table 6-5.)

- Legally required benefits such as Social Security, Medicare, and workers' compensation made up 29 percent of total benefit costs in June 2007. (See Table 6-5.)

NOTES AND DEFINITIONS

EMPLOYMENT COST INDEX

The National Compensation Survey (NCS) provides data for the Employment Cost Index (ECI), the Employer Costs for Employee Compensation (ECEC), an experimental series, the occupational earnings series, and the incidence of employee benefits. Part one of this chapter concerns the ECI.

The ECI is a measure of the change in the cost of labor, free from the influence of employment shifts among occupations and industries. The compensation series includes changes in wages and salaries and employer costs for employee benefits. The wage and salary series and the benefit cost series are the two components of compensation.

Sample establishments are classified by industry categories based on the 2002 North American Industry Classification System (NAICS). Within a sample establishment, specific job categories are selected and classified into about 800 occupational classifications according to the 2000 Standard Occupational Classification (SOC) system. Individual occupations are combined to represent one of ten intermediate aggregations, such as professional and related occupations, or one of five higher-level aggregations, such as management, professional, and related occupations. Due to the new classifications, the historical data shown here begins with 2001.

Concepts and Definitions

Wages and salaries are defined as the hourly straight-time wage rate or, for workers not paid on an hourly basis, straight-time earnings divided by the corresponding hours. Straight-time wage and salary rates are total earnings before payroll deductions, excluding premium pay for overtime and for work on weekends and holidays, shift differentials, and nonproduction bonuses such as lump-sum payments provided in lieu of wage increases. Production bonuses, incentive earnings, commission payments, and cost-of-living adjustments are included in straight-time wage and salary rates.

Benefits covered by the ECI are: paid leave—vacations, holidays, sick leave, and other leave; supplemental pay—premium pay for work in addition to the regular work schedule (such as overtime, weekends, and holidays), shift differentials, and nonproduction bonuses (such as referral bonuses and attendance bonuses); insurance benefits—life, health, short-term disability, and long-term disability; retirement and savings benefits—defined benefit and defined contribution plans; and legally required benefits—Social Security, Medicare, federal and state unemployment insurance, and workers' compensation.

Fixed employment weights are used each quarter to calculate the most aggregate series-civilian, private, and state and local government. These fixed weights are also used to derive all of the industry and occupational series indexes. Beginning with March 2006 estimates, 2002 fixed employment weights from the Bureau's Occupational Employment Statistics survey were introduced. For the series based on bargaining status, census region and division, metropolitan area status, and for series excluding incentive paid occupations, fixed employment data are not available. The employment weights are reallocated within these series each quarter based on the current ECI sample.

The ECI private industry sample is rotated over approximately 5 years, which makes the sample more representative of the economy and reduces respondent burden. The sample is replaced on a cross-area, cross-industry basis.

Sources of Additional Information

Additional information on ECI methodology and more tables are available in Chapter 8 of the *BLS Handbook of Methods* and BLS new releases. The BLS publication *Compensation and Working Conditions* contains articles on all aspects of the NCS. All of these resources are on the BLS Web site at <http://www.bls.gov>.

Table 6-1. Employment Cost Index, Private Industry Workers, Total Compensation[1] and Wages and Salaries, by Industry and Occupation, 2001–2006

(December 2005 = 100.)

Characteristic and year	Total compensation					Wages and salaries				
	Indexes				Percent change for 12 months (ended December)	Indexes				Percent change for 12 months (ended December)
	March	June	September	December		March	June	September	December	
WORKERS BY INDUSTRY										
Total Private										
2001	85.0	85.8	86.7	87.3	4.1	87.6	88.4	89.2	89.9	3.8
2002	88.2	89.2	89.7	90.0	3.1	90.7	91.6	92.0	92.2	2.6
2003	91.4	92.3	93.2	93.6	4.0	93.3	94.0	94.8	95.1	3.1
2004	94.9	95.9	96.7	97.2	3.8	95.7	96.5	97.3	97.6	2.6
2005	98.2	98.9	99.5	100.0	2.9	98.3	98.9	99.5	100.0	2.5
2006	100.8	101.7	102.5	103.2	3.2	100.7	101.7	102.5	103.2	3.2
Goods-Producing[2]										
2001	83.9	84.7	85.3	86.0	3.6	87.9	88.8	89.3	90.0	3.6
2002	87.0	87.7	88.2	89.0	3.5	90.7	91.4	91.9	92.6	2.9
2003	90.5	91.5	92.1	92.6	4.0	93.3	94.1	94.6	94.9	2.5
2004	94.5	95.4	96.5	96.9	4.6	95.6	96.2	97.2	97.2	2.4
2005	98.0	99.0	99.8	100.0	3.2	97.9	98.7	99.5	100.0	2.9
2006	100.3	101.3	102.0	102.5	2.5	100.7	101.8	102.3	102.9	2.9
Service-Providing[3]										
2001	85.4	86.2	87.1	87.8	4.4	87.4	88.3	89.2	89.8	3.8
2002	88.7	89.7	90.2	90.4	3.0	90.7	91.7	92.0	92.1	2.6
2003	91.7	92.5	93.6	94.0	4.0	93.3	93.9	94.9	95.2	3.4
2004	95.1	96.1	96.8	97.3	3.5	95.8	96.6	97.3	97.7	2.6
2005	98.3	98.9	99.5	100.0	2.8	98.4	99.0	99.5	100.0	2.4
2006	101.0	101.8	102.7	103.4	3.4	100.8	101.7	102.6	103.3	3.3
WORKERS BY OCCUPATION										
White-Collar[4]										
2001	84.8	85.7	86.5	87.2	4.4	87.0	87.9	88.7	89.3	3.7
2002	88.1	89.1	89.5	89.8	3.0	90.3	91.2	91.6	91.7	2.7
2003	91.3	92.1	93.2	93.5	4.1	92.9	93.7	94.7	94.9	3.5
2004	94.7	95.7	96.5	97.0	3.7	95.6	96.4	97.3	97.5	2.7
2005	98.2	98.9	99.5	100.0	3.1	98.3	98.9	99.5	100.0	2.6
2006	100.9	101.8	102.7	103.3	3.3	100.8	101.8	102.7	103.3	3.3
White-Collar, Excluding Sales										
2001	84.8	85.7	86.6	87.2	4.6	87.0	87.9	88.8	89.5	4.1
2002	88.2	89.0	89.4	89.8	3.0	90.5	91.3	91.7	91.9	2.7
2003	91.5	92.2	93.2	93.7	4.3	93.3	93.9	94.7	95.1	3.5
2004	94.9	95.7	96.5	97.1	3.6	95.9	96.5	97.2	97.7	2.7
2005	98.4	99.0	99.6	100.0	3.0	98.5	99.1	99.5	100.0	2.4
2006	101.1	101.9	102.9	103.5	3.5	101.0	102.0	102.9	103.5	3.5
Management, Professional, and Related										
2001	85.0	86.0	86.8	87.4	4.5	87.0	88.0	88.9	89.5	4.1
2002	88.3	89.2	89.5	89.7	2.6	90.4	91.3	91.6	91.7	2.5
2003	91.6	92.3	93.3	93.8	4.6	93.3	94.0	94.8	95.3	3.9
2004	94.9	95.7	96.5	97.1	3.5	96.0	96.5	97.3	97.8	2.6
2005	98.5	99.1	99.6	100.0	3.0	98.6	99.2	99.6	100.0	2.2
2006	101.1	101.9	102.9	103.5	3.5	101.1	102.0	103.0	103.6	3.6
Management, Business, and Financial										
2001	86.1	87.1	87.8	88.5	4.4	87.3	88.3	89.1	89.8	4.1
2002	89.5	90.7	90.7	90.6	2.4	90.8	92.2	92.4	92.1	2.6
2003	93.3	93.9	94.9	95.4	5.3	94.8	95.5	96.4	96.7	5.0
2004	95.9	96.8	97.3	97.9	2.6	96.8	97.5	98.1	98.5	1.9
2005	99.1	99.6	99.7	100.0	2.1	99.2	99.7	99.5	100.0	1.5
2006	101.3	102.0	102.7	103.1	3.1	101.3	102.2	102.8	103.1	3.1
Professional and Related										
2001	84.1	85.0	86.0	86.5	4.7	86.9	87.8	88.7	89.3	4.1
2002	87.3	87.9	88.5	89.1	3.0	90.1	90.5	91.0	91.4	2.4
2003	90.3	91.0	92.0	92.6	3.9	92.1	92.7	93.6	94.2	3.1
2004	94.1	94.8	95.8	96.5	4.2	95.3	95.7	96.7	97.2	3.2
2005	98.0	98.8	99.5	100.0	3.6	98.2	98.8	99.6	100.0	2.9
2006	101.0	101.8	103.1	103.9	3.9	100.9	101.8	103.1	104.0	4.0

[1]Includes wages, salaries, and employer costs for employee benefits.
[2]Includes mining, construction, and manufacturing.
[3]Includes the following industries: wholesale trade; retail trade; transportation and warehousing; utilities; information; finance and insurance; real estate and rental and leasing; professional, scientific, and technical services; management of companies and enterprises; administrative and support and waste management and remediation services; education services; health care and social assistance; arts, entertainment, and recreation; accommodation and food services; and other services, except public administration.
[4]Includes the following occupational groups: management, business, and financial; professional and related; sales and related; and office and administrative support.

Table 6-1. Employment Cost Index, Private Industry Workers, Total Compensation[1] and Wages and Salaries, by Industry and Occupation, 2001–2006—*Continued*

(December 2005 = 100.)

Characteristic and year	Total compensation					Wages and salaries				
	Indexes				Percent change for 12 months (ended December)	Indexes				Percent change for 12 months (ended December)
	March	June	September	December		March	June	September	December	
Sales and Office										
2001	84.5	85.4	86.1	86.9	4.1	86.9	87.8	88.4	89.1	3.5
2002	87.8	89.0	89.5	89.8	3.3	90.0	91.2	91.5	91.7	2.9
2003	90.8	91.9	93.0	93.1	3.7	92.4	93.3	94.4	94.3	2.8
2004	94.4	95.7	96.6	96.8	4.0	95.1	96.1	97.2	97.2	3.1
2005	97.8	98.5	99.3	100.0	3.3	97.8	98.5	99.3	100.0	2.9
2006	100.5	101.6	102.3	102.9	2.9	100.4	101.6	102.4	103.0	3.0
Sales and Related										
2001	84.9	86.0	86.3	87.2	3.3	86.8	88.0	87.9	88.6	2.4
2002	87.7	89.7	89.7	89.7	2.9	89.2	91.0	91.0	90.9	2.6
2003	90.6	91.7	93.2	92.9	3.6	91.5	92.5	94.3	93.8	3.2
2004	94.0	95.4	96.8	96.2	3.6	94.4	95.7	97.4	96.6	3.0
2005	97.2	97.9	99.2	100.0	4.0	97.3	97.8	99.2	100.0	3.5
2006	99.9	101.1	101.7	102.3	2.3	99.8	101.3	102.0	102.6	2.6
Office and Administrative Support										
2001	84.2	84.9	85.9	86.6	4.6	87.0	87.7	88.8	89.4	4.2
2002	87.9	88.6	89.3	89.9	3.8	90.7	91.3	91.8	92.4	3.4
2003	91.0	92.0	92.8	93.3	3.8	93.1	93.9	94.4	94.7	2.5
2004	94.7	95.8	96.5	97.2	4.2	95.6	96.4	97.1	97.6	3.1
2005	98.1	98.9	99.5	100.0	2.9	98.2	99.0	99.4	100.0	2.5
2006	100.9	101.9	102.7	103.4	3.4	100.9	101.9	102.6	103.3	3.3
Blue-Collar[5]										
2001	84.8	85.5	86.6	87.1	3.8	88.2	89.0	90.1	90.6	3.9
2002	88.0	88.9	89.5	90.0	3.3	91.3	92.1	92.6	93.0	2.6
2003	91.2	92.2	93.0	93.5	3.9	93.7	94.4	95.0	95.3	2.5
2004	95.2	96.3	97.1	97.5	4.3	95.9	96.7	97.4	97.7	2.5
2005	98.2	99.0	99.6	100.0	2.6	98.1	98.8	99.5	100.0	2.4
2006	100.6	101.5	102.3	102.8	2.8	100.6	101.5	102.2	102.8	2.8
Natural Resources, Construction, and Maintenance										
2001	84.3	85.0	86.4	86.6	4.0	87.6	88.4	89.9	90.0	3.8
2002	87.4	88.5	89.3	89.7	3.6	90.5	91.7	92.3	92.6	2.9
2003	90.8	92.0	92.8	93.3	4.0	93.2	94.1	94.8	95.2	2.8
2004	94.8	96.1	96.5	97.1	4.1	95.8	96.7	97.1	97.5	2.4
2005	97.9	98.9	99.5	100.0	3.0	97.8	98.7	99.4	100.0	2.6
2006	100.8	102.1	103.0	103.6	3.6	100.7	101.8	102.8	103.4	3.4
Construction, Extraction, Farming, Fishing, and Forestry										
2001	84.2	85.1	86.2	86.4	3.8	87.8	88.9	89.8	90.0	3.6
2002	87.3	88.1	88.8	89.5	3.6	90.6	91.3	91.9	92.4	2.7
2003	90.3	91.6	92.5	93.1	4.0	92.7	93.7	94.6	94.9	2.7
2004	94.7	95.8	96.4	97.2	4.4	95.8	96.6	96.9	97.5	2.7
2005	97.7	98.7	99.5	100.0	2.9	97.8	98.5	99.3	100.0	2.6
2006	100.7	102.2	103.1	103.7	3.7	100.7	102.0	103.0	103.7	3.7
Installation, Maintenance, and Repair										
2001	84.4	84.9	86.8	86.8	4.1	87.4	87.9	90.1	90.1	4.3
2002	87.4	89.1	90.0	90.1	3.8	90.4	92.2	92.9	92.9	3.1
2003	91.4	92.5	93.1	93.6	3.9	93.8	94.6	95.1	95.5	2.8
2004	95.0	96.3	96.7	97.0	3.6	95.9	96.8	97.3	97.4	2.0
2005	98.1	99.3	99.6	100.0	3.1	97.8	99.1	99.5	100.0	2.7
2006	100.9	102.1	103.0	103.4	3.4	100.7	101.6	102.6	103.0	3.0
Production, Transportation, and Material Moving										
2001	85.3	85.8	86.7	87.4	3.6	88.7	89.4	90.2	91.0	3.9
2002	88.4	89.1	89.7	90.3	3.3	91.9	92.4	92.8	93.3	2.5
2003	91.5	92.4	93.2	93.6	3.7	94.0	94.6	95.1	95.4	2.3
2004	95.5	96.5	97.4	97.8	4.5	96.0	96.7	97.6	97.8	2.5
2005	98.5	99.0	99.7	100.0	2.2	98.3	98.9	99.6	100.0	2.2
2006	100.4	101.1	101.7	102.3	2.3	100.6	101.2	101.8	102.4	2.4

[1] Includes wages, salaries, and employer costs for employee benefits.
[5] Includes the following occupational groups: farming, fishing, and forestry; construction and extraction; installation, maintenance, and repair; production; and transportation and material moving.

Table 6-1. Employment Cost Index, Private Industry Workers, Total Compensation¹ and Wages and Salaries, by Industry and Occupation, 2001–2006—*Continued*

(December 2005 = 100.)

Characteristic and year	Total compensation					Wages and salaries				
	Indexes				Percent change for 12 months (ended December)	Indexes				Percent change for 12 months (ended December)
	March	June	September	December		March	June	September	December	
Production										
2001	84.9	85.2	86.0	86.7	3.2	88.4	89.1	89.7	90.5	3.7
2002	87.7	88.3	88.8	89.4	3.1	91.3	91.8	92.3	92.8	2.5
2003	91.0	91.7	92.5	93.0	4.0	93.6	94.1	94.8	95.1	2.5
2004	95.3	96.4	97.4	97.7	5.1	95.6	96.5	97.4	97.5	2.5
2005	98.6	99.1	99.6	100.0	2.4	98.3	98.9	99.5	100.0	2.6
2006	100.4	101.0	101.6	102.0	2.0	100.7	101.2	101.7	102.2	2.2
Transportation and Material Moving										
2001	85.8	86.7	87.7	88.5	4.2	89.0	89.9	90.8	91.6	4.1
2002	89.5	90.2	90.9	91.4	3.3	92.6	93.1	93.6	94.0	2.6
2003	92.4	93.4	94.0	94.4	3.3	94.7	95.3	95.6	95.8	1.9
2004	95.7	96.7	97.5	97.9	3.7	96.4	97.1	97.9	98.2	2.5
2005	98.3	99.0	99.8	100.0	2.1	98.5	98.9	99.7	100.0	1.8
2006	100.4	101.2	102.0	102.6	2.6	100.4	101.2	102.0	102.6	2.6
Service										
2001	87.1	87.7	88.2	89.4	3.8	89.7	90.2	90.6	91.7	3.4
2002	90.2	90.6	91.5	92.0	2.9	92.5	92.8	93.4	93.9	2.4
2003	93.0	93.4	94.4	95.0	3.3	94.5	94.8	95.6	96.1	2.3
2004	95.9	96.7	97.2	97.7	2.8	96.4	96.9	97.4	97.9	1.9
2005	98.5	99.0	99.5	100.0	2.4	98.6	99.0	99.6	100.0	2.1
2006	100.8	101.5	102.3	103.1	3.1	100.6	101.3	102.0	102.9	2.9

¹Includes wages, salaries, and employer costs for employee benefits.

Table 6-2. Employment Cost Index, Private Industry Workers, Total Compensation[1] and Wages and Salaries, by Bargaining Status, Industry, Region, and Metropolitan Area Status, 2001–2006

(December 2005 = 100.)

Characteristic and year	Total compensation					Wages and salaries				
	Indexes				Percent change for 12 months (ended December)	Indexes				Percent change for 12 months (ended December)
	March	June	September	December		March	June	September	December	
WORKERS BY BARGAINING STATUS AND INDUSTRY										
Union Workers										
2001	82.0	82.9	83.7	84.8	4.2	86.5	87.4	88.3	89.6	4.3
2002	85.7	86.5	87.5	88.2	4.0	90.2	91.1	91.9	92.6	3.3
2003	89.5	90.7	91.6	92.3	4.6	93.0	93.8	94.4	94.9	2.5
2004	94.5	95.9	96.7	97.3	5.4	95.6	96.4	97.1	97.6	2.8
2005	97.9	98.8	99.6	100.0	2.8	97.9	98.7	99.5	100.0	2.5
2006	100.5	101.8	102.4	103.0	3.0	100.3	101.2	101.7	102.3	2.3
Union Workers, Goods-Producing[2]										
2001	81.9	82.7	83.4	84.0	2.9	87.2	88.2	88.9	89.5	3.5
2002	84.8	85.5	86.4	87.1	3.7	90.0	90.9	91.7	92.4	3.2
2003	88.9	90.2	90.9	91.7	5.3	92.9	94.0	94.5	95.0	2.8
2004	94.6	95.9	96.7	97.2	6.0	95.4	96.3	96.9	97.1	2.2
2005	97.7	98.8	99.6	100.0	2.9	97.5	98.5	99.2	100.0	3.0
2006	99.9	101.2	101.8	102.2	2.2	100.5	101.6	101.9	102.3	2.3
Union Workers, Manufacturing										
2001	81.1	81.4	82.0	83.0	2.7	87.3	88.1	88.8	89.7	3.7
2002	84.1	84.7	85.4	86.5	4.2	90.3	90.8	91.6	92.5	3.1
2003	88.6	89.5	90.1	91.0	5.2	93.3	94.2	94.5	95.0	2.7
2004	95.6	96.7	97.5	97.8	7.5	95.5	96.2	97.0	97.1	2.2
2005	98.3	99.1	99.7	100.0	2.2	97.6	98.3	99.0	100.0	3.0
2006	99.3	100.1	100.5	100.8	0.8	100.6	101.2	101.4	101.7	1.7
Union Workers, Manufacturing, Blue-Collar[3]										
2001	81.4	81.7	82.4	83.3	2.7	87.4	88.1	88.8	89.7	3.7
2002	84.3	85.0	85.6	86.8	4.2	90.2	90.8	91.6	92.6	3.2
2003	88.8	89.7	90.3	91.3	5.2	93.3	94.2	94.6	95.0	2.6
2004	95.9	97.0	97.8	98.2	7.6	95.5	96.2	97.0	97.1	2.2
2005	98.3	99.1	99.7	100.0	1.8	97.6	98.4	99.0	100.0	3.0
2006	99.4	100.2	100.5	100.7	0.7	100.6	101.2	101.2	101.5	1.5
Union Workers, Service-Providing[4]										
2001	82.0	83.0	84.0	85.5	5.2	85.9	86.8	87.8	89.6	4.9
2002	86.4	87.3	88.4	89.1	4.2	90.3	91.2	92.0	92.7	3.5
2003	90.1	91.1	92.3	92.8	4.2	93.1	93.6	94.4	94.8	2.3
2004	94.4	95.8	96.6	97.3	4.8	95.7	96.5	97.3	98.0	3.4
2005	98.1	98.8	99.6	100.0	2.8	98.2	99.0	99.7	100.0	2.0
2006	101.0	102.2	102.9	103.6	3.6	100.1	100.9	101.6	102.2	2.2
Nonunion Workers										
2001	85.5	86.3	87.2	87.8	4.2	87.7	88.6	89.3	89.9	3.7
2002	88.7	89.6	90.0	90.3	2.8	90.8	91.7	92.0	92.2	2.6
2003	91.8	92.5	93.5	93.9	4.0	93.3	94.0	94.9	95.1	3.1
2004	95.0	95.9	96.7	97.2	3.5	95.8	96.5	97.3	97.6	2.6
2005	98.3	98.9	99.5	100.0	2.9	98.3	98.9	99.5	100.0	2.5
2006	100.9	101.7	102.6	103.2	3.2	100.8	101.8	102.7	103.3	3.3
Nonunion, Goods-Producing[2]										
2001	84.7	85.5	86.0	86.7	3.8	88.1	89.0	89.5	90.1	3.6
2002	87.8	88.5	88.8	89.7	3.5	91.0	91.6	91.9	92.7	2.9
2003	91.1	91.9	92.6	92.9	3.6	93.4	94.1	94.6	94.9	2.4
2004	94.5	95.2	96.4	96.8	4.2	95.6	96.2	97.3	97.3	2.5
2005	98.1	99.0	99.9	100.0	3.3	98.0	98.7	99.6	100.0	2.8
2006	100.5	101.4	102.0	102.5	2.5	100.7	101.9	102.4	103.0	3.0
Nonunion Workers, Manufacturing										
2001	84.5	85.3	85.8	86.3	3.6	88.5	89.4	89.8	90.3	3.4
2002	87.6	88.4	88.7	89.4	3.6	91.4	92.0	92.4	92.9	2.9
2003	91.2	91.9	92.6	92.8	3.8	93.9	94.5	94.9	95.2	2.5
2004	94.4	95.3	96.4	96.6	4.1	95.8	96.5	97.5	97.5	2.4
2005	98.2	99.1	99.8	100.0	3.5	98.4	99.0	99.8	100.0	2.6
2006	100.3	101.3	101.7	102.1	2.1	100.7	101.8	102.0	102.5	2.5
Nonunion, Manufacturing, Blue-Collar[3]										
2001	85.7	86.1	86.9	87.6	3.4	88.5	89.4	90.1	90.8	3.9
2002	88.8	89.5	89.8	90.6	3.4	91.8	92.5	92.7	93.4	2.9
2003	92.1	92.7	93.6	94.0	3.8	94.3	94.6	95.2	95.5	2.2
2004	95.5	96.2	97.4	97.7	3.9	96.1	96.5	97.5	97.7	2.3
2005	98.8	99.4	99.7	100.0	2.4	98.6	99.2	99.7	100.0	2.4
2006	100.7	101.3	102.1	102.7	2.7	100.8	101.4	102.3	102.9	2.9

[1]Includes wages, salaries, and employer costs for employee benefits.
[2]Includes mining, construction, and manufacturing.
[3]Includes the following occupational groups: farming, fishing, and forestry; construction and extraction; installation, maintenance, and repair; production; and transportation and material moving.
[4]Includes the following industries: wholesale trade; retail trade; transportation and warehousing; utilities; information; finance and insurance; real estate and rental and leasing; professional, scientific, and technical services; management of companies and enterprises; administrative and support and waste management and remediation services; education services; health care and social assistance; arts, entertainment, and recreation; accommodation and food services; and other services, except public administration.

Table 6-2. Employment Cost Index, Private Industry Workers, Total Compensation¹ and Wages and Salaries, by Bargaining Status, Industry, Region, and Metropolitan Area Status, 2001–2006—*Continued*

(December 2005 = 100.)

Characteristic and year	Total compensation					Wages and salaries				
	Indexes				Percent change for 12 months (ended December)	Indexes				Percent change for 12 months (ended December)
	March	June	September	December		March	June	September	December	
Nonunion, Service-Providing⁴										
2001	85.7	86.5	87.5	88.0	4.1	87.6	88.5	89.3	89.9	3.8
2002	88.9	89.9	90.4	90.5	2.8	90.8	91.7	92.0	92.1	2.4
2003	91.9	92.7	93.7	94.1	4.0	93.3	94.0	94.9	95.2	3.4
2004	95.2	96.1	96.9	97.3	3.4	95.8	96.6	97.3	97.7	2.6
2005	98.3	98.9	99.4	100.0	2.8	98.4	99.0	99.5	100.0	2.4
2006	101.0	101.8	102.7	103.4	3.4	100.8	101.7	102.7	103.4	3.4
CENSUS REGIONS AND DIVISIONS⁵										
Northeast										
2001	84.3	85.3	86.2	86.7	3.8	86.8	87.8	88.6	89.2	3.8
2002	87.7	88.6	88.9	89.3	3.0	90.2	91.0	91.1	91.5	2.6
2003	90.6	91.4	92.4	92.9	4.0	92.4	93.2	94.1	94.5	3.3
2004	94.2	95.5	96.3	96.6	4.0	95.3	96.3	97.1	97.2	2.9
2005	97.6	98.5	99.2	100.0	3.5	97.8	98.6	99.2	100.0	2.9
2006	100.9	101.8	102.5	103.3	3.3	100.8	101.7	102.5	103.1	3.1
New England										
2001	...	...	...	...	...	...	...	...	...	...
2002	...	...	...	...	...	...	...	...	...	...
2003	...	...	...	...	...	...	...	...	...	...
2004	...	...	...	...	...	...	...	...	...	...
2005	...	...	...	...	...	...	...	...	...	...
2006	100.7	101.4	102.1	103.1	3.1	100.7	101.5	102.3	103.1	3.1
Middle Atlantic										
2001	...	...	...	...	...	...	...	...	...	...
2002	...	...	...	...	...	...	...	...	...	...
2003	...	...	...	...	...	...	...	...	...	...
2004	...	...	...	...	...	...	...	...	...	...
2005	...	...	...	...	...	...	...	...	...	...
2006	100.9	101.9	102.6	103.3	3.3	100.8	101.7	102.5	103.1	3.1
South										
2001	86.4	87.2	88.1	88.7	4.2	88.9	89.7	90.5	91.0	3.6
2002	89.5	90.5	91.2	91.2	2.8	91.8	92.7	93.3	93.2	2.4
2003	92.0	92.7	93.6	93.9	3.0	93.5	94.1	94.9	95.0	1.9
2004	95.2	96.2	97.1	97.7	4.0	95.8	96.7	97.5	98.0	3.2
2005	98.9	99.3	99.7	100.0	2.4	98.9	99.3	99.7	100.0	2.0
2006	101.0	101.6	102.8	103.5	3.5	101.0	101.6	102.9	103.6	3.6
South Atlantic										
2001	...	...	...	...	...	...	...	...	...	...
2002	...	...	...	...	...	...	...	...	...	...
2003	...	...	...	...	...	...	...	...	...	...
2004	...	...	...	...	...	...	...	...	...	...
2005	...	...	...	...	...	...	...	...	...	...
2006	101.2	101.9	103.1	103.8	3.8	101.3	101.9	103.2	103.9	3.9
East South Central										
2001	...	...	...	...	...	...	...	...	...	...
2002	...	...	...	...	...	...	...	...	...	...
2003	...	...	...	...	...	...	...	...	...	...
2004	...	...	...	...	...	...	...	...	...	...
2005	...	...	...	...	...	...	...	...	...	...
2006	100.7	100.9	101.5	102.3	2.3	100.7	101.5	102.1	103.1	3.1
West South Central										
2001	...	...	...	...	...	...	...	...	...	...
2002	...	...	...	...	...	...	...	...	...	...
2003	...	...	...	...	...	...	...	...	...	...
2004	...	...	...	...	...	...	...	...	...	...
2005	...	...	...	...	...	...	...	...	...	...
2006	100.7	101.4	102.7	103.4	3.4	100.6	101.2	102.7	103.4	3.4

¹Includes wages, salaries, and employer costs for employee benefits.
⁴Includes the following industries: wholesale trade; retail trade; transportation and warehousing; utilities; information; finance and insurance; real estate and rental and leasing; professional, scientific, and technical services; management of companies and enterprises; administrative and support and waste management and remediation services; education services; health care and social assistance; arts, entertainment, and recreation; accommodation and food services; and other services, except public administration.
⁵The states (including the District of Columbia) that comprise the census divisions are: New England—Connecticut, Maine, Massachusetts, New Hampshire, Rhode Island, and Vermont; Middle Atlantic—New Jersey, New York, and Pennsylvania; South Atlantic—Delaware, District of Columbia, Florida, Georgia, Maryland, North Carolina, South Carolina, Virginia, and West Virginia; East South Central—Alabama, Kentucky, Mississippi, and Tennessee; West South Central—Arkansas, Louisiana, Oklahoma, and Texas; East North Central—Illinois, Indiana, Michigan, Ohio, and Wisconsin; West North Central— Iowa, Kansas, Minnesota, Missouri, Nebraska, North Dakota, and South Dakota; Mountain—Arizona, Colorado, Idaho, Montana, Nevada, New Mexico, Utah, and Wyoming; and Pacific—Alaska, California, Hawaii, Oregon, and Washington.
. . . = Not available.

Table 6-2. Employment Cost Index, Private Industry Workers, Total Compensation[1] and Wages and Salaries, by Bargaining Status, Industry, Region, and Metropolitan Area Status, 2001–2006—*Continued*

(December 2005 = 100.)

Characteristic and year	Total compensation					Wages and salaries				
	Indexes				Percent change for 12 months (ended December)	Indexes				Percent change for 12 months (ended December)
	March	June	September	December		March	June	September	December	
Midwest										
2001	84.8	85.4	86.1	86.7	3.5	86.8	87.6	88.3	88.9	3.3
2002	88.0	88.7	89.0	89.5	3.2	90.3	91.0	91.3	91.7	3.1
2003	92.1	92.8	93.6	94.0	5.0	94.2	94.7	95.2	95.5	4.1
2004	95.0	95.9	96.6	96.9	3.1	95.6	96.1	96.9	97.1	1.7
2005	97.8	98.4	99.5	100.0	3.2	97.8	98.2	99.4	100.0	3.0
2006	100.7	101.7	102.3	102.8	2.8	100.4	101.4	102.0	102.6	2.6
East North Central										
2001	...	...	...	...	...	...	...	...	...	...
2002	...	...	...	...	...	...	...	...	...	...
2003	...	...	...	...	...	...	...	...	...	...
2004	...	...	...	...	...	...	...	...	...	...
2005	...	...	...	...	...	...	...	...	...	...
2006	100.7	101.7	102.3	102.8	2.8	100.3	101.4	101.9	102.5	2.5
West North Central										
2001	...	...	...	...	...	...	...	...	...	...
2002	...	...	...	...	...	...	...	...	...	...
2003	...	...	...	...	...	...	...	...	...	...
2004	...	...	...	...	...	...	...	...	...	...
2005	...	...	...	...	...	...	...	...	...	...
2006	100.6	101.5	102.4	102.7	2.7	100.6	101.5	102.4	102.7	2.7
West										
2001	84.1	85.0	85.9	86.9	5.2	87.4	88.3	89.2	90.2	4.8
2002	87.4	88.5	89.1	89.8	3.3	90.4	91.5	92.0	92.4	2.4
2003	90.9	92.0	93.2	93.8	4.5	93.0	93.9	95.1	95.5	3.4
2004	95.3	96.2	96.9	97.4	3.8	96.4	97.0	97.7	98.0	2.6
2005	98.4	99.3	99.7	100.0	2.7	98.4	99.3	99.6	100.0	2.0
2006	100.6	101.8	102.5	103.0	3.0	100.7	102.1	102.7	103.2	3.2
Mountain										
2001	...	...	...	...	...	...	...	...	...	...
2002	...	...	...	...	...	...	...	...	...	...
2003	...	...	...	...	...	...	...	...	...	...
2004	...	...	...	...	...	...	...	...	...	...
2005	...	...	...	...	...	...	...	...	...	...
2006	101.0	101.8	102.7	103.1	3.1	100.6	101.7	102.8	103.2	3.2
Pacific										
2001	...	...	...	...	...	...	...	...	...	...
2002	...	...	...	...	...	...	...	...	...	...
2003	...	...	...	...	...	...	...	...	...	...
2004	...	...	...	...	...	...	...	...	...	...
2005	...	...	...	...	...	...	...	...	...	...
2006	100.5	101.8	102.5	103.0	3.0	100.8	102.2	102.7	103.3	3.3
Metropolitan Areas										
2001	...	...	...	...	...	...	...	...	...	...
2002	...	...	...	...	...	...	...	...	...	...
2003	...	...	...	...	...	...	...	...	...	...
2004	...	...	...	...	...	...	...	...	...	...
2005	...	...	...	...	...	...	...	...	...	...
2006	100.8	101.7	102.5	103.1	3.1	100.7	101.7	102.5	103.1	3.1
Nonmetropolitan Areas										
2001	...	...	...	...	...	...	...	...	...	...
2002	...	...	...	...	...	...	...	...	...	...
2003	...	...	...	...	...	...	...	...	...	...
2004	...	...	...	...	...	...	...	...	...	...
2005	...	...	...	...	...	...	...	...	...	...
2006	100.8	101.5	102.6	103.3	3.3	100.9	101.6	102.6	103.5	3.5

[1]Includes wages, salaries, and employer costs for employee benefits.
... = Not available.

Table 6-3. Employment Cost Index, State and Local Government Workers, Total Compensation[1] and Wages and Salaries, by Industry and Occupation, 2001–2006

(December 2005 = 100.)

Characteristic and year	Total compensation					Wages and salaries				
	Indexes				Percent change for 12 months (ended December)	Indexes				Percent change for 12 months (ended December)
	March	June	September	December		March	June	September	December	
WORKERS BY INDUSTRY										
Total State and Local Government										
2001	83.6	84.1	85.8	86.2	4.1	87.6	88.0	89.7	90.2	3.8
2002	86.7	87.0	89.0	89.7	4.1	90.5	90.8	92.4	93.0	3.1
2003	90.4	90.7	92.3	92.8	3.5	93.4	93.6	94.6	95.0	2.2
2004	93.5	93.9	95.4	96.1	3.6	95.4	95.6	96.6	97.0	2.1
2005	96.9	97.2	99.1	100.0	4.1	97.6	97.8	99.1	100.0	3.1
2006	100.5	100.9	103.2	104.1	4.1	100.3	100.8	102.8	103.5	3.5
Education and Health Services										
2001	84.3	84.7	86.9	87.1	3.9	87.8	88.1	90.2	90.4	3.6
2002	87.4	87.6	89.7	90.4	3.8	90.6	90.8	92.8	93.3	3.2
2003	90.8	91.1	92.7	93.2	3.1	93.5	93.6	94.7	95.0	1.8
2004	93.7	93.8	95.5	96.1	3.1	95.3	95.4	96.6	97.0	2.1
2005	96.7	97.0	99.0	100.0	4.1	97.4	97.6	99.0	100.0	3.1
2006	100.3	100.8	103.7	104.3	4.3	100.2	100.7	103.1	103.6	3.6
Education Services										
2001	84.4	84.7	86.9	87.2	3.9	87.9	88.2	90.3	90.5	3.4
2002	87.3	87.5	89.7	90.4	3.7	90.6	90.8	92.9	93.3	3.1
2003	90.8	91.1	92.7	93.1	3.0	93.4	93.6	94.7	95.0	1.8
2004	93.6	93.8	95.4	96.1	3.2	95.3	95.4	96.6	96.9	2.0
2005	96.6	96.9	98.9	100.0	4.1	97.3	97.5	98.9	100.0	3.2
2006	100.2	100.5	103.5	104.1	4.1	100.1	100.4	103.0	103.4	3.4
Schools[2]										
2001	84.4	84.7	87.0	87.2	3.9	87.9	88.2	90.3	90.5	3.4
2002	87.3	87.5	89.7	90.4	3.7	90.6	90.8	92.9	93.3	3.1
2003	90.8	91.1	92.7	93.1	3.0	93.4	93.6	94.7	95.0	1.8
2004	93.6	93.8	95.5	96.1	3.2	95.3	95.4	96.6	96.9	2.0
2005	96.6	96.9	98.9	100.0	4.1	97.3	97.5	98.9	100.0	3.2
2006	100.2	100.5	103.5	104.1	4.1	100.1	100.4	103.0	103.4	3.4
Elementary and Secondary Schools										
2001	84.1	84.3	86.5	86.7	3.5	87.8	88.2	90.0	90.3	3.1
2002	86.8	87.0	89.3	89.9	3.7	90.5	90.6	92.8	93.2	3.2
2003	90.3	90.6	92.4	92.7	3.1	93.2	93.4	94.6	94.8	1.7
2004	93.2	93.4	95.3	96.0	3.6	95.1	95.2	96.5	96.9	2.2
2005	96.4	96.6	98.8	100.0	4.2	97.1	97.2	98.9	100.0	3.2
2006	100.2	100.5	103.6	104.2	4.2	100.0	100.3	103.0	103.4	3.4
Health Care and Social Assistance[3]										
2001	83.4	84.5	86.0	86.8	5.0	86.1	87.1	88.6	89.5	4.8
2002	87.8	88.2	89.5	90.6	4.4	90.7	91.1	92.2	93.0	3.9
2003	91.2	91.4	92.9	93.5	3.2	93.5	93.9	94.7	95.3	2.5
2004	94.2	94.7	96.3	96.5	3.2	95.7	96.0	97.1	97.3	2.1
2005	97.6	98.0	99.5	100.0	3.6	98.1	98.5	99.4	100.0	2.8
2006	101.3	102.9	105.1	105.7	5.7	101.0	103.0	104.8	105.5	5.5
Hospitals										
2001	83.0	84.4	85.9	86.6	4.5	85.3	86.6	88.0	88.8	4.3
2002	87.6	88.1	89.3	90.6	4.6	90.0	90.6	91.7	92.8	4.5
2003	91.0	91.1	92.8	93.4	3.1	93.1	93.5	94.5	95.2	2.6
2004	93.9	94.4	96.1	96.7	3.5	95.6	95.9	97.1	97.7	2.6
2005	97.6	98.0	99.5	100.0	3.4	98.3	98.6	99.4	100.0	2.4
2006	100.9	101.3	103.3	104.3	4.3	100.9	101.4	103.1	104.4	4.4
WORKERS BY OCCUPATION										
White-Collar[4]										
2001	83.9	84.4	86.2	86.6	4.1	87.5	88.0	89.7	90.1	3.7
2002	87.0	87.3	89.3	90.1	4.0	90.4	90.6	92.5	93.1	3.3
2003	90.7	91.0	92.6	93.1	3.3	93.4	93.6	94.7	95.0	2.0
2004	93.8	94.1	95.6	96.2	3.3	95.4	95.6	96.6	97.0	2.1
2005	97.0	97.3	99.0	100.0	4.0	97.6	97.8	99.0	100.0	3.1
2006	100.4	100.9	103.3	104.0	4.0	100.3	100.7	102.8	103.5	3.5
Management, Professional, and Related										
2001	84.1	84.6	86.5	86.8	4.1	87.5	88.0	89.8	90.2	3.8
2002	87.2	87.4	89.5	90.3	4.0	90.4	90.6	92.5	93.1	3.2
2003	90.8	91.1	92.6	93.1	3.1	93.4	93.6	94.6	95.0	2.0
2004	93.8	94.0	95.5	96.2	3.3	95.3	95.5	96.6	97.0	2.1
2005	97.0	97.3	99.0	100.0	4.0	97.5	97.8	99.0	100.0	3.1
2006	100.3	100.8	103.3	104.0	4.0	100.2	100.7	102.9	103.5	3.5

[1]Includes wages, salaries, and employer costs for employee benefits.
[2]Includes elementary and secondary schools, junior colleges, colleges, universities, and professional schools.
[3]Includes ambulatory health care services and social assistance, not shown separately.
[4]Includes the following occupational groups: management, business, and financial; professional and related; sales and related; and office and administrative support.

Table 6-3. Employment Cost Index, State and Local Government Workers, Total Compensation[1] and Wages and Salaries, by Industry and Occupation, 2001–2006—*Continued*

(December 2005 = 100.)

Characteristic and year	Total compensation					Wages and salaries				
	Indexes				Percent change for 12 months (ended December)	Indexes				Percent change for 12 months (ended December)
	March	June	September	December		March	June	September	December	
Professional and Related										
2001	84.0	84.4	86.4	86.7	4.0	87.5	87.9	89.8	90.1	3.7
2002	87.0	87.2	89.4	90.2	4.0	90.2	90.5	92.4	93.0	3.2
2003	90.7	91.0	92.5	93.0	3.1	93.3	93.4	94.5	94.9	2.0
2004	93.6	93.9	95.5	96.1	3.3	95.3	95.4	96.6	96.9	2.1
2005	96.8	97.1	98.9	100.0	4.1	97.4	97.7	98.9	100.0	3.2
2006	100.2	100.8	103.4	104.0	4.0	100.2	100.7	103.0	103.6	3.6
Sales and Office										
2001	82.8	83.1	84.5	85.2	3.9	87.4	87.8	89.1	89.6	3.1
2002	86.1	86.5	88.3	89.1	4.6	90.4	90.8	92.3	92.9	3.7
2003	89.8	90.3	92.4	92.8	4.2	93.5	93.8	95.1	95.4	2.7
2004	93.7	94.4	95.7	96.5	4.0	96.0	96.2	97.3	97.6	2.3
2005	97.5	97.6	99.3	100.0	3.6	98.1	98.0	99.4	100.0	2.5
2006	100.9	101.5	103.3	104.1	4.1	100.6	101.2	102.6	103.2	3.2
Office and Administrative Support										
2001	82.6	82.9	84.4	85.1	3.9	87.4	87.8	89.1	89.7	3.1
2002	86.0	86.5	88.2	88.9	4.5	90.5	91.0	92.4	92.8	3.5
2003	89.6	90.0	92.1	92.6	4.2	93.4	93.7	95.0	95.3	2.7
2004	93.5	94.2	95.6	96.4	4.1	95.9	96.1	97.1	97.5	2.3
2005	97.4	97.5	99.2	100.0	3.7	98.0	97.9	99.3	100.0	2.6
2006	101.0	101.6	103.5	104.2	4.2	100.7	101.4	102.7	103.4	3.4
Blue-Collar[5]										
2001	83.5	83.7	84.9	85.8	4.3	87.8	88.1	89.4	90.4	3.9
2002	86.3	86.6	88.4	89.3	4.1	90.9	91.2	92.4	92.8	2.7
2003	90.3	90.5	91.7	92.4	3.5	93.7	94.0	94.8	95.1	2.5
2004	93.3	93.9	95.3	95.8	3.7	95.4	95.7	96.7	97.1	2.1
2005	97.2	97.7	99.5	100.0	4.4	97.9	98.3	99.5	100.0	3.0
2006	100.6	101.0	102.9	104.0	4.0	100.7	101.0	102.6	103.6	3.6
Service										
2001	82.1	82.6	84.1	84.7	4.7	87.8	88.3	89.7	90.3	3.8
2002	85.2	85.8	87.4	88.0	3.9	90.8	91.2	92.1	92.4	2.3
2003	88.8	89.3	91.0	91.6	4.1	93.1	93.6	94.3	94.9	2.7
2004	92.3	92.7	94.9	95.5	4.3	95.3	95.4	96.4	96.8	2.0
2005	96.2	96.7	99.1	100.0	4.7	97.3	97.7	99.3	100.0	3.3
2006	100.6	101.2	103.1	104.5	4.5	100.3	100.8	102.4	103.9	3.9

[1]Includes wages, salaries, and employer costs for employee benefits.
[5]Includes the following occupational groups: farming, fishing, and forestry; construction and extraction; installation, maintenance, and repair; production; and transportation and material moving.

Table 6-4. Employment Cost Index, Benefits, by Industry and Occupation, 2001–2006

(December 2005 = 100.)

Characteristic and year	Indexes				Percent change for 3 months (ended December)
	March	June	September	December	
WORKERS BY INDUSTRY					
Private Industry					
2001	78.8	79.5	80.6	81.5	1.1
2002	82.3	83.3	84.1	85.0	1.1
2003	87.0	88.1	89.4	90.5	1.2
2004	92.9	94.4	95.4	96.5	1.2
2005	98.0	98.8	99.6	100.3	0.7
2006	100.8	101.5	102.5	103.4	0.9
State and Local Government					
2001	75.2	76.3	77.4	78.0	0.8
2002	78.8	79.9	81.4	82.9	1.8
2003	84.1	85.4	86.9	88.0	1.3
2004	89.5	91.1	92.5	93.9	1.5
2005	95.6	96.9	98.4	99.7	1.3
2006	100.8	102.1	103.5	104.9	1.4
Goods-Producing[1]					
2001	76.5	77.0	77.8	78.7	1.1
2002	79.9	80.6	81.2	82.5	1.6
2003	85.2	86.5	87.5	88.4	1.0
2004	92.4	93.8	95.0	96.5	1.6
2005	98.2	99.5	100.3	100.2	-0.1
2006	99.5	100.3	101.2	101.9	0.7
Manufacturing					
2001	75.4	75.8	76.4	77.4	1.2
2002	78.8	79.7	80.3	81.5	1.5
2003	84.7	85.7	86.8	87.5	0.8
2004	92.7	94.1	95.3	96.1	0.8
2005	98.2	99.4	100.0	100.1	0.1
2006	98.9	99.7	100.5	101.0	0.5
Service-Providing[2]					
2001	79.7	80.5	81.7	82.6	1.1
2002	83.2	84.4	85.2	86.0	0.9
2003	87.7	88.8	90.2	91.4	1.3
2004	93.1	94.6	95.5	96.5	1.0
2005	98.0	98.5	99.4	100.3	0.9
2006	101.3	102.0	103.0	104.1	1.1
WORKERS BY OCCUPATION					
White-Collar[3]					
2001	79.0	80.0	81.0	82.1	1.3
2002	82.4	83.5	84.2	85.2	1.2
2003	86.9	88.0	89.4	90.6	1.3
2004	92.1	93.7	94.8	96.1	1.4
2005	97.7	98.6	99.7	100.5	0.8
2006	100.8	101.5	102.6	103.7	1.1
Management, Professional, and Related					
2001	. . .	. . .	. . .	. . .	. . .
2002	82.7	83.7	84.2	85.2	1.2
2003	87.1	87.9	89.5	90.7	1.3
2004	91.8	93.4	94.5	96.0	1.6
2005	97.8	98.8	99.8	100.5	0.7
2006	100.9	101.6	102.8	103.9	1.1
Sales and Office					
2001	. . .	. . .	. . .	. . .	. . .
2002	81.8	83.2	84.2	85.1	1.1
2003	86.6	88.0	89.3	90.4	1.2
2004	92.4	94.2	95.2	96.2	1.1
2005	97.4	98.2	99.4	100.4	1.0
2006	100.6	101.3	102.1	103.2	1.1

[1]Includes mining, construction, and manufacturing.
[2]Includes the following industries: wholesale trade; retail trade; transportation and warehousing; utilities; information; finance and insurance; real estate and rental and leasing; professional, scientific, and technical services; management of companies and enterprises; administrative and support and waste management and remediation services; education services; health care and social assistance; arts, entertainment, and recreation; accommodation and food services; and other services, except public administration.
[3]Includes the following occupational groups: management, business, and financial; professional and related; sales and related; and office and administrative support.
. . . = Not available.

Table 6-4. Employment Cost Index, Benefits, by Industry and Occupation, 2001–2006
   —Continued

(December 2005 = 100.)

Characteristic and year	Indexes				Percent change for 3 months (ended December)
	March	June	September	December	
Blue-Collar[4]					
2001	78.4	78.6	79.8	80.5	0.9
2002	81.6	82.5	83.6	84.7	1.3
2003	86.4	87.9	89.1	90.4	1.5
2004	93.8	95.3	96.4	97.6	1.2
2005	98.3	99.0	99.8	100.4	0.6
2006	100.5	101.4	102.3	103.2	0.9
Natural Resources, Construction, and Maintenance					
2001	. . .	. . .	. . .	. . .	. . .
2002	81.2	82.1	83.3	84.6	1.6
2003	86.0	87.6	88.7	90.3	1.8
2004	92.9	94.4	95.3	97.0	1.8
2005	98.0	98.8	99.7	100.5	0.8
2006	101.1	102.2	103.4	104.5	1.1
Production, Transportation, and Material Moving					
2001	. . .	. . .	. . .	. . .	. . .
2002	81.8	82.7	83.7	84.8	1.3
2003	86.7	88.1	89.4	90.5	1.2
2004	94.4	95.9	97.1	98.1	1.0
2005	98.6	99.1	99.9	100.3	0.4
2006	100.0	100.8	101.5	102.3	0.8
Service					
2001	. . .	. . .	. . .	. . .	. . .
2002	83.5	84.4	86.0	86.8	0.9
2003	88.5	89.4	90.7	92.0	1.4
2004	94.3	95.8	96.7	97.4	0.7
2005	97.9	98.8	99.5	100.4	0.9
2006	101.2	102.1	103.0	104.0	1.0

[4]Includes the following occupational groups: farming, fishing, and forestry; construction and extraction; installation, maintenance, and repair; production; and transportation and material moving.
. . . = Not available.

NOTES AND DEFINITIONS

EMPLOYER COSTS FOR EMPLOYEE COMPENSATION

The Employer Costs for Employee Compensation (ECEC) measures the average cost per employee hour worked that employers pay for wages and salaries and benefits.

Survey Scope

The ECEC consists of data for the civilian economy, obtained from both private industry and state and local government. Excluded from private industry are the self-employed and farm and private household workers. Federal government workers are excluded from the public sector. The private industry series and the state and local government series provide separate data for the two sectors.

The cost levels for June 2007 were collected from a probability sample of about 58,000 occupational observations within over 12,000 sample establishments in private indus-try, and from approximately 3,500 occupations within about 800 sample establishments in state and local governments. Data were collected for the pay period including the 12th day of the survey months of March, June, September, and December.

Current employment weights are used to calculate cost levels. The cost levels were calculated using the employment counts from the Bureau of Labor Statistics's (BLS) Current Employment Statistics (CES) program, benchmarked to the March 2005 universe of all private nonfarm establishments.

Sources of Additional Information

Additional information may be obtained from BLS news release 07-1434 "Employer Costs for Employee Compensation—June 2007," and in various articles in the BLS e-publication, *Compensation and Working Conditions*. These resources are available on the BLS Web site at <http://www.bls.gov>.

Table 6-5. Employer Compensation Costs Per Hour Worked for Employee Compensation and Costs as a Percent of Total Compensation: Private Industry Workers, by Major Industry Group, June 2007

(Dollars, percent of total cost.)

Compensation component	All workers		Goods-producing[1]						Service-providing[2]			
			All goods-producing[1]		Construction		Manufacturing		All service-providing[2]		Trade, transportation, and utilities	
	Cost	Percent	Cost	Percent	Cost	Percent	Cost	Percent	Cost	Percent	Cost	Percent
TOTAL COMPENSATION	25.93	100.0	30.41	100.0	29.12	100.0	30.56	100.0	24.77	100.0	22.15	100.0
WAGES AND SALARIES	18.32	70.6	20.26	66.6	20.15	69.2	20.06	65.6	17.82	71.9	15.72	71.0
TOTAL BENEFITS	7.61	29.4	10.15	33.4	8.98	30.8	10.50	34.4	6.96	28.1	6.43	29.0
Paid Leave	1.77	6.8	1.96	6.4	1.03	3.5	2.39	7.8	1.72	6.9	1.38	6.2
Vacation	0.90	3.5	1.03	3.4	0.58	2.0	1.24	4.1	0.86	3.5	0.70	3.2
Holiday	0.58	2.2	0.69	2.3	0.36	1.2	0.85	2.8	0.55	2.2	0.43	1.9
Sick	0.22	0.8	0.16	0.5	0.07	0.2	0.21	0.7	0.23	0.9	0.19	0.9
Other	0.08	0.3	0.07	0.2	0.02	0.1	0.09	0.3	0.08	0.3	0.05	0.2
Supplemental Pay	0.78	3.0	1.23	4.0	1.05	3.6	1.26	4.1	0.66	2.7	0.56	2.5
Overtime and premium pay[3]	0.27	1.0	0.56	1.8	0.60	2.1	0.52	1.7	0.20	0.8	0.27	1.2
Shift differentials	0.07	0.3	0.10	0.3	(4)	(5)	0.14	0.5	0.06	0.3	0.03	0.1
Nonproduction bonuses	0.44	1.7	0.57	1.9	0.44	1.5	0.60	2.0	0.40	1.6	0.27	1.2
Insurance	1.97	7.6	2.77	9.1	2.15	7.4	3.02	9.9	1.77	7.1	1.75	7.9
Life insurance	0.04	0.2	0.07	0.2	0.05	0.2	0.06	0.2	0.04	0.2	0.03	0.2
Health insurance	1.84	7.1	2.58	8.5	2.04	7.0	2.81	9.2	1.65	6.7	1.65	7.4
Short-term disability	0.05	0.2	0.08	0.3	0.04	0.1	0.10	0.3	0.05	0.2	0.04	0.2
Long-term disability	0.04	0.1	0.04	0.1	(4)	(5)	0.05	0.2	0.04	0.2	0.03	0.1
Retirement and Savings	0.88	3.4	1.38	4.5	1.43	4.9	1.27	4.1	0.75	3.0	0.75	3.4
Defined benefit plans	0.41	1.6	0.82	2.7	0.95	3.2	0.69	2.2	0.30	1.2	0.35	1.6
Defined contribution plans	0.48	1.8	0.57	1.9	0.48	1.7	0.58	1.9	0.45	1.8	0.40	1.8
Legally Required Benefits	2.21	8.5	2.82	9.3	3.31	11.4	2.56	8.4	2.05	8.3	1.99	9.0
Social Security and Medicare	1.54	5.9	1.74	5.7	1.67	5.7	1.75	5.7	1.49	6.0	1.32	5.9
Social Security[6]	1.24	4.8	1.40	4.6	1.35	4.6	1.41	4.6	1.19	4.8	1.06	4.8
Medicare	0.30	1.2	0.34	1.1	0.32	1.1	0.34	1.1	0.29	1.2	0.26	1.2
Federal unemployment insurance	0.03	0.1	0.03	0.1	0.03	0.1	0.03	0.1	0.03	0.1	0.04	0.2
State unemployment insurance	0.16	0.6	0.21	0.7	0.25	0.8	0.19	0.6	0.14	0.6	0.14	0.6
Workers' compensation	0.48	1.8	0.85	2.8	1.36	4.7	0.59	1.9	0.38	1.5	0.50	2.3

Note: Individual items may not sum to totals due to rounding.

[1]Includes mining, construction, and manufacturing. The agriculture, forestry, farming, and hunting sector is excluded.
[2]Includes utilities; wholesale trade; retail trade; transportation and warehousing; information; finance and insurance; real estate and rental and leasing; professional and technical services; management of companies and enterprises; administrative and waste services; education services; health care and social assistance; arts, entertainment, and recreation; accommodation and food services; and other services, except public administration.
[3]Includes premium pay for work in addition to the regular work schedule (such as overtime, weekends, and holidays).
[4]Cost per hour worked is $0.01 or less.
[5]Less than 0.05 percent.
[6]Comprises the Old Age, Survivors, and Disability Insurance (OASDI) program.

Table 6-5. Employer Compensation Costs Per Hour Worked for Employee Compensation and Costs as a Percent of Total Compensation: Private Industry Workers, by Major Industry Group, June 2007—*Continued*

(Dollars, percent of total cost.)

Compensation component	Service-providing[2]											
	Information		Financial activities		Professional and business services		Education and health services		Leisure and hospitality		Other services	
	Cost	Percent	Cost	Percent	Cost	Percent	Cost	Percent	Cost	Percent	Cost	Percent
TOTAL COMPENSATION	39.10	100.0	34.70	100.0	30.41	100.0	27.67	100.0	11.49	100.0	21.58	100.0
WAGES AND SALARIES	26.75	68.4	23.58	68.0	22.30	73.3	19.99	72.3	8.98	78.1	16.01	74.2
TOTAL BENEFITS	12.35	31.6	11.12	32.0	8.11	26.7	7.68	27.7	2.51	21.9	5.57	25.8
Paid Leave	3.62	9.3	2.81	8.1	2.16	7.1	2.12	7.7	0.40	3.5	1.36	6.3
Vacation	1.82	4.7	1.42	4.1	1.07	3.5	1.05	3.8	0.23	2.0	0.62	2.9
Holiday	1.11	2.8	0.90	2.6	0.74	2.4	0.65	2.3	0.12	1.0	0.52	2.4
Sick	0.43	1.1	0.36	1.0	0.27	0.9	0.32	1.1	0.04	0.4	0.16	0.7
Other	0.26	0.7	0.14	0.4	0.08	0.3	0.11	0.4	0.02	0.1	0.06	0.3
Supplemental Pay	1.09	2.8	1.79	5.2	0.84	2.8	0.55	2.0	0.13	1.2	0.39	1.8
Overtime and premium pay[3]	0.36	0.9	0.13	0.4	0.19	0.6	0.21	0.8	0.08	0.7	0.13	0.6
Shift differentials	0.05	0.1	0.02	(5)	0.05	0.2	0.20	0.7	(4)	(5)	(4)	(5)
Nonproduction bonuses	0.68	1.7	1.64	4.7	0.60	2.0	0.14	0.5	0.05	0.4	0.25	1.2
Insurance	3.17	8.1	2.74	7.9	1.83	6.0	2.06	7.5	0.61	5.3	1.37	6.4
Life insurance	0.05	0.1	0.07	0.2	0.06	0.2	0.03	0.1	(4)	(5)	0.05	0.2
Health insurance	2.87	7.3	2.53	7.3	1.66	5.5	1.95	7.0	0.59	5.1	1.27	5.9
Short-term disability	0.17	0.4	0.08	0.2	0.06	0.2	0.04	0.1	(4)	(5)	0.03	0.1
Long-term disability	0.08	0.2	0.06	0.2	0.05	0.2	0.05	0.2	(4)	(5)	0.03	0.1
Retirement and Savings	1.70	4.3	1.46	4.2	0.87	2.9	0.74	2.7	0.11	1.0	0.47	2.2
Defined benefit plans	0.97	2.5	0.56	1.6	0.32	1.0	0.24	0.9	0.02	0.2	0.14	0.6
Defined contribution plans	0.73	1.9	0.90	2.6	0.55	1.8	0.50	1.8	0.09	0.8	0.34	1.6
Legally Required Benefits	2.77	7.1	2.32	6.7	2.41	7.9	2.20	7.9	1.25	10.9	1.97	9.1
Social Security and Medicare	2.26	5.8	1.93	5.6	1.82	6.0	1.67	6.0	0.82	7.1	1.34	6.2
Social Security[6]	1.80	4.6	1.52	4.4	1.45	4.8	1.34	4.8	0.66	5.8	1.08	5.0
Medicare	0.45	1.2	0.41	1.2	0.37	1.2	0.33	1.2	0.16	1.4	0.26	1.2
Federal unemployment insurance	0.03	0.1	0.03	0.1	0.03	0.1	0.03	0.1	0.04	0.4	0.03	0.1
State unemployment insurance	0.19	0.5	0.15	0.4	0.18	0.6	0.13	0.5	0.12	1.1	0.14	0.6
Workers' compensation	0.29	0.7	0.21	0.6	0.38	1.3	0.37	1.3	0.27	2.3	0.46	2.1

Note: Individual items may not sum to totals due to rounding.

[2]Includes utilities; wholesale trade; retail trade; transportation and warehousing; information; finance and insurance; real estate and rental and leasing; professional and technical services; management of companies and enterprises; administrative and waste services; education services; health care and social assistance; arts, entertainment, and recreation; accommodation and food services; and other services, except public administration.
[3]Includes premium pay for work in addition to the regular work schedule (such as overtime, weekends, and holidays).
[4]Cost per hour worked is $0.01 or less.
[5]Less than 0.05 percent.
[6]Comprises the Old Age, Survivors, and Disability Insurance (OASDI) program.

Table 6-6. Employer Compensation Costs Per Hour Worked for Employee Compensation and Costs as a Percent of Total Compensation: Private Industry Workers, by Census Region and Area, June 2007

(Dollars, percent of total costs.)

Compensation component	Census region and division[1]					
	Northeast		Northeast divisions			
			New England		Middle Atlantic	
	Cost	Percent	Cost	Percent	Cost	Percent
TOTAL COMPENSATION	29.71	100.0	29.81	100.0	29.67	100.0
WAGES AND SALARIES	20.69	69.6	21.16	71.0	20.49	69.1
TOTAL BENEFITS	9.03	30.4	8.66	29.0	9.18	30.9
Paid Leave	2.25	7.6	2.19	7.4	2.28	7.7
Vacation	1.11	3.7	1.11	3.7	1.12	3.8
Holiday	0.73	2.5	0.75	2.5	0.73	2.4
Sick	0.30	1.0	0.25	0.8	0.31	1.1
Other	0.11	0.4	0.09	0.3	0.12	0.4
Supplemental Pay	1.03	3.5	0.92	3.1	1.07	3.6
Overtime and premium pay[2]	0.29	1.0	0.27	0.9	0.30	1.0
Shift differentials	0.07	0.2	0.06	0.2	0.07	0.2
Nonproduction bonuses	0.67	2.2	0.59	2.0	0.70	2.4
Insurance	2.20	7.4	2.05	6.9	2.26	7.6
Life insurance	0.05	0.2	0.04	0.1	0.05	0.2
Health insurance	2.04	6.9	1.92	6.4	2.09	7.1
Short-term disability	0.07	0.2	0.05	0.2	0.08	0.3
Long-term disability	0.04	0.1	0.04	0.1	0.04	0.1
Retirement and Savings	1.08	3.6	1.01	3.4	1.11	3.7
Defined benefit	0.50	1.7	0.44	1.5	0.53	1.8
Defined contribution	0.58	1.9	0.57	1.9	0.58	2.0
Legally Required Benefits	2.47	8.3	2.48	8.3	2.47	8.3
Social Security and Medicare	1.74	5.9	1.78	6.0	1.72	5.8
Social Security[3]	1.39	4.7	1.43	4.8	1.38	4.6
Medicare	0.35	1.2	0.35	1.2	0.35	1.2
Federal unemployment insurance	0.03	0.1	0.03	0.1	0.03	0.1
State unemployment insurance	0.22	0.7	0.23	0.8	0.22	0.7
Workers' compensation	0.48	1.6	0.44	1.5	0.49	1.7

Note: Individual items may not sum to totals due to rounding.

[1]The states that comprise the Census divisions are: New England—Connecticut, Maine, Massachusetts, New Hampshire, Rhode Island, and Vermont; Middle Atlantic—New Jersey, New York, and Pennsylvania; South Atlantic—Delaware, District of Columbia, Florida, Georgia, Maryland, North Carolina, South Carolina, Virginia, and West Virginia; East South Central—Alabama, Kentucky, Mississippi, and Tennessee; West South Central—Arkansas, Louisiana, Oklahoma, and Texas; East North Central—Illinois, Indiana, Michigan, Ohio, and Wisconsin; West North Central—Iowa, Kansas, Minnesota, Missouri, Nebraska, North Dakota, and South Dakota; Mountain—Arizona, Colorado, Idaho, Montana, Nevada, New Mexico, Utah, and Wyoming; and Pacific—Alaska, California, Hawaii, Oregon, and Washington.
[2]Includes premium pay for work in addition to the regular work schedule (such as overtime, weekends, and holidays).
[3]Comprises the Old-Age, Survivors, and Disability Insurance (OASDI) program.

Table 6-6. Employer Compensation Costs Per Hour Worked for Employee Compensation and Costs as a Percent of Total Compensation: Private Industry Workers, by Census Region and Area, June 2007—*Continued*

(Dollars, percent of total costs.)

Compensation component	Census region and division[1]							
	South		South divisions					
			South Atlantic		East South Central		West South Central	
	Cost	Percent	Cost	Percent	Cost	Percent	Cost	Percent
TOTAL COMPENSATION	23.21	100.0	24.68	100.0	19.78	100.0	22.70	100.0
WAGES AND SALARIES	16.70	72.0	17.79	72.1	14.01	70.8	16.41	72.3
TOTAL BENEFITS	6.51	28.0	6.89	27.9	5.77	29.2	6.29	27.7
Paid Leave	1.48	6.4	1.59	6.4	1.19	6.0	1.45	6.4
Vacation	0.75	3.2	0.81	3.3	0.65	3.3	0.72	3.2
Holiday	0.49	2.1	0.52	2.1	0.38	1.9	0.49	2.2
Sick	0.18	0.8	0.20	0.8	0.11	0.5	0.18	0.8
Other	0.06	0.3	0.06	0.3	0.05	0.3	0.06	0.2
Supplemental Pay	0.63	2.7	0.63	2.5	0.59	3.0	0.66	2.9
Overtime and premium pay[2]	0.25	1.1	0.25	1.0	0.21	1.1	0.26	1.2
Shift differentials	0.06	0.3	0.07	0.3	0.07	0.4	0.05	0.2
Nonproduction bonuses	0.32	1.4	0.32	1.3	0.31	1.5	0.34	1.5
Insurance	1.72	7.4	1.78	7.2	1.70	8.6	1.63	7.2
Life insurance	0.04	0.2	0.05	0.2	0.04	0.2	0.04	0.2
Health insurance	1.59	6.9	1.64	6.7	1.59	8.0	1.51	6.6
Short-term disability	0.04	0.2	0.05	0.2	0.04	0.2	0.04	0.2
Long-term disability	0.04	0.2	0.04	0.2	0.03	0.2	0.04	0.2
Retirement and Savings	0.77	3.3	0.90	3.6	0.55	2.8	0.69	3.1
Defined benefit	0.34	1.4	0.41	1.7	0.20	1.0	0.28	1.2
Defined contribution	0.44	1.9	0.49	2.0	0.34	1.7	0.41	1.8
Legally Required Benefits	1.91	8.2	2.00	8.1	1.74	8.8	1.86	8.2
Social Security and Medicare	1.39	6.0	1.46	5.9	1.26	6.3	1.36	6.0
Social Security[3]	1.12	4.8	1.17	4.7	1.01	5.1	1.09	4.8
Medicare	0.28	1.2	0.29	1.2	0.24	1.2	0.27	1.2
Federal unemployment insurance	0.03	0.1	0.03	0.1	0.03	0.2	0.03	0.1
State unemployment insurance	0.10	0.4	0.10	0.4	0.08	0.4	0.11	0.5
Workers' compensation	0.39	1.7	0.41	1.6	0.37	1.9	0.37	1.6

Note: Individual items may not sum to totals due to rounding.

[1]The states that comprise the Census divisions are: New England—Connecticut, Maine, Massachusetts, New Hampshire, Rhode Island, and Vermont; Middle Atlantic—New Jersey, New York, and Pennsylvania; South Atlantic—Delaware, District of Columbia, Florida, Georgia, Maryland, North Carolina, South Carolina, Virginia, and West Virginia; East South Central—Alabama, Kentucky, Mississippi, and Tennessee; West South Central—Arkansas, Louisiana, Oklahoma, and Texas; East North Central—Illinois, Indiana, Michigan, Ohio, and Wisconsin; West North Central—Iowa, Kansas, Minnesota, Missouri, Nebraska, North Dakota, and South Dakota; Mountain—Arizona, Colorado, Idaho, Montana, Nevada, New Mexico, Utah, and Wyoming; and Pacific—Alaska, California, Hawaii, Oregon, and Washington.
[2]Includes premium pay for work in addition to the regular work schedule (such as overtime, weekends, and holidays).
[3]Comprises the Old-Age, Survivors, and Disability Insurance (OASDI) program.

Table 6-6. Employer Compensation Costs Per Hour Worked for Employee Compensation and Costs as a Percent of Total Compensation: Private Industry Workers, by Census Region and Area, June 2007—*Continued*

(Dollars, percent of total costs.)

Compensation component	Census region and division[1]					
	Midwest		Midwest divisions			
			East North Central		West North Central	
	Cost	Percent	Cost	Percent	Cost	Percent
TOTAL COMPENSATION	25.08	100.0	26.16	100.0	22.69	100.0
WAGES AND SALARIES	17.50	69.8	18.16	69.4	16.03	70.6
TOTAL BENEFITS	7.58	30.2	8.00	30.6	6.66	29.4
Paid Leave	1.70	6.8	1.79	6.8	1.49	6.6
Vacation	0.88	3.5	0.91	3.5	0.80	3.5
Holiday	0.55	2.2	0.59	2.3	0.47	2.1
Sick	0.18	0.7	0.19	0.7	0.16	0.7
Other	0.09	0.3	0.10	0.4	0.06	0.3
Supplemental Pay	0.74	2.9	0.78	3.0	0.64	2.8
Overtime and premium pay[2]	0.30	1.2	0.32	1.2	0.25	1.1
Shift differentials	0.09	0.3	0.10	0.4	0.07	0.3
Nonproduction bonuses	0.35	1.4	0.36	1.4	0.32	1.4
Insurance	2.12	8.5	2.25	8.6	1.82	8.0
Life insurance	0.05	0.2	0.05	0.2	0.04	0.2
Health insurance	1.97	7.9	2.09	8.0	1.71	7.5
Short-term disability	0.06	0.2	0.07	0.3	0.05	0.2
Long-term disability	0.04	0.2	0.04	0.2	0.03	0.1
Retirement and Savings	0.90	3.6	0.96	3.7	0.75	3.3
Defined benefit	0.46	1.8	0.51	2.0	0.34	1.5
Defined contribution	0.44	1.7	0.45	1.7	0.41	1.8
Legally Required Benefits	2.13	8.5	2.21	8.4	1.96	8.6
Social Security and Medicare	1.49	5.9	1.55	5.9	1.37	6.0
Social Security[3]	1.20	4.8	1.24	4.8	1.10	4.9
Medicare	0.29	1.2	0.30	1.2	0.26	1.2
Federal unemployment insurance	0.03	0.1	0.03	0.1	0.03	0.1
State unemployment insurance	0.16	0.7	0.18	0.7	0.14	0.6
Workers' compensation	0.44	1.8	0.45	1.7	0.42	1.8

Note: Individual items may not sum to totals due to rounding.

[1]The states that comprise the Census divisions are: New England—Connecticut, Maine, Massachusetts, New Hampshire, Rhode Island, and Vermont; Middle Atlantic—New Jersey, New York, and Pennsylvania; South Atlantic—Delaware, District of Columbia, Florida, Georgia, Maryland, North Carolina, South Carolina, Virginia, and West Virginia; East South Central—Alabama, Kentucky, Mississippi, and Tennessee; West South Central—Arkansas, Louisiana, Oklahoma, and Texas; East North Central—Illinois, Indiana, Michigan, Ohio, and Wisconsin; West North Central—Iowa, Kansas, Minnesota, Missouri, Nebraska, North Dakota, and South Dakota; Mountain—Arizona, Colorado, Idaho, Montana, Nevada, New Mexico, Utah, and Wyoming; and Pacific—Alaska, California, Hawaii, Oregon, and Washington.
[2]Includes premium pay for work in addition to the regular work schedule (such as overtime, weekends, and holidays).
[3]Comprises the Old-Age, Survivors, and Disability Insurance (OASDI) program.

Table 6-6. Employer Compensation Costs Per Hour Worked for Employee Compensation and Costs as a Percent of Total Compensation: Private Industry Workers, by Census Region and Area, June 2007—*Continued*

(Dollars, percent of total costs.)

Compensation component	Census region and division[1]						Area[4]			
	West		West divisions				Metropolitan area		Nonmetropolitan area	
			Mountain		Pacific					
	Cost	Percent	Cost	Percent	Cost	Percent	Cost	Percent	Cost	Percent
TOTAL COMPENSATION	27.75	100.0	23.61	100.0	29.53	100.0	27.18	100.0	19.14	100.0
WAGES AND SALARIES	19.66	70.8	16.99	72.0	20.81	70.5	19.20	70.6	13.55	70.8
TOTAL BENEFITS	8.09	29.2	6.62	28.0	8.72	29.5	7.98	29.4	5.59	29.2
Paid Leave	1.88	6.8	1.44	6.1	2.06	7.0	1.90	7.0	1.07	5.6
Vacation	0.96	3.4	0.75	3.2	1.04	3.5	0.96	3.5	0.57	3.0
Holiday	0.61	2.2	0.47	2.0	0.67	2.3	0.62	2.3	0.36	1.9
Sick	0.25	0.9	0.17	0.7	0.28	0.9	0.24	0.9	0.11	0.6
Other	0.06	0.2	0.04	0.2	0.06	0.2	0.08	0.3	0.04	0.2
Supplemental Pay	0.84	3.0	0.72	3.1	0.88	3.0	0.82	3.0	0.58	3.0
Overtime and premium pay[2]	0.26	0.9	0.23	1.0	0.28	0.9	0.27	1.0	0.29	1.5
Shift differentials	0.06	0.2	0.05	0.2	0.06	0.2	0.07	0.3	0.06	0.3
Nonproduction bonuses	0.52	1.9	0.44	1.9	0.55	1.9	0.48	1.8	0.23	1.2
Insurance	2.00	7.2	1.73	7.3	2.12	7.2	2.04	7.5	1.59	8.3
Life insurance	0.04	0.1	0.04	0.2	0.04	0.1	0.05	0.2	0.04	0.2
Health insurance	1.88	6.8	1.63	6.9	1.99	6.7	1.90	7.0	1.50	7.8
Short-term disability	0.04	0.1	0.03	0.1	0.04	0.1	0.06	0.2	0.04	0.2
Long-term disability	0.04	0.1	0.03	0.1	0.04	0.1	0.04	0.2	0.02	0.1
Retirement and Savings	0.86	3.1	0.68	2.9	0.93	3.2	0.94	3.5	0.57	3.0
Defined benefit	0.37	1.3	0.26	1.1	0.42	1.4	0.44	1.6	0.26	1.4
Defined contribution	0.48	1.7	0.42	1.8	0.51	1.7	0.51	1.9	0.31	1.6
Legally Required Benefits	2.52	9.1	2.05	8.7	2.72	9.2	2.28	8.4	1.78	9.3
Social Security and Medicare	1.64	5.9	1.43	6.0	1.73	5.9	1.61	5.9	1.18	6.2
Social Security[3]	1.32	4.7	1.15	4.9	1.39	4.7	1.29	4.7	0.95	5.0
Medicare	0.32	1.2	0.28	1.2	0.34	1.2	0.32	1.2	0.22	1.2
Federal unemployment insurance	0.03	0.1	0.03	0.1	0.03	0.1	0.03	0.1	0.03	0.2
State unemployment insurance	0.18	0.7	0.12	0.5	0.21	0.7	0.16	0.6	0.13	0.7
Workers' compensation	0.66	2.4	0.47	2.0	0.75	2.5	0.48	1.8	0.44	2.3

Note: Individual items may not sum to totals due to rounding.

[1]The states that comprise the Census divisions are: New England—Connecticut, Maine, Massachusetts, New Hampshire, Rhode Island, and Vermont; Middle Atlantic—New Jersey, New York, and Pennsylvania; South Atlantic—Delaware, District of Columbia, Florida, Georgia, Maryland, North Carolina, South Carolina, Virginia, and West Virginia; East South Central—Alabama, Kentucky, Mississippi, and Tennessee; West South Central—Arkansas, Louisiana, Oklahoma, and Texas; East North Central—Illinois, Indiana, Michigan, Ohio, and Wisconsin; West North Central—Iowa, Kansas, Minnesota, Missouri, Nebraska, North Dakota, and South Dakota; Mountain—Arizona, Colorado, Idaho, Montana, Nevada, New Mexico, Utah, and Wyoming; and Pacific—Alaska, California, Hawaii, Oregon, and Washington.
[2]Includes premium pay for work in addition to the regular work schedule (such as overtime, weekends, and holidays).
[3]Comprises the Old-Age, Survivors, and Disability Insurance (OASDI) program.
[4]A metropolitan area can be a metropolitan statistical area (MSA) or a consolidated metropolitan statistical area (CMSA), as defined by the Office of Management and Budget in 1994. Nonmetropolitan areas are counties that do not fit the definitions above.

Table 6-7. Employer Compensation Costs Per Hour Worked for Employee Compensation and Costs as a Percent of Total Compensation: State and Local Government, by Major Occupational and Industry Group, June 2007

(Dollars, percent of total cost.)

Compensation component	All workers		Occupational group[1]						Industry group	
			Management, professional, and related		Sales and office		Service		Service-providing[2]	
	Cost	Percent	Cost	Percent	Cost	Percent	Cost	Percent	Cost	Percent
TOTAL COMPENSATION	38.61	100.0	47.30	100.0	26.59	100.0	30.05	100.0	38.71	100.0
WAGES AND SALARIES	25.73	66.6	33.11	70.0	16.38	61.6	18.09	60.2	25.81	66.7
TOTAL BENEFITS	12.88	33.4	14.18	30.0	10.21	38.4	11.96	39.8	12.90	33.3
Paid Leave	3.05	7.9	3.35	7.1	2.52	9.5	2.75	9.1	3.06	7.9
Vacation	1.07	2.8	0.97	2.1	1.03	3.9	1.18	3.9	1.07	2.8
Holiday	0.98	2.5	1.10	2.3	0.81	3.0	0.85	2.8	0.98	2.5
Sick	0.75	1.9	0.96	2.0	0.52	1.9	0.51	1.7	0.75	1.9
Other	0.25	0.7	0.31	0.7	0.17	0.6	0.20	0.7	0.25	0.7
Supplemental Pay	0.35	0.9	0.21	0.4	0.18	0.7	0.66	2.2	0.35	0.9
Overtime and premium pay[3]	0.18	0.5	0.05	0.1	0.10	0.4	0.37	1.2	0.17	0.5
Shift differentials	0.07	0.2	0.05	0.1	0.02	0.1	0.15	0.5	0.07	0.2
Nonproduction bonuses	0.10	0.3	0.10	0.2	0.07	0.3	0.15	0.5	0.10	0.3
Insurance	4.38	11.4	4.82	10.2	4.16	15.7	3.61	12.0	4.39	11.3
Life insurance	0.07	0.2	0.08	0.2	0.06	0.2	0.05	0.2	0.07	0.2
Health insurance	4.24	11.0	4.66	9.9	4.06	15.3	3.47	11.6	4.25	11.0
Short-term disability	0.03	0.1	0.02	(4)	0.02	0.1	0.05	0.2	0.03	0.1
Long-term disability	0.04	0.1	0.05	0.1	0.03	0.1	0.04	0.1	0.04	0.1
Retirement and Savings	2.86	7.4	3.24	6.9	1.70	6.4	3.06	10.2	2.87	7.4
Defined benefit plans	2.57	6.7	2.90	6.1	1.53	5.7	2.88	9.6	2.57	6.7
Defined contribution plans	0.30	0.8	0.34	0.7	0.17	0.7	0.17	0.6	0.30	0.8
Legally Required Benefits	2.23	5.8	2.57	5.4	1.63	6.1	1.89	6.3	2.24	5.8
Social Security and Medicare	1.70	4.4	2.13	4.5	1.26	4.7	1.13	3.8	1.70	4.4
Social Security[5]	1.30	3.4	1.63	3.4	1.00	3.7	0.85	2.8	1.31	3.4
Medicare	0.40	1.0	0.50	1.1	0.27	1.0	0.28	0.9	0.40	1.0
Federal unemployment insurance	(6)	(4)	(6)	(4)	(6)	(4)	(6)	(4)	(6)	(4)
State unemployment insurance	0.06	0.1	0.06	0.1	0.05	0.2	0.06	0.2	0.06	0.1
Workers' compensation	0.48	1.2	0.38	0.8	0.32	1.2	0.70	2.3	0.48	1.2

Note: Individual items may not sum to totals due to rounding.

[1]This table presents data for the three major occupational groups in state and local government: management, professional, and related occupations, including teachers; sales and office occupations, including clerical workers; and service occupations, including police and firefighters.
[2]Service-providing industries, which include health and education services, employ a large proportion of the state and local government workforce.
[3]Includes premium pay for work in addition to the regular work schedule (such as overtime, weekends, and holidays).
[4]Less than 0.05 percent.
[5]Comprises the Old Age, Survivors, and Disability Insurance (OASDI) program.
[6]Cost per hour worked is $0.01 or less.

Table 6-8. Employer Compensation Costs Per Hour Worked for Employee Compensation and Costs as a Percent of Total Compensation: State and Local Government Workers, by Major Occupational and Industry Group, June 2007

(Dollars, percent of total compensation.)

Characteristic	Total compensation	Wages and salaries	Cost per hour worked					
			Total	Paid leave	Supplemental pay	Insurance	Retirement and savings	Legally required benefits
COSTS PER HOUR WORKED								
State and Local Government Workers	38.61	25.73	12.88	3.05	0.35	4.38	2.86	2.23
Occupational Group								
Management, professional, and related	47.30	33.11	14.18	3.35	0.21	4.82	3.24	2.57
Professional and related	47.01	33.22	13.79	3.02	0.21	4.86	3.16	2.53
Teachers[1]	52.24	37.99	14.25	2.76	0.10	5.03	3.65	2.70
Primary, secondary, and special education school teachers	50.86	36.76	14.11	2.61	0.09	5.30	3.52	2.59
Sales and office	26.59	16.38	10.21	2.52	0.18	4.16	1.70	1.63
Office and administrative support	26.60	16.39	10.21	2.52	0.18	4.16	1.71	1.63
Service	30.05	18.09	11.96	2.75	0.66	3.61	3.06	1.89
Industry Group								
Education and health services	40.95	28.57	12.38	2.81	0.20	4.47	2.67	2.23
Education services	41.59	29.27	12.32	2.62	0.12	4.59	2.77	2.22
Elementary and secondary schools	40.71	28.64	12.07	2.33	0.11	4.78	2.70	2.15
Junior colleges, colleges, and universities	45.29	31.86	13.43	3.77	0.20	3.89	3.08	2.50
Health care and social assistance	37.00	24.28	12.73	4.01	0.68	3.69	2.04	2.31
Hospitals	33.25	21.68	11.57	3.44	0.80	3.35	1.77	2.22
Public administration	35.43	21.84	13.59	3.41	0.54	4.26	3.28	2.11
PERCENT OF TOTAL COMPENSATION								
State and Local Government Workers	100.0	66.6	33.4	7.9	0.9	11.4	7.4	5.8
Occupational Group								
Management, professional, and related	100.0	70.0	30.0	7.1	0.4	10.2	6.9	5.4
Professional and related	100.0	70.7	29.3	6.4	0.4	10.3	6.7	5.4
Teachers[1]	100.0	72.7	27.3	5.3	0.2	9.6	7.0	5.2
Primary, secondary, and special education school teachers	100.0	72.3	27.7	5.1	0.2	10.4	6.9	5.1
Sales and office	100.0	61.6	38.4	9.5	0.7	15.7	6.4	6.1
Office and administrative support	100.0	61.6	38.4	9.5	0.7	15.6	6.4	6.1
Service	100.0	60.2	39.8	9.1	2.2	12.0	10.2	6.3
Industry Group								
Education and health services	100.0	69.8	30.2	6.9	0.5	10.9	6.5	5.4
Education services	100.0	70.4	29.6	6.3	0.3	11.0	6.7	5.3
Elementary and secondary schools	100.0	70.4	29.6	5.7	0.3	11.8	6.6	5.3
Junior colleges, colleges, and universities	100.0	70.4	29.6	8.3	0.4	8.6	6.8	5.5
Health care and social assistance	100.0	65.6	34.4	10.8	1.8	10.0	5.5	6.2
Hospitals	100.0	65.2	34.8	10.3	2.4	10.1	5.3	6.7
Public administration	100.0	61.6	38.4	9.6	1.5	12.0	9.3	6.0

Note: Individual items may not sum to totals due to rounding.

[1]Includes postsecondary teachers; primary, secondary, and special education teachers; and other teachers and instructors.

NOTES AND DEFINITIONS

EXPERIMENTAL ESTIMATES OF COMPENSATION LEVELS AND TRENDS FOR WORKERS IN THE 15 LARGEST METROPOLITAN AREAS, 2004–2005

This section presents new experimental Employment Cost Index (ECI) and Employer Costs for Employee Compensation (ECEC) estimates for the 15 largest metropolitan areas in the United States. The estimates were calculated as part of a research project to determine the feasibility of publishing ECI and ECEC estimates for metropolitan areas. The Bureau of Labor Statistics (BLS) plans to begin regular publication of these kinds of estimates in the coming years.

Since the inception of the two series, the only ECI and ECEC estimates available for geographic areas smaller than the entire United States have been for the broad groups of states that make up Census regions and divisions.

ECI for the 15 Largest Metropolitan Areas

ECI estimates for 15 metropolitan areas were calculated using the same index number formula used by the national ECI. Employment for industry-occupation groups, which the index formula holds constant over time, has a reference period of May 2005 and refers to employment for the industry-occupation groups within the particular area.

Total compensation equals wages and salaries plus employer costs for 18 categories of benefits, so it is designed to be a comprehensive measure of the change in the cost to businesses of employing workers. Although the National Compensation Survey (NCS), which encompass-

es the ECI and ECEC, also includes workers in state and local government, metropolitan area estimates are restricted to workers in private industry.

ECEC for the 15 Largest Metropolitan Areas

ECEC estimates for the 15 largest U.S. metropolitan areas were calculated using procedures that are similar to what is used currently for the national ECEC.

The ECEC estimate for a metropolitan area reflects the local composition of the workforce, so differences in the composition of workers among the areas will affect any comparison of their average total compensation. The National Compensation Survey reported estimates of "pay relatives" for about 80 metropolitan areas for July 2005. Pay relatives compare average hourly earnings among the areas after adjusting for differences in their establishment and occupational characteristics and their occupation composition. For some purposes, they may provide more appropriate comparisons of the average level of pay among metropolitan areas.

Sources of Additional Information

The text and tables in this section are excerpted from the article "Experimental Estimates of Compensation Levels and Trends for Workers in the 15 Largest Metropolitan Areas, 2004–05" by Michael K. Lettau and Christopher J. Guciardo in the September 2007 edition of *Compensation and Working Conditions*. This article contains extensive descriptions of the methodology and estimation procedures and analysis of the data and is available on the BLS Web site at <http://www.bls.gov>.

Table 6-9. Employment Cost Index for Total Compensation for the 15 Largest Metropolitan Areas, Private Industry, Experimental Series, 2004–2005

(Percent.)

Metropolitan area	Percent change for 12 months ending:					Average annual change
	December 2004	March 2005	June 2005	September 2005	December 2005	
All Areas in the United States[1]	3.8	3.5	3.1	2.9	2.9	3.3
Atlanta, GA	5.2	1.9	0.2	0.3	-0.7	2.2
Boston-Worcester-Lawrence, MA-NH-ME-CT	2.8	4.1	4.5	3.9	4.4	3.6
Chicago-Gary-Kenosha, IL-IN-WI	3.3	2.5	3.3	3.9	5.4	4.3
Dallas-Fort Worth, TX	4.0	2.8	2.3	1.7	1.9	2.9
Detroit-Ann Arbor-Flint, MI	5.1	1.9	2.0	2.2	1.4	3.2
Houston-Galveston-Brazoria, TX	4.7	3.5	3.4	5.1	3.6	4.2
Los Angeles-Riverside-Orange County, CA	3.0	2.4	3.6	3.5	3.4	3.2
Miami-Fort Lauderdale, FL	3.7	2.7	3.2	3.5	2.4	3.1
Minneapolis-St. Paul, MN-WI	2.8	2.7	2.6	2.2	2.1	2.4
New York-Northern New Jersey-Long Island, NY-NJ-CT-PA	4.1	3.4	3.0	3.1	3.1	3.6
Philadelphia-Wilmington-Atlantic City, PA-NJ-DE-MD	3.4	3.7	3.4	3.5	4.2	3.8
Phoenix-Mesa, AZ	3.6	4.8	5.2	5.3	5.5	4.5
San Francisco-Oakland-San Jose, CA	2.5	4.2	3.5	2.3	2.1	2.3
Seattle-Tacoma-Bremerton, WA	6.8	5.8	6.2	6.7	8.1	7.4
Washington-Baltimore, DC-MD-VA-WV	4.4	4.3	3.6	3.4	3.1	3.8
STANDARD ERROR						
All Areas in the United States[1]	0.3	0.3	0.2	0.2	0.3	0.2
Atlanta, GA	0.9	0.7	0.7	1.1	0.9	0.3
Boston-Worcester-Lawrence, MA-NH-ME-CT	0.8	0.3	0.4	0.4	0.3	0.4
Chicago-Gary-Kenosha, IL-IN-WI	0.3	0.5	0.3	0.3	0.6	0.3
Dallas-Fort Worth, TX	0.3	0.5	0.4	1.2	0.5	0.2
Detroit-Ann Arbor-Flint, MI	0.4	0.4	0.4	0.4	0.9	0.4
Houston-Galveston-Brazoria, TX	0.8	0.7	0.6	0.6	0.5	0.4
Los Angeles-Riverside-Orange County, CA	1.5	0.9	0.7	0.9	0.8	0.6
Miami-Fort Lauderdale, FL	0.3	0.6	0.7	0.7	0.9	0.4
Minneapolis-St. Paul, MN-WI	0.3	0.4	0.3	0.3	0.4	0.2
New York-Northern New Jersey-Long Island, NY-NJ-CT-PA	0.3	0.3	0.1	0.2	0.2	0.2
Philadelphia-Wilmington-Atlantic City, PA-NJ-DE-MD	0.3	0.3	0.2	0.3	0.2	0.2
Phoenix-Mesa, AZ	0.8	0.3	0.3	0.4	0.4	0.3
San Francisco-Oakland-San Jose, CA	0.7	0.8	0.6	0.7	0.7	0.6
Seattle-Tacoma-Bremerton, WA	0.4	0.3	0.2	0.4	0.5	0.3
Washington-Baltimore, DC-MD-VA-WV	0.4	0.2	0.2	0.6	0.8	0.6

[1]Includes all metropolitan areas and nonmetropolitan counties in the 50 states and the District of Columbia.

Table 6-10. Employer Costs Per Hour Worked for Total Employee Compensation for the 15 Largest Metropolitan Areas, Private Industry, Experimental Series, March 2004 and March 2005

(Dollars, percent.)

Metropolitan area	March 2004		March 2005	
	ECEC for total compensation	Percent relative standard error	ECEC for total compensation	Percent relative standard error
All Areas in the United States[1]	23.29	1.2	24.17	1.5
Atlanta, GA	27.33	4.9	27.68	1.7
Boston-Worcester-Lawrence, MA-NH-ME-CT	29.85	1.6	31.54	2.0
Chicago-Gary-Kenosha, IL-IN-WI	27.36	1.7	28.91	2.2
Dallas-Fort Worth, TX	24.63	2.5	26.70	2.2
Detroit-Ann Arbor-Flint, MI	28.74	3.0	29.04	2.8
Houston-Galveston-Brazoria, TX	25.06	1.9	25.59	4.1
Los Angeles-Riverside-Orange County, CA	26.58	2.6	28.58	2.6
Miami-Fort Lauderdale, FL	20.36	2.8	20.36	3.2
Minneapolis-St. Paul, MN-WI	28.50	1.0	29.38	1.6
New York-Northern New Jersey-Long Island, NY-NJ-CT-PA	30.05	2.7	30.65	2.1
Philadelphia-Wilmington-Atlantic City, PA-NJ-DE-MD	25.54	1.8	27.06	1.9
Phoenix-Mesa, AZ	24.22	2.6	24.39	3.1
San Francisco-Oakland-San Jose, CA	29.49	1.5	31.95	2.0
Seattle-Tacoma-Bremerton, WA	28.22	2.2	28.44	2.6
Washington-Baltimore, DC-MD-VA-WV	26.36	1.6	27.46	2.1

[1]Includes all metropolitan areas and nonmetropolitan counties in the 50 states and the District of Columbia.

NOTES AND DEFINITIONS

EMPLOYEE BENEFITS SURVEY

The Employee Benefits Survey provides data on the incidence and provisions of selected employee benefit plans.

Collection and Coverage

The statistics in this chapter represent the integration of data on employee benefits into the NCS. Prior to 1999, surveys of different sectors of the economy were conducted in alternating years; medium and large private establishments were studied during odd-numbered years, and small private establishments were studied during even-numbered years. Since these surveys have been replaced by the new survey, the tables previously presented in this *Handbook* have been discontinued. Data for all private workers are now collected annually.

Definitions

Incidence refers to different methods of computing the number or percentage of employees who receive a benefit plan or specific benefit feature.

Access to a benefit is determined on an occupational basis within an establishment. An employee is considered to have access to a benefit if it is available for his or her use.

Participation refers to the proportion of employees covered by a benefit. There will be cases where employees with access to a plan will not participate. For example, some employees may decline to participate in a health insurance plan if there is an employee cost involved.

Sources of Additional Information

For more information, see Bureau of Labor Statistics (BLS) news release USDL-06-1482, "Employee Benefits in Private Industry, 2006." For a listing of selected benefit definitions, see the *Glossary of Compensation Terms*. Additional data and further information on methodology and sampling are available in BLS Bulletin 2555, "National Compensation Survey: Employee Benefits in Private Industry in the United States, 2000." These resources are available on the BLS Web site at <http://www.bls.gov>. The NCS was described in an article in the fifth edition of this *Handbook*.

Table 6-11. Percent of Workers with Access to or Participating in Selected Benefits, March 2007

(Percent.)

Characteristic	Retirement benefits			Health care benefits				Life insurance	Disability benefits	
	All plans[1]	Defined benefit	Defined contribution	Medical care	Dental care	Vision care	Outpatient prescription drug coverage	Life insurance	Short-term disability	Long-term disability
ACCESS TO SELECTED BENEFITS										
All workers	61	21	55	71	46	29	68	58	39	31
Worker Characteristics										
Management, professional, and related occupations	76	29	71	85	62	39	82	76	53	56
Service occupations	36	8	32	46	28	20	44	35	22	12
Sales and office occupations	64	19	60	71	47	27	67	58	36	32
Natural resources, construction, and maintenance occupations	61	26	51	76	43	31	72	54	33	21
Production, transportation, and material moving occupations	65	26	56	78	49	30	75	66	48	26
Full-time workers	70	24	64	85	56	35	81	71	46	39
Part-time workers	31	10	27	24	16	11	23	16	14	7
Union workers	84	69	49	88	68	53	85	76	61	33
Nonunion workers	58	15	56	69	44	26	66	56	36	31
Average wage less than $15 per hour	47	11	44	57	34	20	54	45	27	17
Average wage $15 per hour or higher	76	33	69	87	61	39	84	74	53	49
Establishment Characteristics										
Goods-producing	70	29	62	85	54	33	81	69	50	30
Service-providing	58	19	53	67	44	28	64	55	36	31
1 to 99 workers	45	9	42	59	30	19	55	42	27	19
100 workers or more	78	34	70	84	64	40	81	76	52	44
Geographic Areas[2]										
Metropolitan areas[3]	61	22	56	72	47	29	68	58	40	33
Nonmetropolitan areas[3]	57	14	53	66	41	26	64	57	32	23
New England	57	21	53	68	51	23	65	55	38	34
Middle Atlantic	62	27	53	72	46	34	67	56	73	29
East North Central	64	25	56	72	45	25	70	63	42	34
West North Central	63	21	56	67	43	20	66	59	32	29
South Atlantic	62	17	59	72	44	27	69	61	33	33
East South Central	66	14	64	75	52	39	73	. . .	. . .	. . .
West South Central	55	17	51	66	39	21	61	56	29	31
Mountain	63	18	60	70	44	28	68	56	26	29
Pacific	57	21	49	72	54	39	68	52	26	29
PARTICIPATING IN SELECTED BENEFITS										
All workers	51	20	43	52	36	22	49	56	38	30
Worker Characteristics										
Management, professional, and related occupations	69	28	60	67	51	30	64	75	51	54
Service occupations	25	7	20	28	20	14	27	32	21	11
Sales and office occupations	54	17	47	48	33	19	46	55	35	30
Natural resources, construction, and maintenance occupations	51	25	40	61	36	26	58	52	33	20
Production, transportation, and material moving occupations	54	25	41	60	38	24	57	63	47	25
Full-time workers	60	23	50	64	44	27	61	69	45	37
Part-time workers	23	9	18	12	9	7	12	14	13	6
Union workers	81	67	41	78	62	47	75	75	60	32
Nonunion workers	47	15	43	49	33	19	46	54	35	29
Average wage less than $15 per hour	36	10	30	37	23	14	35	41	26	15
Average wage $15 per hour or higher	69	32	57	70	51	31	67	73	52	47
Establishment Characteristics										
Goods-producing	61	28	49	68	45	27	66	66	49	29
Service-providing	48	18	41	47	33	21	45	53	35	30
1 to 99 workers	37	9	33	42	24	14	39	40	26	18
100 workers or more	66	32	53	62	49	31	60	73	51	42
Geographic Areas[2]										
Metropolitan areas[3]	52	21	43	52	36	22	50	56	39	31
Nonmetropolitan areas[3]	44	14	38	48	32	21	46	54	31	22
New England	50	20	44	47	38	16	45	54	37	32
Middle Atlantic	55	26	44	54	36	25	50	54	72	29
East North Central	56	24	45	53	35	20	52	61	41	32
West North Central	55	20	45	52	36	17	50	57	31	28
South Atlantic	50	17	44	52	33	20	49	58	31	31
East South Central	46	13	42	57	42	33	55	. . .	. . .	. . .
West South Central	44	16	38	46	29	15	42	52	28	29
Mountain	50	16	44	48	32	21	47	52	25	27
Pacific	48	20	38	54	43	31	51	49	26	28

Note: Individual items may not sum to totals due to rounding.

[1]Includes defined benefit pension plans and defined contribution retirement plans. The total is less than the sum of the individual items because many employees have access to both types of plans.

[2]The states that comprise the Census divisions are: New England—Connecticut, Maine, Massachusetts, New Hampshire, Rhode Island, and Vermont; Middle Atlantic—New Jersey, New York, and Pennsylvania; South Atlantic—Delaware, District of Columbia, Florida, Georgia, Maryland, North Carolina, South Carolina, Virginia, and West Virginia; East South Central—Alabama, Kentucky, Mississippi, and Tennessee; West South Central—Arkansas, Louisiana, Oklahoma, and Texas; East North Central—Illinois, Indiana, Michigan, Ohio, and Wisconsin; West North Central—Iowa, Kansas, Minnesota, Missouri, Nebraska, North Dakota, and South Dakota; Mountain—Arizona, Colorado, Idaho, Montana, Nevada, New Mexico, Utah, and Wyoming; and Pacific—Alaska, California, Hawaii, Oregon, and Washington.

[3]A metropolitan area can be a metropolitan statistical area (MSA) or a consolidated metropolitan statistical area (CMSA), as defined by the Office of Management and Budget (OMB) in 1994. Nonmetropolitan areas are counties that do not fit the definitions above.

. . . = Not available.

Table 6-12. Percent of Medical Plan Participants and Employer Premiums Per Participant, by Requirements for Employee Contributions for Single and Family Coverage, Private Industry, March 2007

(Dollars, percent.)

Characteristic	Total		Employee contribution not required		Employee contribution required		
	Percent of participating employees	Average flat monthly employer premium	Percent of participating employees	Average flat monthly employer premium	Percent of participating employees	Average flat monthly employer premium	Average flat monthly employee contribution
SINGLE COVERAGE							
All workers	100	293.25	24	382.19	76	265.74	81.37
Worker Characteristics							
Management, professional, and related occupations	100	293.74	21	355.26	79	277.73	79.97
Service occupations	100	272.50	18	395.85	82	246.32	88.89
Sales and office occupations	100	281.24	21	353.90	79	262.06	83.63
Natural resources, construction, and maintenance occupations ..	100	350.37	38	467.49	62	278.37	82.21
Production, transportation, and material moving occupations	100	286.82	26	365.77	74	258.43	75.38
Full-time workers	100	293.71	24	381.90	76	266.38	80.67
Part-time workers	100	285.50	23	387.22	77	254.81	93.04
Union workers	100	408.46	50	479.57	50	337.51	62.45
Nonunion workers	100	272.12	19	334.72	81	257.62	83.51
Average wage less than $15 per hour	100	264.97	18	334.58	82	249.33	84.74
Average wage $15 per hour or higher	100	310.99	27	402.53	73	277.24	79.00
Establishment Characteristics							
Goods-producing	100	316.48	29	423.72	71	272.53	76.48
Service-providing	100	284.66	22	361.53	78	263.46	83.00
1 to 99 workers	100	295.65	31	388.57	69	253.71	89.89
100 workers or more	100	291.49	18	374.16	82	273.16	76.10
Geographic Areas[1]							
Metropolitan areas[2]	100	297.17	24	391.33	76	267.20	81.33
Nonmetropolitan areas[2]	100	270.98	21	321.56	79	257.78	81.56
New England	100	306.88	16	478.99	84	273.42	96.82
Middle Atlantic	100	310.74	27	392.86	73	280.16	79.79
East North Central	100	301.64	23	407.53	77	269.43	81.06
West North Central	100	303.72	25	399.77	75	271.89	77.38
South Atlantic	100	268.39	19	323.38	81	255.49	82.96
East South Central	100	245.03	16	307.96	84	232.61	84.61
West South Central	100	293.21	22	350.70	78	277.24	78.48
Mountain	100	297.90	23	418.44	77	262.47	85.42
Pacific	100	303.50	32	387.57	68	263.44	75.65
FAMILY COVERAGE							
All workers	100	664.04	13	814.44	87	642.02	312.78
Worker Characteristics							
Management, professional, and related occupations	100	702.15	9	810.82	91	691.43	313.42
Service occupations	100	576.28	8	678.24	92	567.06	342.92
Sales and office occupations	100	645.71	9	795.13	91	630.42	333.44
Natural resources, construction, and maintenance occupations ..	100	659.83	26	839.20	74	595.82	314.33
Production, transportation, and material moving occupations	100	683.19	18	844.44	82	648.82	263.68
Full-time workers	100	666.82	13	823.89	87	643.76	311.94
Part-time workers	100	614.21	12	637.67	88	610.93	327.75
Union workers	100	790.21	43	832.68	57	758.15	211.91
Nonunion workers	100	641.65	7	795.63	93	629.33	323.80
Average wage less than $15 per hour	100	602.29	8	705.18	92	593.33	326.84
Average wage $15 per hour or higher	100	702.52	16	849.05	84	675.14	303.21
Establishment Characteristics							
Goods-producing	100	706.84	20	869.49	80	666.51	267.46
Service-providing	100	648.36	10	775.06	90	634.02	327.58
1 to 99 workers	100	608.18	15	804.48	85	572.25	359.49
100 workers or more	100	704.14	11	824.65	89	689.50	280.99
Geographic Areas[1]							
Metropolitan areas[2]	100	670.64	13	815.33	87	648.13	315.15
Nonmetropolitan areas[2]	100	626.35	9	806.67	91	608.87	299.92
New England	100	717.53	9	889.88	91	700.81	319.38
Middle Atlantic	100	711.96	17	792.19	83	695.66	299.81
East North Central	100	723.92	17	898.43	83	687.79	285.19
West North Central	100	658.46	15	790.69	85	635.56	294.00
South Atlantic	100	623.01	7	833.53	93	607.34	334.43
East South Central	100	584.50	6	816.51	94	568.80	294.46
West South Central	100	638.59	6	721.43	94	633.45	334.41
Mountain	100	620.32	11	809.18	89	596.74	359.24
Pacific	100	644.94	19	752.05	81	620.60	312.25

Note: Individual items may not sum to totals due to rounding.

[1]The states that comprise the Census divisions are: New England—Connecticut, Maine, Massachusetts, New Hampshire, Rhode Island, and Vermont; Middle Atlantic—New Jersey, New York, and Pennsylvania; South Atlantic—Delaware, District of Columbia, Florida, Georgia, Maryland, North Carolina, South Carolina, Virginia, and West Virginia; East South Central—Alabama, Kentucky, Mississippi, and Tennessee; West South Central—Arkansas, Louisiana, Oklahoma, and Texas; East North Central—Illinois, Indiana, Michigan, Ohio, and Wisconsin; West North Central—Iowa, Kansas, Minnesota, Missouri, Nebraska, North Dakota, and South Dakota; Mountain—Arizona, Colorado, Idaho, Montana, Nevada, New Mexico, Utah, and Wyoming; and Pacific—Alaska, California, Hawaii, Oregon, and Washington.
[2]A metropolitan area can be a metropolitan statistical area (MSA) or a consolidated metropolitan statistical area (CMSA), as defined by the Office of Management and Budget in 1994. Nonmetropolitan areas are counties that do not fit the definitions above.

NOTES AND DEFINITIONS

NATIONAL COMPENSATION SURVEY: OCCUPATIONAL EARNINGS

Collection and Coverage

The occupational earnings in this section are from the National Compensation Survey (NCS). Private sector establishments with one or more workers are included in the survey. State and local governments with 50 or more workers within a survey area are also included. Agriculture, private households, and the federal government were excluded from the scope of the survey. In 2006, industry and occupations were classified in accordance with the North American Industry Classification System (NAICS) and the Standard Occupational Classification (SOC). The data were collected from December 2005 to January 2007, with June 2006 as the reference period.

The survey covers goods-producing industries (mining, construction, and manufacturing); service-producing industries (transportation, communications, electric, gas, and sanitary services; wholesale trade; retail trade; finance, insurance, and real estate; and services industries); and state and local governments. For purposes of this survey, an establishment is an economic unit that produces goods or services, a central administrative office, or an auxiliary unit providing support services to a company. For private industries in this survey, the establishment is usually at a single physical location and for state and local governments, an establishment is defined as all locations of a government entity. The geographic scope of the NCS includes all 50 states and the District of Columbia.

Identification of the occupations for which wage data were to be collected was a multi-step process:

1. Probability-proportional-to-size selection of establishment jobs

2. Classification of jobs into occupations based on the Census of Population system

3. Characterization of jobs as full time versus part time, union versus nonunion, and time versus incentive

4. Determination of the level of work of each job

For each occupation, wage data were collected for those workers who met the unique set of characteristics identified in the last three steps. Special procedures were developed for jobs for which a level could not be determined.

In step one, the jobs to be sampled were selected at each establishment by the Bureau of Labor Statistics (BLS) field economist during a personal visit. A complete list of employees was used for sampling, with each selected worker representing a job within the establishment.

In step two, the selected jobs were classified into occupations based on their duties. A job may fall into any one of about 800 classifications. For cases in which a job's duties overlapped two or more SOC classification codes, the duties used to set the wage level were used to classify the job.

In step three, other characteristics were identified such as whether the worker was full-time or part-time, a member of a union, or was paid on a time or incentive basis.

In the last step before wage data were collected, the work level of each selected job was determined using a "point factor leveling" process. Point factor leveling matches certain aspects of a job to specific levels of work with assigned point values. Points for each factor are then totaled to determine the overall work level for the job.

Definitions

Earnings. Regular payments from the employer to the employee as compensation for straight-time hourly work, or for any salaried work performed. The following components were included as part of earnings:

• Incentive pay, including commissions, production bonuses, and piece rates

• Cost-of-living allowances

• Hazard pay

• Payments of income deferred due to participation in a salary reduction plan

• Deadhead pay, defined as pay given to transportation workers returning in a vehicle without freight or passengers

Full-time worker. Any employee whom the employer considers to be working full time.

Incentive worker. Any employee whose earnings are at least partly tied to commissions, piece rates, production bonuses, or other incentives based on production or sales.

Level. A ranking of an occupation based on the requirements of the position. (See the description in the technical note on occupational leveling through point factor analysis for more details on the leveling process.)

Nonunion worker. An employee in an occupation not meeting the conditions for union coverage.

Part-time worker. Any employee that the employer considers to be working part time.

Time-based worker. Any employee whose earnings are tied to an hourly rate or salary, and not to a specific level of production.

Union worker. Any employee is in a union occupation when all of the following conditions are met:

- A labor organization is recognized as the bargaining agent for all workers in the occupation

- Wage and salary rates are determined through collective bargaining or negotiations

- Settlement terms, which must include earnings provisions and may include benefit provisions, are embodied in a signed, mutually binding collective bargaining agreement

Sources of Additional Information

An extensive description of the sampling, weighting and estimation steps and many additional detailed tables are available in BLS Bulletin 2590, "National Compensation Survey: Occupational Wages in the United States, June 2006," which is available on the BLS Web site at <http://www.bls.gov>.

Table 6-13. Mean Hourly Earnings[1] and Weekly Hours, by Selected Worker and Establishment Characteristics, National Compensation Survey,[2] June 2006

(Dollars, number of hours.)

Characteristic	Civilian workers		Private workers		State and local government workers	
	Mean hourly earnings	Mean weekly hours[3]	Mean hourly earnings	Mean weekly hours[3]	Mean hourly earnings	Mean weekly hours[3]
TOTAL	19.29	35.6	18.56	35.4	23.99	36.6
Worker Characteristics[4]						
Management, professional, and related occupations	31.45	37.1	31.66	37.5	30.79	35.9
Management, business, and financial occupations	34.89	39.8	35.17	40.0	33.03	38.4
Professional and related occupations	29.76	35.9	29.54	36.2	30.30	35.4
Service occupations	11.31	31.5	9.72	30.5	18.51	37.1
Sales and office occupations	15.46	34.9	15.42	34.7	15.86	37.2
Sales and related occupations	16.57	32.6	16.57	32.6	15.10	33.0
Office and administrative support occupations	14.86	36.3	14.71	36.2	15.87	37.3
Natural resources, construction, and maintenance occupations	19.49	39.4	19.46	39.4	19.84	39.3
Construction and extraction occupations	19.46	39.4	19.46	39.4	19.52	39.5
Installation, maintenance, and repair occupations	19.70	39.6	19.64	39.6	20.39	39.4
Production, transportation, and material moving occupations	14.78	37.3	14.64	37.3	18.33	35.4
Production occupations	15.11	38.9	15.02	38.9	20.75	39.3
Transportation and material moving occupations	14.42	35.6	14.22	35.7	17.60	34.4
Full-time workers	20.44	39.6	19.76	39.7	24.46	38.9
Part-time workers	11.00	20.6	10.61	20.7	16.57	18.8
Union workers	23.33	36.6	21.41	36.4	26.01	36.8
Nonunion workers	18.53	35.4	18.21	35.3	22.07	36.4
Time workers	18.97	35.5	18.13	35.3	23.98	36.6
Incentive workers	24.88	38.0	24.86	38.0	. . .	. . .
Establishment Characteristics						
Goods-producing	([5])	([5])	20.06	39.5	([5])	([5])
Service-providing	([5])	([5])	18.09	34.4	([5])	([5])
1-49 workers	16.19	34.2	16.18	34.2	17.50	36.8
50-99 workers	17.45	35.0	17.36	35.0	19.81	35.3
100-499 workers	18.81	36.2	18.47	36.2	22.00	35.8
500 workers or more	23.93	37.0	23.50	37.2	24.69	36.8

[1]Earnings are the straight-time hourly wages or salaries paid to employees. They include incentive pay, cost-of-living adjustments, and hazard pay. Excluded are premium pay for overtime, vacations, and holidays; nonproduction bonuses; and tips. The mean is computed by totaling the pay of all workers and dividing by the number of workers, weighted by hours.

[2]This survey covers all 50 states. Data collection was conducted between December 2005 and January 2007. The average reference period was June 2006.

[3]Mean weekly hours are the hours an employee is scheduled to work in a week, not including overtime.

[4]Employees are classified as working either a full-time or part-time schedule based on the definition used by each establishment. Union workers are those whose wages are determined through collective bargaining. Wages of time workers are based solely on hourly rate or salary; incentive workers are those whose wages are at least partly based on productivity payments such as piece rates, commissions, and production bonuses.

[5]Classification of establishments into goods-producing and service-producing industries applies to private industry only.

. . . = Not available.

Table 6-14. Mean Hourly Earnings[1] and Weekly Hours of Civilian Workers in Metropolitan and Nonmetropolitan Areas by Worker and Establishment Characteristics, June 2006

(Dollars, percent, hours.)

Characteristic	Civilian		Metropolitan areas		Nonmetropolitan areas	
	Mean hourly earnings	Mean weekly hours[2]	Mean hourly earnings	Mean weekly hours[2]	Mean hourly earnings	Mean weekly hours[2]
ALL WORKERS	19.29	35.6	20.08	35.6	15.01	35.7
Worker Characteristics[3,4]						
Management, professional, and related occupations	31.45	37.1	32.23	37.2	25.17	36.7
Management, business, and financial occupations	34.89	39.8	35.49	39.8	28.91	39.8
Professional and related occupations	29.76	35.9	30.57	36.0	23.74	35.6
Service occupations	11.31	31.5	11.71	31.4	9.65	32.1
Sales and office occupations	15.46	34.9	15.95	34.9	12.33	34.9
Sales and related occupations	16.57	32.6	17.35	32.5	12.00	33.2
Office and administrative support occupations	14.86	36.3	15.20	36.4	12.54	36.0
Natural resources, construction, and maintenance occupations	19.49	39.4	20.17	39.4	16.63	39.4
Construction and extraction occupations	19.46	39.4	20.24	39.4	15.93	39.3
Installation, maintenance, and repair occupations	19.70	39.6	20.24	39.5	17.60	39.7
Production, transportation, and material moving occupations	14.78	37.3	15.03	37.0	13.74	38.1
Production occupations	15.11	38.9	15.38	38.8	14.17	39.3
Transportation and material moving occupations	14.42	35.6	14.68	35.4	13.14	36.6
Full-time workers	20.44	39.6	21.30	39.6	15.80	39.7
Part-time workers	11.00	20.6	11.31	20.6	9.37	20.7
Union workers	23.33	36.6	23.79	36.4	19.93	37.8
Nonunion workers	18.53	35.4	19.35	35.4	14.33	35.5
Time workers	18.97	35.5	19.74	35.4	14.86	35.6
Incentive workers	24.88	38.0	25.93	37.8	18.01	39.2
Establishment Characteristics						
Goods-producing	(^{5})	(^{5})	21.03	39.5	(^{5})	(^{5})
Service-providing	(^{5})	(^{5})	19.69	34.5	(^{5})	(^{5})
1-49 workers	16.19	34.2	16.83	34.3	13.20	33.8
50-99 workers	17.45	35.0	18.01	35.0	14.21	35.0
100-499 workers	18.81	36.2	19.32	36.1	16.14	36.8
500 workers or more	23.93	37.0	24.99	36.9	16.88	38.0

[1]Earnings are the straight-time hourly wages or salaries paid to employees. They include incentive pay, cost-of-living adjustments, and hazard pay. Excluded are premium pay for overtime, vacations, and holidays; nonproduction bonuses; and tips. The mean is computed by totaling the pay of all workers and dividing by the number of workers, weighted by hours.

[2]Mean weekly hours are the hours an employee is scheduled to work in a week, not including overtime.

[3]Employees are classified as working either a full-time or a part-time schedule based on the definition used by each establishment. Union workers are those whose wages are determined through collective bargaining. Wages of time workers are based solely on hourly rate or salary; incentive workers are those whose wages are at least partly based on productivity payments such as piece rates, commissions, and production bonuses.

[4]A classification system including about 800 individual occupations is used to cover all workers in the civilian economy.

[5]Classification of establishments into goods-producing and service-producing industries applies to private industry only.

CHAPTER 7

PRICES

PRICES

HIGHLIGHTS

This chapter examines the movement of prices, which is one of the most important indicators of the state of the economy. Several indexes are covered: the Producer Price Index (PPI), which gives information about prices received by producers; the Consumer Price Index (CPI), which gives information about prices paid by consumers; and the Import Price Index (MPI) and the Export Price Index (XPI), which give information about prices involved in various foreign trade, export, and import price indexes.

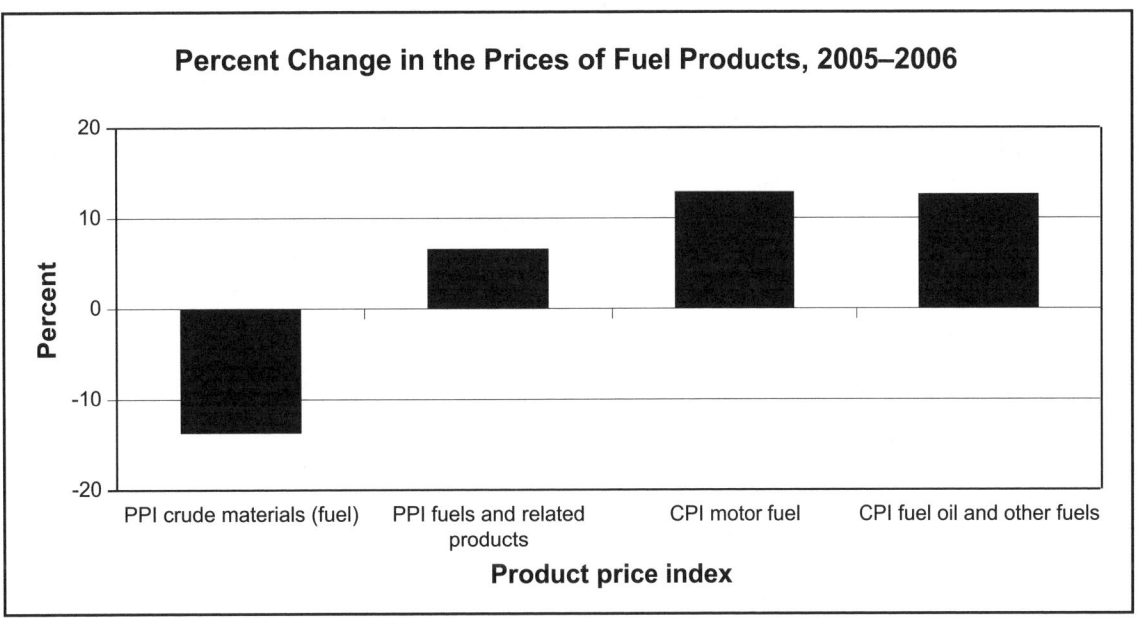

Percent Change in the Prices of Fuel Products, 2005–2006

The increase in the producer prices for processed fuel is reflected in the increase in consumer prices for motor fuel and fuel oil. There is a time lag and other possible factors in the relationship between the price change for crude oil and its products. Although the price of crude fuel declined from 2005 to 2006, it was still 14 percent higher than the price in 2004. (See Tables 7-1 and 7-8.)

OTHER HIGHLIGHTS

- At the intermediate level, the PPI for materials and components for construction rose 6.7 percent in 2006, after an increase of 6.1 percent in 2005. (See Table 7-1.)

- The PPI for consumer goods continued to increase faster than the PPI for capital equipment (3.5 percent compared to 1.6 percent). (See Table 7-1.)

- The PPI for all commodities rose 4.6 percent, with fuels and power, chemicals, metals, and non-metallic minerals each rising between 6.6 percent and 12.9 percent. (See Table 7-2.)

- The MPI for all commodities rose 2.5 percent between December 2005 and December 2006. For industrial supplies and materials, it rose 5.0 percent. The XPI for all commodities rose 4.5 percent, with prices for industrial supplies and materials rising 9 percent. (See Tables 7-12 and 7-13.)

NOTES AND DEFINITIONS

PRODUCER PRICE INDEX

Coverage

The *Producer Price Index (PPI)* measures average changes in prices received by domestic producers of goods and services. Most of the information used in calculating the indexes is obtained through the systematic sampling of nearly every industry in the manufacturing and mining sectors of the economy. The PPI program also includes data from other sectors, including agriculture, fishing, forestry, services, and gas and electricity. As producer price indexes are designed to measure only the change in prices received for the output of domestic industries, imports are not included. The sample currently contains about 100,000 price quotations per month.

Producer price indexes are based on selling prices reported by establishments of all sizes as selected by probability sampling, with the probability of selection proportional to size. Individual items and transaction terms from these firms are also chosen by probability proportionate to size. The Bureau of Labor Statistics (BLS) strongly encourages cooperating companies to supply actual transaction prices at the time of shipment to minimize the use of list prices. Prices are normally reported monthly by mail questionnaire for the Tuesday of the week containing the 13th of the month.

Price data are always provided on a voluntary and confidential basis; only BLS employees, sworn to secrecy, are allowed access to individual company price reports. BLS publishes price indexes instead of unit dollar prices. All producer price indexes are routinely subject to revision four months after the original publication to reflect the availability of late reports and corrections by respondents.

There are three primary systems of indexes within the PPI program: (1) stage-of-processing indexes; (2) indexes for the net output of industries and their products; and (3) commodity indexes. The commodity-based stage-of-processing structure organizes products by class of buyer and degree of fabrication. The entire output of various industries is sampled to derive price indexes for the net output of industries and their products. The commodity structure organizes products by similarity of end-use or material composition.

Within the commodity stage-of-processing system, finished goods are commodities that will not undergo further processing and that are ready for sale to the final demand user—either an individual consumer or a business firm. Consumer foods include unprocessed foods, such as eggs and fresh vegetables, and processed foods, such as bakery products and meats. Other finished consumer goods include durable goods, such as automobiles, household furniture, and appliances; and nondurable goods, such as apparel and home heating oil. Capital equipment includes producer durable goods, such as heavy motor trucks, tractors, and machine tools.

The stage-of-processing category for intermediate materials, supplies, and components includes commodities that have been processed but require further processing, such as flour, cotton, yarn, steel mill products, and lumber. The intermediate goods category also encompasses physically complete nondurable goods purchased by business firms as inputs for their operations, such as diesel fuel, belts and belting, paper boxes, and fertilizers.

Crude materials for further processing are products entering the market for the first time that have not been manufactured or fabricated; these products will not be sold directly to consumers. Crude foodstuffs and feedstuffs includes items such as grains and livestock; examples of crude nonfood materials include raw cotton, crude petroleum, coal, hides and skins, and iron and steel scrap.

Producer price indexes for the net output of industries and their products are grouped according to the Standard Industrial Classification (SIC) and the Census Bureau product code extensions of the SIC. Industry price indexes are compatible with other economic time series organized by SIC codes, such as data on employment, wages, and productivity.

Net output values of shipments are used as weights for industry indexes and refer to the value of shipments from establishments in one industry shipped to establishments classified in another industry. However, *weights for commodity price indexes* are based on gross shipment values, including shipment values between establishments within the same industry. As a result, commodity aggregate indexes, such as the *all commodities index*, are affected by the multiple counting of price change at successive stages of processing. This can lead to exaggerated or misleading signals about inflation. Stage-of-processing indexes partly correct this defect, but industry indexes consistently correct this weakness at all levels of aggregation. Therefore, industry and stage-of-processing indexes are more appropriate than commodity aggregate indexes for economic analysis of general price trends.

Weights for most traditional commodity groupings of the PPI, as well as all indexes calculated from traditional commodity groupings (such as stage-of-processing indexes), are currently weighted by value-of-shipments data contained in the 1997 economic censuses.

With the release of data for January 2004, the PPI program changed its basis for industry classification from the 1987

SIC System to the North American Industry Classification System (NAICS). The PPI treats the SIC-to-NAICS comparison as continuous if 80 percent or more of the weight of the SIC-based index comprises at least 80 percent of the weight of the NAICS-based index. All index series that have passed this test are published under the NAICS structure using the index base date and price index history established by the SIC-based index.

Sources of Additional Information

Additional information is published monthly by the BLS in the Producer Price Index Detailed Report. For information on the underlying concepts and methodology of the Producer Price Index, see Chapter 14 in the *BLS Handbook of Methods*, which is available on the BLS Web site at <http://www.bls.gov>.

Table 7-1. Producer Price Indexes, by Stage of Processing, 1947–2006

(1982 = 100.)

Year	Crude materials for further processing				Intermediate materials, supplies, and components						Finished goods		
	Total	Foodstuffs and feedstuffs	Nonfood materials, except fuel	Fuel	Total	Materials and components for construction	Components for manufacturing	Processed fuels and lubricants	Containers	Supplies	Total	Consumer goods	Capital equipment
1947	31.7	45.1	24.0	7.5	23.3	22.5	21.3	14.4	23.4	28.5	26.4	28.6	19.8
1948	34.7	48.8	26.7	8.9	25.2	24.9	23.0	16.4	24.4	29.8	28.5	30.8	21.6
1949	30.1	40.5	24.3	8.8	24.2	24.9	23.4	14.9	24.5	28.0	27.7	29.4	22.7
1950	32.7	43.4	27.8	8.8	25.3	26.2	24.3	15.2	25.2	29.0	28.2	29.9	23.2
1951	37.6	50.2	32.0	9.0	28.4	28.7	27.6	15.9	29.6	32.6	30.8	32.7	25.5
1952	34.5	47.3	27.8	9.0	27.5	28.5	27.6	15.7	28.0	32.6	30.6	32.3	25.9
1953	31.9	42.3	26.6	9.3	27.7	29.0	28.1	15.8	28.0	31.0	30.3	31.7	26.3
1954	31.6	42.3	26.1	8.9	27.9	29.1	28.3	15.8	28.5	31.7	30.4	31.7	26.7
1955	30.4	38.4	27.5	8.9	28.4	30.3	29.5	15.8	28.9	31.2	30.5	31.5	27.4
1956	30.6	37.6	28.6	9.5	29.6	31.8	32.2	16.3	31.0	32.0	31.3	32.0	29.5
1957	31.2	39.2	28.2	10.1	30.3	32.0	33.5	17.2	32.4	32.3	32.5	32.9	31.3
1958	31.9	41.6	27.1	10.2	30.4	32.0	33.8	16.2	33.2	33.1	33.2	33.6	32.1
1959	31.1	38.8	28.1	10.4	30.8	32.9	34.2	16.2	33.0	33.5	33.1	33.3	32.7
1960	30.4	38.4	26.9	10.5	30.8	32.7	34.0	16.6	33.4	33.3	33.4	33.6	32.8
1961	30.2	37.9	27.2	10.5	30.6	32.2	33.7	16.8	33.2	33.7	33.4	33.6	32.9
1962	30.5	38.6	27.1	10.4	30.6	32.1	33.4	16.7	33.6	34.5	33.5	33.7	33.0
1963	29.9	37.5	26.7	10.5	30.7	32.2	33.4	16.6	33.2	35.0	33.4	33.5	33.1
1964	29.6	36.6	27.2	10.5	30.8	32.5	33.7	16.2	32.9	34.7	33.5	33.6	33.4
1965	31.1	39.2	27.7	10.6	31.2	32.8	34.2	16.5	33.5	35.0	34.1	34.2	33.8
1966	33.1	42.7	28.3	10.9	32.0	33.6	35.4	16.8	34.5	36.5	35.2	35.4	34.6
1967	31.3	40.3	26.5	11.3	32.2	34.0	36.5	16.9	35.0	36.8	35.6	35.6	35.8
1968	31.8	40.9	27.1	11.5	33.0	35.7	37.3	16.5	35.9	37.1	36.6	36.5	37.0
1969	33.9	44.1	28.4	12.0	34.1	37.7	38.5	16.6	37.2	37.8	38.0	37.9	38.3
1970	35.2	45.2	29.1	13.8	35.4	38.3	40.6	17.7	39.0	39.7	39.3	39.1	40.1
1971	36.0	46.1	29.4	15.7	36.8	40.8	41.9	19.5	40.8	40.8	40.5	40.2	41.7
1972	39.9	51.5	32.3	16.8	38.2	43.0	42.9	20.1	42.7	42.5	41.8	41.5	42.8
1973	54.5	72.6	42.9	18.6	42.4	46.5	44.3	22.2	45.2	51.7	45.6	46.0	44.2
1974	61.4	76.4	54.5	24.8	52.5	55.0	51.1	33.6	53.3	56.8	52.6	53.1	50.5
1975	61.6	77.4	50.0	30.6	58.0	60.1	57.8	39.4	60.0	61.8	58.2	58.2	58.2
1976	63.4	76.8	54.9	34.5	60.9	64.1	60.8	42.3	63.1	65.8	60.8	60.4	62.1
1977	65.5	77.5	56.3	42.0	64.9	69.3	64.5	47.7	65.9	69.3	64.7	64.3	66.1
1978	73.4	87.3	61.9	48.2	69.5	76.5	69.2	49.9	71.0	72.9	69.8	69.4	71.3
1979	85.9	100.0	75.5	57.3	78.4	84.2	75.8	61.6	79.4	80.2	77.6	77.5	77.5
1980	95.3	104.6	91.8	69.4	90.3	91.3	84.6	85.0	89.1	89.9	88.0	88.6	85.8
1981	103.0	103.9	109.8	84.8	98.6	97.9	94.7	100.6	96.7	96.9	96.1	96.6	94.6
1982	100.0	100.0	100.0	100.0	100.0	100.0	100.0	100.0	100.0	100.0	100.0	100.0	100.0
1983	101.3	101.8	98.8	105.1	100.6	102.8	102.4	95.4	100.4	101.8	101.6	101.3	102.8
1984	103.5	104.7	101.0	105.1	103.1	105.6	105.0	95.7	105.9	104.1	103.7	103.3	105.2
1985	95.8	94.8	94.3	102.7	102.7	107.3	106.4	92.8	109.0	104.4	104.7	103.8	107.5
1986	87.7	93.2	76.0	92.2	99.1	108.1	107.5	72.7	110.3	105.6	103.2	101.4	109.7
1987	93.7	96.2	88.5	84.1	101.5	109.8	108.8	73.3	114.5	107.7	105.4	103.6	111.7
1988	96.0	106.1	85.9	82.1	107.1	116.1	112.3	71.2	120.1	113.7	108.0	106.2	114.3
1989	103.1	111.2	95.8	85.3	112.0	121.3	116.4	76.4	125.4	118.1	113.6	112.1	118.8
1990	108.9	113.1	107.3	84.8	114.5	122.9	119.0	85.9	127.7	119.4	119.2	118.2	122.9
1991	101.2	105.5	97.5	82.9	114.4	124.5	121.0	85.3	128.1	121.4	121.7	120.5	126.7
1992	100.4	105.1	94.2	84.0	114.7	126.5	122.0	84.5	127.7	122.7	123.2	121.7	129.1
1993	102.4	108.4	94.1	87.1	116.2	132.0	123.0	84.7	126.4	125.0	124.7	123.0	131.4
1994	101.8	106.5	97.0	82.4	118.5	136.6	124.3	83.1	129.7	127.0	125.5	123.3	134.1
1995	102.7	105.8	105.8	72.1	124.9	142.1	126.5	84.2	148.8	132.1	127.9	125.6	136.7
1996	113.8	121.5	105.7	92.6	125.7	143.6	126.9	90.0	141.1	135.9	131.3	129.5	138.3
1997	111.1	112.2	103.5	101.3	125.6	146.5	126.4	89.3	136.0	135.9	131.8	130.2	138.2
1998	96.8	103.9	84.5	86.7	123.0	146.8	125.9	81.1	140.8	134.8	130.7	128.9	137.6
1999	98.2	98.7	91.1	91.2	123.2	148.9	125.7	84.6	142.5	134.2	133.0	132.0	137.6
2000	120.6	100.2	118.0	136.9	129.2	150.7	126.2	102.0	151.6	136.9	138.0	138.2	138.8
2001	121.0	106.1	101.5	151.4	129.7	150.6	126.4	104.5	153.1	138.7	140.7	141.5	139.7
2002	108.1	99.5	101.0	117.3	127.8	151.3	126.1	96.3	152.1	138.9	138.9	139.4	139.1
2003	135.3	113.5	116.9	185.7	133.7	153.6	125.9	112.6	153.7	141.5	143.3	145.3	139.5
2004	159.0	127.0	149.2	211.4	142.6	166.4	127.4	124.3	159.3	146.7	148.5	151.7	141.4
2005	182.2	122.7	176.7	279.7	154.0	176.6	129.9	150.0	167.1	151.9	155.7	160.4	144.6
2006	184.8	119.3	210.0	241.5	164.0	188.4	134.5	162.8	175.0	157.0	160.4	166.0	146.9

Table 7-2. Producer Price Indexes, by Commodity Group, 1913–2006

(1982 = 100.)

Year	All commodities	Farm products	Processed foods and feeds	Industrial commodities													
				Total	Textile products and apparel	Hides, leather, and related products	Fuels and related products and power	Chemicals and related products	Rubber and plastics products	Lumber and wood products	Pulp, paper, and allied products	Metals and metal products	Machinery and equipment	Furniture and household durables	Nonmetallic mineral products	Transportation equipment	Miscellaneous products
1913	12.0	18.0	...	11.9	...	...	...	...	...	...	...	...	...	...	...	...	...
1914	11.8	17.9	...	11.3	...	...	...	...	...	...	...	...	...	...	...	...	...
1915	12.0	18.0	...	11.6	...	...	...	...	...	...	...	...	...	...	...	...	...
1916	14.7	21.3	...	15.0	...	...	...	...	...	...	...	...	...	...	...	...	...
1917	20.2	32.6	...	19.5	...	...	...	...	...	...	...	...	...	...	...	...	...
1918	22.6	37.4	...	21.1	...	...	...	...	...	...	...	...	...	...	...	...	...
1919	23.9	39.8	...	22.0	...	...	...	...	...	...	...	...	...	...	...	...	...
1920	26.6	38.0	...	27.4	...	...	...	...	...	...	...	...	...	...	...	...	...
1921	16.8	22.3	...	17.8	...	...	...	...	...	...	...	...	...	...	...	...	...
1922	16.7	23.7	...	17.4	...	...	...	...	...	...	...	...	...	...	...	...	...
1923	17.3	24.9	...	17.8	...	...	...	...	...	...	...	...	...	...	...	...	...
1924	16.9	25.2	...	17.0	...	...	...	...	...	...	...	...	...	...	...	...	...
1925	17.8	27.7	...	17.5	...	...	...	...	...	...	...	...	...	...	...	...	...
1926	17.2	25.3	...	17.0	...	17.1	10.3	...	47.1	9.3	...	13.7	...	28.6	16.4	...	...
1927	16.5	25.1	...	16.0	...	18.4	9.1	...	35.7	8.8	...	12.9	...	27.9	15.7	...	...
1928	16.7	26.7	...	15.8	...	20.7	8.7	...	28.3	8.5	...	12.9	...	27.2	16.2	...	...
1929	16.4	26.4	...	15.6	...	18.6	8.6	...	24.6	8.8	...	13.3	...	27.0	16.0	...	...
1930	14.9	22.4	...	14.5	...	17.1	8.1	...	21.5	8.0	...	12.0	...	26.5	15.9	...	...
1931	12.6	16.4	...	12.8	...	14.7	7.0	...	18.3	6.5	...	10.8	...	24.4	14.9	...	...
1932	11.2	12.2	...	11.9	...	12.5	7.3	...	15.9	5.6	...	9.9	...	21.5	13.9	...	...
1933	11.4	13.0	...	12.1	...	13.8	6.9	16.2	16.7	6.7	...	10.2	...	21.6	14.7	...	...
1934	12.9	16.5	...	13.3	...	14.8	7.6	17.0	19.5	7.8	...	11.2	...	23.4	15.7	...	...
1935	13.8	19.8	...	13.3	...	15.3	7.6	17.7	19.6	7.5	...	11.2	...	23.2	15.7	...	...
1936	13.9	20.4	...	13.5	...	16.3	7.9	17.8	21.1	7.9	...	11.4	...	23.6	15.8	...	...
1937	14.9	21.8	...	14.5	...	17.9	8.0	18.6	24.9	9.3	...	13.1	...	26.1	16.1	...	...
1938	13.5	17.3	...	13.9	...	15.8	7.9	17.7	24.4	8.5	...	12.6	...	25.5	15.6	...	...
1939	13.3	16.5	...	13.9	...	16.3	7.5	17.6	25.4	8.7	...	12.5	14.8	25.4	15.3	...	...
1940	13.5	17.1	...	14.1	...	17.2	7.4	17.9	23.7	9.6	...	12.5	14.9	26.0	15.3	...	...
1941	15.1	20.8	...	15.1	...	18.4	7.9	19.5	25.5	11.5	...	12.8	15.1	27.6	15.7	...	...
1942	17.0	26.7	...	16.2	...	20.1	8.1	21.7	29.7	12.5	...	13.0	15.4	29.9	16.3	...	...
1943	17.8	30.9	...	16.5	...	20.1	8.3	21.9	30.5	13.2	...	12.9	15.2	29.7	16.4	...	...
1944	17.9	31.2	...	16.7	...	19.9	8.6	22.2	30.1	14.3	...	12.9	15.1	30.5	16.7	...	...
1945	18.2	32.4	...	17.0	...	20.1	8.7	22.3	29.2	14.5	...	13.1	15.1	30.5	17.4	...	...
1946	20.8	37.5	...	18.6	...	23.3	9.3	24.1	29.3	16.6	...	14.7	16.6	32.4	18.5	...	...
1947	25.6	45.1	33.0	22.7	50.6	31.7	11.1	32.1	29.2	25.8	25.1	18.2	19.3	37.2	20.7	...	26.6
1948	27.7	48.5	35.3	24.6	52.8	32.1	13.1	32.8	30.2	29.5	26.2	20.7	20.9	39.4	22.4	...	27.7
1949	26.3	41.9	32.1	24.1	48.3	30.4	12.4	30.0	29.2	27.3	25.1	20.9	21.9	40.1	23.0	...	28.2
1950	27.3	44.0	33.2	25.0	50.2	32.9	12.6	30.4	35.6	31.4	25.7	22.0	22.6	40.9	23.5	...	28.6
1951	30.4	51.2	36.9	27.6	56.0	37.7	13.0	34.8	43.7	34.1	30.5	24.5	25.3	44.4	25.0	...	30.3
1952	29.6	48.4	36.4	26.9	50.5	30.5	13.0	33.0	39.6	33.2	29.7	24.5	25.3	43.5	25.0	...	30.2
1953	29.2	43.8	34.8	27.2	49.3	31.0	13.4	33.4	36.9	33.1	29.6	25.3	25.9	44.4	26.0	...	31.0
1954	29.3	43.2	35.4	27.2	48.2	29.5	13.2	33.8	37.5	32.5	29.6	25.5	26.3	44.9	26.6	...	31.3
1955	29.3	40.5	33.8	27.8	48.2	29.4	13.2	33.7	42.4	34.1	30.4	27.2	27.2	45.1	27.3	...	31.3
1956	30.3	40.0	33.8	29.1	48.2	31.2	13.6	33.9	43.0	34.6	32.4	29.6	29.3	46.3	28.5	...	31.7
1957	31.2	41.1	34.8	29.9	48.3	31.2	14.3	34.6	42.8	32.8	33.0	30.2	31.4	47.5	29.6	...	32.6
1958	31.6	42.9	36.5	30.0	47.4	31.6	13.7	34.9	42.8	32.5	33.4	30.0	32.1	47.9	29.9	...	33.3
1959	31.7	40.2	35.6	30.5	48.1	35.9	13.7	34.8	42.6	34.7	33.7	30.6	32.8	48.0	30.3	...	33.4

. . . = Not available.

Table 7-2. Producer Price Indexes, by Commodity Group, 1913–2006—*Continued*

(1982 = 100.)

Year	All commodities	Farm products	Processed foods and feeds	Industrial commodities													
				Total	Textile products and apparel	Hides, leather, and related products	Fuels and related products and power	Chemicals and related products	Rubber and plastics products	Lumber and wood products	Pulp, paper, and allied products	Metals and metal products	Machinery and equipment	Furniture and household durables	Non-metallic mineral products	Transportation equipment	Miscellaneous products
1960	31.7	40.1	35.6	30.5	48.6	34.6	13.9	34.8	42.7	33.5	34.0	30.6	33.0	47.8	30.4	. . .	33.6
1961	31.6	39.7	36.2	30.4	47.8	34.9	14.0	34.5	41.1	32.0	33.0	30.5	33.0	47.5	30.5	. . .	33.7
1962	31.7	40.4	36.5	30.4	48.2	35.3	14.0	33.9	39.9	32.2	33.4	30.2	33.0	47.2	30.5	. . .	33.9
1963	31.6	39.6	36.8	30.3	48.2	34.3	13.9	33.5	40.1	32.8	33.1	30.3	33.1	46.9	30.3	. . .	34.2
1964	31.6	39.0	36.7	30.5	48.5	34.4	13.5	33.6	39.6	33.5	33.0	31.1	33.3	47.1	30.4	. . .	34.4
1965	32.3	40.7	38.0	30.9	48.8	35.9	13.8	33.9	39.7	33.7	33.3	32.0	33.7	46.8	30.4	. . .	34.7
1966	33.3	43.7	40.2	31.5	48.9	39.4	14.1	34.0	40.5	35.2	34.2	32.8	34.7	47.4	30.7	. . .	35.3
1967	33.4	41.3	39.8	32.0	48.9	38.1	14.4	34.2	41.4	35.1	34.6	33.2	35.9	48.3	31.2	. . .	36.2
1968	34.2	42.3	40.6	32.8	50.7	39.3	14.3	34.1	42.8	39.8	35.0	34.0	37.0	49.7	32.4	. . .	37.0
1969	35.6	45.0	42.7	33.9	51.8	41.5	14.6	34.2	43.6	44.0	36.0	36.0	38.2	50.7	33.6	40.4	38.1
1970	36.9	45.8	44.6	35.2	52.4	42.0	15.3	35.0	44.9	39.9	37.5	38.7	40.0	51.9	35.3	41.9	39.8
1971	38.1	46.6	45.5	36.5	53.3	43.4	16.6	35.6	45.2	44.7	38.1	39.4	41.4	53.1	38.2	44.2	40.8
1972	39.8	51.6	48.0	37.8	55.5	50.0	17.1	35.6	45.3	50.7	39.3	40.9	42.3	53.8	39.4	45.5	41.5
1973	45.0	72.7	58.9	40.3	60.5	54.5	19.4	37.6	46.6	62.2	42.3	44.0	43.7	55.7	40.7	46.1	43.3
1974	53.5	77.4	68.0	49.2	68.0	55.2	30.1	50.2	56.4	64.5	52.5	57.0	50.0	61.8	47.8	50.3	48.1
1975	58.4	77.0	72.6	54.9	67.4	56.5	35.4	62.0	62.2	61.1	59.0	61.5	57.9	67.5	54.4	56.7	53.4
1976	61.1	78.8	70.8	58.4	72.4	63.9	38.3	64.0	66.0	72.2	62.1	65.0	61.3	70.3	58.2	60.5	55.6
1977	64.9	79.4	74.0	62.5	75.3	68.3	43.6	65.9	69.4	83.0	64.6	69.3	65.2	73.2	62.6	64.6	59.4
1978	69.9	87.7	80.6	67.0	78.1	76.1	46.5	68.0	72.4	96.9	67.7	75.3	70.3	77.5	69.6	69.5	66.7
1979	78.7	99.6	88.5	75.7	82.5	96.1	58.9	76.0	80.5	105.5	75.9	86.0	76.7	82.8	77.6	75.3	75.5
1980	89.8	102.9	95.9	88.0	89.7	94.7	82.8	89.0	90.1	101.5	86.3	95.0	86.0	90.7	88.4	82.9	93.6
1981	98.0	105.2	98.9	97.4	97.6	99.3	100.2	98.4	96.4	102.8	94.8	99.6	94.4	95.9	96.7	94.3	96.1
1982	100.0	100.0	100.0	100.0	100.0	100.0	100.0	100.0	100.0	100.0	100.0	100.0	100.0	100.0	100.0	100.0	100.0
1983	101.3	102.4	101.8	101.1	100.3	103.2	95.9	100.3	100.8	107.9	103.3	101.8	102.7	103.4	101.6	102.8	104.8
1984	103.7	105.5	105.4	103.3	102.7	109.0	94.8	102.9	102.3	108.0	110.3	104.8	105.1	105.7	105.4	105.2	107.0
1985	103.2	95.1	103.5	103.7	102.9	108.9	91.4	103.7	101.9	106.6	113.3	104.4	107.2	107.1	108.6	107.9	109.4
1986	100.2	92.9	105.4	100.0	103.2	113.0	69.8	102.6	101.9	107.2	116.1	103.2	108.8	108.2	110.0	110.5	111.6
1987	102.8	95.5	107.9	102.6	105.1	120.4	70.2	106.4	103.0	112.8	121.8	107.1	110.4	109.9	110.0	112.5	114.9
1988	106.9	104.9	112.7	106.3	109.2	131.4	66.7	116.3	109.3	118.9	130.4	118.7	113.2	113.1	111.2	114.3	120.2
1989	112.2	110.9	117.8	111.6	112.3	136.3	72.9	123.0	112.6	126.7	137.8	124.1	117.4	116.9	112.6	117.7	126.5
1990	116.3	112.2	121.9	115.8	115.0	141.7	82.3	123.6	113.6	129.7	141.2	122.9	120.7	119.2	114.7	121.5	134.2
1991	116.5	105.7	121.9	116.5	116.3	138.9	81.2	125.6	115.1	132.1	142.9	120.2	123.0	121.2	117.2	126.4	140.8
1992	117.2	103.6	122.1	117.4	117.8	140.4	80.4	125.9	115.1	146.6	145.2	119.2	123.4	122.2	117.3	130.4	145.3
1993	118.9	107.1	124.0	119.0	118.0	143.7	80.0	128.2	116.0	174.0	147.3	119.2	124.0	123.7	120.0	133.7	145.4
1994	120.4	106.3	125.5	120.7	118.3	148.5	77.8	132.1	117.6	180.0	152.5	124.8	125.1	126.1	124.2	137.2	141.9
1995	124.7	107.4	127.0	125.5	120.8	153.7	78.0	142.5	124.3	178.1	172.2	134.5	126.6	128.2	129.0	139.7	145.4
1996	127.7	122.4	133.3	127.3	122.4	150.5	85.8	142.1	123.8	176.1	168.7	131.0	126.5	130.4	131.0	141.7	147.7
1997	127.6	112.9	134.0	127.7	122.6	154.2	86.1	143.6	123.2	183.8	167.9	131.8	125.9	130.8	133.2	141.6	150.9
1998	124.4	104.6	131.6	124.8	122.9	148.0	75.3	143.9	122.6	179.1	171.7	127.8	124.9	131.3	135.4	141.2	156.0
1999	125.5	98.4	131.1	126.5	121.1	146.0	80.5	144.2	122.5	183.6	174.1	124.6	124.3	131.7	138.9	141.8	166.6
2000	132.7	99.5	133.1	134.8	121.4	151.5	103.5	151.0	125.5	178.2	183.7	128.1	124.0	132.6	142.5	143.8	170.8
2001	134.2	103.8	137.3	135.7	121.3	158.4	105.3	151.8	127.2	174.4	184.8	125.4	123.7	133.2	144.3	145.2	181.3
2002	131.1	99.0	136.2	132.4	119.9	157.6	93.2	151.9	126.8	173.3	185.9	125.9	122.9	133.5	146.2	144.6	182.4
2003	138.1	111.5	143.4	139.1	119.8	162.3	112.9	161.8	130.1	177.4	190.0	129.2	121.9	133.9	148.2	145.7	179.6
2004	146.7	123.3	151.2	147.6	121.0	164.5	126.9	174.4	133.8	195.6	195.7	149.6	122.1	135.1	153.2	148.6	183.2
2005	157.4	118.5	153.1	160.2	122.8	165.4	156.4	192.0	143.8	196.5	202.6	160.8	123.7	139.4	164.2	151.0	195.1
2006	164.7	117.0	153.8	168.8	124.5	168.4	166.7	205.8	153.8	194.4	209.8	181.6	126.2	142.6	179.9	152.6	205.6

. . . = Not available.

Table 7-3. Producer Price Indexes for the Net Output of Selected Industries, 1996–2006

(December 2003 = 100, unless otherwise specified.)

Industry	1996	1997	1998	1999	2000	2001	2002	2003	2004	2005	2006
Agriculture, Forestry, Fishing, and Hunting											
Logging[1]	185.7	191.2	188.1	182.7	177.5	167.5	165.0	168.7	175.2	179.0	176.6
Mining											
Oil and gas extraction[2]	84.8	87.5	68.3	78.5	126.8	127.5	107.0	160.1	192.7	262.0	252.5
Mining (except oil and gas)	...	...	...	...	...	...	...	...	109.5	126.6	147.9
Coal mining[2]	91.4	92.2	89.5	87.3	84.8	91.3	93.9	94.4	104.1	118.2	126.9
Metal ore mining[3]	92.1	85.8	73.2	70.3	73.8	70.8	73.6	81.6	111.8	146.0	204.6
Iron ore mining[3]	95.7	95.3	94.5	94.0	93.9	95.2	94.2	95.0	97.2	115.7	131.2
Gold ore and silver ore mining[3]	78.6	67.9	61.1	58.2	57.0	55.2	62.6	72.6	82.6	89.5	121.3
Copper, nickel, lead, and zinc mining[4]	117.0	110.4	76.8	71.3	88.7	81.7	80.1	90.1	147.7	195.2	350.2
Other metal ore mining[2]	31.9	29.9	27.6	25.9	26.4	24.7	28.9	34.9	80.0	159.1	128.7
Nonmetallic mineral mining and quarrying[3]	127.1	128.8	132.2	134.0	137.0	141.0	143.5	146.4	151.2	161.3	176.0
Stone mining and quarrying[3]	133.2	135.4	138.8	142.1	147.3	152.2	156.1	160.2	166.1	176.7	192.7
Sand, gravel, clay, and refractory minerals mining	...	...	...	...	...	...	...	...	102.4	108.8	117.6
Other nonmetallic mineral mining and quarrying[3]	108.6	107.6	110.1	108.0	106.8	107.1	107.7	108.4	111.4	120.8	133.8
Mining support activities	...	...	...	...	...	...	...	...	104.8	133.9	172.0
Utilities	...	...	...	...	...	...	...	...	104.9	117.6	123.1
Electric power generation, transmission, and distribution	...	...	...	...	...	...	...	...	103.3	111.3	118.8
Electric power generation	...	...	...	...	...	...	...	...	105.2	121.6	128.0
Electric power transmission, control, and distribution	...	...	...	...	...	...	...	...	102.5	107.1	115.1
Natural gas distribution	...	...	...	...	...	...	...	...	107.3	126.6	129.3
Manufacturing											
Food[3]	127.1	127.9	126.3	126.3	128.5	132.8	132.0	137.4	144.3	146.1	146.8
Animal food	...	...	...	...	...	...	...	...	103.3	98.2	101.8
Grain and oilseed milling	...	...	...	...	...	...	...	...	103.1	99.8	104.7
Flour milling and malt	...	...	...	...	...	...	...	...	102.6	100.5	109.1
Starch and vegetable fats and oils	...	...	...	...	...	...	...	...	103.6	97.9	102.4
Breakfast cereal manufacturing	...	...	...	...	...	...	...	...	101.7	105.0	106.9
Sugar and confectionery product[3]	127.7	129.3	128.8	129.4	127.5	129.3	133.7	139.5	141.4	147.3	154.7
Sugar	...	...	...	...	...	...	...	...	99.7	105.6	123.4
Chocolate and confectionery from cacao beans	...	...	...	...	...	...	...	...	100.1	101.7	103.9
Confectionery from purchased chocolate	...	...	...	...	...	...	...	...	100.1	102.2	103.8
Non-chocolate confectionery	...	...	...	...	...	...	...	...	104.0	111.0	113.0
Fruit and vegetable preserving and specialty food[3]	129.7	129.9	130.1	131.7	132.1	133.3	135.2	136.6	139.2	141.7	144.5
Fruit and vegetable canning, pickling, and drying	...	...	...	...	...	...	...	...	100.5	104.0	107.3
Dairy product[3]	125.0	123.9	133.1	133.8	129.9	141.2	133.3	135.8	151.0	151.3	147.4
Ice cream and frozen dessert	...	...	...	...	...	...	...	...	103.3	104.7	106.9
Animal slaughtering and processing[3]	114.6	116.1	109.2	108.9	115.0	120.3	114.0	125.8	134.2	135.8	130.8
Seafood product preparation and packaging	...	...	...	...	...	...	...	...	102.4	106.2	107.0
Bakery and tortilla	...	...	...	...	...	...	...	...	100.8	102.6	105.3
Bread and bakery product	...	...	...	...	...	...	...	...	101.1	103.4	106.6
Cookie, cracker, and pasta	...	...	...	...	...	...	...	...	100.5	101.3	103.2
Tortilla	...	...	...	...	...	...	...	...	100.4	102.5	103.9
Other food	...	...	...	...	...	...	...	...	101.1	105.4	107.0
Snack food	...	...	...	...	...	...	...	...	101.4	108.4	108.5
Coffee and tea	...	...	...	...	...	...	...	...	101.7	115.1	117.3
Flavoring syrup and concentrate	...	...	...	...	...	...	...	...	101.0	103.1	106.5
Seasoning and dressing	...	...	...	...	...	...	...	...	101.1	101.3	102.7
All other food	...	...	...	...	...	...	...	...	100.4	100.8	103.1
Beverage and tobacco product	...	...	...	...	...	...	...	...	101.0	104.8	106.3
Beverage[3]	125.5	126.3	127.2	129.8	134.4	138.6	140.8	142.7	146.4	150.4	153.3
Soft drink and ice	...	...	...	...	...	...	...	...	102.1	104.1	106.8
Breweries	...	...	...	...	...	...	...	...	101.3	105.6	105.6
Wineries	...	...	...	...	...	...	...	...	100.7	104.2	109.8
Distilleries	...	...	...	...	...	...	...	...	100.1	100.6	101.9
Tobacco[3]	199.1	210.8	243.1	325.7	345.8	386.1	401.9	377.9	379.7	401.0	403.8
Tobacco stemming and redrying[5]	109.7	106.5	104.2	104.7	109.0	112.3	114.7	117.5	119.4	119.9	109.4
Tobacco product[6]	210.5	223.3	260.4	356.7	379.3	425.8	442.8	411.7	412.5	436.3	440.2
Textile mills	...	...	...	...	...	...	...	...	101.1	103.6	106.6
Fiber, yarn, and thread mills[3]	113.6	114.1	112.1	106.9	105.5	103.0	99.8	100.9	105.6	108.8	111.1
Fabric mills	...	...	...	...	...	...	...	...	101.0	103.0	105.8
Broadwoven fabric mills	...	...	...	...	...	...	...	...	101.1	103.2	106.7
Narrow fabric mills and schiffli mach embroidery[5]	121.2	122.7	123.8	124.3	125.3	126.2	126.0	125.1	126.2	129.3	131.1
Nonwoven fabric mills	...	...	...	...	...	...	...	...	101.5	105.6	108.1
Knit fabric mills	...	...	...	...	...	...	...	...	100.4	100.5	101.3
Textile and fabric finishing mills	...	...	...	...	...	...	...	...	99.9	102.8	106.5
Fabric coating mills	...	...	...	...	...	...	...	...	100.2	104.9	113.4
Textile product mills	...	...	...	...	...	...	...	...	101.4	105.3	108.4
Textile furnishings mills	...	...	...	...	...	...	...	...	101.1	105.1	108.6
Carpet and rug mills[3]	114.1	115.7	116.3	115.4	117.8	118.9	119.0	121.8	124.6	132.9	140.2
Curtain and linen mills	...	...	...	...	...	...	...	...	100.2	100.3	100.5
Other textile product mills	...	...	...	...	...	...	...	...	102.0	105.4	107.9
Textile bag and canvas mills	...	...	...	...	...	...	...	...	102.7	104.9	107.5
All other textile product mills	...	...	...	...	...	...	...	...	101.7	105.6	108.0

[1]December 1981 = 100.
[2]December 1985 = 100.
[3]December 1984 = 100.
[4]June 1988 = 100.
[5]June 1984 = 100.
[6]December 1982 = 100.
... = Not available.

Table 7-3. Producer Price Indexes for the Net Output of Selected Industries, 1996–2006—*Continued*

(December 2003 = 100, unless otherwise specified.)

Industry	1996	1997	1998	1999	2000	2001	2002	2003	2004	2005	2006
Manufacturing—*Continued*											
Apparel	...	...	...	...	...	...	...	...	100.0	100.0	100.5
Apparel knitting mills[3]	116.6	117.0	116.6	114.0	113.9	113.7	112.7	111.6	110.3	109.6	110.5
Cut and sew apparel	...	...	...	...	...	...	...	...	100.2	100.2	100.6
Cut and sew apparel contractors	...	...	...	...	...	...	...	...	100.2	103.0	105.3
Men's and boys' cut and sew apparel	...	...	...	...	...	...	...	...	99.9	98.4	98.0
Women's and girls' cut and sew apparel	...	...	...	...	...	...	...	...	100.4	100.8	101.0
Other cut and sew apparel	...	...	...	...	...	...	...	...	100.2	102.3	107.1
Accessories and other apparel	...	...	...	...	...	...	...	...	100.5	101.6	102.2
Leather and allied product[3]	134.7	137.1	137.1	136.5	137.9	141.3	141.1	142.8	143.6	144.5	146.6
Leather and hide tanning and finishing[7]	172.4	176.9	171.6	168.8	174.6	191.7	191.4	200.5	205.7	204.8	208.4
Footwear	...	...	...	...	...	...	...	...	100.1	101.1	102.2
Other leather and allied product	...	...	...	...	...	...	...	...	99.8	100.7	102.6
Wood product	...	...	...	...	...	...	...	...	106.7	108.6	108.5
Sawmills and wood preservation	...	...	...	...	...	...	...	...	110.5	110.7	107.9
Plywood, and engineered wood product	...	...	...	...	...	...	...	...	107.0	105.2	99.6
Other wood product	...	...	...	...	...	...	...	...	104.7	108.3	111.4
Millwork	...	...	...	...	...	...	...	...	104.8	105.4	106.7
Wood container and pallet	...	...	...	...	...	...	...	...	102.8	107.1	110.9
All other wood product	...	...	...	...	...	...	...	...	105.0	111.3	115.9
Paper	...	...	...	...	...	...	...	...	102.6	106.9	112.3
Pulp, paper, and paperboard mills	...	...	...	...	...	...	...	...	103.8	109.4	115.7
Pulp mills[6]	135.5	131.0	125.1	122.7	143.4	122.9	116.5	120.9	131.3	137.4	144.8
Paper mills[7]	152.2	143.2	144.5	139.7	148.8	150.5	144.1	145.7	151.1	161.0	168.1
Paperboard mills[6]	169.7	158.2	165.1	166.9	192.2	187.3	179.5	180.2	189.9	196.0	212.7
Converted paper product	...	...	...	...	...	...	...	...	101.9	105.5	110.5
Paper container[3]	140.4	132.9	141.1	144.1	157.1	158.9	157.0	157.3	161.5	167.1	177.1
Paper bag and coated and treated paper	...	...	...	...	...	...	...	...	101.7	105.8	110.4
Stationery product	...	...	...	...	...	...	...	...	101.7	106.8	110.5
Other converted paper product	...	...	...	...	...	...	...	...	97.0	98.7	100.0
Printing and related support activities	...	...	...	...	...	...	...	...	101.1	103.1	105.6
Printing	...	...	...	...	...	...	...	...	101.2	103.3	105.9
Printing support activities	...	...	...	...	...	...	...	...	100.4	100.0	100.4
Petroleum and coal product[3]	87.4	85.6	66.3	76.8	112.8	105.3	98.8	122.0	149.9	200.4	235.5
Petroleum refineries[8]	85.3	83.1	62.3	73.6	111.6	103.1	96.3	121.2	151.5	205.3	241.0
Asphalt paving, roofing, and saturated materials[3]	99.4	102.2	102.0	102.8	113.5	116.9	119.7	125.1	127.1	138.6	164.8
Other petroleum and coal product[3]	140.9	142.0	142.5	142.1	150.3	159.3	160.5	165.3	172.0	197.8	238.3
Chemical[3]	145.8	147.1	148.7	149.7	156.7	158.4	157.3	164.6	172.8	187.3	196.8
Basic chemical[3]	164.0	163.9	160.1	161.4	177.3	173.5	170.6	183.0	197.7	225.9	244.3
Petrochemical	...	...	...	...	...	...	...	...	120.7	151.0	164.7
Industrial gas	...	...	...	...	...	...	...	...	108.3	118.3	123.0
Synthetic dye and pigment	...	...	...	...	...	...	...	...	104.2	108.7	112.0
Other basic inorganic chemical	...	...	...	...	...	...	...	...	103.1	120.4	149.4
Resin, synthetic rubber, and artificial and synthetic fiber and filament[3]	123.1	124.4	115.9	115.4	128.0	126.2	119.7	131.0	145.5	169.4	175.2
Resin and synthetic rubber	...	...	...	...	...	...	...	...	115.1	136.5	141.2
Artificial and synthetic fiber and filament	...	...	...	...	...	...	...	...	101.2	107.8	111.1
Pesticide, fertilizer, and other agricultural chemical[3]	133.4	131.9	128.5	123.2	124.9	132.0	127.0	135.3	142.7	151.3	156.6
Fertilizer	...	...	...	...	...	...	...	...	107.3	118.1	123.5
Pesticide and other agricultural chemical	...	...	...	...	...	...	...	...	100.6	102.2	104.4
Pharmaceutical and medicine[3]	181.2	184.8	203.1	210.1	215.7	220.5	226.3	235.4	244.2	255.2	266.3
Paint, coating, and adhesive	...	...	...	...	...	...	...	...	101.9	108.8	116.9
Adhesive	...	...	...	...	...	...	...	...	100.5	106.4	114.8
Soap, cleaners, and toilet preparation[3]	126.6	127.3	128.7	130.3	132.5	134.2	134.2	134.9	136.9	140.5	144.6
Soap and cleaning compound	...	...	...	...	...	...	...	...	102.0	105.8	110.5
Toilet preparation	...	...	...	...	...	...	...	...	100.0	101.2	102.1
Other chemical product and preparation	...	...	...	...	...	...	...	...	101.6	108.6	114.2
Printing ink	...	...	...	...	...	...	...	...	100.0	103.0	107.2
All other chemical product and preparation	...	...	...	...	...	...	...	...	101.8	109.4	115.3
Plastics and rubber product[3]	123.1	122.8	122.1	122.2	124.6	125.9	125.5	128.4	131.7	141.2	149.7
Plastics product[9]	108.0	107.6	106.8	107.1	109.8	111.0	110.2	113.0	116.2	125.8	134.1
Unsupported plastics film, sheet, and bag	...	...	...	...	...	...	...	...	104.2	116.9	124.4
Plastics pipe, fitting, and unsupported shape	...	...	...	...	...	...	...	...	108.5	122.6	142.8
Laminated plastics plate, sheet, and shape	...	...	...	...	...	...	...	...	101.7	105.0	108.4
Polystyrene foam product	...	...	...	...	...	...	...	...	104.6	117.0	120.8
Foam product (except polystyrene)	...	...	...	...	...	...	...	...	100.2	110.0	136.6
Plastics bottle	...	...	...	...	...	...	...	...	103.1	114.8	119.5
Other plastics product	...	...	...	...	...	...	...	...	101.3	107.1	111.7
Rubber product	...	...	...	...	...	...	...	...	102.1	106.7	111.8
Tire[7]	105.2	103.4	102.0	100.4	100.4	101.5	102.7	105.6	110.5	116.9	123.8
Rubber and plastics hose and belting	...	...	...	...	...	...	...	...	102.3	107.4	111.0
Other rubber product	118.3	119.8	120.2	119.9	120.5	121.3	121.4	121.8	121.9	125.1	130.2
Nonmetallic mineral product[3]	125.8	127.4	129.3	132.6	134.7	136.0	137.1	138.0	142.7	152.0	163.4
Clay product and refractory	...	...	...	...	...	...	...	...	101.5	105.1	110.4
Pottery, ceramics, and plumbing fixture[3]	130.0	131.8	133.5	138.1	139.7	150.2	150.1	150.6	152.1	154.3	159.8
Clay building material and refractories	...	...	...	...	...	...	...	...	102.2	107.8	114.5
Glass and glass product	...	...	...	...	...	...	...	...	100.1	101.6	103.7
Cement and concrete product	...	...	...	...	...	...	...	...	104.2	114.8	126.6
Cement[10]	132.9	138.1	144.2	149.1	148.6	148.7	151.1	150.5	155.4	175.2	197.7

[3]December 1984 = 100.
[6]December 1982 = 100.
[7]June 1981 = 100.
[8]June 1985 = 100.
[9]June 1993 = 100.
[10]June 1982 = 100.
... = Not available.

Table 7-3. Producer Price Indexes for the Net Output of Selected Industries, 1996–2006—*Continued*

(December 2003 = 100, unless otherwise specified.)

Industry	1996	1997	1998	1999	2000	2001	2002	2003	2004	2005	2006
Manufacturing—*Continued*									104.5	117.3	130.6
Ready-mix concrete	...	...	...	...	...	...	...	...	104.5	117.3	130.6
Concrete pipe, brick, and block	...	...	...	...	...	...	...	...	102.5	109.2	116.7
Other concrete products	...	...	...	...	...	...	...	...	104.7	111.3	121.0
Lime and gypsum product	...	...	...	...	...	...	...	...	110.0	124.5	145.1
Lime	...	...	...	...	...	...	...	...	103.5	112.4	121.8
Gypsum product	...	...	...	...	...	...	...	...	111.9	127.9	151.6
Other nonmetallic mineral product[3]	125.6	126.2	127.4	131.3	130.9	132.0	132.6	133.4	137.2	142.5	150.2
Abrasive product	...	...	...	...	...	...	...	...	100.2	103.1	107.2
All other nonmetallic mineral product	...	...	...	...	...	...	...	...	103.5	108.0	114.5
Primary metal[3]	123.7	124.7	120.9	115.8	119.8	116.1	116.2	118.4	142.8	156.3	179.3
Iron and steel mills and ferroalloy	...	...	...	...	...	...	...	...	127.7	136.7	150.9
Steel product from purchased steel	...	...	...	...	...	...	...	...	133.1	146.2	148.2
Iron/steel pipe and tube from purchased steel	...	...	...	...	...	...	...	...	147.9	160.1	164.1
Rolling and drawing of purchased steel	...	...	...	...	...	...	...	...	123.7	137.5	138.1
Nonferrous (except aluminum) production and processing	...	...	...	...	...	...	...	...	113.6	137.6	202.8
Copper rolling, drawing, extruding, and alloying	...	...	...	...	...	...	...	...	118.2	138.9	222.0
Other nonferrous rolling, drawing, extruding, and alloying	...	...	...	...	...	...	...	...	110.3	136.2	181.2
Ferrous metal foundries[3]	127.6	129.2	129.7	130.4	132.1	132.7	133.0	133.5	140.4	152.5	160.1
Nonferrous metal foundries[3]	131.4	133.8	132.7	131.6	133.5	134.1	134.4	135.6	140.0	145.0	160.4
Fabricated metal product[3]	126.2	127.6	128.7	129.1	130.3	131.0	131.7	132.9	141.3	149.5	155.7
Forging and stamping	...	...	...	...	...	...	...	...	107.0	113.3	116.8
Architectural and structural metals	...	...	...	...	...	...	...	...	111.2	118.0	122.6
Plate work and fabricated structural product	...	...	...	...	...	...	...	...	115.2	124.2	128.9
Ornamental and architectural metal product	...	...	...	...	...	...	...	...	108.3	113.5	118.1
Boiler, tank, and shipping container	...	...	...	...	...	...	...	...	106.8	115.7	120.3
Light gauge metal container[3]	103.9	102.7	102.3	100.7	101.0	100.8	102.7	105.4	110.4	117.5	121.0
Hardware	...	...	...	...	...	...	...	...	103.4	107.2	110.7
Spring and wire product	...	...	...	...	...	...	...	...	108.9	114.4	117.9
Machine shops; turned product; and screw, nut, and bolt	...	...	...	...	...	...	...	...	102.8	108.4	113.0
Machine shops	...	...	...	...	...	...	...	...	102.4	107.4	109.8
Turned product and screw, nut, and bolt[3]	121.6	122.6	122.7	121.8	122.9	122.8	123.4	123.6	128.4	136.6	147.1
Coating, engraving, heat treating, and other activity	...	...	...	...	...	...	...	...	102.0	104.2	110.6
Other fabricated metal product	...	...	...	...	...	...	...	...	103.8	109.8	115.7
Metal valve	...	...	...	...	...	...	...	...	103.0	109.8	118.1
All other fabricated metal product	...	...	...	...	...	...	...	...	104.5	109.9	113.7
Machinery	...	...	...	...	...	...	...	...	101.9	105.6	108.8
Agricultural, construction, and mining machinery	...	...	...	...	...	...	...	...	102.4	107.4	111.7
Agricultural implement	...	...	...	...	...	...	...	...	101.8	105.8	107.8
Construction machinery	...	...	...	...	...	...	...	...	102.9	107.7	112.5
Mining and oil and gas field machinery	...	...	...	...	...	...	...	...	102.7	110.6	119.5
Industrial machinery[3]	140.5	143.0	145.4	147.2	148.7	149.9	149.6	150.1	153.0	155.9	158.9
Sawmill and woodworking machinery	...	...	...	...	...	...	...	...	101.5	105.0	108.2
Plastics and rubber industry machinery	...	...	...	...	...	...	...	...	102.8	106.3	109.4
Other industrial machinery[3]	140.5	143.0	145.4	147.2	148.7	149.9	149.6	150.1	152.7	155.3	158.0
Commercial and service industry machinery	...	...	...	...	...	...	...	...	101.3	102.9	103.9
HVAC and commercial refrigeration equipment	...	...	...	...	...	...	...	...	101.9	108.0	112.1
Metalworking machinery	...	...	...	...	...	...	...	...	100.8	103.3	105.8
Turbine, and power transmission equipment[3]	132.3	133.6	133.9	135.7	136.6	137.7	138.9	139.1	140.8	143.2	148.0
Other general purpose machinery	...	...	...	...	...	...	...	...	103.0	107.6	111.2
Pump and compressor	...	...	...	...	...	...	...	...	102.2	108.4	112.6
Material handling equipment	...	...	...	...	...	...	...	...	104.6	110.6	114.4
All other general purpose machinery	...	...	...	...	...	...	...	...	102.5	107.5	108.7
Computer and electronic product	...	...	...	...	...	...	...	...	99.0	97.5	96.5
Communications equipment[2]	115.0	115.7	115.0	113.0	110.4	108.6	105.0	101.7	98.4	97.0	95.9
Telephone apparatus	...	...	...	...	...	...	...	...	95.3	93.2	91.1
Radio/TV broadcast and wireless communication equipment	...	...	...	...	...	...	...	...	99.4	98.7	98.2
Other communications equipment	...	...	...	...	...	...	...	...	99.8	99.7	101.2
Audio and video equipment	...	...	...	...	...	...	...	...	98.1	95.6	93.7
Semiconductor and other electronic component[3]	99.3	95.1	91.9	90.1	88.8	86.4	84.9	81.1	78.3	76.5	75.1
Navigation, measuring, medical, and control instruments	...	...	...	...	...	...	...	...	100.6	101.9	103.5
Manufacturing and reproducing magnetic and optical media	...	...	...	...	...	...	...	...	98.0	97.0	95.5
Electrical equipment, appliance and component	...	...	...	...	...	...	...	...	103.2	108.0	116.6
Electric lighting equipment	...	...	...	...	...	...	...	...	100.8	103.5	105.9
Electric lamp bulb and part	...	...	...	...	...	...	...	...	98.1	100.2	98.6
Lighting fixture	...	...	...	...	...	...	...	...	101.7	104.6	108.2
Household appliance[3]	109.7	108.3	107.5	107.2	106.2	104.6	104.2	103.1	103.1	106.3	107.7
Small electrical appliance	...	...	...	...	...	...	...	...	99.9	101.8	103.0
Major appliance	...	...	...	...	...	...	...	...	100.6	104.2	105.6
Electrical equipment	...	...	...	...	...	...	...	...	101.9	107.2	113.7
Other electrical equipment and component	...	...	...	...	...	...	...	...	106.6	112.5	129.1
Battery	...	...	...	...	...	...	...	...	102.2	105.7	112.6
Communications and energy wire and cable	...	...	...	...	...	...	...	...	106.8	115.8	150.3
Wiring device	...	...	...	...	...	...	...	...	113.6	118.9	128.6
All other electrical equipment and component	...	...	...	...	...	...	...	...	101.7	105.4	109.3
Transportation equipment	...	...	...	...	...	...	...	...	100.9	102.5	103.2
Motor vehicle	...	...	...	...	...	...	...	...	99.4	98.7	96.1
Automobile and light duty motor vehicle	...	...	...	...	...	...	...	...	99.2	98.2	95.1
Heavy duty truck	...	...	...	...	...	...	...	...	102.2	106.4	110.4
Motor vehicle body and trailer	...	...	...	...	...	...	...	...	104.0	109.7	113.7
Motor vehicle parts	...	...	...	...	...	...	...	...	101.4	102.7	104.8
Motor vehicle steering and suspension parts	...	...	...	...	...	...	...	...	101.8	105.1	106.3
Aerospace product and parts[8]	140.8	142.7	143.4	144.8	149.9	154.7	157.3	162.2	168.0	176.0	182.8

[2]December 1985 = 100.
[3]December 1984 = 100.
[8]June 1985 = 100.
. . . = Not available.

Table 7-3. Producer Price Indexes for the Net Output of Selected Industries, 1996–2006—*Continued*

(December 2003 = 100, unless otherwise specified.)

Industry	1996	1997	1998	1999	2000	2001	2002	2003	2004	2005	2006
Manufacturing—*Continued*											
Railroad rolling stock[5]	129.7	127.4	127.6	128.2	128.6	128.3	127.7	129.0	135.8	150.5	158.4
Ship and boat building[3]	138.2	142.0	144.1	145.6	149.0	152.6	156.8	163.0	169.6	175.0	181.4
Other transportation equipment	...	...	...	...	...	...	...	...	101.1	103.6	104.8
Furniture and related product[3]	136.2	138.2	139.7	141.3	143.3	145.1	146.3	147.4	151.5	157.8	162.5
Household and institutional furniture and kitchen cabinet[3]	134.7	136.4	138.4	140.3	142.5	144.4	146.2	147.0	148.6	152.6	157.4
Wood kitchen cabinet and countertop	...	...	...	...	...	...	...	...	101.1	103.2	106.3
Household and institutional furniture	...	...	...	...	...	...	...	...	101.1	104.0	107.4
Office furniture (including fixtures)	...	...	...	...	...	...	...	...	105.1	111.5	113.8
Other furniture-related product	...	...	...	...	...	...	...	...	104.0	110.6	115.2
Mattress	...	...	...	...	...	...	...	...	105.6	115.0	120.6
Blind and shade	...	...	...	...	...	...	...	...	101.3	103.9	106.9
Miscellaneous	...	...	...	...	...	...	...	...	101.2	102.9	104.7
Medical equipment and supplies	...	...	...	...	...	...	...	...	101.3	102.5	103.8
Other miscellaneous[2]	127.8	129.0	129.7	130.3	130.9	132.4	133.3	133.9	135.2	138.4	142.0
Jewelry and silverware[2]	128.0	128.0	127.1	126.4	127.1	128.0	129.1	131.0	134.6	138.7	146.5
Sporting and athletic goods	...	...	...	...	...	...	...	...	101.3	102.0	103.6
Doll, toy, and game	...	...	...	...	...	...	...	...	100.3	101.7	102.7
Office supplies (except paper)[2]	130.2	129.8	130.9	132.0	132.0	131.4	132.8	132.9	133.1	135.8	136.2
Sign	...	...	...	...	...	...	...	...	100.9	104.6	106.9
All other miscellaneous	...	...	...	...	...	...	...	...	101.0	103.7	106.7
Wholesale Trade											
Merchant wholesalers, durable goods	...	...	...	...	...	...	...	...	...	102.0	106.3
Merchant wholesalers, nondurable goods	...	...	...	...	...	...	...	...	...	...	106.2
Retail Trade											
Motor vehicle and parts dealers	...	...	...	...	...	...	...	...	103.5	106.9	112.8
Automobile dealers	...	...	...	...	...	...	...	...	102.9	105.4	110.8
New car dealers[11]	...	...	...	...	99.7	103.1	108.7	111.5	113.5	116.3	122.3
Recreational vehicle dealers[12]	...	...	...	...	...	98.8	112.2	109.7	121.4	133.6	133.8
Automotive parts, accessories, and tire stores[13]	...	...	...	...	...	...	100.9	104.2	109.4	115.1	124.3
Automotive parts and accessories stores	...	...	...	...	...	...	...	...	106.8	110.9	119.7
Tire dealers	...	...	...	...	...	...	...	...	102.0	110.7	119.3
Furniture and home furnishings stores	...	...	...	...	...	...	...	...	102.4	110.7	116.6
Furniture stores	...	...	...	...	...	...	...	...	100.8	108.0	111.0
Floor covering stores	...	...	...	...	...	...	...	...	104.6	114.4	124.3
Electronics and appliance stores	...	...	...	...	...	...	...	...	99.0	98.9	99.4
Appliance, TV, and other electronics stores	...	...	...	...	...	...	...	...	101.8	103.5	103.8
Computer and software stores	...	...	...	...	...	...	...	...	95.2	92.4	91.7
Camera and photographic supplies stores	...	...	...	...	...	...	...	...	88.6	82.0	95.5
Building material and garden equipment and supplies dealers	...	...	...	...	...	...	...	...	108.3	109.9	118.4
Building material and supplies dealers	...	...	...	...	...	...	...	...	108.7	109.9	119.8
Home centers	...	...	...	...	...	...	...	...	107.0	109.6	122.5
Paint and wallpaper stores	...	...	...	...	...	...	...	...	99.5	104.4	106.2
Hardware stores	...	...	...	...	...	...	...	...	103.1	108.2	112.3
Other building material dealers	...	...	...	...	...	...	...	...	111.4	110.8	121.3
Lawn and garden equipment and supplies stores	...	...	...	...	...	...	...	...	105.8	110.3	111.5
Nursery, garden, and farm supply stores	...	...	...	...	...	...	...	...	105.8	110.3	111.5
Food and beverage stores[11]	...	...	...	...	103.8	109.6	113.4	117.6	123.2	131.0	134.7
Grocery stores	...	...	...	...	...	...	...	...	103.5	110.7	114.0
Grocery (except convenience) stores	...	...	...	...	...	...	...	...	103.5	110.7	114.0
Specialty food stores	...	...	...	...	...	...	...	...	107.1	110.2	114.1
Beer, wine, and liquor stores[14]	...	...	...	...	...	102.9	103.5	106.9	110.7	111.0	111.3
Health and personal care stores	...	...	...	...	...	...	...	...	101.7	107.6	118.7
Pharmacies and drug stores[14]	...	...	...	...	...	102.4	112.4	116.6	119.8	127.9	142.0
Optical goods stores	...	...	...	...	...	...	...	...	99.8	100.1	101.5
Gasoline stations[12]	...	...	...	...	...	105.6	66.8	54.1	51.3	51.0	50.9
Gasoline stations with convenience stores	...	...	...	...	...	...	...	...	102.5	104.3	110.0
Other gasoline stations	...	...	...	...	...	...	...	...	132.8	118.1	84.2
Clothing and clothing accessories stores	...	...	...	...	...	...	...	...	100.5	103.3	105.4
Clothing stores	...	...	...	...	...	...	...	...	99.3	102.4	104.4
Men's clothing stores	...	...	...	...	...	...	...	...	100.2	102.1	98.9
Women's clothing stores	...	...	...	...	...	...	...	...	102.9	103.3	108.6
Family clothing stores	...	...	...	...	...	...	...	...	97.8	102.2	104.3
Shoe stores	...	...	...	...	...	...	...	...	103.9	105.0	105.7
Jewelry, luggage, and leather goods stores	...	...	...	...	...	...	...	...	101.8	104.9	108.7
Jewelry stores	...	...	...	...	...	...	...	...	101.8	104.8	108.6
Luggage and leather goods stores	...	...	...	...	...	...	...	...	101.4	106.5	111.0
Sporting goods, hobby, book, and music stores	...	...	...	...	...	...	...	...	96.6	96.6	98.4
Sporting goods, hobby, and musical instrument stores	...	...	...	...	...	...	...	...	97.8	99.0	102.5
Sporting goods stores	...	...	...	...	...	...	...	...	95.0	96.1	99.2
Hobby, toy, and game stores	...	...	...	...	...	...	...	...	100.5	101.7	105.7
Sewing, needlework, and piece goods stores	...	...	...	...	...	...	...	...	103.2	104.7	109.0
Book, periodical, and music stores	...	...	...	...	...	...	...	...	94.7	92.5	91.6
Bookstores and news dealers	...	...	...	...	...	...	...	...	95.0	92.0	94.2
Prerecorded tape, CD, and record stores	...	...	...	...	...	...	...	...	93.9	93.8	84.4
General merchandise stores	...	...	...	...	...	...	...	...	103.1	103.4	106.6
Department stores	...	...	...	...	...	...	...	...	105.4	105.1	105.6
Other general merchandise stores	...	...	...	...	...	...	...	...	97.7	99.5	108.9
Florists	...	...	...	...	...	...	...	...	100.2	100.2	102.8

[2]December 1985 = 100.
[3]December 1984 = 100.
[5]June 1984 = 100.
[11]December 1999 = 100.
[12]June 2001 = 100.
[13]December 2001 = 100.
[14]June 2000 = 100.

Table 7-3. Producer Price Indexes for the Net Output of Selected Industries, 1996–2006—*Continued*

(December 2003 = 100, unless otherwise specified.)

Industry	1996	1997	1998	1999	2000	2001	2002	2003	2004	2005	2006
Retail Trade—*Continued*											
Office supplies, stationery, and gift stores	. . .	. . .	. . .	. . .	. . .	. . .	. . .	. . .	99.7	101.7	104.3
Office supplies and stationery stores	. . .	. . .	. . .	. . .	. . .	. . .	. . .	. . .	100.4	102.9	107.1
Gift, novelty, and souvenir stores	. . .	. . .	. . .	. . .	. . .	. . .	. . .	. . .	98.7	100.0	100.1
Manufactured (mobile) home dealers	. . .	. . .	. . .	. . .	. . .	. . .	. . .	. . .	107.7	116.7	123.2
Nonstore retailers	. . .	. . .	. . .	. . .	. . .	. . .	. . .	. . .	107.5	119.8	118.9
Vending machine operators	. . .	. . .	. . .	. . .	. . .	. . .	. . .	. . .	101.5	104.4	105.7
Fuel dealers[14]	. . .	. . .	. . .	. . .	. . .	120.5	113.8	122.7	129.4	147.3	138.9
Transportation and Warehousing											
Air transportation[15]	121.1	125.3	124.5	130.8	147.7	157.2	157.8	162.1	162.3	171.0	180.4
Scheduled air transportation[16]	145.5	150.8	149.3	157.3	180.1	193.0	193.3	198.5	198.6	209.3	220.5
Nonscheduled air transportation[17]	. . .	97.8	99.2	102.2	107.3	112.7	114.7	117.8	119.9	126.7	136.8
Rail transportation[17]	. . .	100.5	101.7	101.3	102.6	104.5	106.6	108.8	113.4	125.2	135.9
Water transportation	. . .	. . .	. . .	. . .	. . .	. . .	. . .	. . .	101.3	106.4	111.1
Inland water transportation	. . .	. . .	. . .	. . .	. . .	. . .	. . .	. . .	103.2	119.3	144.1
Truck transportation	. . .	. . .	. . .	. . .	. . .	. . .	. . .	. . .	103.1	109.0	113.2
General freight trucking	. . .	. . .	. . .	. . .	. . .	. . .	. . .	. . .	103.5	110.0	114.1
General freight trucking, local	. . .	. . .	. . .	. . .	. . .	. . .	. . .	. . .	105.2	111.5	115.3
General freight trucking, long distance	. . .	. . .	. . .	. . .	. . .	. . .	. . .	. . .	103.2	109.7	113.8
Specialized freight trucking	. . .	. . .	. . .	. . .	. . .	. . .	. . .	. . .	102.3	107.0	111.4
Used household and office goods moving	. . .	. . .	. . .	. . .	. . .	. . .	. . .	. . .	102.6	106.0	107.8
Specialized freight (except used) trucking, local	. . .	. . .	. . .	. . .	. . .	. . .	. . .	. . .	102.7	107.1	112.3
Specialized freight (except used) trucking, long distance	. . .	. . .	. . .	. . .	. . .	. . .	. . .	. . .	101.7	107.5	112.8
Pipeline transportation of crude oil	. . .	. . .	. . .	. . .	. . .	. . .	. . .	. . .	103.9	113.3	122.0
Other pipeline transportation	. . .	. . .	. . .	. . .	. . .	. . .	. . .	. . .	101.4	105.2	108.2
Pipeline transportation of refined petroleum products	. . .	. . .	. . .	. . .	. . .	. . .	. . .	. . .	101.4	105.2	108.2
Transportation support activities	. . .	. . .	. . .	. . .	. . .	. . .	. . .	. . .	101.1	104.1	106.5
Air transportation support activities[17]	. . .	102.5	105.2	108.6	114.2	117.5	121.4	125.1	128.1	134.2	138.6
Airport operations	. . .	. . .	. . .	. . .	. . .	. . .	. . .	. . .	101.1	104.8	108.6
Other air transportation support activities	. . .	. . .	. . .	. . .	. . .	. . .	. . .	. . .	102.0	107.5	110.8
Water transportation support activities	. . .	. . .	. . .	. . .	. . .	. . .	. . .	. . .	101.0	103.5	107.7
Port and harbor operations	. . .	. . .	. . .	. . .	. . .	. . .	. . .	. . .	102.4	105.9	108.8
Marine cargo handling	. . .	. . .	. . .	. . .	. . .	. . .	. . .	. . .	100.5	102.2	105.1
Navigational services to shipping	. . .	. . .	. . .	. . .	. . .	. . .	. . .	. . .	101.5	105.7	113.9
Freight transportation arrangement[17]	. . .	99.4	97.7	97.3	98.3	98.2	97.5	97.9	98.9	99.1	98.8
Postal service[18]	132.3	132.3	132.3	135.3	135.2	143.4	150.2	155.0	155.0	155.0	164.7
Couriers and messengers	. . .	. . .	. . .	. . .	. . .	. . .	. . .	. . .	106.1	113.8	121.5
Couriers	. . .	. . .	. . .	. . .	. . .	. . .	. . .	. . .	106.6	115.0	123.2
Local messengers and local delivery	. . .	. . .	. . .	. . .	. . .	. . .	. . .	. . .	101.1	102.7	104.4
Refrigerated warehousing and storage	. . .	. . .	. . .	. . .	. . .	. . .	. . .	. . .	100.5	101.0	102.4
Farm product warehousing and storage	. . .	. . .	. . .	. . .	. . .	. . .	. . .	. . .	100.2	101.5	103.8
Information											
Publishing industries, except Internet	. . .	. . .	. . .	. . .	. . .	. . .	. . .	. . .	101.5	104.1	106.2
Newspaper, book, and directory publishers	. . .	. . .	. . .	. . .	. . .	. . .	. . .	. . .	102.1	105.5	108.3
Newspaper publishers[19]	306.9	317.7	328.7	339.3	351.3	367.9	381.9	395.7	409.7	426.2	439.0
Periodical publishers[19]	253.1	263.2	276.9	284.9	292.6	305.9	320.4	332.4	339.1	347.6	354.4
Book publishers[3]	169.4	174.0	178.9	184.7	190.2	195.6	201.5	208.2	215.7	224.3	232.8
Directory and mailing list publishers	. . .	. . .	. . .	. . .	. . .	. . .	. . .	. . .	101.3	103.3	105.4
Other publishers	. . .	. . .	. . .	. . .	. . .	. . .	. . .	. . .	100.7	103.9	104.9
Software publishers	. . .	. . .	. . .	. . .	. . .	. . .	. . .	. . .	99.8	99.8	100.1
Broadcasting, except Internet	. . .	. . .	. . .	. . .	. . .	. . .	. . .	. . .	101.2	102.1	102.8
Radio and television broadcasting[12]	. . .	. . .	. . .	. . .	. . .	98.2	97.1	99.8	102.8	101.9	101.1
Radio broadcasting	. . .	. . .	. . .	. . .	. . .	. . .	. . .	. . .	102.7	106.3	105.8
Television broadcasting	. . .	. . .	. . .	. . .	. . .	. . .	. . .	. . .	100.5	97.3	96.3
Cable networks	. . .	. . .	. . .	. . .	. . .	. . .	. . .	. . .	101.4	104.3	106.7
Telecommunications	. . .	. . .	. . .	. . .	. . .	. . .	. . .	. . .	99.8	98.1	98.3
Wired telecommunications carriers[20]	. . .	. . .	. . .	. . .	96.4	93.6	89.9	88.1	86.3	85.8	86.6
Wireless telecommunications carriers	. . .	. . .	. . .	. . .	. . .	. . .	. . .	. . .	98.4	86.4	80.9
Cable and other program distribution	. . .	. . .	. . .	. . .	. . .	. . .	. . .	. . .	102.2	106.5	109.6
Data processing and related services	. . .	. . .	. . .	. . .	. . .	. . .	. . .	. . .	98.8	98.8	99.7
Financial Activities											
Security, commodity contracts, and like activity	. . .	. . .	. . .	. . .	. . .	. . .	. . .	. . .	103.4	109.4	113.8
Security and commodity contracts, intermediation, and brokerage[14]	. . .	. . .	. . .	. . .	. . .	88.1	81.8	82.5	84.2	88.1	90.1
Investment banking and securities dealing	. . .	. . .	. . .	. . .	. . .	. . .	. . .	. . .	102.6	109.1	111.0
Securities brokerage	. . .	. . .	. . .	. . .	. . .	. . .	. . .	. . .	100.0	102.2	105.2
Portfolio management	. . .	. . .	. . .	. . .	. . .	. . .	. . .	. . .	108.1	117.8	124.8
Investment advice	. . .	. . .	. . .	. . .	. . .	. . .	. . .	. . .	102.0	104.8	119.4
Other direct insurance carriers[21]	. . .	. . .	. . .	100.7	101.9	104.3	108.7	115.0	118.7	121.0	121.7
Insurance agencies and brokerages	. . .	. . .	. . .	. . .	. . .	. . .	. . .	. . .	100.8	101.8	102.2
Lessors of nonresidential building (except miniwarehouse)	. . .	. . .	. . .	. . .	. . .	. . .	. . .	. . .	102.3	105.1	107.7
Lessors of miniwarehouse and self-storage units	. . .	. . .	. . .	. . .	. . .	. . .	. . .	. . .	102.0	105.6	109.2
Offices of real estate agents and brokers	. . .	. . .	. . .	. . .	. . .	. . .	. . .	. . .	101.8	108.1	110.9

[3]December 1984 = 100.
[12]June 2001 = 100.
[14]June 2000 = 100.
[15]December 1992 = 100.
[16]December 1989 = 100.
[17]December 1996 = 100.
[18]June 1989 = 100.
[19]December 1979 = 100.
[20]June 1999 = 100.
[21]December 1998 = 100.
. . . = Not available.

Table 7-3. Producer Price Indexes for the Net Output of Selected Industries, 1996–2006—*Continued*

(December 2003 = 100, unless otherwise specified.)

Industry	1996	1997	1998	1999	2000	2001	2002	2003	2004	2005	2006
Financial Activities—*Continued*											
Real estate property managers	...	...	...	...	...	...	...	...	100.9	102.2	102.9
Offices of real estate appraisers	...	...	...	...	...	...	...	...	102.7	104.2	107.6
Automotive equipment rental and leasing[12]	...	...	...	...	...	...	103.9	106.6	107.8	109.0	115.2
Passenger car rental and leasing	...	...	...	...	...	...	...	...	98.2	99.9	108.0
Truck, utility trailer, and RV rental and leasing	...	...	...	...	...	...	...	...	99.9	99.9	101.2
Legal services[17]	...	102.5	106.1	108.7	112.5	117.9	121.7	125.6	131.8	138.5	145.2
Offices of lawyers[17]	...	102.5	106.1	108.7	112.5	117.9	121.7	125.6	131.8	138.5	145.2
Architectural, engineering, and related services[17]	...	102.2	105.1	108.5	111.8	115.9	121.1	124.3	126.8	129.2	134.4
Architectural services	...	...	...	...	...	...	...	...	99.7	102.0	106.0
Engineering services	...	...	...	...	...	...	...	...	101.5	103.4	107.6
Advertising agencies	...	...	...	...	...	...	...	...	100.1	101.4	104.1
Employment services[17]	...	101.0	103.2	105.2	107.3	108.2	108.9	111.4	113.9	116.3	119.2
Employment placement agencies	...	...	...	...	...	...	...	...	102.2	104.4	104.4
Temporary help services	...	...	...	...	...	...	...	...	101.7	104.0	106.9
Employee leasing services	...	...	...	...	...	...	...	...	101.3	102.9	105.4
Travel agencies	...	...	...	...	...	...	...	...	96.9	95.9	99.5
Janitorial services	...	...	...	...	...	...	...	...	100.9	101.9	103.7
Waste collection	...	...	...	...	...	...	...	...	101.3	102.5	104.5
Health Care and Social Assistance											
Offices of physicians[17]	...	101.0	103.2	105.5	107.3	110.4	110.3	112.1	114.3	116.4	117.5
Medical and diagnostic laboratories	...	...	...	...	...	...	...	...	100.0	104.1	104.4
Home health care services[17]	...	103.3	106.2	107.1	111.1	114.0	116.6	117.0	119.8	121.1	121.8
Hospitals[15]	112.6	113.6	114.4	116.4	119.4	123.0	127.5	134.9	141.5	146.9	153.3
General medical and surgical hospitals	...	...	...	...	...	...	...	...	102.9	106.7	111.2
Psychiatric and substance abuse hospitals	...	...	...	...	...	...	...	...	101.1	103.7	106.2
Other specialty hospitals	...	...	...	...	...	...	...	...	103.8	109.6	122.8
Nursing care facilities	...	...	...	...	...	...	...	...	102.6	106.4	109.6
Residential mental retardation facilities	...	...	...	...	...	...	...	...	101.2	104.5	108.5
Accommodations[17]	...	104.2	108.1	112.7	116.2	121.3	121.3	122.0	125.2	131.9	136.7
Hotels (except casino hotels) and motels	...	...	...	...	...	...	...	...	103.5	110.0	114.1
Casino hotels	...	...	...	...	...	...	...	...	105.0	107.5	110.8

[12]June 2001 = 100.
[15]December 1992 = 100.
[17]December 1996 = 100.
. . . = Not available.

CONSUMER PRICE INDEX

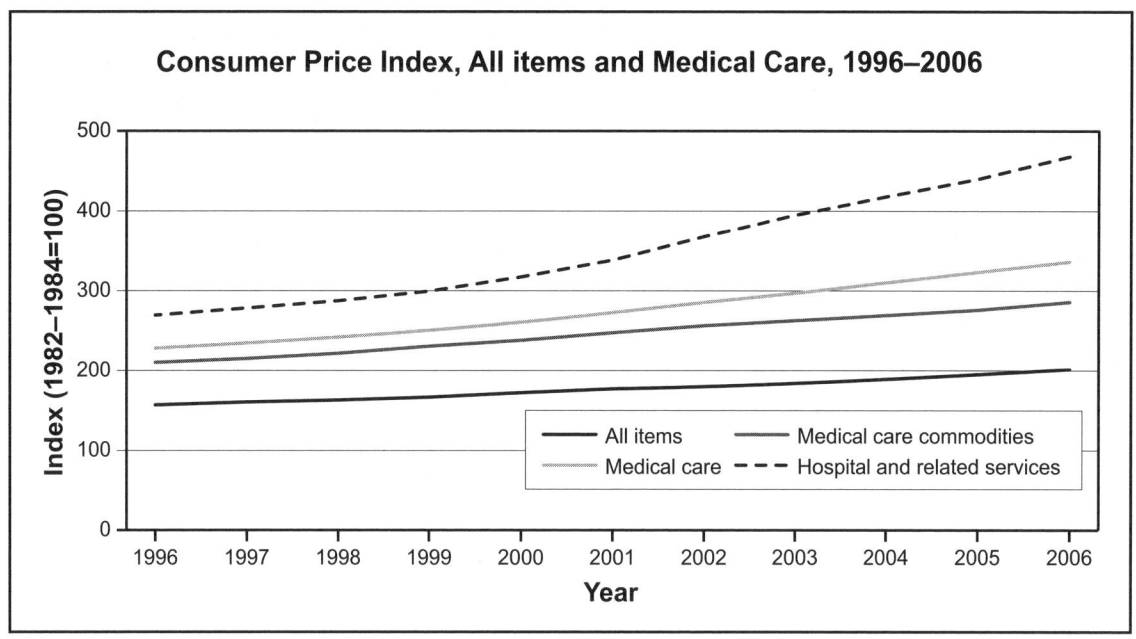

Consumer Price Index, All items and Medical Care, 1996–2006

Prices for hospital and related services continued to be the fastest-growing part of the medical care component of the CPI in 2006. These services rose 6.4 percent, twice as fast as the increase in the total CPI. Medical care commodities rose 3.6 percent, while professional services rose 2.7 percent (See Table 7-8.)

OTHER HIGHLIGHTS

• The CPI-U for all items rose 3.2 percent in 2006. It grew the fastest for all types of gasoline including motor fuel, which rose 12.9 percent, followed by household energy (fuel oil plus gas and electricity), which increased 9.6 percent. (See Table 7-8.)

• Food and beverages, housing, and transportation comprised almost 75 percent of the total CPI in 2006, compared to 73.5 percent in 2001. From 2001 to 2006, the relative importance of housing increased, while the relative importance of food decreased slightly. The relative importance of transportation stayed virtually the same. (See Table 7-9.)

• Among the selected metropolitan statistical areas, the CPI-U for Honolulu, HI, grew the fastest from 2005 to 2006, rising 5.9 percent. It was followed by Miami-Fort Lauderdale, FL, at 4.9 percent. The CPI-U for New York-Northern New Jersey-Long Island, NY-NJ-CT-PA, rose 3.8 percent and the CPI-U for Boston-Brockton-Nashua, MA-NH-ME-CT, rose 3.1 percent. In Chicago and Atlanta, the CPI-U rose much slower than average, increasing at 2.1 and 2.6 percent, respectively. (See Table 7-10.)

NOTES AND DEFINITIONS

CONSUMER PRICE INDEX

Coverage

The Consumer Price Index (CPI) measures the average change in prices of goods and services purchased by urban consumers for day to day living. The weights used in calculating the index, which remain fixed for relatively long periods of time, are based on actual expenditures reported in the Consumer Expenditure Surveys (CE). The quantities and qualities of the sample items in the "market basket" remain essentially the same between consecutive pricing periods. The index measures only the effect of price change on the cost of living and does not measure changes in the total amount families spend for living. Geographic area indexes measure price changes in individual areas over time, not relative differences in prices or living costs between areas.

Periodic Updating

The index for the years 1913–1935 used a study of 1917–1919 spending by households of wage earners and clerical workers as the basis for its weights. Since then, there have been six revisions to bring the "market basket" of goods and services up to date and to revise the weights and improve the sampling methods used in the survey. In the past 20 years, several major changes have been introduced into the CPI.

The 1978 revision of the CPI updated the Consumer Price Index for Urban Wage Earners and Clerical Workers (CPI-W) and introduced a Consumer Price Index for All Urban Consumers (CPI-U), which includes salaried workers, the self employed, the retired, the unemployed, and wage earners and clerical workers. The CPI-W now represents the spending patterns of 32 percent of the population; the CPI-U represents the spending patterns of 87 percent of the population. Before 1978, changes in the CPI-U were based on changes in the CPI-W. The 1978 revision also instituted sampling for all levels of the index, right down to the selection of individual items within each retail outlet.

Beginning with the index for January 1983, the Bureau of Labor Statistics (BLS) changed the way the CPI-U measures homeowners' costs; the CPI-W implemented the same change in January 1985. The change converted the homeownership component from an asset approach, which includes both the investment and consumption aspects of homeownership, to a flow of services approach, which only measures the cost of shelter services consumed by homeowners. The new approach uses a rental equivalence method to calculate homeowner shelter costs by estimating the implicit rent owners would have to pay to rent the homes in which they live. The old method calculated homeowners' costs as home purchase, mortgage interest costs, property taxes, property insurance, and maintenance and repair.

The 1987 major revision of both the CPI-U and the CPI-W introduced weights based upon data from the 1982, 1983, and 1984 CE surveys. The 1998 CPI revision, which went into effect with the index for January 1998, uses expenditure data from the 1993–1995 CE Surveys and population data from the 1990 decennial census.

Current Methodology

The CPI uses 87 pricing areas in 38 different index areas from around the United States. BLS revises the outlets and items in its sample on a five-year rotating basis. Before rotating the sample, the Census Bureau conducts a Point-of-Purchase Survey for BLS. This survey determines the locations of retail outlets at which consumers buy goods and services in various categories; it also determines how much they spend on each category in each reported outlet. BLS then draws outlet samples from the Point-of-Purchase Survey information. Field agents visit the selected retail outlets and sample the applicable item categories with checklists, which exhaustively define these categories of goods and services. A data collector, who uses the checklists in systematic stages, generally selects the items to be priced in a specific retail store. Information provided by the respondent is taken into account at each stage. Outlets may be located outside of the pricing area to represent out of town purchases.

After the initial selection, the same item (or a close substitute) is priced from period to period in order to ensure the greatest extent possible that differences in reported prices are measures of price change only. All taxes directly associated with the purchase, or with the continued use of the items priced, are included in the indexes. Foods, fuels, rents, and other items are priced monthly in all areas. Prices of most other commodities and services are obtained monthly in the three largest geographical areas and every other month in the remaining areas, with half obtained in odd-numbered months and half obtained in even-numbered months. Between scheduled survey dates, prices are held at the level of their last pricing. BLS agents also collect data for a sample of rental units drawn from the Decennial Census of Population and Housing. This sample is heavily augmented with renter-occupied housing units in areas where there are many owner-occupied units. This survey is the basis for the rent and owner-equivalent rent components of the CPI.

BLS calculates basic indexes (elementary aggregates) for the 211 item strata in each of the 38 index areas. Basic indexes are combined with weights based on the 1993–1995 consumer expenditure surveys and the 1990 decennial census.

BLS publishes CPI indexes for a variety of commodities and services by region, by size of city, by cross classifications of regions and population size classes, and for 26 metropolitan areas.

The purchasing power of the consumer dollar for any given date is calculated as the reciprocal of the index for that date, expressed in dollars, with the dollar's value in 1982–1984 equal to $1.00. It shows changes in the value of the dollar resulting from changes in prices of consumer goods and services. Dividing the index for the desired base date by the index for the current date and expressing the result in dollars can calculate the purchasing power of the dollar; this allows for clear comparisons to other base dates.

The relative importance figures are percentage distributions of the cost or value weights used in the index calculation. The cost weights represent average expenditures by consumers for specific classes of goods and services. However, in the subsequent pricing periods, the value weights and the corresponding relative importance figures change as prices change differentially. (In other words, the relative importance increases for an item or group with a greater-than-average price increase and decreases for an item with a lower-than-average price increase). Historically, the weights in the CPI have been updated about once every 10 years. Since 2002, the CPI expenditure weights have been updated every other year to keep the weights more current with consumer spending habits.

Since the CPI traditionally measured price changes for a fixed market basket of goods and services, it was criticized as overstating inflation because it did not account for the fact that consumers can substitute (buy more or less) as relative prices change. In 1999, the CPI began using a geometric mean formula to average the prices within most item categories. This formula assumes a modest degree of substitution within CPI item categories as relative prices change.

In 2002, BLS created an additional price index using a "superlative" formula to be address consumer substitution across CPI item categories. BLS began publishing this index, called the Chained Consumer Price Index for All Urban Consumers effective with release of July data in August 2002. Designated the C-CPI-U, the index will supplement—not replace—the CPI-U and the CPI-W.

The Consumer Price Index Research Series Using Current Methods (CPI-U-RS) presents an estimate of the CPI for all Urban Consumers (CPI-U) from 1978 to the present that incorporates most of the improvements made over that time span into the entire series.

Sources of Additional Information

An extensive description of the methodology is available in the updated version of Chapter 17 in the *BLS Handbook of Methods*. Additional detailed data can be found in the *Consumer Price Index Detailed Report* and in special reports. All of these resources can be found on the BLS Web site at <http://www.bls.gov>.

Table 7-4. Consumer Price Indexes, All Urban Consumers (CPI-U): U.S. City Average, Major Groups, 1967–2006

(1982–1984 = 100, unless otherwise specified.)

Year	All items	Food and beverages	Housing	Apparel	Transportation	Medical care	Recreation[1]	Education and communication[1]	Other goods and services
1967	33.4	35.0	30.8	51.0	33.3	28.2	. . .	. . .	35.1
1968	34.8	36.2	32.0	53.7	34.3	29.9	. . .	. . .	36.9
1969	36.7	38.1	34.0	56.8	35.7	31.9	. . .	. . .	38.7
1970	38.8	40.1	36.4	59.2	37.5	34.0	. . .	. . .	40.9
1971	40.5	41.4	38.0	61.1	39.5	36.1	. . .	. . .	42.9
1972	41.8	43.1	39.4	62.3	39.9	37.3	. . .	. . .	44.7
1973	44.4	48.8	41.2	64.6	41.2	38.8	. . .	. . .	46.4
1974	49.3	55.5	45.8	69.4	45.8	42.4	. . .	. . .	49.8
1975	53.8	60.2	50.7	72.5	50.1	47.5	. . .	. . .	53.9
1976	56.9	62.1	53.8	75.2	55.1	52.0	. . .	. . .	57.0
1977	60.6	65.8	57.4	78.6	59.0	57.0	. . .	. . .	60.4
1978	65.2	72.2	62.4	81.4	61.7	61.8	. . .	. . .	64.3
1979	72.6	79.9	70.1	84.9	70.5	67.5	. . .	. . .	68.9
1980	82.4	86.7	81.1	90.9	83.1	74.9	. . .	. . .	75.2
1981	90.9	93.5	90.4	95.3	93.2	82.9	. . .	. . .	82.6
1982	96.5	97.3	96.9	97.8	97.0	92.5	. . .	. . .	91.1
1983	99.6	99.5	99.5	100.2	99.3	100.6	. . .	. . .	101.1
1984	103.9	103.2	103.6	102.1	103.7	106.8	. . .	. . .	107.9
1985	107.6	105.6	107.7	105.0	106.4	113.5	. . .	. . .	114.5
1986	109.6	109.1	110.9	105.9	102.3	122.0	. . .	. . .	121.4
1987	113.6	113.5	114.2	110.6	105.4	130.1	. . .	. . .	128.5
1988	118.3	118.2	118.5	115.4	108.7	138.6	. . .	. . .	137.0
1989	124.0	124.9	123.0	118.6	114.1	149.3	. . .	. . .	147.7
1990	130.7	132.1	128.5	124.1	120.5	162.8	. . .	. . .	159.0
1991	136.2	136.8	133.6	128.7	123.8	177.0	. . .	. . .	171.6
1992	140.3	138.7	137.5	131.9	126.5	190.1	. . .	. . .	183.3
1993	144.5	141.6	141.2	133.7	130.4	201.4	90.7	85.5	192.9
1994	148.2	144.9	144.8	133.4	134.3	211.0	92.7	88.8	198.5
1995	152.4	148.9	148.5	132.0	139.1	220.5	94.5	92.2	206.9
1996	156.9	153.7	152.8	131.7	143.0	228.2	97.4	95.3	215.4
1997	160.5	157.7	156.8	132.9	144.3	234.6	99.6	98.4	224.8
1998	163.0	161.1	160.4	133.0	141.6	242.1	101.1	100.3	237.7
1999	166.6	164.6	163.9	131.3	144.4	250.6	102.0	101.2	258.3
2000	172.2	168.4	169.6	129.6	153.3	260.8	103.3	102.5	271.1
2001	177.1	173.6	176.4	127.3	154.3	272.8	104.9	105.2	282.6
2002	179.9	176.8	180.3	124.0	152.9	285.6	106.2	107.9	293.2
2003	184.0	180.5	184.8	120.9	157.6	297.1	107.5	109.8	298.7
2004	188.9	186.6	189.5	120.4	163.1	310.1	108.6	111.6	304.7
2005	195.3	191.2	195.7	119.5	173.9	323.2	109.4	113.7	313.4
2006	201.6	195.7	203.2	119.5	180.9	336.2	110.9	116.8	321.7

[1]December 1997 = 100.
. . . = Not available.

Table 7-5. Consumer Price Indexes, All Urban Consumers (CPI-U): U.S. City Average, Commodity, Service, and Special Groups, 1967–2006

(1982–1984 = 100, unless otherwise specified.)

Year	All items less food	All items less shelter	All items less medical care	All items less energy	All items less food and energy	Commodities	Commodities less food and beverages	Commodities less food and energy	Energy commodities	Nondurables	Nondurables less food	Nondurables less food and apparel
1967	33.4	35.2	33.7	34.4	34.7	36.8	38.3	41.3	23.9	35.7	37.6	32.6
1968	34.9	36.7	35.1	35.9	36.3	38.1	39.7	42.9	24.4	37.1	39.1	33.7
1969	36.8	38.4	37.0	38.0	38.4	39.9	41.4	44.7	25.2	38.9	40.9	34.9
1970	39.0	40.3	39.2	40.3	40.8	41.7	43.1	46.7	25.6	40.8	42.5	36.3
1971	40.8	42.0	40.8	42.0	42.7	43.2	44.7	48.5	26.1	42.1	44.0	37.6
1972	42.0	43.3	42.1	43.4	44.0	44.5	45.8	49.7	26.4	43.5	45.0	38.6
1973	43.7	46.2	44.8	46.1	45.6	47.8	47.3	51.1	29.1	47.5	46.9	40.3
1974	48.0	51.4	49.8	50.6	49.4	53.5	52.4	55.0	40.4	54.0	52.9	46.9
1975	52.5	56.0	54.3	55.1	53.9	58.2	57.3	60.1	43.4	58.3	57.0	51.5
1976	56.0	59.3	57.2	58.2	57.4	60.7	60.2	63.2	45.4	60.5	59.5	54.1
1977	59.6	63.1	60.8	61.9	61.0	64.2	63.6	66.5	48.7	64.0	62.5	57.2
1978	63.9	67.4	65.4	66.7	65.5	68.8	67.3	70.5	51.0	68.6	65.5	60.4
1979	71.2	74.2	72.9	73.4	71.9	76.6	75.2	76.4	68.7	77.2	74.6	71.2
1980	81.5	82.9	82.8	81.9	80.8	86.0	85.7	83.5	95.2	87.6	88.4	87.1
1981	90.4	91.0	91.4	90.1	89.2	93.2	93.1	90.0	107.6	95.2	96.7	96.8
1982	96.3	96.2	96.8	96.1	95.8	97.0	96.9	95.3	102.9	97.8	98.3	98.2
1983	99.7	99.8	99.6	99.6	99.6	99.8	100.0	100.2	99.0	99.7	100.0	100.0
1984	104.0	103.9	103.7	104.3	104.6	103.2	103.1	104.4	98.1	102.5	101.7	101.8
1985	108.0	107.0	107.2	108.4	109.1	105.4	105.2	107.1	98.2	104.8	104.1	104.1
1986	109.8	108.0	108.8	112.6	113.5	104.4	101.4	108.6	77.2	103.5	98.5	96.9
1987	113.6	111.6	112.6	117.2	118.2	107.7	104.0	111.8	80.2	107.5	101.8	100.3
1988	118.3	115.9	117.0	122.3	123.4	111.5	107.3	115.8	80.8	111.8	105.8	104.0
1989	123.7	121.6	122.4	128.1	129.0	116.7	111.6	119.6	87.9	118.2	111.7	111.3
1990	130.3	128.2	128.8	134.7	135.5	122.8	117.0	123.6	101.2	126.0	119.9	120.9
1991	136.1	133.5	133.8	140.9	142.1	126.6	120.4	128.8	99.1	130.3	124.5	125.7
1992	140.8	137.3	137.5	145.4	147.3	129.1	123.2	132.5	98.3	132.8	127.6	128.9
1993	145.1	141.4	141.2	150.0	152.2	131.5	125.3	135.2	97.3	135.1	129.3	130.7
1994	149.0	144.8	144.7	154.1	156.5	133.8	126.9	137.1	97.6	136.8	129.7	131.6
1995	153.1	148.6	148.6	158.7	161.2	136.4	128.9	139.3	98.8	139.3	130.9	134.1
1996	157.5	152.8	152.8	163.1	165.6	139.9	131.5	141.3	105.7	143.5	134.5	139.5
1997	161.1	155.9	156.3	167.1	169.5	141.8	132.2	142.3	105.7	146.4	136.3	141.8
1998	163.4	157.2	158.6	170.9	173.4	141.9	130.5	143.2	92.1	146.9	134.6	139.2
1999	167.0	160.2	162.0	174.4	177.0	144.4	132.5	144.1	100.0	151.2	139.4	147.5
2000	173.0	165.7	167.3	178.6	181.3	149.2	137.7	144.9	129.5	158.2	149.1	162.9
2001	177.8	169.7	171.9	183.5	186.1	150.7	137.2	145.3	125.2	160.6	149.1	164.1
2002	180.5	170.8	174.3	187.7	190.5	149.7	134.2	143.7	117.1	161.1	147.4	163.3
2003	184.7	174.6	178.1	190.6	193.2	151.2	134.5	140.9	136.7	165.3	151.9	172.1
2004	189.4	179.3	182.7	194.4	196.6	154.7	136.7	139.6	161.2	172.2	159.3	183.8
2005	196.0	186.1	188.7	198.7	200.9	160.2	142.5	140.3	197.4	180.2	170.1	201.2
2006	202.7	191.9	194.7	203.7	205.9	164.0	145.9	140.6	223.0	186.7	178.2	213.9

Table 7-5. Consumer Price Indexes, All Urban Consumers (CPI-U): U.S. City Average, Commodity, Service, and Special Groups, 1967–2006—*Continued*

(1982–1984 = 100, unless otherwise indicated.)

Year	Total services[1]	Rent of shelter[2]	Gas (piped) and electricity	Transportation services	Medical care services	Other services	Services less medical care	Energy	Services less energy
1967	28.8	. . .	23.7	32.6	26.0	36.0	29.3	23.8	29.3
1968	30.3	. . .	23.9	33.9	27.9	38.1	30.8	24.2	30.9
1969	32.4	. . .	24.3	36.3	30.2	40.0	32.9	24.8	33.2
1970	35.0	. . .	25.4	40.2	32.3	42.2	35.6	25.5	36.0
1971	37.0	. . .	27.1	43.4	34.7	44.4	37.5	26.5	38.0
1972	38.4	. . .	28.5	44.4	35.9	45.6	38.9	27.2	39.4
1973	40.1	. . .	29.9	44.7	37.5	47.7	40.6	29.4	41.1
1974	43.8	. . .	34.5	46.3	41.4	51.3	44.3	38.1	44.8
1975	48.0	. . .	40.1	49.8	46.6	55.1	48.3	42.1	48.8
1976	52.0	. . .	44.7	56.9	51.3	58.4	52.2	45.1	52.7
1977	56.0	. . .	50.5	61.5	56.4	62.1	55.9	49.4	56.5
1978	60.8	. . .	55.0	64.4	61.2	66.4	60.7	52.5	61.3
1979	67.5	. . .	61.0	69.5	67.2	71.9	67.5	65.7	68.2
1980	77.9	. . .	71.4	79.2	74.8	78.7	78.2	86.0	78.5
1981	88.1	. . .	81.9	88.6	82.8	86.1	88.7	97.7	88.7
1982	96.0	. . .	93.2	96.1	92.6	93.5	96.4	99.2	96.3
1983	99.4	102.7	101.5	99.1	100.7	100.0	99.2	99.9	99.2
1984	104.6	107.7	105.4	104.8	106.7	106.5	104.4	100.9	104.5
1985	109.9	113.9	107.1	110.0	113.2	113.0	109.6	101.6	110.2
1986	115.4	120.2	105.7	116.3	121.9	119.4	114.6	88.2	116.5
1987	120.2	125.9	103.8	121.9	130.0	125.7	119.1	88.6	122.0
1988	125.7	132.0	104.6	128.0	138.3	132.6	124.3	89.3	127.9
1989	131.9	138.0	107.5	135.6	148.9	140.9	130.1	94.3	134.4
1990	139.2	145.5	109.3	144.2	162.7	150.2	136.8	102.1	142.3
1991	146.3	152.1	112.6	151.2	177.1	159.8	143.3	102.5	149.8
1992	152.0	157.3	114.8	155.7	190.5	168.5	148.4	103.0	155.9
1993	157.9	162.0	118.5	162.9	202.9	177.0	153.6	104.2	161.9
1994	163.1	167.0	119.2	168.6	213.4	185.4	158.4	104.6	167.6
1995	168.7	172.4	119.2	175.9	224.2	193.3	163.5	105.2	173.7
1996	174.1	178.0	122.1	180.5	232.4	201.4	168.7	110.1	179.4
1997	179.4	183.4	125.1	185.0	239.1	209.6	173.9	111.5	185.0
1998	184.2	189.6	121.2	187.9	246.8	216.9	178.4	102.9	190.6
1999	188.8	195.0	120.9	190.7	255.1	223.1	182.7	106.6	195.7
2000	195.3	201.3	128.0	196.1	266.0	229.9	188.9	124.6	202.1
2001	203.4	208.9	142.4	201.9	278.8	238.0	196.6	129.3	209.6
2002	209.8	216.7	134.4	209.1	292.9	246.4	202.5	121.7	217.5
2003	216.5	221.9	145.0	216.3	306.0	254.4	208.7	136.5	223.8
2004	222.8	227.9	150.6	220.6	321.3	261.3	214.5	151.4	230.2
2005	230.1	233.7	166.5	225.7	336.7	268.4	221.2	177.1	236.6
2006	238.9	241.9	182.1	230.8	350.6	277.5	229.6	196.9	244.7

[1]Includes tenants, household insurance, water, sewer, trash, and household operations services, not shown separately.
[2]December 1982 = 100.
. . . = Not available.

Table 7-6. Consumer Price Indexes, All Urban Consumers (CPI-U): U.S. City Average, Selected Groups and Purchasing Power of the Consumer Dollar, 1913–2006

(1982–1984 = 100, unless otherwise specified.)

Year	All items	Food	Rent of primary residence	Owners' equivalent of primary residence[1]	Apparel	Purchasing power of the consumer dollar[2]
1913	9.9	10.0	21.0	. . .	14.9	10.08
1914	10.0	10.2	21.0	. . .	15.0	9.94
1915	10.1	10.0	21.1	. . .	15.3	9.84
1916	10.9	11.3	21.3	. . .	16.8	9.15
1917	12.8	14.5	21.2	. . .	20.2	7.79
1918	15.1	16.7	21.5	. . .	27.3	6.64
1919	17.3	18.6	23.3	. . .	36.2	5.78
1920	20.0	21.0	27.4	. . .	43.1	4.99
1921	17.9	15.9	31.5	. . .	33.2	5.59
1922	16.8	14.9	32.4	. . .	27.0	5.96
1923	17.1	15.4	33.2	. . .	27.1	5.86
1924	17.1	15.2	34.4	. . .	26.8	5.85
1925	17.5	16.5	34.6	. . .	26.3	5.70
1926	17.7	17.0	34.2	. . .	25.9	5.65
1927	17.4	16.4	33.7	. . .	25.3	5.76
1928	17.1	16.3	32.9	. . .	25.0	5.83
1929	17.1	16.5	32.1	. . .	24.7	5.83
1930	16.7	15.6	31.2	. . .	24.2	5.99
1931	15.2	12.9	29.6	. . .	22.0	6.56
1932	13.7	10.7	26.5	. . .	19.5	7.32
1933	13.0	10.4	22.9	. . .	18.8	7.71
1934	13.4	11.6	21.4	. . .	20.6	7.46
1935	13.7	12.4	21.4	. . .	20.8	7.28
1936	13.9	12.6	21.9	. . .	21.0	7.21
1937	14.4	13.1	22.9	. . .	22.0	6.96
1938	14.1	12.1	23.7	. . .	21.9	7.09
1939	13.9	11.8	23.7	. . .	21.6	7.20
1940	14.0	12.0	23.7	. . .	21.8	7.13
1941	14.7	13.1	24.2	. . .	22.8	6.79
1942	16.3	15.4	24.7	. . .	26.7	6.13
1943	17.3	17.1	24.7	. . .	27.8	5.78
1944	17.6	16.9	24.8	. . .	29.8	5.68
1945	18.0	17.3	24.8	. . .	31.4	5.55
1946	19.5	19.8	25.0	. . .	34.4	5.12
1947	22.3	24.1	25.8	. . .	39.9	4.47
1948	24.1	26.1	27.5	. . .	42.5	4.15
1949	23.8	25.0	28.7	. . .	40.8	4.19
1950	24.1	25.4	29.7	. . .	40.3	4.15
1951	26.0	28.2	30.9	. . .	43.9	3.85
1952	26.5	28.7	32.2	. . .	43.5	3.77
1953	26.7	28.3	33.9	. . .	43.1	3.74
1954	26.9	28.2	35.1	. . .	43.1	3.72
1955	26.8	27.8	35.6	. . .	42.9	3.73
1956	27.2	28.0	36.3	. . .	43.7	3.68
1957	28.1	28.9	37.0	. . .	44.5	3.55
1958	28.9	30.2	37.6	. . .	44.6	3.46
1959	29.1	29.7	38.2	. . .	45.0	3.43

[1]December 1982 = 100.
[2]Purchasing power in 1982–1984 = $1.00.
. . . = Not available.

Table 7-6. Consumer Price Indexes, All Urban Consumers (CPI-U): U.S. City Average, Selected Groups and Purchasing Power of the Consumer Dollar, 1913–2006—Continued

(1982–1984 = 100, unless otherwise specified.)

Year	All items	Food	Rent of primary residence	Owners' equivalent of primary residence[1]	Apparel	Purchasing power of the consumer dollar[2]
1960	29.6	30.0	38.7	. . .	45.7	3.37
1961	29.9	30.4	39.2	. . .	46.1	3.34
1962	30.2	30.6	39.7	. . .	46.3	3.30
1963	30.6	31.1	40.1	. . .	46.9	3.27
1964	31.0	31.5	40.5	. . .	47.3	3.22
1965	31.5	32.2	40.9	. . .	47.8	3.17
1966	32.4	33.8	41.5	. . .	49.0	3.08
1967	33.4	34.1	42.2	. . .	51.0	2.99
1968	34.8	35.3	43.3	. . .	53.7	2.87
1969	36.7	37.1	44.7	. . .	56.8	2.73
1970	38.8	39.2	46.5	. . .	59.2	2.57
1971	40.5	40.4	48.7	. . .	61.1	2.47
1972	41.8	42.1	50.4	. . .	62.3	2.39
1973	44.4	48.2	52.5	. . .	64.6	2.25
1974	49.3	55.1	55.2	. . .	69.4	2.03
1975	53.8	59.8	58.0	. . .	72.5	1.86
1976	56.9	61.6	61.1	. . .	75.2	1.76
1977	60.6	65.5	64.8	. . .	78.6	1.65
1978	65.2	72.0	69.3	. . .	81.4	1.53
1979	72.6	79.9	74.3	. . .	84.9	1.38
1980	82.4	86.8	80.9	. . .	90.9	1.22
1981	90.9	93.6	87.9	. . .	95.3	1.10
1982	96.5	97.4	94.6	. . .	97.8	1.04
1983	99.6	99.4	100.1	102.5	100.2	1.00
1984	103.9	103.2	105.3	107.3	102.1	0.96
1985	107.6	105.6	111.8	113.2	105.0	0.93
1986	109.6	109.0	118.3	119.4	105.9	0.91
1987	113.6	113.5	123.1	124.8	110.6	0.88
1988	118.3	118.2	127.8	131.1	115.4	0.85
1989	124.0	125.1	132.8	137.4	118.6	0.81
1990	130.7	132.4	138.4	144.8	124.1	0.77
1991	136.2	136.3	143.3	150.4	128.7	0.73
1992	140.3	137.9	146.9	155.5	131.9	0.71
1993	144.5	140.9	150.3	160.5	133.7	0.69
1994	148.2	144.3	154.0	165.8	133.4	0.68
1995	152.4	148.4	157.8	171.3	132.0	0.66
1996	156.9	153.3	162.0	176.8	131.7	0.64
1997	160.5	157.3	166.7	181.9	132.9	0.62
1998	163.0	160.7	172.1	187.8	133.0	0.61
1999	166.6	164.1	177.5	192.9	131.3	0.60
2000	172.2	167.8	183.9	198.7	129.6	0.58
2001	177.1	173.1	192.1	206.3	127.3	0.57
2002	179.9	176.2	199.7	214.7	124.0	0.56
2003	184.0	180.0	205.5	219.9	120.9	0.54
2004	188.9	186.2	211.0	224.9	120.4	0.53
2005	195.3	190.7	217.3	230.2	119.5	0.51
2006	201.6	195.2	225.1	238.2	119.5	0.50

[1]December 1982 = 100.
[2]Purchasing power in 1982–1984 = $1.00.
. . . = Not available.

Table 7-7. Consumer Price Indexes, Urban Wage Earners and Clerical Workers (CPI-W): U.S. City Average, Major Groups, 1913–2006

(1982–1984 = 100, unless otherwise specified.)

Year	All items	Food and beverages	Housing	Apparel	Transportation	Medical care	Recreation[1]	Education and communication[1]	Other goods and services
1913	10.0	...	...	15.0	...	...	...	...	...
1914	10.1	...	...	15.1	...	...	...	...	...
1915	10.2	...	...	15.4	...	...	...	...	...
1916	11.0	...	...	16.9	...	...	...	...	...
1917	12.9	...	...	20.3	...	...	...	...	...
1918	15.1	...	...	27.5	...	...	...	...	...
1919	17.4	...	...	36.4	...	...	...	...	...
1920	20.1	...	...	43.3	...	...	...	...	...
1921	18.0	...	...	33.4	...	...	...	...	...
1922	16.9	...	...	27.2	...	...	...	...	...
1923	17.2	...	...	27.2	...	...	...	...	...
1924	17.2	...	...	26.9	...	...	...	...	...
1925	17.6	...	...	26.4	...	...	...	...	...
1926	17.8	...	...	26.0	...	...	...	...	...
1927	17.5	...	...	25.5	...	...	...	...	...
1928	17.2	...	...	25.1	...	...	...	...	...
1929	17.2	...	...	24.8	...	...	...	...	...
1930	16.8	...	...	24.3	...	...	...	...	...
1931	15.3	...	...	22.1	...	...	...	...	...
1932	13.7	...	...	19.6	...	...	...	...	...
1933	13.0	...	...	18.9	...	...	...	...	...
1934	13.5	...	...	20.7	...	...	...	...	...
1935	13.8	...	...	20.9	14.1	10.2	...	...	...
1936	13.9	...	...	21.1	14.2	10.3	...	...	...
1937	14.4	...	...	22.1	14.5	10.4	...	...	...
1938	14.2	...	...	22.0	14.6	10.4	...	...	...
1939	14.0	...	...	21.7	14.2	10.4	...	...	...
1940	14.1	...	...	21.9	14.1	10.4	...	...	...
1941	14.8	...	...	23.0	14.6	10.5	...	...	...
1942	16.4	...	...	26.8	15.9	10.8	...	...	...
1943	17.4	...	...	28.0	15.8	11.3	...	...	...
1944	17.7	...	...	30.0	15.8	11.6	...	...	...
1945	18.1	...	...	31.5	15.8	11.9	...	...	...
1946	19.6	...	...	34.6	16.6	12.6	...	...	...
1947	22.5	...	...	40.1	18.4	13.6	...	...	...
1948	24.2	...	...	42.7	20.4	14.5	...	...	...
1949	24.0	...	...	41.0	22.0	14.9	...	...	...
1950	24.2	...	...	40.5	22.6	15.2	...	...	...
1951	26.1	...	...	44.1	24.0	15.9	...	...	...
1952	26.7	...	...	43.7	25.6	16.8	...	...	...
1953	26.9	...	...	43.3	26.3	17.4	...	...	...
1954	27.0	...	...	43.3	25.9	17.9	...	...	...
1955	26.9	...	...	43.1	25.6	18.3	...	...	...
1956	27.3	...	...	44.0	26.1	19.0	...	...	...
1957	28.3	...	...	44.7	27.6	19.8	...	...	...
1958	29.1	...	...	44.8	28.4	20.7	...	...	...
1959	29.3	...	...	45.2	29.6	21.6	...	...	...

[1]December 1997 = 100.
. . . = Not available.

Table 7-7. Consumer Price Indexes, Urban Wage Earners and Clerical Workers (CPI-W): U.S. City Average, Major Groups, 1913–2006—*Continued*

(1982–1984 = 100, unless otherwise specified.)

Year	All items	Food and beverages	Housing	Apparel	Transportation	Medical care	Recreation[1]	Education and communication[1]	Other goods and services
1960	29.8	...	...	45.9	29.6	22.4	...	...	...
1961	30.1	...	...	46.3	30.0	23.0	...	...	...
1962	30.4	...	...	46.6	30.6	23.6	...	...	...
1963	30.8	...	...	47.1	30.8	24.2	...	...	...
1964	31.2	...	...	47.5	31.2	24.7	...	...	...
1965	31.7	...	...	48.0	31.7	25.3	...	...	...
1966	32.6	...	...	49.2	32.2	26.4	...	...	...
1967	33.6	35.0	31.1	51.2	33.1	28.3	...	...	35.4
1968	35.0	36.2	32.3	54.0	34.1	30.0	...	...	37.2
1969	36.9	38.0	34.3	57.1	35.5	32.1	...	...	39.1
1970	39.0	40.1	36.7	59.5	37.3	34.1	...	...	41.3
1971	40.7	41.3	38.3	61.4	39.2	36.3	...	...	43.3
1972	42.1	43.1	39.8	62.7	39.7	37.5	...	...	45.1
1973	44.7	48.8	41.5	65.0	41.0	39.0	...	...	46.9
1974	49.6	55.5	46.2	69.8	45.5	42.6	...	...	50.2
1975	54.1	60.2	51.1	72.9	49.8	47.7	...	...	54.4
1976	57.2	62.0	54.2	75.6	54.7	52.3	...	...	57.6
1977	60.9	65.7	57.9	79.0	58.6	57.3	...	...	60.9
1978	65.6	72.1	62.9	81.7	61.5	62.1	...	...	64.8
1979	73.1	79.9	70.7	85.2	70.4	68.0	...	...	69.4
1980	82.9	86.9	81.7	90.9	82.9	75.6	...	...	75.6
1981	91.4	93.6	91.1	95.6	93.0	83.5	...	...	82.5
1982	96.9	97.3	97.7	97.8	97.0	92.5	...	...	90.9
1983	99.8	99.5	100.0	100.2	99.2	100.5	...	...	101.3
1984	103.3	103.2	102.2	102.0	103.8	106.9	...	...	107.9
1985	106.9	105.5	106.6	105.0	106.4	113.6	...	...	114.2
1986	108.6	108.9	109.7	105.8	101.7	122.0	...	...	120.9
1987	112.5	113.3	112.8	110.4	105.1	130.2	...	...	127.8
1988	117.0	117.9	116.8	114.9	108.3	139.0	...	...	136.5
1989	122.6	124.6	121.2	117.9	113.9	149.6	...	...	147.4
1990	129.0	131.8	126.4	123.1	120.1	162.7	...	...	158.9
1991	134.3	136.5	131.2	127.4	123.1	176.5	...	...	171.7
1992	138.2	138.3	135.0	130.7	125.8	189.6	...	...	183.3
1993	142.1	141.2	138.5	132.4	129.4	200.9	91.2	86.0	192.2
1994	145.6	144.4	142.0	132.2	133.4	210.4	93.0	89.1	196.4
1995	149.8	148.3	145.4	130.9	138.8	219.8	94.7	92.3	204.2
1996	154.1	153.2	149.6	130.9	142.8	227.6	97.5	95.4	212.2
1997	157.6	157.2	153.4	132.1	143.6	234.0	99.7	98.5	221.6
1998	159.7	160.4	156.7	131.6	140.5	241.4	100.9	100.4	236.1
1999	163.2	163.8	160.0	130.1	143.4	249.7	101.3	101.5	261.9
2000	168.9	167.7	165.4	128.3	152.8	259.9	102.4	102.7	276.5
2001	173.5	173.0	172.1	126.1	153.6	271.8	103.6	105.3	289.5
2002	175.9	176.1	175.7	123.1	151.8	284.6	104.6	107.6	302.0
2003	179.8	179.9	180.4	120.0	156.3	296.3	105.5	109.0	307.0
2004	184.5	186.2	185.0	120.0	161.5	309.5	106.3	110.0	312.6
2005	191.0	190.5	191.2	119.1	173.0	322.8	106.8	111.4	322.2
2006	197.1	194.9	198.5	119.1	180.3	335.7	108.2	113.9	330.9

[1]December 1997 = 100.
... = Not available.

Table 7-8. Consumer Price Indexes, All Urban Consumers (CPI-U): U.S. City Average, by Expenditure Category, 1990–2006

(1982–1984 = 100, unless otherwise specified.)

Expenditure category	1990	1991	1992	1993	1994	1995	1996	1997	1998
ALL ITEMS	130.7	136.2	140.3	144.5	148.2	152.4	156.9	160.5	163.0
Food and Beverages	132.1	136.8	138.7	141.6	144.9	148.9	153.7	157.7	161.1
Food	132.4	136.3	137.9	140.9	144.3	148.4	153.3	157.3	160.7
Food at home	132.3	135.8	136.8	140.1	144.1	148.8	154.3	158.1	161.1
Cereals and bakery product	140.0	145.8	151.5	156.6	163.0	167.5	174.0	177.6	181.1
Meats, poultry, fish, and eggs	130.0	132.6	130.9	135.5	137.2	138.8	144.8	148.5	147.3
Dairy and related product	126.5	125.1	128.5	129.4	131.7	132.8	142.1	145.5	150.8
Fruits and vegetables	149.0	155.8	155.4	159.0	165.0	177.7	183.9	187.5	198.2
Nonalcoholic beverages and beverage materials	113.5	114.1	114.3	114.6	123.2	131.7	128.6	133.4	133.0
Other food at home	123.4	127.3	128.8	130.5	135.6	140.8	142.9	147.3	150.8
Sugar and sweets	124.7	129.3	133.1	133.4	135.2	137.5	143.7	147.8	150.2
Fats and oils	126.3	131.7	129.8	130.0	133.5	137.3	140.5	141.7	146.9
Other food	131.2	137.1	140.1	143.7	147.5	151.1	156.2	161.2	165.5
Other miscellaneous food[1]	. . .	. . .	. . .	. . .	. . .	. . .	. . .	. . .	102.6
Food away from home	133.4	137.9	140.7	143.2	145.7	149.0	152.7	157.0	161.1
Other food away from home[1]	. . .	. . .	. . .	. . .	. . .	. . .	. . .	. . .	101.6
Alcoholic beverages	129.3	142.8	147.3	149.6	151.5	153.9	158.5	162.8	165.7
Housing	128.5	133.6	137.5	141.2	144.8	148.5	152.8	156.8	160.4
Shelter	140.0	146.3	151.2	155.7	160.5	165.7	171.0	176.3	182.1
Rent of primary residence	138.4	143.3	146.9	150.3	154.0	157.8	162.0	166.7	172.1
Lodging away from home[1]	. . .	. . .	. . .	. . .	. . .	. . .	. . .	. . .	109.0
Owners' equivalent rent of primary residence[2]	144.8	150.4	155.5	160.5	165.8	171.3	176.8	181.9	187.8
Tenants' and household insurance[1]	. . .	. . .	. . .	. . .	. . .	. . .	. . .	. . .	99.8
Fuels and utilities	111.6	115.3	117.8	121.3	122.8	123.7	127.5	130.8	128.5
Household energy	104.5	106.7	108.1	111.2	111.7	111.5	115.2	117.9	113.7
Fuel oil and other fuels	99.3	94.6	90.7	90.3	88.8	88.1	99.2	99.8	90.0
Gas (piped) and electricity	109.3	112.6	114.8	118.5	119.2	119.2	122.1	125.1	121.2
Water, sewer, and trash collection services[1]	. . .	. . .	. . .	. . .	. . .	. . .	. . .	. . .	101.6
Household furnishings and operations	113.3	116.0	118.0	119.3	121.0	123.0	124.7	125.4	126.6
Household operations[1]	. . .	. . .	. . .	. . .	. . .	. . .	. . .	. . .	101.5
Apparel	124.1	128.7	131.9	133.7	133.4	132.0	131.7	132.9	133.0
Men's and boys' apparel	120.4	124.2	126.5	127.5	126.4	126.2	127.7	130.1	131.8
Women's and girls' apparel	122.6	127.6	130.4	132.6	130.9	126.9	124.7	126.1	126.0
Infants' and toddlers' apparel	125.8	128.9	129.3	127.1	128.1	127.2	129.7	129.0	126.1
Footwear	117.4	120.9	125.0	125.9	126.0	125.4	126.6	127.6	128.0
Transportation	120.5	123.8	126.5	130.4	134.3	139.1	143.0	144.3	141.6
Private transportation	118.8	121.9	124.6	127.5	131.4	136.3	140.0	141.0	137.9
New and used motor vehicles[1]	. . .	. . .	. . .	91.8	95.5[1]	99.4	101.0	100.5	100.1
New vehicles	121.4	126.0	129.2	132.7	137.6	141.0	143.7	144.3	143.4
Used cars and trucks	117.6	118.1	123.2	133.9	141.7	156.5	157.0	151.1	150.6
Motor fuel	101.2	99.4	99.0	98.0	98.5	100.0	106.3	106.2	92.2
Gasoline (all types)	101.0	99.2	99.0	97.7	98.2	99.8	105.9	105.8	91.6
Motor vehicle parts and equipment	100.9	102.2	103.1	101.6	101.4	102.1	102.2	101.9	101.1
Motor vehicle maintenance and repair	130.1	136.0	141.3	145.9	150.2	154.0	158.4	162.7	167.1
Public transportation	142.6	148.9	151.4	167.0	172.0	175.9	181.9	186.7	190.3
Medical Care	162.8	177.0	190.1	201.4	211.0	220.5	228.2	234.6	242.1
Medical care commodities	163.4	176.8	188.1	195.0	200.7	204.5	210.4	215.3	221.8
Medical care services	162.7	177.1	190.5	202.9	213.4	224.2	232.4	239.1	246.8
Professional services	156.1	165.7	175.8	184.7	192.5	201.0	208.3	215.4	222.2
Hospital and related services	178.0	196.1	214.0	231.9	245.6	257.8	269.5	278.4	287.5
Recreation[1]	. . .	. . .	. . .	90.7	92.7	94.5	97.4	99.6	101.1
Video and audio[1]	. . .	. . .	. . .	96.5	95.4	95.1	96.6	99.4	101.1
Education and Communication[1]	. . .	. . .	. . .	85.5	88.8	92.2	95.3	98.4	100.3
Education[1]	. . .	. . .	. . .	78.4	83.3	88.0	92.7	97.3	102.1
Educational books and supplies	171.3	180.3	190.3	197.6	205.5	214.4	226.9	238.4	250.8
Tuition, other school fees, and childcare	175.7	191.4	208.5	225.3	239.8	253.8	267.1	280.4	294.2
Communication[1]	. . .	. . .	. . .	96.7[1]	97.6	98.8	99.6	100.3	98.7
Information and information processing[1]	. . .	. . .	. . .	97.7	98.6	98.7	99.5	100.4	98.5
Telephone services[1]	. . .	. . .	. . .	. . .	. . .	. . .	. . .	. . .	100.7
Information technology, hardware, and services[3]	93.5	88.6	83.7	78.8	72.0	63.8	57.2	50.1	39.9
Personal computers and peripheral equipment[1]	. . .	. . .	. . .	. . .	. . .	. . .	. . .	. . .	78.2
Other Goods and Services	159.0	171.6	183.3	192.9	198.5	206.9	215.4	224.8	237.7
Tobacco and smoking product	181.5	202.7	219.8	228.4	220.0	225.7	232.8	243.7	274.8
Personal care	130.4	134.9	138.3	141.5	144.6	147.1	150.1	152.7	156.7
Personal care product	128.2	132.8	136.5	139.0	141.5	143.1	144.3	144.2	148.3
Personal care services	132.8	137.0	140.0	144.0	147.9	151.5	156.6	162.4	166.0
Miscellaneous personal services	158.4	168.8	177.5	186.1	195.9	205.9	215.6	226.1	234.7

[1]December 1997 = 100.
[2]December 1982 = 100.
[3]December 1988 = 100.
. . . = Not available.

Table 7-8. Consumer Price Indexes, All Urban Consumers (CPI-U): U.S. City Average, by Expenditure Category, 1990–2006—*Continued*

(1982–1984 = 100, unless otherwise specified.)

Expenditure category	1999	2000	2001	2002	2003	2004	2005	2006
ALL ITEMS	166.6	172.2	177.1	179.9	184.0	188.9	195.3	201.6
Food and Beverages	164.6	168.4	173.6	176.8	180.5	186.6	191.2	195.7
Food	164.1	167.8	173.1	176.2	180.0	186.2	190.7	195.2
Food at home	164.2	167.9	173.4	175.6	179.4	186.2	189.8	193.1
Cereals and bakery product	185.0	188.3	193.8	198.0	202.8	206.0	209.0	212.8
Meats, poultry, fish, and eggs	147.9	154.5	161.3	162.1	169.3	181.7	184.7	186.6
Dairy and related product	159.6	160.7	167.1	168.1	167.9	180.2	182.4	181.4
Fruits and vegetables	203.1	204.6	212.2	220.9	225.9	232.7	241.4	252.9
Nonalcoholic beverages and beverage materials	134.3	137.8	139.2	139.2	139.8	140.4	144.4	147.4
Other food at home	153.5	155.6	159.6	160.8	162.6	164.9	167.0	169.6
Sugar and sweets	152.3	154.0	155.7	159.0	162.0	163.2	165.2	171.5
Fats and oils	148.3	147.4	155.7	155.4	157.4	167.8	167.7	168.0
Other food	168.9	172.2	176.0	177.1	178.8	179.7	182.5	185.0
Other miscellaneous food[1]	104.9	107.5	108.9	109.2	110.3	110.4	111.3	113.9
Food away from home	165.1	169.0	173.9	178.3	182.1	187.5	193.4	199.4
Other food away from home[1]	105.2	109.0	113.4	117.7	121.3	125.3	131.3	136.6
Alcoholic beverages	169.7	174.7	179.3	183.6	187.2	192.1	195.9	200.7
Housing	163.9	169.6	176.4	180.3	184.8	189.5	195.7	203.2
Shelter	187.3	193.4	200.6	208.1	213.1	218.8	224.4	232.1
Rent of primary residence	177.5	183.9	192.1	199.7	205.5	211.0	217.3	225.1
Lodging away from home[1]	112.3	117.5	118.6	118.3	119.3	125.9	130.3	136.0
Owners' equivalent rent of primary residence[2]	192.9	198.7	206.3	214.7	219.9	224.9	230.2	238.2
Tenants' and household insurance[1]	101.3	103.7	106.2	108.7	114.8	116.2	117.6	116.5
Fuels and utilities	128.8	137.9	150.2	143.6	154.5	161.9	179.0	194.7
Household energy	113.5	122.8	135.4	127.2	138.2	144.4	161.6	177.1
Fuel oil and other fuels	91.4	129.7	129.3	115.5	139.5	160.5	208.6	234.9
Gas (piped) and electricity	120.9	128.0	142.4	134.4	145.0	150.6	166.5	182.1
Water, sewer, and trash collection services[1]	104.0	106.5	109.6	113.0	117.2	124.0	130.3	136.8
Household furnishings and operations	126.7	128.2	129.1	128.3	126.1	125.5	126.1	127.0
Household operations[1]	104.5	110.5	115.6	119.0	121.8	125.0	130.3	136.6
Apparel	131.3	129.6	127.3	124.0	120.9	120.4	119.5	119.5
Men's and boys' apparel	131.1	129.7	125.7	121.7	118.0	117.5	116.1	114.1
Women's and girls' apparel	123.3	121.5	119.3	115.8	113.1	113.0	110.8	110.7
Infants' and toddlers' apparel	129.0	130.6	129.2	126.4	122.1	118.5	116.7	116.5
Footwear	125.7	123.8	123.0	121.4	119.6	119.3	122.6	123.5
Transportation	144.4	153.3	154.3	152.9	157.6	163.1	173.9	180.9
Private transportation	140.5	149.1	150.0	148.8	153.6	159.4	170.2	177.0
New and used motor vehicles[1]	100.1	100.8	101.3	99.2	96.5	94.2	95.6	95.6
New vehicles	142.9	142.8	142.1	140.0	137.9	137.1	137.9	137.6
Used cars and trucks	152.0	155.8	158.7	152.0	142.9	133.3	139.4	140.0
Motor fuel	100.7	129.3	124.7	116.6	135.8	160.4	195.7	221.0
Gasoline (all types)	100.1	128.6	124.0	116.0	135.1	159.7	194.7	219.9
Motor vehicle parts and equipment	100.5	101.5	104.8	106.9	107.8	108.7	111.9	117.3
Motor vehicle maintenance and repair	171.9	177.3	183.5	190.2	195.6	200.2	206.9	215.6
Public transportation	197.7	209.6	210.6	207.4	209.3	209.1	217.3	226.6
Medical Care	250.6	260.8	272.8	285.6	297.1	310.1	323.2	336.2
Medical care commodities	230.7	238.1	247.6	256.4	262.8	269.3	276.0	285.9
Medical care services	255.1	266.0	278.8	292.9	306.0	321.3	336.7	350.6
Professional services	229.2	237.7	246.5	253.9	261.2	271.5	281.7	289.3
Hospital and related services	299.5	317.3	338.3	367.8	394.8	417.9	439.9	468.1
Recreation[1]	102.0	103.3	104.9	106.2	107.5	108.6	109.4	110.9
Video and audio[1]	100.7	101.0	101.5	102.8	103.6	104.2	104.2	104.6
Education and Communication[1]	101.2	102.5	105.2	107.9	109.8	111.6	113.7	116.8
Education[1]	107.0	112.5	118.5	126.0	134.4	143.7	152.7	162.1
Educational books and supplies	261.7	279.9	295.9	317.6	335.4	351.0	365.6	388.9
Tuition, other school fees, and childcare	308.4	324.0	341.1	362.1	386.7	414.3	440.9	468.1
Communication[1]	96.0	93.6	93.3	92.3	89.7	86.7	84.7	84.1
Information and information processing[1]	95.5	92.8	92.3	90.8	87.8	84.6	82.6	81.7
Telephone services[1]	100.1	98.5	99.3	99.7	98.3	95.8	94.9	95.8
Information technology, hardware, and services[3]	30.5	25.9	21.3	18.3	16.1	14.8	13.6	12.5
Personal computers and peripheral equipment[1]	53.5	41.1	29.5	22.2	17.6	15.3	12.8	10.8
Other Goods and Services	258.3	271.1	282.6	293.2	298.7	304.7	313.4	321.7
Tobacco and smoking product	355.8	394.9	425.2	461.5	469.0	478.0	502.8	519.9
Personal care	161.1	165.6	170.5	174.7	178.0	181.7	185.6	190.2
Personal care product	151.8	153.7	155.1	154.7	153.5	153.9	154.4	155.8
Personal care services	171.4	178.1	184.3	188.4	193.2	197.6	203.9	209.7
Miscellaneous personal services	243.0	252.3	263.1	274.4	283.5	293.9	303.0	313.6

[1]December 1997 = 100.
[2]December 1982 = 100.
[3]December 1988 = 100.

Table 7-9. Relative Importance of Components in the Consumer Price Index: U.S. City Average, Selected Groups, December 1997–December 2006

(Percent distribution.)

Index and year	All items	Food and beverages	Housing	Apparel	Transportation	Medical care	Recreation	Education and communication	Other goods and services
ALL URBAN CONSUMERS (CPI-U)									
December 1997	100.0	16.3	39.6	4.9	17.6	5.6	6.1	5.5	4.3
December 1998	100.0	16.4	39.8	4.8	17.0	5.7	6.1	5.5	4.6
December 1999	100.0	16.3	39.6	4.7	17.5	5.8	6.0	5.4	4.7
December 2000	100.0	16.2	40.0	4.4	17.6	5.8	5.9	5.3	4.8
December 2001[1]	100.0	16.4	40.5	4.2	16.6	6.0	5.9	5.4	4.9
December 2001[2]	100.0	15.7	40.9	4.4	17.1	5.8	6.0	5.8	4.3
December 2002	100.0	15.6	40.9	4.2	17.3	6.0	5.9	5.8	4.4
December 2003	100.0	15.4	42.1	4.0	16.9	6.1	5.9	5.9	3.8
December 2004	100.0	15.3	42.0	3.8	17.4	6.1	5.7	5.8	3.8
December 2005	100.0	15.1	42.2	3.7	17.7	6.2	5.6	5.8	3.7
December 2006	100.0	15.0	42.7	3.7	17.2	6.3	5.6	6.0	3.5
URBAN WAGE EARNERS AND WORKERS (CPI-W)									
December 1997	100.0	17.9	36.5	5.3	19.8	4.6	6.0	5.4	4.5
December 1998	100.0	18.0	36.7	5.2	19.2	4.7	5.9	5.4	5.0
December 1999	100.0	17.9	36.5	5.0	19.7	4.7	5.8	5.3	5.1
December 2000	100.0	17.8	36.8	4.8	19.9	4.7	5.7	5.2	5.2
December 2001[1]	100.0	18.0	37.3	4.6	18.8	4.9	5.7	5.3	5.4
December 2001[2]	100.0	17.2	38.1	4.8	19.4	4.6	5.6	5.6	4.5
December 2002	100.0	17.1	38.1	4.6	19.7	4.7	5.6	5.6	4.6
December 2003	100.0	17.2	39.1	4.4	19.1	5.0	5.7	5.6	3.9
December 2004	100.0	17.0	39.0	4.2	19.8	5.0	5.5	5.5	3.9
December 2005	100.0	16.8	39.2	4.0	20.1	5.1	5.4	5.4	3.9
December 2006	100.0	16.5	40.5	4.0	19.5	5.2	5.0	5.6	3.7

[1]1993–1995 weights.
[2]1999–2000 weights.

Table 7-10. Consumer Price Indexes, All Urban Consumers (CPI-U), All Items: Selected Metropolitan Statistical Areas, Selected Years, 1965–2006

(1982–1984 = 100, unless otherwise specified.)

Area	1965	1970	1975	1980	1981	1982	1983	1984	1985	1986	1987	1988	1989	1990	1991
NORTHEAST															
Boston-Brockton-Nashua, MA-NH-ME-CT	32.5	40.2	55.8	82.6	91.8	95.5	99.8	104.7	109.4	112.2	117.1	124.2	131.3	138.9	145.0
New York-Northern New Jersey-Long Island, NY-NJ-CT-PA	32.6	41.2	57.6	82.1	90.1	95.3	99.8	104.8	108.7	112.3	118.0	123.7	130.6	138.5	144.8
Philadelphia-Wilmington-Atlantic City, PA-NJ-DE-MD	32.8	40.8	56.8	83.6	92.1	96.6	99.4	104.1	108.8	111.5	116.8	122.4	128.3	135.8	142.2
Pittsburgh, PA	31.4	38.1	52.4	81.0	89.3	94.4	101.1	104.5	106.9	108.2	111.4	114.9	120.1	126.2	131.3
NORTH CENTRAL															
Chicago-Gary-Kenosha, IL-IN-WI	31.7	38.9	52.8	82.2	90.0	96.2	100.0	103.8	107.7	110.0	114.5	119.0	125.0	131.7	137.0
Cincinnati-Hamilton, OH-KY-IN	30.5	37.4	51.8	82.1	87.9	94.9	100.8	104.3	106.6	107.6	111.9	116.1	120.9	126.5	131.4
Cleveland-Akron, OH	29.6	37.2	50.2	78.9	87.2	94.0	101.2	104.8	107.8	109.4	112.7	116.7	122.7	129.0	134.2
Detroit-Ann Arbor-Flint, MI	31.2	39.5	53.9	85.3	93.2	97.0	99.8	103.2	106.8	108.3	111.7	116.1	122.3	128.6	133.1
Kansas City, MO-KS	32.2	39.0	53.2	83.6	90.5	95.0	100.5	104.5	107.7	108.7	113.1	117.4	121.6	126.0	131.2
Milwaukee-Racine, WI	31.0	37.5	50.8	81.4	90.7	95.9	100.2	103.8	107.0	107.4	111.5	115.9	120.8	126.2	132.2
Minneapolis-St. Paul, MN-WI	30.1	37.4	51.2	78.9	88.6	97.4	99.5	103.1	107.0	108.4	111.6	117.2	122.0	127.0	130.4
St. Louis, MO-IL	31.7	38.8	52.6	82.5	90.1	96.6	100.1	103.3	107.1	108.6	112.2	115.7	121.8	128.1	132.1
SOUTH															
Atlanta, GA	31.2	38.6	53.6	80.3	90.2	96.0	99.9	104.1	108.9	112.2	116.5	120.4	126.1	131.7	135.9
Dallas-Fort Worth, TX	29.9	37.6	50.4	81.5	90.8	96.0	99.7	104.3	108.2	109.9	112.9	116.1	119.5	125.1	130.8
Houston-Galveston-Brazoria, TX	29.6	36.4	51.4	82.7	91.0	97.3	100.0	102.7	104.9	103.9	106.5	109.5	114.1	120.6	125.1
Miami-Fort Lauderdale, FL	...	...	...	81.1	90.5	96.7	99.9	103.5	106.5	107.9	111.8	116.8	121.5	128.0	132.3
Tampa-St. Petersburg-Clearwater, FL[1]	...	...	...	...	...	...	...	...	...	...	100.0	103.7	107.2	111.7	116.4
Washington-Baltimore, DC-MD-VA-WV[2]	...	...	...	...	...	...	...	...	...	...	...	...	...	...	...
WEST															
Anchorage, AK	35.3	41.1	57.1	85.5	92.4	97.4	99.2	103.3	105.8	107.8	108.2	108.6	111.7	118.6	124.0
Denver-Boulder-Greeley, CO	28.8	34.5	48.4	78.4	87.2	95.1	100.5	104.3	107.1	107.9	110.8	113.7	115.8	120.9	125.6
Honolulu, HI	34.4	41.5	56.3	83.0	91.7	97.2	99.3	103.5	106.8	109.4	114.9	121.7	128.7	138.1	148.0
Los Angeles-Riverside-Orange County, CA	32.4	38.7	53.3	83.7	91.9	97.3	99.1	103.6	108.4	111.9	116.7	122.1	128.3	135.9	141.4
Phoenix-Mesa, AZ	...	...	...	...	...	...	...	...	...	...	...	...	...	...	...
Portland-Salem, OR-WA	32.3	38.7	53.5	87.2	95.0	98.0	99.1	102.8	106.7	108.2	110.9	114.7	120.4	127.4	133.9
San Diego, CA	28.2	34.1	47.6	79.4	90.1	96.2	99.0	104.8	110.4	113.5	117.5	123.4	130.6	138.4	143.4
San Francisco-Oakland-San Jose, CA	30.8	37.7	51.8	80.4	90.8	97.6	98.4	104.0	108.4	111.6	115.4	120.5	126.4	132.1	137.9
Seattle-Tacoma-Bremerton, WA	31.0	37.4	51.1	82.7	91.8	97.7	99.3	103.0	105.6	106.7	109.2	112.8	118.1	126.8	134.1

Area	1992	1993	1994	1995	1996	1997	1998	1999	2000	2001	2002	2003	2004	2005	2006
NORTHEAST															
Boston-Brockton-Nashua, MA-NH-ME-CT	148.6	152.9	154.9	158.6	163.3	167.9	171.7	176.0	183.6	191.5	196.5	203.9	209.5	216.4	223.1
New York-Northern New Jersey-Long Island, NY-NJ-CT-PA	150.0	154.5	158.2	162.2	166.9	170.8	173.6	177.0	182.5	187.1	191.9	197.8	204.8	212.7	220.7
Philadelphia-Wilmington-Atlantic City, PA-NJ-DE-MD	146.6	150.2	154.6	158.7	162.8	166.5	168.2	171.9	176.5	181.3	184.9	188.8	196.5	204.2	212.1
Pittsburgh, PA	136.0	139.9	144.6	149.2	153.2	157.0	159.2	162.5	168.0	172.5	174.0	177.5	183.0	189.8	195.7
NORTH CENTRAL															
Chicago-Gary-Kenosha, IL-IN-WI	141.1	145.4	148.6	153.3	157.4	161.7	165.0	168.4	173.8	178.3	181.2	184.5	188.6	194.3	198.3
Cincinnati-Hamilton, OH-KY-IN	134.1	137.8	142.4	146.2	149.6	152.1	155.1	159.2	164.8	167.9	170.0	173.4	176.5	181.6	188.6
Cleveland-Akron, OH	136.8	140.3	144.4	147.9	152.0	156.1	159.8	162.5	168.0	172.9	173.3	176.2	181.6	187.9	191.1
Detroit-Ann Arbor-Flint, MI	135.9	139.6	144.0	148.6	152.5	156.3	159.8	163.9	169.8	174.4	178.9	182.5	185.4	190.8	196.6
Kansas City, MO-KS	134.3	138.1	141.3	145.3	151.6	155.8	157.8	160.1	166.6	172.2	174.0	177.0	180.7	185.3	190.1
Milwaukee-Racine, WI	137.1	142.1	147.0	151.0	154.7	157.7	160.3	163.7	168.6	171.7	174.0	177.7	180.2	185.2	189.9
Minneapolis-St. Paul, MN-WI	135.0	139.2	143.6	147.0	151.9	155.4	158.3	163.3	170.1	176.5	179.6	182.7	187.9	193.1	196.2
St. Louis, MO-IL	134.7	137.5	141.3	145.2	149.6	152.9	154.5	157.6	163.1	167.3	169.1	173.4	180.3	186.2	189.5
SOUTH															
Atlanta, GA	138.5	143.4	146.7	150.9	156.0	158.9	161.2	164.8	170.6	176.2	178.2	180.8	183.2	188.9	193.8
Dallas-Fort Worth, TX	133.9	137.3	141.2	144.9	148.8	151.4	153.6	158.0	164.7	170.4	172.7	176.2	178.7	184.7	190.1
Houston-Galveston-Brazoria, TX	129.1	133.4	137.9	139.8	142.7	145.4	146.8	148.7	154.2	158.8	159.2	163.7	169.5	175.6	180.6
Miami-Fort Lauderdale, FL	134.5	139.1	143.6	148.9	153.7	158.4	160.5	162.4	167.8	173.0	175.5	180.6	185.6	194.3	203.9
Tampa-St. Petersburg-Clearwater, FL[1]	119.2	124.0	126.5	129.7	131.6	134.0	137.5	140.6	145.7	148.8	153.9	158.1	162.0	168.5	175.2
Washington-Baltimore, DC-MD-VA-WV[2]	...	...	...	...	...	100.8	102.1	104.2	107.6	110.4	113.0	116.2	119.5	124.3	128.8
WEST															
Anchorage, AK	128.2	132.2	135.0	138.9	142.7	144.8	146.9	148.4	150.9	155.2	158.2	162.5	166.7	171.8	177.3
Denver-Boulder-Greeley, CO	130.3	135.8	141.8	147.9	153.1	158.1	161.9	166.6	173.2	181.3	184.8	186.8	187.0	190.9	197.7
Honolulu, HI	155.1	160.1	164.5	168.1	170.7	171.9	171.5	173.3	176.3	178.4	180.3	184.5	190.6	197.8	209.4
Los Angeles-Riverside-Orange County, CA	146.5	150.3	152.3	154.6	157.5	160.0	162.3	166.1	171.6	177.3	182.2	187.0	193.2	201.8	210.4
Phoenix-Mesa, AZ	...	...	...	...	...	...	...	...	...	...	101.2	103.3	105.2	108.3	111.5
Portland-Salem, OR-WA	139.8	144.7	148.9	153.2	158.6	164.0	167.1	172.6	178.0	182.4	183.8	186.3	191.1	196.0	201.1
San Diego, CA	147.4	150.6	154.5	156.8	160.9	163.7	166.9	172.8	182.8	191.2	197.9	205.3	212.8	220.6	228.1
San Francisco-Oakland-San Jose, CA	142.5	146.3	148.7	151.6	155.1	160.4	165.5	172.5	180.2	189.9	193.0	196.4	198.8	202.7	209.2
Seattle-Tacoma-Bremerton, WA	139.0	142.9	147.8	152.3	157.5	163.0	167.7	172.8	179.2	185.7	189.3	192.3	194.7	200.2	207.6

[1]1987 = 100.
[2]November 1996 = 100.
. . . = Not available.

Table 7-11. Consumer Price Index Research Series, Using Current Methods (CPI-U-RS), by Month and Annual Average, 1977–2006

(December 1977 = 100.)

Year	January	February	March	April	May	June	July	August	September	October	November	December	Annual average
1977	. . .	. . .	. . .	. . .	. . .	. . .	. . .	. . .	. . .	. . .	. . .	100.0	. . .
1978	100.5	101.1	101.8	102.7	103.6	104.6	105.0	105.5	106.1	106.7	107.3	107.9	104.4
1979	108.7	109.7	110.7	111.8	113.0	114.1	115.2	116.0	117.1	117.9	118.5	119.5	114.4
1980	120.9	122.4	123.8	124.8	125.8	126.7	127.6	128.6	130.0	130.8	131.5	132.4	127.1
1981	133.6	135.3	136.4	137.1	137.9	138.7	139.7	140.7	141.8	142.4	142.9	143.4	139.2
1982	144.2	144.7	144.9	145.1	146.1	147.5	148.5	148.8	149.5	150.2	150.5	150.7	147.6
1983	151.1	151.2	151.3	152.4	153.2	153.8	154.4	154.8	155.6	156.0	156.2	156.4	153.9
1984	157.3	158.0	158.4	159.1	159.5	160.0	160.5	161.1	161.9	162.3	162.3	162.4	160.2
1985	162.6	163.3	164.0	164.7	165.3	165.8	166.1	166.4	167.0	167.4	167.9	168.3	165.7
1986	168.8	168.3	167.5	167.1	167.7	168.5	168.5	168.7	169.7	169.7	169.8	169.9	168.7
1987	170.9	171.6	172.3	173.2	173.7	174.3	174.6	175.6	176.4	176.8	176.9	176.8	174.4
1988	177.3	177.6	178.3	179.2	179.8	180.5	181.1	181.9	183.0	183.5	183.6	183.7	180.8
1989	184.6	185.2	186.2	187.5	188.4	188.8	189.3	189.5	190.2	190.9	191.2	191.5	188.6
1990	193.3	194.2	195.2	195.5	195.8	196.9	197.6	199.3	200.9	202.1	202.3	202.4	198.0
1991	203.3	203.5	203.6	203.9	204.4	204.9	205.0	205.6	206.4	206.6	207.1	207.2	205.1
1992	207.5	208.1	209.0	209.3	209.6	210.1	210.4	211.0	211.6	212.2	212.5	212.3	210.3
1993	212.9	213.7	214.3	214.9	215.3	215.5	215.6	216.1	216.4	217.1	217.3	217.1	215.5
1994	217.4	218.0	218.8	219.0	219.2	219.9	220.4	221.1	221.5	221.6	221.9	221.8	220.1
1995	222.6	223.3	224.0	224.7	225.1	225.6	225.7	226.1	226.5	227.1	226.9	226.8	225.4
1996	227.9	228.7	229.8	230.6	231.2	231.3	231.7	232.0	232.7	233.4	233.8	233.8	231.4
1997	234.5	235.2	235.6	235.9	235.8	236.2	236.3	236.7	237.5	237.9	237.8	237.4	236.4
1998	237.8	238.2	238.6	239.1	239.4	239.6	239.8	240.2	240.5	241.0	241.0	240.7	239.7
1999	241.4	241.7	242.4	244.1	244.1	244.2	244.9	245.6	246.7	247.2	247.3	247.3	244.7
2000	248.0	249.4	251.4	251.6	251.8	253.2	253.7	253.8	255.1	255.5	255.7	255.5	252.9
2001	257.1	258.2	258.8	259.8	260.9	261.4	260.6	260.7	261.8	260.9	260.4	259.4	260.0
2002	260.1	261.1	262.5	264.0	264.0	264.2	264.5	265.3	265.8	266.3	266.3	265.7	264.2
2003	266.8	268.9	270.5	269.9	269.5	269.8	270.1	271.1	271.9	271.7	270.9	270.6	270.1
2004	272.0	273.5	275.2	276.1	277.6	278.5	278.2	278.3	278.8	280.4	280.5	279.5	277.4
2005	280.0	281.6	283.8	285.7	285.5	285.6	286.9	288.3	291.9	292.5	290.2	288.9	286.7
2006	291.2	291.8	293.5	295.9	297.3	297.9	298.8	299.5	298.0	296.4	295.9	296.4	296.1

. . . = Not available.

NOTES AND DEFINITIONS

IMPORT AND EXPORT PRICE INDEXES

Collection and Coverage

All indexes use a modified Laspeyres formula. Price indexes for merchandise goods are re-weighted annually, with a two-year lag. Published series use a base year of 2000 = 100 whenever possible and the product categories classified by SITC have been discontinued. The products are now classified by end use as used by the Department of Commerce's Bureau of Economic Analysis (BEA).

The merchandise item price indexes are classified by end use for the Bureau of Economic Analysis System, by industry for the North American Industry Classification System (NAICS), and product category for the Harmonized System (HS). While classification by end use and product category are self-explanatory, a couple of notes are in order for classifying items by industry. In the NAICS tables, for both imports and exports, items are classified by output industry, not input industry. As an example, NAICS import index 326 (plastics and rubber products) would include outputs such as manufactured plastic rather than inputs such as petroleum. The NAICS classification structure also matches the classification system used by the PPI to produce the NAICS primary products indexes.

The Import Price Indexes (MPI) are based on U.S. dollar prices paid by the U.S. importer. The prices are generally either "free on board" (f.o.b.) foreign port or "cost, insurance, and freight" (c.i.f.) U.S. port transaction prices, depending on the practices of the individual industry. The index for crude petroleum is calculated from data collected by the Department of Energy.

The Export Price Indexes (XPI) are classified by end use, determined by BEA. The prices used are generally either "free alongside ship" (f.a.s.) factory or "free on board" (f.o.b.) transaction prices, depending on the practices of the individual industry. Prices used in the grain index, excluding rice, are obtained from the Department of Agriculture.

Prices used in the import indexes by locality of origin are a subset of the data collected for the Import Price Indexes. Beginning with January 2002, the indexes are defined by locality of origin using a nomenclature based upon the North American Industry Classification System (NAICS). Nonmanufactured goods are defined as NAICS 11 and 21, and manufactured goods are defined as NAICS 31–33.

Indexes for air passenger fares and crude oil tanker freight are calculated on a monthly basis. Indexes for air freight and ocean liner freight are calculated on a quarterly basis. The figures for services indexes will not sum up to the aggregate dollar value because not all categories are shown in the tables. Revenue figures for air passenger indexes exclude frequent flyer tickets and those sold by consolidators. Indexes for crude oil tanker freight are calculated from data collected by the Department of Energy and the publication of these indexes is lagged two months.

The Air Passenger Fares Indexes are calculated from data collected from a commercial airliner reservation system. These data exclude frequent flyer tickets and those sold by consolidators. The Crude Oil Tanker Freight Indexes are calculated from data collected by the U. S. Department of Energy, and the publication of these indexes is lagged two months. The Air Freight and Ocean Liner Freight Indexes are calculated from data collected directly from companies.

Sources of Additional Information

Concepts and methodology are described in Chapter 15 of the *BLS Handbook of Methods* and in monthly BLS press releases. These resources are available on the BLS Web site at <http://www.bls.gov>.

Table 7-12. U.S. Export Price Indexes for Selected Categories of Goods, by End Use, 2000–2006

(2000 = 100, unless otherwise indicated.)

Commodity	Relative impor- tance	2000				2001				2002			
		March	June	Septem- ber	Decem- ber	March	June	Septem- ber	Decem- ber	March	June	Septem- ber	Decem- ber
All Commodities	100.0	100.0	100.1	100.4	100.1	100.0	99.4	99.0	97.6	97.6	98.0	98.8	98.6
Foods, Feeds, and Beverages	8.4	100.8	100.8	98.7	101.2	101.0	100.4	102.6	100.7	99.7	101.5	109.8	108.7
Agricultural foods, feeds, and beverages, excluding distilled beverages	7.7	100.9	100.9	98.6	101.5	101.2	101.2	103.6	101.6	100.0	101.7	110.7	109.5
Nonagricultural foods (fish and distilled beverages)	0.7	99.6	99.9	99.7	98.2	99.4	92.6	92.9	92.1	98.3	100.7	101.3	102.3
Industrial Supplies and Materials	30.0	100.1	100.2	101.7	100.0	98.9	97.2	95.2	91.4	91.9	94.6	95.9	96.0
Industrial supplies and materials, durable	11.6	100.7	99.9	100.4	99.5	98.6	97.6	95.9	93.8	94.4	96.0	96.4	96.6
Industrial supplies and materials, nondurable	18.5	99.8	100.4	102.4	100.2	99.0	96.9	94.8	90.0	90.4	93.9	95.8	95.8
Agricultural industrial supplies and materials	1.5	98.0	98.6	103.2	104.6	101.7	99.3	96.8	93.3	93.6	95.8	98.4	101.9
Nonagricultural Industrial Supplies and Materials	28.5	100.3	100.3	101.6	99.7	98.7	97.0	95.1	91.3	91.8	94.5	95.8	95.7
Fuels and lubricants	4.5	103.1	97.3	111.3	104.9	100.3	102.8	103.2	83.5	85.6	86.7	92.9	91.3
Nonagricultural supplies and materials, excluding fuels and building materials	22.9	99.8	100.8	100.2	98.8	98.5	96.1	93.8	92.3	92.6	95.7	96.4	96.4
Selected building materials	1.1	100.5	100.2	99.7	99.2	97.5	97.0	95.5	94.2	94.2	94.2	96.2	96.2
Capital Goods	38.8	99.9	99.9	100.0	100.2	100.6	100.3	100.0	99.4	99.4	98.7	98.4	98.1
Electrical generating equipment	3.6	99.6	100.0	100.7	100.5	100.9	101.7	101.6	101.5	102.1	102.0	102.0	101.9
Nonelectrical machinery	28.1	100.2	100.0	99.8	99.7	99.7	99.1	98.6	97.7	97.5	96.6	96.0	95.4
Transportation equipment, excluding motor vehicles[1]	7.1	. . .	. . .	. . .	. . .	. . .	. . .	. . .	100.0	100.9	100.8	101.7	102.5
Automotive Vehicles, Parts, and Engines	10.4	99.9	99.9	100.3	100.1	100.3	100.4	100.4	100.5	100.9	100.9	101.1	101.3
Consumer goods, excluding automotives	12.4	100.0	99.9	99.9	99.7	99.6	99.4	99.7	99.9	99.1	99.1	99.3	99.3
Nondurables, manufactured	5.9	100.1	99.8	99.8	99.6	99.0	99.0	99.1	99.1	98.1	98.5	98.7	98.7
Durables, manufactured	5.4	99.8	100.1	100.1	99.9	100.2	100.0	100.4	100.5	99.7	99.4	99.6	99.6
Agricultural Commodities	9.2	100.4	100.5	99.4	102.0	101.3	100.9	102.5	100.2	98.9	100.7	108.6	108.2
Nonagricultural Commodities	90.8	100.0	100.0	100.5	99.9	99.9	99.3	98.6	97.4	97.5	97.8	98.0	97.8

[1]December 2001 = 100.
. . . = Not available.

Table 7-12. U.S. Export Price Indexes for Selected Categories of Goods, by End Use, 2000–2006—*Continued*

(2000 = 100, unless otherwise specified.)

Commodity	2003				2004				2005			
	March	June	September	December	March	June	September	December	March	June	September	December
All Commodities	99.7	99.5	99.8	100.8	103.0	103.4	103.8	104.8	106.4	106.7	107.5	107.7
Foods, Feeds, and Beverages	108.2	111.3	115.3	122.4	130.5	129.1	118.7	116.9	120.9	125.2	122.8	121.9
Agricultural foods, feeds, and beverages, excluding distilled beverages	108.1	111.2	116.3	123.8	132.4	131.1	119.3	116.6	120.7	125.6	122.6	121.7
Nonagricultural foods (fish and distilled beverages)	110.0	113.1	106.5	108.5	112.1	110.7	113.0	118.4	121.8	120.1	123.6	123.6
Industrial Supplies and Materials	100.6	100.1	100.2	102.5	108.1	109.9	114.0	118.0	122.3	122.3	127.4	127.9
Industrial supplies and materials, durable	99.2	99.7	100.4	103.3	110.3	111.8	116.0	120.2	122.6	122.7	123.4	129.1
Industrial supplies and materials, nondurable	101.7	100.6	100.4	102.2	107.0	108.9	112.9	116.9	122.2	122.1	129.8	127.4
Agricultural industrial supplies and materials	104.8	104.4	107.3	117.5	117.2	110.7	109.4	109.5	115.6	115.8	116.4	117.4
Nonagricultural Industrial Supplies and Materials	100.3	99.8	99.8	101.7	107.7	109.9	114.3	118.6	122.8	122.8	128.2	128.7
Fuels and lubricants	108.0	97.0	97.6	99.0	108.9	114.9	121.5	125.4	143.8	148.8	184.8	163.4
Nonagricultural supplies and materials, excluding fuels and building materials	99.9	100.7	100.5	102.5	108.1	110.0	114.4	118.9	121.4	120.6	122.2	125.7
Selected building materials	96.4	96.3	98.4	99.5	102.3	103.4	104.0	104.4	105.3	106.2	105.7	106.5
Capital Goods	98.3	97.6	97.5	97.5	98.0	97.8	97.8	98.2	98.4	98.4	97.6	97.7
Electrical generating equipment	101.6	101.6	101.7	101.7	102.0	102.0	102.4	103.6	103.9	103.4	102.6	103.6
Nonelectrical machinery	95.6	94.5	94.3	94.1	94.5	94.1	93.9	93.9	93.9	93.7	92.7	92.5
Transportation equipment, excluding motor vehicles[1]	103.5	104.0	105.1	105.7	106.6	107.2	108.3	109.5	111.1	111.8	112.6	113.8
Automotive Vehicles, Parts, and Engines	101.5	101.6	101.8	101.8	101.9	102.3	102.5	102.9	103.3	103.4	103.7	103.9
Consumer goods, excluding automotives	99.4	99.6	99.4	99.9	100.2	100.4	101.0	101.2	101.6	101.5	101.9	101.9
Nondurables, manufactured	98.7	98.8	98.5	99.2	99.9	100.0	101.0	101.0	101.5	101.2	101.5	101.6
Durables, manufactured	99.7	100.1	100.1	100.3	100.1	100.7	100.9	101.1	101.5	101.5	101.8	101.5
Agricultural Commodities	107.5	110.0	114.7	122.7	129.7	127.4	117.6	115.4	119.9	123.9	121.5	121.0
Nonagricultural Commodities	99.1	98.7	98.6	99.1	100.9	101.5	102.8	104.1	105.4	105.4	106.5	106.8

[1]December 2001 = 100.

Table 7-12. U.S. Export Price Indexes for Selected Categories of Goods, by End Use, 2000–2006—*Continued*

(2000 = 100, unless otherwise specified.)

Commodity	2006			
	March	June	September	December
All Commodities	108.8	111.2	111.7	112.5
Foods, Feeds, and Beverages	121.7	125.6	128.8	138.7
Agricultural foods, feeds, and beverages, excluding distilled beverages	121.5	125.7	129.1	140.5
Nonagricultural foods (fish and distilled beverages)	123.2	125.0	126.0	123.5
Industrial Supplies and Materials	131.3	138.8	139.5	139.4
Industrial supplies and materials, durable	135.7	146.2	146.9	150.1
Industrial supplies and materials, nondurable	129.0	134.9	135.7	133.9
Agricultural industrial supplies and materials	116.8	117.3	118.1	123.9
Nonagricultural Industrial Supplies and Materials	132.3	140.2	140.9	140.5
Fuels and lubricants	173.5	196.3	191.1	183.5
Nonagricultural supplies and materials, excluding fuels and building materials	128.5	134.7	136.3	136.8
Selected building materials	108.5	109.8	110.0	111.5
Capital Goods	98.2	98.4	98.5	98.8
Electrical generating equipment	104.4	104.8	105.1	106.2
Nonelectrical machinery	92.7	92.7	92.6	92.6
Transportation equipment, excluding motor vehicles[1]	116.0	117.1	117.7	119.1
Automotive Vehicles, Parts, and Engines	104.4	104.9	105.2	105.5
Consumer goods, excluding automotives	102.3	103.5	104.0	104.0
Nondurables, manufactured	102.4	103.3	103.8	104.0
Durables, manufactured	101.3	102.4	103.1	102.8
Agricultural Commodities	120.7	124.1	127.1	137.3
Nonagricultural Commodities	108.0	110.3	110.6	110.7

[1]December 2001 = 100.

Table 7-13. U.S. Import Price Indexes for Selected Categories of Goods, by End Use, 2000–2006

(2000 = 100, unless otherwise indicated.)

Commodity	Relative impor- tance	2000				2001				2002			
		March	June	Septem- ber	Decem- ber	March	June	Septem- ber	Decem- ber	March	June	Septem- ber	Decem- ber
All Commodities	100.0	99.9	100.2	101.6	100.5	98.3	97.6	95.9	91.4	92.8	94.1	95.5	95.2
Foods, Feeds, and Beverages	4.4	101.0	99.4	98.9	99.3	98.9	95.4	95.0	94.6	95.0	96.2	99.7	100.2
Agricultural foods, feeds, and beverages, excluding distilled beverages	3.4	102.1	99.2	97.3	99.3	101.0	97.0	97.8	98.3	99.5	101.3	105.4	106.0
Nonagricultural foods (fish and distilled beverages)	1.0	98.5	99.7	102.3	99.2	94.5	92.2	89.2	86.8	85.5	85.1	87.3	87.5
Industrial Supplies and Materials	38.4	99.0	100.7	105.5	102.9	96.0	95.5	91.0	77.6	84.9	89.8	95.2	94.6
Fuels and lubricants	23.3	97.2	101.3	111.3	106.1	91.1	90.9	86.1	61.6	76.4	85.8	96.2	94.7
Paper and paper base stocks	0.8	95.5	100.0	103.2	104.5	104.4	100.0	93.9	90.7	88.0	87.1	90.5	89.1
Materials associated with nondurable supplies and materials	4.6	98.5	99.9	101.1	101.5	102.8	100.3	97.9	96.2	95.9	97.1	99.4	100.1
Selected building materials	1.9	107.1	100.3	94.3	94.7	91.9	111.1	103.7	92.9	100.7	99.1	97.6	95.0
Unfinished metals associated with durable goods	4.5	102.7	100.7	101.5	99.5	99.5	93.6	87.1	82.1	83.8	88.5	89.7	91.5
Finished metals associated with durable goods	1.7	100.6	100.5	100.3	99.4	98.3	99.4	98.2	97.9	97.1	96.5	97.1	96.8
Nonmetals associated with durable goods	1.6	100.2	99.5	99.7	99.7	101.6	100.6	100.4	99.0	97.2	96.7	96.9	97.1
Industrial Supplies and Materials, Durable	38.4	102.9	100.4	99.6	98.5	98.1	99.1	94.1	89.1	91.1	92.3	92.7	92.7
Industrial Supplies and Materials, Excluding Fuels[1]	15.1	. . .	. . .	. . .	. . .	. . .	. . .	. . .	100.0	101.0	102.1	103.4	103.6
Industrial Supplies and Materials, Excluding Petroleum	17.3	98.9	99.9	101.0	105.4	102.1	99.8	94.2	90.0	90.3	92.9	93.9	95.2
Industrial Supplies and Materials, Nondurable, Excluding Petroleum	5.4	94.6	99.3	102.6	112.9	106.4	100.7	94.2	90.9	89.3	93.4	95.2	98.1
Capital Goods	21.0	100.5	100.0	99.7	98.9	98.7	97.7	96.8	96.2	95.2	95.1	94.7	93.9
Electric generating equipment	2.6	98.7	101.1	100.3	99.8	102.1	101.8	101.4	100.6	95.5	95.1	95.7	94.9
Nonelectrical machinery	16.7	100.9	99.9	99.5	98.6	98.0	96.7	95.6	94.9	94.4	94.4	93.7	92.8
Transportation equipment, excluding motor vehicles[1]	1.6	. . .	. . .	. . .	. . .	. . .	. . .	. . .	100.0	100.5	100.4	101.0	101.0
Automotive Parts and Engines	13.4	99.7	100.2	100.0	100.2	100.1	99.8	99.9	100.0	99.9	100.1	100.3	100.5
Consumer Goods, Excluding Automotive	22.8	100.3	99.6	99.8	99.5	99.8	99.3	99.1	98.7	98.2	98.1	98.1	98.0
Nondurables, manufactured	10.6	100.3	99.6	99.8	99.6	100.2	99.8	99.6	99.7	99.2	99.1	99.5	99.7
Nonmanufactured consumer goods	1.1	100.3	98.2	99.8	99.0	99.3	99.2	97.9	96.4	96.1	95.6	95.4	95.4
All Imports, Excluding Fuels	76.7	. . .	. . .	. . .	. . .	. . .	. . .	. . .	100.0	99.7	99.9	100.1	100.0
All Imports, Excluding Petroleum	78.9	100.0	99.9	100.0	100.7	100.0	98.9	97.3	96.2	95.8	96.2	96.4	96.5

[1]December 2001 = 100.
. . . = Not available.

Table 7-13. U.S. Import Price Indexes for Selected Categories of Goods, by End Use, 2000–2006—*Continued*

(2000 = 100, unless otherwise indicated.)

Commodity	2003				2004				2005			
	March	June	September	December	March	June	September	December	March	June	September	December
All Commodities	99.1	96.2	96.2	97.5	100.2	101.7	104.1	104.0	107.8	109.2	114.4	112.3
Foods, Feeds, and Beverages	102.6	100.7	101.8	103.2	105.9	106.9	108.7	111.5	115.9	114.1	114.2	117.5
Agricultural foods, feeds, and beverages, excluding distilled beverages	109.6	107.1	108.3	110.9	113.0	114.3	116.4	120.7	125.7	123.5	122.6	127.2
Nonagricultural foods (fish and distilled beverages)	86.9	86.6	87.6	86.0	90.1	90.3	91.4	91.0	94.0	93.1	95.6	95.9
Industrial Supplies and Materials	109.7	98.2	98.9	103.6	112.7	119.3	128.5	126.4	139.8	145.5	167.2	158.6
Fuels and lubricants	125.2	100.3	99.4	107.2	120.2	130.9	146.2	141.0	165.6	178.0	222.1	202.4
Paper and paper base stocks	91.0	94.1	94.0	93.9	95.6	99.0	101.1	101.3	103.8	103.8	104.3	106.1
Materials associated with nondurable supplies and materials	104.2	103.0	102.5	104.4	105.4	106.0	108.0	109.8	113.0	113.5	117.3	117.8
Selected building materials	96.3	96.7	110.3	108.0	118.4	120.5	125.6	115.6	122.7	118.1	117.6	116.9
Unfinished metals associated with durable goods	92.8	92.2	93.4	99.2	114.9	124.4	133.1	138.5	140.4	139.9	138.2	145.8
Finished metals associated with durable goods	96.1	97.4	99.0	101.0	104.8	108.1	112.4	114.7	115.9	116.6	117.3	117.6
Nonmetals associated with durable goods	97.9	98.2	97.5	98.2	99.3	98.7	98.8	99.7	100.8	100.9	100.7	100.5
Industrial Supplies and Materials, Durable	93.6	93.7	97.3	99.5	108.5	112.8	117.8	118.0	120.8	119.7	119.1	121.4
Industrial Supplies and Materials, Excluding Fuels[1]	105.8	105.7	107.9	110.1	116.5	119.8	124.1	124.8	128.0	127.5	128.5	130.3
Industrial Supplies and Materials, Excluding Petroleum	104.3	99.9	100.3	102.1	107.9	112.5	114.4	118.8	119.9	120.2	126.8	132.2
Industrial Supplies and Materials, Nondurable, Excluding Petroleum	117.1	107.2	103.8	105.0	107.1	112.0	110.2	119.7	118.7	120.7	135.4	144.3
Capital Goods	93.7	93.8	93.5	92.9	93.1	92.2	92.0	92.2	92.3	92.3	91.5	91.0
Electric generating equipment	95.5	96.6	95.8	96.8	97.8	97.0	97.4	98.0	98.8	98.8	99.0	99.3
Nonelectrical machinery	92.5	92.3	92.1	91.1	91.2	90.1	89.8	89.9	89.8	89.8	88.7	88.1
Transportation equipment, excluding motor vehicles[1]	101.6	102.0	102.2	102.8	103.5	104.0	103.9	104.5	105.6	106.0	106.4	106.1
Automotive Parts and Engines	100.5	100.6	100.5	101.4	101.8	102.2	102.7	103.2	103.2	103.4	103.6	103.6
Consumer Goods, Excluding Automotive	97.9	98.1	97.9	98.1	98.7	98.5	98.4	99.0	99.9	99.9	99.7	99.6
Nondurables, manufactured	99.7	99.8	99.7	100.1	101.3	100.9	100.8	101.4	102.8	102.8	103.1	102.7
Nonmanufactured consumer goods	95.7	96.2	95.7	96.2	96.4	96.8	97.9	98.2	100.3	101.8	100.6	101.2
All Imports, Excluding Fuels	100.3	100.3	100.6	101.0	102.4	102.7	103.4	104.0	105.0	104.9	104.8	105.1
All Imports, Excluding Petroleum	98.1	97.3	97.3	97.7	99.1	99.7	100.1	101.3	102.0	102.0	102.8	103.7

[1]December 2001 = 100.

Table 7-13. U.S. Import Price Indexes for Selected Categories of Goods, by End Use, 2000–2006—*Continued*

(2000 = 100, unless otherwise indicated.)

Commodity	2006			
	March	June	September	December
All Commodities	112.7	117.3	116.2	115.1
Foods, Feeds, and Beverages	117.0	118.0	120.9	122.6
Agricultural foods, feeds, and beverages, excluding distilled beverages	125.4	126.8	130.4	133.7
Nonagricultural foods (fish and distilled beverages)	98.3	98.5	99.8	97.9
Industrial Supplies and Materials	160.4	178.1	172.2	166.6
Fuels and lubricants	201.5	230.2	216.3	204.3
Paper and paper base stocks	107.7	111.3	113.1	112.8
Materials associated with nondurable supplies and materials	119.3	120.6	121.8	123.0
Selected building materials	118.0	117.2	115.8	110.6
Unfinished metals associated with durable goods	161.1	193.2	194.4	195.9
Finished metals associated with durable goods	119.2	125.3	128.4	128.9
Nonmetals associated with durable goods	100.8	101.1	101.3	101.7
Industrial Supplies and Materials, Durable	127.2	139.1	139.8	139.2
Industrial Supplies and Materials, Excluding Fuels[1]	134.9	143.7	144.7	144.7
Industrial Supplies and Materials, Excluding Petroleum	128.1	133.9	135.1	138.3
Industrial Supplies and Materials, Nondurable, Excluding Petroleum	128.3	126.7	128.5	136.3
Capital Goods	91.1	91.2	91.3	91.5
Electric generating equipment	100.1	102.1	102.7	103.0
Nonelectrical machinery	88.0	87.8	87.8	87.9
Transportation equipment, excluding motor vehicles[1]	107.0	107.9	108.3	109.1
Automotive Parts and Engines	103.5	103.9	104.1	104.3
Consumer Goods, Excluding Automotive	99.6	99.8	100.5	101.0
Nondurables, manufactured	102.8	102.6	103.0	103.4
Nonmanufactured consumer goods	98.2	98.6	100.5	101.8
All Imports, Excluding Fuels	105.7	107.2	107.8	108.1
All Imports, Excluding Petroleum	103.0	104.2	104.8	105.7

[1]December 2001 = 100.

Table 7-14. U.S. Import Price Indexes for Selected Categories of Goods, by Locality of Origin, 1996–2006

(2000 = 100.)

Category and year	Percent of U.S. imports[1]	Month			
		March	June	September	December
INDUSTRIALIZED COUNTRIES	44.8				
Total Goods					
1996		99.7	98.8	99.3	99.4
1997		97.4	96.5	96.4	96.1
1998		94.6	94.0	93.3	93.8
1999		94.1	94.8	96.4	97.5
2000		99.5	100.1	100.9	101.4
2001		100.2	99.0	96.5	93.7
2002		94.3	95.7	96.9	96.7
2003		100.0	98.4	98.6	100.0
2004		103.4	104.7	106.3	107.5
2005		109.7	110.0	113.5	114.1
2006		113.5	117.4	117.0	116.4
Nonmanufactured Goods	4.6				
1996		71.6	72.3	76.0	84.3
1997		73.3	68.9	69.4	68.5
1998		59.3	56.8	57.2	55.7
1999		56.9	65.1	78.7	83.2
2000		92.7	102.2	107.5	118.2
2001		103.9	97.2	85.2	69.9
2002		82.9	93.8	102.4	102.7
2003		134.3	113.7	108.9	112.4
2004		122.9	133.1	138.7	147.1
2005		156.7	158.0	203.0	199.2
2006		170.9	190.0	183.7	184.9
Manufactured Goods	39.8				
1996		102.1	101.1	101.4	100.7
1997		99.5	98.9	98.8	98.6
1998		97.8	97.5	96.7	97.3
1999		97.6	97.7	98.1	98.9
2000		100.2	99.9	100.2	99.8
2001		99.9	99.2	97.6	96.0
2002		95.6	96.3	96.9	96.7
2003		97.8	97.7	98.2	99.4
2004		102.1	102.8	104.0	104.6
2005		106.3	106.6	106.7	107.7
2006		109.0	111.8	111.8	111.1
OTHER COUNTRIES	55.2				
Total Goods					
1996		99.8	99.0	101.3	102.7
1997		100.6	99.4	98.7	96.6
1998		92.4	90.7	89.5	86.8
1999		87.7	90.3	94.5	96.9
2000		99.8	100.4	102.5	99.5
2001		97.0	96.6	95.0	88.6
2002		90.9	92.2	94.3	93.4
2003		96.7	93.1	93.3	94.1
2004		96.3	97.9	101.5	99.7
2005		105.0	107.0	112.1	109.5
2006		110.8	115.5	114.0	111.8
Nonmanufactured Goods	11.0				
1996		73.7	72.1	80.9	84.5
1997		75.8	72.6	72.2	68.8
1998		57.1	54.9	54.5	46.8
1999		53.0	63.6	80.3	89.2
2000		99.9	102.4	109.2	97.4
2001		88.9	89.7	86.1	65.3
2002		81.3	88.2	99.6	96.4
2003		113.3	98.0	98.8	106.5
2004		118.1	123.2	141.5	130.3
2005		158.0	169.5	199.8	181.3
2006		191.7	215.4	204.6	191.1
Manufactured Goods	44.0				
1996		108.9	108.4	107.9	108.6
1997		108.4	107.8	107.0	105.3
1998		103.5	102.2	100.6	99.6
1999		98.8	98.9	99.0	99.3
2000		99.8	99.7	100.3	100.2
2001		99.6	98.8	97.9	96.0
2002		95.6	95.9	96.2	95.8
2003		96.5	95.1	95.1	94.5
2004		95.2	96.2	97.2	97.1
2005		98.4	98.7	99.3	99.6
2006		99.4	101.2	101.2	100.7

[1]Based on 2005 trade values.

Table 7-14. U.S. Import Price Indexes for Selected Categories of Goods, by Locality of Origin, 1996–2006
—*Continued*

(2000 = 100.)

Category and year	Percent of U.S. imports¹	Month			
		March	June	September	December
CANADA	17.1				
Total Goods					
1996		94.3	93.5	93.8	95.1
1997		93.2	92.6	93.2	92.0
1998		90.1	89.7	89.3	88.7
1999		88.8	90.6	93.5	94.7
2000		97.2	99.8	102.4	105.6
2001		102.6	101.8	97.0	93.2
2002		96.1	97.8	99.6	99.2
2003		106.6	103.1	103.9	104.4
2004		110.0	112.3	114.4	116.6
2005		120.1	119.6	128.2	129.6
2006		125.4	130.6	129.7	129.2
Nonmanufactured Goods	3.9				
1996		70.3	70.7	74.4	84.3
1997		69.9	66.6	68.1	66.4
1998		58.4	56.6	56.5	56.3
1999		56.5	64.2	76.8	79.9
2000		89.3	103.6	107.6	124.4
2001		108.1	97.9	83.1	69.8
2002		83.8	96.8	104.1	104.9
2003		143.1	119.0	111.5	114.0
2004		126.1	138.0	138.9	150.5
2005		157.9	159.8	210.8	207.4
2006		171.3	189.2	183.1	187.1
Manufactured Goods	12.9				
1996		99.0	98.0	97.7	97.4
1997		98.0	98.0	98.3	97.3
1998		96.7	96.6	96.3	95.5
1999		95.5	96.1	96.9	97.7
2000		98.8	98.9	101.3	101.8
2001		101.6	102.8	99.9	98.1
2002		99.1	98.7	99.5	98.9
2003		100.9	101.1	103.2	103.3
2004		107.4	108.2	110.3	110.7
2005		113.7	112.9	113.1	115.6
2006		117.2	120.0	119.9	118.7
EUROPEAN UNION	17.9				
Total Goods					
1996		101.3	101.0	101.7	101.9
1997		100.5	100.0	99.1	100.1
1998		98.9	98.8	98.7	99.4
1999		98.8	99.1	99.9	100.3
2000		100.8	100.1	100.0	98.9
2001		99.0	98.8	98.2	97.4
2002		97.4	99.2	101.0	100.9
2003		103.2	102.8	102.8	104.3
2004		107.4	108.5	110.0	111.6
2005		113.8	114.1	115.7	114.5
2006		117.7	120.4	120.5	119.6
Nonmanufactured Goods	0.4				
1996		78.8	80.6	85.7	91.7
1997		89.3	82.2	76.5	78.4
1998		65.6	58.7	58.8	53.4
1999		53.6	66.6	81.3	88.7
2000		100.4	102.9	107.9	106.2
2001		96.0	99.5	89.1	75.7
2002		86.6	88.7	99.6	104.1
2003		118.8	106.7	111.5	118.8
2004		128.4	135.1	157.9	163.1
2005		177.1	177.5	209.7	191.1
2006		211.4	231.9	219.9	198.7
Manufactured Goods	17.4				
1996		102.3	101.8	102.4	102.3
1997		101.0	100.8	100.1	101.0
1998		100.4	100.6	100.5	101.5
1999		100.9	100.6	100.8	100.8
2000		100.8	99.9	99.6	98.6
2001		99.2	98.8	98.7	98.4
2002		98.1	99.9	101.5	101.4
2003		103.3	103.2	103.2	104.5
2004		107.4	108.4	109.3	110.9
2005		112.8	113.0	113.8	112.9
2006		116.0	118.0	118.4	118.0

¹Based on 2005 trade values.

Table 7-14. U.S. Import Price Indexes for Selected Categories of Goods, by Locality of Origin, 1996–2006 —*Continued*

(2000 = 100.)

Category and year	Percent of U.S. imports[1]	Month			
		March	June	September	December
LATIN AMERICA	17.6				
Total Goods					
1996		. . .	. . .	. . .	. . .
1997		. . .	. . .	. . .	. . .
1998		84.3	83.9	83.0	80.4
1999		81.7	85.3	90.7	94.2
2000		98.9	100.9	103.5	99.5
2001		99.5	98.9	97.2	90.6
2002		94.0	96.2	100.0	98.9
2003		104.8	99.6	99.8	102.6
2004		106.3	108.6	114.7	113.1
2005		122.1	126.3	133.8	131.0
2006		134.0	142.8	140.2	136.4
Nonmanufactured Goods	4.8				
1996		. . .	. . .	. . .	. . .
1997		. . .	. . .	. . .	. . .
1998		60.8	59.7	59.4	51.9
1999		59.3	67.2	82.1	90.2
2000		100.2	103.5	107.8	93.6
2001		89.3	89.0	86.0	67.3
2002		83.5	90.7	103.0	99.3
2003		111.7	103.5	100.9	109.8
2004		121.1	125.9	144.6	130.1
2005		161.0	175.1	205.1	184.6
2006		195.5	217.2	205.7	197.1
Manufactured Goods	12.7				
1996		. . .	. . .	. . .	. . .
1997		. . .	. . .	. . .	. . .
1998		94.8	95.0	93.8	93.5
1999		92.0	93.6	94.6	96.0
2000		98.3	99.6	101.6	102.3
2001		104.2	103.5	102.5	101.4
2002		101.5	102.4	104.2	103.8
2003		108.2	103.6	104.4	105.8
2004		107.5	109.1	112.0	113.9
2005		117.1	118.6	120.1	122.2
2006		123.2	128.9	128.4	125.8
JAPAN	8.3				
Total Goods					
1996		110.1	108.4	107.8	106.5
1997		104.6	103.2	102.7	101.0
1998		99.8	98.2	96.8	98.0
1999		98.2	98.2	98.6	99.6
2000		99.6	100.0	99.9	99.9
2001		99.4	98.6	97.8	97.0
2002		95.6	95.4	95.0	94.6
2003		94.4	94.2	93.8	94.7
2004		95.2	95.1	95.3	95.9
2005		95.9	95.8	95.8	95.2
2006		94.6	94.7	94.4	94.1
ASIAN NEWLY INDUSTRALIZED COUNTRIES[2]	6.1				
Total Goods					
1996		120.6	119.6	118.1	117.3
1997		116.6	115.3	113.8	111.3
1998		108.7	105.2	103.0	102.0
1999		101.3	100.8	100.7	100.8
2000		100.6	99.9	100.0	99.3
2001		97.3	96.4	95.2	93.8
2002		93.3	92.6	92.5	91.3
2003		91.2	91.5	91.7	90.9
2004		90.3	90.6	91.0	90.6
2005					
2006		88.8	89.2	89.3	89.1

[1]Based on 2005 trade values.
[2]The Asian Newly Industrialized Countries are Hong Kong, Korea, Singapore, and Taiwan.
. . . = Not available.

Table 7-15. U.S. International Price Indexes for Selected Transportation Services, 1996–2006

(2000 = 100.)

Category and year	March	June	September	December
AIR FREIGHT				
Import Air Freight				
1996	113.7	112.2	112.0	110.6
1997	104.1	104.5	102.5	100.1
1998	93.0	94.2	92.8	100.2
1999	101.5	98.7	100.6	102.8
2000	100.7	100.1	100.2	99.0
2001	98.9	96.0	95.9	95.6
2002	96.7	99.7	101.2	106.9
2003	110.2	111.5	116.8	114.9
2004	117.1	117.5	120.0	126.8
2005	128.6	128.4	129.7	128.9
2006	129.7	135.2	133.1	131.2
Export Air Freight				
1996	. . .	. . .	. . .	. . .
1997	111.1	110.4	109.0	105.4
1998	107.1	106.6	108.0	109.2
1999	102.1	102.5	100.8	99.1
2000	99.1	100.8	100.8	99.4
2001	99.7	98.4	98.6	97.9
2002	95.5	97.9	98.3	95.2
2003	96.3	95.2	95.1	95.4
2004	97.1	99.1	100.3	106.1
2005	106.4	110.1	110.9	112.0
2006	113.6	115.9	117.9	116.7
Inbound Air Freight				
1996	108.6	107.7	108.2	107.6
1997	101.3	101.8	100.3	97.9
1998	93.9	94.4	92.7	99.0
1999	99.6	97.6	99.5	102.8
2000	100.7	100.1	100.2	99.0
2001	97.9	95.1	94.9	95.1
2002	93.9	98.3	100.3	105.9
2003	108.8	109.4	112.5	112.9
2004	116.2	116.6	118.7	125.1
2005	126.3	125.6	127.5	124.6
2006	124.6	129.2	128.9	127.1
Outbound Air Freight				
1996	107.3	107.6	107.0	107.3
1997	108.0	107.3	107.7	105.7
1998	105.2	103.8	103.7	103.0
1999	100.3	100.4	100.3	99.2
2000	99.2	100.3	100.2	100.2
2001	100.1	98.0	97.6	97.8
2002	95.9	98.4	97.3	95.4
2003	97.2	95.4	95.5	94.9
2004	96.1	99.0	100.7	104.7
2005	103.8	107.2	112.4	112.0
2006	113.5	117.2	116.9	113.8

. . . = Not available.

Table 7-15. U.S. International Price Indexes for Selected Transportation Services, 1996–2006—*Continued*

(2000 = 100.)

Category and year	March	June	September	December
AIR PASSENGER FARES				
Import Air Passenger Fares				
1996	82.0	88.1	86.8	84.3
1997	84.7	95.5	94.0	88.0
1998	87.1	94.9	95.1	88.6
1999	87.5	98.9	99.5	89.7
2000	92.5	103.5	105.1	98.9
2001	101.1	112.8	116.4	105.7
2002	103.1	119.1	125.2	107.2
2003	108.6	122.3	125.9	107.0
2004	103.6	123.1	121.0	111.7
2005	110.0	128.1	124.0	116.3
2006	114.9	136.7	130.9	125.4
Export Air Passenger Fares				
1996	93.0	94.4	97.7	94.7
1997	85.3	97.7	95.0	87.4
1998	89.5	90.2	90.6	93.1
1999	95.5	96.8	100.6	98.6
2000	98.1	101.5	102.6	97.7
2001	99.6	100.4	102.5	98.4
2002	97.5	103.2	108.1	103.2
2003	108.4	117.0	118.0	118.4
2004	123.2	123.8	130.1	134.0
2005	136.3	136.2	139.5	128.3
2006	130.8	139.3	142.4	137.3
CRUDE OIL TANKER FREIGHT				
Inbound Crude Oil Tanker Freight				
1996	78.8	77.3	68.8	74.4
1997	79.7	80.3	72.7	76.7
1998	76.9	64.9	61.5	61.4
1999	55.4	53.0	53.0	57.7
2000	73.2	86.3	107.5	133.0
2001	119.3	96.7	74.3	72.4
2002	60.2	59.9	58.5	77.2
2003	133.2	101.9	73.7	90.2
2004	133.4	104.3	119.1	186.9
2005	130.7	116.8	99.8	154.8
2006	137.6	118.8	130.1	123.7
OCEAN LINER FREIGHT				
Inbound Ocean Liner Freight				
1996	71.9	70.5	69.4	69.7
1997	69.1	68.5	67.2	65.8
1998	65.9	73.1	74.4	73.8
1999	72.7	94.7	104.8	98.7
2000	96.6	101.3	101.1	101.0
2001	102.8	100.8	98.1	92.8
2002	91.7	90.3	93.5	93.3
2003	94.0	116.1	116.2	117.8
2004	119.1	121.1	120.3	122.7
2005	121.3	128.5	127.9	126.8
2006	125.4	114.9	114.2	114.0

Table 7-16. U.S. Export Price Indexes and Percent Change for Travel and Tourism Services, October 2006–October 2007

(December 2006 = 100.)

Category	Relative importance	Index		Percent change				
		September 2007	October 2007	October 2006 to October 2007	June 2006 to July 2007	July 2007 to August 2007	August 2007 to September 2007	September 2007 to October 2007
Total Export Travel and Tourism	100.000	106.3	107.5	. . .	-1.3	0.4	2.1	1.1
From Europe	39.567	106.7	108.3	. . .	-1.3	0.5	2.0	1.5
From Asia	32.125	106.0	106.6	. . .	-1.8	0.2	2.8	0.6
From Latin America/Caribbean	15.275	105.7	107.3	. . .	-1.1	0.2	1.7	1.5
From Canada	8.676	106.3	107.6	. . .	-0.1	0.1	1.3	1.2

. . . = Not available.

CHAPTER 8

CONSUMER EXPENDITURES

CONSUMER EXPENDITURES

HIGHLIGHTS

The principal objective of the Consumer Expenditure (CE) Survey is to collect information about the buying habits of American households. The survey breaks down expenditures for different demographic categories, such as income, age, family size, and geographic location. These data are used in a variety of government, business, and academic research projects and provide important weights for the periodic revisions of the Consumer Price Index (CPI).

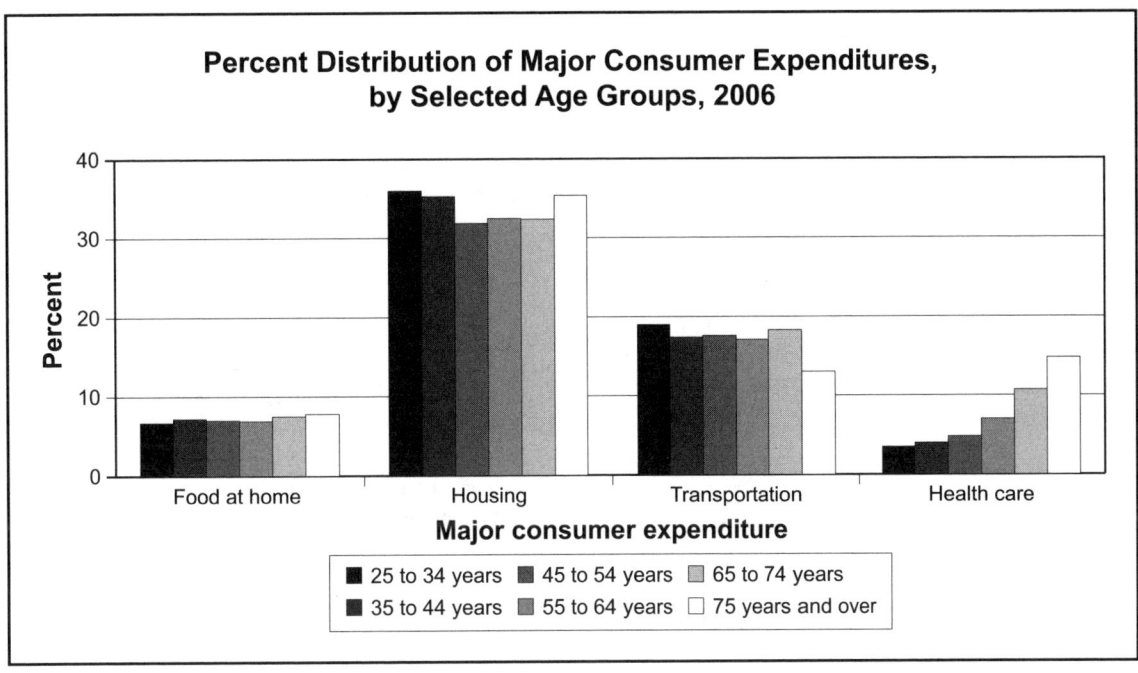

Percent Distribution of Major Consumer Expenditures, by Selected Age Groups, 2006

Legend:
- 25 to 34 years
- 35 to 44 years
- 45 to 54 years
- 55 to 64 years
- 65 to 74 years
- 75 years and over

Two obvious differences between the 75 years old and over age group and the other age groups are the decline in the share spent on transportation and the increase in the share spent on health care costs. Health care costs increase with every age group, rising from 3.5 percent for the 25- to 34-year-old age group to 14.8 percent for the 75 years old and over age group. (See Table 8-10.)

OTHER HIGHLIGHTS

- Average annual expenditures per household rose 4.3 percent in 2006, which was faster than the 3.2 percent increase in consumer prices. The increase in spending for housing—the largest component of total spending—was 7.9 percent, a significant factor in the total increase. (See Table 8-1.)

- Households in the highest income quintile (the top 20 percent of all earners) accounted for 38.9 percent of aggregate expenditures in 2006. (See Table 8-5.)

- The number of households that reported more that $150,000 in annual income increased over 40 percent from 2004 to 2006. (See Table 8-4.)

- Single women spent a higher proportion of income on health care than single men from 2005 to 2006 (8.0 percent compared to 4.6 percent) and less on transportation (13.6 percent compared to 16.6 percent). This is partly because single women included more elderly persons; the average age for single women was 57.6 years, compared to 46.8 years for single men. (See Tables 8-21 and 8-22.)

NOTES AND DEFINITIONS

Purpose, Collection, and Coverage

The buying habits of American consumers change over time because of changes in relative prices, real income, family size and composition, and other determinants of tastes and preferences. The introduction of new products into the marketplace and the emergence of new concepts in retailing also influence consumer buying habits. Data from the Consumer Expenditure Survey (CE), the only national survey that relates family expenditures to demographic characteristics, are of great importance to researchers. The survey data are also used to revise the Consumer Price Index market baskets and item samples.

Until the 1970s, the Bureau of Labor Statistics (BLS) conducted surveys of consumer expenditures approximately once every 10 years. The last such survey was conducted in 1972–1973. In late 1979, in a significant departure from previous methodology, BLS initiated a survey to be conducted on a continuous basis with rotating panels of respondents.

The current CE is similar to its 1972–1973 predecessor in that it consists of two separate components. Each component has its own questionnaire and sample: (1) the Interview Survey, in which an interviewer visits each consumer unit every three months for a twelve-month period; and (2) the Diary Survey, a record-keeping survey completed by other consumer units for two consecutive one-week periods. The Census Bureau, under contract to BLS, collects the data for both components of the survey. Beginning in 1999, the sample was increased from 5,000 to 7,500 households.

In 2003, the survey modified the questions on race and Hispanic origin to comply with the new standards for maintaining, collecting, and presenting federal data on race and ethnicity for federal statistical agencies. Beginning with the data collected in 2003, the CE tables use data collected from the new race and ethnicity questions. A number of new classifications were made with publication of the 2003 data.

Beginning with the publication of the 2004 tables, the CE has been implementing multiple imputations of income data. Prior to 2004, the CE only published income data collected from complete income reporters. The introduction of multiply imputed income data affects the published CE tables in several ways, because income data are now published for all consumer units (instead of for complete reporters only). The most obvious result of this change is seen on the tables showing expenditures categorized by income before taxes, including income by quintile. Starting with the 2004 data, columns describing income, expenditures, and characteristics for "total complete reporting" and "incomplete reporting of income" no longer appear in these tables, and the column entitled "all consumer units" appears on all income tables. Due to the implementation of income imputation, data for 2004 are not strictly com-

parable to those of prior years, especially for the income tables. Averages for demographic characteristics and annual expenditures will change due to differences between the incomplete and complete income reporters in these categories. Furthermore, certain expenditures (such as personal insurance and pensions) are computed using income data. As a result of imputation, average annual values for these expenditures may be substantially different in the 2004 CE tables than in tables for previous years. The regular flow of data resulting from this design substantially enhances the usefulness of the survey by providing more timely information on consumption patterns within different kinds of consumer units.

The *Interview Survey* is designed to collect data on the types of expenditures that respondents can be expected to recall after a period of three months or longer. These include relatively large expenditures (such as those for property, travel, automobiles, and major appliances) and expenditures that occur on a regular basis (such as those for rent, utilities, insurance premiums, and clothing). The interview also obtains "global estimates" of food expenditures for both food at home and food away from home. For food-at-home expenditures, respondents are asked to estimate their typical weekly spending at the grocery store and to determine how much money was spent on nonfood items. Nonfood spending is then subtracted from the total. Convenience and specialty stores are also included in the food-at-home estimates. The survey also collects data for approximately 95 percent of total expenditures. Excluded from the Interview Survey are nonprescription drugs, household supplies, and personal care products.

The *Diary Survey* is designed to collect data on expenditures for frequently purchased items that are more difficult to recall over longer periods of time. Respondents keep detailed records of expenses for food and beverages at home and meals in eating places away from home. Expenditures for tobacco, drugs (including nonprescription drugs), and personal care supplies and services are also collected in the Diary Survey.

Participants in both surveys record dollar amounts for goods and services purchased during the reporting period, regardless of whether payment was made at the time of purchase. Excluded from both surveys are business-related expenditures and expenditures for which the family is reimbursed. Information is collected on demographic and family characteristics at the initial interview for each survey.

The tables in this chapter present integrated data from the Diary Survey and the Interview Survey and provide a complete accounting of consumer expenditures and income, which neither survey component is designed to do alone. Data for some expenditure items are only collected in one of the surveys. For example, the Diary Survey does not collect data for expenditures on overnight travel or information on reimbursements, while the Interview

Survey records these purchases. Examples of expenditures for which reimbursements are netted out include those for medical care, auto repair, and construction, repairs, alterations, and maintenance of property.

For items unique to one survey or the other, the choice of which survey to use as the source of data is obvious. However, there is considerable overlap in coverage between the two surveys. Integrating the data thus presents the problem of determining the appropriate survey component. When data are available from both survey sources, the more reliable of the two (as determined by statistical methods) is selected. As a result, some items are selected from the Interview Survey and others are selected from the Diary Survey.

Research is underway to evaluate survey methodology; it is described in *Consumer Expenditure Survey Anthology, 2005*, which can be found on the BLS Web site at <http://www.bls.gov>.

Data Included in This Book

Data for single characteristics are for calendar year 2006, and data for two cross-classified characteristics are for an average of calendar years 2005 and 2006. Income values from the survey are derived from "complete income reporters" only. Complete income reporters are defined as consumer units that provide values for at least one of the major sources of their income: wages and salaries, self-employment income, retirement income, dividends and interest, and welfare benefits. Some consumer units are defined as complete income reporters, even though they may not have provided a full accounting of all income from all sources.

Consumer units are classified by quintiles of income before taxes, age of reference person, size of consumer unit, region, composition of consumer unit, number of earners in consumer unit, housing tenure, race, type of area (urban or rural), and occupation.

Concepts and Definitions

A *consumer unit* comprises either (1) all members of a particular household related by blood, marriage, adoption, or other legal arrangements; (2) a person living alone, sharing a household with others, living as a roomer in a private home or lodging house or in permanent living quarters in a hotel or motel, but who is financially independent; or (3) two or more persons living together who pool their income to make joint expenditure decisions. Financial independence is determined by the three major expense categories: housing, food, and other living expenses. To be considered financially independent, at least two of the three major expense categories have to be provided by the respondent. The terms "family," "household," and "consumer unit" are used interchangeably in descriptions of the CE.

The *householder or reference person* is the first member of the consumer unit mentioned by the respondent as owner or renter of the premises at the time of the initial interview.

Total expenditures include the transaction costs, including excise and sales taxes of goods and services acquired during the interview period. Estimates include expenditures for gifts and contributions and payments for pensions and personal insurance.

An *earner* is a consumer unit member, 14 years of age or over, who reported having worked at least 1 week during the 12 months prior to the interview date.

Sources of Additional Information

More extensive descriptions and tables can be found in an updated version of Chapter 16 in the *BLS Handbook of Methods* and in an anthology of articles relating to consumer expenditures. These resources can be found on the BLS Web site at <http://www.bls.gov>.

Table 8-1. Consumer Expenditures, Annual Average of All Consumer Units, 1996–2006

(Number, dollar, percent.)

Item	1996	1997	1998	1999	2000	2001	2002	2003	2004	2005	2006
NUMBER OF CONSUMER UNITS (THOUSANDS)	104 212	105 576	107 182	108 465	109 367	110 339	112 108	115 356	116 282	117 356	118 843
CONSUMER UNIT CHARACTERISTICS											
Income Before Taxes	38 014	39 926	41 622	43 951	44 649	47 507	49 430	51 128	54 453	58 712	60 533
Age of Reference Person	47.7	47.7	47.6	47.9	48.2	48.1	48.1	48.0	48.5	48.6	48.7
Average Number in Consumer Unit											
All persons	2.5	2.5	2.5	2.5	2.5	2.5	2.5	2.5	2.5	2.5	2.5
Children under 18 years	0.7	0.7	0.7	0.7	0.7	0.7	0.7	0.6	0.6	0.6	0.6
Persons 65 years and over	0.3	0.3	0.3	0.3	0.3	0.3	0.3	0.3	0.3	0.3	0.3
Earners	1.3	1.3	1.3	1.3	1.4	1.4	1.4	1.3	1.3	1.3	1.3
Vehicles	1.9	2.0	2.0	1.9	1.9	1.9	2.0	1.9	1.9	2.0	1.9
Percent Homeowner	64	64	64	65	66	66	66	67	68	67	67
With mortgage	38	38	39	38	39	40	41	41	42	43	43
Without mortgage	26	26	26	27	27	26	26	26	25	25	24
AVERAGE ANNUAL EXPENDITURES	33 797	34 819	35 535	36 995	38 045	39 518	40 677	40 817	43 395	46 409	48 398
Food	4 698	4 801	4 810	5 031	5 158	5 321	5 375	5 340	5 781	5 931	6 111
Food at home	2 876	2 880	2 780	2 915	3 021	3 086	3 099	3 129	3 347	3 297	3 417
Cereals and bakery products	447	453	425	448	453	452	450	442	461	445	446
Meats, poultry, fish, and eggs	447	453	425	448	453	452	798	825	880	764	797
Dairy products	312	314	301	322	325	332	328	328	371	378	368
Fruits and vegetables	490	476	472	500	521	522	552	535	561	552	592
Other food at home	889	895	858	896	927	952	970	999	1 075	1 158	1 212
Food away from home	1 823	1 921	2 030	2 116	2 137	2 235	2 276	2 211	2 434	2 634	2 694
Alcoholic Beverages	309	309	309	318	372	349	376	391	459	426	497
Housing	10 747	11 272	11 713	12 057	12 319	13 011	13 283	13 432	13 918	15 167	16 366
Shelter	6 064	6 344	6 680	7 016	7 114	7 602	7 829	7 887	7 998	8 805	9 673
Owned dwellings	3 783	3 935	4 245	4 525	4 602	4 979	5 165	5 263	5 324	5 958	6 516
Rented dwellings	1 864	1 983	1 978	2 027	2 034	2 134	2 160	2 179	2 201	2 345	2 590
Other lodging	417	426	458	465	478	489	505	445	473	502	567
Utilities, fuels, and public services	2 347	2 412	2 405	2 377	2 489	2 767	2 684	2 811	2 927	3 183	3 397
Household operations	522	548	546	666	684	676	706	707	753	801	948
Housekeeping supplies	464	455	482	498	482	509	545	529	594	611	640
Household furnishings and equipment	1 350	1 512	1 601	1 499	1 549	1 458	1 518	1 497	1 646	1 767	1 708
Apparel and Services	1 752	1 729	1 674	1 743	1 856	1 743	1 749	1 640	1 816	1 886	1 874
Transportation	6 382	6 457	6 616	7 011	7 417	7 633	7 759	7 781	7 801	8 344	8 508
Vehicle purchases (net outlay)	2 815	2 736	2 964	3 305	3 418	3 579	3 665	3 732	3 397	3 544	3 421
Gasoline and motor oil	1 082	1 098	1 017	1 055	1 291	1 279	1 235	1 333	1 598	2 013	2 227
Other vehicle expenses	2 058	2 230	2 206	2 254	2 281	2 375	2 471	2 331	2 365	2 339	2 355
Public transportation	427	393	429	397	427	400	389	385	441	448	505
Health Care	1 770	1 841	1 903	1 959	2 066	2 182	2 350	2 416	2 574	2 664	2 766
Health insurance	827	881	913	923	983	1 061	1 168	1 252	1 332	1 361	1 465
Medical services	543	531	542	558	568	573	590	591	648	677	670
Drugs	303	320	346	370	416	449	487	467	480	521	514
Medical supplies	97	108	102	109	99	100	105	107	114	105	117
Entertainment	1 834	1 813	1 746	1 891	1 863	1 953	2 079	2 060	2 218	2 388	2 376
Personal Care Products and Services	513	528	401	408	564	465	526	527	581	541	585
Reading	159	164	161	159	146	141	139	127	130	126	117
Education	524	571	580	635	632	648	752	783	905	940	888
Tobacco Products and Smoking Supplies	255	264	273	300	319	308	320	290	288	319	327
Miscellaneous	855	847	860	867	776	750	792	606	690	808	846
Cash Contributions	940	1 001	1 109	1 181	1 192	1 258	1 277	1 370	1 408	1 663	1 869
Personal Insurance and Pensions	3 060	3 223	3 381	3 436	3 365	3 737	3 899	4 055	4 823	5 204	5 270
Life and other personal insurance	353	379	398	394	399	410	406	397	390	381	322
Pensions and Social Security	2 707	2 844	2 982	3 042	2 966	3 326	3 493	3 658	4 433	4 823	4 948

Table 8-2. Shares of Annual Average Consumer Expenditures and Characteristics of All Consumer Units, 1996–2006

(Number, dollar, percent.)

Item	1996	1997	1998	1999	2000	2001	2002	2003	2004	2005	2006
NUMBER OF CONSUMER UNITS (THOUSANDS)	104 212	105 576	107 182	108 465	109 367	110 339	112 108	115 356	116 282	117 356	118 843
CONSUMER UNIT CHARACTERISTICS											
Income Before Taxes	38 014	39 926	41 622	43 951	44 649	47 507	49 430	51 128	54 453	58 712	60 533
Age of Reference Person	47.7	47.7	47.6	47.9	48.2	48.1	48.1	48.4	48.5	48.6	48.7
Average Number in Consumer Unit											
All persons	2.5	2.5	2.5	2.5	2.5	2.5	2.5	2.5	2.5	2.5	2.5
Children under 18 years	0.7	0.7	0.7	0.7	0.7	0.7	0.7	0.6	0.6	0.6	0.6
Persons 65 years and over	0.3	0.3	0.3	0.3	0.3	0.3	0.3	0.3	0.3	0.3	0.3
Earners	1.3	1.3	1.3	1.3	1.4	1.4	1.4	1.3	1.3	1.3	1.3
Vehicles	1.9	2.0	2.0	1.9	1.9	1.9	2.0	1.9	1.9	2.0	1.9
Percent Homeowner	64	64	64	65	66	66	66	67	68	67	67
With mortgage	38	38	39	38	39	40	41	41	42	43	43
Without mortgage	26	26	26	27	27	26	26	26	25	25	24
AVERAGE ANNUAL EXPENDITURES	33 797	34 819	35 535	36 995	38 045	39 518	40 677	40 817	43 395	46 409	48 398
Food	13.9	13.8	13.5	13.6	13.6	13.5	13.2	13.1	13.3	12.8	12.6
Food at home	8.5	8.3	7.8	7.9	7.9	7.8	7.6	7.7	7.7	7.1	7.1
Cereals and bakery products	1.3	1.3	1.2	1.2	1.2	1.1	1.1	1.1	1.1	1.0	0.9
Meats, poultry, fish, and eggs	2.2	2.1	2.0	2.0	2.1	2.1	2.0	2.0	2.0	1.6	1.6
Dairy products	0.9	0.9	0.8	0.9	0.9	0.8	0.8	0.8	0.9	0.8	0.8
Fruits and vegetables	1.4	1.4	1.3	1.4	1.4	1.3	1.4	1.3	1.3	1.2	1.2
Other food at home	2.6	2.6	2.4	2.4	2.4	2.4	2.4	2.4	2.5	2.5	2.5
Food away from home	5.4	5.5	5.7	5.7	5.6	5.7	5.6	5.4	5.6	5.7	5.6
Alcoholic Beverages	0.9	0.9	0.9	0.9	1.0	0.9	0.9	1.0	1.1	0.9	1.0
Housing	31.8	32.4	33.0	32.6	32.4	32.9	32.7	32.9	32.1	32.7	33.8
Shelter	17.9	18.2	18.8	19.0	18.7	19.2	19.2	19.3	18.4	19.0	20.0
Owned dwellings	11.2	11.3	11.9	12.2	12.1	12.6	12.7	12.9	12.3	12.8	13.5
Rented dwellings	5.5	5.7	5.6	5.5	5.3	5.4	5.3	5.3	5.1	5.1	5.4
Other lodging	1.2	1.2	1.3	1.3	1.3	1.2	1.2	1.1	1.1	1.1	1.2
Utilities, fuels, and public services	6.9	6.9	6.8	6.4	6.5	7.0	6.6	6.9	6.7	6.9	7.0
Household operations	1.5	1.6	1.5	1.8	1.8	1.7	1.7	1.7	1.7	1.7	2.0
Housekeeping supplies	1.4	1.3	1.4	1.3	1.3	1.3	1.3	1.3	1.4	1.3	1.3
Household furnishings and equipment	4.0	4.3	4.5	4.1	4.1	3.7	3.7	3.7	3.8	3.8	3.5
Apparel and Services	5.2	5.0	4.7	4.7	4.9	4.4	4.3	4.0	4.2	4.1	3.9
Transportation	18.9	18.5	18.6	19.0	19.5	19.3	19.1	19.1	18.0	18.0	17.6
Vehicle purchases (net outlay)	8.3	7.9	8.3	8.9	9.0	9.1	9.0	9.1	7.8	7.6	7.1
Gasoline and motor oil	3.2	3.2	2.9	2.9	3.4	3.2	3.0	3.3	3.7	4.3	4.6
Other vehicle expenses	6.1	6.4	6.2	6.1	6.0	6.0	6.1	5.7	5.5	5.0	4.9
Public transportation	1.3	1.1	1.2	1.1	1.1	1.0	1.0	0.9	1.0	1.0	1.0
Health Care	5.2	5.3	5.4	5.3	5.4	5.5	5.8	5.9	5.9	5.7	5.7
Health insurance	2.4	2.5	2.6	2.5	2.6	2.7	2.9	3.1	3.1	2.9	3.0
Medical services	1.6	1.5	1.5	1.5	1.5	1.4	1.5	1.4	1.5	1.5	1.4
Drugs	0.9	0.9	1.0	1.0	1.1	1.1	1.2	1.1	1.1	1.1	1.1
Medical supplies	0.3	0.3	0.3	0.3	0.3	0.3	0.3	0.3	0.3	0.2	0.2
Entertainment	5.4	5.2	4.9	5.1	4.9	4.9	5.1	5.0	5.1	5.1	4.9
Personal Care Products and Services	1.5	1.5	1.1	1.1	1.5	1.2	1.3	1.3	1.3	1.2	1.2
Reading	0.5	0.5	0.5	0.4	0.4	0.4	0.3	0.3	0.3	0.3	0.2
Education	1.6	1.6	1.6	1.7	1.7	1.6	1.8	1.9	2.1	2.0	1.8
Tobacco Products and Smoking Supplies	0.8	0.8	0.8	0.8	0.8	0.8	0.8	0.7	0.7	0.7	0.7
Miscellaneous	2.5	2.4	2.4	2.3	2.0	1.9	1.9	1.5	1.6	1.7	1.7
Cash Contributions	2.8	2.9	3.1	3.2	3.1	3.2	3.1	3.4	3.2	3.6	3.9
Personal Insurance and Pensions	9.1	9.3	9.5	9.3	8.8	9.5	9.6	9.9	11.1	11.2	10.9
Life and other personal insurance	1.0	1.1	1.1	1.1	1.0	1.0	1.0	1.0	0.9	0.8	0.7
Pensions and Social Security	8.0	8.2	8.4	8.2	7.8	8.4	8.6	9.0	10.2	10.4	10.2

Table 8-3. Consumer Expenditures, Averages by Income Before Taxes, 2006

(Number, dollar, percent.)

Item	All consumer units	Less than $5,000	$5,000 to $9,999	$10,000 to $14,999	$15,000 to $19,999	$20,000 to $29,999	$30,000 to $39,999	$40,000 to $49,999	$50,000 to $69,999	$70,000 and over
NUMBER OF CONSUMER UNITS (THOUSANDS)	118 843	4 572	6 247	7 585	7 671	14 232	13 304	11 446	17 674	36 112
CONSUMER UNIT CHARACTERISTICS										
Income Before Taxes	60 533	439	8 006	12 551	17 462	24 905	34 685	44 620	59 253	125 688
Income After Taxes	58 101	316	8 019	12 630	17 411	24 743	33 916	43 573	57 358	119 298
Age of Reference Person	48.7	43.2	50.7	56.9	56.1	51.1	48.2	47.5	46.6	46.4
Average Number in Consumer Unit										
All persons	2.5	1.6	1.6	1.7	1.9	2.2	2.3	2.5	2.8	3.0
Children under 18 years	0.6	0.3	0.3	0.4	0.4	0.6	0.6	0.6	0.7	0.8
Persons 65 years and over	0.3	0.2	0.3	0.5	0.5	0.5	0.3	0.3	0.2	0.2
Earners	1.3	0.5	0.5	0.5	0.6	0.9	1.2	1.4	1.6	2.0
Vehicles	1.9	0.8	0.7	1.0	1.2	1.5	1.7	1.9	2.3	2.8
Percent Distribution										
Male	46	41	34	34	38	40	45	48	49	53
Female	54	59	66	66	62	60	55	52	51	47
Percent Homeowner	67	36	32	47	53	55	60	68	75	88
With mortgage	43	14	8	11	17	22	34	42	54	71
Without mortgage	24	22	24	35	37	33	27	26	21	17
AVERAGE ANNUAL EXPENDITURES	48 398	20 709	16 751	20 612	24 422	29 042	35 108	39 573	50 086	82 294
Food	6 111	3 049	2 860	3 099	3 631	4 136	4 689	5 330	6 496	9 300
Food at home	3 417	1 802	1 894	2 159	2 476	2 605	2 719	3 061	3 603	4 798
Cereals and bakery products	446	239	248	277	319	357	346	406	463	627
Meats, poultry, fish, and eggs	797	485	466	525	613	623	634	723	814	1 103
Dairy products	368	188	203	233	259	275	318	333	406	503
Fruits and vegetables	592	293	328	378	428	471	462	537	597	841
Other food at home	1 212	597	649	747	857	878	959	1 061	1 322	1 724
Food away from home	2 694	1 246	966	940	1 155	1 531	1 970	2 269	2 892	4 502
Alcoholic Beverages	497	220	192	202	227	254	384	427	505	833
Housing	16 366	8 037	7 047	8 176	9 408	10 755	12 289	13 970	16 635	26 495
Shelter	9 673	5 037	4 221	4 699	5 399	6 297	7 311	8 057	9 706	15 853
Owned dwellings	6 516	2 024	1 212	1 596	2 232	2 929	3 837	4 752	6 525	12 902
Rented dwellings	2 590	2 742	2 906	2 998	3 020	3 227	3 255	2 999	2 761	1 629
Other lodging	567	272	103	106	147	140	220	306	420	1 322
Utilities, fuels, and public services	3 397	1 827	1 811	2 201	2 531	2 763	2 972	3 275	3 747	4 579
Household operations	948	307	217	361	394	405	513	696	797	1 923
Housekeeping supplies	640	297	379	288	356	409	472	531	667	1 003
Household furnishings and equipment	1 708	570	419	627	729	881	1 021	1 410	1 717	3 137
Apparel and Services	1 874	1 255	883	670	860	1 133	1 297	1 573	1 981	3 078
Transportation	8 508	3 206	2 107	3 299	3 572	5 067	6 770	6 844	9 423	14 500
Vehicle purchases (net outlay)	3 421	1 161	485	1 261	961	1 866	2 781	2 229	3 597	6 331
Gasoline and motor oil	2 227	966	794	980	1 278	1 580	1 897	2 147	2 599	3 319
Other vehicle expenses	2 355	882	667	890	1 107	1 427	1 811	2 193	2 728	3 837
Public transportation	505	197	162	167	225	193	280	275	499	1 013
Health Care	2 766	1 041	948	1 738	2 221	2 411	2 498	2 616	3 006	3 791
Health insurance	1 465	526	488	1 000	1 264	1 335	1 346	1 465	1 629	1 908
Medical services	670	270	197	302	408	476	560	580	676	1 079
Drugs	514	198	232	372	471	508	502	461	588	622
Medical supplies	117	47	31	64	78	92	90	110	114	182
Entertainment	2 376	856	765	833	1 103	1 158	1 579	1 864	2 344	4 371
Personal Care Products and Services	585	230	201	256	346	355	450	481	629	949
Reading	117	48	41	55	65	71	80	99	116	201
Education	888	1 046	441	462	240	285	398	412	681	1 838
Tobacco Products and Smoking Supplies	327	239	265	243	302	331	383	364	382	311
Miscellaneous	846	544	330	515	412	559	572	584	871	1 412
Cash Contributions	1 869	482	359	547	1 222	961	1 181	1 280	1 743	3 580
Personal Insurance and Pensions	5 270	456	311	517	813	1 564	2 537	3 729	5 275	11 635
Life and other personal insurance	322	75	79	108	129	168	171	235	314	629
Pensions and Social Security	4 948	381	232	409	684	1 396	2 365	3 494	4 961	11 005

Table 8-4. Consumer Expenditures, Averages by Higher Income Before Taxes, 2006

(Number, dollar, percent.)

Item	All consumer units	Less than $70,000	$70,000 to $79,000	$80,000 to $99,999	$100,000 and over	$100,000 to $119,000	$120,000 to $149,999	$150,000 and over
NUMBER OF CONSUMER UNITS (THOUSANDS)	118 843	82 730	6 956	10 241	18 915	6 300	5 357	7 258
CONSUMER UNIT CHARACTERISTICS								
Income Before Taxes	60 533	32 093	74 647	88 763	164 452	108 417	132 682	236 545
Income After Taxes	58 101	31 388	72 173	85 269	155 055	103 684	126 314	220 861
Age of Reference Person	48.7	49.7	45.5	46.2	46.9	46.1	46.3	48.1
Average Number in Consumer Unit								
All persons	2.5	2.2	2.8	3.0	3.2	3.2	3.1	3.2
Children under 18 years	0.6	0.6	0.7	0.7	0.8	0.9	0.8	0.9
Persons 65 years and over	0.3	0.4	0.2	0.2	0.2	0.1	0.2	0.2
Earners	1.3	1.1	1.8	1.9	2.1	2.1	2.1	2.0
Vehicles	1.9	1.6	2.5	2.7	2.9	2.7	2.9	3.1
Percent Distribution								
Male	46	43	53	52	54	54	55	53
Female	54	57	47	48	46	46	45	47
Percent Homeowner	67	58	82	85	92	89	92	95
With mortgage	43	31	64	67	76	75	78	77
Without mortgage	24	28	18	18	16	14	14	18
AVERAGE ANNUAL EXPENDITURES	48 398	33 490	57 352	65 810	100 386	78 129	88 647	128 681
Food	6 111	4 660	7 094	8 491	10 547	9 310	10 159	12 029
Food at home	3 417	2 784	3 977	4 482	5 269	4 875	5 169	5 736
Cereals and bakery products	446	364	515	605	680	607	706	733
Meats, poultry, fish, and eggs	797	657	970	1 054	1 179	1 184	1 112	1 224
Dairy products	368	307	419	472	551	499	557	597
Fruits and vegetables	592	479	665	733	963	802	971	1 117
Other food at home	1 212	978	1 408	1 618	1 897	1 782	1 823	2 065
Food away from home	2 694	1 875	3 118	4 009	5 278	4 435	4 990	6 293
Alcoholic Beverages	497	344	562	600	1 059	905	781	1 419
Housing	16 366	11 927	18 832	21 242	32 157	24 337	28 672	41 579
Shelter	9 673	6 976	11 260	12 565	19 323	14 564	17 280	24 963
Owned dwellings	6 516	3 729	8 675	9 870	16 098	11 787	14 715	20 861
Rented dwellings	2 590	3 009	2 074	1 957	1 288	1 622	1 150	1 101
Other lodging	567	238	511	738	1 937	1 155	1 415	3 000
Utilities, fuels, and public services	3 397	2 881	3 921	4 088	5 087	4 525	4 865	5 738
Household operations	948	522	975	1 274	2 623	1 523	1 928	4 090
Housekeeping supplies	640	473	722	953	1 134	940	1 039	1 399
Household furnishings and equipment	1 708	1 075	1 953	2 362	3 990	2 784	3 560	5 388
Apparel and Services	1 874	1 331	2 035	2 405	3 824	2 775	3 596	4 983
Transportation	8 508	5 891	10 921	12 206	17 059	13 601	15 661	21 097
Vehicle purchases (net outlay)	3 421	2 151	4 322	5 155	7 706	5 502	6 805	10 284
Gasoline and motor oil	2 227	1 751	2 909	3 138	3 568	3 318	3 598	3 763
Other vehicle expenses	2 355	1 707	3 115	3 229	4 432	3 732	4 206	5 209
Public transportation	505	282	574	684	1 353	1 049	1 052	1 841
Health Care	2 766	2 318	3 216	3 345	4 244	3 699	3 889	4 984
Health insurance	1 465	1 272	1 727	1 669	2 104	1 983	2 005	2 282
Medical services	670	492	879	947	1 224	946	971	1 654
Drugs	514	466	499	588	685	603	699	748
Medical supplies	117	88	111	141	231	166	214	300
Entertainment	2 376	1 500	2 804	3 225	5 568	4 187	4 434	7 606
Personal Care Products and Services	585	422	747	794	1 107	915	1 054	1 322
Reading	117	80	137	160	247	191	228	309
Education	888	472	843	1 050	2 631	1 704	1 907	3 974
Tobacco Products and Smoking Supplies	327	334	363	348	271	319	290	216
Miscellaneous	846	599	957	1 065	1 768	1 381	1 379	2 390
Cash Contributions	1 869	1 122	1 931	2 171	4 949	3 904	3 208	7 141
Personal Insurance and Pensions	5 270	2 491	6 910	8 709	14 956	10 903	13 388	19 633
Life and other personal insurance	322	188	373	453	819	571	568	1 218
Pensions and Social Security	4 948	2 303	6 537	8 256	14 138	10 332	12 819	18 415

Table 8-5. Consumer Expenditures, Averages by Quintiles of Income Before Taxes, 2006

(Number, dollar, percent.)

Item	All consumer units	Lowest 20 percent	Second 20 percent	Third 20 percent	Fourth 20 percent	Highest 20 percent
NUMBER OF CONSUMER UNITS (THOUSANDS)	118 843	23 738	23 773	23 765	23 770	23 796
CONSUMER UNIT CHARACTERISTICS						
Income Before Taxes	60 533	9 974	26 657	44 933	70 975	149 963
Income After Taxes	58 101	9 969	26 346	43 799	68 497	141 738
Age of Reference Person	48.7	52.3	50.9	47.4	46.1	46.9
Average Number in Consumer Unit						
All persons	2.5	1.7	2.2	2.5	2.8	3.1
Children under 18 years	0.6	0.4	0.5	0.6	0.7	0.8
Persons 65 years and over	0.3	0.4	0.4	0.3	0.2	0.2
Earners	1.3	0.5	1.0	1.4	1.8	2.1
Vehicles	1.9	0.9	1.5	1.9	2.5	2.9
Percent Distribution						
Male	46	36	42	47	51	54
Female	54	64	58	53	49	46
Percent Homeowner	67	42	56	67	80	91
With mortgage	43	13	24	42	62	75
Without mortgage	24	30	32	25	18	17
AVERAGE ANNUAL EXPENDITURES	48 398	20 410	30 224	41 431	55 697	94 150
Food	6 111	3 193	4 307	5 614	7 195	10 243
Food at home	3 417	2 138	2 647	3 210	3 903	5 186
Cereals and bakery products	446	276	354	413	516	673
Meats, poultry, fish, and eggs	797	532	631	749	902	1 172
Dairy products	368	227	291	358	426	540
Fruits and vegetables	592	370	464	547	649	933
Other food at home	1 212	733	907	1 144	1 410	1 867
Food away from home	2 694	1 055	1 660	2 404	3 292	5 058
Alcoholic Beverages	497	213	294	474	534	971
Housing	16 366	8 128	10 973	14 204	18 428	30 071
Shelter	9 673	4 805	6 405	8 269	10 847	18 025
Owned dwellings	6 516	1 719	3 003	4 928	7 949	14 968
Rented dwellings	2 590	2 946	3 240	3 032	2 369	1 363
Other lodging	567	140	162	310	529	1 694
Utilities, fuels, and public services	3 397	2 090	2 782	3 307	3 901	4 902
Household operations	948	310	443	668	916	2 398
Housekeeping supplies	640	331	437	552	779	1 097
Household furnishings and equipment	1 708	591	906	1 406	1 985	3 649
Apparel and Services	1 874	845	1 193	1 680	2 101	3 548
Transportation	8 508	3 038	5 277	7 662	10 120	16 426
Vehicle purchases (net outlay)	3 421	987	1 954	2 940	3 774	7 442
Gasoline and motor oil	2 227	991	1 624	2 182	2 829	3 508
Other vehicle expenses	2 355	879	1 489	2 188	2 968	4 248
Public transportation	505	182	211	352	549	1 228
Health Care	2 766	1 485	2 456	2 647	3 154	4 086
Health insurance	1 465	817	1 347	1 446	1 677	2 036
Medical services	670	290	504	602	776	1 179
Drugs	514	321	520	487	582	658
Medical supplies	117	57	85	112	119	213
Entertainment	2 376	879	1 271	1 898	2 720	5 105
Personal Care Products and Services	585	262	385	513	713	1 050
Reading	117	51	73	98	131	232
Education	888	505	295	477	879	2 281
Tobacco Products and Smoking Supplies	327	266	345	367	374	282
Miscellaneous	846	454	510	674	939	1 652
Cash Contributions	1 869	573	1 117	1 412	1 834	4 403
Personal Insurance and Pensions	5 270	517	1 728	3 712	6 577	13 800
Life and other personal insurance	322	97	164	227	370	752
Pensions and Social Security	4 948	420	1 564	3 485	6 207	13 048

Table 8-6. Consumer Expenditures, Averages by Occupation of Reference Person, 2006

(Number, dollar, percent.)

Item	Self-employed workers	Wage and salary earners						Retired	All others, including those not reporting
		Total wage and salary earners	Managers and professional workers	Technical sales and clerical workers	Service workers	Construction workers and mechanics	Operators, fabricators, and laborers		
NUMBER OF CONSUMER UNITS (THOUSANDS)	5 491	78 242	29 597	21 770	12 796	4 868	9 212	20 186	14 923
CONSUMER UNIT CHARACTERISTICS									
Income Before Taxes	87 362	69 402	94 686	61 161	46 562	54 552	47 220	32 411	42 202
Income After Taxes	84 756	66 298	89 254	59 000	45 449	52 441	46 074	31 613	41 144
Age of Reference Person	47.8	42.9	44.4	42.4	41.8	40.5	42.4	73.7	45.5
Average Number in Consumer Unit									
All persons	2.7	2.6	2.5	2.5	2.7	2.7	2.7	1.7	2.8
Children under 18 years	0.7	0.7	0.7	0.7	0.8	0.8	0.8	0.1	0.9
Persons 65 years and over	0.2	0.1	0.1	0.1	0.1	0.1	0.1	1.2	0.2
Earners	1.8	1.7	1.7	1.7	1.7	1.7	1.7	0.2	0.7
Vehicles	2.1	2.1	2.2	2.0	1.8	2.3	2.1	1.6	1.6
Percent Distribution									
Male	62	50	49	38	43	93	71	41	25
Female	38	50	51	62	57	7	29	59	75
Percent Homeowner	74	66	76	63	53	61	58	81	56
With mortgage	51	51	61	48	38	47	41	19	33
Without mortgage	23	15	15	14	15	13	17	62	23
AVERAGE ANNUAL EXPENDITURES	62 226	52 938	67 541	49 056	38 717	45 382	39 193	33 858	39 375
Food	7 752	6 582	7 758	6 303	5 396	6 162	5 430	4 312	5 577
Food at home	4 255	3 509	3 943	3 323	3 112	3 298	3 259	2 704	3 613
Cereals and bakery products	547	456	525	437	379	410	412	363	476
Meats, poultry, fish, and eggs	1 019	811	841	779	750	801	873	633	870
Dairy products	446	378	433	364	314	366	333	293	394
Fruits and vegetables	804	596	707	535	537	559	507	513	606
Other food at home	1 439	1 268	1 437	1 208	1 131	1 162	1 134	902	1 266
Food away from home	3 497	3 073	3 814	2 980	2 284	2 864	2 170	1 609	1 965
Alcoholic Beverages	716	570	760	504	367	527	427	308	311
Housing	19 419	17 781	22 646	16 519	13 561	14 674	12 707	11 483	14 445
Shelter	11 356	10 703	13 853	9 715	8 178	8 824	7 418	5 957	8 682
Owned dwellings	8 177	7 319	10 405	6 402	4 501	5 635	4 374	4 031	5 059
Rented dwellings	2 329	2 765	2 447	2 786	3 391	2 885	2 807	1 523	3 209
Other lodging	849	619	1 001	527	286	303	236	404	413
Utilities, fuels, and public services	3 870	3 503	3 900	3 408	3 102	3 328	3 102	3 008	3 193
Household operations	1 096	1 074	1 538	1 054	608	568	543	663	617
Housekeeping supplies	1 001	642	823	604	502	434	485	595	561
Household furnishings and equipment	2 095	1 859	2 531	1 739	1 171	1 520	1 160	1 260	1 392
Apparel and Services	2 336	2 095	2 587	1 960	1 599	1 816	1 695	970	1 801
Transportation	10 006	9 551	11 398	9 326	7 210	8 930	7 742	5 617	6 399
Vehicle purchases (net outlay)	3 895	3 891	4 660	3 966	2 814	3 471	2 966	2 286	2 314
Gasoline and motor oil	2 717	2 489	2 698	2 410	2 136	2 657	2 405	1 353	1 859
Other vehicle expenses	2 758	2 627	3 185	2 504	1 945	2 480	2 155	1 573	1 841
Public transportation	636	544	855	446	315	322	216	405	384
Health Care	3 249	2 421	2 981	2 376	1 793	1 988	1 829	4 305	2 321
Health insurance	1 608	1 253	1 496	1 302	928	1 024	931	2 513	1 105
Medical services	966	644	833	578	450	598	486	713	644
Drugs	543	411	492	401	343	292	334	923	489
Medical supplies	133	113	160	96	73	75	78	155	84
Entertainment	3 026	2 629	3 541	2 397	1 690	2 256	1 764	1 625	1 828
Personal Care Products and Services	725	635	836	607	491	393	405	457	451
Reading	155	117	175	104	66	64	62	133	81
Education	1 082	1 026	1 602	862	604	440	462	235	974
Tobacco Products and Smoking Supplies	359	344	238	351	368	527	538	194	404
Miscellaneous	1 207	872	1 112	786	612	878	654	824	608
Cash Contributions	2 742	1 817	2 656	1 403	1 012	1 558	1 355	2 331	1 194
Personal Insurance and Pensions	9 452	6 498	9 250	5 557	3 948	5 169	4 122	1 064	2 981
Life and other personal insurance	450	340	487	297	208	206	224	273	248
Pensions and Social Security	9 002	6 158	8 763	5 260	3 740	4 963	3 898	791	2 733

Table 8-7. Consumer Expenditures, Averages by Number of Earners, 2006

(Number, dollar, percent.)

Item	Single consumer		Consumer units of two or more persons			
	No earner	One earner	No earner	One earner	Two earners	Three or more earners
NUMBER OF CONSUMER UNITS (THOUSANDS)	13 017	22 205	10 000	24 022	39 222	10 377
CONSUMER UNIT CHARACTERISTICS						
Income Before Taxes	16 195	40 562	29 936	55 796	86 421	101 491
Income After Taxes	15 863	38 216	29 380	54 059	82 615	98 014
Age of Reference Person	68.7	43.1	65.3	46.9	42.9	46.1
Average Number in Consumer Unit						
All persons	1.0	1.0	2.3	3.0	3.0	4.4
Children under 18 years	X	X	0.4	1.1	0.9	1.0
Persons 65 years and over	0.7	0.1	1.2	0.3	0.1	0.1
Earners	X	1.0	X	1.0	2.0	3.3
Vehicles	0.8	1.2	1.7	1.9	2.5	3.2
Percent Distribution						
Male	32	53	45	41	49	48
Female	68	47	55	59	51	52
Percent Homeowner	57	49	78	68	75	81
With mortgage	10	33	20	43	60	64
Without mortgage	47	15	58	24	15	17
AVERAGE ANNUAL EXPENDITURES	21 694	33 939	35 594	48 901	62 364	71 597
Food	2 415	3 771	5 253	6 560	7 687	9 820
Food at home	1 616	1 798	3 440	3 912	4 061	5 640
Cereals and bakery products	223	225	471	500	541	701
Meats, poultry, fish, and eggs	345	380	844	944	924	1 428
Dairy products	182	191	359	426	445	575
Fruits and vegetables	307	306	623	675	693	979
Other food at home	559	695	1 142	1 367	1 458	1 958
Food away from home	798	1 973	1 813	2 648	3 626	4 179
Alcoholic Beverages	186	579	363	374	620	707
Housing	8 572	12 533	12 276	17 217	20 489	20 731
Shelter	5 144	8 384	6 107	9 940	12 058	11 918
Owned dwellings	2 325	4 428	4 074	6 566	9 014	9 037
Rented dwellings	2 660	3 572	1 618	2 741	2 306	2 059
Other lodging	159	383	415	633	738	822
Utilities, fuels, and public services	2 087	2 192	3 296	3 718	3 991	4 729
Household operations	441	424	740	1 032	1 442	838
Housekeeping supplies	330	330	646	693	807	926
Household furnishings and equipment	570	1 203	1 488	1 833	2 191	2 320
Apparel and Services	578	1 179	1 258	2 004	2 519	2 907
Transportation	2 918	5 322	5 839	8 539	11 250	14 480
Vehicle purchases (net outlay)	1 154	1 795	2 268	3 432	4 651	6 177
Gasoline and motor oil	690	1 479	1 477	2 274	2 910	3 793
Other vehicle expenses	824	1 618	1 672	2 354	3 056	3 868
Public transportation	250	429	422	478	633	643
Health Care	2 490	1 439	4 607	2 988	2 935	3 021
Health insurance	1 337	720	2 723	1 576	1 524	1 529
Medical services	487	387	687	741	799	840
Drugs	580	270	997	561	480	499
Medical supplies	85	62	200	111	133	154
Entertainment	937	1 776	1 691	2 360	3 171	3 159
Personal Care Products and Services	291	404	480	569	743	900
Reading	81	97	128	109	138	131
Education	371	539	226	759	1 186	2 091
Tobacco Products and Smoking Supplies	167	262	232	357	384	472
Miscellaneous	641	673	755	802	970	1 197
Cash Contributions	1 893	1 446	2 001	1 795	1 943	2 505
Personal Insurance and Pensions	155	3 918	486	4 468	8 329	9 477
Life and other personal insurance	130	140	287	327	449	496
Pensions and Social Security	[1]25	3 778	199	4 141	7 881	8 981

[1]Data are likely to have large sampling errors.
X = Not applicable.

Table 8-8. Consumer Expenditures, Averages by Size of Consumer Unit, 2006

(Number, dollar, percent.)

Item	One person	Two or more persons	Two persons	Three persons	Four persons	Five or more persons
NUMBER OF CONSUMER UNITS (THOUSANDS)	35 221	83 621	37 650	18 445	16 484	11 043
CONSUMER UNIT CHARACTERISTICS						
Income Before Taxes	31 557	72 738	65 632	72 418	82 996	82 190
Income After Taxes	29 955	69 956	62 485	69 865	80 410	79 976
Age of Reference Person	52.5	47.1	53.1	44.2	40.7	41.2
Average Number in Consumer Unit						
All persons	1.0	3.1	2.0	3.0	4.0	5.6
Children under 18 years	X	0.9	0.1	0.8	1.6	2.7
Persons 65 years and over	0.3	0.3	0.5	0.2	0.1	0.1
Earners	0.6	1.6	1.3	1.8	2.0	2.2
Vehicles	1.1	2.3	2.2	2.3	2.5	2.5
Percent Distribution						
Male	45	46	49	43	45	45
Female	55	54	51	57	55	55
Percent Homeowner	52	74	76	70	76	71
With mortgage	25	51	42	53	64	58
Without mortgage	27	23	34	17	12	13
AVERAGE ANNUAL EXPENDITURES	29 374	56 361	50 652	56 382	63 897	64 654
Food	3 249	7 287	6 203	7 195	8 543	9 334
Food at home	1 728	4 109	3 328	4 010	4 833	5 880
Cereals and bakery products	224	538	430	504	654	790
Meats, poultry, fish, and eggs	367	974	768	941	1 120	1 508
Dairy products	188	443	358	429	537	615
Fruits and vegetables	307	710	593	689	818	982
Other food at home	643	1 446	1 179	1 447	1 703	1 985
Food away from home	1 521	3 178	2 875	3 185	3 710	3 454
Alcoholic Beverages	428	526	586	537	483	367
Housing	11 067	18 590	16 507	18 751	21 311	21 361
Shelter	7 187	10 721	9 569	10 767	12 148	12 441
Owned dwellings	3 651	7 723	6 732	7 645	9 375	8 765
Rented dwellings	3 235	2 318	2 058	2 465	2 180	3 163
Other lodging	300	680	778	656	593	513
Utilities, fuels, and public services	2 153	3 921	3 501	3 990	4 347	4 602
Household operations	430	1 165	780	1 328	1 777	1 293
Housekeeping supplies	330	766	708	698	842	961
Household furnishings and equipment	967	2 017	1 949	1 968	2 197	2 064
Apparel and Services	950	2 254	1 877	2 319	2 710	2 796
Transportation	4 433	10 224	8 805	10 471	11 836	12 239
Vehicle purchases (net outlay)	1 558	4 205	3 409	4 424	5 024	5 335
Gasoline and motor oil	1 188	2 665	2 263	2 707	3 146	3 253
Other vehicle expenses	1 324	2 789	2 531	2 813	3 147	3 093
Public transportation	363	564	603	528	520	558
Health Care	1 827	3 161	3 641	2 868	2 824	2 516
Health insurance	948	1 683	1 976	1 492	1 513	1 254
Medical services	424	774	809	700	771	782
Drugs	384	568	702	521	436	381
Medical supplies	70	137	154	155	105	99
Entertainment	1 464	2 758	2 576	2 580	3 232	2 965
Personal Care Products and Services	361	678	619	703	750	735
Reading	91	128	145	111	127	97
Education	477	1 061	632	1 260	1 453	1 602
Tobacco Products and Smoking Supplies	227	369	360	394	347	392
Miscellaneous	662	924	887	990	921	935
Cash Contributions	1 611	1 977	2 211	1 693	1 725	2 032
Personal Insurance and Pensions	2 528	6 425	5 602	6 509	7 634	7 283
Life and other personal insurance	136	400	386	395	446	392
Pensions and Social Security	2 391	6 024	5 216	6 114	7 188	6 891

X = Not applicable.

Table 8-9. Consumer Expenditures, Averages by Composition of Consumer Unit, 2006

(Number, dollar, percent.)

Item	Husband and wife consumer units						Other husband and wife consumer units	One parent, at least one child under 18 years	Single person and other consumer units
	Total	Husband and wife only	Husband and wife with children						
			Total	Oldest child under 6 years	Oldest child 6 to 17 years	Oldest child 18 years or over			
NUMBER OF CONSUMER UNITS (THOUSANDS)	59 428	25 306	29 381	5 763	15 166	8 452	4 741	7 225	52 190
CONSUMER UNIT CHARACTERISTICS									
Income Before Taxes	82 195	73 032	89 351	81 372	89 792	93 999	86 765	34 852	39 422
Income After Taxes	78 787	69 350	86 064	77 848	86 807	90 334	84 065	34 632	37 795
Age of Reference Person	48.8	56.8	42.0	32.1	40.2	52.0	48.1	38.3	50.1
Average Number in Consumer Unit									
All persons	3.2	2.0	3.9	3.5	4.1	3.9	5.0	2.9	1.6
Children under 18 years	0.9	X	1.6	1.5	2.1	0.6	1.5	1.7	0.2
Persons 65 years and over	0.3	0.6	0.1	(1)	(1)	0.2	0.5	(1)	0.3
Earners	1.7	1.2	2.0	1.6	1.8	2.5	2.3	1.0	1.0
Vehicles	2.6	2.4	2.6	2.1	2.6	3.2	2.7	1.2	1.3
Percent Distribution									
Male	53	55	51	54	49	51	52	14	43
Female	47	45	49	46	51	49	48	86	57
Percent Homeowner	83	87	81	73	80	87	78	43	53
With mortgage	58	46	67	68	70	62	59	34	28
Without mortgage	26	41	14	5	10	25	19	9	25
AVERAGE ANNUAL EXPENDITURES	62 503	55 631	68 354	63 416	69 157	70 234	63 614	35 491	33 997
Food	7 920	6 745	8 864	7 121	9 211	9 356	8 836	5 139	4 114
Food at home	4 423	3 571	5 032	4 053	5 088	5 578	5 571	3 046	2 279
Cereals and bakery products	580	461	674	509	708	715	681	412	294
Meats, poultry, fish, and eggs	1 031	816	1 152	788	1 150	1 401	1 535	725	531
Dairy products	483	385	556	518	573	548	590	315	241
Fruits and vegetables	780	650	869	737	868	957	990	446	390
Other food at home	1 549	1 260	1 782	1 500	1 788	1 957	1 775	1 148	824
Food away from home	3 497	3 175	3 831	3 068	4 123	3 777	3 265	2 093	1 835
Alcoholic Beverages	562	628	500	476	506	502	581	232	456
Housing	20 283	17 652	22 502	24 837	22 728	20 522	20 599	13 840	12 233
Shelter	11 635	10 116	12 957	14 092	13 493	11 221	11 548	8 055	7 664
Owned dwellings	9 094	7 838	10 260	11 083	10 681	8 943	8 579	3 926	3 939
Rented dwellings	1 702	1 303	1 939	2 483	2 100	1 281	2 364	3 938	3 414
Other lodging	839	976	758	527	713	997	605	190	311
Utilities, fuels, and public services	4 139	3 680	4 432	3 731	4 488	4 811	4 776	3 331	2 561
Household operations	1 334	816	1 793	3 485	1 585	1 013	1 245	969	505
Housekeeping supplies	863	793	926	754	942	1 011	871	423	404
Household furnishings and equipment	2 312	2 246	2 392	2 775	2 219	2 466	2 158	1 063	1 099
Apparel and Services	2 381	1 878	2 805	2 666	2 852	2 828	2 607	1 863	1 281
Transportation	11 388	9 674	12 787	11 188	12 769	13 909	11 868	5 504	5 644
Vehicle purchases (net outlay)	4 745	3 803	5 553	5 211	5 587	5 725	4 764	1 917	2 121
Gasoline and motor oil	2 901	2 419	3 246	2 609	3 246	3 680	3 331	1 697	1 534
Other vehicle expenses	3 087	2 733	3 381	2 909	3 326	3 800	3 155	1 628	1 621
Public transportation	655	718	608	459	610	705	618	261	367
Health Care	3 713	4 435	3 133	2 726	3 038	3 583	3 446	1 306	1 887
Health insurance	1 976	2 416	1 623	1 449	1 570	1 839	1 809	644	997
Medical services	924	1 000	871	855	864	894	853	383	421
Drugs	653	839	492	336	448	679	638	209	395
Medical supplies	161	180	146	86	156	171	146	70	74
Entertainment	3 124	2 938	3 378	2 879	3 738	3 064	2 552	1 859	1 590
Personal Care Products and Services	749	685	813	747	783	921	727	460	410
Reading	149	172	137	105	144	146	101	63	88
Education	1 236	646	1 769	570	1 633	2 826	1 086	754	510
Tobacco Products and Smoking Supplies	332	315	311	215	319	361	559	259	330
Miscellaneous	969	915	944	774	964	1 026	1 413	644	733
Cash Contributions	2 312	2 681	2 083	1 347	2 116	2 525	1 764	733	1 521
Personal Insurance and Pensions	7 383	6 266	8 330	7 766	8 356	8 666	7 475	2 835	3 201
Life and other personal insurance	487	475	501	363	522	557	468	150	158
Pensions and Social Security	6 895	5 790	7 829	7 403	7 834	8 109	7 007	2 686	3 043

1Value less than 0.05.
X = Not applicable.

Table 8-10. Consumer Expenditures, Averages by Age of Reference Person, 2006

(Number, dollar, percent.)

Item	Under 25 years	25 to 34 years	35 to 44 years	45 to 54 years	55 to 64 years	65 years and over	65 to 74 years	75 years and over
NUMBER OF CONSUMER UNITS (THOUSANDS)	8 167	20 071	23 950	24 696	18 952	23 007	11 764	11 243
CONSUMER UNIT CHARACTERISTICS								
Income Before Taxes	29 057	57 208	75 613	77 043	64 425	37 982	46 064	29 525
Income After Taxes	28 535	55 676	72 445	73 683	60 894	36 753	44 304	28 850
Age of Reference Person	21.5	29.6	39.7	49.3	59.1	75.2	69.1	81.5
Average Number in Consumer Unit								
All persons	2.0	2.9	3.2	2.7	2.0	1.7	1.9	1.5
Children under 18 years	0.4	1.1	1.3	0.6	0.1	0.1	0.1	(¹)
Persons 65 years and over	(¹)	(¹)	(¹)	(¹)	0.1	1.4	1.4	1.3
Earners	1.3	1.5	1.6	1.7	1.3	0.5	0.7	0.2
Vehicles	1.2	1.8	2.1	2.4	2.1	1.6	1.9	1.2
Percent Distribution								
Male	49	47	47	47	46	42	47	37
Female	51	53	53	53	54	58	53	63
Percent Homeowner	20	50	68	75	80	80	83	77
With mortgage	13	42	59	58	46	20	29	10
Without mortgage	7	7	9	17	34	60	54	67
AVERAGE ANNUAL EXPENDITURES	28 181	47 582	57 476	57 563	50 789	35 058	40 960	28 904
Food	3 919	6 104	7 331	7 328	6 132	4 319	5 172	3 437
Food at home	1 946	3 186	4 128	4 036	3 518	2 659	3 062	2 244
Cereals and bakery products	240	406	553	510	453	370	413	325
Meats, poultry, fish, and eggs	434	746	962	972	801	611	723	495
Dairy products	219	352	452	420	370	293	330	256
Fruits and vegetables	319	537	671	683	656	507	572	439
Other food at home	734	1 144	1 490	1 451	1 238	878	1 024	729
Food away from home	1 973	2 918	3 203	3 292	2 613	1 659	2 110	1 193
Alcoholic Beverages	473	657	496	612	477	263	339	184
Housing	9 355	17 139	20 303	18 377	16 529	11 787	13 273	10 236
Shelter	5 923	10 725	12 445	10 896	9 199	6 281	6 934	5 597
Owned dwellings	1 405	6 132	8 965	8 024	6 866	4 210	5 151	3 224
Rented dwellings	4 315	4 286	2 938	2 064	1 460	1 630	1 191	2 090
Other lodging	203	307	541	807	873	441	592	284
Utilities, fuels, and public services	1 781	3 093	3 854	3 912	3 640	3 008	3 297	2 705
Household operations	374	1 130	1 380	793	934	720	718	722
Housekeeping supplies	295	531	761	727	739	554	660	445
Household furnishings and equipment	982	1 660	1 864	2 050	2 017	1 224	1 664	767
Apparel and Services	1 464	2 152	2 368	2 176	1 892	930	1 212	639
Transportation	5 667	9 047	9 977	10 111	8 676	5 658	7 481	3 751
Vehicle purchases (net outlay)	2 396	3 912	4 057	3 983	3 165	2 301	3 273	1 284
Gasoline and motor oil	1 637	2 346	2 636	2 693	2 288	1 359	1 766	934
Other vehicle expenses	1 413	2 342	2 725	2 819	2 638	1 584	1 972	1 179
Public transportation	221	448	559	616	584	414	471	354
Health Care	706	1 652	2 284	2 757	3 556	4 331	4 379	4 282
Health insurance	367	883	1 214	1 310	1 676	2 617	2 718	2 511
Medical services	193	469	634	798	978	663	636	692
Drugs	97	243	345	499	759	887	859	916
Medical supplies	49	58	90	151	143	164	166	163
Entertainment	1 348	2 237	2 966	2 770	2 666	1 584	2 049	1 099
Personal Care Products and Services	348	547	688	696	586	475	527	421
Reading	46	82	112	133	147	136	143	129
Education	1 259	710	857	1 736	662	219	274	162
Tobacco Products and Smoking Supplies	286	318	354	433	370	171	241	97
Miscellaneous	388	615	943	971	1 105	762	966	549
Cash Contributions	632	1 070	1 707	2 118	2 266	2 579	2 121	3 058
Personal Insurance and Pensions	2 291	5 252	7 090	7 346	5 726	1 844	2 782	862
Life and other personal insurance	42	172	364	413	458	299	365	231
Pensions and Social Security	2 249	5 079	6 726	6 933	5 267	1 545	2 417	631

¹Value less than 0.05.

Table 8-11. Consumer Expenditures, Averages by Race of Reference Person, 2006

(Number, dollar, percent.)

Item	White, Asian, and other races			Black
	Total	White and other races	Asian	
NUMBER OF CONSUMER UNITS (THOUSANDS)	104 577	100 479	4 098	14 265
CONSUMER UNIT CHARACTERISTICS				
Income Before Taxes	63 179	62 661	75 865	41 142
Income After Taxes	60 500	60 005	72 641	40 516
Age of Reference Person	49.1	49.2	45.3	46.2
Average Number in Consumer Unit				
All persons	2.5	2.4	2.7	2.6
Children under 18 years	0.6	0.6	0.6	0.8
Persons 65 years and over	0.3	0.3	0.3	0.2
Earners	1.4	1.3	1.5	1.2
Vehicles	2.0	2.0	1.7	1.3
Percent Distribution				
Male	48	47	55	33
Female	52	53	45	67
Percent Homeowner	70	70	63	49
With mortgage	44	44	45	34
Without mortgage	25	26	18	15
AVERAGE ANNUAL EXPENDITURES	50 287	49 994	57 544	34 583
Food	6 329	6 289	7 411	4 530
Food at home	3 503	3 486	3 947	2 796
Cereals and bakery products	458	455	524	366
Meats, poultry, fish, and eggs	791	782	1 022	845
Dairy products	387	390	298	237
Fruits and vegetables	615	605	884	432
Other food at home	1 253	1 254	1 219	916
Food away from home	2 826	2 802	3 463	1 735
Alcoholic Beverages	537	545	302	210
Housing	16 859	16 676	21 332	12 754
Shelter	9 986	9 791	14 782	7 378
Owned dwellings	6 914	6 781	10 168	3 600
Rented dwellings	2 458	2 409	3 655	3 555
Other lodging	614	600	958	223
Utilities, fuels, and public services	3 388	3 395	3 221	3 461
Household operations	1 003	1 003	1 005	545
Housekeeping supplies	661	665	557	482
Household furnishings and equipment	1 820	1 822	1 767	888
Apparel and Services	1 889	1 881	2 117	1 762
Transportation	8 832	8 796	9 722	6 130
Vehicle purchases (net outlay)	3 565	3 555	3 823	2 362
Gasoline and motor oil	2 294	2 298	2 191	1 740
Other vehicle expenses	2 439	2 435	2 519	1 742
Public transportation	535	508	1 189	286
Health Care	2 940	2 967	2 262	1 497
Health insurance	1 538	1 545	1 363	927
Medical services	728	736	523	248
Drugs	547	557	286	272
Medical supplies	127	128	89	49
Entertainment	2 540	2 564	1 941	1 172
Personal Care Products and Services	594	587	772	519
Reading	127	128	100	46
Education	941	885	2 332	495
Tobacco Products and Smoking Supplies	346	353	181	187
Miscellaneous	887	896	670	544
Cash Contributions	1 935	1 950	1 568	1 384
Personal Insurance and Pensions	5 531	5 478	6 837	3 354
Life and other personal insurance	333	330	410	245
Pensions and Social Security	5 198	5 148	6 428	3 109

Table 8-12. Consumer Expenditures, Averages by Hispanic Origin of Reference Person, 2006

(Number, dollar, percent.)

Item	Hispanic[1]	Not Hispanic		
		Total	White, Asian, and other races	Black
NUMBER OF CONSUMER UNITS (THOUSANDS)	13 664	105 178	91 049	14 129
CONSUMER UNIT CHARACTERISTICS				
Income Before Taxes	48 108	62 148	65 417	41 080
Income After Taxes	47 074	59 534	62 495	40 452
Age of Reference Person	42.0	49.6	50.1	46.3
Average Number in Consumer Unit				
All persons	3.2	2.4	2.3	2.6
Children under 18 years	1.1	0.6	0.5	0.8
Persons 65 years and over	0.2	0.3	0.3	0.2
Earners	1.6	1.3	1.3	1.2
Vehicles	1.6	2.0	2.1	1.3
Percent Distribution				
Male	50	46	47	33
Female	50	54	53	67
Percent Homeowner	50	70	73	49
With mortgage	37	44	45	34
Without mortgage	14	26	27	15
AVERAGE ANNUAL EXPENDITURES	43 053	49 093	51 351	34 571
Food	6 170	6 103	6 351	4 522
Food at home	3 719	3 377	3 470	2 787
Cereals and bakery products	427	449	462	365
Meats, poultry, fish, and eggs	999	771	759	844
Dairy products	384	366	387	235
Fruits and vegetables	735	574	596	430
Other food at home	1 173	1 217	1 265	913
Food away from home	2 451	2 726	2 881	1 735
Alcoholic Beverages	326	520	568	212
Housing	15 412	16 490	17 070	12 755
Shelter	9 639	9 678	10 035	7 379
Owned dwellings	5 355	6 667	7 142	3 607
Rented dwellings	4 031	2 403	2 225	3 548
Other lodging	253	608	668	224
Utilities, fuels, and public services	3 224	3 419	3 413	3 464
Household operations	661	985	1 053	545
Housekeeping supplies	529	654	681	482
Household furnishings and equipment	1 359	1 754	1 889	885
Apparel and Services	2 278	1 821	1 829	1 767
Transportation	8 286	8 537	8 913	6 110
Vehicle purchases (net outlay)	3 400	3 423	3 590	2 349
Gasoline and motor oil	2 319	2 216	2 289	1 740
Other vehicle expenses	2 152	2 381	2 481	1 741
Public transportation	414	516	553	280
Health Care	1 659	2 910	3 129	1 501
Health insurance	780	1 554	1 651	929
Medical services	504	692	761	249
Drugs	305	541	582	273
Medical supplies	69	124	135	50
Entertainment	1 568	2 481	2 684	1 175
Personal Care Products and Services	537	591	602	517
Reading	43	127	139	46
Education	633	921	986	499
Tobacco Products and Smoking Supplies	150	350	375	189
Miscellaneous	575	881	934	541
Cash Contributions	1 343	1 937	2 023	1 385
Personal Insurance and Pensions	4 074	5 425	5 747	3 352
Life and other personal insurance	151	344	360	244
Pensions and Social Security	3 923	5 081	5 387	3 108

[1]May be of any race.

Table 8-13. Consumer Expenditures, Averages by Education of Reference Person, 2006

(Number, dollar, percent.)

Item	Less than a college graduate					College graduate or more		
	Total	Less than a high school graduate	High school graduate	High school graduate with some college	Associate's degree	Total	Bachelor's degree	Master's, professional, or doctoral degree
NUMBER OF CONSUMER UNITS (THOUSANDS)	85 598	17 747	31 134	25 135	11 582	33 244	21 277	11 967
CONSUMER UNIT CHARACTERISTICS								
Income Before Taxes	48 219	31 775	45 962	53 809	67 353	92 241	82 860	108 918
Income After Taxes	46 819	31 362	44 780	52 005	64 730	87 151	78 401	102 707
Age of Reference Person	49.2	53.5	50.5	45.5	47.1	47.5	45.7	50.6
Average Number in Consumer Unit								
All persons	2.5	2.6	2.5	2.4	2.5	2.4	2.4	2.4
Children under 18 years	0.6	0.7	0.6	0.6	0.6	0.6	0.6	0.5
Persons 65 years and over	0.3	0.5	0.4	0.2	0.2	0.2	0.2	0.3
Earners	1.3	1.1	1.3	1.4	1.5	1.4	1.5	1.4
Vehicles	1.9	1.4	1.9	2.0	2.2	2.1	2.1	2.2
Percent Distribution								
Male	44	44	44	45	39	52	50	55
Female	56	56	56	55	61	48	50	45
Percent Homeowner	64	55	66	63	75	77	74	82
With mortgage	38	25	36	41	54	56	55	58
Without mortgage	26	29	29	21	20	20	19	24
AVERAGE ANNUAL EXPENDITURES	40 813	28 760	39 305	45 891	52 272	67 836	63 864	74 906
Food	5 544	4 381	5 432	6 046	6 516	7 531	7 353	7 850
Food at home	3 244	2 853	3 251	3 395	3 491	3 847	3 739	4 041
Cereals and bakery products	421	362	423	433	475	510	483	559
Meats, poultry, fish, and eggs	804	742	827	795	853	780	776	788
Dairy products	341	297	337	368	364	436	425	455
Fruits and vegetables	532	503	524	557	546	742	690	836
Other food at home	1 146	948	1 139	1 242	1 253	1 379	1 365	1 404
Food away from home	2 300	1 529	2 181	2 652	3 025	3 684	3 614	3 809
Alcoholic Beverages	390	214	356	483	545	764	721	843
Housing	13 712	10 398	13 195	15 100	17 166	23 181	21 818	25 606
Shelter	7 894	6 006	7 568	8 742	9 822	14 255	13 412	15 754
Owned dwellings	4 926	2 854	4 699	5 643	7 159	10 611	9 820	12 017
Rented dwellings	2 640	3 037	2 599	2 638	2 147	2 460	2 594	2 222
Other lodging	328	116	270	461	516	1 185	998	1 516
Utilities, fuels, and public services	3 218	2 790	3 242	3 301	3 628	3 858	3 724	4 095
Household operations	668	333	560	821	1 142	1 668	1 452	2 052
Housekeeping supplies	557	462	540	597	663	843	781	955
Household furnishings and equipment	1 374	807	1 285	1 640	1 911	2 556	2 449	2 749
Apparel and Services	1 618	1 171	1 513	1 850	2 074	2 519	2 442	2 656
Transportation	7 562	5 043	7 412	8 634	9 495	10 943	10 648	11 467
Vehicle purchases (net outlay)	3 057	1 956	2 979	3 627	3 720	4 356	4 193	4 647
Gasoline and motor oil	2 119	1 575	2 131	2 288	2 553	2 507	2 510	2 502
Other vehicle expenses	2 061	1 326	2 028	2 324	2 703	3 111	3 073	3 177
Public transportation	324	186	274	395	519	968	872	1 141
Health Care	2 479	1 991	2 575	2 498	2 923	3 504	3 349	3 781
Health insurance	1 347	1 123	1 446	1 323	1 473	1 770	1 690	1 912
Medical services	547	368	531	627	690	988	937	1 078
Drugs	485	435	504	442	599	587	577	604
Medical supplies	100	64	94	106	161	160	145	188
Entertainment	1 910	1 134	1 842	2 250	2 542	3 570	3 366	3 933
Personal Care Products and Services	493	311	489	532	692	818	803	844
Reading	84	43	76	104	122	203	171	258
Education	562	151	413	882	897	1 725	1 514	2 101
Tobacco Products and Smoking Supplies	394	390	445	385	288	153	164	132
Miscellaneous	708	409	680	835	973	1 200	988	1 578
Cash Contributions	1 325	879	1 177	1 561	1 893	3 269	2 898	3 928
Personal Insurance and Pensions	4 032	2 245	3 700	4 731	6 147	8 456	7 628	9 928
Life and other personal insurance	256	148	241	308	352	491	426	607
Pensions and Social Security	3 776	2 098	3 459	4 422	5 795	7 965	7 202	9 321

Table 8-14. Consumer Expenditures, Averages by Housing Tenure and Type of Area, 2006

(Number, dollar, percent.)

Item	Housing tenure				Type of area			
	Homeowner			Renter	Urban			Rural
	Total	Homeowner with mortgage	Homeowner without mortgage		Total	Central city	Other urban	
NUMBER OF CONSUMER UNITS (THOUSANDS)	80 035	51 190	28 845	38 808	108 771	35 782	72 990	10 071
CONSUMER UNIT CHARACTERISTICS								
Income Before Taxes	72 988	85 146	51 412	34 847	61 634	53 520	65 612	48 646
Income After Taxes	69 780	81 405	49 148	34 016	59 141	51 351	62 959	46 873
Age of Reference Person	52.2	46.5	62.3	41.5	48.4	46.6	49.3	51.7
Average Number in Consumer Unit								
All persons	2.6	2.9	2.1	2.2	2.5	2.3	2.5	2.5
Children under 18 years	0.6	0.8	0.3	0.6	0.6	0.6	0.6	0.6
Persons 65 years and over	0.4	0.2	0.7	0.2	0.3	0.3	0.3	0.4
Earners	1.4	1.7	0.9	1.2	1.3	1.2	1.4	1.3
Vehicles	2.3	2.5	2.1	1.1	1.9	1.5	2.1	2.5
Percent Distribution								
Male	47	49	43	45	46	46	46	45
Female	53	51	57	55	54	54	54	55
Percent Homeowner	100	100	100	X	66	51	73	84
With mortgage	64	100	X	X	43	33	48	41
Without mortgage	36	X	100	X	23	17	25	43
AVERAGE ANNUAL EXPENDITURES	56 212	64 374	41 292	32 275	49 285	43 780	51 966	38 855
Food	6 843	7 384	5 639	4 597	6 188	5 755	6 391	5 300
Food at home	3 787	4 017	3 265	2 651	3 439	3 199	3 551	3 181
Cereals and bakery products	501	530	437	333	448	407	467	431
Meats, poultry, fish, and eggs	874	930	745	639	804	786	813	723
Dairy products	411	436	354	280	368	328	387	370
Fruits and vegetables	656	683	593	462	602	574	615	494
Other food at home	1 345	1 438	1 135	938	1 217	1 103	1 270	1 163
Food away from home	3 056	3 367	2 374	1 946	2 749	2 556	2 840	2 119
Alcoholic Beverages	542	612	386	405	516	500	523	297
Housing	18 585	22 570	11 478	11 787	16 836	15 312	17 579	11 285
Shelter	10 495	13 769	4 687	7 978	10 088	9 459	10 396	5 197
Owned dwellings	9 623	12 846	3 903	109	6 737	5 062	7 558	4 134
Rented dwellings	120	138	86	7 684	2 760	3 906	2 198	755
Other lodging	753	784	697	185	591	491	640	309
Utilities, fuels, and public services	4 014	4 307	3 494	2 124	3 408	2 991	3 612	3 278
Household operations	1 189	1 363	879	449	975	846	1 038	654
Housekeeping supplies	768	786	725	374	639	579	667	642
Household furnishings and equipment	2 118	2 344	1 693	862	1 726	1 436	1 865	1 513
Apparel and Services	2 067	2 328	1 520	1 475	1 940	1 889	1 964	1 169
Transportation	9 961	11 440	7 332	5 511	8 547	7 024	9 293	8 091
Vehicle purchases (net outlay)	4 030	4 686	2 867	2 164	3 438	2 736	3 782	3 236
Gasoline and motor oil	2 560	2 901	1 954	1 542	2 188	1 756	2 400	2 652
Other vehicle expenses	2 778	3 209	2 009	1 483	2 386	1 978	2 587	2 015
Public transportation	594	644	503	321	534	554	524	188
Health Care	3 414	3 102	3 975	1 431	2 735	2 231	2 982	3 103
Health insurance	1 815	1 620	2 161	743	1 448	1 152	1 593	1 648
Medical services	831	829	835	340	666	549	724	715
Drugs	624	523	813	285	502	424	540	638
Medical supplies	143	130	166	63	119	105	125	101
Entertainment	2 886	3 261	2 203	1 322	2 390	2 101	2 530	2 219
Personal Care Products and Services	681	754	533	385	603	545	631	385
Reading	141	148	130	67	120	107	126	89
Education	1 018	1 229	636	620	938	751	1 030	343
Tobacco Products and Smoking Supplies ...	307	333	260	367	317	279	336	431
Miscellaneous	991	1 066	854	547	866	783	906	634
Cash Contributions	2 298	2 113	2 627	983	1 925	1 886	1 944	1 261
Personal Insurance and Pensions	6 478	8 033	3 718	2 778	5 364	4 618	5 730	4 246
Life and other personal insurance	428	489	321	103	325	252	360	294
Pensions and Social Security	6 049	7 544	3 396	2 675	5 040	4 366	5 370	3 952

X = Not applicable.

Table 8-15. Consumer Expenditures, Averages by Population Size of Area of Residence, 2006

(Number, dollar, percent.)

Item	Outside urbanized area	Urbanized area consumer units						
		Total	Less than 100,000	100,000 to 249,999	250,000 to 999,999	1,000,000 to 2,499,999	2,500,000 to 4,999,999	5,000,000 and over
NUMBER OF CONSUMER UNITS (THOUSANDS)	23 783	95 060	17 903	9 445	19 811	15 832	16 696	15 371
CONSUMER UNIT CHARACTERISTICS								
Income Before Taxes	58 798	60 967	46 969	58 032	58 185	62 068	71 512	70 074
Income After Taxes	56 544	58 490	45 322	55 371	55 889	59 490	68 034	67 702
Age of Reference Person	51.5	48.0	48.1	47.9	48.1	48.8	46.5	48.8
Average Number in Consumer Unit								
All persons	2.6	2.5	2.3	2.5	2.4	2.4	2.5	2.6
Children under 18 years	0.6	0.6	0.6	0.7	0.6	0.6	0.7	0.6
Persons 65 years and over	0.4	0.3	0.3	0.3	0.3	0.3	0.2	0.3
Earners	1.4	1.3	1.2	1.4	1.3	1.3	1.4	1.4
Vehicles	2.7	1.8	1.8	2.0	1.8	1.8	1.7	1.4
Percent Distribution								
Male	45	46	43	46	48	46	47	48
Female	55	54	57	54	52	54	53	52
Percent Homeowner	85	63	62	64	65	66	63	57
With mortgage	46	42	37	44	43	47	46	39
Without mortgage	39	21	24	20	23	19	17	19
AVERAGE ANNUAL EXPENDITURES	46 217	48 948	40 092	47 894	47 842	49 637	55 105	53 939
Food	5 853	6 178	5 403	6 118	6 097	6 175	6 500	6 869
Food at home	3 436	3 412	3 152	3 374	3 265	3 418	3 513	3 800
Cereals and bakery products	453	445	412	450	442	441	451	481
Meats, poultry, fish, and eggs	798	797	709	766	740	792	828	959
Dairy products	388	363	348	359	354	373	366	383
Fruits and vegetables	532	608	521	571	545	589	663	767
Other food at home	1 264	1 199	1 162	1 228	1 184	1 223	1 206	1 210
Food away from home	2 417	2 766	2 251	2 744	2 831	2 757	2 987	3 069
Alcoholic Beverages	364	532	405	444	490	655	582	601
Housing	13 891	16 983	12 731	15 604	15 891	17 066	20 442	20 360
Shelter	7 151	10 304	6 833	9 072	9 134	10 363	13 017	13 607
Owned dwellings	5 609	6 743	4 374	6 206	6 084	7 074	8 625	8 298
Rented dwellings	1 092	2 964	1 986	2 358	2 519	2 690	3 647	4 592
Other lodging	449	597	474	507	531	598	746	717
Utilities, fuels, and public services	3 538	3 362	3 094	3 288	3 332	3 313	3 740	3 397
Household operations	771	992	796	921	853	981	1 255	1 165
Housekeeping supplies	688	627	578	601	646	709	650	565
Household furnishings and equipment	1 742	1 699	1 430	1 723	1 926	1 699	1 780	1 626
Apparel and Services	1 500	1 970	1 597	1 796	1 933	1 925	2 061	2 502
Transportation	9 203	8 334	7 578	8 782	8 217	8 456	9 139	8 091
Vehicle purchases (net outlay)	3 681	3 356	3 438	3 820	3 414	3 502	3 345	2 759
Gasoline and motor oil	2 833	2 076	1 974	2 079	2 064	2 026	2 296	2 020
Other vehicle expenses	2 390	2 346	1 870	2 387	2 256	2 384	2 829	2 429
Public transportation	299	556	296	496	482	543	669	883
Health Care	3 270	2 640	2 494	2 800	2 822	2 665	2 747	2 337
Health insurance	1 728	1 399	1 339	1 489	1 456	1 448	1 386	1 305
Medical services	774	645	557	650	705	608	743	595
Drugs	651	479	491	486	538	490	499	352
Medical supplies	118	117	106	176	123	119	119	84
Entertainment	2 556	2 329	1 972	2 629	2 270	2 606	2 421	2 254
Personal Care Products and Services	473	613	506	563	611	608	692	691
Reading	112	118	99	138	122	124	125	112
Education	567	968	718	692	911	1 037	993	1 405
Tobacco Products and Smoking Supplies	450	296	348	387	302	298	247	223
Miscellaneous	959	818	770	840	803	751	887	872
Cash Contributions	1 890	1 864	1 571	1 901	2 367	1 790	1 921	1 545
Personal Insurance and Pensions	5 129	5 305	3 898	5 200	5 007	5 482	6 349	6 075
Life and other personal insurance	344	317	271	401	314	323	335	295
Pensions and Social Security	4 785	4 988	3 627	4 799	4 693	5 159	6 014	5 780

Table 8-16. Consumer Expenditures, Averages by Region of Residence, 2006

(Number, dollar, percent.)

Item	Region[1]			
	Northeast	South	Midwest	West
NUMBER OF CONSUMER UNITS (THOUSANDS)	22 757	42 457	27 206	26 423
CONSUMER UNIT CHARACTERISTICS				
Income Before Taxes	64 232	56 190	57 980	66 955
Income After Taxes	61 766	54 140	55 902	63 574
Age of Reference Person	49.7	48.9	48.8	47.4
Average Number in Consumer Unit				
All persons	2.4	2.5	2.4	2.6
Children under 18 years	0.6	0.7	0.6	0.7
Persons 65 years and over	0.3	0.3	0.3	0.3
Earners	1.3	1.3	1.4	1.4
Vehicles	1.6	1.9	2.1	2.1
Percent Distribution				
Males	45	44	47	50
Females	55	56	53	50
Percent Homeowner	65	70	70	63
With mortgage	40	43	43	46
Without mortgage	25	27	26	18
AVERAGE ANNUAL EXPENDITURES	49 164	44 501	45 085	57 486
Food	6 220	5 649	5 763	7 158
Food at home	3 463	3 134	3 260	4 018
Cereals and bakery products	477	407	433	499
Meats, poultry, fish, and eggs	818	764	738	899
Dairy products	380	328	365	429
Fruits and vegetables	635	512	530	758
Other food at home	1 153	1 123	1 193	1 433
Food away from home	2 757	2 515	2 503	3 140
Alcoholic Beverages	519	366	523	667
Housing	17 682	14 457	14 660	20 061
Shelter	11 035	7 876	8 220	12 885
Owned dwellings	7 291	5 347	5 868	8 395
Rented dwellings	3 042	2 143	1 812	3 719
Other lodging	701	387	540	770
Utilities, fuels, and public services	3 584	3 554	3 283	3 101
Household operations	932	863	926	1 120
Housekeeping supplies	583	660	606	691
Household furnishings and equipment	1 548	1 504	1 624	2 264
Apparel and Services	2 057	1 737	1 700	2 126
Transportation	7 819	8 497	7 502	10 156
Vehicle purchases (net outlay)	2 894	3 643	2 730	4 230
Gasoline and motor oil	1 910	2 356	2 142	2 382
Other vehicle expenses	2 386	2 182	2 225	2 741
Public transportation	629	316	405	804
Health Care	2 591	2 775	2 816	2 853
Health insurance	1 462	1 459	1 505	1 437
Medical services	596	614	697	798
Drugs	412	594	500	489
Medical supplies	122	109	114	129
Entertainment	2 346	2 096	2 261	2 970
Personal Care Products and Services	557	571	537	681
Reading	132	85	129	144
Education	1 080	707	951	948
Tobacco Products and Smoking Supplies	331	336	355	279
Miscellaneous	883	727	805	1 051
Cash Contributions	1 470	1 762	1 902	2 350
Personal Insurance and Pensions	5 477	4 736	5 179	6 042
Life and other personal insurance	334	313	344	304
Pensions and Social Security	5 144	4 423	4 835	5 738

[1]The states that comprise the Census regions are: Northeast—Connecticut, Maine, Massachusetts, New Hampshire, New Jersey, New York, Pennsylvania, Rhode Island, and Vermont; South—Alabama, Arkansas, Delaware, District of Columbia, Florida, Georgia, Kentucky, Louisiana, Maryland, Mississippi, North Carolina, Oklahoma, South Carolina, Tennessee, Texas, Virginia, and West Virginia; Midwest—Illinois, Indiana, Iowa, Kansas, Michigan, Minnesota, Missouri, Nebraska, North Dakota, Ohio, South Dakota, and Wisconsin; and West—Alaska, Arizona, California, Colorado, Hawaii, Idaho, Montana, Nevada, New Mexico, Oregon, Utah, Washington, and Wyoming.

Table 8-17. Consumer Expenditures, Averages by Selected Metropolitan Statistical Areas: Northeast Region, 2005–2006

(Number, dollar, percent.)

Item	All consumer units in the Northeast[1]	New York	Philadelphia	Boston
NUMBER OF CONSUMER UNITS (THOUSANDS)	22 557	8 155	2 856	3 127
CONSUMER UNIT CHARACTERISTICS				
Income Before Taxes	63 655	73 243	60 304	76 273
Age of Reference Person	49.9	50.6	48.4	47.3
Average Number in Consumer Unit				
All persons	2.4	2.5	2.4	2.3
Children under 18 years	0.6	0.6	0.6	0.6
Persons 65 years and over	0.3	0.3	0.3	0.2
Earners	1.3	1.4	1.3	1.4
Vehicles	1.6	1.4	1.5	1.8
Percent Homeowner	65	58	71	63
AVERAGE ANNUAL EXPENDITURES	48 564	55 137	45 922	53 691
Food	6 357	7 101	6 031	6 865
Food at home	3 554	3 877	3 372	3 760
Cereals and bakery products	493	533	454	561
Meats, poultry, fish, and eggs	851	989	834	866
Dairy products	402	425	382	405
Fruits and vegetables	643	759	620	634
Other food at home	1 165	1 172	1 082	1 295
Food away from home	2 803	3 224	2 659	3 105
Alcoholic Beverages	480	488	437	573
Housing	17 072	20 865	16 417	18 922
Shelter	10 572	13 848	9 722	12 256
Owned dwellings	7 004	8 613	6 748	8 351
Rented dwellings	2 905	4 424	2 510	3 020
Other lodging	663	812	464	885
Utilities, fuels, and public services	3 498	3 709	3 771	3 590
Household operations	849	1 019	877	918
Housekeeping supplies	619	599	634	584
Household furnishings and equipment	1 535	1 689	1 413	1 574
Apparel and Services	2 046	2 746	2 063	1 690
Transportation	7 776	7 792	7 092	9 170
Vehicle purchases (net outlay)	2 902	2 416	2 661	4 011
Gasoline and motor oil	1 836	1 798	1 783	1 958
Other vehicle expenses	2 405	2 555	2 227	2 625
Public transportation	633	1 022	421	576
Health Care	2 586	2 607	2 188	2 794
Entertainment	2 305	2 451	1 871	2 555
Personal Care Products and Services	549	659	575	554
Reading	140	133	108	189
Education	1 232	1 597	1 064	1 779
Tobacco Products and Smoking Supplies	331	245	371	302
Miscellaneous	853	1 132	561	699
Cash Contributions	1 421	1 353	1 301	1 330
Personal Insurance and Pensions	5 416	5 968	5 842	6 269
Life and other personal insurance	354	380	323	360
Pensions and Social Security	5 062	5 588	5 519	5 909

[1]The states in the Northeast include Connecticut, Maine, Massachusetts, New Hampshire, New Jersey, New York, Pennsylvania, Rhode Island, and Vermont.

Table 8-18. Consumer Expenditures, Averages by Selected Metropolitan Statistical Areas: South Region, 2005–2006

(Number, dollar, percent.)

Item	All consumer units in the South[1]	Washington, D.C.	Baltimore	Atlanta	Miami	Dallas-Fort Worth	Houston
NUMBER OF CONSUMER UNITS (THOUSANDS)	42 288	2 194	1 016	2 123	1 628	2 072	1 753
CONSUMER UNIT CHARACTERISTICS							
Income Before Taxes	54 756	88 551	74 508	64 217	51 232	66 261	68 659
Age of Reference Person	48.8	45.9	50.6	46.1	50.4	44.9	45.7
Average Number in Consumer Unit							
All persons	2.5	2.5	2.4	2.5	2.5	2.8	2.8
Children under 18 years	0.7	0.6	0.6	0.7	0.6	0.8	0.8
Persons 65 years and over	0.3	0.2	0.3	0.2	0.4	0.2	0.2
Earners	1.3	1.5	1.3	1.3	1.3	1.6	1.4
Vehicles	1.9	1.7	1.7	1.6	1.5	2.0	1.9
Percent Homeowner	69	68	71	69	63	65	70
AVERAGE ANNUAL EXPENDITURES	43 513	58 236	47 494	43 727	42 379	53 294	56 260
Food	5 570	6 357	4 921	5 289	5 637	6 537	6 063
Food at home	3 073	3 092	2 883	2 506	3 593	3 573	3 231
Cereals and bakery products	404	393	388	323	464	468	382
Meats, poultry, fish, and eggs	748	687	743	661	910	805	784
Dairy products	330	370	286	234	427	392	329
Fruits and vegetables	493	642	467	443	727	596	587
Other food at home	1 097	1 000	999	846	1 066	1 312	1 149
Food away from home	2 498	3 264	2 038	2 783	2 044	2 964	2 832
Alcoholic Beverages	358	572	390	265	255	461	604
Housing	13 938	24 059	17 063	16 158	15 928	17 854	17 198
Shelter	7 529	15 976	10 813	9 539	10 053	9 883	9 427
Owned dwellings	5 130	11 628	7 744	6 467	6 385	6 793	6 501
Rented dwellings	2 028	3 765	2 464	2 523	3 445	2 478	2 293
Other lodging	371	582	605	549	222	611	634
Utilities, fuels, and public services	3 398	3 827	3 424	3 773	3 421	4 424	4 179
Household operations	820	1 447	883	990	856	1 140	1 181
Housekeeping supplies	617	603	503	548	532	714	732
Household furnishings and equipment	1 575	2 206	1 440	1 307	1 065	1 693	1 679
Apparel and Services	1 786	2 195	1 805	1 847	1 242	2 048	2 608
Transportation	8 244	7 341	7 554	7 599	8 186	9 662	11 636
Vehicle purchases (net outlay)	3 593	2 133	2 929	3 146	3 199	3 919	5 305
Gasoline and motor oil	2 213	1 958	2 073	2 124	2 069	2 410	2 743
Other vehicle expenses	2 134	2 503	2 076	1 965	2 480	2 816	3 068
Public transportation	305	747	476	364	437	517	519
Health Care	2 691	2 505	2 551	2 017	2 190	3 075	3 259
Entertainment	2 104	2 480	2 186	1 861	1 523	2 285	2 528
Personal Care Products and Services	540	625	525	460	633	713	737
Reading	89	135	83	72	43	110	114
Education	691	1 446	1 840	652	724	799	998
Tobacco Products and Smoking Supplies	327	187	242	190	168	260	274
Miscellaneous	691	1 039	713	522	524	839	1 025
Cash Contributions	1 736	1 635	1 578	1 207	1 328	2 077	2 736
Personal Insurance and Pensions	4 748	7 661	6 043	5 587	4 000	6 573	6 478
Life and other personal insurance	366	412	463	266	221	382	441
Pensions and Social Security	4 382	7 249	5 580	5 321	3 779	6 191	6 038

[1]The states in the South include Alabama, Arkansas, Delaware, District of Columbia, Florida, Georgia, Kentucky, Louisiana, Maryland, Mississippi, North Carolina, Oklahoma, South Carolina, Tennessee, Texas, Virginia, and West Virginia.

Table 8-19. Consumer Expenditures, Averages by Selected Metropolitan Statistical Areas: Midwest Region, 2005–2006

(Number, dollar, percent.)

Item	All consumer units in the Midwest[1]	Chicago	Detroit	Minneapolis-St. Paul	Cleveland
NUMBER OF CONSUMER UNITS (THOUSANDS)	27 105	3 119	2 192	1 403	1 120
CONSUMER UNIT CHARACTERISTICS					
Income Before Taxes	57 295	73 086	62 834	85 455	55 798
Age of Reference Person	48.7	49.5	48.7	47.7	52.6
Average Number in Consumer Unit					
All persons	2.4	2.6	2.6	2.2	2.5
Children under 18 years	0.6	0.7	0.7	0.5	0.6
Persons 65 years and over	0.3	0.3	0.2	0.2	0.4
Earners	1.4	1.4	1.4	1.4	1.3
Vehicles	2.1	1.8	2.0	2.2	2.0
Percent Homeowner	70	71	75	75	72
AVERAGE ANNUAL EXPENDITURES	45 068	54 757	50 345	61 428	43 611
Food	5 759	6 902	6 614	6 393	5 043
Food at home	3 246	3 730	3 827	3 297	2 996
Cereals and bakery products	443	491	527	470	375
Meats, poultry, fish, and eggs	725	879	931	564	840
Dairy products	378	381	416	431	304
Fruits and vegetables	524	664	638	584	476
Other food at home	1 176	1 315	1 316	1 248	1 001
Food away from home	2 513	3 171	2 787	3 095	2 047
Alcoholic Beverages	493	839	463	688	488
Housing	14 419	19 059	16 831	20 380	14 654
Shelter	8 067	11 755	9 899	11 650	8 546
Owned dwellings	5 792	8 448	7 710	8 879	5 659
Rented dwellings	1 738	2 573	1 543	2 004	2 250
Other lodging	537	733	645	767	636
Utilities, fuels, and public services	3 221	3 620	3 794	3 245	3 624
Household operations	843	1 096	823	2 466	546
Housekeeping supplies	612	695	588	651	550
Household furnishings and equipment	1 676	1 893	1 727	2 368	1 388
Apparel and Services	1 725	2 468	2 057	2 346	1 618
Transportation	7 626	8 453	8 652	8 915	7 596
Vehicle purchases (net outlay)	2 907	3 352	2 252	3 593	2 965
Gasoline and motor oil	2 059	2 092	2 405	2 031	1 825
Other vehicle expenses	2 268	2 302	3 585	2 618	2 487
Public transportation	393	706	411	673	318
Health Care	2 828	2 878	2 349	3 322	3 035
Entertainment	2 322	2 621	2 287	4 070	2 338
Personal Care Products and Services	526	632	584	623	489
Reading	130	141	142	161	153
Education	974	1 513	1 297	1 269	1 070
Tobacco Products and Smoking Supplies	365	312	517	364	380
Miscellaneous	821	817	1 043	1 184	1 056
Cash Contributions	1 885	1 986	1 690	3 687	1 227
Personal Insurance and Pensions	5 196	6 135	5 818	8 026	4 464
Life and other personal insurance	362	358	346	376	361
Pensions and Social Security	4 833	5 777	5 472	7 651	4 103

[1]The states in the Midwest include Illinois, Indiana, Iowa, Kansas, Michigan, Minnesota, Missouri, Nebraska, North Dakota, Ohio, South Dakota, and Wisconsin.

Table 8-20. Consumer Expenditures, Averages by Selected Metropolitan Statistical Areas: West Region, 2005–2006

(Number, dollar, percent.)

Item	All consumer units in the West[1]	Los Angeles	San Francisco	San Diego	Seattle	Phoenix
NUMBER OF CONSUMER UNITS (THOUSANDS)	26 149	5 279	2 923	954	1 915	1 565
CONSUMER UNIT CHARACTERISTICS						
Income Before Taxes	66 452	70 847	90 781	73 846	65 672	65 520
Age of Reference Person	47.4	46.7	47.5	48.7	47.8	44.3
Average Number in Consumer Unit						
All persons	2.6	2.9	2.5	2.6	2.3	2.7
Children under 18 years	0.7	0.8	0.6	0.6	0.5	0.8
Persons 65 years and over	0.3	0.3	0.3	0.3	0.2	0.2
Earners	1.4	1.5	1.4	1.4	1.5	1.4
Vehicles	2.1	1.9	1.9	1.9	2.4	1.9
Percent Homeowner	63	57	58	56	67	68
AVERAGE ANNUAL EXPENDITURES	55 214	58 404	66 344	62 321	55 544	53 570
Food	6 745	7 222	7 942	6 238	6 887	7 187
Food at home	3 769	3 873	4 173	3 261	3 778	3 822
Cereals and bakery products	477	470	527	423	479	482
Meats, poultry, fish, and eggs	832	914	965	711	743	894
Dairy products	415	395	443	376	417	433
Fruits and vegetables	690	795	839	529	662	672
Other food at home	1 356	1 297	1 399	1 222	1 477	1 342
Food away from home	2 975	3 349	3 769	2 977	3 109	3 365
Alcoholic Beverages	585	475	757	755	752	693
Housing	19 064	21 190	26 382	23 034	19 142	16 469
Shelter	12 134	14 312	18 845	15 654	12 279	9 279
Owned dwellings	7 887	8 994	12 442	9 517	8 515	6 249
Rented dwellings	3 560	4 775	5 112	5 374	2 796	2 456
Other lodging	687	543	1 290	763	968	573
Utilities, fuels, and public services	3 013	2 996	2 925	3 001	3 046	3 348
Household operations	1 017	1 235	1 574	1 830	733	899
Housekeeping supplies	660	643	625	499	611	784
Household furnishings and equipment	2 240	2 004	2 414	2 049	2 473	2 158
Apparel and Services	2 050	2 396	2 524	2 111	1 541	2 019
Transportation	10 112	10 716	10 080	11 115	10 127	10 964
Vehicle purchases (net outlay)	4 399	4 443	3 492	4 959	4 145	5 422
Gasoline and motor oil	2 282	2 566	2 309	2 542	2 221	2 217
Other vehicle expenses	2 724	2 980	3 261	2 753	2 950	2 832
Public transportation	707	727	1 017	862	810	493
Health Care	2 751	2 316	2 820	3 421	2 889	3 134
Entertainment	2 960	2 743	3 080	2 774	3 196	2 615
Personal Care Products and Services	652	815	734	866	626	657
Reading	150	141	205	154	179	115
Education	937	1 127	1 106	986	848	794
Tobacco Products and Smoking Supplies	267	199	151	99	289	411
Miscellaneous	1 033	1 014	1 073	1 161	924	919
Cash Contributions	1 993	1 710	1 741	2 470	1 995	1 910
Personal Insurance and Pensions	5 917	6 340	7 748	7 138	6 149	5 683
Life and other personal insurance	315	307	342	425	371	312
Pensions and Social Security	5 602	6 033	7 406	6 713	5 779	5 371

[1]The states in the West include Alaska, Arizona, California, Colorado, Hawaii, Idaho, Montana, Nevada, New Mexico, Oregon, Utah, Washington, and Wyoming.

Table 8-21. Consumer Expenditures, Averages for Single Men by Income Before Taxes, 2005–2006

(Number, dollar, percent.)

Item	All single men	Complete reporting of income						
		Less than $5,000	$5,000 to $9,999	$10,000 to $14,999	$15,000 to $19,999	$20,000 to $29,999	$30,000 to $39,999	$40,000 and over
NUMBER OF CONSUMER UNITS (THOUSANDS)	15 811	1 327	1 613	1 734	1 388	2 458	2 146	5 146
CONSUMER UNIT CHARACTERISTICS								
Income Before Taxes	35 722	1 791	7 726	12 569	17 386	24 412	34 312	71 977
Income After Taxes	33 840	1 764	7 586	12 488	16 991	23 474	32 594	67 545
Age of Reference Person	46.8	38.8	46.6	52.1	51.9	47.8	44.4	46.2
Average Number in Consumer Unit								
All persons	1.0	1.0	1.0	1.0	1.0	1.0	1.0	1.0
Children under 18 years	X	X	X	X	X	X	X	X
Persons 65 years and over	0.2	0.1	0.2	0.3	0.3	0.2	0.1	0.1
Earners	0.7	0.5	0.4	0.5	0.6	0.7	0.9	0.9
Vehicles	1.3	0.7	0.7	1.0	1.2	1.3	1.5	1.7
Percent Homeowner	46	22	23	36	41	43	48	64
With mortgage	25	6	4	10	12	17	30	47
Without mortgage	21	16	19	26	28	26	19	17
AVERAGE ANNUAL EXPENDITURES	30 149	15 510	14 083	17 766	21 423	23 845	29 557	48 319
Food	3 502	2 263	2 209	2 721	2 886	2 812	3 584	4 694
Food at home	1 621	1 040	1 241	1 483	1 606	1 410	1 641	1 936
Cereals and bakery products	204	139	167	180	224	178	232	226
Meats, poultry, fish, and eggs	365	257	264	376	347	310	374	429
Dairy products	172	116	128	172	169	139	177	204
Fruits and vegetables	264	175	208	229	299	252	241	307
Other food at home	616	352	473	526	568	531	618	770
Food away from home	1 880	1 223	968	1 238	1 280	1 403	1 943	2 758
Alcoholic Beverages	552	360	345	338	497	345	536	812
Housing	10 422	5 641	5 252	6 972	7 830	8 781	10 693	15 754
Shelter	6 907	3 920	3 675	4 651	4 804	5 704	6 859	10 611
Owned dwellings	3 165	884	643	1 202	1 339	1 894	3 001	6 374
Rented dwellings	3 464	2 838	2 953	3 357	3 340	3 710	3 681	3 647
Other lodging	277	198	79	92	124	99	178	590
Utilities, fuels, and public services	1 958	1 010	1 079	1 480	1 728	1 949	2 086	2 651
Household operations	339	168	96	202	233	256	314	584
Housekeeping supplies	247	121	145	159	379	194	273	297
Household furnishings and equipment	972	422	257	480	686	678	1 161	1 611
Apparel and Services	858	832	480	499	537	472	782	1 386
Transportation	5 011	2 186	2 149	2 684	3 531	4 627	5 323	7 869
Vehicle purchases (net outlay)	1 806	¹733	¹725	708	1 072	1 833	1 802	2 978
Gasoline and motor oil	1 373	786	713	893	1 126	1 330	1 576	1 895
Other vehicle expenses	1 519	548	558	956	1 110	1 300	1 680	2 405
Public transportation	314	119	154	128	223	163	265	591
Health Care	1 399	479	693	1 207	1 562	1 568	1 297	1 830
Health insurance	750	264	336	668	850	818	759	968
Medical services	340	78	173	291	246	425	278	486
Drugs	264	116	163	195	359	295	239	318
Medical supplies	46	¹21	¹20	54	107	30	20	58
Entertainment	1 626	599	948	832	957	1 093	1 357	2 913
Personal Care Products and Services	193	143	107	136	189	148	203	266
Reading	87	38	33	54	78	70	81	141
Education	569	1 546	784	535	300	270	445	526
Tobacco Products and Smoking Supplies	320	291	334	314	346	321	376	294
Miscellaneous	767	470	184	380	376	719	689	1 298
Cash Contributions	1 759	435	301	535	1 445	1 013	1 271	3 612
Personal Insurance and Pensions	3 085	229	263	559	889	1 606	2 919	6 923
Life and other personal insurance	155	¹22	40	79	97	120	118	299
Pensions and Social Security	2 930	207	223	480	792	1 485	2 801	6 624

¹Data are likely to have large sampling errors.
X = Not applicable.

Table 8-22. Consumer Expenditures, Averages for Single Women by Income Before Taxes, 2005–2006

(Number, dollar, percent.)

Item	All single women	Complete reporting of income						
		Less than $5,000	$5,000 to $9,999	$10,000 to $14,999	$15,000 to $19,999	$20,000 to $29,999	$30,000 to $39,999	$40,000 and over
NUMBER OF CONSUMER UNITS (THOUSANDS)	18 969	1 664	2 660	3 190	2 379	3 168	2 209	3 699
CONSUMER UNIT CHARACTERISTICS								
Income Before Taxes	26 938	1 729	8 028	12 462	17 237	24 579	34 369	68 182
Income After Taxes	25 729	1 717	8 017	12 355	16 892	23 885	32 884	63 788
Age of Reference Person	57.6	44.9	58.5	67.7	65.9	58.8	52.4	50.6
Average Number in Consumer Unit								
All persons	1.0	1.0	1.0	1.0	1.0	1.0	1.0	1.0
Children under 18 years	X	X	X	X	X	X	X	X
Persons 65 years and over	0.4	0.2	0.5	0.7	0.6	0.4	0.3	0.2
Earners	0.5	0.4	0.3	0.2	0.4	0.6	0.8	0.9
Vehicles	0.9	0.6	0.6	0.7	0.9	1.0	1.1	1.2
Percent Homeowner	57	35	35	57	63	61	64	73
With mortgage	24	11	7	10	15	23	37	54
Without mortgage	33	24	29	47	48	39	27	19
AVERAGE ANNUAL EXPENDITURES	26 382	15 519	13 124	17 356	21 886	26 398	30 721	48 458
Food	2 881	2 574	1 910	2 046	2 417	2 744	3 093	4 567
Food at home	1 736	1 361	1 334	1 435	1 611	1 744	1 795	2 403
Cereals and bakery products	243	210	181	215	227	245	242	326
Meats, poultry, fish, and eggs	337	283	312	273	311	343	343	431
Dairy products	205	167	167	174	196	209	209	270
Fruits and vegetables	327	224	237	269	282	345	366	458
Other food at home	623	477	437	504	595	603	634	918
Food away from home	1 145	1 213	577	611	807	1 000	1 298	2 163
Alcoholic Beverages	233	174	77	89	121	223	301	515
Housing	10 497	6 007	5 950	7 320	9 245	10 674	12 501	17 895
Shelter	6 516	3 780	3 616	4 276	5 477	6 675	7 895	11 474
Owned dwellings	3 524	1 459	910	1 743	2 700	3 395	4 599	7 869
Rented dwellings	2 731	2 020	2 639	2 446	2 614	3 084	3 060	2 941
Other lodging	261	300	67	88	163	196	235	664
Utilities, fuels, and public services	2 199	1 349	1 541	1 942	2 297	2 366	2 459	2 914
Household operations	464	174	160	349	438	451	529	900
Housekeeping supplies	390	223	277	256	348	361	480	628
Household furnishings and equipment	928	481	355	498	685	822	1 139	1 980
Apparel and Services	1 054	842	564	477	698	922	1 378	2 077
Transportation	3 587	1 968	1 517	2 155	2 487	4 163	4 314	6 809
Vehicle purchases (net outlay)	1 204	¹671	392	805	¹536	1 591	1 164	2 492
Gasoline and motor oil	892	627	494	577	775	972	1 194	1 397
Other vehicle expenses	1 173	551	529	633	942	1 336	1 590	2 138
Public transportation	317	119	103	139	234	264	366	782
Health Care	2 114	970	1 022	2 161	2 710	2 437	2 154	2 679
Health insurance	1 064	478	530	1 228	1 483	1 277	1 031	1 138
Medical services	494	240	187	340	490	489	614	897
Drugs	470	185	258	532	660	563	421	513
Medical supplies	86	67	48	61	76	107	88	131
Entertainment	1 212	666	510	696	1 090	1 018	1 462	2 477
Personal Care Products and Services	471	237	220	299	396	441	560	897
Reading	105	52	39	72	101	101	140	191
Education	420	1 124	370	376	204	326	276	484
Tobacco Products and Smoking Supplies	149	114	142	156	149	171	165	137
Miscellaneous	485	304	195	413	461	418	632	815
Cash Contributions	1 219	317	395	743	1 193	1 378	1 227	2 500
Personal Insurance and Pensions	1 956	170	213	353	613	1 382	2 520	6 415
Life and other personal insurance	144	51	82	160	133	145	128	234
Pensions and Social Security	1 812	120	131	193	480	1 237	2 392	6 182

¹Data are likely to have large sampling errors.
X = Not applicable.

Table 8-23. Consumer Expenditures, Averages for Age Groups by Income Before Taxes: Reference Person Under 25 Years of Age, 2005–2006

(Number, dollar, percent.)

Item		Complete reporting of income						
	Total	Less than $5,000	$5,000 to $9,999	$10,000 to $14,999	$15,000 to $19,999	$20,000 to $29,999	$30,000 to $39,999	$40,000 and over
NUMBER OF CONSUMER UNITS (THOUSANDS)	8 355	1 319	1 159	920	704	1 271	1 008	1 974
CONSUMER UNIT CHARACTERISTICS								
Income Before Taxes	28 258	2 507	7 369	12 334	17 378	24 610	34 189	68 344
Income After Taxes	27 812	2 556	7 434	12 289	17 364	24 257	33 729	66 872
Age of Reference Person	21.5	20.3	20.7	21.3	21.9	21.8	22.2	22.3
Average Number in Consumer Unit								
All persons	2.1	1.2	1.4	1.7	2.0	2.1	2.4	3.0
Children under 18 years	0.4	0.1	0.3	0.4	0.5	0.6	0.6	0.6
Persons 65 years and over	(1)	. . .	(1)	(1)	(1)	(1)	(1)	(1)
Earners	1.4	0.7	0.9	1.0	1.2	1.4	1.5	2.2
Vehicles	1.2	0.5	0.7	0.8	1.1	1.2	1.5	2.1
Percent Distribution								
Male	48	47	48	46	46	47	50	51
Female	52	53	52	54	54	53	50	49
Percent Homeowner	19	8	7	9	11	12	23	44
With mortgage	13	1	2	3	5	7	17	35
Without mortgage	7	7	5	6	6	5	6	9
AVERAGE ANNUAL EXPENDITURES	27 976	12 653	15 722	18 276	22 164	26 458	33 099	49 292
Food	3 926	2 015	2 351	2 809	3 516	3 611	4 366	6 156
Food at home	1 931	848	1 029	1 431	2 093	1 915	1 918	3 030
Cereals and bakery products	257	128	121	207	269	236	259	410
Meats, poultry, fish, and eggs	442	161	230	276	403	439	404	770
Dairy products	216	86	104	157	236	219	244	334
Fruits and vegetables	308	133	141	235	392	327	275	475
Other food at home	708	340	432	556	793	694	736	1 041
Food away from home	1 995	1 166	1 322	1 378	1 423	1 696	2 448	3 126
Alcoholic Beverages	435	223	300	301	428	344	534	670
Housing	9 144	3 916	5 384	6 412	7 735	9 080	11 020	15 581
Shelter	5 727	2 743	3 583	4 212	4 988	5 716	7 038	9 286
Owned dwellings	1 333	269	298	214	414	541	1 438	3 955
Rented dwellings	4 198	2 195	3 077	3 761	4 456	5 085	5 426	5 106
Other lodging	197	279	208	238	118	90	174	224
Utilities, fuels, and public services	1 768	601	909	1 204	1 534	1 892	2 190	3 102
Household operations	381	97	168	238	353	396	386	759
Housekeeping supplies	267	128	137	181	216	266	280	441
Household furnishings and equipment	1 001	347	587	577	645	810	1 127	1 994
Apparel and Services	1 523	982	844	1 061	1 071	1 448	1 635	2 484
Transportation	5 831	1 658	2 500	3 037	3 804	6 173	7 707	11 402
Vehicle purchases (net outlay)	2 562	[2]450	[2]651	1 002	1 209	3 059	3 507	5 503
Gasoline and motor oil	1 587	690	842	1 044	1 430	1 565	1 994	2 737
Other vehicle expenses	1 476	415	791	820	1 050	1 411	1 889	2 862
Public transportation	206	104	215	170	115	138	317	301
Health Care	705	163	246	221	515	802	919	1 446
Health insurance	372	65	100	93	264	351	524	841
Medical services	195	55	75	68	132	322	198	356
Drugs	98	33	54	34	86	102	144	170
Medical supplies	40	[2]10	[2]17	[2]25	[2]33	27	53	79
Entertainment	1 373	588	954	855	1 751	1 163	1 547	2 272
Personal Care Products and Services	342	206	266	296	226	275	376	542
Reading	47	34	42	41	36	32	51	74
Education	1 310	2 455	1 847	1 723	843	693	590	962
Tobacco Products and Smoking Supplies	297	81	181	231	278	396	421	419
Miscellaneous	323	113	189	270	361	188	515	523
Cash Contributions	510	82	227	267	384	432	614	1 116
Personal Insurance and Pensions	2 210	137	392	752	1 215	1 822	2 801	5 645
Life and other personal insurance	43	[2]2	[2]5	[2]30	[2]14	34	64	106
Pensions and Social Security	2 167	134	386	722	1 201	1 788	2 737	5 540

[1]Value less than 0.05.
[2]Data are likely to have large sampling errors.
. . . = Not available.

Table 8-24. Consumer Expenditures, Averages for Age Groups by Income Before Taxes: Reference Person 25 to 34 Years of Age, 2005–2006

(Number, dollar, percent.)

Item	Total	Complete reporting of income								
		Less than $5,000	$5,000 to $9,999	$10,000 to $14,999	$15,000 to $19,999	$20,000 to $29,999	$30,000 to $39,999	$40,000 to $49,999	$50,000 to $69,999	$70,000 and over
NUMBER OF CONSUMER UNITS (THOUSANDS)	19 853	564	707	880	963	2 548	2 723	2 300	3 521	5 647
CONSUMER UNIT CHARACTERISTICS										
Income Before Taxes	56 149	1 182	7 758	12 613	17 560	25 107	34 647	44 263	58 935	108 532
Income After Taxes	54 480	1 467	8 125	13 003	17 831	25 194	34 069	43 071	56 998	104 417
Age of Reference Person	29.6	29.1	28.8	29.1	29.1	29.2	29.3	29.5	29.6	30.3
Average Number in Consumer Unit										
All persons	2.8	2.3	2.3	2.6	2.6	2.7	2.7	2.8	3.0	3.1
Children under 18 years	1.1	1.0	1.1	1.2	1.2	1.1	1.0	1.1	1.1	1.0
Persons 65 years and over	(^{1})	. . .	. . .	(^{1})	(^{1})	(^{1})	(^{1})	(^{1})	(^{1})	(^{1})
Earners	1.5	0.6	0.8	1.0	1.1	1.3	1.4	1.6	1.7	1.9
Vehicles	1.8	0.7	0.8	1.0	1.1	1.3	1.5	1.8	2.2	2.4
Percent Distribution										
Male	48	32	33	36	39	43	47	49	53	54
Female	52	68	67	64	61	57	53	51	47	46
Percent Homeowner	49	21	18	18	19	25	37	48	60	76
With mortgage	42	12	7	7	10	17	30	41	54	71
Without mortgage	7	10	11	11	9	8	7	7	6	5
AVERAGE ANNUAL EXPENDITURES	46 341	20 450	19 186	23 191	24 356	29 326	35 538	39 300	49 903	72 840
Food	5 871	2 645	3 427	4 086	3 795	4 284	4 858	5 095	6 465	8 061
Food at home	3 065	1 709	2 107	2 708	2 315	2 540	2 566	2 690	3 291	3 889
Cereals and bakery products	397	219	306	354	312	331	340	349	429	491
Meats, poultry, fish, and eggs	700	422	540	715	558	605	606	602	721	864
Dairy products	350	205	251	257	268	277	297	312	404	434
Fruits and vegetables	499	266	337	436	385	432	407	428	509	654
Other food at home	1 119	597	672	947	793	894	916	999	1 228	1 446
Food away from home	2 806	936	1 319	1 378	1 480	1 745	2 292	2 405	3 175	4 172
Alcoholic Beverages	567	153	280	255	330	252	530	412	608	910
Housing	16 342	9 334	7 562	8 764	9 478	10 609	12 607	13 799	17 389	25 201
Shelter	10 121	6 366	4 657	5 236	5 697	6 497	7 889	8 450	10 963	15 563
Owned dwellings	5 681	1 476	747	787	871	1 467	2 819	3 849	6 245	11 976
Rented dwellings	4 166	4 641	3 826	4 384	4 764	4 943	4 969	4 432	4 484	2 980
Other lodging	274	^{2}249	^{2}84	^{2}65	^{2}62	87	101	169	234	606
Utilities, fuels, and public services	3 002	1 871	1 904	2 113	2 269	2 490	2 637	2 892	3 243	3 817
Household operations	1 068	303	302	415	457	503	594	841	1 024	2 049
Housekeeping supplies	517	243	224	298	386	317	394	437	560	767
Household furnishings and equipment	1 634	552	476	702	669	801	1 093	1 180	1 600	3 006
Apparel and Services	2 117	1 259	1 236	1 374	1 191	1 489	1 764	1 742	1 959	3 249
Transportation	8 924	2 255	2 975	3 890	4 926	6 321	7 218	7 972	10 248	13 359
Vehicle purchases (net outlay)	3 930	^{2}471	^{2}1 158	1 358	2 100	2 833	3 060	3 358	4 681	6 014
Gasoline and motor oil	2 236	895	1 000	1 289	1 483	1 717	1 930	2 185	2 617	2 964
Other vehicle expenses	2 351	617	685	1 101	1 175	1 563	1 985	2 206	2 599	3 564
Public transportation	407	272	134	142	169	207	242	223	351	816
Health Care	1 588	427	412	572	630	929	1 112	1 563	1 788	2 579
Health insurance	853	194	246	237	337	441	606	878	1 043	1 354
Medical services	434	81	54	189	144	280	296	378	450	755
Drugs	240	96	97	127	121	165	169	250	239	372
Medical supplies	60	^{2}56	^{2}15	^{2}19	27	43	41	57	56	98
Entertainment	2 345	958	1 321	1 186	1 092	1 227	1 691	1 822	2 474	3 957
Personal Care Products and Services	525	221	243	293	326	337	395	433	562	811
Reading	85	48	30	44	64	48	59	75	85	140
Education	744	1 830	448	937	251	500	744	725	628	919
Tobacco Products and Smoking Supplies	313	416	249	337	241	384	324	346	348	246
Miscellaneous	656	329	387	358	264	342	476	615	778	999
Cash Contributions	1 075	398	237	269	469	640	765	761	1 069	1 954
Personal Insurance and Pensions	5 188	178	379	826	1 301	1 963	2 995	3 940	5 503	10 457
Life and other personal insurance	196	^{2}48	^{2}42	52	55	62	108	135	205	398
Pensions and Social Security	4 992	129	338	774	1 245	1 901	2 887	3 805	5 298	10 059

^{1}Value less than 0.05.
^{2}Data are likely to have large sampling errors.
. . . = Not available.

Table 8-25. Consumer Expenditures, Averages for Age Groups by Income Before Taxes: Reference Person 35 to 44 Years of Age, 2005–2006

(Number, dollar, percent.)

Item	Total	Complete reporting of income								
		Less than $5,000	$5,000 to $9,999	$10,000 to $14,999	$15,000 to $19,999	$20,000 to $29,999	$30,000 to $39,999	$40,000 to $49,999	$50,000 to $69,999	$70,000 and over
NUMBER OF CONSUMER UNITS (THOUSANDS)	23 892	537	689	840	846	2 226	2 576	2 452	4 228	9 498
CONSUMER UNIT CHARACTERISTICS										
Income Before Taxes	74 159	-1 803	7 770	12 664	17 401	25 017	34 879	44 769	59 406	130 091
Income After Taxes	71 035	-1 682	8 025	13 118	17 774	25 130	34 321	43 666	57 543	123 372
Age of Reference Person	39.7	39.7	39.9	39.8	39.9	39.6	39.4	39.8	39.5	39.8
Average Number in Consumer Unit										
All persons	3.2	2.3	2.2	2.6	2.8	2.9	2.9	3.0	3.3	3.6
Children under 18 years	1.3	0.9	0.8	1.2	1.2	1.2	1.2	1.1	1.3	1.4
Persons 65 years and over	(1)	(1)	(1)	(1)	(1)	(1)	(1)	(1)	(1)	(1)
Earners	1.6	0.6	0.6	0.9	1.1	1.3	1.4	1.6	1.8	2.0
Vehicles	2.1	0.8	0.8	1.1	1.2	1.5	1.7	2.1	2.3	2.6
Percent Distribution										
Male	47	35	38	37	41	41	43	46	49	52
Female	53	65	62	63	59	59	57	54	51	48
Percent Homeowner	68	37	28	31	34	43	56	63	72	89
With mortgage	59	22	12	17	20	30	44	51	63	82
Without mortgage	10	15	17	14	14	13	12	12	9	7
AVERAGE ANNUAL EXPENDITURES	56 350	27 002	18 200	23 892	23 532	29 277	36 372	41 000	51 166	84 436
Food	7 345	4 345	3 160	4 972	4 151	4 702	5 436	6 034	7 085	9 800
Food at home	4 125	2 403	2 077	3 588	3 045	3 066	3 232	3 433	3 979	5 186
Cereals and bakery products	559	297	277	459	353	402	416	445	539	724
Meats, poultry, fish, and eggs	963	647	581	879	762	796	804	818	950	1 147
Dairy products	465	244	221	386	314	326	375	368	469	590
Fruits and vegetables	667	429	293	559	537	492	488	574	605	859
Other food at home	1 471	786	706	1 306	1 078	1 049	1 148	1 226	1 416	1 866
Food away from home	3 220	1 942	1 083	1 384	1 105	1 636	2 204	2 602	3 107	4 614
Alcoholic Beverages	504	216	119	188	157	202	361	508	435	738
Housing	19 409	11 042	8 018	9 264	9 643	10 777	13 188	14 543	16 818	28 573
Shelter	11 656	7 460	4 868	5 570	6 054	6 438	7 717	8 753	9 989	17 205
Owned dwellings	8 465	3 871	1 434	1 884	1 743	2 386	4 057	5 126	6 893	14 598
Rented dwellings	2 706	3 385	3 370	3 654	4 257	3 996	3 529	3 388	2 804	1 652
Other lodging	485	[2]203	[2]63	[2]33	[2]53	56	130	239	292	955
Utilities, fuels, and public services	3 712	2 251	2 249	2 352	2 545	2 816	3 092	3 269	3 747	4 602
Household operations	1 263	411	167	299	202	352	442	679	813	2 357
Housekeeping supplies	738	365	376	336	295	415	512	538	646	1 076
Household furnishings and equipment	2 039	555	359	706	547	756	1 425	1 305	1 623	3 332
Apparel and Services	2 366	2 016	1 051	1 290	909	1 602	1 769	1 721	2 326	3 215
Transportation	9 961	4 726	2 549	3 658	3 328	5 527	6 383	6 806	10 207	14 655
Vehicle purchases (net outlay)	4 232	[2]2 177	[2]879	1 169	[2]779	2 187	2 389	2 251	4 409	6 581
Gasoline and motor oil	2 507	980	905	1 284	1 382	1 794	1 954	2 181	2 660	3 252
Other vehicle expenses	2 697	1 342	593	1 091	1 008	1 400	1 834	2 073	2 772	3 883
Public transportation	525	226	173	114	158	146	207	302	367	939
Health Care	2 278	824	661	839	972	1 119	1 489	1 954	2 327	3 265
Health insurance	1 187	423	229	380	602	599	846	1 004	1 342	1 632
Medical services	650	276	173	205	200	273	321	553	552	1 031
Drugs	349	102	234	213	150	214	267	332	352	457
Medical supplies	92	[2]24	[2]25	[2]42	[2]20	33	55	66	82	145
Entertainment	2 866	909	798	929	926	1 112	1 706	1 912	2 430	4 631
Personal Care Products and Services	657	227	224	294	390	344	449	497	626	948
Reading	117	49	26	38	39	41	53	76	92	198
Education	894	567	109	249	262	255	328	431	653	1 612
Tobacco Products and Smoking Supplies	356	380	430	382	496	437	445	397	370	274
Miscellaneous	867	738	351	502	336	369	632	678	815	1 244
Cash Contributions	1 721	267	362	407	604	753	1 088	1 130	1 235	2 885
Personal Insurance and Pensions	7 009	697	340	881	1 320	2 038	3 045	4 311	5 745	12 399
Life and other personal insurance	381	[2]182	[2]59	74	133	122	136	214	301	669
Pensions and Social Security	6 629	515	282	807	1 187	1 916	2 909	4 096	5 444	11 729

[1]Value less than 0.05.
[2]Data are likely to have large sampling errors.

Table 8-26. Consumer Expenditures, Averages for Age Groups by Income Before Taxes: Reference Person 45 to 54 Years of Age, 2005–2006

(Number, dollar, percent.)

Item	Total	Less than $5,000	$5,000 to $9,999	$10,000 to $14,999	$15,000 to $19,999	$20,000 to $29,999	$30,000 to $39,999	$40,000 to $49,999	$50,000 to $69,999	$70,000 and over
					Complete reporting of income					
NUMBER OF CONSUMER UNITS (THOUSANDS)	24 544	654	844	903	974	2 072	2 538	2 274	3 917	10 368
CONSUMER UNIT CHARACTERISTICS										
Income Before Taxes	76 160	-4 325	7 869	12 468	17 399	25 280	34 745	44 675	59 519	131 361
Income After Taxes	72 569	-4 556	7 918	12 711	17 515	24 997	33 645	43 539	57 475	124 186
Age of Reference Person	49.3	49.2	49.5	49.7	49.2	49.3	49.1	49.2	49.6	49.3
Average Number in Consumer Unit										
All persons	2.7	1.8	1.7	2.1	2.3	2.2	2.3	2.5	2.7	3.1
Children under 18 years	0.6	0.4	0.4	0.5	0.6	0.5	0.5	0.6	0.5	0.7
Persons 65 years and over	(1)	(1)	(1)	(1)	(1)	(1)	0.1	(1)	(1)	(1)
Earners	1.7	0.6	0.5	0.8	1.0	1.3	1.4	1.6	1.9	2.2
Vehicles	2.4	1.0	0.8	1.0	1.3	1.6	1.8	2.0	2.5	3.1
Percent Distribution										
Male	48	33	28	43	40	39	44	43	49	54
Female	52	67	72	57	60	61	56	57	51	46
Percent Homeowner	75	43	28	38	44	57	63	71	81	92
With mortgage	58	19	13	15	25	38	45	55	63	77
Without mortgage	17	24	15	23	19	18	18	16	18	16
AVERAGE ANNUAL EXPENDITURES	56 729	25 701	17 188	19 746	23 269	28 069	33 551	38 965	49 753	85 910
Food	7 155	4 150	3 211	3 236	3 473	4 099	4 589	5 111	6 809	10 012
Food at home	3 922	2 672	2 363	2 303	2 252	2 689	2 801	3 024	3 940	5 055
Cereals and bakery products	505	356	305	292	275	340	364	383	493	659
Meats, poultry, fish, and eggs	945	696	624	633	558	696	638	744	995	1 180
Dairy products	426	285	214	251	254	283	316	335	428	550
Fruits and vegetables	649	381	353	377	358	450	432	498	611	867
Other food at home	1 397	954	868	751	808	919	1 051	1 064	1 413	1 800
Food away from home	3 233	1 477	847	933	1 222	1 410	1 788	2 088	2 869	4 957
Alcoholic Beverages	535	229	140	148	242	274	275	357	482	808
Housing	17 837	9 839	7 469	7 767	9 154	10 436	11 574	13 817	15 668	25 552
Shelter	10 606	6 016	4 566	4 617	5 321	6 158	6 938	8 111	9 060	15 322
Owned dwellings	7 871	2 514	1 069	1 263	1 941	3 139	3 880	5 461	6 949	12 696
Rented dwellings	1 946	3 287	3 440	3 299	3 293	2 921	2 882	2 444	1 743	1 038
Other lodging	788	2216	258	254	88	98	177	206	369	1 588
Utilities, fuels, and public services	3 803	2 415	2 047	2 217	2 500	2 879	2 968	3 367	3 730	4 807
Household operations	731	249	166	184	220	277	343	370	615	1 210
Housekeeping supplies	722	357	314	282	440	344	440	484	675	1 039
Household furnishings and equipment	1 975	802	376	468	673	779	884	1 484	1 587	3 174
Apparel and Services	2 247	1 204	973	1 088	888	1 062	1 357	1 469	1 903	3 358
Transportation	9 954	4 208	2 338	2 909	3 560	4 510	6 311	6 757	9 411	15 035
Vehicle purchases (net outlay)	3 964	21 608	2718	2615	2799	1 184	2 322	2 071	3 708	6 436
Gasoline and motor oil	2 559	1 268	766	1 180	1 445	1 649	1 970	2 253	2 581	3 396
Other vehicle expenses	2 835	1 095	659	933	1 158	1 449	1 811	2 222	2 769	4 128
Public transportation	596	237	195	180	157	229	207	212	353	1 074
Health Care	2 715	1 421	531	1 275	1 259	1 810	1 845	2 345	2 594	3 753
Health insurance	1 296	551	225	469	555	788	891	1 206	1 352	1 772
Medical services	784	530	91	475	343	518	489	632	631	1 141
Drugs	497	255	173	282	314	444	371	423	499	629
Medical supplies	137	286	242	49	46	61	95	85	112	210
Entertainment	2 901	921	754	836	937	1 147	1 641	1 759	2 430	4 639
Personal Care Products and Services	662	270	223	198	288	331	434	483	595	977
Reading	138	44	22	25	38	64	71	107	113	220
Education	1 752	438	207	126	455	366	322	422	1 023	3 416
Tobacco Products and Smoking Supplies	430	329	475	457	512	447	501	465	509	365
Miscellaneous	960	881	272	563	572	586	655	576	1 025	1 292
Cash Contributions	2 097	807	295	406	745	849	809	1 110	1 337	3 667
Personal Insurance and Pensions	7 347	959	277	712	1 145	2 088	3 167	4 186	5 852	12 817
Life and other personal insurance	443	101	69	69	132	172	195	278	348	743
Pensions and Social Security	6 904	858	208	643	1 014	1 915	2 972	3 908	5 504	12 074

[1]Value less than 0.05.
[2]Data are likely to have large sampling errors.

Table 8-27. Consumer Expenditures, Averages for Age Groups by Income Before Taxes: Reference Person 55 to 64 Years of Age, 2005–2006

(Number, dollar, percent.)

Item	Total	Complete reporting of income								
		Less than $5,000	$5,000 to $9,999	$10,000 to $14,999	$15,000 to $19,999	$20,000 to $29,999	$30,000 to $39,999	$40,000 to $49,999	$50,000 to $69,999	$70,000 and over
NUMBER OF CONSUMER UNITS (THOUSANDS)	18 528	643	1 000	1 058	1 099	2 057	1 988	1 969	2 900	5 814
CONSUMER UNIT CHARACTERISTICS										
Income Before Taxes	64 293	1 130	8 082	12 527	17 362	24 878	34 599	44 784	59 396	132 386
Income After Taxes	60 979	371	7 935	12 542	17 135	24 189	33 757	43 462	56 627	124 334
Age of Reference Person	59.2	59.2	59.8	59.8	59.6	59.8	59.6	59.4	59.0	58.7
Average Number in Consumer Unit										
All persons	2.1	1.5	1.4	1.7	1.7	1.7	1.9	2.0	2.2	2.5
Children under 18 years	0.2	[1]0.1	[1]0.1	0.2	0.1	0.1	0.2	0.1	0.1	0.2
Persons 65 years and over	0.1	([2])	[1]0.1	0.1	0.1	0.1	0.1	0.1	0.1	0.1
Earners	1.3	0.4	0.3	0.4	0.6	0.9	1.1	1.3	1.5	1.9
Vehicles	2.2	1.2	0.8	1.2	1.6	1.8	2.0	2.1	2.4	3.0
Percent Distribution										
Male	48	48	38	34	36	37	45	48	50	57
Female	52	52	62	66	64	63	55	52	50	43
Percent Homeowner	81	59	39	62	70	73	80	84	89	95
With mortgage	46	25	11	18	30	32	40	46	54	65
Without mortgage	35	34	29	43	40	41	39	38	34	30
AVERAGE ANNUAL EXPENDITURES	50 219	25 975	18 408	21 904	27 650	29 770	36 082	40 800	49 067	82 566
Food	6 165	3 436	3 211	3 350	3 693	3 984	4 368	5 464	6 365	8 954
Food at home	3 504	2 182	2 288	2 163	2 495	2 606	2 663	3 108	3 763	4 643
Cereals and bakery products	459	292	321	293	310	330	365	434	478	603
Meats, poultry, fish, and eggs	813	587	549	526	574	662	620	682	866	1 062
Dairy products	373	248	248	243	257	268	288	350	405	485
Fruits and vegetables	642	399	394	370	450	487	464	574	651	879
Other food at home	1 216	655	776	731	905	859	925	1 068	1 363	1 614
Food away from home	2 662	1 254	923	1 187	1 198	1 378	1 706	2 357	2 602	4 311
Alcoholic Beverages	466	306	76	231	157	245	285	327	435	798
Housing	16 171	10 181	7 489	8 708	9 900	10 352	12 628	13 493	15 519	25 185
Shelter	8 963	6 250	4 428	4 639	5 176	5 759	7 126	7 121	8 293	14 265
Owned dwellings	6 775	3 785	1 559	2 294	3 149	3 693	5 016	5 168	6 615	11 818
Rented dwellings	1 377	1 850	2 701	2 143	1 749	1 807	1 776	1 552	1 103	675
Other lodging	811	615	[1]168	202	278	258	334	402	575	1 772
Utilities, fuels, and public services	3 536	2 408	1 857	2 509	2 900	2 845	3 186	3 432	3 752	4 549
Household operations	815	473	235	280	314	336	440	635	615	1 602
Housekeeping supplies	737	312	419	389	416	467	540	683	837	1 023
Household furnishings and equipment	2 120	738	551	891	1 094	946	1 335	1 622	2 023	3 746
Apparel and Services	1 841	1 194	891	681	1 082	844	1 193	1 321	1 680	3 099
Transportation	8 789	4 473	2 567	3 391	4 730	6 082	6 425	7 405	9 109	14 152
Vehicle purchases (net outlay)	3 454	[1]1 678	[1]873	[1]812	[1]1 373	2 712	2 316	2 760	3 412	5 876
Gasoline and motor oil	2 197	1 113	778	1 176	1 552	1 586	1 900	2 038	2 368	3 154
Other vehicle expenses	2 578	1 334	755	1 213	1 528	1 608	1 940	2 302	2 817	4 001
Public transportation	561	348	161	190	277	175	269	304	512	1 121
Health Care	3 485	2 096	1 471	1 824	2 629	2 675	3 478	3 588	3 555	4 653
Health insurance	1 631	1 050	595	928	1 248	1 399	1 439	1 602	1 753	2 172
Medical services	979	651	522	369	655	556	1 226	1 090	874	1 345
Drugs	736	289	302	474	610	648	734	766	778	922
Medical supplies	139	106	[1]53	52	116	71	79	130	151	215
Entertainment	2 549	1 345	823	1 018	1 344	1 350	1 670	2 050	2 143	4 533
Personal Care Products and Services	569	247	155	270	325	330	362	442	565	940
Reading	157	70	58	63	69	87	123	135	153	263
Education	697	[1]233	[1]83	221	104	187	242	286	441	1 651
Tobacco Products and Smoking Supplies	353	318	376	305	378	337	485	362	356	313
Miscellaneous	1 045	446	295	669	575	552	627	591	1 051	1 854
Cash Contributions	2 116	1 038	463	659	1 616	1 041	1 393	1 362	2 038	3 803
Personal Insurance and Pensions	5 815	592	450	514	1 051	1 704	2 802	3 972	5 657	12 369
Life and other personal insurance	499	137	124	155	246	298	280	358	468	923
Pensions and Social Security	5 316	455	326	360	805	1 406	2 523	3 614	5 189	11 446

[1]Data are likely to have large sampling errors.
[2]Value less than 0.05.

Table 8-28. Consumer Expenditures, Averages for Age Groups by Income Before Taxes: Reference Person 65 Years of Age and Over, 2005–2006

(Number, dollar, percent.)

Item		Complete reporting of income								
	Total	Less than $5,000	$5,000 to $9,999	$10,000 to $14,999	$15,000 to $19,999	$20,000 to $29,999	$30,000 to $39,999	$40,000 to $49,999	$50,000 to $69,999	$70,000 and over
NUMBER OF CONSUMER UNITS (THOUSANDS)	22 927	811	1 935	3 428	3 008	4 297	2 781	1 781	2 076	2 810
CONSUMER UNIT CHARACTERISTICS										
Income Before Taxes	37 461	2 322	8 271	12 623	17 476	24 674	34 579	44 860	58 565	121 510
Income After Taxes	36 381	2 301	8 215	12 464	17 115	24 331	33 980	44 029	57 296	115 908
Age of Reference Person	75.2	76.0	77.2	77.8	77.2	75.3	74.4	73.5	72.9	71.6
Average Number in Consumer Unit										
All persons	1.7	1.4	1.2	1.2	1.4	1.7	1.9	1.9	2.2	2.4
Children under 18 years	0.1	(1)	(1)	(1)	(1)	0.1	0.1	0.1	0.1	0.1
Persons 65 years and over	1.4	1.2	1.1	1.1	1.3	1.4	1.5	1.5	1.6	1.5
Earners	0.5	2 0.1	0.1	0.1	0.1	0.3	0.5	0.7	0.9	1.4
Vehicles	1.6	0.9	0.7	0.9	1.1	1.5	1.7	2.1	2.1	2.6
Percent Distribution										
Male	43	37	29	26	34	42	47	54	55	64
Female	57	63	71	74	66	58	53	46	45	36
Percent Homeowner	80	69	54	67	76	84	88	90	91	95
With mortgage	20	18	8	11	14	16	21	25	28	41
Without mortgage	61	51	46	56	62	68	67	65	63	54
AVERAGE ANNUAL EXPENDITURES	33 978	18 370	14 035	17 788	22 550	28 453	32 886	39 709	48 028	77 880
Food	4 241	2 726	2 438	2 348	2 931	3 664	3 966	4 777	5 808	8 344
Food at home	2 632	1 920	1 835	1 718	2 063	2 442	2 482	2 927	3 263	4 421
Cereals and bakery products	368	267	251	253	304	365	332	417	459	568
Meats, poultry, fish, and eggs	590	522	458	370	510	525	535	665	687	997
Dairy products	300	224	210	214	240	288	309	346	358	445
Fruits and vegetables	499	325	351	333	367	468	481	547	612	842
Other food at home	875	581	565	548	642	795	825	952	1 147	1 568
Food away from home	1 609	806	603	630	867	1 222	1 484	1 850	2 545	3 923
Alcoholic Beverages	255	2 84	150	97	145	205	249	289	346	610
Housing	11 435	8 201	6 084	7 408	9 021	10 349	11 126	13 092	14 461	22 024
Shelter	6 070	3 983	3 393	4 170	4 907	5 594	5 651	6 796	7 655	11 592
Owned dwellings	4 068	2 555	1 420	2 030	2 779	3 658	4 062	4 852	5 708	9 119
Rented dwellings	1 561	1 355	1 934	2 064	1 996	1 673	1 221	1 382	1 202	829
Other lodging	441	2 73	2 38	75	132	263	368	562	745	1 644
Utilities, fuels, and public services	2 911	2 245	1 841	2 136	2 503	2 837	3 077	3 349	3 580	4 396
Household operations	685	344	206	348	468	498	724	732	837	1 863
Housekeeping supplies	544	436	358	298	392	486	532	645	744	932
Household furnishings and equipment	1 225	1 192	286	456	752	933	1 141	1 570	1 644	3 240
Apparel and Services	943	338	516	341	529	686	768	1 018	1 691	2 256
Transportation	5 415	2 435	1 339	2 201	2 840	4 529	5 552	7 003	8 369	13 770
Vehicle purchases (net outlay)	2 155	2 877	2 187	2 796	780	1 714	2 129	2 671	3 213	6 596
Gasoline and motor oil	1 284	837	515	628	798	1 140	1 446	1 693	1 901	2 605
Other vehicle expenses	1 589	660	544	678	1 046	1 423	1 631	2 141	2 373	3 529
Public transportation	388	61	93	98	216	251	345	498	881	1 040
Health Care	4 262	2 115	1 809	2 688	3 499	4 330	4 894	5 202	5 854	6 740
Health insurance	2 462	1 309	1 082	1 629	2 035	2 546	2 887	3 240	3 187	3 642
Medical services	716	218	236	366	520	657	652	737	1 065	1 704
Drugs	932	527	440	619	839	952	1 192	1 031	1 366	1 142
Medical supplies	152	2 62	51	74	105	175	164	194	236	252
Entertainment	1 588	727	511	676	943	1 133	1 486	2 026	2 386	4 241
Personal Care Products and Services	468	239	177	247	327	404	493	583	687	927
Reading	140	56	43	76	103	121	149	169	228	283
Education	215	2 53	2 46	115	39	87	155	258	274	862
Tobacco Products and Smoking Supplies	168	144	104	131	173	159	210	202	198	189
Miscellaneous	800	428	195	388	386	636	822	857	1 151	2 151
Cash Contributions	2 235	630	480	829	1 310	1 502	1 924	2 344	3 568	6 987
Personal Insurance and Pensions	1 810	194	145	242	305	648	1 093	1 890	3 007	8 495
Life and other personal insurance	351	129	116	174	164	230	298	397	427	1 145
Pensions and Social Security	1 459	2 65	28	68	140	418	795	1 493	2 580	7 350

1Value less than 0.05.
2Data are likely to have large sampling errors.

CHAPTER 9

OCCUPATIONAL SAFETY AND HEALTH

OCCUPATIONAL SAFETY AND HEALTH

HIGHLIGHTS

This chapter includes data on work-related illnesses and injuries and fatal work injuries from the annual Survey of Occupational Injuries and Illnesses and the Census of Fatal Occupations. Data are classified by industry and selected worker characteristics.

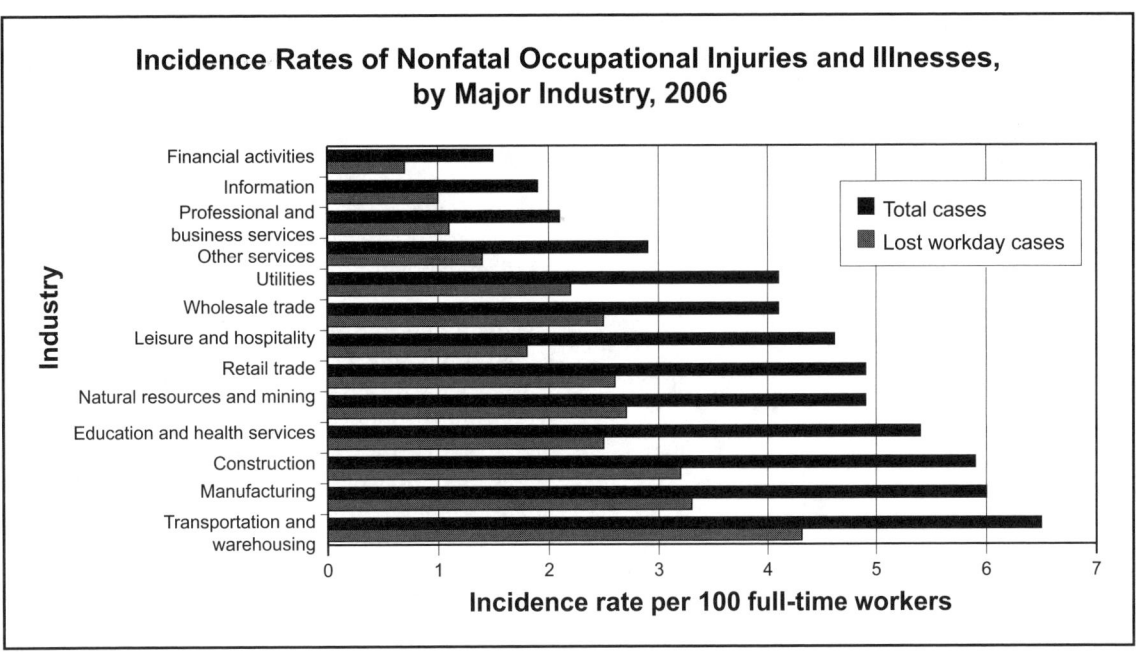

Incidence Rates of Nonfatal Occupational Injuries and Illnesses, by Major Industry, 2006

Among the major industries, transportation and warehousing continued to have the highest incidence of non-fatal occupational injuries and illnesses in 2006. However, there has been a noticeable decline in recent years. The number of non-fatal occupational injuries and illnesses in transportation and warehousing declined from 7.3 per 100 full-time workers in 2004 to 7.0 per 100 full-time workers in 2005, and to 6.5 per 100 full-time workers in 2006. The rates for most industries have declined in the past few years. Financial activities, information, and professional and business services—most of the desk-bound industries—had the lowest rates in 2006. Cases with days away from work were lower, frequently around half of the total of recordable cases. (See Table 9-1.)

OTHER HIGHLIGHTS

- The total number of nonfatal occupational injuries and illnesses in private industry dropped from 4.6 per 100 full-time workers in 2005 to 4.4 per 100 full-time workers in 2006, a decline of 4.3 percent. (See Table 9-1.)

- Within the transportation and warehousing sector, couriers and messengers had the highest rate of nonfatal occupational injuries and illnesses at 10.5 per 100 full-time workers; air transportation was the next highest, with 9.9 cases per 100 full-time workers. (See Table 9-1.)

- Truck drivers had the highest percentage of days-away-from-work cases involving 31 days or more. The median number of days away from work for the private sector was 7 days; for truck drivers, it was 14 days. (See Table 9-3.)

NOTES AND DEFINITIONS

Collection and Coverage

Nonfatal Occupational Injuries and Illnesses

The Survey of Occupational Injuries and Illnesses is a federal/state program that collected employer reports from about 195,200 private industry establishments in 2006. The survey estimates are based on a probability sample and are then processed by state agencies in cooperation with the Bureau of Labor Statistics (BLS). The survey measures only nonfatal injuries and illnesses and excludes the self-employed, farms with fewer than 11 employees, private households, federal government agencies, and, for national estimates, employees in state and local government agencies

BLS has reported annually on the number and rate of days-away-from work injuries and illnesses in private industry since the early 1970s. The 2006 national survey marks the 15th year that BLS has collected additional detailed information concerning worker and case characteristics data, including data on lost work time. On January 19, 2001, the Occupational Safety and Health Administration (OSHA) promulgated revisions to its requirements for recording occupational injuries and illnesses. These revisions became effective January 1, 2002, and were reflected in the 2002 survey.

The term "lost workdays" was eliminated under these revisions, which instead require companies to record days away from work and days of restricted work or transfer to another job. In addition, the new rules for counting rely on calendar days instead of workdays. Employers are no longer required to count days away from work or days of job transfer or restriction beyond 180 days. These changes have affected the calculation of median days away from work from 2002 onward, making data from those years noncomparable to previous years.

The number and frequency (incidence rates) of days-away-from-work cases are based on logs and other records kept by private industry employers throughout the year. These records reflect the year's overall injury and illness experience and the employers' understanding of which cases are work related under the current record-keeping guidelines of the U.S. Department of Labor. The number of injuries and illnesses reported in a given year can be influenced by changes in the level of economic activity, working conditions and work practices, worker experience and training, and the number of hours worked.

The Mine Safety and Health Administration (MSHA) and the Federal Railroad Administration (FRA) furnish mining and railroad data to BLS. These data are therefore noncomparable to data from other industries.

Industry data are classified according to the North American Industry Classification System (NAICS).

Concepts and Definitions

Recordable occupational injuries and illnesses include: (1) nonfatal occupational illnesses; and (2) nonfatal occupational injuries that involve one or more of the following: loss of consciousness, restriction of work or motion, transfer to another job, or medical treatment (other than first aid). The annual survey measures only nonfatal injuries and illnesses. To better address fatalities, BLS implemented the Census of Fatal Occupational Injuries (described elsewhere in these notes).

Occupational injury is any injury—such as a cut, fracture, sprain, or amputation—that results from a work accident or from exposure to an incident in the work environment.

Occupational illness is an abnormal condition or disorder (other than one resulting from an occupational injury) caused by exposure to environmental factors associated with employment. It includes acute and chronic illnesses and diseases that may have been caused by inhalation, absorption, ingestion, or direct contact. Long-term latent illnesses can be difficult to relate to the workplace and are believed to be understated in this survey.

Days away from work are cases that involve days away from work, days of restricted work activity, or both.

The data are presented in the form of incidence rates, defined as the number of injuries and illnesses or cases of days away from work per 100 full-time employees. The formula is (N/EH) x 200,000, where N = number of injuries and illnesses or days away from work, EH=total hours worked by all employees during the calendar year, and 200,000 represents the base for 100 full-time equivalent workers (working 40 hours per week, 50 weeks per year).

Comparable data for individual states are available from BLS's Office of Safety, Health, and Working Conditions.

Fatal Occupational Injuries

Beginning in 1992, BLS has been collecting a comprehensive count of work-related deaths in the Census of Fatal Occupational Injuries (CFOI). The CFOI covers private wage and salary workers, workers on small farms, the self-employed, workers in family businesses, and public-sector workers.

The CFOI program is a cooperative venture between the state and federal governments. The program collects and cross checks fatality information from multiple sources, including death certificates, state and federal workers' compensation reports, OSHA and MSHA records, medical examiner and autopsy reports, media accounts, state motor vehicle fatality records, and follow-up questionnaires to employers.

Fatality counts from the CFOI are combined with annual average employment from the Current Population Survey (CPS) to produce a fatal work injury rate. CFOI data include deaths that resulted from traumatic occupational injuries.

For a fatality to be included in the CFOI, the decedent must have been employed at the time of the event and present at the site of the incident as a job requirement. Due to the latency period of many occupational illnesses and the resulting difficulty associated with linking illnesses to work, it is difficult to compile a complete count of all fatal illnesses in a given year. Thus, information on illness-related deaths are excluded from the basic fatality count.

Industries are classified according to NAICS and occupations according to the Standard Occupational Classification System (SOC).

Sources of Additional Information

For more extensive definitions and description of collection methods see BLS news release USDL 07-1562, "Workplace Injuries and Illnesses in 2006," for injuries and illnesses; USDL 07-1202, "National Census of Fatal Occupational Injuries in 2006," for more information on the CFOI; and occasional articles in *Compensation and Working Conditions*. All of these resources are available on the BLS Web site at <http://www.bls.gov>.

Table 9-1. Incidence Rates of Nonfatal Occupational Injuries and Illnesses Per 100 Full-Time Workers,[1] by Selected Industries and Case Types, 2006

(Number, rate.)

Industry[2]	NAICS code[3]	2006 average annual employment (thousands)[4]	Total recordable cases	Cases with days away from work, job transfer, or restriction			Other recordable cases
				Total	Cases with days away from work[5]	Cases with job transfer or restriction	
PRIVATE INDUSTRY[6]		111 273	4.4	2.3	1.3	1.0	2.1
Goods-Producing[6]		23 285	5.9	3.2	1.7	1.6	2.7
Natural resources and mining[6]		1 573	4.9	2.7	1.7	1.0	2.2
Agriculture, forestry, fishing, and hunting[6]	11	971	6.0	3.2	1.9	1.2	2.8
Crop production[6]	111	420	5.8	3.1	1.8	1.4	2.7
Animal production	112	147	8.1	3.9	2.4	1.5	4.2
Forestry and logging	113	69	5.3	2.4	2.2	0.2	3.0
Fishing, hunting and trapping	114	9	8.4	3.4	3.3	. . .	5.0
Support activities for agriculture and forestry	115	325	5.1	3.0	1.9	1.1	2.1
Mining[7]	21	602	3.5	2.1	1.4	0.7	1.4
Oil and gas extraction	211	132	2.0	0.9	0.5	0.4	1.1
Mining (except oil and gas)[8]	212	218	3.8	2.5	1.9	0.7	1.3
Support activities for mining	213	252	3.9	2.2	1.4	0.8	1.7
Construction	23	7 563	5.9	3.2	2.2	1.0	2.7
Construction of buildings	236	1 782	5.1	2.6	1.8	0.8	2.5
Heavy and civil engineering construction	237	966	5.3	3.0	2.0	1.0	2.3
Specialty trade contractors	238	4 814	6.3	3.5	2.4	1.1	2.9
Manufacturing	31-33	14 150	6.0	3.3	1.4	1.9	2.7
Food	311	1 471	7.4	4.8	1.6	3.2	2.6
Beverage and tobacco product	312	194	8.1	5.5	2.3	3.2	2.6
Textile mills	313	200	4.4	2.3	0.9	1.5	2.0
Textile product mills	314	163	4.5	2.6	0.9	1.7	1.9
Apparel	315	243	2.9	1.4	0.7	0.8	1.4
Leather and allied product	316	37	5.9	3.1	1.2	1.9	2.8
Wood product	321	563	8.5	4.7	2.3	2.4	3.8
Paper	322	472	4.3	2.5	1.2	1.3	1.8
Printing and related support activities	323	635	4.2	2.4	1.2	1.2	1.8
Petroleum and coal products	324	113	2.7	1.4	0.9	0.5	1.3
Chemical manufacturing	325	863	2.9	1.7	0.8	1.0	1.2
Plastics and rubber products	326	798	6.8	3.9	1.6	2.3	2.9
Nonmetallic mineral product	327	511	7.1	4.1	2.0	2.2	3.0
Primary metal	331	464	8.6	4.7	2.1	2.6	3.9
Fabricated metal product	332	1 539	7.6	3.8	1.8	2.0	3.8
Machinery	333	1 173	6.2	3.0	1.4	1.6	3.2
Computer and electronic product	334	1 305	2.0	1.0	0.5	0.6	1.0
Electrical equipment, appliance, and component	335	432	5.1	2.7	1.0	1.6	2.4
Transportation equipment	336	1 764	8.0	4.3	1.6	2.7	3.7
Furniture and related product	337	561	7.5	4.2	1.8	2.4	3.3
Miscellaneous	339	648	4.2	2.1	1.0	1.1	2.1
Service-Providing		87 988	3.9	2.0	1.1	0.8	1.9
Trade, transportation, and utilities[9]		25 914	5.0	2.9	1.6	1.3	2.1
Wholesale trade	42	5 852	4.1	2.5	1.3	1.2	1.6
Merchant wholesalers, durable goods	423	3 052	3.9	2.1	1.2	0.9	1.8
Merchant wholesalers, nondurable goods	424	2 025	5.4	3.7	1.9	1.8	1.7
Wholesale electronic markets and agents and brokers	425	775	1.7	1.0	0.5	0.5	0.7
Retail trade	44-45	15 342	4.9	2.6	1.4	1.2	2.4
Motor vehicle and parts dealers	441	1 908	4.4	1.9	1.3	0.6	2.6
Furniture and home furnishings stores	442	582	4.7	2.8	1.7	1.1	1.9
Electronics and appliance stores	443	548	2.8	1.2	0.6	0.6	1.6
Building material and garden equipment and supplies dealers	444	1 313	7.4	4.3	2.0	2.3	3.1
Food and beverage stores	445	2 812	5.9	3.2	1.7	1.5	2.7
Health and personal care stores	446	960	2.2	1.0	0.6	0.4	1.2
Gasoline stations	447	861	3.6	1.5	0.9	0.6	2.0
Clothing and clothing accessories stores	448	1 438	2.7	1.1	0.8	0.3	1.6
Sporting goods, hobby, book, and music stores	451	655	3.0	1.1	0.6	0.4	2.0
General merchandise stores	452	2 950	6.7	3.9	1.7	2.2	2.8
Miscellaneous store retailers	453	890	3.9	2.0	1.2	0.8	1.9
Nonstore retailers	454	426	4.2	2.6	1.3	1.3	1.6

Note: Components may not sum to totals because of rounding.

[1]The incidence rates represent the number of injuries and illnesses per 100 full-time workers and were calculated as: (N/EH) x 200,000 (where N = number of injuries and illnesses; EH = total hours worked by all employees during the calendar year; 200,000 = base for 100 equivalent full-time workers working 40 hours per week, 50 weeks per year).
[2]Totals include data for industries not shown separately.
[3]North American Industry Classification System—United States, 2002.
[4]Employment is expressed as an average annual value and is derived primarily from the Bureau of Labor Statistics's (BLS) Quarterly Census of Employment and Wages (QCEW) program.
[5]Days away from work cases include those that result in days away from work with or without job transfer or restriction.
[6]Excludes farms with fewer than 11 employees.
[7]Data for mining include establishments not governed by the Department of Labor's Mine Safety and Health Administration (MSHA) rules and reporting, such as those in oil and gas extraction and related support activities. Data for mining operators in coal, metal, and nonmetal mining are provided to BLS by MSHA. Independent mining contractors are excluded from the coal, metal, and nonmetal mining industries. These data do not reflect the changes the Occupational Safety and Health Administration (OSHA) made to its record-keeping requirements effective January 1, 2002; thus, estimates for these industries are not comparable to estimates in other industries.
[8]Data for mining operators in this industry are provided to BLS by MSHA. Independent mining contractors are excluded. These data do not reflect the changes OSHA made to its record-keeping requirements effective January 1, 2002; thus, estimates for these industries are not comparable to estimates in other industries.
[9]Data for employers in rail transportation are provided to BLS by the Department of Transportation's Federal Railroad Administration (FRA).
. . . = Not available.

Table 9-1.   Incidence Rates of Nonfatal Occupational Injuries and Illnesses Per 100 Full-Time Workers,[1] by Selected Industries and Case Types, 2006—*Continued*

(Number, rate.)

Industry[2]	NAICS code[3]	2006 average annual employment (thousands)[4]	Total recordable cases	Cases with days away from work, job transfer, or restriction			Other recordable cases
				Total	Cases with days away from work[5]	Cases with job transfer or restriction	
Service-Providing—*Continued*							
Transportation and warehousing	48-49	4 172	6.5	4.3	2.7	1.6	2.2
Air transportation	481	484	9.9	7.7	5.4	2.2	2.2
Rail transportation[9]	482	. . .	2.3	1.7	1.5	0.2	0.6
Water transportation	483	61	4.4	2.6	1.9	0.7	1.8
Truck transportation	484	1 415	5.8	3.7	2.7	0.9	2.2
Transit and ground passenger transportation	485	390	5.4	3.0	2.2	0.9	2.3
Pipeline transportation	486	39	2.2	0.9	0.6	0.3	1.3
Scenic and sightseeing transportation	487	27	4.3	2.8	2.1	0.6	1.6
Support activities for transportation	488	565	4.5	2.6	1.8	0.9	1.8
Couriers and messengers	492	573	10.5	7.2	3.5	3.7	3.3
Warehousing and storage	493	618	8.0	5.6	2.2	3.4	2.4
Utilities	22	547	4.1	2.2	1.2	1.0	1.9
Information	51	3 046	1.9	1.0	0.7	0.4	0.9
Publishing industries (except Internet)	511	900	2.1	1.1	0.6	0.4	1.0
Motion picture and sound recording industries	512	376	2.0	0.6	0.4	0.2	. . .
Broadcasting (except Internet)	515	327	1.9	1.0	0.6	0.4	1.0
Telecommunications	517	974	2.2	1.4	1.0	0.4	0.8
Internet service providers, Web search portals, and data processing services	518	385	0.9	0.4	0.2	0.2	0.4
Other information services	519	51	2.0	1.0	0.8	0.2	1.0
Financial activities		8 142	1.5	0.7	0.5	0.2	0.8
Finance and insurance	52	5 993	0.9	0.3	0.2	0.1	0.6
Monetary authorities—central bank	521	21	2.7	1.9	1.1	0.8	0.8
Credit intermediation and related activities	522	2 916	1.0	0.3	0.2	0.1	0.6
Securities, commodity contracts, and other financial investments and related activities	523	813	. . .	0.1	0.1	. . .	. . .
Insurance carriers and related activities	524	2 151	1.0	0.4	0.3	0.1	0.7
Funds, trusts, and other financial vehicles	525	92	1.2	0.7	0.5	0.2	0.5
Real estate and rental and leasing	53	2 149	3.3	1.8	1.1	0.7	1.5
Real estate	531	1 484	2.9	1.5	1.0	0.5	1.4
Rental and leasing services	532	637	4.2	2.6	1.5	1.1	1.7
Lessors of nonfinancial intangible assets (except copyrighted works)	533	27	0.8	0.2	0.1	. . .	0.6
Professional and business services		17 334	2.1	1.1	0.7	0.4	1.1
Professional, scientific, and technical services	54	7 305	1.2	0.5	0.3	0.2	0.7
Management of companies and enterprises	55	1 776	2.1	1.1	0.6	0.5	1.1
Administrative and support and waste management and remediation services	56	8 253	3.4	1.9	1.2	0.6	1.5
Administrative and support services		7 908	3.1	1.7	1.1	0.6	1.5
Waste management and remediation services	562	345	6.5	3.9	2.5	1.4	2.5
Education and health services		16 796	5.4	2.5	1.4	1.1	3.0
Education services	61	2 190	2.3	0.9	0.7	0.3	1.4
Health care and social assistance	62	14 606	5.8	2.7	1.5	1.2	3.2
Ambulatory health care services	621	5 239	3.1	1.1	0.8	0.3	2.0
Hospitals	622	4 349	8.1	3.2	1.8	1.4	4.9
Nursing and residential care facilities		2 869	8.9	5.4	2.6	2.7	3.6
Social assistance	624	2 150	3.9	1.9	1.2	0.8	1.9
Leisure and hospitality		12 932	4.6	1.8	1.1	0.7	2.8
Arts, entertainment, and recreation	71	1 891	5.3	2.5	1.3	1.2	2.8
Performing arts, spectator sports, and related industries	711	388	5.8	2.2	1.4	0.8	3.6
Museums, historical sites, and similar institutions	712	120	5.3	2.4	1.5	0.9	2.9
Amusement, gambling, and recreation industries	713	1 382	5.1	2.6	1.2	1.3	2.5
Accommodation and food services	72	11 042	4.5	1.7	1.1	0.6	2.8
Accommodation	721	1 818	5.8	3.1	1.5	1.5	2.8
Food services and drinking places	722	9 223	4.2	1.4	1.0	0.4	2.8
Other services		3 825	2.9	1.4	0.9	0.5	1.5
Other services, except public administration	81	3 825	2.9	1.4	0.9	0.5	1.5
Repair and maintenance	811	1 238	3.5	1.6	1.2	0.4	1.9
Personal and laundry services	812	1 280	2.6	1.5	0.9	0.6	1.1
Religious, grantmaking, civic, professional, and similar organizations	813	1 306	2.7	1.0	0.7	0.4	1.6

Note: Components may not sum to totals because of rounding.

[1]The incidence rates represent the number of injuries and illnesses per 100 full-time workers and were calculated as: (N/EH) x 200,000 (where N = number of injuries and illnesses; EH = total hours worked by all employees during the calendar year; 200,000 = base for 100 equivalent full-time workers working 40 hours per week, 50 weeks per year).
[2]Totals include data for industries not shown separately.
[3]North American Industry Classification System—United States, 2002.
[4]Employment is expressed as an average annual value and is derived primarily from the Bureau of Labor Statistics's (BLS) Quarterly Census of Employment and Wages (QCEW) program.
[5]Days away from work cases include those that result in days away from work with or without job transfer or restriction.
[9]Data for employers in rail transportation are provided to BLS by the Department of Transportation's Federal Railroad Administration (FRA).
. . . = Not available.

Table 9-2. Number of Nonfatal Occupational Injuries and Illnesses Involving Days Away from Work,[1] by Selected Worker Characteristics and Private Industry Division, 2006

(Number.)

Characteristic	Total cases[2]	Goods-producing[2]			
		All goods-producing	Natural resources and mining[3]	Construction	Manufacturing
TOTAL CASES	1 183 500	380 440	26 290	153 180	200 970
Sex					
Men	775 900	328 560	22 740	148 530	157 290
Women	403 740	51 630	3 550	4 650	43 440
Age[4]					
14 to 15 years	170	110	100	. . .	. . .
16 to 19 years	39 330	8 890	860	3 680	4 350
20 to 24 years	132 120	45 200	3 220	21 980	20 000
25 to 34 years	270 670	92 100	7 020	42 170	42 910
35 to 44 years	301 700	99 920	5 960	40 330	53 630
45 to 54 years	266 660	86 700	5 650	30 850	50 200
55 to 64 years	134 030	38 400	2 710	10 520	25 170
65 years and over	25 170	4 740	510	1 650	2 580
Length of Service with Employer					
Less than 3 months	157 740	58 670	5 820	28 990	23 860
3 to 11 months	259 320	84 490	6 110	39 820	38 560
1 to 5 years	394 870	121 790	8 160	53 860	59 770
More than 5 years	361 250	113 620	5 990	30 120	77 500
Race and Hispanic Origin					
White only	523 320	191 560	6 900	83 100	101 550
Black only	94 370	23 220	660	6 770	15 790
Hispanic only[5]	158 760	74 820	9 670	33 930	31 220
Asian only	15 350	3 410	90	410	2 920
Native Hawaiian or Pacific Islander only	3 820	840	30	410	400
American Indian or Alaskan Native only	5 190	1 930	110	820	990
Hispanic[5] and other race	680	190	30	60	100
Multiple races	790	220	. . .	50	160
Not reported	381 230	84 250	8 780	27 640	47 840

Note: Components may not sum to totals because of rounding.

[1]Days away from work cases include those that result in days away from work with or without restricted work activity.
[2]Excludes farms with fewer than 11 employees.
[3]Data for mining include establishments not governed by the Department of Labor's Mine Safety and Health Administration (MSHA) rules and reporting, such as those in oil and gas extraction and related support activities. Data for mining operators in coal, metal, and nonmetal mining are provided to the Bureau of Labor Statistics (BLS) by MSHA. Independent mining contractors are excluded from the coal, metal, and nonmetal mining industries. These data do not reflect the changes the Occupational Safety and Health Administration (OSHA) made to its record-keeping requirements effective January 1, 2002; thus, estimates for these industries are not comparable to estimates in other industries.
[4]Data are not shown separately for injured workers under 14 years of age; these workers accounted for fewer than 50 cases.
[5]May be of any race.
. . . = Not available.

Table 9-2. Number of Nonfatal Occupational Injuries and Illnesses Involving Days Away from Work,[1] by Selected Worker Characteristics and Private Industry Division, 2006—*Continued*

(Number.)

Characteristic	Service-providing							
	All service-providing	Trade, transportation, and utilities[6]	Information	Financial activities	Professional and business services	Education and health services	Leisure and hospitality	Other services
TOTAL CASES	803 060	354 510	18 560	33 300	89 940	182 210	96 910	27 640
Sex								
Men	447 340	251 370	12 840	18 250	61 070	36 800	47 660	19 350
Women	352 110	99 570	5 720	15 050	28 870	145 370	49 240	8 290
Age[4]								
14 to 15 years	70	. . .	. . .	. . .	. . .	. . .	60	. . .
16 to 19 years	30 430	14 980	320	320	2 490	3 150	8 300	880
20 to 24 years	86 920	37 310	960	2 350	11 950	15 420	15 960	2 960
25 to 34 years	178 570	74 670	3 970	7 860	23 830	38 900	23 260	6 070
35 to 44 years	201 770	92 000	5 590	8 990	22 370	44 490	21 460	6 880
45 to 54 years	179 960	80 800	5 130	7 800	18 180	46 310	15 670	6 070
55 to 64 years	95 630	41 470	2 200	4 230	8 230	26 880	8 790	3 820
65 years and over	20 430	9 020	220	1 610	1 650	4 820	2 450	660
Length of Service with Employer								
Less than 3 months	99 070	44 290	840	3 120	14 710	15 740	17 200	3 170
3 to 11 months	174 840	74 130	2 310	8 070	22 280	36 730	25 590	5 720
1 to 5 years	273 090	112 470	4 660	11 570	30 310	69 340	34 200	10 540
More than 5 years	247 630	117 570	10 470	10 490	21 910	59 780	19 340	8 070
Race and Hispanic Origin								
White only	331 760	142 140	6 230	13 790	37 800	80 590	35 210	16 010
Black only	71 150	22 390	980	3 700	7 740	26 340	8 160	1 840
Hispanic only[5]	83 940	28 790	900	4 770	16 510	14 400	15 230	3 350
Asian only	11 940	3 700	260	340	1 100	2 700	3 280	550
Native Hawaiian or Pacific Islander only	2 970	1 370	40	50	230	690	430	170
American Indian or Alaskan Native only	3 260	1 320	50	90	480	700	520	110
Hispanic[5] and other race	490	120	. . .	30	50	50	250	. . .
Multiple races	570	280	. . .	30	40	120	80	. . .
Not reported	296 980	154 400	10 090	10 500	26 000	56 630	33 760	5 600

Note: Components may not sum to totals because of rounding.

[1]Days away from work cases include those that result in days away from work with or without restricted work activity.
[4]Data are not shown separately for injured workers under 14 years of age; these workers accounted for fewer than 50 cases.
[5]May be of any race.
[6]Data for employers in rail transportation are provided to BLS by the Department of Transportation's Federal Railroad Administration (FRA).
. . . = Not available.

Table 9-3. Number and Percent Distribution of Nonfatal Occupational Injuries and Illnesses Involving Days Away from Work,[1] by Selected Occupation and Number of Days Away from Work, Private Industry, 2006

(Number, percent.)

Occupation	Total number of cases	Percent of days away from work cases involving:								Median days away from work
		Total	1 day	2 days	3 to 5 days	6 to 10 days	11 to 20 days	21 to 30 days	31 days or more	
TOTAL	1 183 500	100.0	14.3	11.6	18.5	12.9	11.5	6.8	24.3	7
Labor and freight, stock, and material movers, hand	85 120	100.0	14.8	10.7	19.3	12.4	11.1	7.3	24.3	7
Truck drivers, heavy and tractor-trailer	66 040	100.0	8.3	8.5	16.1	12.5	11.9	8.1	34.8	14
Nursing aides, orderlies, and attendants	49 480	100.0	14.7	16.4	21.5	14.5	10.5	4.8	17.7	5
Construction laborers	40 510	100.0	14.9	12.0	18.6	11.7	11.2	7.0	24.6	7
Retail salespersons	33 210	100.0	14.6	9.5	17.6	15.1	15.3	5.2	22.7	8
Janitors and cleaners, except maids and housekeeping cleaners	28 260	100.0	13.2	12.0	17.6	15.4	11.9	8.5	21.6	7
Carpenters	28 000	100.0	11.7	10.3	17.2	12.2	10.8	9.1	28.6	10
Truck drivers, light or delivery services	26 760	100.0	12.1	9.2	18.0	10.9	13.9	6.1	29.7	10
Maintenance and repair workers, general	21 600	100.0	16.6	12.4	17.6	11.8	11.9	7.9	21.8	6
Stock clerks and order fillers	20 870	100.0	14.7	12.4	19.2	13.1	9.9	7.6	23.3	7
Registered nurses	20 500	100.0	15.4	14.6	17.6	14.0	12.0	6.0	20.4	6
Maids and housekeeping cleaners	17 440	100.0	11.5	10.7	23.3	13.0	11.0	5.7	24.8	7
First-line supervisors/mangers of retail sales workers	15 070	100.0	12.0	13.4	19.4	12.4	12.3	6.3	24.2	7
Cashiers	13 460	100.0	13.2	15.8	16.9	14.4	8.8	5.9	24.9	7
Welders, cutters, solderers, and brazers	12 890	100.0	20.6	13.1	16.7	10.6	12.3	6.2	20.6	5
Automotive service technicians and mechanics	12 770	100.0	19.6	10.7	16.3	12.8	13.2	9.7	17.6	7
Combined food preparation and serving workers, including fast food	12 750	100.0	14.0	16.1	22.1	12.9	14.2	4.1	16.5	5
Landscaping and groundskeeping workers	12 450	100.0	16.3	9.6	24.9	13.0	11.1	5.5	19.6	5
Electricians	12 030	100.0	14.3	12.0	19.0	12.9	11.7	5.6	24.6	7
Plumbers, pipefitters, and steamfitters	11 400	100.0	9.6	13.7	19.0	17.0	8.9	12.4	19.4	8
Cooks, restaurant	11 290	100.0	11.2	19.2	23.4	13.2	11.3	5.0	16.7	5
Customer service representatives	10 300	100.0	12.3	14.2	15.9	10.4	13.0	5.1	29.0	9
Food preparation workers	9 950	100.0	20.2	14.4	17.8	13.0	12.4	5.9	16.4	5
Driver/sales workers	9 640	100.0	11.2	10.9	14.2	13.0	10.9	9.3	30.5	11
Waiters and waitresses	9 520	100.0	14.4	14.4	23.2	13.7	7.6	6.9	19.9	5
First-line supervisors/managers of construction and extraction workers	8 910	100.0	14.0	8.3	17.1	11.9	14.8	7.1	26.8	10

Note: Percentages may not sum to 100 because of rounding.

[1]Days away from work cases include those that result in days away from work with or without restricted work activity.

Table 9-4. Fatal Occupational Injuries, by Selected Worker Characteristics and Selected Event or Exposure, 2006

(Number, percent.)

Characteristic	Fatalities		Selected event or exposure[1] (percent of total for characteristic category)			
	Number	Percent	Highway[2]	Homicides	Falls	Struck by object
TOTAL	5 703	100	23	9	14	10
Employee Status						
Wage and salary workers[3]	4 690	82	26	8	14	10
Self-employed[4]	1 013	18	12	13	14	13
Sex						
Men	5 275	92	23	8	15	11
Women	428	8	30	27	9	2
Age[5]						
Under 16 years	10	([6])	. . .	. . .	. . .	. . .
16 to 17 years	20	([6])	. . .	15	. . .	20
18 to 19 years	104	2	21	10	12	12
20 to 24 years	382	7	19	8	11	10
25 to 34 years	1 016	18	26	11	12	10
35 to 44 years	1 266	22	24	11	12	9
45 to 54 years	1 378	24	23	8	15	10
55 to 64 years	941	17	24	9	17	11
65 years and over	577	10	20	5	17	13
Race and Hispanic Origin						
White	3 945	69	25	6	13	10
Black	552	10	24	21	11	10
Hispanic[7]	937	16	17	8	21	12
American Indian or Alaskan Native	44	1	39	7	7	9
Asian	142	2	15	46	8	4
Native Hawaiian or Pacific Islander	10	([6])	50	. . .	. . .	. . .
Multiple races	10	([6])	30	. . .	. . .	. . .
Other or not reported	63	1	21	11	13	10

Note: Totals for 2006 are preliminary. Totals for major categories may include subcategories not shown separately. Components may not sum to totals because of rounding.

[1]The figure shown is the percentage of the total fatalities for that demographic group.
[2]"Highway" includes deaths to vehicle occupants resulting from traffic incidents that occur on the public roadway, shoulder, or surrounding area. It excludes incidents occurring entirely off the roadway, such as in parking lots or on farms; incidents involving trains; and deaths of pedestrians or other non-passengers.
[3]May include volunteers and other workers receiving compensation.
[4]Includes self-employed workers, owners of unincorporated businesses and farms, paid and unpaid family workers, and members of partnerships; may also include owners of incorporated businesses.
[5]There were seven fatalities for which there was insufficient information to determine the age of the decedent.
[6]Less than or equal to 0.5 percent.
[7]May be of any race.
. . . = Not available.

Table 9-5. Fatal Occupational Injuries, by Occupation and Selected Event or Exposure, 2006

(Number, percent.)

Occupation[1]	Fatalities		Selected event or exposure (percent of total for characteristic category)[2]			
	Number	Percent	Highway[3]	Homicide	Falls	Struck by object
Total	5 703	100	23	9	14	10
Management	543	10	11	9	9	13
Top executives	25	(4)	32	...	...	...
Advertising, marketing, promotions, public relations, and sales managers	12	(4)	50	...	...	...
Operations specialties managers	29	1	10	...	21	...
Other management	477	8	9	10	8	14
Business and financial operations	38	1	26	13	18	...
Business operations specialists	23	(4)	35	13	17	...
Financial specialists	15	(4)	...	...	20	...
Computer and mathematical	16	(4)	19	...	25	...
Computer specialists	15	(4)	20	...	20	...
Architecture and engineering	54	1	26	...	19	6
Architects, surveyors, and cartographers	14	(4)	...	...	21	...
Engineers	29	1	24	...	21	...
Drafters, engineering, and mapping techicians	11	(4)	45	...	...	...
Life, physical, and social science	25	(4)	16	...	20	...
Physical scientists	7	(4)	...	...	...	...
Social scientists and related workers	5	(4)	...	...	...	...
Life, physical, and social science technicians	11	(4)	...	...	...	...
Community and social services	31	1	55	23	10	...
Counselors, social workers, and other community and social service specialists	19	(4)	58	21	...	...
Religious workers	12	(4)	50	25	...	...
Legal	11	(4)	...	45	...	...
Lawyers, judges, and related workers	9	(4)	...	44	...	...
Education, training, and library	23	(4)	30	...	22	...
Postsecondary teachers	11	(4)	27	...	27	...
Primary, secondary, and special education teachers	6	(4)	...	...	...	...
Other teachers and instructors	5	(4)	...	...	...	...
Librarians, curators, and archivists	45	1	9	...	11	...
Arts, design, entertainment, sports, and media	4	(4)	...	...	...	...
Art and design workers	26	(4)	...	...	19	...
Entertainers and performers, sports and related workers	5	(4)	60	...	...	...
Media and communication workers	10	(4)	...	...	...	...
Media and communication equipment workers	54	1	28	19	...	...
Health care practitioners and technical operations	41	1	22	22	...	...
Health diagnosing and treating practitioners	13	(4)	46	...	...	...
Health technologists and technicians	20	(4)	40	15	15	...
Health care support	17	(4)	41	18	...	...
Nursing, psychiatric, and home health aides	3	(4)	...	...	...	...
Protective service	274	5	27	33	1	2
First-line supervisors and managers of protective service workers	21	(4)	24	19	...	...
Fire fighting and prevention workers	44	1	20	...	...	...
Law enforcement workers	131	2	40	38	...	2
Other protective service workers	78	1	12	46	4	...
Food preparation and serving related	78	1	9	54	10	...
Supervisors of food preparation and serving workers	26	(4)	...	73	...	...
Cooks and food preparation workers	14	(4)	...	36	...	...
Food and beverage serving workers	28	(4)	...	57	18	...
Other food preparation and serving related workers	10	(4)	60	...	...	...
Building and grounds cleaning and maintenance	277	5	11	5	29	14
Supervisors of building and grounds cleaning and maintenance workers	36	1	25	...	17	...
Building cleaning and pest control workers	74	1	14	11	39	...
Grounds maintenance workers	167	3	7	2	27	22
Personal care and service	56	1	11	21	11	5
Supervisors of personal care and service workers	5	(4)	...	80	...	...
Animal care and service workers	13	(4)	...	...	...	...
Entertainment attendants and related workers	8	(4)	...	...	...	...
Personal appearance workers	6	(4)	...	67	...	...
Transportation, tourism, and lodging attendants	5	(4)	...	...	...	...
Other personal care and service workers	19	(4)	16	...	16	...
Sales and related	308	5	20	48	6	3
Supervisors of sales workers	132	2	11	52	5	5
Retail sales workers	99	2	13	70	5	...
Sales representatives, services	23	(4)	48	22	17	...
Sales representatives, wholesale and manufacturing	27	(4)	59	...	11	...
Other sales and related workers	27	(4)	30	...	...	...
Office and administrative support	82	1	33	29	10	5
Supervisors of office and administrative support workers	8	(4)	...	50	...	...
Financial clerks	5	(4)	...	...	...	...
Information and record clerks	7	(4)	...	43	...	...
Material recording, scheduling, dispatching, and distributing workers	45	1	38	22	11	7
Secretaries and administrative asistants	6	(4)	...	...	...	...
Other office and administrative support workers	11	(4)	45	27	...	...
Farming, fishing, and forestry	289	5	11	...	4	23
Supervisors of farming, fishing, and forestry workers	11	(4)	27	...	...	36
Agricultural workers	162	3	17	...	6	10
Fishing and hunting workers	51	1	...	...	...	...
Forest, conservation, and logging workers	65	1	...	...	...	71

Note: Totals for 2006 are preliminary. Totals for major categories may include subcategories not shown separately. Components may not sum to totals because of rounding.

[1] Based on the 2000 Standard Occupational Classification (SOC) system.
[2] The figure shown is the percentage of total fatalities for that occupation group.
[3] "Highway" includes deaths to vehicle occupants resulting from traffic incidents that occur on the public roadway, shoulder, or surrounding area. It excludes incidents occurring entirely off the roadway, such as in parking lots or on farms; incidents involving trains; and deaths of pedestrians or other non-passengers.
[4] Less than or equal to 0.5 percent.
. . . = Not available.

Table 9-5. Fatal Occupational Injuries, by Occupation and Selected Event or Exposure, 2006—*Continued*

(Number, percent.)

Occupation[1]	Fatalities		Selected event or exposure (percent of total for characteristic category)[2]			
	Number	Percent	Highway[3]	Homicide	Falls	Struck by object
Construction and extraction	1 258	22	10	1	33	11
Supervisors of construction and extraction workers	113	2	19	4	22	11
Construction trades workers	969	17	9	1	38	9
Helpers—construction trades	10	([4])	. . .	. . .	30	. . .
Other construction and related workers	51	1	12	. . .	22	8
Extraction workers	115	2	10	. . .	6	23
Installation, maintenance, and repair	415	7	12	3	18	20
Supervisors of installation, maintenance, and repair workers	23	([4])	22	13	13	13
Electrical and electronic equipment mechanics, installers, and repairers	20	([4])	20	. . .	35	20
Vehicle and mobile equipment, mechanics, installers, and repairers	137	2	9	4	4	36
Other installation, maintenance, and repair workers	235	4	12	2	25	11
Production	282	5	6	4	9	18
Supervisors of production workers	25	([4])	. . .	. . .	. . .	16
Assemblers and fabricators	21	([4])	. . .	. . .	. . .	29
Food processing workers	8	([4])	. . .	. . .	. . .	. . .
Metal workers and plastics workers	85	1	4	5	15	25
Printing workers	4	([4])	. . .	. . .	. . .	. . .
Textile, apparel, and furnishings workers	11	([4])	. . .	. . .	. . .	27
Woodworkers	14	([4])	. . .	. . .	. . .	57
Plant and system operators	20	([4])	15	. . .	. . .	. . .
Other production workers	94	2	7	3	9	9
Transportation and material moving	1 463	26	50	4	4	7
Supervisors of transportation and material moving workers	15	([4])	27	. . .	. . .	. . .
Air transportation workers	101	2	. . .	. . .	. . .	. . .
Motor vehicle operators	1 021	18	67	4	3	5
Rail transportation workers	16	([4])	. . .	. . .	. . .	. . .
Water transportation workers	27	([4])	. . .	. . .	. . .	11
Other transportation workers	18	([4])	. . .	39	. . .	. . .
Material moving workers	265	5	14	3	11	14
Military	51	1	25	. . .	. . .	14

Note: Totals for 2006 are preliminary. Totals for major categories may include subcategories not shown separately. Components may not sum to totals because of rounding.

[1] Based on the 2000 Standard Occupational Classification (SOC) system.
[2] The figure shown is the percentage of total fatalities for that occupation group.
[3] "Highway" includes deaths to vehicle occupants resulting from traffic incidents that occur on the public roadway, shoulder, or surrounding area. It excludes incidents occurring entirely off the roadway, such as in parking lots or on farms; incidents involving trains; and deaths of pedestrians or other non-passengers.
[4] Less than or equal to 0.5 percent.
. . . = Not available.

CHAPTER 10

LABOR-MANAGEMENT RELATIONS

LABOR-MANAGEMENT RELATIONS

HIGHLIGHTS

This chapter contains information on historical trends in union membership, earnings, and work stoppages.

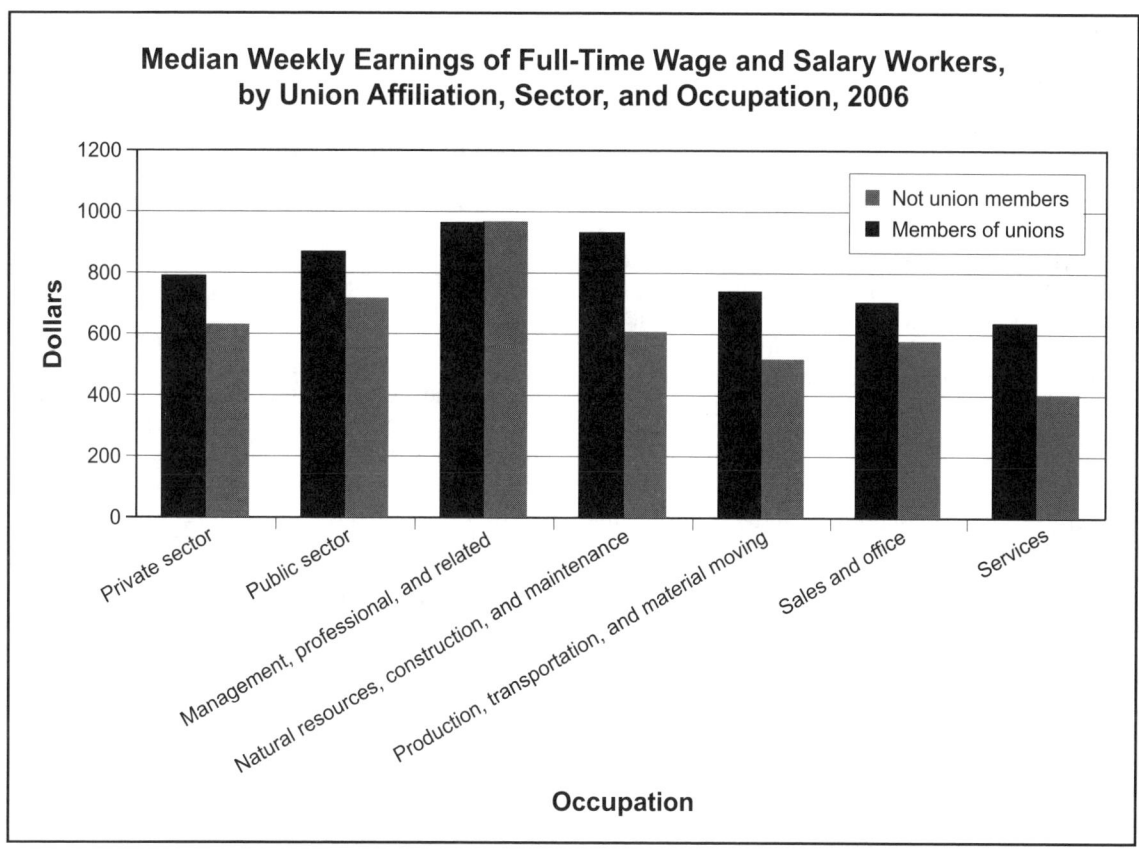

Median Weekly Earnings of Full-Time Wage and Salary Workers, by Union Affiliation, Sector, and Occupation, 2006

Legend: Not union members; Members of unions

Y-axis: Dollars (0 to 1200)

X-axis (Occupation): Private sector; Public sector; Management, professional, and related; Natural resources, construction, and maintenance; Production, transportation, and material moving; Sales and office; Services

In 2006, the median weekly earnings of union members in both the private and public sectors were more than 17 percent higher than the median weekly earnings of non-union members. Union members in national resources, construction, and maintenance earned nearly 35 percent more that non-union workers. However, in management, professional, and related occupations, there was no virtually no difference in earnings. (See Table 10-4.)

OTHER HIGHLIGHTS

- In 2006, the proportion of workers who were union members declined to 12 percent—about half the proportion of union members in 1977. (See Table 10-2.)

- The local government sector, which accounted for over half of public-sector employment in 2006, had the highest proportion of union representation at 45.7 percent. Many of these employees worked in education, training, and library occupations and protective service occupations. (See Table 10-3.)

- At least 20 percent of workers were represented by unions in six states in 2006: Hawaii (25.9 percent), New York (25.4 percent), Alaska (23.8 percent), New Jersey (21.6 percent), Washington (21.0 percent) and Michigan (20.4 percent). (See Table 10-6.)

- The number of workers involved in work stoppages declined in 2006. Although days idle increased from the 2005 total, it remained quite low. (See Table 10-1.)

NOTES AND DEFINITIONS

WORK STOPPAGES

Collection and Coverage

Data on work stoppages measure the number and duration of major strikes or lockouts (involving 1,000 workers or more) during the year, the number of workers involved in these stoppages, and the amount of time lost due to these stoppages.

Information on work stoppages is obtained from reports issued by the Federal Mediation and Conciliation Service, state labor market information offices, Bureau of Labor Statistics (BLS) Strike Reports from the Office of Employment and Unemployment Statistics, and media sources such as the Daily Labor Report and the Wall Street Journal. One or both parties involved in the work stoppage (employer and/or union) is contacted to verify the duration of the stoppage and number of workers idled by the stoppage.

The current series is not comparable with the series terminated in 1981. The former series covered strikes involving six workers or more.

Concepts and Definitions

Major work stoppage includes both worker-initiated strikes and employer-initiated lockouts involving 1,000 workers or more. BLS does not distinguish between lockouts and strikes in its statistics.

Workers involved consists of workers directly involved in the stoppage. This category does not measure the indirect or secondary effect of stoppages on other establishments whose employees are idle from material shortages or lack of service.

Days of idleness are calculated by taking the number of workers involved in the strike or lockout and multiplying it by the number of days workers are off the job.

Sources of Additional Information

Additional information is available in BLS news release USDL 07-0304, "Major Work Stoppages in 2006."

UNION MEMBERSHIP

Collection, Coverage, and Definitions

The estimates of union membership are obtained from the Current Population Survey (CPS). The union membership and earnings data are tabulated from one-quarter of the CPS monthly sample and are limited to wage and salary workers. Excluded are all self-employed workers.

Union members are members of a labor union or an employee association similar to a union.

Represented by unions refers to union members, as well as to workers who have no union affiliation but whose jobs are covered by a union contract.

Sources of Additional Information

Additional information is available in BLS news release USDL 07-0113, "Union Members in 2006."

Table 10-1. Work Stoppages Involving 1,000 Workers or More, 1947–2006

(Number, percent.)

Year	Stoppages beginning during the year		Days idle during the year[1]	
	Number	Workers involved (thousands)[2]	Number (thousands)	Percent of estimated total working time[3]
1947	270	1 629	25 720	. . .
1948	245	1 435	26 127	0.22
1949	262	2 537	43 420	0.38
1950	424	1 698	30 390	0.26
1951	415	1 462	15 070	0.12
1952	470	2 746	48 820	0.38
1953	437	1 623	18 130	0.14
1954	265	1 075	16 630	0.13
1955	363	2 055	21 180	0.16
1956	287	1 370	26 840	0.20
1957	279	887	10 340	0.07
1958	332	1 587	17 900	0.13
1959	245	1 381	60 850	0.43
1960	222	896	13 260	0.09
1961	195	1 031	10 140	0.07
1962	211	793	11 760	0.08
1963	181	512	10 020	0.07
1964	246	1 183	16 220	0.11
1965	268	999	15 140	0.10
1966	321	1 300	16 000	0.10
1967	381	2 192	31 320	0.18
1968	392	1 855	35 367	0.20
1969	412	1 576	29 397	0.16
1970	381	2 468	52 761	0.29
1971	298	2 516	35 538	0.19
1972	250	975	16 764	0.09
1973	317	1 400	16 260	0.08
1974	424	1 796	31 809	0.16
1975	235	965	17 563	0.09
1976	231	1 519	23 962	0.12
1977	298	1 212	21 258	0.10
1978	219	1 006	23 774	0.11
1979	235	1 021	20 409	0.09
1980	187	795	20 844	0.09
1981	145	729	16 908	0.07
1982	96	656	9 061	0.04
1983	81	909	17 461	0.08
1984	62	376	8 499	0.04
1985	54	324	7 079	0.03
1986	69	533	11 861	0.05
1987	46	174	4 481	0.02
1988	40	118	4 381	0.02
1989	51	452	16 996	0.07
1990	44	185	5 926	0.02
1991	40	392	4 584	0.02
1992	35	364	3 989	0.01
1993	35	182	3 981	0.01
1994	45	322	5 021	0.02
1995	31	192	5 771	0.02
1996	37	273	4 889	0.02
1997	29	339	4 497	0.01
1998	34	387	5 116	0.02
1999	17	73	1 996	0.01
2000	39	394	20 419	0.06
2001	29	99	1 151	([4])
2002	19	46	660	([4])
2003	14	129	4 091	0.01
2004	17	171	3 344	0.01
2005	22	100	1 736	0.01
2006	20	70	2 688	0.01

[1]Days idle include all stoppages in effect during the reference period. For work stoppages that are still ongoing at the end of the calendar year, only those days of idleness during the calendar year are counted.
[2]Workers are counted more than once if involved in more than one stoppage during the reference period.
[3]Agricultural and government workers are included in the calculation of estimated working time; private household, forestry, and fishery workers are excluded.
[4]Less than 0.005 percent.
. . . = Not available.

Table 10-2. Union Affiliation of Employed Wage and Salary Workers, by Selected Characteristics, 2001–2006

(Numbers in thousands, percent.)

Characteristic	2001 Total employed	2001 Member of union[1] Total	2001 Member Percent employed	2001 Represented by union[2] Total	2001 Repr Percent employed	2002 Total employed	2002 Member of union[1] Total	2002 Member Percent employed	2002 Represented by union[2] Total	2002 Repr Percent employed	2003 Total employed	2003 Member of union[1] Total	2003 Member Percent employed	2003 Represented by union[2] Total	2003 Repr Percent employed
SEX AND AGE															
Both Sexes, 16 Years and Over	122 482	16 387	13.4	18 114	14.8	121 826	16 145	13.3	17 695	14.5	122 358	15 776	12.9	17 448	14.3
16 to 24 years	19 698	1 015	5.2	1 184	6.0	19 216	995	5.2	1 126	5.9	18 904	966	5.1	1 124	5.9
25 years and over	102 784	15 372	15.0	16 930	16.5	102 610	15 151	14.8	16 569	16.1	103 454	14 810	14.3	16 324	15.8
25 to 34 years	28 809	3 264	11.3	3 659	12.7	28 232	3 172	11.2	3 522	12.5	28 179	3 097	11.0	3 455	12.3
35 to 44 years	31 962	4 733	14.8	5 191	16.2	31 253	4 455	14.3	4 859	15.5	30 714	4 308	14.0	4 717	15.4
45 to 54 years	26 909	5 068	18.8	5 543	20.6	27 040	5 016	18.6	5 446	20.1	27 567	4 848	17.6	5 307	19.3
55 to 64 years	12 032	2 063	17.1	2 265	18.8	12 952	2 256	17.4	2 456	19.0	13 633	2 300	16.9	2 547	18.7
65 years and over	3 072	243	7.9	272	8.9	3 133	251	8.0	285	9.1	3 361	258	7.7	297	8.8
Men, 16 Years and Over	63 756	9 578	15.0	10 410	16.3	63 272	9 325	14.7	10 066	15.9	63 236	9 044	14.3	9 848	15.6
16 to 24 years	10 137	607	6.0	704	6.9	9 857	616	6.3	687	7.0	9 683	595	6.1	685	7.1
25 years and over	53 619	8 971	16.7	9 706	18.1	53 415	8 709	16.3	9 379	17.6	53 553	8 450	15.8	9 163	17.1
25 to 34 years	15 627	1 983	12.7	2 169	13.9	15 284	1 877	12.3	2 061	13.5	15 263	1 826	12.0	2 005	13.1
35 to 44 years	16 657	2 821	16.9	3 028	18.2	16 355	2 631	16.1	2 805	17.1	16 080	2 535	15.8	2 735	17.0
45 to 54 years	13 561	2 840	20.9	3 070	22.6	13 578	2 784	20.5	2 982	22.0	13 723	2 684	19.6	2 891	21.1
55 to 64 years	6 168	1 195	19.4	1 292	20.9	6 570	1 281	19.5	1 376	21.0	6 776	1 271	18.8	1 377	20.3
65 years and over	1 605	131	8.1	148	9.2	1 627	136	8.4	155	9.5	1 710	133	7.8	155	9.0
Women, 16 Years and Over	58 726	6 809	11.6	7 704	13.1	58 555	6 820	11.6	7 629	13.0	59 122	6 732	11.4	7 601	12.9
16 to 24 years	9 561	409	4.3	480	5.0	9 359	378	4.0	439	4.7	9 221	371	4.0	439	4.8
25 years and over	49 166	6 400	13.0	7 224	14.7	49 196	6 441	13.1	7 190	14.6	49 901	6 360	12.7	7 161	14.4
25 to 34 years	13 181	1 281	9.7	1 490	11.3	12 948	1 295	10.0	1 461	11.3	12 916	1 270	9.8	1 451	11.2
35 to 44 years	15 305	1 912	12.5	2 163	14.1	14 898	1 825	12.2	2 055	13.8	14 634	1 773	12.1	1 982	13.5
45 to 54 years	13 349	2 227	16.7	2 474	18.5	13 462	2 232	16.6	2 464	18.3	13 844	2 163	15.6	2 416	17.5
55 to 64 years	5 864	868	14.8	973	16.6	6 383	975	15.3	1 080	16.9	6 857	1 029	15.0	1 170	17.1
65 years and over	1 467	113	7.7	124	8.5	1 506	115	7.6	130	8.6	1 651	125	7.6	142	8.6
RACE, HISPANIC ORIGIN, AND SEX															
White, 16 Years and Over[3]	101 546	13 209	13.0	14 574	14.4	100 923	12 958	12.8	14 178	14.0	100 589	12 535	12.5	13 849	13.8
Men	53 731	7 909	14.7	8 585	16.0	53 198	7 689	14.5	8 284	15.6	52 827	7 378	14.0	8 016	15.2
Women	47 815	5 300	11.1	5 989	12.5	47 725	5 269	11.0	5 894	12.3	47 762	5 157	10.8	5 834	12.2
Black, 16 Years and Over[3]	14 261	2 409	16.9	2 668	18.7	14 108	2 386	16.9	2 624	18.6	13 928	2 298	16.5	2 540	18.2
Men	6 488	1 221	18.8	1 330	20.5	6 493	1 183	18.2	1 281	19.7	6 302	1 153	18.3	1 249	19.8
Women	7 773	1 188	15.3	1 338	17.2	7 615	1 204	15.8	1 343	17.6	7 626	1 145	15.0	1 291	16.9
Asian, 16 Years and Over[3]	...	...	...	...	...	...	...	...	...	...	5 096	581	11.4	659	12.9
Men	...	...	...	...	...	...	...	...	...	...	2 669	296	11.0	346	12.8
Women	...	...	...	...	...	...	...	...	...	...	2 397	285	11.9	313	13.1
Hispanic, 16 Years and Over[4]	15 174	1 679	11.1	1 876	12.4	15 486	1 639	10.6	1 810	11.7	16 068	1 712	10.7	1 913	11.9
Men	8 997	1 032	11.5	1 136	12.6	9 098	1 006	11.1	1 100	12.1	9 567	1 050	11.0	1 160	12.1
Women	6 177	647	10.5	740	12.0	6 387	633	9.9	710	11.1	6 501	662	10.2	753	11.6
FULL- OR PART-TIME STATUS[5]															
Full-time workers	101 187	14 921	14.7	16 445	16.3	100 081	14 622	14.6	16 005	16.0	100 302	14 263	14.2	15 732	15.7
Part-time workers	21 057	1 437	6.8	1 637	7.8	21 513	1 492	6.9	1 654	7.7	21 809	1 479	6.8	1 679	7.7

Note: Beginning in January 2006, data reflect revised population controls used in the household survey.

[1]Data refer to members of a labor union or to an employee association similar to a union.

[2]Data refer to members of a labor union or to an employee association similar to a union, as well as to workers who report no union affiliation but whose jobs are covered by a union or an employee association contract.

[3]Beginning in 2003, persons who selected this race group only; persons who selected more than one race group are not included. Prior to 2003, persons who reported more than one race group were included in the group they identified as their main race. Additionally, estimates for the above race groups (White, Black, and Asian) do not sum to totals because data are not presented for all races.

[4]May be of any race.

[5]The distinction between full- and part-time workers is based on hours usually worked. Data will not sum to totals because full- or part-time status on the principal job is not identifiable for a small number of multiple job holders.

. . . = Not available.

Table 10-2. Union Affiliation of Employed Wage and Salary Workers, by Selected Characteristics, 2001–2006—*Continued*

(Numbers in thousands, percent.)

Characteristic	2004					2005					2006				
	Total employed	Member of union[1]		Represented by union[2]		Total employed	Member of union[1]		Represented by union[2]		Total employed	Member of union[1]		Represented by union[2]	
		Total	Percent employed	Total	Percent employed		Total	Percent employed	Total	Percent employed		Total	Percent employed	Total	Percent employed
SEX AND AGE															
Both Sexes, 16 Years and Over	123 554	15 472	12.5	17 087	13.8	125 889	15 685	12.5	17 223	13.7	128 237	15 359	12.0	16 860	13.1
16 to 24 years	19 109	890	4.7	1 019	5.3	19 283	878	4.6	1 019	5.3	19 538	857	4.4	978	5.0
25 years and over	104 444	14 581	14.0	16 069	15.4	106 606	14 808	13.9	16 204	15.2	108 699	14 502	13.3	15 883	14.6
25 to 34 years	28 202	2 982	10.6	3 316	11.8	28 450	3 044	10.7	3 368	11.8	28 805	2 899	10.1	3 195	11.1
35 to 44 years	30 470	4 173	13.7	4 590	15.1	30 654	4 211	13.7	4 579	14.9	30 526	3 997	13.1	4 356	14.3
45 to 54 years	28 039	4 771	17.0	5 233	18.7	28 714	4 731	16.5	5 158	18.0	29 401	4 710	16.0	5 131	17.5
55 to 64 years	14 239	2 390	16.8	2 617	18.4	15 158	2 496	16.5	2 732	18.0	16 095	2 568	16.0	2 832	17.6
65 years and over	3 495	264	7.5	314	9.0	3 631	325	8.9	366	10.1	3 872	328	8.5	370	9.5
Men, 16 Years and Over	64 145	8 878	13.8	9 638	15.0	65 466	8 870	13.5	9 597	14.7	66 811	8 657	13.0	9 360	14.0
16 to 24 years	9 835	557	5.7	627	6.4	9 860	523	5.3	603	6.1	10 130	543	5.4	608	6.0
25 years and over	54 310	8 321	15.3	9 010	16.6	55 606	8 347	15.0	8 994	16.2	56 682	8 114	14.3	8 752	15.4
25 to 34 years	15 391	1 722	11.2	1 873	12.2	15 559	1 754	11.3	1 915	12.3	15 677	1 650	10.5	1 793	11.4
35 to 44 years	16 035	2 449	15.3	2 658	16.6	16 196	2 422	15.0	2 582	15.9	16 159	2 309	14.3	2 488	15.4
45 to 54 years	14 026	2 699	19.2	2 903	20.7	14 421	2 658	18.4	2 849	19.8	14 867	2 617	17.6	2 807	18.9
55 to 64 years	7 117	1 309	18.4	1 414	19.9	7 606	1 346	17.7	1 458	19.2	7 990	1 370	17.1	1 474	18.4
65 years and over	1 741	142	8.2	163	9.4	1 824	167	9.1	190	10.4	1 989	167	8.4	190	9.6
Women, 16 Years and Over	59 408	6 593	11.1	7 450	12.5	60 423	6 815	11.3	7 626	12.6	61 426	6 702	10.9	7 501	12.2
16 to 24 years	9 274	333	3.6	391	4.2	9 423	354	3.8	417	4.4	9 408	315	3.3	370	3.9
25 years and over	50 134	6 260	12.5	7 058	14.1	51 000	6 461	12.7	7 210	14.1	52 018	6 388	12.3	7 131	13.7
25 to 34 years	12 811	1 261	9.8	1 443	11.3	12 891	1 290	10.0	1 454	11.3	13 127	1 249	9.5	1 401	10.7
35 to 44 years	14 435	1 725	11.9	1 931	13.4	14 457	1 790	12.4	1 997	13.8	14 368	1 687	11.7	1 867	13.0
45 to 54 years	14 014	2 072	14.8	2 330	16.6	14 293	2 073	14.5	2 309	16.2	14 534	2 093	14.4	2 325	16.0
55 to 64 years	7 122	1 081	15.2	1 203	16.9	7 552	1 150	15.2	1 274	16.9	8 106	1 198	14.8	1 358	16.8
65 years and over	1 753	121	6.9	151	8.6	1 806	158	8.8	176	9.8	1 883	160	8.5	180	9.5
RACE, HISPANIC ORIGIN, AND SEX															
White, 16 Years and Over[3]	101 340	12 381	12.2	13 657	13.5	102 967	12 520	12.2	13 755	13.4	104 668	12 259	11.7	13 424	12.8
Men	53 432	7 260	13.6	7 854	14.7	54 462	7 275	13.4	7 858	14.4	55 459	7 115	12.8	7 668	13.8
Women	47 908	5 121	10.7	5 803	12.1	48 505	5 245	10.8	5 897	12.2	49 209	5 144	10.5	5 756	11.7
Black, 16 Years and Over[3]	14 090	2 130	15.1	2 355	16.7	14 459	2 178	15.1	2 391	16.5	14 878	2 163	14.5	2 391	16.1
Men	6 409	1 085	16.9	1 185	18.5	6 603	1 062	16.1	1 166	17.7	6 788	1 056	15.6	1 158	17.1
Women	7 681	1 045	13.6	1 170	15.2	7 857	1 115	14.2	1 225	15.6	8 090	1 107	13.7	1 233	15.2
Asian, 16 Years and Over[3]	5 280	603	11.4	670	12.7	5 479	614	11.2	666	12.2	5 703	592	10.4	657	11.5
Men	2 815	328	11.7	371	13.2	2 881	314	10.9	337	11.7	3 015	286	9.5	316	10.5
Women	2 465	275	11.1	299	12.1	2 598	299	11.5	329	12.7	2 688	306	11.4	340	12.7
Hispanic, 16 Years and Over[4]	16 533	1 676	10.1	1 888	11.4	17 191	1 793	10.4	1 981	11.5	18 121	1 770	9.8	1 935	10.7
Men	9 857	1 016	10.3	1 130	11.5	10 324	1 093	10.6	1 185	11.5	10 842	1 064	9.8	1 144	10.6
Women	6 676	661	9.9	758	11.4	6 866	700	10.2	796	11.6	7 279	706	9.7	791	10.9
FULL- OR PART-TIME STATUS[5]															
Full-time workers	101 224	14 029	13.9	15 463	15.3	103 560	14 207	13.7	15 551	15.0	106 106	13 938	13.1	15 244	14.4
Part-time workers	22 047	1 406	6.4	1 587	7.2	22 052	1 441	6.5	1 630	7.4	21 863	1 382	6.3	1 573	7.2

Note: Beginning in January 2006, data reflect revised population controls used in the household survey.

[1]Data refer to members of a labor union or to an employee association similar to a union.

[2]Data refer to members of a labor union or to an employee association similar to a union, as well as to workers who report no union affiliation but whose jobs are covered by a union or an employee association contract.

[3]Beginning in 2003, persons who selected this race group only; persons who selected more than one race group are not included. Prior to 2003, persons who reported more than one race group were included in the group they identified as their main race. Additionally, estimates for the above race groups (White, Black, and Asian) do not sum to totals because data are not presented for all races.

[4]May be of any race.

[5]The distinction between full- and part-time workers is based on hours usually worked. Data will not sum to totals because full- or part-time status on the principal job is not identifiable for a small number of multiple job holders.

Table 10-3. Union Affiliation of Wage and Salary Workers, by Occupation and Industry, 2005–2006

(Thousands of people, percent.)

Occupation and industry	2005					2006				
	Total employed	Member of union[1]		Represented by union[2]		Total employed	Member of union[1]		Represented by union[2]	
		Total	Percent of employed	Total	Percent of employed		Total	Percent of employed	Total	Percent of employed
OCCUPATION										
Management, professional, and related	42 226	5 639	13.4	6 385	15.1	43 105	5 522	12.8	6 288	14.6
Management, business, and financial operations	15 955	793	5.0	939	5.9	16 471	802	4.9	964	5.9
Management	10 921	485	4.4	585	5.4	11 260	478	4.2	595	5.3
Business and financial operations	5 034	308	6.1	354	7.0	5 210	324	6.2	369	7.1
Professional and related	26 271	4 845	18.4	5 447	20.7	26 635	4 721	17.7	5 324	20.0
Computer and mathematical	3 067	142	4.6	172	5.6	3 069	133	4.3	172	5.6
Architecture and engineering	2 593	221	8.5	259	10.0	2 669	197	7.4	236	8.9
Life, physical, and social science	1 305	125	9.6	140	10.7	1 315	130	9.9	155	11.8
Community and social service	2 100	346	16.5	376	17.9	2 099	327	15.6	356	17.0
Legal	1 261	71	5.6	83	6.6	1 282	68	5.3	73	5.7
Education, training, and library	7 813	3 006	38.5	3 354	42.9	7 888	2 942	37.3	3 287	41.7
Arts, design, entertainment, sports, and media	1 957	152	7.8	171	8.8	1 930	124	6.4	140	7.2
Health care practitioner and technical	6 175	782	12.7	892	14.4	6 383	800	12.5	904	14.2
Services	21 074	2 446	11.6	2 659	12.6	21 569	2 460	11.4	2 658	12.3
Health care support	2 971	286	9.6	317	10.7	2 999	312	10.4	340	11.3
Protective service	2 843	1 051	37.0	1 109	39.0	2 919	1 012	34.7	1 067	36.6
Food preparation and serving related	7 361	316	4.3	362	4.9	7 478	321	4.3	353	4.7
Building and grounds cleaning and maintenance	4 525	504	11.1	553	12.2	4 703	507	10.8	561	11.9
Personal care and service	3 373	288	8.5	317	9.4	3 471	307	8.9	337	9.7
Sales and office	32 541	2 385	7.3	2 671	8.2	32 986	2 319	7.0	2 573	7.8
Sales and related	13 630	451	3.3	519	3.8	13 883	430	3.1	489	3.5
Office and administrative support	18 911	1 934	10.2	2 152	11.4	19 103	1 889	9.9	2 084	10.9
Natural resources, construction, and maintenance	12 907	2 129	16.5	2 238	17.3	13 366	2 138	16.0	2 248	16.8
Farming, fishing, and forestry	898	35	3.9	38	4.3	880	31	3.5	33	3.7
Construction and extraction	7 296	1 283	17.6	1 348	18.5	7 617	1 337	17.6	1 396	18.3
Installation, maintenance, and repair	4 713	811	17.2	851	18.1	4 870	771	15.8	820	16.8
Production, transportation, and material moving	17 142	3 086	18.0	3 271	19.1	17 211	2 920	17.0	3 094	18.0
Production	9 007	1 539	17.1	1 617	17.9	8 964	1 392	15.5	1 468	16.4
Transportation and material moving	8 135	1 547	19.0	1 655	20.3	8 247	1 528	18.5	1 626	19.7
INDUSTRY										
Private sector	105 508	8 255	7.8	8 962	8.5	107 846	7 981	7.4	8 688	8.1
Agriculture and related industries	1 021	28	2.7	30	3.0	1 059	25	2.3	27	2.6
Nonagricultural industries	104 487	8 227	7.9	8 931	8.5	106 786	7 957	7.5	8 660	8.1
Mining	600	48	8.0	57	9.5	632	48	7.5	56	8.8
Construction	8 053	1 057	13.1	1 111	13.8	8 444	1 097	13.0	1 146	13.6
Manufacturing	15 518	2 017	13.0	2 127	13.7	15 643	1 827	11.7	1 949	12.5
Durable goods	9 845	1 310	13.3	1 382	14.0	10 072	1 190	11.8	1 263	12.5
Nondurable goods	5 673	707	12.5	746	13.1	5 571	637	11.4	686	12.3
Wholesale and retail trade	18 989	1 021	5.4	1 122	5.9	19 245	957	5.0	1 023	5.3
Wholesale trade	4 017	236	5.9	259	6.4	4 100	201	4.9	215	5.2
Retail trade	14 973	785	5.2	864	5.8	15 145	756	5.0	808	5.3
Transportation and utilities	5 212	1 252	24.0	1 309	25.1	5 299	1 227	23.2	1 287	24.3
Transportation and warehousing	4 379	1 024	23.4	1 071	24.4	4 459	991	22.2	1 042	23.4
Utilities	833	228	27.4	239	28.6	840	237	28.2	245	29.1
Information[3]	2 934	398	13.6	422	14.4	3 105	372	12.0	404	13.0
Publishing, except Internet	765	68	8.8	74	9.7	833	58	7.0	63	7.5
Motion pictures and sound recording	277	42	15.0	43	15.5	296	30	10.3	32	10.6
Broadcasting, except Internet	534	46	8.6	48	9.0	522	31	5.9	40	7.6
Telecommunications	1 096	234	21.4	248	22.6	1 183	245	20.7	261	22.1
Financial activities	8 619	195	2.3	238	2.8	8 841	168	1.9	206	2.3
Finance and insurance	6 304	102	1.6	132	2.1	6 503	92	1.4	123	1.9
Finance	4 114	59	1.4	77	1.9	4 308	52	1.2	73	1.7
Insurance	2 190	44	2.0	54	2.5	2 195	40	1.8	50	2.3
Real estate and rental and leasing	2 315	92	4.0	107	4.6	2 338	77	3.3	82	3.5
Professional and business services	10 951	292	2.7	341	3.1	11 398	274	2.4	329	2.9
Professional and technical services	6 468	98	1.5	120	1.9	6 601	90	1.4	116	1.8
Management, administrative, and waste services	4 483	194	4.3	221	4.9	4 798	184	3.8	213	4.4
Education and health services	17 357	1 434	8.3	1 632	9.4	17 853	1 483	8.3	1 694	9.5
Education services	3 312	435	13.1	511	15.4	3 540	478	13.5	562	15.9
Health care and social assistance	14 045	999	7.1	1 121	8.0	14 313	1 005	7.0	1 132	7.9
Leisure and hospitality	10 658	333	3.1	377	3.5	10 638	326	3.1	370	3.5
Arts, entertainment, and recreation	1 869	118	6.3	134	7.2	1 781	112	6.3	126	7.1
Accommodation and food services	8 790	215	2.4	243	2.8	8 857	214	2.4	244	2.8
Accommodation	1 459	122	8.3	130	8.9	1 422	131	9.2	141	9.9
Food services and drinking places	7 331	93	1.3	113	1.5	7 436	83	1.1	103	1.4
Other services[3]	5 596	181	3.2	194	3.5	5 689	177	3.1	198	3.5
Other services, except private households	4 799	175	3.7	188	3.9	4 873	172	3.5	191	3.9
Public sector	20 381	7 430	36.5	8 262	40.5	20 392	7 378	36.2	8 172	40.1
Federal government	3 427	954	27.8	1 134	33.1	3 381	960	28.4	1 139	33.7
State government	5 874	1 838	31.3	2 056	35.0	6 102	1 843	30.2	2 049	33.6
Local government	11 080	4 638	41.9	5 071	45.8	10 908	4 575	41.9	4 984	45.7

Note: Beginning in January 2006, data reflect revised population controls used in the household survey. Data refer to the sole or principal job of full- and part-time workers. Excluded are all self-employed workers, regardless of whether or not their businesses are incorporated.

[1]Data refer to members of a labor union or an employee association similar to a union.
[2]Data refer to members of a labor union or an employee association similar to a union, as well as to workers who report no union affiliation but whose jobs are covered by a union or an employee association contract.
[3]Includes other industries, not shown separately.

Table 10-4. Median Weekly Earnings of Full-Time Wage and Salary Workers, by Union Affiliation, Occupation, and Industry, 2005–2006

(Dollars.)

Occupation and industry	2005				2006			
	Total	Member of union[1]	Represented by union[2]	Non-union	Total	Member of union[1]	Represented by union[2]	Non-union
OCCUPATION								
Management, professional, and related	937	942	937	937	967	966	962	968
Management, business, and financial operations	997	1 015	1 029	995	1 045	1 042	1 060	1 044
Management	1 083	1 137	1 146	1 076	1 127	1 144	1 154	1 125
Business and financial operations	871	854	866	872	930	950	947	928
Professional and related	902	932	924	894	928	956	948	921
Computer and mathematical	1 132	1 009	1 029	1 141	1 166	1 057	1 103	1 170
Architecture and engineering	1 105	1 133	1 133	1 101	1 155	1 148	1 157	1 155
Life, physical, and social science	965	978	1 011	959	984	1 114	1 086	977
Community and social service	725	880	865	693	740	886	872	707
Legal	1 052	1 147	1 155	1 042	1 144	1 422	1 415	1 136
Education, training, and library	798	913	898	710	819	929	917	725
Arts, design, entertainment, sports, and media	819	983	925	808	841	968	964	823
Health care practitioner and technical	878	932	932	867	905	995	979	889
Services	413	643	629	392	422	638	629	404
Health care support	410	466	462	405	423	484	481	417
Protective service	678	896	886	568	693	918	913	585
Food preparation and serving related	356	439	442	350	371	484	482	366
Building and grounds cleaning and maintenance	394	528	518	378	406	524	520	393
Personal care and service	409	558	549	397	407	530	529	397
Sales and office	575	681	675	562	589	706	697	578
Sales and related	622	623	625	622	628	671	656	627
Office and administrative support	550	689	682	528	572	713	705	549
Natural resources, construction, and maintenance	623	910	903	585	653	934	925	608
Farming, fishing, and forestry	372	(3)	(3)	369	387	(3)	(3)	383
Construction and extraction	604	913	903	554	619	941	933	582
Installation, maintenance, and repair	705	915	913	666	742	931	922	709
Production, transportation, and material moving	540	709	704	510	557	741	733	519
Production	538	698	693	511	559	730	723	525
Transportation and material moving	543	721	717	508	556	752	743	512
INDUSTRY								
Private sector	625	757	752	615	645	792	785	631
Agriculture and related industries	402	(3)	(3)	402	422	(3)	(3)	420
Nonagricultural industries	629	758	753	617	648	793	786	634
Mining	885	(3)	989	870	912	(3)	1 044	899
Construction	619	933	926	590	642	969	956	610
Manufacturing	676	722	719	667	702	755	753	692
Durable goods	704	751	747	695	729	785	780	719
Nondurable goods	624	676	672	618	650	694	697	640
Wholesale and retail trade	566	615	610	562	578	637	632	575
Wholesale trade	692	678	676	694	725	780	778	720
Retail trade	515	590	585	513	520	583	582	518
Transportation and utilities	726	864	860	676	739	876	876	697
Transportation and warehousing	688	829	827	640	700	831	828	661
Utilities	941	960	954	931	978	1 041	1 051	939
Information[4]	832	931	925	810	871	998	990	841
Publishing, except Internet	755	860	867	740	848	(3)	950	830
Motion pictures and sound recording	751	(3)	(3)	691	813	(3)	(3)	748
Broadcasting, except Internet	749	(3)	(3)	738	737	(3)	(3)	722
Telecommunications	927	937	935	923	947	986	982	928
Financial activities	741	698	696	743	757	674	691	759
Finance and insurance	765	692	696	767	794	657	674	799
Finance	765	650	667	768	811	(3)	673	817
Insurance	764	(3)	729	766	767	(3)	(3)	769
Real estate and rental and leasing	653	711	696	649	663	701	700	660
Professional and business services	739	663	673	743	749	744	752	749
Professional and technical services	961	770	858	963	996	940	966	996
Management, administrative, and waste services	488	586	578	485	504	653	643	499
Education and health services	627	731	736	617	648	751	745	635
Education services	737	818	809	718	750	816	806	737
Health care and social assistance	607	684	692	601	620	703	700	614
Leisure and hospitality	409	513	510	405	417	538	533	412
Arts, entertainment, and recreation	521	652	618	515	545	617	604	537
Accommodation and food services	388	487	486	384	399	515	515	395
Accommodation	455	515	510	438	490	567	570	481
Food services and drinking places	372	400	406	372	382	480	481	381
Other services[4]	535	694	698	524	568	816	794	550
Other services, except private households	579	698	701	572	597	824	800	588
Public sector	758	850	842	692	773	871	865	717
Federal government	882	873	879	887	919	896	900	938
State government	733	802	798	684	746	835	824	699
Local government	738	858	844	633	754	876	868	656

Note: Beginning in January 2006, data reflect revised population controls used in the household survey. Data refer to the sole or principal job of full- and part-time workers. Excluded are all self-employed workers, regardless of whether or not their businesses are incorporated.

[1]Data refer to members of a labor union or an employee association similar to a union.
[2]Data refer to members of a labor union or an employee association similar to a union, as well as to workers who report no union affiliation but whose jobs are covered by a union or an employee association contract.
[3]Data not shown where base is less than 50,000.
[4]Includes other industries, not shown separately.

Table 10-5. Union or Employee Association Members Among Wage and Salary Employees, 1977–2006

(Numbers in thousands, percent.)

Year	Total wage and salary employment	Union or employee association member	Union or association members as a percent of total wage and salary employment
1977	81 334	19 335	23.8
1978	84 968	19 548	23.0
1979	87 117	20 986	24.1
1980	87 480	20 095	23.0
1981	. . .	. . .	. . .
1982	. . .	. . .	. . .
1983[1]	88 290	17 717	20.1
1984	92 194	17 340	18.8
1985	94 521	16 996	18.0
1986	96 903	16 975	17.5
1987	99 303	16 913	17.0
1988	101 407	17 002	16.8
1989	103 480	16 980	16.4
1990	103 905	16 740	16.1
1991	102 786	16 568	16.1
1992	103 688	16 390	15.8
1993	105 087	16 598	15.8
1994[2]	107 989	16 748	15.5
1995	110 038	16 360	14.9
1996	111 960	16 269	14.5
1997	114 533	16 110	14.1
1998	116 730	16 211	13.9
1999	118 963	16 477	13.9
2000	120 786	16 258	13.5
2001	122 482	16 387	13.4
2002	121 826	16 145	13.3
2003	122 358	15 776	12.9
2004	123 554	15 472	12.5
2005	125 889	15 685	12.5
2006	128 237	15 359	12.0

Note: Beginning in January 2006, data reflect revised population controls used in the household survey.

[1] Annual average data beginning in 1983 are not directly comparable with the data for 1977–1980.

[2] Data beginning in 1994 are not strictly comparable with data for 1993 and earlier years because of the introduction of a major redesign of the Current Population Survey questionnaire and collection methodology and the introduction of 1990 census–based population controls.

. . . = Not available.

Table 10-6. Union Affiliation of Employed Wage and Salary Workers, by State, 2005–2006

(Numbers in thousands, percent.)

State	2005					2006				
	Total employed	Member of union[1]		Represented by union[2]		Total employed	Member of union[1]		Represented by union[2]	
		Total	Percent of employed	Total	Percent of employed		Total	Percent of employed	Total	Percent of employed
UNITED STATES	125 889	15 685	12.5	17 223	13.7	128 237	15 359	12.0	16 860	13.1
Alabama	1 909	195	10.2	223	11.7	1 930	170	8.8	194	10.0
Alaska	275	63	22.8	66	24.1	280	62	22.2	67	23.8
Arizona	2 366	145	6.1	181	7.7	2 584	197	7.6	250	9.7
Arkansas	1 138	54	4.8	68	6.0	1 130	58	5.1	67	6.0
California	14 687	2 424	16.5	2 610	17.8	14 501	2 273	15.7	2 444	16.9
Colorado	2 052	170	8.3	193	9.4	2 154	165	7.7	186	8.6
Connecticut	1 550	247	15.9	263	17.0	1 591	247	15.6	263	16.5
Delaware	386	46	11.8	50	12.9	396	43	10.8	45	11.4
District of Columbia	259	29	11.3	33	12.8	246	25	10.3	30	12.2
Florida	7 389	401	5.4	532	7.2	7 676	397	5.2	497	6.5
Georgia	3 765	190	5.0	226	6.0	3 974	176	4.4	230	5.8
Hawaii	545	141	25.8	145	26.7	562	139	24.7	146	25.9
Idaho	606	31	5.2	38	6.3	620	37	6.0	45	7.2
Illinois	5 473	927	16.9	965	17.6	5 684	931	16.4	979	17.2
Indiana	2 789	346	12.4	368	13.2	2 787	334	12.0	362	13.0
Iowa	1 369	157	11.5	185	13.5	1 424	161	11.3	199	14.0
Kansas	1 210	85	7.0	115	9.5	1 236	99	8.0	115	9.3
Kentucky	1 696	164	9.7	184	10.8	1 752	172	9.8	196	11.2
Louisiana	1 778	114	6.4	132	7.4	1 676	107	6.4	121	7.2
Maine	582	69	11.9	79	13.6	584	69	11.9	79	13.5
Maryland	2 530	337	13.3	379	15.0	2 614	342	13.1	386	14.8
Massachusetts	2 886	402	13.9	431	14.9	2 859	414	14.5	438	15.3
Michigan	4 288	880	20.5	916	21.4	4 299	842	19.6	879	20.4
Minnesota	2 494	392	15.7	410	16.4	2 479	395	16.0	416	16.8
Mississippi	1 089	77	7.1	105	9.7	1 065	60	5.6	78	7.3
Missouri	2 532	290	11.5	319	12.6	2 610	284	10.9	310	11.9
Montana	391	42	10.7	48	12.2	397	48	12.2	52	13.1
Nebraska	830	69	8.3	79	9.5	831	66	7.9	79	9.5
Nevada	1 051	145	13.8	158	15.1	1 124	167	14.8	191	17.0
New Hampshire	627	65	10.4	72	11.5	620	63	10.1	70	11.3
New Jersey	3 868	791	20.5	838	21.7	3 827	770	20.1	825	21.6
New Mexico	777	63	8.1	83	10.7	796	62	7.8	92	11.5
New York	8 008	2 090	26.1	2 201	27.5	8 115	1 981	24.4	2 060	25.4
North Carolina	3 631	107	2.9	143	3.9	3 810	126	3.3	155	4.1
North Dakota	289	21	7.3	26	9.2	300	20	6.8	24	8.0
Ohio	5 039	804	16.0	866	17.2	5 170	734	14.2	801	15.5
Oklahoma	1 432	77	5.4	91	6.4	1 453	93	6.4	112	7.7
Oregon	1 470	213	14.5	231	15.7	1 527	211	13.8	225	14.7
Pennsylvania	5 456	753	13.8	818	15.0	5 457	745	13.6	802	14.7
Rhode Island	494	79	15.9	83	16.8	498	76	15.3	79	16.0
South Carolina	1 739	40	2.3	58	3.3	1 775	59	3.3	74	4.2
South Dakota	350	21	5.9	29	8.2	351	21	5.9	25	7.2
Tennessee	2 368	128	5.4	156	6.6	2 550	153	6.0	174	6.8
Texas	9 485	506	5.3	590	6.2	9 751	476	4.9	576	5.9
Utah	1 035	51	4.9	63	6.1	1 121	61	5.4	69	6.1
Vermont	287	31	10.8	37	13.0	305	34	11.0	39	12.9
Virginia	3 406	165	4.8	211	6.2	3 446	139	4.0	179	5.2
Washington	2 746	523	19.1	559	20.4	2 772	549	19.8	583	21.0
West Virginia	688	99	14.4	107	15.5	710	101	14.2	110	15.5
Wisconsin	2 551	410	16.1	438	17.2	2 587	386	14.9	415	16.1
Wyoming	228	18	7.9	22	9.5	235	19	8.3	24	10.0

Note: Beginning in January 2006, data reflect revised population controls used in the household survey. Data refer to the sole or principal job of full-and part-time workers. Excluded are all self-employed workers, regardless of whether or not their businesses are incorporated.

[1]Data refer to members of a labor union or an employee association similar to a union.
[2]Data refer to members of a labor union or an employee association similar to a union, as well as to workers who report no union affiliation but whose jobs are covered by a union or an employee association contract.

CHAPTER 11

FOREIGN LABOR FORCE STATISTICS

FOREIGN LABOR FORCE STATISTICS

HIGHLIGHTS

This chapter compares several summary statistics of labor force status, manufacturing productivity, and consumer prices for the United States with similar statistics for other countries. Different concepts and methodologies can make comparisons between countries difficult, but the Bureau of Labor Statistics (BLS) makes adjustments to reconcile as much of the data as possible.

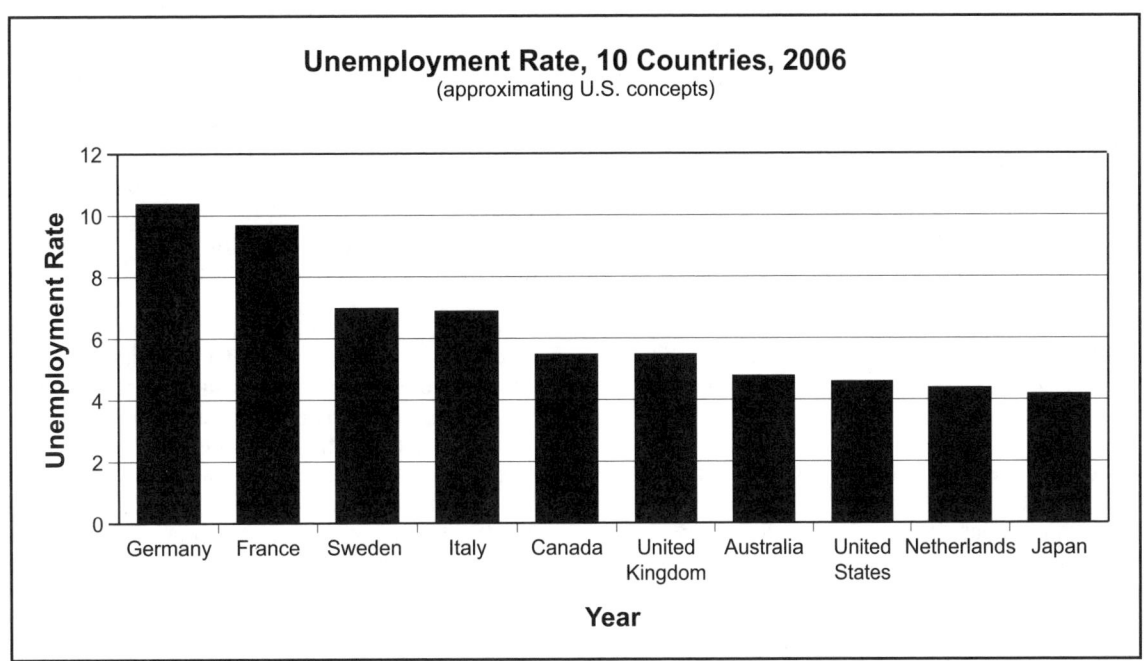

All countries except the United Kingdom had lower unemployment rates in 2006 than in 2005. However, counties in Western Europe continued to struggle with high unemployment rates—particularly Germany, at 10.4 percent, and France, at 9.7 percent (See Table 11-1.)

OTHER HIGHLIGHTS

- Labor force participation rates in 2006 were highest in Canada (67.4 percent) and lowest in Italy (48.9 percent). (See Table 11-1.)

- In 2006, output per hour in manufacturing rose the fastest in Korea (10.8 percent) and Taiwan (6.8 percent). In the United States, it rose 2.4 percent, while in Canada, it remained the same. Output per hour in Australia only rose 0.3 percent. (See Table 11-2.)

- Inflation remained relatively low in all of the countries in 2006, with price increases ranging from 0.3 percent in Japan to 3.5 percent in Australia. Prices increased 3.2 percent in the United States. (See Table 11-5.)

- Stated in U.S. dollars, the United States had the second highest real gross domestic product (GDP) per capita in 2006 ($39,682), exceeded only by Norway ($39,869). All of the measured countries had increases from 2005 (data adjusted for price differences reflecting purchasing power parity.) (See Table 11-6.)

NOTES AND DEFINITIONS

Collection and Coverage

From its inception, the Bureau of Labor Statistics (BLS) has conducted a program of research and statistical analysis that compares labor conditions in the United States with those in selected foreign countries. The principal comparative measures cover the labor force, employment, and unemployment; trends in labor productivity and unit labor costs in manufacturing; and hourly compensation costs for manufacturing production workers. All of the measures are based upon statistical data and other source materials from (a) the statistical agencies of the foreign countries studied; (b) international and supranational bodies such as the United Nations, the International Labour Office (ILO), the Organisation for Economic Co-operation and Development (OECD), and the Statistical Office of the European Communities (EUROSTAT), which attempt to obtain comparable country data; and (c) other secondary sources.

International statistical comparisons should be made with caution, as the statistical concepts and methods in each country are primarily fashioned to meet domestic (rather than international) needs. Whenever possible, BLS adjusts the data to improve comparability.

The first table in this chapter provides BLS comparative measures of the civilian labor force participation rate, employment, and unemployment, approximating U.S. concepts. The second table provides trend indexes of manufacturing labor productivity (output per hour), hourly compensation, unit labor costs (labor compensation per unit of output), and related measures for the United States and 14 other countries. The third table is limited to production workers in manufacturing and shows hourly compensation costs in U.S. dollars for the United States and 32 other countries.

The fourth and fifth tables provide Consumer Price Indexes for selected countries. No adjustments for comparability are made in the total indexes except to convert them to a uniform base year (1982–1984 = 100). The final tables present comparative levels and trends in real gross domestic product (GDP) per capita and per employed person for 16 countries. All GDP series are converted to U.S. dollars through the use of purchasing power parities.

U.S. data in this chapter have been revised from 1998 forward and are based on the 1997 North American Industry Classification System (NAICS). Output, a value-added measure, is based on a new methodology that balances and reconciles industry production with commodity usage. Canadian data are also on a NAICS basis for 1997 onward.

Labor productivity is defined as real output per hour worked. Although the labor productivity measure presented in this release relates output to the hours worked of persons employed in manufacturing, it does not measure the specific contributions of labor as a single factor of production. It instead reflects the joint effects of many influences, including new technology, capital investment, capacity utilization, energy use, managerial skills, and the skills and efforts of the workforce. Unit labor costs are defined as the cost of labor input required to produce one unit of output. They are computed as compensation in nominal terms divided by real output.

Sources of Additional Information

An extensive description of the methodology can be found in Chapter 12 in the *BLS Handbook of Methods*. For more information on manufacturing productivity, see BLS news release USDL 07-1456, "International Comparisons of Manufacturing Productivity and Unit Labor Costs Trends, 2006." Special reports on the BLS Web site at <http://www.bls.gov> describe the adjustments made to each country to conform the country's data to U.S. definitions.

Table 11-1. Employment Status of the Working-Age Population, Approximating U.S. Concepts, 10 Countries, 1970–2006

(Numbers in thousands, percent.)

Category and year	United States	Canada	Australia	Japan	France	Germany[1]	Italy	Nether-lands	Sweden	United Kingdom
Employed										
1970	78 678	7 919	5 388	50 140	20 270	26 100	19 080	. . .	3 850	[2]24 330
1971	79 367	8 104	5 517	50 470	20 420	26 220	19 020	. . .	3 854	[2]24 315
1972	[2]82 153	8 344	5 601	50 590	20 540	26 280	18 710	. . .	3 856	24 385
1973	85 064	8 761	5 765	51 920	20 840	26 590	18 870	5 050	3 873	24 777
1974	86 794	9 125	5 891	51 710	21 030	26 240	19 280	5 100	3 956	24 849
1975	85 846	9 284	5 866	51 530	20 860	25 540	19 400	5 070	4 056	24 758
1976	88 752	[2]9 652	5 946	52 030	21 030	25 400	19 500	5 100	4 082	24 611
1977	92 017	9 825	6 000	52 720	21 220	25 430	19 670	5 210	4 093	24 638
1978	[2]96 048	10 124	6 038	53 370	21 320	25 650	19 720	5 260	4 109	24 774
1979	98 824	10 561	6 111	54 040	21 390	26 080	19 930	5 350	4 174	25 031
1980	99 303	10 872	6 284	54 600	21 440	26 490	20 200	5 520	4 226	24 917
1981	100 397	11 192	6 416	55 060	21 330	26 450	20 280	5 550	4 219	24 256
1982	99 526	10 847	6 415	55 620	[2]21 390	26 150	20 250	5 520	4 213	23 781
1983	100 834	10 936	6 300	56 550	21 380	[2]25 770	20 320	[2]5 420	4 218	23 607
1984	105 005	11 211	6 494	56 870	21 200	25 830	20 390	5 490	4 249	24 115
1985	107 150	11 526	6 697	57 260	21 150	26 010	20 490	5 650	4 293	24 422
1986	[2]109 597	11 873	[2]6 984	57 740	21 240	26 380	[2]20 610	5 740	4 326	24 578
1987	112 440	12 221	7 142	58 320	21 320	26 590	20 590	[2]5 756	[2]4 340	25 072
1988	114 968	12 591	7 413	59 310	21 520	26 800	20 870	5 917	4 410	25 905
1989	117 342	12 876	7 734	60 500	21 850	27 200	20 770	6 048	4 480	26 588
1990	[2]118 793	12 964	7 877	61 700	[2]22 075	27 950	21 080	6 251	4 513	26 713
1991	117 718	12 754	7 698	62 920	22 113	[2]36 871	[2]21 360	6 427	4 447	26 007
1992	118 492	12 643	7 660	63 620	22 000	36 390	21 230	[2]6 559	4 265	25 384
1993	120 259	12 705	7 699	63 820	21 715	35 989	[2]20 549	6 554	4 027	25 158
1994	[2]123 060	12 975	7 942	63 860	21 746	35 756	20 176	6 614	3 990	25 685
1995	124 900	13 210	8 256	63 900	21 955	35 780	20 034	6 821	4 053	25 691
1996	126 708	13 338	8 364	64 200	22 036	35 637	20 124	6 966	4 014	25 941
1997	[2]129 558	13 637	8 444	64 900	22 176	35 508	20 169	7 189	3 969	26 413
1998	[2]131 463	13 973	8 618	64 450	22 597	36 059	20 370	7 408	4 033	26 686
1999	[2]133 488	14 331	8 762	63 920	23 080	[2]36 042	20 617	7 605	4 110	27 051
2000	[2]136 891	14 681	8 989	63 790	23 714	36 236	20 973	7 781	4 222	27 368
2001	136 933	14 866	9 086	63 460	24 167	36 350	21 359	7 875	4 295	27 599
2002	136 485	15 223	9 264	62 650	24 311	36 018	21 666	7 925	4 303	27 812
2003	[2]137 736	15 586	9 480	62 510	24 337	35 615	21 972	7 895	4 293	28 073
2004	[2]139 252	15 861	9 668	62 640	24 330	35 604	22 124	7 847	4 271	28 358
2005	141 730	16 080	9 975	62 910	24 392	[2]36 185	22 290	7 860	[2]4 334	28 628
2006	144 427	16 393	10 186	63 210	24 600	36 978	22 721	8 005	4 415	28 859
Unemployed										
1970	4 093	476	91	590	530	140	640	. . .	59	770
1971	5 016	535	107	640	580	160	640	. . .	101	[2]1 059
1972	4 882	553	150	730	610	190	740	. . .	107	1 116
1973	4 365	515	136	680	590	190	720	160	98	946
1974	5 156	514	162	730	630	420	620	190	80	949
1975	7 929	690	303	1 000	910	890	690	270	67	1 174
1976	7 406	[2]716	298	1 080	1 020	890	790	290	66	1 414
1977	6 991	836	358	1 100	1 160	900	840	270	75	1 470
1978	6 202	898	405	1 240	1 220	870	850	280	94	1 453
1979	6 137	831	408	1 170	1 390	780	920	290	88	1 432
1980	7 637	854	409	1 140	1 490	770	920	350	86	1 833
1981	8 273	887	394	1 260	1 760	1 090	1 040	540	108	2 609
1982	10 678	1 298	495	1 360	[2]1 930	1 560	1 160	630	137	2 875
1983	10 717	1 437	697	1 560	2 020	[2]1 900	1 270	[2]700	151	3 081
1984	8 539	1 377	641	1 610	2 360	1 970	1 280	710	136	3 241
1985	8 312	1 309	603	1 560	2 470	2 010	1 310	600	125	3 151
1986	8 237	1 216	[2]601	1 670	2 520	1 860	[2]1 680	640	117	3 161
1987	7 425	1 123	612	1 730	2 570	1 800	1 760	[2]622	[2]97	2 940
1988	6 701	999	558	1 550	2 460	1 810	1 790	609	84	2 445
1989	[2]6 528	982	490	1 420	2 320	1 640	1 760	558	72	2 082
1990	[2]7 047	1 083	563	1 340	[2]2 084	1 590	1 460	516	81	2 053
1991	8 628	1 386	788	1 360	2 210	[2]2 204	[2]1 580	490	144	2 530
1992	9 613	1 507	897	1 420	2 443	2 615	1 680	[2]478	255	2 823
1993	8 940	1 533	914	1 660	2 776	3 113	[2]2 227	437	416	2 930
1994	[2]7 996	1 372	829	1 920	2 926	3 318	2 421	492	426	2 433
1995	7 404	1 246	739	2 100	2 787	3 200	2 544	523	404	2 439
1996	7 236	1 285	751	2 250	2 946	3 505	2 555	489	440	2 298
1997	[2]6 739	1 248	759	2 300	2 940	3 907	2 584	423	445	1 987
1998	[2]6 210	1 162	721	2 790	2 837	3 693	2 634	337	368	1 788
1999	[2]5 880	1 072	652	3 170	2 711	[2]3 333	2 559	277	313	1 726
2000	[2]5 692	956	602	3 200	2 385	3 065	2 388	231	260	1 584
2001	6 801	1 026	[2]658	3 400	2 226	3 110	2 164	223	227	1 486
2002	8 378	1 143	629	3 590	2 334	3 396	2 062	261	234	1 524
2003	[2]8 774	1 147	599	3 500	2 585	3 661	2 048	360	264	1 484
2004	[2]8 149	1 093	553	3 130	2 631	4 107	1 960	422	300	1 417
2005	7 591	1 028	531	2 940	2 682	[2]4 575	1 889	432	[2]361	1 459
2006	7 001	958	512	2 750	2 647	4 272	1 673	367	332	1 666

[1]Unified Germany from 1991 onward; data for previous years relate to the former West Germany.
[2]Break in series.
. . . = Not available.

Table 11-1. Employment Status of the Working-Age Population, Approximating U.S. Concepts, 10 Countries, 1970–2006—*Continued*

(Numbers in thousands, percent.)

Category and year	United States	Canada	Australia	Japan	France	Germany[1]	Italy	Netherlands	Sweden	United Kingdom
Civilian Labor Force Participation Rate										
1970	60.4	57.8	62.1	64.5	57.5	56.9	49.0	. . .	64.0	61.1
1971	60.2	58.1	62.2	64.3	57.4	56.5	48.7	. . .	64.2	[2]62.8
1972	60.4	58.6	62.3	63.8	57.2	56.2	47.7	. . .	64.1	62.9
1973	60.8	59.7	62.6	64.0	57.3	56.3	47.6	53.4	64.1	63.1
1974	61.3	60.5	63.0	63.1	57.4	55.7	47.7	53.5	64.8	63.1
1975	61.2	61.1	63.2	62.4	57.2	55.0	47.7	54.5	65.9	63.1
1976	61.6	[2]62.5	62.7	62.4	57.5	54.6	48.0	54.1	66.0	63.0
1977	62.3	62.8	62.7	62.5	57.8	54.4	48.2	54.2	65.9	62.7
1978	63.2	63.7	61.9	62.8	57.7	54.4	47.8	54.0	66.1	62.6
1979	63.7	64.5	61.6	62.7	57.8	54.5	48.0	54.2	66.6	62.7
1980	63.8	65.0	62.1	62.6	57.5	54.7	48.2	55.4	66.9	62.8
1981	63.9	65.6	61.9	62.6	57.5	54.7	48.3	56.7	66.8	62.7
1982	64.0	64.9	61.7	62.7	[2]57.5	54.6	47.7	56.6	66.8	61.9
1983	64.0	65.2	61.4	63.1	57.2	[2]54.3	47.5	[2]55.7	66.7	61.6
1984	64.4	65.5	61.5	62.7	57.2	54.4	47.3	55.7	66.6	62.7
1985	64.8	65.9	61.7	62.3	56.8	54.7	47.2	55.5	66.9	62.9
1986	65.3	66.4	[2]62.8	62.1	56.7	54.9	[2]47.8	56.0	67.0	62.9
1987	65.6	66.8	62.9	61.9	56.5	55.0	47.6	[2]55.2	[2]66.4	63.2
1988	65.9	67.1	63.3	61.9	56.2	55.1	47.4	55.9	66.9	63.8
1989	66.5	67.5	64.1	62.2	56.1	55.2	47.3	56.1	67.3	64.3
1990	[2]66.5	67.4	64.7	62.6	[2]55.7	55.3	47.2	57.0	67.3	64.3
1991	66.2	66.8	64.2	63.2	55.8	[2]58.8	[2]47.7	57.7	67.0	63.7
1992	66.4	65.9	63.9	63.4	55.7	58.1	47.5	[2]58.3	65.7	62.9
1993	66.3	65.5	63.5	63.3	55.5	57.8	[2]48.3	57.5	64.5	62.6
1994	[2]66.6	65.2	63.9	63.1	55.6	57.4	47.6	58.0	63.7	62.4
1995	66.6	64.9	64.5	62.9	55.5	57.1	47.3	59.6	64.0	62.4
1996	66.8	64.8	64.6	63.0	55.7	57.1	47.3	60.2	63.9	62.4
1997	67.1	65.1	64.3	63.2	55.6	57.3	47.3	61.1	63.2	62.5
1998	67.1	65.4	64.3	62.8	56.0	57.7	47.7	61.8	62.8	62.5
1999	67.1	65.9	64.0	62.4	56.4	[2]56.9	47.9	62.5	62.7	62.8
2000	67.1	66.0	64.4	62.0	56.6	56.7	48.1	63.0	63.7	62.9
2001	66.8	66.1	64.4	61.6	56.8	56.7	48.3	63.3	63.6	62.7
2002	66.6	67.1	64.3	60.8	56.9	56.4	48.5	63.5	63.9	62.9
2003	66.2	67.7	64.6	60.3	57.0	56.0	49.1	63.7	63.8	63.0
2004	66.0	67.7	64.6	60.0	56.7	56.4	49.1	63.6	63.6	63.0
2005	66.0	67.4	65.3	60.0	56.6	[2]57.6	48.7	63.4	[2]64.8	63.1
2006	66.2	67.4	65.6	60.0	56.4	58.2	48.9	63.8	64.9	63.5
Unemployment Rate										
1970	4.9	5.7	1.7	1.2	2.5	0.5	3.2	. . .	1.5	3.1
1971	5.9	6.2	1.9	1.3	2.8	0.6	3.3	. . .	2.6	[2]4.2
1972	5.6	6.2	2.6	1.4	2.9	0.7	3.8	. . .	2.7	4.4
1973	4.9	5.6	2.3	1.3	2.8	0.7	3.7	3.1	2.5	3.7
1974	5.6	5.3	2.7	1.4	2.9	1.6	3.1	3.6	2.0	3.7
1975	8.5	6.9	4.9	1.9	4.2	3.4	3.4	5.1	1.6	4.5
1976	7.7	[2]6.9	4.8	2.0	4.6	3.4	3.9	5.4	1.6	5.4
1977	7.1	7.8	5.6	2.0	5.2	3.4	4.1	4.9	1.8	5.6
1978	6.1	8.1	6.3	2.3	5.4	3.3	4.1	5.1	2.2	5.5
1979	5.8	7.3	6.3	2.1	6.1	2.9	4.4	5.1	2.1	5.4
1980	7.1	7.3	6.1	2.0	6.5	2.8	4.4	6.0	2.0	6.9
1981	7.6	7.3	5.8	2.2	7.6	4.0	4.9	8.9	2.5	9.7
1982	9.7	10.7	7.2	2.4	[2]8.3	5.6	5.4	10.2	3.1	10.8
1983	9.6	11.6	10.0	2.7	8.6	[2]6.9	5.9	[2]11.4	3.5	11.5
1984	7.5	10.9	9.0	2.8	10.0	7.1	5.9	11.5	3.1	11.8
1985	7.2	10.2	8.3	2.7	10.5	7.2	6.0	9.6	2.8	11.4
1986	7.0	9.3	[2]7.9	2.8	10.6	6.6	[2]7.5	10.0	2.6	11.4
1987	6.2	8.4	7.9	2.9	10.8	6.3	7.9	[2]9.8	[2]2.2	10.5
1988	5.5	7.4	7.0	2.5	10.3	6.3	7.9	9.3	1.9	8.6
1989	5.3	7.1	6.0	2.3	9.6	5.7	7.8	8.4	1.6	7.3
1990	[2]5.6	7.7	6.7	2.1	[2]8.6	5.0	7.0	7.6	1.8	7.1
1991	6.8	9.8	9.3	2.1	9.1	[2]5.6	[2]6.9	7.1	3.1	8.9
1992	7.5	10.6	10.5	2.2	10.0	6.7	7.3	[2]6.8	5.6	10.0
1993	6.9	10.8	10.6	2.5	11.3	8.0	[2]9.8	6.3	9.4	10.4
1994	[2]6.1	9.6	9.4	2.9	11.9	8.5	10.7	6.9	9.6	8.7
1995	5.6	8.6	8.2	3.2	11.3	8.2	11.3	7.1	9.1	8.7
1996	5.4	8.8	8.2	3.4	11.8	9.0	11.3	6.6	9.9	8.1
1997	4.9	8.4	8.3	3.4	11.7	9.9	11.4	5.6	10.1	7.0
1998	4.5	7.7	7.7	4.1	11.2	9.3	11.5	4.4	8.4	6.3
1999	4.2	7.0	6.9	4.7	10.5	[2]8.5	11.0	3.5	7.1	6.0
2000	4.0	6.1	6.3	4.8	9.1	7.8	10.2	2.9	5.8	5.5
2001	4.7	6.5	[2]6.8	5.1	8.4	7.9	9.2	2.8	5.0	5.1
2002	5.8	7.0	6.4	5.4	8.8	8.6	8.7	3.2	5.2	5.2
2003	6.0	6.9	5.9	5.3	9.6	9.3	8.5	4.4	5.8	5.0
2004	5.5	6.4	5.4	4.8	9.8	10.3	8.1	5.1	6.6	4.8
2005	5.1	6.0	5.1	4.5	9.9	[2]11.2	7.8	5.2	[2]7.7	4.8
2006	4.6	5.5	4.8	4.2	9.7	10.4	6.9	4.4	7.0	5.5

[1]Unified Germany from 1991 onward; data for previous years relate to the former West Germany.
[2]Break in series.
. . . = Not available.

Table 11-2. Indexes of Manufacturing Productivity and Related Measures, 15 Countries, 1970 and 1990–2006

(1992 = 100.)

Category and year	United States	Canada	Japan	Korea, Republic of	Taiwan	Belgium	Denmark	France	Germany[1]	Italy	Nether-lands	Norway	Sweden	United Kingdom	Australia
Output Per Hour															
1970	52.4	53.5	37.7	...	...	32.9	47.6	42.9	52.0	40.0	38.7	59.5	52.2	45.4	...
1990	93.5	94.7	94.4	82.7	89.8	96.8	98.5	95.3	99.0	97.3	98.0	98.3	94.6	90.1	92.4
1991	96.3	95.7	99.0	92.7	96.8	99.1	99.7	97.8	98.3	96.5	98.3	98.7	95.5	94.3	95.8
1992	100.0	100.0	100.0	100.0	100.0	100.0	100.0	100.0	100.0	100.0	100.0	100.0	100.0	100.0	100.0
1993	102.8	104.5	101.7	108.3	101.3	102.5	100.3	101.8	101.0	102.8	103.7	99.9	107.3	104.1	104.5
1994	108.2	110.4	103.3	118.1	105.2	107.9	112.7	109.5	108.5	107.6	113.3	99.9	118.2	106.7	107.0
1995	112.3	111.7	111.0	129.7	112.9	112.7	112.7	114.9	110.2	111.1	117.7	98.7	125.1	105.0	106.4
1996	116.7	111.2	116.1	142.6	121.5	114.3	109.0	115.5	113.3	112.5	120.3	101.6	130.2	104.1	112.3
1997	121.7	116.3	120.2	160.8	126.5	121.5	117.7	122.3	119.9	113.3	120.7	101.8	142.0	105.1	115.4
1998	130.1	121.8	121.4	179.3	132.7	122.9	117.1	128.7	120.4	112.5	124.2	99.2	150.7	106.4	118.5
1999	136.7	127.0	124.7	199.4	140.9	121.5	119.0	134.4	123.4	112.5	129.3	102.7	164.1	111.6	119.7
2000	147.1	134.7	131.4	216.4	148.4	125.7	123.2	143.7	132.0	116.1	138.6	105.9	176.8	117.2	128.1
2001	148.6	132.2	128.6	214.8	155.1	126.9	123.4	146.0	135.4	116.6	139.2	108.9	172.6	122.2	131.4
2002	164.4	134.8	133.3	235.8	169.0	131.1	124.2	152.0	136.7	114.8	143.5	111.9	190.7	125.7	137.1
2003	174.8	134.0	142.4	252.2	174.5	134.5	129.3	158.7	141.6	112.1	146.5	121.6	204.5	132.1	140.1
2004	186.8	134.1	152.2	281.2	183.2	141.0	138.8	162.3	146.6	110.4	156.3	128.8	227.9	140.0	142.3
2005	193.2	139.1	158.2	300.4	196.5	144.9	141.6	169.2	154.8	110.3	161.7	132.0	241.9	145.0	143.7
2006	197.9	139.1	161.9	332.7	209.9	147.9	147.2	175.4	165.1	111.8	166.8	136.3	257.7	151.5	144.1
Output															
1970	54.5	57.3	39.4	6.4	12.9	57.6	73.7	64.1	70.9	41.7	60.1	91.6	80.7	90.3	...
1990	98.2	106.7	97.1	88.1	91.0	101.0	101.7	100.5	99.1	100.5	98.3	101.7	110.1	105.3	104.2
1991	96.8	99.0	102.0	96.0	96.4	100.7	100.3	100.6	102.4	100.2	99.1	99.4	104.1	100.1	100.7
1992	100.0	100.0	100.0	100.0	100.0	100.0	100.0	100.0	100.0	100.0	100.0	100.0	100.0	100.0	100.0
1993	104.2	105.4	96.3	105.1	100.9	97.0	97.0	96.6	92.0	97.6	99.4	102.0	101.9	101.4	103.8
1994	112.2	113.5	94.9	117.1	106.9	101.4	107.5	100.7	94.9	104.1	104.7	104.7	117.5	106.2	109.1
1995	117.3	118.7	98.9	130.8	112.7	104.2	112.7	105.2	94.0	109.1	108.6	105.2	132.5	107.9	108.5
1996	121.6	120.3	103.0	139.2	118.7	104.6	107.5	105.2	92.0	107.8	110.2	109.4	137.1	108.6	111.9
1997	129.0	127.8	105.6	146.0	125.5	109.5	116.3	110.1	96.1	109.6	111.7	114.1	147.6	110.6	114.5
1998	137.7	134.3	100.1	134.5	129.5	111.3	117.2	115.4	97.2	109.9	115.5	113.3	159.5	111.3	117.8
1999	143.7	145.5	99.7	163.7	139.0	111.2	118.2	119.3	98.2	109.6	119.8	113.2	173.9	112.3	117.5
2000	152.7	160.1	104.9	191.5	149.2	115.7	122.5	124.8	104.8	112.9	127.8	112.6	189.7	115.0	123.1
2001	144.2	153.9	99.1	196.7	138.1	115.7	122.5	126.0	106.6	111.8	127.6	111.8	185.6	113.5	121.9
2002	148.2	155.2	97.6	210.5	150.4	114.8	119.0	125.9	104.4	110.4	127.7	111.2	196.4	110.5	127.8
2003	149.9	154.2	102.8	222.2	158.4	113.4	115.7	128.3	105.2	107.8	126.2	114.9	203.6	110.7	130.1
2004	159.6	157.1	108.8	246.8	173.8	117.9	119.6	129.4	108.8	106.4	130.6	121.4	224.4	113.0	130.1
2005	163.0	158.3	111.7	264.3	185.3	117.3	121.6	131.2	112.3	103.7	130.6	125.8	233.5	111.6	130.3
2006	168.5	156.2	117.1	286.5	198.7	120.2	127.7	133.2	118.5	107.6	133.7	131.4	246.8	113.1	128.7
Total Hours															
1970	104.0	107.1	104.3	...	...	174.7	154.9	149.6	136.3	104.0	155.4	154.1	154.7	198.6	...
1990	104.9	112.6	102.9	106.4	101.4	104.3	103.3	105.5	100.1	103.3	100.4	103.4	116.4	116.9	112.7
1991	100.5	103.4	103.1	103.6	99.6	101.5	100.6	102.9	104.1	103.8	100.8	100.7	109.0	106.2	105.1
1992	100.0	100.0	100.0	100.0	100.0	100.0	100.0	100.0	100.0	100.0	100.0	100.0	100.0	100.0	100.0
1993	101.3	100.9	94.7	97.1	99.6	94.7	96.8	94.8	91.1	95.0	95.9	102.1	94.9	97.4	99.3
1994	103.7	102.8	91.9	99.2	101.7	94.0	95.4	91.9	87.5	96.8	92.5	104.8	99.4	99.5	102.0
1995	104.4	106.3	89.1	100.9	99.8	92.4	100.0	91.6	85.3	98.2	92.3	106.6	105.9	102.7	101.9
1996	104.2	108.1	88.8	97.6	97.7	91.5	98.6	91.0	81.3	95.8	91.6	107.7	105.3	104.4	99.7
1997	106.0	109.9	87.9	90.8	99.2	90.2	98.8	90.1	80.1	96.7	92.6	112.1	103.9	105.2	99.2
1998	105.8	110.2	82.4	75.0	97.6	90.5	100.1	89.7	80.8	97.7	93.0	114.2	105.9	104.6	99.4
1999	105.1	114.5	79.9	82.1	98.7	91.5	99.4	88.7	79.6	97.4	92.7	110.3	106.0	100.6	98.2
2000	103.8	118.9	79.8	88.5	100.5	92.1	99.4	86.8	79.4	97.2	92.2	106.4	107.3	98.1	96.0
2001	97.0	116.4	77.1	91.1	89.0	91.2	99.3	86.3	78.7	95.9	91.7	102.7	107.5	92.9	92.8
2002	90.1	115.1	73.3	89.3	89.0	87.5	95.8	82.8	76.4	96.2	89.0	99.3	103.0	88.0	93.2
2003	85.7	115.0	72.2	88.1	90.8	84.3	89.5	80.8	74.3	96.1	86.2	94.5	99.6	83.8	92.8
2004	85.4	117.2	71.5	87.8	94.9	83.6	86.2	79.7	74.2	96.4	83.5	94.2	98.5	80.7	91.4
2005	84.4	113.8	70.6	88.0	94.3	80.9	85.9	77.5	72.6	94.1	80.8	95.3	96.5	77.0	90.7
2006	85.1	112.3	72.3	86.1	94.6	81.3	86.8	75.9	71.8	96.2	80.2	96.4	95.8	74.6	89.3

[1]Unified Germany from 1991 onward; data for previous years relate to the former West Germany.
. . . = Not available.

Table 11-2. Indexes of Manufacturing Productivity and Related Measures, 15 Countries, 1970 and 1990–2006—Continued

(1992 = 100.)

Category and year	United States	Canada	Japan	Korea, Republic of	Taiwan	Belgium	Denmark	France	Germany[1]	Italy	Nether-lands	Norway	Sweden	United King-dom	Australia
Compensation Per Hour, National Currency Basis															
1970	24.0	17.2	16.4	...	...	13.7	10.8	9.2	20.7	5.3	19.4	11.9	10.7	6.8	...
1990	90.5	89.2	90.6	68.0	85.2	90.1	93.6	88.5	89.4	87.7	89.8	92.3	87.8	88.7	87.5
1991	95.6	95.5	96.5	85.5	93.5	97.3	97.8	93.9	91.4	94.3	94.8	97.5	95.5	99.8	94.0
1992	100.0	100.0	100.0	100.0	100.0	100.0	100.0	100.0	100.0	100.0	100.0	100.0	100.0	100.0	100.0
1993	102.0	101.2	102.7	115.9	105.9	104.8	102.4	104.3	106.2	105.7	104.4	101.5	97.4	104.5	105.2
1994	105.3	104.1	104.7	133.1	111.1	105.6	106.0	108.0	111.0	107.3	108.9	104.5	99.8	107.0	106.1
1995	107.3	106.6	108.3	161.6	120.2	108.6	108.2	110.7	117.0	112.0	111.8	109.2	106.8	108.9	113.5
1996	109.3	108.2	109.1	188.1	128.2	110.6	112.6	112.5	122.5	120.0	113.8	113.8	115.2	108.7	121.7
1997	112.2	110.8	112.8	204.5	132.1	114.7	116.5	116.3	124.9	124.1	116.4	118.8	121.0	112.3	126.0
1998	118.7	116.5	115.6	222.7	137.1	116.5	119.6	117.2	126.7	123.3	121.4	125.8	125.5	121.2	128.4
1999	123.4	119.0	115.5	223.9	139.6	118.0	122.6	121.0	129.6	125.6	125.7	133.0	130.1	128.3	132.9
2000	134.7	123.0	114.9	239.1	142.3	120.1	125.0	127.0	136.3	128.7	132.1	140.5	136.7	133.8	140.2
2001	137.8	126.7	116.4	246.7	151.4	126.4	130.9	130.6	140.6	134.0	138.1	149.0	143.8	140.7	149.2
2002	147.8	131.2	117.2	271.6	146.7	131.9	136.5	136.9	144.0	137.5	146.1	157.9	151.6	149.0	156.0
2003	158.2	135.2	114.6	285.0	149.1	135.8	145.7	141.0	147.2	141.6	151.9	164.3	159.2	156.9	161.4
2004	161.5	136.9	115.7	325.5	151.6	138.8	150.6	144.6	148.0	145.7	158.1	169.7	163.4	165.1	169.1
2005	168.3	142.1	117.0	351.5	158.2	144.6	153.7	143.7	149.7	150.2	161.3	176.2	167.2	172.2	177.6
2006	172.4	145.9	117.6	375.5	161.5	147.7	157.6	147.5	153.2	152.9	165.8	184.3	172.1	184.2	189.2
Compensation Per Hour, U.S. Currency Basis															
1970	24.0	19.9	5.8	...	...	8.9	8.7	8.8	8.9	10.4	9.4	10.3	12.1	9.2	...
1990	90.5	92.4	79.2	75.0	79.6	86.6	91.2	86.0	86.4	90.2	86.7	91.7	86.4	89.6	92.9
1991	95.6	100.7	90.9	91.1	87.9	91.5	92.2	88.0	86.0	93.6	89.1	93.3	91.9	99.9	99.6
1992	100.0	100.0	100.0	100.0	100.0	100.0	100.0	100.0	100.0	100.0	100.0	100.0	100.0	100.0	100.0
1993	102.0	94.8	117.2	112.9	100.9	97.4	95.3	97.5	100.3	82.8	98.8	88.8	72.8	88.8	97.2
1994	105.3	92.1	129.9	129.5	105.6	101.6	100.7	103.1	106.9	82.1	105.3	92.0	75.3	92.8	105.6
1995	107.3	93.9	146.1	164.1	114.2	118.5	116.6	117.5	127.6	84.7	122.6	107.1	87.1	97.3	114.3
1996	109.3	95.9	127.2	183.4	117.4	114.8	117.2	116.4	127.2	95.8	118.7	109.4	100.1	96.0	129.6
1997	112.2	96.7	118.1	169.3	115.5	103.0	106.4	105.4	112.5	89.8	104.9	104.2	92.2	104.1	127.4
1998	118.7	94.9	111.9	124.8	102.8	103.1	107.7	105.1	112.5	87.5	107.6	103.5	92.0	113.8	109.8
1999	123.4	96.8	128.8	147.6	108.7	100.2	105.9	104.0	110.3	85.1	106.9	105.8	91.6	117.5	116.6
2000	134.7	100.0	135.1	165.9	114.6	88.3	93.2	94.6	100.5	75.6	97.4	99.1	86.8	114.8	110.9
2001	137.8	98.9	121.4	149.8	112.6	90.2	94.9	94.3	100.5	76.3	98.7	102.9	81.0	114.7	104.9
2002	147.8	101.0	118.6	170.4	106.9	99.4	104.5	104.5	108.7	82.7	110.2	122.9	90.8	126.8	115.3
2003	158.2	116.7	125.3	187.6	109.0	122.5	133.7	128.8	133.1	102.0	137.3	144.2	114.8	145.2	143.2
2004	161.5	127.1	135.6	223.0	114.3	137.5	151.8	145.2	147.0	115.4	157.0	156.5	129.6	171.4	169.4
2005	168.3	141.8	134.7	269.4	123.8	143.5	154.7	144.4	148.8	119.0	160.3	170.0	130.4	177.4	184.2
2006	172.4	155.5	128.1	308.7	125.0	147.9	160.1	149.6	153.7	122.2	166.3	178.6	136.0	192.3	193.8
Unit Labor Costs, National Currency Basis															
1970	45.8	32.2	43.6	8.6	23.3	41.7	22.8	21.4	39.8	13.2	50.1	20.0	20.6	14.9	...
1990	96.7	94.2	95.9	82.1	94.9	93.0	95.0	92.8	90.3	90.2	91.7	93.9	92.9	98.5	94.6
1991	99.2	99.8	97.4	92.2	96.5	98.1	98.1	96.0	93.0	97.6	96.4	98.8	100.1	105.9	98.1
1992	100.0	100.0	100.0	100.0	100.0	100.0	100.0	100.0	100.0	100.0	100.0	100.0	100.0	100.0	100.0
1993	99.2	96.9	101.0	107.0	104.6	102.3	102.2	102.4	105.2	102.9	100.7	101.6	90.8	100.4	100.6
1994	97.3	94.3	101.4	112.7	105.6	97.9	94.1	98.6	102.4	99.8	96.2	104.6	84.5	100.2	99.2
1995	95.5	95.4	97.6	124.6	106.5	96.4	96.0	96.3	106.2	100.8	95.0	110.7	85.3	103.7	106.6
1996	93.7	97.3	94.0	131.9	105.5	96.8	103.3	97.4	108.2	106.6	94.6	112.0	88.5	104.4	108.4
1997	92.2	95.3	93.8	127.1	104.5	94.5	98.9	95.0	104.2	109.5	96.5	116.7	85.2	106.8	109.2
1998	91.2	95.6	95.2	124.2	103.4	94.8	102.1	91.0	105.2	109.6	97.7	126.8	83.3	113.9	108.4
1999	90.3	93.7	92.7	112.3	99.1	97.2	103.0	90.0	105.1	111.7	97.3	129.5	79.3	115.0	111.0
2000	91.6	91.3	87.5	110.5	95.9	95.6	101.4	88.4	103.3	110.9	95.3	132.7	77.3	114.2	109.4
2001	92.7	95.8	90.5	114.8	97.6	99.6	106.1	89.4	103.8	114.9	99.2	136.8	83.3	115.1	113.6
2002	89.9	97.4	87.9	115.2	86.8	100.6	109.9	90.1	105.3	119.8	101.8	141.0	79.5	118.6	113.8
2003	90.5	100.9	80.5	113.0	85.5	101.0	112.7	88.9	104.0	126.3	103.7	135.1	77.8	118.8	115.2
2004	86.4	102.0	76.0	115.8	82.7	98.4	108.5	89.1	100.9	132.0	101.2	131.7	71.7	117.9	118.9
2005	87.1	102.2	73.9	117.0	80.5	99.8	108.5	85.0	96.7	136.2	99.8	133.5	69.1	118.7	123.6
2006	87.2	104.9	72.6	112.8	76.9	99.9	107.0	84.1	92.8	136.7	99.4	135.2	66.8	121.6	131.2

[1]Unified Germany from 1991 onward; data for previous years relate to the former West Germany.
. . . = Not available.

Table 11-2. Indexes of Manufacturing Productivity and Related Measures, 15 Countries, 1970 and 1990–2006—*Continued*

(1992 = 100.)

Category and year	United States	Canada	Japan	Korea, Republic of	Taiwan	Belgium	Denmark	France	Germany[1]	Italy	Nether-lands	Norway	Sweden	United King-dom	Australia
Unit Labor Costs, U.S. Currency Basis															
1970	45.8	37.3	15.4	21.7	14.6	27.0	18.3	20.5	17.1	26.0	24.4	17.4	23.1	20.2	. . .
1990	96.7	97.5	83.9	90.7	88.7	89.5	92.7	90.2	87.3	92.7	88.5	93.3	91.4	99.5	100.5
1991	99.2	105.2	91.8	98.2	90.8	92.3	92.5	90.0	87.5	96.9	90.6	94.5	96.3	106.0	104.0
1992	100.0	100.0	100.0	100.0	100.0	100.0	100.0	100.0	100.0	100.0	100.0	100.0	100.0	100.0	100.0
1993	99.2	90.7	115.3	104.2	99.6	95.1	95.1	95.7	99.3	80.6	95.2	88.9	67.9	85.3	93.0
1994	97.3	83.4	125.8	109.6	100.4	94.2	89.4	94.1	98.6	76.3	93.0	92.1	63.8	86.9	98.7
1995	95.5	84.0	131.7	126.5	101.1	105.2	103.5	102.2	115.8	76.2	104.1	108.6	69.6	92.7	107.4
1996	93.7	86.3	109.6	128.6	96.7	100.4	107.6	100.7	112.3	85.2	98.6	107.7	76.8	92.3	115.4
1997	92.2	83.2	98.3	105.3	91.3	84.8	90.4	86.2	93.8	79.2	86.9	102.3	64.9	99.0	110.4
1998	91.2	77.9	92.2	69.6	77.5	83.9	92.0	81.7	93.4	77.7	86.6	104.3	61.0	106.9	92.7
1999	90.3	76.2	103.3	74.0	77.2	82.5	89.0	77.4	89.4	75.7	82.7	103.1	55.9	105.3	97.5
2000	91.6	74.3	102.9	76.7	77.2	70.3	75.6	65.8	76.2	65.1	70.2	93.6	49.1	98.0	86.5
2001	92.7	74.8	94.4	69.7	72.6	71.1	76.9	64.6	74.2	65.5	70.9	94.5	46.9	93.8	79.8
2002	89.9	74.9	89.0	72.3	63.2	75.8	84.2	68.7	79.5	72.1	76.8	109.8	47.6	100.9	84.1
2003	90.5	87.1	88.0	74.4	62.5	91.1	103.4	81.2	94.0	91.0	93.7	118.6	56.1	109.9	102.2
2004	86.4	94.7	89.1	79.3	62.4	97.5	109.4	89.5	100.2	104.5	100.4	121.4	56.9	122.4	119.1
2005	87.1	102.0	85.1	89.7	63.0	99.0	109.3	85.4	96.1	107.9	99.1	128.8	53.9	122.3	128.2
2006	87.2	111.8	79.2	92.8	59.5	100.0	108.7	85.3	93.1	109.3	99.7	131.1	52.8	126.9	134.5
Exchange Rates[2]															
1970	100.0	115.8	35.4	252.7	62.9	64.7	80.5	95.7	42.8	196.5	48.6	86.9	112.3	135.6	152.3
1990	100.0	103.6	87.4	110.4	93.5	96.2	97.5	97.2	96.6	102.8	96.6	99.4	98.4	101.0	106.3
1991	100.0	105.5	94.2	106.5	94.0	94.0	94.3	93.7	94.0	99.3	93.9	95.7	96.3	100.1	106.0
1992	100.0	100.0	100.0	100.0	100.0	100.0	100.0	100.0	100.0	100.0	100.0	100.0	100.0	100.0	100.0
1993	100.0	93.7	114.1	97.4	95.2	93.0	93.1	93.4	94.4	78.3	94.6	87.5	74.7	85.0	92.5
1994	100.0	88.4	124.1	97.2	95.1	96.2	95.0	95.4	96.3	76.5	96.7	88.1	75.5	86.7	99.5
1995	100.0	88.1	134.9	101.5	95.0	109.1	107.8	106.2	109.1	75.6	109.6	98.1	81.6	89.4	100.7
1996	100.0	88.6	116.5	97.5	91.6	103.8	104.1	103.5	103.8	79.9	104.3	96.2	86.8	88.4	106.5
1997	100.0	87.3	104.7	82.8	87.4	89.8	91.3	90.7	90.0	72.3	90.1	87.7	76.2	92.7	101.1
1998	100.0	81.5	96.8	56.0	75.0	88.5	90.1	89.7	88.8	70.9	88.7	82.3	73.3	93.8	85.6
1999	100.0	81.3	111.5	65.9	77.8	84.9	86.4	86.0	85.1	67.8	85.0	79.6	70.4	91.6	87.8
2000	100.0	81.4	117.6	69.4	80.5	73.6	74.6	74.5	73.7	58.7	73.7	70.5	63.5	85.8	79.1
2001	100.0	78.0	104.3	60.7	74.4	71.3	72.5	72.2	71.5	57.0	71.4	69.1	56.3	81.5	70.3
2002	100.0	77.0	101.2	62.8	72.9	75.3	76.6	76.3	75.5	60.2	75.4	77.8	59.9	85.1	73.9
2003	100.0	86.3	109.3	65.8	73.1	90.2	91.8	91.4	90.4	72.0	90.3	87.8	72.1	92.5	88.7
2004	100.0	92.8	117.2	68.5	75.4	99.1	100.8	100.4	99.3	79.2	99.3	92.2	79.3	103.8	100.2
2005	100.0	99.8	115.1	76.6	78.3	99.2	100.7	100.5	99.4	79.2	99.4	96.5	78.0	103.1	103.7
2006	100.0	106.6	109.0	82.2	77.4	100.1	101.6	101.4	100.3	79.9	100.3	97.0	79.0	104.4	102.5

[1]Unified Germany from 1991 onward; data for previous years relate to the former West Germany.
[2]Index of value of foreign currency relative to the U.S. dollar.
. . . = Not available.

Table 11-3. Hourly Compensation Costs in U.S. Dollars for Production Workers in Manufacturing, 33 Countries and Selected Areas, Selected Years, 1975–2005

(Dollars.)

Region and country	1975	1980	1985	1990	1995	2000	2002	2003	2004	2005
Americas										
United States	6.16	9.63	12.71	14.81	17.17	19.65	21.33	22.20	22.82	23.65
Brazil	...	...	...	...	...	3.50	2.57	2.74	3.15	4.09
Canada	6.11	8.87	11.20	16.33	16.50	16.48	16.72	19.53	21.77	23.82
Mexico	1.46	2.20	1.59	1.57	1.70	2.07	2.49	2.44	2.44	2.63
Asia and Oceania										
Australia	5.60	8.44	8.18	13.09	15.36	14.40	15.38	19.79	23.38	24.91
Hong Kong SAR[1]	0.75	1.50	1.73	3.22	4.80	5.45	5.66	5.54	5.51	5.65
Israel	2.02	3.41	3.65	7.69	9.41	11.41	11.00	11.62	12.01	12.42
Japan	2.97	5.46	6.27	12.59	23.47	21.93	18.60	20.26	21.84	21.76
Korea, Republic of	0.32	0.95	1.23	3.70	7.28	8.23	8.77	9.69	11.13	13.56
New Zealand	3.28	5.44	4.55	8.48	10.35	8.38	9.10	11.69	13.65	14.97
Singapore	0.83	1.53	2.52	3.74	7.57	7.18	6.71	7.18	7.38	7.66
Sri Lanka	0.28	0.22	0.28	0.35	0.48	0.48	0.49	0.51	0.52	...
Taiwan	0.38	1.03	1.51	3.91	5.99	6.19	5.64	5.69	5.98	6.38
Europe										
Austria	4.50	8.87	7.57	17.91	25.26	19.14	20.71	25.51	28.53	29.42
Belgium	5.77	11.74	8.21	17.85	25.67	20.13	21.77	26.55	30.01	30.79
Czech Republic	...	...	...	...	2.63	2.83	3.83	4.72	5.45	6.11
Denmark	6.24	10.77	8.10	18.35	25.28	21.87	24.31	30.22	34.46	35.47
Finland	4.63	8.30	8.20	21.15	24.31	19.44	21.78	27.10	30.67	31.93
France	4.50	8.90	7.48	15.36	19.26	15.46	17.13	21.14	23.89	24.63
Germany[2]	...	...	...	...	30.10	22.67	24.22	29.64	32.50	33.00
Greece	1.69	3.73	3.67	6.82	9.07	...	...	...	...	...
Hungary	...	...	...	...	2.69	2.79	3.92	4.76	5.63	6.07
Ireland	3.06	6.02	6.00	11.77	13.75	12.72	15.26	19.09	21.94	22.76
Italy	4.64	8.09	7.56	17.28	15.69	13.84	14.75	18.11	20.48	21.05
Luxembourg	6.22	11.51	7.48	16.00	23.56	17.51	18.71	23.12	26.57	27.68
Netherlands	6.58	12.05	8.73	17.98	24.03	19.33	22.12	27.47	30.76	31.81
Norway	6.90	11.80	10.47	21.76	24.84	22.56	27.93	32.73	36.41	39.14
Poland	...	...	...	...	...	2.81	3.29	3.52	3.85	4.54
Portugal	1.52	1.98	1.46	3.59	5.09	4.49	5.07	6.24	7.02	7.33
Spain	2.52	5.86	4.64	11.30	12.70	10.65	11.95	15.01	17.14	17.78
Sweden	7.14	12.44	9.61	20.81	21.68	20.18	20.23	25.19	28.42	28.73
Switzerland	6.03	10.96	9.55	20.63	28.90	20.95	23.77	27.78	30.21	30.50
United Kingdom	3.35	7.52	6.22	12.61	13.79	16.84	18.36	21.33	24.76	25.66
Trade-Weighted Measures[3,4]										
All foreign economies	3.82	6.49	6.61	11.83	14.99	13.66	13.90	16.19	17.95	18.89
OECD[5,6]	4.13	7.00	7.08	12.62	15.85	14.59	14.92	17.47	19.43	20.43
Europe[6]	4.87	9.49	7.72	16.80	21.19	17.77	19.48	23.70	26.62	27.33
European Union-15[7]	4.80	9.40	7.61	16.58	21.07	17.89	19.53	23.83	26.81	27.52
Asian NIEs[8]	0.49	1.15	1.62	3.71	6.62	7.06	7.04	7.49	8.16	9.28

[1]Hong Kong Special Administrative Region of China.
[2]Unified Germany from 1995 onward; data for previous years relate to the former West Germany.
[3]Since data for Germany are not available before 1993, data for the former West Germany are only included in the trade-weighted measures.
[4]The trade weights used to compute the average compensation cost measures for selected economic groups are weights based on the relative dollar value of U.S. trade in manufactured commodities (exports plus imports) with each country or region in 2004. The trade data are compiled by the U.S. Census Bureau.
[5]Organisation for Economic Co-operation and Development.
[6]Data are not included for the Czech Republic or Hungary from 1975 to 1990 or for Poland from 1975 to 1995.
[7]European Union-15 refers to European Union member countries prior to the European Union's expansion to 25 countries on May 1, 2004. It consisted of Austria, Belgium, Denmark, Finland, France, Germany, Greece, Ireland, Italy, Luxembourg, the Netherlands, Portugal, Spain, Sweden, and the United Kingdom.
[8]The Asian Newly Industrialized Economies (NIEs) are Hong Kong SAR, the Republic of Korea, Singapore, and Taiwan.
. . . = Not available.

Table 11-4. Consumer Price Indexes, 16 Countries, 1950–2006

(1982–1984 = 100.)

Year	United States[2]	Canada[3]	Japan[4]	Australia[5]	Austria	Belgium[6]	Denmark[7]	France[8]	Germany[9]	Italy	Netherlands	Norway[10]	Spain[11]	Sweden	Switzerland[12]	United Kingdom
1950	24.1	21.6	14.7	12.6	...	24.0	12.3	11.1	...	...	...	13.6	5.5	13.4	33.2	9.8
1951	26.0	23.9	17.2	15.1	...	26.3	13.5	13.0	...	...	...	15.7	6.0	15.5	34.8	10.7
1952	26.5	24.5	18.0	17.7	...	26.5	14.0	14.6	...	...	...	17.1	5.9	16.7	35.7	11.7
1953	26.7	24.2	19.2	18.4	...	26.4	14.1	14.4	...	10.3	...	17.5	6.0	16.9	35.4	12.1
1954	26.9	24.4	20.4	18.5	...	26.9	14.2	14.3	...	10.6	...	18.2	6.1	17.1	35.7	12.3
1955	26.8	24.4	20.2	18.9	...	26.8	15.0	14.5	...	10.9	...	18.4	6.3	17.5	36.0	12.9
1956	27.2	24.8	20.3	20.1	...	27.4	15.8	14.8	...	11.2	...	19.1	6.7	18.4	36.5	13.5
1957	28.1	25.6	20.9	20.6	...	28.2	16.1	15.3	...	11.4	...	19.6	7.4	19.2	37.3	14.0
1958	28.9	26.3	20.8	20.9	31.6	28.6	16.3	17.6	...	11.7	...	20.6	8.4	20.0	37.9	14.4
1959	29.1	26.6	21.0	21.3	32.0	29.0	16.5	18.7	...	11.7	...	21.0	9.0	20.2	37.7	14.5
1960	29.6	26.9	21.8	22.1	32.6	29.1	16.7	19.4	...	11.9	...	21.1	9.1	21.0	38.2	14.6
1961	29.9	27.1	23.0	22.6	33.8	29.3	17.4	20.0	...	12.2	...	21.6	9.2	21.5	38.9	15.1
1962	30.2	27.4	24.5	22.6	35.3	29.8	18.8	21.0	43.1	12.7	...	22.8	9.7	22.5	40.6	15.8
1963	30.6	27.9	26.4	22.7	36.2	30.4	19.8	22.0	44.4	13.7	...	23.4	10.6	23.2	42.0	16.1
1964	31.0	28.4	27.4	23.2	37.6	31.7	20.5	22.7	45.4	14.5	...	24.7	11.3	23.9	43.3	16.6
1965	31.5	29.1	29.5	24.1	39.5	32.9	21.8	23.3	46.9	15.2	...	25.7	12.8	25.1	44.8	17.4
1966	32.4	30.2	31.0	24.9	40.3	34.3	23.3	23.9	48.6	15.5	...	26.6	13.6	26.8	46.9	18.1
1967	33.4	31.3	32.2	25.7	41.9	35.3	25.0	24.6	49.4	16.1	...	27.8	14.5	27.9	48.8	18.5
1968	34.8	32.5	33.9	26.3	43.1	36.3	27.0	25.7	50.2	16.3	...	28.7	15.2	28.4	50.0	19.4
1969	36.7	34.0	35.7	27.1	44.4	37.6	27.9	27.3	51.1	16.7	40.6	29.6	15.5	29.2	51.3	20.5
1970	38.8	35.1	38.4	28.2	46.4	39.1	29.8	28.8	52.8	17.5	42.1	32.8	16.4	31.3	53.1	21.8
1971	40.5	36.2	40.9	29.9	48.5	40.8	31.5	30.3	55.6	18.4	45.3	34.8	17.7	33.6	56.6	23.8
1972	41.8	37.9	42.9	31.6	51.6	43.0	33.6	32.2	58.7	19.4	48.9	37.3	19.2	35.6	60.4	25.5
1973	44.4	40.7	47.9	34.6	55.5	46.0	36.7	34.6	62.8	21.6	52.9	40.1	21.4	38.0	65.7	27.9
1974	49.3	45.2	59.0	39.9	60.8	51.9	42.3	39.3	67.2	25.7	58.1	43.8	24.8	41.7	72.1	32.3
1975	53.8	50.1	65.9	45.9	65.9	58.5	46.4	43.9	71.2	30.0	63.8	49.0	29.0	45.8	76.9	40.1
1976	56.9	53.8	72.2	52.1	70.8	63.8	50.5	48.2	74.2	35.1	69.6	53.5	34.1	50.5	78.2	46.8
1977	60.6	58.1	78.1	58.5	74.6	68.4	56.1	52.7	77.0	41.0	74.1	58.3	42.4	56.3	79.2	54.2
1978	65.2	63.3	81.4	63.1	77.3	71.4	61.8	57.5	79.0	46.0	77.2	63.1	50.8	61.9	80.1	58.7
1979	72.6	69.1	84.3	68.8	80.2	74.6	67.7	63.6	82.3	52.8	80.5	66.1	58.8	66.4	83.0	66.6
1980	82.4	76.1	91.0	75.8	85.3	79.6	76.1	72.3	86.7	64.0	86.1	73.3	67.9	75.5	86.3	78.5
1981	90.9	85.6	95.3	83.2	91.1	85.6	85.0	82.0	92.2	75.4	91.9	83.3	77.8	84.6	91.9	87.9
1982	96.5	94.9	98.1	92.4	96.0	93.1	93.6	91.6	97.1	87.8	97.2	92.7	89.0	91.9	97.1	95.4
1983	99.6	100.4	99.8	101.8	99.2	100.3	100.0	100.5	100.3	100.7	99.8	100.5	99.9	100.0	100.0	99.8
1984	103.9	104.7	102.1	105.8	104.8	106.6	106.4	107.9	102.7	111.5	103.0	106.8	111.1	108.1	102.9	104.8
1985	107.6	108.9	104.2	112.9	108.2	111.8	111.4	114.2	104.8	121.8	105.3	112.9	120.9	116.0	106.4	111.1
1986	109.6	113.4	104.8	123.2	110.0	113.3	115.4	117.2	104.7	129.0	105.6	121.0	131.5	121.0	107.2	114.9
1987	113.6	118.4	104.9	133.7	111.6	115.0	120.0	120.9	104.9	135.1	105.1	131.6	138.5	126.1	108.8	119.7
1988	118.3	123.2	105.6	142.9	113.8	116.4	125.5	124.2	106.3	141.9	106.1	140.4	145.1	133.4	110.8	125.6
1989	124.0	129.3	108.0	154.1	116.6	120.0	131.5	128.6	109.2	150.8	107.1	146.8	155.0	142.0	114.3	135.4
1990	130.7	135.5	111.3	165.3	120.5	124.1	135.0	133.0	112.1	160.5	109.9	152.8	165.4	156.7	120.5	148.2
1991	136.2	143.1	115.1	170.7	124.4	128.1	138.2	137.2	81.9	170.6	113.3	158.0	175.2	171.5	127.5	156.9
1992	140.3	145.3	117.0	172.4	129.5	131.2	141.1	140.6	86.1	179.4	116.9	161.7	185.6	175.6	132.7	162.7
1993	144.5	147.9	118.5	175.5	134.1	134.8	142.9	143.5	89.9	187.5	120.0	165.4	194.1	183.9	137.0	165.3
1994	148.2	148.2	119.2	178.8	138.2	138.0	145.8	145.9	92.3	195.0	123.3	167.7	203.3	187.8	138.3	169.3
1995	152.4	151.4	119.1	187.1	141.3	140.1	148.8	148.4	93.9	205.1	125.7	171.8	212.8	192.4	140.8	175.2
1996	156.9	153.8	119.2	192.0	143.9	142.9	151.9	151.3	95.3	213.4	128.2	174.0	220.3	193.5	141.9	179.4
1997	160.5	156.2	121.5	192.5	145.8	145.3	155.3	153.2	97.1	217.7	131.0	178.5	224.8	194.8	142.5	185.1
1998	163.0	157.7	122.2	194.1	147.1	146.7	158.2	154.3	98.0	222.0	133.6	182.5	228.8	194.2	142.7	191.4
1999	166.6	160.5	121.8	197.0	147.9	148.3	162.0	155.0	98.6	225.7	136.5	186.7	234.2	195.1	143.8	194.3
2000	172.2	164.8	120.9	205.8	151.4	152.1	166.8	157.7	100.0	231.4	140.0	192.5	242.1	196.9	146.0	200.1
2001	177.1	169.0	120.1	214.8	155.5	155.8	170.8	160.3	102.0	237.8	145.9	198.4	250.8	201.6	147.4	203.6
2002	179.9	172.8	119.0	221.2	158.2	158.4	174.8	163.4	103.4	243.7	150.7	200.9	259.6	206.0	148.4	207.0
2003	184.0	177.6	118.7	227.4	160.3	160.9	178.5	166.8	104.5	250.3	153.9	205.9	267.6	209.9	149.3	213.0
2004	188.9	180.9	118.7	232.7	163.7	164.3	180.7	170.3	106.2	255.8	155.7	206.8	275.7	210.7	150.5	219.4
2005	195.3	184.9	118.3	238.9	167.4	168.8	183.9	173.3	108.3	260.8	158.4	210.1	285.0	211.7	152.2	225.6
2006	201.6	188.6	118.6	247.4	170.0	171.9	187.4	176.2	110.1	266.3	160.2	214.9	295.0	214.6	153.9	232.8

[1] The figures may differ from official indexes published by national statistical agencies because of rounding.
[2] Urban worker households prior to 1978.
[3] All households from January 1995, all urban households from September 1978 to December 1994, and middle-income urban households prior to September 1978.
[4] Excluding imputed rent for owner-occupied households prior to 1970.
[5] Urban worker households prior to September 1998.
[6] Excluding rent and several other services prior to 1976.
[7] Excluding rent prior to 1964.
[8] Urban worker households prior to 1991; worker households in Paris only prior to 1962.
[9] Unified Germany from 1991 onward; data for previous years relate to the former West Germany.
[10] Urban worker households prior to 1960.
[11] All family households from 1993; middle-income family households prior to 1963.
[12] Urban worker households prior to May 1993.
. . . = Not available.

Table 11-5. Consumer Price Indexes, Percent Change from the Previous Year, 16 Countries, 1955–2006

(Percent.)

Year	United States[2]	Canada[3]	Japan[4]	Australia[5]	Austria	Belgium[6]	Denmark[7]	France[8]	Germany[9]	Italy	Netherlands	Norway[10]	Spain[11]	Sweden	Switzerland[12]	United Kingdom
1955	-0.4	0.0	-1.5	2.2	...	-0.4	5.6	1.4	...	2.8	...	1.1	3.3	2.3	0.8	4.9
1956	1.5	1.5	0.4	6.3	...	2.9	5.3	1.9	...	3.4	...	3.7	5.9	5.0	1.5	4.9
1957	3.3	3.2	3.1	2.7	...	3.1	2.2	3.5	...	1.3	...	2.7	10.8	4.3	1.9	3.7
1958	2.8	2.6	-0.5	1.1	...	1.3	0.7	15.1	...	2.8	...	4.8	13.4	4.4	1.8	3.0
1959	0.7	1.1	1.1	1.9	1.3	1.2	1.8	6.1	...	-0.4	...	2.2	7.3	0.8	-0.7	0.6
1960	1.7	1.2	3.7	4.0	1.9	0.3	1.2	3.6	...	2.3	...	0.3	1.2	4.1	1.4	1.0
1961	1.0	0.9	5.3	2.6	3.6	1.0	4.2	3.3	...	2.1	...	2.6	1.1	2.1	1.9	3.4
1962	1.0	1.2	6.8	-0.3	4.4	1.4	7.5	4.8	...	4.7	...	5.3	5.7	4.8	4.3	4.3
1963	1.3	1.8	7.6	0.5	2.7	2.1	5.3	4.8	2.9	7.5	...	2.5	8.8	2.9	3.4	2.0
1964	1.3	1.8	3.8	2.4	3.8	4.2	3.6	3.4	2.4	5.9	...	5.7	7.0	3.4	3.1	3.3
1965	1.6	2.4	7.6	4.0	5.0	4.1	6.5	2.5	3.1	4.6	...	4.3	13.2	5.0	3.4	4.8
1966	2.9	3.7	5.1	3.0	2.2	4.2	6.7	2.7	3.7	2.3	...	3.2	6.2	6.4	4.7	3.9
1967	3.1	3.5	4.0	3.2	4.0	2.9	7.5	2.7	1.7	3.7	...	4.4	6.4	4.2	4.0	2.5
1968	4.2	4.1	5.3	2.7	2.8	2.8	8.0	4.5	1.5	1.4	...	3.5	4.9	1.9	2.4	4.7
1969	5.5	4.5	5.2	2.9	3.1	3.7	3.5	6.4	1.9	2.7	...	3.1	2.2	2.7	2.5	5.4
1970	5.7	3.3	7.7	3.9	4.4	3.9	6.5	5.2	3.4	4.9	3.7	10.6	5.7	7.0	3.6	6.4
1971	4.4	2.9	6.3	6.1	4.7	4.3	5.8	5.5	5.3	4.8	7.6	6.2	8.2	7.4	6.6	9.4
1972	3.2	4.8	4.9	5.9	6.3	5.5	6.6	6.2	5.5	5.7	8.0	7.2	8.3	6.0	6.7	7.1
1973	6.2	7.5	11.7	9.5	7.6	7.0	9.3	7.3	6.9	10.8	8.1	7.5	11.5	6.8	8.7	9.2
1974	11.0	10.9	23.2	15.1	9.5	12.7	15.2	13.7	7.0	19.1	9.8	9.4	15.7	9.9	9.8	16.0
1975	9.1	10.8	11.7	15.1	8.4	12.8	9.6	11.8	6.0	17.0	9.9	11.7	17.0	9.8	6.7	24.2
1976	5.8	7.5	9.4	13.5	7.3	9.2	9.0	9.6	4.3	16.8	9.0	9.1	17.6	10.3	1.7	16.5
1977	6.5	8.0	8.1	12.3	5.5	7.1	11.1	9.4	3.7	17.0	6.4	9.1	24.5	11.4	1.3	15.8
1978	7.6	9.0	4.2	7.9	3.6	4.4	10.1	9.1	2.7	12.1	4.2	8.1	19.8	10.0	1.1	8.3
1979	11.3	9.1	3.7	9.1	3.7	4.5	9.6	10.8	4.1	14.8	4.3	4.8	15.7	7.2	3.6	13.4
1980	13.5	10.1	7.7	10.2	6.4	6.6	12.3	13.6	5.4	21.2	7.0	10.9	15.5	13.7	4.0	18.0
1981	10.3	12.5	4.9	9.7	6.8	7.6	11.7	13.4	6.3	17.8	6.7	13.6	14.6	12.1	6.5	11.9
1982	6.2	10.8	2.8	11.2	5.4	8.7	10.1	11.8	5.3	16.5	5.7	11.3	14.5	8.6	5.6	8.6
1983	3.2	5.8	1.9	10.1	3.3	7.7	6.9	9.6	3.3	14.7	2.7	8.4	12.2	8.9	2.9	4.6
1984	4.3	4.4	2.3	4.0	5.6	6.3	6.3	7.4	2.4	10.8	3.2	6.2	11.3	8.1	3.0	5.0
1985	3.6	4.0	2.0	6.7	3.2	4.9	4.7	5.8	2.1	9.2	2.3	5.7	8.8	7.3	3.4	6.1
1986	1.9	4.1	0.6	9.1	1.7	1.3	3.6	2.7	-0.1	5.9	0.2	7.2	8.8	4.3	0.7	3.4
1987	3.6	4.4	0.1	8.5	1.4	1.6	4.0	3.1	0.2	4.7	-0.4	8.7	5.3	4.2	1.5	4.2
1988	4.1	4.1	0.7	6.9	2.0	1.2	4.6	2.7	1.3	5.0	0.9	6.7	4.8	5.8	1.8	4.9
1989	4.8	5.0	2.3	7.9	2.5	3.1	4.8	3.6	2.8	6.3	1.0	4.6	6.8	6.5	3.2	7.8
1990	5.4	4.8	3.1	7.3	3.3	3.5	2.6	3.4	2.7	6.5	2.6	4.1	6.7	10.4	5.4	9.5
1991	4.2	5.6	3.3	3.2	3.3	3.2	2.4	3.2	3.7	6.3	3.1	3.4	6.0	9.4	5.8	5.9
1992	3.0	1.5	1.6	1.0	4.1	2.4	2.1	2.4	5.1	5.2	3.2	2.3	5.9	2.4	4.0	3.7
1993	3.0	1.8	1.3	1.8	3.6	2.8	1.2	2.1	4.4	4.5	2.6	2.3	4.6	4.7	3.3	1.6
1994	2.6	0.2	0.7	1.9	3.0	2.4	2.0	1.7	2.7	4.0	2.7	1.4	4.8	2.1	0.9	2.4
1995	2.8	2.1	-0.1	4.6	2.2	1.5	2.1	1.7	1.7	5.2	2.0	2.4	4.6	2.5	1.8	3.5
1996	3.0	1.6	0.1	2.6	1.9	2.1	2.1	2.0	1.5	4.0	2.0	1.3	3.6	0.5	0.8	2.4
1997	2.3	1.6	1.8	0.3	1.3	1.6	2.2	1.2	1.9	2.0	2.2	2.6	2.0	0.7	0.5	3.1
1998	1.6	0.9	0.6	0.9	0.9	1.0	1.9	0.7	0.9	2.0	2.0	2.3	1.8	-0.3	0.1	3.4
1999	2.2	1.7	-0.3	1.5	0.6	1.1	2.5	0.5	0.6	1.7	2.2	2.3	2.3	0.5	0.8	1.5
2000	3.4	2.7	-0.7	4.5	2.3	2.5	3.0	1.7	1.4	2.5	2.6	3.1	3.4	0.9	1.5	3.0
2001	2.8	2.6	-0.7	4.4	2.7	2.5	2.4	1.7	2.0	2.7	4.5	3.0	3.6	2.4	1.0	1.8
2002	1.6	2.2	-0.9	3.0	1.8	1.6	2.3	1.9	1.4	2.5	3.5	1.3	3.5	2.2	0.7	1.7
2003	2.3	2.8	-0.3	2.8	1.3	1.6	2.1	2.1	1.1	2.7	2.1	2.5	3.0	1.9	0.6	2.9
2004	2.7	1.9	0.0	2.3	2.1	2.1	1.2	2.1	1.6	2.2	1.2	0.5	3.0	0.4	0.8	3.0
2005	3.4	2.2	-0.3	2.7	2.3	2.8	1.8	1.8	2.0	2.0	1.7	1.5	3.4	0.5	1.2	2.8
2006	3.2	2.0	0.3	3.5	1.5	1.8	1.9	1.6	1.7	2.1	1.1	2.3	3.5	1.4	1.1	3.2

[1]The figures may differ from official percent changes published by national statistical agencies because of rounding.
[2]Urban worker households prior to 1978.
[3]All households from January 1995, all urban households from September 1978 to December 1994, and middle-income urban households prior to September 1978.
[4]Excluding imputed rent for owner-occupied households prior to 1970.
[5]Urban worker households prior to September 1998.
[6]Excluding rent and several other services prior to 1976.
[7]Excluding rent prior to 1964.
[8]Urban worker households prior to 1991; worker households in Paris only prior to 1962.
[9]Unified Germany from 1991 onward; data for previous years relate to the former West Germany.
[10]Urban worker households prior to 1960.
[11]All family households from 1993; middle-income family households prior to 1963.
[12]Urban worker households prior to May 1993.
. . . = Not available.

Table 11-6. Real Gross Domestic Product (GDP) Per Capita, 16 Countries, 1960–2006

(2002 U.S. dollars.)

Year	United States	Canada	Australia	Japan	Korea, Republic of	Austria	Belgium	Denmark	France	Germany¹	Italy	Netherlands	Norway	Spain	Sweden	United Kingdom
1960	14 420	11 451	12 304	5 344	1 684	9 301	8 766	11 256	9 259	11 343	8 150	11 463	10 320	...	11 458	11 967
1961	14 516	11 576	11 919	5 979	1 730	9 741	9 172	11 838	9 616	11 712	8 760	11 639	10 862	...	12 038	12 143
1962	15 161	12 139	12 373	6 432	1 718	9 914	9 611	12 397	10 091	12 115	9 241	11 971	11 065	...	12 486	12 158
1963	15 598	12 523	12 858	6 926	1 823	10 252	9 955	12 355	10 545	12 336	9 688	12 197	11 398	...	13 071	12 600
1964	16 278	13 094	13 440	7 619	1 948	10 799	10 547	13 357	11 112	13 026	9 878	13 070	11 879	8 092	13 840	13 200
1965	17 107	13 690	13 816	7 887	2 008	11 036	10 823	13 889	11 545	13 572	10 115	13 575	12 410	8 507	14 226	13 406
1966	18 014	14 319	13 973	8 710	2 196	11 577	11 091	14 097	12 051	13 826	10 637	13 774	12 777	9 026	14 392	13 591
1967	18 267	14 483	14 667	9 564	2 272	11 837	11 457	14 767	12 546	13 751	11 319	14 340	13 464	9 305	14 783	13 846
1968	18 958	15 024	15 221	10 583	2 472	12 302	11 891	15 491	13 003	14 449	11 984	15 146	13 652	9 820	15 247	14 359
1969	19 351	15 600	15 923	11 709	2 751	13 029	12 645	16 413	13 824	15 380	12 643	15 991	14 152	10 570	15 864	14 593
1970	19 162	15 786	16 632	12 650	2 928	13 908	13 443	16 462	14 539	15 999	13 244	16 692	14 330	10 886	16 731	14 874
1971	19 557	16 127	16 520	13 027	3 107	14 554	13 904	16 868	15 155	16 318	13 422	17 219	15 029	11 242	16 818	15 093
1972	20 374	16 794	16 612	13 926	3 186	15 368	14 584	17 473	15 719	16 905	13 838	17 497	15 699	12 013	17 173	15 585
1973	21 342	17 783	17 103	14 837	3 506	16 030	15 399	18 020	16 616	17 623	14 724	18 210	16 288	12 806	17 821	16 657
1974	21 040	18 263	17 102	14 461	3 694	16 634	15 981	17 790	17 247	17 636	15 433	18 807	16 806	13 405	18 319	16 425
1975	20 797	18 397	17 275	14 726	3 849	16 618	15 700	17 522	17 001	17 478	15 020	18 679	17 553	13 356	18 714	16 326
1976	21 694	19 154	17 722	15 155	4 188	17 409	16 548	18 543	17 680	18 498	16 010	19 357	18 483	13 637	18 848	16 758
1977	22 468	19 586	17 825	15 672	4 536	18 240	16 608	18 849	18 226	19 065	16 351	19 723	19 167	13 831	18 478	17 165
1978	23 470	20 183	18 011	16 351	4 882	18 229	17 048	19 218	18 864	19 660	16 820	20 093	19 830	13 850	18 762	17 723
1979	23 944	20 824	18 559	17 104	5 135	19 260	17 399	19 927	19 446	20 479	17 771	20 324	20 623	13 754	19 439	18 175
1980	23 615	20 842	18 863	17 450	4 980	19 603	18 132	19 828	19 673	20 611	18 343	20 499	21 483	13 859	19 728	17 765
1981	23 970	21 218	19 343	17 834	5 206	19 524	18 070	19 663	19 744	20 592	18 476	20 252	21 741	13 762	19 683	17 496
1982	23 282	20 367	19 016	18 199	5 501	19 890	18 172	20 406	20 104	20 413	18 538	19 902	21 688	13 859	19 903	17 848
1983	24 115	20 715	18 672	18 368	6 005	20 533	18 230	20 965	20 235	20 845	18 748	20 172	22 452	14 038	20 269	18 467
1984	25 623	21 713	19 605	18 820	6 412	20 530	18 680	21 850	20 437	21 519	19 349	20 722	23 709	14 230	21 110	18 908
1985	26 445	22 545	20 457	19 655	6 781	21 045	18 983	22 722	20 684	22 010	19 884	21 177	24 903	14 507	21 530	19 524
1986	27 114	22 862	20 592	20 134	7 427	21 496	19 321	23 816	21 084	22 510	20 452	21 721	25 816	14 933	22 060	20 246
1987	27 780	23 521	21 171	20 800	8 170	21 813	19 751	23 848	21 493	22 839	21 103	21 976	26 153	15 723	22 709	21 118
1988	28 667	24 372	21 677	22 115	8 952	22 537	20 577	23 804	22 353	23 546	21 977	22 585	25 968	16 488	23 173	22 124
1989	29 402	24 564	22 281	23 198	9 461	23 228	21 255	23 930	23 147	24 158	22 705	23 446	26 119	17 250	23 605	22 536
1990	29 620	24 242	22 287	24 325	10 226	24 113	21 857	24 245	23 631	25 055	23 151	24 262	26 531	17 876	23 687	22 632
1991	29 179	23 452	21 775	25 040	11 077	24 732	22 175	24 495	23 754	23 570	23 483	24 654	27 225	18 288	23 280	22 246
1992	29 752	23 378	21 932	25 189	11 606	25 039	22 423	24 897	23 961	23 912	23 656	24 887	28 022	18 398	22 748	22 240
1993	30 152	23 662	22 564	25 177	12 194	24 916	22 121	24 787	23 641	23 550	23 431	25 022	28 632	18 152	22 194	22 697
1994	30 987	24 527	23 462	25 388	13 102	25 481	22 764	26 074	24 078	24 103	23 931	25 610	29 907	18 534	22 874	23 613
1995	31 389	24 955	24 036	25 823	14 160	25 928	25 577	26 747	24 501	24 487	24 607	26 273	30 998	19 001	23 711	24 237
1996	32 174	25 095	24 701	26 471	15 008	26 571	25 833	27 337	24 688	24 659	24 776	27 053	32 414	19 415	24 010	24 844
1997	33 221	25 896	25 451	26 824	15 559	27 029	26 676	28 091	25 153	25 057	25 231	28 064	33 977	20 113	24 561	25 533
1998	34 208	26 734	26 425	26 208	14 388	27 961	27 066	28 599	25 940	25 573	25 586	28 987	34 682	20 938	25 442	26 314
1999	35 324	27 984	27 298	26 131	15 642	28 833	27 927	29 236	26 663	26 068	26 074	30 141	35 143	21 756	26 572	27 013
2000	36 225	29 174	27 885	26 824	16 828	29 729	28 903	30 166	27 522	26 872	26 996	31 106	36 051	22 599	27 656	27 946
2001	36 111	29 377	28 085	26 791	17 344	29 859	29 032	30 272	27 835	27 155	27 464	31 466	36 583	23 045	27 869	28 494
2002	36 311	29 903	28 919	26 826	18 450	29 963	29 339	30 310	27 922	27 108	27 471	31 288	36 933	23 221	28 325	28 978
2003	36 856	30 157	29 443	27 162	18 927	30 163	29 506	30 347	28 032	27 045	27 268	31 246	37 089	23 549	28 693	29 634
2004	37 934	30 846	30 212	27 887	19 748	30 684	30 246	30 916	28 539	27 388	27 325	31 752	38 295	23 925	29 758	30 458
2005	38 778	31 447	30 663	28 420	20 535	31 088	30 402	31 771	28 855	27 650	27 148	32 159	39 057	24 349	30 499	30 853
2006	39 682	31 991	31 053	29 030	21 489	31 900	31 233	32 678	29 253	28 426	27 536	32 907	39 869	24 948	31 621	31 618

¹Unified Germany from 1991 onward; data for previous years relate to the former West Germany.
. . . = Not available.

Table 11-7. Real Gross Domestic Product (GDP) Per Employed Person, 16 Countries, 1960–2006

(2002 U.S. dollars.)

Year	United States	Canada	Australia	Japan	Korea, Republic of	Austria	Bel-gium	Den-mark	France	Ger-many[1]	Italy	Nether-lands	Norway	Spain	Sweden	United Kingdom
1960	38 168	32 520	30 420	10 719	...	17 604	22 794	24 176	21 704	24 126	19 552	28 560	24 256	...	23 646	25 962
1961	39 041	33 025	30 165	11 832	...	18 438	23 751	25 229	22 786	24 897	21 023	28 966	25 336	...	24 789	26 285
1962	40 687	34 343	31 141	12 703	...	18 969	24 609	26 218	24 353	25 967	22 393	29 618	25 872	...	25 705	26 433
1963	41 883	35 278	32 072	13 703	6 571	19 879	25 500	26 019	25 687	26 634	24 048	30 184	26 732	...	26 940	27 504
1964	43 365	36 318	33 058	15 012	7 080	21 114	26 891	27 773	27 056	28 384	24 806	32 215	27 982	...	28 370	28 630
1965	45 044	37 300	33 575	15 621	7 105	21 864	27 741	28 583	28 292	29 735	26 258	33 636	29 218	...	29 252	28 979
1966	46 587	38 167	33 124	16 859	7 766	23 292	28 516	28 765	29 565	30 659	28 291	34 311	30 190	...	29 822	29 475
1967	46 654	38 219	34 535	18 348	7 939	24 390	29 752	30 387	30 950	31 594	29 949	36 241	31 859	...	31 158	30 554
1968	47 898	39 552	35 576	20 150	8 413	25 819	31 036	31 868	32 417	33 288	31 925	38 314	32 537	...	31 953	31 985
1969	48 190	40 419	37 073	22 342	9 347	27 491	32 542	33 289	34 226	35 223	34 117	40 249	33 708	...	32 934	32 651
1970	48 003	41 052	37 960	24 360	9 815	29 390	34 584	33 342	35 837	36 535	35 763	42 033	33 836	...	34 392	33 475
1971	49 425	42 364	38 548	25 251	10 272	30 557	35 603	34 394	37 541	37 500	36 401	43 641	35 441	26 845	34 785	34 175
1972	50 553	43 381	38 827	27 234	10 283	32 216	37 563	35 125	39 055	38 939	37 842	45 193	36 882	28 679	35 465	35 290
1973	51 760	44 319	39 442	28 772	10 928	33 324	39 433	35 996	41 047	40 354	39 973	47 395	38 261	30 142	36 734	37 230
1974	50 554	44 335	39 629	28 539	11 222	34 194	40 442	35 995	42 514	40 929	41 526	48 860	39 204	31 720	37 172	36 640
1975	51 027	44 553	40 609	29 494	11 615	34 324	40 425	36 029	42 470	41 532	40 627	49 324	40 499	32 536	37 383	36 558
1976	52 049	46 079	41 678	30 418	12 097	35 774	42 907	37 587	43 998	43 976	43 086	51 261	41 459	33 983	37 649	37 739
1977	52 570	46 858	41 712	31 377	12 890	37 044	43 284	38 427	45 185	45 163	44 054	51 466	42 010	35 175	36 973	38 611
1978	53 227	47 322	42 571	32 712	13 458	36 809	44 433	39 020	46 742	46 141	45 331	52 234	42 888	36 595	37 480	39 658
1979	53 413	47 240	43 587	34 154	14 170	38 659	44 970	40 177	48 147	47 294	47 504	52 277	44 140	37 458	38 361	40 307
1980	53 033	46 518	43 610	34 878	13 877	38 993	46 972	40 336	48 832	47 032	48 433	51 541	45 037	38 862	38 573	39 624
1981	53 768	46 584	44 496	35 630	14 375	39 089	47 719	40 644	49 471	47 129	48 882	50 996	45 155	39 763	38 447	40 075
1982	53 160	46 746	44 519	36 318	15 046	40 402	48 638	42 020	50 613	47 249	48 984	50 601	45 198	40 607	38 970	41 653
1983	54 846	47 676	45 113	36 353	16 522	41 919	49 292	43 129	51 377	48 774	49 397	52 459	47 042	41 470	39 613	43 434
1984	56 490	49 199	46 532	37 359	17 955	41 948	50 606	44 269	52 258	50 067	50 994	53 428	49 442	43 176	40 975	43 612
1985	57 661	50 108	47 733	39 046	18 483	42 895	51 157	44 987	53 562	50 705	51 929	53 341	50 684	44 636	41 440	44 590
1986	58 350	49 783	46 768	39 997	19 740	43 712	51 745	46 109	54 671	51 185	53 049	54 151	51 057	45 044	42 316	46 063
1987	58 818	50 442	47 757	41 351	20 794	44 411	52 663	46 036	55 606	51 569	54 618	55 116	50 930	45 370	43 385	47 218
1988	59 945	51 382	47 900	43 642	22 304	45 555	54 361	46 337	57 637	53 075	56 304	55 420	51 124	46 067	43 904	47 996
1989	60 843	51 566	48 010	45 284	22 872	46 598	55 379	46 810	59 044	54 209	57 817	56 710	53 147	46 602	44 435	47 799
1990	61 263	51 309	47 871	46 857	24 241	47 826	56 293	47 770	60 126	55 647	58 079	57 209	54 657	46 595	44 511	47 924
1991	61 733	51 130	48 460	47 462	25 716	48 933	57 264	48 677	60 671	48 813	57 886	57 109	56 918	47 214	44 689	48 553
1992	63 456	52 090	49 655	47 389	26 711	49 804	58 405	50 233	61 860	50 637	58 760	56 919	59 047	48 325	45 954	49 855
1993	64 289	53 050	51 357	47 327	28 018	50 203	58 281	50 984	62 094	50 905	59 846	57 705	60 266	49 223	47 600	51 484
1994	65 426	54 467	52 353	47 796	29 469	51 523	60 390	53 998	63 377	52 312	62 157	59 013	62 457	50 635	49 908	52 658
1995	66 140	54 999	52 253	48 666	31 279	52 604	67 537	54 696	64 150	53 180	64 042	59 125	63 747	51 059	51 072	54 232
1996	67 655	55 365	53 707	49 795	32 763	53 788	68 131	55 513	64 619	53 856	64 134	59 918	65 671	51 553	52 198	55 216
1997	69 184	56 506	55 432	50 228	33 704	54 291	69 888	56 433	65 776	54 879	65 142	60 555	67 240	52 030	54 120	55 906
1998	71 053	57 397	57 004	49 785	33 403	55 525	69 718	56 758	67 061	55 332	65 432	61 147	67 251	52 314	55 248	57 191
1999	73 117	59 057	58 605	50 408	35 935	56 443	71 166	57 585	67 902	55 691	65 976	62 328	67 986	52 881	56 557	58 133
2000	73 944	60 642	59 084	52 174	37 391	57 780	72 389	59 277	68 714	56 421	67 039	63 351	69 801	53 679	57 610	59 657
2001	74 455	60 973	59 648	52 669	38 077	57 919	73 629	59 135	68 766	56 871	66 892	63 780	70 941	53 921	57 144	60 560
2002	75 845	61 275	60 938	53 647	39 634	58 484	74 483	59 400	69 042	57 191	65 993	63 451	71 731	54 188	58 195	61 337
2003	76 983	60 951	61 389	54 583	40 917	59 144	75 220	60 438	69 705	57 632	65 043	63 921	73 213	54 137	59 388	62 371
2004	79 127	61 877	62 390	55 961	42 058	60 603	76 153	61 714	71 351	58 124	65 537	65 550	75 688	54 043	62 204	63 775
2005	80 289	62 816	62 131	56 806	43 250	61 557	75 223	63 149	72 248	58 731	65 388	66 443	76 957	53 901	63 755	64 419
2006	81 454	63 311	62 482	57 794	44 831	62 684	77 071	63 954	73 134	59 870	65 477	67 324	76 825	54 314	65 412	65 684

[1]Unified Germany from 1991 onward; data for previous years relate to the former West Germany.
. . . = Not available.

Table 11-8. Employment-Population Ratios, 16 Countries, 1960–2006

(Percent.)

Year	United States	Canada	Australia	Japan	Korea, Republic of	Austria	Bel-gium	Den-mark	France	Ger-many[1]	Italy	Nether-lands	Norway	Spain	Sweden	United Kingdom
1960	37.8	35.2	40.4	49.9	. . .	52.8	38.5	46.6	42.7	47.0	41.7	40.1	42.5	. . .	48.5	46.1
1961	37.2	35.1	39.5	50.5	. . .	52.8	38.6	46.9	42.2	47.0	41.7	40.2	42.9	. . .	48.6	46.2
1962	37.3	35.3	39.7	50.6	. . .	52.3	39.1	47.3	41.4	46.7	41.3	40.4	42.8	. . .	48.6	46.0
1963	37.2	35.5	40.1	50.5	27.7	51.6	39.0	47.5	41.1	46.3	40.3	40.4	42.6	. . .	48.5	45.8
1964	37.5	36.1	40.7	50.8	27.5	51.1	39.2	48.1	41.1	45.9	39.8	40.6	42.5	. . .	48.8	46.1
1965	38.0	36.7	41.1	50.5	28.3	50.5	39.0	48.6	40.8	45.6	38.5	40.4	42.5	. . .	48.6	46.3
1966	38.7	37.5	42.2	51.7	28.3	49.7	38.9	49.0	40.8	45.1	37.6	40.1	42.3	. . .	48.3	46.1
1967	39.2	37.9	42.5	52.1	28.6	48.5	38.5	48.6	40.5	43.5	37.8	39.6	42.3	. . .	47.4	45.3
1968	39.6	38.0	42.8	52.5	29.4	47.6	38.3	48.6	40.1	43.4	37.5	39.5	42.0	. . .	47.7	44.9
1969	40.2	38.6	43.0	52.4	29.4	47.4	38.9	49.3	40.4	43.7	37.1	39.7	42.0	. . .	48.2	44.7
1970	39.9	38.5	43.8	51.9	29.8	47.3	38.9	49.4	40.6	43.8	37.0	39.7	42.4	. . .	48.6	44.4
1971	39.6	38.1	42.9	51.6	30.2	47.6	39.1	49.0	40.4	43.5	36.9	39.5	42.4	41.9	48.3	44.2
1972	40.3	38.7	42.8	51.1	31.0	47.7	38.8	49.7	40.2	43.4	36.6	38.7	42.6	41.9	48.4	44.2
1973	41.2	40.1	43.4	51.6	32.1	48.1	39.0	50.1	40.5	43.7	36.8	38.4	42.6	42.5	48.5	44.7
1974	41.6	41.2	43.2	50.7	32.9	48.6	39.5	49.4	40.6	43.1	37.2	38.5	42.9	42.3	49.3	44.8
1975	40.8	41.3	42.5	49.9	33.1	48.4	38.8	48.6	40.0	42.1	37.0	37.9	43.3	41.0	50.1	44.7
1976	41.7	41.6	42.5	49.8	34.6	48.7	38.6	49.3	40.2	42.1	37.2	37.8	44.6	40.1	50.1	44.4
1977	42.7	41.8	42.7	49.9	35.2	49.2	38.4	49.1	40.3	42.2	37.1	38.3	45.6	39.3	50.0	44.5
1978	44.1	42.6	42.3	50.0	36.3	49.5	38.4	49.3	40.4	42.6	37.1	38.5	46.2	37.8	50.1	44.7
1979	44.8	44.1	42.6	50.1	36.2	49.8	38.7	49.6	40.4	43.3	37.4	38.9	46.7	36.7	50.7	45.1
1980	44.5	44.8	43.3	50.0	35.9	50.3	38.6	49.2	40.3	43.8	37.9	39.8	47.7	35.7	51.1	44.8
1981	44.6	45.5	43.5	50.1	36.2	49.9	37.9	48.4	39.9	43.7	37.8	39.7	48.1	34.6	51.2	43.7
1982	43.8	43.6	42.7	50.1	36.6	49.2	37.4	48.6	39.7	43.2	37.8	39.3	48.0	34.1	51.1	42.8
1983	44.0	43.5	41.4	50.5	36.3	49.0	37.0	48.6	39.4	42.7	38.0	38.5	47.7	33.9	51.2	42.5
1984	45.4	44.1	42.1	50.4	35.7	48.9	36.9	49.4	39.1	43.0	37.9	38.8	48.0	33.0	51.5	43.4
1985	45.9	45.0	42.9	50.3	36.7	49.1	37.1	50.5	38.6	43.4	38.3	39.7	49.1	32.5	52.0	43.8
1986	46.5	45.9	44.0	50.3	37.6	49.2	37.3	51.7	38.6	44.0	38.6	40.1	50.6	33.2	52.1	44.0
1987	47.2	46.6	44.3	50.3	39.3	49.1	37.5	51.8	38.7	44.3	38.6	39.9	51.4	34.7	52.3	44.7
1988	47.8	47.4	45.3	50.7	40.1	49.5	37.9	51.4	38.8	44.4	39.0	40.8	50.8	35.8	52.8	46.1
1989	48.3	47.6	46.4	51.2	41.4	49.8	38.4	51.1	39.2	44.6	39.3	41.3	49.1	37.0	53.1	47.1
1990	48.3	47.2	46.6	51.9	42.2	50.4	38.8	50.8	39.3	45.0	39.9	42.4	48.5	38.4	53.2	47.2
1991	47.3	45.9	44.9	52.8	43.1	50.5	38.7	50.3	39.2	48.3	40.6	43.2	47.8	38.7	52.1	45.8
1992	46.9	44.9	44.2	53.2	43.5	50.3	38.4	49.6	38.7	47.2	40.3	43.7	47.5	38.1	49.5	44.6
1993	46.9	44.6	43.9	53.2	43.5	49.6	38.0	48.6	38.1	46.3	39.2	43.4	47.5	36.9	46.6	44.1
1994	47.4	45.0	44.8	53.1	44.5	49.5	37.7	48.3	38.0	46.1	38.5	43.4	47.9	36.6	45.8	44.8
1995	47.5	45.4	46.0	53.1	45.3	49.3	37.9	48.9	38.2	46.0	38.4	44.4	48.6	37.2	46.4	44.7
1996	47.6	45.3	46.0	53.2	45.8	49.4	37.9	49.2	38.2	45.8	38.6	45.2	49.4	37.7	46.0	45.0
1997	48.0	45.8	45.9	53.4	46.2	49.8	38.2	49.8	38.2	45.7	38.7	46.3	50.5	38.7	45.4	45.7
1998	48.1	46.6	46.4	52.6	43.1	50.4	38.8	50.4	38.7	46.2	39.1	47.4	51.6	40.0	46.0	46.0
1999	48.3	47.4	46.6	51.8	43.5	51.1	39.2	50.8	39.3	46.8	39.5	48.4	51.7	41.1	47.0	46.5
2000	49.0	48.1	47.2	51.4	45.0	51.5	39.9	50.9	40.1	47.6	40.3	49.1	51.6	42.1	48.0	46.8
2001	48.5	48.2	47.1	50.9	45.6	51.6	39.4	51.2	40.5	47.7	41.1	49.3	51.6	42.7	48.8	47.1
2002	47.9	48.8	47.5	50.0	46.6	51.2	39.4	51.0	40.4	47.4	41.6	49.3	51.5	42.9	48.7	47.2
2003	47.9	49.5	48.0	49.8	46.3	51.0	39.2	50.2	40.2	46.9	41.9	48.9	50.7	43.5	48.3	47.5
2004	47.9	49.9	48.4	49.8	47.0	50.6	39.7	50.1	40.0	47.1	41.7	48.4	50.6	44.3	47.8	47.8
2005	48.3	50.1	49.4	50.0	47.5	50.5	40.4	50.3	39.9	47.1	41.5	48.4	50.8	45.2	47.8	47.9
2006	48.7	50.5	49.7	50.2	47.9	50.9	40.5	51.1	40.0	47.5	42.1	48.9	51.9	45.9	48.3	48.1

[1]Unified Germany from 1991 onward; data for previous years relate to the former West Germany.

. . . = Not available.

Table 11-9. Real Gross Domestic Product (GDP) Per Capita and Per Employed Person, 16 Countries, Selected Years, 1979–2006

(Average annual percent change.)

Category and country	1979–2006	1979–1990	1990–1995	1995–2000	2000–2006	2001–2002	2002–2003	2003–2004	2004–2005	2005–2006
Real GDP Per Capita										
United States	1.9	2.0	1.2	2.9	1.5	0.6	1.5	2.9	2.2	2.3
Canada	1.6	1.4	0.6	3.2	1.5	1.8	0.8	2.3	1.9	1.7
Australia	1.9	1.7	1.5	3.0	1.8	3.0	1.8	2.6	1.5	1.3
Japan	2.0	3.3	1.2	0.8	1.3	0.1	1.2	2.7	1.9	2.1
Korea, Republic of	5.4	6.5	6.7	3.5	4.2	6.4	2.6	4.3	4.0	4.6
Austria	1.9	2.1	1.5	2.8	1.2	0.3	0.7	1.7	1.3	2.6
Belgium	2.2	2.1	3.2	2.5	1.3	1.1	0.6	2.5	0.5	2.7
Denmark	1.8	1.8	2.0	2.4	1.3	0.1	0.1	1.9	2.8	2.9
France	1.5	1.8	0.7	2.4	1.0	0.3	0.4	1.8	1.1	1.4
Germany[1]	1.6	1.9	1.5	1.9	0.9	-0.2	-0.2	1.3	1.0	2.8
Italy	1.6	2.4	1.2	1.9	0.3	0.0	-0.7	0.2	-0.6	1.4
Netherlands	1.8	1.6	1.6	3.4	0.9	-0.6	-0.1	1.6	1.3	2.3
Norway	2.5	2.3	3.2	3.1	1.7	1.0	0.4	3.3	2.0	2.1
Spain	2.2	2.4	1.2	3.5	1.7	0.8	1.4	1.6	1.8	2.5
Sweden	1.8	1.8	0.0	3.1	2.3	1.6	1.3	3.7	2.5	3.7
United Kingdom	2.1	2.0	1.4	2.9	2.1	1.7	2.3	2.8	1.3	2.5
Real GDP Per Employed Person										
United States	1.6	1.3	1.5	2.3	1.6	1.9	1.5	2.8	1.5	1.5
Canada	1.1	0.8	1.4	2.0	0.7	0.5	-0.5	1.5	1.5	0.8
Australia	1.3	0.9	1.8	2.5	0.9	2.2	0.7	1.6	-0.4	0.6
Japan	2.0	2.9	0.8	1.4	1.7	1.9	1.7	2.5	1.5	1.7
Korea, Republic of	4.4	5.0	5.2	3.6	3.1	4.1	3.2	2.8	2.8	3.7
Austria	1.8	2.0	1.9	1.9	1.4	1.0	1.1	2.5	1.6	1.8
Belgium	2.0	2.1	3.7	1.4	1.1	1.2	1.0	1.2	-1.2	2.5
Denmark	1.7	1.6	2.7	1.6	1.3	0.4	1.7	2.1	2.3	1.3
France	1.6	2.0	1.3	1.4	1.0	0.4	1.0	2.4	1.3	1.2
Germany[1]	1.5	1.5	2.2	1.2	1.0	0.6	0.8	0.9	1.0	1.9
Italy	1.2	1.8	2.0	0.9	-0.4	-1.3	-1.4	0.8	-0.2	0.1
Netherlands	0.9	0.8	0.7	1.4	1.0	-0.5	0.7	2.5	1.4	1.3
Norway	2.1	2.0	3.1	1.8	1.6	1.1	2.1	3.4	1.7	-0.2
Spain	1.4	2.0	1.8	1.0	0.2	0.5	-0.1	-0.2	-0.3	0.8
Sweden	2.0	1.4	2.8	2.4	2.1	1.8	2.0	4.7	2.5	2.6
United Kingdom	1.8	1.6	2.5	1.9	1.6	1.3	1.7	2.3	1.0	2.0

[1]Unified Germany from 1995–2000 onward; data for previous years relate to the former West Germany.

Table 11-10. Purchasing Power Parities (PPPs), Exchange Rates, and Relative Prices, 16 Countries, 2002

(United States = 1.0.)

Country	PPPs for gross domestic product (GDP)	Exchange rates	Relative prices[1]
United States	1.000	1.000	1.00
Canada	1.229	1.570	0.78
Australia	1.337	1.839	0.73
Japan	143.7	125.2	1.15
Korea, Republic of	778.8	1 250.3	0.62
Austria	0.912	1.058	0.86
Belgium	0.883	1.058	0.83
Denmark	8.425	7.886	1.07
France	0.900	1.058	0.85
Germany	0.959	1.058	0.91
Italy	0.825	1.058	0.78
Netherlands	0.921	1.058	0.87
Norway	9.142	7.984	1.15
Spain	0.743	1.058	0.70
Sweden	9.365	9.723	0.96
United Kingdom	0.610	0.666	0.92

[1]A number below 1.00 indicates that prices are lower in the specified country than in the United States, and a number greater than 1.00 indicates that prices are higher in the specified country than in the United States.

CHAPTER 12

AMERICAN TIME USE SURVEY

AMERICAN TIME USE SURVEY

HIGHLIGHTS

This chapter presents data from the new American Time Use Survey (ATUS). The survey was introduced in the sixth edition of the *Handbook of U.S. Labor Statistics*. Its purpose is to collect data on the activities people do during the day and the amount of time they spend on each one.

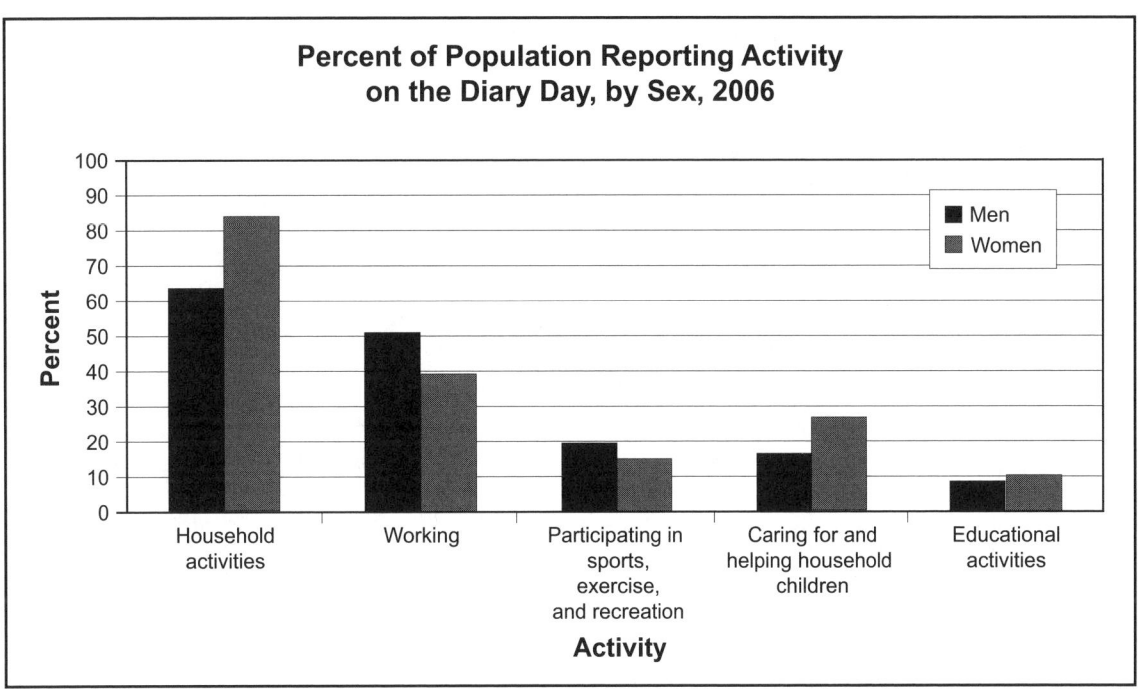

The time spent on various activities has changed little in the last two years. Despite the increased labor force participation of women, there is still a considerable difference between the number of men and women who reported working on the diary day. In 2006, 51 percent of men and 39 percent of women reported working. However, 83.6 percent of women reported participating in household activities on the diary day, compared with 63.7 percent of men. (See Table 12-1.)

OTHER HIGHLIGHTS

• Not only did more men report working on the average diary day, they reported working longer hours. On average, men worked 8.04 hours on the diary day, compared with 7.04 hours for women in 2006. More women than men worked part time. (See Table 12-1.)

• A higher proportion of women (10.1 percent) than men (8.6 percent) reported engaging in educational activities. (See Table 12-1.)

• Women spent more time caring for children, regardless of employment status or the age of the children. (See Table 12-8.)

• Persons employed in transportation and material moving and installation, maintenance, and repair worked more hours per day (8.32 hours and 8.16 hours, respectively) than workers in any other occupation. (See Table 12-4.)

NOTES AND DEFINITIONS

Survey Methodology

While the Bureau of Labor Statistics (BLS) has long produced statistics about the labor market, including information about employment, hours, and earnings, the American Time Use Survey (ATUS) marks the first time that a federal statistical agency has produced estimates on how Americans spend another critical resource—their time. Data collection for the ATUS began in January 2003. Sample cases for the survey are selected monthly, and interviews are conducted continuously throughout the year. In 2006, approximately 13,000 individuals were interviewed.

ATUS sample households are chosen from the households that have completed their eighth (final) interview for the Current Population Survey (CPS), the nation's monthly household labor force survey. (See Chapter 1 of this *Handbook* for a description of the CPS.) ATUS sample households are selected to ensure that estimates will be representative of the nation.

An individual age 15 years or over is randomly chosen from each sample household. This "designated person" takes part in a one-time telephone interview about his or her activities on the previous day (the "diary day").

Concepts and Definitions

Average hours per day. The average number of hours spent in a 24-hour day (between 4 a.m. on the diary day and 4 a.m. on the interview day) doing a specified activity.

Average hours per day, population. The average number of hours per day spent on a particular activity is computed using all responses from the sample population, including those from respondents who did not do the particular activity on their diary day. These estimates reflect the total number of respondents engaged in an activity and the total amount of time they spent on the activity.

Average hours per day, persons reporting the activity on the diary day. The average number of hours per day spent on a particular activity is computed using responses only from those engaged in the particular activity on the diary day.

Diary day. The diary day is the day about which the designated person reports. For example, the diary day of a designated person interviewed on Tuesday would be Monday.

Employment Status

Employed. All persons who, at any time during the seven days prior to the interview: 1) did any work at all as paid employees, worked in their own business professions, or on their own farms, or usually worked 15 hours or more an unpaid workers in family-operated enterprises; and 2) all those who were not working but had jobs or businesses from which they were temporarily absent due to illness, bad weather, vacation, childcare problems, labor-management disputes, maternity or paternity leave, job training, or other family or personal reasons, whether or not they were paid for the time off or were seeking other jobs.

Employed full time. Full-time workers are those who usually work 35 hours or more per week at all jobs combined.

Employed part time. Part-time workers are those who usually work fewer than 35 hours per week at all jobs combined.

Not employed. Persons are not employed if they do not meet the conditions for employment. Not employed workers include those classified as unemployed as well as those classified as not in the labor force (using CPS definitions).

The numbers of employed and not employed persons in this report do not correspond to published totals from the CPS. While the information on employment from the ATUS is useful for assessing work in the context of other daily activities, the employment data are not intended for analysis of current employment trends. Compared to the CPS and other estimates of employment, the ATUS estimates are based on a much smaller sample and are only available with a substantial lag.

Household children. Household children are children under 18 years of age who reside in the household of the ATUS respondent. The children may be related to the respondent (such as their own children, grandchildren, nieces, nephews, brothers, or sisters) or not related (such as foster children or children of roommates). For secondary childcare calculations, respondents are asked about care of household children under 13 years of age.

Primary activity. A primary activity is the main activity of a respondent at a specified time.

Major Activity Category Definitions

Personal care activities. Personal care activities include sleeping, bathing, dressing, health-related self-care, and personal or private activities. Receiving unpaid personal care from others (for example, "my sister put polish on my nails") is also captured in this category.

Eating and drinking. All time spent eating or drinking (except when identified by the respondent as part of a work or volunteer activity), whether alone, with others, at home, at a place of purchase, in transit, or somewhere else, is classified in this category.

Household activities. Household activities are those done by respondents to maintain their households. These include housework, cooking, yard care, pet care, vehicle maintenance and repair, and home maintenance, repair, decoration, and renovation. Food preparation is always classified as a household activity. Household management and organizational activities—such as filling out paperwork, balancing a checkbook, or planning a party—are also included in this category.

Purchasing goods and services. This category includes the purchase of consumer goods as well as the purchase or use of professional and personal care services, household services, and government services. Most purchases and rentals of consumer goods, regardless of mode or place of purchase or rental (in person, via telephone, over the Internet, at home, or in a store), are classified in this category. Time spent obtaining, receiving, and purchasing professional and personal care services provided by someone else is also classified in this category, which also includes time spent arranging for and purchasing household services provided by someone else.

Caring for and helping household members. Time spent doing activities that involve caring for or helping to care for or help any child or adult in the respondent's household, regardless of the relationship to the respondent or the physical or mental health status of the person being helped, are classified in this category. Household member are considered children if they are under 18 years of age. Caring for and helping household members also includes a range of activities done to benefit adult members of households, such as providing physical and medical care or obtaining medical services.

Caring for and helping non-household members. Time spent caring for and helping any child or adult who is not part of the respondent's household, regardless of the relationship to the respondent or the physical or mental health status of the person being helped, is classified in this category.

Working and work-related activities. This category includes time spent working, doing activities as part of one's job, engaging in income-generating activities (not as part of one's job), and job search activities. "Working" includes hours spent doing the specific tasks required of one's main or other job, regardless of location or time of day. Travel time related to working and work-related activities includes time spent commuting to and from one's job, as well as time spent traveling for work-related activities, generating income, and job searching.

Educational activities. Educational activities include taking classes (including Internet and other distance-learning courses), doing research and homework, and taking care of administrative tasks, such as registering for classes or obtaining a school ID. For high school students, before- and after-school extracurricular activities (except sports) also are classified as educational activities.

Organizational, civic, and religious activities. This category captures time spent volunteering for or through an organization, performing civic obligations, and participating in religious and spiritual activities.

Leisure and sports. The leisure and sports category includes sports, exercise, and recreation; socializing and communicating; and other leisure activities, such as watching television, reading or attending entertainment events.

Telephone calls, mail, and e-mail. This category captures telephone communication and handling household or personal mail and e-mail. Telephone and Internet purchases are classified in purchasing goods and services.

Other activities, not elsewhere classified. This residual category includes security procedures related to traveling, traveling not associated with a specific activity category, ambiguous activities that could not be coded, or missing activities that were considered too private to report.

Sources of Additional Information

Additional information, including expanded definitions and estimation methodology, is available from BLS news release USDL 07-0930, "American Time Use Survey, 2006"; the June 2005 edition of the *Monthly Labor Review*; and the *ATUS User's Guide*, June 2007. All of these resources are available on the BLS Web site at <http://www.bls.gov>.

Table 12-1. Average Hours Per Day Spent in Primary Activities[1] for the Total Population and for Persons Reporting the Activity on the Diary Day, by Activity Category and Sex, 2006 Annual Averages

(Number, percent.)

Activity	Hours per day, total population			Percent of population reporting the activity on the diary day			Hours per day, persons reporting the activity on the diary day		
	Both sexes	Men	Women	Both sexes	Men	Women	Both sexes	Men	Women
All Activities[2]	24.00	24.00	24.00	X	X	X	X	X	X
Personal care activities	9.41	9.21	9.59	100.0	100.0	100.0	9.41	9.22	9.59
Sleeping	8.63	8.56	8.69	99.9	99.9	100.0	8.63	8.57	8.69
Eating and drinking	1.23	1.25	1.22	96.0	96.0	96.1	1.29	1.31	1.27
Household activities	1.79	1.33	2.23	74.0	63.7	83.6	2.42	2.09	2.66
Housework	0.61	0.25	0.95	36.1	19.5	51.8	1.69	1.27	1.83
Food preparation and cleanup	0.53	0.29	0.75	51.6	37.1	65.2	1.02	0.79	1.15
Lawn and garden care	0.20	0.26	0.14	10.3	11.8	8.9	1.92	2.22	1.55
Household management	0.13	0.11	0.14	18.5	15.4	21.4	0.68	0.70	0.67
Purchasing goods and services	0.81	0.64	0.96	45.5	40.3	50.3	1.78	1.60	1.91
Consumer goods purchases	0.40	0.29	0.51	41.1	36.3	45.6	0.98	0.80	1.12
Professional and personal care services	0.09	0.06	0.11	8.8	6.4	11.0	0.98	0.98	0.99
Caring for and helping household members	0.53	0.33	0.71	25.2	19.9	30.2	2.09	1.64	2.37
Caring for and helping household children	0.41	0.24	0.57	21.6	16.5	26.4	1.90	1.48	2.15
Caring for and helping non-household members	0.21	0.18	0.24	13.1	11.3	14.8	1.63	1.63	1.62
Caring for and helping non-household adults	0.07	0.07	0.08	8.1	7.5	8.7	0.92	0.93	0.91
Working and work-related activities	3.75	4.53	3.02	46.5	52.6	40.8	8.06	8.60	7.40
Working	3.40	4.10	2.74	44.8	51.0	39.0	7.59	8.04	7.04
Educational activities	0.49	0.45	0.53	9.4	8.6	10.1	5.20	5.19	5.21
Attending class	0.30	0.29	0.32	6.8	6.4	7.1	4.51	4.55	4.47
Homework and research	0.15	0.12	0.17	6.0	5.2	6.8	2.42	2.35	2.46
Organizational, civic, and religious activities	0.30	0.29	0.31	13.3	12.0	14.5	2.26	2.39	2.16
Religious and spiritual activities	0.12	0.11	0.13	7.7	6.5	8.8	1.57	1.62	1.54
Volunteering (organizational and civic activities)	0.13	0.13	0.13	6.7	6.2	7.1	2.00	2.14	1.88
Leisure and sports	5.09	5.47	4.72	96.4	96.4	96.4	5.28	5.68	4.90
Socializing and communicating	0.76	0.71	0.80	40.4	37.4	43.2	1.87	1.90	1.84
Watching television	2.58	2.80	2.36	79.5	80.8	78.2	3.24	3.46	3.02
Participating in sports, exercise, and recreation	0.28	0.38	0.18	17.1	19.5	14.8	1.64	1.96	1.24
Telephone calls, mail, and e-mail	0.19	0.12	0.26	25.9	19.2	32.3	0.73	0.63	0.79
Other activities n.e.c.	0.21	0.20	0.22	13.9	12.2	15.5	1.50	1.64	1.39

Note: Data refer to respondents age 15 years and over, unless otherwise specified.

n.e.c. = Not elsewhere classified.

[1]A primary activity is designated by a respondent as his or her main activity. Other activities done simultaneously are not included.
[2]All major activity categories include related travel time.
X = Not applicable.

Table 12-2. Average Hours Per Day Spent in Primary Activities[1] for the Total Population, by Age, Sex, Race, Hispanic Origin, and Educational Attainment, 2006 Annual Averages

(Number.)

Characteristic	Hours per day spent in primary activities[2]											
	Personal care activities	Eating and drinking	Household activities	Purchasing goods and services	Caring for and helping household members	Caring for and helping non-household members	Working and work-related activities	Edu-cational activities	Organiza-tional, civic, and religious activities	Leisure activities	Telephone calls, mail, and e-mail	Other activities n.e.c.
Both Sexes, 15 Years and Over	9.41	1.23	1.79	0.81	0.53	0.21	3.75	0.49	0.30	5.09	0.19	0.21
15 to 19 years	10.30	1.07	0.76	0.56	0.15	0.21	1.39	3.29	0.34	5.40	0.33	0.22
20 to 24 years	9.64	1.21	1.05	0.67	0.51	0.20	4.23	0.80	0.21	5.03	0.19	0.24
25 to 34 years	9.31	1.19	1.55	0.81	1.07	0.12	4.77	0.39	0.16	4.30	0.14	0.17
35 to 44 years	9.12	1.18	1.87	0.87	0.98	0.19	4.96	0.15	0.30	4.09	0.13	0.16
45 to 54 years	9.10	1.17	1.97	0.82	0.36	0.24	5.06	0.09	0.29	4.52	0.17	0.20
55 to 64 years	9.19	1.31	2.11	0.91	0.16	0.28	3.80	0.04	0.39	5.41	0.18	0.20
65 to 74 years	9.68	1.44	2.64	0.93	0.13	0.30	0.94	0.05	0.38	6.97	0.24	0.29
75 years and over	9.83	1.50	2.32	0.80	0.12	0.21	0.34	0.06	0.43	7.82	0.30	0.27
Men, 15 Years and Over	9.21	1.25	1.33	0.64	0.33	0.18	4.53	0.45	0.29	5.47	0.12	0.20
15 to 19 years	10.26	1.02	0.61	0.38	0.10	0.20	1.53	3.08	0.34	6.02	0.24	0.23
20 to 24 years	9.36	1.23	0.84	0.46	0.12	0.22	4.62	0.65	0.23	5.80	0.17	0.27
25 to 34 years	9.10	1.20	1.03	0.62	0.50	0.11	6.00	0.38	0.15	4.66	0.10	0.16
35 to 44 years	8.93	1.22	1.28	0.66	0.66	0.14	6.13	0.06	0.28	4.42	0.07	0.15
45 to 54 years	8.85	1.21	1.50	0.64	0.32	0.21	5.85	0.06	0.29	4.81	0.09	0.18
55 to 64 years	8.97	1.34	1.70	0.79	0.13	0.21	4.26	0.03	0.37	5.90	0.11	0.20
65 to 74 years	9.74	1.51	2.20	0.87	0.12	0.30	1.07	0.02	0.34	7.36	0.13	0.33
75 years and over	9.60	1.52	1.77	0.75	0.17	0.19	0.61	0.04	0.44	8.49	0.18	0.23
Women, 15 Years and Over	9.59	1.22	2.23	0.96	0.71	0.24	3.02	0.53	0.31	4.72	0.26	0.22
15 to 19 years	10.34	1.11	0.92	0.74	0.19	0.23	1.24	3.51	0.33	4.75	0.42	0.21
20 to 24 years	9.93	1.20	1.26	0.87	0.91	0.17	3.83	0.96	0.19	4.24	0.21	0.22
25 to 34 years	9.53	1.18	2.08	0.99	1.64	0.14	3.54	0.40	0.18	3.95	0.19	0.18
35 to 44 years	9.31	1.15	2.45	1.07	1.30	0.24	3.81	0.23	0.32	3.77	0.18	0.18
45 to 54 years	9.35	1.12	2.42	1.00	0.40	0.27	4.31	0.12	0.29	4.25	0.24	0.23
55 to 64 years	9.40	1.28	2.49	1.01	0.19	0.35	3.37	0.05	0.42	4.96	0.25	0.21
65 to 74 years	9.63	1.39	3.01	0.97	0.14	0.30	0.83	0.07	0.41	6.65	0.34	0.26
75 years and over	9.98	1.48	2.68	0.83	0.09	0.22	0.17	0.07	0.43	7.38	0.37	0.30
White, 15 Years and Over	9.30	1.28	1.85	0.81	0.53	0.21	3.76	0.47	0.29	5.09	0.18	0.21
Men	9.11	1.31	1.37	0.64	0.33	0.19	4.61	0.42	0.28	5.42	0.11	0.21
Women	9.49	1.25	2.31	0.98	0.71	0.24	2.96	0.52	0.30	4.76	0.25	0.22
Black, 15 Years and Over	10.08	0.87	1.38	0.75	0.46	0.20	3.54	0.43	0.37	5.49	0.25	0.18
Men	9.93	0.81	0.98	0.64	0.22	0.18	3.97	0.50	0.36	6.10	0.17	0.14
Women	10.19	0.92	1.72	0.83	0.67	0.21	3.19	0.38	0.38	4.99	0.32	0.20
Hispanic,[3] 15 Years and Over	9.67	1.18	1.85	0.77	0.60	0.15	3.92	0.69	0.23	4.63	0.13	0.18
Men	9.60	1.20	1.17	0.56	0.31	0.14	4.95	0.71	0.19	4.92	0.11	0.15
Women	9.75	1.16	2.58	0.99	0.92	0.16	2.81	0.67	0.28	4.31	0.15	0.21
Marital Status and Sex												
Married, spouse present	9.12	1.28	2.09	0.88	0.75	0.21	4.08	0.11	0.33	4.79	0.14	0.21
Men	8.90	1.31	1.49	0.73	0.51	0.18	5.04	0.07	0.33	5.16	0.08	0.21
Women	9.35	1.25	2.69	1.04	1.00	0.24	3.12	0.15	0.32	4.41	0.20	0.22
Other marital statuses	9.75	1.18	1.43	0.72	0.25	0.22	3.34	0.94	0.27	5.45	0.25	0.20
Men	9.63	1.18	1.13	0.53	0.09	0.19	3.86	0.93	0.23	5.87	0.17	0.19
Women	9.86	1.17	1.70	0.88	0.39	0.24	2.89	0.95	0.30	5.08	0.32	0.21
Educational Attainment, 25 Years and Over												
Less than a high school diploma	9.86	1.10	2.38	0.80	0.50	0.20	2.57	0.04	0.25	6.01	0.10	0.17
High school graduate, no college[4]	9.42	1.19	2.05	0.76	0.46	0.25	3.58	0.07	0.28	5.57	0.15	0.21
Some college or associate degree	9.21	1.24	1.94	0.92	0.58	0.23	4.25	0.22	0.29	4.76	0.19	0.18
Bachelor's degree and higher[5]	8.94	1.41	1.77	0.91	0.71	0.18	4.72	0.22	0.37	4.33	0.22	0.23

Note: Data refer to persons age 15 years and over, unless otherwise specified

n.e.c. = Not elsewhere classified.

[1]A primary activity is designated by a respondent as his or her main activity. Other activities done simultaneously are not included.
[2]All major activity categories include related travel time.
[3]May be of any race.
[4]Includes persons with a high school diploma or equivalent.
[5]Includes persons with bachelor's, master's, professional, and doctoral degrees.

Table 12-3. Average Hours Worked Per Day by Employed Persons on Weekdays and Weekends, by Selected Characteristics, 2006 Annual Averages

(Number, percent.)

Characteristic	Total employed (thousands)	Worked on an average day			Worked on an average weekday			Worked on an average Saturday, Sunday, or holiday[1]		
		Number (thousands)	Percent	Hours per day[2]	Number[3] (thousands)	Percent	Hours per day[2]	Number[4] (thousands)	Percent	Hours per day[2]
Both Sexes[5]	151 175	104 048	68.8	7.60	126 176	83.5	7.99	52 673	34.8	5.43
Full-time worker	117 880	85 035	72.1	8.12	104 111	88.3	8.54	40 760	34.6	5.59
Part-time worker	33 295	19 012	57.1	5.30	22 067	66.3	5.40	11 914	35.8	4.87
Men[5]	80 637	57 426	71.2	8.04	69 041	85.6	8.47	30 198	37.4	5.75
Full-time worker	68 954	50 722	73.6	8.44	61 214	88.8	8.89	25 697	37.3	5.82
Part-time worker	11 684	6 704	57.4	5.08	7 747	66.3	5.01	4 491	38.4	5.34
Women[5]	70 538	46 622	66.1	7.06	57 124	81.0	7.41	22 506	31.9	5.00
Full-time worker	48 926	34 314	70.1	7.65	42 891	87.7	8.03	15 146	31.0	5.21
Part-time worker	21 611	12 308	57.0	5.42	14 320	66.3	5.60	7 390	34.2	4.55
Multiple Job Holding Status										
Single job holder	135 379	91 292	67.4	7.53	112 022	82.7	7.90	43 576	32.2	5.40
Multiple job holder	15 795	12 756	80.8	8.08	14 130	89.5	8.75	9 317	59.0	5.55
Educational Attainment, 25 Years and Over										
Less than a high school diploma	11 035	7 301	66.2	7.87	9 279	84.1	7.96	2 713	24.6	([6])
High school graduate, no college[7]	36 699	24 815	67.6	8.05	30 589	83.4	8.28	11 539	31.4	6.67
Some college or associate degree	34 941	24 388	69.8	7.74	29 668	84.9	8.13	11 780	33.7	5.38
Bachelor's degree or higher[8]	44 584	32 735	73.4	7.38	39 511	88.6	8.06	17 335	38.9	3.87

Note: Data refer to persons age 15 years and over, unless otherwise specified.

[1]Holidays are New Year's Day, Easter, Memorial Day, the Fourth of July, Labor Day, Thanksgiving Day, and Christmas Day.
[2]Includes work at main and other job(s) and excludes travel related to work.
[3]Number was derived by multiplying the "total employed" by the percentage of employed persons who worked on an average weekday.
[4]Number was derived by multiplying the "total employed" by the percentage of employed persons who worked on an average Saturday, Sunday, or holiday.
[5]Includes workers whose hours vary.
[6]Data not shown where base is less than 1.2 million.
[7]Includes persons with a high school diploma or equivalent.
[8]Includes persons with bachelor's, master's, professional, and doctoral degrees.

Table 12-4. Average Hours Worked Per Day at Main Job Only by Employed Persons on Weekdays and Weekend Days, by Selected Characteristics, 2006 Annual Averages

(Number, percent.)

Characteristic	Total employed (thousands)	Worked on an average day			Worked on an average weekday			Worked on an average Saturday, Sunday, or holiday[1]		
		Number (thousands)	Percent	Hours per day[2]	Number[3] (thousands)	Percent	Hours per day[2]	Number[4] (thousands)	Percent	Hours per day[2]
Class of Worker										
Wage and salary workers	139 901	94 208	67.3	7.61	115 885	82.8	7.95	43 855	31.3	5.51
Self-employed workers	11 115	7 964	71.6	6.40	9 031	81.3	6.92	5 458	49.1	4.40
Occupation										
Management, business, and financial operations	21 568	16 135	74.8	7.69	19 626	91.0	8.33	8 103	37.6	4.17
Professional and related	32 540	22 872	70.3	7.21	28 124	86.4	7.79	10 336	31.8	3.48
Services	25 897	15 804	61.0	7.07	18 051	69.7	7.19	10 355	40.0	6.56
Sales and related	17 208	11 879	69.0	7.28	13 530	78.6	7.60	8 234	47.9	6.11
Office and administrative support	20 337	12 669	62.3	7.32	16 287	80.1	7.54	4 075	20.0	5.21
Farming, fishing, and forestry	(5)	(5)	(5)	(5)	(5)	(5)	(5)	(5)	(5)	(5)
Construction and extraction	8 202	5 338	65.1	8.08	7 274	88.7	8.34	1 331	16.2	(5)
Installation, maintenance, and repair	5 510	3 880	70.4	8.16	4 871	88.4	8.37	1 441	26.1	(5)
Production	9 745	6 627	68.0	8.13	8 560	87.8	8.39	2 590	26.6	(5)
Transportation and material moving	9 055	6 300	69.6	8.32	7 824	86.4	8.32	2 705	29.9	(5)
Earnings of Full-Time Wage and Salary Earners[6]										
$0 to $460	26 950	18 575	68.9	7.73	22 950	85.2	7.86	8 662	32.1	6.92
$461 to $710	26 514	17 650	66.6	8.05	22 026	83.1	8.34	6 772	25.5	5.76
$711 to $1,100	27 002	19 427	71.9	8.24	24 633	91.2	8.58	7 462	27.6	5.66
$1,101 and higher	26 546	19 256	72.5	8.08	23 784	89.6	8.72	9 022	34.0	4.26

Note: Data refer to persons age 15 years and over, unless otherwise specified.

[1]Holidays are New Year's Day, Easter, Memorial Day, the Fourth of July, Labor Day, Thanksgiving Day, and Christmas Day.
[2]Includes work at main job only and excludes travel related to work.
[3]Number was derived by multiplying the "total employed" by the percentage of employed persons who worked on an average weekday.
[4]Number was derived by multiplying the "total employed" by the percentage of employed persons who worked on an average Saturday, Sunday, or holiday.
[5]Data not shown where base is less than 1.2 million.
[6]These values are based on usual weekly earnings. Each earnings range represents approximately 25 percent of full-time wage and salary workers.

Table 12-5. Average Hours Worked Per Day at All Jobs by Employed Persons at Workplaces or at Home, by Selected Characteristics, 2006 Annual Averages

(Number, percent.)

Characteristic	Total employed (thousands)	Employed persons who reported working on an average day[1]								
		Number (thousands)	Percent	Hours of work	Location of work[2]					
					Persons who reported working at their workplaces on an average day			Persons who reported working at home on an average day[3]		
					Number (thousands)	Percent	Hours of work at workplace	Number (thousands)	Percent	Hours of work at home
Full and Part-time Status and Sex										
Both sexes[4]	151 175	104 048	68.8	7.60	89 664	86.2	7.87	21 980	21.1	2.64
Full-time worker	117 880	85 035	72.1	8.12	74 487	87.6	8.31	17 729	20.8	2.76
Part-time worker	33 295	19 012	57.1	5.30	15 177	79.8	5.74	4 251	22.4	2.17
Men[4]	80 637	57 426	71.2	8.04	49 741	86.6	8.28	12 386	21.6	2.60
Full-time worker	68 954	50 722	73.6	8.44	44 428	87.6	8.61	10 828	21.3	2.69
Part-time worker	11 684	6 704	57.4	5.08	5 313	79.2	5.59	1 558	23.2	2.01
Women[4]	70 538	46 622	66.1	7.06	39 923	85.6	7.36	9 594	20.6	2.70
Full-time worker	48 926	34 314	70.1	7.65	30 059	87.6	7.87	6 901	20.1	2.87
Part-time worker	21 611	12 308	57.0	5.42	9 865	80.1	5.82	2 693	21.9	2.27
Multiple Job Holding Status										
Single job holder	135 379	91 292	67.4	7.53	79 351	86.9	7.85	17 054	18.7	2.47
Multiple job holder	15 795	12 756	80.8	8.08	10 313	80.8	8.05	4 926	38.6	3.24
Educational Attainment, 25 Years and Over										
Less than a high school diploma	11 035	7 301	66.2	7.87	6 869	94.1	7.92	402	5.5	(5)
High school graduate, no college[6]	36 699	24 815	67.6	8.05	22 402	90.3	8.15	3 227	13.0	2.94
Some college or associate degree	34 941	24 388	69.8	7.74	21 212	87.0	8.04	4 983	20.4	2.39
Bachelor's degree or higher[7]	44 584	32 735	73.4	7.38	25 496	77.9	7.88	12 104	37.0	2.71

Note: Data refer to persons age 15 years and over, unless otherwise specified.

[1]Includes work at main and other job(s) and excludes travel related to work.
[2]Respondents may have worked at more than one location.
[3]"Working at home" includes any time the respondent reported doing activities that were identified as "part of one's job"; this category is not restricted to persons whose usual workplace is their home.
[4]Includes workers whose hours vary.
[5]Data not shown where base is less than 1.2 million.
[6]Includes persons with a high school diploma or equivalent.
[7]Includes persons with bachelor's, master's, professional, and doctoral degrees.

Table 12-6. Average Hours Worked Per Day at Main Job Only by Employed Persons at Workplaces or at Home, by Selected Characteristics, 2006 Annual Averages

(Number, percent.)

Characteristic	Total employed (thousands)	Employed persons who reported working on an average day[1]								
		Number (thousands)	Percent	Hours of work	Location of work[2]					
					Persons who reported working at their workplaces on an average day			Persons who reported working at home on an average day[3]		
					Number (thousands)	Percent	Hours of work at workplace	Number (thousands)	Percent	Hours of work at home
Class of Worker										
Wage and salary worker	139 901	94 208	67.3	7.61	84 013	89.2	7.85	15 557	16.5	2.27
Self-employed worker	11 115	7 964	71.6	6.40	4 565	57.3	7.10	4 447	55.8	3.51
Occupation										
Management, business, and financial operations	21 568	16 135	74.8	7.69	12 757	79.1	8.13	5 206	32.3	2.91
Professional and related	32 540	22 872	70.3	7.21	18 739	81.9	7.69	7 592	33.2	2.03
Services	25 897	15 804	61.0	7.07	13 981	88.5	7.21	1 918	12.1	4.28
Sales and related	17 208	11 879	69.0	7.28	10 164	85.6	7.68	2 415	20.3	2.44
Office and administrative support	20 337	12 669	62.3	7.32	11 725	92.5	7.65	1 039	8.2	([4])
Farming, fishing, and forestry	([4])	([4])	([4])	([4])	([4])	([4])	([4])	([4])	([4])	([4])
Construction and extraction	8 202	5 338	65.1	8.08	4 861	91.1	8.13	776	14.5	([4])
Installation, maintenance, and repair	5 510	3 880	70.4	8.16	3 618	93.2	8.19	423	10.9	([4])
Production	9 745	6 627	68.0	8.13	6 395	96.5	8.23	249	3.8	([4])
Transportation and material moving	9 055	6 300	69.6	8.32	5 670	90.0	8.35	384	6.1	([4])
Earnings of Full-Time Wage and Salary Earners[5]										
$0 to $460	26 950	18 575	68.9	7.73	17 561	94.5	7.81	1 431	7.7	3.03
$461 to $710	26 514	17 650	66.6	8.05	16 328	92.5	8.23	1 954	11.1	1.70
$711 to $1,100	27 002	19 427	71.9	8.24	17 613	90.7	8.46	3 155	16.2	1.77
$1,101 and higher	26 546	19 256	72.5	8.08	16 212	84.2	8.49	5 576	29.0	2.25

Note: Data refer to persons age 15 years and over, unless otherwise specified.

[1]Includes work at main job only and excludes travel related to work.
[2]Respondents may have worked at more than one location.
[3]"Working at home" includes any time the respondent reported doing activities that were identified as "part of one's job"; this category is not restricted to persons whose usual workplace is their home.
[4]Data not shown where base is less than 1.2 million.
[5]These values are based on usual weekly earnings. Each earnings range covers approximately 25 percent of full-time wage and salary workers.

Table 12-7. Average Hours Per Day Spent by Persons Age 18 Years and Over Caring for Household Children Under 18 Years, by Sex of Respondent, Age of Youngest Household Child, and Day, 2003–2006 Annual Averages

(Number.)

Activity	Hours per day caring for household children								
	Total			Weekdays			Weekends and holidays[1]		
	Both sexes	Men	Women	Both sexes	Men	Women	Both sexes	Men	Women
Persons in Households with Children Under 18 Years									
Caring for household children as a primary activity	1.31	0.82	1.73	1.40	0.79	1.92	1.31	0.82	1.73
Physical care	0.45	0.22	0.64	0.48	0.21	0.70	0.45	0.22	0.64
Education-related activities	0.10	0.06	0.13	0.13	0.08	0.17	0.10	0.06	0.13
Reading to/with children	0.04	0.02	0.05	0.04	0.02	0.05	0.04	0.02	0.05
Talking to/with children	0.05	0.03	0.07	0.06	0.03	0.08	0.05	0.03	0.07
Playing/doing hobbies with children	0.25	0.22	0.28	0.24	0.19	0.28	0.25	0.22	0.28
Looking after children	0.07	0.06	0.09	0.07	0.05	0.08	0.07	0.06	0.09
Attending children's events	0.06	0.05	0.06	0.05	0.04	0.05	0.06	0.05	0.06
Travel related to care of household children	0.17	0.11	0.23	0.21	0.12	0.28	0.17	0.11	0.23
Other childcare activities	0.12	0.06	0.17	0.14	0.06	0.21	0.12	0.06	0.17
Persons in Households with Youngest Child 6 to 17 Years									
Caring for household children as a primary activity	0.78	0.49	1.02	0.86	0.51	1.16	0.78	0.49	1.02
Physical care	0.15	0.07	0.23	0.17	0.07	0.26	0.15	0.07	0.23
Education-related activities	0.12	0.07	0.16	0.15	0.09	0.20	0.12	0.07	0.16
Reading to/with children	0.02	0.01	0.02	0.02	0.01	0.02	0.02	0.01	0.02
Talking to/with children	0.07	0.03	0.10	0.08	0.04	0.11	0.07	0.03	0.10
Playing/doing hobbies with children	0.05	0.07	0.05	0.05	0.06	0.04	0.05	0.07	0.05
Looking after children	0.04	0.03	0.05	0.04	0.03	0.05	0.04	0.03	0.05
Attending children's events	0.07	0.06	0.08	0.06	0.05	0.07	0.07	0.06	0.08
Travel related to care of household children	0.16	0.10	0.21	0.19	0.12	0.25	0.16	0.10	0.21
Other childcare activities	0.10	0.05	0.13	0.11	0.05	0.17	0.10	0.05	0.13
Persons in Households with Youngest Child Under 6 Years									
Caring for household children as a primary activity	1.96	1.22	2.58	2.06	1.15	2.83	1.96	1.22	2.58
Physical care	0.81	0.41	1.15	0.85	0.39	1.23	0.81	0.41	1.15
Education-related activities	0.08	0.05	0.10	0.10	0.06	0.14	0.08	0.05	0.10
Reading to/with children	0.06	0.03	0.08	0.06	0.03	0.09	0.06	0.03	0.08
Talking to/with children	0.03	0.02	0.04	0.04	0.02	0.05	0.03	0.02	0.04
Playing/doing hobbies with children	0.49	0.41	0.56	0.47	0.35	0.57	0.49	0.41	0.56
Looking after children	0.12	0.10	0.13	0.11	0.08	0.13	0.12	0.10	0.13
Attending children's events	0.04	0.03	0.04	0.03	0.02	0.04	0.04	0.03	0.04
Travel related to care of household children	0.18	0.11	0.25	0.23	0.12	0.32	0.18	0.11	0.25
Other childcare activities	0.15	0.07	0.22	0.18	0.07	0.27	0.15	0.07	0.22

Note: Universe includes respondents age 18 years and over living in households with children under 18 years of age, whether or not they provided childcare.

[1]Holidays are New Year's Day, Easter, Memorial Day, the Fourth of July, Labor Day, Thanksgiving Day, and Christmas Day. Data were not collected for Christmas Day in 2003 or Thanksgiving Day from 2003 to 2005.

Table 12-8. Average Hours Per Day Spent in Primary Activities[1] by the Total Population Age 18 Years and Over, by Activity Category, Employment Status, Presence and Age of Household Children, and Sex, 2006 Annual Averages

(Number.)

Activity	Hours spent per day in primary activities								
	Household with children under 6 years			Household with children 6 to 17 years			Household with no children under 18 years		
	Both sexes	Men	Women	Both sexes	Men	Women	Both sexes	Men	Women
TOTAL									
All Activities[2]	24.00	24.00	24.00	24.00	24.00	24.00	24.00	24.00	24.00
Personal care activities	9.22	8.90	9.48	9.29	9.08	9.48	9.42	9.22	9.61
Sleeping	8.60	8.35	8.80	8.51	8.42	8.60	8.59	8.55	8.64
Eating and drinking	1.16	1.23	1.10	1.14	1.15	1.13	1.31	1.32	1.30
Household activities	1.94	1.25	2.49	1.93	1.36	2.43	1.82	1.43	2.21
Housework	0.73	0.26	1.12	0.70	0.26	1.09	0.58	0.25	0.90
Food preparation and cleanup	0.69	0.33	0.99	0.61	0.33	0.87	0.50	0.30	0.70
Lawn and garden care	0.15	0.23	0.09	0.17	0.25	0.11	0.23	0.29	0.18
Household management	0.11	0.09	0.13	0.12	0.09	0.14	0.14	0.12	0.16
Purchasing goods and services	0.83	0.63	0.99	0.90	0.71	1.06	0.81	0.67	0.94
Consumer goods purchases	0.45	0.33	0.55	0.46	0.30	0.60	0.39	0.29	0.48
Professional and personal care services	0.07	0.04	0.09	0.07	0.04	0.10	0.10	0.08	0.12
Caring for and helping household members	1.98	1.24	2.57	0.81	0.55	1.03	0.07	0.05	0.08
Caring for and helping household children	1.76	1.09	2.30	0.61	0.40	0.80	X	X	X
Caring for and helping non-household members	0.12	0.10	0.14	0.16	0.16	0.16	0.26	0.22	0.31
Caring for and helping non-household adults	0.06	0.04	0.08	0.06	0.07	0.04	0.09	0.08	0.10
Working and work-related activities[3]	4.21	6.06	2.71	4.44	5.44	3.57	3.68	4.24	3.13
Working[3]	3.82	5.46	2.49	4.03	4.90	3.26	3.35	3.87	2.84
Educational activities	0.16	0.13	0.18	0.27	0.20	0.32	0.29	0.23	0.34
Attending class	0.07	0.05	0.09	0.12	0.11	0.12	0.14	0.11	0.17
Homework and research	0.08	0.07	0.08	0.12	0.08	0.16	0.12	0.11	0.14
Organizational, civic, and religious activities	0.24	0.22	0.25	0.32	0.29	0.34	0.30	0.29	0.31
Religious and spiritual activities	0.10	0.09	0.11	0.12	0.10	0.14	0.12	0.10	0.14
Volunteering (organizational and civic activities)	0.10	0.10	0.10	0.15	0.14	0.15	0.13	0.13	0.13
Leisure and sports	3.86	4.04	3.71	4.38	4.71	4.08	5.63	5.99	5.26
Socializing and communicating	0.75	0.72	0.78	0.75	0.72	0.77	0.74	0.70	0.79
Watching television	1.97	2.02	1.92	2.20	2.39	2.03	2.92	3.18	2.66
Participating in sports, exercise, and recreation	0.21	0.29	0.15	0.27	0.39	0.17	0.26	0.33	0.18
Telephone calls, mail, and e-mail	0.12	0.05	0.18	0.14	0.10	0.18	0.21	0.13	0.29
Other activities n.e.c.	0.17	0.14	0.19	0.23	0.24	0.23	0.21	0.20	0.22
EMPLOYED									
All Activities[2]	24.00	24.00	24.00	24.00	24.00	24.00	24.00	24.00	24.00
Personal care activities	8.98	8.73	9.31	9.08	8.79	9.37	9.12	8.89	9.38
Sleeping	8.34	8.19	8.54	8.31	8.17	8.46	8.31	8.19	8.44
Eating and drinking	1.18	1.24	1.10	1.14	1.16	1.13	1.28	1.31	1.24
Household activities	1.49	1.16	1.92	1.68	1.30	2.07	1.39	1.15	1.66
Housework	0.51	0.24	0.86	0.55	0.22	0.89	0.39	0.21	0.61
Food preparation and cleanup	0.48	0.29	0.73	0.52	0.31	0.74	0.36	0.23	0.51
Lawn and garden care	0.15	0.21	0.07	0.18	0.24	0.11	0.17	0.20	0.14
Household management	0.11	0.10	0.13	0.11	0.09	0.13	0.12	0.11	0.13
Purchasing goods and services	0.78	0.63	0.98	0.82	0.69	0.95	0.75	0.59	0.94
Consumer goods purchases	0.41	0.33	0.52	0.42	0.31	0.54	0.37	0.27	0.49
Professional and personal care services	0.06	0.03	0.10	0.06	0.04	0.09	0.08	0.06	0.10
Caring for and helping household members	1.60	1.20	2.13	0.72	0.53	0.91	0.04	0.03	0.05
Caring for and helping household children	1.40	1.05	1.86	0.54	0.39	0.70	X	X	X
Caring for and helping non-household members	0.09	0.09	0.09	0.15	0.17	0.14	0.23	0.20	0.27
Caring for and helping non-household adults	0.03	0.04	0.03	0.06	0.07	0.04	0.09	0.08	0.10
Working and work-related activities	5.78	6.61	4.70	5.66	6.44	4.86	5.88	6.26	5.45
Working	5.29	5.98	4.38	5.18	5.84	4.50	5.40	5.75	4.99
Educational activities	0.14	0.12	0.16	0.21	0.16	0.26	0.26	0.20	0.33
Attending class	0.06	0.05	0.09	0.08	0.08	0.08	0.12	0.09	0.16
Homework and research	0.06	0.06	0.06	0.12	0.07	0.16	0.12	0.10	0.14
Organizational, civic, and religious activities	0.23	0.21	0.25	0.31	0.30	0.31	0.24	0.26	0.22
Religious and spiritual activities	0.10	0.10	0.11	0.11	0.10	0.13	0.09	0.09	0.09
Volunteering (organizational and civic activities)	0.09	0.08	0.10	0.15	0.16	0.14	0.10	0.11	0.09
Leisure and sports	3.51	3.85	3.06	3.90	4.17	3.63	4.49	4.84	4.08
Socializing and communicating	0.73	0.71	0.75	0.67	0.63	0.71	0.66	0.63	0.70
Watching television	1.71	1.90	1.46	1.93	2.12	1.74	2.26	2.46	2.02
Participating in sports, exercise, and recreation	0.22	0.29	0.12	0.24	0.33	0.15	0.26	0.33	0.19
Telephone calls, mail, and e-mail	0.10	0.05	0.16	0.11	0.08	0.14	0.17	0.11	0.23
Other activities n.e.c.	0.14	0.12	0.16	0.21	0.20	0.22	0.16	0.16	0.15

n.e.c. = Not elsewhere classified.

[1]A primary activity is designated by a respondent as his or her main activity. Other activities done simultaneously are not included.
[2]All major activity categories include related travel time.
[3]Estimates include a small amount of work time done by persons who do not meet the American Time Use Survey (ATUS) definition for employed.
X = Not applicable.

Table 12-8. Average Hours Per Day Spent in Primary Activities[1] by the Total Population Age 18 Years and Over, by Activity Category, Employment Status, Presence and Age of Household Children, and Sex, 2006 Annual Averages—*Continued*

(Number.)

Activity	Hours spent per day in primary activities								
	Household with children under 6 years			Household with children 6 to 17 years			Household with no children under 18 years		
	Both sexes	Men	Women	Both sexes	Men	Women	Both sexes	Men	Women
NOT EMPLOYED									
All Activities[2]	24.00	24.00	24.00	24.00	24.00	24.00	24.00	24.00	24.00
Personal care activities	9.84	10.62	9.71	10.04	10.61	9.75	9.90	9.90	9.90
Sleeping	9.26	9.97	9.14	9.21	9.72	8.95	9.06	9.27	8.90
Eating and drinking	1.12	1.22	1.10	1.12	1.09	1.13	1.36	1.35	1.38
Household activities	3.08	2.13	3.24	2.80	1.72	3.35	2.53	1.98	2.94
Housework	1.32	0.43	1.47	1.21	0.44	1.60	0.89	0.35	1.30
Food preparation and cleanup	1.24	0.69	1.33	0.94	0.42	1.21	0.72	0.42	0.95
Lawn and garden care	0.15	0.43	0.10	0.16	0.26	0.11	0.34	0.49	0.22
Household management	0.11	0.03	0.13	0.15	0.13	0.16	0.18	0.14	0.20
Purchasing goods and services	0.95	0.63	1.00	1.17	0.85	1.33	0.90	0.82	0.96
Consumer goods purchases	0.56	0.39	0.59	0.59	0.25	0.77	0.41	0.34	0.46
Professional and personal care services	0.08	0.07	0.09	0.10	0.04	0.13	0.14	0.12	0.15
Caring for and helping household members	2.94	1.68	3.15	1.11	0.63	1.36	0.12	0.10	0.13
Caring for and helping household children	2.67	1.53	2.86	0.86	0.47	1.06	X	X	X
Caring for and helping non-household members	0.21	0.18	0.21	0.18	0.13	0.20	0.32	0.27	0.36
Caring for and helping non-household adults	0.12	0.06	0.13	0.06	0.07	0.05	0.09	0.09	0.10
Working and work-related activities[3]	0.18	0.56	0.12	0.20	0.23	0.19	0.10	0.15	0.07
Working[3]	0.04	0.10	0.03	0.03	0.00	0.04	0.02	0.05	0.00
Educational activities	0.22	0.25	0.22	0.44	0.41	0.46	0.33	0.30	0.35
Attending class	0.09	0.03	0.10	0.25	0.26	0.24	0.17	0.15	0.18
Homework and research	0.12	0.19	0.10	0.15	0.12	0.17	0.13	0.12	0.14
Organizational, civic, and religious activities	0.26	0.31	0.25	0.35	0.22	0.41	0.39	0.34	0.43
Religious and spiritual activities	0.11	0.07	0.12	0.16	0.11	0.18	0.16	0.13	0.19
Volunteering (organizational and civic activities)	0.12	0.22	0.10	0.14	0.06	0.18	0.17	0.17	0.18
Leisure and sports	4.76	5.97	4.56	6.02	7.55	5.25	7.48	8.33	6.83
Socializing and communicating	0.81	0.75	0.82	1.03	1.23	0.93	0.87	0.84	0.89
Watching television	2.63	3.22	2.53	3.14	3.79	2.80	4.00	4.64	3.51
Participating in sports, exercise, and recreation	0.20	0.31	0.18	0.38	0.71	0.21	0.24	0.35	0.16
Telephone calls, mail, and e-mail	0.18	0.04	0.20	0.26	0.15	0.31	0.27	0.16	0.36
Other activities n.e.c.	0.25	0.40	0.22	0.31	0.44	0.24	0.30	0.29	0.30

n.e.c. = Not elsewhere classified.

[1]A primary activity is designated by a respondent as his or her main activity. Other activities done simultaneously are not included.
[2]All major activity categories include related travel time.
[3]Estimates include a small amount of work time done by persons who do not meet the American Time Use Survey (ATUS) definition for employed.
X = Not applicable.

Table 12-9. Average Hours Per Day Spent in Leisure and Sports Activities for the Total Population, by Selected Characteristics, 2006 Annual Averages

(Number.)

Characteristic	Total, all leisure and sports activities			Participating in sports, exercise, and recreation		Socializing and communicating		Watching TV	
	Total, all days	Weekdays	Weekends and holidays[1]	Weekdays	Weekends and holidays[1]	Weekdays	Weekends and holidays[1]	Weekdays	Weekends and holidays[1]
Sex									
Men	5.47	4.83	6.98	0.35	0.47	0.57	1.05	2.49	3.53
Women	4.72	4.26	5.80	0.18	0.20	0.64	1.17	2.22	2.69
Age									
Total, 15 years and over	5.09	4.54	6.37	0.26	0.33	0.60	1.11	2.35	3.10
15 to 19 years	5.40	4.85	6.68	0.58	0.69	0.76	1.32	1.96	2.45
20 to 24 years	5.03	4.45	6.42	0.38	0.54	0.77	1.26	1.95	2.66
25 to 34 years	4.30	3.64	5.86	0.20	0.30	0.57	1.22	1.92	2.85
35 to 44 years	4.09	3.56	5.34	0.21	0.28	0.48	1.04	1.88	2.65
45 to 54 years	4.52	3.90	5.98	0.20	0.34	0.57	1.05	2.11	3.03
55 to 64 years	5.41	4.78	6.90	0.21	0.25	0.57	1.05	2.59	3.59
65 to 74 years	6.97	6.64	7.75	0.29	0.16	0.64	1.08	3.75	4.07
75 years and over	7.82	7.66	8.18	0.18	0.16	0.69	0.90	4.15	4.28
Race and Hispanic Origin									
White	5.09	4.51	6.43	0.27	0.35	0.62	1.12	2.31	3.12
Black	5.49	5.10	6.39	0.19	0.22	0.59	1.02	2.85	3.44
Hispanic[2]	4.63	4.09	5.90	0.26	0.31	0.58	1.32	2.38	2.98
Employment Status									
Employed	4.18	3.51	5.74	0.22	0.33	0.52	1.07	1.77	2.75
Full-time workers	4.09	3.36	5.78	0.21	0.33	0.48	1.08	1.72	2.79
Part-time workers	4.52	4.06	5.58	0.26	0.36	0.67	1.04	1.96	2.60
Not employed	6.75	6.42	7.55	0.32	0.32	0.76	1.19	3.41	3.76
Earnings of Full-Time Wage and Salary Earners[3]									
$0 to $460	4.25	3.56	5.81	0.17	0.21	0.44	1.14	1.88	2.92
$461 to $710	4.22	3.56	5.85	0.18	0.26	0.51	0.99	1.78	3.02
$711 to $1,100	4.15	3.37	5.96	0.20	0.32	0.50	1.15	1.79	2.91
$1,101 and higher	3.88	3.12	5.61	0.30	0.48	0.49	1.03	1.48	2.38
Presence and Age of Children									
No household children under 18 years	5.63	5.09	6.90	0.25	0.31	0.61	1.06	2.66	3.47
Household children under 18 years	4.27	3.71	5.57	0.27	0.36	0.59	1.19	1.88	2.55
Children 13 to 17 years, none younger	4.92	4.40	6.24	0.41	0.45	0.73	1.14	1.97	2.87
Children 6 to 12 years, none younger	4.24	3.63	5.65	0.27	0.37	0.54	1.18	1.97	2.50
Youngest child under 6 years	3.92	3.36	5.17	0.20	0.32	0.55	1.21	1.77	2.42
Marital Status and Sex									
Married, spouse present	4.79	4.23	6.10	0.21	0.27	0.57	1.14	2.24	3.01
Men	5.16	4.52	6.71	0.25	0.35	0.53	1.06	2.45	3.55
Women	4.41	3.95	5.50	0.18	0.19	0.62	1.22	2.02	2.48
Other marital status	5.45	4.91	6.68	0.31	0.40	0.64	1.07	2.49	3.20
Men	5.87	5.24	7.31	0.47	0.62	0.62	1.03	2.54	3.50
Women	5.08	4.62	6.12	0.18	0.22	0.66	1.11	2.45	2.93
Educational Attainment, 25 Years and Over									
Less than a high school diploma	6.01	5.54	7.13	0.13	0.18	0.56	1.14	3.51	4.13
High school graduate, no college[4]	5.57	5.06	6.76	0.17	0.22	0.58	1.03	2.97	3.78
Some college or associate degree	4.76	4.23	6.02	0.23	0.22	0.55	1.08	2.15	2.99
Bachelor's degree or higher[5]	4.33	3.69	5.78	0.28	0.41	0.57	1.09	1.62	2.40

Note: Data refer to respondents age 15 years and over, unless otherwise specified.

[1]Holidays are New Year's Day, Easter, Memorial Day, the Fourth of July, Labor Day, Thanksgiving Day, and Christmas Day.
[2]May be of any race.
[3]These values are based on usual weekly earnings. Each earnings range covers approximately 25 percent of full-time wage and salary workers.
[4]Includes persons with a high school diploma or equivalent.
[5]Includes persons with bachelor's, master's, professional, and doctoral degrees.

Table 12-9. Average Hours Per Day Spent in Leisure and Sports Activities for the Total Population, by Selected Characteristics, 2006 Annual Averages—*Continued*

(Number.)

Characteristic	Reading		Relaxing/thinking		Playing games and computer use for leisure		Other leisure and sports activities, including travel[6]	
	Weekdays	Weekends and holidays[1]	Weekdays	Weekends and holidays[1]	Weekdays	Weekends and holidays[1]	Weekdays	Weekends and holidays[1]
Sex								
Men	0.28	0.38	0.31	0.34	0.40	0.48	0.43	0.73
Women	0.38	0.51	0.28	0.33	0.21	0.27	0.36	0.63
Age								
Total, 15 years and over	0.33	0.44	0.29	0.33	0.30	0.37	0.40	0.68
15 to 19 years	0.11	0.11	0.15	0.13	0.69	1.00	0.61	0.98
20 to 24 years	0.14	0.24	0.18	0.22	0.40	0.61	0.64	0.89
25 to 34 years	0.15	0.19	0.17	0.20	0.30	0.37	0.33	0.72
35 to 44 years	0.20	0.26	0.26	0.26	0.18	0.26	0.34	0.58
45 to 54 years	0.29	0.40	0.25	0.27	0.20	0.25	0.28	0.64
55 to 64 years	0.50	0.65	0.32	0.46	0.25	0.29	0.35	0.60
65 to 74 years	0.70	0.90	0.49	0.59	0.28	0.28	0.50	0.66
75 years and over	0.97	1.35	0.86	0.83	0.41	0.20	0.40	0.45
Race and Hispanic Origin								
White	0.35	0.48	0.26	0.31	0.30	0.38	0.40	0.68
Black	0.24	0.23	0.50	0.54	0.36	0.26	0.36	0.69
Hispanic[2]	0.12	0.12	0.21	0.23	0.22	0.32	0.31	0.63
Employment Status								
Employed	0.24	0.31	0.19	0.25	0.23	0.32	0.34	0.70
Full-time workers	0.20	0.31	0.19	0.26	0.22	0.30	0.33	0.72
Part-time workers	0.35	0.32	0.19	0.21	0.26	0.42	0.37	0.63
Not employed	0.50	0.68	0.49	0.48	0.44	0.47	0.50	0.64
Earnings of Full-Time Wage and Salary Earners[3]								
$0 to $460	0.20	0.21	0.23	0.32	0.26	0.31	0.37	0.71
$461 to $710	0.15	0.27	0.23	0.30	0.28	0.35	0.43	0.67
$711 to $1,100	0.20	0.29	0.20	0.27	0.15	0.33	0.33	0.69
$1,101 and higher	0.26	0.49	0.11	0.18	0.20	0.26	0.27	0.80
Presence and Age of Children								
No household children under 18 years	0.44	0.60	0.35	0.41	0.34	0.38	0.45	0.68
Household children under 18 years	0.17	0.21	0.22	0.22	0.25	0.37	0.32	0.67
Children 13 to 17 years, none younger	0.24	0.28	0.25	0.19	0.34	0.47	0.46	0.83
Children 6 to 12 years, none younger	0.17	0.24	0.20	0.24	0.24	0.43	0.25	0.69
Youngest child under 6 years	0.13	0.16	0.21	0.21	0.20	0.27	0.30	0.58
Marital Status and Sex								
Married, spouse present	0.34	0.47	0.30	0.33	0.24	0.26	0.34	0.61
Men	0.32	0.45	0.34	0.35	0.27	0.29	0.35	0.66
Women	0.36	0.50	0.25	0.31	0.20	0.24	0.32	0.57
Other marital status	0.32	0.41	0.29	0.33	0.38	0.50	0.47	0.76
Men	0.23	0.29	0.27	0.32	0.57	0.72	0.54	0.83
Women	0.40	0.51	0.31	0.34	0.22	0.31	0.41	0.69
Educational Attainment, 25 Years and Over								
Less than a high school diploma	0.26	0.21	0.64	0.79	0.16	0.14	0.29	0.54
High school graduate, no college[4]	0.32	0.49	0.39	0.42	0.28	0.28	0.36	0.54
Some college or associate degree	0.44	0.47	0.26	0.28	0.27	0.33	0.32	0.64
Bachelor's degree or higher[5]	0.44	0.66	0.17	0.19	0.24	0.32	0.38	0.73

Note: Data refer to respondents age 15 years and over, unless otherwise specified.

[1]Holidays are New Year's Day, Easter, Memorial Day, the Fourth of July, Labor Day, Thanksgiving Day, and Christmas Day.
[2]May be of any race.
[3]These values are based on usual weekly earnings. Each earnings range covers approximately 25 percent of full-time wage and salary workers.
[4]Includes persons with a high school diploma or equivalent.
[5]Includes persons with bachelor's, master's, professional, and doctoral degrees.
[6]Includes other leisure and sports activities, not elsewhere classified, and travel related to leisure and sports activities.

CHAPTER 13

INCOME IN THE UNITED STATES (CENSUS BUREAU)

INCOME IN THE UNITED STATES (CENSUS BUREAU)

HIGHLIGHTS

This chapter presents data on income collected by the Census Bureau for the Current Population Survey (CPS). Income, as distinguished from earnings, also includes income from pensions, investments, and other sources and is measured as real income in 2006 dollars.

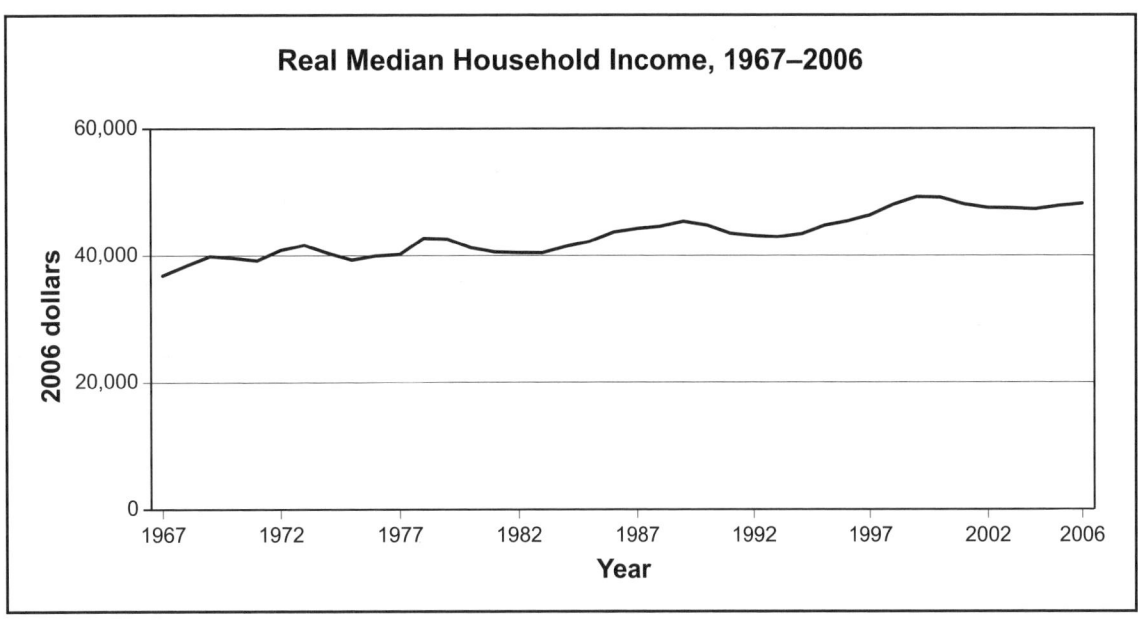

Real median income for the nation increased slightly in 2006 for the second year in a row rising from $47,845 to $48,201, or 0.7 percent. (See Table 13-1.)

OTHER HIGHLIGHTS

- Although real median income increased, earnings of full-time, year-round workers decreased for the second year in 2006 in a row for both men and women. (See Table 13-1.)

- Black households continued to have the lowest median income in 2006. Their median income also increased at a lower-than-average rate. Earnings of White non-Hispanic households stayed virtually the same, and Asian households continued to have the highest median income. The median income for Asians was 22.5 percent higher than that for White non-Hispanic households. (See Table 13-1.)

- In 2006, the income of households in which the head of household was under 65 years old was $54,726, while it was $27,798 for households in which the head was 65 years old or over. However, income grew at a much faster rate from 2005 to 2006 (3.4 percent, compared to 1.3 percent) for households in which the head of household was 65 years old or over. (See Table 13-1.)

- The highest quintile of household income continued to account for about 50 percent of total income in 2006. (See Table 13-1.)

- In 2006, Asians (alone) had the highest percentage of households with income over $100,000—30.8 percent, up from 28.9 percent in 2005. Among non-Hispanic Whites (alone), 21.6 percent of households had median incomes of over $100,000, up from 20.7 percent in 2005. In 2006, 9.1 percent of Black (alone) households had incomes over $100,000, up from 8.5 percent in 2005. (See Table 13-2.)

NOTES AND DEFINITIONS

Collection and Coverage

Data on income in the United States in this chapter are based on information collected in the 2007 and earlier Annual Social and Economic Supplements (ASEC) to the Census Bureau's Current Population Survey (CPS). The CPS is also the basis for the employment and unemployment data shown in Chapter 1 of this *Handbook*, which are collected by the Census Bureau for BLS. The basic CPS is described in the notes and definitions for Chapter 1. The sample universe for the CPS ASEC is slightly larger than that for the basic CPS, as it includes military personnel who live in a household with at least one other civilian adult, regardless of whether they live on post or off post.

For each person in the sample age 15 years and over, the ASEC asks questions about the amount of income received from all sources during the preceding calendar year from all sources. In addition to wage and salary earnings, which represent the largest component of income, other sources include Social Security, pensions, interest, dividends, and other money income. Excluded are certain money receipts, such as capital gains.

Although the income statistics refer to receipts during the previous calendar year, the demographic characteristics, such as age and household composition, are as of the survey date.

Concepts and Definitions

Data on income cover money income received before payments for personal income taxes, Social Security, Medicare, union dues, and the like. Therefore money income does not reflect the fact that some families receive noncash benefits, such as food stamps, health benefits, subsidized housing, and the like. In addition, money income does not reflect noncash benefits such payments by business for retirement programs, medical expenses, and other benefits.

The Census Bureau uses the research series of the BLS Consumer Price Index (CPI-U-RS) to adjust for changes in the cost of living. These indexes are shown in Table 7-11 of this Handbook.

Additional Information

Additional information is available in the Census publication "Income, Poverty, and Health Insurance Coverage in the United States: 2006," which can be found on the Census Bureau Web site at <http://www.census.gov/hhes>.

Table 13-1. Income and Earnings Summary Measures, by Selected Characteristics, 2005 and 2006

(Numbers in thousands, dollars, percent; income in 2006 dollars.)

Characteristic	2005			2006			Percent change in real median income (2006 less 2005)	
		Median income (dollars)			Median income (dollars)			
	Number	Estimate	90 percent confidence interval[1] (+/-)	Number	Estimate	90 percent confidence interval[1] (+/-)	Estimate	90 percent confidence interval[1] (+/-)
Households								
All households	114 384	47 845	263	116 011	48 201	341	0.7	0.73
Type of Household								
Family households	77 402	59 156	343	78 425	59 894	403	1.2	0.73
Married-couple	58 179	68 233	415	58 945	69 716	559	2.2	0.84
Female householder, no husband present	14 093	31 655	445	14 416	31 818	433	0.5	1.59
Male householder, no wife present	5 130	48 289	1 065	5 063	47 078	1 026	-2.5	2.44
Nonfamily households	36 982	28 222	275	37 587	29 083	368	3.1	1.34
Female householder	20 230	23 432	426	20 249	23 876	411	1.9	2.06
Male householder	16 753	35 164	729	17 338	35 614	439	1.3	2.03
Race[2] and Hispanic Origin of Householder								
White	93 588	50 146	360	94 705	50 673	242	1.1	0.72
White, not Hispanic	82 003	52 449	292	82 675	52 423	309	-	0.65
Black	14 002	31 870	511	14 354	31 969	396	0.3	1.65
Asian	4 273	63 097	1 210	4 454	64 238	2 754	1.8	4.11
Hispanic[3]	12 519	37 146	607	12 973	37 781	831	1.7	1.92
Age of Householder								
Under 65 years	90 926	54 001	250	92 282	54 726	426	1.3	0.76
15 to 24 years	6 795	29 713	802	6 662	30 937	620	4.1	2.85
25 to 34 years	19 120	48 932	590	19 435	49 164	735	0.5	1.57
35 to 44 years	23 016	59 988	914	22 779	60 405	528	0.7	1.48
45 to 54 years	23 731	64 471	748	24 140	64 874	781	0.6	1.36
55 to 64 years	18 264	53 973	705	19 266	54 592	821	1.1	1.63
65 years and over	23 459	26 890	297	23 729	27 798	332	3.4	1.36
Nativity of Householder								
Native	99 579	48 435	280	100 603	49 074	375	1.3	0.79
Foreign-born	14 806	43 418	700	15 408	43 943	956	1.2	2.23
Naturalized citizen	6 990	51 670	1 385	7 210	51 440	948	-0.4	2.66
Not a citizen	7 815	37 945	804	8 198	39 497	1 061	4.1	2.89
Region								
Northeast	21 054	52 550	630	21 261	52 057	568	-0.9	1.24
Midwest	26 351	47 457	598	26 508	47 836	643	8.0	1.46
South	41 805	43 520	360	42 587	43 884	549	8.0	1.25
West	25 174	51 641	629	25 656	52 249	540	12.0	1.35
Metropolitan Status								
Inside metropolitan statistical areas	95 107	50 063	372	96 739	50 616	240	1.1	0.74
Inside principal cities	38 008	42 516	365	38 488	42 627	515	0.3	1.22
Outside principal cities	57 098	55 300	549	58 251	55 775	433	0.9	1.03
Outside metropolitan statistical areas[4]	19 278	38 796	705	19 272	38 293	767	-1.3	2.15
Shares of Household Income, Quintiles, and Gini Index[5]								
Lowest quintile	22 877	3.4	0.04	23 202	3.4	0.04	-	1.27
Second quintile	22 877	8.6	0.10	23 202	8.6	0.10	-	1.27
Third quintile	22 877	14.6	0.16	23 202	14.5	0.16	-0.7	1.25
Fourth quintile	22 877	23.0	0.26	23 202	22.9	0.25	-0.4	1.25
Highest quintile	22 877	50.4	0.56	23 202	50.5	0.55	0.2	1.26
Gini index of income inequality	114 384	0.469	0.0047	116 011	0.470	0.0047	0.2	1.14
Earnings of Full-Time Year-Round Workers								
Men with earnings	61 500	42 743	153	63 055	42 261	145	-1.1	0.41
Women with earnings	43 351	32 903	138	44 663	32 515	304	-1.2	0.89
Per Capita Income[6]								
All races[2]	293 834	25 857	165	296 824	26 352	168	1.9	0.77
White	235 903	27 365	194	237 892	27 821	192	1.7	0.84
White, not Hispanic	195 893	29 895	226	196 252	30 431	224	1.8	0.90
Black	36 965	17 427	313	37 369	17 902	357	2.7	2.31
Asian	12 599	28 227	860	13 194	30 474	1 142	8.0	4.38
Hispanic[3]	43 168	14 958	262	44 854	15 421	299	3.1	2.00

[1]A 90-percent confidence interval is a measure of an estimate's variability. The larger the confidence interval in relation to the size of the estimate, the less reliable the estimate.
[2]Federal surveys now give respondents the option of reporting more than one race. Therefore, there are two basic ways of defining a race group. A group such as Asian may be defined as those who reported Asian and no other race (the race-alone or single-race concept) or as those who reported Asian regardless of whether they also reported another race (the race-alone-or-in-combination concept). This table shows data using the race-alone concept. The use of the single-race population does not imply that it is the preferred method of presenting or analyzing data; the Census Bureau uses a variety of approaches. Information on people who reported more than one race, such as White and American Indian and Alaska Native or Asian and Black or African American, is available from Census 2000 through American FactFinder. About 2.6 percent of respondents reported more than one race in Census 2000.
[3]May be of any race.
[4]The "outside metropolitan statistical areas" category includes both micropolitan statistical areas and territory outside of metropolitan and micropolitan statistical areas.
[5]The data shown in this section are shares of aggregate household income, the Gini index, and their respective confidence intervals. See the article by Paul Allison entitled "Measures of Inequality" from American Sociological Review 43 (December 1977), pp. 865–880, for an explanation of inequality measures.
[6]The data shown in this section are per capita incomes and their respective confidence intervals. Per capita income is the mean income computed for every man, woman, and child in a particular group. It is derived by dividing the total income of a particular group by the total population in that group (excluding patients or inmates in institutional quarters).
- = Quantity represents or rounds to zero.

Table 13-2. Households, by Total Money Income, Race, and Hispanic Origin of Householder, 1967–2006

(Numbers in thousands, percent, dollars; income in 2006 CPI-U-RS adjusted dollars.)

Race and Hispanic origin of householder and year	Number	Percent distribution										Median income (dollars)		Mean income (dollars)	
		Total	Under $5,000	$5,000 to $9,999	$10,000 to $14,999	$15,000 to $24,999	$25,000 to $34,999	$35,000 to $49,999	$50,000 to $74,999	$75,000 to $99,000	$100,000 and over	Value	Standard error	Value	Standard error
All Races															
1967[1]	60 813	100.0	4.4	7.8	7.1	13.1	15.1	21.2	20.1	6.5	4.7	36 847	134	41 212	134
1968	62 214	100.0	3.9	7.4	6.7	13.4	14.2	21.4	21.0	7.3	4.7	38 404	139	43 448	139
1969	63 401	100.0	3.6	7.5	6.5	12.7	13.2	20.8	21.8	8.4	5.5	39 871	147	45 361	143
1970	64 778	100.0	3.6	7.6	6.7	12.9	12.9	20.6	21.1	8.7	5.9	39 604	145	45 349	145
1971[2]	66 676	100.0	3.4	7.6	7.0	13.3	13.7	19.5	21.1	8.3	6.0	39 196	152	45 079	143
1972[3]	68 251	100.0	3.0	7.1	7.1	13.0	12.9	18.4	21.9	9.4	7.2	40 843	156	47 536	147
1973	69 859	100.0	2.8	6.6	7.2	13.2	12.1	18.6	21.8	10.1	7.7	41 668	159	48 189	147
1974[4,5]	71 163	100.0	2.4	6.7	7.5	13.4	12.9	19.0	21.5	9.4	7.0	40 383	155	47 225	148
1975[5]	72 867	100.0	2.5	7.1	8.0	14.1	13.5	18.2	21.0	9.3	6.3	39 302	160	45 894	143
1976[6]	74 142	100.0	2.4	7.0	7.4	14.0	13.3	17.7	21.7	9.6	6.9	39 961	148	47 004	145
1977	76 030	100.0	2.3	7.0	7.7	13.9	12.5	17.7	21.5	9.8	7.4	40 187	151	47 672	145
1978	77 330	100.0	2.2	6.5	7.4	13.1	12.6	16.8	21.7	11.0	8.8	42 725	173	50 286	193
1979[7]	80 776	100.0	2.4	6.4	7.1	12.9	12.8	16.6	21.7	10.9	9.2	42 606	202	50 611	192
1980	82 368	100.0	2.5	6.7	7.4	13.6	12.6	17.0	21.2	10.3	8.6	41 258	212	49 070	179
1981	83 527	100.0	2.7	6.7	7.6	13.8	13.0	16.8	20.7	10.2	8.5	40 573	213	48 471	177
1982	83 918	100.0	2.9	6.7	7.8	13.7	12.7	17.2	20.2	9.9	8.9	40 465	183	48 766	181
1983[8]	85 290	100.0	3.0	6.8	7.2	13.8	13.0	16.8	19.7	10.4	9.2	40 438	183	49 271	183
1984	86 789	100.0	2.8	6.5	7.5	13.3	12.5	16.9	19.7	10.7	10.2	41 430	189	50 762	187
1985[9]	88 458	100.0	2.8	6.4	7.3	12.8	12.5	16.4	20.0	11.1	10.6	42 205	229	51 940	206
1986	89 479	100.0	2.9	6.4	6.8	12.6	11.8	16.2	20.2	11.4	11.8	43 699	226	53 988	219
1987[10]	91 124	100.0	2.6	6.2	6.9	12.5	12.0	15.4	20.3	11.5	12.5	44 247	211	55 026	226
1988	92 830	100.0	2.6	6.3	6.6	12.5	11.7	15.8	19.9	11.7	12.8	44 587	218	55 710	249
1989	93 347	100.0	2.5	5.7	6.7	12.4	11.8	15.7	19.9	11.8	13.7	45 382	250	57 336	250
1990	94 312	100.0	2.6	6.1	6.6	12.3	12.0	16.2	19.9	11.3	13.0	44 778	229	55 934	236
1991	95 669	100.0	2.6	6.2	7.0	12.8	12.1	15.8	19.6	11.2	12.7	43 492	209	54 747	225
1992[11]	96 426	100.0	2.8	6.4	7.0	13.1	11.7	16.1	19.3	11.1	12.5	43 135	204	54 686	230
1993[12]	97 107	100.0	3.0	6.2	7.0	13.2	12.2	15.7	18.5	10.9	13.3	42 926	201	56 923	308
1994[13]	98 990	100.0	2.9	5.9	7.1	13.1	12.2	15.4	18.4	11.1	14.0	43 405	198	58 027	312
1995[14]	99 627	100.0	2.6	5.6	6.7	13.1	11.7	15.7	19.0	11.3	14.2	44 764	259	59 033	323
1996	101 018	100.0	2.6	5.6	6.6	12.9	11.9	14.8	19.0	11.8	14.7	45 416	229	60 299	338
1997	102 528	100.0	2.7	5.3	6.2	12.5	11.5	14.9	18.8	11.9	16.1	46 350	214	62 241	348
1998	103 874	100.0	2.7	5.1	6.0	12.1	11.1	15.1	18.9	11.9	17.1	48 034	284	64 056	346
1999[15]	106 434	100.0	2.4	4.6	5.9	12.0	11.0	14.9	18.5	12.2	18.3	49 244	230	66 235	344
2000[16]	109 297	100.0	2.8	4.6	6.3	11.7	11.5	14.7	18.3	12.1	18.1	48 091	147	66 290	264
2001	111 278	100.0	2.9	4.8	6.5	12.0	11.5	14.3	18.2	12.0	17.8	47 530	156	64 837	243
2002	108 209	100.0	2.6	4.6	5.9	11.7	10.9	15.1	18.6	12.3	18.3	49 163	155	66 895	263
2003	112 000	100.0	3.2	4.8	6.4	12.0	11.3	14.7	17.8	11.8	18.1	47 488	206	64 753	237
2004[17]	113 343	100.0	3.3	4.6	6.4	12.1	11.6	14.3	18.5	11.4	17.8	47 323	209	64 542	243
2005	114 384	100.0	3.2	4.7	6.3	12.1	11.1	14.8	18.3	11.4	18.2	47 845	160	65 421	247
2006	116 011	100.0	3.1	4.4	5.9	11.8	11.5	14.6	18.2	11.3	19.1	48 201	207	66 570	257
White Alone[18]															
2002	91 645	100.0	2.3	4.1	6.1	11.6	11.3	14.2	18.8	12.6	19.0	50 530	205	67 431	275
2003	91 962	100.0	2.6	4.0	6.0	11.7	11.2	14.7	18.2	12.3	19.3	50 023	196	67 515	271
2004[17]	92 880	100.0	2.7	3.9	6.2	11.8	11.4	14.3	18.9	12.0	18.9	49 803	195	67 150	276
2005	93 588	100.0	2.6	3.9	6.0	11.7	11.1	14.8	18.7	11.9	19.3	50 146	219	68 125	282
2006	94 705	100.0	2.5	3.7	5.6	11.5	11.3	14.6	18.8	11.8	20.2	50 673	147	69 107	288

[1]Implementation of a new Curent Population Survey (CPS) Annual Social and Economic Supplements (ASEC) processing system.
[2]Introduction of 1970 census sample design and population controls.
[3]Full implementation of 1970 census–based sample design.
[4]Implementation of a new CPS ASEC processing system. Questionnaire expanded to ask 11 income questions.
[5]Some of these estimates were derived using Pareto interpolation and may differ from published data that were derived using linear interpolation.
[6]First-year medians were derived using both Pareto and linear interpolation. Before this year, all medians were derived using linear interpolation.
[7]Implementation of 1980 census population controls. Questionnaire expanded to show 27 possible values from a list of 51 possible sources of income.
[8]Implementation of Hispanic population weighting controls and introduction of 1980 census–based sample design.
[9]Recording of amounts for earnings from longest job increased to $299,999. Full implementation of 1980 census–based sample design.
[10]Implementation of a new CPS ASEC processing system.
[11]Implementation of 1990 census population controls.
[12]Data collection method changed from paper and pencil to computer-assisted interviewing. In addition, the 1994 ASEC was revised to allow for the coding of different income amounts on selected questionnaire items. Limits either increased or decreased in the following categories: earnings limits increased to $999,999, Social Security limits increased to $49,999, Supplemental Security Income and public assistance limits increased to $24,999, veterans' benefits limits increased to $99,999, and child support and alimony limits decreased to $49,999.
[13]Introduction of 1990 census sample design.
[14]Full implementation of 1990 census–based sample design and metropolitan definitions, 7,000 household sample reduction, and revised editing of responses on race.
[15]Implementation of the 2000 census–based population controls.
[16]Implementation of a 28,000 household sample expansion.
[17]Data revised to reflect a correction to the weights in the 2005 ASEC.
[18]Beginning with the 2003 CPS, respondents were allowed to choose one or more races. White alone refers to people who reported White and did not report any other race category. The use of this single-race population does not imply that it is the preferred method of presenting or analyzing the data; the Census Bureau uses a variety of approaches. Information on people who reported more than one race, such as White and American Indian and Alaska Native or Asian and Black or African American, is available from Census 2000 through American FactFinder. About 2.6 percent of respondents reported more than one race in Census 2000.

Table 13-2. Households, by Total Money Income, Race, and Hispanic Origin of Householder, 1967–2006
—Continued

(Numbers in thousands, percent, dollars; income in 2006 CPI-U-RS adjusted dollars.)

Race and Hispanic origin of householder and year	Number	Percent distribution										Median income (dollars)		Mean income (dollars)	
		Total	Under $5,000	$5,000 to $9,999	$10,000 to $14,999	$15,000 to $24,999	$25,000 to $34,999	$35,000 to $49,999	$50,000 to $74,999	$75,000 to $99,000	$100,000 and over	Value	Standard error	Value	Standard error
White[19]															
1967[1]	54 188	100.0	4.0	7.2	6.4	12.4	14.9	22.0	21.1	6.9	5.0	38 426	139	42 718	144
1968	55 394	100.0	3.5	6.8	6.2	12.6	14.1	22.1	22.0	7.8	5.0	39 986	149	45 010	149
1969	56 248	100.0	3.2	6.9	6.1	11.9	12.8	21.3	22.9	9.0	6.0	41 611	152	47 043	157
1970	57 575	100.0	3.2	6.9	6.3	12.3	12.7	21.1	22.1	9.2	6.3	41 250	159	46 936	154
1971[2]	59 463	100.0	3.1	6.9	6.5	12.7	13.4	20.1	22.1	8.8	6.4	40 998	156	46 712	152
1972[3]	60 618	100.0	2.7	6.4	6.4	12.3	12.7	18.8	22.9	10.0	7.8	42 848	164	49 385	160
1973	61 965	100.0	2.4	6.0	6.7	12.5	11.8	18.9	22.7	10.7	8.3	43 670	166	50 052	159
1974[4][5]	62 984	100.0	2.1	5.9	6.9	12.8	12.7	19.4	22.5	9.9	7.6	42 233	159	48 974	159
1975[5]	64 392	100.0	2.3	6.2	7.4	13.7	13.3	18.5	21.9	9.9	6.8	41 101	150	47 589	157
1976[6]	65 353	100.0	2.2	6.2	6.8	13.4	13.2	17.9	22.6	10.3	7.4	41 860	173	48 812	158
1977	66 934	100.0	2.1	6.1	7.2	13.3	12.3	18.1	22.5	10.4	8.1	42 259	178	49 535	160
1978	68 028	100.0	1.9	5.6	6.9	12.6	12.4	17.0	22.6	11.5	9.4	44 415	196	52 149	210
1979[7]	70 766	100.0	2.0	5.5	6.6	12.4	12.6	16.9	22.5	11.4	10.0	44 671	212	52 607	210
1980	71 872	100.0	2.0	5.8	6.9	13.0	12.6	17.3	22.1	10.9	9.3	43 527	224	51 050	196
1981	72 845	100.0	2.3	5.7	7.0	13.3	12.9	17.2	21.6	10.8	9.3	42 869	198	50 503	191
1982	73 182	100.0	2.4	5.7	7.3	13.1	12.7	17.5	21.0	10.5	9.7	42 363	193	50 776	199
1983[8]	74 170	100.0	2.4	5.8	6.7	13.3	13.0	17.3	20.5	11.0	9.9	42 395	190	51 330	198
1984	75 328	100.0	2.3	5.4	7.0	12.7	12.5	17.3	20.7	11.3	10.9	43 707	220	52 856	205
1985[9]	76 576	100.0	2.3	5.5	6.9	12.3	12.3	16.7	20.8	11.6	11.5	44 510	238	54 072	227
1986	77 284	100.0	2.4	5.4	6.4	12.1	11.7	16.5	21.0	12.0	12.6	45 942	223	56 236	240
1987[10]	78 519	100.0	2.1	5.2	6.3	12.0	11.9	15.8	21.3	12.2	13.3	46 619	236	57 378	248
1988	79 734	100.0	2.1	5.2	6.1	12.0	11.7	16.2	20.7	12.4	13.6	47 135	278	58 087	273
1989	80 163	100.0	1.9	4.7	6.2	12.0	11.6	15.9	20.6	12.3	14.6	47 737	232	59 724	276
1990	80 968	100.0	2.0	5.1	6.1	12.1	12.0	16.5	20.5	12.0	13.8	46 705	214	58 191	260
1991	81 675	100.0	2.0	5.2	6.5	12.5	12.0	16.1	20.3	11.9	13.6	45 576	221	57 059	248
1992[11]	81 795	100.0	2.2	5.2	6.6	12.6	11.7	16.3	20.0	11.8	13.5	45 350	220	57 156	255
1993[12]	82 387	100.0	2.4	5.2	6.5	12.8	12.0	15.9	19.4	11.5	14.3	45 287	264	59 474	344
1994[13]	83 737	100.0	2.4	4.8	6.7	12.7	12.1	15.7	18.9	11.7	14.9	45 778	257	60 584	352
1995[14]	84 511	100.0	2.1	4.7	6.3	12.8	11.6	15.8	19.6	11.8	15.3	46 985	246	61 386	356
1996	85 059	100.0	2.0	4.8	6.1	12.5	11.8	14.9	19.7	12.5	15.7	47 551	246	62 693	371
1997	86 106	100.0	2.2	4.6	5.9	12.1	11.3	15.0	19.2	12.5	17.2	48 814	309	65 009	396
1998	87 212	100.0	2.2	4.2	5.7	11.7	10.9	15.1	19.5	12.5	18.2	50 538	253	66 962	394
1999[15]	88 893	100.0	1.9	3.9	5.6	11.7	10.9	15.0	18.9	12.8	19.2	51 215	259	68 641	388
2000[16]	90 030	100.0	2.1	4.0	5.7	11.3	10.8	15.1	18.9	12.9	19.4	51 418	227	69 376	297
2001	90 682	100.0	2.2	4.0	6.0	11.4	11.2	14.7	18.7	12.6	19.2	50 698	238	68 914	296
White Alone, Not Hispanic[18]															
2002	81 166	100.0	2.2	4.0	6.0	11.0	10.8	13.9	19.0	13.0	20.2	52 563	206	69 615	296
2003	81 148	100.0	2.4	3.8	5.9	11.1	10.7	14.4	18.4	12.7	20.6	52 376	253	70 037	297
2004[17]	81 628	100.0	2.5	3.7	6.0	11.2	10.9	13.9	19.1	12.5	20.2	52 207	239	69 657	303
2005	82 003	100.0	2.4	3.7	5.8	11.1	10.5	14.5	18.9	12.4	20.7	52 449	178	70 852	313
2006	82 675	100.0	2.4	3.5	5.4	10.9	10.9	14.2	19.0	12.2	21.6	52 423	188	71 745	317

[1]Implementation of a new Curent Population Survey (CPS) Annual Social and Economic Supplements (ASEC) processing system.
[2]Introduction of 1970 census sample design and population controls.
[3]Full implementation of 1970 census–based sample design.
[4]Implementation of a new CPS ASEC processing system. Questionnaire expanded to ask 11 income questions.
[5]Some of these estimates were derived using Pareto interpolation and may differ from published data that were derived using linear interpolation.
[6]First-year medians were derived using both Pareto and linear interpolation. Before this year, all medians were derived using linear interpolation.
[7]Implementation of 1980 census population controls. Questionnaire expanded to show 27 possible values from a list of 51 possible sources of income.
[8]Implementation of Hispanic population weighting controls and introduction of 1980 census–based sample design.
[9]Recording of amounts for earnings from longest job increased to $299,999. Full implementation of 1980 census–based sample design.
[10]Implementation of a new CPS ASEC processing system.
[11]Implementation of 1990 census population controls.
[12]Data collection method changed from paper and pencil to computer-assisted interviewing. In addition, the 1994 ASEC was revised to allow for the coding of different income amounts on selected questionnaire items. Limits either increased or decreased in the following categories: earnings limits increased to $999,999, Social Security limits increased to $49,999, Supplemental Security Income and public assistance limits increased to $24,999, veterans' benefits limits increased to $99,999, and child support and alimony limits decreased to $49,999.
[13]Introduction of 1990 census sample design.
[14]Full implementation of 1990 census–based sample design and metropolitan definitions, 7,000 household sample reduction, and revised editing of responses on race.
[15]Implementation of the 2000 census–based population controls.
[16]Implementation of a 28,000 household sample expansion.
[17]Data revised to reflect a correction to the weights in the 2005 ASEC.
[18]Beginning with the 2003 CPS, respondents were allowed to choose one or more races. White alone refers to people who reported White and did not report any other race category. The use of this single-race population does not imply that it is the preferred method of presenting or analyzing the data; the Census Bureau uses a variety of approaches. Information on people who reported more than one race, such as White and American Indian and Alaska Native or Asian and Black or African American, is available from Census 2000 through American FactFinder. About 2.6 percent of respondents reported more than one race in Census 2000.
[19]For 2001 and earlier years, the CPS allowed respondents to report only one race group.

Table 13-2. Households, by Total Money Income, Race, and Hispanic Origin of Householder, 1967–2006
—Continued

(Numbers in thousands, percent, dollars; income in 2006 CPI-U-RS adjusted dollars.)

Race and Hispanic origin of householder and year	Number	Percent distribution										Median income (dollars)		Mean income (dollars)	
		Total	Under $5,000	$5,000 to $9,999	$10,000 to $14,999	$15,000 to $24,999	$25,000 to $34,999	$35,000 to $49,999	$50,000 to $74,999	$75,000 to $99,000	$100,000 and over	Value	Standard error	Value	Standard error
White, Not Hispanic[19]															
1972[3]	58 005	100.0	2.7	6.4	6.3	12.0	12.4	18.7	23.2	10.3	8.1	43 459	206	49 958	223
1973	59 236	100.0	2.4	6.0	6.6	12.2	11.6	18.8	22.9	11.0	8.6	44 054	206	50 611	214
1974[4,5]	60 164	100.0	2.1	5.9	6.8	12.5	12.5	19.4	22.8	10.1	7.8	42 594	209	49 518	216
1975[5]	61 533	100.0	2.2	6.1	7.3	13.4	13.2	18.6	22.2	10.2	7.0	41 411	220	48 162	233
1976[6]	62 365	100.0	2.1	6.1	6.6	13.1	13.1	17.9	22.9	10.5	7.7	42 714	249	49 455	221
1977	63 721	100.0	2.0	6.1	7.0	13.0	12.1	18.0	22.8	10.7	8.3	43 097	243	50 159	237
1978	64 836	100.0	1.9	5.5	6.8	12.4	12.2	17.0	22.8	11.8	9.7	45 252	238	52 753	227
1979[7]	67 203	100.0	2.0	5.4	6.5	12.2	12.4	16.9	22.8	11.7	10.3	45 300	251	53 215	233
1980	68 106	100.0	1.9	5.6	6.8	12.7	12.4	17.3	22.4	11.1	9.6	44 299	108	51 718	233
1981	68 996	100.0	2.2	5.6	6.9	13.1	12.7	17.1	21.8	11.0	9.6	43 488	221	51 137	213
1982	69 214	100.0	2.3	5.6	7.0	12.8	12.6	17.6	21.2	10.8	10.1	43 073	217	51 517	221
1983[8]	. . .	100.0	2.3	5.5	6.4	13.1	12.8	17.4	20.8	11.3	10.3	. . .	. . .	. . .	. . .
1984	70 586	100.0	2.2	5.2	6.8	12.5	12.4	17.2	20.9	11.6	11.3	44 615	248	53 767	240
1985[9]	71 540	100.0	2.2	5.2	6.6	12.0	12.2	16.7	21.1	11.9	12.0	45 510	232	55 128	250
1986	72 067	100.0	2.2	5.2	6.2	11.7	11.5	16.4	21.3	12.4	13.1	46 986	242	57 360	263
1987[10]	73 120	100.0	1.9	4.9	6.1	11.7	11.7	15.7	21.6	12.5	13.8	47 901	278	58 507	272
1988	74 067	100.0	1.9	4.9	5.9	11.6	11.5	16.1	21.0	12.8	14.2	48 434	272	59 269	278
1989	74 495	100.0	1.8	4.5	6.1	11.8	11.4	15.9	20.9	12.6	15.2	48 764	239	60 916	298
1990	75 035	100.0	1.9	4.9	5.8	11.7	11.8	16.4	20.7	12.4	14.4	47 772	223	59 474	269
1991	75 625	100.0	1.9	4.9	6.2	12.1	11.9	16.0	20.6	12.2	14.2	46 664	230	58 282	260
1992[11]	75 107	100.0	2.0	4.9	6.3	12.2	11.4	16.2	20.4	12.2	14.2	46 872	290	58 608	270
1993[12]	75 697	100.0	2.3	4.9	6.1	12.4	11.8	15.8	19.8	11.9	15.1	46 954	275	61 042	364
1994[13]	77 004	100.0	2.2	4.4	6.4	12.3	11.9	15.7	19.3	12.0	15.7	47 255	250	62 127	369
1995[14]	76 932	100.0	1.8	4.3	5.9	12.2	11.3	15.8	20.1	12.3	16.2	48 839	255	63 388	380
1996	77 240	100.0	1.8	4.4	5.9	11.9	11.5	14.9	20.1	13.0	16.6	49 632	340	64 589	. . .
1997	77 936	100.0	2.0	4.1	5.6	11.7	10.9	14.8	19.5	13.0	18.2	50 824	266	67 092	. . .
1998	78 577	100.0	2.0	3.9	5.4	11.1	10.5	14.9	19.8	13.0	19.3	52 425	301	69 106	422
1999[15]	79 819	100.0	1.8	3.7	5.4	11.2	10.5	14.6	19.1	13.2	20.4	53 432	338	70 892	420
2000[16]	80 527	100.0	2.0	3.8	5.5	10.8	10.4	14.7	19.0	13.2	20.6	53 416	214	71 487	321
2001	80 818	100.0	2.1	3.8	5.8	10.9	10.8	14.4	18.8	13.0	20.4	52 734	219	71 114	322
Black Alone or in Combination															
2002	13 778	100.0	6.3	9.4	9.1	15.3	13.3	15.0	14.7	8.3	8.6	32 700	430	45 204	527
2003	13 969	100.0	6.5	9.5	9.0	15.0	13.3	15.0	15.1	8.0	8.5	32 547	409	44 197	468
2004[17]	14 151	100.0	7.3	9.4	8.7	15.2	13.8	14.8	15.2	7.8	7.9	32 273	296	43 507	462
2005	14 399	100.0	6.7	9.9	8.8	16.0	12.2	15.0	15.4	7.3	8.6	31 969	305	44 128	480
2006	14 709	100.0	6.6	9.1	8.6	15.1	13.4	14.9	15.3	7.7	9.3	32 132	238	45 493	558
Black Alone[20]															
2002	13 465	100.0	6.3	9.5	9.2	15.3	13.3	15.0	14.7	8.3	8.5	32 531	438	44 842	518
2003	13 629	100.0	6.6	9.7	8.9	15.1	13.3	15.1	15.1	8.0	8.4	32 499	423	43 994	471
2004[17]	13 809	100.0	7.3	9.5	8.8	15.2	13.8	14.7	15.1	7.7	7.9	32 124	334	43 372	470
2005	14 002	100.0	6.7	9.9	8.8	16.0	12.3	15.1	15.3	7.3	8.5	31 870	311	43 846	476
2006	14 354	100.0	6.6	9.2	8.6	15.2	13.5	14.8	15.2	7.7	9.1	31 969	241	45 127	558

[3]Full implementation of 1970 census–based sample design.
[4]Implementation of a new CPS ASEC processing system. Questionnaire expanded to ask 11 income questions.
[5]Some of these estimates were derived using Pareto interpolation and may differ from published data that were derived using linear interpolation.
[6]First-year medians were derived using both Pareto and linear interpolation. Before this year, all medians were derived using linear interpolation.
[7]Implementation of 1980 census population controls. Questionnaire expanded to show 27 possible values from a list of 51 possible sources of income.
[8]Implementation of Hispanic population weighting controls and introduction of 1980 census–based sample design.
[9]Recording of amounts for earnings from longest job increased to $299,999. Full implementation of 1980 census–based sample design.
[10]Implementation of a new CPS ASEC processing system.
[11]Implementation of 1990 census population controls.
[12]Data collection method changed from paper and pencil to computer-assisted interviewing. In addition, the 1994 ASEC was revised to allow for the coding of different income amounts on selected questionnaire items. Limits either increased or decreased in the following categories: earnings limits increased to $999,999, Social Security limits increased to $49,999, Supplemental Security Income and public assistance limits increased to $24,999, veterans' benefits limits increased to $99,999, and child support and alimony limits decreased to $49,999.
[13]Introduction of 1990 census sample design.
[14]Full implementation of 1990 census–based sample design and metropolitan definitions, 7,000 household sample reduction, and revised editing of responses on race.
[15]Implementation of the 2000 census–based population controls.
[16]Implementation of a 28,000 household sample expansion.
[17]Data revised to reflect a correction to the weights in the 2005 ASEC.
[19]For 2001 and earlier years, the CPS allowed respondents to report only one race group.
[20]Black alone refers to persons who reported Black and did not report any other race category.
. . . = Not available.

Table 13-2. Households, by Total Money Income, Race, and Hispanic Origin of Householder, 1967–2006
—Continued

(Numbers in thousands, percent, dollars; income in 2006 CPI-U-RS adjusted dollars.)

Race and Hispanic origin of householder and year	Number	Percent distribution										Median income (dollars)		Mean income (dollars)	
		Total	Under $5,000	$5,000 to $9,999	$10,000 to $14,999	$15,000 to $24,999	$25,000 to $34,999	$35,000 to $49,999	$50,000 to $74,999	$75,000 to $99,000	$100,000 and over	Value	Standard error	Value	Standard error
Black[19]															
1967[1]	5 728	100.0	8.4	13.7	12.8	20.0	17.1	14.0	10.3	2.1	1.7	22 311	371	26 809	299
1968	5 870	100.0	7.3	13.5	11.5	21.4	15.2	15.7	11.2	3.0	1.2	23 579	342	28 717	303
1969	6 053	100.0	7.4	13.3	10.8	19.5	16.3	16.0	11.9	3.6	1.3	25 152	371	29 943	318
1970	6 180	100.0	7.4	13.2	11.2	18.7	15.0	16.6	12.3	4.1	1.6	25 107	345	30 657	331
1971[2]	6 578	100.0	6.7	13.6	12.2	19.0	15.9	15.4	12.2	3.7	1.4	24 218	360	30 009	308
1972[3]	6 809	100.0	6.0	13.2	12.4	18.4	15.3	14.9	13.5	4.3	1.9	25 011	375	31 594	337
1973	7 040	100.0	5.7	12.3	12.0	19.2	14.3	16.1	13.9	4.4	2.1	25 706	400	31 921	317
1974[4,5]	7 263	100.0	5.1	13.8	12.2	19.0	15.0	16.0	12.9	4.5	1.6	25 116	303	31 237	278
1975[5]	7 489	100.0	5.1	14.8	13.3	17.7	14.7	15.6	13.1	4.1	1.6	24 674	363	30 799	273
1976[6]	7 776	100.0	4.7	14.0	12.6	19.1	14.0	15.5	13.9	4.3	2.0	24 891	309	31 802	284
1977	7 977	100.0	4.3	14.7	12.1	19.6	14.3	14.8	13.4	4.6	2.2	24 938	335	31 952	284
1978	8 066	100.0	4.2	14.6	12.1	16.7	13.8	15.2	14.2	6.0	3.0	26 692	564	34 111	445
1979[7]	8 586	100.0	5.0	14.0	11.7	17.7	14.4	14.1	14.6	5.9	2.8	26 227	479	33 653	414
1980	8 847	100.0	5.7	14.9	11.7	18.4	13.3	14.5	13.5	5.2	2.7	25 076	473	32 545	401
1981	8 961	100.0	6.0	15.3	12.4	17.8	13.8	13.9	13.1	5.2	2.5	24 056	404	31 601	383
1982	8 916	100.0	6.7	14.9	11.9	18.3	12.9	14.5	13.9	4.7	2.2	24 009	385	31 590	395
1983[8]	9 243	100.0	7.0	15.3	11.6	17.4	14.1	13.4	13.2	5.4	2.6	23 998	448	31 965	392
1984	9 480	100.0	6.1	14.7	12.0	18.1	13.3	14.1	12.2	5.8	3.6	24 899	479	33 207	408
1985[9]	9 797	100.0	6.1	14.4	11.0	16.5	14.6	13.5	14.0	6.4	3.5	26 481	515	34 551	449
1986	9 922	100.0	7.3	14.2	10.2	16.4	12.5	14.4	14.4	5.7	4.7	26 468	520	35 511	483
1987[10]	10 192	100.0	6.3	14.7	11.1	15.7	13.7	13.9	13.6	6.0	4.9	26 608	513	35 928	494
1988	10 561	100.0	5.9	15.3	10.6	16.1	12.3	13.9	13.6	7.0	5.2	26 870	560	36 811	537
1989	10 486	100.0	6.4	13.7	10.0	15.4	13.2	14.2	14.3	7.0	5.6	28 390	578	37 672	512
1990	10 671	100.0	6.7	14.0	11.0	14.8	12.6	14.3	15.0	6.0	5.7	27 929	637	37 108	501
1991	11 083	100.0	7.0	14.2	11.0	15.4	12.4	14.3	14.7	6.2	4.9	27 151	570	36 154	472
1992[11]	11 269	100.0	7.3	14.8	10.0	16.2	12.4	14.4	13.9	6.1	4.9	26 407	539	35 833	486
1993[12]	11 281	100.0	7.3	13.3	11.1	16.1	13.2	14.3	12.7	6.5	5.5	26 839	530	37 413	621
1994[13]	11 655	100.0	6.3	13.4	9.9	16.6	13.0	12.9	14.4	7.3	6.4	28 288	526	39 362	565
1995[14]	11 577	100.0	6.0	11.8	9.7	16.0	13.3	14.9	15.3	7.2	5.8	29 417	502	39 935	683
1996	12 109	100.0	6.0	11.1	9.8	16.4	13.2	14.7	15.0	7.2	6.6	30 048	591	41 536	811
1997	12 474	100.0	5.7	10.9	9.1	15.6	13.3	14.9	16.1	7.6	6.8	31 376	540	41 287	592
1998	12 579	100.0	6.1	11.5	8.6	16.0	12.7	14.8	14.8	7.5	8.1	31 316	490	42 172	563
1999[15]	12 838	100.0	5.2	9.9	8.7	14.9	12.7	14.8	15.9	8.0	10.0	33 773	629	46 541	668
2000[16]	13 174	100.0	5.4	9.0	7.9	15.2	12.8	16.0	16.6	8.2	8.8	34 735	460	45 870	465
2001	13 315	100.0	6.0	9.2	8.5	14.8	13.8	14.9	16.1	8.3	8.4	33 562	395	44 697	471
Asian Alone or in Combination															
2002	4 079	100.0	4.0	2.6	4.2	9.4	9.6	12.2	18.9	13.0	25.9	58 598	887	77 865	1 481
2003	4 235	100.0	4.7	4.5	4.7	9.4	6.5	12.8	16.9	14.0	26.4	60 582	1 351	76 094	1 309
2004[17]	4 346	100.0	3.6	3.6	3.7	8.6	8.6	12.1	19.6	12.7	27.7	61 322	1 236	81 263	1 534
2005	4 500	100.0	4.3	3.3	4.5	8.0	7.1	11.7	19.1	13.2	28.8	63 050	753	82 620	1 442
2006	4 664	100.0	3.3	3.1	3.9	7.6	8.5	13.0	17.3	12.8	30.6	63 900	1 617	87 528	1 832
Asian Alone[21]															
2002	3 917	100.0	4.1	2.5	4.2	9.5	9.7	12.1	18.8	13.0	26.2	58 980	1 032	78 505	1 531
2003	4 040	100.0	4.8	4.6	4.6	9.4	6.3	12.9	16.7	14.1	26.8	61 061	1 199	76 709	1 358
2004[17]	4 123	100.0	3.6	3.5	3.8	8.6	8.5	11.9	19.6	12.6	28.0	61 380	1 304	81 675	1 580
2005	4 273	100.0	4.3	3.4	4.6	8.1	7.1	11.3	19.4	13.0	28.9	63 097	735	82 722	1 459
2006	4 454	100.0	3.4	3.1	3.9	7.7	8.5	12.8	17.0	12.8	30.8	64 238	1 674	88 293	1 908

[1]Implementation of a new Curent Population Survey (CPS) Annual Social and Economic Supplements (ASEC) processing system.
[2]Introduction of 1970 census sample design and population controls.
[3]Full implementation of 1970 census–based sample design.
[4]Implementation of a new CPS ASEC processing system. Questionnaire expanded to ask 11 income questions.
[5]Some of these estimates were derived using Pareto interpolation and may differ from published data that were derived using linear interpolation.
[6]First-year medians were derived using both Pareto and linear interpolation. Before this year, all medians were derived using linear interpolation.
[7]Implementation of 1980 census population controls. Questionnaire expanded to show 27 possible values from a list of 51 possible sources of income.
[8]Implementation of Hispanic population weighting controls and introduction of 1980 census–based sample design.
[9]Recording of amounts for earnings from longest job increased to $299,999. Full implementation of 1980 census–based sample design.
[10]Implementation of a new CPS ASEC processing system.
[11]Implementation of 1990 census population controls.
[12]Data collection method changed from paper and pencil to computer-assisted interviewing. In addition, the 1994 ASEC was revised to allow for the coding of different income amounts on selected questionnaire items. Limits either increased or decreased in the following categories: earnings limits increased to $999,999, Social Security limits increased to $49,999, Supplemental Security Income and public assistance limits increased to $24,999, veterans' benefits limits increased to $99,999, and child support and alimony limits decreased to $49,999.
[13]Introduction of 1990 census sample design.
[14]Full implementation of 1990 census–based sample design and metropolitan definitions, 7,000 household sample reduction, and revised editing of responses on race.
[15]Implementation of the 2000 census–based population controls.
[16]Implementation of a 28,000 household sample expansion.
[17]Data revised to reflect a correction to the weights in the 2005 ASEC.
[19]For 2001 and earlier years, the CPS allowed respondents to report only one race group.
[21]Asian alone refers to persons who reported Asian and did not report any other race category.

Table 13-2. Households, by Total Money Income, Race, and Hispanic Origin of Householder, 1967–2006
—Continued

(Numbers in thousands, percent, dollars; income in 2006 CPI-U-RS adjusted dollars.)

Race and Hispanic origin of householder and year	Number	Percent distribution										Median income (dollars)		Mean income (dollars)	
		Total	Under $5,000	$5,000 to $9,999	$10,000 to $14,999	$15,000 to $24,999	$25,000 to $34,999	$35,000 to $49,999	$50,000 to $74,999	$75,000 to $99,000	$100,000 and over	Value	Standard error	Value	Standard error
Asian and Pacific Islander[19]															
1987[10]	...	100.0	4.3	3.4	5.5	12.6	9.3	11.5	19.2	13.2	21.0	54 714	2 034	...	...
1988	1 913	100.0	3.0	4.1	3.9	12.0	9.2	14.8	20.5	11.3	21.2	52 844	2 172	66 067	1 973
1989	1 988	100.0	2.9	2.6	5.7	8.7	9.3	14.5	20.4	15.2	20.7	56 680	1 532	70 461	2 050
1990	1 958	100.0	3.8	3.0	5.0	9.4	8.2	13.5	22.1	13.3	21.7	57 500	1 703	69 407	1 965
1991	2 094	100.0	3.3	4.6	4.6	9.6	11.1	14.5	18.6	13.3	20.2	52 621	1 698	66 811	1 969
1992[11]	2 262	100.0	3.7	3.7	5.5	10.7	9.2	14.4	20.7	12.8	19.4	53 223	1 536	65 964	1 813
1993[12]	2 233	100.0	4.5	4.7	6.7	9.8	10.1	12.8	16.5	14.8	20.2	52 689	2 591	69 036	2 780
1994[13]	2 040	100.0	4.3	4.0	4.7	10.4	9.1	14.0	18.6	14.1	20.9	54 460	2 064	70 712	2 520
1995[14]	2 777	100.0	4.5	3.2	6.5	10.2	7.4	15.0	19.8	14.1	19.3	53 353	1 339	72 551	2 927
1996	2 998	100.0	3.4	4.8	4.7	9.5	9.1	13.8	18.2	14.0	22.6	55 376	1 985	72 358	2 595
1997	3 125	100.0	3.9	3.8	4.5	8.9	9.1	13.3	18.8	14.1	23.5	56 676	1 576	73 762	2 286
1998	3 308	100.0	4.2	3.7	3.7	9.3	8.6	14.5	17.7	13.9	24.4	57 610	1 603	74 375	2 148
1999[15]	3 742	100.0	3.9	2.9	4.6	7.9	7.8	14.8	17.4	13.2	27.3	61 664	2 173	81 542	2 067
2000[16]	3 963	100.0	3.4	2.6	3.9	7.8	8.4	13.1	17.7	14.9	28.2	65 281	1 113	85 232	1 769
2001	4 071	100.0	4.0	2.8	4.0	8.9	9.3	12.8	18.4	12.5	27.4	61 082	1 458	83 317	1 967
Hispanic[22]															
1972[3]	2 655	100.0	3.0	6.6	9.9	18.5	17.9	21.0	16.0	4.5	2.6	32 335	632	37 166	632
1973	2 722	100.0	3.2	6.3	9.0	18.6	17.3	20.1	17.9	5.2	2.5	32 282	733	37 506	610
1974[4,5]	2 897	100.0	2.5	7.4	9.5	19.3	16.2	20.4	16.9	5.3	2.6	32 120	703	37 209	606
1975[5]	2 948	100.0	3.5	9.2	10.2	20.0	16.6	18.3	15.8	4.2	2.3	29 527	653	35 052	623
1976[6]	3 081	100.0	3.0	9.6	10.3	18.6	16.7	17.7	16.7	4.7	2.6	30 142	643	35 620	580
1977	3 304	100.0	3.1	7.8	9.9	18.5	16.6	19.2	16.5	5.4	3.0	31 526	554	37 205	574
1978	3 291	100.0	3.0	7.3	9.4	16.8	16.7	18.0	18.8	6.3	3.8	33 476	811	39 542	800
1979[7]	3 684	100.0	3.0	7.4	8.7	16.3	16.6	18.3	18.1	6.9	4.8	33 756	973	40 843	820
1980	3 906	100.0	3.8	8.6	9.1	18.3	15.5	17.4	16.8	6.7	3.9	31 802	862	38 845	773
1981	3 980	100.0	3.5	7.5	10.2	17.1	15.1	18.5	16.6	7.4	4.0	32 545	891	39 082	747
1982	4 085	100.0	4.2	8.7	11.5	17.6	15.0	16.9	15.9	6.7	3.5	30 449	804	37 578	762
1983[8]	4 666	100.0	4.3	9.6	10.8	16.6	16.2	16.8	15.3	6.5	3.9	30 387	775	37 221	716
1984	4 883	100.0	4.5	9.5	10.1	16.5	13.9	17.5	16.6	6.7	4.7	31 407	787	39 053	762
1985[9]	5 213	100.0	4.0	9.0	10.6	17.3	14.0	16.8	16.4	7.0	4.8	31 209	729	38 997	634
1986	5 418	100.0	4.4	8.8	9.4	17.2	13.5	17.0	16.5	7.3	5.9	32 211	839	40 673	669
1987[10]	5 642	100.0	4.2	9.1	9.3	16.9	14.1	16.1	16.4	7.5	6.3	32 829	720	42 082	779
1988	5 910	100.0	4.4	9.2	8.4	16.5	14.1	16.7	17.1	7.2	6.4	33 342	822	42 569	902
1989	5 933	100.0	4.2	8.3	7.9	15.6	15.2	16.2	17.4	8.5	6.8	34 416	667	43 947	755
1990	6 220	100.0	3.6	8.4	9.9	16.2	14.1	17.6	17.2	6.8	6.2	33 394	685	41 831	689
1991	6 379	100.0	3.7	8.5	9.9	16.9	14.2	16.6	16.7	7.3	6.2	32 759	681	41 682	667
1992[11]	7 153	100.0	4.0	9.0	9.9	17.0	14.2	17.5	15.5	7.3	5.6	31 816	658	40 581	638
1993[12]	7 362	100.0	3.9	8.9	10.1	17.3	15.2	17.0	14.2	7.6	5.8	31 446	632	41 620	875
1994[13]	7 735	100.0	4.0	9.5	10.5	16.8	14.8	15.8	14.7	7.3	6.7	31 508	585	42 487	1 060
1995[14]	7 939	100.0	4.4	9.6	9.8	18.4	14.7	16.0	14.5	6.8	5.9	30 030	654	40 988	920
1996	8 225	100.0	3.8	8.9	8.6	18.3	14.9	15.4	15.9	7.4	6.8	31 870	618	43 513	1 007
1997	8 590	100.0	4.0	8.8	8.4	16.0	14.6	16.5	16.6	7.4	7.6	33 353	595	44 945	907
1998	9 060	100.0	4.2	7.7	8.3	16.0	14.2	17.0	16.6	7.9	8.2	34 996	674	47 287	1 006
1999[15]	9 579	100.0	3.3	5.9	7.5	16.1	14.3	17.5	17.1	9.4	9.0	37 204	541	48 874	868
2000[16]	10 034	100.0	3.1	5.7	6.9	15.6	13.4	18.0	18.3	9.9	9.1	38 834	560	51 490	741
2001	10 499	100.0	3.6	5.3	7.3	15.5	14.2	17.4	17.4	9.6	9.7	38 225	485	50 545	639
2002	11 339	100.0	3.9	5.5	7.2	15.8	15.0	16.4	17.6	9.0	9.5	37 100	540	50 307	672
2003	11 693	100.0	4.2	5.5	7.2	16.1	15.3	17.5	16.1	8.9	9.2	36 173	503	48 749	539
2004[17]	12 178	100.0	4.2	5.8	7.3	16.1	14.9	16.5	17.4	8.3	9.5	36 581	512	48 970	599
2005	12 519	100.0	3.8	5.8	7.4	15.9	14.6	17.1	17.5	8.5	9.4	37 146	369	48 684	490
2006	12 973	100.0	3.5	5.7	7.1	15.5	14.0	17.5	17.3	8.9	10.5	37 781	505	50 575	580

[3]Full implementation of 1970 census–based sample design.
[4]Implementation of a new CPS ASEC processing system. Questionnaire expanded to ask 11 income questions.
[5]Some of these estimates were derived using Pareto interpolation and may differ from published data that were derived using linear interpolation.
[6]First-year medians were derived using both Pareto and linear interpolation. Before this year, all medians were derived using linear interpolation.
[7]Implementation of 1980 census population controls. Questionnaire expanded to show 27 possible values from a list of 51 possible sources of income.
[8]Implementation of Hispanic population weighting controls and introduction of 1980 census–based sample design.
[9]Recording of amounts for earnings from longest job increased to $299,999. Full implementation of 1980 census–based sample design.
[10]Implementation of a new CPS ASEC processing system.
[11]Implementation of 1990 census population controls.
[12]Data collection method changed from paper and pencil to computer-assisted interviewing. In addition, the 1994 ASEC was revised to allow for the coding of different income amounts on selected questionnaire items. Limits either increased or decreased in the following categories: earnings limits increased to $999,999, Social Security limits increased to $49,999, Supplemental Security Income and public assistance limits increased to $24,999, veterans' benefits limits increased to $99,999, and child support and alimony limits decreased to $49,999.
[13]Introduction of 1990 sample design.
[14]Full implementation of 1990 census–based sample design and metropolitan definitions, 7,000 household sample reduction, and revised editing of responses on race.
[15]Implementation of the 2000 census–based population controls.
[16]Implementation of a 28,000 household sample expansion.
[17]Data revised to reflect a correction to the weights in the 2005 ASEC.
[19]For 2001 and earlier years, the CPS allowed respondents to report only one race group.
[22]Because Hispanics may be of any race, data in this report for Hispanics overlap with data for racial groups. Hispanic origin was reported by 12.7 percent of White householders who reported only one race, 3.1 percent of Black householders who reported only one race, and 1.4 percent of Asian householders who reported only one race. Data users should exercise caution when interpreting aggregate results for the Hispanic population and for race groups, because these populations consist of many distinct groups that differ in socioeconomic characteristics, culture, and recentness of immigration. Data were first collected for Hispanics in 1972.
. . . = Not available.

INDEX

INDEX